D1501574

Contents

[†] deceased

Contents

SECTION 2   THE CREATION, DIFFUSION, AND UTILIZATION OF KNOWLEDGE

[†] deceased

[†] deceased

Preface

This volume, *Educational Research, Methodology and Measurement: An International Handbook*, seeks to provide an up-to-date overview of the methods of inquiry that are employed in the investigation of problems which arise in the field of education. During the past 25 years different research strategies have been developed, not only in different parts of the world, but also as scholars drawn from different disciplines have endeavoured to examine educational problems with the approaches that customarily have been employed in specific disciplinary areas. The result has been great variety in the methods, theoretical perspectives, and approaches that have been used to investigate the processes and practices, the context and conditions, as well as the products and the procedures which occur in the field of education. Nevertheless, in spite of this variety, it is the claim of this *International Handbook* that there is an essential unity in these endeavours that justifies the many different tactics and strategies of investigation being brought together in one volume. Moreover, this unity supports the view of the field of inquiry as one of educational research, rather than accepting the contention that the disparities are so great that the field can only be seen as one of research into educational problems.

The purpose of this Preface is to answer five questions in order to explain the principles that have guided the development of this *International Handbook*.

(a) Why is there a need for a volume concerned with the methods of educational research?

(b) What are the relationships between the areas referred to in the title of the volume, namely methodology and measurement, and the four sections into which the volume is divided?

(c) What are the links between this volume and *The International Encyclopedia of Education*, and what principles were followed in the preparation of this *International Handbook*?

(d) How have the contents of this volume been organized?

(e) How can this volume and the various sources of information incorporated within it best be used?

Before addressing these five questions, it is necessary to recognize the marked growth and development that has occurred in the field of educational research during the past 25 years. The opening article of this volume by De Landsheere examines the *History of Educational Research* and reports on a third phase of development in this field of inquiry which took place in the 1960s and 1970s and involved an unprecedented expansion of investigatory activity into educational problems. During this period educational research gained from the massive support provided by both governmental and private agencies. Scholars were drawn from many disciplinary areas in the social and behavioural sciences to undertake research into educational problems. This expansion of research activity took place not only in the affluent industrialized countries, but spread to the Soviet Union and to less developed countries that were establishing or rapidly expanding their national educational systems. However, the late 1960s were also marked by the growth of an epistemological debate in the social sciences in reaction to the strident emphasis on a scientific approach that had occurred as a result of access to computers to carry out complex calculations and statistical analyses. These developments were accompanied by the student revolt in the universities of the more prosperous nations and by a challenge to institutionalized schooling together with a questioning of the value of traditional approaches to education. The confrontation that took place has in some ways damaged systematic research into educational problems. Nevertheless, it is now widely recognized that a rigid scientific approach to educational research is both incomplete and inadequate and that alternative approaches have much to contribute.

1. The Need for a Single Volume Concerned with the Methods of Educational Research

In the previous paragraph reference has been made to the conflict that has taken place between the two main perspectives employed in the investigation of educational problems, namely, the scientific and humanistic approaches. These issues are considered in greater detail in the second article in this volume by Husén concerned with *Research Paradigms in Education*. The scientific paradigm has been built on the approaches employed in the natural sciences and has emphasized the use of empirical, quantifiable observations in order to provide causal explanations of educational phenomena. The alternative paradigm has been developed from the humanities. Within this second paradigm there is an emphasis on holistic and qualitative information, and the purposes of research are to provide understanding and an interpretative account of educational phenomena. Moreover, it is argued that education is concerned with unique, goal-seeking individuals for whom the causal relationships of the scientific paradigm do not apply. The difference between these two paradigms is contained in the distinction made by Dilthey (1833–1911) in the field of psychology between *Erklären* and *Verstehen*, between explaining and understanding. He maintained that there were two kinds of psychology; the one employed experimental procedures and sought to generalize and predict, while the other used humanistic approaches and sought to interpret and understand. These alternative approaches to investigation can be viewed as forming one dimension of inquiry into educational problems.

In part as a consequence of the greater financial support for educational and social science research that has occurred during the past 25 years, there has been increasing interest in and concern for the usefulness of the findings of research. Of particular importance has been the emergence of an area addressed by Nisbet, namely that of *Policy-oriented Research*. It is, however, necessary to recognize that the investigation into educational problems can be undertaken from a perspective that is concerned with either the promotion of change, or alternatively the conservation of an existing situation. It is argued that there is a further dimension concerned with the uses of educational and social science research within which the advancement or retardation of change is considered. The purposes of inquiry extend beyond the cumulation of knowledge about education processes and the explanation or understanding of phenomena. Thus the policy or applied orientation of investigation involves a second dimension that necessarily interacts with the first and is concerned with the uses of inquiry for the solution of educational and social problems.

The emergence of a second dimension and the multiplicity of alternative approaches to the investigation of educational problems, together with a growing interest in undertaking studies that involve evaluation have generated, during the 25-year period from 1960 to 1985, great diversity in the tactics and strategies that can be employed in educational research. While the distinctions which lie beneath the scientific and humanistic approaches are maintained throughout this *International Handbook*, it is argued that the field of inquiry of educational research is more complex than a simple dichotomy would permit and that the differences which can be identified are essentially ones of degree rather than of kind. The purpose of this volume is to bring what is known about the many disparate approaches to research into educational problems together into one volume, so that the full diversity in methods is revealed. However, it is also claimed that there is a unity in the field that arises both from the epistemological bases of inquiry into educational problems (see *The Epistemological Unity of Educational Research*), as well as a coherence that arises from recent changes in social theory (see *Social Theory and Educational Research*). An emphasis on both the unity and diversity within the field of inquiry into educational problems is seen to meet the urgent need for reconciling the conflicts that currently exist in the field and for the development of a more coherent approach to research. The publication of the many different perspectives in a single volume should be seen as a contribution towards this goal.

This *International Handbook* seeks to be a truly international publication, providing coverage of the many different research traditions that are used in different parts of the world as well as looking forward to the future. It is clear that educational research is a dynamic enterprise. Its methods and procedures are changing, sometimes quite rapidly. This *International Handbook* aims at capturing this changing nature of educational inquiry and at assisting the enterprise to move ahead rapidly and with strength in a way that will contribute both to the creation of knowledge about educational processes and to the use of the findings of inquiry to improve both educational policy and practice.

2. Relationships between Methodology and Measurement and the Four Sections of the Volume

An important influence on educational research over the 25 years from the early 1960s has been the electronic computer, which has provided a remarkable boost for empirical and quantitative research into educational problems. This *International Handbook* has been assembled after a 25-year period of creative activity in the field of educational research. Initially in the early 1960s educational research workers reacted against the historical and philosophical approaches to inquiry of the 1940s and 1950s, which they saw to be highly conservative and unrelated to the practical problems of education. However, after a resurgence of empirical research conducted within the scientific perspective, the humanistic approach reemerged in more constructive forms with a concern for innovation and change. As a consequence of these oscillations in orientation this *International Handbook* seeks to adopt a flexible perspective that takes into account the variations which might be expected to occur in the future in the approaches adopted towards the investigation of educational problems. Since the future cannot be foretold with accuracy, approaches and procedures that have yet to be widely accepted, as well as those that are the subject of some controversy are presented alongside those that are well-established. Thus the traditional approaches and the alternative approaches that are being employed by some research workers in some countries are both presented.

Relationships between research methodology and measurement strategies are commonly technical in nature. Nevertheless, it is important to recognize that new approaches to measurement are being gradually introduced and are replacing the classical approach that has so far dominated educational research throughout the twentieth century. Some of the shortcomings of norm-referenced tests, which rely heavily on comparisons between individuals within groups, have been overcome in the new approaches of domain sampling and latent trait theories. Two questions face those concerned with the use of measurement procedures in educational research and evaluation studies. The first involves a choice in the construction of achievement tests and attitude scales of either classical test theory, domain sampling theory, or latent trait theory. A sound understanding of the strengths and weaknesses of each theoretical approach is necessary before a choice can be made as to which approach is most appropriate in measuring achievement and attitudes in specific research situations. The second question involves the use of generalizability or latent trait models in the investigation of particular research questions. The application of these approaches to measurement in situations concerned, for example, with the investigation of change, have not been adequately appreciated or explored. Relatively little use has been made of these measurement procedures in the investigation of major problems as opposed to illustrative examples. The task ahead is concerned with the use of these models in intervention studies and inquiry into the development of human characteristics. Latent trait models would appear to have the potential to reform investigative strategies where measures of change are required.

This *International Handbook* contains articles which have been clustered into four sections, namely:

(a) the methods of educational inquiry;

(b) the creation, diffusion, and utilization of knowledge;

(c) measurement for educational research; and

(d) research techniques and statistical analysis.

Within each section the articles are grouped in such a way as to provide a coherent view across the topics which are presented. In general, a pluralistic perspective is adopted and it is contended that the different approaches to research are complementary to each other.

In the *Introduction* to each section, issues that have arisen in research are addressed. These issues are concerned with the problems faced by educational research workers in the use of the different strategies presented in the articles within the section. In addition, an overview of the articles included in the section is provided.

3. The Preparation of the International Handbook

This *International Handbook* has been developed from *The International Encyclopedia of Education* which was edited by Torsten Husén and Neville Postlethwaite, with the assistance of an editorial board of 17 persons, and published in 1985. The *Encyclopedia* was organized around 18 areas of scholarly specialization related to education. Two key areas of the *Encyclopedia* were: evaluation and assessment, and research policy and methodology. After the *Encyclopedia* was published it was recognized that there was a need for a series of reference books and textbooks for university teachers and graduate students who were reading and studying in different areas of educational inquiry. Thus it was proposed that a volume should be prepared which cut across the two areas referred to above and would be concerned with research methodology and measurement. During the five-year period from when the *Encyclopedia* was planned in March 1981 at a meeting of the

Section Editors with the Editors-in-Chief, to when the contents of this *International Handbook* were determined, there were many important developments in the areas of research methodology and measurement. As a consequence, it was necessary to commission a significant number of new articles related to these developments which could be published together with the substantial number of relevant articles that had been included in the *Encyclopedia*. Of the 139 articles contained in this *International Handbook*, 115 were drawn from the *Encyclopedia*, and 24 were specially prepared for this volume in order to reflect the developments that had taken place during recent years. Further comment on such developments has been provided in the *Introductions* to each of the four sections of this *International Handbook*.

In the preparation of articles for both the *Encyclopedia* and this *International Handbook* authors were provided with a booklet of *Guidelines to Authors* on format and style. In addition, authors were given the opportunity to use either British or American spelling according to their own practice, and were requested to avoid sex bias in their use of language. All articles that were submitted were received by the Section Editors and the Editors-in-Chief and were commonly sent to an eminent scholar in the field who was asked to appraise the article for balance and accuracy of content.

Prior to the publication of the *Encyclopedia* the Section Editor for the area concerned with Evaluation and Assessment, Bruce H. Choppin, died while on a lecturing tour in Chile. The emphasis on the new approaches to educational measurement associated with the use of latent trait theory reflects his strong interest in this field. While the implications of these developments for both student assessment and research methodology have not been widely recognized, there is a rapidly growing interest in this area both with respect to research into theory and the application of the procedures to educational problems. As a consequence these approaches are likely to be more extensively used in the future, as the article by Carroll on *Future Developments in Educational Measurement* suggests. The preparation of this *International Handbook* owes a great debt to Bruce Choppin whose untimely death cut short his distinguished contribution to the field of educational measurement.

4. The International Handbook's Structure

As mentioned above this *International Handbook* is divided into four sections. The first section seeks to provide a broad coverage of topics related to the methods of educational inquiry. The introductory articles are concerned with general research perspectives. They are followed by articles that consider the two major approaches to research, namely, the humanistic perspective and the scientific perspective. It is not the purpose of this volume to advocate the use of one approach in preference to the other but rather to present the pluralism of views and perspectives that are employed in educational research. Moreover, as discussed above, this volume seeks to emphasize the unity and coherence that exists in the field of educational research rather than to emphasize the differences in outlook and the divisions that have arisen. The first section concludes with four articles on different aspects of policy-oriented research, one of which, a key article by Tyler on *Evaluation for Utilization*, describes both the new directions being followed in evaluation as well as the practical applications of evaluation. These four articles recognize that educational policy and practice are not independent of the cultural and social context in which they operate, and that educational researchers are rarely able to adopt a completely neutral perspective which is independent of problems relating to existing policy and practice.

The second section of this *International Handbook* is concerned with the creation, diffusion, and utilization of knowledge. It is increasingly being recognized, although it was probably never denied, that the creation of new knowledge and understanding of educational processes is not enough. The work of educational researchers extends beyond the building of coherent bodies of knowledge, however intellectually stimulating and challenging this might be. It has become clear that funding is available only for research studies that are seen to be useful and related to the problems of educational policy and practice. As a consequence consideration is increasingly being given to the dissemination of the findings of research and to the utilization of the theories and products of research in the provision of education.

The third section of this *International Handbook* is concerned with measurement for educational research. The emphasis of this section is primarily on the improvement of measurement which is attainable as a consequence of recent advances in measurement theory. Developments in measurement theory have important applications for achievement testing and the measurement of attitudes, both areas being of importance for educational practice as well as for further research. There are, however, many additional areas where recent development in both measurement theory and the techniques of measurement are capable of advancing the quality and the accuracy with which measurements are made in educational research. Some of these areas that are of importance for educational research, such as the use of census data and statistics, environmental measurement, the measurement of social background, classroom observation techniques, and the use of questionnaires and rating scales have been considered in articles contained in the closing pages of this section.

The fourth section includes articles on research techniques and statistical analysis, with the purpose of increasing the strength of the inferences that can be drawn from evidence collected in educational research. Consideration is given to the procedures employed in the use of both the humanistic and scientific approaches, as well as to a wide range of techniques of statistical analysis.

The articles in this section reveal the efforts undertaken since the 1960s largely by scholars working within the scientific perspective to improve their research techniques and increase the validity of their conclusions. The availability of computers has greatly facilitated their efforts and the considerable number of articles concerned with statistical procedures reflects the developments in this area that have occurred during the past 25 years, particularly in the United States, but more recently in European countries, such as Sweden, Denmark, and the Netherlands. There are relatively few articles within this section that address the question of drawing inferences from evidence based on research conducted from the humanistic perspective. Without the development and use of clearly identifiable methods, there would seem to be no way in which the conclusions of research undertaken in this context could be verified. Thus there would appear to be an urgent need for work in this area of investigation.

The collection of articles assembled in the four sections of this *International Handbook* is unique, and the range and depth of treatment of the articles goes well beyond that previously brought together in other works on educational research, methods, and measurement.

5. How to Use this International Handbook

Educational research, as pointed out above, draws on diverse disciplines that have bearings on problems in the field of education. While it is the Editor's contention that there is a unity and coherence running through this volume, it must be seen as a compendium of articles, written by different scholars with different research traditions, drawn from different countries across the world. Thus the volume is intended as a reference or source book for university and college teachers to use in the preparation of lectures; for graduate students to use as a first introduction to a procedure or research technique; and for practising research workers to obtain information on a research strategy that they might employ in their work or might explore in greater depth, if the strategy is likely to serve their needs. As a consequence of the inclusion of articles on so many separate topics in a single volume, it will be clear that no article can be complete in itself. Thus each article seeks not only to be relevant and up-to-date, but also to provide reference, through a concise bibliography, to key articles or publications likely to be readily available, from which a scholar, student, or research worker could obtain further information.

To emphasize the unity and the coherence of educational research as an investigatory activity the articles have been grouped into the four sections and into areas within each of the sections. Nevertheless, there is likely to be a need for information on a topic that is treated within one or more articles in the volume. In order to facilitate the search for information, references are provided within each article to other articles in the volume where related information has been presented.

The compilers of both the *Encyclopedia* and the *International Handbook* were fortunate to have advanced computer technology available for processing the articles through the various stages of publication, which has made possible the composition of an exhaustive Subject Index based on key words or phrases indentified by the authors as cornerstones in the structure of the information they wished to convey. As a consequence, the user of this *International Handbook* who wants information on a specific topic could begin by looking up appropriate key words in the Subject Index in order to locate either an article related to the topic or to identify articles where the topic, as referenced by the key words, is considered. In a similar way, the Name Index can be used to locate references to the writings of a particular author who is known to have made a significant contribution to a field of research related to the topic on which information is sought. To facilitate this task, page numbers are given both for the bibliographic reference and for the point at which the reference is cited in the text.

6. Acknowledgements

No work of the size of this *International Handbook* could be published without considerable effort by many people. To several of these people a special debt of gratitude is due. First, I am grateful to Neville Postlethwaite and Torsten Husén who guided the preparation of this *International Handbook* and the earlier *Encyclopedia*. Second, I am grateful to the many authors who prepared articles, carefully checked galley proofs and in many cases acted as consultants for other articles in the volume. Third, I am grateful to Barbara Barrett, Editorial Director at Pergamon Press, who directed work on both the *Encyclopedia* and the *International Handbook*, and to Priscilla Chambers, Clare Watkins and Joan Burks, who assisted her at different stages of the production enterprise. Finally, I am grateful to Marjorie Balloch and Anne Pettigrove and to many secretarial assistants who have undertaken the typing of articles and correspondence in connection with the preparation of this volume. To them all, my sincere thanks.

August 1988

John P. Keeves
Parkville, Australia

Section 1

The Methods
of
Educational Inquiry

Section 1

The Methods
of
Educational Inquiry

Introduction

Towards a Unified Approach

The aim of this section is to present an account of the different methods of inquiry that are employed in the investigation of educational and related social problems in a way that will contribute towards the resolution of the conflict that has emerged since the late 1960s among scholars in the social and behavioural sciences concerned with the nature of educational and social science research.

1. Research Perspectives

The opening article in this *International Handbook* is concerned with the *History of Educational Research* and it traces the development of educational research as a disciplined inquiry since the late nineteenth century. While the interest is primarily in empirical research, it is evident that the emphases for the conduct of inquiry have changed both over time and place. There was a blooming of educational research activity during the 1960s and 1970s, with much of this research being carried out within the scientific approach. This peak in activity was relatively short-lived. As a consequence it need not surprise us to observe differences across countries or across time in the manner in which educational research has been conducted.

The article on *Research Paradigms in Education* discusses the growth of an epistemological debate that developed between the proponents of the two major paradigms which guide the conduct of educational research. These paradigms have their origins in the two

3

major philosophical traditions that have influenced the quest for knowledge concerning the world in which we live. The humanistic paradigm, which had its origins in the views advanced by Aristotle, seeks an interpretation or understanding of events in terms of intentions, motives, and stated reasons. The scientific paradigm, which began with the investigations of Galileo, has sought causal explanations. These paradigms were seen as being mutually exclusive. Modern empirical research in the field of science has traditionally been conducted within the scientific paradigm. However, it is now widely recognized that the scientific or positivistic approach, while highly successful in many areas of inquiry, cannot take into account all the many aspects of human behaviour and the influences of the social context on that behaviour. These issues are examined and discussed in the article on *Social Theory and Educational Research*. Recently, the research community in the field of education has come to recognize that in the investigation of educational problems consideration must be given to both approaches to inquiry. However, there is normally common ground within the problem being investigated, and the two approaches are complementary to each other in the search for knowledge which involves both an explanation in terms of causes and an interpretation or understanding in terms of motives and intentions. Although this section of the *International Handbook* is concerned with the methods of educational research, the core of the debate does not lie within procedural differences but with questions that are concerned with the nature of knowledge.

The epistemological bases of educational research are complex, as the article on *The Epistemological Unity of Educational Research* indicates. During recent decades understanding of the epistemological foundations of knowledge within the two perspectives has advanced significantly, so that no longer can the two approaches to educational research be seen to be substantially different, but rather to have a common base. It is argued that there is a unity to educational inquiry derived from its epistemological origins, whatever the approach followed. The essentially pragmatic or problem-oriented character of educational research enables a nonfoundational theory of knowledge to utilize either or both quantitative–statistical and humanistic–qualitative methods in educational research depending on the kind of problem to be investigated. Conceived of in this way, educational research can thus make the best use of the strengths of both the scientific and humanistic approaches and consequently establish its unity as a theoretical enterprise.

Popkewitz (1984) draws attention to the fact that investigation into educational problems is carried out by people who are seeking an understanding of those problems and who are striving to improve educational institutions and processes. First, he contends that educational research, like other forms of scientific and social inquiry, possesses a quality that emerges from the communal context in which investigation is conducted. Furthermore, the processes of inquiry that are employed are influenced by the "norms, beliefs and patterns of social conduct of that community". Second, he argues that the social conditions in which the investigation is carried out give rise to contradictions and unresolved problems from which the methods to be employed in research emerge. Third, inquiry into educational and social problems is influenced by the social role of the researcher with respect to social movements that generate ideas and that reformulate issues for research. Depending on the social setting in which research is conducted differences will emerge in the methodologies employed. Consequently, it is not the purpose of this section of the *International Handbook* to advance one method in preference to others, but to argue that a range of methods is available from which the researcher into educational and social problems must select those most appropriate to the task in hand, the social situation, and indeed the researcher's own capabilities.

4

Two key characteristics of educational research must be recognized. First, the range of problematic situations encountered in the field of education cannot be viewed in terms of one and only one disciplinary field. Educational research is essentially multidisciplinary in nature, drawing upon such disciplines as psychology, sociology, anthropology, philosophy, history, political science, law, linguistics, economics, and demography. There have been times in the United States during this century when psychology has dominated the field of educational research, and although psychology can contribute to the investigation of many problems, other disciplinary perspectives are frequently more useful. While it is argued that educational research is multidisciplinary and the bodies of knowledge as well as the methods employed in the different disciplines listed above can be used in the investigation of educational problems, it is not appropriate to view educational research as a field in which the basic knowledge of a particular discipline is applied. Nor is it meaningful to argue that problems which are investigated in the field of educational research should always be tackled from an interdisciplinary perspective, although some inquiries may profit from the employment of such an approach. However, it is necessary to recognize that educational research is not dependent on a single disciplinary field and the methods of inquiry used within that field.

The second key characteristic of educational research arises from the complex nature of educational problems. It is rare that a problematic situation in education can be reduced in such a way that it can be viewed in terms of only two constructs or variables. In general, many variables are necessary to describe antecedent forces, mediating conditions, and the products or outcomes of the educational process. Thus educational research is multivariate in so far as many factors are customarily involved in each problematic situation. The procedures employed in educational research must be capable of examining many variables at the same time, and not necessarily through the use of complex statistical procedures, although these have their place. Anthropologists have evolved procedures for analysing and presenting information from a problematic situation which involves many variables that are very different from those used by psychologists, and different again from those that might be employed by economists. It is the complex multivariate nature of research situations in education that has led educational research workers to develop their own procedures, many of which are not drawn from any particular disciplinary field.

These characteristics, together with the domains of human activity from which educational researchers draw their problems, have helped to give educational research an identity of its own. A plurality of views about society, about the bodies of knowledge that can be brought to bear on educational problems, and about the methods of investigation that can be employed, is necessary to provide flexibility to tackle the wide range of educational problems that are open to investigation. The conflict between alternative perspectives and approaches provides the growing-points from which imaginative inquiry develops, and without which stagnation in thought and repetition in investigative activity would occur. Nevertheless, there is the risk that disagreements on theoretical and methodological questions can be counterproductive if strongly linked to ideologies and political purposes. Consequently, it is important that all who are engaged in the research enterprise in education should understand and appreciate the full range of intellectual resources available, and the extent to which their use might be restricted by the social context, so that outstanding problems in the field of education are tackled in productive ways. The essential unity of the enterprise and the complementary nature of alternative views must be recognized.

2. Humanistic Research Methods

After the presentation of the four background articles which consider the past and more recent developments that have taken place in the field of educational research, there is a collection of articles that examine the methods employed in humanistic research. The opening article discusses *Research Methodology: Historical Methods*. This links with an article on *Oral History* which is concerned with the use of oral sources in the examination of educational questions from a historical perspective. The article on *Hermeneutics* examines how this type of research seeks to develop interpretation and understanding in different kinds of human contexts. *Critical Theory* is also concerned with the detailed analysis of ideas and their influence on a society to enlighten and to emancipate people in their lives in that society. *Action Research* is a form of research that is carried out by practitioners into their own practices in order to improve these practices. A related approach is considered in an article on *Teachers as Researchers*. This type of research is undertaken by teachers not only to improve practice, but also to devise strategies for change in educational processes.

The article on *Case Study Methods* discusses the different types of case studies that can be conducted from the perspectives of cultural and social anthropology, in the development of understanding of educational processes, in action research, or in evaluation studies. The first named type is related to an approach to research in education that has gained in strength during recent decades and is referred to as *Ethnographic Research Methods*. A further and emerging field of research is *Metacognition*, a field that bridges the humanistic and scientific approaches and is concerned with the study of the understandings acquired by individual human beings as the result of both formal learning and experience. The concluding article, on *Naturalistic and Rationalistic Enquiry*, contrasts the different approaches to research which is conducted within a natural setting (referred to as naturalistic research) with those approaches to research that are conducted within the scientific perspective. However, it should be noted that the term *naturalistic* as used in this article differs from a use of the term that relates this approach to research to the philosophical view of naturalism, a view that is commonly adopted by biological and behavioural scientists in their investigations.

3. Scientific Research Methods

The opening article in this collection on scientific research methods examines *Research Methodology: Scientific Methods* and provides a concise account of both the more general techniques and more concrete aspects of philosophy necessary for the conduct of inquiry in the behavioural sciences. The articles that follow provide an account of the major types of investigations that are undertaken within a scientific research perspective. On the one hand there is the article on *Experimental Studies* which examines both fully randomized experimental investigations as well as quasi-experimental investigations. On the other hand there are several related articles on cross-sectional survey studies (see *Survey Studies, Cross-Sectional*), *Survey Research Methods*, *Longitudinal Research Methods*, and *Tracer Studies*. This difference in emphasis reflects, probably in an accurate way, the difficulties encountered in conducting truly experimental investigations into educational problems. An interesting and commonly fruitful method of investigation involves the study of twins, and the article on *Twin Studies* examines this type of research that seeks to tease out the relative contributions of genetic and environmental influences on behaviour and development.

A comparatively new and sophisticated research strategy is addressed in an article on *Simulation as a Research Technique*. Simulation studies seek to obtain approximate solutions to many statistical and related problems that are difficult to examine using more conventional techniques, because appropriate data are not available.

4. Policy Research

The final set of articles in this section is concerned with policy research which is a field of inquiry in education that has emerged since the mid-1960s as one of growing interest and importance. The introductory article is on *Policy-oriented Research*. When research into educational problems is carried out with the specific purpose of informing decisions related to policy, or with the aim of monitoring the implementation of policy, the term *policy-oriented research* is generally employed. Some research in this area is primarily involved with the initiation and the support of processes of change. The article on *Participatory Research* is concerned with the methods of research conducted with the purpose of promoting change. However, it is also possible for research to be designed, managed, and reported with the specific purpose of conserving an existing situation. Here the methods seek to legitimate existing policies and practices or to confirm decisions that have already been taken. The express purpose of this type of research and the methods it employs are involved with maintaining an existing system or institution rather than promoting change. An article on *Legitimatory Research* examines investigations of this type. In the field of evaluation the extent to which a study is concerned with conservation or with change will depend on the social and political context within which the evaluation is conducted, which will also influence the model of evaluation chosen. The final article by Tyler on *Evaluation for Utilization* presents a reconsideration of the theory of evaluation that he first presented in the late 1940s which was very influential in the United States and elsewhere. This article emphasizes the uses made of evaluation studies in school settings.

5. Conclusion

Throughout this *International Handbook* we recognize the two major approaches within which educational research is conducted, namely the scientific approach and the humanistic approach. Wilhelm Dilthey (1833–1911) in the 1890s developed the important distinction between *Erklären* and *Verstehen* in connection with research conducted in the field of psychology. The task of research undertaken within the scientific perspective is to establish causal relationships and to explain (*Erklären*), while the task of research carried out within the humanistic perspective is to provide an interpretation or understanding of events (*Verstehen*). Each approach operates within identifiable and established traditions. This distinction provides a dimension along which the methods of inquiry employed in educational research can be mapped, since according to the social context within which the research is conducted the emphasis on one approach or the other will vary. There will be on the one hand a strong tendency for investigations within the scientific perspective to employ quantified data, to seek a high level of reliability in the evidence collected by accurate measurement, to analyse the data using mathematical or statistical procedures, to seek replicability in the data and the analyses carried out, to emphasize the nomothetic nature of inquiry, and to present the findings of research in terms of generalizations. On the other hand, for studies undertaken within the humanistic perspective there will be a greater tendency to use holistic and qualitative information, to deny the relevance of replication, to emphasize the idiographic nature of the findings, and to refrain from generalization by providing a unique interpretation of events.

There would appear to be, however, a second dimension concerned with the methods employed in educational research. This dimension involves the ideological component of the research and relates to the policy orientation of an investigation. On the one hand there are methods of research such as *Action Research, Teachers as Researchers, Critical Theory,* and *Participatory Research* whose function is not merely to describe and provide an understanding of the role of education in society in terms of the relations between values, interest, and actions, but also through inquiry to change society and to provide opportunities for emancipation. On the other hand there are approaches to research that seek to minimize change and to conserve an existing situation. The article on *Legitimatory Research* provides an account of this type of research. The long-term consequences of the emergence of this ideological component in educational and social science research are difficult to foresee.

Bibliography

Popkewitz T S 1984 *Paradigm and Ideology in Educational Research.* Falmer Press, London

Research Perspectives

History of Educational Research

G. De Landsheere

Educational research as disciplined inquiry with an empirical basis was first known as "experimental pedagogy". This term was analogous to that of "experimental psychology", an expression coined by Wundt in Leipzig around 1880. Experimental pedagogy was founded around 1900 by Lay and Meumann in Germany; Binet and Simon in France; Rice, Thorndike, and Judd in the United States; Claparède in Switzerland; Mercante in Argentina; Schuyten in Belgium; Winch in England; and Sikorsky and Netschajeff in Russia. Some years earlier, three publications—*The Mind of the Child* by Preyer, a German psychologist, in 1882; *The Study of Children* by Stanley Hall from America in 1883; and articles by an English psychologist, Sully, in 1884 concerned with children's language and imagination—marked the beginning of the child study movement. Although progress was slow during the 1880s the foundations were laid through this movement for research into related educational problems. From 1900 onwards, the study of educational questions developed rapidly and three movements can be identified: (a) the child study movement, where educational research was associated with applied child psychology; (b) the New Education or progressive movement where philosophy took precedence over science, and life experience over experimentation; and (c) the scientific research movement with a positivist approach. This article is primarily concerned with the third movement which involves empirical research.

In the first major identifiable period (1900–1930), Cronbach and Suppes (1969) speak of a "heyday of empiricism", empirical educational research focused on rational management of instruction, challenging the concept of transfer of training, psychology of school subjects, development of new curricula, psychological testing, administrative surveys (school attendance, failure rates, etc.), and normative achievement surveys. Descriptive statistics were already well-established and in the 1920s and 1930s inferential statistics and multivariate data analysis developed rapidly.

In the second period (1930 to the late 1950s), however, the strict scientific approach to education lost impetus to make room, practically all over the developed world, for the more philosophically oriented and innovative progressivism. Behind this shift were three factors: (a) the atomistic character of most educational research; (b) a questioning of the scientific approach to the management of education at a time when there was an economic crisis soon to be followed by war; and (c) the charisma of the progressive movement with its combination of empirical research and a social and political philosophy merging the free enterprise, liberal spirit with humanistic socialism.

Nevertheless, during this period interest in cognitive development and language studies continued with the work of Piaget in Switzerland, and Vygotsky, who died in 1934, and his associates Luria and Leontief in the Soviet Union. In addition, a new strand of enquiry was opened up in the field of the sociology of education with the publication in 1944 of *Who Shall be Educated* by Warner, Havighurst, and Loeb in the United States. These authors brought together a substantial body of research to establish that schooling in the United States favoured white children from an urban middle-class background. Other studies into adolescence and adolescent development soon followed.

In the third period (1960s and 1970s) the knowledge "explosion" took place and its applications to technology really began. Educational research was soon influenced by this dynamic development. Challenged by the Soviet technological advance (e.g., Sputnik) and being economically affluent, United States governmental and private agencies supported educational research to an unprecedented extent. A similar development, although not so spectacular, occurred in other highly industrialized countries. During the 1960s the computer added a new dimension to educational research leading to the introduction of sophisticated experimental design since data processing and data analysis were no longer limited by calculation time as in the precomputer era. From this, new ways of thinking about educational issues developed, which were concerned with assessing probabilities, the interaction of the influences of many factors on educational outcomes, and the introduction of mathematical and causal modelling to predict and explain educational phenomena (see *Models and Model Building*).

The Anglo–Saxon world led the field in educational research followed by the Scandinavian countries, while West European countries tended to move more slowly.

The profound impact of the Anglo–Saxon research methodology has been felt all over the world since the 1960s. But the 1960s were also marked by the beginning of an epistemological debate in the social sciences, perhaps a reaction to the strident empiricism which had developed. It is now fully realized that the rigid scientific ideal, embodied in the neopositivist approach, cannot take into account the multifaceted aspects of human behaviour and all its environment-bound subtle nuances.

Confrontation took place. Just as the student movement and revolt can now be considered as part of an emerging, new human culture, the positivistic versus the anthropological or hermeneutic debate can be conceived as a new era in the social sciences. The answer of educational researchers of the 1980s is not either–or, but both. The research community has come to realize that sound inquiry develops in a spiral way combining methods or approaches that some would earlier have considered as incompatible: the scientific or hard data approach is seen to be complementary to the anthropological, historical, phenomenological, or soft data approaches.

Thus, it took empirical educational research approximately a century to reach its present status of maturity. For the first time in the history of humankind, the art of education can rely upon a sound and increasingly comprehensive basis.

In tracing the development of educational research this article will examine the successive periods: pre-1900 era, 1900 to 1930s, 1930s to late 1950s, the 1960s and 1970s, and developments in the 1980s.

1. Pre-1900

It is certainly not incidental that within a period of about 25 years empirical educational research was born and began to tackle most of the pervasive educational problems which are today still under study throughout the Western world. The foundations for this sudden rise were laid during centuries of educational experience and philosophical thinking, and were inspired by the explosion of the natural sciences during the nineteenth century. More specifically, longitudinal observations of individual children were recorded during the nineteenth century and attained a high-quality level with the pioneering study, in 1882, by Preyer, *Die Seele des Kindes* [The Mind of the Child]. This was the first textbook on developmental psychology. The idea of an experimental school and of experimentation in education is present in the writings of Kant, Herbart, and Pestalozzi, but this idea implied field experiences and not experimentation according to an elaborated design.

In the second part of the nineteenth century, several signs show that developments in the natural sciences slowly began to influence psychology and education. In 1859, in *The Emotions and the Will,* Bain considered the construction of aptitude tests. Five years later, G. Fisher proposed, in his *Scalebook,* a set of scales for the rating of ability and knowledge in major school subjects including handwriting. Fisher also introduced statistics

into educational research by using the arithmetic mean as an index of achievement of a group of students. In 1870, Bartholomaï administered a questionnaire to 2,000 children entering primary school in order to know the "content of their mind" at that moment. Three years later, the first experimental study of attention was published by Miller in Göttingen. In 1875, James opened the first psychological laboratory of the United States at Harvard in order to carry out systematic observation, but not experimentation. The year 1879, saw the publication of Bain's *Education as a Science.*

It is clear that the immediate origin of modern educational research (and of experimental psychology) is not to be found in the emerging social sciences, but in the natural sciences. With his *Origin of Species* (1859), Darwin linked research on humans with physics, biology, zoology, and geography. Six years later, Bernard published his *Introduction to the Study of Experimental Medicine,* the guide to modern scientific research. In 1869, Galton suggested, in *Hereditary Genius,* applying statistics to the study of human phenomena and began work on the concepts of standardization, correlation, and operational definition. Carroll (1978) saw in Galton's *Inquiry into Human Faculty and its Development* (1883) the invention of the concept of mental testing.

Experimental psychology—soon to be followed by experimental pedagogy—was created in German physics laboratories by scholars with a strong philosophical background. Wundt, a student of one of these scholars, Helmholtz, founded the first laboratory of experimental psychology in 1879. Wundt's laboratory had a considerable impact, and the scientific leadership of the German universities at the end of the 1800s must be recognized in order to understand what happened between 1880 and 1900. At that time, many students, particularly from the United States, completed their advanced education at the universities of Berlin, Leipzig, Heidelberg, or Jena. This explains the extraordinarily rapid dissemination of Wundt's ideas: Cattell, Hall, Judd, Rice, and Valentine were among his students. His work was immediately known in France by Ribot and Binet, in Russia by Netschajeff, in Japan by Matsumoto, in Santiago, Chile by Mann, and in Argentina by Mercante. Psychological laboratories were soon opened on both sides of the Atlantic.

In the meantime, certain key events were associated with the birth of modern educational research:

1885 Ebbinghaus's study on memory drew the attention of the education world to the importance of associations in the learning process.

1888 Binet published his *Etudes de Psychologie Experimentales;* at that time he was already working in schools.

1890 The term mental test was coined by Cattell.

1891 Stanley Hall launched the review *Pedagogical Seminary.*

1894 Rice developed a spelling test to be administered to 16,000 pupils. He published the results of his testing in his *Scientific Management of Education* in 1913.

1895 In the United States, the *National Society for the Scientific Study of Education* was founded (initially called the National Herbart Society for the Scientific Study of Teaching).

1896 In Belgium, Schuyten published a report of his first educational research study on the influence of temperature on school children's attention.
Dewey, a student of Stanley Hall, opened a laboratory school at the University of Chicago.

1897 Thorndike studied under James at Harvard and there discovered the works of Galton and Binet.
Ebbinghaus published his so-called completion test to measure the effect of fatigue on school performance. This can be considered to be the first operational group test.
In the same year Binet began to work on his intelligence scale.

1898 Lay suggested distinguishing experimental education from experimental psychology.
Binet and Henri condemned traditional education in their book *La Fatigue Intellectuelle* and indicated the need for experimental education.

1899 Schuyten opened a pedological laboratory in Antwerp (Belgium) to study experimentally, among other things, group teaching methods.

Who is the father of "experimental pedagogy"? The answer to this question differs whether the activity covered by the term or the term itself is considered. Empirical research in education definitely existed before 1900. Many American authors regard Rice as the founder because of his research on the effect of spelling drills (1895–1897), but other names: Binet, Lay, Mercante, or Schuyten, could also qualify. As for the term itself, it was coined by Meumann (Wundt's former student) in 1900, in the German *Zeitschrift für Pädogogik* where he dealt with the scientific study of schooling. In 1903, Lay published his *Experimentelle Didaktik* where he made his famous statement about "...experimental education will become all education". In 1905, Lay and Meumann together published the review *Die Experimentelle Pädagogik*. Subsequently, Meumann's three-volume work *Einführung in die Experimentelle Pädagogik* (1910, 1913, 1914) emphasized both the strict scientific and quantitative side of the laboratory, while Lay continued to emphasize both quantitative and qualitative approaches (empathy, intention) in classroom research.

When did modern educational research appear in France? There is no doubt that Binet inspired it. In his introduction to his book *La Fatigue Intellectuelle* (1898), he wrote:

Education must rely on observation and experimentation. By experience, we do not mean vague impressions collected by persons who have seen many things. An experimental study includes all methodically collected documents with enough detail and precise information to enable the reader to replicate the study, to verify it and to draw conclusions that the first author had not identified. (Simon 1924 p. 5)

It is obvious throughout the whole psychological work of Binet that he had a strong interest in education. In 1905, he founded the School Laboratory in rue Grande-aux-Bettes in Paris. With him were Vaney, who in 1907 published the first French reading scale and Simon, the coauthor of the *Intelligence Scale* (1905) and later author of the *Pédagogie Expérimentale*. Binet and Simon's *Intelligence Scale* presented in Rome at the 1905 International Conference of Psychology was the first truly operational mental test covering higher cognitive processes. Like Wundt's ideas, Binet's test became known throughout the world within a very few years. But beyond its intrinsic value, this test had a far greater historical significance. It was now acknowledged that a test could be a valid measurement instrument both in psychology and education.

In 1904, Claparède, a medical doctor, founded the Laboratory for Experimental Psychology at the University of Geneva with his uncle Flournoy. In 1892, Claparède had visited Binet in Paris and in the following year was, for a short time, Wundt's student in Leipzig. In 1905, he published the first version of his *Psychologie de l'enfant et pédagogie expérimentale* that was the only French educational research methods handbook until 1935 when Buyse published his *Expérimentation en Pédagogie*. In 1912, Claparède established the J. J. Rousseau Institute in Geneva which over the next 50 years was to make a marked contribution to child study and education through the work of Jean Piaget. However, Claparède remained mostly psychologically and philosophically oriented. With his theory of functional education, he was the European counterpart of John Dewey. Together they were seen as the two main leaders of progressive education.

Among many interesting features in the work of Claparède (following Dilthey's work in 1892 on *Verstehen* vs. *Erklären*) is his analysis, in 1903, of the explaining (positivist, nomothetic approach) versus the understanding (hermeneutic) approach. This elicited a debate which still lasts today.

At the end of *Les Idées modernes sur les enfants*, Binet (1924 p. 300) mentioned that "it is specially in the United States that the remodelling of education has been undertaken on a new, scientific basis". In fact, at the beginning of the century, education research advanced at an extraordinarily quick pace in the United States.

At Columbia University, Cattell, who had obtained his Ph.D. under Wundt and had known Galton in Cambridge, had, in 1890, as mentioned above, coined the term mental test in the philosophical journal *Mind*. In 1891, he established his psychological laboratory just above the laboratory for electricity. Under his supervision Thorndike completed his Ph.D. in 1898 on animal intelligence. Like many psychologists of the time he soon developed a keen interest in education. In this period, so much attention was focused on objective measurement that the experimental education movement was sometimes called "the measurement movement" (Joncich 1962).

Thorndike can be considered as the most characteristic representative of the scientific orientation in education. During the following decades, he dealt with all aspects of educational research. He was the first person to conceive of teaching methods in terms of an explicitly formulated and experimentally tested learning theory. In so doing, he opened a new teaching era. The influence of Thorndike in the field of educational research can probably be compared with the influence of Wundt in experimental psychology.

2. The Flourishing of Quantitative Research, from 1900 to 1930

During this period, most educational research was quantitatively oriented and geared to the study of effectiveness. For a while, Taylorism and the study of efficiency, became a component of educational thinking. The behaviouristic and antimentalist study of human behaviour was regarded as the best weapon against the formalism of the past.

The following aspects of research activities, although not comprehensive, are representative illustrations of the era.

2.1 Statistical Theory

It has sometimes been said that there is an inconsistency between the limitations of measurement in the social sciences and the rapidly increasing sophistication of the statistical techniques resorted to. However, it can be argued that many statistical advances were achieved by researchers in education precisely because they were aware of the complexity and the instability of most phenomena they had under study and had to look for increasingly sophisticated methods to obtain sufficient validity of measurement or else indicate the limitations of their conclusions.

The applicability of the Gaussian probability curve to biological and social phenomena was suggested at the beginning of the 1800s by Quetelet, who coined the term statistics. Galton was the first to make extensive use of the normal curve to study psychological problems. He sometimes preferred to express the same distributions with his ogive because this representation gave a better picture of the hierarchy of characteristics. Galton also suggested percentile norms. In 1875, he drew the first regression line, and developed the concept of correlation in 1877. In 1896, Pearson, who worked under Galton, published the formula for the product–moment correlation coefficient. In the first decade of the 1900s, the essentials of the correlational method, including the theory of regression, were well-developed, especially by British statisticians, Pearson and Yule. In the same period, Pearson developed the chi-square technique and

the multiple correlation coefficient. Reliability was measured with the Spearman–Brown Formula. In 1904, Spearman published his analysis of a correlation matrix to sustain his two-factor theory and factor analysis began to emerge.

Researchers were also aware of the statistical significance of differences. They used rather crude methods indeed, but did not take many chances. Carroll has written:

> Fortunately, American psychologists in the early days, tended to employ such a conservative standard in testing statistical differences (a "critical ratio" of four times the probable error, corresponding to $p < 0.007$) that at least it can be said that they only infrequently made "Type 1 errors." (Carroll 1978 p. 20)

In 1908, under the name of Student, Gossett showed how to measure the standard error of the mean and the principle of the t-test was formulated.

Experimental design was also used. In 1903, Schuyten used experimental and control groups. In 1916, McCall, a student of Thorndike and probably the first comprehensive theorist of experimentation in education, recommended the setting up of random experimental and control groups. In a research study with Thorndike and Chapman (Thorndike et al. 1916), he applied 2×2 and 5×5 latin square designs. This was 10 years before the work of R. A. Fisher in England.

The contribution of Sir Ronald Fisher was critical. With the publication of his *Statistical Methods for Research Workers* in 1925, small-sample inferential statistics became known, but were not immediately utilized. In the same work, Fisher reinforced Pearson's chi-square by adding the concept of degrees of freedom, demonstrated the t-test, and explained the technique of analysis of variance. In 1935, Fisher crowned his scientific career with his famous *The Design of Experiments*, originally conceived for agriculture, and not widely applied in educational research before the late 1940s.

A look at some of the statistical texts available in the 1920s is often a surprise for today's students: Thorndike (1913), McCall (1922), Otis (1925), Thurstone (1925) in the United States; Yule (1911), Brown and Thomson (1921) in the United Kingdom; Claparède (1911) in Switzerland; Decroly and Buyse (1929) in Belgium had a surprisingly good command of descriptive parametric statistics and also a keen awareness of the need for testing the significance of differences.

2.2 Testing and Assessment

It has been shown that both mental and achievement tests already existed at the turn of the century. Between 1895 and 1905 tests were administered in schools in the United States, Germany, France, Belgium, and many other countries. Perhaps the critical moment was the appearance in 1905 of Binet and Simon's test, the first valid and operational mental measurement instrument. Group testing began in England in Galton's laboratory in 1905, and Burt and Spearman assisted him. In 1911, the United States National Education Association approved the use of tests for school admission and final examinations. A breakthrough occurred with the development and wide-scale, efficient use of tests by the United States Army, which were quickly constructed in 1917 mostly by drawing upon existing mental tests. Soon after the war, these tests were modified for school use (Carroll 1978).

The 1918 *Yearbook* of the National Society for the Study of Education was entirely devoted to the measurement of educational products. In 1928, about 1,300 standard tests were available in the United States. By the 1930s, normative-test construction techniques could be considered to be fully developed: item formats, order of items, parallel forms, scoring stencils and machine scoring, norms, reliability, and validity. The psychometric advance of the United States, at that time, was such that standardized tests were often referred to as "American tests".

Mental tests were soon used in all industrialized countries. In particular, Binet's scale was used in Europe, North and South America, and Australia, and was tried out in some African countries. This was far from being the case with achievement tests. Some fairly crude tests were used as research instruments but frequently remained unknown to the classroom teacher. It is, for instance, surprising to observe the lack of sophistication of the achievement tests developed in France after Binet and Simon. This continued until the 1940s, and the situation is particularly well-illustrated in the book by Ferré, *Les Tests a l'école*, a fifth edition of which appeared in 1961. It is all the more surprising since in the 1930s traditional examinations (essay and oral tests) were sharply criticized in England and in France where Piéron coined the French word *docimologie*, meaning "science of examinations". Lack of validity, of reliability, and sociocultural bias were denounced with documented evidence. In Continental Europe, standardized achievement tests were not extensively used in schools.

2.3 Administrative and Normative Surveys

Among educational research endeavours, surveys are the oldest. In 1817, Marc Antoine Jullien de Paris became the founder of comparative education by designing a 34-page national and international questionnaire covering all aspects of national systems of education. The questions were posed, but unfortunately not answered, at that time.

The modern questionnaire technique was developed by Stanley Hall at the end of the 1800s to show, among other things, that what is obvious for an adult is not necessarily so for a child. This observation has, of course, direct educational implications.

In 1892, Rice visited 36 towns in the United States and interviewed some 1,200 teachers about curriculum content and teaching methods. Subsequently he carried out a spelling survey (1895–1897) on 16,000 pupils and found a low correlation between achievement and time invested in drill. This survey was repeated in 1908 and in 1911 (Rice 1913). Thorndike's 1907 survey of dropouts

was followed by a series of other surveys of school characteristics: differences in curricula, failure rate, teaching staff qualifications, school equipment and the like. The most comprehensive survey of the period was the Cleveland Schools Survey undertaken in 1915–16 by L. P. Ayres and a large team of assistants. The study was reported in 25 volumes each dealing with different aspects of urban life and education.

In Germany, France, Switzerland, and Belgium, similar but smaller surveys were carried out by "pedotechnical" offices such as that opened in 1906 in the Decroly School in Brussels.

Several large-scale psychological surveys were undertaken: the Berkeley Growth Study (1928), the Fell's Study of Human Development (1929), and the Fourth Harvard Study (1929). In 1932, the Scottish Council for Research in Education carried out its first *Mental Survey* on a whole school population which provided a baseline for later surveys and for determining the representativeness of samples of the population of the same age.

A landmark in the history of experimental education was the *Eight-year Study* (1933–1941) conducted in the United States by the Progressive Education Association. The initial purpose of the study, which was carried out using survey research methodology, was to examine to what extent the college entrance requirements hampered the reform of the high-school curriculum and to demonstrate the relevance and effectiveness of progressive ideas at the high-school level. In this study students from 30 experimental schools were admitted to college irrespective of subjects they had studied in high school. The by-products of this project were probably more important than the project itself. Tests covering higher cognitive processes and effective outcomes were developed by an evaluation team directed by Ralph Tyler. The careful definition of educational objectives was advanced. In 1950, influenced by the *Eight-year Study*, Tyler wrote *Basic Principles of Curriculum and Instruction*, in which he presented his model for the definition of objectives. It was followed by Bloom's first taxonomy in 1956 (see *Taxonomies of Educational Objectives*), and this marked the beginning of the contemporary thinking on the definition of objectives and on curriculum development and evaluation.

2.4 Curriculum Development and Evaluation

Curriculum was one focus of attention of empirical educational research from its very beginning. The article, in 1900, in which Meumann used the term "*experimentelle Pädagogik*" for the first time dealt with the scientific study of school subjects. Shortly afterwards, Thorndike introduced a radical change in curriculum development by conceptualizing teaching methods in terms of a "psychology of school branches", and by demonstrating through his work on the transfer of learning the lack of validity of the prevailing theories of formal education, and how it ignored the needs of contemporary society. This psychological approach was perfectly compatible with the new pragmatic philosophy and the attempts to rationalize work and labour. Some years later, Decroly and Buyse hoped to "taylorize instruction to save time for education". The psychology of school subjects was also dealt with by other leading scholars such as Judd. But, as far as research on curriculum, in the broad sense of the word is concerned, the work of Thorndike on content, teaching methods, and evaluation of material is second to none.

During the same period, the progressive movement, partly inspired by Dewey, remained in close contact with these specific developments, although it soon rejected—as William James had done earlier—a strictly quantitative experimental approach to educational phenomena. According to Thorndike's scientific approach, there could only be one standard curriculum at a given time, the best one that scientific research could produce. Most important to the movement was the rejection of formalism for functionality. The main criteria for curriculum content became individual needs in a new society, as conceived by liberal, middle-class educators of the time.

In 1918, Bobbitt published *Curriculum*, soon to be followed by Charters' *Curriculum Construction* (1923). This led to a series of studies with increasingly strong emphasis on a systematic and operational definition of educational objectives. On the European side, the Belgian *Plan d'études* (1936), written by Jeunehomme, can be considered as a curricular masterpiece, built on contributions of both strict empirical research and the progressive philosophy.

3. From the 1930s to the late 1950s

The economic crisis of the 1930s made research funds scarce. The need for a new social order was interpreted differently: fascism in some countries (Germany, Italy, Japan); socialism in others (the *front populaire* in France and Spain). Progressivism, advocated by the New Education movement outside the United States, seemed to be an obvious educational solution in most democratic countries and a guarantee for the future of democracy.

The Second World War and the years immediately following froze most educational research activities in European countries. Freedom of research was (and still is) not acceptable to dictators. In the Soviet Union, the utilization of tests (as incompatible with political decisions) and more generally the "pedological movement" were officially banned in 1936 by a resolution of the Communist Party, and this situation lasted until Stalin's death. However, other forms of research continued, arising from the publication in 1938 of *Thought and Language* by L. S. Vygotsky four years after his death in 1934, and the subsequent work of his associates such as Luria and Leontief in the development of Pavlov's ideas. In occupied countries, school reorganization was planned by underground movements which tried to draw conclusions from previous experiments and to design educational systems for peace and democracy.

The *Plan Langevin–Wallon*, for the introduction of comprehensive secondary education in France is an example.

Conditions were different in the United States, Australia, and in Sweden. Even if no spectacular advances occurred in educational research in those countries, the maturation of ideas went on and prepared the way for the postwar developments. Warfare had again raised problems of recruitment and placement and the role of military psychology and the development of selection tests is exemplified by the work of Guilford in the United States and Husén and Boalt (1968) in Sweden.

The strong field of interest in the 1940s and 1950s was without doubt in sociological studies. The seminal investigations were those concerned with social status and its impact on educational opportunity. A series of studies in the United States showed the pervasive existence of the school's role in maintaining social distinctions and discriminatory practices. From this research it was argued that schools and teachers were the purveyors of middle-class attitudes and habits. These effects of schooling were particularly evident at the high-school stage, and this trend of research became closely linked to the study of adolescent development. This work spread to England in the mid-1950s and subsequently to other parts of the world and led to challenging the maintenance of selective schools and to establishing comprehensive high schools. This research emphasis on issues associated with educational disadvantage has continued subsequently, with concern for disparities in the educational opportunities provided for different racial and ethnic groups, for inner urban and rural groups and, in particular, for girls.

4. The 1960s and 1970s

During the first part of the 1960s in affluent countries educational research enjoyed for the first time in its history the massive support necessary for it to have a significant impact. This development was particularly marked in the United States. At that time money for research and curriculum development, particularly in mathematics and science, was readily available in the United States. In 1954, federal funds were first devoted through the Cooperative Research Act to a programme of research and development in education (Holtzman 1978). The big, private foundations also began to sponsor educational research on a large scale. The civil rights movement, Kennedy's New Frontier, and Johnson's Great Society continued the trend.

In 1965, the Elementary and Secondary Education Act was passed which authorized funding over a five-year period for constructing and equipping regional research and development (R & D) centres and laboratories. President Johnson implemented developments that had been planned under Kennedy and in 1968, federal support for educational research reached its peak: 21 R & D centres, 20 regional laboratories, 100 graduate training programmes in educational research, and thousands of demonstration projects, represented a total federal investment of close to 200 million dollars per year.

On a much smaller scale, a similar development took place in England. Wall (1968 p. 16) wrote:

In 1958, it was possible to demonstrate that expenditure of all kinds on research relating to education represented no more than 0.1 per cent of all expenditure on education: in 1967 the proportion may well be thirty times as much and will probably grow over the next decade.

A similar expansion took place in the Soviet Union. Between 1960 and 1970 the professional staff engaged in educational research increased considerably. In 1966, the Soviet Academy of Pedagogical Sciences took on its present status. Initially under the name of the Academy of the Russian Republic it was founded in 1943. In 1967, the *Institut Pédagogique Nationale* of France, for the first time, received significant funding for educational research. Girod de l'Ain (1967) considered 1967 as the Year 1 of educational research in France.

By the late 1960s, all highly industrialized countries were in the midst of a cultural crisis which had a deep impact on scientific epistemology and thus affected the research world. There was also talk about a "world crisis" (Coombs 1968) in education which applied in the first place to the imbalance between demand and supply of education, particularly in Third World countries. Deeply disappointed in their hope for general peace, wealth, and happiness, people realized that neither science and technology nor traditional—mostly middle-class—values had solved their problems. An anti-intellectualist counterculture developed, emphasizing freedom in all respects, rejecting strict rationality, glorifying community life. The value of "traditional" education was questioned. "Deschooling", nondirectivity, group experience, and participation seemed to many the alpha and omega of all pedagogy. This trend did not leave socialist countries unaffected. In May 1976, a group of researchers in the Soviet Union regretted a too rationalistic approach in educational research (Novikov 1977).

At the same time, scholars also began to question science, some with great caution and strong argumentation, others superficially in the line of the Zeitgeist. Kerlinger (1977) condemned the latter with ferocity: "mostly bizarre nonsense, bandwaggon climbing, and guruism, little related to what research is and should be".

This was not the case in the crucial epistemological debate inspired by scholars like Polanyi, Popper, Kuhn, and Piaget. Fundamentally, the world of learning acknowledged both the contemporary "explosion" of knowledge and the, still very superficial, comprehension of natural, human phenomena.

While Piaget (1972) showed in his *Epistémologie des sciences de l'homme,* that nomothetic and historical (anthropological) approaches are not mutually exclusive but complementary, in 1974, two of the best-known American educational researchers Cronbach (1974) and Campbell (1974), without previous mutual consultation, chose the annual meeting of the American Psychological Association to react against the traditional positivist emphasis on quantitative methods and stressed the critical importance of alternative methods of inquiry.

Since the 1960s, the computer has become the daily companion of the researcher. For the first time in the history of humankind, the amount and complexity of calculation are no longer a problem. Already existing statistical techniques, like multiple regression analysis, factor analysis, multivariate analysis of variance, that previously were too onerous for desk calculation suddenly became accessible in a few moments. Large-scale research projects became feasible. Simultaneously, new statistical methods and techniques were developed (see *Statistical Analysis in Educational Research*).

Huge surveys, such as Project Talent in the United States and the mathematics and six subject surveys of the International Association for the Evaluation of Educational Achievement (IEA) would have been unthinkable without powerful data processing units. Campbell and Stanley's (1963) presentation of experimental and quasiexperimental design for educational research can be considered to be a landmark.

Scientific developments in the field of educational research were not only stimulated by access to funds and to powerful technology, but also by the "explosion" of knowledge in the physical and social sciences, especially in psychology, linguistics, economics, and sociology.

Many scientific achievements in the field of education can be mentioned for the 1960s: the new ideas on educational objectives, the new concepts of criterion-referenced testing, formative and summative evaluation, teacher–pupil interaction analysis, research on teacher effectiveness, compensatory education for socioculturally handicapped children, the study of cognitive and affective handicaps, research into the importance and methods of early education, social aspects of learning aptitudes, deschooling experiments, adult education, the development of new curricula and of an empirical methodology of curriculum development and evaluation, and developments in research methodology.

5. Developments in the 1980s

With the advent of the last quarter of the twentieth century, the scientific status of educational research has attained a level of quality comparable to that of other disciplines. The epistemological debate of the previous decade clarified considerably the respective strengths and weaknesses of the qualitative and the quantitative approaches. It is now widely acknowledged that no one research paradigm can answer all the questions which arise in educational research.

A clear impact of this scientific maturity can also be spotted in educational practice. Both the scientific quest for the most efficient standard teaching method and the progressivist improvisation (for a while replaced by nondirectivity) have been succeeded by subtle classroom management including careful definition and negotiation of objectives, consideration of student and teacher's characteristics, of cognitive and affective styles, and of economic and social needs. Thanks to the advancement of developmental and educational psychology it is now understood, for instance, how the Piagetian constructivist theory implies that many crucial educational objectives can only be defined by or with the learner, while interacting with his or her environment. The naive concept of individualized teaching and the dogma of group work is replaced by flexible group structuring and flexible scheduling. Beyond the original model of mastery learning now appears the more general concept of a school making sensible use of time and of all human and technological resources available. Opportunities to learn are multiplied. The future appears to belong to a more modular system of education. The new perspectives opened by the computer technology are also more clearly perceived and are probably best illustrated by the "Logo environment" (Papert 1972), which is a challenge to intellectual creativity and development. These new developments, given as examples among many others, still have to be disseminated to the majority of schools, their validity and feasibility in terms of daily practice having been established.

6. Conclusion

Like medicine, education is an art. That is why advances in research do not produce a science of education, in the positivist meaning of the term, but yield increasingly powerful foundations for practice and decision making. In this perspective, it can be said that from 1900 to 1980, educational research has gathered a surprisingly large body of knowledge containing valuable observations and conclusions.

See also: Educational Research and Policy Making

Bibliography

Binet A 1924 *Les Idées modernes sur les enfants.* Flammarion, Paris
Brown W, Thomson G H 1921 *The Essentials of Mental Measurement.* Cambridge University Press, Cambridge
Campbell D T 1974 Qualitative knowing in action research. Paper, American Psychological Association, Los Angeles, California
Campbell D T, Stanley J C 1963 Experimental and quasi-experimental designs for research on teaching. In: Gage N L (ed.) 1963 *Handbook of Research on Teaching.* Rand McNally, Chicago, Illinois, pp. 171–246
Carroll J B 1978 On the theory–practice interface in the measurement of intellectual abilities. In: Suppes P (ed.) 1978 *Impact of Research of Education.* National Academy of Education, Washington, DC

Claparède E 1911 *Psychologie de l'enfant et pédagogie expérimentale,* Vol. 2: *Les Méthodes.* Delachaux and Niestlé, Neuchâtel
Connell W F 1980 *A History of Education in the Twentieth Century World.* Teachers College Press, New York
Coombs P H 1968 *The World Educational Crisis: A Systems Analysis.* Oxford University Press, London
Cronbach L J 1974 Beyond the two disciplines of scientific psychology. Paper, American Psychological Association, Los Angeles, California
Cronbach L, Suppes P (eds.) 1969 *Research for Tomorrow's Schools: Disciplined Inquiry for Education: Report.* Macmillan, New York
Decroly O, Buyse R 1929 *Introduction à la pédagogie quantitative: Eléments de statistiques appliqués aux problèmes pédagogiques.* Lamertin, Brussels
De Landsheere G 1982 *La Recherche expérimentale en éducation.* International Bureau of Education, UNESCO, Geneva
de l'Ain G 1967 L'an I de la recherche pédagogique. *Le Monde* 5th Sept. 1967
Holtzman W H 1978 Social change and the research and development movement. In: Glaser R (ed.) 1978 *Research and Development and School Change.* Erlbaum, Hillsdale, New Jersey, pp. 7–18
Husén T, Boalt G 1968 *Educational Research and Educational Change: The Case of Sweden.* Wiley, New York
Husén T, Kogan M 1983 *Researchers and Policy-makers in Education.* Pergamon, Oxford
Joncich G 1962 Wither thou, educational scientist? *Teach. Coll. Rec.* 64: 1–12
Kerlinger F N 1977 *The Influence of Research on Educational Practice.* University of Amsterdam, Amsterdam
McCall W A 1922 *How to Measure in Education.* Macmillan, New York
Novikov L 1977 Probleme der Planung und Organisation der pädagogischen Forschung in der Sowjetunion. In: Mitter W, Novikov L (eds.) 1977 *Pädagogische Forschung und Bildungspolitik in der Sowjetunion: Organisation, Gegenstand, Methoden.* Deutsches Institut für Internationale Pädagogische Forschung, Frankfurt/Main
Otis A S 1925 *Statistical Method in Educational Measurement.* World Book, Yonkers-on-Hudson, New York
Papert S 1972 Teaching children thinking. *Program. Learn. Educ. Technol.* 9: 245–55
Piaget J 1972 *Epistémologie des sciences de l'homme.* Gallimard, Paris
Rice J M 1913 *Scientific Management in Education.* Hinds, Noble and Eldredge, New York
Simon T 1924 *Pédagogie expérimentale: Ecriture, lecture, orthographe.* Colin, Paris
Thorndike E L 1913 *An Introduction to the Theory of Mental and Social Measurements,* 2nd edn. Teachers College Press, New York
Thorndike E L, McCall W A, Chapman J C 1916 *Ventilation in Relation to Mental Work.* Teachers College Press, New York
Thurstone L L 1925 *The Fundamentals of Statistics.* Macmillan, New York
Wall W D 1968 The work of the National Foundation for Educational Research in England and Wales. In: Butcher H J (ed.) 1968 *Educational Research in Britain.* University of London Press, London, pp. 15–32
Yule G U 1911 *An Introduction to the Theory of Statistics.* Griffin, London

Research Paradigms in Education

T. Husén

Thomas Kuhn, himself a historian of science, contributed to a fruitful development in the philosophy of science with his book *The Structure of Scientific Revolutions* published in 1962. It mapped out how established thinking, research strategies, and methods in a scientific field, in Kuhn's terminology "normal science," were established. It brought into focus two streams of thinking about what could be regarded as "scientific," the Aristotelian tradition with its teleological approach and the Galileian with its causal and mechanistic approach. It introduced the concept of "paradigm" in the philosophical debate.

"Paradigm" derives from the Greek verb for "exhibiting side by side." In lexica it is given with the translations "example" or "table of declensions and conjugations." Although Kuhn himself used paradigm rather ambiguously, the concept has turned out to be useful in inspiring critical thinking about "normal science" and the way shifts in basic scientific thinking occur. A paradigm determines the criteria according to which one selects and defines problems for inquiry. Young scientists tend to be socialized into the precepts of the prevailing paradigm which to them constitutes "normal science." In that respect a paradigm could be regarded as a cultural artifact, reflecting the dominant notions about scientific behavior in a particular scientific community, be it national or international, and at a particular point in time. Paradigms determine scientific approaches and procedures which stand out as exemplary to the new generation of scientists—as long as they do not oppose it.

A "revolution" in the world of scientific paradigms occurs when one or several researchers at a given time encounter anomalies, for instance, make observations, which in a striking way do not fit the prevailing paradigm. Such anomalies can give rise to a crisis after which the universe under study is perceived in an entirely new light. Previous theories and facts become subject to thorough rethinking and reevaluation.

In well-defined disciplines which have developed over centuries, such as the natural sciences, it is relatively easy to point out dramatic changes in paradigms, such as in astronomy from Ptolemy through Copernicus to Galileo or in physics from Aristotle via Galileo and Newton to Einstein. When the social sciences emerged in the nineteenth century, they tended to regard the natural sciences as scientific models, but without awareness that the social scientist is part of a process of social self-understanding. Educational research faces a particular problem, since education, as William James pointed out, is not a well-defined, unitary discipline but a practical art. Research into educational problems is conducted by scholars with many disciplinary affiliations. Most of them have a background in psychology or other behavioral sciences, but quite a few of them have a humanistic background in philosophy and history. Thus there cannot be any prevailing paradigm or "normal science" in the very multifaceted field of education research. However, when empirical research conducted by behavioral scientists, particularly in the Anglo–Saxon countries, in the 1960s and early 1970s began to be accused of dominating research with a positivist paradigm that prevented other paradigms of a humanistic or dialectical nature being employed, the accusations were directed at those with a behavioral science background.

1. The Two Main Paradigms

The twentieth century has seen the conflict between two main paradigms employed in researching educational problems. The one is modeled on the natural sciences with an emphasis on empirical quantifiable observations which lend themselves to analyses by means of mathematical tools. The task of research is to establish causal relationships, to explain (*Erklären*). The other paradigm is derived from the humanities with an emphasis on holistic and qualitative information and to interpretive approaches (*Verstehen*).

Briefly, the two paradigms in educational research developed historically as follows. By mid-nineteenth century when Auguste Comte (1798–1857) developed positivism in sociology and John Stuart Mill (1806–1873) empiricism in psychology, there was a major breakthrough in the natural sciences at the universities with a development of a particular logic and methodology of experiments and hypothesis testing. They therefore came to serve as models and their prevailing paradigm was taken over by social scientists, particularly in the Anglo–Saxon countries. However, on the European Continent there was another tradition from German idealism and hegelianism. The "Galilean," mechanistic conception became the dominant one, particularly with mathematical physics as the methodological ideal. Positivism was characterized by methodological monism. Philosophers at the University of Vienna (such as Neurath), referred to as the Vienna Circle, developed what is called "neopositivism" or "logical empiricism." Around 1950 they founded a series of publications devoted to the study of what they called unified science. Positivism saw the main task for the social sciences as being the making of causal explanations and the prediction of future behavior on the basis of the study of present behavior. Neopositivism emanated from the strong influence of analytical philosophy.

There are at least three strands for the other main paradigm in educational research. The Continental idealism of the early nineteenth century has been mentioned. Around the turn of the century it had a dominant influence at German universities with philosophers, such as Wilhelm Dilthey (1833–1911) who in the 1890s published a classical treatise in which he made the distinction between *Erklären* and *Verstehen*. He maintained that the humanities had their own logic of research and pointed out that the difference between natural sciences and humanities was that the former tried to explain, whereas the latter tried to understand. He also maintained that there were two kinds of psychology, the one which by means of experimental methods attempted to generalize and predict, and the one that tried to understand the unique individual in its entire, concrete setting. Other philosophers with similar conceptions were Heinrich Rickert and Wilhelm Windelband. A counterpart in France was Henri Bergson (1859–1941) who maintained that the intellect was unable to grasp the living reality which could only be approached by means of intuition. In Sweden, John Landquist advanced an epistemology of human knowledge about human affairs.

A second strand was represented by the phenomenological philosophy developed by Edmund Husserl (1859–1938) in Germany. It emphasized the importance of taking a widened perspective and of trying to "get to the roots" of human activity. The phenomenological, and later the hermeneutic, approach is holistic, it tries by means of empathy (*Einfühlung*) to understand the motives behind human reactions. By widening the perspective and trying to understand human beings as individuals in their entirety and in their proper context it tries also to avoid the fragmentation caused by the positivistic and experimental approach that takes out a small slice which it subjects to closer scrutiny.

The third strand in the humanistic paradigm consists of the critical philosophy, not least the one of the Frankfurt school (Adorno, Horckheimer and Habermas) which developed with a certain amount of neo-Marxism. Marx himself would probably have felt rather ambivalent in an encounter between the two main scientific philosophies. On the one hand, he felt attracted to positivism and it is typical that Pavlovian behaviorism enjoyed a strong support in the Soviet Union. On the other hand, Marx belonged to the German philosophical tradition and the neo-Marxists have not had great difficulties in accepting hermeneutics and merging it with a dialectical approach.

The paradigm determines how a problem is formulated and methodologically tackled. According to the traditional positivist conception, problems that relate, for example, to classroom behavior should be investigated primarily in terms of the individual actor, either the pupils, who might be neurotic, or the teacher, who might be ill prepared for his or her job. The other conception is to formulate the problem in terms of the larger setting, that of the school, or rather that of the society at large. Furthermore, one does not in the first place, by means of such mechanisms as testing, observation, and the like, try to find out why the pupil or the teacher deviates from the "normal" or the established rules. Rather an attempt is made to study the particular individual as a goal-directed human being with particular and unique motives.

The belief that science, particularly social science, would "save us," was expressed as late as in the 1940s by George Lundberg (1947), a sociologist who represented a consistent positivist approach. In the long run the study of human beings would map out the social reality and provide a knowledge base for vastly improved methods of dealing with human beings, be they pupils in the classroom or workers in the factory. A similar hope still guided the establishment of Research and Development Centers with massive resources at some North American universities in the 1960s. What experience and enlightened empathy could tell was somehow regarded as inferior to the knowledge provided by systematic observations and measurements.

2. An Historical Note

In his *Talks to Teachers on Psychology,* given in the 1890s, William James pointed out: "To know psychology ... is absolutely no guarantee that we shall be good teachers." An additional ability is required, something that he calls the "happy tact and ingenuity," the "ingenuity in meeting and pursuing the pupil, the tact for the concrete situation." He mentions the demands of making systematic observations that some "enthusiasts for child study" have burdened the teachers with, including "compiling statistics and computing the percent." In order to avoid such endeavors resulting in trivialities they must be related to the "anecdotes and observations" which acquaint the teachers more intimately with the students.

What James refers to is something that in the terminology of today would be characterized as a conflict between two main research paradigms. By the turn of the century the scientific paradigm emerged that has since then been the prevailing one, at least in the Anglo–Saxon world. It was part of a larger movement towards "scientific management" in industry.

The new scientific approach emerging at the turn of the century was spelled out by the leading educational psychologist, Edward Lee Thorndike of Columbia University, in the preface to his seminal book *Educational Psychology* in 1903. He set out to apply "the methods of exact science" to educational problems, reject "speculative opinions," and emphasize "accurate quantitative treatment" of information collected. He acknowledged the influence on his thinking of people who have advocated the quantitative and experimental approach, like James McKeen Cattell and R. S. Woodworth in the United States and Francis Galton and Karl Pearson in England. In a brief concluding chapter he dealt with the problem of education as a science and presented the main characteristics of what he regarded as scientific in education:

> It is the vice or the misfortune of thinkers about education to have chosen the methods of philosophy or of popular thought instead of those of science.... The chief duty of serious students of the theory of education today is to form the habit of inductive study and learn the logic of statistics. (Thorndike 1903 p. 164)

Part of the new scientific paradigm was to make a clearcut distinction between the descriptive and the normative. Research conducted according to "logic" was supposed to be neutral with regard to policy making.

The prevailing paradigm in North America spelled out by Edward Lee Thorndike was further developed by John Franklin Bobbitt, professor at the University of Chicago, who in 1912 advanced the notion that schools could be operated according to the methods of "scientific management" which had been developed in industry by Frederick Taylor. Bobbitt also played an important role in attempts to determine empirically the content of curriculum by analyzing what people needed as holders of occupations and as citizens in order to arrive at a common denominator of skills and specific pieces of knowledge with which the school had to equip them.

With an eye on the natural sciences, social science has for more than two centuries made the claim to be an "objective" and "explaining" science. It purported to be able to make a clearcut distinction between aims and means of achieving these aims. It maintained that in handling social realities it was able to do it without any moral commitments. Its representatives claim to reside outside the system they observe. Such a claim has been brought into question. Gunnar Myrdal (1969) did so in a book (first published in Swedish in the 1930s) on science and politics in economics. He showed that the social researcher could not be free from his or her own values and political convictions, but could arrive at more valid conclusions and gain in credibility by making his or her value premises explicit and by making clear what those biases were in describing reality. Thereby the researcher can also give the "consumers" of his or her research an instrument for correction.

Social research, not least that in education, consists of data collection and reflection about societal problems, with their dilemmas and paradoxes, tensions, and so on, as well as alternatives for political action which offer themselves. Not even in the ideal case can a consensus be expected around theoretical paradigms as separated from practical problems. Social science researchers are part of the social process which they set out to investigate. They share social and political values of the surrounding society. In a way, they participate in the process of social self-understanding. This means that there is no such thing as a "social technology" in the same sense as a technology based on natural science. This does not imply, however, that educational research endeavors are of very limited value or entirely futile. The "aloofness" of the researchers in terms of dependence on interest groups and politics with shared social values is a relative matter. The task of the academic of "seeking the truth" can become institutionalized. This is what happens when fundamental, discipline-oriented research is established in institutions where the researchers can pursue their tasks of critical review without jeopardizing their positions.

There were those who, in contrast to William James, thought that it would be possible to make education a

science. One of them was Charles H. Judd, who in his book *Introduction to the Scientific Study of Education* in 1918 tried to explain how research was related to teacher training and educational practice. In 1909 the Department of Education at the University of Chicago had abandoned course requirements for prospective teachers in the history of education and psychology. These courses had been replaced by one course called "Introduction to Education" and one in "Methods of Teaching." Thereby the teacher candidates could be introduced to the school problems in "a more direct, concrete way." Each chapter in Judd's book presents practical school problems and gives sources of information for the solution of these problems. Much of this information is very incomplete, but as a whole Judd thinks that it is justified to speak about a "science of education." To use the term "science" he thinks would be justified, even when the information available is very scanty, "for the essence of science is its methods of investigation, not its ability to lay down a body of final rules of action" (Judd 1918 p. 299).

A research paradigm similar to the one advanced by Galton, Pearson, and Thorndike developed in Germany and France under the influence of experimental psychology. Ernst Meumann, a student of Wilhelm Wundt, a leading experimental psychologist, published at the beginning of the century his monumental three-volume work *Vorlesungen zur Einführung in die experimentelle Pädagogik* [Introduction to Experimental Pedagogy]. He meant by "experimental education" largely the application of the systematic, empirical, and statistical methods to educational data. Alfred Binet in France had a similar influence in both child study and intelligence testing.

3. The Need for Pluralism in Approaches

In the late 1960s and early 1970s critical, dialectical, hermeneutical, and neo-Marxian paradigms were advanced as alternatives or even replacements for the prevailing neopositivist paradigm of quantification, hypothesis testing, and generalizations. The latter had dominated the scene of social science research in the Anglo–Saxon countries for many decades and had taken the lead at many Continental universities as well. The new approaches were espoused by many from these universities to the extent that a group of younger researchers in education even prepared an international handbook of educational research that deliberately challenged the prevailing Anglo–Saxon research paradigms. The behavioral sciences have equipped educational researchers with an arsenal of research tools, such as observational methods and tests, which help them to systematize observations which would otherwise not have been considered in the more holistic and intuitive attempts to make, for instance, informal observations, or to conduct personal interviews.

Those who turn to social science research in order to find out about the "best" pedagogy or the most "efficient" methods of teaching are in a way victims of the traditional science which claimed to be able to arrive at generalizations applicable in practically every context. But, not least through critical philosophy, researchers have become increasingly aware that education does not take place in a social vacuum. Educational researchers have also begun to realize that educational practices are not independent of the cultural and social context in which they operate. Nor are they neutral to educational policies. Therefore, dogmatic evangelism for particular philosophies and ideologies espoused as "scientific" and not accessible to criticism is detrimental to the spirit of inquiry. The two main paradigms are not exclusive, but complementary to each other.

See also: Policy-oriented Research; Hermeneutics; History of Educational Research; Educational Research and Policy Making

Bibliography

Fritzell C 1981 *Teaching, Science and Ideology: A Critical Inquiry into the Sociology of Pedagogy.* Gleerup, Lund
Fromm E (ed.) 1965 *Socialist Humanism: An International Symposium.* Doubleday, Garden City, New York
Galtung J 1977 *Essays in Methodology*, Vol. 1: *Methodology and Ideology.* Ejlers, Copenhagen

Habermas J 1972 *Knowledge and Human Interests.* Heinemann, London
Heidegger M 1962 *Being and Time.* Harper, New York
Judd C 1918 *Introduction to the Scientific Study of Education.* Ginn, Boston, Massachusetts
Kuhn T S 1962 *The Structure of Scientific Revolutions.* University of Chicago Press, Chicago, Illinois
Lindholm S 1981 *Paradigms, Science and Reality: On Dialectics, Hermeneutics and Positivism in the Social Sciences.* Department of Education, University of Stockholm, Stockholm
Lundberg G 1947 *Can Science Save Us?* Longmans Green, London
Meumann E 1911 *Vorlesungen zur Einführung in die experimentelle Pädagogik und ihre Psychologischen Grundlagen.* Engelmann, Leipzig
Myrdal G 1969 *Objectivity in Social Research.* Pantheon, New York
Palmer R E 1969 *Hermeneutics: Interpretation Theory in Schleiermacher, Dilthey, Heidegger, and Gadamer.* Northwestern University Press, Evanston, Illinois
Rapoport A 1950 *Science and the Goals of Man: A Study in Semantic Orientation.* Harper, New York
Thorndike E L 1903 *Educational Psychology.* Scientific Press, New York
Wright G H von 1971 *Explanation and Understanding.* Routledge and Kegan Paul, London

Social Theory and Educational Research

J. P. Keeves

For much of the last 100 years, since the field of empirical research in education was first established, there was a stereotyped view that the research worker, trained in the discipline of psychology was well placed to prescribe for pedagogical practice the "do's" and "don'ts" which could be derived from the laws of generalizations of psychological theory. The audiences for the counsel of the educational research worker and psychologist were practising classroom teachers who sought to improve both student learning and the efficiency of their daily work (Jackson and Kiesler 1977). It is perhaps not surprising that this view should have been advanced at a time when psychology was developing as a science and when empirical research in education was being established as a systematic activity. However, with the growth of the field of educational research after the Second World War, and more particularly as a result of the injection of substantial funds for educational research in the 1960s, scholars from disciplines other than psychology became active in the investigation of educational problems. These scholars came, in the main, from the social science disciplines of sociology, political science, economics, demography, anthropology, and linguistics. They brought with them different perspectives and they frequently saw educational problems in terms of social theory.

The dominant view of social processes in the 1960s was that of structural functionalism, which was a perspective where the influence of Parsons in the United States had been highly significant. Parsons interpreted the social theories of European scholars of the nineteenth and early twentieth centuries, including Durkheim, Weber and Pareto and to a lesser degree Marx. In addition, he developed the functionalist conception of sociology. Although his writings were complex, his ideas had considerable appeal and influence. From this perspective educational inquiry could no longer be seen as a field where psychological principles only would be applied. For example, Feinberg has argued recently that the appropriate perspective for educational inquiry is that of social reproduction, since:

Education is best understood by recognizing that one of the functions of any society is that of maintaining intergenerational continuity — that is, of maintaining its identity as a society across generations and even in the context of many possible and significant changes, and that it is the activity and institution of education, both formal and informal, that carries on this function. (Feinberg 1983 p. 6)

While these views involving an emphasis in educational research on social theory were not new, since they were shared with Plato, Marx, and Dewey, they have had a growing influence on the conduct of inquiry into educational problems.

Nonetheless, from the 1970s functionalism as an approach to research in the social sciences has been under siege. The perspectives provided by positivism and the scientific approach, which underpinned both functionalism and an alternative but related approach of naturalism, were based on the strategies of inquiry of the natural sciences, particularly the biological sciences. They were strongly challenged as being inappropriate for inquiry in the social sciences and for educational research. An alternative approach has emerged with a humanistic perspective. In addition critical theory has become established and has sought not only to understand the relations between value, interest, action, and power, but also to change society. These new approaches have also advanced new research perspectives and methodologies including those of ethnomethodology, ethnography, symbolic interactionism, historical materialism, action research, participatory research, cultural anthropology, social phenomenology, dramaturgical sociology, as well as critical social science. During the past 15 years the many alternative approaches to the study of society and to research in the field of education have generated both conflict and confusion, as they have competed against one another for scholarly acceptance.

The recent debate that has taken place with respect to both educational and social science research has been concerned with the merits and demerits of quantitative or qualitative research, with issues of the value-free or value-laden nature of investigation in the social sciences, and with the roles of understanding (*Verstehen*) as contrasted with explanation (*Erklären*). The view has been advanced that the humanistic and scientific approaches should be seen as complementary to one another rather than in direct opposition (see *Research Paradigms in Education*). However, important theoretical developments have taken place during recent years that have clarified the nature of social theory and as a consequence the nature of social research. These developments, as exemplified in the writings of Giddens (1984), are leading to a unification of the alternative views of social science and educational research. The advancement of a coherent approach to investigation in these fields, that recognizes the shortcomings of structural functionalism, and makes provision for the key ideas contained in the many different research strategies which have been proposed during the past 15 years, is an important and in many ways exciting development. Before considering these changes in the field of social theory it is necessary to examine three aspects of the differences which are said to exist between investigation in the social and natural sciences.

1. The Social and the Natural Sciences

Three aspects of inquiry in the social and natural sciences are of interest at this time. First, there is concern for the nature of the worlds of inquiry. Secondly, there is concern for the epistemological origins of inquiry.

Thirdly, there is concern for the nature of the generalizations that can be made within the two approaches to inquiry of the scientific and humanistic research traditions.

1.1 The Worlds of Inquiry

Popper and Eccles (1977) have distinguished between three worlds of inquiry. The entities of the real world are World 1. The products of the human mind that are built into a corpus of knowledge form World 3. World 3 contains within it propositional knowledge. The important point is that World 3 objects acquire a reality of their own. There is in addition, however, a world of individual mental states, which comprises the states of consciousness and psychological dispositions as well as the unconscious states of individuals. Popper and Eccles refer to this as World 2. Contained within World 2 is personal knowledge. Educational research in the area of metacognition seeks to map certain aspects of this personal knowledge, recognizing that it is heavily overlaid by the mental state of each individual. Personal knowledge about education and society is acquired in part from experience and in part from corporate bodies of knowledge, commonly presented in propositional form. Inquiry conducted from the humanistic perspective contributes very directly to personal knowledge through the interpretations it provides of social and educational processes. Information obtained through these strategies is presented in such a way as to appeal to individual readers. In so far as it is commonly concerned with motives and expressed reasons this information can interact readily with existing personal knowledge. It seeks to build directly new personal knowledge for each individual. Subsequently, it may prove possible to develop theory from this personal knowledge and transfer ideas to a corporate body of propositional knowledge concerned with causal explanation which resides in World 3. It should be noted that World 3 also contains works of art, music, and literary writings that are parts of the world of shared knowledge.

The body of propositional knowledge that has been assembled by the natural sciences can be used to transform the real world through technology. Moreover, it has been the marked success of research and development strategies in the physical and biological sciences acting through technology that has enhanced the standing of both scientific research and technological development not only in the field of scholarly inquiry but also in daily life. Furthermore, it has been the apparent failure of the social and behavioural sciences, and of educational inquiry, to use their findings through technology and strategies of research, development and dissemination that has led to disillusionment and a serious questioning of the relevance of educational and social science research.

Figure 1 presents in diagrammatic form some of the relationships that exist between these three worlds of inquiry, and technology.

From the perspectives of both functionalism and naturalism there are no essential differences between

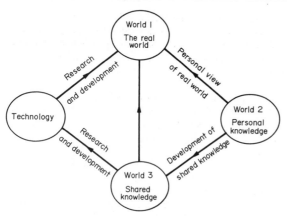

Figure 1
The worlds of inquiry

inquiry in the natural sciences and the social sciences. Both fields of inquiry are considered to be involved in the development of a shared body of knowledge about the real world. The real world is knowable through direct observation or through the use of instrumentation, and the research worker seeks to eliminate personal values from the observations made and the measurements recorded by complex instruments. However, during the past 15 years in educational and social science research, the approaches of both functionalism and naturalism have been questioned.

1.2 Epistemological Origins of Inquiry

Recently our understanding of the epistemological origins of knowledge that is developed within both the scientific and humanistic perspectives has changed. It is argued that no longer can these two approaches be seen to be substantially different. Furthermore, it is acknowledged that both scientific and social science research workers are influenced by their previous knowledge and theories which guide what they observe and record from the real world. In neither field is it possible to contend that the real world can be apprehended independent of our previous knowledge and theories of the world. Thus Quinean philosophy argues that either field of inquiry belongs to the same coherent "web of belief" (Quine and Ullian 1970). While the extent to which a personal view of the real world is permitted to intrude on inquiry may differ between different fields of investigation, the differences that occur are ones of degree and not of kind.

Furthermore, while the extent to which abstraction occurs, and the extent to which measurement is employed, may differ between the two fields, both quality and quantity are misconceived if they are considered to be alternatives and antithetical to one another and are employed to differentiate between the two fields (Kaplan 1964 p. 207). Thus it is argued that there is a unity of inquiry, in social science and educational research, derived from the epistemological basis of

inquiry whatever approach is taken, namely, the scientific perspective or the humanistic perspective. Furthermore, the methods that are employed in both the sciences and the social sciences are determined by the problem in need of resolution. The goal of inquiry is to develop answers to the questions being investigated and to solve problems.

1.3 Laws and Generalizations

The success of the natural sciences would appear to arise from the capacity of inquiry to advance generalizations that possess a universality which entitles them to be classified as laws. In this respect the social sciences have not experienced the same degree of success. However, it is necessary to recognize that the laws of science are not absolute truths which are established after the facts have been obtained. They have initially been developed from theory which has a role in the process of determining what the facts are. In these matters the generalizations of science do not differ from those of the social sciences. However, the major findings of science are concerned with relationships where a very large number of elementary units is involved. Such relationships are essentially probabilistic statements, where the probability of a statement holding in any particular situation is unity not because of inherent certainty but because with very large numbers the probabilities are extremely close to 1.0. In the social sciences the situations being investigated rarely involve such very large numbers of elementary units so that probabilities of 1.0 could not be expected. However, social science research workers have over the past two decades learnt to work with probabilities of less than unity, and computers have become available so that a large enough number of cases can be investigated for stable estimates of probabilities to be recorded.

In addition, recent developments in statistical analysis have made it possible for statistical control to be exercised in order to make allowance for the many factors that operate in any particular situation in educational and social science investigations. The differences between the natural and the social sciences lie not in the approaches to investigation but in the large number of factors over which some control must be exercised in the social sciences and in education. The differences between the natural sciences and the social sciences are not essentially differences in kind but rather differences in degree.

There are, however, differences between the social sciences and the natural sciences that recent inquiry into social theory has exposed. These differences do not arise from the epistemological foundations of research, where an essential unity exists. However, it is recognized that the universality of the laws of science is in marked contrast to the limited nature of the generalizations that can be established in the social sciences. These recent developments in social theory are considered in the next section

2. Recent Changes in Social Theory

Giddens in an unpublished address given at the University of Melbourne, August 1986, has identified four areas of social theory where important developments have emerged which, if recognized, help to resolve the conflicts that have arisen between the alternative approaches to research in the social sciences and education.

2.1 The Nature of the Human Agent

It must be acknowledged that in social science and educational research the individual person, with his or her unique personal knowledge that constitutes World 2, has a very different role in the study of problems in society and education from the role played by the individual in the investigation of phenomena in the natural sciences. However, the widely held view during the years when functionalism dominated inquiry in the social sciences was that human beings, in the main, did not understand why they behaved as they did and that the purpose of the social sciences was to investigate and to explain the behaviour of groups of human beings. In the famous sociological study of suicide by Durkheim, it was found that suicide rates remained constant across years within particular countries, but differed significantly between countries. This finding was used to argue that social causes were required to explain the factors that lead individuals to kill themselves. Likewise, in the educational field, it is found that retention rates at the terminal year of schooling not only differ between countries, between school types, between social class groups, and between schools, but also remain remarkably constant across years within any particular group. Clearly, different students are involved in deciding whether to leave school or remain to Year 12 each year, yet a surprising degree of regularity is observed between schools and other groups over time. On the surface it would appear that sociological factors should be invoked to provide an explanation of such data, and that an account in terms of purely psychological principles would be inadequate.

This oversimplified view, which is quite commonly advanced in explanations of social class differences in educational outcomes and practices has been largely discredited. Individuals cannot be regarded as passive units in the analysis of evidence from a sociological perspective or even as neutral subjects in psychological research. Human beings must be considered rather as active agents, who know what they are doing in most situations and are making conscious decisions with regard to their actions. In this respect they differ in significant ways from animals, which are the units of much biological research concerned with the effects of environmental and ecological forces. It must also be acknowledged that not only do most individuals know what they are doing most of the time but, as those philosophers influenced by Wittgenstein have shown, they have, and can provide, reasons for their decisions. Human beings are not just puppets operated within a social system by social forces. What happens to them in society is at least to some extent the consequence of deliberate efforts by the individuals to make it happen. From the perspectives of naturalism there would be a search for the underlying causes for both group and individual behaviour. However, a new perspective of human agency is emerging that seeks to investigate both the reasons and intentions of individuals as agents as well as those institutional and social phenomena that influence individuals independently of their own volition.

As an example of these newer perspectives, Giddens (1984) has reexamined the findings which Willis (1977) reported in his study of working-class boys at school in a poor district of Birmingham, England. Willis treats the boys as actors who have a considerable tacit and discursive knowledge of the school and social environment of which they are a part. The behaviour of the boys is influenced by the knowledge that they will take up unskilled and unrewarding jobs when they leave. As a consequence, they develop rebellious attitudes towards the authority system of the school that are consistent with the attitudes they will develop towards authority in the workplace and on the shop floor, and which they learn from their parents and older mates. They employ humour, banter and aggressive sarcasm in a single-minded way to challenge and test authority. They are purposeful agents in their social activities exploring the intended and unintended consequences of their actions. Thus the behaviour of individual agents is influenced by the larger social setting and constrained by the smaller cultural setting of which they are part. However, such agents know what they are doing and can provide an account of their actions.

It is necessary to recognize that much of what is known to human agents is not known in the form of reasoned argument. A high level of skill is required to be an effective member of society, but many of the skills developed cannot be readily stated, since language is extremely complicated. The fact that much knowledge is tacit does not mean that it does not influence the actions of an individual. This, in part, renders inaccessible some of the reasons for the decisions that an individual makes, but it also provides a new perspective with respect to language.

2.2 The Nature of Language

During recent years there have been significant advances in both philosophy and social theory with respect to the use of language. The traditional view of language and its relationship to human activity has been that language was a medium used by human beings to describe things. From this perspective language was a symbol system that enabled us to communicate with each other and to generate a description of the world in which we live Wittgenstein in his earlier writings accepted this view that language was a medium of description and to a considerable degree, reflected what the world was like. Subsequently Wittgenstein proposed radical changes to this view. He has argued that language is all the things you do with language. In daily life, language is used to get things done in a social context in which actions must be taken in conjunction with other human beings. The consequence of this new understanding of language is that the written text and the spoken word have no essence of their own. They can only be interpreted within the context of the practical actions involved where language is a form of social activity.

The change in emphasis and understanding of the nature of language is all the more important when it is recognized that in everyday life the use of language commonly occurs at a tacit level. Day to day actions are taken through a form of language that presumes a great deal more than is actually said. Furthermore, those things that are not said must necessarily be done. Language is a substitute for action, and action replaces the things that cannot be said. When viewed from this perspective, language has a very different role from that where it is used merely for descriptive purposes. This changing view of language is related to the examination and study of meaning which will be discussed at a later section of this article. It also leads to a changing view of the nature of social action.

2.3 The Nature of Social Action

During the last 100 years many different views of the nature of social inquiry have been held, including the perspectives of Marxism and pragmatism. However, those research workers who were conducting inquiry in the social sciences within the perspectives of functionalism or naturalism sought universal generalizations about the social world. Knowledge of these generalizations would allow the introduction of change for the betterment of society. These views were particularly strongly held in the field of educational research. The research, development and dissemination model was seen to apply both in the field of education as well as the other social sciences, and this model was considered to operate in much the same way as technology generated by the natural sciences was seen to provide control and to permit change of the natural world. The dream of some research workers in the social sciences was that by obtaining knowledge about the processes of human society, it would be possible to control the social world. They sought to provide a social technology and to engage in social engineering that paralleled the scientific technology of the nineteenth century. Because of the success of inquiry in the physical and biological sciences this has been the dominant view in most discussions about the practical implications of the social sciences, and it is this approach that has been involved in the current accusations by administrators, politicians and natural scientists of the paucity of practical results arising from educational and social science research. Furthermore, it is the view that seeks to identify tangible evidence of the applications of educational and social science research in practice.

In the mid-1950s it was possible to answer the critics of educational and social science research with proposals for both increased funding and significant expansion of research activity. In addition, it was commonly claimed that with increased resources and effort both important generalizations and significant practical applications would emerge. Today, we are coming to recognize that such a view was simplistic and naive. However, there is no doubt that the increased resources for educational research, in particular, transformed this area of inquiry in the period of 20 years from the early 1960s to the early 1980s. An immense body of knowledge about educational and social processes was assembled that is only now being assimilated in a purposeful and meaningful way. Nevertheless, it is also apparent that few universal generalizations have emerged that can be directly applied to benefit either educational practice or the operation of society.

Giddens (1984) argues that we have failed to understand in an adequate way the nature of social action in the context of a new social theory. He contends that the technological view of the application of social science research is grossly inadequate, and that there is a sense in which such a view has seriously underestimated the practical impact of research in education and the social sciences on the world in which we live.

In the quest for universal generalizations in the study of educational processes and in social research we have failed to recognize the existence of World 2 and the role of human agents in society. Furthermore, Giddens (1984) argues that we have misunderstood the nature of the relationships associated with language as a form of practical action or praxis. In the study of educational problems and societal processes, human beings as a group do not remain as passive subjects of inquiry. They comprehend the debate which arises during the formulation of ideas, and they not only assimilate these ideas but they also accommodate to them and are changed. Thus as we have indicated in Fig. 1, World 3, the world of shared ideas, interacts with World 2, the world of personal knowledge, to such an extent that the views and perceptions of World 1, the world of real things, held by human agents, are changed. Since the real world is itself unknowable without these views and perceptions which are held by human beings, and thus the very foundations of our knowledge are without certainty, we are confronted with a situation in which generalizations are advanced, but their existence has been generated from the social theories held by research workers.

It is clear that Popper and Eccles (1977) are concerned with these same issues, approaching these problems from the perspective of the natural scientist. However, the problems are of greater magnitude in the social sciences because, as recent developments in social theory have proposed, human beings act as social agents. Furthermore, universal schooling and widespread higher education have during recent decades greatly facilitated the dissemination of advances in social theory through paperback publication, journal articles and the mass media. As a consequence the rate of change of social and educational processes has been significantly increased.

An example drawn from the field of education is informative of how such processes work. In the years following the Second World War, initially in the United States, scales of socioeconomic status (SES) were developed and it was soon shown convincingly that there was a clearly identifiable relationship between the SES level of the home and achievement of children at school. Research of this kind was repeated in the United Kingdom and the general relationship confirmed. Soon this relationship was found to have a generality that was sustained in most developed countries, although variations were detected in some less developed countries. It was clear that where large random samples of students were drawn from age populations in which all children in an age group were still at school, this general relationship was observed. It was argued that children from homes of low socioeconomic status were educationally deprived and compensatory programmes to overcome educational disadvantage were needed. However, when the recipients of such programmes learnt of the purposes of these compensatory programmes and the emergent theory concerned with cultural and social deprivation, they resented these perspectives and the labels which were attached. Consequently, the emphasis of the programmes was changed. There was concern for equity rather than equality, since the recipients of the programmes commonly did not wish to be equal, but rather to share more fully in the rewards of society on their own terms. While the general relationships recorded several decades ago remain, the social theory has changed and the nature and administration of such programmes have been modified in significant ways.

Keeves (1986) has reviewed these changes in programmes for educational disadvantage in Australia. There is no doubt that social theory has had a significant influence on the establishment of such programmes of social action. However, in the process of introducing these programmes the views of the recipients have changed both the nature of the programmes and the underlying social theory associated with these aspects of social reality. Similar accounts could be given of the changes that have occurred in the fields of equal opportunity according to sex, and multiculturalism in those societies where significant variation in ethnic mix occurs. These are fields where the world of educational inquiry interacts with that of sociology and social inquiry.

There are important reasons why it is not possible to point to a substantial number of universal generalizations which have been generated by educational and social science research. When from a study of human action, new ideas and concepts emerge which explain a social process in a clearer way than members of society are themselves able to provide, these ideas are appropriated by those members of society and incorporated back into their social lives. Sometimes these ideas have the effect of changing social life, and sometimes the effect of changing the nature of the ideas and concepts of social theory. It is not the case that the initial views and generalizations associated with the educational and social processes were necessarily wrong, but rather that the ideas were so powerful that they changed both the social processes as well as perceptions of them. The original ideas were not trivial or of little consequence but, as a result of their formulation and dissemination by the social scientist, society itself was changed. However, the impact of new ideas and theories in the social sciences depends upon how human agents assimilate and accommodate to these new ideas and theories, and this view leads us to consider a changing approach to hermeneutic inquiry.

2.4 The Nature of the Double Hermeneutic

The hermeneutic approach to inquiry in education and the social sciences has long been established in continental Europe. It involves the study of meaning and comprises the theory and practice of interpretation and understanding in the different social contexts in which human beings live and work. It has developed from many different facets of scholarly inquiry in the social sciences, and its goal is that of understanding (*Verstehen*) in the study of human conduct within a social context. Moreover, this approach recognizes that in order to obtain meaning with respect to how and why humans act it is necessary for an investigator to enter into dialogue with the human agents. Furthermore, the changing view of language extends the range of hermeneutic inquiry to include the use of language in daily life at the tacit level as well as at the discursive level. Thus, inquiry may be concerned with the meaning of action for which language is a substitute. However, the changes that have occurred in social theory with respect to the nature of social action and the influence of ideas and social theory on personal knowledge require further changes in the hermeneutic approach to inquiry.

Giddens (1984) argues that a double hermeneutic is involved. There is not only the frame of meaning provided by individuals as they view the real world, or the interaction between World 2 and World 1 as shown in Fig. 1. There is also a second frame of meaning provided by the same individuals as they view the world of shared meaning and assimilate the ideas and concepts developed by social scientists. In Fig. 1 this would require an arrow from World 3 to World 2. Thus, an investigation of the meanings given by lay persons to both the events of the real world and the ideas and concepts of the social sciences is necessary. In the situation discussed earlier, where there was concern for equality of educational opportunity, the social scientists and educational research workers involved employed such phrases as "educationally disadvantaged" and "culturally deprived" as metalanguage terms to describe human agents in specific situations. However, those human agents saw the context in which they lived very differently. They did not regard themselves as deprived or disadvantaged, but rather lacking the power to obtain social justice. As a consequence they sought greater equity in their treatment by those in power, and greater empowerment and thus greater control over their own lives. The intersection of the two frames of meaning generated a change both in the ideas employed in relation to equality or equity in society as well as change in praxis and the administration of the programmes. In the past, hermeneutic inquiry has explored the meaning of social reality from one direction only. There is, however, a double hermeneutic involved and meaning must be examined from two different perspectives, since the ideas and concepts of the social sciences circulate back into the world in which they were developed and become part of the processes of observing and describing that world.

2.5 Summary

The four changes outlined above help to map out a new approach to social theory in which there are possibilities of a synthesis taking place across the many apparently conflicting alternative theoretical and methodological perspectives that have been advanced during the past 15 years. In addition, it is evident that this emerging synthesis carries across the wide range of disciplines that comprise the field of the social sciences and the humanities. Because education has a key role in the processes of social reproduction, the four areas of change — namely, the nature of the human agent, the nature of language, the nature of social action, and the nature of the double hermeneutic — are all closely related to educational processes. Consequently, the domain of educational sociology and the activity of educational research assume within this new perspective an even more central position than they have previously held. Nonetheless, it must be acknowledged that the ideas and changes discussed in this article are presented from the perspective of sociology and social theory. No consideration has so far been given to human learning and the processes by which it occurs. It is clear that the contribution of learning to social reproduction cannot be overlooked, and that the viewpoint of psychology cannot be ignored. In the main, psychological research workers have adopted a positivist perspective. Whether this perspective can be maintained in view of the recent changes to social theory is uncertain. The changes described above with respect to the nature of the human agent provide human beings with greater autonomy than has commonly been granted to them in the past by existing psychological theories.

Giddens (1984) has developed a "theory of structuration" that incorporates and extends some of the ideas presented in this article, in which he has attempted to overcome many of the unwanted and unwarranted dualisms that have arisen between earlier social theories. Giddens accepts the Parsonian view that the problem of order in the social world is the central problem confronting social theory, but a strictly deterministic perspective is necessarily rejected in a conception which grants human agents greater autonomy. Thus, a stochastic perspective would appear to be required to permit causal relationships to be examined in situations where strict determinism must be abandoned. In the past 20 years social science and educational research have advanced in directions that would permit such a perspective to be maintained not only in theory but also

from the standpoint of systematic investigation. Whether or not Giddens's theory of structuration would permit the investigation of causal relationships from this perspective is not clear. However, it is evident that the forced dualism between the quantitative and qualitative approaches to inquiry is being rejected in the social sciences. This leaves the way clear for an alternative to be advanced that unifies the divergent approaches that currently exist in educational and social science research.

3. Towards the Future

If we accept the changes outlined above, then it is possible to consider where social science and educational inquiry might proceed in the future. If these changes are rejected in whole or in part we are forced back to the situation of conflict and confusion that has beset investigation in this area during the past 15 years. The emergent synthesis that Giddens has advanced would seem to draw strength from its potential to resolve conflict and from its capacity to account for the unresolved issues that have confronted philosophers and social theorists during recent decades. Several signposts which point the way ahead for future research and inquiry can be advanced.

3.1 Nonrecursive Systems

Most of the causal models that have been employed to examine in probabilistic or stochastic terms the influence of individual and group variables on educational outcomes have been recursive models that have made no allowances for interactive effects. If human agents are influenced by forces in their environment and in turn interact with and change the environment, then a recursive model is inappropriate. Until recently it has been difficult to examine and estimate the parameters of nonrecursive models. However, it is now possible in particular circumstances to develop and test by a variety of analytical techniques causal models that include such interaction effects, provided an instrumental variable can be identified and the model is fully specified. The techniques that have been employed in educational research include indirect regression analysis (Hauser 1973, Larkin and Keeves 1984), or two-stage least squares regression analysis when included in partial least squares path analysis (Sellin 1986). The increased availability of appropriate computer programs is likely to lead to increased use of this type of analysis, and the possibility of investigating the magnitudes of relationships associated with reciprocal effects involving human agents must be welcomed.

3.2 Multilevel Analysis

The concept of a human agent acting within a specified context that involves both individual level as well as group level factors has in the past been difficult to investigate. This has been a consequence of:

(a) the known effects of aggregation bias;

(b) the conceptual problems of disaggregation of data from the group level to the individual level;

(c) the ecological fallacy associated with analysis undertaken at the group level when inferences at the individual level are required; and

(d) the lack of meaning and instability of estimates of contextual effects in individual level analysis using an aggregated variable.

Recently in both social science and educational research, work has been undertaken to investigate strategies of multilevel analysis that would permit individual level effects to be disentangled from group level effects. The long-term prospects of this development are highly promising and the implications for the sociology of education where both sociological and psychological factors are being examined is considerable.

3.3 Inquiries into Metacognition

During recent years investigations have been conducted in the area of metacognition. A great deal more needs to be known about how the concepts and theories of the social sciences modify the personal knowledge of individuals and how such personal knowledge not only influences individual action but in turn changes social concepts and theory. This is now a potentially fruitful field of inquiry with consequences in the longer term for educational practice, particularly if allowance can be made for the autonomy of the individual when engaged in learning.

3.4 Studies of Social Action

Giddens's (1984) review of recent changes in theories of social action helps to account for the paradox as to why social science and educational research have appeared so unrewarding for those who have invested both time and resources in this enterprise. In order to provide support for Giddens's ideas it would seem desirable that a series of case studies in different disciplinary areas should be undertaken to show how the theories developed in the different disciplines have had a substantial influence on the operation of modern society and the daily lives of human agents. The field of education and, in particular, the sociology of education is a potentially rich one for such investigation since the striking phenomena of the past 100 years have been the development of universal primary education, the moves towards a high level of participation in secondary education, the expansion of tertiary education, and the recent emergence of lifelong or recurrent education. These developments have their origins in changes in social theory. In turn, these developments have led to marked advances in social theory itself. Connell (1980) has documented this development, but the interpretation of this remarkable story in terms of Giddens's ideas remains.

4. Conclusion

The apparent failure of social science and educational research to produce universal generalizations should not be overemphasized. The application of the technique of meta-analysis is starting to bear fruit and the past few years have seen an assimilation of findings from disparate sources and the assembling of a substantial body of knowledge about educational processes in particular. Nevertheless, Giddens has argued that the emergence of new ideas and relationships in the fields of the social sciences and education is commonly accompanied by the widespread acceptance of those ideas by human agents in society, and that the ideas are brought back into the praxis of everyday life and have the effect of changing society. Thus, contrary to common belief, the concepts of the social sciences have helped in a highly significant way to restructure society, and consequently to change the circumstances under which the general relationships were established. Thus generalizations which are reported in the fields of education and the social sciences must be considered to be less immutable and to lack the permanence of generalizations reported in the natural sciences. Currently, we live in a world of quite tremendous social change, much of which has resulted probably not from scientific research and the accompanying technological development, but from research in the social sciences and a greater understanding of the social and educational processes which have served to reshape the world they have sought both to interpret and explain.

Bibliography

Connell W F 1980 *A History of Education in the Twentieth Century World*. Teachers College Press, New York

Feinberg W 1983 *Understanding Education. Toward a Reconstruction of Educational Inquiry*. Cambridge University Press, Cambridge

Giddens A 1984 *The Constitution of Society*. Polity Press, Cambridge and Blackwell, Oxford

Hauser R M 1973 *Sociological Background and Educational Performance*. American Sociological Association, Washington, D.C.

Jackson P W, Kieslar S B 1977 Fundamental research in education. *Educ. Res.* 6(8): 13–18

Kaplan A 1964 *The Conduct of Inquiry*. Chandler, San Francisco, California

Keeves J P 1986 *Equitable Opportunities in Australian Education*. Victorian Government Printer, Melbourne

Larkin A I, Keeves J P 1984 *The Class Size Question: A Study at Different Levels of Analysis*. Australian Council for Educational Research (ACER), Hawthorn, Victoria

Popper K R, Eccles J C 1977 *The Self and Its Brain*. Routledge and Kegan Paul, London

Quine W V O, Ullian J S 1970 *The Web of Belief*. Random House, New York

Sellin N 1986 Partial least squares analysis. *Int. J. Educ. Res.* 10(2): 189–200

Willis P 1977 *Learning to Labour*. Saxon House, Farnborough, England

The Epistemological Unity of Educational Research

J. C. Walker and C. W. Evers

Epistemology is the study of the nature, scope, and applicability of knowledge. Educational research, in being concerned with the conduct of educational inquiry and the development and evaluation of its methods and findings, embodies a commitment to epistemological assumptions. At least it does if its findings are expected to command attention, serve as a sound basis for action, or constitute legitimate knowledge claims. These matters are the subject of epistemological theories which deal more systematically with such general corresponding issues as justification, truth, and the accessibility of reality in the search for knowledge.

In educational research, obviously, there are different methods of inquiry, ranging from controlled laboratory experiments through participant observation to action research, from historical studies to logical analysis. These have been organized in different research traditions, such as "quantitative" and "qualitative", or associated with different theoretical positions, such as behaviourism and critical theory. Of course, in practice, the categories of method, tradition, and theoretical position cut across each other to some extent.

The major epistemological question here is whether these distinctions are associated with different ways of knowing or forms of knowledge, which partition educational research so that research traditions, for example, turn out to be radically distinct epistemologically, each having its own theories and rules of justification, meaning, and truth. If so, the next question is whether findings produced by the different traditions can be rationally integrated, rendered coherent, or even compared. For this to be possible, for traditions to be commensurable, there will have to be some shared concepts and standards of justification, meaning, and truth: some epistemological touchstone. If, however, the traditions are so fundamentally disparate that any choice between them in educational research is arbitrary or the result of nonrational commitment — an act of faith — there is no touchstone. The research traditions are incommensurable.

There has long been controversy over these issues, in educational research and the social sciences generally, as advocates of research traditions variously described as "scientific", "humanistic", "quantitative", "qualitative", "positivist" and "interpretative" have tried to sort out the respective epistemological merits of these approaches and the methodological, practical, and even political relations between them.

There are three major views available, which have emerged in educational research in more or less the following historical order. First, it can be asserted that there are epistemologically different paradigms, which are incommensurable in that neither educational research nor any other form of inquiry can provide a rational method for judging between them. Moreover,

they are mutually incompatible, competitive ways of researching the same territory. Let us call this the "oppositional diversity thesis". Second, we could decide that there are epistemologically distinct paradigms, but that though incommensurable they are complementary, not competitive: equally appropriate ways of approaching different, overlapping, or perhaps even the same research problems. Let us call this the "complementary diversity thesis". The first and the second views agree that there is a fundamental epistemological diversity in educational research. The third alternative, the unity thesis, denies this. It disagrees with the view that different research methods can be grouped under incommensurable paradigms, and asserts that the very idea of such paradigms is mistaken, even incoherent. It claims there is touchstone for judging the respective merits of different research traditions and bringing them into a productive relationship with one another. It asserts a fundamental epistemological unity of educational research, derived from the practical problems addressed.

This article argues for the unity thesis. After a discussion of the term "paradigm", and of the oppositional and complementary diversity theses, we show that the theory that there are research paradigms — call it the "P-theory" — is largely responsible for both forms of diversity thesis. We then give some reasons for believing that P-theory is incoherent, and argue that a coherent epistemology sustains the thesis of the epistemological unity of educational research. A feature of this epistemology is its account of touchstone in educational research.

1. Epistemology and Paradigms

Numerous educational researchers have been drawn to the view that research traditions are best regarded as different paradigms. Indeed, as Shulman (1985 p. 3) observes, in writing about the different research programmes of communities of scholars engaged in the study of teaching, "the term most frequently employed to describe such research communities, and the conceptions of problem and method they share, is *paradigm*".

As the quantitative/qualitative debate shows, many recent writers in education distinguish two fundamental paradigms of research: the "scientific", which is often erroneously identified with positivism, and the "interpretative" or "humanistic". Husén (*Research Paradigms in Education* p. 17) associates the distinction with divergent forms of explanation and understanding:

> The twentieth century has seen the conflict between two main paradigms employed in researching educational problems. The one is modeled on the natural sciences with an emphasis on empirical quantifiable observations which lend themselves to analyses by means of mathematical tools. The task of research is to establish causal relationships, to explain (*Erklären*). The other paradigm is derived from the

humanities with an emphasis on holistic and qualitative information and to interpretive approaches (*Verstehen*).

In offering a broader, three-way, taxonomy of research to account for diversity in inquiry, Popkewitz (1984 p. 35) says: "...the concept of paradigm provides a way to consider this divergence in vision, custom and tradition. It enables us to consider science as having different sets of assumptions, commitments, procedures and theories of social affairs". He assumes that "in educational sciences, three paradigms have emerged to give definition and structure to the practice of research". After the fashion of "critical theory" (Habermas 1972), he identifies the paradigms as "empirical–analytic" (roughly equivalent to quantitative science), "symbolic" (qualitative and interpretative or hermeneutical inquiry), and "critical" (where political criteria relating to human betterment are applied in research).

Noting the influence of positivism on the formation of research traditions and the paradigms debate, Lincoln and Guba (1985 p. 15) mention another common three-way distinction, which they apply to "paradigm eras", "periods in which certain sets of basic beliefs have guided inquiry in quite different ways", rather than directly to paradigms as such. They identify these paradigm eras as "prepositivist", "positivist" and "postpositivist". Now the term "positivist" also has a history of varied usage (Phillips 1983) but, because of the practice common among educational researchers of defining their perspectives in relation to one or more of the varieties of positivism, it is important to note some of the issues involved in the transition to postpositivism.

In philosophy of science, views of the nature of science commonly described as positivist have characterized science as value-free, basing its theories and findings on logically simple and epistemically secure observation reports, and using empirical concepts themselves deriving directly from observation (Hooker 1975). Positivism in this sense, as a form of empiricism, involves a *foundational* epistemology. Knowledge claims are justified when they are shown to be based on secure foundations, which for positivistic empiricism are the sense data acquired through empirical observation. Some positivists — the logical positivists — maintained that only the sentences of science *thus conceived*, and the "conceptual truths" of logic and mathematics, were objectively meaningful, and that therefore here were to be drawn the limits of genuine knowledge, not simply scientific knowledge. Thus delimited, the domain of knowledge excluded morals, politics, and indeed any field where value judgments were made, which would include much educational research. The movement to postpositivist philosophy of science has occurred because of the undermining of all such doctrines.

This use of "positivist" needs to be clearly distinguished from use of the term to describe *any* view that science (and perhaps conceptual truths of logic and mathematics), even if conceived nonpositivistically (in the first sense), is the only way to knowledge, and that

the task of philosophy, which is not sharply distinguished from but continuous with empirical science, is to find general principles common to all sciences and even to extend the use of such principles to the regulation of human conduct and the organization of society. The move to a postpositivist (in the first sense) philosophy of science is quite compatible with such a view of the nature of science and its role in human affairs.

Unfortunately, this distinction is not always clearly observed in epistemological discussions of educational research. It is one thing to say, with Lincoln and Guba (1985), that since it has been recognized that science is more complex than building on theory-free and value-free observations, qualitative inquiry may be recognized as a legitimate approach; that the latest paradigm era sanctions more than one paradigm. It is another thing to identify science with positivism (in the first sense) and on the basis of this identification to attack all views suggesting an epistemological continuity between the natural and the social sciences including educational research. Ironically, many writers, while they claim to reject positivism (in both senses), retain a positivist (in the first sense) view of *natural* science (e.g. Habermas 1972). In this article we use *positivist* in the first sense, to refer to positivistic empiricism, including logical positivism.

In summary, the move from a positivist to a postpositivist philosophy of science has been paralleled by a move from a view of educational research dominated by the quantitative tradition to a more pluralistic view. The advent of the postpositivist era has been characterized by an acceptance of epistemological diversity which, however, insofar as it is formulated in terms of P-theory, leaves educational research epistemologically divided. The question, then, if there are such divisions as we have noted, is whether the diversity must be oppositional, or can be harmonious.

2. The Oppositional Diversity Thesis

Quantitative researchers have often seen qualitative research as lacking in objectivity, rigour, and scientific controls (Kerlinger 1973 p. 401). Lacking the resources of quantification, qualitative research cannot produce the requisite generalizations to build up a set of laws of human behaviour, nor can it apply adequate tests for validity and reliability. Moreover, the positivist fact/value distinction is often employed to discredit the claims of qualitative inquiry to produce knowledge, since knowledge is value-free whereas qualitative research is irreducibly value-laden and subjective. In short, qualitative research falls short of the high standards of objectivity and the tight criteria for truth of the quantitative, or "scientific", paradigm. Given the prestige of science, and a positivist view of science, it is easy to see why quantitative researchers have sometimes even seen qualitative research as opposed to sound scientific method.

In reply, many qualitative researchers, invoking the explanation/understanding distinction, claim that the genuinely and distinctively human dimension of education cannot be captured by statistical generalizations and causal laws. Knowledge of human affairs is irreducibly subjective. It must grasp the meanings of actions, the uniqueness of events, and the individuality of persons. From this perspective, it is easy to see the quantitative tradition as an intrusive, even alien and antihuman, approach to the study of education. "Science" may be appropriate to the study of nature, but it distorts the study of human affairs. It is easy to see why, given a perceived de facto domination of educational research by the quantitative tradition, qualitative researchers have sometimes seen it in oppositional, even antagonistic, terms.

Thus the debate over whether so-called quantitative research methodology is in conflict with qualitative research methodology does not revolve simply around the use of numbers, of mathematical and statistical procedures. Rather, it concerns the relation of quantification to more basic questions about objectivity, validity, reliability, and criteria for truth. For example, according to Smith and Heshusius (1986 p. 9), who have reasserted the oppositional diversity thesis against the increasing popularity of the other two: "For quantitative inquiry, a logic of justification that is epistemologically foundational leads to the position that certain sets of techniques are epistemologically privileged in that their correct application is necessary to achieve validity or to discover how things really are out there." On the other hand they say: "From the perspective of qualitative inquiry, this line of reasoning is unacceptable. The assumptions or logic of justification in this case are not foundationalist and, by extension, do not allow that certain sets of procedures are epistemologically privileged." There are two key epistemological distinctions here. First, "logic of justification" (our grounds for making claims) is distinguished from research procedures (techniques used to gather, analyse and interpret data). Second, foundational epistemologies, which provide a logic of justification basing our knowledge claims on supposedly secure or certain foundations (such as empirical observations), are distinguished from non-foundational epistemologies whose logic of justification involves no foundations. Later we shall query the assumption that quantitative inquiry must be foundationalist.

The key epistemological dilemma posed by Smith and Heshusius is that for the quantitative researcher there exists a mind-independent reality "out there" that is, to some extent, knowable. Disciplined observation of it provides our epistemic foundations. Qualitative researchers, they assert, are committed to denying this. By following certain practices of inquiry that enjoy a cluster of related theoretical advantages — the advantages of internal and external validity, reliability, and objectivity — the quantitative researcher increases the likelihood of discovering something important about that reality. Its properties and the causal structures governing the orderly behaviour of its interrelated parts constitute typical goals of quantitative inquiry. What makes these goals possible, and indeed holds together

the theoretical features of such inquiry, is a belief that we can *know* when a correspondence obtains between the sentences of a theory and the world "out there". It is this correspondence that makes our knowledge claims *true*.

It is precisely this belief that is most often questioned by qualitative researchers. Reality, or at least social reality, they frequently maintain, is something that we construct with our minds as a product of our theorizing. Theorizing shapes reality, rather than the other way around. There is simply no mind-independent or theory-independent reality to match up with or correspond to our sentences, to serve as a check on their acceptability. Under this assumption, the theoretical apparatus we employ to characterize epistemically virtuous inquiry will apparently have little use for familiar quantitative notions. Instead, distinctly alternative networks of theoretical requirements for qualitative research will need to be devised, tied to procedures for getting at subjective, or intersubjective, symbols, meanings, and understandings.

Critical theorists go one step further in this philosophical opposition to the "intrusion" of the quantitative tradition into the search for knowledge of the "genuinely human". In addition to being unable to capture the necessary relation between the human mind and social reality, critical theorists maintain that the quantitative (or empirical-analytic) tradition cannot capture the essential role of *values* in that kind of knowledge we need to improve the human condition. Thus Bates (1980) argues that epistemically adequate educational research must be research that makes for *human betterment*. The "praxis" tradition in epistemology, well exemplified in recent theory by the writings of Freire (1972) and more particularly in the action research tradition (Carr and Kemmis 1983), provides a rich theoretical context for elaborating further nonquantitative criteria to replace quantitative notions of validity, reliability, and objectivity. In contrast to the usual lines drawn in the quantitative/qualitative debate, the elimination of social injustice, for example, is not merely a matter of constructing alternative realities, or alternative theories. Nor is validity simply a matter of establishing a correspondence between theory and the world, when the goal is social improvement. Rather, what counts as valid inquiry, as epistemically progressive, is limited to what the surrounding epistemology counts as promoting human well-being.

3. The Complementary Diversity Thesis

Within the epistemologically softer climate of the postpositivist era, many educational researchers nowadays believe that the various research traditions, even if incommensurable, are equally legitimate and in no necessary conflict. The "scientific" and "humanistic" approaches, "are not exclusive, but complementary to each other" (*Research Paradigms in Education* p. 20). Indeed Shulman (1985 p. 4) goes so far as to suggest that "the danger for any field of social science or educational research lies in its potential corruption... by a single paradigmatic view". Against what they have regarded as the unwarranted "positivist", quantitative, domination of educational research, proponents of the qualitative/interpretative paradigm have succeeded in convincing a number of scholars whose work has been within the quantitative tradition (e.g. Campbell 1982, Cronbach 1975) that the qualitative approach has its own merits.

Some writers have suggested that complementarity must be recognized in view of various distinct desiderata in educational research, not all of which can be met by any one single paradigm. For example, there are pressing educational and social problems requiring policy and practical responses. The information necessary for policy formulation might not be available from controlled laboratory experiments of limited generalizability (or external validity), but might be provided by "quasi-experiments" (Cook and Campbell 1979) or qualitative research. Moreover, given the rate of social change, or the constant interactive effects of educational treatments and student aptitudes, generalizations yielded by a quantitative approach might become rapidly out of date. The project of developing a stable set of scientific educational laws may not be viable (Cronbach 1975).

For other writers espousing complementary diversity, the multi-factorial complexity of educational problems supports epistemological pluralism. Keeves (1986 p. 390) acknowledges that some approaches are more holistic, embracing greater complexity than others:

> The techniques employed in educational research must be capable of examining many variables at the same time, but not necessarily through the use of complex statistical procedures...although these have their place. Anthropologists have evolved procedures for analyzing and presenting information from a situation which involves many factors that are very different from those used by psychologists, and different again from those that might be employed by economists and sociologists.

Nevertheless, according to Campbell (1982), P-theoretical differences are still unavoidable because there remains a need for the kind of research produced by "the tools of descriptive science and formal logic", which cannot embrace the value judgments characteristic of much nonquantitative educational inquiry. For other writers, fundamental epistemological differences between explanation and interpretation, of course, remain.

In educational research acceptance of the epistemological integrity of a nonquantitative paradigm has largely been the result of efforts by qualitative researchers to spell out alternative networks of theoretical requirements for qualitative research. These have tended to run parallel to elements in the received epistemological scheme of quantitative research (validity, reliability, etc.) One influential example, elaborated by Lincoln and Guba (1985), employs the notions of credibility, applicability (or transferability), consistency, and neutrality,

as analogues respectively for internal validity, external validity, reliability, and objectivity.

The point here, however, is not so much that there is some loose analogical connection between corresponding terms in these sets. Rather, despite détente, the point to note is the persisting apparent epistemological *distinctiveness* of these theoretically interanimated clusters and their respective embeddings in different epistemologies. Some complementary diversity theorists might think that they can have fundamental *epistemological* diversity without subscribing to something as strong as the P-theory and its incommensurability doctrine. Here, perhaps, epistemological diversity is being confused with *methodological* diversity, a diversity of techniques of inquiry. Of course the latter is possible but, we maintain, is best underwritten by a "touchstone" account of epistemic justification, not several incommensurable epistemologies. Such an account does not have to be fixed and absolute; it can change. The point is that at any given time it embraces those epistemological commitments that are shared by researchers. This is the unity thesis. If complementary diversity theorists wish to eschew such epistemological touchstone, then they remain committed to P-theory.

It should be noted that many advocates of equal rights for qualitative research have wished to play down the epistemological differences (Lincoln and Guba 1985, Le Compte and Goetz 1982, Miles and Huberman 1984). It may be that exponents of the complementary diversity thesis who persist with the term "paradigm" do not embrace P-theory's doctrine of incommensurability, although this is rarely made explicit. If they disavow incommensurability, their position would seem to collapse into the unity thesis, with revisionary consequences for the way they draw the distinctions between paradigms. These may be more drastic than at first appears. In the case of the explanation/understanding distinction, for instance, Keeves (see *Social Theory and Educational Research*), in arguing for complementarity has adopted Giddens's (1984) reworking of this distinction. But not all complementarists have recognized the seriousness of the problem. As Smith and Heshusius (1986 p. 7) put it, there has been a tendency to "de-epistemologize" the debate or even ignore paradigmatic differences. Given that paradigms exist, Smith and Heshusius may well be right. But do paradigms exist?

4. Criticisms of the Paradigms Theory

It is apparent that there is some confusion over both the term "paradigm" and the problem of unambiguously identifying paradigms of educational research. Some of the confusion comes from the ambiguity of the term "paradigm" itself. On the one hand, as Husén (*Research Paradigms in Education* p. 17) points out, there would be wide agreement that the most influential use of "paradigm" stems from the work of Kuhn (1970a). However, Masterman (1970) has identified some 22 different uses of the term in Kuhn's book; Kuhn has subsequently published revisions, some substantial, to his original theory (e.g. Kuhn 1970b, Kuhn 1970c, Kuhn 1974); and finally, not all methodologists embrace Kuhn's ideas uncritically.

Kuhn (1970a pp. 109-10) has also put the principal argument for regarding paradigms as incommensurable, as incapable of being compared or measured against some touchstone standard:

In learning a paradigm the scientist acquires theory, methods, and standards together, usually in an inextricable mixture. Therefore when paradigms change, there are usually significant shifts in the criteria determining the legitimacy both of problems and of proposed solutions.

That observation...provides our first explicit indication of why the choice between competing paradigms regularly raises questions that cannot be resolved by the criteria of normal science...[scientists] will inevitably talk through each other when debating the relative merits of their respective paradigms. In the partially circular arguments that regularly result, each paradigm will be shown to satisfy more or less the criteria that it dictates for itself and to fall short of a few of those dictated by its opponent.

The key claim being made here is that paradigms include both substantive theories and the standards and criteria for evaluating those theories, or *paradigm-specific epistemologies*. As such, it is also claimed, there is no privileged epistemic vantage point from which different paradigms can be assessed; there are only the rival epistemic standards built into each paradigm.

Kuhn's early comments on the task of adjudicating the merits of competing paradigms are instructive: "...the proponents of competing paradigms practise their trade in different worlds" (Kuhn 1970a p. 150); "the transfer of allegiance from paradigm to paradigm is a conversion experience that cannot be forced" (Kuhn 1970a p. 151); such a transition occurs relatively suddenly, like a gestalt switch "just because it is a transition between incommensurables" (Kuhn 1970a p. 150).

Moreover, the belief that some research traditions are incommensurable can be made to look initially plausible by noting the kind of tradition-specific vocabularies that are used to characterize matters epistemological. As we have seen, methodological reflection on quantitative research commonly trades in such terminology as "scientific", "positivist", "foundational", "correspondence truth", "objective", "realist", "validity", "reliability", "reductionist" and "empiricist". The qualitative network of such terms includes "nonpositivist", "antifoundational", "interpretation", "understanding", "subjective", "idealist", "relativist" and "anti-reductionist". The fact that key terms of epistemic conduct in one cluster are formed by negating terms in the other cluster readily suggests no common basis for the conduct and assessment of inquiry, and hence the incommensurability of these traditions.

Clearly, for a defence of the epistemological unity of educational research, the most important obstacle is this P-theoretical analysis of research traditions. In beginning our defence of the unity thesis we note that in philosophy, and philosophy of science in particular, P-theory is widely regarded as false. In a major review of the literature following a 1969 symposium on the structure of scientific theories, Suppe (1977 p. 647) remarks: "Since the symposium Kuhn's views have undergone a sharply declining influence on contemporary work in philosophy of science". He goes on to claim that contemporary work in philosophy of science, that is, *postpositivist* philosophy of science, "increasingly subscribes to the position that it is a central aim of science to come to know how the world *really is*" (Suppe 1977 p. 649). In social and educational research, on the other hand, especially among qualitative researchers and critical theorists, antirealist belief in paradigms remains strong. In our view, the apparent ubiquity of "paradigms" in educational research occurs because the epistemological assumptions of the P-theory itself, or its P-epistemology, are largely responsible for structuring differences among research traditions into putative paradigms.

Of course epistemologists in general agree that inquiry structures our knowledge of the objects of inquiry; this is part of what is involved in maintaining that all experience is theory-laden. Contrary to Smith and Heshusius (1986), it is not a feature peculiar to qualitative inquiry. The interesting question is whether there is any reason to believe that different research traditions partition into paradigms the way P-theory requires. However, it is rarely noted that whether it is even *appropriate* to give reasons, to marshall evidence, to analyse research practices and inquiry contexts in order to justify such a belief, will depend on whether P-theory is, by its own lights, a paradigm (or part of a paradigm), or not. If it is, then the relevant standards of reasoning, evidence and analysis will be peculiar to P-theory (or its encompassing paradigm) and so will have rational epistemic purchase on none but the already committed. To the unbeliever, P-theory would literally have nothing to say for itself. For one to believe that educational research comes in paradigms would require an act of faith; to come to believe it after believing the contrary would require a conversion experience.

There are interesting problems with this view. For example, what happens if we are converted to it? Do we now say that it is *true* that educational research divides into paradigms? Unfortunately the term "true" is P-theoretical and so we need to determine first whether, for example, the sentences of P-theory correspond to a world of real educational researchers really engaged in incommensurable research practices. If so, then P-theory is not after all a paradigm distinct from those that employ correspondence-truth. If not, then there is a genuine equivocation over the term "true" which will permit the following claims to be made without contradiction: (a) it is correspondence-true that the different research traditions are not epistemologically distinct; and (b) it is P-true that the different research traditions are epistemologically distinct.

But in conceding the equal legitimacy of incommensurable rivals (whether oppositional or complementary), particularly a correspondence-truth rival, the P-theorist seems to be surrendering the capacity to say anything about actual educational research practices and the historical and theoretical context of current research traditions. Worse still, in eschewing any schema for determining the ontological commitments of P-theory, there seems to be no way of knowing what the P-theorist is talking *about*. As such, P-theory hardly provides a challenge to a realist view of the unity of educational research.

To avoid the dilemma that threatens when P-theory becomes self-referential, several options are available. We shall consider two. First, a less parsimonious attitude to rival epistemologies can be adopted by maintaining that correspondence-truth theories, which caused all the trouble, are false, wrong or, as hard-hitting relativists are fond of saying, inadequate. Indeed, getting rid of correspondence truth may be a condition for meaningful P-theoretical claims about theorists' living in different worlds; after all, talk of a real world tends to make other worlds pale into nonexistence. A second, opposite, strategy is to say that P-theory is not a distinct paradigm at all, but rather a set of carefully argued, evidentially supported, correspondence-true claims about the existence of paradigmatic divisions among the major research traditions. It is instructive to note that some methodologists run both these strategies simultaneously (e.g. Lincoln and Guba 1985, Eisner 1979, Eisner 1981. For damaging criticism of Eisner's running the two strategies together, see Phillips 1983.)

Arguments for the first option are by now familiar enough. Correspondence-truth is assumed to be located in a network of terms usually associated with the quantitative research tradition. Valid and reliable knowledge about the world is said to be that which is, in some way, derivable from some epistemically secure (or even certain) foundation; in positivistic empiricism usually observations or first person sensory reports. Objectivity consists in intersubjectively agreed matchings between statements and experience. And, of course, these objectively known statements are correspondence-true just in case the required matching occurs (although often the only reality admitted was sense data).

There are many objections to foundational empiricist epistemologies (e.g. Feyerabend 1975, Kuhn 1970a, Hesse 1974, Churchland 1979), but a version of the earlier argument from self-reference will suffice to illustrate the problems. Although this is not widely recognized in positivistic empiricism, epistemology is a task that requires (as Kant saw) a theory of the powers of the mind. What we can know will depend, to some extent, on what sort of creature we are and, in particular, on what sort of perceptual and cognitive capacities we have. A theory of the mind, however, is something we have to get to *know*. In the case of empiricist foundationalism, what we need to know is that our own sensory experiences will provide us with epistemically secure foundations. Unfortunately for the foundationalist, the theory of mind required to underwrite this claim is not itself an item of sensory experience, nor an observation report. This means that our knowledge of how we know the class of epistemically privileged items is not

itself epistemically privileged. Indeed, the sophisticated neurophysiological models of brain functioning now typical of accounts of perception and cognition are quite ill-suited to serving the regress pattern of foundational justification. For they so far outrun the purported resources of any proposed foundation that the whole point of foundational justification here collapses. More generally, our knowledge of our perceptual powers, or possible foundations, like our knowledge of everything, is theory-laden. The result is that there is no epistemically privileged, theory-free, way of viewing the world. There is thus no reality that can be seen independent of competing theoretical perspectives. This applies as much to the empirical sciences (and the quantitative tradition in educational research) as to other areas. (See Walker and Evers 1982, Walker and Evers 1986.)

But from the fact that all experience is theory-laden, that what we believe exists depends on what theory we adopt, it does not follow that all theories are evidentially equivalent, or equally reasonable. There is more to evidence than observation, or as Churchland (1985 p. 35) argues: "observational excellence or 'empirical adequacy' is only one epistemic virtue among others of equal or comparable importance". The point is that some theories organize their interpretations of experience better than others. A humdrum example employing subjectivist scruples on evidence will illustrate this point. A theory which says that I can leave what I interpret to be my office by walking through what I interpret to be the wall will cohere less well with my interpreted desire to leave my office than a theory which counsels departure via what I take to be the door. It is all interpretative, of course, but some organized sets of interpretations, or theories, are better than others. The theory that enables a person to experience the desired success of departing the perceived enclosure of an office enjoys certain epistemic advantages over one that does not. With all experience interpreted, though, the correct conclusion to draw is not that we have no adequate objective standard of reality, but that objectivity involves more than *empirical* adequacy. Theoretically motivated success in getting in and out of rooms is about as basic as objectivity ever gets. There are superempirical, theoretical, tests which can be couched in a "coherence epistemology". One advocate of coherence epistemology, the postpositivist philosopher Quine, sums up this standard of reality:

> Having noted that man has no evidence for the existence of bodies beyond the fact that their assumption helps him organize experience, we should have done well, instead of disclaiming evidence for the existence of bodies, to conclude: such, then, at bottom, is what evidence is, both for ordinary bodies and molecules. (Quine 1960a p. 251)

Quine's point here foreshadows a significant epistemological consequence of this attack on foundationalism. According to Quine, and many coherence theorists, we need to distinguish sharply between the theory of *evidence* and the theory of *truth* (Quine 1960a, Quine

1960b, Quine 1969, Quine 1975, Williams 1977, Williams 1980). Theory of evidence is concerned with the global excellence of theory, and involves both empirical adequacy, inasmuch as this can be achieved; and the superempirical virtues of simplicity, consistency, comprehensiveness, fecundity, familiarity of principle, and explanatory power. Once we have our best theory according to these coherence criteria, it is the resulting theory itself that we use to tell us what exists and how the theory's sentences match up with that posited reality. What corresponds to true sentences is therefore something that is determined *after* the theory of evidence has done its work. It is not something that figures a priori, or in some privileged foundational way in the determination of the best theory.

This conclusion suggests that P-theory critiques of foundationalism draw too radical a conclusion. In terms of the quantitative/qualitative debate, for example, the coherence epistemology sanctioned by the most powerful criticisms of empiricist foundationalism cuts across the familiar methodological (putatively paradigmatic) bifurcation. In acknowledging the theory-ladenness of all experience it is nonpositivist and nonfoundational. It agrees that our window on the world is mind-dependent and subject to the interpretations of theorists. On the other hand, it can be realist, scientific, objective, reductionist, and embrace correspondence-truth. This possibility raises serious doubts about P-theorists' claims concerning the diversity of educational research, whether oppositional or complementary.

A more systematic objection to P-theory can be raised, however, by examining the epistemological warrant for incommensurability. The belief that research methodologies comprising incommensurable networks of theoretical terms are epistemically autonomous is sustained in large measure by a particular theory of meaning, notably that terms gain what meaning they possess in virtue of their role in some network or conceptual scheme. Where conceptual schemes or theories are said to be systematically different, no basis exists for matching the terms of one theory with those of another. So expressions such as "validity" or "truth", which appear as orthographically equivalent across different schemes, are really equivocal, with systematic differences emerging as differences in conceptual role.

Both Kuhn and Feyerabend maintain versions of the conceptual role theory of meaning. The trouble, however, is that they maintain implausibly strong versions of it, for if meaning is determined *entirely* by conceptual role then incommensurable theories become unlearnable. This all turns on the modest empirical fact that as finite learners we need some point of entry into an elaborate systematically interconnected vocabulary like a theory. But in order to learn some small part of a theory, say a handful of expressions, P-epistemology requires us to have mastered the *whole* theory in order to appreciate the conceptual role played by these expressions. It is at this point that the theory of meaning begins to outrun its own epistemological resources: it posits learned antecedents of learning that cannot themselves be learned. We cannot understand the parts unless we have mastered the whole, and we lack the resources to master the whole without first scaling the parts. An implicit feature of the epistemology driving P-theory's account of meaning as conceptual role is thus an implausibly strong theory of the powers of the mind. (We should note in passing that a P-theoretical attack on correspondence-truth appears to depend on a correspondence-true theory of mind.)

Once again we have observed P-theory getting into difficulty over self-reference. In this case an epistemology should come out knowable on its own account of knowledge. The chief advantage of arguments from self-reference is that they focus directly on the superempirical virtues or weaknesses of a theory.

Inasmuch as we are impressed by such theoretical shortcomings as inconsistency, lack of explanatory power in relation to rivals, arbitrary use of ad hoc hypotheses, and so on, we are allowing these criteria to function as touchstone in the evaluation of epistemologies and research methodologies. Of course we can ignore these vices in theory-construction: they are not extra-theoretical privileged foundations by which all theorizing can be assessed. But methodologists in the main research traditions who expect their inquiries to command attention, serve as a sound basis for action, or constitute a particular or definite set of knowledge claims have, as a matter of fact, been unwilling to play fast and loose with such virtues as consistency (usually on the formal ground that a contradiction will sanction *any* conclusion whatever) or simplicity and comprehensiveness (on the ground that ad hoc, or arbitrary addition of hypotheses can be used to explain anything whatsoever, and hence nothing at all). Indeed a theory cannot be empirically significant unless it is consistent. With P-theory's theory of meaning exhibiting the superempirical weakness of lack of explanatory power in relation to what it sets itself to explain, and with that weakness being traceable to a theory of mind, we should observe that whether epistemologies or methodologies are incommensurable turns on such things as empirical theories of mind or brain functioning, theories of learning and cognition. Epistemology itself is therefore continuous with, and relies upon, empirical science. In Quine's words (1969), epistemology is "naturalized". One consequence is that interpretative theorists, for example, must, incoherently, rely on the "scientific" paradigm in order to show the incommensurability of their own paradigm with the "scientific".

5. The Unity Thesis

Although the paradigms perspective is seriously flawed, some account of the kind of unity educational research actually enjoys still needs to be given. In arguing against P-theory, we have already drawn on coherence epistemology. To conclude this article we shall briefly outline a particular version of coherentism, or epistemological holism, which has achieved considerable prominence in postpositivist philosophy (Quine 1975) and has more recently been applied to educational philosophy (Walker and Evers 1982). In particular, it has been argued that there is no logically consistent way to partition the domain of knowledge into radically distinct forms of knowledge (Evers and Walker 1983).

We note that a more positive epistemological agenda for educational research can be provided by responding to the second strategy a P-theorist can adopt in defending diversity. Recall that this strategy involved denying P-theory was a distinct paradigm, conceding correspondence-truth, but arguing that fundamental epistemological diversity still occurred in educational research. In replying to this claim we can note that the strategy will need to employ superempirical epistemic virtues to be persuasive. To be effective against a wide range of theoretical perspectives these virtues (consistency, simplicity, fecundity, etc.) will need to be recognized as such by rival epistemologies and hence function as touchstone. As a result the P-theorist's strategy is already compromised. To complete the job, however, we need a coherence epistemology that yields a touchstone-coherent account of itself and its own epistemic virtues, that is unproblematically self-referential in scope, and that can account for the touchstone-recognized successes of alternative epistemologies and their research extensions.

In our view, the epistemology that best accounts for knowledge, its growth, and evaluation is a form of holistic scientific naturalism (in Quine's "epistemology naturalized" sense of "naturalism") — a theory that makes ready use of our best or most coherent theories of perception and cognition. Our term for this is "materialist pragmatist" epistemology (Walker and Evers 1984). On this view, we are acquiring our theory of the world from infancy onward. Indeed, as Quine (1960b) has shown, theory precedes all learning and hence commences with our innate complement of dispositions to respond selectively to the environment. What we can know is dependent on the kind of creature that we are and, as human beings, we are all one kind of creature. We share genetically derived, though culturally expressed, refined and modified touchstone standards and procedures. Added to these are further culturally produced touchstone we acquire as social beings sharing material problems in concrete social contexts. Our knowledge is made up of our theories, whose existence is to be explained causally, as problem-solving devices. There are numerous philosophical accounts (e.g. Popper 1972, Lakatos 1970, Laudan 1977) of how theories can be analyzed as problem-solving devices. In the case of epistemological theories, the problems arise from theoretical practice, including empirical (e.g. educational) research. Clearly, there are certain issues concerning whether a theory is addressing the right problem, and we will need a theory of how to distinguish between real problems and pseudoproblems, and between better and worse formulations of problems. Here our epistemology would lean on a theory of evidence and experiment, on the pragmatic relations between "theory" and "practice" (Walker 1985a).

One real problem, shared by all educational researchers, is how best to conduct inquiry into human learning itself. Without this problem there could be no debate about whether educational research is epistemologically diverse. For there to be an issue at all presupposes at least some sharing of language, including general epistemological terminology such as "truth", "meaning", "adequacy", "interpretation", "paradigm", and so on.

Competition remains, of course, but competition between theories, including theories of educational research methodology, not paradigms. Competition arises because, in addition to touchstone, there are unshared (which is not to say incommensurable) concepts, hypotheses, and rules of method. Indeed, this is part and parcel of our being able to distinguish one theory from another in a competitive situation. There can be genuine competition between theories, however, only when they have an issue over which to compete, some shared problem(s). Theory A is in competition with theory B when one or more of its sentences is contrary to sentences in theory B. For this situation to obtain, theories A and B must be attempts at solving at least one common problem. To identify a shared problem involves some conceptual common ground and, if only implicitly at first, some shared method: the concepts have to be deployed. Thus we begin to discover and negotiate touchstone theory which, unlike the privileged epistemic units of foundational epistemologies, is merely the shifting and historically explicable amount of theory that is shared by rival theories and theorists. Beginning with identification of common problems, we can proceed to identify further touchstone and elaborate the touchstone frameworks within which theories compete.

Having identified common ground between theories, we next rigorously set out their differences and test them against the touchstone by empirical research and theoretical analysis, seeking to identify the strengths and weaknesses of each, and reach a decision on the theory which is strongest under present circumstances (Walker 1985b), taking into account past achievements and likely future problems (Churchland 1979).

Other features of this epistemology include its capacity to survive its own test of self-reference (Quine 1969), its unified account of validity and reliability (Walker and Evers 1986), its denial that all science consists of sets of laws, and of any fundamental epistemological distinction between explanation and understanding (Walker 1985c) or between fact and value judgments (Evers 1987).

Finally, although we have maintained that such a materialist pragmatist epistemology is a sound way of underwriting the epistemological unity of educational research, achieved through touchstone analysis, it should be stressed that it is as much a competing theory as any other, and subject to touchstone testing (Walker 1985a). Granted that it shares touchstone with other epistemologies, arguments can of course be mounted against it. But to engage in such arguments, all participants would be implicitly conceding the epistemological unity of research.

35

Bibliography

Bates R J 1980 New developments in the new sociology of education. *Br. J. Sociol. Educ.* 1(1): 67–79

Campbell D T 1982 Experiments as arguments. In: House E (ed.) 1982 *Evaluation Studies Review Annual.* Sage, Beverly Hills, California

Carr W, Kemmis S 1983 *Becoming Critical. Knowing Through Action Research.* Deakin University Press, Geelong, Victoria

Churchland P M 1979 *Scientific Realism and the Plasticity of Mind.* Cambridge University Press, London

Churchland P M 1985 The ontological status of observables. In: Churchland P M, Hooker C A (eds.) 1985 *Images of Science.* University of Chicago Press, Chicago, Illinois, pp. 35–47

Cook T D, Campbell D T 1979 *Quasi-Experimentation. Design and Analysis Issues for Field Settings.* Rand McNally, Chicago, Illinois

Cronbach L J 1975 Beyond the two disciplines of scientific psychology. *Am. Psychol.* 30(2): 116–26

Eisner E 1979 *The Educational Imagination.* Macmillan, New York

Eisner E 1981 A rejoinder. *Educ. Res. AERA* 10(10): 25–26

Evers C W 1987 Epistemology and the structure of educational theory: Some reflections on the O'Connor–Hirst debate. *J. Philos. Educ.* 21(2): 3–13

Evers C W, Walker J C 1983 Knowledge, partitioned sets, and extensionality. *J. Philos. Educ.* 17(2): 155–70

Feyerabend P K 1975 *Against Method.* Verso, London

Freire P 1972 *Cultural Action for Freedom.* Penguin, Harmondsworth

Giddens A 1984 *The Constitution of Society.* Polity Press, Cambridge, and Blackwell, Oxford

Habermas J 1972 *Knowledge and Human Interests.* Heinemann, London

Hesse M 1974 *The Structure of Scientific Inference.* Macmillan, London

Hooker C A 1975 Philosophy and meta-philosophy of science. Empiricism, Popperianism and realism. *Synthèse* 32: 177–231

Keeves J P 1986 Theory, politics and experiment in educational research methodology. A response. *Int. Rev. Educ.* 32(4): 388–92

Kerlinger F N 1973 *Foundations of Behavioral Research. Educational and Psychological Inquiry*, 2nd edn. Holt, Rinehart and Winston, New York

Kuhn T S 1970a *The Structure of Scientific Revolutions*, 2nd edn. University of Chicago Press, Chicago, Illinois

Kuhn T S 1970b Postscript — 1969. In: Kuhn (1970a), pp. 174–210

Kuhn T S 1970c Reflections on my critics. In: Lakatos and Musgrave (1970), pp. 321-78

Kuhn T S 1974 Second thoughts about paradigms. In: Suppe (1977), pp. 459–82

Lakatos I 1970 Falsification and the methodology of scientific research programmes. In: Lakatos and Musgrave (1970), pp. 91–196

Lakatos I, Musgrave A (eds.) 1970 *Criticism and the Growth of Knowledge.* Cambridge University Press, London

Laudan L 1977 *Progress and its Problems. Towards a Theory of Scientific Growth.* Routledge and Kegan Paul, London

Le Compte M, Goetz J 1982 Problems of validity and reliability in educational research. *Educ. Res. AERA* 52: 31–60

Lincoln Y S, Guba E G 1985 *Naturalistic Inquiry.* Sage, Beverly Hills, California

Masterman M 1970 The nature of a paradigm. In: Lakatos and Musgrave (1970), pp. 59–89

Miles M, Huberman M 1984 Drawing valid meaning from qualitative data. Towards a shared craft. *Educ. Res. AERA* 13: 20–30

Phillips D C 1983 After the wake: Postpositivistic educational thought. *Educ. Res. AERA* 12(5): 4–12

Popkewitz T 1984 *Paradigm and Ideology in Educational Research.* Falmer Press, London

Popper K R 1972 *Objective Knowledge.* Oxford University Press, Oxford

Quine W V 1960a Posits and reality. In: Uyeda S (ed.) 1960 *Bases of Contemporary Philosophy*, Vol. 5. Waseda University Press, Tokyo. Cited as reprinted in Quine W V 1976 *The Ways of Paradox and Other Essays*, 2nd edn. Harvard University Press, Cambridge, Massachusetts, pp. 246–54

Quine W V 1960b *Word and Object.* MIT Press, Cambridge, Massachusetts

Quine W V 1969 Epistemology naturalized. In: Quine W V 1969 *Ontological Relativity and Other Essays.* Columbia University Press, New York, pp. 69–90

Quine W V 1975 The nature of natural knowledge. In: Guttenplan S (ed.) 1975 *Mind and Language.* Oxford University Press, Oxford, 67–81

Shulman L 1985 Paradigms and research programs in the study of teaching. A contemporary perspective. In: Wittrock M C (ed.) 1985 *Handbook of Research on Teaching*, 3rd edn. Macmillan, New York, pp. 3–36

Smith J K, Heshusius L 1986 Closing down the conversation. The end of the qualitative/quantitative debate among educational inquirers *Educ. Res. AERA* 15(1): 4–12

Suppe F (ed.) 1977 *The Structure of Scientific Theories*, 2nd edn. University of Illinois Press, Chicago, Illinois

Walker J C 1985a The philosopher's touchstone. Towards pragmatic unity in educational studies. *J. Philos. Educ.* 19(2): 181–98

Walker J C 1985b Philosophy and the study of education. A critique of the commonsense consensus. *Aust. J. Educ.* 29(2): 101–14

Walker J C 1985c Materialist pragmatism and sociology of education. *Br. J. Sociol. Educ.* 6(1): 55–74

Walker J C, Evers C W 1982 Epistemology and justifying the curriculum of educational studies. *Br. J. Educ. Stud.* 30(2): 312–29

Walker J C, Evers C W 1984 Towards a materialist pragmatist philosophy of education. *Educ. Res. Perspect.* 11(1): 23–33

Walker J C, Evers C W 1986 Theory, politics, and experiment in educational research methodology. *Int. Rev. Educ.* 32(4): 373–87

Williams M 1977 *Groundless Belief.* Blackwell, Oxford

Williams M 1980 Coherence justification and truth. *Rev. Metaphys.* 34(2): 243–72

Humanistic Research Methods

Research Methodology: Historical Methods [1]

C. F. Kaestle

Historians often observe that their discipline is both a science and an art. When they say that history is a science, they mean that historians adhere to certain procedures of investigation and argument that allow them to agree on some generalizations about the past, even though their personal values and their understanding of human nature may differ. In many cases they can agree simply because the evidence is ample and clear, and because they agree on the ground rules. Factual statements like "Jean-Jacques Rousseau was born in 1712" occasion little debate as long as it is the same Rousseau being spoken about and as long as the surviving records are not contradictory. More complex statements are also capable of verification and may attract wide consensus among historians. Examples are such statements as the following: "The average white fertility rate was declining during the period from 1800 to 1860," or "Most educators in 1840 believed that state-funded schooling would reduce crime."

However, the rules of investigation and analysis help less and less as historians attempt to make broader generalizations about the past, or make judgments about its relation to the present, and this is part of what is meant by saying that history is also an art. Consider such statements as: "Slavery destroyed the American black family," or "Schooling was a major avenue of social mobility in France." These claims are not only immensely difficult to study empirically; they also involve problems of definition and problems of implicit value judgments. The process of broad generalization is thus not simply inductive; it remains an act of creative and often normative interpretation, within the limits established by the evidence. To a considerable degree, history remains stubbornly subjective.

The history of education shares the methodological problems of the field of history in general. There is no single, definable method of inquiry, and important historical generalizations are rarely beyond dispute. Rather they are the result of an interaction between fragmentary evidence and the values and experiences of the historian. It is a challenging and creative interaction, part science, part art.

It is important for educators to understand this problematic nature of historical methodology because historical statements about education abound far beyond textbooks or required history courses in schools of education. Beliefs about the historical role of schooling in America are encountered every day as arguments for educational policies. For example, during the debates in America about the decentralization of urban school control in the 1960s, advocates of decentralization argued that centralization was a device by which social elites in the early twentieth century had gained control of urban education, protected the social structure, and tried to impose their particular values on public school children. The decentralizers argued that centralization had been an undemocratic means of social control, and therefore it deserved to be reversed. Opponents of decentralization claimed that it would lead to inefficiency and corruption. Besides, they said, a common, uniform school system has been a successful tool in creating a cohesive, democratic society in America. They too cited history as their authority. Behind these contending positions is a mass of complex evidence and conflicting values. The historian has no magic formula to tell you which analysis is correct.

The uncertain nature of historical generalization has been particularly apparent in the history of education since the early 1960s. During this period the traditional methods and assumptions of educational historians have come increasingly under attack. The controversy has led to fresh insights, new questions and, more than ever, a heightened sense of the precariousness of historical generalizations.

1. The Traditional Framework

Current methodological issues in the history of education are best understood in the light of the assumptions

1   This article also appears under the title "Recent methodological developments in the history of American education" which was published in Jaeger R (ed.) 1985 *Alternative Methodologies in Educational Research*. American Educational Research Association, Washington, DC. Copyright 1985, American Educational Research Association.

and conclusions of traditional educational historians. Until the 1950s most writers of educational history shared two basic assumptions: first, that the history of education was concerned centrally, indeed, almost exclusively, with the history of school systems; and second, that state-regulated, free, tax-supported, universal schooling was a good thing. These assumptions were largely unquestioned, partly because many educational historians performed a dual role as educational administrators or professors of education, and therefore they had a vested interest in seeing state schooling in a good light. But also there was widespread popular agreement that free, universal schooling was an unquestionably positive institution.

There were several unstated corollaries to these assumptions, and they provided the framework—what some might call the paradigm—for research in educational history. Four elements will be mentioned in this paradigm which helped determine methodology and which occasioned later criticism. The first has to do with the focus on schooling. Because they tended to equate education with schooling, traditional historians rated the educational well-being and enlightenment of earlier societies by assessing how much formal schooling there was, and to what extent it was organized under state control. Because their view of historical development was dominated by their present conception of desirable educational policy, they spent much effort trying to explain the lack of enthusiasm for state-regulated schooling prior to the 1830s, and they underestimated the importance of the family, the workplace, the churches, and other educational agencies in preindustrial society.

Related to this problem of focus is the problem of intent. Traditional historians of education saw those who favored state-regulated school systems as enlightened leaders working for the common good; they portrayed people who opposed educational reform as ignorant, misled, or selfish. The attribution of human motivation is a very difficult methodological problem in historical writing; it involves careful comparison of public and private statements; and it requires the separation, if possible, of attempts to determine the historical actor's personal motivation from moral judgments on the effects of an event or a policy. Moral judgments may be timeless, but the historical actor's motivation must be understood in the context of the social values and scientific knowledge of the day. The value bias of most traditional educational historians prejudiced them against recognizing self-interest on the part of school reformers or legitimate, principled objection on the part of their opponents. On the other hand, some recent so-called "revisionist" historians have simply reversed the bias, making school reformers the villains and their opponents the heroes. Either value bias tends to collapse the complexity of educational history and to side-step methodological problems in determining intent.

A third corollary of the assumption that state schooling was a good thing is the equation of growth with progress. Methodologically this prompted historians to glory in numerical growth, often without controlling for parallel population growth or monetary inflation, and without taking seriously the differential educational opportunities of different groups. The tendency is seen equally in the traditional history of Roman Catholic schooling, which is largely a chronicle of increasing schools, children, and budgets.

A fourth corollary of the goodness theme is the focus on leadership and organization rather than on the educational behavior and attitudes of ordinary people. The methodological implication of this focus on the governors rather than on the clients of schooling is to give central attention to public records created by elites rather than attempting to tease out of scanty evidence some inkling of the educational lives of the inarticulate, as recent social historians of education have been attempting to do.

The great majority of books and doctoral dissertations written prior to 1950 on the history of education adhered to this paradigm, focusing on the progressive and beneficial evolution of state school systems. There were some notable exceptions, and even within the paradigm, many excellent legal, institutional, and intellectual studies were written. Nonetheless, the traditional framework had long outlived its usefulness by the late 1950s and early 1960s, when it came under attack.

2. Two Strands of Revisionism

The two major thrusts of revision in the history of education resulted from rather distinct critiques of the two major tenets of the traditional paradigm: that is, that the history of education is essentially the history of schooling and second, that state-regulated schooling was benign and desirable. The first critique broadened the focus of education history to look at various agencies of instruction other than schools in America; it has yielded its finest fruits in the works of Bernard Bailyn and Lawrence Cremin on the colonial period, when schooling was much less important than today in the transmission of knowledge. It remains to be seen whether this broader focus can be applied successfully to the history of education in more recent periods. It will be more difficult to research and construct a coherent account of all the ways children learn in twentieth-century society. Merely broadening the definition to include every aspect of socialization would leave the historian of education hopelessly adrift; each historian must therefore now decide carefully what definition of education lurks in his or her work, and this must depend upon what questions are being asked. If one is asking questions about how children acquire skills and beliefs in a society, then the definition of education must be quite broad indeed. If, on the other hand, one is asking questions about the origins of state policy toward education, it is legitimate to focus on schooling, because past policy makers, like past historians, have equated schooling with education. Society as a whole educates in many ways; but the state educates through schools.

There has been a second, quite different, strand of revision in recent educational history, one which has caused considerable commotion among educators. These revisionists have questioned the assumption that state-regulated schooling has been generated by democratic and humanitarian impulses, and the assumption that it has resulted in democratic opportunity. Their work has emphasized variously the exploitative nature of capitalism and how schools relate to it, the culturally abusive nature of values asserted by the schools, and the negative aspects of increasingly bureaucratic school systems. This reversal of ideological perspective on the development of school systems has not always resulted in methodologically sophisticated work, although as a whole the works labeled "radical revisionism" have raised important questions about the gloomier aspects of educational systems and have made some persuasive statements about the educational failures of state schooling in industrial nations. Since this article is about methodology, not ideology, it is not the place to argue the merits of the radical view of school history.

3. Quantitative Methods

A newer brand of revisionism has been pursued by historians of various ideological persuasions. Their methods and their subject matter may help answer some of the questions raised by the radicals. These quantitative, social historians have devised the most substantial and problematic methodological innovations. Two aspects of the inadequate traditional framework summarized above were a naive use of numerical data and a focus on the leaders rather than on the clients of educational institutions. Recent social historians of education have taken these problems as their starting point. They have adopted techniques from sociology and statistics to map out in some detail patterns of literacy, school attendance, years of schooling, school expenditures, voter characteristics on school issues, and other characteristics and have tried to chart changes over time. Much of this work would have been impossible in the early 1960s. It has been made possible by the development of computer programs for social scientists and by the availability of microfilmed sources of information, such as the manuscript United States censuses of the nineteenth century. The inspiration and the models have been provided by historical demographers and by other social historians, who have been charting changing family structures, mobility patterns, wealth distribution, and other phenomena that affect common people. The new emphasis on parents and children in educational history also parallels similar emphases in other fields of educational research: sociologists are studying family background and schooling outcomes, lawyers are studying students' rights, and philosophers are studying the ethics of child–adult relations.

Hopefully, the complex description provided by quantitative historical studies will help develop understanding about educational supply and demand in the past, about the role of schooling in different types of communities, about the different school experiences of different social groups, and about the impact of schooling on later life in different historical periods. The great virtue of quantitative educational history is that it places historians in touch with the realities of schooling in the past; it provides a way to start doing history from the bottom up, as it were, and a way to compare popular behavioral patterns with the opinions and policies of educational leaders. However, the quantitative social historian of education also faces problems, problems so numerous and frustrating that they cause some researchers to shun the techniques altogether. Others feel compelled by questions that demand quantitative answers, and they are groping toward a more adequate descriptive social history of education, and to theories that will help explain the patterns they are discovering.

Here is a short list of the problems they encounter. First, statistics and computers are unfamiliar, even alien, to many historians. Even for those who learn the techniques, the work is still very time consuming and expensive. Experts are constantly devising improved and more arcane statistical techniques. Social historians have trailed along behind sociologists and economists, picking and choosing the techniques that seem most appropriate. Some have moved from simple cross-tabulations and graphs into multiple regression analysis and its various offspring. The social historian who can solve these problems of time, money, and expertise then has to worry about the audience. Most readers of history balk at simple tables; but statistical adequacy demands detailed documentation and detailed presentation of results. This creates problems of style. Methodological sophistication is not worth much if it cannot reach the audience it is aimed at, but it is difficult to serve a technical audience and a general audience in the same work.

As serious as these matters of training and style are, there are more substantive methodological problems in quantitative educational history. First, the data are crude and incomplete. Often the available school and population censuses were ambiguous on crucial matters, or failed to ask the questions that are of most interest now. Most of the data are cross-sectional; they provide only a snapshot of a group at a given moment; but education is a process, and many important questions about educational careers, or the influence of education on people's lives, can be answered only by data that trace individuals over time. Similarly, questions about the role of education in economic development require comparable aggregate data over time. Some historians have taken up this challenge and have developed longitudinal files by linking data from different sources, but that task is prodigious, and the attrition rate in studies of individuals (the cases lost by geographical mobility, death, and the ambiguity of common names) is so great as to render many conclusions dubious. More commonly, historians have tried to infer process from cross-sectional data. For example, they have examined length of schooling among different social groups by calculating the school-entry and school-leaving ages of different individuals in sample years; or, they have made inferences about the impact of industrialization on communities' educational practices by comparing communities at different stages of industrialization in a given year. Although the questions are about process, in neither case do the data trace individual children or communities over time. The logical and methodological problems of inferring process from static information are serious, and they constitute a central problem in quantitative history today.

Even within legitimate cross-sectional analysis—that is, in pursuing questions about a population at a given moment in time—there is a conflict between statistical adequacy and conceptual adequacy. Limits on research resources and on available data often result in small historical samples. In order to attain statistically significant results, it is sometimes necessary to collapse categories that should remain distinct. For example, if an attempt is being made to relate ethnic background and teenage school attendance while controlling for parental occupation, it may be necessary to combine immigrant groups with quite different cultural and economic features, in order to achieve statistically significant comparisons between children of immigrants and nonimmigrants. The best solution, of course, is to provide the reader with both the significant statistics for the grossly aggregated categories, as well as the descriptively useful information about the smaller subcategories. Here again, though, there are problems of space limits or sheer tedium in presentation.

There are numerous other problems in this new area of research in educational history. For instance, it is difficult to know how conscientiously the data were reported in the first place, or what biases operated; caution on this matter is reinforced when substantial contradictions are found between different sources that claim to measure the same variable in the same population. It is also difficult to create time series on educational variables like attendance, teachers' salaries, educational expenditures, or length of school year, because often the items were defined differently in different periods or omitted altogether.

Despite these many problems, however, some impressive work is beginning to emerge, work which helps to locate the history of education more solidly in the context of social structure and economic development. It is hardly a time for methodological self-congratulation, but neither is it a time for despair. One of the important by-products of this quantitative work in educational history has been to sustain the methodological self-consciousness that began with the critiques of the traditional paradigm in the early 1960s. When the historian does not take methodology for granted, and when his or her methodology is critically scrutinized by other researchers, and when historians are constantly searching for new sources of evidence and techniques of analysis, better work should result.

Not all questions are amenable to quantitative research. It is important to remember that history of education is still vitally concerned with the history of educational ideas. Much good work remains to be done on popular attitudes, on the quality of educational experience in the past, and on the intellectual and institutional history of education. The excitement since the early 1960s has not resulted in a new single methodology, nor in a new, broadly accepted interpretation of educational history. However, the collapse of the old consensus has caused educational historians to explore new questions, discard old assumptions, try new techniques, and attempt to meet more rigorous standards of evidence and argument.

4. Conclusion: Pervasive Methodological Concerns

There are four key problems to watch for when assessing arguments about the history of education, problems that have been highlighted by recent work in the social history of education, but which are also pertinent to the intellectual history of education, the institutional history of education, and other approaches.

The first problem is the confusion of correlations and causes, a problem particularly salient in quantitative work, but certainly not unique to it. To demonstrate that two phenomena occur together systematically is not, of course, to prove that one causes the other, but historians as well as social scientists are constantly tempted into this kind of argument. For example, Irish families in nineteenth-century urban America sent their children to school less often and for fewer years, on the average, than many other groups. This does not, however, demonstrate that "Irishness" (whatever that is) caused low school attendance. First it must be asked whether Irish immigrants also tended to be poor, because it might be poverty that caused low attendance. Then it would be necessary to control for family structure, religion, and other factors. If, in the end, after controlling for all other measurable factors, Irish status was independently associated with low school attendance, a causal relationship would still not have been established. It would be necessary to investigate, and speculate on, why and how being Irish affected schoolgoing. Correlations are just concerned with proximate occurrence; causality is about how things work, and correlations don't indicate much about how things work. Because human motivation is often multiple and vague and because society is not very much like a clock, historians must exercise great caution in moving from systematic statistical associations to assertions of causality.

The second problem to which critical readers must give close attention is the problem of defining key terms. The problem of definition can be subdivided into two common pitfalls: vagueness and presentism. As an example of vagueness, the notion that industrialization caused educational reform is a commonplace in educational history. However, the statement has almost no analytical value until the meanings of the umbrella terms "industrialization" and "educational reform" are specified. In contrast, consider the statement: "The expansion of wage labor in nineteenth-century communities or regions was followed by an expansion of annual school enrollment." This is much more precise, has important causal implications, and is amenable to empirical research.

By "presentism" is meant the danger of investing key terms from the past with their present connotations, or, conversely, applying to past developments present-day terms that did not exist or meant something else at the time. A classic example in American educational history involves the use of the word "public." In the eighteenth century a "public" educational institution was one in which children learned collectively, in contrast with private tutorial education, and it was one devoted to education for the public good, as opposed to mere selfish gain. Thus the colonial colleges, which were controlled by self-perpetuating trustees and financed mainly by tuition, were thoroughly "public" and were called so at the time, as in England. In today's terminology they would be called "private" in America, but calling them "private" in historical work greatly muddies understanding of eighteenth-century society. Avoiding presentism thus means paying close attention to the etymology of key terms, and it is a methodological imperative in good history.

A third problem that critical consumers of educational history should keep in mind is the distinction between ideas about how people should behave and how ordinary people in fact behaved. Too often evidence of the latter is lacking and evidence of the former is allowed to stand in its place, that is, it is assumed that people did as they were told. The methodological dilemma is posed by the following problem: if the legal and legislative bodies of a society constantly passed rules requiring school attendance, is it evidence that the society valued schooling highly, expressing this value in their legislation, or is it evidence of a society that did not value schoolgoing very much, thus alarming its leaders into coercive efforts? To answer the question, something needs to be known about school attendance patterns by different groups. Here is a more specific example. There was widespread agreement among professional educators and physicians beginning in the late 1830s in the northeastern part of the United States that school attendance by very young children was unwise, even dangerous to their health, as well as being a nuisance to teachers. Parents were constantly urged to keep their children under 5 or 6 at home. This campaign continued throughout the 1840s and 1850s. To infer from this that children normally began school at age five or six during these decades, however, would be incorrect. Parents resisted the conventional expertise. As is now known from analysis of manuscript censuses and statistical school reports, they persisted in sending 3- and 4-year-old children to school, for reasons that can only be guessed at, until they were coerced to keep them home by local regulations on age of school entry in the 1850s and 1860s. Only then did the aggregate average age of entry rise substantially. Here, then, is an example of the lag between elite opinion and popular behavior, one which warns against equating literary sources with popular behavior. Child-rearing manuals may not cause or even reflect actual child-rearing practices; and exhortations about educational policies often fall on deaf ears.

The fourth and final problem has to do with the distinction between intent and consequences. No matter how wise educational leaders have been, their powers of foresight have rarely equalled the historians' powers of hindsight. It is an inherent advantage in historical analysis—and yet it is a problem too: historians know how things turned out. The problem lies in the danger of assuming that the historical actors could have (and should have) foreseen the full consequences of their ideas and of the institutions they shaped. It is undoubtedly true that many of the consequences of educational leadership have been precisely as the leaders intended; it does not follow, however, that intent can be inferred from consequences. The fact that large bureaucracies are effective instruments of racial discrimination does not necessarily mean that their creators had a racist intent. The fact that schooling has done an unimpressive job in reducing crime does not mean that school reformers who touted it for that purpose were hypocrites. Intent cannot be inferred from consequences. Direct evidence is needed of intent at the time an act occurred.

No historian can completely transcend or resolve these four problems, but each must recognize the problems and the associated methodological challenges when trying to make meaningful generalizations about the educational past. Historians have always been scavengers. Since history involves all human experience and thought, historians have constantly raided other disciplines for new techniques of analysis and for new insights into society and human nature. This helps explain why there is no single methodology in history, and why historians love their craft so much: because it is so complex and so all-encompassing. Recent trends in the history of education—the effort to see education as broader than schooling, the effort to see school systems in the context of social and economic development, and the effort to study popular attitudes and behavior as well as the history of elite intentions and actions—have greatly accelerated the borrowing process in this historical subfield. Historians of education have reached out and become involved in the history of the family, of childhood, and of reform institutions, for example, in addition to deepening their traditional commitment to economic and political history as a context for educational development. They have also explored recent sociology, anthropology, psychology, and statistics for new ideas and techniques. Because this period of exploration and revision has resulted in a diverse, eclectic methodology, because no new methodological or ideological consensus has emerged—in short, because there is no successful paradigm in educational history today, it is all the more important that each reader of educational history be critically alert and independent.

See also: History of Educational Research

Bibliography

Bailyn B 1960 *Education in the Forming of American Society.* University of North Carolina Press, Chapel Hill, North Carolina

Baker D N, Harrigan P J (eds.) 1980 *The Making of Frenchmen: Current Directions in the History of Education in France, 1679–1979.* Wilfred Laurier University Press, Waterloo, Ontario

Butterfield H 1931 *The Whig Interpretation of History.* Bell, London

Carnoy M 1974 *Education as Cultural Imperialism.* McKay, New York

Craig J 1981 The expansion of education. In: Berliner D (ed.) 1981 *Review of Research in Education.* American Educational Research Association, Washington, DC, pp. 151–213

Cremin L A 1970 *American Education: The Colonial Experience, 1607–1783.* Harper and Row, New York

Cubberley E P 1934 *Public Education in the United States: A Study and Interpretation of American Educational History.* Houghton-Mifflin, Boston, Massachusetts

Dore R F 1967 *Education in Tokugawa, Japan.* Routledge and Kegan Paul, London

Johansson E 1973 *Literacy and Society in a Historical Perspective.* University Press, Umea

Kaestle C F, Vinovskis M A 1980 *Education and Social Change in Nineteenth-century Massachusetts.* Cambridge University Press, New York

Katz M B 1968 *The Irony of Early School Reform: Educational Innovation in Mid-nineteenth Century Massachusetts.* Harvard University Press, Cambridge, Massachusetts

Laqueur T W 1976 *Religion and Respectability: Sunday Schools and Working-class Culture, 1780–1850.* Yale University Press, New Haven, Connecticut

Maynes M J 1979 The virtues of archaism: The political economy of schooling in Europe, 1750–1850. *Comp. Stud. Soc. Hist.* 21: 611–25

Ringer F K 1979 *Education and Society in Modern Europe.* Indiana University Press, Bloomington, Indiana

Simon B 1960 *Studies in the History of Education, 1780–1870.* Lawrence and Wishart, London

Spaull A 1981 The biographical tradition in the history of Australian education. *Aust. N.Z. Hist. Educ. Soc. J.* 10: 1–10

Stone L 1969 Literacy and education in England, 1640–1900. *Past and Present* 42: 61–139

Thabault R 1971 *Education and Change in a Village Community, Mazières-en-Gâtine, 1848–1914.* Schocken, New York

Tyack D B 1974 *The One Best System: A History of American Urban Education.* Harvard University Press, Cambridge, Massachusetts

Action Research

S. Kemmis

Action research is a form of research carried out by practitioners into their own practices. In this article, the definition and character of action research is outlined with reference to its history. The resurgence of interest in educational action research is discussed. Action research is then distinguished from other forms of contemporary educational research through an examination of the "objects" of action research: educational practices. These are not understood by action researchers as "phenomena", "treatments", or expressions of practitioners' perspectives, but rather as praxis. Examples of practices studied by action researchers are given. Research techniques employed by action researchers are noted; it is argued that action research is distinguished not by technique but in terms of method. Criteria for evaluation of action research are then outlined. The role of outside facilitators in educational action research is discussed, and different kinds of intervention by outsiders are shown to influence the form of action research studies. The article concludes with a discussion of the relationship between action research, policy research, and the control of education, suggesting that action research is a participatory democratic form of educational research for educational improvement.

1. The Definition and Character of Action Research

Action research is a form of self-reflective enquiry undertaken by participants in social (including educational) situations in order to improve the rationality and justice of (a) their own social or educational practices, (b) their understanding of these practices, and (c) the situations in which the practices are carried out. It is most rationally empowering when undertaken by participants collaboratively, though it is often undertaken by individuals, and sometimes in cooperation with "outsiders". In education, action research has been employed in school-based curriculum development, professional development, school improvement programmes, and systems planning and policy development. Although these activities are frequently carried out using approaches, methods, and techniques unrelated to those of action research, participants in these development processes are increasingly choosing action research as a way of participating in decision making about development.

In terms of method, a self-reflective spiral of cycles of planning, acting, observing, and reflecting is central to the action research approach. Kurt Lewin, who coined the phrase "action research" in about 1944, described the process in terms of planning, fact finding, and execution.

Planning usually starts with something like a general idea. For one reason or another it seems desirable to reach a certain objective. Exactly how to circumscribe this objective and how to reach it is frequently not too clear. The first step, then, is to examine the idea carefully in the light of the means available. Frequently more fact-finding about the situation is required. If this first period of planning is successful, two items emerge: an "over-all plan" of how to reach the objective and a decision in regard to the first step of action. Usually this planning has also somewhat modified the original idea.

The next period is devoted to executing the first step of the overall plan. In highly developed fields of social management, such as modern factory management or the execution of a war, this second step is followed by certain fact-findings. For example, in the bombing of Germany a certain factory may have been chosen as the first target after careful consideration of various priorities and of the best means and ways of dealing with this target. The attack is pressed home and immediately a reconnaissance plane follows with the one objective of determining as accurately and objectively as possible the new situation.

This reconnaissance or fact-finding has four functions: It should evaluate the action by showing whether what has been achieved is above or below expectation. It should serve as a basis for correctly planning the next step. It should serve as a basis for modifying the "overall plan". Finally, it gives the planners a chance to learn, that is, to gather new general insight, for instance, regarding the strength and weakness of certain weapons or techniques of action.

The next step again is composed of a circle of planning, executing, and reconnaissance or fact-finding for the purpose of evaluating the results of the second step, for preparing the rational basis for planning the third step, and for perhaps modifying again the over-all plan. (Lewin 1952 p. 564)

Lewin documented the effects of group decision in facilitating and sustaining changes in social conduct, and emphasized the value of involving participants in every phase of the action research process (planning, acting, observing, and reflecting). He also saw action research as based on principles which could lead "gradually to independence, equality, and cooperation" and effectively alter policies of "permanent exploitation" which he saw as "likely to endanger every aspect of democracy" (Lewin 1946 p. 46). Lewin saw action research as being essential for the progress of "basic social research". In order to "develop deeper insights into the laws which govern social life", mathematical and conceptual problems of theoretical analysis would be required, as would "descriptive fact-finding in regard to small and large social bodies"; "above all", he argued, basic social research "would have to include laboratory and field experiments in social change" (Lewin 1946 p. 35).

Lewin thus presaged three important characteristics of modern action research: its participatory character, its democratic impulse, and its simultaneous contribution to social science and social change. In each of these three areas, however, action researchers of the 1980s would take exception to Lewin's formulation of the significance of action research. First, they would regard group decision making as important as a matter of principle rather than as a matter of technique; that is, not merely as an effective means of facilitating and maintaining social change but also as essential for authentic commitment to social action. Second, though this is partly a matter of changing historical conditions, contemporary exponents of action research would object to the notion that participants should or could be "led" to

more democratic forms of life through action research. Action research should not be seen as a recipe or technique for bringing about democracy, but rather as an embodiment of democratic principles in research, allowing participants to influence, if not determine, the conditions of their own lives and work, and collaboratively to develop critiques of social conditions which sustain dependence, inequality, or exploitation in any research enterprise in particular, or in social life in general. Third, contemporary action researchers would object to the language in which Lewin describes the theoretical aims and methods of social science ("developing deeper insights into the laws that govern social life" through mathematical and conceptual analysis and laboratory and field experiments); this language would now be described as belonging to positivistic science (determinist, technicist) and incompatible with the aims and methods of an adequate and coherent view of social science, especially educational science.

Carr and Kemmis (1983 p. 158) argue that there are five formal requirements for any adequate and coherent educational science:

(a) it must reject positivist notions of rationality, objectivity, and truth;

(b) it must employ the interpretive categories of teachers (or the other participants directly concerned with the practices under enquiry);

(c) it must provide ways of distinguishing ideas and interpretations which are systematically distorted by ideology from those which are not, and provide a view of how distorted self-understandings can be overcome;

(d) it must be concerned to identify and expose those aspects of the existing social order which frustrate rational change, and must be able to offer theoretical accounts which enable teachers (and other participants) to become aware of how they may be overcome; and

(e) it must be based on an explicit recognition that it is practical, in the sense that the question of its truth will be determined by the way it relates to practice.

Unlike a number of other forms of contemporary educational research, contemporary action research meets these requirements.

2. The Resurgence of Interest in Action Research

Lewin's early action research work was concerned with changes in attitudes and conduct in a number of areas of social concern (for example, in relation to food habits and factory production in the later years of the Second World War, and in relation to prejudice and intergroup relations immediately after the War). His ideas were quickly carried into education, when his co-workers and students (and often Lewin himself) began working with educationists on issues of curriculum construction and the professional development of teachers. Teachers College, Columbia University became a centre for action research in education. Stephen Corey, at one time Dean of Teachers College, became an influential advocate (Corey 1953). Kenneth Benne, Hilda Taba, and Abraham Shumsky were other early exponents of educational action research.

After enjoying a decade of growth, educational action research went into decline in the late 1950s. Although some action research work in education has continued in the United States, Nevitt Sanford (1970) argued that the decline was attributable to a growing separation of research and action (or, as it might be put today, of theory from practice). As academic researchers in the social sciences began to enjoy unprecedented support from public funding bodies, they began to distinguish the work (and the status) of the theorist–researcher from that of the "engineer" responsible for putting theoretical principles into practice. The rising tide of post-Sputnik curriculum development, based on a research–development–diffusion (R,D, and D) model of the relationship between research and practice, legitimated and sustained this separation. Large-scale curriculum development and evaluation activities, based on the cooperation of practitioners in development and evaluation tasks devised by theoreticians, diverted legitimacy and energy from the essentially small-scale, locally organized, self-reflective approach of action research. By the mid-1960s, the technical R,D, and D model had established itself as the pre-eminent model for change and practically inclined educationists were increasingly absorbed into R,D, and D activities.

Perhaps the greatest impetus to the resurgence of contemporary interest in educational action research came from the work of the 1973–1976 Ford Teaching Project in the United Kingdom, under the direction of John Elliott and Clem Adelman. This project, initially based at the Centre for Applied Research in Education, University of East Anglia, involved teachers in collaborative action research into their own practices, in particular in the area of inquiry/discovery approaches to learning and teaching (Elliott 1976–77). Its notion of the "self-monitoring teacher" was based on Lawrence Stenhouse's (1975) views of the teacher as a researcher and as an "extended professional". It seems that Stenhouse had been influenced by certain action research work carried out at the Tavistock Institute of Human Relations. Lewin and his co-workers at the Research Center for Group Dynamics (established at the Massachusetts Institute of Technology and subsequently moved, after Lewin's death in 1947, to the University of Michigan) had collaborated with Tavistock social psychologists in founding the *Journal of Social Issues*.

Since his involvement in the Ford Teaching Project, John Elliott has continued to develop action research theory and practice, and has established the *Classroom Action Research Network* (publishing its own *Bulletin*) from the Cambridge Institute of Education.

Interest in action research is also growing in Australia and in continental Europe, and, once again, in the United States.

There are a number of reasons for this resurgence of interest. First, there is the demand from within an increasingly professionalized teacher force for a research role, based on the notion of the extended professional investigating her or his own practice. Second, there is the perceived irrelevance to the concerns of these practitioners of much contemporary educational research. Third, there has been the revival of interest in "the practical" in curriculum, following the work of Schwab and others on "practical deliberation" (Schwab 1969). This work has revived interest in, and provided legitimacy for, practical reasoning (as against technical or instrumental reasoning) as the basis for decisions about educational practice. Fourth, action research has been assisted by the rise of the "new wave" methods in educational research and evaluation (interpretive approaches, including illuminative evaluation, democratic evaluation, responsive evaluation, case study methods, field research, ethnography, and the like), with their emphasis on participants' perspectives and categories in shaping educational practices and situations. These methods place the practitioner at centre stage in the educational research process: actors' understandings are crucial in understanding educational action. From the role of critical informant to an external researcher, it is but a short step for the practitioner to become a self-critical researcher into her or his own practice. Fifth, the accountability movement has galvanized and politicized practitioners. In response to the accountability movement, practitioners have adopted the self-monitoring role as a proper means of justifying practice and generating sensitive critiques of the working conditions in which their practice is conducted (conditions often created by the policy makers who hold them accountable for their actions). Sixth, there is the growing solidarity of the teaching profession in response to the public criticism which has accompanied the postexpansion educational politics of the 1970s and 1980s; this, too, has fostered the organization of support networks of concerned professionals interested in the continuing development of education even though the expansionist tide has turned. And finally, there is the increased awareness of action research itself, which is perceived as providing an understandable and workable approach to the improvement of practice through critical self-reflection.

3. The Objects of Action Research

The "objects" of educational action research are educational practices. These are not construed by action researchers as "phenomena" (by analogy with the objects of physical science, as if their existence was somehow independent of practitioners), nor as "treatments" (by analogy with technical or agricultural research, as if they were mere techniques, valued only as alternative and more or less efficient means to a single set of known and universally desired ends), nor as expressions of practitioners' intentions and perspectives (by analogy with the objects of interpretive research, as if their significance could be understood solely by reference to the points of view of practitioners as these meanings emerged in response to historical circumstances).

Practice, as it is understood by action researchers, is informed, committed action: *praxis*. Praxis has its roots in the commitment of the practitioner to wise and prudent action in a practical (concrete historical) situation. It is action which is informed by a "practical theory", and which may, in its turn, inform and transform the theory which informed it. Practice is not to be understood as mere behaviour, but as strategic action undertaken with commitment in response to a present, immediate, and problematic action context. Practical action is always risky; it requires wise judgment by the practitioner.

As one theorist of practical action remarks, "practical problems are problems about what to do...their solution is only found in doing something". In this sense the significance of practices can only be established in context: only under the "compulsion" to act in a real historical situation can a commitment have force for the practitioner, on the one hand, and definite historical consequences for actors and the situation, on the other. Action is thus both a "test" of commitment and the means by which practitioners can determine the adequacy of their understandings and of the situations in which practice occurs.

Since only the practitioner has access to the commitments and practical theories which inform praxis, only the practitioner can study praxis. Action research, as the study of praxis, must thus be research into one's own practice. The action researcher will embark on a course of action strategically (deliberately experimenting with practice while aiming simultaneously for improvement in the practice, understanding of the practice and the situation in which the practice occurs); monitor the action, the circumstances under which it occurs, and its consequences; and then retrospectively reconstruct an interpretation of the action in context as a basis for future action. Knowledge achieved in this way informs and refines both specific planning in relation to the practice being considered and the practitioner's general practical theory. The interpretations of other participants in the situation will be relevant in the process of reconstruction; they may be treated as the perspectives of relevant "others", in which case they inform the practitioner about the social consequences of the practice, or be regarded as the perspectives of coparticipants in the action, in which case they can inform collaborative reconstruction and contribute to the discourse of a community of practitioners researching their joint (collaborative) practices. The crucial point, however, is that only the practitioner can have access to the perspectives and commitments that inform a particular action as praxis, thus praxis can only be researched by the actor him/herself. The dialectic of action and understanding is a uniquely personal process of rational reconstruction and construction.

If it is only practitioners who can research their own practice, a problem seems to arise about whether the practitioner can understand his or her own praxis in an undistorted way—whether understandings reached will be biased, idiosyncratic (some would say "subjective"), or systematically distorted by ideology. This problem is illusory. First, this way of construing the problem suggests that there is some medium in which praxis can be described and analysed in ways which are entirely unrelated to the values and interests of those doing the observing (for example, value-free, neutral, or "objective" observation categories). This is an illusion created by the image of a value-free, "objective" social science which cannot by definition be a science of human praxis which must always embody values and interests. Moreover, the study of praxis (informed action) is always through praxis (action with and for understanding)—it, too, is an embodiment of values and interests (in the improvement of praxis). Second, this way of construing the problem fails to acknowledge that the purpose of the critical self-reflection undertaken by the practitioner is to discover previously unrecognized distortions of interpretation and action (for example, the taken-for-granted assumptions of habit, custom, precedent, and coercive social structures and the limitations on action these assumptions produce). It is important to recognize that the medium in which these distortions are expressed (language) is itself social praxis and always subject to influence by values and interests. In short, the dialectic of reconstituting meanings from actions by interpretation is always a process of relative emancipation from the dictates of habit, custom, precedent, and bureaucratic systematization; it is never a complete emancipation from injustice and irrationality. Undistorted communication is purely ideal–typical: it is never achieved, though the practitioner seeking to understand her or his praxis is bound to pursue the ideal in order to discover concrete and particular distortions influencing his or her practice. This dialectical process of reconstruction is a key part of the critical self-reflection of the action researcher.

A range of practices have been studied by educational action researchers. Some examples may suffice to give a picture of how action research has helped practitioners to understand their own practices more deeply. In studies of inquiry/discovery teaching, practitioners have come to understand how, even despite their aspirations, they have used questioning strategies which maintain student dependency on teacher authority rather than create the conditions for autonomy. In studies of the organization of remedial reading, practitioners have come to understand the contradictions of withdrawal practices that preserve rather than overcome the labelling of students as in need of "remediation", which mystify the reading process rather than make it transparent to students, and which deskill students in terms of progress in other subjects by interrupting subject teaching to focus on reading skills out of context. In studies of teacher–student negotiation of curriculum, practitioners have come to understand that an overemphasis on student interest as the basis for curriculum formation may fragment the social relations of teaching and learning, and deny students access to the discourse of established fields of knowledge. Studies of assessment practices have helped practitioners to understand that notions of ability and achievement can confirm students in failure rather than create the conditions for further learning. Investigations of learning in the classroom, undertaken by students, have helped them to understand how their roles as learners may either imprison them in dependency on teachers or create the conditions for self-directed and collaborative learning. And studies of teaching and learning in higher education, undertaken collaboratively by students and teachers, have helped them to revise their working relationships so as to achieve their joint aspirations more completely.

4. Methods, Techniques, and the Evaluation of Action Research

Action research is not distinguished by the use of a particular set of research techniques. While it is common for educational action researchers to keep focused diaries about specific aspects of their practice, to make audiotape records of verbal interactions in classrooms or meetings, to carry out group interviews with students after particular lessons, and so forth, these techniques for recording are not particularly distinctive. Similarly, the techniques for analysis of data (such as content analysis of artefacts like audiotapes of interactions or portfolios of student work, analysis of the relative frequencies of different classroom events, or critical–historical analyses of classroom records to produce interpretations of the interdependence of circumstance, action, and consequence in the classroom) are not unique to action research. It is true, however, that in general the techniques for generating and accumulating evidence about practices, and the techniques for analysing and interpreting this evidence more closely resemble the techniques employed by interpretive researchers (ethnographers, case study researchers, historians, etc.) than empirical–analytic researchers (correlational analysis, comparative experiments, etc.). This is so primarily because the "objects" of research are actions (practices) and the viewpoints and historical circumstances that give these actions meaning and significance; the "objects" of action research are not mere behaviours .

What distinguishes action research is its method, rather than particular techniques. The method is based on the notion of a spiral of self-reflection (a spiral of cycles of planning, acting, observing, and reflecting). It is essentially participatory in the sense that it involves participants in reflection on practices. It expresses a commitment to the improvement of practices, practitioners' understandings, and the settings of practice. And it is collaborative, wherever possible involving coparticipants in the organization of their own enlightenment in relation to social and political action in their own situations.

The rigour of action research does not derive from the use of particular techniques of observation or analysis (for example, measuring instruments or statistical analyses) or the use of particular metatechniques (for example, techniques for establishing the reliability or validity of measures, or for ascertaining the power of tests). Rigour derives from the logical, empirical, and political coherence of interpretations in the reconstructive moments of the self-reflective spiral (observing and reflecting) and the logical, empirical, and political coherence of justifications of proposed action in its constructive or prospective moments (planning and acting).

As in Habermas's (1974) critical social science, three separate functions in the mediation of theory and practice must be distinguished in action research. These supply criteria for the evaluation of action research studies. Separate criteria are relevant for evaluation in relation to each function, and each requires certain preconditions. First, at the level of scientific discourse, action researchers are engaged in the formation and extension of critical theorems about their practices and their situations, that is, in the formulation and articulation of their own practical theories. This can take place only under the precondition of freedom of discourse. Here the criterion is true statements; the truth of statements is evaluated through discourse which raises, recognizes, and redeems "validity claims": claims that what is stated is comprehensible, true (accurate), truthfully or sincerely stated, and right or appropriate (in its normative context). Second, at the level of enlightenment of those engaged in the self-reflective process, action researchers are involved in applying and testing their practical theories in their own action in their own situations. This can take place only under the precondition that those involved commit themselves to proper precautions and assure scope for open communication aimed at mutual understanding. Here the criterion is authentic insights, grounded in participants' own circumstances and experience. Finally, at the level of the organization of action, action researchers are engaged in the selection of strategies, the resolution of tactical questions, and the conduct of "political struggle" (that is, social and strategic action in a social and political context). This can only occur if decisions of consequence depend on the practical discourse of participants. Here the criterion is prudent decisions. Evaluating the quality of action research requires analysis at each of these "levels" of discourse, the organization of enlightenment, and the organization of action.

These criteria provide the most stringent basis for the evaluation of action research. Typically, however, action research in progress tends not to be evaluated formally in this way. Variants of the questions "Is it true?", "Does it make sense in terms of our experience?", and "Is it prudent?" are more likely to be asked by action researchers in the course of their work. This is an important observation since action research as it is actually practised by teachers and others is a part of their own social process. As such, it tends to be informal and convivial rather than formalistic and overtly "theoretical".

5. *"Facilitating" Action Research*

Since action research is research into one's own practice, it follows that only practitioners and groups of practitioners can carry out action research. It is common, however, for "outsiders" to be involved in action research, providing material, organizational, emotional, and intellectual support to practitioners. The relationships established between outside "facilitators" and action researchers can have profound effects on the character of the action research undertaken, however. To varying degrees, they influence the agenda of issues being addressed in the research and the "ownership" (authenticity) of the questions asked, the data-gathering and analytic techniques employed, and the interpretations and findings of particular studies. The intervention of outsiders may introduce significant distortions in each of the three definitive characteristics of action research: the degree to which it is practical, collaborative, or self-reflective. Indeed, it can be argued that some of what passes for action research today is not action research at all but merely a species of field experimentation or "applied" research carried out by academic or service researchers who coopt practitioners into gathering data *about* educational practices for them. This point needs to be emphasized since the rising popularity of action research in the 1980s (as in the late 1950s) has prompted many educational researchers aspiring to "relevance" to go out into the field to work with practitioners in the investigation of contemporary educational practices. Forgetting the origins of action research, they have appropriated the term and carried out studies paradigmatically opposed to the nature and spirit of action research.

At worst, these facilitators have coopted practitioners to work on externally formulated questions and issues which are not based in the practical concerns of practitioners. To the extent that it can be described as action research at all, this form may be described as technical action research. It employs techniques (for example, techniques based on a technology of group dynamics) to create and sustain commitment to investigation of issues raised by the outsider, and it frequently concerns itself with the relative efficiency and effectiveness of practices (instrumental reasoning). It is sometimes carried out in order to test the applicability of findings from studies undertaken elsewhere. Such studies may contribute to the improvement of practices, of practitioners' understandings, and the situations of practice (both from an external point of view and from practitioners' own perspectives), but they run the risk of being inauthentic for the practitioners involved, and they may create conditions for the legitimation of practices by reference to outsiders' reputations or ascribed status as "experts" or "authorities" rather than being based in the practical discourse of practitioners themselves.

More often, outsiders form cooperative relationships with practitioners, helping them to articulate their own concerns, plan strategic action, monitor the action, and reflect on processes and consequences. This is sometimes described as a "process consultancy" role. In such cases, outsiders may work with individual practitioners or with groups of practitioners interested in common practices. Where the aim is the improvement of individuals' own practices however, the relationships between participants may still be mediated by the outsider. In these situations, the research may be described as practical action research (action research which sharpens individual practical reasoning). It can and typically does contribute to the improvement of practices, practitioners' understandings, and the situations in which practice occurs, but it need not develop collaborative responsibility for practices within participant groups.

Emancipatory action research, by contrast, shifts responsibility for practice and the action research process to the participant group. In this case, the group takes joint responsibility for action and reflection. The work of the group expresses a joint commitment to the development of common practical theories, authentic insights, and prudent decision making (based on mutual understanding and consensus). This kind of action research may be described as "emancipatory" because the group itself takes responsibility for its own emancipation from the dictates of irrational or unjust habits, customs, precedents, coercion, or bureaucratic systematization. Here outsiders are unnecessary; where they do participate in the work of the group, they do so on the basis that they share responsibility equally with other members (not as legitimating authorities nor merely as process facilitators).

Historically, it is possible to discern a shift from technical to practical to emancipatory action research from the late 1940s to the early 1980s, judging from reports of educational action research over the period. Arguably, the ideal of emancipatory action research has existed from the beginning; as the "ownership" of the idea of action research has shifted from the academy to the profession itself, so the concrete relationship between outsiders and practitioners in particular action research projects has changed (from cooption to cooperation to collaboration). In some places in the world, the profession has sufficiently well-developed organizational structures to foster the development of emancipatory action research which can exist without conspicuous support from outsiders; in these areas, the profession is able to resist the legitimating role of the academy with respect to practice and to take a nondoctrinaire, critical, and self-reflective stance on the bureaucratic control of curriculum and pedagogy (and, in particular, the nexus of policy making and policy research).

6. *Action Research, Policy Research, and the Control of Education*

The choice of research methods depends on the presumed character of the object of the research (e.g. a "natural" phenomenon, a product of "subjective" views of participants, a product of historical and ideological processes). Moreover, these presumptions will tend to be confirmed by the conduct of educational inquiries not because of any principle "correctness" of the presumptions, but because the presumptions will appear to be vindicated merely by the practice of research. In this way, research practice alone (and ultimately research traditions) conventionalizes and legitimates the paradigmatic presumptions of researchers.

Educational research is generally justified by reference to its contribution to educational reform. In this sense, almost all educational research is policy research; that is, it has the aim of influencing educational practices through influencing local or systemwide policies about curriculum and pedagogy. Three points need to be made about this nexus of research and reform: (a) it assumes that researchers understand the nature of education as an object of research (including its nature as a social enterprise); (b) it assumes that researchers understand the social nature and consequences of educational reform; and (c) it assumes that researchers understand the research enterprise itself as inherently social and political, that is, as an ideological activity.

Different approaches to educational research have different perspectives on how reform relates to research. Put at its simplest, different approaches to educational research have different theories of educational change which underpin them. These theories of educational change embody different assumptions about the control of education.

Empirical–analytic research views educational events and practices as "phenomena" susceptible to "objective" treatment. It views schooling as a delivery system whose effectiveness and efficiency can be improved by improvements in the technology of the system. Its form of reasoning is technical, instrumental (means–ends) reasoning. Its interest is in the technical control of education systems, and this technical rationality readily expresses itself in an interest in hierarchical bureaucratic control of the social relations between systems personnel and between teachers and students.

Interpretive research sees education as a historical process and as a lived experience for those involved in educational processes and institutions. Its form of reasoning is practical; it aims to transform the consciousness of practitioners and, by so doing, to give them grounds upon which to reform their own practices. Its interest is in transforming education by educating practitioners; it assumes a relationship between educational researchers and educational practitioners based on mutual trust which leaves practitioners free to decide how to change their practices in the light of their own informed practical deliberation.

Critical social scientific research, including emancipatory action research, views education as a historical and ideological process. Its form of reasoning is practical (like that of interpretive research) but also critical: it is shaped by the emancipatory intent to transform educational organizations and practices to achieve rationality and social justice. It is predisposed towards ideology–critique: the recognition and negation of educational ideologies which serve the interests of specific groups at the expense of others and which mask oppression and domination with the appearance of liberation.

Empirical–analytic and interpretive research preserve a "gap" between theory and practice. They institutionalize the separation of theory and practice in the separate roles of the researcher–theorist and the practitioner. Critical social scientific research requires the development of self-reflective communities of practitioner–theorists committed to critically examining their own practices and improving them in the interests of rationality and social justice. While the first two forms of educational research employ theories of change which are concretely realized in political relationships which seek to bring practitioners' practices into line with theorists' theories (explicitly in the case of empirical–analytic research and implicitly in the case of interpretive research), critical educational research does not. In this latter case, the development of practical theories is carried out by practitioners as part of the process of change; indeed, all change in the latter case is transformation by practitioners of existing conditions, perspectives, and practices in the interests of rationality and social justice.

Educational action research is a form of educational research which places control over processes of educational reform in the hands of those involved in the action. In principle, this control can be shared collaboratively by communities of teachers, students, administrators, parents, and others. In practice, most action research projects have involved only one or two, and occasionally three, of these groups.

It would be an exaggeration to argue that emancipatory action research in education is the only defensible form of educational research or the only form of educational research capable of bringing about stable transformations of educational practice towards more rational and more just educational arrangements in contemporary society. An argument can be mounted, however, that educational action research is grossly underutilized as an approach to educational reform in a democratic society and that it is, or should be, a key part of the role of the professional educator. Participatory democracy involves substantial control by people over their own lives, and within that, over their work. Emancipatory action research is one means by which this ideal can be approached.

See also: Teachers as Researchers; Knowledge Utilization

Bibliography

Carr W, Kemmis S 1983 *Becoming Critical: Knowing through Action Research*. Deakin University Press, Geelong, Victoria
Corey S M 1953 *Action Research to Improve School Practices*. Teachers College, Columbia University, New York
Elliott J 1976–77 Developing hypotheses about classrooms from teachers' practical constructs: An account of the work of the Ford Teaching Project. *Interchange* 7(2): 2–22

Habermas J 1974 *Theory and Practice*. Heinemann, London
Lewin K 1946 Action research and minority problems. *J. Soc. Issues* 2(4): 34–46
Lewin K 1952 Group decision and social change. In: Swanson G E, Newcomb T M, Hartley E L (eds.) 1952 *Readings in Social Psychology*. Holt, New York, pp. 459–73

Sanford N 1970 Whatever happened to action research? *J. Soc. Issues* 26(4): 3–23
Schwab J J 1969 The practical: A language for curriculum. *Sch. Rev.* 78: 1–23
Stenhouse L 1975 *An Introduction to Curriculum Research and Development*. Heinemann, London

Case Study Methods

L. Stenhouse

Case study methods involve the collection and recording of data about a case or cases, and the preparation of a report or a presentation of the case. The collection of data on site is termed "fieldwork", and it involves: (a) generally, participant or nonparticipant observation and interviewing; (b) probably, the collection of documentary evidence and descriptive statistics, and the administration of tests or questionnaires; and (c) possibly, the use of photography, motion pictures, or videotape recording.

Sometimes, particularly in evaluation research, which is commissioned to evaluate a specific case, the case itself is regarded as of sufficient interest to merit investigation. However, case study does not preclude an interest in generalization, and many researchers seek theories that will penetrate the varying conditions of action, or applications founded on the comparison of case with case. Generalization and application are matters for judgment rather than for calculation, and the task of case study is to produce ordered reports of experience which invite judgment and offer evidence to which judgment can appeal. In this, case study resembles history, and, like history, its appeal to judgment often demands the representation or quotation of persons. This element of naturalistic presentation or portrayal raises in case study ethical problems regarding the use of data identifiably associated with living persons.

This article does not cover the case study of individual subjects in psychology, narrative historical studies of individual schools, or documentary films of cases.

1. Case Study and the Psychostatistical Paradigm

The psychostatistical paradigm of educational research is expressed in field experiments and surveys based on sampling. It is founded on the insight that to draw a sample from a population randomly rather than by judgment permits the use of the mathematics of probability to estimate the reliability and validity of results obtained in the sample. This entails the expression of observations as quantitative indices. The paradigm is elegant, but in practice many educational problems involve such a complex interaction of variables that they elude quantitative techniques which reduce disparate observed phenomena to the homogeneity of traits or types. This suggests the need for analyses based on close observation.

Case study may be seen as a response to this need for a return to close natural observation, or as a reaction against the positivist epistemology implied in the psychostatistical paradigm. Case study methods are often described as naturalistic, qualitative, descriptive, responsive, interpretative, hermeneutic, or idiographic by way of contrast to the abstracted, quantitative, nomothetic approach of psychostatistical methods that strip observation to indices. However, quantitative indices are often used in case study, though generally descriptively and in a subordinate role, and there is some scope for the use of single-case experimental designs.

2. Styles of Case Study

Although case study methods are in flux, for the purpose of exposition it is worth describing four broad styles of work. The first of these, ethnography, is located within the social sciences. The others, evaluation, educational case study, and action research, are closely related to educational action and are differently modulated derivations from the curriculum movement.

2.1 Ethnographic Case Study

In ethnography, a single case is studied in depth by participant observation supported by interview, after the manner of cultural or social anthropology, which concentrates on the understanding of human societies and cultures, particularly through the observation and interpretation of inter-personal relations in the context of an emphasis on custom and institutions. Some would restrict the term ethnography to those studies conceived within the theoretical framework of cultural anthropology. However, the term is also generally applied to case studies conducted in the neoethnographic tradition of the Chicago school of sociologists and their successors, and set within sociological, rather than anthropological, theory. Of ethnographic case study it may be said that it calls into question the apparent understandings of the actors in the case and offers from the outsider's standpoint explanations that emphasize causal or structural patterns of which participants in the case are unaware. It does not generally relate directly to the practical needs of the actors in the case, though it may affect their perception and hence the tacit grounding of their actions. Examples of the use of such methods have been reported by Hargreaves (1967), Wolcott (1967), and Peshkin (1978).

2.2 Evaluative Case Study

In evaluative case studies a single case or a collection of cases is studied in depth with the purpose of providing educational actors or decision makers (administrators, teachers, parents, pupils, etc.) with information that will help them to judge the merit and worth of policies, programmes, or institutions. Case study styles of evaluation developed in the curriculum movement and examples of such research have been reported by Stake and Gjerde (1974) and MacDonald (1981).

Evaluative case studies are caught in the time scale of the programmes they are evaluating and the decisions they are informing and this has led to the development of "condensed fieldwork", in which interview typically dominates participant observation, since the latter is essentially a long-term, in-depth technique. In evaluation, the case to be evaluated is commonly a programme or policy expressed in a number of institutions or settings and the evaluator is thus concerned with multiple case studies in a number of sites: hence multisite case study (Stake and Easley 1978).

2.3 Educational Case Study

Many researchers using case study methods are concerned neither with social theory nor with evaluative judgment, but rather with the understanding of educational action. They may adopt a strategy close to that of the ethnographer (Smith and Keith 1971) or close to that of the evaluator (Hamilton 1977). They are concerned to enrich the thinking and discourse of educators either by the development of educational theory or by the refinement of prudence through the systematic and reflective documentation of experience.

It seems likely that multisite approaches will have an increasing part to play in educational case study (Stenhouse 1982).

2.4 Case Study in Action Research

Action research is concerned with contributing to the development of the case or cases under study by feedback of information which can guide revision and refinement of the action. In the curriculum movement, action research was extensively used in research and development projects to produce curricular specifications and materials. When teaching strategies were important in the development, teachers were heavily involved in developing their own teaching through self case study.

3. Teacher as Researcher

A significant development in the field of educational case study is the teacher-as-researcher movement. In evaluative case study, this has led to school self-evaluation within the framework of the accountability movement. In educational case study, practising teachers have produced studies of their own classrooms or

schools, mainly in unpublished research degree dissertations. Such case studies present particular problems and advantages because of the status of the observer as a responsible participant. The teacher action research movement has gathered pace in England and Wales and Australia in particular, and is also beginning to evoke considerable interest in Scandinavia.

4. The Conduct of Case Studies

The conduct of case studies falls naturally into four phases: selecting cases and negotiating access, fieldwork, the organization of records, and the writing of a report.

4.1 Selecting Cases and Negotiating Access

Most single case studies are opportunistic: a matter of seeing interest in a case to which one has access. However, each case studied adds to the collection of cases, and ideally the choice of case should be made bearing in mind its relation to the corpus of cases available. In multisite case study, the collection of cases should cover the range of variables judged to be the most important in relation to the theme of the study.

A high proportion of case-study workers cite the advice offered by Glaser and Strauss (1967 p. 55):

> By maximizing or minimizing differences among comparative groups, the sociologist can control the theoretical relevance of his data collection. Comparing as many differences and similarities in data as possible tends to force the analyst to generate categories, their properties, and their inter-relations as he tries to understand his data.

Random sampling is only applicable where case studies conducted within a sample run alongside quantitative methods deployed within the psychostatistical paradigm. Normally the external validity of case study hinges on judgmental comparison or the generation of theory rather than on calculations that premise randomness.

Once a case is selected, it is necessary to negotiate access. In educational research this process is complicated by the hierarchical structure of accountability. The researcher may need to negotiate with the administrative authority before approaching an institution, with the head of the institution before approaching staff, with staff before approaching pupils. At each stage there is danger that the fieldworker might be seen as sponsored by the higher authority with consequent risks of distortion of data. It is crucial that access to data is not conceded to authorities in return for access to the case, thus exposing the subjects of study and influencing their responses (see *Ethical Considerations in Research*).

4.2 Fieldwork

Fieldwork is that process of evoking, gathering, and organizing information which takes place on, or in close proximity to, the site of the events or phenomena being studied. This definition is intended to cover not simply the work done on site, but also that done during evenings and weekends that are intervals within a period of on-site study. Fieldwork includes: collecting and evoking documents; observing; and measuring or collecting statistics.

(a) *Collecting and evoking documents.* "It is," wrote the Webbs (1897), "a peculiarity of human, and especially of social, action that it secretes records of facts, not with any view to affording material for the investigator, but as data for the future guidance of the organisms themselves." Such documents as log books, minutes and school timetables, letters, and memos are, for many research purposes, invaluable. Also valuable, though more subject to distorting influences, are statements for audiences, such as brochures addressed to parents or school magazines.

In addition to such records, written testimony may be available in the form of diaries, autobiographies, memoirs, and letters, though these are relatively uncommon in educational case studies. However, such documents may be evoked by the researcher: in particular, participants may be asked to keep diaries or engage in correspondence.

It is also possible that there will be visual records such as architects' plans or photographs of school classes or perhaps even films or videotapes about an institution such as a school or college.

Documents are readily collected as a rule, do not raise problems of record keeping for the researcher, are not usually so prolific in an educational setting as to overburden the researcher, and are subject to well-established canons of critical appraisal which have been worked out by historians.

(b) *Observing.* By observing is meant perceiving appearances, events, or behaviour (including speech). The observer may be fully participant, that is, filling an available role in the social setting under observation; aspirant participant, that is, seeking to achieve acceptance in an unusual participant role such as researcher; nonparticipant, that is, seeking to minimize participant interaction with those observed; or covert, that is, hidden from those observed by such a device as a one-way screen. Fully participant observation can itself be covert if the research interest of the observer is screened from those research, though this limits the observer's capacity to engage in direct inquiry.

Close and thoughtful observation of others is always an important and intensive feature of participant observation, and this includes, as an important element, observation of speech in natural settings.

Observation clearly calls for some kind of recording, and the field notebook is the classic form. But it is not easy to keep a good record. Taking notes during observation is generally intrusive, and field notes are usually written up from memory as soon as possible after the event. Clear indications are desirable to distinguish paraphrase from quotation. Sometimes photography can be used either as a record or as a stimulus for writing. A trained memory is at a premium.

As fieldwork becomes more condensed, the participant observer role is attenuated, and observation becomes located within a study where the main weight is carried by interviewing. Observation often provides cues for the agenda of interview or follows from remarks made by an interviewer. The crucial issue in such fieldwork is whether to trust observation over interview or interview over observation. In some cases one is clearly more reliable than the other: in other cases the matter is contentious. It is clear, however, that, as fieldwork becomes condensed, influence based on observation becomes more precarious because of the observer's limited acquaintance with the site.

(c) *Interviewing.* Observation of speech behaviour shades across into interview, as the spoken transaction becomes initiated and managed by the researcher, who becomes the audience for what is spoken. Many participant observers try to keep interviewing as informal and as close to observation as possible, making their interviews many and short and conducting them in informal settings—walking along a corridor or driving in a car, for example. One problem of such interviews is their recording. Most often they are recorded from memory in a notebook at the earliest opportunity.

As fieldwork becomes more interview based and less observation based, interviews tend to become more formal. For example, they are often arranged by appointment. Generally, however, interviews are not structured by a schedule, though the interviewer will commonly have an agenda in mind. Early questions are usually broadly framed, later questions tend to be more focused. The style of an interviewer is largely a matter of personality. The aim is to establish a relaxed conversation—whether it be relatively formal or relatively informal. Learning to listen well is important.

Seating arrangements are significant. To sit side-by-side or obliquely facing one another is, as it were, to look out on the world together, a good position for a collaborative interview. Face-to-face seating favours interrogation. However, the effects of seating interact with the styles of the persons involved.

How to record an interview is a matter of contention. Some feel that tape recording is more intrusive than note taking, others take the opposite view. Formally, it is clear that tape recording provides the most reliable record, though with the disadvantage that tape recordings are themselves not easy to use as sources for later work. If time and resources allow, tapes are generally transcribed. Where limited resources make this impossible, a good procedure is to play the tape through and make notes on pages ruled into three columns: one column contains the tape recorder counter number, the second contains a running index of content, and the third is devoted to verbatim quotations.

The process of interviewing and recording the interview creates a "document" in the sense that historians use that word. At the extreme of participant observation, interpretation in the field is at a premium: the extreme of interviewing produces a document for subsequent critical interpretation at leisure.

(d) *Measuring or collecting statistics.* Many are involved in case study as a reaction against the psychostatistical paradigm, and have regarded case study as qualitative. However, the contrast is not between quantitative and qualitative, but between samples and cases (Stenhouse 1982).

Thus the emphasis in statistical applications would be on the description of the case and its comparison with other cases rather than on statistical inference based on sampling. A reading of Ball (1981) will show how far case study has gone in the use of indices. There is plenty of room for development and work on social indicators, on unobtrusive measures, and on exploratory data analysis, where relevant.

4.3 Organization of Records

As a result of the processes described above, it is now possible to imagine the researcher having a substantial collection of documents, observer's notes, interview transcripts, statistics, and the like. Perhaps these materials extend to 1,000 pages or more. The task may be to write up the case or to write across a number of cases of which this is one. This raw material produced by case study may be termed the "case record" (Stenhouse 1982).

Experience shows that case studies are inclined to falter at this point. In particular, social scientists used to handling data reduced by quantitative techniques find the sheer bulk of the record daunting, though historians commonly deal with the problem in yet more acute form.

Two strategies are: progressive reduction of the record and indexing. Progressive reduction selects from the record a smaller record, perhaps photocopied, and then further reduces that by weeding. It is important to take notes during such reduction so that the relation of the reduced record is kept in mind. The alternative, indexing, also requires note taking and a gradual build-up of an interpretation, but the indexing of the record allows selection without actual pruning. Marginal colour codings can also be useful.

It is good practice to make two copies of the record if possible, one to stand as primary source, the other to use as a working copy.

4.4 Reporting and Writing a Report

There is not really enough experience of the problem of writing up this kind of material in educational research. For present purposes a good starting point is to consider the use of narrative, portrayal, vignette, and analysis.

Narrative reporting has two great strengths: directness and subtlety. Its directness comes partly from the familiarity of its conventions to readers, and partly because the narrative form constrains the author from presenting his or her own logic in the teeth of resistance from the story. Its subtlety lies in a capacity to convey ambiguity concerning cause and effect by selecting information that invites the reader to speculate about alternative interpretations.

Portrayal reporting is an attempt to preserve some of the qualities of narrative in descriptive writing that lacks a natural story line. As in documentary film, characters,

incidents, and descriptions of an environment in which they are set are juxtaposed to provide a portrayal which is interpretative of the case as a whole.

Vignette reporting has the status of a sketch compared to a fully worked picture. The selection of the subject of a vignette is an interpretative act, for a vignette crystallizes some important aspect of a case. Commonly a vignette is used to concretize an analysis by relating an incident or offering a snapshot of a person or a place.

Analysis reporting debates its points explicitly, wherever possible reviewing evidence. Most often the conceptual framework is contributed by its author and draws on the social sciences. Though cruder than narrative, it is more explicit. Whereas the words of narrative are crowded with connotations and derivations, those of analysis tend to be starker and more denotative in the light of their definitions. Analysis favours the search for precision in terminology and in theory.

Interesting problems in the reporting of case study research are set by multisite case study. Stake and Easley in *Case Studies in Science Education* (1978) offer in one volume portrayals of each case and in another an overview which attempts to look across the cases. It could be argued that the overview is too concerned to generalize as opposed to contrast, but there is a lack of examples of attempts to use contrast to highlight variables.

5. Case Study Theory and Explanation

Case study is pitched between science and history, and the role of theory and the nature of explanation is debatable. Polar positions can be illustrated by quotation. Popper speaks for the scientific pole:

> A scientist, whether theorist or experimenter, puts forward statements, or systems of statements, and tests them step by step. In the field of the empirical sciences, more particularly, he constructs hypotheses, or systems of theories, and tests them against experience by observation and experiment. (1959 p. 27)

Gardiner speaks for the historical pole:

> We do explain human actions in terms of reaction to environment. But we also explain human actions in terms of thoughts, desires, and plans. We may believe that it is in principle possible to give a full causal explanation of why people think, desire, or plan the things they do in terms of their past experience or training or perhaps in terms of the working of their bodies. But, even if the latter proposition is true, it still does not follow that explanation in terms of thoughts and desires has been rendered superfluous, or that it has been "reduced" to cause–effect explanation. (1961 p. 139)

Between these two poles lies theory in the social sciences.

Glaser and Strauss (1967) characterized case study methods as generative of theory grounded in the study of the case rather than as capable of testing theory, and their position has been very influential among researchers. However, their reserve must be related to the weakness of theory in the social sciences, since strong theory can readily be falsified or shown to be paradoxical on the basis of a single case.

Case study workers with a strong interest in theory have generally been attracted by phenomenology and symbolic interactionism which stress the status of experience and of meaning, as contrasted with the residual behaviourism of much social theory. Recently some case studies have been set within Marxist theory (Willis 1977).

Case study in educational research might reasonably be thought of as giving priority to educational practice as compared to social theory, and this issue has divided researchers. Marxist standpoints are attractive as offering a dialectical resolution of this conflict in the concept of praxis, which in Marxist theory expresses the problem of the unity of theory and practice.

Habermas, who has a central concern with this problem, also builds on Vico:

> Vico retains the Aristotelian distinction between science and prudence, episteme and phronesis: while science aims at "eternal truths", making statements about what is always and necessarily so, practical prudence is only concerned with the "probable". Vico shows how this latter procedure precisely because it makes less theoretical claims, brings greater certainty in practice. (Habermas 1971 p. 45)

If educational case study appeals to the experience of participation and consequently tends towards the vernacular because it recognizes "the task of entering into the consciousness and the conviction of citizens prepared to act" (Habermas 1971 p. 75), then both its theoretical basis and its contribution to theory are likely to continue to be the subject of lively debate.

6. Ethics and Educational Case Study

The problem of ethics particular to case study arises principally because of the portrayal of persons or institutions in forms that subject them to the possibility of recognition. There are social scientists who take the view that ethical considerations of this sort should not normally be allowed to block the pursuit of truth and there are also researchers who place ethical considerations in the context of accountability and the "right to know". Judging by the statements of the ethics committees of various associations of social and psychological scientists, those who take a hard line are in a minority.

However, there is a basic dispute as to whether data gathered about people are to be regarded as owned by them and hence to a high degree open to their control or whether they are owned by the researchers who have gathered the data and subject only to their ethical principles.

Various procedures are used by those who believe the data in principle belong to the subjects in order to negotiate contracts for the conduct of case study and clearance of data gathered. It has become evident that subjects cannot always see clearly the implications of their consent and many workers thus feel that, though contract may be necessary, it does not exempt the researcher from further ethical considerations.

It might be thought a reasonable principle that no data used in such a way as to threaten disadvantage to the persons portrayed, but this is difficult to interpret both in terms of anticipation of risk and in terms of what counts as a recognizable disadvantage.

In educational case study where the purpose of the research is to improve educational practice and hence the lot of children and the professionalism of teachers, there is at least some room for a consideration of the responsibility of subjects to take some risks on professional grounds.

What is clear is that no researcher should embark on research by case study methods without a thoughtful review of ethical problems and a study of the relevant literature.

Bibliography

Ball S J 1981 *Beachside Comprehensive: A Case-study of Secondary Schooling*. Cambridge University Press, Cambridge

Gardiner P 1961 *The Nature of Historical Explanation*. Oxford University Press, London

Glaser B G, Strauss A L 1967 *The Discovery of Grounded Theory: Strategies for Qualitative Research*. Aldine Press, Chicago, Illinois

Habermas J 1971 *Theorie und Praxis*. Suhrkamp, Frankfurt

Hamilton D 1977 *In Search of Structure: Essays from a New Scottish Open-plan Primary School*. Hodder and Stoughton, London

Hargreaves D H 1967 *Social Relations in a Secondary School*. Routledge and Kegan Paul, London

MacDonald B 1981 *The Experience of Innovation*. CARE, University of East Anglia, Norwich

Peshkin A 1978 *Growing Up American: Schooling and the Survival of Community*. University of Chicago Press, Chicago, Illinois

Popper K R 1959 *The Logic of Scientific Discovery*. Hutchinson, London

Smith L M, Keith P M 1971 *Anatomy of Educational Innovation: An Organizational Analysis of an Elementary School*. Wiley, New York

Stake R E, Easley J 1978 *Case Studies in Science Education*. CIRCE, University of Illinois, Urbana, Illinois

Stake R E, Gjerde C 1974 *An Evaluation of T. City*. American Educational Research Association (AERA) Monograph Series in Curriculum Evaluation No 7. Rand McNally, Chicago, Illinois

Stenhouse L 1982 *Papers on Case-study Research in Education*. CARE, University of East Anglia, Norwich

Webb S, Webb B 1897 *Industrial Democracy*. Longmans Green, London

Willis P E 1977 *Learning to Labour: How Working Class Kids get Working Class Jobs*. Saxon House, Farnborough

Wolcott H F 1967 *A Kwakiutl Village and School*. Holt, Rinehart and Winston, New York

Critical Theory [1]

G. Lakomski

Among the various theories currently competing for acceptance, if not dominance, in the field of education, critical theory is a vigorous and ambitious contender. It is the purpose of this article to ask just how serious a contender critical theory is by examining its validity as a theory and its usefulness as an approach to educational research.

As a relative newcomer to educational theory, the critical theory of society, whether in its original, or later Habermasian, form has already marshalled significant support and won over a dedicated group of educators. Its arrival in educational research was greeted enthusiastically by writers such as Bredo and Feinberg (1982), for example, who believe that critical theory is able to transcend the distance between the dominant positivist school and its challenger, the interpretivist paradigm. Both schools of educational research have come under attack. Positivist research has been challenged both from within analytic philosophy of science and from interpretivists who criticize its reductionism, while the implicit relativism of the interpretivist approach is said to make it an unsuitable successor to positivism. Critical theory, as seen by its advocates, promises to solve the problems of both schools in a higher-order synthesis which allocates the empirical–analytic and the historical–hermeneutic sciences to their own, mutually exclusive, object domains, complete with their respective methodologies.

In addition to relegating the sciences to their respective spheres of influence and thus deflating any claims for the superiority of one or the other methodology, critical theory has a distinctive political orientation. It suggests that the current dominance of science and the rise of technology and bureaucracy are developmental tendencies of late capitalism which increasingly encroach on the domain of social life (Habermas 1976b). As a result of such imperialism which is accompanied by the decline and erosion of traditional institutions and legitimations, the legitimatory vacuum thus created is filled by the new belief in science (Habermas 1972c). What is obliterated in this process, according to Habermas, is the possibility of raising questions about social norms and values, and questions about "the good life" in the public domain. Where they are raised, they can only be perceived through the distorting lens of instrumental action, or the technical interest, which makes them appear solvable by the application of Weber's means–end scheme. Unmasking the illegitimate intrusion of science into the realm of social norms, Habermas believes, makes critical theory "critical" in the sense Marx understood the term, since science and

technology have thus been shown to be ideological. The perspective which makes such insight possible is that of critical reflection which liberates or emancipates actors from false beliefs and subsequently leads to concrete proposals for overcoming oppression.

It is not difficult to see the attraction of critical theory for a number of educators who, critical of positivism, wary of the implicit relativism and conservatism of the interpretive school, and disenchanted with the so-called economism of Marxist education theory (e.g. Bowles and Gintis 1976), have been searching for a more appropriate foundation for a socially-just educational theory and practice. Critical theory, consequently, has found application in curriculum theory (Apple 1982, Young and Whitty 1977), educational administration (Bates 1983, Foster 1980a, Foster 1980b, Giroux 1983), action research (Carr and Kemmis 1983, Kemmis et al. 1983), and has been used to explain the crisis in formal schooling (e.g. Shapiro 1984).

Employing the critical theory, Huebner (1975 p. 223) describes contemporary approaches to curriculum-making as reflecting:

> almost completely, a technical value system. It [curricular ideology] has a means–end rationality that approaches an economic model. End states, end products, or objectives are specified as accurately as possible, hopefully in behavioral terms. Activities are then designed which become the means to these ends or objectives.

This assessment is echoed by Van Manen (1977 p. 209) who notes that "Curriculum is approached as a nexus of behavioral modes which must be monitored, objectified, rationalized, and made accountable". Questions about the practical relevancy of, for example, teacher education programmes in Van Manen's view are then directly translatable into demands for increasing teacher competency and curriculum effectiveness.

In educational administration, writers such as Bates, Foster, and Giroux argue that the administration of schools, when carried out from within the scientific theory of administration (which they equate with positivism), merely emphasizes the technical-procedural aspects of their operations which are then taken as the only relevant and legitimate foci of analysis. They contend that schools ought to be studied in all their interactional complexities. This is to be done by the method of "cultural analysis" with its emphasis on understanding and critical reflection. The rationale for cultural analysis is that, in Giroux's words, "the notion of culture [is]...a political force... a powerful moment in the process of domination" (Giroux 1983 p. 31).

1   Sections of this article have appeared in Critical theory and educational administration, by G Lakomski which was published in the *Journal of Educational Administration* Vol. 25, no. 1, pp. 85–100. It appears here with permission from *Journal of Educational Administration* © 1987.

The advantages of critical theory as seen by those who adopt its central concepts are, as Foster (1980a p. 499) notes, that "it is possible to have a social science which is neither purely empirical nor purely interpretative", on the assumption that critical theory thus escapes the criticisms levelled at positivism and interpretivist theory respectively.

The stakes, then, are high, and the goal ambitious. For if critical theory could achieve what is claimed on its behalf, and what it claims for itself, then it would indeed be an outstanding candidate for a new, comprehensive social theory in general, and for education in particular.

The version of critical theory to be considered here is that presented in the work of Habermas since it is his version which provides the source material for most educators interested in critical theory, Giroux's emphasis on the older school notwithstanding. The task is then not only to examine critical theory's central claims, but also to explicate briefly what it sets itself to achieve. This is important since critical theory is presented by its advocates as both theoretically superior to positivist social and educational theory and as practically and politically more desirable as well. While neither claim is considered justified, it is the first which is to be examined since the validity of any theory depends on the justification not only of its claims to knowledge but also on the grounds on which these claims are made. If these are inadequate, then any claims derived from them, be they "practical" or "political", are equally unjustified. If critical theory turns out to be incoherent, so is any educational theory which seeks to derive its justification from it.

This article examines two central doctrines of the theory: (a) the conception of interests, and (b) the notion of communicative competence which culminates in the "ideal speech situation". The first concept provides the justification of the theory as knowledge and the second is Habermas's proposed solution to the "theory–practice" problem, that is, the proposal for overcoming domination.

1. Habermasian Interests

Central to understanding Habermas's approach to social theory is what he takes to be the fundamental problem of contemporary social science: the relationship between theory and practice (Habermas 1974). He means by this that the connection between knowledge and social action has become an instrumentalist one, a relation which assumes the neutrality of science. Because science is considered to be free of values, it cannot give us any guidance on how to conduct our lives. This development is the result of the victory of "scientism", or positivism, which, Habermas argues, presents itself as the only valid form of knowledge. As a consequence, it has become impossible, he suggests, to reflect critically on current forms of domination since even they appear as problems which are solvable by technical means. Habermas's aim is to restore to theory the

dimension of reflection eclipsed by positivism and present a social theory which, as "ideology–critique", reunites theory with practice.

The quest for a comprehensive theory of social evolution as a theory of rationality leads Habermas to examine recent developments in the social sciences and in the analytic philosophy of science on the one hand (Habermas 1966-67), and to investigations in the field of philosophy of language and theoretical linguistics on the other (Habermas 1972a, Habermas 1972b, Habermas 1976a, Habermas 1979). In addition, he also reexamines the crisis potential of late capitalism (Habermas 1976b, Habermas 1976c) and the foundations of the older school of critical theory (Habermas 1982). These issues are outside the scope of this article. For present purposes the conception of "interests" (*Interessen*) is most important since it is the cornerstone of critical theory, aiming as it does at the reexamination of the connection between knowledge and human interests in general.

Interests, Habermas contends, are not like any other contingent empirical fact about human beings; neither are they rooted in an ahistorical subjectivity. Rather, they are grounded in the fundamental human conditions of *work* (following Marx) and *interaction*. What Habermas also calls a *cognitive* interest is consequently:

> a peculiar category, which conforms as little to the distinction between empirical and transcendental or factual and symbolic determinations as to that between motivation and cognition. For knowledge is neither a mere instrument of an organism's adaptation to a changing environment nor the act of a pure rational being removed from the context of life in contemplation. (Habermas 1972a p. 197)

Cognitive, or knowledge-constitutive, interests are hence ascribed a *quasitranscendental* status, an ascription Habermas acknowledges as being problematic (Habermas 1974 p. 8 ff.). Critical theory claims three such interests: the technical, the practical, and the emancipatory. These three are asserted to correspond to the three types of sciences. The natural sciences, in Habermas's view, incorporate a technical interest; the historical-hermeneutic sciences the practical interest; and the critical sciences (such as sociology and Freudian psychoanalysis) the emancipatory. The technical interest guides work, the practical guides interaction, and the emancipatory guides power. Work, or purposive-rational action, is defined as:

> either instrumental action or rational choice or their conjunction. Instrumental action is governed by technical rules based on empirical knowledge. In every case they imply conditional predictions about observable events, physical or social. These predictions can prove correct or incorrect. The conduct of rational choice is governed by strategies based on analytic knowledge. They imply deductions from preference rules (value systems) and decision procedures; these propositions are either correctly or incorrectly deduced. Purposive rational action realizes defined goals under given conditions. But while instrumental action organizes means that are appropriate or inappropriate according to criteria of an effective control of reality, strategic action depends only on the correct evaluation of possible alternative choices, which

results from calculation supplemented by values and maxims. (Habermas 1972c pp. 91-92)

The second cognitive interest, the practical, enables grasping reality through understanding in different historical contexts (Habermas 1972a Chaps. 7 and 8). It involves interaction patterns which provide a reliable foundation for communication. What Habermas terms "interaction", or "communicative action", is, like the technical interest, also a distinct, nonreducible kind of action which demands specific categories of description, explanation, and understanding. It is this conception which provides the justification for the method of "cultural analysis" employed by some writers in education.

Habermas argues that just as human beings produce and reproduce themselves through work, so they shape and determine themselves through language and communication in the course of their historical development. While he emphasizes with Marx the historically determined forms of interaction, he nevertheless insists that symbolic interaction, together with cultural tradition, forms a "second synthesis" and is the "only basis on which power (*Herrschaft*) and ideology can be comprehended" (Habermas 1972a p. 42). Marx is accused of not understanding the importance of communicative action since it does not play a separate role in, and is subsumed under, the concept of social labour which, Habermas claims, fits his own notion of instrumental action. Nevertheless, undistorted communication which, in his view, is the goal of the practical interest inherent in the hermeneutic sciences, requires the existence of social institutions which are free from domination themselves. On Habermas's own admission, these do not yet exist. By adding the model of symbolic interaction, he wishes to expand epistemologically Marx's conception of labour.

Finally, the notion of the emancipatory cognitive interest leads us to the most fundamental, yet also derivative, interest. It must be understood in the context of the German idealist tradition whose underlying theme, Habermas asserts, is that reason, once properly understood, "means the will to reason. In self-reflection knowledge for the sake of knowledge attains congruence with the interest in autonomy and responsibility. The emancipatory cognitive interest aims at the pursuit of reflection as such" (Habermas 1972a p. 314). It is this interest which provides the epistemological basis for Habermas's notion of critique which is alleged to be the function of the critical social sciences. Consequently, this interest is of equal importance for educational theory which aims to be "interested" in just this way.

2. Interests and their Epistemological Status

Habermas's conception of interests was developed in critical response to positivism. The peculiar status of the interests resulted from his desire to avoid a naturalistic reduction of quasitranscendental interests to empirical ones. Habermas wants to say, on the one hand, that humans *have* transformed nature, built social systems,

and developed science in the course of their evolution, a process which is analogous to the evolution of claws and teeth in animals (Habermas 1972a p. 312). On the other hand, he is not content with such naturalism and claims that these achievements of human evolution are not merely accidental or contingent but have developed the way they have because of a priori knowledge-constitutive interests. These cognitive interests are described as being of "metalogical necessity...that we can neither prescribe nor represent, but with which we must instead come to terms" (Habermas 1972a p. 312). They are "innate" and "have emerged in man's natural history" (Habermas 1972a p. 312) and are located in "deeply rooted (invariant) structures of action and experience — i.e. in the constituent elements of social systems" (Habermas 1972a p. 371). But from the observation that humans have *in fact* transformed nature, built social systems, and created science it does not follow that they have done so because of transcendental interests. In other words, there is no equivalence between asserting that the technical, practical, and emancipatory interests have emerged in human natural history and asserting that they are true, and provide the transcendental framework for all human knowledge. How could such a transcendental framework be justified?

Two alternatives are possible. Habermas can resort to another transcendental framework or, alternatively, concede that there is a framework which exists a priori. In the case of the first alternative, Habermas argues, as we saw, that cognitive interests are rooted in the depth structures of the human species. But this is merely another transcendental, anthropological, concept which is itself in need of justification. This solution leads to an infinite regress of transcendental frameworks since we can press the point of justification with each new framework. This means that in the end, no justification is provided. If this regress is to be avoided one would need to fall back on an a priori framework, a solution Habermas wants to avoid. It would seem that no matter which of these two alternatives is chosen, the status of interests which are neither amenable to empirical demonstration nor to be sought in the transcendental realm, being "*quasi*-transcendental" entities, remains unclear. Now if the epistemological status of the interests remains in such jeopardy, the consequences for critical theory are serious since the interests were meant to provide the foundation for the claims made on behalf of the sciences. This means that Habermas's assertion of the existence of two *categorially distinct* forms of knowledge and inquiry lapses for want of adequate justification.

In the light of the various criticisms of the epistemological status of the interests (e.g. McCarthy 1981) Habermas felt compelled to note recently (Habermas 1982 p. 233), "My view is today that the attempt to ground critical theory by way of the *theory of knowledge,* while it did not lead astray, was indeed a roundabout way". This assessment leads him in recent work to "ground" his theory in the theory of language instead (Habermas 1979).

3. Communicative Competence and the Ideal Speech Situation

The concept of communicative competence culminating in the ideal speech situation is the centrepiece of critical theory, since here the various strands of Habermas's investigations are drawn together. Parallel to Marx's critique of political economy, Habermas attempts to elucidate contemporary forms of alienation expressed in distorted communication. He wants to show that the potential for emancipation *inheres* in ordinary language which both presupposes and anticipates an ideal speech situation in which communication free from domination is possible. The full impact of Habermas's theory of communicative competence cannot be grasped adequately without taking recourse to its three underlying tenets which need further explication: (a) the notion of discourse and its relation to interaction, (b) the consensus theory of truth, and (c) the conception of an ideal speech situation.

Habermas argues that we can proceed from the fact that functioning language games, in which speech acts are exchanged, are based on an underlying consensus which is formed in the reciprocal recognition of at least four claims to validity. These claims comprise the "comprehensibility of an utterance, the truth of its propositional component, the correctness and appropriateness of its performatory component, and the authenticity of the speaking subject" (Habermas 1974, p. 18, Habermas 1979 Chap. 1). Habermas contends that in normal communication these claims are accepted uncritically. Only when a background consensus is challenged can *all* claims be questioned. Their justification is subject to *theoretical discourse* which is an intersubjective enterprise within a community of inquirers. This concept is adapted from Habermas's interpretation of Peirce's model of empirical science (Habermas 1972a Chaps. 5 and 6). Although theoretical discourse demands the "virtualization of constraints on action", it still remains implicitly presupposed in interaction because Habermas assumes that the subjects are in fact capable of justifying their beliefs *discursively*. Such a capability is characteristic of a functioning language game. Yet he is also aware of the fact that there is no complete symmetry of power among the partners of communication.

But if we consider a consensus to be rational and discover after further reflection and argumentation that it is not, how are we to decide what does constitute a *rational* consensus? Habermas claims that the only recourse we have is to discourse itself. He is aware that this answer might lead into a vicious circle and contends that not every achieved agreement is a consensus, that is, can be considered a criterion for truth. If, for example, an agreement is reached on the basis of what Habermas calls (covert or open) "strategic" action, then that consensus is a "pseudo-consensus" (Habermas 1982 p. 237). Strategic action is that which is undertaken primarily to safeguard an individual's personal success by means of conscious or unconscious deception. In the case of systematically distorted communication, that is,

unconscious deception, Habermas believes that "at least one of the participants is deceiving *himself* or *herself* regarding the fact that he or she is actually behaving strategically, while he or she has only apparently adopted an attitude orientated to reaching understanding" (Habermas 1982 p. 264). Even in this case, he contends, the actors themselves can know — even though only "vaguely and intuitively" which of the two attitudes they were adopting. Both kinds are seen as "genuine types of interaction" and may be mixed up with each other in practice. As a result, Habermas asserts, ". . . it is often difficult for an observer to make a correct ascription" (Habermas 1982 p. 266). If we want to reach a true (or "founded") consensus, he argues, we must admit as the only permissible compulsion the force of the argument and consider as the only permissible motive the cooperative search for truth (Habermas 1972a p. 363).

An argument, then, qualifies as rational when it is cogent and motivates us in our search for truth. Implicit in this thesis is Habermas's belief that there must be increased freedom for discourse to reach higher levels, that truth claims and claims to correctness of problematic statements and norms must be able to be assessed discursively, and in the course of assessment, also be able to be changed or rejected. The conditions under which such freedom can be attained are, in Habermas's view, given in the *ideal speech situation* because "the design of an ideal speech situation is necessarily implied with the structure of potential speech; for every speech, even that of intentional deception, is oriented towards the idea of truth" (Habermas 1972b p. 144). The ideal speech situtation is attained when the requirements of symmetrical relations obtain which involve that all speakers have equal chances of selecting and employing "speech acts" and when they can assume interchangeable dialogue roles. But since practical discourse is generally distorted according to Habermas, and since the ideal speech situation can only be anticipated, it is difficult to assess empirically whether or not, or to what extent, the conditions of an ideal speech situation actually obtain. This problem, Habermas contends, cannot be solved in any a priori way. There is no single decisive criterion by which we can judge whether a consensus reached is "founded", *even under ideal conditions*; we can only determine in retrospect whether the conditions for an ideal speech situation obtained. This difficulty resides in the fact that

the ideal speech situation is neither an empirical phenomenon nor simply a construct, but a reciprocal supposition or imputation (*Unterstellung*) unavoidable in discourse. This supposition can, but need not be, contra-factual; but even when contra-factual it is a fiction which is operatively effective in communication. I would therefore prefer to speak of an anticipation of an ideal speech situation. . . .This anticipation alone is the warrant which permits us to join to an actually attained consensus the claim of a rational consensus. At the same time it is a critical standard against which every actually reached consensus can be called into question and checked. (Habermas as quoted in McCarthy 1976 p. 486)

What, exactly, does this notion amount to? Stripped of its abstractions, we are left with a *procedural* model of negotiation which has the following characteristics in practice: (a) not everyone can participate in a given negotiation because of the existing power differential in society; (b) even when we reach agreement practically, we are not sure whether it *really is* a consensus, nor do we have the means to check this (presuming that that is a worthwhile thing to do in the first place); and (c) the language we use to reach consensus is itself a carrier of ideology. While Habermas emphasizes that his model is only an "anticipation" possessing the status of a "practical hypothesis" which does not refer to any *historical* society (see Habermas 1982 pp. 261-62), one is nevertheless entitled to press the point regarding its potential for realization in the here and now. Recall that the solution to this dilemma is that we can only determine with hindsight whether or not its conditions obtained. Recall further that these are the postulates of symmetrical relations in which all speakers have equal chances of "selecting and employing speech acts". But this does not solve the problem because we have to repeat the question of how we would ever know that these "equal chances" did obtain. Since all we have to go by are self-reports which may be consciously or unconsciously misleading, or plain false, even a retrospective assessment would not get us out of the sceptical regress.

Habermas calls his model a "constitutive illusion" and an "unavoidable supposition of discourse" which, however, is possibly always counter-factual! From this, McCarthy (1981 p. 309) draws the conclusion that:

> Nonetheless this does not itself render the ideal illegitimate, an ideal that can be more or less adequately approximated in reality, that can serve as guide for the institutionalization of discourse and as a critical standard against which every actually achieved consensus can be measured.

While this is not an uncommon defence of the ideal speech situation, it is nevertheless invalid. This is so because the ideal speech situation is *in principle* unrealizable. It cannot be "more or less" adequately approximated in reality because the condition of retrospectivity does not get Habermas out of the problem of stopping an infinite sceptical regress, as was argued above. It follows that we cannot even achieve what self-reflection and the emancipatory interest promised us: the liberation from dogmatic *attitudes* which is, in any case, only the formal precondition for practical, political action in Habermas's scheme of things. For his theory to work, we must assume as already given, what, on his own account, does not yet exist but is supposed to come into existence as the result of the theory: namely, a world in which power and control are equalized. On the issue of social change then, this theory, which makes so much of its historical-materialist heritage, is silent.

4. Conclusion

It is perplexing that this model of rationality, i.e. rational persons discussing their differences in an ideal speech situation, has been hailed as at least potentially the solution to the so-called theory/practice problem which holds that traditional (positivist) theory is incapable of informing and guiding practice. If the preceding analysis is correct, it seems that critical theory is similarly incapable of doing so. While the reasons outlined above go a considerable way towards explaining the problems of the theory of communicative competence, and hence critical theory, it finally fails because truth-as-consensus is removed from direct confrontation with the "objects of possible experience". In other words, the consensus theory of truth rules out the possibility of making true statements about empirical reality. If we cannot, in principle, *know* whether or not there is, as Habermas asserts, distorted communication and oppression in contemporary society, then we are left with mere speculation. However intuitively convincing this may be, speculation comes a poor second to knowledge.

These fundamental problems need to be resolved if the critical theory of society is to be relevant for *this* world.

See also: Action Research; Participatory Research; Research Paradigms in Education

Bibliography

Apple M W 1982 *Education and Power*. Routledge and Kegan Paul, London

Bates R J 1983 *Educational Administration and the Management of Knowledge*. Deakin University Press, Geelong, Victoria

Bowles S, Gintis H 1976 *Schooling in Capitalist America*. Basic Books, New York

Bredo E, Feinberg W (eds.) 1982 *Knowledge and Values in Social and Educational Research*. Temple, Philadelphia, Pennsylvania

Carr W, Kemmis S 1983 *Becoming Critical: Knowing Through Action Research*. Deakin University Press, Geelong, Victoria

Foster W P 1980a Administration and the crisis of legitimacy: A review of Habermasian thought. *Harvard Educ. Rev.* 50 (4): 496–505

Foster W P 1980b The changing administrator: Developing managerial praxis. *Educ. Theory* 30 (1): 11–23

Giroux H 1983 *Critical Theory and Educational Practice*. Deakin University Press, Geelong, Victoria

Habermas J 1966–67 Zur Logik der Sozialwissenschaften. Beiheft 5, *Philosoph. Rundsch.* 14: 1–195

Habermas J 1972a *Knowledge and Human Interests*. Heinemann, London

Habermas J 1972b Towards a theory of communicative competence. In: Dreitzel H P (ed.) 1972 *Recent Sociology*, No. 2, *Patterns of Communicative Behaviour*. Macmillan, New York, pp. 114–48

Habermas J 1972c *Toward a Rational Society*. Heinemann, London

Habermas J 1974 *Theory and Practice*. Heinemann, London

Habermas J 1976a Systematically distorted communication. In: Connerton P (ed.) 1976 *Critical Sociology*. Penguin, Harmondsworth, pp. 348–87

Habermas J 1976b *Legitimation Crisis*. Heinemann, London

Habermas J 1976c *Zur Rekonstruktion des Historischen Materialismus*, 2nd edn. Suhrkamp Verlag, Frankfurt

Habermas J 1979 *Communication and the Evolution of Society.* Beacon Press, Boston, Massachusetts

Habermas J 1982 A reply to my critics. In: Thompson J B, Held D (eds.) 1982 *Habermas: Critical Debates.* Macmillan, London, pp. 219–83

Huebner D 1975 Curricular language and classroom meanings. In: Pinar W (ed.) 1975 *Curriculum Theorizing: The Reconceptualists.* McCutchan, Berkeley, California, pp.217–36

Kemmis S, Cole P, Suggett D 1983 *Towards The Socially-Critical School.* Victorian Institute of Secondary Education, Melbourne

McCarthy T A 1976 A Theory of communicative competence. In: Connerton P (ed.) 1976 *Critical Sociology.* Penguin, Harmondsworth, pp.470–97

McCarthy T A 1981 *The Critical Theory of Jürgen Habermas.* MIT Press, Cambridge, Massachusetts

Shapiro S 1984 Crisis of legitimation: Schools, society and declining faith in education. *Interchange* 15 (4): 26–39

Van Manen M 1977 Linking ways of knowing with ways of being practical. *Curric. Inq.* 6 (3): 205–28

Young M, Whitty G 1977 *Society, State and Schooling.* Falmer Press, Guildford

Ethnographic Research Methods

R. Taft

Some educational researchers have recently advocated the adoption of the ethnographic methods employed by cultural and social anthropologists in their field studies of social groups and communities. These methods are considered to be particularly appropriate for empirical research on the relatively bounded system of a school or classroom but they also have their place in the study of the role of the family, social organizations, or ethnic communities in education. Ethnographic research consists essentially of a description of events that occur within the life of a group, with special regard to the social structures and the behaviour of the individuals with respect to their group membership, and an interpretation of the meaning of these for the culture of the group. Thus ethnography is used both to record primary data and to interpret its meaning. It is naturalistic enquiry as opposed to controlled, and a qualitative, as opposed to quantitative, method. In ethnography the researcher participates in some part of the normal life of the group and uses what he or she learns from that participation to produce the research findings. It is consequently often treated as being equivalent to participant observation, in contrast with nonparticipant observation in which the observer as an outsider records the overt behaviour of the subjects, but it involves more than that. Participation in a group provides investigators with an understanding of the culture and the interactions between the members that is different from that which can be obtained from merely observing or conducting a questionnaire survey or an analysis of documents. The investigators' involvement in the normal activities of the group may be treated as a case of partial acculturation in which they acquire an insider's knowledge of the group through their direct experience with it. These experiences provide them with tacit knowledge which helps them to understand the significance to the group members of their own behaviour and that of others and enables them to integrate their observations about that behaviour with information obtained from other sources such as interviews with informants and documentary material.

1. The Development of Ethnographic Methods

Field research was employed by anthropologists and sociologists in the nineteenth and early twentieth centuries, but the first to stress the need for a systematic approach to its conduct was the Polish–British scholar Malinowski, who emphasized the need for ethnographers to employ controls in their assembly of data in a manner that he described as analogous, although by no means similar, to those of the natural scientists. Malinowski laid down the requirement that observers should tabulate the data on which their conclusions are based, including verbatim statements, and should indicate whether they are derived from direct or indirect sources, a method that he called "concrete statistical documentation" (see the introductory chapter on methodology in Malinowski 1922). He stressed the need for the investigator to establish "trustworthiness" in respect of the study. Malinowski described the goal of ethnographic studies as "to grasp the native's point of view, his relation to life, to realise his view of his world" (p. 25). In order to achieve this, the investigator should learn the language of the community being studied, reside for a protracted period in the community—preferably out of contact with "white" people, and use both observation and informed interviews with selected informants from within the community as sources of data.

The field methods laid down by Malinowski have, to a greater or lesser degree, been adapted for studies of segments of modern, urbanized societies which have provided a model for the application of the methods to educational research. For example, studies have been carried out of the unemployed in Austria, industrial organizations (Tavistock Institute), urban areas in the United States (Middletown, Yankee City), hobos, gangs, and dance musicians, to name just a few. These studies each raised their own peculiar problems of research strategy, but what they all have in common is their method of research in which the investigator becomes closely involved over a prolonged period in the everyday life of the members of a designated group or community in order to understand its culture. This contact enables the researchers not only to obtain an intimate and a broad knowledge of the group but also to test and refine hypotheses about the phenomena being studied.

Ethnographic methods of research came to education fairly late. The team of sociologists from the University of Chicago who studied medical students (Becker et al. 1961) were probably the pioneers in the field of education, while Smith and Geoffrey (1968) were the first to base a study of classroom processes on anthropological field studies using a method which they described as microethnography. They stated that their "primary intent was to describe the silent language of a culture, a classroom in a slum school, so that those who have not lived in it will appreciate its subtleties and complexities" (p. 2). Smith observed the classroom every day for one semester and kept copious field notes, which he used as a basis for his daily discussions with the class teacher, Geoffrey, with the purpose of clarifying the intentions and motives behind the teacher's behaviour in order to move towards a conceptualization in abstract terms of the teaching process. Both of the investigators were participants in the classroom, although one was more of an observer and the other more of an initiator and an informant.

A word should be added about the terms used in describing ethnographic studies in education. Smith and Geoffrey seem to have simply meant an intensive field study by their term microethnography, while Erickson (1975) confines it more narrowly to studies that use extensive observation and recording to establish the interactional structures in the classroom, a usage which Mehan (1978) prefers to call constitutive ethnography. For the purposes of this present article, the term ethnography is interpreted liberally to include case studies, the concept preferred by the ethnographers in the United Kingdom. The intensive study of a bounded community is a clear example of a simple case study, even though there are many individuals who make up that community.

2. The Scientific Status of the Ethnographic Method

The use of ethnographic methods involves some important questions relating to the tactics, ethics, and validity of the study.

2.1 The Social Role of the Investigator

The description of the investigator as a participant in the life of the group implies that he or she has some role in it which is recognized by the group. Sometimes this role is simply that of participant observer, a role which does not usually exist in most formal group structures, but one which does have a meaning in many classrooms where outsiders come to observe the class on occasions for one purpose or another. Thus, Louis Smith was introduced to both the children and the teachers as

someone from the university who was interested in children's learning, a role which is understood and accepted in modern classrooms. In other cases the investigator fills a normal role in the group other than that of a researcher. For example, a study of an orthodox Jewish school was conducted while the researcher concerned was a regular classroom teacher in the school, a situation that represents participant observation in the fullest sense of the word. Another example would be a student who studies his or her college or professors on the basis of his or her normal personal experience with them. The role of participant observer has some advantages as a viewing point over that of the participant who plays the additional role of observer. The former is expected by the group to share, probe, ask questions, take notes, and so on because this is consistent with his or her role as an observer whereas the latter has tactical and ethical problems in doing so because of his or her obligations as a participant. On the other hand there is a danger that a participant observer can become so much absorbed into the group after a time that his or her status as an observer may be compromised.

The group member who also acts as an investigator may do so overtly or covertly, or as a mixture of both where it is known to some members of the group that he or she is observing for research purposes but not to others. Covert observation raises serious ethical issues as does semicovert, but, on the other hand, overt observation by a person who has another role in the group can place him or her in an anomalous position with regard to the carrying out of a normal group role. Furthermore, colleagues are likely to respond to him or her as an observer in a biased fashion because of their other involvement with him or her. A distinction is often made between obtrusive and unobtrusive methods of research according to whether the subjects of the research are aware that they are being studied. A participant observer, by definition, plays an obtrusive role and this fact may influence the behaviour of the group whereas the observer participant may or may not be obtrusive as a researcher.

2.2 The Inside–Outside View

One of the main advantages of the ethnographic method is that, in the course of becoming involved in the group, the investigator becomes acculturated to it. This means that he or she develops personal knowledge about the rules of the group and begins to perceive the same meanings in events as do the members of the group. The investigator learns what behaviour is expected when, where, and in response to what situations. This process of acculturation is sometimes described as transition from the status of a "stranger" to that of "a friend", that is, a person who knows the "silent language" of the group and is in intimate communication with its members. It is, however, significant that a scholar who is studying the subculture of a school in his or her own society is unlikely to be as complete a stranger at the beginning as an anthropologist studying a traditional society.

Nevertheless, being an insider has its drawbacks as a method of studying a group. First, as already indicated, there are constraints imposed by propriety and ethics on an insider revealing to others the secrets of the group (see *Ethical Considerations in Research*). There may, of course, be the same constraints on an outsider but, at least, the group can usually control his or her access to information by barring entry.

Second, the insider may not always have even as much access to information as an outsider. He or she may have personal knowledge of only a segment of the group's life, sometimes without being aware of the limitation. He or she may even be denied access to the other segments: for example, a teacher may not be permitted to study the classroom of a colleague. In contrast, a stranger who is accepted as an observer may be deliberately informed and invited to observe just because he or she is a stranger. Futhermore, an outsider is more likely to be able to take steps to obtain a representative sampling of people, occasions, and settings in the group and thus can help to offset the suspicion of biased observation. A third drawback that may arise as a result of being an insider is that highly salient data may be overlooked just because it is so familiar. Strangers will notice events that stand out as a result of their contrast with the expectations that they have brought with them from their own cultural background and may therefore be better placed to infer their meaning and significance for other events in the group. Some element of surprise aids awareness. A further problem is the one mentioned earlier of the subjects' reactivity to being studied, particularly when the observer is a full participant in the group. Whether or not the observation is obtrusive, it is reactive observation; that is, the observer affects the behaviour of the people being studied and consequently will have to take into account his or her own influence when assessing the group. As Everhart puts it "the fieldworker, rather than appearing to be one of many in the audience observing the drama on stage, is himself on stage, interacting with the other actors in 'his' setting and playing a role in the resolution of the production" (1977 p. 14). In order to take into account their own contributions and to assess what the situation would be if it were not for the fact that their presence is influencing the group, investigators need a great deal of self-awareness and a thorough understanding of the group processes. This necessity for playing the dual roles of participant and detached observer can impose a severe strain on the ethnographic investigator and calls for continual monitoring of the effect the investigator has on others.

2.3 Subjectivity, Reliability, and Validity

The fact that investigators have a role in the group not only requires them to be aware of their own influence but also may give them an emotional stake in a particular research outcome. For example, if the observer is also a teacher, there may be a tendency for observation to be slanted towards a justification of the style of teaching normally used. Since ethnographic researchers use themselves as the instrument through which they observe the group, the method lends itself to extreme subjectivity; that is, the interpretation may be idiosyncratic to the observer with all of the associated limitations, eccentricities, and biases and is not matched by the interpretation of other observers. This raises questions concerning the reliability of the observations and the validity of the conclusions. The difficulty is that the observations are not easily subject to public scrutiny. Observations and interpretations are by their very nature subjective but they still can be made susceptible to reliability checks and it is still possible for the investigation to follow rules that can increase the validity of the conclusions.

Reliability, that is accuracy, of the observations can be enhanced by following the prescription laid down by Malinowski of recording wherever possible the concrete data in the form of a "synoptic chart" on which the inferences are to be based, including verbatim utterances and opinions. Modern audiovisual methods of recording events so that they can be examined at leisure offer ethnographers unprecedented possibilities today of attaining accuracy, but there are still sampling problems in the selection of the data and limitations to accuracy due to bias and lack of opportunity, as well as tactical and ethical considerations in making the recordings.

The reliability of the observations is assisted by the long period of exposure to the data in ethnographic research which provides opportunities for investigators to cross check their observations over time and to reconcile inconsistencies. Cross checks may also be made by triangulation, a procedure in which multiple sources are used to obtain evidence on the same phenomenon. Thus, the observations may be supplemented by interviews, feedback to the members of the group for their comment, and documentary evidence such as school notices, correspondence, minutes, and other archives. An additional source of reliability is to have more than one observer as, for example, in the study by Smith and Geoffrey (1968), a situation which is relatively rare in traditional anthropological studies. In the typical case, the multiple observers may be members of a team who are exposed to the same events and are then able to cross check each other's data.

Validity is a quality of the conclusions and the processes through which these were reached, but its exact meaning is dependent on the particular criterion of truth that is adopted. In ethnographic research the most appropriate criterion is credibility although even that term is subject to fuzziness in meaning. Here the concern will be only with the steps that ethnographic research workers can take to improve the credibility of their analyses. Credibility is dependent on the apparent accuracy of the data and all the steps described above that are intended to increase reliability are relevant. Much depends on the way in which the study is communicated to the scientific audience. A report in which the investigator describes the precautions that have been taken to ensure the accuracy of the observations has more credibility than one in which the reader is merely asked to take the data and findings "on faith". The report should contain indications that the investigator is aware of the need to convince the audience of the validity of the study. The interpretations made from the data are more credible when the researcher describes the evidence on which they are based and also any efforts made to test for evidence that would tend to disconfirm any tentative conclusions. One of the procedures that is often followed in ethnographic studies to confirm the validity of interpretations is to feed them back for comment to selected members of the group or to other persons who know the group. In the case of literate participants such as are found in educational research, the research workers may submit to the members drafts of sections of their reports as well as oral accounts of their impressions. If necessary, the interpretations can be "negotiated" with the participants so that the final product is more likely to represent the situation as they see it, but there is always a danger in this procedure that the participants may exercise distortion and cover-up for their own reasons or that the researcher finds it impossible to obtain consensus. Different members of the group may hold different perceptions of the events, for example, teachers and students, or boys and girls. Some researchers have attempted to overcome these problems by setting up small groups of about four participants to engage in discussions towards establishing their shared meanings by acting as "checks, balances, and prompts" for each other, but in practice there are distinct limitations to the possible application of this procedure.

2.4 The Role of Theory, Hypotheses, and Generalizations

Malinowski specifically recommends that a field worker should commence with "foreshadowed problems" arising from his or her knowledge of theory, but should not have "preconceived ideas" in which he or she aims to prove certain hypotheses. The ethnographic method is qualitative and holistic, making use of the investigator's intuition, empathy, and general ability to learn another culture. The investigator is more concerned with discovery than with verification and this requires preparedness to formulate, test, and, if necessary, discard a series of hunches. As investigators develop hypotheses in the course of pursuing a foreshadowed problem they should be alert for data which refute, support, or cast doubts on their hypotheses and should be prepared to alter them in accordance with increased acquaintance with the phenomena. Research workers as they puzzle over the meaning of the behaviour of the group, and perhaps seek help from informants, are likely to obtain illumination through a sudden shaft of understanding. Thus there is a continual dialogue between an orientation towards discovery and one towards verification. Gradually a theoretical basis for the understanding of the group processes may emerge through the process often described as grounded theory, that is, grounded in the research process itself. Theory that emerges from exposure to the data is more likely to fit the requirements

than theory that is preconceived on an abstract basis. Also the actual data are more likely to produce categories that are appropriate for describing the particular case. The main problem that arises from grounded theory derived from a case study is that of making generalizations beyond the particular case viewed at a particular time. A straight out description of concrete happenings has some value as an addition to the corpus of information that is available to the investigator and to other interested people—including members of the group itself. However, its value is greatly enhanced when the case can be "located as an instance of a more general class of events" (Smith 1978 p. 335). To achieve this, the investigator treats the case in point as either a representative of, or a departure from, a particular type. Sometimes the actual group or groups that are studied have been chosen initially as representatives of a designated type of case and this facilitates generalizations based on it but they should still be treated with reserve.

2.5 Ethnography as a Case Study Method

The problem of the relationship between the One and the Many, a perennial one in philosophy, arises in different guises in the social sciences—idiographic versus nomothetic treatments of data, -emic versus -etic approaches to comparative studies, and the case study versus the sample survey research design. In order to generalize from an individual case study of behaviour in one group to behaviour in others it is necessary to reach sufficient understanding about the significance of the events in relation to the context in which they occur in order to extend interpretations to other contexts and other groups. In the process of generalizing it is necessary to violate somewhat the full integrity of any one group by describing events in some language that extends beyond the bounds of the culture of that group. The ethnographers are partially acculturated to the group that they are studying, but they are also familiar with other groups with which they compare their experience of the group. To maintain the analogy, an ethnographer is multicultural with respect to the object of study. When an investigator attempts to understand one group, he or she is aided by knowledge of other ones and his or her impressions are partially consolidated with the others. Thus, generalizations are built up through the investigator being able to mediate between one group and others; an ethnographic account of a school, then, derives its value largely from the fact that the investigator—and also the readers—are familiar with other schools, and with schools in general. Diesing refers to this as "pluralism" which he describes as follows: "one might say the method is relativistic in its treatment of individual cases and becomes gradually absolutistic as it moves toward broader generalizations" (1971 pp. 297–98).

In ethnographic studies no generalization can be treated as final, only as a working hypothesis for further studies which may again be ethnographic, or may consist of a survey by means of interviews, questionnaires, or tests. The ethnographic method gains credibility when it combines both subjective and objective methods but it need not be regarded as deriving its value only as a preliminary and exploratory procedure prior to the use of more conventional semiobjective techniques. It can make its own legitimate independent contribution at any stage of a research including the confirmation of hypotheses that have emerged out of other sources provided that the basic principles on which its credibility rests are observed.

See also: Naturalistic and Rationalistic Enquiry; Classroom Observation Techniques

Bibliography

Becker G S, Geer B, Hughes E, Strauss A 1961 *Boys in White: Student Culture in Medical School.* University of Chicago Press, Chicago, Illinois

Diesing P 1971 *Patterns of Discovery in the Social Sciences.* Aldine-Atherton, Chicago, Illinois

Erickson F 1975 Gatekeeping and the melting pot: Interaction in counseling encounters. *Harvard Educ. Rev.* 45: 44–70

Everhart R B 1977 Between stranger and friend: Some consequences of "long term" fieldwork in schools. *Am. Educ. Res. J.* 14: 1–15

Malinowski B 1922 *Argonauts of the Western Pacific: An Account of Native Enterprise and Adventure in the Archipelagoes of Melanesian New Guinea.* Routledge, London

Mehan H 1978 Structuring school structure. *Harvard Educ. Rev.* 48: 32–64

Roberts J I, Akinsanya S K (eds.) 1976 *Educational Patterns and Cultural Configuration: The Anthropology of Education.* McKay, New York

Smith L M 1978 An evolving logic of participant observation, educational ethnography, and other case studies. In: Shulman L S (ed.) 1978 *Review of Research in Education*, Vol. 6. Peacock, Ithaca, Illinois, pp. 316–77

Smith L M, Geoffrey W 1968 *The Complexities of an Urban Classroom: An Analysis Toward a General Theory of Teaching.* Holt, Rinehart and Winston, New York

Spradley J P, McCurdy D W 1972 *The Cultural Experience: Ethnography in Complex Society.* SRA, Chicago, Illinois

Wilson S 1977 The use of ethnographic techniques in educational research. *Rev. Educ. Res.* 47: 245–65

Hermeneutics

P-J. Ödman

The most common meaning of the term "hermeneutics" formerly was "the art (or science) of interpretation (especially of the Bible)." As a consequence of the contributions by Schleiermacher, Dilthey, and late existential philosophers like Heidegger and Gadamer the meaning of the term has changed. An alternative definition is therefore suggested here, namely the theory and practice of interpretation and understanding (*Verstehen*) in different kinds of human contexts (religious as well as secular, scientific as well as those of everyday life). This definition implies, for instance, that hermeneutics has developed into more elaborate theories of interpretation and that the act of understanding has become more central in hermeneutical thought, though it, of course, always has been present in interpretive practice. The definition also indicates that understanding and its significance as a fundamental part of existence has been emphasized in a more decisive way through the development of hermeneutics as existential philosophy.

Hermeneutics does not, however, constitute a unitary tradition. Instead, it includes several different lines of thought. Palmer (1969), for example, mentions six main branches: (a) the theory of biblical exegesis; (b) general philological methodology; (c) the science of linguistic understanding; (d) the methodological foundation of human sciences (*Geisteswissenschaften*); (e) phenomenology of existence and of existential understanding; and (f) systems of interpretation, used by human beings to reach the meaning behind myths, symbols, and actions. To this list could be added: (g) theories of the process and validity of interpretation; (h) empirically oriented schools of hermeneutics, studying people in a social context.

1. Differences in Relation to Other Traditions of Thought

Some distinctive features of hermeneutics in relation to other traditions of thought can help to clarify the issue further.

1.1 Positivism

Hermeneutics is more directed toward qualitative analysis and more language oriented than positivism. The possibilities of human manifestations play a greater role in hermeneutics, in comparison with the stress on observable entities in positivism. Dialectical logic is consequently more important than formal logic. Dilthey stressed that the main purpose of the human sciences is understanding (*Verstehen*), not explanation (*Erklären*), though the latter could be a useful tool in the hermeneutical process (Apel 1972).

1.2 Marxism

The underlying theory of hermeneutics is not primarily materialistic, but an ontological theory of understanding (Heidegger 1977). Moreover, hermeneutics does not focus on the question of historical determinism; there is a greater stress on the freedom of human action.

1.3 Critical Theory

Hermeneutics is not primarily preoccupied with the question of revealing the ideologies behind human actions, products, and life styles, but rather with understanding their meaning. It can consequently bring about an understanding of a certain life-style and still remain a part of it, whereas the purpose of critical theory is to put itself and its proponents in a perspective outside the phenomenon criticized.

1.4 Phenomenology

Whereas phenomenology is primarily oriented towards the immediate phenomena of human experience, such as thinking and feeling, hermeneutics is more context directed. In interpreting human "traces," hermeneutics often tries to go beyond the observable in order to "read between the lines." It can therefore be characterized as more transphenomenal.

Hermeneutics is often closely linked with other approaches, especially with that of critical theory. However, from a hermeneutical point of view, understanding is in itself the most fundamental task even if the interaction with other approaches can be very close.

2. Purpose of Hermeneutics

The purpose of hermeneutics is consequently to increase understanding as regards other cultures, groups, individuals, conditions, and life-styles, both in the present as well as the past. The process must be mutual and imply an increase of self-understanding on the part of the subject.

From the academic viewpoint, the purpose of hermeneutics is to contribute to this development. A subgoal is to increase the scientific self-understanding of hermeneutics, for instance by the clarification of working principles. Beside this methodological goal, applied hermeneutics must be developed, in order to fulfill the chief purpose mentioned above. Existential issues must thereby be brought in focus, because of their close connection with the world view (*Weltanschauung*) of hermeneutics.

The hermeneutical approach is considered adequate for practical educational work as well as for educational research. It stresses, for instance, the importance of understanding various groups of pupils and their life-styles. It also accentuates the significance of mutual understanding, like, for instance, between teachers and their pupils or between pupils with different backgrounds.

As far as educational research is concerned, the purpose of hermeneutics can, for example, be to try to detect the meaning underlying specific educational practices. By means of hermeneutical research it is possible, for example, to get answers to questions like: How should certain administrative school practices be understood? What are their hidden meanings? Or—as some French educational sociologists in the 1970s asked themselves—how should educational practice be interpreted in a broader cultural context? Is the concept of violence still relevant, even though it is manifesting itself in a more symbolic form? The answers to questions like these are often given as interpretations, through which understanding is promoted.

3. Understanding, Pre-understanding, and Interpretation

The concept of "understanding" can only be defined with the help of analogy or by the use of synonyms. The original literal meaning of the word may have been "to stand close to, or under, something" or "to place something close to, or under, oneself." Now, to stand close to something gives a sense of familiarity. You know well that which you are close to, you are understanding it. Often you can even see it. The analogy of seeing is appropriate, because it coincides with linguistic practice; the verb "see" is often used as synonymous with understanding. Thus to "see" something in this meaning is not only to perceive it; it is also to understand it.

The concept of "pre-understanding" is very important in hermeneutical thinking. Often it refers to the concept of the hermeneutical circle and the fact that it is not possible to understand something if a person has not, at least partially, already understood it. In other words, it is necessary to have a pre-understanding in order to understand. Pre-understanding means therefore such understanding which is already accomplished; it is understanding as history. It functions as a structure, a whole within the limits of which it is possible to understand something new. This structure is through understanding re-experienced and revitalized. In other cases, the pre-understanding of something familiar could be changed through the development of a new structure of understanding. At the moment of understanding, pre-understanding and understanding thus are functioning as a dialectical entity, in which both parts are depending on each other. In teaching practice, for example, pre-understanding can manifest itself as a tendency, because of superficial similarities, to perceive and treat a new group of pupils in the same way as those belonging to another class. In spite of its insufficiency, pre-understanding, even in cases like this, functions as an indispensable point of departure for a new understanding. As time passes, contradictory evidence will appear and the structures of the teacher's pre-understanding will be modified. In later confrontations with the group, the teacher's pre-understanding will facilitate his or her interaction with the pupils; he or she sees them more as they are.

Interpretation is, according to Heidegger (1977), to place in the open what is already understood. But it is not the pure mirroring of understanding. Interpretation and understanding are interacting much more closely, since making something explicit often implies a change in the understanding of it. The whole thing gets clearer by its being said.

Interpretation could also be regarded as translation. The interpreter is transferring the meaning of something from one reality to another. Translation in the literal sense is, however, primarily concerned with verbal meaning and has consequently that archeological purpose of hermeneutics, of which Ricoeur speaks. Here Heidegger's definition of interpretation, mentioned above, seems more suitable.

Interpretation, understanding, and pre-understanding are dialectically coupled with our existence as human beings. People's self-definitions and definitions of life are a result of their understanding and their understanding develops through their experiences. The understanding of their lives is the ultimate hermeneutical circle.

4. Historical Background

The concept of hermeneutics has its roots in the Greek antiquity. The Greek verb "hermeneuein," "to interpret," and the noun "hermeneia," "interpretation," are the sources of the modern concept, as well as the name of Hermes, the messenger and also the interpreter among the gods. With Hermes was also connected the discovery of language and writing, the most important tools for grasping meaning and conveying it to others, as Palmer (1969) has pointed out.

4.1 Hermeneutics as Biblical Exegesis

Biblical exegesis has a very long tradition going back to Old Testament times. In fact, the tradition of interpretation even in earlier times was so strong, that canons for interpretation of the Old Testament had already been developed by the second century AD.

Two standards of interpretation can be discerned during these early periods. The first is known as literal interpretation, the purpose of which is to spell out the messages, which are more or less explicit in the text itself. The second style of interpretation was more concerned with the symbolic content. Since the text also was looked upon as a message from God, it had to be interpreted allegorically. The purpose was to reconstruct or create the divine meanings which were not there in a literal sense.

These two traditions of interpretation are characteristic of even later stages of biblical exegesis, in which literal interpretation gradually became more directed towards reconstructing the historical meaning of the biblical texts. Thus, literal interpretation became a bridge between biblical exegesis and interpretation used as a tool for scientific purposes.

During the Enlightenment, the tradition of literal interpretation therefore broadened in scope. It was especially in the field of philological research that hermeneutics took its first step into the world of modern science. The Bible gradually came to be regarded as one among many other objects of interpretation.

4.2 Hermeneutics as "The Art of Understanding"

Friedrich Schleiermacher (1768–1834) was the first to formulate a new hermeneutical approach in a more decisive way. Opening his lectures on hermeneutics in 1819 he declared that his main purpose was to establish a general hermeneutics as the art of understanding (Palmer 1969 p. 84). What had been missing was the examination of the act of understanding as the intuitive act of the existing individual.

For Schleiermacher, interpretation consists of two elements, one grammatical and one psychological. The relationship between these two elements is dialectical. In grammatical interpretation, the work is interpreted in terms of its linguistic principles. Psychological interpretation, on the other hand, implies that the text should be analyzed as regards the thoughts and feelings of the author through identification with or transformation into the other person.

Schleiermacher's conception of understanding was founded on the idea of the hermeneutical circle. Understanding is always relating to a context, in terms of which its elements can be understood and which in turn make their context intelligible. Understanding is also founded on intuition, it has an important element of divination in order to transcend the paradox of understanding previously mentioned, namely that the act of understanding always must build on prior understanding.

4.3 Hermeneutics as the Theoretical Foundation of the Human Sciences

Wilhelm Dilthey (1833–1911) extended the application of hermeneutics to the whole field of humanities. His lines of thought led in ontological as well as methodological directions.

Dilthey's thinking can be summarized as an enormous widening of the idea of the hermeneutical circle. His central concepts were experience, expression, and understanding (*Verstehen*). Experience, for Dilthey, had a much broader connotation than it has today: ". . . one may call each encompassing unity of parts of life bound together through a common meaning for the course of life an 'experience'—even when the several parts are separated from each other by interrupting events" (translation by Palmer 1969). In the context of such an overall experience you can interpret a singular experience and assign to it a special meaning in relation to the whole. For example, a teacher with long experience can more easily interpret a pupil's shortcomings in different subjects by putting them in the context of his or her overall experience. The teacher has previously seen that lack of interest on the part of the parents influences children's progress in school a great deal. When he or she finds out that a certain child has very cold relations with his or her parents, the teacher's understanding of the child's achievement in school will increase.

And inversely, one singular experience can totally change a person's self-conception and perception of meaning. There is, in other words, a continuous interaction between the parts and the whole of life. The hermeneutical circle is at work.

By "expression" Dilthey meant all manifestations of human consciousness, even such expressions that are nonverbal or nonintentional. The expressions cannot be understood solely from themselves. As manifestations of culture and history they always have transindividual connotations, which must be interpreted.

Understanding is "the combined activity of all the mental powers in apprehending" (translation by Palmer

1969). What is understood is the living human experience. Understanding is a part of life and as such its own purpose, pleasure, and necessity.

Dilthey sees human beings and self-understanding as essentially historical: "What man is, only history can tell him." The expressions of life that are left behind tell us who we are. Our "historicality" is inescapable; understanding is always taking place in a historical context.

To summarize Dilthey's theory: the task of the interpreter—and also the purpose of hermeneutics—is to unite the past with the present through a process of reconstruction. In this way the connections between expressions, experience, structure of meaning, and life are clarified (Engdahl et al. 1977). The interpreter thus can make it possible to understand not only the concrete expression but also the life-world to which it belonged. The following is an illustration. A Swedish educational historian gives an interpretation of the financial accounts which a gymnasium student in the seventeenth century has given to his headmaster. The accounts tell how much money the scholar collected during one of his wanderings among more or less distant villages (wanderings like this were very usual and formed an important source of income for Scandinavian schools at that time). The interpreter's first task is to clarify the expressions, that is, the meaning of the symbols used in the accounts. Secondly, an attempt should be made to detect the underlying experiences, for instance the overwhelming experience of necessity and need, of which the wandering was a function. Furthermore, the interpreter has to reconstruct the context of forgotten meanings characterizing the practice and must also show how the life of these students during the seventeenth century was formed. By doing this the interpreter, according to Dilthey's scheme, is uniting the past, that is the scholar and his life-world, with the present of modern readers.

5. Hermeneutics as a Phenomenology of Existence and Understanding

With Martin Heidegger (1889–1976) and Hans-Georg Gadamer (b. 1900), Dilthey's thoughts develop into philosophies of existence. Hermeneutics is regarded as interwoven with existence and intrinsic to it. By understanding and interpretation people present the things of the world to themselves. They can be seen as this or that. Understanding is in itself an integral part of being-in-the-world. The process of existing is inseparable from the process of understanding.

Understanding is constantly referring to the future. At the same time it is conditioned by a person's situation. Furthermore, it works within a totality of already interpreted relations. This totality could be called the "world." A teacher entering a class can serve as an example. His or her understanding of the situation is future referenced, when he or she anticipates how the pupils will react to instruction, or when there is a fear that some of them are going to be troublesome. But the teacher's understanding is also conditioned by former experiences of this class, or by earlier experiences during the day. His or her understanding is, in other words, working within a framework of already interpreted relations. Even in referring to the future it is conditioned by the past. The teacher's understanding of the class constitutes, of course, a very important part of his or her "world."

The interplay between understanding and interpretation is permanent, for example in language. Interpretations are expressed in language, but one understands through the categories of thought that language has provided. Language therefore is both interpretation and a way of understanding.

Gadamer (1972) accentuates the linguistic character of understanding. He even claims that language forms the boundaries of understanding and interpretation. It is possible, however, to transcend time and space through language. Ancient texts can, for instance, make the past come very close.

This, however, demands openness on the part of the interpreter, the same kind of openness which often characterizes the situation of experiencing great works of art. Gadamer uses this situation as a model for what he calls "the hermeneutical encounter." This is an experience that by-passes the limits of pre-understanding. In the ideal case a dialectic is started between a "horizon" of understanding and the world of what is being seen. The situation can be described in terms of genuine questioning, which is founded on open expectancy and readiness for change. An example is a historian working with a diary written by an elementary-school teacher in the nineteenth century. The teacher—as he describes himself in his diary—seems to have been a nice man, free from several prejudices typical of his time. However, in some passages of the diary this teacher mentions that he has subjected some of his pupils to corporal punishment. When confronting this information the interpreter experiences a clash between his or her "horizon" of understanding and the "world" of the teacher. The historian could react by shutting off further understanding. Instead he or she asks: "How should I understand these actions, when performed by such a nice person?" In order to reduce conflict, the historian reads books about the role of corporal punishment in earlier stages of education. Gradually he or she understands that the teacher from the past only did as he was told to do by other teachers and contemporary school authorities. The historian also learns that children a century ago were not looked upon in the same way as in the present day. Through a series of questions, for which there is a real need to know the answers, the historian develops a new understanding, which by-passes the limits of pre-understanding and prejudices.

Every hermeneutical endeavour must, according to Gadamer, build on these principles. The interpreter must not therefore take possession of the thing being interpreted. Instead he or she must let it reveal its own world.

6. The Model of the Text

The contribution of Paul Ricoeur (1971) to the development of hermeneutics and interpretation theory could be described as an effort to make a synthesis of hermeneutical thinking from Schleiermacher to the present day. His thinking is strikingly constructive, the question of application being, for instance, more crucial to Ricoeur than to many other hermeneutical theorists.

Ricoeur defines hermeneutics as "the theory of rules that governs an exegesis, that is to say, an interpretation of a particular text or collection of signs susceptible of being considered as a text."

The literal meaning of a text or another system of symbols represents a closed world. This view is parallel, for example, to that of structural analysis, where different aspects of language are reduced and language can be studied as a closed system of signs.

But a text not only refers to itself. Considered as a written discourse and not as language, it refers to a certain situation in a way that is reminiscent of the situation of oral discourse, with all its nonverbal signs, which all refer to a world both within and outside the discourse itself.

A written discourse, or a work, can therefore be looked upon in two ways. First, it can be regarded as a closed system and an attempt can be made to detect its underlying meanings. This is the archaeological aspect of hermeneutics. Secondly, people can make themselves susceptible to the world of the work, which expresses itself in the references to an existential space. Ricoeur thus is opposing "meaning," the "what" of the discourse, to "reference," the "about what?" of the discourse.

What, then, is happening when a text is being interpreted? Ricoeur means that a text or work is world-referring rather than referring to the specific situation of oral discourse. The text is freed from the limits of the speech act. What is met is the nonsituational references which have survived and are given as potential ways of life. What has to be understood then is the "about what?" of the text, which points to a possible world and to ways of orientation in this world.

According to this approach, understanding and interpretation are directed toward the world of the work rather than toward the mentality of the author. In understanding, the dynamics of a work are followed, its movement from what it is saying to what it is speaking about. Something alien becomes a part of the world of the interpreter. This is not identification with an unknown mentality. On the contrary, the interpreter understands himself or herself in a new way when faced with the world of the work. The hermeneutical circle is moving between the interpreter's way of being and the being that is disclosed by the text.

Considering that Ricoeur regards all traces of human activity as in many respects analogous to texts, the relevance of this theory of interpretation becomes obvious. Even the social, cultural, and behavioral sciences can be encompassed by its scheme.

7. Other Contemporary Schools of Hermeneutics

Besides the above-mentioned schools of hermeneutical thought, there are today also some strongly empirically oriented schools.

Emilio Betti and E. D. Hirsch (1967), for example, try to adjust hermeneutical theory to modern scientific principles of objectivity and validity. Betti thinks that a great mistake in existential hermeneutics is made when the two interpretive functions of placing meaning in the open and attributing meaning to a phenomenon (i.e., meaning and significance) are mixed together, which, according to him, leads to complete anarchy of interpretation. Concerning the first function, Betti claims that there are possibilities of finding objective rules of verification, because there is objectively verifiable meaning in the object. And since human expressions are objectifications of the human spirit, the purpose of interpretation must be to reconstruct the meaning which the author intended.

Hirsch stresses this purpose perhaps even more with his principle that the author's intentions must be the norm for interpretation. An essential objection to this, however, is that the meaning of a text could be interpreted even if the intentions of its author were completely unknown to the reader. Texts thus have a dimension which is set free from the mastery of intentions. As Ricoeur has pointed out, a text could be seen as a part of the closed world of language itself. The intentions of the author can of course give important clues, but they are not the sole criterion in the process of interpretation.

As has been learnt from Ricoeur, a text can also be interpreted with special regard to the world in which it was created and which it is disclosing. This dimension of interpretation seems to be somewhat elided in Betti's and Hirsch's approaches. The world of a text is something else, something wider and more lucid than the intention of the author. A decisive point in this context is the fact that this world is also often easier to check than the mysterious mentality of the person behind the text.

In spite of this criticism, Betti's and Hirsch's writings have been a healthy challenge to the development of hermeneutics, which tended to turn into pure philosophy during the first half of this century.

Another tendency to make hermeneutics a more empirical pursuit has also been observable in Europe in the 1960s and 1970s, for instance in Scandinavia. However, this direction of hermeneutics has not the validation school as a point of departure, but uses existential theorists like Gadamer (1972) and Heidegger (1977) as well as the thinking of Ricoeur (1971). The empirical character of this trend may—so far as Scandinavia is concerned—partly be explained by the fact that many of its adherents were initially trained in the scientific principles of positivism, which has been very influential in the social and behavioral sciences in Scandinavia. Perhaps this twofold scientific heritage can contribute to a synthesis of the philosophical and empirical trends in the hermeneutics of today.

Contributions to hermeneutically oriented research in Scandinavia have been made by, for instance, Yngvar Løchen, Arne Trankell, and Johan Asplund.

8. *The Present Position of Hermeneutics*

Habermas (1968) sees three main streams in the development of knowledge and science today, all of which are connected with human existence and survival but with different facets of it. The first of them is the technical interest of knowledge. This is connected with work as its existential mode. The necessity of it is obvious, and its dominance in the world of science is consequently very great.

The other two interests of knowledge which Habermas mentions are the hermeneutical one and critical theory. Hermeneutics is primarily concerned with language, communication, and dialogue as existential modes, while critical theory focuses on the autonomy of the individual. Its ultimate purpose is the emancipation of the individual, which is described as the process whereby the individual becomes more and more autonomous and gradually develops ego-identity and self-consciousness. The individual is freed from dependencies and powerlessness by means of criticism of organizations, standards, and ways of life. The criticism thus points to alternative life-styles, new ways of thinking, and new ways of organizing society.

A study of a school for adult gypsies (Ödman 1980) can illustrate some aspects of critical theory. Many of the gypsies in the investigation—which was conducted in Stockholm in the late 1960s—seemed ambitious and said that they were eager to learn, yet their progress was rather slow, and their teachers often perceived their own situation as very frustrating. The gap between the expressed attitudes of the students and their actual behavior confused the teachers. However, one of the researchers came up with an interpretation which threw light on the problem: the gypsies were defending their cultural autonomy by means of sophisticated forms of passive resistance. What all the teachers, their authorities, and the researchers had failed to see was that the school was "ideology-producing." It was gradually influencing its adult pupils by means of Swedish history, Swedish interests, attitudes, and habits. In short, the gypsies saw the school as a place where they, in a subtle way, were taught to be and behave like Swedes. They had disclosed a "hidden ideology" of the school, which was difficult to discover for the teaching staff itself. In order to keep their identities as independent gypsies intact, they therefore passively refused to accept what the Swedish society through the school had to offer; the silence of their protest was explained by their intentions to remain friends with teachers and authorities. One step on the part of the researchers was to describe the "hidden ideology" and demonstrate its relationships with school practice.

Criticism is only sparsely represented in the sciences and then mostly in the form of Marxian criticism.

Each one of the interests of knowledge is very strongly needed and ought to be given a place in every scientific society. They are concerned with different aspects of the human situation, and since reality in fact must be seen in different ways in order to get a diversified view of it, the different traditions ought to be regarded as complementary to each other (Apel 1972).

However, hermeneutics has a rather weak position in the English-speaking countries, especially in the social and behavioral branches of the human sciences. In Central Europe the influence of hermeneutics is much greater, due to the long tradition of humanities and existential philosophy there.

In the Scandinavian countries the tradition of hermeneutics has been much weaker than on the European continent. The interest from scientists is, however, steadily growing, in so far as the social and behavioral sciences are concerned. Since this trend is associated with a growing familiarity with the continental tradition, it is to be expected that hermeneutics will secure a stronger position in those countries.

9. *Criteria of Interpretation*

The correctness of meaning is decided by judgment, which must always be more vague and diffuse than the figures, for example, of statistical testing. But there are intersubjective meanings, pre-understandings, and interpretations of reality, which have been agreed upon for a long time. Therefore, meaning is often intersubjectively controllable. However, it is seldom necessary for people to check their interpretations with each other. Instead controls are made by means of logical operations. The main principle for this is the canon of the "hermeneutical circle": the parts and its whole must be checked against each other.

A text can be interpreted mainly in two ways. It can be interpreted literally or an attempt can be made to reconstruct the world of the text. Literal interpretation is parallel to interpretation of meanings in the external world. Like language, this also has its grammar, its laws, and restrictions. Clearly, since the logic of sentences and events is often rather strict, it is also possible to apply rather strict logic when their corresponding interpretations are being judged.

First, an interpretation cannot be accepted unless it explains all relevant information available (Trankell 1972). If some important action or meaning is excluded or diffusely reconstructed, the interpretation must be rejected.

Secondly, an interpretation cannot be fully accepted unless it is the only interpretation left to explain the events or phenomena interpreted. In many cases, this second canon is very difficult to satisfy. And even in those successful situations when only one interpretation is left, there is no guarantee that it will remain the correct one.

These two canons of interpretation are most useful when judging reconstructions of such events or chains of events which, at least in principle, are observable. Such events are exemplified by the sequence of questions, replies, and instructions during a regular lesson at school or, to take another example, by the series of actions constituting a mobbing incident on the playground. Processes of this kind can be referred to the category of overt behavior, in which events have or have not happened, and the chain of actions is irreversible.

Interpretations of the literal meanings of texts can also be judged by help of the two canons. Literal meaning is often very accurate, which is often experienced by historians trying to understand old documents. It may shift from century to century, but at a given moment it often has an accuracy, which in the case of a correct interpretation can elucidate a sentence or even a whole document. Inversely, a misinterpretation or bad translation of a word can totally mislead the reader as regards the text as a whole.

Feelings, emotions, and thinking could be seen as kinds of internal events, whose similarity with external events or literal meaning can very clearly be seen. Those events are not observable but leave their own traces in memory, attitudes, and actions. Furthermore, they can be verbalized or expressed in many ways. Many of these phenomena are also very distinct. It is therefore possible to identify them rather easily. A teacher in front of a crying pupil receives, for example, a very clear emotional message: the pupil is sad. Even if there could be several explanations to this reaction, the interpretation "grief" is in itself most plausible.

Hence, it seems possible to discern a triple analogy, that between the literal meaning of texts, and the "immediate" meaning of external and internal events. The interpretations of those kinds of meaning corresponds to what Ricoeur has called the "archeological" aspect of hermeneutics. It is a question of bringing to the surface something which in a certain sense is already there, even if it is impossible to claim that those meanings are inherent in the words or actions themselves. Thus, the meaning is there because of a long tradition of intersubjectivity, which makes it possible for this kind of meaning to be attributed in a rather straightforward way, as is, for instance, the case when people react to traffic signals.

The mistake must not be made, however, of mixing together this kind of "immediate" meaning with the meaning in a broader biographical or cultural context, because this corresponds to another level of interpretation. There the concern is with the symbolic and contextual messages behind a feeling, a text, or its world. Something which is not self-evidently there is being interpreted, a "not-given." Meanings must be created in quite another way. Such meanings do not follow the same type of logic as sentences or observable events, and hence it is not possible to apply the same rigid rules. They are, however, functions of the "grammar" of human consciousness and culture. Though the field of this grammar is very broad, cultural and historical contexts are forming what Schleiermacher refers to as "hermeneutical circles," which can be used in order to understand or check the meanings of texts and events.

In the case of the crying pupil, the teacher is able to relate the grief to the fact that the pupil has failed an examination. But such an interpretation is often insufficient. In many cases it is necessary to go back to the biography of the pupil, for instance to earlier experiences of teachers, schools, and parents. Furthermore, the cultural context with its dominating value systems concerning success and failure has to be taken into consideration.

But on what grounds can interpretations of this kind be accepted or rejected? It is, of course, still possible to use the canon of the circle. And since interpretations on this level are built on arguments and descriptions, which in turn are founded on cultural, political, and existential knowledge, the opportunity exists to ask: Are those references based on good knowledge? Do the interpretations make sense? Is there a preference for one frame of interpretation at the cost of complexity and ontological depth? Are the contexts for interpretation sufficiently realistic and subtle?

From this it follows that there are no absolute standards of judging interpretations on this level. This often contrasts very sharply with the intuitively based experience of evidence which is felt when a good interpretation is being confronted. And often there is a consensus too. Why is it so? It may be because what is recognized is that ontological acuteness of human mind when it is manifesting itself in a good interpretation.

See also: Research Paradigms in Education; Participatory Research

Bibliography

Apel K-O 1972 The a priori of communication and the foundation of the humanities. *Man and World.* 5: 3–37
Betti E 1967 *Allgemeine Auslegungslehre als Methodik der Geisteswissenschaften.* Mohr, Tübingen
Engdahl H et al. 1977 *Hermeneutik. En antologi.* Rabén and Sjögren, Stockholm
Gadamer H-G 1972 *Wahrheit und Methode: Grundzüge einer philosophischen Hermeneutik,* 3rd edn. Mohr, Tübingen
Habermas J 1968 *Erkenntnis und Interesse.* Suhrkamp, Frankfurt
Heidegger M 1977 *Sein und Zeit.* Vittorio Klostermann, Frankfurt/Main
Hirsch E D 1967 *Validity in Interpretation.* Yale University Press, New Haven, Connecticut
Ödman P-J 1979 *Tolkning, Förståelse, Vetande: Hermeneutik i teori och praktik* [Interpretation, Understanding, Science: Hermeneutics in Theory and Practice]. AWE/Gebers, Stockholm
Ödman P-J 1980 *En skolas framåtskridande och tillbakagång. Utvecklingen på zigenarskolan i Årsta läsåren 1967/68 och 1968/69* [Progress and regress of a school for adult gypsies in Stockholm during two years]. Bokförlaget Korpen, Göteborg
Palmer R E 1969 *Hermeneutics: Interpretation theory in Schleiermacher, Dilthey, Heidegger, and Gadamer.* Northwestern University Press, Evanston, Illinois
Radnitzky G 1970 *Contemporary Schools of Metascience,* 2nd edn. Akademiförlaget, Göteborg

Ricoeur P 1971 The model of the text: Meaningful action considered as a text. *Soc. Res.* 38: 529–62

Trankell A 1972 *Reliability of Evidence: Methods for Analyzing and Assessing Witness Statements.* Beckman, Stockholm

Metacognition

R. T. White

Metacognition refers to awareness of one's own thoughts. It has recently become a popular topic for theorizing and empirical research, and is of interest because it implies that modes of teaching might be devised that lead to more effective learning than the general level currently attained in schools. Both theory and research are hampered by difficulties that have been encountered in defining metacognition and in assessing the degree of it in an individual. This article describes these difficulties and some attempts to cope with them.

1. Background Issues

Research invoking the term "metacognition", or one of its derivatives such as "metalearning" or "metamemory", is young. The terms were not used until the 1970s, and metacognition did not become a descriptor in the Educational Resources Information Center (ERIC) system until 1980. However, other older words from the history of psychology dealt with similar conceptions. The fate of those words creates some nervousness about the future of metacognition. For instance, Flavell's definition of metacognition as "knowledge concerning one's own cognitive processes and products or anything related to them" (Flavell 1976 p. 232) might remind psychologists of introspection and the arguments that have surrounded it since at least the seventeenth century. The temporary victory of behaviourism over the introspective methods of Wundt, Titchener, and the gestalt school was aided by the methodological difficulties inevitable in research on a phenomenon that could not be observed and that involved subjective and unverifiable reports. Those difficulties remain, and are of concern to researchers into metacognition.

Despite the difficulties associated with research on it, the concept of metacognition has been taken up with enthusiasm as part of the general surge of interest in cognition, and as a notion that fits more readily with the currently popular theories of information processing than two alternative conceptions of ability, the notion of intelligence that has prevailed throughout most of the twentieth century and Piaget's levels of operational thinking. Intelligence has seen many controversies, and recently was shaken by the furore that greeted Jensen's interpretation of his results (Jensen 1969) as indicating that black Americans are less able than white, and by the demonstration by Kamin (1974) and Hearnshaw (1979) that Burt had invented the data in his influential studies on the inheritance of intelligence. Although

Piaget's interpretations of his observations have not suffered comparable shocks, his stage notion has been criticized (e.g., Donaldson 1978, Isaacs 1930, White and Tisher 1986; see also the Introduction in Gruber and Vonèche (1977), for a discussion of the status of stages in Piaget's theory).

A positive reason for educationists to turn to metacognition and away from the intelligence and stage notions is that the last two deny the value of intervention to improve ability. In those notions ability is a relatively fixed characteristic, while the notion of metacognition, in contrast, holds out the promise of being able to train people at almost any age so that the quality of their learning in future will rise. They will become more able. Naturally many people find that promise exciting, since it presents the possibility of a beneficial revolution in education. However, early experience in research on metacognition shows that the promise will not be trivial to fulfil.

Among the problems to be overcome in research and in implementing its results in practice are those of defining metacognition, of deriving from theory potentially effective teaching methods, of finding valid ways of determining whether people are being metacognitive, and of devising suitable procedures of investigation. These problems are demonstrated by the relatively small number of investigations, given the quantity of discussion of metacognition in articles like the present one; by the diversity of forms of investigation, to the extent that there are few parallel studies or anything like a replication by an independent researcher; and by a lack of consensus about what should be done.

Though the small quantity of studies is unfortunate, diversity and lack of consensus are of less concern. Indeed, in the first stage of research on a topic as complex as metacognition they are rather to be welcomed, since too early a conformity would reflect a sterile narrowness in which effort is concentrated on one aspect to the neglect of others equally important. Early diversity and fumbling are better than conformity and certainty, but eventually some sorting out is necessary. We may now be at that point, for the scene is certainly confusing. Without even considering differences in definition and measurement, the diversity of styles of investigation is remarkable: experiments in which treatments are controlled by the experimenter contrast with descriptive studies in which they are not; in some experiments treatments run for a few minutes only, in others they go on for years; in some, people learn artificial tasks and in others meaningful ones; sometimes people learn from texts, sometimes from a teacher; sometimes the study is run in a psychological laboratory, sometimes in a school. The first attempts to derive order from that diversity are unlikely to synthesize many coherent principles, but will be useful if they make clear the nature of the problems. That will be a step towards their solution.

The two main sources of problems in research on metacognition are the conceptions of it and the model that has it as a factor intervening between training or other experience and the quality of learning. The first leads to difficulties in determining what methods of training should be tried and in devising informative methods of assessment for metacognitive activity, while the second complicates experimental design since it means that metacognition has to be considered both as an outcome (of training) and a cause (of learning). Although these problems are intertwined, for clarity it is best to discuss them separately.

2. Conceptions of Metacognition

While Flavell's (1976) definition of metacognition as awareness of what one is thinking is clear, as with other abstract concepts extensions and alternatives are possible. Should, for instance, metacognition encompass not only awareness but also the control of thinking? Awareness does not guarantee control: one might, for instance, be like a subject in a case study by Baird and White (1982) who was aware of being compulsive in jumping to conclusions but was unable to resist doing so. A legalistic reading of Flavell's definition would exclude regulation of thinking, though regulation is too important to ignore. It is what matters in practice, since unless one can control one's cognitive processes and harness them to learning there is not much use in merely being aware of them. Flavell recognized this, for later on the same page as his definition he wrote: "Metacognition refers, among other things, to the active monitoring and consequent regulation and orchestration of these processes in relation to the cognitive objects or data on which they bear . . . . " (Flavell 1976 p. 232). Probably no one investigating metacognition proposes that regulation of thinking should be ignored. The issue is rather one of definition, about whether regulation should be kept separate from the conception of metacognition. When Brown writes about metacognition, she refers to both awareness and regulation: "Metacognition refers to the deliberate conscious control of one's own cognitive actions" (Brown 1980 p. 453). Cavanaugh and Perlmutter (1982) prefer to exclude regulation from their meaning:

Calling both what the person knows and how she or he uses it "metamemory" reflects a failure to make an explicit distinction between knowledge about memory and processes orchestrating this knowledge . . . . Inclusion of executive processes as an aspect of metamemory is counterproductive, since it adds little to understanding of memory knowledge per se and heightens perceptual confusion. (Cavanaugh and Perlmutter 1982 pp. 15-16)

While authors are free to give whatever meaning they choose to a word, their readers are likely to misunderstand or be confused if they are not aware of the differences in meaning.

A further question in defining metacognition is whether the ability to regulate thoughts guarantees that the person will apply that ability. In other words, is regulation spontaneous or does it often have to be stimulated by an external agent? Do people who do not regulate their thinking productively not know how to, or not choose to do so, or need an applied stimulus to do so? Should such matters of choice and spontaneity be included in our conception of metacognition?

Yet another issue is whether propositional knowledge about metacognition should be part of the concept. Many authors might exclude that knowledge, since even a comprehensive understanding of what has been written about metacognition does not guarantee awareness of one's own thoughts. Others might choose to include it.

To sum up, there are at least four possible facets to metacognition: propositional knowledge about it, awareness of personal thinking, ability to regulate thinking, and readiness to apply that ability. It is essential to know which of these are meant when an author refers to metacognition in order for communication to be clear.

Whatever exclusions and inclusions of the four facets are accepted in the definition of metacognition, the relations between them are suitable targets for research. Is awareness of cognitive processes essential for their regulation? Does training in awareness transfer to regulation? Does knowing about what is involved in metacognition aid awareness of one's own thinking? What conditions promote and what inhibit application of an ability to regulate cognition? Progress with these questions should speed the development of a consensus about the definition of metacognition.

As well as the four facets, or whatever number other authors identify, metacognition has a further dimension that needs clarifying, a dimension that centres on the question: What is the nature of cognition, and how is it regulated in metacognition? I will not go into the first part of the question here, for it is a large area that has received much attention in theories of information processing. The second part, though, must be attended to.

Most authors describe regulation as the application of sets of strategies or general skills. For example, Paris et al. (1986) refer to comprehension strategies in reading such as skimming, rereading, paraphrasing, and summarizing; while Ellis (1986) refers to some in problem solving of planning, checking, testing, revising, and evaluating; and Baird (1986) to some in learning the establishment of a topic, evaluating knowledge and feelings about it, reviewing the structure of the message and picking out important parts, evaluating the outcome of the learning, and several others.

Brown (1978) raised the further question of whether strategies are anything other than glorified (perhaps over-glorified) cognitive skills. That is, whether there is any need for the concept of metacognition at all, or whether knowing that one knows is any different from knowing other facts. Although the question is apparently philosophical, the distinction between metacognition and cognition was tackled empirically by Slife et al. (1985). By an ingenious procedure they matched two groups of children on mathematical skills and performance, so, they claimed, equating them on relevant cognition. One group consisted of rather older children who were enrolled in a programme for disabled learners with large differences between their mental ages and arithmetic achievement ages, while the other was of children in a regular school programme. Though equal on mathematics skills and achievement, the children in the learning disabled programme fared worse on the metacognitive tasks of predicting how many arithmetic exercises they would get correct and of identifying which ones they actually did get correct. Slife et al. are aware that their procedure is open to the criticism that the groups might differ on relevant factors other than those for which they were matched, and state that, "The evidence reported in this article is not dramatic proof of the separability of cognition and metacognition" (Slife et al. 1985 p. 444). However, their study is, as they say, an example of an empirical way of tackling the issue and an indication that more elaborate procedures such as multitrait–multimethod designs are worth undertaking.

Conception of metacognition as involving strategies brings out a further issue: Can a comprehensive set of metacognitive strategies be defined? Experience with other psychological concepts suggests that the answer is a qualified no. For example, within the psychometric tradition of intelligence the wide range of test types reflects a wide range of conceptions. Raven's matrices differ from Stanford–Binet items, and they in turn from the Weschler Intelligence Scale for Children (WISC), and so on. Still, some consensus is desirable, and may be attained for metacognition to about the same extent as it has been for intelligence. The initial procedure, before empirical comparisons are attempted, would be to carry out frequent reviews of articles on metacognition to compile lists of strategies. Equivalent but differently named strategies could be identified, to reduce redundancy. Perhaps overoptimistically, one hopes that a generally accepted terminology and list of strategies would emerge.

Faced with diversity and confusion, humans try to group things, and will certainly do that to lists of strategies. This is demonstrated by Weinstein and Mayer (1986), who identify eight categories of learning strategies. Part of the process of reaching consensus about metacognition could be debate about which of the categories are metacognitive. The debate should sharpen the criteria for a mental act to be graded metacognitive. Must, for example, the person be conscious that he or she is applying the strategy? For an example of their first category, rehearsal strategies for basic learning tasks, Weinstein and Mayer cite the naming of objects in lists that are to be memorized, which is evidenced by

moving of lips (Flavell et al. 1966). The people who move their lips may not be aware that they do it. Is it then metacognition? Another criterion is whether application of the strategy is deliberate. A strategy that has been used for millenia is to attach each object in the list to a well-established sequence of images, such as houses along a familiar street (Yates 1966). This can be done deliberately, but Luria's famous mnemonist, S, (Luria 1968) appears to have applied it automatically and indeed was often hampered by his inability to "turn off" his images. Is an uncontrolled strategy metacognitive?

Towards the other end of the sequence of strategies that Weinstein and Mayer (1986) propose are less contentious skills. Weinstein and Mayer equate their category of comprehension monitoring strategies with metacognition, though they do not specifically exclude their other categories from metacognition.

Systems like that of Weinstein and Mayer are helpful in framing debates about criteria for metacognition. They are useful further in seeing how comprehensive are current notions of metacognition. As new metacognitive strategies are listed and described, they should be fitted into the system. If they do not fit any category, yet meet the criteria for metacognition, the system (or the criteria) must be amended. Gradually a stable system should evolve, useful until a conceptual revolution brings an entirely new way of thinking about metacognition.

3. The Two-Stage Model

The second major source of problems in research on metacognition is its conception as a mental state that intervenes between experience and learning (or other performance). The presumption is that people can be trained in metacognitive strategies, and that when they apply them they will learn better than they used to. Thus investigations of metacognition can have two parts, one in which it is an outcome of training and one in which it is a cause of better learning. Approaches in these two parts must differ, because in the first the independent variable or cause is directly under the control of the experimenter while in the second it is not.

Since training is controllable, its influence on metacognition can be studied using one or other of the true experimental designs described by Campbell and Stanley (1963). The paradigm is a study in which subjects are assigned randomly to a treatment group that receives training in metacognition or to a control group whose time is occupied in some other way; after a suitable interval the groups are compared on the amount of metacognition they display.

Studies of the second part of the model would have to be correlational, since experimenters cannot assign people to high or low metacognitive groups any more than they can to high or low intelligence ones. However, because metacognition may, unlike intelligence, be amenable to instruction, it is possible to design studies in which both stages are investigated. One way would be to employ a design that is represented, using Campbell and Stanley's symbols, in Fig. 1.

$$R \quad X_1 \quad 0_1 \quad 0_3$$
$$R \quad X_2 \quad 0_2 \quad 0_4$$

Figure 1
Symbolic representation of design of investigations of metacognition

In Fig. 1, the Rs stand for random allocation of people to two groups, X_1 and X_2 represent the training and control treatments, 0_1 and 0_2 measures of metacognitive activity, and 0_3 and 0_4 measures of quality of learning. The analyses would consist of a comparison of 0_1 with 0_2 to check on the effect of training, and correlations of 0_1 with 0_3 and 0_2 with 0_4 to see whether differences in metacognition affect learning. Hardly any researcher would be able to resist comparing 0_3 with 0_4 also. For assurance about the longevity of the effect of the training, the fours 0s could be repeated later.

In practice, the neat representation of research in Fig. 1 is complicated by two further issues, the nature of training methods and the way in which metacognition is to be assessed.

4. Training Methods

Lacking a mature theory of metacognition from which they could deduce potentially effective methods of training, researchers have had to try commonsense methods. For instance, since metacognition concerns awareness of one's own thinking, training people to check on their thinking through self-questioning might appear to have promise. Wong (1985) reviewed 27 studies of self-questioning, though only four were based obviously on a metacognitive perspective. In most of the 27 studies the self-questioning was content directed, for example generating questions about details or implications of stories or texts. Because it is not aimed at arousing consciousness of the learner's own thoughts, many people may not want to count this sort of self-questioning as metacognition. More direct raising of awareness may occur through questions like: What do I already know about this topic? How much am I interested in it? Do I understand this information? What should I do to understand it better? The distinction between the two types of self-question is blurred: "What are the key points in this text?" and "Do I know what the key points in this text are?" are related. Nevertheless, the second form of question is more personal, and training in it might be found to have more effect than the first on metacognition.

As well as self-questioning, feedback on effectiveness of strategies (see Lodico et al. 1983, for a list of studies) and training in monitoring the utility of strategies (Ghatala et al. 1985) have been tried. Ellis (1986) suggests other treatments. However, rather than attempting a comprehensive list, I shall turn to other characteristics of training methods: their length, site, and integration with normal lessons.

The self-questioning investigations that Wong (1985) reviewed generally involved brief training treatments. The shortest took less than half an hour, and even three

of the four studies with a metacognition perspective used short treatments: a single 50 minute session (André and Anderson 1978-1979); two sessions of unspecified length a day apart (Dreher and Gambrell 1982); and two sessions of two hours each (Wong and Jones 1982). The fourth study (Palincsar 1982) involved 18 sessions. Hindsight suggests that it is optimistic to expect brief training to effect lasting changes in styles of thinking and learning that have been established over years of experience by each individual. Certainly Baird and White (1982) had very limited success in changing the learning styles of college students in an intervention that was much more intensive than that in any of the foregoing studies.

The belief that training in metacognition must be intense and long lies behind studies by Paris (e.g., Paris et al. 1984, Paris and Jacobs 1984, Paris et al. 1986) and Baird (Baird 1986, Baird and Mitchell 1986). Long studies can hardly be run in a laboratory; they must occur in a school or college. In Paris's studies, children in eight elementary school classes, whose teachers volunteered to help, were taught for a year by the experimenters and the teachers about strategies that are effective in reading. Baird (1986) worked for six months with one teacher and three of his classes to improve students' application of learning strategies, while the Project to Enhance Effective Learning (Baird and Mitchell 1986) is on an even larger scale, involving 10 high school teachers and their classes in its first year and 12 in its second. It is an action research study in which the teachers are the experimenters. In contrast to brief laboratory investigations, the Paris and the Baird studies trade tight control over treatment for gains in effect and in ecological validity. Though the trade involves costs in time and effort, it is defensible because although brief laboratory studies may tell us something about potentially effective methods and about ways of assessing metacognition, it seems certain that long-term training is required to bring about permanent improvements in metacognition and we need to find out as much as we can about the implementation of lengthy interventions in functioning institutions.

5. Measurement of Metacognition

Though it may be trite to say that all mental measurement involves inference, in that it consists of making a judgment about an unobservable construct from overt performance that one hopes is related validly to it, that is the essence of the problem of assessing metacognition. Metacognition is an inner awareness or process, not an overt behaviour. The two commonly used ways of assessing it, self-report and observation of its products, have weaknesses.

Self-report is obtained through interviews and questionnaires, both of which are open to the criticism that the report may not be honest or accurate. There is no need to add here to the extensive literature on interviews and questionnaires and the techniques that are applied to overcome their weaknesses, but it is worth pointing out that both involve introspection, which was mentioned earlier along with the note that one of the chief objections to it was that it was not defined precisely. As has been discussed, metacognition suffers from the same problem. Despite their weaknesses, interviews and questionnaires have been used to assess level of metacognition (e.g., Baird 1986, Paris et al. 1986).

Observations of products of metacognition may appear more objective than self-report. Eye movements, for instance, could be monitored to see whether a learner pays more attention to key points in a text than to peripherals. Less direct methods include how often subjects generate questions that relate to important parts of a lesson or text (e.g., André and Anderson 1978-1979, Wong and Jones 1982).

As observations of products become less direct, two weaknesses increase. One is possible reduction in validity of the measure through glib performance of the behaviour without basing it on metacognition. For example, one consequence of metacognition could be for learners to ask more questions in school lessons. If this behaviour were rewarded, students could develop formulas for generating questions such as "What use is this substance?" and "Is there anything in (another subject or topic) that relates to this topic?", that could be applied in many situations without reflection (Arzi and White 1986). No doubt this weakness could be minimized, but it exists.

The second weakness of less direct methods is the circularity that they introduce into studies of the second stage of the model that has metacognition intervening between experience and performance. The products are evidence both of the existence of metacognition and of the relation between metacognition and quality of learning. The relation cannot really be tested with indirect measures of metacognition; all that is involved is a test of whether two products are related.

The solution to the problem of assessing metacognition is to use as many methods as possible with each subject. Though each method is weak, the constellation of evidence from them will be more reliable and valid than each alone.

6. Recommendations

In this discussion of issues in research on metacognition several recommendations have been made that can now be listed. First, we need to attend to the definition of metacognition, debating what facets are to be covered by the term and developing a comprehensive list of strategies. Then we need to develop a theory of the relation between training methods and experiences and the development of metacognition, and of the relation between metacognition and specific aspects of learning. More investigations should study both relations. In assessing the presence of metacognition, researchers should use broad ranges of tasks. Though there may be some value in short-term studies, long-term studies in natural settings are essential.

Bibliography

André M E D A, Anderson T R 1978–1979 The development and evaluation of a self-questioning study technique. *Read. Res. Q.* 14: 605–23

Arzi H J, White R T 1986 Questions on students' questions. *Res. Sci. Educ.* 16: 82–91

Baird J R 1986 Improving learning through enhanced metacognition: A classroom study. *Eur. J. Sci. Educ.* 8: 263–82

Baird J R, Mitchell I J (eds.) 1986 *Improving the Quality of Teaching and Learning: An Australian Case Study—The Peel Project.* Monash University, Melbourne

Baird J R, White R T 1982 Promoting self-control of learning. *Instr. Sci.* 11: 227–47

Brown A L 1978 Knowing when, where, and how to remember: A problem of metacognition. In: Glaser R (ed.) 1978 *Advances in Instructional Psychology*, Vol. 1. Erlbaum, Hillsdale, New Jersey

Brown A L 1980 Metacognitive development and reading. In: Spiro R J, Bruce B C, Brewer W F (eds.) 1980 *Theoretical Issues in Reading Comprehension: Perspectives from Cognitive Psychology, Linguistics, Artificial Intelligence, and Education.* Erlbaum, Hillsdale, New Jersey

Campbell D T, Stanley J C 1963 Experimental and quasi-experimental designs for research on teaching. In: Gage N L (ed.) 1963 *Handbook of Research on Teaching.* Rand McNally, Chicago, Illinois

Cavanaugh J C, Perlmutter M 1982 Metamemory: A critical examination. *Child Dev.* 53: 11–28

Donaldson M 1978 *Children's Minds.* Croom Helm, London

Dreher M J, Gambrell L B 1982 (April) Training children to use a self-questioning strategy for studying expository prose. Paper presented at the annual meeting of the American Educational Research Association, New York

Ellis E S 1986 The role of motivation and pedagogy on the generalization of cognitive strategy training. *J. Learn. Disabil.* 19: 66–70

Flavell J H 1976 Metacognitive aspects of problem solving. In: Resnick L B (ed.) 1976 *The Nature of Intelligence.* Erlbaum, Hillsdale, New Jersey

Flavell J H, Beach D R, Chinsky J M 1966 Spontaneous verbal rehearsal in a memory task as a function of age. *Child Dev.* 37: 283–99

Ghatala E S, Levin J R, Pressley M, Lodico M G 1985 Training cognitive strategy-monitoring in children. *Am. Educ. Res. J.* 22: 199–215

Gruber H E, Vonèche J J (eds.) 1977 *The Essential Piaget.* Routledge and Kegan Paul, London

Hearnshaw L S 1979 *Cyril Burt: Psychologist.* Hodder and Stoughton, London

Isaacs S 1930 *Intellectual Growth in Young Children.* Routledge and Kegan Paul, London

Jensen A R 1969 How much can we boost IQ and scholastic achievement? *Harvard Educ. Rev.* 39: 1–123

Kamin L J 1974 *The Science and Politics of I.Q.* Erlbaum, Potomac, Maryland

Lodico M G, Ghatala E S, Levin J R, Pressley M, Bell J A 1983 The effects of strategy-monitoring training on children's selection of effective memory strategies. *J. Exp. Child Psychol.* 35: 263–77

Luria A R 1968 *The Mind of a Mnemonist* [Translated by Solotaroff L]. Basic Books, New York

Palincsar A S 1982 Improving the reading comprehension of junior high students through reciprocal teaching of comprehension-monitoring strategies. Doctoral dissertation, University of Illinois, Urbana, Illinois

Paris S G, Cross D R, Lipson M Y 1984 Informed strategies for learning: A program to improve children's reading awareness and comprehension skills. *Child Dev.* 55: 2083–93

Paris S G, Jacobs J E 1984 The benefits of informed instruction for children's reading awareness and comprehension skills. *Child Dev.* 55: 2083–93

Paris S G, Saarnio D A, Cross D R 1986 A metacognitive curriculum to promote children's reading and learning. *Aust. J. Psychol.* 38: 107–23

Slife B D, Weiss J, Bell T 1985 Separability of metacognition and cognition: Problem solving in learning disabled and regular students. *J. Educ. Psychol.* 77:437–45

Weinstein C E, Mayer R E 1986 The teaching of learning strategies. In: Wittrock M C (ed.) 1986 *Handbook of Research on Teaching*, 3rd edn. Macmillan, New York

White R T, Tisher R P 1986 Research on natural sciences. In: Wittrock M C (ed.) 1986 *Handbook of Research on Teaching*, 3rd edn. Macmillan, New York

Wong B Y L 1985 Self-questioning instructional research: A review. *Rev. Educ. Res.* 55: 227–68

Wong B Y L, Jones W 1982 Increasing metacomprehension in learning-disabled and normally-achieving students through self-questioning training. *Learn. Disabil. Q.* 5: 228–40

Yates F A 1966 *The Art of Memory*. Routledge and Kegan Paul, London

Oral History

A. D. Spaull

Oral history, or strictly the use of oral sources in history, was the first kind of historical inquiry. It has been rediscovered after being unjustly dismissed by several generations of professional historians. The sources of this rediscovery, their influence on the study of history of education and its use of oral history are surveyed. Special attention is paid to the evidential problems associated with oral sources, and although some problems remain they should not be seen as a deterrent against the use of oral history by educational researchers.

1. Oral History in General

The recent growth in the use of oral history methods by historians has risen from several sources.

1.1 Contemporary History

The revival and popularity of contemporary history, that is, history since circa 1920, has broken the professional resistance to studying the contemporary period and to using methods and techniques appropriate to the period. The movement towards contemporary history has been due to several factors: (a) the momentum of the twentieth century, with periods of rapid social change and episodic experiences, has meant that the "present" becomes the "past" much faster than before; (b) the popular demand for the historian to explain these changes, assisted by the film sources, as found in television histories; and (c) the easing of official restrictions on public records (Schlesinger 1971). The need to understand the contemporary past has made the collection of oral sources imperative to both the "lay" historians of local communities, and the professional historians, especially in the fields of political and military history, biography, and twentieth-century science.

1.2 Sociological Approaches to History

Historians have increasingly adopted sociological methods; in particular there has been a revival of interest in life histories, whether Scandinavian folk studies or European labour histories, of workers' communities or rural and industrial occupations. The life history method is closely akin to the oral history interview (Bertaux 1981).

1.3 The New Social History

There has been a dramatic increase in the study of the historical dynamics of social structures, and the attitudes, experience, and daily lives of ordinary people. The new social history aims to look at these aspects of the "forgotten people" in history. Various methodologies have been employed, including placing an emphasis on quantification for pre-twentieth-century studies, looking at structuralist–cultural approaches which study collective mentalities of communities, and carrying out studies which analyse the personal experiences of individuals and groups.

Most advocates of oral history claim that it is a valuable addition, not just a supplement, to the tools of historical investigation. Others hold more buoyant expectations for oral history. Paul Thompson who directed the English project on Edwardian life argues that oral history widens the scope for a "radical transformation of the social meaning of history" (Thompson 1978 p. 18). Although this level of expectations has not been realized, oral historians have challenged the mandarins of academic history.

2. Education and Oral History

History of education studies have tracked these recent developments in oral history, but with a discernible lag, and at times, lack of appreciation. The use of oral sources is not new to the history of education, especially in the use of interviews with, or about, educational leaders. The use of interviews has increased in recent years with historians' interest in the expansion of modern public education or in areas of educational policy making, that are essentially twentieth-century developments, for example, state secondary schooling, preschooling, teacher unionization, or central government finance of schooling, and so on. Oral history has also become important as a supplementary source in modern policy studies, often because documentary evidence is unavailable, inaccessible because of restrictions, or the study requires insights into personal and group motives and attitudes. Examples of the extensive use of oral records can be found in "instant" histories such as the analysis of the St. Louis teachers' strike (Cortinovis 1974). Edinburgh University's project on Scottish education policy making in the period 1939–70 (McPherson and Raab 1981) consists of a collection of interviews with retired members of the education system which analyse and document relationships between governmental processes and changes in the curriculum, patterns of innovation, teacher training, and teacher supply.

Sociologists of education have used oral history techniques for many years, particularly when studying student groups, teachers, or educational changes. Studies in the early 1960s of English working-class children and schooling and of American disadvantaged children, which drew heavily on oral narratives, still provide inspiration for later sociologists (Connell et al. 1982). However there are complaints that life histories are neglected in other sociological studies of schooling (Goodson 1981).

There has been a swing towards the systematic collection and use of oral sources in the preparation of institutional histories of individual schools and universities. This type of activity has been extended to the study of particular developments such as Cornell University's Black Studies programme. Other universities have established education collections in their oral history programmes: the University of California at Los Angeles; the Hebrew University at Jerusalem; Monash University, Australia; and Columbia University, New York—the last being part of a collection holding nearly 3,000 interviews. Columbia's education section includes collections on twentieth-century American educators, the Children's Television Workshops ("Sesame Street"), a history of the American Association of Physics Teachers, and the educational work of the Carnegie Corporation Endowment. These projects are within the original tradition of retrieving the career histories of representative public figures for future use by historians.

The use of oral history methods in studies of the history of education has received its greatest stimulus from the new social history. Much of the pioneering work has been undertaken by those historians interested in wider questions of social class, family, local community structures, or ethnic history. The life history interview runs through many of these aspects so that educational topics such as schooling, growing up, acculturation, can be found in Negro oral history projects and immigrant studies. Similarly, French, Italian, or Scandinavian oral history projects of working-class regions or labour processes contribute incidently to studies of working-class children's schooling and, deliberately, to knowledge of their preparation for work and industrial training. Radical labour history, which draws increasingly on oral history, encounters theoretical ambiguities in the classroom teacher. Despite the discovery of teachers' written recollections of their working conditions during France's Third Republic (Ozouf 1967), Marxists are reluctant to place the teacher in the proletariat class.

Studies of national and local communities or family history (Thompson 1978) have provided insights into the experience of schooling, teachers' behaviour, and the educational development of children. Building on this, a new history of education has appeared in an exciting oral history of working-class childhood and youth in England (Humphries 1981). The study draws on the "Edwardian data" at Essex University, a larger collection at Manchester Polytechnic, and the author's own Bristol People's Oral History Project. Nearly half the book examines working-class responses to compulsory schooling, locating a strong resistance to the school as an agent of middle-class socialization. In Australia a similar study has confirmed earlier quantitative studies on working-class opposition to schools, and concludes that connections between school and work were tenuous and ill-defined (Broomhill and Davey 1980). One of the intellectual barriers to the growth of oral history in studies of the history of education is that the new social history of education has focused on nineteenth-century schooling, often using quantitative sources. However, as studies of schooling and social class edge towards the twentieth century, the availability of oral sources will add new research dimensions to the history of education.

3. Problems of Method

The status of oral history still remains suspect to many professional historians, because of the character and nature of its evidence. A censorious view is that oral history sources have an inferior ranking to that of written transactional records and selective records. A more liberal view is that oral history has the same degree of acceptance for reliability as a range of sources, all of which have special limitations, and to which in some cases, oral sources can offer relief. The extreme case for oral history is that it is intrinsically different to other forms of history, "in that the narrator from outside the narration, is pulled inside and becomes part of it" (Portelli 1981). Ultimately it depends upon the historian's assumptions about social inquiry; is the historian prepared to move beyond positivist training to acceptance of the personal narrative?

The credibility of oral history hinges on three major problems in collecting oral sources. These problems must be acknowledged by the historian, but they should not become obstacles in the collection and writing of oral histories.

3.1 Representativeness of Sources

A common argument raised against oral history is that its sources are unrepresentative of the range of human experience, or rely too much on a few individual sources, so that they distort social reality. There is concern that major sampling errors will occur due to natural shortages of older people, or people who cannot recall early childhood. This type of argument is rebutted in general terms. All historians are faced with problems of representativeness; historians are forced to select, especially when writing from a mass of documentary sources. Frequently they resort to constructing a small number of representative stereotypes to portray the response of groups and communities to social forces. Oral historians complain that their problems are not shortages or distortions, but abundance; how best to utilize the many people willing to be interviewed. Where surveying of national, social, or community groups is required, normal techniques of quota sampling are available to the oral historian, methods not always available to historians of earlier periods. Finally, oral historians should not become obsessive about representativeness to the extent that they miss the uniqueness or vividness of the interview (Thompson 1978).

3.2 Recollections

Oral history sources are not the product of an earlier historical period, but how the interviewee, a product of today's experience, recalls or thinks life was for that period. As memory is essentially a process of reconstruction, oral historians are faced with two methodological problems. First, there is the question of perception and the comprehension of past events and feelings. Memory is a highly selective process—it distorts, diverts, and desists, and is unable to provide direct access to past emotions. There is speculation on the reliability of recalling subjective experiences, because, unlike the recollection of events, there is no opportunity for external validation. Also there is a tendency to equate the descriptive label of an emotion, for example, pain, with the emotion itself. These are positions in a debate, best answered by recourse to the analogy of historical inferences; historians are forced to draw inferences about feelings and attitudes from fragmentary traces of the past (Hay 1981). This leads to the question of whether painful experiences are blocked from recall. Such experiences are often central to an investigation, for example historical studies of adolescents or of school policies and practice, including corporal punishment, left-handedness, and so on. Psychiatry, based on repression theories, and early efforts at group psychohistory (children in socially deprived situations) question whether painful experiences can be recalled. However, recent oral histories of wartime orphans (Hay 1981), wartime youth (Spaull 1980), or working-class school students (Humphries 1981) suggest that distressful personal experiences are recoverable, although not without distortion. Yet it is the selectivity of memory that continually challenges the oral historian. This in itself is important because the recalled interests of the interviewee provide social indicators as to what was important to individuals in the past and over time. Second, there is the question of memory over time. The oral historian's credo that "forgetting is not a problem", is not always shared by psychologists of memory. They have more confidence in the reliability of short-term memory, with the accuracy of recall after declining rapidly, continuing to decline more slowly over time, coinciding when aging accelerates reminiscing. The oral historian tends to be involved in this third phase, and with older people, expecting that the social facts retained in individual memories are recoverable and are a reliable historical source. The theory of information processing within studies of long-term memory is attractive to the oral historian. It sees memory as a large store-house of semantic and episodic traces. Semantic traces are verbal symbols that record nonaffective information. Episodic traces are recorded events and actions which seem to be stored as a timetable, as well as rehearsed memories and reminiscences (Neuenschwander 1978). These episodic traces become the historian's primary targets in the gathering of additional empirical material, interpretative narratives, or exploring an individual's meanings and beliefs about the past, although memory on beliefs is less reliable.

There is then some compatibility between the psychologists' view of memory and the oral historians' work in recovering the past. However, more systematic attention by historians to the psychology of memory, to interdisciplinary aspects of oral source methodology, experimental interviewing, and skilful interviewing will reduce, but not entirely overcome, these methodological problems.

3.3 Interviewing

Skill in interviewing is the basis of any successful social investigation. Its centrality to some of the methodological problems involved in collecting oral sources has been indicated above. This subsection will not be an exposition of the interview and inter viewing; instead it will raise issues pertinent to oral history.

The interview is a social relationship, although an unequal one, because of the social position of the interviewer as researcher and in some cases, the different class positions. The successful interview can become the privileged means which takes the researcher (and interviewee) beyond the normal attempts to obtain information. Oral history is a unique means of forcing people into history, because it enables older generations of people to become part of the writing of history. For many this is their first opportunity to think about history as a discipline, to justify their past actions, and to recall past beliefs. For some, it will be the first time that they have been invited to participate in a public programme, or in a scholarly or community activity, and subjected to recording equipment that is not the part of their normal household facilities. Within these situations, the interviewer must attempt to overcome the natural modesty, courteous restraint, and social or language inhibitions of the interviewee, to elicit information, which is accurate and reliable, and volunteered with candour and vividness. Ironically the same expectations of outcomes are not present when interviewing public figures, even retired ones, who are more guarded with an eye to public image or history, and therefore are not as reliable as an oral source.

Whatever the case, the basis for an interviewing relationship must be built on trust, not only to satisfy legal or personal requirements, but to establish a meaningful working situation, dedicated, if only momentarily, to the notion of historical inquiry. The onus for establishing such a relationship rests with the project designer, who must decide on strategies such as the personality and social characteristics of interviewers (should men interview women?), whether to use group rather than individual interviews, the recording technology, and the locality of the interview. The choice of recording equipment is not always possible or considered; the topic and interviewee may preclude anything but a notebook. There are times when expensive film or television film is required to record expression and actions. Locality also requires preliminary judgment. Institutional localities such as the old neighbourhood, school yard, or classroom, "sight, sound, and smells of the past", and even the use of reunions or textbooks, may be valuable in prompting recall. These can be artificially presented from audiovisual material, old film, and so on, or by interviewing in a school museum.

After considerations of strategies, matched by extensive background research (including work on newspapers or newsreels of the period) and armed with a battery of conversational questions on major themes, the interview can commence. The interviewer should listen without judging; converse in the language of the interviewee and the period; question without interrogating or leading; observe with regard for style and rhythm, and the physical signs of fatigue (often), overexcitement, boredom (rarely), and/or anxiety about the direction of the interview or the recollection of the past itself.

4. Presentation

There are several different forms that the presentation of oral sources can take. There must be duplication of recordings (transcription is now too expensive), indexing, cataloguing, storing of the recordings, and so on.

There must be reporting publicity and administration of the collection. But above all else, the records of the interviews must be used in the writing of history. To repeat the repeat of a dictum: "There will be more oral history and less tape recording."

Bibliography

Bertaux D (ed.) 1981 *Biography and Society: The Life History Approach in the Social Sciences.* Sage, London

Broomhill R, Davey J 1980 *The Hindmarsh (S. Aust.) Oral History Project.* Report to ERDC, Canberra

Connell R W et al. 1982 *Making the Difference, Schools, Families and Social Division.* Allen and Unwin, Sydney

Cortinovis I E 1974 Documenting an event with manuscripts and oral history: The St. Louis teachers' strike, 1973. *Oral History Rev.* 1974: 59–63

Goodson I 1981 Life histories and the study of schooling. *Interchange* 11(4): 62–76

Hay C 1981 The pangs of the past. *Oral History* (UK) 9(1): 41–46

Humphries S 1981 *Hooligans or Rebels? An Oral History of Working Class Childhood and Youth 1889–1939.* Blackwell, Oxford

McPherson A, Raab C 1981 *Notes on Oral History Project on Scottish Education Policy-making.* Centre for Educational Sociology, Edinburgh University, Edinburgh

Neuenschwander J 1978 Remembrance of things past: Oral historians and long-term memory. *Oral History Rev.* 1978: 45–53

Ozouf J 1967 *Nous, les maîtres d'écoles: Autobiographies d'instituteurs de la belle époque.* Juillard, Paris

Portelli A 1981 The peculiarities of oral history. *History Workshop* 12: 96–107

Schlesinger J R A 1971 The historian as participant. *Daedalus* 100: 339–49

Spaull A D 1980 Oral history and history of education. *OH Aust. J.* 2: 81–83

Thompson P R 1978 *The Voice of the Past: Oral History.* Oxford University Press, Oxford

Teachers as Researchers

J. Elliott

The idea of teachers as researchers is usually associated with Stenhouse, director of the Schools Council's Humanities Project (1967–72). Stenhouse integrated the idea into an imaginative conception of the curriculum project as a concrete expression of educational ideas for teachers to reflect upon as they attempted to implement it in practice. The "curriculum project" was conceived as a device for linking theory to practice, and holding theorists accountable to teachers. These ideas were elaborated as an alternative process model of curriculum development, to the objectives model (Stenhouse 1975).

The two models constituted different solutions to a dilemma centrally funded developers faced in the United Kingdom during the late 1960s and early 1970s. Their curricula were being misused by teachers, who adapted them to match their traditional pedagogy and the assumptions about knowledge and teaching which underpinned it. This problem was exacerbated by the prevailing ideology of teacher autonomy, which gave developers little control over the use of their products. All they could do was to market them with "suggestions". So the dilemma was how to effect change in classrooms while respecting teachers' autonomy of judgment.

The objectives model (Tyler 1949) was used to establish a rational foundation for the adoption of curriculum projects. Its emphasis on analysing broad curricular aims into quantifiable learning outcomes as a basis for developing and evaluating curriculum activities, opened the possibility of rationally demonstrating their effectiveness.

A major assumption underlying the use of the objectives model as a basis for securing "rational adoption" was that curricula, like washing machines, can be mass produced. The influence of contextual factors on the way curricula "shape up" in different settings was ignored. In spite of positive evaluation findings teachers continued to misuse innovations.

Stenhouse's solution to the dilemma was a highly original one. Rather than developing a curriculum which appealed to teachers as rational adopters the Humanities Project addressed them as pragmatic sceptics.

Instead of analysing the teaching aim of the project—"to develop an understanding of controversial value issues"—into behavioural objectives, Stenhouse claimed it could be logically analysed into the following procedural principles governing the way teachers handle controversial issues with students.

(a) Discussion rather than instruction should be the core activity in the classroom.

(b) Divergence of view should be protected.

(c) Procedural neutrality should be the criterion governing the teachers' role.

(d) Teachers have responsibility for quality and standards in learning, for example by representing criteria for understanding evidence about peoples' views.

These principles are not couched as precise technical rules governing exactly what teachers ought to do in classrooms. They constitute an operational philosophy mediating between a rather abstract ideal or aim and the practicalities of teaching. Stenhouse's logic provided an orientation for classroom practice but left questions about how it was to shape up in particular circumstances for teachers' own research. They were encouraged to tape or video-record episodes of classroom interaction and elicit students' perceptions of the extent to which their teaching exemplified or negated the principles of procedure. Teachers were asked to use this data as a basis for formulating and testing hypotheses about strategies which either negated or enabled the realization of the principles. Since the work in schools involved groups, teachers were encouraged to share and discuss each others' data, and thereby generate hypotheses collaboratively.

The initiative for hypothesis generation came, at least initially, from central team members, who assisted the teacher groups to collect observational data and elicit feedback from students. At a midpoint in the trials the central team identified a number of hypotheses which might be generalizable to a variety of contexts, and teachers were asked to test them in the second half of the trials. At the end, a number of teachers produced

detailed case studies of their work (Elliott and MacDonald 1975), and on the basis of these the author (a member of the Humanities Project from 1967–72) distilled a number of general hypotheses about the problems of implementing the project's logic of teaching in secondary schools. These not only referred to concrete teaching strategies, but also to factors in the institutional context which constrained and facilitated classroom implementation.

The Humanities Project has been emphasized in order to clarify certain features of the context in which the idea of teachers as researchers emerged.

First, it emerged as one solution to the problems of implementing curriculum innovations in classrooms. Secondly, it was linked with a process model of curriculum development, which posited curriculum and teacher development as one and the same enterprise. Within the terms of this model, teachers develop the curriculum and themselves through cycles of action research—of reflection upon action followed by action upon reflection. It is important to grasp the contrasting views of professional development implicit in the process and objectives models.

Aristotle long ago made a distinction in his "Ethics" (1955) between activities of doing and making. The latter involves the application of precise technical rules to the production of quantifiable results. Precise technical rules can be prescribed because the product can be clearly specified in advance. Therefore what constitutes competent performance can be discovered and prescribed independently of the performer, who can simply be trained to apply the rules correctly. Technical rules cannot be applied to activities of doing, Aristotle claimed, because ends here refer to abstract ethical ideals which constitute qualities to be realized in the activities themselves rather than quantities to be produced as a result of them. No perfect method of doing is possible. What constitutes the best method is always something of a shot in the dark, and therefore a subject for deliberative reflection and discussion by participants in the light of their particular circumstances. Although practical knowledge (wisdom) of what worked in the past is a resource for such deliberation it cannot determine its outcome. The context of practice is always changing and requires continuous innovation. Moreover, it is only through retrospective reflection about their strategic responses that participants develop their understanding of the ends-in-view. By identifying negative and positive instances of good practice, participants clarify the ideals which constitute it. Thus the improvement of practice proceeds interactively with a developing understanding of the ideals which guide it; means and ends are joint objects of reflection. Practical deliberation integrates empirical with theoretical/philosophical inquiry.

Aristotle's idea of practical deliberation has inspired a tradition of curriculum theorizing in the United States and the United Kingdom (Schwab 1971, Reid 1978) which has only recently begun to link with the literature stemming from the classroom action-research movement. But the link is obvious.

Aristotle's distinction illuminates understanding of the different implications of objectives and process models of curriculum for teacher education. On the former model, curriculum development is a technology requiring an hierarchical system of specialized roles. Educational theorists clarify objectives; empirical researchers discover rules (or correlations) through process–product studies; developers translate rules into methods; and teacher technicians implement them correctly. The model provides another group of specialists, staff developers, with standardized criteria for identifying and rectifying deficiencies in performance. Construed as technicians, teachers become objects to be developed by experts.

When curriculum development is viewed as a doing activity it constitutes a professional practice guided by an ethic or logic. Here teachers develop themselves as a professional group through collegial deliberation about their curricular practices. This process assumes an absence of hierarchical control through a system of specialized roles. From the standpoint of the teachers as researchers movement theorizing about, researching into, deciding upon, and implementing the curriculum are integral components of professional practice.

The teachers as researchers movement entails a radically different role for external change agents; one of facilitation rather than control. Curriculum theorizing and research by external agents is a legitimate part of facilitation, providing it focuses on teachers' conceptions of ends and means and helps them to clarify and extend their ideas through dialogue. Facilitation also involves helping teachers learn techniques for collecting, sharing, and analysing data about their practical problems.

The Ford Teaching Project (Elliott 1976) provided ample illustrations of the facilitating role. Groups of teachers in the United Kingdom investigated the implementation of inquiry/discovery-based curricula. Working from tape-recorded discussions of classroom situations Adelman and Elliott identified a number of key concepts teachers employed. They then analysed the logical relationships between the teachers' concepts and the aim of inquiry/discovery teaching, which teachers defined as "enabling independent reasoning". This logic was specified as a set of pedagogic principles, and after discussion with teachers, used as a common framework for the study of classrooms.

Teachers were helped to use a triangulation procedure (Adelman 1980) for generating a database consisting of teachers', students', and observers' perceptions. The database was then subjected to collaborative analysis by all three parties, in dialogue—a process often extended to involve other project teachers and schools. This collaborative reflection led to further refinements of the initial logic and the generation of a commonly agreed set of hypotheses concerning implementation problems and strategies.

In generating a logic of teaching in dialogue with teachers, rather than specifying it in advance, the Ford Project anticipated the mid-1970s trend in the United

Kingdom towards school-based curriculum development. This tendency to give teachers greater responsibility for theory generation was pushed even further in Elliott's work with Ebbutt on the Schools Council's TIQL Project (Elliott 1985).

During the latter half of the 1970s the teachers as researchers movement mushroomed with the growth of school-based curriculum development in the United Kingdom and Australia. As a result an international classroom action research network (CARN) was established to promote exchanges of ideas between teacher researchers and facilitators. It holds an annual conference and produces regular bulletins (Elliott and Whitehead 1980, 1982).

There exists an increasing amount of second-order action research into the problems of facilitating teachers' research (Brown et al. in Elliott and Whitehead 1982). Some of the major facilitation problems being addressed are:

(a) *Data analysis.* Winter (1982) claimed that although much has been written on data collection methods in action research, little has emerged on data analysis. His "dilemma analysis" focuses on the practitioner's experiences of conflicting action requirements in the classroom.

(b) *Producing written accounts.* Increasingly teachers' accounts of their research are being published (Nixon 1981). Many reflective teachers however, are reluctant to make their deliberations public, claiming that private reflection is sufficient as a basis for improvement. However, in as much as action research involves discussion with professional peers, it must be accountable to some degree, and should be differentiated from purely private self-evaluation activities.

(c) *Institutionalizing and utilizing teachers' research.* In order to reduce the dependence of teacher groups on external facilitators, attention is now being given to the institutionalization and utilization of action research in schools. Increasingly attempts are being made to give major facilitation responsibilities to school staff. The Schools Council TIQL Project was structured around school based coordinators who are both senior teachers and trained action researchers (Ebbutt 1982). Some have already begun to make major contributions to second-order educational action research (Holly and Wakeman in Elliott and Whitehead 1982).

As facilitators reflect upon their practices they are also beginning to refine the theory of educational action research. In Australia, Grundy and Kemmis (1981) have argued that action research must focus on the structural determinants of practice as well as on those elements which teachers can change. By entertaining critical theorems about "structures of domination" teachers can begin to collaboratively devise strategies for emancipating themselves from them. Educational action research is not only practical but emancipatory. As the educational context of the teachers as researchers movement becomes more bureaucratized and hierarchized, so action-research theory develops a political dimension.

See also: Action Research; Ethical Considerations in Research

Bibliography

Adelman C 1980 On first hearing In: Adelman C (ed.) 1980 *Uttering, Muttering.* Grant McIntyre, London
Aristotle 1955 *The Ethics of Aristotle,* Book 6. Penguin, Harmondsworth
Ebbutt D 1982 *Teachers as Researchers: How Four Teachers Co-ordinate the Process of Research in Their Respective Schools.* Cambridge Institute of Education, Cambridge
Elliott J 1976 *Developing Hypotheses about Classrooms from Teachers' Practical Constructs.* North Dakota Group on Evaluation, University of North Dakota, North Dakota
Elliott J 1985 Facilitating action-research in schools: Some dilemmas. In: Burgess R E (ed.) 1985 *Field Methods in the Study of Education.* Falmer, London
Elliott J, MacDonald B (eds.) 1975 *People in Classrooms: Teacher Evaluations of the Humanities Curriculum Project.*
Occasional Publications, No. 2. Centre for Applied Research in Education, University of East Anglia, Norwich
Elliott J, Whitehead D 1980 CARN Bulletin No. 4. Cambridge Institute of Education, Cambridge
Elliott J, Whitehead D 1982 CARN Bulletin No. 5. Cambridge Institute of Education, Cambridge
Grundy S, Kemmis S 1981 *Educational Action-research in Australia: The State of the Art.* Deakin University, Victoria
Nixon J (ed.) 1981 *A Teachers' Guide to Action Research.* Grant McIntyre, London
Reid W H 1978 *Thinking About the Curriculum: The Nature and Treatment of Curriculum Problems.* Routledge and Kegan Paul, London
Schwab J J 1971 The practical: A language for curriculum. In: Schwab J J 1971 *Science, Curriculum, and Liberal Education.* University of Chicago Press, Chicago, Illinois
Stenhouse L 1975 *An Introduction to Curriculum Research and Development.* Heinemann, London
Stenhouse L et al. 1970 *The Humanities Project: An Introduction.* Heinemann, London
Tyler R W 1949 *Basic Principles of Curriculum and Instruction.* University of Chicago Press, Chicago, Illinois
Winter D 1982 Dilemma analysis: A contribution to methodology for action research. *Camb. J. Educ.* 12(3): 161–74

Naturalistic and Rationalistic Enquiry

E. G. Guba and Y. S. Lincoln

Persons concerned with disciplined enquiry have tended to use what is commonly called the scientific paradigm—that is, model or pattern—of enquiry. A second paradigm, also aimed at disciplined enquiry, is currently emerging; this paradigm is commonly known as the naturalistic paradigm, although it is often referred to (mistakenly) as the case study or qualitative paradigm. Its distinguishing features are not, however, its format or methods, or even, as its title might suggest, the fact that it is usually carried out in natural settings. What differentiates the naturalistic from the scientific (or, as it is sometimes referred to, the rationalistic paradigm) approach is, at bottom, the different interpretations placed on certain basic axioms or assumptions. In addition, the two approaches characteristically take different postures on certain issues which, while not as basic as axiomatic propositions, are nevertheless fundamental to an understanding of how the naturalistic enquirer operates.

1. Axiomatic Differences Between the Naturalistic and Rationalistic Paradigms

Axioms may be defined as the set of undemonstrated (and undemonstrable) propositions accepted by convention or established by practice as the basic building blocks of some conceptual or theoretical structure or system. As such they are arbitrary and certainly not "self-evidently true." Different axiom systems have different utilities depending on the phenomenon to which they are applied; so, for example, Euclidean geometry as an axiomatic system has good fit to terrestial phenomena but Lobachevskian geometry (a non-Euclidean

form) has better fit to interstellar phenomena. A decision about which of several axiom systems to employ for a given purpose is a matter of the relative "fit" between the axiom sets and the characteristics of the application area. It is the general contention of naturalists that the axioms of naturalistic enquiry provide a better fit to most social/behavioral phenomena than do the rationalistic axioms.

1.1 Axiom 1: The Nature of Reality

Rationalists assume that there exists a single, tangible reality fragmentable into independent variables and processes, any of which can be studied independently of the others; enquiry can be caused to converge onto this single reality until, finally, it is explained. Naturalists assume that there exist multiple realities which are, in the main, constructions existing in the minds of people; they are therefore intangible and can be studied only in wholistic, and idiosyncratic, fashion. Enquiry into these multiple realities will inevitably diverge (the scope of the enquiry will enlarge) as more and more realities must be considered. Naturalists argue that while the rationalist assumptions undoubtedly have validity in the hard and life sciences, naturalist assumptions are more meaningful in studying human behavior. Naturalists do not deny the reality of the objects, events, or processes with which people interact, but suggest that it is the meanings given to or interpretations made of these objects, events, or processes that constitute the arena of interest to investigators of social/behavioral phenomena. Note that these constructions are not perceptions of the objects, events, or processes but of meaning and interpretation. The situation is very much approximated, the naturalist would say, by the ancient tale of the blind men and the elephant—provided it is conceded that there is no elephant.

1.2 Axiom 2: The Enquirer–Respondent Relationship

The rationalist assumes that the enquirer is able to maintain a discrete and inviolable distance from the "object" of enquiry; but concedes that when the object is a human being, special methodological safeguards, must be taken to prevent reactivity, that is, a reaction of the object to the conditions of the enquiry that will influence the outcome in undesirable ways. The naturalist assumes that the enquirer and the respondent in any human enquiry inevitably interact to influence one another. While safeguards need to be mounted in both directions, the interaction need not be eliminated (it is impossible to do that anyway) but should be exploited for the sake of the inquiry.

Naturalists point out that the proposition of subject–object independence is dubious even to areas like particle physics, as exemplified in the Heisenberg Uncertainty Principle. The effect is certainly more noticeable in dealing with people, they assert. Nor should it be supposed that the interpolation of a layer of apparently objective instrumentation (paper and pencil or brass) solves the problem. Enquirers react to the mental images they have of respondents in developing the instrumentation; respondents answer or act in terms of what they perceive to be expectations held for their behavior as they interpret the meaning of the items or tasks put before them; enquirers deal with responses in terms of their interpretation of response meaning and intent, and so on. Nor, say the naturalists, is interactivity a generally undesirable characteristic; indeed, if interactivity could be eliminated by some methodological tour de force, the trade off would not be worthwhile, because it is precisely the interactivity that makes it possible for the human instrument to achieve maximum responsiveness, adaptability, and insight.

1.3 Axiom 3: The Nature of Truth Statements

Rationalists assert that the aim of inquiry is to develop a nomothetic body of knowledge; this knowledge is best encapsulated in generalizations which are truth statements of enduring value that are context free. The stuff of which generalizations are made is the similarity among units; differences are set aside as intrinsically uninteresting. Naturalists assert that the aim of inquiry is to develop an idiographic body of knowledge; this knowledge is best encapsulated in a series of "working hypotheses" that describe the individual case. Generalizations are not possible since human behavior is never time or context free. Nevertheless, some transferability of working hypotheses from context to context may be possible depending on the similarity of the contexts (an empirical matter). Differences are as inherently impor-

tant as (and at times more important than) the similarities. Naturalists well-understand the utility of generalizations such as $f = ma$ or $e = mc^2$ in physics, although even in the hard or life sciences, as Cronbach (1975) has pointed out, generalizations are much like radioactive materials, in that they decay and have a halflife. Surely it is unreasonable to suppose that analogous tendencies do not exist in the social and behavioral sciences?

1.4 Axiom 4: Causality

For the rationalist, the determination of cause–effect relationships is of prime importance; for each effect, it is assumed, there is a cause which can, given sufficiently sophisticated enquiry, be detected. The ultimate form for demonstrating cause–effect relationships is the experiment. The naturalist asserts that the determination of cause–effect is often a search for the Holy Grail. Human relationships are caught up in such an interacting web of factors, events, and processes that the hope that "the" cause–effect chain can be sorted out is vain; the best the enquirer can hope to establish are plausible patterns of influence. Naturalists point out that there have been a variety of cause–effect theories proposed since the simplistic "if–then" formulation was critiqued by Hume in the early eighteenth century, including Hume's own constant conjunction or regularity theory, "law" theories, formulations about "necessary and sufficient" conditions, and more recently, various attributional and semantic theories of causation. All have flaws in the opinion of epistemologists; however, the attributional and semantic formulations provide some insight into the possibility that if the realities with which humans deal are constructed, so, most likely, are their ideas of causation. If causality demonstrations are intended by rationalists to be compelling, naturalists feel the best they can do is to be persuasive. Causality can never be demonstrated in the "hard" sense; only patterns of plausible influence can be inferred.

1.5 Axiom 5: Relation to Values

Rationalists assume that enquiry is value free and can be guaranteed to be so by virtue of the "objective" methodology which the rationalist employs. The naturalist asserts that values impinge upon an enquiry in at least five ways, in terms of: the selection made by the investigator from among possible problems, theories, instruments, and data analysis modes; the assumptions underlying the substantive theory that guides the enquiry (for example, a theory of reading or an organizational theory); the assumptions underlying the methodological paradigm (as outlined in the preceding section on axioms); the values that characterize the respondents, the community, and the culture in which the enquiry is carried out (contextual values); and, finally, the possible interactions among any two or more of the preceding, which may be value consonant or value dissonant. Of particular interest is the possibility of resonance or dissonance between the substantive and methodological assumptions which can produce quite misleading results. Naturalists in particular take the position that many of the ambiguities and other irresolutions that tend to characterize social and behavioral research can be traced to such dissonances. So long as methodologies are assumed to be value free, naturalists assert, the problem of dissonance will not be recognized, since by definition it cannot exist. But once the role that values play in shaping enquiry is recognized, the problem becomes very real.

2. Postural Differences Between the Naturalistic and Rationalistic Paradigms

Postures differ from axioms in that they are not logically necessary to the integrity of the paradigm nor are they important to assess in determining fit between a paradigm and the area proposed to be studied. Nevertheless they characterize the "style" of the two positions and are, for a variety of reasons, "congenial" or reinforcing to the practice of each. Some writers who have been anxious to compromise the two paradigms—what might be called an attempt at conceptual ecumenicism—have pointed out that these postures may be seen as complementary, and have urged that both rationalists and naturalists attempt a middle course. But despite good intentions, neither group seems to have been able to respond to this advice, which gives rise to the possibility that, unless one wishes to write off enquirers of both camps as obstinate or intransigent, there must be some more fundamental reason for the failure. That reason is simply that there exists a synergism among the postures as practiced by either camp that virtually precludes compromise. In fact, the arguments that might be made by naturalists, say, in defense of their choices depend in the case of every posture on the choices made among the other postures. And so with rationalists.

Consider first the postures themselves; six are of special importance:

2.1 Preferred Methods

Rationalists tend to prefer quantitative methods probably because of their apparently greater precision and objectivity and because of the enormous advantage of being mathematically manipulable. Naturalists prefer qualitative methods, probably because they appear to promise the most wholistic products and they seem more appropriate to the use of a human as the prime data collection instrument. The distinction between quantitative and qualitative methods is often mistakenly taken to be the chief mark of distinction between the paradigms; in fact, the two dimensions are orthogonal. Either methodology is appropriate to either paradigm, even though in practice there is a high correlation between quantitative and rationalistic, on the one hand, and qualitative and naturalistic on the other.

2.2 Source of Theory

Rationalists insist on a priori formulations of theory; indeed, they are likely to assert that enquiry without a priori theory to guide it is mindless. The naturalist believes that it is not theory but the enquiry problem itself that guides and bounds the enquiry; that a priori theory constrains the enquiry to those elements recognized by the investigator as important, and may introduce biases (believing is seeing). In all events, theory is more powerful when it arises from the data rather than being imposed on them. The naturalist does not, of course, insist on grounding theory afresh in each and every enquiry; what the naturalist does insist on is that the theory to be used shall have been grounded at some time in experience.

2.3 Knowledge Types Used

Rationalists constrain the type of knowledge admissible in an enquiry to propositional knowledge; that is, knowledge that can be stated in language form. In view of their commitment to a priori theory and their interest in shaping enquiry preordinately about particular questions and hypotheses, this is not surprising. The naturalist, often intent on the use of the human-as-instrument, also admits tacit knowledge—insights, intuitions, apprehensions that cannot be stated in language form but which are nevertheless "known" to the enquirer. Of course naturalists seek to recast their tacit knowledge into propositional form as quickly as possible. It is equally clear that rationalists depend upon tacit knowledge at least as much as do their naturalist counterparts; however, the reconstructed logic of rationalism militates against exposing this dependency publicly.

2.4 Instruments

The rationalist prefers nonhuman devices for data collection purposes, perhaps because they appear to be more cost efficient, have a patina of objectivity, and can be systematically aggregated. The naturalist prefers humans as instruments, for reasons such as their greater insightfulness, flexibility, and responsiveness, the fact that they are able to take a wholistic view, are able to utilize their tacit knowledge, and are able simultaneously to acquire and process information. Obviously both sets of advantages are meaningful.

2.5 Design

The rationalist insists on a preordinate design; indeed, it is sometimes asserted that a "good" design makes it possible for the enquirer to specify in dummy form the very tables he or she will produce. The naturalist, entering the field without a priori theory, hypotheses, or questions (mostly), is unable to specify a design (except in the broadest process sense) in advance. Instead, he or she anticipates that the design will emerge (unfold, roll, cascade) as the enquiry proceeds, with each step heavily dependent on all preceding steps. Clearly, the naturalist is well-advised to specify as much in advance as possible, while the rationalist should seek to keep as many options open as possible.

2.6 Setting

The rationalist prefers to conduct studies under laboratory conditions, probably because the laboratory represents the epitome of control. The naturalist prefers natural settings (it is this propensity that has lent its name to the paradigm), arguing that only in nature can it be discovered what does happen rather than what can happen. Moreover, studies in nature can be transferred to other, similar contexts, whereas laboratory studies can be generalized only to other laboratories. Clearly both kinds of studies have utility—it may be just as important to know what can happen as what does happen.

While it might appear that compromise is indeed possible on these six postures, in fact the postures are bound together by a synergism such that each posture requires a counterpart position to be taken on all other postures. Consider rationalists, for example. Begin with a posture, say their preference for a priori theory. Rationalists do not exhibit this preference by accident, however. In part they prefer a priori theory because they deal in propositional language, and theory is the best means for formulating and clarifying their propositional statements. The hypotheses or questions are propositional deductions from theory. Because of the precision of these hypotheses or questions it is possible to imagine a design for testing them, and to devise appropriate instruments. Having such instruments makes it unnecessary to interpolate a "subjective" human between data and respondents. Moreover, these instruments can best be used in the highly controlled environment of the laboratory. And precise instruments yield data that can conveniently be expressed in quantitative form, a marked advantage since numbers can be easily manipulated statistically. Hence quantitative methods. And of course numbers can be aggregated and summarized, yielding apparent generalizations, expressions of causality, and so on. The sum exhibits a synergism such that each posture depends on every other one.

Similar observations can be made about the naturalists' preference. Naturalists are forced into a natural setting because they cannot tell, having no a priori theory or hypotheses, what is important to control, or even to study. They could not set up a contrived experiment because they do not know what to contrive. If theory is to emerge from the data, the data must first be gathered. Since the nature of those data is unknown, an adaptive instrument is needed to locate and make sense of them—the "smart" human. Humans find certain data collection means more congenial than others; hence they tend toward the use of qualitative methods such as observation, interview, reading documents, and the like, which come "naturally" to the human. These methods result in insights and information about the specific instance being studied but make it difficult to produce aggregations, generalizations, or cause–effect statements. Again, the naturalists' behavior demonstrates a kind of synergism among postures which is understandable and defensible only in terms of the totality of positions.

3. The Trustworthiness of Naturalistic Enquiries

Because of its unusual axioms and the apparent "softness" of its postures, naturalistic enquiry is often attacked as untrustworthy, in contrast to rationalistic enquiry which has well-developed standards of trustworthiness.

Recently, serious efforts have been undertaken to develop standards which are parallels of those commonly used by rationalists, that is, counterparts to standards of internal and external validity, reliability, and objectivity. Analogous terms have been proposed, viz., (respectively) credibility, transferability, dependability, and confirmability.

Credibility is seen as a check on the isomorphism between the enquirer's data and interpretations and the multiple realities in the minds of informants. Transferability is the equivalent of generalizability to the extent that there are similarities between sending and receiving contexts. Dependability includes the instability factors typically indicated by the term "unreliability" but makes allowances for emergent designs, developing theory, and the like that also induce changes but which cannot be taken as "error." Confirmability shifts the emphasis from the certifiability of the enquirer to the confirmability of the data.

It is premature to expect that adherents of the naturalistic paradigm would have evolved as sophisticated a methodology for dealing with trustworthiness questions as have the rationalists, who have had centuries of experience to shape their standards. However, some suggestions have emerged for handling trustworthiness questions.

With respect to credibility it is proposed that the following techniques may be profitably used: (a) prolonged engagement at a site to overcome a variety of possible biases and misperceptions and to provide time to identify salient characteristics; (b) persistent observation, to understand salient characteristics as well as to appreciate atypical but meaningful features; (c) peer debriefing, to test growing insights and receive counsel about the evolving design, discharge personal feelings and anxieties, and leave an audit trail (see below); (d) triangulation, whereby a variety of data sources, different investigators, different perspectives (theories), and different methods are pitted against one another; (e) referential adequacy materials, whereby various documents, films, videotapes, audio recordings, pictures, and other "raw" or "slice-of-life" materials are collected during the study and archived for later use, for example, in member or auditor checks (see below); and (f) members checks, whereby data and interpretations are continuously checked with members of the various groups from which data were solicited, including an overall check at the end of the study.

With respect to transferability, it is proposed to use theoretical or purposive sampling to maximize the range of information which is collected and to provide the most stringent conditions for theory grounding; and thick description, furnishing enough information about a context to provide a vicarious experience of it, and to facilitate judgments about the extent to which working hypotheses from that context might be transferable to a second, similar context.

With respect to dependability, it is proposed to use overlap methods, one kind of triangulation which undergirds claims of dependability to the extent that the methods produce complementary results; stepwise replication, a kind of "split-halves" approach in which enquirers and data sources are divided into halves to pursue the enquiry independently, provided, however, that there is sufficient communication between the two teams to allow for the articulated development of the emergent design, and the dependability audit, a process modelled on the fiscal audit. A fiscal auditor has two responsibilities: first, to ascertain that the accounts were kept in one of the several modes that constitute "good practice," and second, to ascertain that every entry can be supported with appropriate documentation and that the totals are properly determined. The dependability audit serves the first of these functions.

With respect to confirmability it is proposed to use triangulation (as above); to keep a reflexive journal that can be used to expose epistemological assumptions and to show why the study was defined and carried out in particular ways; and the confirmability audit, which carries out the second of the two auditor functions mentioned above.

It is generally understood that the use of even all of these techniques cannot guarantee the trustworthiness of a naturalistic study but can only contribute greatly to persuading a consumer of its meaningfulness.

4. Summary

Naturalistic enquiry is one of two paradigms currently being used by investigators within the framework of disciplined research. While this paradigm has distinguished antecedents in anthropology and ethnography, it is nevertheless relatively emergent and not as much is known about its properties as might be desired.

Naturalistic enquiry differs from rationalistic enquiry in terms of interpretations based on five basic axioms; reality, enquirer–object relationship, generalizability, causality, and value freedom. In addition, a number of salient postures also play important roles; methods, sources of theory, knowledge types used, instruments, design, and setting.

As a relatively new paradigm, naturalism suffers in not having yet devised as solid an approach to trustworthiness as has its rationalistic counterpart. Nevertheless important strides are being made. It seems likely that, given several decades in which to develop, the naturalistic paradigm will prove to be as useful as the rationalistic paradigm has been historically. The major decision to be made between the two paradigms revolve about the assessment of fit to the area under study, rather than to any intrinsic advantages or disadvantages of either.

See also: Ethnographic Research Methods; Classroom Observation Techniques; Participant Observation; Hermeneutics

Bibliography

Cook T D, Campbell D T 1979 *Quasi-experimentation: Design and Analysis Issues for Field Settings.* Rand McNally, Chicago, Illinois

Cook T D, Reichardt C S 1979 *Qualitative and Quantitative Methods in Evaluation Research.* Sage, Beverly Hills, California

Cronbach L J 1975 Beyond the two disciplines of scientific psychology. *Am. Psychol.* 30: 116–27

Cronbach L J, Suppes P (eds.) 1969 *Research for Tomorrow's Schools: Disciplined Inquiry for Education.* Macmillan, New York

Filstead W J (ed.) 1970 *Qualitative Methodology: Firsthand Involvement with the Social World.* Rand McNally, Chicago, Illinois

Glaser B G, Strauss A L 1967 *The Discovery of Grounded Theory: Strategies for Qualitative Research.* Aldine, Chicago, Illinois

Guba E G 1978 *Toward a Methodology of Naturalistic Inquiry in Educational Evaluation.* Center for the Study of Evaluation, University of California, Los Angeles, California

Guba E G 1981 Criteria for assessing the trustworthiness of naturalistic inquiries. *Educ. Comm. Tech. J.* 29(2): 75–92

Guba E G, Lincoln Y S 1982 *Effective Evaluation.* Jossey-Bass, San Francisco, California

Kaplan A 1964 *The Conduct of Inquiry: Methodology for Behavioral Science.* Chandler, San Francisco, California

Polani M 1966 *The Tacit Dimension.* Doubleday, Garden City, New York

Scriven M 1971 Objectivity and subjectivity in educational research In: Thomas L G (ed.) 1971 *Philosophical Redirection of Educational Research.* University of Chicago Press, Chicago, Illinois

Scientific Research Methods

Research Methodology: Scientific Methods

A. Kaplan

Methodology as a discipline lies between two poles. On the one hand is technics, the study of specific techniques of research—interpreting a Rorschach protocol, conducting a public opinion survey, or calculating a correlation coefficient. On the other hand is philosophy of science, the logical analysis of concepts presupposed in the scientific enterprise as a whole—evidence, objectivity, truth, or inductive inference. Technics has an immediate practical bearing, but only on the use of specific techniques. Philosophy of science, though quite general in application, has only remote and indirect practical bearings. Though philosophy is much exercised about the problem of induction, for instance, behavioral scientists would be quite content to arrive at conclusions acceptable with the same confidence as the proposition that the sun will rise tomorrow.

Methodology is a generalization of technics and a concretization of philosophy. It deals with the resources and limitations of general research methods—such as observation, experiment, measurement, and model building—with reference to concrete contexts of inquiry. No sharp lines divide methodology from technics or from philosophy; particular discussions are likely to involve elements of all three.

The behavioral sciences' concern with methodology has lessened: more and more the researchers do their work rather than working on how they should do it. There has been a corresponding lessening of belief in the myth of methodology, the notion that if only the student of human behavior could find "the right way" to go about research, the findings would be undeniably "scientific."

Anxious defensiveness heightened vulnerability to the pressure of scientific fashions. Scientism is an exaggerated regard for techniques which have succeeded elsewhere, in contrast to the scientific temper, which is open to whatever techniques hold promise for the particular inquiry at hand. Computers, mathematical models, and brass instruments are not limited to one subject matter or another; neither is their use necessary for scientific respectability.

Methodology does not dictate that the soft sciences be hardened or abandoned. Neither does methodology exclude human behavior from scientific treatment. The task is to do as well as is made possible by the nature of the problem and the given state of knowledge and technology.

Fashions in science are not intrinsically objectionable, any more than fashions in dress, nor are they intrinsically praiseworthy. What is fashionable is only one particular way of doing things; that it is in the mode neither guarantees nor precludes effectiveness. Cognitive style is a characteristic way of attaining knowledge; it varies with persons, periods, cultures, schools of thought, and entire disciplines. Many different styles are identifiable in the scientific enterprise; at different times and places some styles are more fashionable than others. Successful scientists include analysts and synthesizers; experimenters and theoreticians; model builders and data collectors; technicians and interpreters. Problems are often formulated to suit a style imposed either by fashion or by personal predilection, and are investigated in predetermined ways. Scientism in the behavioral sciences is marked by the drunkard's search—the drunkard hunts for the dropped house key, not at the door, but under the corner streetlamp, "because it's lighter there." Widespread throughout the sciences is the law of the instrument: give a small child a hammer and it turns out that everything the child sees needs pounding. It is not unreasonable to do what is possible with given instruments; what is unreasonable is to view them as infallible and all-powerful.

1. Scientific Terms

Closely associated with the myth of methodology is the semantic myth—that all would be well in the behavioral sciences if only their terms were defined with clarity and precision. The myth does not make clear precisely how this is to be done. Scientists agree that scientific terms must bear some relation to observations. There is no consensus on exactly what relation, nor even on whether a useful scientific purpose would be served by a general formulation of a criterion of cognitive meaning. In particular cases the issue is not whether a term has meaning but just what its meaning might be.

For some decades the behavioral sciences were dominated by operationism, which held that terms have meaning only if definite operations can be performed to decide whether the terms apply in any given case, and that the meaning of the terms is determined by these operations. "Intelligence" is what is measured by an intelligence test; "public opinion" is what is disclosed in a survey. Which details are essential to the operation called for and which are irrelevant presupposes some notion of what concept the operations are meant to delimit. The same presupposition underlies attempts to improve tests and measures. A more serious objection is that the validation of scientific findings relies heavily on the circumstances that widely different measuring operations yield substantially the same results. It is hard to avoid the conclusion that they are measuring the same magnitude. Most operations relate terms to observations only by way of other terms; once "symbolic operations" are countenanced, the semantic problems which operationism was meant to solve are reinstated.

Ambiguities abound in the behavioral sciences. The behavioral scientist is involved with the subject matter in distinctive ways, justifiably so. The involvement makes for widespread normative ambiguity, the same term being used both normatively and descriptively—"abnormal" behavior, for example, may be pathological or merely deviant. Also widespread is functional ambiguity, the same term having both a descriptive sense and an explanatory sense—the Freudian "unconscious" may be topographical or dynamic. Ambiguity is a species of openness of meaning, perhaps the most objectionable. Vagueness is another species. All terms are more or less vague, allowing for borderline cases to which it is uncertain whether the term applies—not because what is known about the case is insufficient, but because the meaning of the term is not sufficiently determinate. All terms have some degree of internal vagueness, uncertainties of application, not at the borderline but squarely within the designation; some instances are better specimens of what the term designates than others (closer to the "ideal type"), and how good a specimen is meant is not wholly determinate. Most terms have also a systemic vagueness: meanings come not singly but in more or less orderly battalions, and the term itself does not identify in what system of meanings (notably, a theory) it is to be interpreted. Significant terms are also likely to exhibit dynamic openness, changing their meanings as contexts of application multiply and knowledge grows.

As dangerous as openness is the premature closure of meanings. The progressive improvement of meanings—the semantic approximation—is interwoven with the growth of knowledge—the epistemic approximation. The advance of science does not consist only of arriving at more warranted judgments but also of arriving at more appropriate concepts. The interdependence of the two constitutes the paradox of conceptualization: formulating sound theories depends on having suitable concepts, but suitable concepts are not to be had without sound theoretical understanding. The circle is not vicious; it is broken by successive approximations, now semantic and now epistemic.

Meanings are made more determinate by a process of specification of meaning. This is sometimes loosely called "definition"; in a strict sense definition is only one way of specifying meanings—providing a combination of terms, whose meaning is presumed to be already known, which in that combination have a meaning equivalent to that of the given term. Definitions are useful for formal disciplines, like mathematics; for empirical disciplines, their usefulness varies inversely with the importance of the term.

In simple cases, meanings can be specified by ostension: making what is meant available to direct experience. Empiricism regards ostensions as the fundamental anchorage for theoretical abstractions. Meanings in the behavioral sciences are often specified by description of the thing meant, especially when this is included in or is close to everyday experience. Most scientific terms have a meaning specified by indication: a set of indices, concrete or abstract, often the outcomes of specified tests and measures, which constitute, not *the* meaning of the term, but some of the conditions which provide ground for applying the term. Each index carries its own weight; each case exhibits a profile, whose weight is not necessarily the sum of the weights of the constituent indices. As contexts of application change as well as what knowledge is available, so do the indications and their weight, and thereby also the meaning specified. Premature closure of meaning by definition is likely to provide false precision, groundless or unusable.

Which type of specification is appropriate depends on the scientific purposes the term is meant to serve. Observables, terms denoting what can be experienced more or less directly, invite ostension. Indirect observables lend themselves to description of what would be observed if our senses or other circumstances were different from what they are: in the behavioral sciences such terms are sometimes known as "intervening variables." Constructs have meanings built up from structures of other terms, and so are subject to definition. Theoretical terms have a core of systemic meaning which can be specified only by an open and ever-changing set of indications. Many terms have sufficient functional ambiguity to exhibit characteristics of several or all of these types of terms; they call for various types of specification of meaning.

2. Classes

Empirical terms determine classes; because of openness of meaning these classes are only approximations to well-defined sets in the sense of mathematical logic, where everything in the universe of discourse definitely belongs to or is excluded from the class. The approximation to a set can be made closer (the term made more precise) by restricting its meaning to what is specifiable by easily observable and measurable indices. The danger is that such classes are only artificial, delimiting a domain which contributes to science little more than knowledge of the characteristics by which it is delimited. Natural classes correspond to an articulation of the subject matter which figures in theories, laws, or at least in empirical generalizations inviting and guiding further research. Artificial and natural classes lie at two poles of a continuum. A classification closer to being artificial is a descriptive taxonomy; one closer to being natural is an explanatory typology. Growth of concepts as science progresses is a movement from taxonomies to typologies—Linnaeus to Darwin, Mendeleef to the modern periodic table, humors to Freudian characterology.

3. Propositions

Knowledge of a subject matter is implicit in how it is conceptualized; knowledge is explicit in propositions. Propositions perform a number of different functions in science.

First are identifications, specifying the field with which a given discipline deals, and identifying the unit elements of the field. In the behavioral sciences "idiographic" disciplines have been distinguished from "nomothetic," the former dealing with individuals, the latter with general relationships among individuals (history and sociology, for instance, or clinical and dynamic psychology). Both equally involve generalizations, because both demand identifications—the same "state" with a new government, or different personalities of the same "person": sameness and difference can be specified only by way of generalizations. Which units are to be selected is the locus problem; political science, for instance, can be pursued as the study of governments, of power, or of political behavior. What is to be the starting point of any given inquiry cannot be prejudged by other disciplines, certainly not by methodology. It is determinable only in the course of the inquiry itself—the principle of the autonomy of the conceptual base.

Other propositions serve as presuppositions of a given inquiry—what is taken for granted about the conceptual and empirical framework of the inquiry. Nothing is intrinsically indubitable but in each context there is always something undoubted. Assumptions are not taken for granted but are taken as starting points of the inquiry or as special conditions in the problem being dealt with. Assumptions are often known to be false, but are made nevertheless because of their heuristic usefulness. Hypotheses are the propositions being investigated.

4. Generalizations

Conclusions of an inquiry, if they are to be applicable to more than the particular context of the inquiry, are stated as generalizations. According to the logical reconstruction prevailing in philosophy of science for some decades (but recently coming under increasing criticism), generalizations have the form: "For all x, if x has the property f, then it has the property g." The content of the generalization can be specified only in terms of its place in a more comprehensive system of propositions.

A simple generalization moves from a set of propositions about a number of individual cases to all cases of that class. An extensional generalization moves from a narrower class to a broader one. Both these types are likely to be only descriptive. An intermediate generalization moves from propositions affirming relations of either of the preceding types to one affirming a relation of both relata to some intermediate term. It begins to be explanatory, invoking the intermediate term to account for the linkage recorded in its premises. A theoretical generalization is fully explanatory, putting the original relata and their intermediates into a meaningful structure. The conclusion of a successful inquiry may produce any of these types of generalization, not only the last.

All empirical findings, whether appearing as premises or as conclusions, are provisional, subject to rejection in the light of later findings. Philosophy of science divides propositions into a priori and a posteriori; for methodology it is more useful to replace the dichotomy by degrees of priority, the weight of evidence required before a finding is likely to be rejected. In increasing order of priority are conjectures, hypotheses, and scientific laws. A law strongly supported by theory as well as by the empirical evidence may have a very high degree of priority, often marked by calling the law a principle. In a logical reconstruction of the discipline in which it appears it may be incorporated in definitions, and so become a priori in the strict sense.

5. Observations and Data

Unless a proposition is a definition or a logical consequence of definition, it must be validated by reference, sooner or later, to observations. Reports of observation—data—must themselves be validated; what was reported might not in fact have been observed. A magician's performance can never be explained from a description of the effect, for the effect is an illusion; a correct description would not call for an explanation.

Errors of observation are virtually inevitable, especially in observations of human behavior; in the fashionable idiom, there is noise in every channel through which nature tells us something. In some contexts, observation can be insulated, to a degree, from error—it might be made, for instance, through a one-way mirror, so that data would not be contaminated by the intrusiveness of the observer. Error can sometimes be cancelled—reports from a large number of observers are likely to cancel out personal bias or idiosyncrasy. In special cases error can be discounted: its magnitude, or at least its direction, can be taken into account in drawing conclusions from the data—memories are likely to be distorted in predictable ways.

There is a mistaken notion that the validity of data would be guaranteed if interpretations were scrupulously excluded from reports of what is actually seen. This mistake has been called "the dogma of immaculate perception." Observation is inseparable from a grasp of meanings; interpretation is intrinsic to perception, not an afterthought. It has been well said that there is more to observation than meets the eye.

Two levels of interpretation can be discriminated (in the abstract) in behavioral science. First is the interpretation of bodily movements as the performance of certain acts—the grasp of an act meaning. Raised hands may be interpreted as voting behavior rather than as involuntary muscular contractions (such contractions may be act meanings for a physiologist). A second level of interpretation sees observed acts in the light of some theory of their causes or functions—the grasp of an action meaning. Dress and hairstyle may be seen as adolescent rebelliousness.

Both levels of interpretation are hypothetical in the literal sense—they rest on hypotheses as to what is going on. Such hypotheses in turn rest on previous observations. This is the paradox of data: hypotheses are necessary to arrive at meaningful data, but valid hypotheses can be arrived at only on the basis of the data. As with the paradox of conceptualization, the circle is broken by successive approximation.

Because observation is interwoven with interpretation, what is observed depends on the concepts and theories through which the world is being seen. Whatever does not fit into the interpretive frame remains unseen—invisible data, like pre-Freudian male hysteria and infantile sexuality. The data may be noted but be dismissed as meaningless—cryptic data, like dreams and slips of the tongue. Observation also depends on what instruments of observation are available. Techniques like mazes, projective tests, and opinion surveys have had enormous impact on behavioral science research.

6. Experiments

Creating circumstances especially conducive to observation is an experiment. Not all experiments are probative, meant to establish a given hypothesis or to select between alternative hypotheses (crucial experiment). Some may be methodological, like pilot studies or the secondary experiments performed to determine factors restricting the interpretation of the primary experiment. Heuristic experiments may be fact finding or exploratory. Other experiments are illustrative, used for pedagogy or to generate ideas, a common function of simulations.

The significance of experiments sometimes appears only long after they were performed. Experiments have meaning only in a conceptual frame. Scientific advance may provide a new frame in which the old experiment has a new and more important meaning. The secondary analysis of an experiment already performed may be more valuable than a new experiment.

Experiments in the behavioral sciences have often been criticized on the basis of an unfounded distinction between the laboratory and "life." There are important differences between the laboratory and other life situations—for instance, significant differences in scale. Only moderate stresses are produced—subjects may be given, say, only a small amount of money with which to play an experimental game, whose outcome may therefore have only questionable bearings on decisions about marriage, surgery, or war. Secondary experiments may be useful to assess the effect of the differences in scale. All observations, whether in the laboratory or not, are of particular circumstances; applying the findings to other circumstances always needs validation.

Not all experiments are manipulative; in some, the manipulation is only of verbal stimuli—administering a questionnaire can be regarded as an experiment. Events especially conducive to observation even though they were not brought about for that purpose are sometimes called nature's experiments—disaster situations or identical twins separated at birth. The relocation of workers or refugees, school bussing, and changes in the penal code are instances of social experiments. Experimentation and field work shade off into one another.

7. Measurement

The more exact the observations, the greater their possible usefulness (possible, but not necessary). Widespread is a mystique of quality—the notion that quantitative description is inappropriate to the study of human behavior. True, quantitative description "leaves something out"—precision demands a sharp focus. But what *is* being described is more fully described by a quantitative description. Income leaves out of account many important components of a standard of living, but a quantitative description says more about income than "high" or "low."

There is a complementary mystique of quantity—the notion that nothing is known till it has been weighed and measured. Precision may be greater than is usable in the context or even be altogether irrelevant. Because quantitative data are more easily processed, they may be taken more seriously than the actually more important imponderables. The precision may be spurious, accurate in itself but combined with impressionistic data. Fashion in the behavioral sciences may invite the use of quantitative idioms even if no measurements are available to determine the implied quantities.

Measurement is the mapping of numbers to a set of elements in such a way that certain operations on the numbers yield results which consistently correspond to certain relations among the elements. The conditions specifying the mapping define a scale; applications of the scale produce measures which correspond to magnitudes. Just what logical operations on the numbers can be performed to yield empirical correspondence depends on the scale.

Numbers may be used only as names—a nominal scale—in which case nothing can be inferred about the elements save that they are the same or different if their names are such. The numbers may be used so as to take into account relations of greater and less—an ordinal scale—allowing the corresponding elements to be put into a definite order. An interval scale defines a relation of greater and less among differences in the order. Operations may be defined allowing measures to be combined arithmetically, by which magnitudes can be compared quantitatively—a ratio or additive scale.

Scales can be freely constructed, but there is no freedom to choose what they logically entail. Equally restrictive are the empirical constraints imposed by the operations coordinating measures and magnitudes.

One measuring operation or instrument is more sensitive than another if it can deal with smaller differences in the magnitudes. One is more reliable than another if repetitions of the measures it yields are closer to one another. Accuracy combines both sensitivity and reliability. An accurate measure is without significance if it does not allow for any inferences about the magnitudes save that they result from just such and such operations. The usefulness of the measure for other inferences, especially those presupposed or hypothesized in the given inquiry, is its validity.

8. Statistics and Probability

No measures are wholly accurate. Observations are multiple, both because data are manifold and because findings, to be scientific, must be capable of replication by other observers. Inevitably, not all the findings are exactly alike. Inferences drawn from any measure are correspondingly inconclusive. Statistics are the set of mathematical techniques developed to cope with these difficulties.

A problematic situation is one inviting inquiry. The situation itself does not predetermine how the problem is to be formulated; the investigator must formulate it. A problem well-formulated is half solved; badly formulated, it may be quite insoluble. The indeterminacy of a situation, from the point of view of statistics, is its uncertainty. When a specific problem has been formulated, the situation is transformed to one of risk. A card game involves risk; playing with strangers, uncertainty. Moving from uncertainty to risk is the structuring problem; it may be more important than computing and coping with risk once that has been defined. How to compute risk is the subject matter of the theory of probability; how to cope with it, the theory of games, and more generally, decision theory.

The calculation of probabilities rests on three different foundations; alternatively, three different conceptions or probability may be invoked. Mathematical probability is expressed as the ratio of "favorable" cases (those being calculated) to the total number of (equally likely) cases. Statistical probability is the (long-run) frequency of favorable cases in the sequence of observations. Personal probability is an expression of judgments of likelihood (or degree of confidence) made in accord with certain rules to guarantee consistency. For different problems different approaches are appropriate. Mendelian genetics or the study of kinship systems makes use of mathematical probability. Studies of traffic accidents or suicides call for statistical probabilities. Prediction of the outcome of a particular war or labor dispute is a matter of personal probability.

Statistics begin where assignment of probabilities leaves off. A multiplicity of data are given. The first task is that of statistical description: how to reduce the multiplicity to a managable unity with minimal distortion. This is usually done by giving some measure of the central tendency of the data, and specifying in one way or another the dispersion of the data around that central measure (like the mean and the standard deviation). Inferences drawn from the data are statable as statistical hypotheses, whose weight is estimated from the relation between the data and the population about which inferences are being made (sampling theory). Depending on the nature of the sample and of its dispersion, statistical tests assign a measure of the likelihood of the hypothesis in question. Explanatory statistics address themselves to the use of statistical descriptions and hypotheses in formulating explanations (for instance, by way of correlations).

9. Theories and Models

Once a problematic situation has been structured and the data measured and counted, a set of hypotheses may be formulated as possible solutions to the problem. Generalized, the hypotheses are said to constitute a theory. Alternatively, it is possible to begin with a set of hypotheses formulated in the abstract, then interpret them as applying to one or another problematic situation. Such a set is called a model.

Often the result of structuring the problematic situation is called a model. Structure is the essential feature of a model. In an interpretation of the model, a correspondence is specified between the elements of the model and those of some situation, and between certain relations holding within each set of elements, so that when two elements of the model are in a certain relation the corresponding elements stand in the corresponding relation, and vice versa. A set of elements related in certain ways is a system; a structure is what is shared by corresponding systems (or it may be identified with the set of all possible systems corresponding to a given one and thus to each other).

A model can be a physical system (like an airplane model in a wind tunnel), in which case it is an analog. An analog computer is a device which allows such systems to be easily constructed—systems consisting, for instance, of electrical networks with certain voltages, resistances, and current flow. Operations on the analog which preserve its structure show what would happen in any other system having the same structure. If the model is a system of symbols it may be called a map. Behavioral science models are maps of human systems.

When the correspondences are only suggested rather than being explicitly defined, the symbolic system is an extended metaphor; intermediate between a metaphor and a model is an analogy, in which correspondences are explicit but inexact. All three have roles in the actual conduct of inquiry; the view that only models have a place in science makes both terms honorific.

In another honorific usage "model" is a synonym for "theory" or even "hypothesis." The term is useful only when the symbolic system it refers to is significant as a structure—a system which allows for exact deductions and explicit correspondences. The value of a model lies in part in its abstractness, so that it can be given many interpretations, which thereby reveal unexpected similarities. The value lies also in the deductive fertility of the model, so that unexpected consequences can be predicted and then tested by observation and experiment. Here digital computers have already shown themselves to be important, and promise to become invaluable.

Two dangers in the use of models are to be noted. One is map reading, attaching significance to features of the model which do not belong to its structure but only to the particular symbolization of the structure (countries are not colored like their maps; psychoanalytic models do not describe hydrodynamic processes of a psychic fluid: "psychic energy" is not equal to mc^2).

The other danger is, not that something is read into the map which does not belong to the structure, but that something is omitted from the map which does. This error is called oversimplification. All models simplify, or they would not have the abstractness which makes them models. The model is oversimplified when it is not known by how much nor even in what direction to correct the outcomes of the model so that they apply to the situation modelled. In an economic model, ignoring differences in the worth of money to the rich and to the poor is likely to be an oversimplification; ignoring what exactly the money is spent on may not be.

Theories need not be models; they may present a significant content even though lacking an exactly specified structure—as was done by the theory of evolution, the germ theory of disease, and the psychoanalytic theory of the neuroses. A theory is a concatenation of hypotheses so bound up with one another that the proof or disproof of any of them affects that of all the others. The terms in which the hypotheses are couched are likely to have systemic meaning, specifiable only by reference to the entire theory. Knowledge may grow by extension—applying a theory to wider domains. It may also grow by intension—deepening the theory, specifying more exactly details previously only sketched in or even glossed over.

Theory is not usefully counterposed to practice; if it is sound, a theory is of practice, though the theoretical problems may be so simplified that the theory provides only an approximate solution to the problems of practice, and then only under certain conditions. A theory, it has been said, is a policy, not a creed. It does not purport to provide a picture of the world but only a map. It guides decisions on how best to deal with the world, including decisions on how to continue fruitful inquiry. It raises as many questions as it answers; the answers themselves are proposed directives for action rather than assertions for belief.

10. Explanation, Interpretation, and Validation

Validation of a theory is a matter, first, of coherence with knowledge already established. A new theory may raise difficulties of its own, but it must at least do justice to the facts the older theory accounted for. Validation means, second, a certain correspondence with the world as revealed in the continually growing body of data—it must successfully map its domain. Validation, finally, lies in the continued usefulness of the theory in practice, especially in the conduct of further inquiry.

A valid theory provides an explanation of the data, not merely a shorthand description of them. The latter, even if comprehensive, is only an empirical generalization; a theory gives grounds for expecting the generalization to be indefinitely extendable to data of the same kind. A dynamic tendency is quite different from a statistical trend. The theory may allow the prediction of data not yet observed, though it may be valid without successful prediction if this is precluded by the intervention of factors outside the theory, or by cumulation of the inexactness to be found in all theories when applied to empirical findings. Conversely, an empirical generalization may suggest successful predictions even though it is unable to say why the predictions should succeed.

Deductive explanation deduces predictions from the premises postulated by the theory (together with the initial conditions of the particular situation). This type of explanation is characteristic of models. Pattern explanation makes the data intelligible by fitting them into a meaningful whole (predictions might then be made of what would fit the gaps). This is characteristic of disciplines concerned with action meanings.

Behavioral interpretation is grasping such meanings, as distinguished from model interpretation, which is setting up correspondences that give content to an abstract structure. In behavioral interpretation actions are understood as purposive, goal directed. Goals need not be conscious, deliberate, intentional—in short, motivational; they may be purely functional, as are the telic mechanisms of cybernetic systems. Interpretation in the behavioral sciences often suffers from mistaking functions for motives, then introducing abstract agents to have the putative motives—neuroses are said to defend themselves, ruling classes to perpetuate a social order, economies to seek to expand.

All explanations, at best, leave something to be desired. They are partial, dealing with only a limited class of situations. They are conditional, depending on special circumstances in those situations. They are approximate—no explanation is wholly precise. They are indeterminate, having only a statistical validity—there are always apparent exceptions. They are inconclusive, never validated beyond any possibility of replacement or correction. They are intermediate, pointing always to something which needs to be explained in turn. They are limited, serving in each instance only some of the purposes for which explanations might be sought—a psychologist's explanation of a death (as, say, a suicide) is very different from a pathologist's explanation (as, say, a poisoning). Both explanations may be equally valid. All this openness of theory corresponds in the epistemic approximation to the openness of meaning in the semantic approximation.

11. Values and Bias

Inquiry itself is purposive behavior and so is subject to behavioral interpretation. The interpretation consists in part in specifying the values implicated in specific processes of conceptualization, observation, measurement, and theory construction. That values play a part in these processes does not in itself make the outcomes of these processes pejoratively subjective, nor otherwise invalidate them. A value which interferes with inquiry is a bias. Not all values are biases; on the contrary, inquiry is impossible without values.

A distinction between facts and values remains; the distinction is functional and contextual, not intrinsic to any given content. Descriptions may be used normatively. They are also shaped by norms which guide not only what is worth describing but also what form the description should take—for instance, the degree of precision which is worthwhile, the size of sample which is worth taking, the confidence level to be demanded, and the like. Values play a part not only in choosing problems but also in choosing patterns of inquiry into them. The behavioral sciences have rightly become concerned with the ethics of the profession, as bearing, for instance, on experimentation with human beings.

A myth of neutralism supposes that scientific status requires rigorous exclusion of values from the scientific enterprise. Even if this exclusion were desirable (a value!), it is impossible. The exclusion of bias, on the other hand, *is* an operative ideal. Bias is only hidden by the pretense of neutrality; it is effectively minimized only by making values explicit and subjecting them in turn to careful inquiry.

The danger that values become biases is especially great when values enter into the assessment of the results of inquiry as distinct from what is being inquired into and how. A truth may be unpleasant, even downright objectionable, yet remain true for all that. Science must be granted autonomy from the dictates of political, religious, and other extrascientific institutions. The content of the pursuit of truth is accountable to nothing and no-one not a part of that pursuit.

All inquiries are carried out in specific contexts. Validation of the results of any particular inquiry by reference to the outcomes of other inquiries is important. How important varies with the distance between their respective subject matters, concepts, data, and other components of the process of inquiry. The behavioral sciences have become increasingly willing to affirm their autonomy with respect to the physical and biological sciences. Science suffers not only from the attempts of church, state, and society to control its findings but also from the repressiveness of the scientific establishment itself. In the end, each scientist must walk alone, not in defiance but with the independence demanded by intellectual integrity. That is what it means to have a scientific temper of mind.

See also: Research Paradigms in Education; History of Educational Research; Measurement in Educational Research

Bibliography

Bailey K D 1978 *Methods of Social Research*. Free Press, New York
Black J A, Champion D J 1976 *Methods and Issues in Social Research*. Wiley, New York
Braithwaite R B 1953 *Scientific Explanation: A Study of the Function of Theory Probability and Law in Science*. Cambridge University Press, Cambridge
Campbell N R 1928 *Measurement and Calculation*. Longman, New York
Durkheim E 1950 *The Rules of Sociological Method*, 8th edn. Free Press, New York
Ellingstad V S, Heimstra N W 1974 *Methods in the Study of Human Behavior*. Brooks Cole, Monterey, California
Gellner E 1973 *Cause and Meaning in the Social Sciences*. Routledge and Kegan Paul, London
Hanson N R 1972 *Observation and Explanation: A Guide to Philosophy of Science*. Harper and Row, New York
Hempel C G 1965 *Aspects of Scientific Explanation, and Other Essays in the Philosophy of Science*. Free Press, New York
Kaplan A 1964 *The Conduct of Inquiry: Methodology for Behavioral Science*. Chandler, New York
Kuhn T S 1970 *The Structure of Scientific Revolutions*. University of Chicago Press, Chicago, Illinois
Lachenmeyer C W 1973 *Essence of Social Research: A Copernican Revolution*. Free Press, New York
Myrdal G 1969 *Objectivity in Social Research*. Pantheon, Westminster, Maryland
Nachmias D, Nachmias C 1976 *Research Methods in the Social Sciences*. St. Martin's Press, New York
Nagel E 1961 *The Structure of Science: Problems in the Logic of Scientific Explanation*. Harcourt Brace, and World, New York
Neale J M, Liebert R M 1973 *Science and Behavior: An Introduction to Methods of Research*. Prentice-Hall, Englewood Cliffs, New Jersey
Popper K R 1959 *The Logic of Scientific Discovery*. Basic Books, New York
Runkel P J, McGrath J E 1972 *Research on Human Behavior: A Systematic Guide to Method*. Holt, Rinehart and Winston, New York
Weber M 1949 *Methodology in the Social Sciences*. Free Press, New York

Experimental Studies

R. Tate

Experimental studies attempt to ensure valid causal inferences from randomized experiments conducted within practical constraints of available resources and time. This design process must first consider whether an experiment is, in fact, feasible. If so, the design process continues and attempts are made to anticipate possible threats to the validity of conclusions and to eliminate or minimize those threats. It should be noted that there is another, more narrow, methodological literature often labeled "experimental design" which is concerned with the associated statistical design and analysis. Important concepts in this statistical literature are included as one component in the broader framework considered here with respect to experimental studies.

1. The Experiment

A "true" or randomized experiment is defined as an inquiry in which experimental units have been randomly assigned to different experimental treatments. A sense of the versatility of the experiment is offered by consideration of each of the elements in this definition. An "inquiry" might be a research study to improve theoretical understanding or an evaluation seeking a pragmatic comparison of different instructional programs. Such inquiries can be conducted either in laboratory settings or in real "field" settings. The experimental "unit" is usually the focus of the inquiry. Thus, in studies of variables influencing the behavior and achievement of individual students, the unit would be the student, while the class would be the appropriate unit in studies of class-level variables on average class outcomes. In other words, an experiment can be used to understand phenomena at any level of the educational hierarchy. The experimental "treatments" may be different levels of a single theoretical construct or variable, for example "degree of structure in instruction," or they may be several instructional programs which differ on many dimensions. Often, one of the treatments is a "control" treatment, that is, a group with no implemented treatment at all. Finally, the random assignment of subjects ("subjects" will be used for "units" hereafter for concreteness) to treatments will result in experimental groups associated with each of the treatments.

An experiment can also be defined as an inquiry in which there are one or more active treatment variables or factors. An active variable is one which has been manipulated in the inquiry, where "manipulation" consists of the random assignment of subjects to different levels of the variable. This definition illustrates that a study may have more than one treatment variable, each variable having multiple treatment levels. For example, an investigator may wish to consider simultaneously the variable "degree of structure" having the three levels of low, medium, and high structure and a second variable "feedback to student" with two levels of "daily feedback" and "no feedback." The subjects would be randomly assigned to each of the resulting six treatment combinations of low structure/daily feedback, and so on. The simultaneous consideration of multiple treatment variables allows the identification and description of interactions between the variables.

The goal of an experiment is causal inference. "Causation," in this context, is defined in a commonsense fashion; if a treatment variable is manipulated or changed while holding constant all other possible determinants of the outcome of interest, and there is a subsequent change in the outcome, then it is said that there is a causal relationship between the manipulated variable and the outcome. There is no implication that the manipulated variable is the only cause of the outcome, only that it is one of probably many causes. It should be noted that use of the concept of causation is sometimes challenged, with some arguing that the concept is "prescientific." There should be little difficulty, however, with the relatively narrow definition used here, a definition which is compatible with utilitarian inquiry seeking understanding of those variables which can be manipulated in the attempt to improve society.

Typical outcomes or dependent variables of interest in educational inquiry which focuses on the individual student include academic achievement, attitudes, traits, self-perceptions, and job performance. The analysis of outcome data for individuals almost always describes the treatment effect on the central tendency (often the mean) of the outcome; it is also usually of interest to determine any effects on the variability and the shape of the distribution of the outcome variable. When the unit is some aggregate like the class or the school, the investigator will be interested in within-aggregate characteristics like the mean or variability of an individual-level outcome or the correlation between several variables within each class or school. The study of the aggregates may also consider various global outcomes like measures of group or organizational harmony and efficiency.

The experiment, when it is feasible, is a particularly efficacious mode of inquiry for causal inference. This is due to the random assignment of subjects to treatments. Generally, outcome differences across different treatment groups can be the result of two factors —differences in the attributes of the subjects in the different groups and the differential effects of the various treatments. Random assignment creates treatment groups which are initially comparable (in a probabilistic sense) on all subject attributes; it can then be concluded in an experiment that any final outcome differences are due to the treatment effects alone, assuming that other possible threats to validity to be discussed below have been controlled.

2. Threats to Validity

The design of an experiment should ensure adequate validity or truthfulness of conclusions. Cook and Campbell (1979), restructuring somewhat the classical discussion of Campbell and Stanley (1963), have identified four different validities which may be pertinent. These are associated with different aspects of the general experimental goal of concluding that a causal relationship between treatment and outcome constructs does or does not exist in specified populations of units, settings, and times. This conclusion will typically be based on the observed relationship between experimental operationalizations of the constructs of interest for a sample of units, settings, and times. The different validities, then, refer to the following component questions leading to the general conclusion (validity type given in parentheses): (a) Does an empirical relationship between the operationalized variables exist in the population (statistical conclusion validity)? (b) If the relationship exists, is it causal (internal validity)? (c) Can the relationship between the operationalized variables be generalized to the treatment and outcome constructs of interest (construct validity of cause and effect)? (d) Can the sample relationship be generalized to or across the populations of units, settings, and times of interest (external validity)?

Design can be viewed, in part, as the process of anticipating different possible threats to the validity of conclusions and seeking study procedures which will eliminate or minimize those threats. Some of the many common threats which have been discussed in detail by Campbell and Stanley (1963), Cook and Campbell (1979), and others will now be briefly considered.

2.1 Statistical Conclusion Validity

The statistical conclusion about the presence or absence of a relationship in the population is often based on statistical hypothesis testing. Statistical conclusion validity results, then, from the use of the appropriate test procedure with acceptable error probabilities. The probability of a false rejection of the null hypothesis of no relationship in the population, that is, the significance level, must be set before the test is conducted, with values of 0.01 or 0.05 usually being considered acceptable. A second error probability is the probability of failing to reject the null hypothesis when it is false. Alternatively, the power of the test defined as the probability of correctly rejecting a false null hypothesis can be considered. For a given significance level and effect size (i.e., strength of relationship), it is possible to determine the sample size required to produce an acceptable power.

The "fail to reject" decision from a test can sometimes be taken further. If the test has adequate power (say 0.90) for the "threshold" effect size defining an effect of practical importance, then a "fail to reject" outcome results in confidence that a practically important relationship does not exist in the population. That is, adequate power allows a decision to "accept," for all practical purposes, the null hypothesis.

Inadequate power is one of the most common threats to statistical conclusion validity when the researcher wishes to be able to detect an effect of practical importance. If the power for the threshold effect size is low, then it is, of course, incorrect to interpret "fail to reject" as implying there is no relationship of practical importance. There are many possible reasons for low power; these reasons and some approaches for ensuring adequate power are discussed in Sect. 4. Another threat is the use of an inappropriate statistical procedure. For example, if important assumptions of the procedure being used are violated by the study data, then the

actual error rates may be different from the nominal rates set for the study. Statistical analysis procedures will be discussed briefly in Sect. 5

2.2 Internal Validity

The threats to validity of a conclusion that final outcome differences in a study are due to the treatment effect would consist of any other reasonable explanations for the outcome differences. For example, as indicated in Sect. 1, the primary purpose of random assignment of subjects to treatments is to control the "selection" threat to internal validity, that is, the threat that final outcome differences may simply reflect initial group attribute differences. Randomization also controls some other threats to internal validity. First, once the selection threat is controlled, then a series of threats based on interaction with selection are also controlled. For example, different maturation rates for initially different groups (i.e., the selection × maturation interaction) are not a threat in an experiment. Also, since initial selection is not based on a prescore (e.g., to create "highs" and "lows"), statistical regression to the mean is not a problem.

Cook and Campbell (1979) point out, however, that random assignment may often aggravate other threats to internal validity. Treatment-related attrition and atypical behavior on the part of subjects are two threats which are often due to the differences in desirability typically found across different treatments in an experiment. Subject attrition which is related to the treatment variable may mean the initially comparable groups are no longer comparable at the end of the study; the resulting group attribute differences then represent an alternative explanation for any final outcome differences. Atypical behavior might include either "compensatory rivalry" (the "underdog" trying harder) or "resentful demoralization" on the part of subjects in the less desirable treatments or control groups (see *Unintended Effects in Educational Research*).

2.3 Construct Validity of Causes and Effects

It is important that the treatment and outcome constructs of interest are adequately fitted by the operational manipulations and measures actually used. Construct validity is questioned when there is a "possibility that the operations which are meant to represent a particular cause or effect construct can be construed in terms of more than one construct" (Cook and Campbell 1979 p. 59). Consider a possible study of the effect of "degree of structure" which randomly assigns students to different treatments based on varying structure. If other instructional variables, such as amount of time devoted to helping individuals or amount of diagnostic testing, are also inadvertently varied across the treatments, there will be a question about the "real" reason for any final outcome differences. Threats to construct validity would consist of any reasons for an operation either underrepresenting all of the aspects of a construct or overrepresenting a construct by including irrelevant aspects. For example, since it can be argued that a construct is seldom precisely represented by a single operation, a "mono-operation bias" may result unless multiple operations are used to define both treatment and outcome.

2.4 External Validity

External validity refers to the validity of the generalization of study results to explicit or implicit target populations of subjects, settings, and times. The validity of such generalizations depends, of course, on the degree to which the samples of persons, settings, and times used in the study are representative of the populations of interest. Formal random sampling procedures (e.g., simple random, stratified random, and cluster sampling) and the associated statistical inferential procedures are available and, if used, allow precise statements about the probability of any degree of nonrepresentativeness due to chance.

For many research and evaluation studies, however, the assessment of external validity is not so formal and precise (e.g., Bracht and Glass 1968). Often, sampling is not directly from the ultimate target population of interest, but rather from some subpopulation which is accessible to the investigator. This distinction between accessible and target populations means that external validity must then be concerned with the validity of two inferential leaps, one from the sample to the accessible population, and the other from the accessible population to the target population. If the sample is the result of a formal random sampling procedure, then precise statements can be made about the validity of the first inferential leap. Sample size is a critical factor here, as with statistical conclusion validity, with larger sample sizes resulting in an increased confidence in sample representativeness. The validity of the second inference, generalizing from the accessible population to the target population, also depends on representativeness. However, this is not ensured by the use of a formal sampling procedure, but must be demonstrated by adequate similarity between the two populations on all characteristics which might be important contextual variables for the relationship of interest.

A judgment of external validity is also required when a researcher wishes to generalize across different populations or subpopulations. For example, a goal may be to demonstrate that a certain treatment effect is found in both boys and girls and across several grade levels. Of course, such a generalization also implies the researcher must be able to generalize separately to each of the individual subpopulations.

External validity is threatened when there is a combination of two factors: (a) a question about representativeness of the sample, and (b) a possibility of interaction between treatment and subjects, settings, or times. The first factor is present when representativeness has not been ensured through use of an appropriate sampling procedure and/or demonstrated through empirical comparisons. The second factor, interaction, refers to the possibility that the effect of a treatment may vary across the different persons, settings, and times comprising the target population. Thus, any treatment effect found in some ill-defined portion of the target population may not be the same as the effect of interest in the total population. Since in most cases, adequate theory or empirical evidence which convincingly argues against such interaction does not exist, a serious question about representativeness is all that is needed to conclude that external validity has not been demonstrated.

3. The Decision to Use an Experiment

The decision concerning which mode of inquiry to use for a planned causal study involves three questions. (a) Which of the available modes of inquiry, including the experimental, are feasible? (b) What can be achieved with each of the feasible modes under the constraints of allowed resources and time? (c) Which mode is best for the purposes of the inquiry? Consider, first, two of the possible alternative approaches for a quantitative causal inquiry. One alternative is a quasiexperimental approach (Cook and Campbell 1979) in which there is a treatment intervention but no assumption of random assignment of subjects to treatments. One variation of this approach is the "nonequivalent group" design in which treatments are introduced to existing groups. Another variation is the "interrupted time series" design involving assessment of a treatment effect with a series of measures before and after introduction of the treatment. Second, when there is no treatment intervention, that is, in correlational or natural-setting studies, path analysis allows an investigator to determine whether a hypothesized causal model is consistent with observed empirical correlations.

The question of the feasibility of an experiment for the planned inquiry depends in large part on the feasibility of random assignment of the subjects to different treatments. First, many individual attribute variables such as sex, race, age, IQ, personality traits, and so on cannot be experimentally manipulated. Researchers in sociology of education, for example, are often interested in the effects of individual and family attributes, and must use techniques like path analysis in their search for causal models. Also, high levels of variables like pain, fear, and stress could not be included in experiments for obvious ethical reasons, and controversial programs concerning, say, sex education or training in political protest, may not be allowed in some communities for political reasons. Thus, the experiment is not, by definition, an option when manipulation of the treatment variable is not technically, ethically, or politically feasible.

Another aspect of feasibility is whether it is possible in practice to obtain permission to randomly assign subjects. In laboratory settings, this is usually not difficult, since only the agreement of each volunteer subject is necessary, and volunteers understand before the experiment that assignment to different treatments will be involved. In field settings, however, the same task is often much more difficult. When it is desired to study individuals, such as students or teachers, in their "everyday" work or study environment, it is necessary to obtain permission from both administrative "gatekeepers" of the environment of interest and the subjects themselves. Gatekeepers may often be reluctant to grant such permission because of their concern about possible inconvenience and disruption of work, or their doubts about the value of the treatments being studied. If the gatekeepers do perceive a proposed treatment as being valuable, they may object to the random assignment of some teachers and students to control groups or less desirable treatments. Finally, even if the gatekeepers do permit access to the teachers and students, the potential subjects themselves may choose not to participate for the same reasons given above.

An experiment, if feasible, is usually superior to the alternatives for controlling certain critical threats to internal validity (i.e., the validity of causal inference). This is, of course, an important consideration when conducting a causal inquiry. Random assignment in an experiment does not guarantee correct causal conclusions, but it usually does result in fewer assumptions being required for a causal inference. For example, "selection" is a critical threat for the nonequivalent group design because of the use of intact groups. The investigator must therefore attempt to explicitly model all of the important group differences to allow the necessary statistical adjustments, and there is usually some question about the assumption that the causal modeling is appropriate. Selection (or, in causal modeling terminology, misspecification) is also a serious threat to causal inferences from path analysis in correlational studies. "History" is a potential threat in the interrupted time series design, and it is necessary to assume (with adequate empirical support) that the introduction of the treatment did not coincide with some other event which could have been the real reason for change in the outcome. Both of these threats, selection and history, are controlled by the random assignment in an experiment.

The degree of intervention associated with the different modes of inquiry ranges from the strong intervention of the experiment to the weak or nonexistent intervention in a correlational study. This variation may have important implications. There may be situations, especially in field settings, where overt intervention may distort or change the setting and the behavior of subjects from those of interest (as with, for example, the resentful demoralization or compensatory rivalry mentioned in Sect. 2). Also, since a greater degree of intervention may often take more time to plan and implement and may therefore cost more, the choice of inquiry mode may be partially constrained by available resources and time. Thus, it may be said that the experiment is superior for causal inquiry, other things being equal, but of course the "other things" in the qualification are often not equal.

Since the difficulty of obtaining permission for random assignment often depends on the setting, it is perhaps best to consider the laboratory versus field decision simultaneously with the inquiry mode decision. The dominant factor in selecting the setting is often external validity. If (a) the target setting for the inquiry is a real field setting, (b) the setting is viewed as important in influencing the phenomena of interest, and (c) it is not feasible to design a laboratory setting to adequately simulate the field setting, then a field setting is clearly needed for acceptable external validity. For example, the basic premise in research on "contextual effects" in the school setting is that context is an important determinant of individual teacher or student behavior; such research would thus usually require field research in school settings. On the other hand, many instructional treatments are designed for efficiently teaching specific topics to small groups of students and often might best be studied in laboratory settings.

The laboratory versus field decision also has other implications. For example, the greater control of irrelevant factors which is allowed in the laboratory setting would provide, for the same sample size, greater statistical power than would be found in the relatively "noisy" field setting, thus improving statistical conclusion validity. The tighter control on the implementation of treatments in the laboratory would also contribute to construct validity. Finally, the arrangement for and implementation of studies in field settings, especially when there are multiple widespread sites, will often be more time consuming and costly than a laboratory study.

The interaction of the laboratory versus field decision with the inquiry mode decision can be illustrated with a situation where both the laboratory and the field settings may be viable options for an inquiry. Depending on the circumstances, the choice may be difficult. Assume, for example, the gatekeepers for the field setting of interest will allow a treatment intervention but not random assignment. The investigator is then faced with the choice between a laboratory experiment or a field quasiexperiment. Some of the factors involved in such a choice would include the extent to which the laboratory setting simulates the target setting, the comparability of intact groups available in the field setting, the potential for systematic attrition and atypical behavior in each of the settings, the resources and time required to conduct the inquiry in each setting, and the relative importance of the different validities for the study.

In summary, there is no suggestion here that an experimental approach, assuming it is feasible, should always be used. Rather, the choice of the optimal approach should involve an estimation of the validities of conclusions which could be obtained under each of the feasible alternatives. The different inquiry modes and settings typically offer different strengths and weaknesses, and the final choice will be the setting/mode combination which best fits the purpose of the inquiry.

4. Design of the Experiment

The "decision to use an experiment" and the "design of the experiment" may at first appear to be two separate steps in the conduct of an inquiry. As indicated in the previous section, however, the choice of a mode of inquiry implies at least a partial design for each of several approaches to predict the relative strengths and weaknesses of each. The current section, then, is concerned with the continuation and refinement of the design process already underway, assuming that an experiment is to be used.

Design is concerned with anticipating and eliminating or minimizing important threats to validity within the constraints of available resources and time. It is not possible here to discuss design considerations associated with all of the many possible validity threats, but the process can be illustrated with several of the more common design concerns. First, different approaches to ensuring adequate statistical power will be discussed. Relatively more space is devoted to this topic, not because it is logically more important than other topics, but because it has proven to be more amenable to quantification and elaboration and has been considered extensively in the literature. Next, the internal validity threat of treatment-related attrition of subjects will be discussed. Finally, the importance of detailed descriptive information for validity will be emphasized.

4.1 Power

Consider a simple experiment with two treatments. The treatment effect size is defined here as the difference in the outcome means for the two populations associated with the treatments. As indicated in Sect. 2, the investigator can define a threshold value of the effect size which represents a difference of practical or scientific importance. Once the level of significance is specified, there are two remaining parameters which influence the power of the hypothesis test (in this case, a t-test) to detect an effect equal to the threshold value. One is the sample size, n; an increase in n, other things being equal, results in an increase in power. The second is the error variability, often represented with the standard error of estimate. For the simple two-group t-test, this is just the estimated standard deviation of the outcome variable, Y, for each of the two populations. It can also be understood by reference to the analysis model which underlies the test of interest, a model which expresses Y as a function of one or more independent variables. (The model for the t-test consists simply of a single "dummy" variable representing the active treatment variable.) The error variability, then, is the variability of Y which is not explained by the independent variables in the model. Since error variability can also be viewed as background noise in which the treatment effect is embedded, increasing error variability makes it more difficult to detect the effect, that is, it decreases the power.

The most direct route to ensuring adequate power for a test is simply to determine and use the sample size required for a power of, say, 0.90 to detect the threshold effect size. This is easily accomplished with available tables (e.g., Cohen 1977) and adequate resources. An estimate of the anticipated size of the standard error of estimate is required, but otherwise the determination is straightforward. Unfortunately, the required sample

size for an analysis model consisting of just the active treatment variable(s) can often be larger than study resources will allow. Also, even if the required n would be allowed by the study budget, most investigators would still be interested in improving the efficiency of the inquiry to achieve the same power with smaller n and less cost.

The key to improving the efficiency of a test lies in the control of and reduction of the error variability. There are two general approaches to this goal. Consider, first, the different contributors to error for an analysis model containing just the active treatment variables. The error variability is due to measurement error in Y, the inherent variability associated with the target populations of subjects and settings, and variability due to extraneous study factors such as undesired variation in treatment implementation or the occurrence of atypical events during the study. Two obvious ways to improve efficiency, then, would be to improve the reliability of the Y measure and to minimize extraneous factors operating in the study. Also, the investigator may choose to use subject and/or setting subpopulations which are more homogeneous than the target populations. The increase in power associated with this last approach, however, would be accompanied by a threat to external validity of the study.

The second basic approach to error reduction attacks the problem of population heterogeneity, not by using a more homogeneous subpopulation, but by expanding the analysis model to include one or more attribute variables which are related to the outcome variable. The addition of such "control" variables to the model already containing the active treatment variables will result in an increase of the Y variability which is explained by the model and a corresponding decrease in the unexplained or error variability. Randomized block designs and analysis of covariance (ANCOVA) designs are two main variations on this theme which have been developed in the experimental statistical design literature (e.g., Kirk 1968, Myers 1979, Neter and Wasserman 1974, Winer 1971).

The randomized block design can be illustrated with a simple experiment involving one active treatment variable with k levels. If there is large variability of ability in the population of students of interest and a strong relationship between Y and ability, then the investigator may elect to block on ability. The sample of students would be ranked on ability and grouped into homogeneous blocks of size k based on this ranking. Then, the k students in each block would be randomly assigned, one to each of the k treatment levels. Randomization within the blocks is often referred to as a restriction in randomization. The associated analysis model consists of two independent variables, the treatment variable and the categorical blocking variable, with the addition of the blocking variable resulting in the desired reduction in error variability.

A blocking variable is most effective when subjects within blocks are very homogeneous and there is great

heterogeneity between blocks. Since the blocking variable is a categorical variable, it can be formed in many
different ways. In addition to using a ranking on a single
interval variable (as in the example above), blocks can
also be created by combining several interval, ordinal,
or nominal variables. Another way to create blocks is to
expose each subject to each of the k treatments, considering each individual subject to be a block. This
repeated measures design may be said to permit each
subject to "act as his/her own control," and can provide
very efficient tests; it should only be used, however,
when there is confidence that there is no "carry-over"
effect from treatment to treatment.

Analysis of covariance is similar to a randomized
block design in that it reduces error variability and
increases power by adding one or more control variables
(called covariates or concomitant variables) to the analysis model. It is also different, however, in several
important aspects. Analysis of covariance does not
involve any initial restriction on randomization like that
in randomized block designs. That is, subjects are randomly assigned to the different treatment levels without
regard to covariate values. Also, ANCOVA assumes the
covariate is an interval rather than categorical variable;
thus, it is necessary to properly specify the functional
nature of the relationship between Y and the covariate
(i.e., whether it is linear or nonlinear). It is assumed that
the covariates are measured before implementation of
the treatments or, if not, that they have not been
affected by the treatments. In addition to increasing
power, ANCOVA also allows an adjustment of outcome
differences to compensate for any initial group differences resulting from the random assignment.

When a potential control variable is an interval variable, the investigator may chose to use it either as a
covariate or to create a blocking variable. Since (a) analogous randomized block and ANCOVA designs provide
roughly the same power for typical Y–control variable
correlations, (b) both designs in their classical form have
similar assumptions (e.g., that there is no interaction
between the treatment and control variables), and (c)
both can be modified to handle violations of these
assumptions (see Sect. 5), it makes little difference for
these considerations which design is used. One possible
basis for a choice between the two would lie in the
assumed measurement level of the control variable. If
the investigator does not wish to be concerned about the
nature of the functional relationship between the outcome and control variables, the randomized block
design would be chosen. On the other hand, use of an
ANCOVA will allow an explicit description of the
Y–covariate relationship, a description which may be of
interest in its own right when nonlinear relationships are
discovered. A second basis of choice is that the decision
to use the randomized block design must be made
before the start of the study because of the required
restriction in randomization. In contrast, the decision to
use an ANCOVA can be made at any time during or after
the study, as long as appropriate covariate measures are
available.

In summary, there are many approaches to the
improvement of the power of a test. The goal usually is
to provide acceptable power for detecting the threshold
effect size. However, it should be noted that even when
this goal cannot be realized because of limited resources
and a small sample size, continuation of the inquiry is
still legitimate as long as the limitations are recognized.
In this situation, the investigator is gambling that the
real effect size is sufficiently greater than the threshold
value so that there is a good chance of detecting it. Also,
it must be recognized that the "fail to reject" conclusion
in this case offers little information about whether an
effect of practical importance really exists.

Finally, the above discussion assumes that hypothesis
testing is the inferential mode being used to make decisions about the presence or absence of a relationship in
the population. Interval estimation can also be used
with (or instead of) hypothesis testing to describe the
treatment effects. All of the above discussion also
applies to interval estimation, except the criterion is,
instead of adequate power, the desired maximum width
of the confidence intervals on treatment contrasts (see
Analysis of Variance and Covariance).

4.2 Treatment-related Attrition

Even when initial comparability of treatment groups has
been achieved through random assignment, the presence
of treatment-related attrition of the subjects can result
in groups which are no longer comparable at the end of
the study, a nonequivalence which may be the real reason for any outcome differences. One important facet of
the attack on this problem is the avoidance of any
unnecessary burden, inconvenience, or frustration for
subjects which may result in their leaving the study. For
example, efforts to work within the schedule of each
subject or to provide necessary transportation may pay
off in reduced attrition. It is more difficult to avoid differences in the desirability of different treatments in a
study, differences which are probably the major reason
for treatment-related attrition. This may be especially
true for control groups which do not have the benefit of
any treatment at all. One possible way to improve the
retention of subjects in control groups and less desirable
treatment groups is to promise that these subjects may
have the superior treatment at some later date.

When some attrition does occur in a study, it is
important to gather the necessary information to determine if it is related to the treatments. Thus, each subject
leaving the study could be asked, in a nonthreatening
way, for the reason. Also, the extent to which attrition is
treatment-related can be described quantitatively. The
attrition rate and various subject attribute variables can
be tested as a function of the treatment variable during
and at the end of the study.

The investigator should plan a back-up analysis when
there is a possibility that treatment-related attrition will
occur. The logical backup for an experiment consists of
the various analyses associated with the nonequivalent
group design for quasiexperimental inquiry. Since these
analyses depend on adequate quantitative modeling of

the ways in which the groups differ, the investigator anticipating attrition should always attempt to collect relevant subject attribute data, before the study starts. Even if there is some question about the precise nature of final group differences in the presence of treatment-related attrition, it is still sometimes possible to draw conclusions if the general direction of those differences is known. Consider, for example, a simple treatment group versus control group comparison; if (a) it is clear that there has been systematic attrition and that the final control group is generally more able and motivated than the treatment group, and (b) the mean achievement for the treatment group is still higher than that for the control group, then there is little question about the superiority of the treatment group even though the exact degree of superiority cannot be determined.

4.3 Description for Validity

Detailed descriptions of subjects, treatments, and settings are a critical element in establishing the validity of conclusions from a study. The description of subject attributes provides a basis for establishing external validity, making covariate adjustments to improve power, determining if any attrition is treatment related, and conducting quasiexperimental analyses if necessary. Detailed description of each treatment as implemented is important for construct validity. It is of little value to know precisely the size of a treatment effect without knowing precisely what treatment was responsible for the effect. And, of course, it is not uncommon for a treatment as implemented to be very different from the treatment as planned. Description of the setting is valuable for external validity, with pertinent aspects including physical dimensions such as lighting and noise level and organizational characteristics like school discipline policy and grading procedures. Finally, the interaction of subjects with the treatments should be described in the search for unanticipated treatment effects. Such process description will also often provide important clues when the treatments are not working as expected.

In summary, the design of an experiment may include the considerations briefly discussed here plus many others. Design is further complicated by the possibility that attempts to minimize one threat to validity may simultaneously aggravate another threat. For example, the use of extensive observation and measurement to provide the detailed description suggested above may, because of associated distraction of the subjects, drastically alter the setting from the one of interest. Clearly, the optimal design of an inquiry can be a complex and subjective task, a process not easily represented by mechanical formulas or guidelines.

5. Statistical Analysis of Data

The appropriate analysis model for an experiment can often be found in the traditional analysis of variance (ANOVA) and analysis of covariance (ANCOVA) literature (e.g., Kirk 1968, Myers 1979, Winer 1971). There are many models and associated considerations of potential interest; only some can be mentioned here. For example, completely randomized ANOVA models like one-way ANOVA (for a single treatment variable) or a k-way factorial design (for k treatment variables) may be used when it is not necessary to include control variables. When control variables are required to ensure adequate power, many variations of the randomized block design and ANCOVA are available. Block designs may include multiple blocking variables, and when the numbers of treatment variables and levels increase, there are incomplete block and fractional replication designs which provide efficient tests with blocks of reasonable size. ANCOVA models can also be elaborated by including multiple treatment variables and multiple covariates.

The simplicity of computations for these models will depend on the pattern of cell sizes in the design. All fixed effects ANOVA and ANCOVA models are special cases of the general linear model (e.g., Neter and Wasserman 1974). In general, it is not feasible to compute general linear model results by hand. However, the computational procedure simplifies drastically for ANOVA designs with only one factor or factorial designs with equal or unequal but proportional cell sizes, producing the simple computational equations found in standard ANOVA texts. On the other hand, when a factorial ANOVA/ANCOVA design has unequal and disproportionate cell sizes, the factors of the resulting "nonorthogonal" design are correlated, and the general computerized procedure for the linear model must be used for an exact solution.

It is not uncommon to find that the assumptions associated with standard analyses are violated for the study data at hand. Fortunately, there is evidence that significance tests are relatively robust to the violation of some assumptions. For example, moderate violations of the homogeneity of variance and normality assumptions in the presence of approximately equal cell sizes can usually be tolerated. In contrast, other violations may be more critical, requiring adjustments or use of a different analysis technique. Thus, drastic violations of the homogeneity and normality assumptions may require the consideration of transformations of the outcome variable or the use of an alternative analysis like generalized least squares or a nonparametric procedure. As another example, there may be evidence of the existence of an interaction between a treatment variable and a control variable, a violation of an important assumption in both the standard randomized block design with a cell size of one and the ANCOVA design. Interaction terms must then be added to the analysis model, using either a generalized randomized block design with cell size larger than one or a general linear model representation of ANCOVA. It should be noted that this last model no longer produces an ANCOVA in the conventional sense, but is identical to the aptitude-treatment–interaction (ATI) model mentioned briefly below. It may also be found in ANCOVA that the relationship between Y and the covariate is nonlinear, another violation of the standard analysis. Again, a general linear model with added polynomial terms would allow adequate fit of the model to study data.

There are some designs of interest in educational research and evaluation which are not fitted precisely by standard ANOVA/ANCOVA models. For example, ATI research attempts to identify and describe interactions between active instructional treatment variables and student aptitudes. An ATI analysis model would typically consist of a categorical treatment variable, one or more interval aptitude variables, and the necessary interaction terms. Another nonstandard design is one with interval treatment variables such as amount of study time allowed in class or the number of homework problems required. A general linear model with any required polynomial or interaction variables would allow the estimation of a multidimensional "response surface" describing the treatment effects.

Finally, there are sometimes multiple outcomes of interest in a study. Often, the investigator will simply conduct multiple analyses, one for each of the outcome variables. If the number of outcomes is relatively large, however, the investigator will be confronted with an inflation of error rate due to the many tests and a cumbersome and complex description based on numerous results. In this situation, the multivariate general linear model (e.g., Timm 1975) may be used. Multivariate global hypotheses and simultaneous inference procedures provide the necessary control of error rates and confidence levels, while the associated generalized discriminant analysis may provide a more parsimonious

description of the effect in terms of derived optimal variates.

See also: Statistical Analysis in Educational Research; Multivariate Analysis

Bibliography

Bracht G, Glass G 1968 The external validity of experiments. *Am. Educ. Res. J.* 5: 437–74
Campbell D T, Stanley J C 1963 *Experimental and Quasi-experimental Designs for Research.* Rand McNally, Chicago, Illinois
Cohen J 1977 *Statistical Power Analysis for the Behavioral Sciences,* rev. edn. Academic Press, New York
Cook T D, Campbell D T 1979 *Quasi-experimentation: Design and Analysis Issues for Field Settings.* Rand McNally, Chicago, Illinois
Kerlinger F N 1973 *Foundations of Behavioral Research,* 2nd. edn. Holt, Rinehart and Winston, New York
Kirk R E 1968 *Experimental Design: Procedures for the Behavioral Sciences.* Brooks/Cole, Belmont, California
Myers J L 1979 *Fundamentals of Experimental Design,* 3rd edn. Allyn and Bacon, Boston, Massachusetts
Neter J, Wasserman W 1974 *Applied Linear Statistical Models: Regression, Analysis of Variance, and Experimental Designs.* Irwin, Homewood, Illinois
Phillips D C 1981 Toward an evaluation of the experiment in educational contexts. *Educ. Res.* AERA 10: 13–20
Timm N H 1975 *Multivariate Analysis with Applications in Education and Psychology.* Brooks/Cole, Monterey, California
Winer B 1971 *Statistical Principles in Experimental Design.* McGraw-Hill, New York

Survey Studies, Cross-sectional

D. A. Walker and P. M. Burnhill

No single definition of a survey is completely satisfactory. There are many different types of survey, but in general they all attempt to obtain measurements from a sample of individuals selected from a predefined finite population in their natural setting. In many instances the individuals are people, but they might be, for example, books in a library. In the cross-sectional type of survey, with which this article is concerned, the measurements are obtained at or about a particular time, and for the most part the purpose is to describe situations and estimate frequencies rather than to establish causal patterns. In a longitudinal survey, on the other hand, measurements of the same individual are made at intervals over a period of time which may cover several years. Although the techniques of survey methods have been largely developed outside the field of education it is possible to highlight the main issues arising in surveys by illustrations drawn from educational surveys. These issues include the definition of the population to be surveyed, the methods of collecting the data, techniques of sampling, the basis for making inferences from the

sample to the population, and the control and measurement of the various errors that arise in every survey.

The two central concepts in survey design are cost and error, and account must be taken of each in planning a survey. What follows is only a brief guide to these concepts. The literature on survey design is large, but a study of at least part of it will repay anyone proposing to use survey methods. Some of the literature covers a wide range of topics (e.g., Moser and Kalton 1971), some is especially suitable for the nonmathematical reader (e.g., Hoinville et al. 1978, Kalton 1983, Stuart 1976, Sudman 1976), while some provides more technical details (e.g., Kish 1965, O'Muircheartaigh and Payne 1977, Ross 1978). The book by O'Muircheartaigh and Payne is one of the few general books in survey analyses of samples from finite populations.

1. Purposes of Surveys

A survey may be largely descriptive in purpose, the findings consisting mainly of statements of the values of the variable measured. For example, the purpose of the first

Scottish Mental Survey in 1932 was to ascertain the distribution of intelligence among children in Scottish schools who were born in 1921. The published results showed that the scatter of intelligence quotients was greater than had been expected, and that it was greater among boys than among girls. The Australian Studies in School Performance (Bourke and Keeves 1977) were designed to "estimate for Australia the number of children who were failing to attain the basic skills of literacy and numeracy as assessed by the tests of reading, writing, and numeration and to specify relationships between other factors...and the attainment of competence".

On the other hand, a survey may be conducted to test hypotheses arising from studies of smaller, selected groups and to seek explanations for relationships that have been found, or are expected to be found, between variables. For example, it had been observed in the United Kingdom that there was a negative correlation between intelligence test score and size of family. This gave rise to the fear that the national average of intelligence might be falling. The second Scottish Mental Survey (Scottish Council for Research in Education 1949) was therefore conducted to test this hypothesis, and the opportunity was taken to measure a number of sociological variables with a view to examining the interrelationships between these and test scores.

The researcher intending to conduct a survey must be very clear about the purpose the survey is intended to serve. The purpose will determine the population to be surveyed, the variables to be included, and the methods of obtaining the data. The international surveys conducted by the International Association for the Evaluation of Educational Achievement (IEA) (Husén 1967, Peaker 1975) were not intended to provide "league tables" of national achievement, but to relate these achievements to a variety of variables describing the characteristics of the national groups. In this way, it was hoped, the participating countries would be able to ascertain what changes in their systems would benefit their students. The surveys were then designed with these purposes in mind.

2. The Population to be Surveyed

The researcher must also be clear on the population to be surveyed and the nature of the units composing that population if the findings are to have the intended generality; the intended or target population should be defined. There must also be some means of identifying and locating units (or members) of the population in order that a sample may be selected and then surveyed.

The problem of defining the population can be especially difficult when interest is in the upper reaches of the secondary school. The dividing line between "secondary" and "tertiary" education can be arbitrary and often corresponds with institutional divisions in the type of education: academic/general or technical/vocational. Students in both sectors may be studying science and mathematics to the same standard, and may belong to the same birth cohort. A population of interest defined carefully in the planning stages will greatly facilitate the drawing of conclusions.

There may be more than one way in which a target population can be defined. It might be all children in a given area born in a particular year. An alternative target population could be all children in that area at a particular stage in the school system. This is a different population, though there may be a large overlap, and findings from one population will not necessarily apply to the other. It should also be understood that the target population applies to a specified unit of interest. A population of students has a corresponding population of teachers who teach them, but that group of teachers is not necessarily representative of the body of teachers.

To select a sample, a listing or frame of the target population is required; if none exists, a means of constructing the whole or part of this sampling frame has to be found. Deficiencies in the sampling frame can severely undermine the best laid sample designs. In almost all studies of children of school age it may be appropriate to define an excluded population. This may be quite a small group (e.g., the mentally handicapped) or involve a substantial proportion of an age group (e.g., those who have already left school). However, there are other excluded subgroups who cannot be so easily identified. Lists constructed in schools may omit truants or those absent through illness, and school registers can be out of date and so effectively exclude some students. Defects in the sampling frame limit inference in much the same ways as the other errors of noncoverage discussed later.

3. Techniques of Survey Sampling

A population census is a survey. Often a population census will involve the whole of a specified population: the sampling fraction is 100 percent. Similarly, in education it is possible to approach a complete population. In the Scottish Mental Surveys over 90 percent of the two populations, which numbered 85,000 and 70,800, were tested, and in the Scottish Scholastic Survey of 1953 about 95 percent of the population of 76,000 took the tests. Whether such a heavy burden of testing, correction, and analysis with its accompanying costs is justifiable depends on the purposes of the survey, but in many cases the information required does not have to be completely accurate: some error is allowable as long as the extent of the error can be estimated. In these cases only a sample of the target population need be involved.

How then should a sample be selected and what is meant by accurate information? Accurate estimates are defined as having small bias and small variable error. If the researcher has extensive knowledge of the population it may well be that a judgment sample, that is, one selected in the light of the previous knowledge of the population, may give more precise estimates than would a sample of the same size drawn at random. However, there is no way of knowing whether greater precision has been achieved and the estimates may be biased. The same objection applies to a quota sample, again because of the lack of random selection of the sample members which quota sampling may provide. Randomization methods in sampling offer protection against bias in the selection of the sample members. A random method of selection gives each of the units in the population a known chance or probability, of selection, hence the term probability sampling, which is commonly used to distinguish it from nonrandom methods. Moreover, because the probability of selection is known, not only does random sampling protect against bias, it also enables the researcher to estimate from the sample data the extent of the error due to sampling.

In practice, the degree of randomness is often restricted by refinements of the sampling process. One such refinement is stratification. In most countries schools vary in size. If a sample of schools were selected completely at random it might be that the sample would contain an excessive proportion of large (or small) schools, and thus would not be adequately representative of the population of schools. The population of schools could be divided into subpopulations or strata according to the number of pupils enrolled, and the sample then selected from the strata in such a way that the different strata are adequately represented. Stratification by size can be accompanied by stratification by other variables, for example the religious affiliation of the school.

Systematic sampling is an administratively easy way of sampling which can also offer some degree of implicit stratification. For example, if the task is to select a 10 percent sample of students from within a school, this may be done on the basis of the school's registers of students. Suppose that the students have been streamed by ability into different classes and that a register is kept of each class. Then every 10th student may be selected from a list of the classes; the starting point being chosen at random. In this way the students from each class are represented in the sample in roughly the desired proportions of ability, that is, there has been some stratification. Care has to be taken that the register list has not been prepared in such a way that the sampling interval has special properties; for example if the list contained boys and girls in alternating positions then selecting every 10th student would produce a highly unrepresentative sample.

It may be very costly to prepare a complete listing or sampling frame, especially in a large country. Recourse may then be had to multistage sampling. For example, in the United States a possible sampling scheme would be to select a random sample of states (the primary sampling units) and within each of these a random sample of school districts. These in turn could provide a random sample of schools and these in turn a random sample of students. The advantage of this method is the saving in costs, since detailed information is not required about units not selected. Multistage sampling of this type was used in some of the countries taking part in the IEA investigations.

One form of multistage sampling which warrants separate mention is cluster sampling, which occurs when all members of the selected primary sampling units are included in the sample. This has advantages and disadvantages which can best be illustrated by an example. The 10-year-old children who were to be the population surveyed in the second Scottish Scholastic Survey were known to be in about 2,600 schools. A simple random sample would have involved correspondence with and entry to most, if not all, of these schools. It was therefore decided that the primary sampling unit would be the school and that all 10-year-olds in the selected schools would be tested. This involved only 169 schools with corresponding economies in cost. The disadvantage was that the estimates of mean score obtained from the sample were much less precise than those which would have been obtained from a simple random sample of the same size. In fact, the 5,000 pupils tested provided the precision that would have been available from about 670 pupils selected in a completely random fashion (Scottish Council for Research in Education 1968). This is due to the resemblances within clusters (in this case schools) which detract from the independence which simple random sampling entails. This point is taken up again in the section on errors.

A refinement which has been widely used in the IEA surveys is to select schools with probability proportional to size, and then to select a sample of students within these schools with probability inversely proportional to size. The net effect is that all students have the same chance of selection, but the number in each school is kept reasonably small and the cluster effect is reduced. It is, however, essential that the selection within schools be random, and precise instructions must be given as to how this is done. In the Six Subject Study carried out by the IEA in 1970 and 1971, the average number of students tested in each school was 26 (Peaker 1975).

These are examples of complex sampling, which when properly used may increase the efficiency and decrease the cost of a survey.

4. Methods of Collecting Data

In educational research the usual method of collecting data is through tests and self-completion questionnaires, though interviewing has also been used. Access to the school system has long been a privilege of the researcher, but it is subject to the school authorities being satisfied that the project is worthwhile, has been adequately planned, and will not throw too heavy a burden on students and teachers. Interviewing may be carried out by teachers, psychologists, health visitors, social workers, or by specially trained interviewers. The use of professionals can be especially valuable in obtaining data on family and social backgrounds.

A useful development has been the use of postal surveys, where the questionnaires are distributed and collected through the postal system, thus giving access to a wider sample of the population than could be reached at the same cost by other methods. This method has been successfully used in the Scottish National School Leaver Survey (Gray et al. 1982, Raffe 1984).

5. *The Pretest and the Pilot Survey*

The need for pretesting the items in tests and questionnaires is already well-known but must be stressed. Designing tests and questionnaires is not easy and demands thought and systematic testing. Each item should be tried out on a reasonably large number of students from a roughly equivalent population. This gives the opportunity to detect and remove ambiguities, to ascertain the range of possible responses, especially to items which are open ended and will require coding or will be changed to closed items in the final survey, and to ensure that the items are yielding the information desired.

When the requisite number of items has been obtained and a draft test or questionnaire constructed, it is very desirable if not essential that a pilot run (sometimes called a dry run) be organized, again with an equivalent group, to test the final form and all the procedures that will be followed in the main survey, including any follow-ups to ensure that measurements are obtained from as many as possible of those selected. The pilot run also gives an opportunity to learn what the results of the main survey are likely to be. It is worthwhile devoting say one-tenth of the resources available for a survey to mounting a pilot run and thus avoiding expensive mistakes in the main survey.

6. *Sources of Error*

It is a truism that the findings of almost all surveys are subject to errors, but it is important that the source of error be identified and as far as possible quantified, so that the researcher may be able to state how accurate are the findings. The errors may be variable or systematic and may arise from nonobservation, from the mode of measurement, or may be attributable to sampling.

6.1 *Errors of Nonobservation*

The extent to which membership of the achieved sample falls short of the target sample, arises from several sources. If the data defining the population have been derived from material collected some time previously, changes may have occurred by the time the actual survey takes place. In some cases it will be possible to make the necessary adjustments during the survey. A greater difficulty is likely to be nonresponse, the most extreme form being unit nonresponse (for example, refusal to cooperate) and the less extreme being missing data or item nonresponse (where items or questions in tests or questionnaires have produced no reply). The threat of nonresponse is that respondents and nonrespondents are not alike, and inferences based solely on replies from respondents will be biased. One method of dealing with direct refusals and those "away from school" is for the researcher, when selecting the sample, to draw a second sample as a reserve list, members of which can be

invited to serve if one of the original sample refuses. The difficulty here is that the sample is then no longer a straightforward probability sample and the threat of bias remains. Where refusal rates are high, as was the case in some of the countries taking part in the IEA surveys, this will create problems. Methods of poststratifying, that is weighting subgroups differentially, may lead to a reduction of this bias. Where the problem is item nonresponse it may be possible to fill some of the gaps from other sources or by making certain assumptions. Algorithms for this missing data problem include "mean value", "cold deck", "hot deck", and "nearest neighbour" replacement.

6.2 *Errors of Measurement*

These arise from a variety of sources. If the tests or questionnaires are poorly designed the questions may be misunderstood. If the data are collected by interviewers, for example where psychologists administer individual tests, a certain amount of the variance of scores is attributable to differences between testers. If items are of open-ended type, where responses have to be coded, errors of coding occur. Methods of reducing these errors are in some cases obvious, but in others not easy to design or employ. Separate measurement of response variance is not generally possible: instead the response variance inflates the estimated sampling variance.

6.3 *Sampling Errors*

These are, in principle, quantifiable where the sample is a probability sample. The standard error of a statistic is a measure of the discrepancy between the value estimated in the sample and the mean value that would be obtained from a very large number of such samples. Assuming unbiased sampling methods like the latter is equivalent to the "true" value in the population. The size of a standard error depends partly on the size of the sample but also on the sample design. Unfortunately, too few of the authors of statistical packages pay sufficient attention to the effect of sample design on the estimation of standard errors. In fact, most packages compute the standard error as though the design were simple random sampling from an infinite population. Since in practice many surveys are based on selection without replacement from finite populations and may make use of stratification and multistage sampling, these computed estimates of the standard errors will be biased.

Reference was made earlier to the variety of sampling schemes. Stratification was used to make the samples more representative of the population in the expectation that this would lead to greater precision in estimation. The change in precision is measured by the design effect, which is the ratio of the sampling variance produced by the complex sample design to that which would be produced by a simple random sample of the same size. An alternative form of the same definition is the ratio of the number of sampling units in the complex sample to the number required in a simple random sample to produce the same standard error. If the design effect is less than 1 there has been a gain in precision, and this is usually the effect of stratification. Multistage or cluster sampling on the other hand produces design effects greater than 1. The loss of precision has to be weighed against the financial and administrative savings effected by the complex design.

The point has already been made that this feature of cluster sampling arises from the fact that resemblances within clusters are greater than resemblances outside clusters. One measure of the within-cluster homogeneity is the intraclass correlation (*roh*) and there is an approximate relationship between design effect and *roh*. It is expressed in the equation

$$\text{design effect} = 1 + (m - 1)roh$$

where m is the average number of units in a cluster. The important point to note here is the influence of m. Even for low values of *roh*, say 0.1, small clusters of size 11 produce a design effect of 2, but clusters of size 51 produce a design effect of 6. It is therefore advisable to reduce as far as possible the size of clusters even if that involves increasing their number. For higher value of *roh*, where there is a high degree of within-cluster homogeneity, it is all the more important to select a large number of clusters. Gains in precision are, however, achieved at extra financial cost.

The formulas for the standard errors of simple statistics such as means and totals are known for complex designs but are more complicated than for simple random sample designs. The formulas for the standard errors of other statistics, for example regression coefficients, are problematic for data complex designs and in some cases are not known. One way round this difficulty is to make use of generalized but approximate estimators of the sampling variance which implicitly take into account the sample design employed and may be used for any statistic. In the simple replicated estimator the sample is divided into a number of subsamples (called replicates), each of equivalent design. The statistic of interest is then calculated for each replicate, and the variation in the value of the statistic across the replicates is used to estimate the standard error. A related technique called the Tukey–Quenouille jackknife procedure was used in the Australian Studies in School Performance (Bourke and Keeves 1977) and the IEA Six Subject Survey (Peaker 1975).

To sum up, methods of reducing errors in the findings of surveys range from the careful construction and pretesting of tests and questionnaires, through the selection of appropriate sampling designs, to the elimination as far as possible of response errors and coding errors and the use of the appropriate methods of estimating sampling errors.

7. Analysis and Interpretation of Survey Data

In this section reference is made to two (possibly related) debates about the analysis of survey data. The first concerns the relevance of survey design in the analysis—does design matter? The second concerns the search for causation—is causal inference possible in cross-sectional survey data?

Cross-sectional surveys are often thought of as descriptive in purpose, and in general the findings usually include point estimates of totals, means, and so on. Measures of association between two or more variables may also be computed. If these statistics have been derived from probability samples then the population values and the standard errors can be estimated from the sample data by employing the probabilities of selection alone. This school of inference is called the randomization or design-based school and is predominant among survey samplers. An alternative approach taken is to propose a probability model to represent the structure in the population, and to derive the random mechanism used in making the leap from sample to population from this probability model. A useful discussion of design-based versus model-based inference is contained in Smith (1976). The default option is to ignore the design and the structure in the population, and to assume implicitly that the data were drawn from an infinite population by simple random sampling: this can, for reasons stated earlier, result in misleading conclusions but is the approach adopted in most standard statistical packages and hence in much published work.

Attempts to establish causation on the basis of empirical data are fraught with problems. Many of these reside in the substantive field in question, but there are several of a methodological nature and some relate to cross-sectional surveys in particular. Consider the assessment of the effects of different teaching strategies on pupil performance. In a true experiment pupils would be assigned randomly to the different treatments. Generally, survey data consists of observations made in natural settings where no attempt has been made to exercise experimental control. It should then be recognized that the allocation of pupils to teaching strategies was not random but was the result of some unknown, and not simple random, mechanism and that this threat of selection bias undermines strict causal inference. Because X (the teaching strategy) and Y (reading achievement) are highly correlated it does not follow that X causes Y (or that Y causes X). A third (confounding) factor may be at work. Causal interpretation consists of the specification of the order of causation, derived from theory or from presumed time ordering, and the attempt to control statistically the influence of confounding factors. Such problems are the subject for other articles in this Handbook. Suffice it to say that in cross-sectional surveys measurements are taken at, or about, one particular time. Establishing the order of causation is not straightforward. To overcome this difficulty questions of a retrospective nature are sometimes asked in surveys, but these are subject to errors of recall, and these errors may themselves be associated with the other variables.

When interpreting survey data, the researchers should take care to state the population to which they wish to generalize, indicate the means by which they make the inference, and respect the reader by suggesting the threats to the inference and by providing the means by which these threats may be evaluated.

There is also much to be said for the judicious combination of experimental method with the cross-sectional survey. The strength of the experimental method lies in the testing and measurement of an effect; methods of sample selection used in cross-sectional surveys provide a basis for generalizing the results of the experiment beyond the sample.

8. The Usefulness of Cross-sectional Surveys, with Examples

The preceding sections may have given the impression that cross-sectional surveys are so hazardous and prone to errors of execution and interpretation that their use can hardly be justified. This is not the case and many successful and useful cross-sectional surveys have been carried out.

Consideration of the value and usefulness of surveys involves an appraisal of the purposes to be served by the survey and an assessment of the design and execution of the survey, that is, of the credibility of the survey's findings. The more important the purpose of the survey the higher the standard demanded of the survey design, and hence the higher the cost. The purposes to which the survey method has been put in the field of education are many and vary along several dimensions. A small-scale one-off exploratory survey, requiring little in the way of resources, may be sufficient to stimulate hypothesis generation. A large-scale continuous survey may be necessary to secure evidence in major policy decision making. There have also been large-scale one-off surveys of great importance in educational research, one of the most notable being that conducted in the United States under Section 402 of the 1964 Civil Rights Act, which provided the basis of a report (Coleman et al. 1966) to the President and to Congress on racial equality of educational opportunity. While the survey was of major policy importance, the analysis of this survey has contributed to academic argument on the effectiveness of schools.

Reference has already been made to the Australian Studies in School Performance, which covered all states and territories and schools of all types at both primary and secondary school levels. The sampling procedures incorporated stratification, cluster selection, and weighting, and the jackknife procedure was used to calculate the sampling errors of the estimates of performance. The results and details of the techniques are described in the three volumes published by the Australian Government Publishing Service in 1976 and 1977.

Reference has also been made to the Scottish Mental and Scholastic Surveys, reports on which have been published by the Scottish Council for Research in Education. The Scottish Education Department and the Centre for Educational Sociology in the University of Edinburgh have been successful in mounting a regular series of National School Leaver Surveys despite the lack of a sampling frame. Their postal questionnaires

have enjoyed a high response rate (86 percent) and through stratification have achieved design effects of 0.6.

The second volume of the Plowden Report (Central Advisory Council 1967) gives detailed information on a number of surveys carried out in England and Wales. These include the 1964 survey of parents of school children, surveys of standards in reading conducted between 1958 and 1964, and the first report of the National Child Development Study, 1958 cohort.

In the United States a programme for the National Assessment of Educational Progress has since 1969 covered science, writing (composition), mathematics, music, literature, social studies, art, reading, and career and occupational development. A series of reports has been published and a bimonthly newsletter is circulated from the office in Princeton, New Jersey. Most states also have their own assessment programmes which involve cross-sectional surveys.

The International Association for the Evaluation of Educational Achievement (IEA) has published a series of International Studies in Evaluation, describing cross-sectional surveys of science, reading comprehension, literature, civic education, and English and French as foreign languages.

A large number of surveys are also conducted by, or on behalf of, governments in order that statistical accounts of the education system are available.

9. A Concluding Remark

A distinction was made earlier between surveys that were descriptive in purpose and those that were analytical; both requiring inference to a predefined target population—the latter involving some degree of causal explanation. In practice, there should be no such clear dichotomy. Attempts to provide adequate descriptions necessarily require categorizations which invoke theoretical constructs and invite causal interpretation. However, these interpretations can never be of better quality than the data on which they are based. Considerations of theory and purpose should motivate attention to all aspects of data generation by survey method.

See also: Longitudinal Research Methods; Sampling; Sampling Errors; Interviews in Sample Surveys

Bibliography

Bourke S F, Keeves J P 1977 *Australian Studies in School Performance*, Vol. 3. Australian Government Publishing Service, Canberra

Central Advisory Council for Education (England) 1967 *Children and their Primary Schools*, Vol. 2: *Research and Surveys*. (Plowden Report.) Her Majesty's Stationery Office (HMSO), London

Coleman J S et al. 1966 *Equality of Educational Opportunity.* Office of Education, United States Department of Health, Education and Welfare, Washington, DC

Gray J M, McPherson A F, Raffe D (eds.) 1982 *Reconstructions of Secondary Education: Theory, Myth and Practice Since the War*. Routledge and Kegan Paul, London

Hoinville G, Jowell R, Airey C, Brook L, Courtenay G, Hedges B, Kalton G, Marton-Williams J, Walker D, Wood D 1978 *Survey Research Practice*. Heinemann, London

Husén T (ed.) 1967 *International Study of Achievement in Mathematics: A Comparison of Twelve Countries*. Almqvist and Wiksell, Stockholm

Kalton G 1983 *Introduction to Survey Sampling*. Sage, Beverly Hills, California

Kish L 1965 *Survey Sampling*. Wiley, New York

Moser C A, Kalton G 1971 *Survey Methods in Social Investigation*. Heinemann, London

National Assessment of Educational Progress (NAEP) *Newsletters*. NAEP, Princeton, New Jersey

O'Muircheartaigh C A, Payne C (eds.) 1977 *The Analysis of Survey Data*. Wiley, New York

Peaker G F 1975 *An Empirical Study of Education in Twenty-one Countries: A Technical Report*. Almqvist and Wiksell, Stockholm

Raffe D (ed.) 1984 *Fourteen to Eighteen: The Changing Pattern of Schooling in Scotland*. Aberdeen University Press, Aberdeen

Ross K N 1978 Sample design for educational survey research. *Eval. Educ.* 2(2): 105–95

Scottish Council for Research in Education 1949 *The Trend of Scottish Intelligence: A Comparison of the 1947 and 1932 Surveys of the Intelligence of Eleven-year-old Pupils*. University of London Press, London

Scottish Council for Research in Education 1968 *Rising Standards in Scottish Primary Schools 1953–63: Attainments of 10-year-olds in English and Arithmetic*. University of London Press, London

Smith T M F 1976 The foundations of survey sampling: A review. *J. Roy. Stat. Soc. (A)* 139: 183–204

Stuart A 1976 *Basic Ideas of Scientific Sampling*, 2nd edn. Griffin, London

Sudman S 1976 *Applied Sampling*. Academic Press, New York

Survey Research Methods

M. J. Rosier

Survey research in education involves the collection of information from members of a group of students, teachers, or other persons associated with the educational process, and the analysis of this information to illuminate important educational issues. Most surveys are based on samples of a specified target population—the group of persons in whom interest is expressed. The researcher often wishes to generalize the results obtained from the samples to the populations from which the samples were drawn.

The starting point for a survey is a clear statement of the questions which the survey is designed to answer. The finishing point is a set of results which address these questions. There is a logical set of procedures which is usually adopted in order to proceed from the questions to the results. In this article the procedures are linked together by reference to the survey research cycle, and the sections of the article follow the stages of the cycle.

1. Purposes of Surveys

The purposes of surveys fall into two main categories. First, surveys may be used to obtain descriptive information about a target population. Occasionally, the entire population may be included in the survey, as in a census of school enrolments. More commonly, a sample is selected, and results obtained from the sample are generalized to the population. Examples include surveys to provide norms for standardized tests, and surveys to measure levels of literacy and numeracy in a school, a region, or a country. Second, a survey may be designed to examine relationships between various factors, typically seeking to explain differences between students, on some criterion, in terms of a range of explanatory factors: for example, to explain differences in the mathematics achievement of students in terms of their age, sex, exposure to the mathematics curriculum, and amount of time spent in class on learning mathematics

(Rosier 1980). Underlying surveys of the second type are conceptual models which the researcher wishes to test, with the aim of improving understanding of the network of factors influencing educational processes.

Sometimes a researcher may wish to fulfil both purposes in a single survey: for example, in evaluating an innovative educational programme the researcher may wish to describe characteristics of students and teachers and levels of student achievement (the descriptive purpose), and also to examine the ways in which these characteristics are related to achievement (the explanatory purpose). Such a dual-purpose survey is valid, and may be less expensive than conducting two separate studies. However, the structure of the survey may be more complicated, especially in terms of sampling designs and analyses. An efficient sample used to provide descriptive characteristics of a population (population parameters) may not be as efficient for estimating the strength of the relationships in an explanatory model.

The aims of a particular survey project should be clearly identified before the design and execution of the survey are undertaken. The researcher responsible for the survey should be confident that these aims can be achieved, and should have a clear idea of how to do so. Many surveys are proposed or sponsored by persons responsible for the administration of education systems. In this case the researchers and the administrators may need to negotiate in order to reach agreement about the aims of the survey so that the intentions of the administrators may be met by the survey.

2. Survey Research Cycle

The methodology of survey research has now been well-established under the influence of three main factors. First, the technology of sampling has reached a high level. The theoretical aspects of probability sampling have been extensively investigated, and the relationships between random samples and the target populations from which they have been taken may now be readily expressed quantitatively in terms of sampling errors (standard errors of sampling). Second, many techniques have been developed for collecting valid and reliable information from survey respondents. Third, the availability of computers and sophisticated survey research computer programs (software) have facilitated the analysis of this information.

One helpful way to understand the range of components of a typical project is in terms of a survey research cycle; a detailed description of one version is given in Runkel and McGrath (1972). Thinking about survey research in terms of a cycle highlights the need to consider a given survey project as an entity. Each stage has implications for later stages. Both in its planning and execution, a survey may be conducted more efficiently by reference to the logical demands of the cycle, which are summarized in Fig. 1.

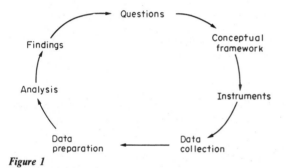

Figure 1
Survey research cycle

3. Questions

The starting point for a survey is, as was previously mentioned, the statement of the questions to be addressed by the investigation, set in the demographic, social, and administrative contexts in which the questions were identified. If the questions are pertinent to real problems, it should be possible to pose them in the language of ordinary people, rather than in statistical language. As the study proceeds through its cycle it becomes necessary to move into the language of statistics, but ultimately the study must return to ordinary language with its answers to the original questions.

4. Conceptual Framework

At the next stage of the cycle, the factors or components included in the original questions should be defined more precisely in conceptual terms. Where an explanatory survey is being undertaken, the hypothesized relationships between concepts should be expressed in terms of a conceptual framework, from which models to be tested can be derived. The conceptual framework should be based on an examination of previous research studies, usually involving a search of relevant research literature. Most researchers operate within an incremental

mode of scientific method, in which each study adds its increment of knowledge to what was previously known. Where the basic conceptual framework is complex it may also be desirable to proceed by forming a series of reduced frameworks. The incremental approach could operate here as well, by enabling a complex model to be examined in stages corresponding to the reduced frameworks or models.

One suggestion for clarifying this stage of a study, which also links back to the original questions, is to develop a set of propositions to be examined at the analysis stage. A proposition may be defined as a statement of expected results, to be confirmed or negated by the analyses.

5. Instruments

The general term instruments refers to the range of questionnaires, tests, attitude scales, and so on used for the collection of data in a survey. The instruments should be linked to the concepts included in the conceptual framework. They should be selected or designed for the collection of data suitable for conversion into variables for subsequent analysis. The numbers associated with a variable represent a quantification of the quality associated with the underlying concept. The subsequent statistical analyses do not involve the concepts themselves, but the quantitative representations of the concepts.

The researcher has the choice of using existing instruments or of developing new instruments to measure the concepts included in the conceptual framework. The advantage of existing instruments is that the work of development and validation has already been undertaken and published. On the other hand, the instruments may not adequately operationalize the concepts. More work is involved in creating new instruments, or in making modifications to existing instruments, but the researcher may then have greater confidence in the ability of the instruments to measure the concepts.

Instruments may be classified into four broad categories, concerned with the measurement of background characteristics, knowledge, attitudes, and behaviour. The term background characteristics refers to the range of personal, social, economic, and demographic characteristics that are typically used as explanatory factors in research on educational outcomes: for example, the sex of a student, the educational level of a parent, the age of a teacher, the enrolment of a school, or the population of a town. The collection of information on background characteristics is usually undertaken by means of a standardized set of questions, administered as an interview, or as a questionnaire completed by the respondents themselves.

In educational settings, knowledge is typically measured by tests requiring written answers, although other measures of performance are possible: for example, science concepts may be measured by means of practical laboratory exercises requiring manipulation of equipment. Attitudes and opinions are often measured by setting out a range of statements on a topic, and asking the respondents to indicate the extent to which they agree or disagree with the statements. Attitudes and knowledge both manifest themselves in behaviour. The measurement of behaviour usually requires direct observation, with the respondent's acts being coded according to a defined protocol. In this area, for example, many instruments have been developed for measuring the behaviour of teachers and students during their lessons.

Whether existing or new instruments are used, they should be adequately pretested on respondents similar to those who will be included in the survey sample. The pretesting provides the opportunity to check that the respondents understand the meaning of the questions or statements, to gauge whether test items are at an appropriate level of difficulty, to develop suitable code values for responses, and so on. It is highly desirable that the pretesting should be extended to follow the complete cycle, so that procedures for data collection, data preparation, and analyses can be refined prior to the commitment of resources to the main data collection programme.

6. Data Collection

The data collection stage of the research cycle involves identifying the survey respondents and collecting the desired information from them. In a survey information is collected from persons in their natural surroundings: for example, from students in their normal classes. To this extent surveys differ from experiments, in which the participants are assigned to specified treatment groups for the purposes of the research. However, it is possible to link studies involving other research methods to a survey. For example, information from a survey may be used to identify specified types of persons from the survey sample for use in a case study requiring detailed observation.

6.1 Target Population

Prior to preparing plans for selecting respondents, it is necessary to define the target population carefully, in order to set the administrative limits for the study as well as to specify the population to which the results of the study may be generalized. Where the student is to be the unit of sampling, a typical population may be initially defined as: "all 14-year-old students". The initial definition should then be progressively refined, usually by setting regional limits, and by excluding students who may not have the ability to participate satisfactorily in the testing programme. In addition it may often be necessary to exclude some students because the costs of collecting data from them may be disproportionately high. The final definition may then be: "all 14-year-old students in year 8, year 9, and year 10 in normal schools in region X, excluding those in special schools for handicapped children, those undertaking their education by correspondence, and those in schools where the total

enrolment is less than 10 students in year 8, year 9, and year 10".

6.2 Sampling Design

The selection of respondents from the target population is based on a sampling plan or design, except where information is to be collected from all members of the population. Most sampling plans assume random sampling, so that each member of the sample is selected with a known probability. It is then possible to use data derived from the sample itself to estimate statistical characteristics of the population (see *Sampling*). The sample and the population are linked by the sampling error (the standard error of sampling) which may be derived from the sample data. It is important to note that the sampling error depends primarily on the size and structure of the sample, not on the size of the population or the proportion of the population sampled. In order to decrease the sampling error by half, it may be necessary to increase the sample size by four times. There are always administrative and cost constraints on the size of the sample. The art of sampling lies in preparing a design to minimize the sampling error within these constraints.

6.3 Stratified Sampling

For most larger studies, the target population is divided into strata, such as regions and types of schools. This is often necessary because information about schools and students, which is needed for sampling purposes, is collected at the level of administrative units corresponding to these strata. There are no agreed rules about the number and type of strata to be established, although the strata would often be distinct administrative units. Strata may also be formed at more than one level: for example, the first level may involve regions and the second level may involve types of schools within regions (such as government-funded schools and private schools). The most efficient stratified sampling designs involve using the same sampling fraction for each stratum. This means that the total sample would be self-weighting, in the sense that it would not be necessary in the later analyses to apply weights to compensate for differences in the sampling fractions for the different strata.

6.4 Multistage Sampling

Many sampling designs in education involve two-stage sampling, where schools are selected at random at the first stage, and students are selected at random from these schools at the second stage. The calculation of sampling errors for these designs should take into account the intraclass correlation of the students in the clusters selected from the schools. This procedure may be extended to multistage sampling. For example, in a large country the initial stage of sampling may require the random selection of areas or regions, with the selection of schools at the second stage, and students at the third stage.

6.5 Administration

Development of the sampling designs inevitably involves other aspects of the administration of a survey. At an early stage the authorities responsible for the education system should be approached for their support for the survey, which may also require their permission to collect data from students or teachers. It may be necessary to approach several distinct administrative units for their support. The authorities should also be asked for census data about schools, teachers, or students, since these data are necessary for the preparation of the sampling plans for the selection of respondents, and for subsequent testing of the adequacy of the achieved sample.

6.6 Cooperation

Adequate resources should be devoted to obtaining the cooperation of the authorities who provide the support, and of the respondents who provide the data. Both the authorities and the respondents should be persuaded that the survey is relevant and important. Surveys depend initially on high response rates, in terms of the percentage of persons in the designed sample from whom data are actually obtained. Surveys also depend on the quality of the data, in the sense that the respondents cooperate well in responding to the instruments. For surveys in which data are collected from students in schools, the testing programmes or other data collection procedures should be designed to be interesting for the students, but also to minimize the disruption to the normal school programme. One way to enhance the collection of data is by holding meetings of the persons responsible for the school testing programmes, at which the aims of the survey are explained and the data collection procedures are described in detail. Schools would usually expect to receive feedback about the performance of their sample students on any achievement tests.

6.7 Confidentiality

An important aspect of the contact with respondents is the assurance that information provided would be used only for the stated purposes of the survey, with any published reports presenting findings in a manner that would prevent the identification of individual respondents. This is not the same as advocating that all information should be provided anonymously. Where the names of respondents are known, it is much easier to apply follow-up procedures to urge nonrespondents to reply. It is advisable to keep all lists of names and addresses of respondents separate from files containing data collected from the respondents.

6.8 Response Rates

The final task in the process of collecting data is to assess the adequacy of the procedure. In practice there are usually differences between the sampling plans as originally developed and the actual administration. Reports of a survey should contain a comparison of the designed and achieved numbers of respondents, from which response rates can be calculated. If the response rates differ across strata, the sample may deviate from an intended constant sampling fraction. The balance may be restored by weighting procedures based on the size of the target population and the size of the achieved sample for each stratum, although weighting procedures may not substitute for data lost due to low response rates.

6.9 Marker Variables

The adequacy of the achieved sample may also be examined by comparing known characteristics of the target population with corresponding characteristics of the sample. Such marker variables may include the percentage of male students, the mean enrolment of schools, the level of teacher qualifications, and so on.

No item of information should be collected in a survey without a clear idea of where it fits into the logic of the research cycle. Each item of information should have a specified place in the analyses that are linked to the original questions posed by the study. It is easy to spoil a survey by attempting to collect too much information, which may alienate the respondents and hence cast doubts on the validity and reliability of their responses. It may also delay the subsequent stages of the cycle, and of the presentation of the results.

7. Data Preparation

The data preparation stage of the cycle starts with the raw information as collected from the respondents, and concludes with the data carefully organized as computer files ready for analysis. This stage is concerned with checking and coding data, and building the data files. The respondents intended responses must be transferred as accurately as possible into a form in which they may be analyzed. This section outlines the basic components of data preparation. Further details may be found in Lansing and Morgan (1971), Moser and Kalton (1971), or Sonquist and Dunkelberg (1977).

7.1 Coding

Most of the data collected in educational survey research is in the form of the respondent's own written responses to the survey instruments. Often the items in the instruments are precoded, so that the respondent selects one of the options presented, as in multiple-choice items for achievement tests. No matter what methods are used for collecting data, the responses must be transferred to a computer file. This is usually accomplished by punching coded responses on to punch cards that can be read by a computer, or by marking sheets or cards that can be read by optical scanning methods.

Prior to the reading process, the responses are coded (if necessary) and checked. For many surveys the items have precoded responses, so that the respondents select the desired option. The precoded responses should be refined at the earlier stage of instrument development, which must also anticipate how the coded values are to be used in the analyses. Where the respondents have given open responses postcoding will be needed. Codes will be supplied as part of the data preparation process. Typical examples are where students are asked to give the answer to a mathematics problem without being prompted by a set of possible responses, or where students are asked to write down the occupations of their fathers, an item of information for which it is very difficult to supply precoded categories.

7.2 Editing and Verifying

Once the coding of responses has been completed, it is advisable to include an editing stage where anomalies and omissions may be detected. It may be possible to return to the respondents for the resolution of anomalies, or for the completion of omitted items. More commonly, the researcher develops a set of rules to resolve these problems at the coding stage. Where responses are transferred to punched cards, it is also important to develop procedures to verify the accuracy of the transfer. At one extreme this may involve an independent punching of all responses with a comparison of the two versions in order to resolve any conflicts. More commonly, a sample of the completed instruments is selected for independent verification.

7.3 Codebook

In association with the reading of data into the computer, a codebook is prepared which specifies the location of each item of the data on the computer file, together with a description of characteristics of each variable: the name of the variable, the valid code values, the code values for missing data, and so on.

7.4 Checking

Once the initial data file has been established, two further checking procedures are available. Checking for wild codes may readily be carried out by the computer to detect cases which have codes values outside the valid range. It is then necessary to return to the original responses to find the valid value, after which the file should be corrected. It is also desirable to include checks of logical consistency: for example, to ensure that educational qualifications are consistent with stated occupations. Small computer programs can readily be prepared to identify logical inconsistencies, which should also be resolved by reference to the original responses.

7.5 Variable Construction

The final stage in building a computer file is to construct new variables from the raw data. For achievement test data this may involve the development of test scores according to defined rules. For attitude scales this may result in scale scores, often based on factor analysis. For questionnaires, a typical generated variable would be an index of socioeconomic level. The variable generation procedures should be carefully documented, preferably including details in the codebook.

7.6 Data Archives

There is increasing recognition that carefully documented data files, especially from larger surveys, should be lodged in data archives. National centres for data archives exist in most countries, and there are also international networks. The lodging of data files with a data archives system facilitates the use of the data by other researchers for secondary analysis.

The strength of the survey analysis depends largely on the quality of the data. A vital contribution to this quality is made by the careful coding and checking of the data which constitute the data file to be used for analysis.

8. Analysis

Analysis can commence once the data file has been adequately prepared. In terms of the logic of the survey cycle, the earlier stages of the cycle should anticipate the analysis stage. The construction of instruments and the coding of responses should anticipate the manipulation of numerical data. The sampling design should also ensure that there are sufficient cases or respondents for the planned analysis.

The plans for a study will include a description of the analysis to be undertaken. The range of analytic methodologies is too wide to be considered here, although a few general comments may be offered. Analysis may be classified in terms of the number of variables involved. Univariate analysis deals with the variables individually. Bivariate analysis involves pairs of variables. Multivariate analysis is concerned with the simultaneous effects of more than two variables.

8.1 Univariate Analysis

All surveys should prepare a set of basic univariates for all variables. For data recorded at the categorical level, the univariates would display the number of cases for each code value for each variable. For continuous data, such as test scores, the corresponding basic univariates would be the mean and standard deviation for each variable. Means may also be calculated for categorical data at the ordinal level of measurement where quantitative meanings have been assigned to the numbers representing code values. For example, consider the following question with its associated coded responses:

Do you like mathematics?
   3 Mathematics is my favourite subject.
   2 I have a moderate liking for mathematics.
   1 I do not like mathematics at all.

If the code values (or other numbers) are considered to represent the amount of liking for mathematics, a mean value for liking mathematics may be calculated. It may not have much meaning in absolute terms, but may be useful for examining relative differences between students in terms of their attitude to mathematics.

The univariates enable the researcher to gain an initial view of the data for each variable. This should be done before submitting the data to further analysis, since weaknesses in given variables may distort the results of more complex analysis. Weaknesses include highly skewed variables, and variables with large amounts of missing data.

8.2 Bivariate Analysis

The main bivariate statistics are cross-tabulations and correlation coefficients. With modern computers it is tempting to generate large numbers of cross-tabulations, often involving several nested levels. Classification of data by using cross-tabulations may assist the researcher to gain a good overview of the data, but the method is rather inefficient for establishing relationships. Most situations in education are complex, involving many interrelated variables. It is not efficient to analyse or present results by carrying out a large number of cross-tabulations of pairs of variables.

Matrices of correlation coefficients are very useful for summarizing bivariate relationships. In particular, they provide an initial opportunity to assess which explanatory variables are strongly associated with each other and with criterion variables. From the correlation matrix it is easy to identify variables that are weakly linked to a criterion, since there is little value in including these variables in explanatory analyses. The correlation matrices may also provide the starting point for multivariate analyses, such as multiple linear regression analysis or factor analysis (see *Correlational Procedures*).

8.3 Multivariate Analysis

Many multivariate analysis techniques are available. One of the most common is multiple regression analysis, which is used to estimate the relative strengths of several explanatory variables acting simultaneously on a criterion. Underlying the regression analysis should be a theoretical model of the relationships between the explanatory variables and the criterion. Care is needed in the selection of variables to include in a regression analysis. Particular attention should be paid to the criterion variable, which should have high reliability and validity. The criterion usually involves continuous level data, although a dichotomous criterion may be used if problems associated with its use are adequately dealt with (Rosier 1978 p. 58–59). The explanatory variables should be linearly related to the criterion, and any interaction effects should be identified and controlled. Explanatory variables should only be included if they have sufficiently strong zero-order correlation coefficients with the criterion.

The number of explanatory variables to be included in an analysis depends largely on the number of cases, since this determines the reliability of the estimated regression weights in terms of the standard errors of the regression coefficients. Kerlinger and Pedhazur (1973 p. 442) suggest at least 100 cases, and preferably more than 200 cases, for an analysis involving a small number of variables with low intercorrelations. This is not usually a problem where students are the units of analysis,

but may be a serious problem where classrooms or schools are used as the units of analysis (see *Units of Analysis*). One way to test the effect of adding an extra variable to a regression analysis is to measure its marginal contribution. If the analysis were run twice: first, excluding the extra variable and second, including it, the marginal contribution of the extra variable would be the additional amount of variance explained on the second occasion. The researcher must then make a judgment about the value or usefulness of including the extra variable in the analysis (see *Regression Analysis*).

Other variations of multiple regression analysis have been developed. Multiple classification analysis (MCA) is designed to handle categorical level explanatory variables with a continuous level criterion (Andrews et al. 1973). Path analysis techniques have been designed to estimate the relative strengths of the direct and indirect paths linking explanatory variables in a causal sequence to each other and to the criterion (Duncan 1975) (see *Path Analysis*; *Structural Equation Models*). Path analysis is particularly useful for testing causal models. Interaction effects between variables, which could invalidate a regression analysis, may be identified by means of the automatic interaction detector (AID) program, as described by Sonquist et al. (1973). This technique may also be used for sorting a sample into subgroups that are more homogeneous with respect to the criterion, and is more efficient than cross-tabulation procedures for classification purposes (see *Detection of Interaction*; *Interaction Effects*).

In some larger surveys, the researcher may carry out analyses separately for each stratum or group of strata, particularly where these strata or groups represent independent administrative units. In effect, each separate analysis is itself a replication of the survey. Strong generalizations may be made where patterns of relationships are similar across the replicated analyses.

Where analyses are conducted on the total sample, rather than separately by strata, it is often useful to include the strata themselves as explanatory variables. This follows logically if the strata were established as distinct administrative units, and may therefore have differential effects on the criteria under examination.

The ultimate purpose of the analysis stage is to produce sets of statistics which summarize the data: frequencies, proportions, percentages, means, standard deviations, correlation coefficients, regression coefficients, and so on. These should relate back to the original conceptual frameworks or models. The statistics serve to confirm or negate the models and the associated propositions. It is important that reports of the survey should contain sufficient information, in the body of the report or in appendices, to enable interested readers to make their independent judgments about the reliability of the data that were collected, the appropriateness of the analysis that was undertaken, and the statistical conclusions that were drawn.

9. Findings

The last stage of the survey research cycle involves the presentation of the findings, which should link back to the original questions. The analysis concludes with a set of statistics, expressed in statistical language. The findings should then be prepared by taking these statistics and providing an interpretation of them in ordinary language. This should be the language of the original questions and concepts: for example, factors rather than variables, relationships rather than correlations, variability rather than variance. This final stage should also include a discussion of the strength of the findings, and of the extent to which they may be generalized. Distinctions should be made between findings that are strong and those that are tentative, and between findings of high generality and those that are limited in scope.

The underlying theme of this article is that the conduct of survey research should follow a logical process, interpreted here as a cycle. Each stage of the cycle has implications for later stages. Thinking in terms of a cycle encourages the researcher to anticipate the later stages, and hence improve the efficiency of the study. To follow the cycle is not to guarantee the success of a survey, but it may provide confidence that the study can be accomplished satisfactorily by following a path that many others have taken. No single study can ever identify all the important questions or find all the helpful answers. So the cycle continues at another level. Findings from one survey lead to questions for others.

See also: Survey Studies, Cross-sectional; Longitudinal Research Methods

Bibliography

Andrews F M, Morgan J N, Sonquist J A, Klem L 1973 *Multiple Classification Analysis: A Report on a Computer Program for Multiple Regression Using Categorical Predictors*, 2nd edn. University of Michigan, Ann Arbor, Michigan
Duncan O D 1975 *Introduction to Structural Equation Models.* Academic Press, New York
Kerlinger F N, Pedhazur E J 1973 *Multiple Regression in Behavioural Research.* Holt, Rinehart and Winston, New York
Lansing J B, Morgan J N 1971 *Economic Survey Methods.* University of Michigan, Ann Arbor, Michigan
Moser C A, Kalton G 1971 *Survey Methods in Social Investigation*, 2nd edn. Heinemann, London
Rosier M J 1978 *Early School Leavers in Australia: Family, School and Personal Determinants of the Decision of 16-year-old Australians to Remain at School or to Leave.* Almqvist and Wiksell, Stockholm
Rosier M J 1980 *Changes in Secondary School Mathematics in Australia 1964–1978.* Australian Council for Educational Research, Hawthorn, Victoria
Runkel P J, McGrath J E 1972 *Research on Human Behavior: A Systematic Guide to Method.* Holt, Rinehart and Winston, New York
Sonquist J A, Dunkelberg W C 1977 *Survey and Opinion Research: Procedures for Processing and Analysis.* Prentice-Hall, Englewood Cliffs, New Jersey
Sonquist J A, Baker E L, Morgan J N 1973 *Searching for Structure: An Approach to Analysis of Substantial Bodies of Micro-data and Documentation for a Computer Program*, rev. edn. University of Michigan, Ann Arbor, Michigan

Longitudinal Research Methods

J. P. Keeves

Longitudinal research studies, that is, investigations conducted over time, are of growing importance in the social and the behavioural sciences and, in particular, in the field of education. In the past investigations conducted over time have been relatively rare, although some important studies have been undertaken. In Sweden, the Malmö study conducted by Husén and his colleagues has been in progress for nearly 60 years. Data were initially collected in 1928 and many reports from this study have been published (Husén 1969, Fägerlind 1975). In the United Kingdom, two major series of studies have been conducted. The first investigation was started shortly after the Second World War, when all children born in one week in March 1946 formed the sample and detailed medical records as well as information on their educational development were collected (Douglas 1964). The second investigation is the ongoing National Child Development Study which was started 12 years later with a sample of all children born in the United Kingdom during the first week of March 1958 (Davie et al. 1972, Fogelman 1983, Butler and Golding 1986). In the United States, there have been at least eight major longitudinal studies that have investigated well-defined samples of children and that have sought to obtain a large variety of measurements on different characteristics of human development: these particular studies have been reviewed by Bloom (1964) in a study titled *Stability and Change in Human Characteristics*.

In all these studies, which have collected data at many points in time, significant problems have inevitably been encountered in maintaining contact or tracing the members of the chosen samples. As a consequence these investigations are sometimes referred to as "tracer studies". This name emphasizes the strategies that are employed for preventing bias which would distort the findings of an investigation as a consequence of substantial losses over time from the sample. In recent years there has been an increased interest in the problems associated with the design of longitudinal research studies and the strategies used in the analysis of the data collected, as well as with the sources of bias that could invalidate the findings. This work has led to significant advances in the methodology associated with such investigations, particularly in the areas of design and analysis. Educational research is concerned with the processes of change, and the study of change requires that observations are made for at least two points in time. While it is possible to describe the practice of education by means of a cross-sectional study undertaken at a single point in time, it is necessary to conduct investigations which are longitudinal in nature in order both to describe and explain the influence of educative processes on the constancy and change of related events. Thus the methods of longitudinal research are central to the empirical study of education, whether there is concern for individuals, classrooms, schools, social subgroups, or educational systems. Although there are substantial problems associated with the investigation of change (see, for example, Cronbach and Furby 1970), the importance to education cannot be denied of providing a detailed description of patterns of stability and change and a coherent explanation of how and why change has occurred or failed to occur. This article is concerned with the methods of longitudinal research and addresses the problems associated with the investigation of both stability and change. It is important to recognize that, while longitudinal methods are frequently contrasted with cross-sectional methods, a detailed comparison between the two methods is largely inappropriate because constancy and change can only be examined through repeated observation which is the key characteristic of the longitudinal method.

1. Explaining Stability and Change

Three major systems of influence can be identified in the field of education which affect stability and change in human development (see Baltes and Nesselroade 1979). Using these systems an explanation or causal analysis of human development can be attempted. While educational research is commonly concerned with the investigation of educational processes at the classroom, school, social subgroup or systemic levels, it is necessary to recognise that the investigation of stability and change in human development must be carried out at the individual level at which the three systems of influence operate. The three sets of influences on human development have their origins in: (a) biological factors, (b) environmental factors, and (c) planned learning experiences or interventions. These three sets of influences interact with each other in significant ways. In particular, since each individual has the opportunity to choose, at least to some degree, whether or not a response will be made to both environmental and intervention influences, and given that such choices may in part be biologically determined, the nature and extent of interactions between the three sets of influences are highly complex. The nature of these three types of influence warrants further consideration.

(a) *Biological influences.* These refer to those determinants that show a strong correlation with chronological age both across historical periods and across a wide range of individuals from different social groups. Development under these influences is ontogenetic and age graded. Normative age-related developments should be seen as largely biological in origin.

(b) *Environmental influences.* These refer to nonbiologically based determinants of development that have a pervading effect on those individuals experiencing a particular environment. Bloom (1964) has considered the meaning of the term "environment" and has suggested that it refers to:

> ...the conditions, forces and external stimuli which impinge on the individual. These may be physical, social, as well as intellectual forces and conditions. We conceive of a range of environments from the most immediate social interactions to the more remote cultural and institutional forces. We regard the environment as providing a network of forces and factors which surround, engulf and play on the individual. (Bloom 1964 p. 187)

The environment as conceived by Bloom is the total stimulus situation, both latent and actual, that interacts, or is capable of interacting, with the individual. Thus while individuals will experience common environments, significant variations will occur as individuals interact with their environments. As a consequence invariant sequences of development will not occur. Development under environmental influences will be largely nonnormative, although common patterns will occur in so far as a common environment is experienced.

(c) *Intervention influences.* These include those planned learning experiences provided by a wide range of educational institutions that are deliberately designed and form the educative process. They differ in kind from the pervasive influences of the environment, in so far as they are designed for a particular stage of development and are directed towards highly specific outcomes. The effects of planned learning experiences are assessed in terms of the achievement of particular outcomes rather than in terms of normative and nonnormative development. Whereas biological and environmental influences may result in either stability or change in specific characteristics, intervention influences, if successfully administered, lead to change. Constancy in characteristics involves lack of success in the administration of the intervention.

The interaction between these three types of influence gives rise to analytical problems when attempts are made to identify the effects of particular influences over time. The administration of an intervention under experimental conditions, in which subjects have been randomly assigned to treatment groups and control groups, provides the most appropriate methodology for the investigation of the effects of an intervention, in so far as the cause of change can be identified. However, in many situations within which educational research is conducted, either it is not physically possible to undertake random allocation to treatment or control groups, or alternatively, randomization and the application of the intervention so affects the educational process that significant distortion from the natural setting occurs. In addition, it must be recognized that even where random assignment to treatment and control groups takes place, prior experiences, as well as genetic and environmental influences, can so interact with the administration of the intervention that the nature of the intervention might be changed significantly by these prior and concurrent influences. Some interactions of this type are amenable to analysis where the models being examined can be derived from theoretical considerations (Campbell and Stanley 1963). However, other interactions, more particularly those between biological and environmental influences would not at this time appear to be always amenable to rigorous analysis.

A specific problem which arises involves the confounding of biological age-graded effects and environmental non-age-graded effects as a result of a changing environment across the different time periods or age levels at which biological influences are being investigated. Moreover, in so far as some environmental influences may be age related, a similar confounding can arise between different classes of environmental effects. Attempts to unravel such interactions have given rise to specific designs in the conduct of longitudinal investigations. It will be evident from the above comments that while investigation at different points of time is the key characteristic of longitudinal research, from which it gains its strength, the use of different time points gives rise to certain problems in the conduct of longitudinal studies and the subsequent analysis of the data collected.

2. The Status of Time in Longitudinal Research

Baltes and Nesselroade (1979 p. 2) have stated that "the study of phenomena in their time-related constancy and change is the aim of longitudinal methodology". Furthermore, where repeated observations are made of individuals or groups in order to describe or explain both stability and change, time acts not only as the logical link between the repeated observations, but also as a variable that is a characteristic of the individuals or groups.

Thus the use of time in longitudinal research studies takes place in two distinct ways. First, time is used as a subject characteristic. Second, time is used as a design characteristic (von Eye 1985). Examples of the first usage occur when chronological age is employed as the basis for the selection of an individual or a group for study, or when the members of an age cohort are studied at successive intervals during their life span. In addition, in retrospective studies events that occurred at particular times in the life of an individual are not only readily identified, but also have special significance. A major limitation on the use of time in this way is that it is not a manipulable variable and subjects cannot be randomly assigned to different time values. The second use of time is as a design characteristic, which occurs in learning studies, when the extent of learning is measured after successive time periods. Fortunately, in this use of time in a longitudinal study, time is an alterable variable

and the effects of time are amenable to analysis. The strength of time in longitudinal studies as a design characteristic arises from the role played by time in the underlying substantive theory. Increasingly, there is recognition that the effects of environmental and intervention influences are time related, in so far as exposure to the environment or to the intervention has significant consequences for the magnitudes of measurable outcomes. Nevertheless, length of exposure is only one of many factors: for example, the intensity of exposure, or the nature and intensity of opposing forces can influence educational outcomes. Thus the effects of time are commonly concealed by the effects of these alternative forces.

Time is not only a continuous variable, but equal time intervals are also readily determined. In addition, in many situations a starting point at which time is zero can be identified. Thus it is possible to collect data in the form of a time series and to examine the constancy or change in particular characteristics with respect to time as recorded on an interval scale. Moreover, because time is a continuous variable, which is measured on an interval scale, it is commonly possible to investigate time samples of behaviour in order to study and compare practices which occur under different conditions. In the investigation of classroom behaviour extensive use is made of time samples in order to compare the practices of different teachers, or the effects of different teaching and learning conditions on student behaviours.

Perhaps the most significant characteristic of time lies in its relationship to causal influence, since earlier events influence later events but not vice-versa. Thus while it cannot be assumed that measurements made on a variable obtained at an initial point in time can be causally related to an outcome measure obtained at a later time, it is clear that unless the appropriate time sequence exists it is not possible to argue logically for a possible causal relationship. The *possibility* of investigating causal relationships between variables measured at different points in time is the important contribution that longitudinal research methods have made to the exploration of causal explanations based on theory and the testing of path models and structural equation models, and this has led to the increased emphasis on longitudinal research in education during the 1970s.

3. Types of Longitudinal Research

Inferences concerning the nature and extent of change over time and the factors influencing change are, in general, obtained from five design strategies (Kessler and Greenberg 1981 pp. 2–3): simultaneous cross-sectional studies, trend studies, time series studies, intervention studies, and panel studies.

3.1 Simultaneous Cross-sectional Studies

Within this strategy, two or more related cross-sectional studies are conducted at the same point in time with different age groups being sampled by each cross-sectional study. The same predictor and criterion variables

Table 1
Simultaneous cross-sectional data matrix[a]

Age group	Sample	Time point	Observed variables
A_1	S_1	T_1	$V_1, V_2, V_3 \cdots\cdots\cdots V_e$
A_2	S_2	T_1	$V_1, V_2, V_3 \cdots\cdots\cdots V_e$
..	..	..	..
..	..	..	..
..	..	..	..
A_m	S_m	T_1	$V_1, V_2, V_3 \cdots\cdots\cdots V_e$

a Source: von Eye 1985 p. 3141

are observed for each age sample. Moreover, the age samples are each drawn from the same larger population. However, each sample is drawn independently of the other. Table 1 describes the data matrix for the simultaneous cross-sectional design where there are m groups of subjects (= m age samples) which are observed with respect to e variables, (see von Eye 1985 p. 3141). The longitudinal dimension in the design of studies of this type is achieved by consideration of the different chronological ages associated with the independent samples. This design has been employed in the studies carried out by the International Association for the Evaluation of Educational Achievement (IEA). However, only two of the many reports issued by IEA have made significant use of the longitudinal element in this design (Comber and Keeves 1973, Carroll 1975). Because in these studies three age groups, the 10-year-old, the 14-year-old, and the terminal secondary-school levels, were tested, it was not possible to employ identical tests at each age level. However, overlapping tests were administered and standardization procedures were employed to bring the achievement outcomes to a common scale. This design has also been employed in the Australian Studies in School Performance (Keeves et al. 1978) and in the National Assessment of Educational Progress in the United States (Tyler 1985). In these two studies comparisons across age levels, which involved the longitudinal component of the design, employed in the main individual items or small clusters of items that were common to the different age groups tested. The scaling and measurement issues associated with such comparison will be considered in Sect. 5. As von Eye (1985) has pointed out, this design is both simple and economical to execute and, since only one point in time is involved, the confounding effects of environmental influences are reduced and the effects of intervention influences such as retention differences across countries (Comber and Keeves 1973) and years spent in foreign language learning (Carroll 1975) are more clearly evident. Nevertheless, there are some specific deficiencies in this type of design which arise from the fact that only one time point is employed (von Eye 1985 p. 3141). The conclusions which can be derived from this design are only valid under the following assumptions: (a) the age samples have been drawn from the same common population; and (b) the factors influencing change in the criterion variables and their effects have remained constant across the time span during which the different age samples have been exposed to those factors.

3.2 Trend Studies

Within this strategy, two or more related cross-sectional studies are conducted with identical age groups at points of time that are sequential. Similar sampling procedures are employed at each time, so that sound comparisons can be drawn over time, and identical or related measures are employed on each occasion. Perhaps the strongest and most widely discussed set of trend data has been associated with the scores on the Verbal and Quantitative Scholastic Achievement Tests in the United States (Donlon 1984). To obtain these sets of data common test items were employed across occasions, so that the data could be accurately chained from one occasion to the next. Widespread debate has taken place in attempts to explain the highly significant decline in Scholastic Aptitude Test (SAT) scores and the more recent rise that has occurred. However, while many competing explanations have been advanced, none has gained clear support over the others.

In Table 2 the data matrix associated with trend studies is presented. It illustrates that at successive points in time new samples are drawn. In addition, the age group under survey remains constant and the same variables are observed, so that constancy and change in characteristics of interest in the changing populations can be examined. Further examples of research studies which have investigated trends in educational achievement are those carried out by the Assessment of Performance Unit (APU) in England and Wales (Black et al. 1984), the Australian Studies in Student Performance (ASSP) in Australia (Bourke et al. 1981), and the National Assessment of Educational Progress (NAEP) in the United States (Tyler 1985). Two sets of problems arise in such studies. First, there are the problems of the meaningfulness and validity of achievement test items in circumstances where the curriculum of the schools is changing and new curricular emphases are evolving. These problems can be allowed for in part by the removal of obsolete test items and their replacement with new and more appropriate items. Nevertheless, uncertainties remain as to whether the reduced number of test items that are common across occasions are equally valid for successive samples of students over time, in order to provide a trend that could be used to guide future curriculum planning and educational practice. A second set of problems is concerned with the statistical procedures

Table 2
Trend data matrix

Age group	Sample	Time point	Observed variables
A_1	S_1	T_1	$V_1, V_2, V_3 \cdots\cdots\cdots V_e$
A_1	S_2	T_2	$V_1, V_2, V_3 \cdots\cdots\cdots V_e$
..	..	..	..
..	..	..	..
..	..	..	..
A_1	S_m	T_m	$V_1, V_2, V_3 \cdots\cdots\cdots V_e$

that are employed to scale a constantly changing sample of test items to obtain a reliable measure of educational achievement. While latent trait scaling techniques have been developed in recent years (Morgan 1982, Spearritt 1982, Donlon 1984), which could be employed for this purpose, the issue remains as to whether with a changing curriculum a single latent trait can be considered to exist that covers an area of the school curriculum and that remains unchanged across time.

The major shortcoming of the trend studies referred to above has been that they were not designed initially in such a way as to permit any trends which might have been detected to be explained through the use of biological, environmental, or intervention variables. A study which has been conducted by the International Association for the Evaluation in Educational Achievement in ten countries in the curriculum field of science in 1970 and 1984 provides a major attempt to examine the possibility of undertaking a trend study in which change in educational achievement across time might be accounted for by changing educational influences.

3.3 Time Series Studies

This type of longitudinal study has its origins in developmental psychology over a hundred years ago. A very large number of such studies have been reported from many parts of the world. Bloom (1964) undertook an integrative work to examine stability and change in human characteristics which sought to draw from the major studies which had been reported in the United States the patterns of growth associated with physical and intellectual characteristics. These longitudinal studies assume that human development is a continuous process which can be meaningfully examined by a series of "snapshots" recorded at appropriate points in time. They do not necessarily involve equal time intervals between successive observational points. Development can be examined in a valid way through the use of the continuous time scale which has strong metric properties. In Table 3 the research data matrix for such longitudinal studies has been recorded, from which it will be seen that the same sample is followed at successive time points with corresponding increases in the age of the group under survey. Information is collected on a wide range of variables relevant to the aspects of human development being investigated.

Von Eye (1985) has drawn attention to five advantages which this type of design has over the simultaneous cross-sectional design and the trend design referred

to above. First, it is possible to identify intra-individual constancy or change directly, thereby reducing the confounding that arises from changing environmental circumstances, since repeated observations are made of the same subjects. Von Eye (1985 p. 3142) states that evidence supporting this advantage has been found repeatedly in the differences in the growth curves obtained from time series longitudinal designs compared with those obtained from simultaneous cross-sectional designs. Second, by observing more than one individual or one group of individuals, differences between individuals or groups in the intra-individual sequences of development become clear. This enables homogeneity or variability in development to be examined between individuals or groups. Third, since each group of individuals possesses characteristics that are used to identify individuals as members of the group, the time series design permits the constancy or change in the dimensions characterizing membership of a class to be examined through the investigation of relationships associated with such characteristics both within classes as well as between classes. The two further advantages of the time series design involve the identification of time related influences on development. Since this design does not include the examination of the effects of time-specific interventions on development, only those influences that occur naturally over time are involved. The fourth advantage is associated with the study of linkages between such influences and intra-individual or intra-group constancy or change in particular characteristics. Finally, the fifth advantage is concerned with the investigation of relationships between time-based influences on interindividual and intergroup constancy or change in specific characteristics.

The conduct of time series studies is expensive since it is commonly very costly to maintain contact with a significant number of sample members over an extended period of time, and sample losses can give rise to substantial distortions of observed relationships. A further problem is that a limited sequence of observations, either through starting with an age group at some time after birth, or through premature limitation of the observation sequence might mean that critical information is not available to reveal either a coherent pattern of development or to identify the effects of factors that influence development.

The costs associated with the conduct of prospective time series studies have led many research workers to employ a retrospective time series design in which a sample is selected and the members of the sample are invited to recall events in their lives at particular times or when they were at specific ages. Retrospective studies suffer from two major shortcomings. First, the sample selected is necessarily biased, because only those who have survived are available for interrogation, and the losses through death, migration, and residential mobility might distort in significant ways the relationships that are derived from the data. Secondly, the recall by subjects of events that took place at earlier stages in their lives can also be distorted either deliberately or

Table 3
Time series data matrix

Age group	Sample	Time point	Observed variables
A_1	S_1	T_1	$V_1, V_2, V_3 \cdots\cdots\cdots V_e$
A_2	S_1	T_2	$V_1, V_2, V_3 \cdots\cdots\cdots V_e$
..	..	..	..
..	..	..	..
..	..	..	..
A_m	S_1	T_m	$V_1, V_2, V_3 \cdots\cdots\cdots V_e$

unintentionally, because in changing circumstances individuals prefer to present a favourable view of their past lives.

The report of the study of the development of talent in young people reported by Bloom (1985) presents striking findings of how 120 young men and women who reached the highest levels of accomplishment in their chosen fields as Olympic swimmers, world-class tennis players, concert pianists, sculptors, research mathematicians, and research neurologists, were influenced by their homes and educative processes. This study made use of the retrospective time series design, but inevitably was unable to include those who aspired towards such goals, but did not achieve them.

3.4 Intervention Studies

Intervention studies involve a variation of the time series design, but differ with respect to the insertion of a planned learning experience or intervention at a selected time or across a period of time in the lives of individuals. Such intervention designs may involve the selection of probability samples, the random allocation of subjects or groups to treatments, the administration of experimental and control treatments, the monitoring of treatment conditions, and the use of immediate and delayed posttests. In Table 4 the data matrix for a simple intervention design has been presented. There are of course a large number of variations on the basic design shown in Table 4 that might have been employed and Kratochwill (1978 pp. 34-35) presents the range of design variations for single-subject and multiple-subject time series investigations.

In the design in Table 4 the samples associated with both the experimental and control groups remain constant throughout the investigation. Initial data on sets of predictor and criterion variables are obtained at time T_1 when all subjects are at age A_1. Between times T_1 and T_2 the treatment conditions are administered to the experimental group and no treatment is given to the control group. At time T_2, when subjects are at age A_2, immediate posttests are given to both the experimental and the control groups and again at time T_m delayed posttests are given to both the experimental and the control groups. Many studies have employed the intervention design in the field of educational research. Important studies to use this design have been the Ypsilanti Perry Pre-School Project conducted by the High/Scope Educational Research Foundation and reported by Weikart and his colleagues (Schweinhart and

Weikart 1980, Weikart 1984) to evaluate Head Start Programs in the United States; the Sustaining Effects Study concerned with the evaluation of Title I Programs for educational disadvantage in the United States (Carter 1984); and the Mount Druitt Study supported by the Bernard Van Leer Foundation, a study which involved the evaluation of early childhood intervention programs in disadvantaged schools in Sydney, Australia (Braithwaite 1983). There are many problems associated with the analysis of data from such studies, since few major investigations of this type are able to allocate subjects randomly to experimental and control groups, or to constrain the administration of the intervention or treatment, so that characteristics of the experimental group do not influence the nature of the treatment applied. Thus biological and environmental influences can interact with intervention influences to such a degree in intervention studies that the assumptions associated with analysis of variance or analysis of covariance techniques are not sustained, and these procedures cannot always be safely used in the analysis of the data collected through intervention designs. Greater use has been made during recent years of structural equation models to tease out the complex interrelationships which exist within the bodies of data collected in such studies. In spite of these analytical problems, it must be recognized that through the administration of a treatment to an experimental group and the withholding of a treatment from a control group, it is possible to make stronger inferences about the influence of factors associated with such intervention designs than could be achieved from studies in natural settings.

3.5 Panel Studies

In trend studies relationships associated with time of measurement are examined while the age of the group under investigation is held constant. In simultaneous cross-sectional studies, the time of measurement is held constant and the age of the group being surveyed is allowed to vary, while in the time series design a single cohort is selected and the time of measurement and the age of the cohort are allowed to covary together. All three designs have their shortcomings, in so far as effects associated with time of measurement, age of group being investigated, and the cohort chosen cannot be completely separated from each other. This has led to the development of panel studies in which an attempt is made to unravel the effects of factors associated with age, time of measurement, or cohort.

Table 4
Intervention data matrix

Age	Experimental group	Control group	Sample	Time point	Observed variables
A_1	E_1	C_1	S_1	T_1	$V_1, V_2, V_3 \cdots\cdots V_e$
	Treatment	No Treatment			
A_2	E_1	C_1	S_1	T_2	$V_1, V_2, V_3 \cdots\cdots V_e$
A_m	E_1	C_1	S_1	T_m	$V_1, V_2, V_3 \cdots\cdots V_e$

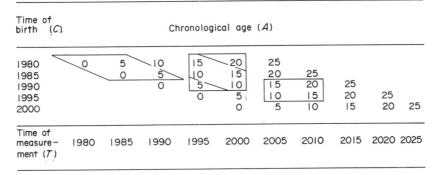

Figure 1
Panel design showing ages of five-year cohorts measured at five-year intervals [a]

a Source: adapted from Schaie (1965 p. 23)

Schaie (1965) has advanced a general model for the study of longitudinal bodies of data that combines the three aspects of time, namely, cohort (C), time of measurement (T) and age (A). In this model, a measure obtained on variable V is a function of cohort, time of measurement and age, that is, $V = f(C, T, A)$. This function includes the interactions between the three aspects of time, $C \times T$, $T \times A$, $C \times A$, and $C \times T \times A$. In Fig. 1, the design of a panel study in which the ages of five-year cohorts which are measured at five-year intervals has been presented. The entries recorded in each column correspond to the simultaneous cross-sectional design. The entries in the constant age diagonals correspond to the trend design, and entries in each row correspond to the time series design. In time-sequential analyses, chronological age (A) and time of measurement (T) are combined. In such studies at least three cohorts have to be measured in one investigation (see rectangular boxed data points for years of measurement of 1995 and 2000). In this way complete data are obtained for two time points, 1995 and 2000, and two age levels, 10 years and 15 years, so that an $A \times T$ interaction can be tested. However, the cohort factor (C) is confounded with age and time of measurement. A similar problem arises in a cohort-sequential analysis in which chronological age and cohort are considered as independent factors. In this case three separate time points are required for the collection of data (see diamond boxed data points for years of measurement 1980, 1985, and 1990). Here the 1980 and 1985 cohorts are being investigated at ages of 0 years and 5 years, and the $A \times C$ interaction can be tested, but it follows that time of measurement is confounded. In a similar way the cross-sectional analysis permits the study of the $C \times T$ interaction, but three age levels have to be investigated (see square box for the 1990 and 1995 cohorts, which are surveyed in years 2005 and 2010). Here the age factor is confounded with cohort and time of measurement.

Schaie (1965) considered that age factors were primarily concerned with biological influences associated with ontogenetic development, and that cohort factors involved environmental influences which operated prior to the first time point of an investigation. The time factors were considered to involve environmental effects which were common to all subjects being studied. The interaction effects arose from interactions between environmental factors and genetic factors. However, if the assumption of a common population was violated then cohort factors could include genetic differences between cohorts together with the more commonly accepted environmental differences.

Baltes et al. (1979) have proposed a modified version of Schaie's General Developmental Model which is presented in Fig. 2. The figure shows the birth cohorts at five-year intervals from 1980 to 2010 for ages 0 to 30 years and at times of measurement from 1980 to 2040. The simple designs, namely, the simultaneous cross-sectional, conducted in year 2010, the trend, for age 30 years, and the time series for the 2010 cohort are shown in Fig. 2a. A second strategy is presented in Fig. 2b, where simultaneous cross-sectional sequences, trend sequences and time series sequences are shown. Each involves a replication of a basic design illustrated in Fig. 2a. The simultaneous cross-sectional sequence involves the collection of replicated information on each age group, while the time series sequences involve the examination of two cohorts.

Whereas the basic designs were considered to be primarily descriptive in nature, the sequence designs were seen by Schaie (1965) also to permit explanation. The distinction between description and explanation is recognized as an important one. Nevertheless, it is clearly not possible to test all three factors, cohort, age, and time of measurement in the one analysis. Nor is it possible to examine the three way interaction, however extensive the data collection might be. The explanatory analysis of data would seem to involve rather more than the investigation of the three factors and their two-way interactions. The construction of structural equation models from theory and the testing of the models using data that permits the examination of cohort related influences, age-related influences, and time of measurement would appear to be necessary. Where the same cohort is involved in the collection of data at different

Age in years

Cohort	0	5	10	15	20	25	30
							SC
1980	1980	1985	1990	1995	2000	2005	2010
1985	1985	1990	1995	2000	2005	2010	2015
1990	1990	1995	2000	2005	2010	2015	2020
1995	1995	2000	2005	2010	2015	2020	2025
2000	2000	2005	2010	2015	2020	2025	2030
2005	2005	2010	2015	2020	2025	2030	2035
2010	TS 2010	2015	2020	2025	2030	2035	2040
							TR

(a)

Age in years

Cohort	0	5	10	15	20	25	30
						SCS	
1980	1980	1985	1990	1995	2000	2005	2010
1985	1985	1990	1995	2000	2005	2010	2015
1990	1990	1995	2000	2005	2010	2015	2020
1995	1995	2000	2005	2010	2015	2020	2025
2000	2000	2005	2010	2015	2020	2025	2030
2005	2005	2010	2015	2020	2025	2030	2035
2010	TSS 2010	2015	2020	2025	2030	2035	2040
							TRS

(b)

Figure 2[ab]
(a) A modified version of Schaie's General Developmental Model illustrating simultaneous cross-sectional (SC, diagonal band), trend (TR, upright rectangle) and time series (TS, horizontal band) designs
(b) Simultaneous cross-sectional sequences (SCS), trend sequences (TRS) and time series sequences (TSS) design strategies

a Based on Baltes et al. 1979 p. 64   b Cell entries refer to dates of measurement

time points, the different time points can be incorporated into the model. However, the explanation of trends and relationships exhibited across simultaneous cross-sectional studies would appear to demand new analytical strategies. As increasingly large bodies of data become available, for example in the Sustaining Effects Study (Carter 1984), the reduction with age in the magnitude of such influences as the effects of school factors on achievement in a simultaneous cross-sectional study clearly warrants more thorough investigation.

In the field of education, relatively few panel studies have been undertaken over time periods that are long enough for age and cohort effects to be distinguished. The Plowden Follow-up Study (Peaker 1971, Marjoribanks 1975) was an important study that involved three grade groups which were investigated on two occasions. Moreover, Peaker (1971) was the first educational research worker to use path analysis as a technique for the examination of longitudinal data using causal models. Subsequently, Marjoribanks (1975) undertook a further examination of the same body of data using more elaborate path models. Another study

of interest has been the Australian Studies of School Performance (Keeves et al. 1978) in which two parallel groups of students aged 10 and 14 years were initially tested in 1975, and were traced and followed from 1978 to 1984 with detailed information obtained on their career expectations and their transition from education into the workforce (Williams et al. 1980, 1981). Matching cohorts are available from a repeated testing program which was conducted in 1980 and the samples are being followed.

4. Validity Issues in Longitudinal Studies

The complex nature of longitudinal studies makes them particularly vulnerable to uncontrolled factors that can threaten their experimental validity. Like other empirical investigations longitudinal studies can yield meaningful results only in so far as the measurements recorded and the data analysed are both valid and reliable, and the samples employed are both randomly generated and remain representative of the populations from which they were derived. Without the maintenance of these essential conditions sound generalizations cannot be made beyond the particular groups under investigation. While the pattern of results associated with both the descriptive and explanatory analyses of data from nonrepresentative samples could appear informative, unless these findings were generalizable beyond the situation in which the data were generated, the effort involved in collecting and analysing the data would be largely wasted. Kratochwill (1978) has identified two classes of validity, internal and external validity, and has listed the different types of threat that are likely to occur in longitudinal studies and which arise from these two sources. Internal validity is concerned with the degree of certainty with which measurements associated with the predictor or explanatory variables are capable of accounting for the observed constancy and change in the criterion variables. It will be evident that high levels of reliability and validity of the predictor variables are necessary preconditions for the interpretation and explanation of time-related observations. External validity refers to the manner and extent to which the findings from the analyses carried out could be generalized to different situations beyond those in which the specific body of data was collected. Kratochwill (1978 p. 11) notes that the quest for both high internal and external validities can operate against each other. The requirement to obtain a high level of internal validity can demand the exercising of tight experimental controls on the collection of data which might so distort the natural setting in which development occurs that the external validity of the investigation was threatened. Fortunately the development and testing of causal models derived from theory and the exercising of statistical controls that are consistent with the structure of these models have greatly reduced the demand for rigid experimental designs, so that random allocation to experimental and control groups and the administration of treatment conditions according to rigid specifications is no longer considered to be as important as it was in former decades.

4.1 Threats to Internal Validity

In longitudinal studies where time plays a key role, consideration must be given at the design stage to the temporal order in which data are gathered on predictor variables with respect to the criterion measures. There are, however, other less obvious threats to internal validity which arise from the conduct of an investigation over an extended period of time.

(a) *History*. Events that are unrelated to a predictor variable but that take place at the same time may be undetected, but may give rise to change in the criterion variable. Alternatively events which have occurred at an earlier time may have influenced both the predictor variable and at a later time the criterion variable. Such threats to validity are reduced if some control is exerted both over the manipulation of the predictor variable through planned intervention, and over the time at which the intervention is administered with respect to

other factors believed or known to influence development.

(b) *Maturation*. Changes within subjects of a physical or psychological nature due to maturation may occur over time and may also influence performance on the criterion variables. Such changes may remain undetected and thus may confound findings that could be ascribed to other causes. As with historical influences these threats to validity are reduced by an effective design and by attention being given to the collection of appropriate data.

(c) *Practice effects in testing*. If similar or identical tests are employed at successive points in time in the collection of data in longitudinal studies, the performance of subjects may increase due to practice effects. These effects may influence the performance of some subjects to a greater extent than others, and thus a confounding occurs in the data collected on the criterion measures.

(d) *Reliability of instruments*. Some measurements of developmental changes such as those associated with physical growth, can be obtained with a high degree of reliability, while other measurements, such as those associated with attitudes and values, commonly have a substantially lower level of reliability. In longitudinal studies, where not only a range of instruments but also many observers must be used at different points in time, it is desirable to ensure that both standardization of instruments and thorough training of observers take place not only to reduce random error but also systematic error or bias in the measurements made over time.

(e) *Multiple intervention interference*. Any investigation intrudes to some extent on the lives of individuals and longitudinal studies are particularly vulnerable in this regard. It is possible that individuals are affected differentially either positively or negatively by investigation, especially where intervention has occurred. In addition, delayed effects produced on some criterion measures may be falsely ascribed to a later treatment when the effect was caused by an earlier treatment.

(f) *Instability in the subject being measured*. In studies of teaching behaviour, errors of measurement not only arise from the unreliability of observation, but also as a consequence of instability in the behaviour of both teachers and students. Certain aspects of teacher behaviour are time related, being dependent on the time of day, the day of the week, or the month of the school year. Under these circumstances what might be either natural variation or systematic variation in behaviour, might be viewed as a consequence of intervention and in turn as mediating between the intervention and the criterion measures of student performance.

(g) *Changes in the composition of samples*. One of the major problems in the conduct of a longitudinal study is the loss from samples over time. It is highly likely that such losses could introduce substantial bias, since those subjects who are lost from a study are commonly the more mobile, frequently of high or low rather than average socioeconomic status, or involve those who are less highly motivated to take part in such a study. While it is commonly possible in a longitudinal study to present information on the characteristics of subjects who have been lost from the study, and it is sometimes possible to weight the data used in the analyses to correct in part for such bias, in general, such losses have an unknown confounding influence on the findings.

(h) *Reactive interventions.* In longitudinal studies it is not uncommon for the research worker to become aware of events in the lives of individuals that cannot be ignored or left without some action. Under such circumstances, although prejudicial to the results of an investigation, the research worker is frequently required to intervene and thus confound or contaminate all subsequent measurements made on predictor and criterion variables.

(i) *The use of natural groups.* It is rarely possible in longitudinal studies in educational research to randomly assign subjects to experimental and control groups, and it is commonly necessary to employ natural groups in an investigation. These natural groups may differ from the outset with respect to the predictor variables used in the study, and in addition the groups might react differently in ways that would influence the nature of the treatments administered to them. Both the initial differences between the natural groups and the consequent variations introduced in the treatments administered to them may confound the results of a study.

Some types of longitudinal study are more vulnerable to these threats to internal validity than are others. While the simultaneous cross-sectional design suffers from severe limitations in the nature of the information that can be derived from it, this design has the advantage that it does not involve the conduct of a study over an extended period, and is not subjected to the threats to internal validity that clearly exist for more complex designs.

4.2 Threats to External Validity

Educational research is a field of investigatory activity that is evolving over time as new tactics and strategies for research are developed and as new procedures for the analysis of data are introduced. Even though a well-designed and controlled investigation might have been planned, there is the risk that during the conduct of the study, the procedures employed will be challenged in the light of new knowledge and new understandings. Alternatively, new analytical procedures might become available that could have been employed if a different design had been used or if different information had been collected. As a consequence the conduct of a longitudinal study and the analysis of the data collected that were beyond challenge at the time of its conception might be seriously threatened at the time of its completion. Pedhazur's (1982) questioning of the validity of the data analyses for the IEA Six Subject Study involved a challenge of this kind.

(a) *Population validity.* Educational policies and practice are subject to constant change, both as new knowledge becomes available and as responses occur to political pressures. Longitudinal studies require time to

conduct, to analyse the data collected, and to report the findings. As a consequence both of the inevitable time-lag and the politicization of the field of education, it has been argued that when the findings of major longitudinal studies in the field of education were released, the characteristics of the population and the circumstances under which the studies were conducted had changed to such an extent that the findings were no longer valid or relevant. The Sustaining Effects Study in the United States (Carter 1984) suffered this fate. Nevertheless, it must be recognized that while superficial changes are commonly experienced in education, there is a natural conservatism of the teaching profession and in the community that enables the findings of research to maintain their validity for longer periods than are generally acknowledged. Furthermore, the findings from studies conducted in many different parts of the world support the view that there is some universality across populations, across countries, and across time. It is nevertheless necessary to establish the ecological validity of research conducted at different times and in different settings so that the relevance beyond a particular setting and at a particular time is accepted. There are many threats to ecological validity; the discussion which follows is derived from that presented by Kratochwill (1978) and is based on the work of Bracht and Glass (1968).

(b) *Explicit statement of treatment conditions.* The validity of research findings and their applicability to other situations depend on a detailed knowledge of the treatment conditions. This requires that a complete and specific description of the predictor variables and the treatment conditions under which the longitudinal investigation was carried out are provided, so that readers and reviewers of the research findings are able to assess the extent to which the findings can be generalized to other situations. The widely used techniques of meta-analysis assist in the combining of the results from similar studies to obtain more general findings.

(c) *Multiple intervention interference.* In the discussion above of threats to internal validity it was pointed out that multiple interventions might confound the findings obtained from a particular longitudinal study. Likewise multiple interventions might be expected to increase the difficulty with which results from such studies might be compared with the findings from investigations where only a single intervention was administered. Similar problems arise in the extent to which the findings from multiple intervention studies might be generalized to other settings.

(d) *Hawthorne effect.* When subjects are aware that they are taking part in a long-term investigation, it would seem that their behaviour, particularly in the longer term aspects, might be significantly affected. Such behaviour might be influenced in ways that are either favourable or unfavourable to the investigation. Moreover, different subjects might respond in different ways.

(e) *Use of appropriate criterion variables.* In longitudinal studies where biological, environmental, and intervention influences are being investigated, there is a risk that a particular criterion variable will be employed that is not sensitive to the different influences that are present. Consequently, it is common in longitudinal studies to employ a battery of criterion variables in the expectation that the range of outcomes which arise from the different influences will be covered. Thus, in general, longitudinal studies are multivariate in nature, and analytical procedures have to be employed in the examination of the data that will take into consideration the many criterion measures on which information has been obtained. Nevertheless, it must be recognized that longitudinal studies, by their nature, must be thoroughly planned in advance and thus lack flexibility to handle unexpected outcomes.

(f) *The effects of critical events on individuals.* Not only is development influenced by biological, environmental, and intervention factors, but critical events in the lives of individual subjects, such as a road accident, or a breakup of the family, may have significant effects on a subject's development. In longitudinal studies conducted over a period of time, the probability of the occurrence of a critical event is significantly greater than in other types of studies, and such events which occur naturally in the lives of substantial numbers of people, serve to distort the data collected. Furthermore, since they are unique, although relatively common events, they are difficult to allow for in the analysis of data and could confound the findings derived from a study.

(g) *The effects of historical events on groups.* In a similar manner, events of an historical nature can affect in significant ways the development of groups. Political unrest and natural disasters can occur during the conduct of a longitudinal study under such circumstances as to confound the effects of an intervention or to affect differentially certain subgroups involved in the investigation and thus distort the overall validity of the study and prevent its findings being generalized to other settings.

(h) *The effects of publication.* Longitudinal studies must maintain support from funding agencies, and this requires them to publish interim reports of their findings. The effects of publication are commonly to make the subjects of an investigation more conscious of their involvement and more aware of the nature of the study. Publication of results can prove damaging to a study if the findings are controversial and attract widespread publicity. Not only is it possible that the subjects of the investigation might distort the information that they provide on occasions subsequent to the release of findings, but some subjects might withdraw from further participation in the investigation. Some longitudinal studies have sought to use the publicity gained in the media to maintain the involvement of the subjects in the study. However, this approach carries with it the significant risk of reducing the validity of the information collected.

Perhaps the greatest threat to the validity of longitudinal studies in educational research, is the magnitude of the task of conducting such a study. In order to sustain an investigation over many years, immense commitments in the form of highly skilled personnel and financial resources are required. Changes in the personnel involved in the conduct of a longitudinal study can be prejudicial to the administration and the rigour with which the investigation is carried out. This poses a major threat to the validity of a study. Likewise the high costs of longitudinal research can result in fluctuations in the financial support provided over time, with the consequent need to change in significant ways both the nature of a study and its conduct in order to contain costs. This can damage substantially the validity of the findings of longitudinal research studies.

5. Analysis of Longitudinal Research Data

The analysis of the data collected in a longitudinal research study has two primary aims: descriptive analysis and explanatory analysis. However, before any analyses can be undertaken attention must be given to the problems of measuring attributes on appropriate scales.

5.1 Measurement of Change

The particular problem encountered in educational research studies that employ a longitudinal design is that it is commonly inappropriate to use the same instrument across different age groups and at different points in time. The procedures employed for equating the measurements obtained using two different instruments by bringing the scores to a common scale require either that (a) the two instruments are administered to a common sample, or (b) the two instruments contain common components or common items when administered to different samples. Three procedures are employed to bring these scores to a common scale.

(a) *Linear scaling.* In this procedure it is assumed that both the test items and the persons tested represent appropriate samples in the measurement of an underlying trait that is normally distributed with respect to both test items and persons. The scores are standardized, commonly to a mean of zero and a standard deviation of one, and the line of equivalence is used to equate one set of scores with the other. Figure 3(a) illustrates the use of this procedure (see Thorndike 1971 p. 569).

(b) *Equipercentile scaling.* In this procedure it is similarly assumed that both the test items and the persons tested represent appropriate samples for the measurement of an underlying trait. In using this procedure cumulative frequency distributions are calculated, the scores obtained at equal percentile points for each test, and a line of equivalence is plotted (see Thorndike 1971 p. 571). Figure 3(b) illustrates the use of this procedure which has the advantage over the linear scaling procedure that no assumptions need be made with respect to the shape of the distributions.

(c) *Latent trait measurement.* It is also possible to employ models based on the assumption of an unobservable, but underlying latent trait which exhibits a relationship with age, for example, as represented by a

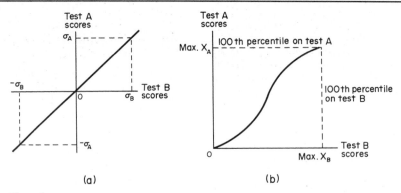

Figure 3
(a) Line of equivalence for linear scaling
(b) Line of equivalence for equipercentile scaling

logistic function. One-parameter, two-parameter (Birnbaum 1968) and three-parameter (Lord 1980) models have been developed. The one-parameter model relates to either item difficulty or person ability. The two-parameter model allows for variability in item discrimination and the three-parameter model also allows for guessing in multiple-choice items where several alternative responses are provided. Goldstein and Blinkhorn (1977) have questioned the use of latent trait procedures in the development of a common scale of measurement over time particularly in educational research, because of the problems of finding sensible interpretations of any results from such models for other than narrowly defined psychological attributes. Linear scaling was used by Comber and Keeves (1973) in the development of an international scale for achievement in science across 10-year old, 14-year old and terminal secondary-school age groups. A variation of the equipercentile scaling technique was used in the scaling of Scholastic Aptitude Test (SAT) scores over time in the United States (Donlon 1984) and latent trait measurement procedures using a modified three-parameter model have been employed in the scaling of scores in the National Assessment of Educational Progress (NAEP) in the United States (Beaton 1987, Bock et al. 1982). However, Sontag (1983) has provided evidence to support the use of the one-parameter model in the scaling of achievement test scores.

5.2 Univariate Models of Change

Statistical time series models have been used to describe a great variety of patterns of change in which measurements have been related to age or to another time scale. Goldstein (1979) has listed procedures for the fitting of growth curves to individual records. The most widely used model assumes that relative rate of change in size decreases proportionately to increases in size. Thus where size is very small the relative growth rate is high, but the actual growth rate is low because of small size. However, as size increases the growth rate increases, and when size approaches the final size, the relative and actual growth rates slow down.

The equation for rate of growth is expressed in the following form:

$$\frac{k}{y}\frac{dy}{dt} = b(k - y) \qquad (1)$$

where b is a constant, and k is the final size (a constant).

The equation for the growth curve is given by the logistic function:

$$y = c + \frac{k}{1 + e^{a - bt}} \qquad (2)$$

where a is a constant, and $y = c$ is the value of the lower asymptote and $y = c + k$ is the value of the upper asymptote.

The curves for rate of growth and growth are shown in Fig. 4(a) and 4(b) respectively.

An alternative model for the measurement of growth is provided by the Gompertz curve in which the relative rate of change in size decreases exponentially with time, and thus in equally small intervals of time there are equal proportional decreases in relative growth rate.

The equation for rate of growth is expressed in the following form:

$$\frac{1}{y}\frac{dy}{dt} = b\ e^{a - bt} \qquad (3)$$

where a and b are constants, and the equation for growth is given by:

$$y = k\ \exp[-\exp(a - bt)] \qquad (4)$$

Although research workers in the fields of child and adolescent development have considered the use of other types of curves, the logistic and the Gompertz curves have found most extensive use, including the combining of curves across different age ranges. Burt (1937) found, for example, that the growth in the height of girls from birth to 18 years could be represented by the sum of three logistic curves.

More powerful mathematical models are likely to become useful in the analysis of data in educational research as the accuracy of measurement increases and

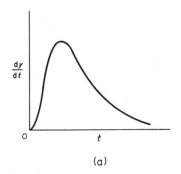
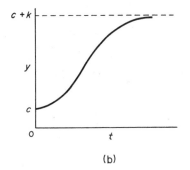

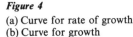

Figure 4
(a) Curve for rate of growth
(b) Curve for growth

thus the quality of the data included in the analysis increases. Overviews of the mathematical models and statistical procedures which might be used to describe change in longitudinal research studies have been provided by Goldstein (1979), Nesselroade and Baltes (1979), and Coleman (1981).

5.3 Multivariate Models of Change

In longitudinal research, the costs of carrying out the processes of data collection and maintaining contact with the sample under survey are so great that, in general, there is little to be gained by collecting data on only one criterion measure. As a consequence data are commonly available on a wide range of characteristics rather than on an isolated variable. Under these circumstances multivariate procedures of analysis are widely used in longitudinal research studies. This has also led to the use of techniques in an exploratory way to condense the large bodies of data and to examine for change more simplified data structures. Techniques that are widely used include exploratory factor analysis, multidimensional scaling, cluster analysis, and configural frequency analysis. Variation in the factor patterns or cluster patterns over time are taken to indicate change and development, while stability in factor and cluster patterns over time would seem to imply the measurement of a dimension that is unaffected by environment or biological influences.

5.4 Explanatory and Causal Analysis

In empirical research in education two strategies are available for the investigation of causal relationships, and in general, both involve the use of longitudinal designs. First, in experimental studies in which subjects are randomly selected from a population and are randomly assigned to experimental and control groups multivariate analysis of variance techniques are appropriate. Such studies which do not demand the collection of data at two points in time are rare in the investigation of educational processes. Secondly, in intervention studies where some degree of randomization in the allocation of subjects to treatments has been achieved, it may be possible to use multivariate analysis of covariance

techniques in the examination of data. However, it is necessary to establish that antecedent conditions are unrelated both logically and empirically to the application of the intervention before covariance procedures can be used. Moreover, since time and time-related factors cannot be manipulated under experimental conditions and applied as interventions or treatments, in studies where more than one time-related variable is being investigated, analysis of variance and covariance techniques cannot be employed because such effects remain confounded.

A variety of techniques are, however, available for the examination of data to provide explanation in terms of causal relationships. These techniques make full use of the time relationships which are present in longitudinal designs. The analytical procedures which are employed require the development of causal models from prior research studies and established theory, and the testing of these models for fit using the available data. Among the procedures now available which are capable of analysing complex bodies of scaled data are Linear Structural Relations Analysis (LISREL) and Partial Least Squares Path Analysis (PLS). For the examination of less complex bodies of qualitative and categorical data log-linear modelling and configural frequency analysis techniques are gaining acceptance. The use of these explanatory analytical procedures requires that the longitudinal study should be designed with a clearly stated theoretical formulation from which causal hypotheses and causal models involving structural relationships between variables are developed for testing. These hypotheses and models are tested and accepted as plausible explanations of the available evidence or are rejected. The incorporation of accepted models into substantive theory that is coherent and is useful for further exploration is seen as the outcome of enquiry. Longitudinal research has an important role to play in this regard within the field of educational research.

Bibliography

Baltes P B, Nesselroade J R 1979 History and rationale of longitudinal research. In: Nesselroade and Baltes 1979, pp. 1–39

Baltes P B, Cornelius S M, Nesselroade J R 1979 Cohort effects in developmental psychology. In: Nesselroade and Baltes 1979

Beaton A E 1987 Implementing the New Design: The NAEP 1983–84 Technical Report. National Assessment of Educational Progress/Educational Testing Service, Princeton, New Jersey

Birnbaum A 1968 Some latent trait models and their use in inferring an examinee's ability. In: Lord F M, Novick M R (eds.) 1968 *Statistical Theory in Mental Test Scores*. Addison-Wesley, Reading, Massachusetts

Black P, Harlen W, Orgee A 1984 *Standards of Performance—Expectation and Reality*, Assessment of Performance Unit (APU), Occasional Paper 3. Department of Education and Science, London

Bloom B S 1964 *Stability and Change in Human Characteristics*. Wiley, New York

Bloom B S (ed.) 1985 *Developing Talent in Young People*. Ballantine, New York

Bock R D, Mislevy R, Woodson C 1982 The next stage in educational assessment. *Educ. Res.* AERA 11(3): 4–11

Bourke S F, Mills J M, Stanyon J, Holzer F 1981 *Performance in Literacy and Numeracy: 1980*. Australian Government Publishing Service for the Australian Education Council, Canberra

Bracht G H, Glass G V 1968 The external validity of experiments. *Am. Educ. Res. J.* 5: 437–74

Braithwaite J 1983 *Explorations in Early Childhood Education*. Australian Council for Educational Research, Hawthorn, Victoria

Burt C B 1937 *The Backward Child*. University of London Press, London

Butler N R, Golding J (eds.) 1986 *From Birth to Five: A Study of the Health and Behaviour of Britain's Five Year Olds*. Pergamon, Oxford

Campbell D T, Stanley J C 1963 Experimental and quasi-experimental designs for research on teaching. In: Gage N L (ed.) 1963 *Handbook of Research on Teaching*. Rand McNally, Chicago, Illinois

Carroll J B 1975 *The Teaching of French as a Foreign Language in Eight Countries*. Wiley, New York

Carter L F 1984 The sustaining effects study of compensatory and elementary education. *Educ. Res.* 13(7): 4–13

Coleman J S 1981 *Longitudinal Data Analysis*. Basic Books, New York

Comber L C, Keeves J P 1973 *Science Education in Nineteen Countries: An Empirical Study*. Wiley, New York

Cronbach L J, Furby L 1970 How we should measure 'change': Or should we? *Psychol. Bull.* 74(1): 68–80

Davie R, Butler N, Goldstein H 1972 *From Birth to Seven: A Report of the National Child Development Study*. Longmans, London

Donlon T F 1984 *The College Board Technical Handbook for the Scholastic Aptitude Test and Achievement Tests*. College Entrance Examination Board, New York

Douglas J W B 1964 *The Home and the School*. MacGibbon and Kee, London

Fägerland I 1975 *Formal Education and Adult Earnings: A Longitudinal Study on the Economic Benefits of Education*. Almqvist and Wiksell, Stockholm

Fogelman K (ed.) 1983 *Growing Up in Great Britain: Collected Papers from the National Child Development Study*. Macmillan, London

Goldstein H 1979 *The Design and Analysis of Longitudinal Studies. Their Role in the Measurement of Change*. Academic Press, New York

Goldstein H, Blinkhorn S 1977 Monitoring educational standards: An inappropriate model. *Bull. Br. Psychol. Soc.* 30: 309–11

Husén T 1969 *Talent, Opportunity and Career*. Almqvist and Wiksell, Stockholm

Keeves J P, Matthews J K, Bourke S F 1978 *Educating for Literacy and Numeracy*. Australian Council for Educational Research, Hawthorn, Victoria

Kessler R C, Greenberg D F 1981 *Linear Panel Analysis: Models of Quantitative Change*. Academic Press, New York

Kratochwill T R (ed.) 1978 *Single Subject Research. Strategies for Evaluating Change*. Academic Press, New York

Lord F M 1980 *Applications of Item Response Theory to Practical Testing Problems*. Erlbaum, Hillsdale, New Jersey

Marjoribanks K 1975 Cognitive performance: A model for analysis. *Aust. J. Educ.* 19(2): 156–66

Morgan G 1982 The use of the Rasch latent trait measurement model in the equating of Scholastic Aptitude Tests. In: Spearritt D (ed.) *The Improvement of Measurement in Education and Psychology*. Australian Council for Educational Research, Hawthorn, Victoria

Nesselroade J R, Baltes P B 1979 *Longitudinal Research in the Study of Behavior and Development*. Academic Press, New York

Peaker G F 1971 *The Plowden Children Four Years Later*. National Foundation for Educational Research, Slough

Pedhazur E J 1982 *Multiple Regression in Behavioral Research. Explanation and Prediction*, 2nd edn. Holt, Rinehart and Winston, New York

Schaie K W 1965 A general model for the study of developmental problems. *Psychol. Bull.* 64: 92–107

Schweinhart L J, Weikart D P 1980 *Young Children Grow Up: The Effects of the Perry Preschool Program on Youths through Age Fourteen*. High Scope Press, Ypsilanti, Michigan

Sontag L M 1983 Vertical equating methods: A comparative study of their efficacy. Ph.D. thesis, Teachers College, Columbia University, New York

Spearritt D (ed.) 1982 *The Improvement of Measurement in Education and Psychology*. Australian Council for Educational Research, Hawthorn, Victoria

Thorndike R L (ed.) 1971 *Educational Measurement*, 2nd edn. American Council on Education, Washington, DC

Tyler R W 1985 National Assessment of Educational Progress (NAEP). In: Husén T, Postlethwaite T N (eds.) 1985 *The International Encyclopedia of Education*. Pergamon, Oxford, Vol. 6, pp. 3478–80

von Eye A 1985 Longitudinal research methods. In: Husén T, Postlethwaite T N (eds.) 1985 *The International Encyclopedia of Education*. Pergamon, Oxford, Vol. 5, pp. 3140–52

Weikart D P (ed.) 1984 *Changed Lives: The Effects of the Perry Preschool Program on Youths through Age Nineteen*. High Scope Press, Ypsilanti, Michigan

Williams T R, Clancy J, Batten M, Girling-Butcher S 1980 *School Work and Career: 17 Year Olds in Australia*. Australian Council for Educational Research, Hawthorn, Victoria

Williams T R, Batten M, Girling-Butcher S, Clancy J 1981 *School and Work in Prospect: 14 Year Olds in Australia*. Australian Council for Educational Research, Hawthorn, Victoria

Tracer Studies

E. Schiefelbein and J. P. Farrell

Although there are several variants, which will be discussed below, in general the term "tracer study" refers to investigations in which a sample of individuals are studied at a given time, and then located and studied again at one or more successive stages in their lives. The essential feature of such studies is that characteristics of the same subjects (and often changes in those characteristics) are observed at two or more points in time. Although such longitudinal studies of the same set of individuals have been occasionally carried out in the past (though only in developed nations until very recently), there has occurred during the last few years a marked increase in the number of such studies either reported or underway. This article is concerned with those tracer studies which deal explicitly with education, tracing individuals through the educational system, and/or tracing their transition from studenthood to adulthood—almost always focusing upon entrance to and degree of success within the labour market.

1. Recent Interest

The increased popularity of such studies may be attributed to the confluence of several factors. Educational research has long been plagued by the "value added" problem. It is recognized that education is a long-term and cumulative process (a) which begins only after children have already acquired a number of essential characteristics (genetic inheritance, prenatal influences, family background characteristics as translated into child-rearing practices, etc.), which have a continuing and long-term effect upon a child's destiny; (b) during which the effect of any particular educational intervention (new policy, change in teaching style, additional didactic materials, structural change, etc.) is constrained by the effects of previous schooling experience; and (c) wherein the effects of many alterations in policy or procedure are expected to be observable only after many years. This essentially dynamic nature of the educational process cannot be captured well, if at all, by cross-sectional studies and is dealt with only imperfectly by most experimental pretest posttest studies of the effects of particular educational treatments because of their limited time frames and small samples. It has become increasingly apparent that only long-term tracer studies can effectively deal with this problem.

At the same time it has become more and more obvious during recent years that the enormous investments in education since the 1960s, particularly in developing nations, have not been producing the types of skilled personnel or productivity increases that had been expected. Rather in many cases rising unemployment levels among school leavers and serious mismatches between education and the labour market have arisen. Thus both educators and economists have become more interested in understanding in greater detail how the educational process influences job search behaviour, the probability of finding a job, the kind of job acquired, and long-term productivity on the job. From this has arisen a substantial interest in tracing school leavers into the labour market (Psacharopoulos 1981).

The influence of the World Bank has been very important in stimulating interest in tracer studies. Faced with the need to evaluate the effectiveness of its many educational investment projects and influenced by the opinions of both educators and economists who are concerned with increasing the quality and efficiency of education, the World Bank has selected tracer studies as the most effective way to evaluate more than 100 of its educational loans in developing nations.

Finally, because tracer studies typically generate very large and complex data sets, and present difficult technical problems in linking two or more data sets, most would have been difficult to contemplate without the enormous development in computer facilities and software packages since the early 1970s. This is particularly true in advanced nations, but many developing nations have also been acquiring the domestic computing facilities required in recent years.

2. Types of Tracer Studies

As has been suggested above, the only element which is unique to a tracer study is that the same subjects are contacted at more than one point in time. "Tracer studies" is not a new concept, but a new phrase to describe a style of study, usually called longitudinal or follow-up, which has been around in limited number for a long time. In this sense there are potentially as many types of tracer studies as there are any other kinds of investigation of human behaviour. However, such studies can usefully be categorized along several different dimensions.

2.1 Short Term Versus Long Term

Tracer studies differ both in the length of time between observations of individuals and the total length of time encompassed by the entire study. At one extreme there are studies that cover a time span of only a few months or at most a year. Here one finds studies which, for example, initially observe a group of school leavers and then observe their success in the labour market anywhere from 3 to 9 months thereafter, and studies which observe a particular educational intervention (for example a new teaching method) at one point in time and measure changes in student behaviour a few months to a year thereafter. At the other extreme one has studies which have followed the same individuals for 10 or more years. The current outer limit of this latter type is a study which started in 1938 with several thousand grade 3 students in the city of Malmö, Sweden. Data have been collected from the same individuals at several points in time during the succeeding years, and the study still continues. Indeed, investigators are now observing the characteristics of the second generation—the children of the original 1938 cohort, and are searching historical archives for data on the pre-1938 family background of the original subjects (Fägerlind 1975).

2.2 Focus on Education Versus Focus on the Labour Market

Most tracer studies are concerned with labour market entry. In such studies major effort is focused upon collecting relatively detailed information regarding entrance into the labour market, and the data collected regarding characteristics of the schooling process are typically very scanty (usually consisting of nothing more than years of schooling completed or year of graduation or school leaving). Other studies are concerned mainly with the educational system, observing the flow of children through the system and the factors which affect their destiny at various points within the schooling process (Flanagan and Cooley 1966). Such studies tend to have relatively rich data regarding the schooling process itself, but minimal or no data regarding the postschool life of the subjects, such as labour market entrance.

2.3 Data Type

To date, most tracer studies have depended upon quantitative data, usually derived from questionnaires or other kinds of survey instruments. There are, however, a few studies which have used qualitative data, based upon detailed life histories or ethnographic observations of the same subjects over a period of time.

2.4 Sample Size

Most tracer studies involve fairly large sample sizes, ranging anywhere from 1,000 or 2,000 up to 10,000 or 20,000 individuals or more. However, this is not a necessary characteristic as there exist in the literature tracer studies which deal with as few as 12, or even 6, individuals.

2.5 Planned Versus Unplanned

Some of the tracer studies available in the literature have clearly been planned from the outset to follow a group of individuals for a considerable period of time (e.g., Project Talent and the longitudinal study of the high-school class of 1972 in the United States). However, most are "accidental", in the sense that the individuals who collected the original data did not expect (or at least had only minimal hopes) that they would be able to contact the same subjects on one or more subsequent occasions.

As one would expect, most extant tracer studies represent combinations of these various dimensions. For example, an 8-year tracer study in Chile focuses both upon the school system itself and the labour market, and combines questionnaire data with relatively detailed interview data (Schiefelbein and Farrell 1981). Similarly, the Malmö study in Sweden has drawn upon a variety of data sources, including not only tests and questionnaires administered to the subjects themselves, but official statistics and government records.

3. Methodology

The only methodological problem which is unique to tracer studies is the process of location, some months or years thereafter, of an originally observed group of subjects. The complexity of this problem depends primarily upon the length of time between observations and the extent to which a society has well-developed administrative and record-keeping systems, an efficient postal service, and so on. The fact that it has proven possible to carry out a few long-term tracer studies in developing societies indicates that these location problems, while difficult, are not insuperable. What is required of the investigator is a knowledge of the local system, and a great deal of ingenuity.

4. Empirical Findings

Although the number of tracer studies, compared with other kinds of educational investigations, is still rather limited, the results which have been obtained to date indicate that one can indeed obtain from this kind of study information that is simply unavailable from other kinds of research activities. For example, the Malmö study in Sweden was able to demonstrate that Jencks's conclusion regarding the limited effects of education upon later variations in income was erroneous. In this study it was found that although different levels of education had little effect upon income levels among individuals between 25 and 35 years of age, education was extremely important in explaining income variance after 40 years of age. Only a long-term study could have discovered this result, which directly contradicts the outcome of cross-section analysis. Similarly, the continuing tracer studies of children who were in Head Start programmes in the United States (special preschool programmes) have indicated that the positive effects did not show up during the early years of primary schooling but have begun to show up very strongly during the later years of schooling. One study has shown that the type of teacher students had in the first grade affected both their income and family relationships 30 years later (Pedersen et al. 1978).

Tracer studies have also permitted taking into account, in studies of the effect of education on intergenerational occupational mobility, changes in the occupational structure between parents' and childrens' generations. In one such study it is clearly seen that most of the intergenerational mobility, conventionally attributed to education, was accounted for by massive changes in the occupational structure. These results suggest that standard path analytic studies of intergenerational mobility may be fatally flawed when applied in countries which have experienced large changes in occupational structure (as have, for example, Ireland, Italy,

Finland, Japan, and many developing nations, in the 1960–78 period) (Farrell 1981).

Tracer studies have also raised some interesting new questions. For example, the Swedish data from Malmö show that students whose achievement levels as rated by teachers were lower than their scores on independent tests died earlier than those whose teacher ratings were higher than their objectively measured performance. Several other studies have shown that early achievement, both as measured on tests and as perceived by teachers, have complex effects upon a child's further development. These results generate a new set of questions regarding the interaction between genetic and environmental influences on an individual's life.

Turning specifically to developing societies, a study in Zambia discovered that university graduates in some fields, such as medicine, engineering, science, or law, are more likely to pursue careers in the fields for which they were specifically trained than are graduates from education and the social sciences (Bardouille 1981). A study in Swaziland revealed that only certain types of school examinations are associated with postschool activities (Sullivan 1981). Several tracer studies have been able to disaggregate socioeconomic status into distinct variables, some of which (e.g., preschool education, nutrition, coaching at home) have long-term effects upon students' achievement levels and are "alterable" by policy.

Finally, the study in Chile has discovered a number of educational variables operating at the primary level (e.g., eighth-grade test scores, textbook availability, characteristics of the classroom group) which have very long-term effects, for example upon performance at the end of secondary schooling, and indeed upon labour market entry. These too could only have been discovered by following the same students for a number of years. Equally important, that study has found a number of educational variables, operating at the primary level, which have effects upon changes in performance between primary and secondary schooling, which again could only be discovered by a longitudinal study which takes account of the value-added problem in educational research.

In sum, the results of the limited number of tracer studies which have been completed clearly indicate that this style of investigation can produce results which are either (a) not derivable from cross-sectional studies, or (b) contrary to the results of cross-sectional studies. These suggest that this particular investigative technique is extremely promising, and cast doubt upon the results of educational investigations which are either cross-sectional or deal with only a short period of time. They suggest that studies that consciously take into account the fact that education is a long-term and aggregative process are likely to produce results which are far more useful than the results of studies which observe individuals at only one point in time.

See also: Longitudinal Research Methods

Bibliography

Bardouille R 1981 A trace study of University of Zambia graduates: Implications for planning. Paper presented at the International Workshop on the Role of Tracer Studies in Education and Employment Research, December, 1981. International Institute for Educational Planning, Paris

Douglas J W B, Ross J M, Simpson H R 1968 *All Our Future: A Longitudinal Study of Secondary Schooling.* Davies, London

Fägerlind I 1975 *Formal Education and Adult Earnings: A Longitudinal Study on the Economic Benefits of Education.* Almqvist and Wiksell, Stockholm

Farrell J P 1981 Some observations on the implications of an 8-year tracer study. Paper presented at the International Workshop on the Role of Tracer Studies in Education and Employment Research, December, 1981. International Institute for Educational Planning, Paris

Flanagan J C, Cooley W W 1966 *Project Talent: One-Year Follow-Up Studies.* University of Pittsburgh School of Education, Pittsburgh, Pennsylvania

Hilton T et al. 1973 *The Base-Year Survey of the National Longitudinal Study of the High School Class of 1972.* Educational Testing Service, Princeton, New Jersey

Pedersen E, Faucher T A, Eaton W W 1978 A new perspective on the effects of first-grade teachers on children's subsequent adult status. *Harvard Educ. Rev.* 48: 1–31

Psacharopoulos G 1981 Lifetime profiles of earnings and employment: A survey. *Inf. Sci. Soc.* 20: 743–85

Schiefelbein E, Farrell J P 1981 *Eight Years of Their Lives: Through Schooling to the Labour Market in Chile.* International Development Research Centre, Ottawa, Ontario

Sewell W H, Hauser R M 1975 *Education, Occupation and Earnings: Achievement in the Early Career.* Academic Press, New York

Sullivan 1981 An "ex-post" appraisal of the Swaziland school leaver tracer project: Institutional and methodological problems—policy indicators and implementation. Paper presented at the International Workshop on the Role of Tracer Studies in Education and Employment Research, December, 1981. International Institute for Educational Planning, Paris

Willis P E 1978 *Learning to Labour: How Working Class Kids Get Working Class Jobs.* Saxon House, Farnborough

Twin Studies

S. E. C. Fischbein

It would seem advisable to differentiate between the study of twins as a matter of interest in itself, and as a research method for investigating heredity and environment interaction and its implications for education. The former type of study is concerned with comparisons of twins and singletons in different respects, but also with the specific relationship that a twin pair possesses both before and after birth. In the second type of study, which will be the main topic of this article, within-pair differences of monozygotic (MZ) and dizygotic (DZ) pairs are compared for different variables and ages. Reduced to its simplest form, the twin method thereby assumes that any difference within MZ pairs must be due to environmental or at least nongenetic causes, whereas differences within DZ pairs are due to both environmental and genetic factors.

Twin studies are of course not the only method used to investigate genetic and environmental influences on behavior and development. Effects of selective breeding have for instance been studied in different species. For human beings, individuals with more or less of an inherited trait in common, for instance parents and children or nontwin siblings, have been the object of study. Of special interest has also been the study of twins reared apart (Shields 1962, Bouchard et al. 1981, Langinvainio et al. 1981). In recent years biological and adoptive family members have also been compared in different respects (Scarr and Weinberg 1977, Scarr and Weinberg 1978, Horn et al. 1981, Scarr et al. 1981).

1. Fields of Research

Twin studies have been of major interest in different research fields, such as medical science, epidemiological studies, behavioral sciences, as well as in behavior genetics as a collaborative field for behavior scientists and geneticists.

1.1 Twin Biology and Multiple Pregnancy

This field of study examines the incidence and factors of twinning, embryology of twinning, and multiple pregnancy. The research results indicate a general decrease in both MZ and DZ twin births. Possible explanations could be decreased average maternal age, decreased fertility, and reduced parity because of contraception.

Many studies in this field have also examined the effects of multiple pregnancy on the mother and her offspring. Apart from the specific strains on the foetuses caused by the prenatal twin situation, mothers of twins generally seem more susceptible to a wider variety of disorders than do mothers giving birth to one child (Gedda et al. 1981 Part A).

1.2 Epidemiological and Clinical Studies

In these types of studies the twins are often used as matched pairs. This implies selecting pairs where one of the twins differs from the other on a recognized experience, measurement, or trait. These discordant pair members are then compared on another target, measurement, or trait that may be simultaneous with, follow, or predate the one that distinguished the twins initially (Gedda et al. 1981 Part C).

Epidemiological and clinical studies have been particularly concerned with health risk factors such as smoking, drinking, or substance exposure. Twin studies thereby help clarify the different roles played by the environment and by genetics in the variation of these habits and the contribution they make to different types of diseases, for instance cancer or coronary heart disease.

1.3 Behavioral Sciences

The study of twins in the behavioral sciences has been specifically used as a method to estimate heritability. These studies have encompassed different areas, such as personality, school achievement, and studies of intelligence. The results have mostly shown a higher within-pair similarity for MZ twins in comparison to DZ twins. The interpretation of these results has been that this is due to genetic factors, since the heritability estimates of course tend to be high. In 1969 Arthur Jensen published an article in the *Harvard Educational Review* entitled "How much can we boost IQ and scholastic achievement?" (Jensen 1969). He maintained, on the basis of results from previous twin studies, that the heritability for IQ is around 0.80. Since the mean IQ of different socioeconomic groups varies over a range of about two standard deviations, it is most unlikely that those groups would not also differ in their genetic endowment. This generalization from individual to group differences has been criticized both on methodological and ideological grounds. During the 1970s, the use of heritability estimates were debated in numerous articles, dealing with for instance the difficulty of generalizing results from one twin population to another, the inadequacy of the traditional additive model in twin research, and the necessity to take interactional and correlational effects into account (Fischbein 1980).

In the following section, some of these criticisms will be further elaborated and attempts to tackle these problems will be presented.

2. Methodological Problems

The additive model for interpreting twin data implies that an environmental change will contribute to a comparable change in all genotypes. Interactional effects, on the other hand, will lead to different reactions in genotypes exposed to the same environmental impact. Heredity–environment correlation can be defined as a "function of the frequency with which certain genotypes and certain environments occur together" (Plomin et al. 1977 p. 310). The additive model was originally borrowed from agricultural genetics, where it has been found useful. It is, however, a plausible assumption that interactional and correlational effects will play a more prominent role for human beings, who, for instance, can store experiences by means of a common language. If this is true, the additive model has obvious shortcomings, since it confuses genetic and interactional effects in interpreting data from different types of twins, who differentially react to and construct their own environment.

It will be necessary to define specifically what is meant by interactional and correlational effects, since these concepts tend to have quite different meanings depending on the preferred model of explanation.

2.1 Genotype–Environment Interaction

Genotype–environment interaction can for instance be estimated within the frame of an additive model of assessing the proportional contribution of genetic and environmental variance to human behavioral traits (Eaves et al. 1977). This interaction term is calculated for groups of individuals in an analysis of variance design and implies that individuals high in a trait will react differently from individuals low in a trait. It is thus connected to genotypic level which presupposes a quantification of genetic contribution.

There is an obvious difference between the above-mentioned population concept and the organismic type of interaction previously mentioned. The latter connotes something more than the statistical type of interaction. It presupposes a reciprocal relationship and focuses upon the psychological environment and the individual as these affect and are affected by each other. This implies that the "same" environment will be differently interpreted by different genotypes and thus lead to different reactions.

2.2 Genotype–Environment Correlation

Genotype–environment correlations, like genotype–environment interactions, can be of different kinds. Plomin et al. (1977 p. 310) have defined the following types.

(a) *Passive G × E correlation.* This is present when endowment and environment covary, so that for instance bright children tend to live in a home conducive to their intellectual development. This type of correlation is called "passive" because it occurs independently of the activities of the individual in question.

(b) *Reactive G × E correlation.* This signifies that people can react differently to persons of different genotypes, thus creating conspicuously dissimilar environmental circumstances. An example of this type of correlation is when certain personality traits are reinforced by particular persons in the environment. The reactive G × E correlation has often been discussed in connection with twin studies. It has been maintained that MZ twins tend to be treated more alike than DZ twins, which would make it unwarranted to assume that environments are the same for both categories. Another pertinent question is whether the twin situation as such creates such a specific environment that it cannot be generalized to singletons.

(c) *Active G × E correlation.* This occurs as a result of the individual's own action. People tend to create for themselves different environments related to their genetic potentials. For instance, in the same home a brighter child may choose to read more books than a

less bright child, thereby creating for himself or herself a more stimulating environment.

Both Plomin et al. (1977) and Eaves et al. (1977) have stressed the difficulty of distinguishing between the active type of G × E correlation and G × E interaction. This is a matter of definition, and it is probably impossible to maintain a clearcut distinction between these two concepts. A definition of interaction in the dynamical sense, that has been previously described, would be as follows: "Genotypes can be shown to interpret the same environmental treatment in different ways." A definition of the active type of correlation, on the other hand, would be: "Genotypes can be shown to react to the same environmental impact in different ways thereby creating different environments for themselves." As can be seen the distinction is arbitrary since a divergent interpretation of the same environment probably will induce a divergent reaction.

3. Recent Developments in Twin Studies

Different methods have been proposed for tackling the methodological problems outlined above. The two major attempts are models of biometrical genetics which involve studying different types of genetically related individuals, and developmental models of twin comparisons.

3.1 Models of Biometrical Genetics

In 1960, Cattell published his multiple abstract variance analysis (MAVA) (Cattell 1960). This was a model for testing nature–nurture influences on the variation of quantitatively measured characteristics. Jinks and Fulker (1970) and Eaves et al. (1977), among others, have further elaborated this model. The basic assumption is that by comparing only within-pair similarity for twins in the form of intraclass correlations, vital information is lost, and it will be impossible to estimate the relative contributions of genetical and environmental effects and their covariation. Instead, the model building relies upon an analysis of variance and covariance for twins brought up together and apart or for other types of relatives with more or less of their genes in common. The model should embody a testable null hypothesis. In addition to testing for general genetic or environmental effects, a specification can be made in terms of assortative mating, dominance, or, for instance, cultural transmission and sibling effects. The most pertinent question concerns, however, the possibility of using biometrical models to test for genotype–environment interaction and correlation. Eaves et al. (1977) have discussed this in great detail. They maintain that with a sufficient number of individuals representing different types of relationships it would be theoretically possible to detect both different kinds of interaction as well as correlation effects. It could be questioned, however, whether the models will not also have to include more sophisticated environmental measures as well as a longitudinal approach to study the dynamic interactional and correlational effects described earlier. If at all, this would only be possible in the type of quantitative statistical design mentioned above. Another pertinent matter for discussion is of course whether it would be practically feasible to carry out a study with the number of individuals and measurements required for testing all possible solutions of the model.

3.2 Multivariate Behavioral Genetics and Development

Plomin and DeFries (1981) have used multivariate behavioral genetics in a developmental model applied to twin data. This model consists of a path diagram of longitudinal stability. It depicts the relationship between the measured phenotype at a given age and a measurement of the same character at a later stage in development. With the help of twin data the correlation between these two measurements can be partitioned into genetic and environmental parts. The authors conclude that "the finding of a large genetic correlation between measures at two different ages would indicate that individual differences in the two measures are due to many of the same genes. Likewise, a large environmental correlation would suggest that similar environmental influences are being manifested." A factor analysis of genetic and environmental correlations could also provide useful information about the organization and timing of developmental stages.

Genotype–environment interactional and correlational effects are not included in the model. Since it has not been applied to actual developmental data, it is premature to decide whether such effects could be detected and subsequently built into the model.

3.3 Development in Twins Before Puberty

In the Louisville twin study, MZ and DZ pairs have been followed from birth onwards (Wilson 1981). Both physical and mental development have been studied. Wilson has used a repeated-measures analysis of variance model specifically designed for twin data to estimate the developmental consistency of each pair.

The model is developed in terms of the expected values for the variance components representing twin concordance, and the derivation is provided for computing within-pair correlations and for estimating the percent of variance explained by each component.

This method gives both an overall measure of concordance over ages and concordance for spurts and lags in development. The results suggest the presence of synchronized developmental pathways in both physical and mental growth for MZ twins but not for DZ. Wilson interprets this as an effect of powerful chronogenetic influences on development. There is, however, no linkage in the pattern of growth spurts and lags for physical and mental development, which therefore seem to occur largely independently of each other.

Wilson also specifically studied MZ twins with large birth-weight differences. When they were examined at 6 years of age, height and weight differences between the

twins were still noticeable but they showed no IQ differences. It therefore seems as though the mental development has "a high degree of buffering against the effects of nutritional deficit in the prenatal period."

3.4 Development in Twins at Adolescence

A Swedish longitudinal twin study, called the SLU-project, has been conducted on twins during puberty for approximately a 10-year period. Height and weight measurements as well as intelligence and school achievement test scores were collected at regular time intervals. A more detailed description of the project has been given by Ljung et al. (1977).

A model for analyzing intrapair similarity in MZ and DZ twins over time has been worked out in this project (Fischbein 1979). The model tries to encompass both a comparison of different characteristics and different types of environments. Fuller and Thompson (1961) have outlined possible outcomes of practice effects on the relative contributions of genetic and environmental factors during a time period. The "divergence" hypothesis predicts that "subjects free to exploit their environment in a variety of fashions will by chance light upon quite different modes of adaptation." It is evident that this description leaves room for considerable interactional and correlational effects of the dynamic type. The "convergence" hypothesis, on the other hand, predicts that "when one specific response is reinforced, other responses will be extinguished, and all subjects will converge upon a common pattern" (Fuller and Thompson 1961 pp. 91–92).

The convergence and divergence hypotheses thus imply a difference in genetic contribution to a variable, depending on the amount of freedom given the phenotype to interact with environmental factors. In a restrictive environment, interactional and correlational effects will contribute less to variation than in a permissive environment. Figure 1 presents the model described above. Hypothetical intrapair correlations (R) are given for MZ and DZ pairs under the assumption that the twins in a pair are living in the same environment and are exposed to a similar environmental impact. Figure 1(a) illustrates the development of a characteristic primarily controlled by genetic factors, where environmental effects are assumed to be constant and additive. MZ twins, because of their identical inheritance, tend to be more similar than DZ twins, and this difference tends to be of the same magnitude as long as the twins are exposed to the same environmental impact. No lowering of the intrapair correlations with increasing age is hypothesized. Figure 1(b) illustrates the divergence hypothesis proposed by Fuller and Thompson (1961). Under permissive circumstances, MZ twins are affected and react similarly to the same environmental influences, whereas DZ twins are affected and react differently and thus get progressively less similar. A lowering of the intrapair correlations for DZ but not for MZ twins with increasing age is hypothesized. Figure 1(c) illustrates the convergence hypothesis. Owing to restrictive environmental influences, negatively reinforcing genetic

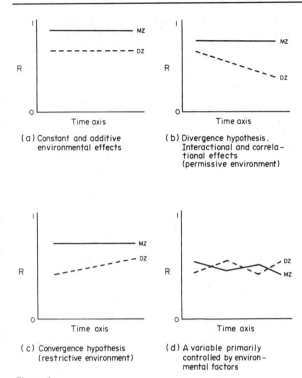

Figure 1
Hypothetical intraclass correlations for MZ and DZ twins
assuming similar environments, and varying nature–nurture
contribution

differences, DZ twins will get progressively more similar
with increasing age. The intrapair correlations will thus
increase with age for DZ twins and remain constant for
MZ. Figure 1(d) illustrates unsystematic environmental
effects largely counteracting genetic differences. Since
the identical inheritance of MZ twins does not predis-
pose them for greater similarity, it will be rather incidental if the intrapair correlations are higher or lower for
MZ than for DZ twins.

A short summary of actual results obtained by applying the above-mentioned model (Fischbein 1979) will be
presented here.

Height growth was measured every half year from age
10 to 16 for twin girls and from age 10 to 18 for twin
boys. The intrapair correlations for MZ and DZ twins
show a parallel trend in accordance with Fig. 1(a) in the
model. MZ twins are very similar in height (around
$R = 0.95$) during puberty while DZ twins are less similar
(around $R = 0.70$). No lowering of the intrapair correlations is evident. It therefore seems as though height
growth in the sample studied was primarily controlled
by genetic factors.

For weight, the correlations for MZ co-twins tended
to be practically as high as for height (around
$R = 0.80–0.90$). For the DZ pairs, however, there
seemed to be a divergent trend consistent with Fig. 1(b)
so that the twins are more similar in weight at age 10
than at age 16 or 18. This is especially evident for girls

where the intrapair correlation decreases to around 0.20
at age 16. Weight growth thus seems to be much more
susceptible to interactional and correlational influences.
Evidently DZ twins and particularly girls are affected
and react differently to the same environmental influences in matters related to the regulation of their weight
growth during puberty.

Verbal and inductive reasoning ability was measured
at age 12 and 18 for the boys. The trends for the two
types of abilities seem to be slightly different. For verbal
ability there is a divergent trend so that MZ twins get
more similar and DZ twins get less similar during this
period. For inductive reasoning ability, on the other
hand, the correlations slightly increase for both MZ and
DZ but the trend is mainly parallel. This would seem to
imply that interactional and correlational effects
are more important for explaining the variation in
verbal ability test scores than for inductive reasoning
ability.

The examples presented so far have been selected to
illustrate heredity–environment influences for *different*
characteristics. It is also of interest, of course, to study
the *same* characteristic in permissive and restrictive environments. A standardized achievement test in mathematics has been given to the twins in grades 3 and 6.
The correlations for the total group show a divergent
trend, so that the correlation increases for MZ twins and
decreases for DZ twins. When socioeconomic background is taken into consideration, however, the divergent trend is much more conspicuous for working-class
children than for the other group. This indicates a more
restrictive environment as regards school achievement
for the children coming from higher socioeconomic
strata.

4. Concluding Comments

It is evident from this article, that there has been a trend
towards more developmental studies in the field of twin
studies. These studies have demonstrated the importance of genetic factors on development during childhood and adolescence. It is also evident that longitudinal studies will be necessary to investigate different types
of heredity–environment interaction and correlation.

This field of research has been largely dominated by
biologists, which has resulted in a certain neglect of
environmental factors which have been treated as
unspecified sources of variation. Environmental distinctions have rarely been observed in twin studies. What
seems to be a fruitful approach by natural and behavioral scientists in this field, however, is to differentiate
between environments that are more or less permissive
in the sense that they allow different genotypes to be
affected and react differently.

Ideally the cooperational activity of natural and
behavioral scientists encompassing a developmental
design as well as environmental distinctions and a rigorous statistical model for testing would be hoped for as
regards twin research in the future.

Bibliography

Bouchard T J Jr, Heston L, Eckert E, Keyes M, Resnick S 1981 The Minnesota study of twins reared apart: Project description and sample results in the developmental domain. In: Gedda L, Parisi P, Nance W E (eds.) 1981, Part B, pp. 227–33

Cattell R B 1960 The multiple abstract variance analysis equations and solutions: For nature–nurture research on continuous variables. *Psychol. Rev.* 67: 353–72

Eaves L J, Last K, Martin N G, Jinks J L 1977 A progressive approach to non-additivity and genotype–environmental covariance in the analysis of human differences. *Brit. J. Math. Stat. Psychol.* 30: 1–42

Fischbein S 1979 *Heredity–Environment Influences on Growth and Development During Adolescence: A Longitudinal Study of Twins.* Liber Läromedel, Lund

Fischbein S 1980 IQ and social class. *Intelligence* 4: 51–63

Fuller J L, Thompson W R 1961 *Behavior Genetics.* Wiley, New York

Gedda L, Parisi P, Nance W E (eds.) 1981 *Twin Research 3.* 3rd Int. Cong. on Twin Studies, Jerusalem, June 16–20, 1980. Part A: *Twin Biology and Multiple Pregnancy.* Part B: *Intelligence, Personality, and Development.* Part C: *Epidemiological and Clinical Studies.* Liss, New York

Horn J M, Loehlin J C, Willerman L 1981 Generalizability of heritability estimates for intelligence from the Texas Adoption Project. In: Gedda L, Parisi P, Nance W E (eds.) 1981 pp. 17–19

Husén T 1959 *Psychological Twin Research: A Methodological Study.* Almqvist and Wiksell, Stockholm

Jensen A R 1969 How much can we boost IQ and scholastic achievement? *Harvard Educ. Rev.* 39: 1–123

Jinks J L, Fulker D W 1970 A comparison of the biometrical genetical, MAVA, and classical approaches to the analysis of human behavior. *Psychol. Bull.* 73: 311–49

Langinvainio H, Koskenvuo M, Kaprio J, Lönnqvist J, Tarkkonen L 1981 Finnish twins reared apart: Preliminary characterization of rearing environment. In: Gedda L, Parisi P, Nance W E (eds.) 1981, Part B, pp. 189–98

Ljung B–O, Fischbein S, Lindgren G 1977 A comparison of growth in twins and singleton controls of matched age followed longitudinally from 10 to 18 years. *Am. Hum. Biol.* 4: 405–15

Plomin R, DeFries J C 1981 Multivariate behavioral genetics and development: Twin studies. In: Gedda L, Parisi P, Nance W E (eds.) 1981, Part B, pp. 25–33

Plomin R, DeFries J C, Loehlin J C 1977 Genotype–Environment interaction and correlation in the analysis of human behavior. *Psychol. Bull.* 84: 309–22

Scarr S, Weinberg R A 1977 Intellectual similarities within families of both adopted and biological children. *Intelligence* 32(8): 170–91

Scarr S, Weinberg R A 1978 The influence of "family background" on intellectual attainment. *Am. Sociol. Rev.* 43: 674–92

Scarr S, Webber P L, Weinberg R A, Wittig M A 1981 Personality resemblance among adolescents and their parents in biologically related and adoptive families. In: Gedda L, Parisi P, Nance W E (eds.) 1981 Part B, pp. 99–120

Shields J 1962 *Monozygotic Twins, Brought Up Apart and Brought Up Together: An Investigation into the Genetic and Environmental causes of Variation in Personality.* Oxford University Press, London

Wilson R S 1981 Synchronized developmental pathways for infant twins. In: Gedda L, Parisi P, Nance W E (eds.) 1981 Part B, pp. 199–209

Simulation as a Research Technique

R. R. Wilcox

Simulation studies are a relatively simple way of getting approximate solutions to many statistical and related problems that are difficult to analyze using conventional techniques. The best way to describe how simulations work is to give some examples of how they are applied. Before doing this, however, some introductory remarks are in order.

In research settings, simulations have two major components. The first is a system that is of interest to the investigator, and the second is a model that represents the system. The system can be almost any set of interrelated elements. For example, it might be the traffic flow in a city, or the operations of a large computer. In education, the system might be an individual learning a skill, or perhaps an examinee responding to an item. The corresponding model can be descriptive, but usually it is mathematical. For instance, in the traffic flow example, the Poisson distribution is frequently used to represent the probability that an automobile will arrive at an intersection during a particular time interval. Learning models are sometimes based on a probability model known as a Markov chain, and several mathematical models have been proposed for describing the probability that an examinee will give a correct response to a test item.

Models have been classified in several ways, but for present purposes the most important distinction is deterministic versus stochastic. Deterministic models refer to situations where all mathematical and logical relationships among the elements of a system are fixed. In a stochastic model, at least one variable is random. In education, stochastic models are by far the most common, but deterministic models are important in certain situations.

1. Monte Carlo Studies

Simulating a stochastic model is generally known as a Monte Carlo study although the technique can be used to solve deterministic problems as well. The term "Monte Carlo" was originally a code word for the secret work on the atomic bomb during the Second World War; the goal was to simulate actions related to random neutron diffusion in fissionable materials. Although a Monte Carlo study generally requires a high-speed computer to be of any practical use, the idea is not a modern one. In fact, it can be traced as far back as Babylonian times (Hammersley and Handscomb 1964).

Whether addressing a deterministic or stochastic problem, all Monte Carlo studies require a set of observations generated according to some probability function. The most basic and commonly used probability function is the uniform distribution over the unit interval. This means that a sequence of real numbers between zero and one must be generated such that for any generated number, say x, the probability that x is less than or equal to x_0 is x_0 where x_0 is any constant between zero and one. Symbolically, $Pr(x \leqslant x_0) = x_0$ is required for any x_0, where $0 < x_0 < 1$.

In practice, generating truly random numbers is impossible, and so approximations are used instead. One of the earliest approximations was proposed by J. von Neumann and his colleagues (von Neumann 1951). Today, however, congruential generators are typically used. These procedures produce a nonrandom sequence of numbers according to some recursive formula. Generally, this formula is given by $x_{i+1} = ax_i + c - mk_i$ where k_i is the largest integer that is less than or equal to $(ax_i + c)/m$, and where the constants a, c, and m are chosen so that the sequence has certain optimal properties. For binary computers, $m = 2^{35}$, $a = 2^7$, and $c = 1$ are known to yield good statistical results (Hull and Dobell 1964, McLaren and Marsaglia 1965, Olmstead 1946). The starting value, or seed, is chosen according to the particular generator being used (Rubinstein 1981 Chap. 2).

Congruential generators are deterministic in the sense that a fixed seed and specific generator will always produce the same sequence of numbers. This is contrary to commonsense notions about randomly generated numbers, but it can be shown that the sequence appears to be uniformly distributed and statistically independent (Knuth 1969). Also, this reproducibility of a sequence facilitates the "debugging" of a computer program designed to simulate a particular model.

Currently, there are several pseudorandom number generators to choose from, but unfortunately there is some confusion about which is best for general use. One of the best known and most frequently used is the IBM subroutine RANDU. According to Rubinstein (1981 p. 26) statistical tests indicate that RANDU is very satisfactory. However, Dudewicz (1976) compared RANDU to several other generators and found it to be relatively inadequate. He recommends using subroutine RANDOM (Learmonth and Lewis 1973a) or subroutine UNI. For additional criticisms of RANDU, see Learmonth and Lewis (1973b) as well as Marsaglia (1968).

2. Testing the Appropriateness of Pseudorandom Sequences

Many statistical tests of pseudorandom number generators have been proposed (Rubinstein 1981).

Among these, the chi-square goodness-of-fit test is probably the most "obvious" one to use, but there are no clear guidelines on how to proceed. For example, suppose a pseudorandom number generator passes most of the six tests listed by Rubinstein (1981). Is it acceptable? Even if a generated sequence passes all six tests, there are many other tests that it might fail. It should be noted that the comparison of the generators made by Dudewicz (1976) was based only on a chi-square test and the speed of the computer subroutines.

When judging the adequacy of a pseudorandom number generator, two points deserve special mention. First, it has been argued that every finite sequence, even if it is quite acceptable as a sample, will contain subsequences which are clearly unrepresentative and computationally undesirable. Thus, it is unreasonable to expect a sequence of numbers to pass a battery of tests since it is to be expected that the sequence is unsuitable on some grounds. Second, even if a generated sequence passed every test ever proposed, in principle, the sequence should be used only once. All pseudorandom number generators eventually will repeat exactly the sequence of numbers that they produced. To get a new sequence, an appropriately chosen starting value must be determined. It appears, however, that the choice of a new seed has received little or no attention. In addition, the extent to which this is a serious practical problem is not clear.

3. Some Illustrations

Monte Carlo procedures have been applied to problems in numerous fields including quantum mechanics, cell population studies, operations research, combinatorics, and traffic flow problems. This section illustrates how Monte Carlo studies can be applied to problems in mental test theory.

Understanding why and how Monte Carlo studies work requires an understanding of the weak law of large numbers. Suppose, for example, a probability model is being investigated where the probability of observing a value x is determined by some unknown parameter, say τ. Further suppose that a statistic $\hat{\tau}$, which is a function of x, has been proposed for estimating τ. The question arises as to how accurately $\hat{\tau}$ estimates τ for various values of τ. The law of large numbers says that if observations are randomly generated according to the probability model and a particular value of τ, and if the process is repeated yielding a sequence of $\hat{\tau}$ values, say $\hat{\tau}_1, \hat{\tau}_2, \ldots$, then $\Sigma_{i=1}^{k} \tau_i / k$ approximates the expected (or average) value of $\hat{\tau}$. If, for example, $\hat{\tau}$ is intended to be an unbiased estimate of τ, $\tau - \Sigma \hat{\tau}_i / k$ gives a reasonably accurate estimate of the bias—assuming, of course, k is large. By repeating this process with various τ values, an investigator can approximately determine how well $\hat{\tau}$ estimates τ no matter what τ happens to be. Many related problems can be solved, and some illustrations are given below.

A relatively simple example will help clarify matters. Suppose an examinee responds to n dichotomously scored test items. Further assume, as is frequently done, that the probability that the examinee gets x items correct is

$$\binom{n}{x} p^x (1-p)^{n-x} \tag{1}$$

where

$$\binom{n}{x} = \frac{n(n-1)\ldots(n-x+1)}{(n-x)(n-x-1)\ldots 2} \tag{2}$$

and p is the unknown probability of a correct response to a randomly selected item. The most common estimate of p is $\hat{p} = x/n$ which is known to have several optimal properties.

Suppose an investigator is interested in determining how well $\hat{p}$ estimates p. As a measure of accuracy, suppose $E(\hat{p} - p)^2$ is used. In other words, accuracy is measured as the average squared difference between $\hat{p}$ and p, the average being taken over an infinite sequence of independent random samples of n items. It is known that $E(\hat{p} - p)^2 = p(1-p)/n$, but for the sake of illustration, suppose this is not known. For any n and p, the value of $E(\hat{p} - p)^2$ can be approximated as follows.

(a) *Step 1.* Generate a random number between zero and one, that is, a number from the uniform distribution on the unit interval. If this number is less than p, set $y_1 = 1$; otherwise, $y_1 = 0$. Repeat this process n times which yields a sequence of y_i's ($i = 1, \ldots, n$).

(b) *Step 2.* Let $x = \sum_{i=1}^{n} y_i$. It is known that the probability function of x is given by Eqn. (1).

(c) *Step 3.* Compute $\hat{\tau} = (\hat{p} - p)^2 = (x/n - p)^2$. Since n and p are chosen by the investigator, $\hat{\tau}$ can be determined.

(d) *Step 4.* Repeat Steps 1 through 3 until k values of $\hat{\tau}$, say $\hat{\tau}_1, \ldots, \hat{\tau}_k$, are available. Because the $\hat{\tau}_i$ values are independent, the weak law of large numbers implies that $k^{-1}\sum\hat{\tau}_i$ approaches $E(\hat{p} - p)^2$ (in probability) as k gets large. Thus, $E(\hat{p} - p)^2$ can be approximated for any n and p that is of interest to the investigator.

There remains the problem of deciding how large k should be. For Monte Carlo studies in general, a conservative choice, one that is frequently recommended, is $k = 10,000$. In practice, however, this can be costly, particularly when the probability model being simulated is somewhat complex. To minimize the chances of highly erroneous results, k is usually chosen to be at least 1,000, but there are studies reported in the statistical literature where k is as small as 100.

As another illustration, suppose that a randomly sampled examinee responding to an n-item test gets x items correct with probability

$$\binom{n}{x} \frac{B(r+x, s+n-x)}{B(r, s)} \tag{3}$$

where B is the beta function given by

$$B(r, s) = \int_0^1 t^{r-1}(1-t)^{s-1}\, dt \tag{4}$$

and where $r, s > 0$ are unknown parameters. This model might appear to be somewhat complex, but it is fairly easy to apply, particularly with the aid of a computer, and it has proven to be very useful in practice.

To apply this model, it is necessary to estimate the parameters r and s. Skellman (1948) proposed an estimate based on the method of moments, and Griffiths (1973) suggests an approximation to the maximum likelihood estimate. The accuracy of both procedures has not been determined analytically, and Griffiths' procedure appears to be particularly intractable when trying to determine its accuracy via standard techniques. This suggests, therefore, that Monte Carlo procedures be used to compare the two estimates for various combinations of r, s, and n. This can be done by following the steps in the previous illustration. However, Step 1 requires that observations be generated according to Eqn. (3) and this can be accomplished via the inverse transform method.

4. Generating Random Variates

As indicated in the previous section, an integral part of a Monte Carlo study is generating observations that have a specific distribution. Moreover, efficient algorithms for accomplishing this goal can have great practical importance. There are several methods of generating observations all of which are based on the uniform pseudorandom number generators described earlier. Some of these procedures are outlined here.

The inverse transform method can be used to generate observations according to any discrete distribution, and it is useful when generating observations according to certain continuous distributions as well. The procedure is implemented as follows. Let F be the cumulative distribution function being used in a particular study, and let

$$F^{-1}(y) = \inf\,[x: F(x) \geqslant y] \tag{5}$$

where inf means the greatest lower bound and $0 < y < 1$. If u is randomly generated from the uniform distribution over the unit interval, the cumulative distribution function of $s = F^{-1}(y)$ is F. If, for example, the density of $f(x) = 3x^2$, $0 \leqslant x \leqslant 1$, then $F(x) = x^3$, and $F^{-1}(y) = y^{1/3}$. This means that if u is randomly generated from say RANDU, where $0 < u < 1$, then $x = u^{1/3}$, and the cumulative distribution function of x will be F.

Another approach is the composition method. Suppose a particular study requires generating observations according to the density $f(x)$, and that $f(x)$ is given by

$$f(x) = \int g(x|\theta) h(\theta)\, d\theta \tag{6}$$

where h is a density function of θ, and g is a probability density function that depends on θ. In other words, the density function $f(x)$ can be given the following interpretation. Suppose a value for θ is generated according to the probability density function h, and that once θ is determined (which determines g), x is generated according to the probability function g. Then the probability density function of x is f.

Consider, for example, a model that requires generating observations according to

$$f(x) = n \int_{1}^{\infty} \theta^{-n} e^{-x\theta} \, d\theta \qquad (7)$$

Simply set $h(\theta) = n\theta^{-n-1}$ and $g(x|\theta) = \theta e^{-\theta x}$. The inverse transform method can be used to generate observations according to h, and once θ is determined, the inverse transform method is applied again to the resulting expression for g. Thus, for this particular example, the method can be summarized as follows. Generate two pseudorandom numbers, say u_1 and u_2. Compute $\theta = u_1^{1/n}$ and $x = -(1/\theta) \ln u_2$. Then the density of x will be f. Additional values of x can be generated by generating two new values for u_1 and u_2 and repeating the process.

A fourth generating procedure is the acceptance–rejection method. Again assume that observations are to be generated according to $f(x)$, and suppose $f(x) = ch(x)g(x)$ for some constant $c \geqslant 1$, $0 \leqslant g(x) \leqslant 1$ and where $h(x)$ is a probability density function. The method is to generate a pseudorandom number u and an observation x according to $h(x)$. If $u \leqslant g(x)$, x is accepted as being generated according to $f(x)$; if $u > g(x)$, u and x are rejected and new u and x values are generated. This procedure can have practical value if $1/c$ is close to one, and if it is easy to generate observations from $h(x)$.

Another generating procedure that should be mentioned is one proposed by Box and Muller (1958) for the case of a standard normal random variable. The procedure is easily implemented. Simply generate two pseudorandom numbers, say u_1 and u_2 and compute

$$z_1 = (-2 \ln u_1)^{1/2} \cos(2\pi u_2) \qquad (8)$$

and

$$z_2 = (-2 \ln u_1)^{1/2} \sin(2\pi u_2) \qquad (9)$$

It is known that z_1 and z_2 are independent and normally distributed with mean zero and variance one. For several alternative procedures see Rubinstein (1981). Rubinstein also summarizes generating methods for the more commonly used distributions in educational statistics, including the multivariate normal case with an arbitrary variance–covariance matrix.

5. Summary

Monte Carlo studies are usually conducted as outlined in previous sections. Once observations can be generated according to the probability function of interest, researchers with even a moderate statistical background find the technique reasonably easy to apply and understand. There are, however, ways of improving the accuracy of a Monte Carlo study that are far from obvious. Frequently, however, these techniques are relatively complex and difficult to apply. For a recent discussion of these procedures, see Rubinstein (1981). For a relatively simple application of this technique, see Koehler (1981).

See also: Experimental Studies

Bibliography

Box G E P, Muller M E 1958 A note on the generation of random normal deviates. *Annu. Math. Stat.* 29: 610–11

Dudewicz E J 1976 Speed and quality of random numbers for simulation. *J. Qual. Tech.* 8: 171–78

Griffiths D A 1973 Maximum likelihood estimation for the beta-binomial distribution and an application to the household distribution on the total number of cases of a disease. *Biometrics* 29: 637–48

Hammersley J M, Handscomb D C 1964 *Monte Carlo Methods.* Methuen, London

Hull T E, Dobell A R 1964 Mixed congruential random number generators for binary machines. *J. Complex Mach.* 11: 31–40

Knuth D E 1969 *The Art of Computer Programming*, Vol. 2: *Seminumerical Algorithms.* Addison-Wesley, Reading, Massachusetts

Koehler K J 1981 An improvement of a Monte Carlo technique using asymptotic moments with an application to the likelihood ratio statistic. *Commun. Stat. Sim. Comp.* 10: 343–57

Learmonth G P, Lewis P A W 1973a *Naval Post Graduate School Number Generator Package LLRANDOM.* Technical Report. Naval Postgraduate School, Monterey, California

Learmonth G P, Lewis P A W 1973b Statistical tests of some widely used and recently proposed uniform random number generators. In: Kennedy W J (ed.) 1973 *Computer Science and Statistics. Proc. Seventh Annu. Symp. on the Interface,* Iowa, Oct. 18–19, 1973. Statistical Laboratory, Iowa State University, Ames, Iowa, pp. 163–71

McLaren M D, Marsaglia G 1965 Uniform random number generators. *J. Assoc. Complex Mach.* 12: 83–89

Marsaglia G 1968 Random numbers fall mainly in the planes. *Proc. Nat. Acad. Sci.* 61: 25–28

Olmstead P S 1946 Distribution of sample arrangements for runs up and down. *Annu. Math. Stat.* 17: 24–33

Rubinstein R Y 1981 *Simulation and the Monte Carlo Method.* Wiley, New York

Skellman J G 1948 A probability distribution derived from the binomial distribution by regarding the probability of success as variable between the sets of trials. *J. Roy. Stat. Soc.* B10: 257–61

von Neumann J 1951 Various techniques used in connection with random digits. *Applications Maths. Series* 12: 36–38

Policy Research

Policy-oriented Research

J. D. Nisbet

Policy-oriented research is best defined in terms of its instrumental function rather than by the topics of study. When research in education is designed, managed, and reported with the specific purpose of informing policy decisions or assisting or monitoring their implementation, the term "policy-oriented" is used to distinguish this approach from "fundamental" research which is primarily designed to extend the frontiers of knowledge. This definition of policy-oriented research may be extended to include evaluation. It may also be applied to research which is closely tied to educational practice as well as policy.

In this approach, educational issues which are of current concern are accepted as priority topics for research. The function of this research is to provide an information base for decision making; administrators, politicians, or teachers then add the necessary value judgments, supposedly so that policy and practice are firmly based on empirical evidence from experiment and survey. The implicit model in this perception of the relation of research to policy is that the task of research is to establish the "facts", which are then used to inform judgment. This instrumental view of the function of research, however, is limited, and it makes naive and simplistic assumptions about how policy and practice are determined. If adopted uncritically, the emphasis on relevance constrains inquiry within the limits of existing policy and risks a trivialization of research. But with a clearer understanding of the function of research and with enlightened administration of research funding, the present trend towards policy-oriented studies could enable research to make a more effective contribution to educational practice.

1. Definitions

The definition of policy-oriented research is usually expressed by contrasting it with fundamental research. A variety of terms can be used to express the contrast: applied versus basic or pure research, policy-oriented versus curiosity-oriented studies, work directed towards decision or action versus work directed towards knowledge or theory. Less charitably, "relevant" research may be contrasted with "academic" research. Whichever terms are used, they carry value judgments which can be misleading if they are not made explicit. The distinction between pure and applied research in education is itself misleading. "From one point of view, *all* educational research is applied research, designed to bring about changes in the way education is carried on, rather than simply to add to our existing stock of knowledge" (Taylor 1973). Defined narrowly, policy-oriented research is research which has direct application to current issues in educational policy or practice. A wider definition (and, to anticipate the argument of this analysis, a better one) is that policy-oriented research consists of careful, systematic attempts to understand the educational process, and through understanding to improve its efficiency. However, as this definition could apply to all forms of educational research, its main virtue is that it blurs these misleading distinctions among various kinds of research.

Listing the processes involved (see Sect. 3) is one way of defining. Policy-oriented research includes survey work or any comparable data gathering which enables policy makers or practitioners to base their decisions on evidence rather than prejudice or guesswork. Thus policy-oriented studies include the search for solutions to pressing educational or social problems, identifying and resolving the problems involved in implementing policy decisions, monitoring and evaluating initiatives in educational practice, and experimental studies to compare alternative educational methods. They also include policy studies and retrospective analyses of past policy, the purpose of which is to help make better policy decisions in the future.

Thus, the essential distinction between policy-oriented and other forms of educational research is in terms of purpose, rather than in choice of subject or method. Since the perception of educational issues as being of current concern is subject to volatile, popular fashions, an aspect of children's learning may be regarded as a theoretical issue this year but a topic for policy-oriented research next year. The end products of policy-oriented research are decisions or recommendations for action. The products of fundamental research are contributions to knowledge, understanding, or theory. Since decisions and action necessarily imply the adoption of some theory or interpretation, and theory likewise has long-term implications for action, the distinction between the two categories is not as sharp as is sometimes assumed. Though policy-oriented research usually operates within the context of accepted theory, and does not aim to modify theory, it may do so incidentally. Similarly, fundamental research does not aim to affect practice, but it may do so indirectly. Policy-oriented research is responsive, whereas fundamental research is autonomous.

Autonomous educational research, which does not have to be accountable in the sense of producing useful or usable findings, runs the risk of pursuing topics which are of interest only to other researchers. In its extreme, it is concerned with attacking other people's theories or findings, irrespective of whether the points at issue are of any importance outside the research sphere. Responsive research, designed as a response to a practical need, is no less likely to raise and illuminate fundamental issues, and there is the added bonus that it can be useful at the same time. It runs the risk of being left behind by the rapid course of events, since by the time results are available the problem which they were designed to answer is liable to have changed, or to be no longer seen as important.

Since responsive research operates within the context of existing policy or practice, it is limited in its generalizability, but it is more likely to have an impact on the specific policy or practice for which it is designed. The impact of this kind of research, however, is incremental rather than radical. It is for reasons such as this that those who provide funds for research projects in education are likely to favour, or even to demand, a policy orientation. Policy-oriented research modifies (and hopefully improves) the existing situation, protecting it from running into trouble by identifying or anticipating problems. It may, however, challenge established policy by demonstrating its impracticability, and may even develop or explore alternative policies. But it is essentially concerned with movement from a present situation, and therefore it obliges researchers to relate their work to "reality", usually in the form of empirical studies or field work.

2. Trends

Although pressure towards policy-related work has become more extreme since the early 1970s, many of the early educational research studies had a strong practical orientation. Binet's work, for example, which laid the foundations of psychometry, began with the problem of early identification of slow-learning children. The work of Thorndike and others in the 1920s on the psychology of the elementary-school curriculum aimed to influence educational policy and classroom practice. The "scientific movement" in educational research envisaged the creation of a science of education based on experimentation, which could then be used to improve decision making at all levels, from the day-to-day practice of the teacher in the classroom to the long-term planning of educational provision, resources, and training. Large-scale national studies such as the Eight-year Study in the 1930s (to test the feasibility of accreditation of schools)

and the international programme of research on examinations also in this period, were directed to produce practical recommendations for improvement of the system. But the distinction between practical and theoretical research was not stressed at this time. The two kinds of inquiry were seen as complementary, and since there was practically no direct public finance involved, the conduct of research was left wholly to the academic researchers whose salaries were paid by universities and colleges. Even the national councils for educational research founded in this period (in Scotland, Australia, and New Zealand in the 1930s and England later) prided themselves on producing results useful to teachers as well as works of scholarship.

The growth of research in the years after 1950 can be divided into four phases: 1955–65, the beginning of publicly financed research on a substantial scale; 1965–70, a period of massive expansion; 1970–75, the growth of accountability; and from 1975, a trend towards central control of research.

The first phase was initiated by awareness that educational research could make a significant contribution to policy and practice. The social sciences had come of age and their potential value was recognized. (Perhaps it was merely that administrators found themselves at a disadvantage in controversies if they could not produce empirical evidence to support their decisions or express their policies in the context of social science concepts which were becoming more widely accepted.) In Sweden, the linking of research to policy began in the late 1940s. In the early 1960s, in the United States and the United Kingdom (and subsequently in many other countries), formal institutional structures were created for channelling public funds into educational research and development, particularly for curriculum development and for intervention programmes. As a result, between 1964 and 1969, expenditure on research in education in the United Kingdom multiplied tenfold; in the United States, expenditure doubled in each year from 1964 through 1967. The increase in funding soon led to a demand for accountability, and for a greater say in how the funds were to be spent. In 1970 in the United Kingdom, politicians demanded that research policy in education "had to move from a basis of patronage—the rather passive support of ideas which were essentially other people's related to problems which were often of other people's choosing—to a basis of commission...the active initiation by the Department [of Education] on problems of its own choosing, within a procedure and timetable which were relevant to its needs".

Perhaps too much had been expected, or promised, and disillusionment was allied with suspicion of "academic drift", in which preoccupations with theories were being given priority over pressing practical issues. In the United Kingdom this trend was most evident, expressed in the crude customer–contractor principle of the 1971 Rothschild Report: "The customer says what he wants; the contractor (the researcher) does it if he can; and the customer pays." This method of deciding how research should be funded was widely challenged at the time. A policy statement by the United Kingdom Social Science Research Council argued: "It is not so much a matter of an ordered hierarchy of priorities, as a process of grasping at opportunities presented by an almost accidental coagulation of interest among a group of able research workers around a chosen problem in order to shift a frontier of knowledge forward." But the idea of "an almost accidental coagulation", however accurate as a description of the research process, could not survive the energy crisis of 1973 and the economic constraints of the years which followed. The need to cut back expenditure made decisions on priorities inevitable, and increasingly these decisions were made by central government. Now research which is not linked to policy is at risk of being seen as a dispensable luxury, and researchers have to be ready to tackle major policy issues as legitimate topics for inquiry, and sometimes even as the only topics worth studying.

Thus, to quote from a review of developments in eight countries,

Across the world, educational research is now an integral part of modern administrative procedure. Increased investment in research has led to...a concern that the conduct, organisation, and funding of research should be directed towards maximising its effect on policy and practice. The major questions to which answers are still sought are, What forms of research should have priority? and, Who is to decide? (Nisbet 1981)

3. Utilization

The analysis of policy has become an academic study of growing importance in recent years. Weiss (1977), reviewing the contribution of social research to public policy, allots to research only a limited influence in decision making: its more important effect is indirect and long-term through "a gradual accumulation of research results", shaping the context within which these decisions are made. Thus research is only one of many inputs to policy making, one contribution to a complicated process in which there are many other competing forces. The policy maker seeks to establish a policy which is acceptable to those with power to influence its implementation. Their concern is not so much a matter of being "right" (for there are different "right" solutions, depending on one's values) but rather of reconciling divergent views in a solution which is seen as "fair" by a maximum number of those affected by it. It is therefore impossible to describe a policy as correct, except in relative terms as correct for some stated aims or values. Since the aims and values of all those with some access to power are bound to be in conflict, it is not possible to find policies which are correct for everyone.

In this amorphous process of policy making, there are several functions which research can perform. First, insofar as information conveys power, research strengthens the hand of any group which can produce research findings to support its preferred viewpoint. (Even to describe assertions as "research" strengthens

their impact, until the speaker is challenged for "evidence": the scientific model is implicit throughout this interaction.) Administrators commission policy-oriented research to strengthen their hand against the many pressure groups in the policy-making arena. In the view of the administrators, pressure groups are those who seek to further their own policies, whereas administrators see themselves as neutral to the policy they implement. Information thus weakens the power of those who play on ignorance or twist facts to suit their private ends. This however assumes that research is value free, or at least that research makes explicit the values on which it is based.

A second function for research is to ensure that action will achieve what is intended by a policy. For this purpose, research is used to work out the details of how to implement decisions, by identifying obstacles, including the opinions and attitudes of those who are likely to oppose implementation of a policy, and perhaps testing out solutions to overcome these obstacles in trials with pilot groups. There are other functions which Weiss (1977) also identifies: for example, the use of research to legitimate policies which have already been decided, or to procrastinate by offering research as an alternative to action, and similar improper uses against which the researcher should guard.

The underlying assumptions in this view of policy-oriented research are considered in the next section. Accepting for the moment this view of research, a range of types of research can be listed which fall within the scope of policy-oriented studies.

(a) *Surveys to gather relevant "facts" as a database for decision.* In the United Kingdom, for example, every major educational report since the 1950s has been accompanied by a research programme: the 1960 Crowther Report and the 1963 Newsom Report on secondary education, the 1963 Robbins Report on higher education, the 1967 Plowden Report on primary education, the 1976 Warnock Report on handicapped children, and so on. The American practice has been to commission an expert or team of experts to produce independent reports which are made available for public debate and which help to create a favourable climate for decision.

(b) *Experimental studies to resolve controversies.* For example, are open-plan schools better than traditional buildings? Is class size related to educational achievement? Since issues like these cannot readily be resolved by laboratory experiments, they usually involve surveys of existing practice, and therefore overlap with (a), but they are more narrowly focused and specify the hypotheses they are designed to test.

(c) *Development studies for implementing policies.* The introduction of an innovation accepted as desirable, such as a new examination procedure or computer-assisted learning, requires pilot studies to establish feasibility and identify likely obstacles to success.

(d) *Evaluation studies.* Whereas (c) is a monitoring of institutions to provide guidance for future decisions, the traditional use of evaluation is a retrospective review of past decisions: Did it work? How could it have been improved? The distinction between (c) and (d) however, is not clear, since formative evaluation falls more readily into category (c).

In all four types, the most valuable research design is one which focuses on analysis of problems, rather than simply seeking to supply answers to questions. There are of course some who still hold the unrealistic expectation that research should provide ready-made incontrovertible solutions. In 1976, for example, the Secretary of the English Department of Education and Science complained: "It is exceptional to find a piece of research that really hits the nail on the head and tells you pretty clearly what is wrong or what should be done." Weiss (1977) describes this as the "linear model" of research utilization and criticizes its "instrumental naivete". The sequence is: "A problem exists; information or understanding is lacking; research provides the missing knowledge; a solution is reached." There are relatively few situations in which this model can be applied. The essential feature of policy-oriented research is that it is designed to contribute towards a solution either by producing recommendations for action, describing as fully as possible the complexity of implications and complications, or by establishing conceptual frameworks which enable decisions to be made with fuller insight and understanding.

The belief that educational decisions can be guided by the results of scientific inquiry carries with it the corollary that the value of research can be judged by evidence of its impact, or at least by evidence that it has clear implications for action. Good research on this interpretation is research which influences (or can influence) policy or practice. Is there evidence that education is any better as a result of research? There has been no shortage of sceptics, even in the 1950s. In 1955, for example, Lamke wrote that if research over the past three years in medicine, agriculture, physics, or chemistry were wiped out, our lives would be changed materially; "but if research on teacher personnel over the same three years were to vanish, educators and education would continue much as usual" (Nisbet and Broadfoot 1980 p. 14). If research, after all its vast expenditures, has not resulted in visible improvement in the educational system, then either the system is at fault (or the teachers are to blame) for being unable to make use of the findings, or the money is being spent wrongly and the research itself is faulty. (There is, of course, another explanation, that this view of how research affects the system is over-simple.) Sometimes there has been the suspicion that the only ones who have derived benefit from the investment in educational research and development are the researchers themselves. Being isolated from the practical realities of the "outside world", as it was termed, they diverted public money to academic interests of their own instead of to the problems which required solutions. The solution adopted was to take the decisions on research priorities out of the hands of the researchers and put them in the hands of the administrators. Since research could not give direction to policy,

then the influence should be reversed and policy makers should be given control of research, allowing policy priorities to determine the choice and design of research. If those who are in contact with the "real world" take over the management of research, so the assumption goes, impact will be improved, relevance will be greater, and the risk of wasted money will be avoided.

Consequently, decisions on research priorities are now often made by those who are not themselves directly involved in research. This mode of working is familiar to the economist, the engineer, and the agricultural specialist but less common in legal and medical matters. The administrator who controls research funds now expects to be involved in the initial decisions on the topic of inquiry, the time scale, the personnel required, the design, and of course the cost. When the project is funded, there will be continuing interest (or interference, as it may appear) in monitoring what is being done through an advisory committee (sometimes a steering committee) and regular reporting. Tighter control may sometimes be imposed by "stepped funding" in which funds for each stage are conditional on approval of a report on the previous one (an impossible procedure to operate without year-long delays between the stages). The mode of reporting and arrangements for publishing and discussing the findings may also be specified in the contract (though the more common complaint is that research sponsors fail to set aside money, time, or staff for diffusion). The contract may require surrender of copyright to the sponsors and acceptance of their right to veto should they find the results not to their liking.

It is difficult to stand against these pressures. Not only can sponsors withhold funds: even the access to schools is usually made conditional on approval of the research project as a whole and the research instruments in detail. Thus policy-oriented research can become wholly directed and censored by people who are not themselves researchers and who have a vested interest in the outcomes. The researcher is put in the position of servant to the policy maker. Clearly, the dangers here are that criticism of a policy is not likely to be encouraged; that important issues are organized out of debate; and that researchers, obliged to undertake studies which they do not see as most urgent, most interesting, or most promising, will work less intensively and move on when they can to other less restrictive fields of study. Fortunately, many of those responsible for the funding of research projects are aware of these dangers. The picture above of the research slave is a caricature, though each element in it has been experienced by those who undertake commissioned research. In most countries, as yet, the relationship between researchers and the providers of funds for research is quite close, both sides understanding the requirements and constraints of the other (as will be shown in the concluding Sect. 5).

4. Analysis

The contrast between policy-oriented and fundamental research in education derives partly from the field of science. The long-standing debate over the relative value of pure and applied science mirrors many of the arguments discussed here. Pressure for more applied studies in educational research reflects the positivist belief that, in education as in science, there are solutions to problems, existing somewhere or other but hidden at present because the information or the techniques or the resources to discover them are lacking. Though seldom explicitly stated, the positivist assumption appears in policies for research funding and in the disillusionment if results are disappointing.

This kind of assumption underlies the early history of educational research when there was no public funding. Educational research had its origins, as pointed out above, in the "scientific movement" in education which was in its hey-day during the first 40 years of this century. By research, a science of education would be established, an organized body of empirical evidence from which would be derived theories and principles refined and tested by experiment. From such a science, it would be possible to derive answers to problems, or at least to develop methods to discover answers. The scientific movement treated education as unproblematic. It assumed that the state of "being an educated person" was not a matter for discussion, that there were "best methods" of teaching and learning, and that these methods could be identified by experiment. What is the optimum time to be devoted to spelling? At what age should a foreign language be taught? Which typeface is most legible? Some of these questions have straight answers; others do not. The position is tenable in areas where "the processes and outcomes of inquiry are independent of their social and historical context" (Becher and Kogan 1980 p. 93). There are issues of this kind in education, and not all of them are merely concerned with miniscule detail. Where there is consensus on values, where decisions on aims are relatively noncontroversial, the researcher's task is "to pursue generalisations about the most effective means of achieving desired goals" (Broadfoot and Nisbet 1981 p. 116). It is here that research is most readily policy oriented and has its most evident impact.

> In topics where there is a general consensus on values, research findings seem to be particularly effective: they are readily incorporated into policy or action. But when basic assumptions are challenged, then research...is treated merely as one more pressure group with vested interests. (Broadfoot and Nisbet 1981 p. 117)

In contrast, there are topics

> ...in which there can be no possibility of maintaining that the processes and outcomes can be separated from, or evaluated outside, their social and historical context. Here...knowledge depends on the development of a refined judgment rather than on incontrovertible demonstration. (Becher and Kogan 1980 p. 93)

This is the relativist end of the continuum.

> A positivist perspective makes two assumptions. First, that there is a fixed and unchanging reality based on constant

relationships which is amenable to scientifically modelled, objective research. Second, that the formulation of the research question itself is part of an objective process. The relativist rejection of this position...emphasises the problematic nature of education itself. (Broadfoot 1979 p. 127)

The distinction may be illustrated using an applied science like engineering. The design and improvement of pyramids, canals, engines, or central heating raise issues which can be decided by scientific inquiry. The decisions, however, are not always infallible when the context changes, and what is needed is a new insight rather than an incremental modification. Berlyne (Dockrell and Hamilton 1980 p. 8) illustrates the point by relating the response of an imaginary advisory committee in 1810, just before the beginning of the railway age, asked to forecast the development of the transport system. "One thing", the committee concluded, "has stood the test of time over several thousand years: the horse has come to stay. Authorities as diverse as Genghis Khan, Dick Turpin, Julius Caesar, and Buffalo Bill, all agree on one thing from long experience, that there is no better way of getting from one place to another than on a horse."

This illustrates the weakness of the criterion of "relevance". Relevance in educational research is liable to mean finding results which are capable of being implemented within the existing system. Hence, if the direction of research is assigned to those whose interest (in both senses of the word) is in the existing system, there is a risk that they may choose only those new ideas or findings which leave their prejudices undisturbed, resulting in innovation without change. This was what Rousseau had in mind in 1762 when he wrote: "People are always telling me to make practical suggestions. You might as well tell me to suggest improvements which can be incorporated with the wrong methods at present in use."

The pressure towards "relevance" may thus operate in a reactionary way. This has led some radical reformers to reject all "contamination" from working within the system, even opposing attempts to ameliorate present conditions, because this is to patch over the cracks, to bolster a system which should be brought to collapse. No administrator can adopt such a standpoint. Administration is committed to incrementalism: if not to piecemeal change, at least to that degree of reform which is demonstrably achievable. Consequently, it is argued, researchers must be given guidance or direction from those who face directly the problem of the "real" world, to avoid the risk of producing work which cannot be exploited.

Difficulties involved in policy-oriented research can be categorized under three types of explanation, adapted from Caplan et al.'s (1975) explanations of the nonutilization of research in policy formation.

The "knowledge-specific" explanation attributes the difficulty of relating research to policy to the kind of information which is provided by research because of its methodology. This is too narrow and limited to be of direct value to policy makers. Research tackles problems by focusing on selected aspects, eliminating other factors in order to achieve generalizable conclusions. Policy has to make decisions in a given context.

The "two-communities" explanation contrasts the different worlds of the researcher and the policy maker. These two worlds have different and even conflicting values, different reward systems, and even different languages.

The "policy-maker constraint" explanation emphasizes the pressures for immediate and acceptable decisions in the formulation of policy. Information for decision making is usually required sooner than research can provide it. Consequently, attempts are made to predict future relevance. Since the framework within which such predictions are made is the current position, itself the product of historical factors, these lists of priority topics are liable to come up with yesterday's problems, especially if they are compiled on the advice of senior members of the education profession. They are almost certain to be out-of-date by the time that research can be mounted to deal with them. Policy makers also have to ensure that their decisions are acceptable, and so they must take account of factors outside the traditional realm of research, including political feasibility. Research findings may appear to be unrealistically impractical. The point can be illustrated by the story of the traveller who asked a local the way to a neighbouring village. "Well, if I were you", was the reply, "I wouldn't start from here." This is how the policy maker often sees the advice of the researcher.

Policy-oriented research tends to rely on a rational analysis model for solving social problems. This model assumes a sequence of stages: establish the facts, specify the objectives, define the problem, canvass a range of solutions, work out the implications of each solution, make a choice, communicate the decision, and plan its implementation. Cronbach et al. (1980 pp. 94–95) criticize this process of rational decision making applied to educational issues.

All the strings are in the hands of the decision maker... Rationalism is dangerously close to totalitarianism ...Concentrating information and, therefore, power in the hands of control management is seen as the sovereign remedy at some moments in history, yet, at those very times, some observers of the system have warned that the "efficiency" so achieved is illusory. The larger the role of experts in governance, the more difficult it becomes for ordinary citizens to give direction to action. When information is closely held, what reaches the public is filtered so that it supports policies that the authorities favour. Insofar as information is a source of power, evaluations carried out to inform a policy maker have a disenfranchising effect. An open society becomes a closed society when only the officials know what is going on.

The closed circle of research restricted to questions which are relevant to currently accepted procedures may thus become an obstacle to radical reform. This argument can also be applied generally in the field of science. According to Kuhn (1970), a major part of scientific research is directed towards solving routine problems in which a dominant paradigm is applied, thus supporting or reinforcing established theories; and this proceeds

until a scientific revolution overthrows accepted beliefs, only to establish a new orthodoxy which then dominates the pattern of research. Thus research, which is commonly regarded as a force for change, may often operate as a restrictive or reactionary influence. In education, if research is confined to processes in the existing system or to problems as defined by current policy, it will result only in marginal change. Indeed,

...by reinforcing the importance of the framework of thought which identifies certain aspects as 'problems', legitimating their priority in the agenda of concern, it has a stabilising effect which discourages alternative perspectives. Challenging interpretations are seen as less relevant...are less likely to be funded, and less likely to be accepted by editors for publication, and if published, less likely to be read or quoted. (Broadfoot and Nisbet 1981 p. 119)

In a complementary way, the indirect, long-term influence of fundamental research is to create the theoretical context in which day-to-day issues are perceived, to write an agenda of concern. New concepts or structures or theories are introduced and gradually absorbed into popular thought and discussion, until they become a new climate of opinion, variously described as a "prevailing view" (Cronbach and Suppes 1969), "a cumulative altering of conceptions of human behaviour" (Getzels), "ideas in good currency" (Schon), "sensitizing" (Taylor), or "a gradual accumulation of research results which can lead to far-reaching changes in the way people and governments address their problems" (Weiss 1977). Administrators and politicians respond to the "resonance" of research findings. Often these research findings have been filtered, are out of date and highly popularized. As Keynes observed in the field of economics: "Practical men who believe themselves to be quite exempt from any intellectual influence, are usually the slaves of some defunct economist."

5. Implications

Thus two functions of research can be distinguished: one long-term, creating or changing the prevailing view; the other more immediate, working out the routine problems within the context of the current prevailing view. These are the basic and policy-oriented styles of research, but the distinction between them is not as sharp as has been suggested. The applied sciences have often contributed as much to pure science as they have received from it.

Academic status tends to be accorded to those who make contributions to pure science. They are the aristocrats of research, a small elite who provide the model to which many aspire. Why should a lesser status be given to the proletariat workers who are prepared to have their research skills used as an instrument of management and control, to identify stress points so that policy and practice may be trimmed accordingly? Research of this kind can be a powerful weapon of reform, testing out new ideas, modifying or rejecting them if they are at fault, and if the evidence shows them to be feasible, establishing their credibility all the more widely and quickly. This style of research attracts funds; it is difficult in a time of financial constraint and accountability to justify the expenditure of public funds on any other kind of research in education. Since failure is immediately evident, it can be used to remedy the past weaknesses of educational research and improve its techniques. The results are more likely to have impact and thus to create in the long-term a favourable climate of opinion as to the value of educational research.

The danger of this line of action is of accepting a purely technocratic role for research, creating an elite group of researchers in alliance with bureaucrats to manage the system. Though at first sight this is an attractive role for the researcher, it is potentially divisive, since it divides the researcher and his or her powerful partner from the teaching profession and the public. An alternative style of research is the "teachers as researchers" movement, or "action research". This is a school-based form of research, in which teachers are encouraged to apply the techniques of research to their own practical work. The teachers define the problems to be researched and they investigate and reflect on their own practice. This style of research also has its risks. It could merely aggravate the present situation, if teachers were to study only what is of immediate concern to them. It could then restrict research even further within the limits of inflexible classroom traditions and narrow professional perspectives. But it could also lead out of the constraints in which educational research is now caught.

It may be that the very act of teachers addressing their own classroom problems from a research perspective will be the most fertile soil for educational research to grow in. Fundamental research can grow from modest questioning. Collaborative research can be developed in quite a different way, retaining its democratic devolution of responsibility so as to prevent the emergence of an elite group of researchers in alliance with those responsible for management and control. If it can be developed so as to provide teachers (and administrators and parents and all those concerned with education) with the means of improving their own understanding, then its effect will be to put educational studies into a questioning framework. To do this, it must go beyond "routine problems", and be concerned instead with the parameters used for thinking about education, redefining issues, and restructuring perceptions. This is no small task, but one well worth attempting. (Broadfoot and Nisbet 1981 p. 121)

This interactionist model for educational research applies also to the relation of research to policy. The association of policy, administration, and research can be developed in such a way that each illuminates the others. Cronbach et al. (1980), quoting Elmore and Caplan, argue for an intermediate structure between research and application, "some institutional means of arguing about the policy relevance of ambiguous results". Cronbach suggests a "collegial group", rather like an advisory council. However, this bridging element could readily be created by a change in the relationships

of researchers to their various partners in the educational enterprise. The 1975 Annual Report of the Scottish Council for Research in Education (Simon and Taylor 1981 p. 171) describes a procedure of "negotiated research", in preference to a customer merely specifying his or her requirements on the Rothschild model. The negotiation of a research commission is developed out of an extended discussion of what is sought and what can be offered, in which (ideally) researchers and customers each accept the other's contribution to the proposal. This Cronbach describes as a "context of accommodation" rather than a "context of command" (1980 pp. 83–84); and with specific reference to evaluation, he argues for the research worker to "learn to serve in a context of accommodation and not dream idly of serving a Platonic guardian" (p. 100). A balance needs to be found between the autonomous and responsive modes of research in education.

If policy-oriented studies can be implemented in this enlightened way, educational research stands to gain from its closer association with both policy and practice. "Two worlds of educational research may be distinguished, the practical and the theoretical, pure and applied; but we are more likely to have a balanced attitude if we can have a foot in both worlds" (Simon and Taylor 1981 p. 175). The contributions of research to policy, to practice, and to theory are not easily reconciled, but the research enterprise in education would suffer if any one of these three is regarded as of lesser importance.

See also: Educational Research and Policy Making; Research Needs and Priorities

Bibliography

Becher T, Kogan M 1980 *Process and Structure in Higher Education.* Heinemann, London
Broadfoot P M 1979 Educational research through the looking glass. *Scottish Educ. Rev.* 11: 133–42
Broadfoot P M, Nisbet J 1981 The impact of research on educational studies. *Br. J. Educ. Stud.* 29: 115–22
Caplan N S, Morrison A, Stambaugh R J 1975 *The Use of Social Science Knowledge in Policy Decisions at the National Level: A Report to Respondents.* University of Michigan, Ann Arbor, Michigan
Cronbach L J, Suppes P (eds.) 1969 *Research for Tomorrow's Schools: Disciplined Inquiry for Education.* Macmillan, New York
Cronbach L J et al. 1980 *Toward Reform of Program Evaluation.* Jossey-Bass, San Francisco, California
Dockrell W B, Hamilton D (eds.) 1980 *Rethinking Educational Research.* Hodder and Stoughton, London
Husén T, Boalt G 1968 *Educational Research and Educational Change: The Case of Sweden.* Wiley, New York
Husén T, Kogan M (eds.) 1984 *Educational Research and Policy: How Do They Relate?* Pergamon, Oxford
Kogan M 1974 *The Politics of Education.* Penguin, Harmondsworth
Kuhn T S 1970 *The Structure of Scientific Revolutions*, 2nd edn. Chicago University Press, Chicago, Illinois
Nisbet J D 1981 The impact of research on policy and practice in education. *Int. Rev. Educ.* 27: 101–04

Nisbet J D, Broadfoot P M 1980 *The Impact of Research on Policy and Practice in Education*. Aberdeen University Press, Aberdeen

Simon B, Taylor W (eds.) 1981 *Education in the Eighties: The Central Issues*. Batsford, London

Suppes P (ed.) 1978 *Impact of Research on Education: Some Case Studies*. National Academy of Education, Washington, DC

Taylor W (ed.) 1973 *Research Perspectives in Education*. Routledge and Kegan Paul, London

Weiss C H (ed.) 1977 *Using Social Research in Public Policy Making*. Heath, Lexington, Massachusetts

Legitimatory Research

J. P. Keeves

The rapidly growing interest in policy-oriented research has led to the need to distinguish between those programmes of research that are associated with the generation of change, and those that serve to maintain and consolidate existing situations. Educational organizations hold considerable power over the lives of the individuals within them, and it is not surprising that in education there should be a strong reciprocal relationship between power and knowledge. Power on the one hand controls the use and flow of knowledge. On the other hand knowledge is used to support existing arrangements for the exercising of power. Legitimatory research is that type of research which is undertaken to strengthen and maintain existing power structures in educational systems as well as the policies and practices operating within those systems. The term "legitimatory" is used because the research is conducted with the express purpose of legitimating existing arrangements for the exercising of power from the perspectives of the institution supporting the research and controlling the release of the findings.

1. Policy-oriented Research

Investigations in the field of education are increasingly being planned with a strong policy orientation. The purpose of such research is to provide information for decision making with respect to educational policy and practice. Administrators and politicians recognize the usefulness of evidence to which they can add their own value judgments before embarking on a course of action that involves the development and implementation of new policy. When research into an educational problem is designed, conducted and reported with the specific aim of providing information for the making of policy, or for monitoring the implementation of policy, or for examining the effects of existing policy, then the term "policy-oriented research" is used. Research of this type in the field of education is becoming more common as politicians and administrators seek and achieve greater control over the allocation of the funds available for research and evaluation studies. Consequently it is not surprising that Weiss (1979), in a classification of ways in which social science research might be utilized, has identified a political approach and a tactical approach that are related to the legitimatory research discussed in this article. Husén (1984), however, argues that Weiss's seven models may be merged into only two major ones,

and that the political and tactical approaches are best combined. It is this combined model that we would refer to as a legitimatory approach to research utilization. In addition, Suchman (1970) has listed the possible misuses of evaluation, which correspond to a legitimatory approach to evaluative research. The growing incidence of such research has led to this more detailed examination of its nature and purpose.

There are types of policy-oriented research in education that have been developed with the particular purpose of introducing change. They combine investigation, educational development and, in general, the promotion of social change. Two important types of research in this area are known as "action research" and "participatory research". In participatory research, for example, the researcher with specialized knowledge and training commonly joins people in the workplace, and together they undertake an investigation which seeks primarily to improve education and, through education, to improve the lives of those people involved. It is clear that people undertaking this type of policy-oriented research are not neutral in the value judgments which they bring to the conduct of an investigation. Thus, in participatory research in particular, there is a commitment to the processes of change in order to benefit and sometimes emancipate those engaged in the investigation.

It is also possible for research to be carried out with the specific purpose of preventing change or obtaining evidence to support an existing institution or to maintain an existing policy. The systematic collection of educational statistics on the numbers of schools of different kinds; the numbers of enrolled students, teachers and ancillary staff; as well as the average numbers of students in daily attendance; can be seen as a simple example of this type of legitimatory research. Commonly, although this information is collected and tabulated, it is generally published in part and not in a form that would permit the evidence being used against the educational organizations involved. The data are held and used in situations and in ways that would support the organization and would not permit the organization to be challenged.

This type of research that is frequently neither conspicuous nor publicized is commonly undertaken within large educational bureaucracies that have not only the necessary resources to support such research, but also the responsibility to maintain an educational system.

Since, in general, such investigations are carried out to legitimate existing policies and practices, the term "legitimatory research" is appropriate. The findings from research conducted within this perspective are commonly not released as a scholarly publication. They remain as "in house" reports that are summarized in a few pages for administrators and policy makers to read.

An example arising from the compilation of educational statistics may contribute to an understanding of how this type of research activity operates. If the information on the average numbers of students by age in daily attendance in some educational systems were examined by critics, they would probably note a very high level of absenteeism at age levels near the end of compulsory schooling. Since it is generally not in the interest of schools and school systems that disruptive students should be present in classrooms, it is considered preferable that this information should not be released, even though it is relevant in a significant way to educational and social problems related to juvenile delinquency. In addition, such absenteeism might be perceived to be a consequence of inadequate teaching or of irrelevant curricula.

In some countries, this type of research has very limited visibility, although it is relatively widespread and obtains regular funding, at the expense of more impartial and scholarly work. Within most large educational organizations, such as universities, local educational authorities, national and state offices of education and indeed within teacher unions, there are research units that seek to maintain existing policies and support established institutions. The research conducted within these units is often of a legitimatory nature. A very wide variety of investigatory activity is involved. It may range from the examination of pass rates and studies of prediction of success in universities, to the monitoring of standards of educational achievement in state and national systems, or studies of teacher stress by teacher unions. The findings from such investigations are only released and widely publicized when it is of value politically to use the information available to sustain existing policies and practices.

Giddens has discussed certain aspects of the dissemination of research findings. He suggests that an investigation can be undertaken from perspectives where:

> ...the new knowledge or information is used to sustain existing circumstances. This may, of course, happen even where the theories or findings concerned could, if utilized in certain ways, modify what they describe. The selective appropriation of social science material by the powerful, for example, can turn that material to ends quite other than those that might be served if they were widely disseminated. (Giddens 1984 p. 342)

This article discusses the characteristics of research carried out within this perspective. It is also concerned with the nature of the process of legitimation. In addition, it considers an example of legitimatory research, and examines the functions of research in the legitimatory process.

2. Power and Knowledge

Legitimation is a social process. Power and authority are not, in general, assigned or transmitted at a single point in time to an educational organization, or an individual within an organization, but are acquired gradually over time. Power and authority can never be taken for granted. They are constantly being challenged and exposed to competing claims. Consequently, legitimation becomes a continuously operating process. Without legitimation, power and authority are insecure and impermanent.

The concept of legitimation owes much to the writings of Weber, who was concerned with belief in a legitimate order:

> Action, especially social action which involves social relationships, may be oriented by the actors to a *belief* (*Vorstellung*) in the existence of a "legitimate order". The probability that action will actually empirically be so oriented will be called the "validity" (*Geltung*) of the order in question. (Henderson and Parsons 1947 p. 124)

In addition, the writings of Habermas (1975) have sounded a warning about the legitimacy crisis faced by public administration. This work has supported an attack on established views of institutional governance, particularly in the field of education.

The link between these ideas and the development and use of knowledge was made by Berger and Luckmann (1967 p. 110). They saw legitimation as a "second-order" process that operated on the "first-order" ideas and relationships concerning society and social institutions in such a way as to develop new meanings that would make this knowledge "objectively available and subjectively plausible". In this sense it validates institutionalized knowledge and an institutional order. Thus it is possible to speak not only of the legitimation of a social institution but also of the legitimation of knowledge through the production of new knowledge.

Research is concerned with organized and systematic activities which are designed to produce knowledge. Consequently legitimatory research involves the compilation of new knowledge that will strengthen a social institution and will validate institutionalized knowledge. In the field of education, research can contribute in a significant way to the legitimation of social institutions and to the support of educational organizations and their policies, programmes and practices. However, educational research is a pursuit that is itself in need of validation, and the support for research provided by educational organizations serves to legitimate research as an activity. Thus educational institutions both validate and are validated by educational research. The dependence of research on educational organizations for financial and operational support, as well as the contribution of research towards maintaining the educational organizations pose certain problems for educational research. Consequently, research that is undertaken at the request of, and with financial support from, an educational organization in order to support the continuance and to maintain the operation of that organization as well as its existing policies and practices, can appropriately be referred to as "legitimatory research".

3. Characteristics of Legitimatory Research

Relatively few studies have been carried out to examine the processes and characteristics of legitimatory research. Although it has had a long-standing presence in many educational organizations, it has only been with the emergence of the field of policy-oriented research that its nature and function have become clear. Some characteristics of legitimatory research and the processes through which such research is conducted are considered below.

The characteristics of legitimatory research are as follows:

(a) The *problem* to be investigated arises from existing policies and practices within an educational organization. This, of course, is not unique to legitimatory research.

(b) The major *aim* of the research is to maintain the existing structure of an educational organization, and the continuance of its existing policies and practices.

(c) Legitimatory research is generally *conducted* by people with competence in research who are employed by the educational organization, so that the organization maintains control over the entire investigation.

(d) In general, the focus of the research is on the *operation* of the organization, on the activities of the people within it, or on the characteristics of those who seek entry into the organization.

(e) Central to the operation of legitimatory research is its role in providing information in a concise form for the senior educational administrators in order to *consolidate their position of power* within an organization.

(f) The release of the findings of the research is, in general, *controlled* by a senior administrator to occur at a time to optimize the impact that the findings might have on the legitimation of a particular policy or practice.

(g) It is rare for the findings of legitimatory research to be *published* in a form that would enable both the methods of investigation and the inferences drawn from the research to be examined critically and challenged. The reports are commonly only circulated in summary form on the grounds that the likely readers are interested only in the main conclusions of the investigation, and would not be interested in examining the available evidence in any detail.

(h) Where the investigation is undertaken by research workers who are outside the day-to-day operation of the organization, a *steering committee* is commonly set up to exercise control over the conduct of the investigation.

(i) If the research workers are external to the organization problems may arise over the publication of the reports of a study. Lynn and Jay (1982 pp. 97-99) draw a distinction between the *suppression of a research report* and the making of a decision not to publish it. In addition, they list the steps that can be taken to discredit research reports and so prevent their publication.

(j) Frequently, legitimatory research is conducted under the guise of an *evaluation study*, since the need for evaluation is widely acknowledged on the grounds of accountability, yet what is being sought is information to sustain a programme or policy in its existing form.

To illustrate these characteristics of legitimatory research an example is provided below.

4. A Study of Staffing and Resources: An Example

In this example, where an independent research organization was commissioned to work with eight educational organizations, some of the problems that can arise in a legitimatory research study were encountered.

The major expenditure in Australian schooling, as with other countries, is on the salaries of teachers, which commonly comprise between 75 and 80 percent of the total budget allocated to the provision of education in schools. Since education in Australia is a responsibility of the states and not of the commonwealth or federal government, the proportion of the total state budgets allocated to education in schools is high, generally of the order of 30 percent. Overall, a little under 6 percent of gross domestic product (GDP) is spent on education in Australia. Clearly the total expenditure on the salaries of the teaching service is a matter of considerable significance.

Following a long period of militancy by the teacher unions in Australia during the late 1960s and early 1970s directed towards decreasing class sizes, funds were made available for marked reductions in student–teacher ratios and thus class sizes. As could be anticipated, this was accompanied by a very substantial increase in the costs of education that had to be provided at the expense of other activities conducted by the state governments. The ministers of education within New Zealand and each of the Australian state and commonwealth governments, together with their advisers, who are the senior administrators in their educational bureaucracies, meet regularly as members of the Australian Education Council to develop common policies for the conduct of education in their regions. The ministers of education and, to a lesser extent, the directors-general of education recognized that if they were to pursue policies for the broad general development of their regions as well as for the general growth of education, it would be necessary to contain the pressure from the teacher unions for further reductions in class sizes. Thus they were placed in a position of seeking to maintain current policies and practices, and the existing structures of their organizations, without becoming committed to policy changes that would involve a further reduction in student–teacher ratios and class sizes.

As a first step, a review of previous research into class size was commissioned (Lafleur et al. 1974). This review found that little research work had been carried out in Australia, and there were inconclusive findings with regard to the effects of class size on achievement and attitude. However, it should be noted that in Australia the First International Mathematics Study conducted by the International Association for the Evaluation of Educational Achievement (IEA) in 1964, and the First IEA Science Study in 1970 had found relationships which indicated that, at the 13- and 14-year-old levels respectively, the larger the classes the higher the average levels of achievement of the students. These relationships remained significant even after other relevant factors on which data were collected had been taken into account. Although it was difficult to account for these findings, they left much to be explained with regard to the sustained demand for further reductions in class sizes.

In 1978, the results of the meta-analysis by Glass and Smith (1978) into the relationships between class size and achievement were published. The findings from this study had received widespread publicity and were hailed with acclaim by the teacher unions. More recently, the criticisms of the work of Glass and Smith that have been made by Slavin (1984a, 1984b) have thrown doubt on the findings of a meaningful relationship between class size and achievement. However, for a period of several years the work of Glass and Smith was accepted as authoritative throughout Australia and New Zealand and gradual reductions in class size took place.

The Australian Education Council, at its meeting in early 1978, expressed interest in the complex questions associated with student–teacher ratios and class sizes and commissioned a study into these problems which would be undertaken in collaboration with the staff of the research branches of the education departments in each of the regions. This study became known as the "Staffing and Resources Study". The initial reports of the work of Glass and Smith had a significant impact on the planning of this study. It was argued by some that further investigations of a non-experimental kind to examine relationships between class size and achievement were of doubtful value. Nevertheless, it was considered that if a study of teaching behaviour could be undertaken which would examine relationships between such behaviours and class size it would be relevant. However, the main thrust of the study would be to examine policies and practices at the level of school systems and schools.

The ministers of education sought a study that would examine the costs of education and, in particular, relationships involving the contribution of reductions in class size to the costs and to the benefits, if any, in terms of achievement outcomes and students' and teachers' attitudes. Immediately after work on this study into a highly sensitive area was authorized, pressures were mounted to distort the study and its design so that only peripheral issues would be investigated. Thus the ministers and some of the senior administrators sought a study which would legitimate existing policies. However, the forces for change in Australian education, such as the teacher unions, and some staff at the middle and lower management levels in the bureaucracies sought to modify the plans for the study so that it would generate change. The research workers who were members of an independent educational research organization and who had accepted responsibility for the conduct of the study, were not fully aware at the time the study was commissioned of the tensions that were likely to develop in the study. These tensions were a result of the conflict between the forces of conservatism that sought a legitimatory research study, and innovative educational practitioners who sought to alter the design of the investigation and the conduct of research in ways that focused on the need for change and the directions in which change should proceed.

The legitimatory nature of this study which was carried out at the request of the ministers of education, who were responsible for eight educational systems, led to sustained attacks on the study from both inside and outside these eight systems. While the senior administrators within the eight systems were willing for a detailed examination of policies and practices to be carried out within each system by their own staff, some were unwilling for this information to be made available to the other systems or to external investigators who would be comparing and contrasting the operations of the eight systems. Moreover, in one system a teacher union prevented the undertaking of a survey of schools in that system.

In due course carefully written reports were prepared and published. The reports covered the following areas: (a) a review of policies in the eight systems (McKenzie and Keeves 1982), (b) a survey of practices in 600 schools (Ainley 1982), (c) a report on critical issues associated with practices in 15 schools that were innovative in their organizational structures (Sturman 1982), (d) a study of relationships between class size, teacher and student behaviour and educational outcomes of achievement and attitudes (Larkin and Keeves 1984), and (e) an executive summary report of the first three volumes listed above (Ainley et al. 1982). In reviewing the study several years after its completion, it was found that some changes flowed from the study. However, the changes introduced were towards an increase in the efficiency of each system rather than educational reform. By and large, the reports of the study were made to serve the purpose of reducing the rate of change in the eight systems.

Several implications may be drawn from this study for the conduct of legitimatory research into a major policy area.

(a) If the issues being investigated are in conflict with the *policies of the teacher unions*, moves are made to block the conduct of a study.

(b) If the issues examined by the study challenge aspects of the *operation of the bureaucracies*, then ways are found to distort the conduct of the study.

(c) Legitimatory research is susceptible to interference from administrators and others who wish to *control the investigation*.

(d) The *findings of legitimatory research* will only be used by senior administrators and politicians at times and in ways that will achieve their previously determined purposes.

(e) Major research studies frequently take *several years* to bring to a satisfactory conclusion. During that time both the political and administrative officials who proposed the study may have been replaced and new officials may see issues from very different political perspectives.

(f) Legitimatory research exists because politicians and senior administrators need *evidence to support and legitimate* their policies and the educational organizations in which they work. The findings from such research are used only if they can be directed towards these ends.

5. Conclusion

It is common for legitimatory research to lead only to a summary report which does not permit an adequate examination of the conduct of the investigation on which the findings are based. As a consequence, although research of a legitimatory nature is relatively widespread within educational bureaucracies, little has been written about this type of research. More detailed analyses of its characterisitcs and its influence are urgently needed.

Bibliography

Ainley J G 1982 *Six Hundred Schools: A Study of Resources in Australian and New Zealand Government Schools*. Australian Council for Educational Research (ACER), Hawthorn, Victoria

Ainley J G, Keeves J P, McKenzie P A, Sturman A 1982 *Resource Allocation in the Government Schools of Australia and New Zealand*. Australian Council for Educational Research (ACER), Hawthorn, Victoria

Berger P L, Luckmann T 1967 *The Social Construction of Reality*. Penguin, London

Giddens A 1984 *The Constitution of Society*. Polity Press, Cambridge, UK; Blackwell, Oxford

Glass G V, Smith M L 1978 *Meta-Analysis of Research on the Relationship of Class Size and Achievement*. Far West Laboratory for Educational Research and Development, San Francisco, California

Habermas J 1975 *Legitimation Crises*. Beacon Press, Boston, Massachusetts

Henderson A M, Parsons T 1947 *Max Weber: The Theory of Social and Economic Organization*. Free Press, New York; Oxford University Press, Oxford

Husén T 1984 Issues and their background. In: Husén T, Kogan M (eds.) 1984 *Educational Research and Policy: How Do They Relate?* Pergamon, Oxford, pp. 14–20

Lafleur C D, Sumner R J, Witton E 1974 *Class Size Survey*. Australian Government Publishing Service, Canberra

Larkin A I, Keeves J P 1984 *The Class Size Question: A Study at Different Levels of Analysis*. Australian Council for Educational Research (ACER), Hawthorn, Victoria

Lynn J, Jay A (eds.) 1982 *Yes Minister. The Diaries of a Cabinet Minister by the Rt. Hon. James Hacker MP*, Vol. 2. British Broadcasting Corporation, London

McKenzie P A, Keeves J P 1982 *Eight Education Systems: Resource Allocation Policies in the Government School Systems of Australia and New Zealand*. Australian Council for Educational Research (ACER), Hawthorn, Victoria

Slavin R E 1984a Meta-analyses in education: How has it been used? *Educ. Res. AERA* 13 (8): 6–15

Slavin R E 1984b A rejoinder to Carlberg et al. *Educ. Res. AERA* 13(8):24–27

Sturman A 1982 *Patterns of School Organization: Resources and Responses in Sixteen Schools*, Australian Council for Education Research (ACER), Hawthorn, Victoria

Suchman E A 1970 Action for what? A critique of evaluative research. In: O'Toole R (ed.) 1970 *The Organization, Management and Tactics of Social Research*. Schenkman, Cambridge, Massachusetts

Weiss C 1979 The many meanings of research utilization. *Public Admin. Rev.* 39:426–31

Participatory Research

B. L. Hall and Y. Kassam

Participatory research is most commonly described as an integral activity that combines social investigation, educational work, and action. The combination of these elements in an interrelated process has provided both stimulation and difficulty for those who have become engaged in participatory research or who have tried to understand it. Some of the characteristics of the process are listed below.

(a) The problem to be studied originates in the community or workplace itself.

(b) The ultimate goal of the research is fundamental structural transformation and the improvement of the lives of those involved. The beneficiaries are the workers or people concerned.

(c) Participatory research involves the people in the workplace or the community who control the entire process of the research.

(d) The focus of participatory research is on work with a wide range of exploited or oppressed groups; immigrants, labour forces, indigenous peoples, women.

(e) Central to participatory research is its role of strengthening the awareness in people of their own abilities and resources and its support for mobilizing or organizing.

(f) The term "researcher" can refer to both the community or workplace persons involved as well as those with specialized training.

(g) Although those with specialized knowledge and training often come from outside the situation, they are committed participants and learners in a process that leads to militancy rather than detachment.

1. The Origins of Participatory Research

It is important to recognize that, while the term "participatory research" may be new, the concerns being expressed have a history and continuity in social science. Many of the ideas that are finding new opportunities for expression can be traced as far back as the early field work of Engels in his alignment with the working classes of Manchester during his early period. Marx's use of the structured interview—*L'Enquête Ouvrière*—with French factory workers is another sometimes forgotten antecedent. More recently, aspects of the work of Dewey, George Herbert Mead, and the Tavistock Institute in London have outlined methods of social investigation that are based on other than a positivistic epistemology.

By the late 1950s and early 1960s, the dominant international research paradigm was a version of the North American and European model based on empiricism and positivism and characterized by an attention to instrument construction and rigour defined by statistical precision and replicability. Through the elaborate mechanisms of international scholarships, cultural exchanges, and training of researchers in Europe and North America, this dominant paradigm was extended to the Third World. Research methods, through an illusion of objectivity and scientific credibility, become one more manifestation of cultural dependency .

The reaction from the Third World—beginning in Latin America—has taken many forms. Dependency theorists, such as Dos Santos, Frank Amin, and Leys outlined some of the mechanisms of economic and cultural dependency. Hence, in the field of research methods, Third World perspectives have grown out of a reaction to approaches developed in North America and Europe; approaches that have been not only created in different cultural settings but that contribute to already existing class distinctions. The Third World's contribution to social science research methods represents an attempt to find ways of uncovering knowledge that

work better in societies where interpretation of reality must take second place to the changing of that reality.

Practical experience in what was becoming known as participatory research occurred in the work of the Tanzanian Bureau of Resource Allocation and Land Use Planning. Here, Marja-Liisa Swantz and teams of students and village workers were involved in the questions of youth and employment in the Coast region and later in studies of socioeconomic causes of malnutrition in Central Kilimanjaro. A visit by Paulo Freire to Tanzania in 1971 was a stimulus to many social scientists who might not otherwise have been as impressed by the existing experience of many adult educators or community development workers.

What happened in Tanzania in a small way, had already begun in Latin America in the early 1960s. Stimulated in part by the success of the Cuban revolution, Latin American social scientists began exploring more committed forms of research. One of the most useful roles of Paulo Freire has been to bring some of the current ideas of Latin American social scientists to the attention of persons in other parts of the world. His work on thematic investigation, first in Brazil and later in Chile, was an expression of this search. Others, such as Beltran and Gerace Larufa, have explored alternatives through concepts of horizontal communication (Beltran 1976, Gerace Larufa 1973). Fals Barda (1980) and others in Colombia have been engaged in *investigación y acción*, while the Darcy de Oliveiras have made people aware of the value of militant observation (Darcy de Oliveira and Darcy de Oliveira 1975).

2. Not the Third World Alone

While the specific term "participatory research" developed in the Third World, due to crises caused by dysfunctional concepts of one-way, detached research in a world of immediate and urgent problems, a consciousness was growing in Europe and North America. The Frankfurt School was rediscovered through Habermas and Adorno. Action sociology was placed on the agenda of most academic meetings. In Switzerland, researchers in curriculum development adapted methodologies from political research to their needs. In Canada, Stinson developed methods of evaluation along action research lines for community development (Stinson 1979). In the Netherlands, Jan de Vries has explored alternatives from a firm philosophical base. The National Institute for Adult Education in the United Kingdom pioneered participatory research through its evaluation of the United Kingdom adult literacy campaign (Holmes 1976). In Italy, Paolo Orefice and colleagues at the University of Naples have been applying the methodology to their investigations of community and district awareness of power and control (Orefice 1981). In the United States, the Highlander Center in Tennessee has been using approaches similar to participatory research for many years, most recently to deal with issues of land ownership and use (Horton 1981).

3. Feminist Research

Feminist critiques of research have been part of the larger search for a form of working with people in a way that empowers them rather than prolongs the status quo. Both feminist research and participatory research seek to shift the centre from which knowledge is generated. Dale Spender has described the field of women's studies:

> Its multi-disciplinary nature challenges the arrangement of knowledge into academic disciplines; its methodology breaks down many of the traditional distinctions between theoretical and empirical and between objective and subjective. It is in the process of redefining knowledge, knowledge gathering and making....(Spender 1978)

In addition, Callaway has demonstrated that women have been largely excluded from producing the dominant forms of knowledge and that the social sciences have been not only a science of male society but also a male science of society (Callaway 1981). Spender urges women "to learn to create our own knowledge". It is crucially important, she states,

> ...that women begin to create our own means for producing and validating knowledge which is consistent with our own personal experience. We need to formulate our own yardsticks, for we are doomed to deviancy if we persist in measuring ourselves against the male standard. This is our area of learning, with learning used in a widely encompassing, highly charged, political and revolutionary sense. (Spender 1978)

4. Debate and Discussion

Many of the developments at both the theoretical and the practical levels were reviewed at an International Forum on Participatory Research which took place in Yugoslavia in April, 1980. The forum brought together about 60 activists and practitioners from all regions and, rare for international seminars, nearly half of the participants were women. The forum's objectives were: (a) sharing and consolidating experiences in participatory research; (b) development of practical guidelines; (c) strengthening of international linkages among regional networks; and (d) development of future strategies. A number of key issues, or themes, emerged from these deliberations. Whether in working group discussions or theoretical plenaries, participants addressed these issues with a sense of exploration, self-clarification, commitment, and mutual respect.

5. The Researcher as Learner

The role of the researcher is an important issue. It has been suggested that the researcher must (a) be committed to seeing the participatory research process through to the end, (b) avoid actions that endanger community members, and (c) see clearly, and support changes improving the situation of the subordinate groups within the community. It was recognized that these commitments were likely to run counter to the interests of the professional researcher, but that the researcher,

along with the community, learns and develops through the educative process. The researcher can make significant contributions by building new understandings and realities so that he or she is no longer an outsider, by bringing new information, and by helping to find funds for the development of technical skills. In all cases, the outside researcher is involved particularly in building an indigenous capacity for collective analysis and action and for the generation of new knowledge by the people concerned.

There has been considerable discussion about the role of the organic intellectual in participatory research. The term comes from Antonio Gramsci, the Italian political activist and theoretician who wrote from his prison cell in the 1930s. Although the term sounds awkward when not placed within Gramsci's overall framework, the idea is not very far removed from what many adult educators mean by "the empowerment of people through learning". The adjective organic means that such leadership arises from, and is nourished by, the actual situation of workers and peasants; such a person is not an outsider, although someone outside the situation can facilitate the necessary growth, awareness, and knowledge.

The term organic intellectual is really a collective expression for the new consciousness of the working class through its own social organization, such as the formation of political parties. Although participatory research may support and help such organizations, it should never seek to replace them. Organic intellectuals are also viewed as individual members of the peasant/working class whose consciousness and technical expertise has been raised through active struggle, of which participatory research may be one means. A third position argues that organic intellectuals may be middle-class intellectuals who have been radicalized through action and struggle and who may be located along a continuum from those engaged only in intellectual work—such as participatory research—to those engaged in a considerable amount of manual, as well as intellectual work. The first two positions are generally favoured. However, further examination of the relationship of the organic intellectual to participatory research is of high priority.

6. Nature of Participation

Participation has been used to cover microactivities, such as the learning of literacy skills, and macroactivities, such as the popular organization for class struggle at a national level. The particular role of participatory research, it has been argued, lies in the process of mobilization of people for their collective creation of new knowledge about themselves and their own reality. Again, this is part of the educative component of the process.

An important distinction has been advanced between participation and manipulation. Under the guise of participation rhetoric, and strategies to involve the people, outside interests might attempt to manipulate communities or workplace groups for purposes of domestication, integration, and exploitation. In contrast, participatory research is seen as a front line against such manipulation since it advocates and provides training in critical and collective analysis of the kind that establishes and maintains control and learning in the hands of the people, and explicitly rejects manipulation. Participatory forms of social action that lead from such collective analyses have also been advocated. A key methodological issue is the problem of how collective a participatory research process should become in view of the internal power relations within communities and workplace groups and the degree of new learning that individuals within a group must engage in.

7. Popular Knowledge

The creation of popular knowledge has emerged as a goal of participatory research. For many, participatory research is a process by which the "raw" and somewhat unformed—or at least, unexpressed—knowledge of ordinary people is brought into the open and incorporated into a connectable whole through discussion, analysis, and the "reflected" knowledge gained with or without allied intellectuals and those who have both broader and deeper insights.

Discussions of these matters have highlighted the dynamic interaction between the kind of practical technology and expertise that people who live in the situation have and the kind known as official technology and expertise. The identification of the various means of controlling this process of interaction that can be made available to local community or workplace groups is central to such discussions.

A further critical question is how the creation and dissemination of new knowledge is linked to social transformation. One position is that participatory research can, through successive movements of popular analysis over time, move people from looking at more peripheral contradictions in the local reality to focusing more clearly on central contradictions that actually influence and control their lives. In the process, they become more aware of how power groups can divert their attention to peripheral and short-term issues so that the inequitable status quo can be maintained. Thus, the linking of action to such analysis moves from action that addresses short-term needs to action based on strategies for bringing about fundamental social change.

8. Historical Materialism

The relationship between historical materialism and participatory research is also of interest. A strong position has been taken by some that the historical materialist method, in contrast to a pragmatic approach, is essential to the participatory research process. Here, class analysis and class struggle are fundamental ideas; popularly created knowledge in interaction with historical materialistic methodology can be regarded as yielding rich potential for social change. Another position

held is that participatory research must embrace a variety of analytic approaches and that historical materialism has sometimes been an alienating, elitist endeavour. However, there is considerable agreement on two related points. First, the use of the historical materialist method should be nondogmatic, given the fact that participatory research is a generative process. Secondly, the historical materialist method can be used in strategic ways, such as to study the dominant class forces (state, corporate) both globally and locally. An important challenge is to popularize such knowledge, to interpret it, and see it placed in the minds and hands of the people the dominant class seeks to exclude and to dominate.

9. Local Autonomy and Broader Struggles

Several tensions exist in the field. For example, there is tension between the requirement of local autonomy for a given participatory research process and the demand for coordinated social action at the national or regional levels. A national struggle must be more than an aggregate of participatory research experiences at the local level; forms of popular organizations developed by social movements are complex and variable and are rooted in local political and economic conditions. It must be noted that, at certain critical moments, a local-level participatory research process may, in fact, hinder the progress of broader social movements by overemphasizing the localized nature of the problems. Consequently there is a need to set ground rules across different levels of struggle. Again, participatory research is not seen as a panacea. However, there is general recognition that, at certain stages, participatory research can enrich broader social organizations.

10. A Question of Power

Emerging from the discussions, debates, and activities of participatory research is the central question of power. Participatory research can only be judged in the long run by whether or not it has the ability to serve the specific and real interests of the working class and other oppressed peoples. For Gaventa of the Highlander Research and Education Center in the Appalachian region of the United States, power can be described as follows: "A exercises power over B when A affects B in a manner contrary to B's interests." In this idea, A may exercise power over B by getting B to do what he does not want to do; A also exercises power by influencing, shaping, or determining B's very wants (Gaventa 1981).

How, then, can participatory research be useful in shifting more power into the hands of popular groups and oppressed peoples? There are at least three possibilities.

10.1 Unmasking the Myths

Vio Grossi (1981) has given considerable thought to the task of participatory research as initiating a process of disindoctrination that allows people to detach themselves from the myths imposed on them by the power structure that have prevented them from seeing their own oppression or from seeing possibilities for breaking free. In Marxian terms, participatory research leads to the analysis of secondary contradictions that exist within society (how does oppression look in our world?) to the location of primary contradictions (what are the hidden structures that shape society?), and then to a process of action.

In this context, structural transformation can be seen as the strategic goal to be reached in the medium or long term. A participatory research process carried out in conjunction with popular groups (and under their control) is designed to facilitate the analysis of stages towards that goal.

10.2 The Creation of Popular Knowledge

The stages of disindoctrination that Vio Grossi (1981) has outlined are discussed in working papers on methods that have been used over the past years by the Toronto-based Participatory Research Group. The papers describe a variety of methods for developing and activating collective analysis. These include drama, drawing, thematic photographs (both still and in photo-novel form), videotape, meetings, radio, and interview surveys as a means of helping people to examine the deeper layers of the social structure. Such action can lead to systematization of new knowledge; knowledge not generated by the dominant ideological producers in the superstructure but generated by and consistent with the experiences and world view of ordinary people.

Fals Barda has contributed to the discussion of popular knowledge in his paper on *Science and the Common People* (Fals Barda 1980). He says the creation of knowledge that comes from the people contributes to the realization of a people's science which serves and is understood by the common people, and no longer perpetuates the status quo. The process of this new paradigm involves: (a) returning information to the people in the language and cultural form in which it originated; (b) establishing control of the work by the popular and base movements; (c) popularizing research techniques; (d) integrating the information as the base of the organic intellectual; (e) maintaining a conscious effort in the action/reflection rhythm of work; (f) recognizing science as part of the everyday lives of all people; and (g) learning to listen.

The creation of popular knowledge is a form of antihegemonic activity, an instrument in the struggle to control what the social agenda is. In Gaventa's terms, popular knowledge can be seen as preventing those in power from maintaining the monopoly of determining the wants of others, thus, in effect, transferring power to those groups engaged in the production of popular knowledge (Gaventa 1981).

10.3 Contribution to Organizing

Participatory research is conceived to be an integral process of investigation, education, and action. When one addresses the question of power it is clearer than ever that the first two aspects are empty without the third.

But action must be explained still further. From several years of sharing information and results it has become clear that the most common action and the critical necessity is that of organizing, in its various phases. It has meant supporting the efforts of farmers' or womens' groups, or workers' health committees, or neighbourhoods, or campesinos to get together to understand issues and discuss options. It has meant building alliances with other social movements and strengthening the links within various progressive sectors. Action is not, however, a substitute for the organizing of the popular movements themselves. With its stress on collective analysis and on the working out of options and solutions together, the participatory research process reinforces the organizing potential of the base groups which use it.

11. Power for Whom?

It would be an error to assume that naive or uncontrolled use of participatory research results in strengthening the power of the powerless at the base of society. Without control over the participatory research process, experience has shown that power can easily accrue to those already in control. There has been a certain lack of clarity in some earlier writings on participatory research around this issue, and it has resulted in misunderstanding and manipulation.

11.1 Professional Researchers

Participatory research has been used by some researchers to provide them with insights and views that they could not ordinarily have had access to or know about. Some writings, with an emphasis on an increased scientific accuracy, have inadvertently encouraged abuses of participatory research, including the manipulation of groups by researchers. Participatory research has become the key by which these researchers have gained more power for themselves within the academic status quo, even admitting that the academic world allows for a wide range of ideological positions. In these cases, participatory researchers have fed the process of ideological control by giving more power to the institutions of the state for which they work. In fairness, participatory research has also legitimized the work of certain researchers in support of various popular groups, thereby resulting in a shift of skills and resources from the institution to the community or workplace.

11.2 The State

Some activists and social workers have seen participatory research as a way to get people to agree to a position, an action, a policy that social workers, adult educators, or others, feel is important for their purposes. Moreover, participatory research can be debased as a powerful tool for getting the predominant view of the state into the hearts and minds of a particularly meddlesome sector of the population. Many organizations use studies or commissions as excuses for not taking action. They are usually promoted as "taking the pulse of the people". However, hours of debate, scores of witnesses, piles of money can go up in smoke—and the real problems are not dealt with. The question remains as to what happens after people have spoken up on such issues, have made alliances, or have had a taste of countering the dominant forces of the day? Is there a memory of power which will resurface at a later time? Is one role of adult education to not let such memories fade and to build on the momentum, the learning, the collective analysis that inquiries can generate?

11.3 Popular Groups and Links to Social Movements
Under circumstances of control by popular groups, participatory research processes have produced increased power for some groups. The recently completed Appalachian Land Use Study, carried out by a coalition of citizen groups with some support from the Highlander Research and Education Center, has produced dramatic evidence of unequal taxation policies—and is leading to legislation and action in several states.

One often finds that the researcher and the base group are not the only parties involved; usually there is a third: the funder. In some experiences, the funder has presented the most difficulty in maintaining the integrity of the work. Funding policies of governments can, for example, expand into procedures that regulate certain groups in the society, such as immigrants and native peoples. Research with popular groups that is funded by the state will often be subject to such intervention and influence. Also, what happens when independent researchers apply for funds as an intermediary group for popular organizations is not entirely satisfactory. This has led, at times, to an unsavoury situation where the needs and weakness of some parts of the population are presented to funders for grants, with the result that the funds got to the researchers and intermediary group but not always to the actual base groups that the work was to serve.

At present, the most promising results for work might be found through better integration with groups that represent basic progressive interests and which can be characterized as social movements. This means working in conditions where the movement has an ability to control and shape the larger organizational and political process, independent of possible participatory research activities. Working with such social movements gives a natural channel for the mobilizing and creative energies of participatory research to feed the larger struggle. It would mean, for example, working within the framework of the women's movement, labour unions, native peoples' political organizations, public interest research groups, tenant associations, or groups of landless labourers.

See also: Research Paradigms in Education; Naturalistic and Rationalistic Enquiry

Bibliography

Beltran L R 1976 Alien premises, objects, and methods in Latin American communication research. *Commun. Res.* 3: 107–34
Callaway H 1981 Women's perspectives: Research as re-vision. In: Reason P, Rowan J (eds.) 1981 *Human Inquiry: A Sourcebook of New Paradigm Research.* Wiley, London
Darcy de Oliveira R, Darcy de Oliveira M 1975 *The Militant Observer: A Sociological Alternative.* Institut d'Action Culturelle, Geneva
Fals Barda O 1980 *Science and the Common People.* International Forum on Participatory Research, Yugoslavia
Gaventa J 1981 *Power and Powerlessness: Quiescence and Rebellion in an Appalachian Valley.* University of Illinois Press, Urbana, Illinois
Gerace Larufa F 1973 *Comunicación Horizontal.* Librería Studium, Lima
Holmes J 1976 Thoughts on research methodology. *Stud. Adult Educ.* 8: 149–63
Horton B D 1981 On the potential of participatory research: An evaluation of a regional experiment. Paper prepared for annual meeting of the Society for the Study of Social Problems, Toronto, Canada, 21–24 August
Orefice P 1981 Cultural self-awareness of local community: An experience in the south of Italy. *Convergence* 14: 56–64
Spender D 1978 Editorial. *Women's Stud. Int. Q.* 1: 1–2
Stinson A (ed.) 1979 *Canadians Participate: Annotated Bibliography of Case Studies.* Centre for Social Welfare Studies, Ottawa, Ontario
Vio Grossi F 1981 The socio-political implications of participatory research. International Forum on Participatory Research, Yugoslavia. *Convergence* 14(3): 43–51

Evaluation for Utilization [1]

R. W. Tyler

The practice of evaluating educational achievement has a very long history, but the systematic study of testing and other forms of educational appraisal is less than 100 years old. Yet in that time profound changes in education have taken place that are greatly influencing the conceptions of educational evaluation. However, the procedures and instruments of evaluation have thus far only partly responded to these changes.

The accepted conceptions of education generally and schooling in particular are changing profoundly, largely in response to the great changes characteristic of modern industrial nations. The increased demand in the

1 This article is a condensed version of the monograph 'Changing concepts of educational evaluation', by R W Tyler which was published in the *International Journal of Educational Research*, Vol. 10, no. 1. It appears here with permission from Pergamon Press plc. © 1986

economy for educated persons has stimulated an expanded view of universal education. The struggle of the common people for civil rights has fueled their aspirations for education and led schools to focus efforts to educate children from homes where parents have had little or no formal education. The studies that demonstrate that many children heretofore thought to be uneducable are learning what the schools are teaching has given new meaning to educability and raised serious questions about trying to define the limits of the educational potential of children.

The recognition that modern industrial society is in a state of continuing change has led schools to emphasize new objectives, especially those involving the development of the attitudes, knowledge, and skills required for problem-solving and those central to the development of self-directed learners. At the same time research on learning by cognitive psychologists, and by those concerned with personality development, has helped to construct a model of conscious human learning that furnishes a theoretical basis to guide the development of educational programs to implement the new expectations. Finally, schools, colleges, and educational evaluation practitioners are finding useful tools to assist teachers in the more complex tasks on which many are engaged.

1. Changes in Conceptions of Evaluation

The recent profound changes in the accepted views of education influenced corresponding changes in conceptions of educational evaluation. Standardized testing developed to serve primarily the purpose of sorting students. Sorting for college admission and for other types of selection is still an important function of testing but it is only one of many other purposes for which systematic appraisal could contribute significantly to the improvement of education. The need for comprehensive and dependable appraisals of education programs is widely recognized. Since the late 1950s, massive financial support has been given to projects concerned with the development of new courses in science, mathematics, and foreign languages. Those supporting the construction of the new courses, and teachers and administrators who are considering the use of them in their schools, are contracting for appraisals of these courses in relation to other courses in the same fields. Most tests on the market were not constructed to furnish relative appraisals of different courses, and they have been found inadequate for the task. Similarly, the evaluation of compensatory educational programs has been handicapped by the lack of instruments and procedures for appraising programs of this sort.

The recent rapid increase in the number and availability of technological devices in education, such as television, tape recorders, and computers, has brought to attention the need to evaluate the effectiveness of these devices for various kinds of educational tasks. Traditional test theory has not been sufficiently relevant to design evaluative studies of technological devices, nor

have the available achievement tests been satisfactory for this purpose.

New knowledge about education is also influencing evaluation. For example, the recent findings of many studies regarding the powerful effects of student's home culture and community environment upon their school learning have revealed the need for assessing these factors in order to guide and improve education. New theories were necessary to rationalize procedures for appraising home and community environment and new instruments had to be developed.

As another illustration, a series of investigations *like* those of Newcomb (1966) and Coleman (1966) have shown the strong influence of peer-group attitudes, practices, and interests upon the learning of its members. These investigations have also shown the need for evaluating the nature, direction, and amount of peer-group influences in developing effective school programs.

Although from the time that achievement tests were first used, writers have emphasized the need for tests to assist the classroom teacher, few standardized tests have served that purpose. Teachers recognize the need for more dependable appraisals in connection with the planning and conduct of their work. They could use tests or other evaluative procedures for assessing the needs of the students in their classes, for furnishing pretest information for each instructional unit, for unit mastery tests, diagnostic tests, appraisals to be used at the conclusion of several units of instruction, and the like.

Principals and district office personnel are asking for evaluation procedures that enable them to monitor the progress of the students within their area of responsibility in order to identify problems on which assistance and additional resources can be focused. Many parents are asking for information about what their children are learning and what difficulties they are meeting. Many of them ask for evidence that the school is "accountable," a term frequently used in the United States to refer in a general sense to the school's recording and reporting on the educational progress and problems of its students. The general public and particularly those persons who are responsible for educational policies need appropriate and dependable information about educational achievements of students in their area, together with analyses of the data that help them to understand what students are learning and what problems are evident. They need information that serves to identify where, with what kinds of students, and under what conditions, the expected achievement levels are not being reached.

One of the most profound changes taking place in educational evaluation is in the increased generalization of meaning attached to this term and others used as synonyms such as educational testing, educational assessment, educational appraisal. It is coming to mean the process of checking the ideas and plans in education with the realities to which these ideas and plans refer. For example, by the end of the third grade, teachers may expect their students to have mastered the mechanics of reading. Tests may be used to find out how many and which children are really able to read simple material. As another example, a new educational program has been developed for the school. It is assumed that the program is being followed in all classes. By using an observation checklist and an interview schedule with teachers, one finds out the extent to which the program is being implemented. As a third example, a remedial reading class is being planned for adolescent students. It is assumed that they will try to read things in which they are interested. An interest inventory or other means for appraising student interests can furnish information about the interests these students really have, and an observation checklist and a self-report schedule can help to find out whether students do try to read materials that deal with their own interests.

This change to a more generalized meaning has both positive and negative possibilities. On the positive side, it may result in a wider scope for collecting evidence to support or negate ideas that guide us in working in schools and colleges. On the negative side, the terms may be used so vaguely that they are slogans rather than meaningful conceptions of the important process of educational evaluation. Whether the broader scope of meaning will be understood and used thoughtfully will depend on the actions and discussions of evaluation practitioners. Clearly the changing conceptions of education in industrialized societies have influenced many changes in the conceptions of educational evaluation.

2. Paradigm of Early Test Theory

Although group achievement testing is common throughout the western world, and program evaluation is increasing, the evaluation instruments and procedures have changed very little since the 1940s. Among the probable causes for the slow response to the changing conceptions are the continuance of a test theory that is not appropriate to the variety of demands and the continuance of test construction techniques that have not been designed with different particular educational uses in mind. The following examples illustrate these two impediments to the needed changes in practice.

Developing from the original uses of standardized tests for selecting individuals for employment, or for educational or training opportunities, a paradigm that guided the development of testing was formulated. In terms of this paradigm, the function of the testing is to arrange those who take the test along a single continuum from the ones most qualified for the particular selection to those least appropriate. To arrange the scores on a single continuum it is necessary to summarize an individual's performance on the test exercises in terms of a single score, most frequently the sum of the items correctly answered, although less frequently, weights are used for different items or sections to produce a single score. This score is viewed as a predictor of the individual's success in performance in the job or in the educational or training program. Hence, the validity

of the test is estimated by the correlation between the test scores of those taking the test and a criterion which is some obtainable indication of their performance in the job or in the educational or training program. The test can be improved by eliminating items that do not correlate with the criterion and substituting others which, in trials, do correlate positively with the criterion.

There are 18 assumptions that are specified by or associated with the early paradigm guiding test theory but these have been found inadequate to guide the changing roles of educational evaluation. The effort to arrange test takers on a continuum from best performers to the poorest is not required for most of the current uses of achievement tests. Teachers want to know who have learned what has been taught and who had difficulties, and what did they fail to master? Parents want to know what their children have learned and what they are having difficulties with. The central administrators of the school district want to know in what schools children are making expected progress in learning, in which schools a considerable number of children are failing to reach the goals that have been set, and what kinds of problems these schools are having. The public wants to know what students are expected to learn in the primary grades, the middle grades, and the high school and what proportion of students are learning these things.

None of the answers to these questions require the arrangement of students on a continuum based on the results of a test. In fact, that kind of reporting encourages people to think of schooling as a contest rather than a social institution seeking to help all students learn what is essential or helpful to constructive participation in the society.

The practice of describing a student's test performance by assigning a single score greatly oversimplifies the complexity of the student's behavior and of the learning process. Instead of seeking to aggregate many items of data about the student's test performance, such as the approach he or she used in attacking the problem, the mode of solution, the recall of relevant data, whether or not the answer was checked, and the time required to complete the exercise, a more helpful appraisal provides the teacher with all the relevant information obtained from each student's test performance, and helps him or her to redesign the instructional program to aid the student in learning. Furthermore, a single score does not inform the teacher, the parent, the school administrator, or the public what the students have learned. The score is only an abstract number which is designed to distinguish those who have learned more from those who have learned less but it is not nearly as helpful as a report which informs the user, for example, that this sample exercise represents what 82 percent of the third-grade children were able to do correctly, while this sample exercise represents what only 20 percent of the third-grade children did correctly.

The scoring of a test in terms of numbers of correct answers or some combination of the number of correct and the number of incorrect answers does not provide a defensible basis for assessing most of the kinds of learning that school teaches, and the score sheds little light on the child's pattern of learned behavior. A child's written work can be scored by counting the number of errors he or she has made in the application of the conventions of grammar, spelling, and syntax but, unless each kind of error is reported in relation to the number of opportunities for such an error, very little useful information is provided and such scoring is not appropriate for assessing such things as the comprehensibility, the organization, and the persuasiveness of the writing.

The notion that the validity of a test is shown by the accuracy of its prediction of success in further educational programs or in employment involves two assumptions that are no longer acceptable. One is that the test is designed primarily to serve a static institution (school or employer) and the other is that individuals cannot be expected to change significantly as they encounter environments new to them. In contrast to earlier years, educational institutions are expected to modify their practices so as to reach effectively the wider range of students now seeking admission. The older paradigm assumed a static institution and the test was to identify the students who would get good grades in the static institution. Now the admission tests are expected to identify the range of significant assets that the student has developed and to report these assets to the institution so that the institution can better design its programs to build on their assets. This new view is also spreading through employing institutions. They are increasingly expected to modify their practices so as to capitalize on the assets of new groups of employees and minimize the dependence upon characteristics not possessed in large measure by the new groups.

Evidence obtained from all levels of schooling from preschool to college indicates that children and youth can and do change their performance when there are new opportunities for learning which are seen by the learners as challenges. Similar results are being reported in studies of women and minority groups in new employment situations. There is no longer justification to try to validate an aptitude test or an achievement test by correlating its results with success in subsequent educational or employing institutions. A more direct effect to identify the individual's assets and limitations is necessary.

An essential principle in all kinds of testing is that the test be based on a representative and adequate sample of the behavior to be assessed. Representativeness in statistical terms means that the sample is either a random sample of the behavior or is a stratified random sample, that is random samples from each stratum of the universe of behavior being assessed. "Adequate" is defined as a large enough representative sample to allow for the estimated variations to be expected among the units of the random sample and still provide a measure that is sufficiently stable to serve the purpose intended. Even when a test is constructed by sampling randomly from the universe of relevant behavior, when it is modified by eliminating items that do not correlate with an external criterion and by adding items that do correlate, then the test items are no longer a representative sample of the test taker's behavior. Hence the results of the modified test no longer provide a reliable description of the individual's behavior.

3. The New Paradigm

The new paradigm of educational evaluation is constructed around the new expectations in education in contemporary society. The old paradigm assumed that educational opportunities had to be rationed because of the limited resources available for schooling. It was also assumed that many children were relatively uneducable and they should be identified early and guided into work at an early age while the more educable should be encouraged to continue their schooling on through high school and college.

The new paradigm assumes that all persons who are not seriously damaged by brain injuries can learn what the schools are responsible for teaching. It recognizes that contemporary society is realizing that its members need increasing amounts of school learning in order that they may become civilized persons, effective citizens, supportive family members, helpful members of their communities, and constructive participants in the economic life of the society.

The old paradigm assumed that the practices of educational institutions were largely static and a role for educational evaluation was to identify persons who would fit into these practices and achieve what the institutions expected of them. The new paradigm assumes that institutional practices can change as the schools and colleges seek to provide real educational opportunities for all of their students. A role of educational evaluation in this connection is to help identify the assets of students on which effective educational programs can be built, and the characteristics which are likely to interfere with the student's learning so that the school or college may help the student overcome these difficulties.

The old paradigm assumed that the task of vocational guidance was to identify the student's present characteristics that most nearly fitted particular job requirements and to advise him or her how to proceed with training which would best prepare the student to fit into this niche. The early slogan was "A round peg should fit into a round hole while a square peg fits in a square hole."

The new paradigm conceives guidance as encouraging and helping students to explore their life options. Every increment of education is viewed as expanding one's life options and increasing one's ability to make wise judgments about the next steps. There are few rigid job characteristics. Most jobs are partly defined by the persons who perform them. Hence, the individual's task in vocational development is continually to learn more about vocations, their missions, their principles, their social conditions, their opportunities for intellectual development and social contributions, and to learn more about himself or herself so as better to estimate performance in these occupational roles. In this connection, educational evaluation seeks to obtain information about significant characteristics of occupations and relevant information about the student.

In brief, this new paradigm conceives the role of educational evaluation to be that of providing information about the realities of the educational arena that can help the institutions to improve educational opportunities and help individuals gain education of high quality and to become self-directed in continuing their education throughout the life cycle. The phrase, "information about the realities of the educational arena," distinguishes between reality and perceived reality. All human beings appear to have a view of the situations they encounter: they think they usually know what is going on. Some of the notions they have are in harmony with objective reality, but some are not. For instance a teacher thinks he or she has made a clear explanation but a simple questioning of the class may show that few of the students understood it. By the same token a supervisor may think that the curriculum guide is being followed as intended in the classroom but observers may find that the activities in some of the classrooms are quite different from those specified in the guide. Evaluation has become a broader process than simply giving tests or examinations to students. It is now viewed as the process for finding out what is really happening in educational situations to guide plans and actions.

This broader conception means that educational evaluation seeks not only to appraise relevant behavior of the students, their knowledge, skills, attitudes, habits, interests, and appreciations but also to assess the learning activities of the school: What are the learning tasks and their appropriateness both to the learning objectives and to the student's present activities? What rewards and feedback does the learner receive as he or she attempts the learning tasks? What are the opportunities for sequential practice? How is transfer assured?

The contemporary view of evaluation also includes assessing the influences on learning outside the classroom. What behavior does the family consider important? How is effective school learning rewarded in the home? What opportunities does the home furnish for transfer of what is learned in school? What opportunities are there in the home for learning some of the behavior which the school emphasizes? This kind of assessment may also be focused on peer-group activities outside the school, and on the other associations and institutions in the community which influence school learning by being supportive or in conflict or in distracting the student's attention from the school learning activities.

Those professionally involved in education are often ignorant of the learning conditions in which students are involved outside the school or the campus so that evaluation, that is, information about relevant realities can be very helpful in enabling them to build on constructive conditions and seek to change those that interfere with student learning. Sometimes, the research or the experience of other situations can be suggestive about what to evaluate in their own situation to confirm or refute the validity in this situation of the information obtained elsewhere. Thus, in planning an educational program for students from families in which the adults have had very little education, one may learn of a research investigation which reported that most uneducated parents did not value education for their children. This is possible in the educator's own situation but a sample survey found that 85 percent of the parents of the children for which the new program is planned considered education for their children the chief means for the children to survive. They urged their children to work hard and do well in school.

To implement this broadened conception of educational evaluation requires a reexamination of purposes, plans, and procedures in order to develop instruments and practices that serve the variety of uses to which evaluation results are to be put. The techniques of instrument construction developed by psychometrists are no longer adequate, because the focus of educational evaluation is now on the dynamics of education rather than on the individual psyche. The following rationale outlines steps to be taken in developing evaluation instruments that are more nearly adequate to the variety of purposes than the older practices involved in test construction.

4. Rationale for Instrument Construction

This rationale includes the following eight steps:

(a) Identifying the questions to be answered and the relevant information to be obtained from the use of the evaluation procedure and instruments.

(b) Defining the behavior to be appraised in order to obtain the needed information.

(c) Identifying situations in which the persons have opportunity to express the behavior.

(d) Selecting or constructing situations which evoke the behavior.

(e) Deciding on the aspects of the behavior to be described or measured, and the terms or units to use.

(f) Trying out the proposed procedure and instruments.

(g) Checking on the validity, objectivity, reliability, and practicability of the procedure and instruments.

(h) Revising the procedures and instruments.

The preceding eight steps are suggested as one coherent rationale to guide the development of procedures and instruments for educational evaluation. It is a natural outgrowth from the changing uses of evaluation that are emerging in response to the changes in education that have been evolving with increased rapidity since the end of the Second World War. These educational changes have necessitated changes in the paradigm that has been the intellectual model for test theory.

The systematic study and development of test theory was the work of psychologists who sought to understand the mental activity and processes of individual human beings. Their effort to probe the psyche was guided by the older paradigm which they constructed. It is now becoming increasingly clear that the process of education and the stimulation and guidance of human learning is a practical endeavor. Whatever may be the composition of the psyche, students of all kinds have been learning and becoming educated persons. To guide this practical activity and to understand it more fully is the test of educators. The paradigm to guide them is not the same as the one that is most useful to psychologists.

Correspondingly, the appraisal of student learning and of the aspects of the environment which influence it requires a conception of educational evaluation appropriate to this task. The focus of educational evaluation is not the same as that of psychometrists, and the assumptions that are consistent with educational purposes and programs are different at several major points. If educational evaluation is to serve schools, colleges, and other formal and informal educational institutions, the conceptual paradigm and the rationale guiding the construction of tests and other evaluative devices and procedures must be consistent with the purposes and essential conditions under which education operates. The foregoing discussion is an initial effort to suggest the kind of thinking which needs to become central to developing a sound and useful program of educational evaluation.

5. Shortcomings in Current Reporting Procedures

Most reports of educational evaluations are not understood by laypeople and are widely misinterpreted. In fact, they are not generally understood by teachers and administrators and, as a result, the information that could provide a basis for improving the educational program or institution is not communicated. Basic to this failure of communication are several practices devised by psychometrists and adapted without careful consideration by those engaged in educational evaluation.

Psychometrists, seeking to measure aspects or factors of the psyche, focus on the appraisal of characteristics of the person rather than on what the person has learned. They hypothesize the existence of abilities, aptitudes, or other factors within the individual, and seek to devise ways of identifying and measuring these characteristics. The teacher, on the other hand, is expected to help students of many different backgrounds and with various observable characteristics learn what the schools try to teach, such as to read, write, compute, explain natural phenomena, become interested in intellectual activities and aesthetic objects, perceive things in new perspectives, and so forth. The teacher's task is to help children learn these things as effectively as possible. What the teacher really wants to know from the results of an educational evaluation are the answers to such questions as: What have the students learned? Where are they having difficulty in learning? The teacher is interested in knowing about those hypothetical abilities, aptitudes, and other factors assumed to be within the individual only when they are shown to be causal variables that can be altered by the teacher so as to improve student learning. Otherwise, the report of test results in terms of individual characteristics is not used by the teacher or is misinterpreted, as in using aptitude test results to justify the practice of not encouraging students whose scores are low to try to learn.

The focus on individual characteristics leads psychometrists to treat test results as indicators of factors rather than direct evidence of learning. This leads to the prevailing practice of reporting test results in abstract numbers, such as numerical scores, without explaining the concrete referents from which the scores are derived. An even greater source of misinterpretation arises from translating "raw" scores into grade equivalents, or percentiles which have the appearance of clarity but, in fact, are interpretations of hypothetical referents that are often different from the actual situation.

In high school subjects, the usual practice is to report standardized achievement test results in terms of percentile ranks, based on a hypothetical normal distribution in which all of the scores obtained from the norming administration of the test are placed. A review of typical standardized tests indicates that the items in a test that deals with things taught in any particular school represent only a fraction of what that school is teaching. This is due to the fact that high school courses vary from school to school in the particular content taught. In the construction of a test for national use, the test makers examine textbooks and available curriculum guides to identify topics that are common to many of the books and guides. Test items are then constructed for these common topics. The topics that are not common, however, are more numerous than those for which test items are written. Hence the report, for example, that "the mean of the scores that the students of teacher A obtained on the test was at the 40th percentile of the norming population" gives no dependable indication of what these students have learned nor even how well they have learned what they have been taught.

6. Suggested Improvements for Reporting Results of Schools Learning

It is, of course, necessary to use abstract numbers in studies that seek to identify hypothetical variables that are not directly observable, since their form and extent of functioning must be estimated from observed differences in individual behavior. But the results of school learning can be much more directly defined, identified, and described in meaningful terms that are relatively concrete.

In reading, for example, learning to *comprehend* reading material is commonly defined in terms that are easily understood. In the primary grades, the behavior associated with the term "comprehend" is often defined as reading aloud accurately, or telling in one's own words what the selection says, or doing what the printed directions tell one to do. In the middle grades the definition of "comprehend" takes into account that reading at that level involves getting information from the printed page.

The definition of the *reading material* which the student is expected to comprehend is also easily understood. In the primary grades the reading material usually includes children's stories, newspaper items, directions for assembling and using toys and games. If a test in reading for children in the primary grades has been constructed by sampling the kinds of comprehension and the several kinds of reading material, the results can be reported in terms of what the children comprehend: fairy tales, newspaper items, directions for toys and games. If desired, the test could sample several levels of complexity in the reading materials, such as range of vocabulary and complexity of syntax. Then results can be reported in terms of the levels of complexity of the reading materials that each child comprehended. Concrete examples of each level can be included in the report so that the user can make his or her own judgment of what the levels of complexity mean.

To take an example in arithmetic, the definition of "computation" with whole numbers is often given as: adding, subtracting, multiplying and dividing with whole numbers; and the content and contexts in which the elementary school child is expected to use computation is often defined as: planning personal and group activities in which quantities are estimated, making retail purchases, estimating sales taxes on purchases, and measuring familiar objects and areas.

Levels of complexity in the behavior associated with the term "computation" are usually defined by increasing numbers of digits in the numbers involved in the computation. Most arithmetic courses do not categorize contents and contexts in terms of difficulty or levels of complexity for children learning to compute. Hence, if a test in arithmetic has been constructed by sampling the kinds of computation and the several contents and contexts in which the students can be expected to use computation with whole numbers, the results can be reported in terms of what kinds of computation they performed accurately—addition, subtraction, multiplication, and division, and in which contexts they solved the computational exercises accurately. If desired, the test could sample computation with one-digit numbers, with two-digit numbers and with numbers of three or more digits. The results could then be reported in these terms representing levels of complexity for children learning to compute.

As an example from another subject and at the high school level, the field of high school biology is typical. One of the major objectives for this subject as presented in curriculum guides is to *understand and explain in scientific terms* common phenomena of plants and animals. The behavior associated with this objective is often defined as the student perceiving a biological phenomenon as involving relevant scientific concepts and principles and using them appropriately in his or her explanation. In most biology courses, there are from 20 to 40

concepts used and from 50 to 70 principles presented. The presentations in textbooks and laboratory exercises include several phenomena involving each of the concepts and principles. The student is expected to generalize from these examples and to understand and explain many other biological phenomena encountered in his or her environment.

An evaluation of student learning in relation to this objective should include test situations in which the student encounters biological phenomena and seeks to explain them in scientific terms. The results of such a test can be reported in terms of the use of each concept and principle if each one has been reliably sampled in the test exercises. More commonly, the concepts and principles will be grouped into classes each of which is reliably sampled. In that case, the results can be reported in terms of the proportion of the test exercises in each class in which the concepts and principles were appropriately used in the explanations. If desired, the phenomena could be classified into levels of complexity and results reported in terms of the proportion of exercises appropriately explained for each level of complexity.

An evaluation of the products of learning furnishes a somewhat different example of the reporting of results. In evaluating the written work of students, several criteria are usually used, such as clarity, logical organization, and coherence, and each paper is appraised in terms of each criterion. Furthermore, to reduce individual idiosyncrasy in assessment, one or more examples of each level of the criterion are established by a panel of judges and used as a standard to guide all the appraisals. The prevailing practice has been to report the mean levels for each group of students. This furnishes little information of use to teachers, parents, school administrators, and others. A more useful report would present an example of each level for each criterion and state the percentage of the group whose written work was judged to be at that level. To illustrate: In class X, 15 percent of the students' writing was judged to be in the (example) top level in *clarity*, 60 percent in the (example) middle level in *clarity*, and 25 percent in the (example) low level in *clarity*. And so on with the other criteria. By presenting concrete examples of products, parents and other laypeople can understand more clearly what schools are teaching and students are expected to learn than abstract scores can ever provide.

The foregoing examples are by no means exhaustive. They are presented only to illustrate certain major guidelines in reporting the results of an educational evaluation. The first of these is to report results that tell *what has been learned and what of the expected learning has not taken place*. To report these things there should have been clear definitions of what students are expected to learn. From these definitions, suggestions are obtained about useful terms for reporting the results.

Second, since an educational evaluation is focused on what students have learned, the use of indicators should be avoided wherever more direct assessment of the learning can be made, and abstract numbers in reporting should be avoided wherever what students have learned can be reported more concretely. This reduces the dependence upon untested assumptions in deriving a score.

Third, the user of the results should be presented with as much information as can be obtained from the evaluation but in no more detail than he or she can use. This guideline requires considerable elaboration to suggest its practical employment.

7. Reports for Different Users

7.1 For Teachers and Parents

The teacher or parent who works with individual students can use information about each individual whose learning he or she is guiding. Hence, reports of an evaluation for the teacher or parent should not only indicate which children have learned what they have been taught but also the particular kinds of learned behavior with what content and in what contexts they demonstrated effectiveness, and what difficulties were evidenced.

For a general report to parents, this information needs to be presented clearly but in nontechnical terms. The purpose is two-fold: to give parents information about the particular things the child is expected to learn and information about what the child is learning and where difficulties are being encountered. Most parents have not understood the test scores that have been reported, and this has led to misinterpretations that have often hampered constructive efforts of the home.

Some test users have reported the results item by item but this item analysis commonly leads to another misunderstanding. The item analysis reports the number or percentage of test takers who responded to the item in a particular way—usually the percentage who answered the item correctly. But a single item is rarely, if ever, a representative sample of a defined behavior, or a defined content, or a defined context. Teachers often treat item analyses as though the response to an item indicated probable responses to the kind of behavior that item represents. To draw any dependable inference about a kind of behavior requires information from enough appropriate items to evaluate a representative sample of that behavior. Failing to understand this, some teachers modify their educational efforts to deal with what they thought they could infer from the item analysis.

The reliability of the item analysis is based on estimates of the variability among students responding to the item; it is not an estimate of the variation among items that could be constructed to represent a kind of behavior that can be estimated from actually giving a sample of such exercises to the students.

7.2 For School Principals

The principal of a school does not usually need to have information about the learning of an individual child. When that is needed on occasion, the teacher can be asked to supply it. The principal needs to know about the progress of learning in each classroom so that assistance can be provided where needed. For example, the principal is usually expected to take the leadership in developing educational goals for each year. These goals should be established after reviewing the educational achievements of the past year, then the school's teaching staff deliberate on goals for the next year which are substantially beyond the achievements of the past year but seem to the teachers to be obtainable for the next year. The review of the results of the last educational evaluation will reveal the objectives that were not reached by most students and other indications of problems that need correction and for which the plan for next year represents a substantial improvement over the past year.

For the purposes of setting annual goals, the educational evaluation results can be helpfully expressed in terms of the proportion of the class group who reached or exceeded the goals set for that year. As an example, consider an elementary school enrolling children from homes in which the parents have had little education and where the opportunities to develop and apply what is learned in school are limited. At the end of the third grade, most children from middle-class homes have learned the mechanics of reading, that is they can get the plain-sense meaning of written material that deals with content and contexts with which they are familiar. But in a school in the inner city, the educational evaluation showed that only 25 percent of the children at the end of the third grade could read and comprehend this simple material.

After staff discussion and deliberation the goal in reading set for the third grade the following year was for 35 percent of the students to reach this standard. Thus, reporting results in terms of the percentage of students reaching accepted and defined standards provided the principal and all the school staff with the information needed to set annual goals and to monitor progress toward them. Reporting the percentage of students exhibiting behavior that interferes with school learning can also be useful in goal setting and monitoring. For example, the percentage of students who were absent 5 days, 10 days, 15 days and 20 days in a term furnishes information helpful in setting goals representing improved attendance.

7.3 For School Districts

Most local school districts include a number of schools. The district personnel do not need data from an educational evaluation that is as detailed as that needed by the principal of each school. The officers of the district—administrators, coordinators, supervisors, resource persons, whatever they may be called, cannot perform the daily functions of teachers, principals, and parents. They must depend on the persons in the local schools to perform these functions. Persons from the district office can stimulate the efforts of the teachers and principals in the schools, they can assist and train local personnel in goal setting, monitoring, and revising goals and plans, they can provide other kinds of assistance, but they cannot take the place of the local school personnel nor depend on their authority to get compliance with their ideas.

To furnish assistance in depth, district personnel need to identify problems serious enough, or opportunities great enough, to justify a considerable commitment of their time. The results of evaluations should indicate what proportion of the students in the local school are attaining the learning objectives and what proportion are having difficulties. The district personnel may ask for breakdowns in these proportions in terms of student demography or sex, or other variables thought to have a causal connection to student achievement. The district personnel also need to know the evidence used by the local school staff in setting the annual goals. But usually district personnel do not need data on individual students, nor even on particular classrooms within the school. The school is the basic unit for monitoring and reporting. Further breakdowns may be needed, however, to guide the appropriate inquiries of the district.

Periodically, the district office needs an appraisal of learning that is independent of the evaluations carried on by personnel in the local school. This is necessary to assure the validity of the data submitted by the school. A few principals may not be able to resist the temptation to doctor results so that their schools will look good. The periodic independent appraisal has the same function in relation to local evaluations that an independent financial audit has to the accounts and accounting activities of an institution. As in the financial audit, only a sample of checks are made and if they are not in harmony with the results presented by the local school personnel, a further investigation is undertaken to obtain valid results at the level of detail required.

There are technical problems in conducting an independent appraisal that utilizes a limited amount of students' time, requires modest expenditures, and obtains valid and reliable samples of the various kinds of learning objectives from reliable samples of students from each local school. If only a fraction of the important objectives are sampled, local teachers interpret them as the only ones. So they focus their teaching efforts on these few objectives and neglect the others. If only a fraction of the students are sampled, the reliability of the results may be too low and the reason some students are not tested is not easily explained to the local school staff and parents. An answer to these technical problems is a process often called matrix sampling, since the allocation of test exercises to particular students is often done by making a matrix chart with individual students in the one axis and the test exercises on the other. By the use of matrix sampling, the reliability of the test exercises as representative samples of the learned behavior applied to representative samples of relevant content in representative samples of appropriate context, does not need to be reduced. All of the test exercises constructed for use in making evaluations useful to the local school are presented to the students but not one student responds to all the exercises. If the completion of all the test exercises would require five hours for one student to do them all, the test can be broken into five subtests

each taking an hour of the student's time. One-fifth of the students is given one subtest, another fifth of the students is given a second subtest, and so on. Every student completes test results for the equivalent of one-fifth of all the students in the school.

The results of this independent appraisal can be reported in terms of each kind of educational objective, and the proportion of the students in each school who made expected progress in attaining the objective and the proportion having difficulty. As with other tests, where representative samples of different levels of behavior are obtained, these can be reported in terms of the percentage of the students reaching or exceeding each level. The report of these results can be compared with the results submitted by each school. Where there are serious discrepancies, inquiries should be undertaken to seek to obtain more dependable data.

7.4 For State, Regional, and National Agencies

Reports of educational evaluation results that are useful to state agencies, regional organizations, and state and national policy makers need to be even less detailed than those for school district personnel. State, regional, and national groups do not work directly with individual children and they need no more information about the child's educational progress and problems than does the Surgeon General of the United States need to know about the health progress and problems of an individual child. The responsibility for working directly with individual children on their educational progress and problems is that of the teacher and parent.

It is helpful for policy development as well as for state oversight in education to know what children in their area of jurisdiction are learning, what learning is expected of these children at various stages of their development, what progress they are making and what problems they are encountering. Since the answers to these questions are thought to vary in relation to demographic factors, the questions need to be asked in relation to each major demographic factor. What can the results of evaluation contribute to answering these questions?

In the United States, the constitutional responsibility for public education is left to the government of each state. Most states delegate a great deal of this responsibility to local school districts. Although many of the states have adopted courses of study, none of them define in clear terms the behavior that students are expected to learn. The courses of study usually specify subjects to be taught, sometimes topics to be covered, but no definition is clearly given as to what students are to learn in these subjects or about these topics. These actual definitions are usually developed by individual teachers, although there is increasing agreement among educators that the teaching staff of a school needs to work as a team to define and agree on the definition of what students are to learn in different subjects and at different levels of their development.

Although in practice, individual teachers or local schools define learning objectives, there is a good deal of consensus among the educated public on the definition of what students should learn in the public elementary and secondary schools. This has been documented in the experience of getting agreement on the learning objectives to be appraised in the National Assessment of Educational Progress (Tyler 1986). In developing an evaluation program to inform policy makers and the public in a state or region, the procedure followed in developing the National Assessment is a practicable one. It is also possible to gain a more informed consensus by arranging for discussion groups to discuss at some length the issues of desirable learning goals and to bring together for further discussion and deliberation the reports of the conclusions reached in many smaller discussion groups. One way of doing this is to invite public participation through invitations to many local groups, such as church groups, labor groups, Chambers of Commerce, service clubs, and hobby groups. When the self-selected members come together in a large auditorium, they are presented with an explanation of the project. Then the large group is broken up into discussion groups with about 20 in each. Each discussion group is moderated by a person who has participated in three brief training sessions. The discussions are directed by a discussion guide that raises the major issues as questions to be discussed and deliberated, and tentative conclusions are reached. The discussion groups usually meet in three or four two-hour sessions. Each discussion group prepares a report of its recommendations which are reproduced for all participants. Then a final meeting is held with the members of all the groups. At this final meeting consensus is sought on the recommendations as they are revised and reformulated to satisfy most participants. This is a time-consuming procedure but it has developed a clearer understanding of what schools are expected to do, and thus furnishes a basis for guiding an evaluation and reporting results.

The report of the results of assessments should take into account what the policy makers understand to be the things students are expected to learn. The reports can help further to clarify the meaning of these expectations by presenting an exercise or two that was used to appraise this kind of learning. Where it is appropriate, the report should present examples of different levels of skill, complexity, or breadth of learning, giving for each the percentage of particular groups who performed at that level or breadth. Where possible, the degree of progress can be reported in terms of the proportion who performed at that level or breadth in previous years. The proportion of students who demonstrated difficulties in performance can be an additional kind of information where this result is obtained from other responses and is not simply the proportion who did not perform at the reported level. Where the learning is thought to be influenced by certain demographic factors, the proportions should be reported for each demographic group for which there was a representative sample taking the test.

8. Concluding Remarks

These examples are not complete. They are presented only as illustrations of efforts to report the results of educational evaluation in terms that are understood by the users as concrete evidence about the learning of clearly defined behavior. From the need for detailed reports by those who work with individual students to the need by policy makers for reports of learning achievements on a large scale, one can select the data and report the results so as to be responsive as far as possible to the kinds of questions different groups are asking.

Bibliography

Coleman J S 1966 Peer cultures and education in modern society. In: Newcomb T M, Wilson E K (eds.) 1966 *College Peer Group*. Aldine Publishing, Chicago, Illinois, pp. 244–69
Newcomb T M 1966 The general nature of peer-group influence. In: Newcomb T M, Wilson E K (eds.) 1966 *College Peer Group*. Aldine Publishing, Chicago, Illinois, pp. 2–16
Tyler R W 1986 Changing concepts of educational evaluation. *Int. J. Educ. Res.* 10(1): 91–96

Section 2

The Creation, Diffusion, and Utilization of Knowledge

Section 2

The Creation, Diffusion, and Utilization of Knowledge

Introduction

Issues in the Creation, Diffusion, and Utilization of Knowledge

This section of the *International Handbook* contains articles that are concerned with the development of knowledge about educational processes and the implementation of change in educational policy and practice arising from that knowledge. It is important to recognize that in the field of educational inquiry there is a necessary unity between the processes of the creation, diffusion, and utilization of knowledge. Although there are many ways in which these three processes can occur, creation presupposes utilization, and without diffusion or dissemination creation and utilization remain unlinked. Moreover, failure to recognize the ways in which knowledge about educational processes change both policy and practice and the ways in which problems in practice generate a quest for new knowledge, has given rise to criticisms of educational research as well as ineffective and inappropriate change in policy and practice. This collection of articles seeks to provide new perspectives for the field of educational research by emphasizing the unity of the inquiry process.

The strategies employed in the field of educational research have fluctuated markedly since its beginnings approximately 100 years ago. In the early years of the twentieth century an approach to the investigation of educational problems within the empirical or scientific perspective was firmly established and with some significant successes, particularly in the field of mental measurement. However, the period from the 1930s to the late 1950s was accompanied by a loss of impetus in the empirical and scientific approach to

167

educational research in most parts of the western world, in favour of innovative progressivism and the widespread use of analytical philosophy in inquiry. Feinberg (1983) has argued that while analytical philosophy sought to clarify the concepts that guided research it failed to consider the value implications of its own approach. As a consequence its contribution to educational inquiry was limited.

In part, this change in emphasis in educational research arose from the economic crisis of the 1930s and the freezing of research activity in European countries during the years of the Second World War. In this setting the progressive movement had a strong appeal to a liberal humanistic spirit that sought to rebuild European society after the Second World War. Nonetheless, as De Landsheere states in the article on the *History of Educational Research* in Section 1 of this *International Handbook*, during the Second World War the issues of selection and recruitment led to the development of appropriate tests and the study of many problems of educational measurement. Furthermore, during the 1940s and 1950s the emerging field of interest was without doubt that of sociological research. Seminal investigatory work was carried out in the areas of social status, the discriminatory practices of schools, and the social distinctions existing within schools. This work supported the concern for equality of educational opportunity in the 1960s.

During the 1960s and 1970s, particularly in the industrialized countries, educational research experienced widespread support that led to a marked increase in the amount of research undertaken. The advent of the electronic computer changed approaches to empirical research, because for the first time it became possible to examine fully large bodies of data. The scientific perspective again became firmly established in the field of educational inquiry. However, this was soon to be challenged by alternative approaches to social science research. Changing circumstances and conflict between different approaches led in most countries to substantial reductions in the funds available for educational inquiry, as well as a demand by policy makers and their advisers that educational research should be directed towards policy questions and evaluation studies. These developments were based on an inadequate understanding of the nature of educational inquiry and the manner in which the creation, diffusion, and the utilization of knowledge are interrelated to form a coherent whole. Undue emphasis on one aspect can be to the detriment of the others as well as to the total field of educational inquiry.

1. The Development of Shared Knowledge

All individuals experience education in some form or another. The view of education as social reproduction (Feinberg 1983) considers that not only do individuals develop skills to meet socially defined needs, but they also develop an understanding of the nature of the society in which they live in order that they might enjoy membership of that society. Knowledge of educational processes, like all knowledge, can then be viewed as existing at two levels: namely, *individual or personal knowledge* and *shared knowledge*. The latter may or may not be formally articulated, but it establishes the basis for the common provision of education by society. Shared knowledge about education is related to individual knowledge about education in so far as it is that knowledge which is accepted by a sufficient proportion of individuals to enable educational programmes to function effectively.

There is an important third form of knowledge about education, perhaps best referred to as *propositional knowledge*, that has been built up over the past 100 years. One aim of educational inquiry is to add to this corpus of propositional knowledge about education, with rigorous tests of coherence and consistency being applied as new knowledge is added and erroneous knowledge is removed from the corpus. Kaplan (1964) has maintained that such knowledge grows in two ways: by extension and by intension. In the growth of knowledge by extension an explanation of a small domain is carried over to provide an explanation of adjacent domains. In the growth of knowledge by intension, an incomplete and partial explanation of a whole domain is made more coherent and more adequate. In testing ideas and evidence for coherence the rules of logic necessarily apply and in establishing whether or not evidence is accepted for consideration the rules provided by statistics can give guidance. The scientific approach with its emphasis on causal explanation seeks to contribute towards adding to propositional knowledge. As the established findings of propositional knowledge about education are disseminated across a society they become accepted by individuals as personal knowledge about education, as well as becoming accepted by society as part of shared knowledge.

Moreover, education, if viewed as social reproduction, is a social process which impacts on individuals. From this perspective education is concerned with building shared knowledge from personal knowledge, and the development of such shared knowledge must be viewed as a social process. In this process the humanistic approach to inquiry makes a marked contribution by providing interpretation and understanding of educational phenomena.

Both approaches to the development of educational knowledge, the scientific and the humanistic, have contributed significantly since the mid-1960s to a body of knowledge that has not been widely disseminated or accepted by those members of societies who are interested in and have the capacity to modify educational processes. Consequently, this substantial body of knowledge has not had the influence on educational policy and practice that might have been expected. The validity of propositional knowledge and the extent to which it coheres to form an integrated body of knowledge are very different issues from that of the degree of consensus in society with respect to shared knowledge which would enable it to be used to change educational policy or practice. There are thus two important tasks which must be achieved with the results of educational inquiry, namely, (a) the building of a body of propositional knowledge about educational processes, and (b) the establishment of a consensus with respect to shared knowledge that would enable change to take place in educational policy or practice. It is possible to accomplish one without having accomplished the other. However, the second task is necessary for effective educational change. Thus if the first task has been achieved, the second still remains. Yet it is possible as an outcome of experience in education to seek to accomplish the second without having attempted to achieve the first. In the process of educational inquiry the creation of knowledge is clearly separate from the diffusion and utilization of knowledge and may require separate agents. Nevertheless, all are part of the one social process.

2. Models of Educational Inquiry

A model of the processes of educational inquiry involves the three basic elements, namely, (a) the creation of knowledge by educational research workers, (b) the utilization of knowledge which involves educational policy makers and practitioners, and (c) the diffusion of knowledge, a process which is associated with a variety of mechanisms that link together the creation of knowledge and its utilization. Four basic models of educational inquiry have been identified. Each element is strongly emphasized in a particular model of inquiry.

(a) *Knowledge-driven or research, development, and diffusion model.* In this model research is commonly conducted within a scientific approach and generates new knowledge which is integrated into a propositional framework. Sometimes, this research can be viewed as basic research which is followed by applied research concerned with the development of applications of the knowledge for practical purposes. Following their establishment, the findings and their applications are disseminated to educational practitioners who use this knowledge to improve educational practice. The links between the components of the model are unidirectional from the research worker to the developer and then to the user of the research. This model is sometimes challenged as being largely inappropriate for the field of education.

(b) *The enlightenment model.* Within this model, research workers maintain a continuing programme of research and systematically build up a coherent body of knowledge about educational processes. Such research can be conducted from a scientific or empirical perspective. Alternatively research can be carried out from a humanistic perspective and reports which provide an interpretation of the findings are prepared. There is a gradual dissemination of the ideas by a variety of channels. These include the actions of innovative practitioners who develop the ideas for practice. The most effective approach to dissemination is through social interaction and the informal discussion of new ideas and their application. In this way an interactive network is established and gradual enlightenment and widespread acceptance of the new ideas are achieved.

(c) *The problem-solving model.* In this model the starting point is with the user who identifies a particular problem and makes a decision to solve the problem in order to improve policy or practice. The user may seek the advice of a research worker who could draw on an accumulated body of knowledge which is relevant to the problem and propose an appropriate solution. In addition, the research worker might examine alternative solutions to the problem through experimental studies, and develop an effective programme for resolving the problem. Case study procedures could also be employed to assess different possible solutions. Alternatively, a solution might be developed and monitored by evaluation techniques. This model would not appear to be widely used in educational practice.

(d) *Action research model.* In this approach the research worker and the user join and work together to investigate a problem identified by the user. It is not uncommon for the user to undertake the research with the trained research worker occupying a subordinate role. A search for existing knowledge relevant to the problem could take place. Since the problem is commonly viewed as requiring urgent resolution, change is implemented and the consequences of change examined. In general, the emphasis in such research is on the implementation of change rather than on the development of new knowledge.

It is clear from the four models presented above, that there is no single approach to the conduct of educational research, which involves the creation of knowledge, the dissemination of ideas, and the utilization of the findings of research, that provides rapid and sure progress. The failure to recognize these features of educational inquiry has led to questioning of the strategies and tactics of research in a manner that denigrates research efforts. This has, in part at least, been responsible for disillusionment with research in the field of education and for the withdrawal of financial support for such research (see *Social Theory and Educational Research*).

3. Articles in this Section

In Section 2 of this *International Handbook* many of the articles elaborate on the points made in this introduction. Since educational research is influenced by political circumstances, and is expected to contribute to policy making, articles by Husén on *Educational Research and Policy Making* and by Timpane on the *Politics of Educational Research* address questions of policy making and politics respectively. It is also essential that ethical issues should be taken into consideration, and articles by Dockrell on *Ethical Considerations in Research* and by House on the *Ethics of Evaluation Studies* examine these questions. Where resources are limited it is clearly essential that the needs for research should be examined and identified and priorities established, and an article on *Research Needs and Priorities* is concerned with these questions. In addition the article by Trow on *Policy Analysis* examines the contribution of this work to inquiry and policy making.

Two articles on *Documentation in Educational Research*, and *Information for Educational Research* discuss the problems of the storage of knowledge that has been generated by research. An article on *Knowledge Utilization* considers the uses made of knowledge derived from research and inquiry. Further articles on the *Dissemination of Educational Research* and *Knowledge Diffusion in Education* report on the work that has been done to examine this important phase in the conduct of investigation which links the research workers and the findings of research with the user who is concerned with innovation and change.

During recent years many major studies have collected more data than could be analysed in an initial round of analysis and, as a consequence, procedures have been developed which have been discussed in the article on *Data Banks and Data Archives* that are used for the storing of data for the purposes of secondary analysis. Moreover, the complexity of the research enterprise requires that educational research workers should be trained to undertake research and studies in education, and Härnqvist examines issues relating to the *Training of Research Workers in Education*.

4. Conclusion

During the 1960s and 1970s there was marked growth in research effort in the field of education in all parts of the world, and Walberg (1979) has written of a "quiet revolution in educational research". The extent of this work was so great that even in the late 1980s the findings generated during this period have not been fully incorporated into coherent bodies of knowledge, although many have contributed to this task; the techniques of meta-analysis were developed to facilitate this work. *The International Encyclopedia of Education* sought to assemble knowledge from all parts of the world, to review the knowledge, and to make the information more readily available to scholars in the field of educational inquiry as well as to the users of educational research. Nevertheless, much challenging work remains to be done in the revision of theory, the refinement of key concepts, and the reformulation of propositional knowledge according to the canons of simplicity and coherence so that a stronger knowledge base would be available both for the design of future research and for improvement of policy and practice in education.

Bibliography

Feinberg W 1983 *Understanding Education. Towards a Reconstruction of Educational Inquiry*. Cambridge University Press, Cambridge

Kaplan A 1964 *The Conduct of Inquiry. Methodology for Behavioral Sciences*. Chandler, San Francisco, California

Walberg H J 1979 The quiet revolution in educational research. *Phi Delta Kappan* 61(3): 179–82

Educational Research and Policy Making

T. Husén

Educational research has two constituencies of practitioners: (a) teachers and school administrators, and (b) policy makers in education. Classroom practitioners expect educational research to help them improve the planning and execution of teaching. At the turn of the century the emerging psychology with its empirical and experimental methods was expected to provide guidelines for educational practice by identifying the facts and laws of learning, and by providing an understanding of individual development, and individual differences. In his *Talks to Teachers on Psychology* (1899) William James underlined that education being an art and not a science could not deduce schemes and methods of teaching for direct classroom application out of psychology. "An intermediary inventive mind must make the application, by using its originality." In order to bridge the gap between theory and practice, James tried over and over again to make his presentation of psychology less technical. In the preface to his book which appeared several years after the lectures were given for the first time he says:

> I have found by experience that what my hearers seem least to relish is analytical technicality, and what they most care for is concrete practical application. So I have gradually weeded out the former, and left the latter reduced; and now, that I have at least written out the lectures, they contain a minimum of what is deemed 'scientific' psychology and are practical and popular in the extreme.

In general, there is a similar relationship between research and practice in policy making. For a long time this relationship was, by both partners involved, conceived of in a rather simplistic way. Policy makers wanted research that primarily addressed their pressing problems within the framework of their perceptions of the world of education. They wanted findings that could be more or less directly applied to issues and problems under their consideration. Researchers conceived of their role as expert problem solvers who advised policy makers what to do.

The problem of how research in education is related to policy making was hardly studied before the 1960s. However, after this date, resources given to educational research grew markedly. Governments and private foundations within a period of a decade massively increased the funds for research in education, most of which was conducted by behavioral scientists. Hopes grew correspondingly high about what research might achieve in broadening the knowledge base for educational practice. Research was expected to provide recipes for the successful solution to classroom problems. Policy makers expected educational research to help them in the planning and execution of reforms that would improve the quality of a nation's schools. Typically, the enormous increase of funds for educational research under the provisions of the Elementary and Secondary Education Act passed by the United States Congress in 1965 was part of a big package of legislation on compensatory education being in its turn part of the Great Society program (Husén 1979).

In the 1960s the research and development (R & D) model which had been developed in science and technology was extended to the fields of education and social welfare. The model assumes a linear relationship between fundamental research, applied research, development of a prototype, its mass production, and dissemination in the field. The high hopes easily led to frustrations. Researchers began to be accused of coming up with "findings" which were "useless" to practitioners, be they school teachers or administrators, in schools or governments. There was a growing demand for "relevance."

The simplistic model of "linear" or "direct" application does not work in education for two main reasons. In the first place, education is like other areas in the social realm imbued with values. Educational research deals with a reality which is perceived differently depending upon ideological convictions and values held by both practitioner and researcher. The way a problem is conceptualized, how it is empirically studied and analyzed, and how the findings from studies are interpreted often depends very much on tacit or overt value assumptions. One typical example is research on bilingual education, the extent to which a minority child in a country with a main language should have an opportunity to be instructed in his or her mother tongue. Secondly, and often overlooked, are the widely different conditions under which researchers and policy makers operate. Studies of these conditions began in the 1970s.

The value problem in educational research has begun to be analyzed by educational philosophers. It is highlighted by the controversy between logical positivism or neopositivism which has dominated the social science scene since the 1940s and critical philosophies of various brands. The former takes the social reality educational research deals with as a fact and takes for granted that research can advance "objectively" valid statements about that reality. The role of the researcher vis-à-vis the policy maker is that of a technician: he or she provides the instrument or the expertise that policy makers and practitioners "use" in framing and implementing their plans and policies. The latter type of philosophy sees critical studies as a means of changing society and thereby more or less explicitly allows value premises to enter into the research process.

In the following, the different conditions under which policy makers and researchers operate will be analyzed and the differences in ethos which guide endeavors in the respective categories will be described. After that, various research utilization models will be dealt with.

1. The Setting for Policy Making

Tensions between researchers and policy makers depend on certain constraints under which policy is shaped and implemented. Some of these have been discussed by Levin (1978).

Policy makers are primarily or even exclusively interested in research that addresses problems which are on their agenda. This means that what researchers conceive as fundamental research which bears no or only a very remote relationship to the issues of the day is of little or no interest, if change in political regime or administration can mean a rearrangement of issues. For instance, the issues of private schools, educational vouchers, and busing have taken on quite a different importance under the Reagan than under the Carter administration in the United States. In Europe after the Second World War the central issue in many countries was to what extent the structure of the mandatory school should be comprehensive with regard to intake of students and programs. In countries like Sweden, England and Wales, and the Federal Republic of Germany many studies pertaining to the pedagogical and social aspects of comprehensiveness have been conducted and have been referred to extensively in the policy debate. In England the 1944 Education Act with its provisions for tripartite, secondary education in grammar, technical, and modern schools, and the selection for grammar school (the so-called 11 + examination) became an issue of the first order and gave rise to a large body of research on methods of selection and their effects. The issue of equality of educational opportunity has been a major one in Europe and the United States since the 1950s and recently in many developing countries as well. It has consequently inspired a large volume of research (Husén 1975).

Politicians have party allegiances which influence not only what they regard as relevant, innocuous, or even dangerous research but also their willingness to take research findings into account. Research, even if it addresses itself to a major issue on the political agenda, can be discarded or even rejected by one side in a political controversy if it does not support its views. Politicians, in the same way as court advocates, tend to select the evidence which they interpret as supporting their views.

Policy makers have their particular time horizon which in a parliamentary democracy tends to be rather narrow and determined not only by regular general elections but also by the flow of policy decisions. Research which takes years to complete cannot be considered if the policy maker's timetable requires the outcomes of a research project or program to be available "here and now." Research findings have to be made available in time for the decisions that by necessity have to be taken, irrespective of the nature of the "knowledge base" on which the decision maker stands. He or she needs immediate access to findings. This is a dilemma which planners and policy makers in a government agency continuously have to face. On the one hand, strategic planning with a relatively broad time perspective goes on. On the other hand, operational decision making is a continuous process which cannot wait for specially commissioned research to produce "relevant facts" of a rather simple, straightforward nature. This had led many administrators involved in policy making to demand that research should be strictly decision or policy oriented and address problems "in the field" only.

Policy makers are concerned only with policies in a particular area of their own experience as politicians or administrators. They therefore tend to disregard the connections with other areas. Educational policies have been advanced in order to solve what basically are problems in the larger social context. For example, in the United States in the mid-1960s compensatory education programs with enormous federal funds were made available to local schools. The intention was to "break the poverty cycle" by providing better education and thereby enhancing the employability of the economically disadvantaged (Husén 1979).

Policy makers are in most cases not familiar with educational research or social science research in general. In particular, they are not familiar with the language researchers use in communicating with each other, a language that ideally serves precision in presenting theories and methods, but by laypersons is often perceived as empty jargon. The problem then is to disseminate research findings in such a way that they can be understood by "ordinary people."

2. The Setting for Research

Researchers operate under conditions that in several respects differ from those under which people of practical affairs in politics and administration operate. There are differences of background, social values, and institutional settings.

Researchers in education have traditionally been performing their tasks at teacher-training institutions, most frequently at universities. As a result of growing government involvement, research units have more recently been established by public agencies as instruments of planning and evaluation. Researchers conduct their work according to paradigms to which they have become socialized during their graduate studies. They are in the first place anxious to preserve their autonomy as researchers from interferences by politicians or administrators. Secondly, their allegiance is more to fundamental or conclusion-oriented research than to applied or decision-oriented research. Thirdly, and as a consequence of this orientation, they pay much more attention to how their research is received by their peers in the national or international community of scholars in their field of specialization than by their customers in public agencies. This means among other things that once a technical report has been submitted, the researcher tends to lose interest in what happens to his or her findings.

Researchers are much less constrained than policy makers with regard to what problems they can tackle, what kind of critical language they can employ, and, not least, how much time they can use in completing a study. An investigation by the Dutch Foundation for Educational Research (Kallen et al. 1982) found that the great majority of projects financed by the Foundation lagged behind the timetable agreed upon for their completion. In order to conduct an empirical field study properly several years are required. The relevant literature on the "state of the art" has to be reviewed, methods have to be developed, data have to be collected in the field, data have to be processed and analyzed, sufficient time has to be allowed for writing the report, and finally, it takes some time for critical reviews in scholarly journals to appear. This is a process which typically takes about four to six years. Thus, the researcher has a different time horizon to that of the policy maker, both in terms of how much time he or she can allow for a study but also in terms of how his or her study fits into the ongoing research in the field. He or she perceives the study as an often humble contribution to an increasingly growing body of knowledge in a particular problem area.

Status in the research system depends upon the reputation that crystallizes from the continuously ongoing review of a researcher's work by colleagues inside or outside his or her own institution. Whereas in an administrative agency status depends on seniority and position in the organizational hierarchy, it is in the long run the quality of a person's research and the recognition of this that determines the reputation in the scholarly community to which the researcher relates himself or herself.

3. Disjunctions between Researchers and Policy Makers

The differences in settings and in value orientation between policy makers and educational researchers constitute what could be referred to as different kinds of ethos. It is even possible to speak of "two cultures." The research customers, the politicians, and/or the administrators/planners in a public agency, are by necessity pragmatists. They regard research almost entirely as an instrument for achieving a certain policy or for use in planning or implementing certain administrative goals. They want research to be focused on priority areas of current politics.

University-based researchers are brought up in the tradition of "imperial, authoritative, and independent" Research with a capital R. In order to discharge properly what they regard as their task, academics tend to take an independent and critical attitude, not least toward government. They tend to guard anxiously their academic autonomy.

These differences in value orientation and outlook tend to influence the relationship between the policy maker and the researcher all the way from the initiation of a research project to the interpretation of its findings. The "researchworthiness" of a proposed study is assessed differently. The policy maker looks at its relevance for the issues on the agenda, whereas the

researcher in the first place tends to assess it on the basis of "research-immanent" criteria, to what extent the proposed research can contribute to fundamental knowledge. The researcher wants to initiate studies without any particular considerations to the applicability of the findings and with the purpose of extending the frontiers of fundamental knowledge.

The fact that education by necessity deals with values anchored in various ideologies easily brings educational research into the turmoil of political controversy. Most regimes and administrations in power tend to perceive social science research with suspicion because of its critical nature. Those who want to preserve the status quo often tend to regard research as subversive radicalism. It is, however, in the nature of research to be in a literal sense "radical," that is to say, to go to the root (Latin *radix*).

The close relationship between education and certain political and social philosophies has made it tempting for social scientists to become ideological evangelists. This has had an adverse effect on their credibility. The common denominator of what is understood by "academic ethos" is critical inquiry that does not spare partisan doctrines, not even the ones of the party to which the researcher belongs.

In the 1960s, social science and behavioral research on an unprecedented scale began to be supported by the government in countries such as the United States, Sweden, the United Kingdom, and the Federal Republic of Germany. Social scientists began to have a strong appeal and provided the arguments liberal politicians needed in favor of programs in education and social welfare. The liberals had a strong confidence in what social science could achieve. This meant that economists, sociologists, and psychologists were commissioned to conduct research that was part of the implementation of various programs in education (Aaron 1978). At the same time there was a quest for evaluation of these programs and increasingly a component of evaluation was included in planning them.

Soon discrepancies between expectations and actual research performances began to be aired and led to demands for accountability. There have since the early 1970s been indications of a decreasing credibility on the part of policy makers vis-à-vis researchers. Expert testimonies on major policy issues have been seen as inconclusive and inconsistent. James Coleman's 1966 survey of equality of educational opportunity was interpreted to support desegregation in the public schools of the United States (Coleman 1966). His subsequent studies of busing were interpreted as providing counterevidence. Policy makers want, as President Truman once expressed it in talking about his economic advisors, "one-handed" advice and are not happy with "on the one hand—on the other hand." Furthermore, the credibility gap has been widened by allegations of ideologically imbued professional advice. In some countries social scientists working in education have been accused of "Leftist leanings" and subversive intentions. Political preferences among social scientists have even led to the establishment of research institutions with different political orientations, such as Brookings Institution and the American Enterprise Institute in the United States.

There are some inherent difficulties for educational research to prove its usefulness. The committee which at the end of the 1970s evaluated the National Institute of Education pointed out that improvements in the learning and the behavior of students as a result of research endeavors are difficult to demonstrate. The committee gave three main reasons for this: (a) a low level of sophistication in the social sciences in comparison with the physical sciences does not allow it "the luxury of predictable results"; (b) problems of bringing about and measuring changes in human learning and behavior are "vastly more complex" than those in the field of technological change; (c) the need for improvement in education is so great that expectations on educational R & D have been set much higher than is possible to achieve.

The crucial problem behind many of the frustrations felt by customers of educational research is that research cannot provide answers to the value questions with which social issues, including those in education, are imbued. This means that research even of the highest quality and "relevance" can only provide partial information that has to be integrated with experience and human judgment. The Australian Minister of Education (Shellard 1979) quoted Gene Glass as saying that there is more knowledge stored in the nervous systems of 10 excellent teachers about how to manage classroom learning than what an average teacher could distill from all existing educational research journals.

Implied in what has been said so far are three major reasons for a "disjunction" between policy making and research.

Research does not "fit" a particular situation. It might not at a given point in time be related to any political issue. Women's equal rights were for a long time a dead issue. But when they became an issue, they rapidly began to spur an enormous amount of research. But research addressing itself to issues on the agenda might come up with evidence that is out of phase with the policy-making process. As pointed out above, policy makers, like advocates, want to use research in order to support or legitimize a "prefabricated position." Often the situation occurs whereby research findings are in contradiction with or at least do not support the policy that a decision-making body or an agency wants to take or has already taken.

Research findings are from the policy maker's point of view not particularly conclusive. Furthermore, it is in the nature of the research process that in order to make a public issue "researchable" the overall problem has to be broken down into parts that more readily lend themselves to focused investigations.

A third major reason for the disjunctions between researchers and policy makers is ineffective dissemination. Research findings do not by themselves reach decision makers and practitioners. Researchers seek recognition in the first place among their peers. They place high premium on reports that can enhance their academic reputation and tend to look with skepticism upon popularization. It has been suggested that this problem can be dealt with by middlepersons who can serve in the role of "research brokers" or policy analysts and can communicate to practitioners what appears to be relevant to them. A particular type of research broker is the one who conducts meta-analyses of research, that is to say, reviews critically the existing research in a particular field in order to come up with relatively valid conclusions from the entire body of research.

4. Models of Research Utilization

The way research, in particular social science research, is "utilized" in educational policy making, in general has been studied in the first place by political scientists. Important contributions to the conceptualization have been made by Weiss (1979, 1980) and to the empirical study of the problem by both her and Caplan (1976).

In the first place, Weiss points out that "decisions" on policies or policy actions are not taken in the orderly and rational way that many think, namely that individuals authorized to decide sit down and ponder various options, consider relevant facts, and choose one of the options. Policies are decided upon in a much more diffuse way. What occurs is a complicated dynamic interaction between various interest groups, where by means of arguments advanced by them, administrative considerations, and, not least, the inertia in the system, guidelines for action begin to emerge. The best way to characterize this process is to talk about "decision accretion."

Not least researchers have been caught in rational and "knowledge-driven" models of how research findings relate to policy making. Research findings rather "percolate" through public opinion to policy makers. Instead of the latter taking into consideration particular studies, they tend to be influenced by the total body of research in a particular field. Findings usually do not reach those in positions of influence via scientific and technical reports but to a large extent via the popular press and other mass media. A body of notions that forms a *commune bonum* of "what research has to say" is built up via diverse channels of popularization. Theoretical conceptions and specific findings are "trickling" or "percolating" down and begin to influence enlightened public opinion and, in the last run, public policy.

Weiss (1979) distinguishes between seven different "models" or concepts of research utilization in the social sciences. The first model is the research and development (R & D) model which has dominated the picture of how research in the physical sciences is utilized. It is a "linear" process from basic research via applied research and development to application of new technology. There was a time in the 1960s and early 1970s when the R & D model was expected to apply in education by the development of programmed instruction and material for individualized teaching. Weiss points out that its applicability in the social sciences is heavily limited, since knowledge in this field does not readily lend itself to "conversion into replicable technologies, either material or social."

The second model is the problem-solving one, where results from a particular research project are expected to be used directly in a pending decision-making situation. The process can schematically be described as follows: identification of missing knowledge → acquisition of research information either by conducting a specific study or by reviewing the existing body of research → interpretation of research findings in the context given policy options → decision about policy to pursue.

This is the classical "philosopher-king" conception. Researchers are supposed to provide the knowledge and wisdom from which policy makers can derive guidelines for action. Researchers, not least in Continental Europe, for a long time liked to think of themselves as the ones who communicated to policy makers what "research has to say" about various issues. The problem-solving model often tacitly assumes consensus about goals. But social scientists often do not agree among themselves about the goals of certain actions, nor are they in agreement with the policy makers.

The third model is the interactive model which assumes "a disorderly set of interconnections and back-and-forthness" and an ongoing dialogue between researchers and policy makers.

The fourth model is the political one. Research findings are used as ammunition to defend a standpoint. An issue, after having been debated for quite some time in a controversial climate, leads to entrenched positions that will not be changed by new evidence. A frequent case is that policy makers in power have already made their decision before they commission research that will legitimize the policy for which they have opted.

The fifth model is the tactical one, whereby a controversial problem is "buried" in research as a defense against taking a decision at the present moment.

The sixth model is the "enlightenment" one, which according to Weiss is the one through which "social science research most frequently enters the policy arena." Research tends to influence policy in a much more subtle way than is suggested by the word "utilization," which implies more or less direct use according to the first model. In the enlightenment model research "permeates" the policy process, not by specific projects but by its "generalizations and orientations percolating through informed publics and coming to shape the way in which people think about social issues." Furthermore, without reference to any specific piece of evidence, research can sensitize policy makers to new issues, help to redefine old ones, and turn "nonproblems into policy problems." Empirical evidence appears to support this model. In a study where she was interviewing 155 policy makers in Washington, DC, Weiss found that 57 percent of them felt that they "used" research but only 7 percent could point to a specific project or study that had had an influence.

The seventh model in Weiss's taxonomy, finally, is referred to as "research-as-part-of-the-intellectual-enterprise-of-society" (research-oriented) model. Social science research together with other intellectual inputs, such as philosophy, history, journalism, and so on, contribute to widening the horizon for the debate on certain issues and to reformulating the problems.

5. Overcoming Disjunctions

The conclusion from analyses and studies of the relationships between research and educational policy making is that the former has an influence in the long run but not usually in the short term following specific projects at specific points in time. The impact of research is exercised by the total body of information and the conceptualization of issues that research produces. It does not yield "products" in the same way as research in the physical sciences. In spite of misgivings about research as "useless" to practitioners and allegations that it contributes little or nothing to policies and practice, research in the social sciences tends to "creep" into policy deliberations. The "linear" R & D model of research utilization derived from science and technology does not apply in the field of social sciences relevant to educational issues. Nor does the problem-solving model which presupposes either value-free issues or consensus about the values implied.

Research "percolates" into the policy-making process and the notion that research can contribute is integrated into the overall perspective that policy makers apply on a particular issue. Research contributes to the enlightenment of those who prepare decisions which usually are not "taken" at a given point in time but are rather accretions (Husén and Kogan 1984).

See also: Knowledge Utilization; Politics of Educational Research; Policy-oriented Research; History of Educational Research

Bibliography

Aaron J H 1978 *Politics and the Professors: The Great Society in Perspective.* Brookings Institution, Washington, DC
Caplan N 1976 Social research and national policy: What gets used by whom, for what purposes, and with what effects? *Int. Soc. Sci. J.* 28: 187–94
Coleman J S et al. 1966 *Equality of Educational Opportunity.* United States Department of Health, Education and Welfare, Washington, DC
Cronbach L J, Suppes P (eds.) 1969 *Research for Tomorrow's Schools: Disciplined Inquiry for Education: Report.* Macmillan, New York
Dutch Foundation for Educational Research 1978 *Programming Educational Research: A Framework for the Programming of Research Within the Context of the Objectives of the Foundation for Educational Research in the Netherlands.* Stichting voor Onderzoek van het Onderwijs (SVO), Dutch Foundation for Educational Research, Staatsuitgeverij, 's-Gravenhage
Her Majesty's Stationery Office (HMSO) 1971 *The Organisation and Management of Government R and D* (The Rothschild Report). Her Majesty's Stationery Office, London

Husén T 1968 Educational research and the state. In: Wall W D, Husén T (eds.) 1968 *Educational Research and Policy-making*. National Foundation for Educational Research, Slough

Husén T 1975 *Social Influences on Educational Attainment: Research Perspectives on Educational Equality*. Organisation for Economic Co-operation and Development (OECD), Paris

Husén T 1979 Evaluating compensatory education. *Proceedings of the National Academy of Education*, Vol. 6. National Academy of Education, Washington, DC

Husén T, Boalt G 1968 *Educational Research and Educational Change: The Case of Sweden*. Almqvist and Wiksell, Stockholm

Husén T, Kogan M (eds.) 1984 *Educational Research and Policy: How Do They Relate?* Pergamon, Oxford

James W 1899 *Talks to Teachers on Psychology: And to Students on Some of the Life's Ideals*. Longmans, Green, London

Kallen D, Kosse G B, Wagenar H C (eds.) 1982 *Social Science Research and Public Policy Making: A Re-appraisal*. National Foundation for Educational Research, Slough; Nelson, London

Kogan M (ed.) 1974 *The Politics of Education: Edward Boyle and Anthony Crosland in Conversation with Maurice Kogan*. Penguin, Harmondsworth

Kogan M, Korman N, Henkel M 1980 *Government's Commissioning of Research: A Case Study*. Department of Government, Brunel University, Uxbridge

Levin H M 1978 Why isn't educational research more useful? *Prospects* 8(2)

Lindblom C E, Cohen D K 1979 *Usable Knowledge: Social Science and Social Problem Solving*. Yale University Press, New Haven, Connecticut

Rein M 1980 Methodology for the study of the interplay between social science and social policy. *Int. Soc. Sci. J.* 32: 361–68

Rule J B 1978 *Insight and Social Betterment: A Preface to Applied School Science*. Oxford University Press, London

Shellard J S (ed.) 1979 *Educational Research for Policy Making in Australia*. Australian Council for Educational Research, Hawthorn, Victoria

Suppes P (ed.) 1978 *Impact of Research on Education: Some Case Studies: Summaries*. National Academy of Education, Washington, DC

United States Office of Education 1969 *Educational Research and Development in the United States*. United States Government Printing Office, Washington, DC

Weiss C H 1979 The many meanings of research utilization. *Public Admin. Rev.* Sept.–Oct.

Weiss C H 1980 Knowledge creep and decision accretion. *Knowledge: Creation, Diffusion, Utilization* 1: 381–404

Politics of Educational Research

M. Timpane

A distinct politics of educational research was created worldwide during the 1960s and 1970s, as the support of such inquiry became established government policy in many developed and developing nations (Myers 1981, King 1981). This spread is part—usually a modest part—of the broad development of government support for research in many areas of national significance, ranging from defense and space to physical science, health, agriculture, economics, and other social-policy concerns.

Modern governments support research on education and other social services for a variety of reasons. Policy makers today are more likely to seek and absorb information from research in considering new policies and programs; they understand that information from research can raise important new questions about policies, help improve program performance, and help control program activities; more cynically, they also understand that research results can be used to legitimate policies, and vindicate choices—including the choice to delay (Weiler 1983).

At the same time, policy makers have placed only modest confidence in the saving power of educational research. Educational research has been considered a "soft science," unpersuasive either in prospect or product. There were extremely limited numbers of first-rate research scholars or institutions to be enlisted in the enterprise. Equally limited was the political support that educational research enjoyed from the politically more powerful educational associations, such as teachers'

unions, associations of administrators, and regional, state, and local educational policy makers (Timpane 1982).

Within this general setting, the politics of educational research operate at three levels: in the establishment of government research institutions and agendas of study, in the selection and conduct of specific research studies, and in the utilization of the results of research. The most visible of these is the first.

1. Establishing Institutions and Agendas

As public institutions and research agendas have emerged in educational research, so has a complicated and fragile politics. A series of related questions are always under political consideration: from what source shall goals and priorities be derived; to whom shall the available resources be allocated; what type of research will best accomplish the agenda? These questions range from the mostly political to the substantially scientific, but politics is absent from none of them.

There is, to start with, no obvious single source from which goals and priorities for educational research may be derived. Goals and priorities may be suggested by government policy makers themselves, but these are multiple in all national political systems. In the United States these include, at least, federal, state, and local officials and officials in the executive, legislative, and judicial branches—and probably more than one agency in each instance. Moreover, the individual researchers and the institutes and universities in which they work have obvious standing to help determine what research is important and possible. So, too, do the field practitioners, such as teachers and local officials, and the concerned publics, for example, parents, taxpayers, and the representatives of special educational interest groups such as the disadvantaged, the handicapped, and the victims of discrimination.

No national government has allocated sufficient resources to carry out any substantial part of the research agenda that these parties of interest might establish in a negotiated political process. Even in the United States, with by far the most ambitious educational research program, funding for the National Institute of Education (NIE) has never been more than a fraction of that suggested in the initial studies proposing its agenda (Levien 1971). In consequence, the politics of educational research are, at this level, typically a desperate attempt to spread resources too thinly over some representative set of research projects, punctuated by the more or less arbitrary selection of one or two politically and substantively important topics—be they reading or vocational preparation, school finance or organization, bilingual or science education—for concentrated attention and support. The choices made typically disappoint more constituents than they encourage. They also leave government research agencies such as the NIE exposed to continual political attack: for not being "useful to the field" or for "doing bad science"; for being a "tool of the Right" (as Democrats charged during and after the Nixon Administration) or for inveterate "funding of the Left" (as the supporters of President Reagan have claimed); for neglecting local realities or for ignoring emerging national problems. The most consistent (and predictable) criticism of the choices that has been made across time and nations is that the research supported is too much applied in character and thereby of too little value with respect to fundamental policy change and to intellectual progress (Nisbet 1982, Kiesler and Turner 1977). Some critics have gone further, to note inherent conflicts between the requirements of politics for timeliness, relevance, and self-protection and the requirements of research for elegance, parsimony, and objectivity, concluding that the research enterprise requires strong protection from the diurnal incursions of public and governmental interest (Coleman 1972, 1978).

2. Selecting and Conducting Studies

The actual conduct of educational research is infested with a similar swarm of political dilemmas. Once governmental research agencies or offices and their priorities are established, there remain a host of questions having no completely "rational" or "scientific" answers. An important set of methodological questions turn out to be political. For the most important areas of educational research, there are no a priori grounds for choosing a disciplinary approach; historians, ethnographers, sociologists, and several varieties of psychologists, for example, have important contributions to make in solving education's most vexing riddles. Inter- and multidisciplinary approaches can bridge some, but only some, of the chasms in perspective amongst these disciplines. More often, choices must be made among them, and representatives of the disciplines must enter bureaucratic politics to secure consideration of their proposed inquiries. Similarly, proponents of the several functional forms of research must promote their longitudinal and cross-sectional case studies, surveys, experiments, evaluations, ethnomethodologies, data reanalyses, meta-analyses, development activities, or other qualitative and quantitative designs in a context where many arguments are plausible but only a few will be successful. Finally, in many cases, individuals qualified to perform or assist in the research may operate in diverse settings—in colleges and universities, in research institutes, in regional and local agencies, in professional associations, and at the very site of schooling or education. Each institution will provide technical assistance and political support for their candidates seeking to participate in the supported research.

The government research agency has a few strategies available to deal with these political dilemmas: it may adhere to a "free grant" process that distributes resources to traditional places in research, in accordance with the procedures and canons of the disciplines (study groups, peer review, etc.); it may sharply define and manage its research requirements through in-house or contract research; or it may establish a process for negotiation with all or some of the prospective recipients seeking to establish some mix of research activities serving various educational agendas. The selection of any such strategy places the research policy makers and program directors at risk. Each has the goal of sustaining effective research programs, but must do so through the development of successively more imaginative bureaucratic processes involving service to higher political authority, the continual taking of outside advice, the extension of selection and review processes to include all pertinent perspectives, and the creation and administration of justificatory documents—in a context where political support for the entire enterprise is at best unreliable. The result, in the United States at least, has been the segmentation of the research agenda into an array of topically significant programs (reading, teaching bilingual education, desegregation, educational organization, finance, and so forth) within which are nested continuing grant programs for individuals and small groups of investigators and selected directed studies performed mostly by institutions—all undergirded by published research plans and broad field participation in project review and selection. There is important emphasis at every stage on the ultimate significance that the research may have for the national educational enterprise: the basic political objective is to create a balanced portfolio of basic and applied studies of sufficient significance, quality, and utility to satisfy, if not delight, all important constituencies.

3. Utilizing Results

Political perspectives concerning the use of educational research have developed swiftly since the early 1960s. Two developments which precipitated this change were: (a) the collapse of linear models of research, development, testing, demonstration, and evaluation as explanations of the progress of educational research results into program operations (Cronbach and Suppes 1969); and (b) the parallel collapse of systematic planning models as explanations of the progress of educational research results into new educational policy (Cohen and Garet 1975).

Each of these two models has been replaced by a more political view. The delivery of new knowledge to classroom teachers and other educators is now usually understood as part of an extended process of synthesis (where bodies of related research results are gathered and made interpretable) and of introduction into an actual process of classroom or school improvement. The program improvements suggested by the research are considered along with the insights of artful practice and the opinion of respected peers, with the entire process dependent upon consistent administrative encouragement and community support (Mann 1978). The emphasis has shifted from "design" of educational innovation to the "mobilization" of a receptive staff. The process is fundamentally political, and only secondarily technical.

Similarly, new research knowledge enters policy deliberations by the compatible processes of "knowledge creep" and "decision accretion" (Weiss 1980). That is to say, research results from many studies are absorbed irregularly as part, but only part of the information environment of decision makers, who arrive at their conclusions on given policy issues over an extended period of time, not at one decisive moment. Careful policy analysis may sometimes have a significant impact at an opportune time, but the decision is most often substantially formed by the more gradual process of "accretion" and "creep." In such a view, there is wide play for political forces. The value of research information becomes bound up with the credibility, political influence, and interpretive skill of its bearer.

These new understandings spotlight one of the most important weaknesses in the political system of educational research—the lack of authoritative interpreters who can speak both objectively and practically about both policy and practice from positions grounded in the state of current knowledge (e.g., Wildavsky 1979). These commentators are especially missed because they can simultaneously perform two additional functions essential to the political survival of educational research: to translate many of the significant issues of educational policy and practice into appropriate questions for fundamental and applied research; and to be witness, by their own effectiveness, to the contribution educational research can make to the public interest which supports it.

See also: Educational Research and Policy Making; Policy-oriented Research; Knowledge Diffusion in Education; Knowledge Utilization

Bibliography

Cohen D K, Garet M S 1975 Reforming educational policy with applied social research. *Harvard Educ. Rev.* 45: 17–43
Coleman J S 1972 *Policy Research in the Social Sciences.* General Learning Press, Morristown, New Jersey
Coleman J S 1978 The use of social science research in the development of public policy. *Urban Rev.* 10: 197–202
Cronbach L J, Suppes P (eds.) 1969 *Research for Tomorrow's Schools: Disciplined Inquiry for Education: Report.* Macmillan, New York
Kiesler S B, Turner C F (eds.) 1977 *Fundamental Research and the Process of Education.* National Academy of Sciences, Washington, DC
King K 1981 Dilemmas of research aid to education in developing countries. *Prospects* 11: 343–51
Levien R E 1971 *National Institute of Education: Preliminary Plan for the Proposed Institute.* A Report Proposed for the Department of Health, Education, and Welfare. Rand, Santa Monica, California
Mann D (ed.) 1978 *Making Change Happen?* Teachers College Press, New York
Myers R G 1981 *Connecting Worlds: A Survey of Development in Educational Research in Latin America.* International Development Research Centre, Ottawa, Ontario
Nisbet J 1982 The impact of research: A crisis of confidence. *Aust. Educ. Res.* 9(1): 5–22
Timpane P M 1982 Federal progress in educational research. *Harvard Educ. Rev.* 52: 540–48
Weiler H N 1983 West Germany: Educational policy as compensatory legitimation. In: Thomas R M (ed.) 1983 *Politics and Education: Cases from Eleven Nations.* Pergamon, Oxford, pp. 35–54
Weiss C H 1980 Knowledge creep and decision accretion. *Knowledge: Creation, Diffusion, Utilization* 1(3): 381-404
Wildavsky A B 1979 *Speaking Truth to Power: The Art and Craft of Policy Analysis.* Little, Brown, & Co., Boston, Massachusetts

Ethical Considerations in Research

W. B. Dockrell

Concern with ethical considerations in educational research has grown in recent years, whereas in earlier years the emphasis was on technical standards. This concern can be viewed as relating to the subjects of study, to the customers for a particular investigation, to the scientific community, and finally to society in general. These sets of concerns are not independent but are interrelated, posing questions for researchers themselves and for all those concerned with research.

1. The Growth of Concern

Most books on educational research published in the 1970s (Butcher and Pont 1973, Kerlinger 1973, Taylor 1973), not only do not include a chapter or section on ethics but do not even include the term in their indexes. There is, however, a discussion of ethics as they apply to social research in general in a book published in 1979 (Barnes 1979), and a later book (Dockrell and Hamilton 1980) does have a chapter which includes ethics in its contents (Walker 1980), but even in this book the term does not appear in the index.

There has been, since the early 1970s, an increased awareness of ethical questions in research involving people. Earlier concern was with technical issues as manifested in such volumes as the *Technical Recommendations for Achievement Tests* (American Educational Research Association 1955) prepared by a committee of the American Educational Research Association and the National Council on Measurement Used in Education and a similar one, *Technical Recommendations for Psychological Tests and Diagnostic Techniques*, prepared by a committee of the American Psychological Association (American Psychological Association 1954). These two volumes were replaced by one prepared by a committee representative of the three organizations, on standards for educational and psychological tests (American Psychological Association 1966). More recently the emphasis has shifted. In 1973, a book on ethical principles in research with human participants (American Psychological Association 1973) was published as well as a substantial volume on standards for evaluation of educational programmes (Joint Committee on Standards 1981). This latter report continued the concern with technical matters but also included a section on propriety standards, which was largely ethical.

Technical standards are an important aspect of ethics in educational research. Whatever procedures are used must be valid, that is, they must provide accurate information relevant to the purposes for which they are used. Accuracy is relative. In most measurements, physical as well as educational, there is some error. Precise accuracy is not possible. The scales used in a maternity hospital for weighing new-born infants need to be more accurate than those used for measuring overweight middle-aged adults in a gymnasium. Each needs to be accurate enough for its purpose. Much of the 1966 volume issued by the American Psychological Association is devoted to this question of the validity of instruments and the rest to other related matters like the reliability of instruments, scales and norms used, instructions for scoring, and the general adequacy of the manuals.

The 1981 report of the Joint Committee on Standards for Educational Evaluations goes beyond this even in technical matters. Additional questions are raised with ethical implications.

2. Ethics in Relation to Subjects

The focus of the manual on ethical principles (American Psychological Association 1973) is exclusively on the subjects of an experiment. This is a major area of concern, but not the only one. The first question for the researcher in relation to his or her subjects is, do they understand fully what is being asked of them? The researcher must not minimize or indeed exaggerate the demands that are to be made in terms of time, effort, or stress on subjects.

It is easiest to be clear about the amount of time that will be required. It is sometimes difficult for a researcher to appreciate the stress that may be induced, for example, in school pupils by a test which proves to be too difficult for them. School children do not always understand the distinction between data which are being gathered anonymously for research purposes and assessments which are being made of them personally.

It may be easier for teachers to make this distinction. However, at the beginning of a study of the effects of different teaching styles, the extent to which their actual classroom practices will be monitored by an outsider may not be clear to the teachers involved. Whatever disclaimers may be made, the observer may appear to be a figure of some authority or at least in close contact with people in authority. The presence of a student in the classroom for a prescribed period may be quite acceptable. The presence of a researcher over a considerable period of time may be a source of considerable stress.

The mere presence of a researcher in a classroom or indeed in a school studying the use of corporal punishment may be a source of stress both to those who would wish to use corporal punishment but are constrained from doing so and to those who wish to see it eliminated but fear their discipline may not be tight enough. The researcher cannot be expected to anticipate the amount of stress in each case but can reasonably be expected to make clear precisely what is being expected and to ensure as far as possible that there is no misunderstanding about what will be involved.

The second area in which the researcher has obligations concerning the subjects of the study is the confidentiality of the information obtained. It is up to the researcher to ensure that the subjects know and agree what will be disclosed about them. Many research organizations have rules about the identification of schools or school districts, teachers, or pupils in published reports (as does the Scottish Council for Research in Education, for example). The application of this principle is easier in the traditional survey-type studies where information is disclosed only about categories of schools, teachers, or pupils. It is only in those rare circumstances where there are only a few cases in any one category that it is possible to identify individuals. However, with case studies which rely on providing substantial information about a limited number of subjects it may not be possible to disguise the individuals concerned. The use of a fictional name as in Elmstown (Hollingshead 1949) or Hightown Grammar (Lacey 1970) may not be sufficient to disguise the source of the information. It may be necessary in those cases to do as Richardson did in her Nailsea study (Richardson 1973), that is, to negotiate with all concerned before the publication of a report.

Whether an attempt is made to disguise individual persons or institutions by the use of a fictional name, or a number, or a letter, or whether their identity is fully disclosed, all concerned must have a chance to read the material before it is published. Should they also have the right to require the removal of any material about themselves to which they object even if this were to weaken the report to the point of rendering it valueless? What is the balance between the rights of the subjects in the study and of the community for whose benefit the study was carried out?

With unpublished materials a similar problem may arise. Information about an individual, whether he or she is explicitly identified or not, may be used as a basis of discussion for clarification or for explanation with colleagues or superiors. The individuals clearly have a right to know beforehand that this may happen to them. Do they equally have a right to exclude from such discussion any material about themselves which they find unacceptable?

The first concern outlined above was about the effects on the subjects. A second concern is about the benefits of research to them. A researcher must specify what return there will be to the subjects and not mislead them about the benefits of the investigation to themselves. It is not unusual for researchers to offer to provide the results of tests to participants in a study. If the test scores are to be meaningful to the participants it may be necessary to provide an interpretation which is not required for research purposes. For example, a test of academic achievement may be administered which provides only raw scores for experimental purposes. That information might be all that the researcher needs. Those scores, however, might be quite meaningless to teachers, pupils, or administrators unless they were related in some way to the objectives of the teaching or the performance of a reference group. If the subjects are to be offered benefits for themselves those benefits must be real.

A serious dilemma may arise when there is concern about the effect on subjects of knowledge of the object of the research. It may be important to know whether classrooms following a particular regime are more likely to induce persistence in their pupils than those adopting an alternative approach. It might be possible to devise an acceptable measure of persistence but what would the effect be on that measure of informing the children that this is what was being measured and not level of attainment? The same problem arises with classroom

observation studies which are concerned with particular aspects of teacher behaviour. If teachers are told precisely what it is that the researchers are looking for, are they more likely to act in that way than if they were simply given general information? If the researcher believes that full disclosure would affect the behaviour of the subjects, under what circumstances is he or she free to withhold relevant information and by doing so mislead? Is it ever legitimate to make false statements in order to disguise the true objective of an investigation?

It is incumbent on the researcher to be explicit in the definition of the role of both sets of participants in a study, researchers and subjects. In some cases the responsibility of each is clear enough. In others, for example in action research, it is sometimes not clear what the subjects can expect of the researchers by way of support for their activities. By contrast there are some research designs which require the researcher to take an authoritarian role and to ensure that certain actions are carried out. It should be clear to all participants what they can expect of each other. This does not mean that they need to follow a rigidly predefined path. Flexibility may be essential for the progress of the research. What is required is that at each stage the mutual expectations be explicit.

A final consideration with respect to the subjects is general cost effectiveness. Is the value that is to be gained from the investigation commensurate with what is being asked of the subjects? It is very rarely that educational research would involve actual psychological harm to children. However, parents sometimes raise this question when a new curriculum is being tried out in the schools. They are concerned that their children may be put at a disadvantage in comparison with others. It is a question which arises with experimental studies rather than with observation of variation in current practice. If a researcher introduces a change in practice he or she is depriving children of something they would otherwise have had, and providing a substitute. In what circumstances is the informed consent of parents required for such an experiment? Does a school have to get consent before trying a new reading scheme, a new form of grouping, a new teaching method? The existence of laboratory schools (Turney 1985) which parents choose to send their children to, provides one answer. However, it is not an alternative that is universally available.

It is also important not to make an excessive demand on the time or resources of pupils or schools. Excessive in this context means not commensurate with any foreseeable benefit from the studies.

3. Ethics in Relation to Customers

A second set of concerns relates to the customers of research. In this context, customer refers to someone who has commissioned the research. At its simplest this can be summarized by saying that researchers should not promise more than they can deliver and that consequently they should deliver what they have promised. This principle applies whether the customer is looking for guidance about a specific course of action, or for better understanding of some theoretical issue. In this section the focus will be on customers whose interest is in research as a basis for action.

Ethical considerations in relation to customers refer primarily to communication. The first concern must be that the customers understand the limits of the information that will be made available. Research findings are rarely prescriptive. They never pre-empt careful consideration of the issues. It is unlikely that research will tell an administrator or teacher what to do. Usually it can only contribute to the examination of the options. The researcher therefore must be clear about what the data from a specific study can and cannot contribute to the thinking about a particular issue or set of issues.

The conclusions from research may range from a plausible hypothesis to a substantiated generalization. Whitehead's distinction in his paper on the rhythm of education (Whitehead 1932) may be applied to research (Dockrell and Hamilton 1980). He talks about the stage of romance which is when the researcher has an insight into the possible interpretation of a set of facts, the stage of precision where he or she attempts to specify the circumstances where the insight might apply, and finally the stage of generalization where the researcher can assert a particular principle or a particular set of relationships that will be of universal application. There is a risk that a research report which is at the stage of romance or indeed at the stage of attempted precision will be misconstrued as at the stage of generalization, even when the authors are careful to point out the limitations of their work as did Rutter and his colleagues (Rutter et al. 1979). The researchers must make clear to the customer what is the status of their conclusions.

It is in this area of relationships with customers that the traditional concern with technical questions is relevant. Researchers understand the meaning of statistical significance, that is, the probability of findings being other than accidental, but the customer may not. He or she may be presented with tables of relationships between groups and assume that the sample findings can be safely generalized to the population. Professional journals would insist on the inclusion of probability levels. They may, however, be excluded from unpublished reports to customers. Even some published reports have presented results which were not statistically significant in a way that might mislead a reader.

One of the conventional distinctions in discussion of educational research is between statistical significance and educational significance. Relationships which it is reasonable to assume actually exist in the population might be so small as to be irrelevant for practical purposes. A customer who is told that results are significant might assume that this means important and not merely probable. The importance of relationships is a matter of judgment and it is therefore the responsibility of the researcher to see that the customer understands the probable size of the differences as well as the likelihood of them being found in the parent population. A customer who thinks that a correlation of 0.5 is high might

not do so if he or she appreciated the extent of the covariation that it indicated.

The measures used in research are frequently not direct measures of the variables which are of concern to the customers. Researchers might talk easily of achievement in mathematics or science, of intelligence or social class, always understanding that what is being referred to is a score on a particular measure. Whether that measure adequately represents what the customer means by the variable in his or her particular set of circumstances needs clarification. Scores on any test of attainment in, for example, physics, will cover only a sample of the skills and concepts which might legitimately be thought of as included in physics. As long as the sets used in the research coincide with those the customer had in mind for this purpose, no problems arise. It is up to the researcher to ensure that the customer understands the nature and content of the test and is consequently in a position to judge for himself or herself whether the measure is appropriate.

The problem is particularly acute in studies where surrogates are used. It is not easy, for example, to define social class and even where a definition is attempted it is the practice to use some surrogate like a scale of occupations. Surrogates may be satisfactory for research purposes but quite unsuitable for policy making. It is probably wisest to avoid using a general label like reading or physics or social class as far as possible and to be specific in saying what the scale assesses.

Where do the researchers' responsibilities end? Have they met their commitments when they present a set of results, or have they a responsibility to their customers to interpret their findings, to say what they mean in a particular context? The extent to which researchers can do this will vary from project to project, but it will be done by somebody and researchers do not absolve themselves from responsibility by saying that they have presented their results. Rather, their responsibility is to facilitate and participate in interpretation, ensuring that any conclusions are in accord with their understanding of the data.

If researchers do accept responsibility for interpreting and explaining their findings, they have the further responsibility of distinguishing between their findings and their extrapolations from them. It is legitimate to interpret results in the light of theory. It is important too to specify which of the researchers' opinions arise from the specific set of findings and which from theoretical or other considerations.

The researcher has a final responsibility to the customer, that is, to ensure that he or she is understood. Researchers frequently use terms which have limited or extended meaning. That may be a convenient form of communication for people who share a particular background. It may be misleading to a customer who does not share the researcher's knowledge or assumptions. Many research organizations employ editors whose job it is to translate research findings into the language of the customers. Where researchers do not have this professional service available to them, they should be particularly alert to the needs and problems of their readers.

4. Ethics in Relation to Colleagues

The researchers' obligations to their colleagues are twofold. One is to them as scientists to ensure that they can make the fullest use of their researches and second, as members of the research community to ensure that what they say does not detract from the status of the community.

Research data are not private property. They are an individual contribution to a common wealth of knowledge and understanding. The first set of responsibilities are those most frequently specified and indeed frequently enforced by colleagues through the medium of reviewing research proposals for funding, articles for publication, and books once they have been published.

In technical reports which are addressed to the research community, far more detail about the way the data have been gathered and how the analyses have been made is called for than in a report to customers so that an adequate professional evaluation of findings may be made. Some research institutions prepare several reports on the same study, designed for different audiences. The report to colleagues should be sufficiently detailed for them to understand the limitations in the data and their analysis. The kind of interpretation and perhaps simplification which is involved in a popular report can be avoided and replaced with specific detail.

One common way of dealing with the question of analysis is to make data available for reanalysis. Social science archives are one way of doing this, though it may be appropriate for some kinds of data to be held in confidence and only made available in carefully controlled circumstances. This does not of course answer all the questions. It only makes available the data on file. It does not answer questions about how the data were gathered. It is important therefore to retain copies of tests, questionnaires, and other material.

In the case of ethnographic studies, the raw data may well be field notes including reports of interviews, descriptions of observations, and so on. In this case the raw data should be available for other scholars to read and interpret but so should a description of the circumstances in which the encounters took place.

Some researchers achieve fame or have it thrust upon them. It is in these circumstances that the researchers' responsibility to the research community is greatest. What is written will be seen as "research". When they are reported it will be "researcher says". They will be taken as representing the whole research community. The clearest responsibility is not to make statements which will bring research into disrepute. This does not mean that they must not participate or indeed provoke debate on important issues. If they do not make clear the significance of their findings for general issues who

will? Researchers must not, however, overstate their cases—and must not assert the infallibility of research findings, particularly of their interpretation of their own findings.

5. Ethics in Relation to the Community

Finally, the researcher has responsibilities to the community as a whole. One of them is implicit in the last consideration of responsibility to colleagues. It may well be the responsibility of researchers to draw attention to the implications of their researches for policy. If they do not, they may be neglected or misinterpreted and the community as a whole may suffer. Important improvements that could have been made might not be made because of a researcher's reluctance to take part in social debate.

It is at this stage that researchers can be the voices of the voiceless. The customer in educational research is more likely to be an administrator with resources than teachers, parents, or pupils. The researcher can be the advocate of a different set of clients—the pupils who might suffer educationally from an apparently efficient set of arrangements or the teachers who might be forced into practices which have been evaluated from only one perspective and that one not their own.

There is a final consideration for the researchers. That is, whether it is appropriate to carry out a particular piece of research in specific social circumstances. A researcher like everyone else is responsible for the foreseeable consequences of his or her actions. In some societies simply to raise certain issues about racial or social differences might now or in the past have been a basis for the abridgement of human rights. The researcher has the obligation to ask questions fearlessly. He or she also has the obligation to be aware of the consequences of raising certain issues.

The relevance of a broad range of ethical questions to the conduct of research has been recognized in fields like medicine for many cultures. In physics, the development of nuclear weapons provided a jolt that led to soul searching and laid the old certainties open to question. As educational research has become less an academic pursuit and more directly a guide to educational practice, ethical issues have become more prominent and concern with them a topic of discussion among researchers.

See also: Teachers as Researchers; Ethics of Evaluation Studies

Bibliography

American Educational Research Association/National Council on Measurements Used in Education 1955 *Technical Recommendations for Achievement Tests.* National Educational Association, Washington, DC

American Psychological Association 1954 *Technical Recommendations for Psychological Tests and Diagnostic Techniques.* American Psychological Association, Washington, DC

American Psychological Association 1966 *Standards for Educational and Psychological Tests and Manuals*. American Psychological Association, Washington, DC

American Psychological Association 1973 *Ethical Principles in the Conduct of Research with Human Participants*. American Psychological Association, Washington, DC

Barnes J A 1979 *Who Should Know What? Social Science, Privacy and Ethics*. Penguin, Harmondsworth

Butcher H J, Pont H B (eds.) 1973 *Educational Research in Britain, 3*. University of London Press, London

Dockrell W B, Hamilton D (eds.) 1980 *Rethinking Educational Research*. Hodder and Stoughton, Dunton Green, Kent

Hollingshead A B 1949 *Elmstown's Youth: The Impact of Social Classes on Adolescents*. Wiley, New York

Joint Committee on Standards for Educational Evaluation 1981 *Standards for Evaluations of Educational Programmes, Projects, and Materials*. McGraw-Hill, New York

Kerlinger F N (ed.) 1973 *Review of Research in Education*, Vol. 3. Peacock, Itasca, Illinois

Lacey C 1970 *Hightown Grammar: The School as Social System*. Manchester University Press, Manchester

Richardson E 1973 *The Teacher, the School and the Task of Management*. Heinemann, London

Rutter M, Maughan B, Mortimore P, Ousten J, Smith A 1979 *Fifteen Thousand Hours: Secondary Schools and Their Effects on Children*. Open Books, London

Taylor W (ed.) 1973 *Research Perspectives in Education*. Routledge and Kegan Paul, London

Turney C 1985 Laboratory schools and teacher education. In: Husén T, Postlethwaite T N (eds.) 1985 *The International Encyclopedia of Education*, Vol. 5. Pergamon Press, Oxford, pp. 2853–60

Walker R 1980 The conduct of educational case studies: Ethics, theory and practice. In: Dockrell W B, Hamilton D (eds.) 1980, pp. 30–63

Whitehead A N 1932 *The Aims of Education, and Other Essays*. Williams and Norgate, London

Ethics of Evaluation Studies

E. R. House

Ethics are the rules or standards of right conduct or practice, especially the standards of a profession. What ethical standards have been proposed for the conduct of educational evaluation? What general principles underlie standards? Are these standards and principles sufficient to ensure an ethical practice? These are the questions this article will address. The extent to which evaluation studies actually meet these ethical standards is not addressed here, except by implication.

The ethics of evaluation studies are a subset of ethics or morality in general but, of course, ethics applied to much narrower problems than those of general morality. "In the narrow sense, a morality is a system of a particular sort of constraints on conduct—ones whose central task is to protect the interests of persons other than the agent and which present themselves to an agent as checks on his natural inclinations or spontaneous tendencies to act" (Mackie 1977 p. 106).

Thus the task of an ethics of evaluation is to check the "natural inclinations" of evaluators that may injure the interests of another person, a task made all the more formidable by the fact that these inclinations may be unconscious, built into the very techniques and methods employed by the evaluator. Given the relative power of the evaluator over those evaluated, the ethics of evaluation are critical to the establishment of a responsible evaluation practice.

According to Sieber,

If there were a field of applied ethics for program evaluation, that field would study how to choose morally right actions and maximize the value of one's work in program evaluation. It would examine the kinds of dilemmas that arise in program evaluation; it would establish guidelines for anticipating and resolving certain ethical problems and encompass a subarea of scientific methodology for performing evaluation that satisfies both scientific and ethical requirements;

and it would consider ways to promote ethical character in program evaluators. (Sieber 1980 p. 52)

There is yet another requirement for an ethics of evaluation: it must be rationally persuasive to evaluators. It seems reasonable to treat evaluators themselves as moral persons. "Thus to respect another as a moral person is to try to understand his aims and interests from his standpoint and try to present him with considerations that enable him to accept the constraints on his conduct" (Rawls 1971 p. 338).

Recently several codes of ethics and standards of practice have been proposed for educational evaluation in particular and for social science research in general. Many of these rules and standards are methodological directives but some are concerned with ethical behavior. For example, in the most elaborate and widely disseminated set of standards, there are four areas of concern—utility, accuracy, feasibility, and propriety. Under propriety the standards are formal obligations, conflict of interest, full and frank disclosure, the public's right to know, rights of human subjects, human interactions, balanced reporting, and fiscal responsibility. These standards relate mostly to privacy, protection of human subjects, and freedom of information. Generally the picture that emerges is that the evaluator should forge a written contract with the sponsor and adhere to that contract. He or she should beware of conflicts of interest in which the evaluator's personal interests are somehow involved. Openness, full disclosure, and release of information are the main ways of dealing with these problems. The limitations on full disclosure are the commonly understood rights of subjects. Ordinarily this means informed consent of the subjects must be obtained. There is also a call for respecting others who are engaged in the evaluation itself, a general admonition to decency.

Anderson and Ball (1978) have compiled a list of ethical responsibilities for the evaluator, as well as a list of ethical obligations for the commissioner of the evaluation. The evaluator is expected to acquaint the sponsor with the evaluator's orientation and values, develop a contract with the sponsor, fulfill the terms of the contract, adhere to privacy and informed consent standards, acquaint the sponsor with unsound program practices, present a balanced report, make the results available to legitimate audiences, allow for other professionals to examine the procedures and data, and publish rejoinders to misinterpretations of the evaluation results. The commissioner of the evaluation has obligations to cooperate in the various tasks of the evaluation. To the degree that they deal with ethics at all, other formal codes of ethics and standards suggest similar ethical principles and sets of problems. Mutual agreement of the evaluator and sponsor is emphasized in most codes.

Ethical issues also emerge from the use of particular techniques in designs, such as the use of control groups. For example, two ethical issues that are of concern in use of control groups are the potential for denying a valuable service to eligible clients who might not be chosen for the beneficial treatment and the equitable allocation of scarce resources to a large group of eligible recipients. Acceptance of the clients as equals is one proposed way of dealing with these problems, and multiple treatment groups is another.

A review of the literature suggests four basic ethical problems: (a) withholding the nature of the evaluation research from participants or involving them without their knowledge; (b) exposing participants to acts which would harm them or diminish their self-esteem; (c) invading the privacy of participants; and (d) withholding benefits from participants. These are all intrusions against the individual's person somehow, or infringements against personal rights.

What principles underlie these ethical concerns? The National Commission for the Protection of Human Subjects of Biomedical and Behavioral Research has identified three underlying principles—beneficence, respect, and justice. Beneficence means avoiding unnecessary harm and maximizing good outcomes. In the opinion of the commission this principle is served by the research or evaluation being valid, by evaluators being competent, by the participants being informed, by the results being disseminated, and by the consequences of the evaluation being weighed with others. The evaluation is supposed to be beneficial.

Respect means respecting the autonomy of others by reducing the power differential between the evaluator and participants, having participants volunteer, informing participants, and giving participants a choice in matters that affect them. Justice, in the commission's view, means equitable treatment and representation of subgroups within society. Justice is operationally defined by equitable design and measurement, and equitable access to data for reanalysis. These three principles constitute

the rationale for ethical human research, including evaluation.

For the most part these ethical codes concentrate upon infringements to personal rights. The codes assume that there are inherent individual rights prior to the conduct of the evaluation, that the participants must be accorded these rights, and that the individual must voluntarily agree to participation. Almost all these codes of ethics require that the evaluator enter into a contractual agreement with the sponsor and adhere to the agreement as a matter of ethics. Not adhering to the agreement would be considered unfair. Those who are not a party to the agreement have certain personal rights, such as the rights to be informed about the study and the right to volunteer.

Fairness suggests that people are obligated to uphold their part of an agreement when they have voluntarily accepted the benefits of an arrangement or taken advantage of its opportunities to further their own interests. People are not to benefit from the efforts of others without doing their fair share.

Not just any agreement is considered binding, however. House and Care (1979) have asserted that a binding agreement must meet certain conditions. For example, a party cannot be coerced into signing the agreement. All parties must be rational, equally informed, and have a say in the agreement itself. Only under certain conditions can the agreement be considered an appropriate basis for the evaluation.

The fundamental ethical notion is that of a contractual ethics, the establishment of an implicit or explicit contract as the basis for conduct. This is consistent and, indeed, entailed by viewing society as a collection of individuals. "The essence of liberalism. . . is the vision of society as made up of independent, autonomous units who co-operate only when the terms of cooperation are such as make it further the ends of the parties" (Barry 1973 p. 166). Voluntary consent of the participants is essential to ethical conduct in this framework, and intrusions upon people without their consent is considered unethical and immoral. Individual autonomy is a primary principle within this conceptual framework, and autonomy is reflected in establishment of agreements, informing participants, and requesting consent. The ethics are essentially personal and contractual.

While these principles capture many of the concerns of those who have codified ethical principles for evaluation, other theorists have held that these notions of ethics are too restricted. Ideology plays an important role in how evaluation studies are conducted. In fact, Sjoberg contends that evaluation studies usually take for granted the structural constraints of the social system. Evaluations are used for effectiveness, efficiency, and accountability within the dominant bureaucratic hierarchies. The categories used by evaluators are those of the status quo, and the social indicators employed are allied to the political power structure. To the degree to which this is true, the formalized ethics of evaluation are limited to concerns which do not threaten the ideological status quo. Many ethical problems are beyond the recognition of evaluators because they are excluded by the prevailing ideology. People are usually not aware of the limits of this ideological consensus until they step outside it.

For example, MacDonald has carried the principle of autonomy a step beyond the prevailing consensus. He has contended that evaluations usually serve the interests and purposes of bureaucratic sponsors or an academic reference group at the expense of those being evaluated. He has proposed that those being evaluated be shown the information collected from them and be given veto power over what is said about them in the evaluation report. Individual autonomy is carried to the extent that "people own the facts of their lives." This is a right not usually accorded to respondents. Within this framework knowledge of social action is the private property of practitioners, and truth is relative to the different interpretive frameworks by which social agents guide their conduct. This position is too extreme for most evaluators but is based upon an extension of an accepted principle. Another unusual ethical position is that evaluators should make themselves more vulnerable to those evaluated, thus redressing the balance of power between the two parties.

Underlying all these various notions of correct behavior in evaluation are contrasting conceptions of justice. The dominant implicit conception of justice is utilitarian, the idea being to maximize satisfaction in society. Any action which maximizes the total or average satisfaction is the right thing to do. Although such a notion seems remote from the practice of evaluation, indicators such as test scores are often taken as surrogate measures of satisfaction and the right thing to do is determine which educational programs maximize these scores. This thinking ultimately leads to a particular kind of evaluation study and technology, even though evaluators may not be fully cognizant of the underlying philosophical assumptions or ethical implications. For example, Schulze and Kneese have shown that the results of a cost–benefit analysis can vary dramatically depending upon which overall ethical system one adopts. They contrast utilitarian, egalitarian, elitist, and libertarian ethical views. As they note, the philosophical underpinnings of current cost–benefit analyses are utilitarian.

Contrasted to utilitarian justice are pluralist conceptions of justice which presume that there are multiple ultimate principles of justice. Such notions often translate into including the perceptions of various interest groups in the evaluation and distinguishing how different groups are served by the program. Pluralist/intuitionist conceptions of justice hold that there are several principles of justice and no overriding endpoint or measure of the general welfare. In practical terms, evaluations based on pluralist ideas treat interest groups as several in number and as having distinct interests from one another.

From different perspectives some theorists have argued that the interests of the disadvantaged and the lower classes are ordinarily neglected in an evaluation

and that such interests should be represented or even given priority as an ethical matter. Such an obligation edges into the political and is quite different from an admonition to respect the rights of individuals. Current formal codes of ethics for evaluators restrict their content to individual rights within a contractual framework.

An expanded view of the ethics of evaluation would be based upon more principles than that of individual autonomy. Autonomy suggests that no-one should impose his or her will upon others by force or coercion or illegitimate means. No-one should be imposed upon against his or her will. Autonomy is intimately tied to the notion of choice and is manifested in the notion of individual rights and the social contract. Presumably a person's autonomy has not been violated if he or she chooses freely what to do.

However, autonomy alone is not sufficient as a moral basis for evaluation. Each person should have an equal right to advance his or her own interests for satisfaction. The fundamental notion of equality is that all persons should be taken as members of the same reference group and consequently should be treated the same. The satisfaction of each person's interests is worthy of equal consideration in the public determinations of wants. Individual rights are a protection against imposition by others but do not guarantee equal consideration. It is here particularly that social-class differences play a most significant but neglected role in evaluation. Often powerless groups are not entitled to consideration or representation of their interests in evaluation. Too often only the interests of the powerful are represented.

Of course, if each individual and group is allowed to advance its own interests, there are inevitable conflicts, and these conflicts must be settled impartially. An evaluation must be impartial, that is, in its procedures it must be fair to all interests. Sometimes impartiality is confused with objectivity, but it is possible to employ an objective procedure which is reproducible but biased against a particular social group. It is possible to have a test which discriminates in a systematic, reproducible but biased fashion against certain social groups. Impartiality is a moral principle that ensures fair consideration.

Impartiality is especially difficult when the evaluator must face a situation in which there are conflicting values. To what degree should the evaluator become involved with the participants? Eraut has suggested two moral principles in such a situation. First, people have a right to know what an evaluation is doing and why. Second, all those who might be considered as clients have a right to some stake in the evaluation. This position proposes the involvement of participants somewhat beyond the negotiation phase, even to the point of helping with data collection. However, even in such an expanded notion of participant involvement, the evaluator is not expected to side with one group or endorse a particular set of values.

There is one other principle worth considering as a moral basis for evaluation. On the basis of equality, autonomy, and impartiality a person could advance his or her own interests equally, not impose on others, and join others in settling conflicts impartially. Yet what about the losers in such a decision process? The winners have no responsibility for the losers, strictly speaking. Intuitively, a person is disturbed at such a situation. Reciprocity, treating others as you would like to be treated, adds an element of humanity. Reciprocity makes winners at least partially responsible for the losers. Reciprocity is not a primary value of liberalism because it suggests a sense of community which extends beyond the notion of separate individuals who cooperate with each other only to seek their own advantage. One of liberalism's deficiencies is this lack of caring and sense of belonging to a larger community.

Finally, there is the formidable problem of the applications of these principles in the actual conduct of evaluation. Ethical principles are rather abstract notions, and it is not always obvious how such principles should be applied in a given situation. Concrete examples and guidelines are essential if a person is to model his or her behavior on such principles.

Even if a person endorsed all the ethical principles discussed here, their application would not be straightforward. Some of the most intractable ethical problems result from a conflict among principles, the necessity of trading off one against the other, rather than disagreement with the principles themselves. For example, both liberals and conservatives endorse the principles of

autonomy and equality but weigh these principles differently in actual situations. The balancing of such principles against one another in concrete situations is the ultimate act of ethical evaluation.

See also: Ethical Considerations in Research

Bibliography

Anderson S B, Ball S 1978 *The Profession and Practice of Program Evaluation.* Jossey-Bass, San Francisco, California
Barry B 1973 *The Liberal Theory of Justice: A Critical Examination of the Principal Doctrines in 'A Theory of Justice' by John Rawls.* Clarendon Press, Oxford
Evaluation Research Society Standards Committee 1982 Evaluation Research Society standards for program evaluation, *New Directions for Program Evaluation* 15: 7–19
House E R 1980 *Evaluating with Validity.* Sage, Beverly Hills, California
House E R, Care N S 1979 Fair evaluation agreement. *Educ. Theory* 29: 159–69
Joint Committee on Standards for Educational Evaluations 1981 *Standards for Evaluations of Educational Programs, Projects, and Materials.* McGraw-Hill, New York
Mackie S L 1977 *Ethics.* Penguin, London
Rawls J 1971 *A Theory of Justice.* Harvard University Press, Cambridge, Massachusetts
Sieber J E 1980 Being ethical? Professional and personal decisions in program evaluation. *New Directions for Program Evaluation* 7: 51–61

Research Needs and Priorities

S. Marklund and J. P. Keeves

The need for research into educational issues would seem to be unlimited. Although knowledge in this field continues to increase, the demand for further research in order to understand and thus to improve the quality of education remains. Some issues in education are more important and more urgent than others and could be given priority, which involves listing the issues for research in a rank order. However, there are other aspects of the issues under consideration that must be examined before priorities are set. One such aspect involves making judgments on the researchability of an issue. Another involves consideration of whether the particular problem could be resolved by making administrative changes. Nevertheless, each individual research worker, each research institution, and each administrative body in education must identify priorities, because the time available to undertake research within the life of an individual research worker is limited, as are personnel and resources for the administration of a research institution, as well as funds available for sponsoring research. The question of determining priorities for research in education is of concern to all who are associated as doers, planners, users, and supporters of research studies or research programmes. This article is concerned with the nature of the research process and

its products in the field of education and the way in which they influence the setting up of priorities for research.

1. The Dangers of Priority Lists

It is important to recognize that the setting up of priorities for research carries with it certain dangers. Superficially it may seem a relatively simple task to rationalize research effort in education through the establishment of guidelines and statements of policy. However, the major problem associated with any attempt to establish priorities and to rationalize research effort comes at the point of making a decision to check the development of one project to the benefit of another, or to transfer support for a research and development enterprise from one institution to another. Snow (1969) has discussed in detail a critical incident that occurred in England in the years immediately prior to and during the Second World War. The incident involved a choice between two research enterprises, one concerned with the development of radar, the other with long-range bombing programmes, at a time when resources were very limited. The issues arose from the different views and perspectives of the scientific evidence available, as well as from long-term personal differences between two individuals in key positions. Only by chance was disaster avoided as the result of a sudden and complete change in priorities. The lessons from this incident for the funding and support for research are clear. In an open environment where there are many avenues to be followed to obtain funding for research and many places to be found where the research might be pursued, if one course of action is closed then it is always possible to turn elsewhere for support. It is apparent that if there is one individual or even a committee with sole power, the situation is potentially dangerous when that individual or that committee makes an error of judgment. The solution must lie in the provision of alternatives in both sources of funding and in locations where research might be carried out. Without alternatives there is no way in which errors of judgment in establishing priorities can be exposed. Other problems associated with the setting of priorities are both the possible ossification of research directions and the risk of being unable to respond quickly to developments that were unknown at the time priorities were set.

These comments on the rationalization of research effort should not be taken to imply that the setting up of priorities and the need for rationalization from time to time are not important. What is essential is the rejection of a universal listing of priorities and the denial of alternative avenues which might be pursued for the funding and conduct of research. Furthermore, it is important that the groups responsible for the establishment of priorities should be broadly based and that there should be mechanisms for the regular review of the appropriateness of the priorities which have been laid down.

2. The Nature of Educational Research

In recent years many research workers in education and in the social and behavioural sciences have examined the nature of the research enterprise, its functions, antecedents, processes, outcomes, and uses. It is necessary in the determining of research priorities in education to take into consideration the nature of research in this field. Unless this is done there is the danger that one perspective will dominate to the exclusion of all others.

2.1 The Functions of Research in Education

It is well-established practice in the physical and biological sciences to make distinctions between fundamental or basic scientific research and applied research. Underlying this perspective is the view of a chain starting with basic research, leading to applied research and translation into practice, and the dissemination and promotion of the findings of research. However, this differentiation between basic and applied research in education can become counterproductive if it involves the claim that research in education is primarily the field for the application of psychological theory which has been developed through basic research. Cronbach and Suppes (1969) have seen as useful a distinction between conclusion-oriented and decision-oriented educational

research, but such a categorization is also to some degree artificial as it is rooted in an approach to educational research from the viewpoint of the psychologist. More recently Coleman (1972) in a discussion of research in the social sciences has distinguished between discipline research and policy research. While there is much to be said in support of Coleman's categorization it is important to recognize that educational research can rarely be viewed in terms of a single discipline, perhaps an educational science, since it draws frequently from such disciplines as psychology, sociology, anthropology, philosophy, history, political science, law, economics, and demography. A sound appreciation of these many facets of educational research is necessary, because, in any proposal for the setting of priorities or for rationalization, the perspectives of the individuals or groups making the seemingly rational decisions must be taken into consideration.

2.2 The Outcomes of Research in Education

It can be suggested that educational research and development can give rise to outcomes that fall into three distinct categories. From a study of the use of social science information by administrators, Rich (1977) has distinguished between the instrumental and conceptual utilization of knowledge. In a similar way Fullan (1980) has suggested that there are two main forms in which knowledge is used in education. In the first type, knowledge is applied to a particular problem and that knowledge may be derived from a specific research study or from a series of studies. The second type of knowledge is cumulative knowledge. A third and important form or outcome of educational research and development is the preparation of a tangible product for direct use in schools, classrooms, and homes that incorporates the findings of educational research. It will be seen that these three outcomes of research are associated with the three stages in the linear chain of research functions considered above, namely basic or fundamental research, applied research, and development. Here, however, the emphasis is on the outcomes and not the functions of research.

It is important that clear recognition of the functions and outcomes of educational research should be maintained by those responsible for the establishment of priorities and for the rationalization of research effort. There is a danger that educational research is seen as essentially policy research or research oriented towards the needs of the decision maker. If this were the context in which the establishment of priorities or the rationalization of research effort were being carried out, then it might be expected that the sole criterion for determining priorities would be the importance of the policy question for educational practice. The setting of priorities in this way without full consideration of the many facets of the research enterprise in education could quickly stultify research efforts. In addition, there would be the all too obvious danger of providing a simple answer for the purposes of decision making in the shortest possible time and ultimately a failure to develop new knowledge about the educational process. In addition, it is necessary to caution against the ever present danger of basing policy and practice on a single empirical result obtained from an isolated study. Unless there is confirmation of the result from theoretical perspectives and from other research studies, inferences for the making of policy or the changing of practice derived from a single piece of research should be strongly questioned.

3. Towards a Body of Knowledge

In educational research a tension exists between responding to the immediate needs of practitioners and the building of a cumulative body of knowledge about the educational process. Tyler (1980) has argued that priorities should be given to problems teachers consider important and that teachers are, in general, sceptical of problems for research that have been identified by groups outside the schools. On the other hand, Sanders (1981) has claimed that educational research has become excessively atheoretical and has not produced an accumulating body of systematic knowledge. Perhaps the danger lies in viewing these two approaches as alternatives. Unless the attention of research workers in education is focused on problems confronting teachers there is a danger that important questions for research will be ignored and the good will of the schools towards research and researchers will disappear. However, unless educational research can add to cumulative knowledge about education, there is the danger that after massive research effort over a long period no progress will have been made and each new generation of research workers will have to start afresh.

In the attempts that must be made to build a body of knowledge about the educational process it is necessary to recognize two important key characteristics of research in education, namely that it is carried out across the many disciplines, and that it is essentially multivariate in nature.

3.1 Cross-disciplinary Research

The stereotyped view is still held by many that the educational research worker has been trained in the discipline of psychology and he or she prescribes for pedagogical practice the "dos" and "don'ts" which may be derived from the laws and generalizations of psychological theory. The audience for the counsel of the educational research worker and psychologist is seen to be the practising classroom teacher who seeks to improve the effectiveness and efficiency of his or her daily work (Jackson and Kieslar 1977). It is not surprising that this view should have become established at a time when psychology was developing as a science and when schools of education were being created. A more appropriate perspective is to consider educational research as cross-disciplinary in nature, cutting across or transcending a variety of disciplines. It would seem to be unduly restrictive to advance the claim that educational

research should command a discipline of its own, forming a field of educational or pedagogical science. In recent years many developments in educational research have taken place as a result of thinking about educational problems from the perspectives of the social sciences, the humanities, and the behavioural sciences. Each field can contribute to an examination of educational questions. Furthermore, perhaps the most interesting advances occur at the borders between two or more disciplines. In addition, educational problems that warrant investigation, and for which solutions must be sought, are not simply those that occur in the classroom. Education takes place not only in the classroom but also within the home, and the peer group, and through the mass media, in libraries and museums, at work, and at play. The multifaceted nature of education means that there is a broad variety of groups to whom the findings of educational research are of concern. Those wishing to contribute to educational policy and practice must draw upon the cumulative body of knowledge about the many different and relevant aspects of education.

3.2 The Many Variables of the Educational Process

The second key characteristic of educational research is that it must deal with very complex relationships involving many variables that are operating simultaneously. It is rare that a high-quality study of an educational problem can be reduced to the investigation of a relationship between only two variables. One of the strategies that is commonly employed to examine the simultaneous action of many variables is to undertake intensive case studies of a situation in which many factors are at work and to report in detail the full complexity and circumstances of the events observed. This approach is admirable if it contributes to the accumulation of a body of knowledge about education through the understandings that were achieved. However, if the case study is idiosyncratic and unique it will add little. A frequently used alternative strategy involves the use of high-speed computers to analyse simultaneously considerable bodies of data which contain many variables. Because of the capabilities of computers to undertake the statistical control of specific factors in the analysis of data, it is no longer essential to design an experiment to remove the effects of many unknown variables by randomization procedures. The educational research worker is rarely able to design a controlled experiment to test a specific hypothesis because it frequently involves interfering in the lives of people. The alternative that has emerged is to develop a complex multivariate statistical model, to test the structure of the model, and then to estimate its parameters through the statistical control of variables rather than through random allocation. Nevertheless, it must be recognized that a truly experimental approach, if it were a practicable alternative, would provide more soundly based conclusions than can be obtained from a nonexperimental study in a natural situation.

4. Factors Influencing the Direction of Research

Some understanding of the factors that influence developments in educational research has emerged from the studies reported by Suppes (1978). Three factors can be identified, namely: (a) a response to critical issues, (b) the impact of technology on research and practice, and (c) new ideas and new paradigms which are derived from other disciplinary areas.

4.1 Research in Response to Critical Issues

During the 1970s the changes in employment patterns in the Western world exposed a critical problem with regard to youth unemployment, the transition from school to work, and the nature of the educational programmes provided by secondary schools. The emergence of these problems has led to research which has addressed these issues. In the past, such issues have arisen from time to time that have changed the direction of educational research while the problems were being investigated. Not only does public concern for the issues release funds for such work, but the public debate about the issues also helps to generate ideas about the nature of the problems and to identify those aspects that are amenable to research.

Those responsible for the determination of research priorities must attempt to anticipate such problems and to have work at least in progress at the time the issues emerge as critical. Nevertheless, in the coordination or rationalization of research in education there is the danger that priorities will be determined solely by critical issues, and that the more significant the issue, the higher the problem on the list of priorities that is drawn up. Educational research workers should not ignore the needs of society, but it should be recognized that some issues which are purported to be educational matters are not amenable to research in an educational context because the issues are in essence societal problems.

4.2 The Impact of Technology on Research and Practice

Since at least the early 1930s, much of the mathematical knowledge necessary for the examination of the interrelations between many predictor variables and many outcomes has been available. However, until the mid-1960s very little progress was made in developing these ideas for use in the analysis of educational data, although sometimes techniques of approximation were employed to obtain partial results. As a consequence of technological development and the availability of the computer, the procedures for the analysis of data changed and both the types of problems that could be investigated and the ways of thinking about the problems changed. It was recognized that some of the formerly intractable problems associated with the simultaneous examination of the effects of many variables had become amenable to investigation. This led to the development of causal and mathematical models to examine educational questions. However, these developments also contributed to the relatively widespread rejection by some of a positivist approach to research and a turning to the use of alternative methods for the investigation of educational problems (see *Action Research*; *Case Study Methods*; *Hermeneutics*; *Ethnographic Research Methods*; *Naturalistic and Rationalistic Enquiry*; *Participatory Research*).

In the immediate future the increased availability of the microcomputer must change both the tactics and strategies that can be employed to study human behaviour, and in particular to investigate human thought processes. Enquiry into the functioning of the brain and its relationship to behaviour would appear to be becoming increasingly amenable to research as a consequence of the introduction of microcomputers. Developments in this field of what must be considered basic research could in the long run have profound consequences for education.

A less dramatic example, in a field where the potential for change in educational practice has not been fully recognized, is associated with the use of the calculator in the classroom. The electronic calculator has become widely used in the market place and industry, but its use in the classroom has been accepted slowly and with considerable resistance. In the long term its availability must change the way in which both arithmetic and mathematics is taught. However, there has been little research and development work carried out in some countries to examine how best to reorient the teaching of mathematics to make allowance for the availability of calculators in schools.

4.3 The Cross-disciplinary Contribution

There is little doubt that new paradigms and strategies for educational research will continue to evolve from fertilization across disciplines, as developments in these disciplines are seen to apply to educational problems. In establishing priorities for educational research, it is essential that the interdisciplinary nature of research into educational problems should be acknowledged and that the need to attract creative and imaginative research workers from the behavioural and social sciences to work with educators on the study of educational problems should be recognized. There is the danger that persons involved in the establishment of priorities for research in education will be isolated from the developments in the many contributing disciplines and will only promote work within their own disciplinary setting. Unless they recognize that priorities must be determined not only by the critical nature of a problem, but also by the availability of appropriate conceptual and methodological paradigms for the tackling of a problem, they are in danger of advancing problems for research that are not amenable to effective investigation.

Hence the determination of priorities solely through reference to the magnitude and the consequences of the issue involved is unwise. Sometimes it would be of greater benefit to consider the researchability of a problem and whether the development of new technology, or the availability of new methodology or new conceptual frameworks from other disciplines would now make the problem more amenable to investigation than it was previously.

5. Determining Priorities

Politicians and the policy makers and administrators they employ are charged with the providing of educational services. They have a more or less clear notion of the kind of schooling and education they want, but they often lack knowledge of the possibilities and the conditions necessary for the realization of their objectives. Consequently, they frequently call upon research to provide information which would assist with policy making. The undertaking of research for policy purposes, policy-oriented research, must, however, be clearly distinguished from the making of policy. Research provides an information base for policy making; the policy makers according to their understanding of the issues and their response to political pressures must make policy. Nevertheless, it is commonly the policy makers who must provide the resources for research, and as a consequence they could develop an expectation that research would produce not only the information base for the making of decisions, but also the answers to the particular problems under consideration. There is frequently disappointment and disillusionment when research does not provide simple answers. However, the complex nature of research, its function, outcomes, and uses, as well as the factors influencing its progress must be recognized and emphasis must be placed on the need for research to be involved with the gradual accumulation of bodies of knowledge about the many facets of the educational process, so that adequate information is available on which decisions might be based.

In the determination of priorities for research in education it is essential that the research workers should interact with the users of research, namely the policy makers and the practitioners. A further group who can contribute significantly to the determination of priorities are change agents who mediate between the resource system which develops and holds knowledge about the educational process and the user system concerned with the making of policies and the conduct of education in the schools and elsewhere. The change or linkage agents are likely to be aware of the views of both the research workers and the users and are well-placed to interpret the views of one group to the other and vice versa. Priorities should be determined by procedures that permit interaction to the full between research workers and users. Sometimes extensive debate will be required before one group can appreciate the views of the other, and both parties can advance together to develop consensus about priorities. This is of course what commonly happens. Nevertheless, the restrictions and reductions that occurred in the funding of educational research in many parts of the world during the early 1980s would appear to indicate that after a period of strong support for research by policy makers, a breakdown in the interaction between the research workers and the users occurred to the detriment of many research programmes. This may have been a consequence of a failure in the dissemination process.

6. Statements of Priorities: Some Examples

Statements of priorities for research in education can be made at many levels, including cross-national, national, institutional, and the individual research worker levels. Some examples of research priorities that have been developed at different levels are given below. In addition, examples will also be given of statements of priorities developed by research workers for programmes of research in specific areas.

6.1 Cross-national Programmes

The Department of Education of the World Bank has drafted a paper called *Research Strategy and Program in Education* (World Bank 1981). This paper contained a broad discussion of the general considerations involved in setting educational research priorities and an explicit description of priorities for research in education. The paper was later reviewed by external experts, who emphasized the importance of making long-term plans for a research strategy and for training programmes to be undertaken by the World Bank. According to this strategy one-third of the studies should deal with efficiency of learning, another third with external educational efficiency, and the last third with access to education, equity, cost and finance, and national capacity building.

The Council of Europe, through its Education Research Committee in 1973 developed a paper on *General Issues of European Co-operation in Educational Research and Development* (Marklund 1974). Research needs and priorities were here categorized in educational stages: precompulsory, compulsory, and postcompulsory education, teacher training, and general and overall educational questions. In each one of these categories development trends and special research needs were listed as fields of prospective European cooperation. Strategic research planning, it was said, must be the task of the individual country. Nevertheless, the committee mentioned five areas of research, which not only were of high priority but also were areas where the European countries could achieve better and quicker results on a joint basis than by separate efforts. These were: (a) adult education, (b) vocational education, (c) precompulsory education, (d) educational progress of poorly motivated pupils, and (e) evaluation of different forms of organization.

6.2 Cross-national Cooperative Research

In the planning of cross-national cooperative research studies the International Association for the Evaluation of Educational Achievement (IEA) has given priority to a series of projects extending beyond the initial programmes of the IEA which involved comparative studies in the areas of primary and secondary school learning in mathematics, science, reading, literature,

French as a foreign language, English as a foreign language, and civic education. Current priorities are for five studies: (a) mathematics, involving the investigation of the effects of a range of teaching practices on mathematics learning; (b) science, involving an examination of science curricula and their relationships to achievement and attitudinal outcomes; (c) classroom environment, involving both a survey study and an experimental investigation into the effects of teaching behaviours on student learning; (d) written composition, involving a study of the factors that influence writing styles and quality of expression in written composition in the classroom; and (e) item banking, involving an exchange of information and test materials associated with the development of item banks. Priorities have been established for future studies in the following areas; (a) a longitudinal study of transition from school to employment; (b) the processes of preprimary school education for children of 4 years of age and under; (c) development and assessment associated with the acquisition of practical and vocational skills; and (d) assessment of the effects of various programmes associated with instruction through a second language (Rosier 1982). The IEA General Assembly in identifying these five current studies and four future studies has taken into consideration the needs for research in these areas in both the more developed and the less developed countries, previous experience by some IEA national centres in the conduct of studies in these areas, the feasibility of studies in these areas in member countries, the training value associated with the conduct of these studies for some countries with less experience in educational research methods, the employment of a variety of research strategies in the conduct of research, and the desirability of cooperative and replicated research in these areas.

7. National Priorities

Special agencies for the funding of educational research now exist in most industrialized and in some developing countries. These agencies define research needs and priorities and determine largely the programmes of educational research in those countries. In the United States, in a report titled *Reflections and Recommendations*, issued in 1978, the National Council on Educational Research (United States NCER 1978) identified five areas of applied research which were given high priority, namely: (a) basic skills, (b) educational equity, (c) financial productivity and management, (d) dissemination of research results, and (e) school capacity for problem solving. To this list of NCER-mandated research was added a corresponding list of basic research relevant to education in which eight areas were given priority: (a) cognitive development, (b) out-of-school education, (c) reading, (d) brain and nerve processes, (e) institutional innovations, (f) opportunities for higher education, (g) multicultural students, and (h) social environment.

In Sweden a corresponding funding agency is the National Board of Education which since 1962 has been responsible for the funding of the major part of policy-oriented educational research. A planning model has been applied (Sweden NBE 1976), according to which research projects are categorized into programme areas: (a) precompulsory, (b) compulsory, (c) upper secondary (including vocational training), (d) adult education, (e) teacher training, and (f) general and overarching problems. The last area has gradually become the biggest one. This defining of programme areas aimed at coordinating research and development projects under each of the different administrative units of the board, so as to avoid the problem of having research and development workers operating independently of each other as well as to facilitate the dissemination and use of the outcomes of research and development. Priorities within each of the six programme areas have since 1977 been structured in 18 problem areas, agreed upon by the administrators of the board (that is the policy makers) and research workers for the commissioning of external projects: (a) documentation and analysis of the Swedish educational system, (b) educational systems and lifelong learning, (c) educational planning and evaluation, (d) school and physical environment, (e) inservice training and personnel development, (f) education and society, (g) the inner work at school (practical school-day work), (h) cognitive development, (i) communication skills, (j) socioemotional and physical development, (k) testing and grading in educational evaluation, (l) regional and local development work, (m) the connection between preschool and primary school, (n) subject-oriented research and development, (o) handicapped children, (p) immigrants and cultural minorities, (q) curriculum development work, and (r) teaching aids. As can be seen, this list, which is a result of a compromise between different interests, includes a mixture of policy-oriented and basic research. The categorization of research and development needs by programme areas as well as by problem areas gives a two-dimensional matrix, where priorities can be drawn up both between and within each one of the two dimensions.

In a Swedish government report on educational research and development (R&D) for the years to come, the following needs and priorities were advanced as guidelines for the R&D programme: (a) the objectives of educational R&D should be based not only on issues concerned with changes within the educational system but also on external conditions; (b) it is important for educational R&D to find instruments to realize the aims and objectives of politically stated curricular guidelines; (c) educational R&D should be carried on in close contact with everyday school situations and be directed to problems experienced in the everyday school situation; (d) long-range projects should be promoted, but the focus should be on problem-oriented R&D related to actual school questions; (e) it is important that R&D should be done in close collaboration with the schools; and (f) it is important with project planning to ensure some projects are finished to provide opportunities for initiating new ones. Although proposals are submitted by independent research workers, the research programmes drawn up by funding agencies and the research strategies recommended by decision makers in education involve the enhancement of a policy orientation in research.

8. Priorities for a National Research Organization

Each national research body is required either implicitly or preferably explicitly to formulate the priorities for the conduct of its own programmes of research. Keeves (1981) taking into account the three factors influencing the direction of research considered above, namely: (a) research in response to critical issues, (b) the likely impact of technology on research, and (c) the cross-disciplinary nature of educational research, identified for the Australian Council for Educational Research, as well as for other research workers in Australia, seven areas in which he believed that research might be undertaken with profit during the 1980s.

8.1 Studies of the Thought Processes of Children

A new strand of research in the study of the thought processes of children is becoming established that builds on the work carried out over a long period by Piaget in Geneva, but in many ways it has received new orientations from information processing. The cross-disciplinary fertilization from information processing and cognitive psychology to education, together with the use of microcomputers to present appropriate stimulus materials, and to record not only the nature of the response but also the time required to generate a response would appear to hold promise for educational research.

8.2 Studies of Schools and School Learning

The impetus for work in this field comes from the need to increase the cost efficiency of school learning at a time when the costs of education are rising rapidly. Again the advent of new technology brings with it the possibility of the introduction of new teaching and learning strategies.

8.3 Studies of Curriculum and Curriculum Change

As a consequence of greater devolution of responsibility to schools for the development of their own curricula at the same time as there has been a rapid expansion in the range of knowledge and skills required from students when they leave school, there is a critical need to investigate the curriculum changes that are occurring in schools and their consequences for student learning.

8.4 Studies of Cost Effectiveness of Education

While the provision of education is a major component of the budget of most countries and most states that assume responsibility for education, little research has been undertaken into the economics of education or into an examination of alternative educational policies and their cost effectiveness. With the development of computerized accounting procedures, information of a sufficiently detailed kind is beginning to become available that would enable cost-effectiveness studies to be

carried out in education. Thus the impact of new technology, the emergence of a critical problem at a time of rapidly rising costs, the limited resources available for education, and the investigation of these educational problems by persons trained in economics, makes this area a promising one for research.

8.5 Studies in the Transition from School to a Constructive Adult Life

Attention has already been drawn to the problem confronting societies throughout the Western world of rising youth unemployment. Furthermore, it is evident that these problems are likely to be present for a number of years. It is clear that research studies are needed into the use of leisure time, into work and the preparation for work, and into education, not merely as an initial preparation for life but also as a lifelong process. Of particular importance are problems associated with the interaction between education, work, and leisure and the need for youth to develop an appropriate balance between all three areas as the basis for a constructive adult life.

8.6 Studies of the Educational Environment of the Home

The structure of the family has changed very considerably since the early 1970s. However, relatively little sustained research has been undertaken to investigate the effects of these changes on the education of children. Here the collaboration of educators with psychologists and with persons from the fields of health and welfare would appear to be necessary if effective research is to be undertaken into these problems.

8.7 Problems in Educational Measurement

With the introduction of the high-speed computer, and with the likelihood that microcomputers will gradually change the measurement techniques that can be employed in the assessment of classroom learning, there are certain problems associated with student, curriculum, and school evaluation that are likely to be more amenable to solution than they have been in the past. The development of appropriate techniques to grapple with these problems of measurement of learning are a challenge to educational research workers.

The task of identifying priority areas within which research studies might be conducted is both difficult and perilous. Nevertheless, in every research institution a similar searching for priority areas for the allocation of limited resources must be carried out. Not only must significant problems be identified, but there must be sound reasons why it is believed that studies in the chosen areas are feasible and why substantial progress is likely to occur through research in the area. In identifying problems for research in education, the choices between research that is basic or applied, discipline- or policy-oriented, and conclusion- or decision-oriented rarely seem to occur. These distinctions are perhaps less than useful except in a classification of research studies at a very broad level. What would appear to be required in educational research is a fruitful interaction between theoretical perspectives and practice.

9. Priorities for Research in Specific Areas

9.1 Educational Change

Heathers (1974) has pointed out that planned educational change is in search of a research tradition. Little attention has been paid to the implementation of change programmes, and he suggests that future research should focus on consumer-referenced rather than product-referenced changes. This could help education agencies in their attempts to plan and conduct significant change programmes, identify needs, and evaluate the consequences. Another model of educational innovation has been presented by Klitgaard (1973). He distinguishes four basic elements of change: (a) setting the objectives, (b) implementation, (c) the production possibilities, and (d) evaluation. Specific needs for research are local objectives and circumstances versus the national ones, the former more precisely stated but giving low productivity, the latter inherently vague and with little evidence of the production possibilities.

9.2 Vocational Education

The United States Office of Vocational Adult Education has sponsored work to identify priorities for research in the field of vocational education. Lewis (1980) has reported the conclusion that in the future, vocational education will be a more diversified enterprise than it has been in the past. There will be more older clients and proportionally more minority groups and individuals in need of special services. Rapid introduction of technological innovation and limited resources for modernization of equipment would seem to indicate that planners of vocational education programmes will have to cooperate more extensively with employers.

9.3 Adult Education

Delker (1979) has pointed out that in the 20 years following the early 1980s, an expanding adult population and a decreasing youth population will make adult learning an increasing concern of educational research. How adults learn, what they want to learn, and when they want to learn are problems for research. Significant research questions are: (a) Who is responsible for the planning of learning? (b) What motivates adults to learn? (c) Where does learning take place? and (d) Does this learning merely confirm the learning behaviour of educated adults? More knowledge based on research is needed in the self-direction of learning.

9.4 Teacher Education

Hall (1979) has summarized the findings of a planning project which undertook the delineation and determination of priorities of crucial, researchable issues in teacher education. The following needs were identified: (a) What does research and development suggest for the content of preservice, induction, and inservice teacher education? (b) What does research say on the design and delivery of teacher education? (c) What does research say about teachers and teacher educators as learners? (d) How do the various roles of teacher educators and students, the various substantive areas, and the various instruction strategies best combine to design, deliver, and assess teacher education programmes? (e) How do social, political, economic and cultural realities affect teacher education, and how can theory development and research address these realities? (f) What are the present strategies, promises, and limitations of research for contributing to the design, development, and evaluation of teacher education? and (g) How can research knowledge and products be shared collaboratively and effectively with constituent groups and how can practical application to improve teacher education practice be facilitated? Another relevant area is concerned with the determination of the characteristics of effective teachers.

9.5 Dissemination Research

Policy-oriented research and other kinds of educational research of an applied nature imply new needs for dissemination and therefore for research into the diffusion or dissemination process. Hull (1978) has identified a number of research studies that are concerned with the dissemination and utilization of knowledge, such as the difference between national and local needs, the practitioner's capability to use research findings, methods of evaluating the impact of research, and the issue of selective versus comprehensive information systems.

9.6 Educational Administration

Getzels (1980) has pointed to a number of special research areas in educational administration. The development of new models of educational research that are more flexible and less heavily formalized demands high quality conceptual and empirical research, and Getzels has identified four priority areas. The first area, the administrator as a problem finder, is based on the idea that the first step towards problem solving is reformulating unmanageable dilemmas into manageable problems. The second proposed area of research is the administrator and the ecology of the school, such as the spatial arrangements of the school. As a third area he proposes research into the many meanings of the administrator–educational community relationship. The fourth issue is associated with the need to examine educational administration problems from a comparative and cross-national perspective.

From time to time in each major area of investigation, research workers and policy makers have prepared statements of needs and priorities which are similar to the ones identified above. Nevertheless, it would appear that insufficient attempts are being made currently to survey areas of investigation, using the techniques of meta-analysis and documentation searches to identify all relevant studies, and to prepare coherent and integrated bodies of knowledge about the educational processes operating in each area. Since the early 1970s a massive amount of knowledge has been generated, derived from the findings of educational research, and the synthesis of this knowledge together with the development of related theory is now an urgent task. The planning of further research is necessarily dependent on carrying out the analyses and syntheses of this knowledge.

10. Conclusion

It is neither possible nor desirable to attempt to develop universal research needs and priorities either today or in the foreseeable future. However, it is not possible for individuals, research institutions, educational administrators, or for those who have responsibility for funding educational research, to operate without their own sets of priorities. Moreover, it would seem that research issues associated with the costs of education, adult education, vocational education, and education in a lifelong perspective are now frequently in the minds of policy makers. This would seem to indicate that there is a great need today for knowledge of how the heavily formalized systems of education which have been established throughout the world can be improved to become more flexible in order to meet new and emerging needs or eventually to be replaced by a less formal system of education. It is, however, important to recognize that, as Levin (1978) has pointed out, after examining certain persistent educational dilemmas, educational research cannot and should not be expected to solve problems that are basically political or social problems.

Advances in educational research will take place in the same manner as they have occurred in other fields of knowledge (Conant 1947). First, they will arise from the demand to find solutions to new problems that have arisen from changing conditions in society, secondly from the impact of new technologies on the way people think and the way in which research is conducted, and thirdly, they will arise from the infusion of new ideas coming from a cross-disciplinary attack on a problem. Thus progress is not necessarily dependent on the provision of greater resources to undertake research, although frequently the availability of sufficient resources permits the tackling of problems that would otherwise be ignored. Advances would appear to come from the interplay of these three factors of the emergence of new problems, the advent of new technology, and cross-disciplinary debate which gives rise to new conceptual and methodological paradigms. If these are the ways in which educational research advances, then in the setting of priorities, cognizance must be taken of the ways in which progress is made and support must be given to those studies or those proposals to investigate issues that not only are associated with societal problems but also have a likelihood of contributing successfully to new conceptual knowledge, new policy or practice, or new products for use in educational work.

See also: Policy-oriented Research; Educational Research and Policy Making

Bibliography

Coleman J S 1972 *Policy Research in the Social Sciences.* General Learning Press, Morristown, New Jersey
Conant J B 1947 *On Understanding Science: An Historical Approach.* Yale University Press, New Haven, Connecticut
Cronbach L J, Suppes P C (eds.) 1969 *Research for Tomorrow's Schools: Disciplined Inquiry for Education: Report.* Macmillan, New York
Delker P V 1979 *Adult Education 1980 and Beyond: Implications for Research and Development.* Occasional Paper No. 59. National Center for Research in Vocational Education. Ohio State University, Columbus, Ohio
Fullan M 1980 An R and D prospectus for educational reform. In: Mack D P, Ellis W E (eds.) 1980 *Interorganizational Arrangements for Collaborative Efforts: Commissioned Papers.* Northwest Regional Educational Laboratory, Portland, Oregon
Getzels J W 1980 Alternative directions for research in educational administration. In: Farquhar R, Housego I (eds.) 1980 *Canadian and Comparative Educational Administration.* Centre for Continuing Education, Vancouver, British Columbia
Hall G E 1979 *A National Agenda for Research and Development in Teacher Education 1979–1984.* Research and Development Center for Teacher Education, University of Texas, Austin, Texas
Heathers G 1974 *Planned Educational Change in Search of a Research Tradition.* Research for Better Schools, Philadelphia, Pennsylvania
Hull W L 1978 *Research Needs in Diffusion, Change and Information Systems.* National Center for Research in Vocational Education. Ohio State University, Columbus, Ohio
Jackson P, Kieslar S B 1977 Fundamental research and education. *Educ. Res.* 6(8): 13–18
Keeves J P 1981 Societal change and its implications for educational research in Australia. In: Karmel P H (ed.) 1981 *Education, Change and Society.* The Australian Council for Educational Research Golden Jubilee Year International Conf. Australian Council for Educational Research, Hawthorn, Victoria
Klitgaard R E 1973 *Models of Educational Innovation and Implications for Research.* Rand, Santa Monica, California
Levin H M 1978 Why isn't educational research more useful? *Prospects Q. Rev. Educ.* 8: 2
Lewis M V 1980 *An R and D Agenda to Respond to Future Needs in Vocational Education.* National Center for Research in Vocational Education, Ohio State University, Columbus, Ohio
Marklund S 1974 General issues of European cooperation in educational research and development. *Council of Europe Information Bulletin 1974/2.* Council of Europe, Strasbourg
Rich R F 1977 Uses of social science information by federal bureaucrats: Knowledge for action versus knowledge for understanding. In: Weiss C H (ed.) 1977 *Using Social Research in Public Policy Making.* Heath, Lexington, Massachusetts, pp. 199–211
Rosier M J (ed.) 1982 *Brochure of The International Association for the Evaluation of Educational Achievement.* Pergamon, Oxford
Sanders D P 1981 Educational inquiry as developmental research. *Educ. Res.* 10(3): 8–13
Snow C P 1969 *Science and Government. With a Postscript.* Oxford University Press, Melbourne
Suppes P C (ed.) 1978 *Impact of Research on Education: Some Case Studies: Summaries.* National Academy of Education, Washington, DC
Sweden National Board of Education (NBE) 1976 *Educational*

Research and Development NBE. National Board of Education, Stockholm

Tyler R W 1980 On integrating research development, dissemination and practice in science education. Position paper. *Journal Announcement: RIE* July 1981

United States Department of Health, Education and Welfare,

National Council for Educational Research (NCER) 1978, *Reflections and Recommendations. Fourth Annual Report of the National Council on Educational Research.* National Institute of Education, Washington, DC

World Bank Education Department 1981 *Research Strategy and Program in Education.* World Bank, Washington, DC

Policy Analysis [1]

M. Trow

Husén (1984) has argued that the relation of research to policy is far more complex, far more indirect than it formerly appeared. Drawing on the informed writings of Weiss (1979) and Kogan et al. (1980) among others, and from rich experience, he dismisses as irrelevant, at least to the field of education, two classical models of the application of research to policy that Weiss lists among seven different models or concepts of research utilization: the "linear" model, which leads neatly from basic knowledge to applied research to development to application, and the "problem-solving" model, in which research is done to fill in certain bodies of knowledge needed to make a decision among policy alternatives. These are dismissed on the grounds that they simply do not even roughly describe what happens in the real world. The remaining models are merged into two. One is an "enlightenment" or "percolation" model, in which research somehow (and just how is of greatest interest) influences policy indirectly, by entering into the consciousness of the actors and shaping the terms of their discussion about policy alternatives. The second, the "political model," refers to the intentional use of research by political decision makers to strengthen an argument, to justify positions already taken, or to avoid making or having to make unpopular decisions by burying the controversial problem in research.

Of these two models, the first or "percolation" model is the more interesting, since it is the way through which research actually has an influence on policy, rather than merely being used to justify or avoid making decisions. Moreover, the percolation model and its mechanisms and processes are so subtle that they challenge study and reflection.

1. Researchers and Policy Analysts

The decade since the mid-1970s has seen in the United States, and to some extent elsewhere, the emergence of a profession, that of the policy analyst, whose training, habits of mind, and conditions of work are expressly designed to narrow the gap between the researcher and the policy maker and to bring systematic knowledge to bear more directly, more quickly, and more relevantly on the issues of public policy. This article attempts to compare and contrast the researcher and the policy analyst to see how this breed of staff analyst/researcher, inside as well as outside government, may affect the ways in which research comes to bear on policy. The comparison is not intended to be invidious, that is, there is no implication that the invention of policy analysis has in any way solved the problems of the relation of research to policy that Husén, Weiss, and others have identified. But it may be of interest to see how this emerging profession affects that process, and how it generates new problems — intellectual, political, and moral — as it solves some of the old.

Policy analysis developed as a formal discipline in the mid-1970s through the coming together of a number of strands of work and thought in the social sciences. These included operations research developed during the Second World War on a strongly mathematical basis for improving the efficiency of military operations — the deployment of submarines, bombing raids, and convoy management. Added to this were new forms of microeconomics developed in the 1950s and 1960s; the long-standing tradition of work in public administration; the newer and increasingly strong strain of behaviorism in the political sciences; organizational theory; certain lines of applied sociology and social psychology; and the emerging interest in the role of law in public policy. Graduate schools of public policy were established in a number of leading American universities around 1970. Twelve leading universities now have genuine graduate schools of public policy; there are literally hundreds of others which offer programs which include some measure of policy analysis in their schools of management, public administration, or business administration. To the mix of social science and law, some schools have added scientists, engineers, and others interested in public policy problems. These graduate schools for the most part offer a 2-year postgraduate professional degree, ordinarily the Master of Public Policy. Their graduates go directly into public service at national, state, or local levels, or get jobs in think-tanks or private agencies concerned with public issues — for example, organizations concerned with the preservation of the environment, with education, overseas trade, and so forth. These latter "private" organizations, however, are directly

1 This is an edited version of the article, 'Researchers, policy analysts, and policy intellectuals', by Martin Trow which was published in *Educational Research and Policy: How Do They Relate?* (1984) edited by T Husén and M Kogan. It appears here with permission from Pergamon Press plc. © 1984

involved for the most part in public policy — indeed, much of what they do is to try to influence public policy, so the conditions of work for public policy analysts in them resemble those of analysts who enter governmental service itself.

There are several aspects of the training of policy analysts that need to be emphasized. As must already be clear, the training of the policy analyst is intensely interdisciplinary. This is required first because of the diverse nature of its intellectual antecedents; the field itself reflects the coming together of diverse currents in what Lasswell (Lerner and Lasswell 1951) called the "policy sciences". But more important, the training has to be interdisciplinary because that is the way the problems present themselves to decision makers. Real decisions, as we all know, do not respect the boundaries of the academic disciplines: they always have political, economic, and organizational components; they may well also have legal, educational, biological, or other technical implications as well.

Perhaps the most important distinguishing characteristic of policy analysts as contrasted with academic research social scientists is that they are trained, indeed required, to see and to formulate problems from the perspectives not of the academic disciplines, but of the decision makers. In their work, they accept the constraints and values of decision makers — the political pressures on them, the political feasibility of a proposal, its financial costs, the legal context within which it will operate, the difficulties of implementing it, of shaping organizations, and of recruiting, training, and motivating people to work in the service of its purposes. They are, if effectively trained, sensitive to the costs and benefits of programs, to the trade-offs in any decision, and to the alternative advantages of government and the market in achieving social purposes. In a word, they try to see problems from the perspective of the decision maker, but with a set of intellectual, analytical, and research tools that the politician or senior civil servant may not possess. They are, and are trained to be, the researchers in government at the elbow of the decision makers, or if not in government, then serving the "government in opposition" or some think-tank or interest group which hopes to staff the next administration or agency on the next swing of the political pendulum. Of course, not all policy analysts are "researchers," as the university conceives of research. But what they do, bringing ideas and information to bear on social "problems" in a search for "solutions," is the kind of "research" that has the most direct influence on public policy.

By contrast, the faculty members of schools of public policy are not, for the most part, like the students that they train: the former are almost without exception academics with PhDs, trained in and drawn from the social science disciplines, specialists originally who have a particular interest in public policy, and who do research on policy issues, but not on the whole like the research that their students will be doing in their government or quasi-government jobs. The faculty members of these schools are for the most part what Wilson (1981 p. 36) has called "policy intellectuals," while their students are policy analysts — the staff people and bureaucrats serving their policy-oriented clients in and out of governments. The relationship of the policy intellectual in the university to the policy analyst in government bears on the issue of "knowledge creep" and "research percolation" that Husén and Weiss speak of, and to which this article will return.

Let us look at some of the characteristics of "researchers" as Husén describes them, and at some of the "disjunctions" between research and policy that the nature of the researcher in the university gives rise to. The field of policy analysis and the new profession of policy analyst were, one might say, invented precisely to meet the need of policy makers for analysis and research carried out within the same constraints that the policy maker experiences. Policy analysis thus aims to narrow those "disjunctions" between research and policy of which Husén speaks. He describes three conditions under which researchers work that are different for policy analysts:

(a) Researchers are usually performing their tasks at...universities....They tend to conduct their research according to the paradigms to which they have become socialized by their graduate studies. Their achievements are subjected to peer reviews which they regard as more important than assessments made by the customers in a public agency. (Husén 1984 p. 10)

Analysts, by contrast, work for the most part in government or in shadow governmental agencies, or in large private business organizations. The paradigms of research that they acquire in graduate school emphasize the importance of serving the client, of defining or clarifying the nature of the problem, or identifying the policy options available, of evaluating those alternatives in terms of their cost, probable effectiveness, political feasibility, ease of implementation, and the like — the same criteria which the decision maker would use in planning and choosing a course of action. The analyst is trained then to make recommendations among the action alternatives that have been identified, supporting the recommendations made with appropriate arguments and evidence.

Much, perhaps most, of what such analysts do is not published, is not reviewed by peers, and will almost certainly appear, if at all, in greatly modified form, either anonymously or under someone else's name. The analyst's reputation will be made *not* in an academic setting, but in his or her agency, and more importantly among the small but active community of analysts in government agencies, on legislative staffs, in think-tanks, and special interest organizations who know of the analyst's work and its quality. Incidentally, it is in that arena of discussion and assessment — the analyst's analog to the scholar's "invisible college" — that we need to look for the mechanisms of information "drift" and "creep," and for the processes of percolation through which research and evidence come to influence policy.

(b) Researchers operate at a high level of training and specialization, which means that they tend to isolate a "slice" of a problem area that can be more readily handled than more complicated global problems. (Husén 1984 p. 10)

By contrast, analysts are trained to be as interdisciplinary as possible, to follow the requirements of a problem in their choice of ideas, theories, and research methods, rather than to allow the theories and methods of their discipline select and shape their problems. This is not wholly successful, in part because their teachers in these schools are not themselves equally familiar with the variety of research methods and perspectives across disciplinary lines, and because their students, the fledgling analysts, inevitably come to be more familiar and comfortable with some kinds of analysis rather than others. Nevertheless the requirement that they see problems as the policy makers would were they analysts, requires analysts to transcend the constraints of a single discipline and to tackle problems as wholes rather than by "slices."

(c) Researchers are much less constrained than policy makers in terms of what problems they can tackle, what kind of critical language they can employ and how much time they have...at their disposal to complete a study. (Husén 1984 p. 10)

Analysts, by contrast, ordinarily are assigned their studies, or do them within circumscribed policy areas. That does not wholly preclude their exercise of discretion; and indeed, they may exercise very important amounts of initiative in how they formulate their problems, and in the range of responses to the problems they consider (Meltsner 1976 pp. 81–114). From the researcher's perspective, the captive analyst is merely "a hired gun" doing what he or she is told by political or bureaucratic superiors. But from the perspective of the analyst, discretion, even within the constraints of a given policy problem or area, may be very considerable. How to control air pollution in a given area, for example, allows a variety of regulatory solutions, from setting standards for allowable emissions for different kinds of plants and industries to setting charges on pollutants requiring polluters to pay for each unit of pollutant emitted. The issues are political, technical, economic, legal, and normative — and they are not always decided a priori by political or administrative decision makers.

It is true that analysts are ordinarily held to a closer time frame than are academic researchers; it is not unusual for students to become accustomed to doing analyses of various policy problems, drawing upon the best available data, research, and advice, within 48 or 72 hours, exercises designed to prepare them for the fierce time pressures of legislative hearings or the negotiations that accompany the writing and revision of legislation. Other exercises allow them a week, and a major piece of research equivalent to a master's essay will take up to six months. Time constraints on the job also vary; analysts become skillful in knowing who has been working on a given problem area, and where published or unpublished research or data on the issue can be found.

For the analyst, knowledgeable people are a central research resource, and the telephone is part of the student's equipment alongside computers and the library.

But as they develop the skill of rapidly bringing ideas to bear on data, and data on ideas, analysts become heavily dependent upon existing statistics and on research done by others. They are often skillful, and even bold, in drawing analogies between findings in different areas of social life, allowing them thus to use the findings of research in one area for informing decisions in another. These analysts cannot often meet the scholar's standards of depth and thoroughness in their research — for example, in the review of the research literature, or in the critical evaluation of the findings of relevant research. Yet working under time and other pressures in the political milieu, the analysts know that the alternative to what they are doing is not a major university-based research project, but more commonly the impressions, anecdotes, and general wisdom of a staff conference. Their own reports, which include discussions of alternative lines of action based on data regarding their comparative costs and benefits, must, they believe, be better than an unsystematic discussion among friends and advisers.

Policy analysts in government as we have described them have some of the characteristics of researchers, but are more narrowly constrained by their bureaucratic roles. They also have some of the characteristics of Kogan's middle-men, professionals who serve a liaison function (Kogan et al. 1980 pp. 36–38), though they are more active and ready to take research initiatives than the term "middle-man" implies. But they also are not infrequently the decision makers themselves.

2. An Example from the Field of Education

One almost always talks about research *influencing* decision makers — and if the researcher is a university social scientist then the decision maker is almost certainly someone a distance away with his or her own concerns, political commitments, interests, and prejudices. But the policy analyst has the advantage of acting within the bureaucracy to make or directly affect a myriad of administrative decisions that rarely get into the newspapers, are not debated by politicians or on floors of legislatures, but nevertheless have very large consequences.

One illustration comes from the University of California, half of whose budget — the half which pays the operating costs of the University, faculty salaries, and the like — comes from the State of California. The preparation of the University's budget and its incorporation into the governor's budget is a complicated procedure. Very substantial parts of the University's budget are governed by formulas, relating, for example, support levels to enrollment levels, that have been negotiated over the years between the budget analysts in the central administration of the University and their counterparts in the State Department of Finance. These formulas, essentially bureaucratic treaties, are mutual understandings which give the university a greater degree of fiscal security and predictability than one would ever guess from reading the newspapers, which almost never report these matters, but only the visible debates in the legislature and speeches by the governor.

The formulas, of course, do not cover all contingencies, especially in an institution as fluid and diverse as the University of California with so many different sources of energy and initiative creating new programs, facilities, and claims on public funds all the time. Claims for resources, old and new, are argued out or negotiated annually between the University analysts and the State Department of Finance analysts; they speak each other's language, and often have been trained in the same. graduate schools and departments, not infrequently in Berkeley's School of Public Policy. In these negotiations, "good arguments" by the University are rewarded; that is, requests for additional support funds that are supported by a good bureaucratic argument are often accepted, and new activities are built into the governor's budget. The arguments made for these programs are the arguments of analysts, often based on analogies with existing state-funded activities, and backed by data showing the actual nature of the activity and its costs. For example, the University wants the State to revise the formula allocating funds for the replacement of scientific equipment used in teaching; it wants more generous provision for teaching assistants; it wants the State to assume the costs of certain athletic facilities; it wants the State to support remedial courses for underprepared students; and so on. In support of these claims the University analysts do research on the actual useful life of laboratory instruments in different scientific departments and on how that record compares with the life of instruments in other universities and in commercial labs; it studies the use and distribution of teaching assistants in the University and how their work contributes to the instructional program; it studies who uses the athletic facilities and for what purposes; and so on. These are not matters of high principle; there exists a broad area of value consensus between the negotiators, but the quality of the research backing those claims is crucial to whether they are accepted, and indeed whether they ought to be accepted. The sums of money that are allocated in these ways are in the aggregate very large. There are many areas of public life in which civil servants exercise wide discretion in decision making, though they are often wise enough to deny that they are in fact making policy or decisions, but merely "implementing" them. Nevertheless, when we reflect on the influence of research on policy, we should not neglect the realm of bureaucratic and technocratic decision making in the public sector where researcher and decision maker come together in the person of the policy analyst. University-based researchers need to be reminded that not all research has to percolate down through a complex network of relationships to enter another complex process of "decision accretion"; some research has access to decision makers quickly and directly, and is done for and by them.

The newly emergent field of policy analysis seems to be thriving in the United States, at least in a modest way, even in the face of budget cuts and hiring freezes in the federal and in many state and local governments. Policy analysts are in demand whether public expenditures are rising or falling; the problems posed to government by budgetary constraints are even more severe than those posed by expansion and the proliferation of public programs and services. And with all the cuts, most governments are not reducing the absolute level of public expenditures on social services, but merely reducing their rates of growth. In any event, public life is becoming increasingly more complex and there is no shortage of work for policy analysts.

3. Four Problems Facing the Policy Analyst

It should not be thought that the emergence of policy analysis, and of the infrastructure of graduate schools, journals, professional associations and meetings which give it definition and self-consciousness, solve all the problems of the relation of research to policy. For if policy analysts solve some of those problems, they also create new ones. This section outlines four such problems in the realm of policy analysis as currently practiced, though this does not imply that there are only four. These are all problems which in significant ways affect the quality of the analyst's work and his or her influence on policy and decision making.

First, and this is a problem that the analyst shares with academic research in education, policy analysis makes relatively little use of ethnographic research methods, the method of direct observation of customary behavior and informal conversation. One consequence of this is that the policy analyst is a captive of existing and usually official statistics; where those statistics are wrong or misleading or inadequate, the analyst's work is flawed, misleading, and inadequate also. By contrast, university researchers are more likely to question the quality of research data, though it is likely that they rarely question the quality of official statistics.

Second, the outcome of public policy analysis, its reports and recommendations, is affected not only by the analyst's own preferences and biases and those of the client, but also by how the analyst bounds the problem, the phenomena and variables that will be taken into account. These boundaries are sharply constrained by the analyst's position within the bureaucratic work setting, more so than for the university-based researcher.

Third, for every policy analyst outside the university there is tension between the needs and requirements of the client, on one hand, and their own professional commitments to intellectual honesty, to the searching out of negative evidence, and to their freedom to speak and publish what is known or has been learnt, on the other. Bureaucratic research settings put severe strains on those scholarly and professional values. Indeed, the moral issue of how policy analysts deal with dual loyalty to their professional identity as analysts and to their political masters and clients is at the heart of policy analysis and not, as moral issues often are, at the margins.

Finally, there is the relation between policy analysts and policy intellectuals which bears on the nature of communication and persuasion in the political arena, and more broadly on the processes of "decision accretion" through enlightenment and the percolation of research findings, ideas, and assumptions in the decision-making process.

4. Policy Intellectuals and Policy Analysts

In his paper identifying several models of connections between research and policy, Husén (1984) is drawn to the enlightenment or "percolation" model. He quotes Weiss to describe research as permeating the policy making process, entering the policy arena not through specific findings or recommendations, but by its "generalizations and orientations percolating through informed publics in coming to shape the way in which people think about social issues" (Weiss 1979).

There is, I think, broad agreement that much of the impact of research on policy (I would not say all) occurs in this subtle, difficult-to-measure way. But is this not at variance with the image of the policy analyst directly at the policy maker's elbow, preparing papers and reports at his or her request, speaking to issues and problems that the policy maker will be facing even if not yet recognizing their character or the available options? This image of the policy analyst is in fact compatible with the metaphor of the "percolation" of research, and of the notion of research entering into the general debate and discussion about an issue going on among interested publics, an ongoing debate that crystallizes into policy at a moment when a political actor chooses to place it on the agenda for action and not merely discussion. The analyst in government cannot often do basic research or long-range studies; he or she is to a large extent a consumer and adapter of research, part of the attentive audience for research, and among the most active participants in the critical discussion about the issue and the literature that grows up around it. In the United States, analysts who are educated at schools of public policy are especially trained to take part in that discussion because their teachers and their teachers' peers in other policy schools and professional and academic departments do the research and comment on the research of others in such journals as *The Public Interest, Policy Analysts, Public Choice, Policy Studies Journal*, and *The Journal of Policy Analysis and Management*, among others. These university-based writers and researchers, some of whom teach in the schools of public policy, are what Wilson calls "policy intellectuals." And his view of their influence on policy is not far from that of Weiss and Husén's notion of the percolation model. Reviewing the role of policy intellectuals over the past decade, Wilson observes that

If the influence of intellectuals was not to be found in the details of policy, it was nonetheless real, albeit indirect. Intellectuals provided the conceptual language, the ruling paradigms, the empirical examples. . .that became the accepted assumptions for those in charge of making policy. Intellectuals framed, and to a large degree conducted, the debates about whether this language and these paradigms were correct. The most influential intellectuals were those who managed to link a concept or a theory to the practical needs and ideological dispositions of political activists and governmental officials. (Wilson 1981 p. 36)

Wilson goes further than most of us in downplaying the role of research per se as against the power of the arguments of skillful intellectuals.

At any given moment in history, an influential idea — and thus an influential intellectual — is one that provides a persuasive simplification of some policy question that is consistent with a particular mix of core values then held by the political elite. . .Clarifying and making persuasive those ideas is largely a matter of argument and the careful use of analogies; rarely. . .does this process involve matters of proof and evidence of the sort that is, in their scholarly, as opposed to their public lives, supposed to be the particular skill and obligation of the intellectual in the university. (Wilson 1981 p. 36)

The role of the policy intellectual in policy debates, independent of his or her research, is of great importance and deserves to be studied more closely. The influence of such informed discussion and argument will, I think, vary in different policy fields. But of special interest is the combined effect of policy intellectuals based in the universities and the policy analysts whom they have trained, or who were trained to read them, to understand them, and to use their arguments in the preparation of their reports for decision makers in government. These staff papers, reports, and memoranda give the policy intellectuals' ideas and work access, in ways that the intellectuals themselves do not always have, to the committee rooms and governmental conversations where decisions are made.

5. Policy Analysts Versus Interest Groups.

The structure of government in the United States, both in Washington and in the state capitols, is changing, becoming even more open and responsive than it has been to vocal, well-organized special interest groups, less and less managed by traditional elites. In the field of education, states Murphy,

State policy systems, no longer the captive of state education establishments, are now far more accessible to interest groups and open to public view. The adoption of a large number of policy reforms reflects a new responsiveness on the part of state government to these groups.

Within government, the most important change is the heavy involvement of legislators and governors in educational matters. Spurred on by worries about money, school quality, and social issues (e.g., integration), general state government has used its new staff and expertise to challenge education professionals and to remove education from its privileged perch "above politics."

There's a different cast of participants outside government as well...Some of the new lobbies promote equality, representing such interests as urban areas, the poor, blacks, Hispanics, the disadvantaged, the handicapped, girls. Reform of state school finance laws has been promoted for the past decade by a network of scholars, foundation executives, lawyers, government officials, community organizers, and citizen groups. Other groups work for efficiency and effectiveness, lobbying for comprehensive planning, improved budgeting, accountability laws, standards for graduation, competency tests for students and teachers. More recently, some of these groups have been promoting tax limitation measures and controls on expenditures. Still other lobbies promote "the public interest". (Murphy 1981 p. 128)

All this energy and activity (in part a consequence of mass higher education) generates an extraordinary level of noise, demands, charges and counter-charges, court actions, and so forth. Pressures of every kind are felt by legislators, elected officials, and their staffs. Policy analysts inside government provide some counterweight, some degree of stability, predictability, and rationality through their professional patterns of response to these pressures and demands. This is not to say that the political activists and their pressure groups are not often successful. But how a government agency responds to organized political pressure may well be shaped by the anonymous analysts in the executive and legislative staffs and agencies. And it is through them that a larger or at least a different, set of ideas comes into play in these discussions, and these ideas at their best are less narrow and parochial, more likely to be illuminated by historical and comparative perspectives and by the ongoing discussion that policy intellectuals carry on among themselves in the professional journals.

The structure of politics, the character of the policy areas in which discussions and debate about policies are carried on, are quite different in, for example, Sweden than they are in the United States. Careful studies of actual policy formulation and implementation in specific areas must illuminate the patterns of "social interaction" that more often than not are the major determinants of outcomes in the policy arena. In these increasingly complex networks of social interaction, the relations between policy analysts in government and policy intellectuals in the university are of large and growing importance in the United States, with close analogues in Sweden and other western societies.

6. Conclusion: Research and the Rhetoric of Politics

It is natural that members of the research community are concerned that the research they do provides true and illuminating accounts of the institutions and processes that they study. Some researchers are also interested in whether research has any influence on the shaping of policy and the making of decisions, and if it does, how it enters the decision process and affects the outcomes of those decisions.

But it may be useful, and not wholly subversive of the research itself, to reflect that policy research has value independent of its truth or quality or its influence on policy. That is because social research is one of the ways in which political discussions are carried on in democratic societies, a way that is supportive of liberal democratic politics. Political argument is increasingly conducted in the language of research and analysis; concepts like "cost-benefit" and "trade-off" have found their way into the daily language of politicians and bureaucrats. Moreover, social research and democratic politics have some close affinities. For one thing, like democratic politics, social research is a process not of assertion or demonstration, but of persuasion. Moreover, it is a form of persuasion that appeals to reason and evidence rather than to supernatural authority, or tradition, or the charisma of an individual, or the authority of a legal order. The appeal to research findings is very far from the coercive domination of others by force or threat, and equally far from political manipulations which depend on the exploitation of a differential of knowledge and awareness between manipulator and the manipulated. The appeal to "research findings" is the appeal to the authority of reason, to a rationality that connects means and ends in ways that are consistent with strongly held social values. Max Weber has said that the contribution of sociology to politics is not to affirm ultimate ends, but to help clarify, if possible to "make transparent," the connections between means and ends so that choices can be made in greater awareness of the consistency of the means chosen with the ends intended. Insofar as social science attempts to do that, it becomes part of the persuasive mechanism of politics, rooting politics, at least in part, in persuasion based on an appeal to reason and knowledge. It need not weaken professional concern for the quality and truth of research to suggest that social research makes its largest contribution to liberal society not through its findings, but by its steady affirmation of the relevance of reason and knowledge to the politics of democracy.

See also: Knowledge Diffusion in Education; Legitimatory Research; Educational Research and Policy Making

Bibliography

Husén T 1984 Issues and their background. In: Husén T, Kogan M (eds.) 1984 *Educational Research and Policy: How do They Relate?* Pergamon, Oxford pp. 1–36
Kogan M, Korman N, Henkel M 1980 *Government's Commissioning of Research: A Case Study.* Department of Government, Brunel University, Uxbridge
Lerner D, Lasswell H (eds.) 1951 *The Policy Sciences.* Stanford University Press, Stanford, California
Meltsner A J 1976 *Policy Analysts in the Bureaucracy.* University of California Press, Berkeley, California
Murphy J T 1981 The paradox of state government reform. *Public Interest* 64:124–39
Weiss C H 1979 The many meanings of research utilization. *Pub. Admin. Review* 39:426–31
Wilson J Q 1981 Policy intellectuals and 'public policy'. *Public Interest* 64:31–46

Documentation in Educational Research

E. Ekman

Documentation is the collecting, classifying, retrieving, and distributing of all kinds of information. Documentation involves not only the analysis and utilization of information, but also the study of methods facilitating the search of information and the various ways of using documents.

The enormous flow of information makes it difficult for educational researchers to survey the existing relevant research material. Researchers must adopt "proper" methods and search strategies as well as identifying their own information needs when wishing to review the published research products as well as the so-called "grey literature"—mimeographed reports existing in many institutions. They must also prepare their own documentation.

The educational researcher has a special interest in documentation problems when starting an investigation or planning a project. It is particularly important to identify up-to-date research results published in scientific journals or research reports.

A distinction, on the basis of general availability, has to be made between conventional and nonconventional material. Conventional material covers:

(a) books, including encyclopedias, bibliographies, and abstract publications;

(b) printed articles in professional magazines and research journals;

(c) textbooks, including teacher guides and teaching aids and media;

(d) tests and other measurement instruments;

(e) governmental publications, committee reports, laws, parliamentary proceedings and reports, and official curricular outlines.

Nonconventional material includes:

(a) interim research reports and related material;

(b) innovation reports and papers;

(c) development plans;

(d) statistical compilations and data;

(e) school-building plans and descriptions;

(f) lectures, conferences, personal contacts;

(g) proceedings from congresses;

(h) newsletters.

Conventional material is to be found in the researchers' own bookshelves, the department library, the university library, and a special education library or documentation center (International Bureau of Education 1982). An increasing number of databases are available and many are in preparation. The university libraries, special libraries, and documentation centers often employ documentalists, who can help select among and within databases because they are familiar with the content and aims of the different databases as well as their terminology. Until now the database ERIC from the Educational Resources Information Center in Washington, DC, has predominated, but European databases are increasing in number and importance.

As a starting point in documenting research in a particular topic, it is important to know:

(a) aims and volume of the research;

(b) the audience—researchers, students, teachers, policymakers, or laymen;

(c) language barriers—important material can often be found in other languages in the form of abstracts or in the reference lists of journal articles. Journals in minor languages often have summaries in major languages or simply a translation of the title (as in the *Sovetskaja Pedagogika*). There are also journals with translation of articles, for instance *Chinese Education* and *Soviet Education*, published in New York by Sharpe.

In documenting educational research it is important to plan a systematic survey of search strategies and sources, and to evaluate the information collected. Certain handbooks (Burke and Burke 1967, Travers 1978) are helpful.

Libraries are, of course, useful information centers, but the user must learn how to use the library efficiently with its various catalogues and systems. In using a subject catalogue one must know the meaning of basic terms. There are different library classification systems, such as the Dewey system and the Library of Congress system. Descriptions in detail are given in various handbooks and in library guides. The alphabetical catalogue provides information about authors and titles. If references are given to publications which are not available in the user's library it is often possible to obtain them through an interlibrary loan system.

Up-to-date handbooks and encyclopedias are important but there may be reasons for searching in older ones (Deighton 1971, Knowles 1977, Rombach 1970–1971, Mitzel 1982, Lenzen 1982).

The results from new research, the different educational systems of the world, new curricula, different educational methods and their problems, as well as political decisions and discussions are presented in professional and scholarly journals, some for teachers, and some for researchers. The following with a comparative orientation can be mentioned:

(a) *Comparative Education* (Carfax, Oxford);

(b) *Comparative Education Review* (University of Chicago Press, Chicago, Illinois);

(c) *International Review of Education* (UNESCO, Hamburg);

(d) *European Journal of Education* (Carfax, Oxford);

(e) *Prospects* (UNESCO, Paris);

(f) *International Journal of Educational Development* (Pergamon, Oxford);

(g) *International Journal of Educational Research* (Pergamon, Oxford).

Among national journals the following can be mentioned:

(a) *American Educational Research Journal* (American Educational Research Association, Washington, DC);

(b) *Australian Journal of Education* (Australian Council for Educational Research, Melbourne);

(c) *Educational Research* (National Foundation for Educational Research, Slough);

(d) *Educational Researcher* (American Educational Research Association, Washington, DC);

(e) *Nouvelle Revue de Pédagogie* (Nathan, Paris);

(f) *Pädagogik* (Volk and Wissen, Berlin, German Democratic Republic);

(g) *Review of Educational Research* (American Educational Research Association, Washington, DC);

(h) *Sovetskaja Pedagogika* (Akademiya Pedagogicheskikh, Nauk, SSSR);

(i) *Zeitschrift für Pädagogik* (Beltz, Weinheim).

Many research institutions produce newsletters, giving information on research and published reports, for example, the Scottish Council for Research in Education. The same is true of associations for educational research such as the International Association for the Evaluation of Educational Achievement (IEA) and the American Educational Research Association (AERA).

Bibliographies are also useful to researchers. In many countries there are national bibliographies, usually very complete, and with an alphabetical and classified section. The classification is often unsophisticated but the bibliographic references are given in detail. Examples are:

(a) *Education Index* (published in Australia, Brazil, the United Kingdom, and the United States);

(b) *Awareness List/Bulletin Signalétique*, P. 520: Sciences de l'Education (from UNESCO, International Bureau of Education);

(c) *Bulletin Signalétique*, P. 520: Sciences de l'Education (from Centre National de la Recherche Scientifique in Paris);

(d) *Bibliographie Pädagogik* (from Dokumentationsring Pädagogik);

(e) *Erziehungswissenschaftliche Dokumentation, Pädagogischer Jahresbericht* (from the Federal Republic of Germany);

(f) *Magyar Pedagóiai Információ* (from Hungary).

Special bibliographies are mostly published in book form and have special subjects (Altbach et al. 1981, Parker and Totter 1971–81). The journal *Educational Documentation and Information*, published by UNESCO, International Bureau of Education in Geneva has a special topic for every number and carries abstracts of the bibliographic items.

The borderline between bibliographies and abstract publications is often not quite clear. The most important abstract publications are periodicals. They cover international and national material. Books and journals are indexed and include: author, title, bibliographic reference, publication date, number of pages, abstract, and key words. The abstract must give essential information about content and character, problems, methods, and results. The key words are useful for a subject index in a printed publication or for computerized searches. The choice of keywords is important for retrieval purposes. Several thesauri are published, for example by ERIC, UNESCO, International Bureau of Education (IBE), and the Council of Europe (European Documentation and Information System for Education—EUDISED). The two last-mentioned present equivalents in several languages.

Important periodical abstract publications are:

(a) *Bulletin Signalétique*, P. 520: *Sciences de l'Education* (Centre National de la Recherche Scientifique, Paris);

(b) *Current Index to Journals in Education*, ERIC (Oryx Press, Phoenix, Arizona);

(c) *Exceptional Child Education Resources* (Council for Exceptional Children, Reston, Virginia);

(d) EUDISED R & D *Bulletin* (Council of Europe) (National Foundation for Educational Research, Slough);

(e) LLBA (Language and Language Behavior Abstracts) (Sociological Abstracts, San Diego, California);

(f) *Psychological Abstracts* (American Psychological Association, Washington, DC);

(g) *Resources in Education*, ERIC (Oryx Press, Phoenix, Arizona);

(h) *Sociology of Education Abstracts* (Carfax, Oxford).

Most of these periodicals are available as databases.

A special kind of abstract publication are the lists of projects of interest to the researcher who may wish to contact other researchers for discussion and actual information. The EUDISED R & D *Bulletin* is a very good example. Other publications of this type include *Research Bulletin, Journal for the South African Plan for Research in the Human Sciences* (SAPRHS) from the Human Science Research Council, Institute for Research and Development in Pretoria, South Africa, and *Permanent Inquiry into Educational Research* from the Swiss Coordination Centre for Research in Education in Aarau, Switzerland. The "grey literature," mostly mimeographed research reports, is often difficult to locate, but from lists of projects it is possible to identify the author or institution to be contacted.

Bibliography

Altbach P G, Kelly G P, Kelly D H 1981 *International Bibliography of Comparative Education.* Praeger, New York

Burke A J, Burke M A 1967 *Documentation in Education.* Teachers College Press, New York

Buros O K 1978 *The Eighth Mental Measurements Yearbook.* Gryphon Press, Highland Park, New Jersey

Centro Interamericano de Investigación y Documentación sobre Formación Profesional (CINTERFOR) 1976 *Catalogo de publicaciones didacticos Latinoamericanos de formación profesional.* CINTERFOR, Montevideo

Deighton L C (ed.) 1971 *The Encyclopedia of Education.* Macmillan, New York

De Landsheere G 1982 *Empirical Research in Education.* UNESCO, Paris

Desvals H 1975 *Comment organiser sa documentation scientifique.* Gauthier-Villars, Paris

Diccionario de las ciencias de la educación 1983 Santillana, Madrid

Dockrell W B, Hamilton D (eds.) 1980 *Rethinking Educational Research.* Hodder and Stoughton, London

Ebel R L (ed.) 1969 *Encyclopedia of Educational Research: A Project of the American Research Association,* 4th edn. Macmillan, New York

Foundation for Educational Research in the Netherlands 1983 *Directory of Educational Research Information Sources,* 2nd edn. Stichting voor Onderzoek van het Onderwijs (SVO), The Hague

Gage N L 1963 *Handbook of Research on Teaching: A Project of the American Educational Research Association.* Rand McNally, Chicago, Illinois

Hassenforder J, Lefort G 1977 *Une Nouvelle Manière d'enseigner pédagogie et documentation.* Cahiers de l'enfance, Paris

Holmes B 1979 *International Guide to Education Systems.* UNESCO, Paris

Idenburg J 1971 *Theorie van het onderwijsbeleid.* Wolters-Noordhoff, Groningen

International Bureau of Education 1982 *Educational Documentation and Information.* UNESCO, Paris

International Colloquium on Designing Educational Information Systems (EDICO) 1975 *Designing Information Systems in the Field of Education, Prague, 1974.* Institute of Educational Information, Prague

International Colloquium on Designing Educational Information Systems (EDICO) 1978 *Exchange of Educational Information as a Means for Further Advancement of European Cooperation in the Field of Education, Bratislava, 1977.* Institute of Educational Information, Bratislava

Johnson M C 1977 *A Review of Research Methods in Education.* Rand McNally, Chicago, Illinois

Kairov I A (ed.) 1964–1968 *Enciklopedija pedagogičeskaja.* Sovetskaja Enciklopedija, Moscow

Knowles A S (ed.) 1977 *International Encyclopedia of Higher Education.* Jossey-Bass, San Francisco, California

Lenzen D (ed.) 1982 *Enzyklopädie Erziehungswissenschaft: Ein Integriertes Hand- und Wörterbuch der Erziehung.* Klett-Cotta, Stuttgart

Mitzel H E (ed.) 1982 *Encyclopedia of Educational Research,* 5th edn. Macmillan, New York

Ness E (ed.) 1974 *Pedagogisk Oppslagsbok.* Gyldendal, Oslo

Parker F, Totter H L 1971–81 *American Dissertations on Foreign Education: A Bibliography of 356 Doctoral Dissertations.* Troy, New York

Peterson P L, Walberg H J (eds.) 1979 *Research on Teaching: Concepts, Findings and Implications.* McCutchan, Berkeley, California

Richmond W K 1972 *The Literature of Education: A Critical Bibliography, 1945–1970.* Methuen, London

Rombach H (ed.) 1970–1971 *Lexikon der Pädagogik.* Herder, Freiburg

Schmidt H 1968 *Erziehungswissenschaftliche Dokumentation.* Beltz, Weinheim

Schütz H 1975 *Function and Organization of a National Documentation Centre in a Developing Country.* UNESCO, Paris

Sciacca M F 1969–1971 *Enciclopedia Italiana della Pedagogia e della Scuola.* Curcio, Rome

Sekretariat der Ständingen Konferenz der Kultusminister der Länder in der Bundesrepublik Deutschland 1977 *Dokumentationsdienst Bildungswesen, 1977.* Luchterhand, Neuwied

Selltiz C, Wrightman L S, Cook S W, Balch G I, Hofstetter R, Bickman 1981 *Research Methods in Social Relations,* 4th edn. Holt-Saunders, Tokyo

Sire M 1975 *Le Document et l'information: Leur rôle dans l'éducation.* Bourrelier, Paris

Skowronek H, Schmied D 1977 *Forschungstypen und Forschungsstrategien in der Erziehungswissenschaft.* Hoffmann und Campe, Hamburg

Travers R M W 1978 *An Introduction to Educational Research,* 4th edn. Macmillan, New York

Tuckman B W 1978 *Conducting Educational Research,* 2nd edn. Harcourt, Brace, Jovanovich, New York

UNESCO *World Survey of Education, 1955–1971.* UNESCO, Paris

UNESCO 1971 *International Guide to Educational Documentation, 1960–1965,* 2nd edn. UNESCO, Paris

Unwin D, McAleese R 1978 *The Encyclopaedia of Educational Media Communications and Technology.* Macmillan, London

Wilson J A R 1976 *Research Guide in Education.* General Learning Press, Morristown, New Jersey

Woodbury M 1976 *A Guide to Sources of Educational Information.* Information Resources Press, Washington, DC

Information for Educational Research

M. A. Findlay

Information is a valuable resource which is essential to the progress of research and development. In order for information to be effectively utilized, it should be identified, managed, and disseminated in a systematic and efficient manner. Information systems have been devised to store and provide access to data. Modern computer technology together with developments in the telecommunications field have resulted in storage and retrieval services from which the user can obtain information from the computer at low cost with almost negligible delays. In this article, the transfer of education information from source to user will be discussed. Special emphasis will be given to bibliographic information services or systems which have been developed to manage the vast range of information in the field of education together with information exchange arrangements which have been established both internationally and nationally.

1. Information Transfer

Educational information or knowledge is presented in a variety of forms which can be categorized into five groups, namely "facts" which are small but true pieces of knowledge; "ideas" or perceptions of existing systems or innovations which can be creative or original as well as developmental and relevant; "methods" by which facts are collected and ideas are implemented; "frameworks" which are complex packages of ideas and methods merged together logically; and "combinations" of other knowledge types which are derived from various groupings of facts, ideas, methods, or frameworks. Information is obtainable from a variety of sources and can also be classified according to these sources. Havelock and Huberman (1977) suggest at least five generic categories of sources, which include "settings", "institutions", "vendors", "knowledge storage centres", and "personal networks". Information storage is assuming greater importance with the need to control the vast quantities of available information. The 1,000 databases in the United States, 600 of which are available online (i.e., by direct interaction with the computer), are evidence of the quantity of current information in all fields of knowledge and its control by modern technology. Furthermore, in Europe there are now 1,400 databases of which 500 are accessible online. The role of the storage centre or information service is to act as an interface between the user and the range of information resources in printed or other forms and to manage the channels of communication by which information is retrieved and disseminated. These mainly autonomous services have the advantages of being unbiased, of covering a range of needs and situations, and of affording the user freedom of access and freedom to choose his or her own information selectively according to his or her own pattern of needs. Finally, information must take form in a certain medium before transfer to its destination for assimilation by the receiver for further utilization and development. Table 1 summarizes the transfer of information.

The *Directory of Educational Research Information Sources* (Foundation for Educational Research in the Netherlands 1979) provides an overview of the main bibliographical publications and databases in the field of educational research and related areas in the social sciences in as many countries as possible. This first edition of the directory lists 293 data files and includes registers of educational and social science research, theses and dissertations listings, abstracting and indexing journals, bibliographies and directories of documentation, and research institutions. Further editions are planned.

2. Information Services

The ERIC (Educational Resources Information Center) is the largest and most diversified information system in education in the world. The United States Office of Education established the ERIC programme in 1966 to acquire, select, abstract, index, and disseminate the rapidly increasing fugitive literature in the field of education—research findings, conference proceedings, papers presented at professional meetings, and so on—and to accelerate widespread adoption of research-based educational programmes. The utilization of high-speed computer technology has enabled the bibliographical citations to be produced, sorted, and disseminated in a variety of forms for searching both manually and by computer. Documents are gathered and processed in 16 decentralized clearinghouses connected to organizations and institutions throughout the United States. The ERIC clearinghouses are subject oriented and contracts for clearinghouse operations are granted on the basis of subject-specialist capabilities. The clearinghouses have responsibility within the network for acquiring the significant educational literature within their particular scope, selecting the highest quality and most relevant material, and processing the selected items for input to the database. In addition, the ERIC clearinghouses provide reference and retrieval services, develop information analysis products, conduct workshops and make presentations, and generate other types of communication links with the educational community. As well as the computer database consisting of all ERIC files, which is available on the major online network services, two monthly publications, *Resources in Education* and *Current Index to Journals in Education*, are produced. By June 1982, the computer database of the ERIC file contained half a million records of documents and journal articles and is available on the major online network services. All noncopyrighted documents and any others for which reproduction permission is obtained are reproduced on microfiche and are available either on demand or on a subscription basis. There are currently over 700 organizations throughout the world that subscribe to the entire ERIC collection on a continuing basis.

The diversity of information retrieval systems reflects the individuality and differences of databases available in the field of education. There is no coordination of accessible files and researchers must familiarize themselves with the files, including the scope of subject or geographic coverage and time period, the format of presentation (whether hard copy or machine readable), and methods of accessing machine-readable files. There are at least eight online services, each offering a variety of databases and with differing accessibility and restrictions of use, in addition to utilizing differing software and search languages. These services include:

(a) AUSINET—Australian Information Network.

(b) BLAISE—British Library Automated Information Service.

(c) BRS—Bibliographic Retrieval Service.

(d) DIALOG—Lockheed Information Systems (US).

(e) DIMDI—Deutsches Institut für Medizinische Dokumentation und Information.

(f) EISO—Educational Information Systems for Ontario.

(g) IRS—Information Retrieval Service ESRIN (Italy).

(h) ORBIT—System Development Corporation (US).

Many countries support national educational indexes and databases as well as research registers. A selection from the *Directory of Educational Research Information Sources* includes:

(a) African Source Research (Institute of African Studies, Zambia).

(b) Australian Education Index (Australian Council for Educational Research). Database online through AUSINET.

(c) BIB Report; Bibliographischer Index Bildungswissenschaften und Schulwirklichkeit (Verlag für Pädagogische Dokumentation).

(d) British Education Index (British Library). Database online through BLAISE.

(e) Canadian Education Index (Canadian Education Association).

(f) Indian Education Abstracts (India, Ministry of Education and Social Welfare).

In addition, the Ontario Ministry of Education in Canada maintains a computer-developed file of research and reports from school board research units across the province, and from the Ontario Educational Communications Authority (OECA), the Ontario Institute for Studies in Education (OISE), and the Ontario Educational Research Council (OERC). This file is available as *ONTERIS Abstracts* from 1978 and as machine-readable file through the Educational Information Systems for Ontario (EISO) network.

Other specific subject-oriented databases together with related subject files offer further access to educational documentation. Major files are:

(a) Comprehensive Dissertation Index (University Microfilms International, US). Database online through BRS, Dialog, Orbit.

(b) Exceptional Child Education Resources (Council for Exceptional Children, US). Database online through Dialog.

(c) Labour Documentation (International Labour Organization, Switzerland). Database online through Orbit.

(d) Language and Language Behavior Abstracts (Sociological Abstracts, US). Database online through Dialog.

(e) National Center for Child Abuse and Neglect (US). Database online through Dialog.

(f) Programs Appliqué à la Selection et à la Compilation Automatique de la Literature (Centre National de la Recherche Scientifique, France). Database online through IRS.

(g) PsychInfo (Psychological Abstracts, US). Database online through Dialog, Orbit.

(h) Social SciSearch (Institute for Scientific Information, US). Database online through Dialog, Orbit.

(i) Sociological Abstracts (Sociological Abstracts, US). Database online through Dialog.

A unique service is offered to social science researchers by the Institute of Scientific Information in addition to its database Social SciSearch. The weekly issues of *Current Contents: Social and Behavioral Sciences* present the titles of papers and all other substantive material from more than 1,300 journals reporting worldwide research and practice in the social and behavioural sciences. Copies of the issues are airmailed to subscribers

Table 1
Model of information or knowledge transfer[a]

| Sources | Information or knowledge transfer | | |
	Knowledge types	Forms/media	Uses
Settings	Facts	Observation	Diagnosis Awareness
Institutions	Ideas	Oral expression	Goal setting Management
Vendors	Methods	Print	Construction– fabrication
Knowledge storage centres	Frameworks	Electronic	Installation Evaluation
Personal networks	Combinations	Training (combination)	Diffusion Adaptation

a Source: Havelock and Huberman 1977 p. 182

throughout the world ensuring the rapid dissemination of information. The selection of journals scanned is determined by an editorial advisory board with representatives from seven countries.

3. International Exchange

Between 1971 and 1976, the activities undertaken by the UNESCO International Bureau of Education (IBE) in the field of educational documentation and information established the bases for the development of the International Network for Educational Information (INED) which began to take form as a result of decisions made during the 36th session of the International Conference on Education and expressed in Recommendation No. 71 adopted at that conference. The recommendation sets forth the underlying principles of recognition of the importance of educational information to the policy-making process and to the improvement of educational systems and practices, and confirms as further underlying principles the concepts of cooperative networking, standardization, professionalization, and international cooperation. Practical measures at the national level are then recommended in the fields of policy and legislative provisions, services and programmes, and status and training of educational information personnel. All relevant national, regional, and international authorities, organizations, and agencies were requested to cooperate in improving regional and international exchanges of information so as to establish a world information network in education (International Conference on Education, 36th Session, 1977). Seventy countries have agreed to participate in the exchange and in coordinating the activities of regional and national networks. The fourth edition of the *Directory of Educational Documentation and Information Services* (UNESCO/IBE 1982) reflects the development of INED and lists 102 national services, seven regional services, and five international services in operation. A quarterly publication, *IBEDOC Information* reporting worldwide activities, is also issued.

The International Educational Reporting Service (IERS) Awareness List includes abstracts of recent documents of educational innovations, particularly those taking place in developing countries and is published quarterly by UNESCO/IBE. A select bibliography series under the title of *Educational Documentation and Information* is also compiled and published quarterly by UNESCO/IBE. Number 221 of the series on educational research was prepared for the international colloquium on "Research and practice in education: How to strengthen links between research and practice in order to strengthen general education" which was organized by UNESCO in 1980 in Bucharest, Romania. In 1980, UNESCO/IBE adapted the computer system CDS/ISIS (Computerized Documentation System/Integrated Scientific Information) for its information activities, coordinating the bureau's activities with the UNESCO's integrated documentation network through the UNESCO computer system. The sectoral documentation centres

within the network reflect the discipline-oriented (education, social sciences, documentation, etc.) nature of UNESCO. The following databases at UNESCO are currently operated under CDS/ISIS:

(a) CDS—UNESCO Bibliographic Database, UNESCO Publications and Documents, UNESCO Library Acquisitions.

(b) CDTHES—UNESCO Thesaurus.

(c) DARE—Experts, institutions, research projects, documents, and journals in the field of the social sciences.

(d) ISORID—Research projects and reports in the field of libraries, documentation, and archives.

(e) EDFAC—Basic references on educational facilities.

(f) IEEN—Experts and institutions in the field of environmental education.

(g) UNED—Industry and environment (operated by the Paris office of UNEP).

(h) DESDATA—Project descriptive data.

(i) PEDPROF—Personnel roster.

Member countries of the Council for Cultural Cooperation support the European Documentation and Information System in Education which was established following a survey of the educational documentation and information systems in Europe by the Documentation Centre for Education in Europe in 1967. An experimental programme for a European network for educational documentation and information, which involved the collection of information on research in progress and completed research, and on national pilot projects of educational reform in various member countries was initiated and the first listing of projects and abstracts, *EUDISED R & D Bulletin* appeared in 1975 and continues to be the only access to the computer-originated files (Davies 1978, 1980).

Also in Europe, a programme was developed within the framework of the CMEA scientific and technical information system to coordinate activities between educational documentation and information centres. Seminars are held every three years with the support of UNESCO/IBE to consider the exchange of educational information and the means of further advancement of European cooperation. The third seminar, EDICO-3 was held in Prague in October 1980 and attended by experts from 14 European countries. The Institute of Educational Sciences at the University of La Laguna, Tenerife, Spain has initiated a project concerned with bibliographic control of books in the field of education published in English, French, German, Italian, Portuguese, and Spanish. Support has been received from UNESCO to publish the first edition in 1982.

As one of its functions, the UNESCO Regional Office for Education in Asia and Oceania provides clearinghouse services to member states through the Asian Centre of Educational Innovation for Development in

Bangkok, Thailand. The centre supports the activities of the Asian Programme of Educational Innovation for Development (APEID) and collects and disseminates information on innovative projects and programmes through a variety of publications and services: *Inventory of Educational Innovations in Asia and Oceania; Experiences in Educational Innovation in Asia; ACEID Newsletter*. A Regional Educational Media Resource Exchange Service (REMRES) has been established to disseminate information on media materials.

The Department of Education of the Arab Educational Cultural and Scientific Organization (ALECSO) is responsible for projects of cooperation in the development of education in all Arab countries. The Department of Documentation and Information provides services by gathering and processing documents, preparing material for basic research, supplying institutions in the Arab world with journals, documents, and statistical and bibliographical bulletins, and assisting Arab countries in developing library and documentation services.

In conclusion, the rapid expansion of educational research in recent decades has been accompanied by an effective control of the flow of information. There is continued advancement in the mechanics for the efficient management and low-cost access to information. Utilization of computer-based videotex systems such as PRESTEL in the United Kingdom and TELDON in Canada is well-advanced and provides access to information through telephone and television systems. Furthermore, cooperation at the international and national levels by information centres and systems benefits all researchers by providing access to the world's rich information resources, improving communication between the researcher and practitioner, and improving educational research and development.

See also: Knowledge Diffusion in Education; Dissemination of Educational Research; Documentation in Educational Research

Bibliography

Bina J V 1978 *Databases and Clearinghouses: Information Resources for Education*. National Center for Research in Vocational Education, Columbus, Ohio. ERIC Document No. ED 162 634
Davies J 1978 The educational policy information centre: An introduction and a review of the background of European co-operation. *Educ. Libr. Bull.* 21(2): 19–29
Davies J 1980 EUDISED: Image and reality: A crisis of identity. *Educ. Libr. Bull.* 23(3): 1–15
Foundation for Educational Research in the Netherlands 1979 *Directory of Educational Research Information Sources*. Foundation for Educational Research, The Hague
Havelock R G 1969 *Planning for Innovation through Dissemination and Utilization of Knowledge*. Institute for Social Research, Ann Arbor, Michigan
Havelock R G, Huberman A M 1977 *Solving Educational Problems: The Theory and Reality of Innovation in Developing Countries*. UNESCO, Paris
Hudson B M, Davis R E 1980 *Knowledge Networks for Educational Planning: Issues and Strategies*. International Institute for Educational Planning, Paris
Institute of Educational Information 1977 *Exchange of Educational Information: A Means of Further Advancement of European Co-operation in the Field of Education*. Proc. of the European colloquium: EDICO-2. Bratislava
International Bureau of Education 1981 *Education Research*. Educational Documentation and Information No. 221. UNESCO, Paris
International Conference on Education (36th Session) 1977a *Final report, Geneva, 30 August–8 September 1977*. UNESCO, Paris
International Conference on Education (36th Session) 1977 *International Information Networks and their Role in the Transfer of Educational Experience*. UNESCO, Paris
Lancaster F W 1979 *Information Retrieval Systems: Characteristics, Testing and Evaluation*, 2nd edn. Wiley, New York
Mellor W L 1982 Information storage and retrieval systems. In: Rao B A, Ravishankar S (eds.) 1982 *Readings in Educational Technology*. Himalaya, Bombay, pp. 176-96
Schmittroth J, Kruzas A T (eds.) 1980 *Encyclopedia of Information Systems and Services*, 4th edn. Gale Research, Detroit, Michigan
UNESCO/International Bureau of Education 1977 *Current Bibliographical Sources in Education*. UNESCO, Paris
UNESCO/International Bureau of Education 1978 International information networks and their role in the transfer of educational experience. UNESCO *Bull. Libr.* 32: 232–51
UNESCO/International Bureau of Education 1982 *Directory of Educational Documentation and Information Services*, 4th edn. UNESCO, Paris
United Nations 1980 *Directory of United Nations Information Systems*. Inter-organization Board for Information Systems, Geneva
Williams M E (ed.) 1981 *Computer-readable Data Bases: A Directory of Data Sourcebook*. American Society for Information Science, Urbana, Illinois

Dissemination of Educational Research

K. King

Dissemination will be considered here as the process whereby research results reach different audiences. In the case of educational research findings it is useful to think of at least three possible audiences that may be the objects of the dissemination process: (a) other researchers; (b) practitioners in the schools, colleges, and other parts of the education system; and (c) policy makers, including politicians, responsible for decisions about education at the national or local levels. It will also be valuable conceptually to look at dissemination in a North–South perspective, since there are many concerns about the present structures of dissemination, and the extent to which these are influenced by the relative power of Northern industrialized nations over the majority of less industrialized, developing countries of the South.

In both North and South, there are similarities between the relative difficulty of dissemination to the different audiences mentioned above. By far the easiest of the three is the dissemination of research results from the original researcher to other researchers; much more difficulty arises when trying to spread new educational findings to practitioners, whether school teachers, teacher trainers, or adult educators. Finally, the greatest difficulty is for new and important research to reach policy makers and politicians in Ministries of Education and regional or local councils. In part these differences are explained by the fact that for many researchers their preferred audience is other researchers. Their first inclination is the presentation of results in learned journals, or in specialist conferences of other researchers. The language of these communications is usually the technical language of their particular field. All this is to be expected, given that researchers seek recognition and eventual promotion in their professions by this first form of dissemination. The transfer of their findings to practitioners is normally left to the educational weekly newspapers, or if some research is particularly topical, it can be disseminated by the more serious daily papers. This question of topicality is equally important for dissemination into the policy process. Occasionally, independent research results are coincidentally to hand when a particular educational crisis sparks public and political attention, but there is little likelihood of the bulk of educational research being disseminated to the decision-making level. The principal obstacle to dissemination both with practitioners and policy makers is that the technical language of research is not accessible to those audiences and in addition, the task of "translating" research language into a commonsense summary is seldom undertaken. One way around this problem of poor dissemination from individual researchers to government bodies has been for the government agency itself to sponsor research on themes which it feels are important; as a corollary, an increasing amount of attention is given by some researchers to "policy research"—conducting research quite deliberately on issues upon which government can be expected to review policy options backed by research. It is possible to see three important dimensions in the dissemination of research in the North and in the South.

1. Dissemination in the North

In many ways this is the most active of the three dimensions. Researchers in the North are supported by the apparatus necessary to research communication. Journals both general and specialized are abundant and they appear with regularity. Copies of new research articles are readily available either from the original scholars or from data banks on educational research. Reprographic facilities are almost everywhere taken for granted and

university and research libraries are committed to acquiring current books and periodicals. Despite this developed infrastructure for dissemination in the North, language remains a major barrier to the flow of information between industrialized countries. There is, for example, much more rapid diffusion amongst anglophone Canada, the United Kingdom, Ireland, and the United States than there is amongst Japan, the Soviet Union, France, the Federal Republic of Germany, Scandinavia, or Spain. To a limited extent, the language barrier can be overcome by multilingual data banks, and by the existence of small international networks of researchers in the North who meet on a disciplinary basis, and act as informal translators of research across language groups.

As far as dissemination to practitioners and policy makers in the North is concerned, it is again the case that many channels are available and open for the flow of research communication. Policy research centres and contracted research aid this process, as does the existence of research funding which frequently builds support to dissemination into the educational research grant itself.

2. Dissemination in the South

This covers dissemination of research within a particular developing country on the one hand, and from one country to another across the South. Both within and across countries of the South, there are major problems of research dissemination with all three types of audiences under discussion. In addition to many of the difficulties experienced in the North, notably language barriers, there are a series of dissemination obstacles which make the situation qualitatively different in many, but by no means all, of the developing countries of the South. Dissemination within the nation itself is often hindered by the absence or irregularity of scholarly journals, infrequent professional meetings, and the relatively small size and consequent isolation of some research communities. In some countries, the educational research community is extremely small, but this does not necessarily make it any more likely that research will be satisfactorily disseminated than where there are large numbers of competing research findings. It seems that some kind of critical mass is almost essential to afford researchers an audience to address in the first instance.

At the regional level or across continents, the situation is in general worse. Even within the same language group, there is not necessarily much research dissemination at all amongst anglophone East, West, Central, or Southern Africa, nor even much amongst neighbouring countries in East or West Africa. Indeed, without funding for regional meetings on a regular basis and the frequent interchange of national journals, the present very weak South–South dissemination cannot rapidly improve.

The very strength of the dissemination process in the North interferes with the improvement of dissemination in the South. Although scholars in the South may wish to have their findings read locally and regionally, their own local journals are frequently less regular, and less likely to be purchased by the national and university libraries than international journals in the field. Hence, many researchers prefer Northern journals for their findings and it is thus sometimes the case that research is disseminated from South to South via a journal of international standing in a Northern capital.

This seems certainly not to be the case as far as much of Spanish-speaking Latin America is concerned. Research is communicated through some journals across the continent and this is aided by an organization of Spanish language research summaries (*Resumenes Analiticos*). There is a widely based concern in the region with the dissemination of educational research, and an interest in exploring ways that researchers can communicate with both policy makers and practitioners.

The pattern is different again in South and Southeast Asia. In some countries, the existence of strongly centralized government research centres brings the research process much nearer to the decision-making process. There remains, however, a problem for university-based research to gain recognition in this situation.

Finally, on this South–South dimension, it has to be acknowledged that some countries, for example India, have a very large local research production, and many hundreds of educational journals. These may well have some direct policy impact within the country itself but there seems to be very little dissemination of Indian research findings in education to audiences outside India, either in the North, or to other anglophone countries in the South.

3. Dissemination between the North and the South

As a result of the long-standing patterns of communication between metropolis and colony during the colonial period, and their continuation after formal independence from the colonial empires, whole sections of the world look Northwards not only to disseminate their findings, but also to select the kind of research to undertake in the first place. Such is the influence of Northern university research centres, their links to funding, and to the dissemination infrastructure, that new research themes and findings are disseminated rapidly and effectively. A powerful channel for their dissemination North–South has been the presence of very large numbers of developing country scholars in Northern universities since the early 1950s. Long-term doctoral training in the North has predisposed Southern scholars to work on topics and methodologies of interest in the North,

and also to the reproduction (or dissemination) of these results in their own universities. The corollary of this has been very significant numbers of Northern scholars doing research in the Third World, often with more adequate funding than those they worked amongst. In many cases, the natural outlet for such Northern research upon the South has been Northern journals, or the bilateral and multilateral agencies concerned with education in developing countries. As a consequence both of the South–North movement of Third World scholars and the North–South movement of Northern scholars, the comparative advantage of dissemination via the industrialized countries has been strengthened. To some extent, therefore, the research dissemination situation is an analogue of the larger pattern of Northern dominance in information processing, storage, and communication.

It should be noted, however, that there have been some critical influences in research which have flowed from the South to the North. These would include insights into the conduct of participatory and action research, in which Latin America has been a particularly powerful disseminator Northwards of methodology and approaches. Another example would be methodologies for literacy, with Freire being only one of many sources of inspiration. Together, these do a little to correct the balance of Northern influence on the South. But although small in scope, some of these Southern successes in dissemination may also be instrumental in suggesting ways in which the research community can reach and involve practitioners, particularly teachers, in the research process. Collaborative research with teachers is of course by no means a Southern monopoly, but it does suggest some new ways of altering some aspects of educational research from being a specialist activity of the professional researcher to being also a part-time enthusiasm of the practising teacher. In this situation, the task of research dissemination is greatly altered, and collaborative research with teachers becomes the counterpart of the policy research mode with decision makers. Both, in different ways, reduce significantly the gap between the researchers and two of the principal audiences.

Bibliography

Husén T, Kogan M (eds.) 1984 *Education Research and Policy: How Do They Relate?* Pergamon, Oxford
Myers R 1981 *Connecting Worlds of Research.* International Development Research Centre, Ottawa, Ontario
Nisbet J, Broadfoot P 1980 *The Impact of Research on Policy and Practice in Education.* Aberdeen University Press, Aberdeen

Knowledge Diffusion in Education

J. P. Keeves

This article is concerned with the transmission of knowledge about education from those who are involved in

research and development to those who must employ that knowledge in their daily work. Just as knowledge in many fields of human endeavour has increased greatly, so too, in education as a consequence of the very significant growth in expenditure on research and development since the early 1960s, has there been a substantial increase in the knowledge about the educational processes for diffusion or dissemination to all those who have use for such knowledge. However, as Huberman and his colleagues have pointed out (Huberman et al. 1981), it is evident that the dissemination of knowledge in education is far more complex and far less manageable than in other fields which would superficially appear similar, such as agriculture or public health.

Related to the increase in knowledge in education and in other fields, there has been widespread recognition of a need for research and investigation into the processes of transmission of knowledge. While diffusion research is emerging as an area of study which is attracting research workers from several disciplines in an attempt to form a single integrated body of concepts and generalizations about the diffusion process, it is important to recognize that the overall area is still very fragmented because of the wide range of disparate elements associated with the creation and utilization of knowledge in different fields of endeavour. One important source of this fragmentation is associated with the different disciplinary perspectives from which the knowledge under consideration has been created. Rogers and Shoemaker (1971) classified the 2,750 items in their diffusion bibliography in seven major and seven minor disciplinary traditions, but they noted that a transfer of ideas was taking place across disciplines in many of the studies under survey. From this review Rogers and Shoemaker were able to revise previous work on the identification of factors which affected the rate of adoption of an innovation. They noted that adoption was not the only outcome, since in reality rejection was also likely to occur; that evaluation of innovations took place either formally or informally at all stages; and that even after adoption had occurred, further evaluation might lead to subsequent rejection. In addition they noted four stages in the innovation–decision process which are as follows: (a) knowledge—the individual is exposed to the innovation's existence and gains some understanding of how it functions; (b) persuasion—the individual forms a favourable or unfavourable attitude towards the innovation; (c) decision—the individual engages in activities which lead to a decision to adopt or reject the innovation; and (d) confirmation—the individual seeks reinforcement for the innovation–decision which has been made, but a previous decision may be reversed if conflicting information about the innovation is received (Rogers and Shoemaker 1971 p. 103).

From research into the diffusion process there has started to emerge a conceptual paradigm related to the transmission of knowledge that is relevant to many disciplines. Since most social scientists, including educators, are interested in social change, the broad area of diffusion research offers a convenient framework within which to develop such understandings, because a general approach to diffusion has something to offer each

discipline. It is necessary before examining the processes of transmission of knowledge in the field of education to consider first the particular characteristics of both the creation and utilization of knowledge in education and how these relate to the processes of diffusion.

1. Creation of Educational Knowledge

It is important to recognize that in the field of education, by and large, the body of knowledge that has the most profound influence on policy and practice is derived not from research or from scholarly analysis but from the accumulated wisdom of teachers and administrators working in schools and administrative units throughout the world. Systematic and cumulative research and development in education is a relatively recent phenomenon, commencing only during the twentieth century and only gaining sufficient strength to make a substantial contribution on a worldwide basis during the late 1960s and the 1970s. It has, however, been possible to document the impact of research and development on education through a series of case studies which establish beyond doubt the contribution that research has made during this century to educational policy and practice (Suppes 1978) (see *Educational Research and Policy Making*).

Educational research and development yield outcomes that are of three distinct types. Rich (1977), from a study of the use of social science information by administrators in the United States, found it of value to differentiate between the instrumental and the conceptual utilization of knowledge: between what he termed knowledge for action and knowledge for understanding. Likewise, Fullan (1980) has suggested that there are two main types of knowledge available for use. The first refers to knowledge that can be applied to a particular problem and is derived from a specific research study or from a collection of studies. The second refers to cumulative knowledge.

From these perspectives it can be seen that there is firstly knowledge together with the use of knowledge in the field of education, which has been derived from research and study in education, that is associated with principles, broad conceptions, and fundamental paradigms, and that provides a basis for an understanding of the educational process. It must be recognized that such knowledge which is largely of a theoretical nature, is nevertheless important, even if it does not appear to have any immediate application. Contrary to common belief, one of the major outcomes of the very substantial investment in educational research that has taken place since the early 1970s has been the gradual assembling of a considerable body of knowledge about schools and how they function that is only now being built into a coherent conceptual framework.

Secondly, there are findings arising from educational research that have direct applications in educational policy and practice. Nevertheless, it is rare for an individual research study to yield findings that can be used alone to change either policy or practice. The complexity of most educational activities and of the settings in which such activities are carried out will restrict the applicability of the findings derived from a single investigation. However, if several similar studies have been undertaken in a variety of situations, there frequently emerges a more general finding that gains are to be made through the implementation of a new policy or practice.

A third and important type of outcome of educational research and development is the preparation of a tangible product that incorporates the findings of research and has a direct use in schools and classrooms. The marked increase in research and development that occurred in many parts of the world during the late 1960s and the 1970s resulted in the production of a number of educational materials for classroom use, each of which was derived from a particular body of research. The acceptance of these materials varied according to the quality of the research, the quality of the materials, and, in particular, the extent to which the ideas underlying the development of the materials were disseminated to the teachers using particular materials in their classrooms.

These three types of outcome of educational research and development, concerned with principle and paradigm, with policy and practice, and with products that have immediate and direct application in schools are different in kind. They are also associated with different types of utilization and with different approaches to diffusion and dissemination.

2. Utilization of Educational Research

As a consequence of the increased body of research-based knowledge in education it has become clearer how such knowledge might be used in the making of policies, the development of practice, and the introduction of tangible products. Weiss (1979) has identified seven ways of utilization of social science research, and all seven approaches would seem to apply in the field of education. What is envisaged is a classification of type of knowledge or product combined with an approach to utilization in the form of a two-way matrix with the three types of knowledge along one axis and the seven approaches to utilization along the other. While not all cells of this matrix will be associated with a specific application, this systemization of the creation of knowledge with the utilization of knowledge would appear to be an appropriate framework within which to consider in detail the mediating process of diffusion or transmission. Moreover, it would seem likely that certain models of the diffusion process will relate to either specific categories of creation of knowledge, or categories of utilization of knowledge, or possibly to a specific cell within the creation–utilization classificatory grid. The seven approaches to utilization of knowledge are considered below.

(a) *Knowledge-driven approach.* Underlying this approach is the view that basic research reveals some findings that have direct application in practice. While this approach would seem highly applicable in the fields of the natural and medical sciences, it is less relevant to education. However, the findings relating to the teaching of subtraction and division have influenced the methods of instruction used in schools in both the United Kingdom and the United States. They provide clear examples of how specific knowledge can be applied in the field of education.

(b) *Problem-solving approach.* In educational policy and practice, a commonly held view of research utilization envisages research as providing empirical evidence and conclusions to help to solve a particular policy problem. In this approach the problem exists and is identified and a decision has to be made to solve the problem, but information and understanding are lacking on how the problem might be solved. Under these circumstances it is appropriate to recognize that research could provide the missing knowledge and understanding.

(c) *Interactive approach.* In this approach neither the researcher involved in the creation of knowledge, nor the practitioner with a problem to be solved, work independently of the other. They interact with one another in a manner that involves both a search for knowledge as well as a solution to a problem. Sometimes the necessary knowledge is obtained through a search for and reconceptualization of findings already available and sometimes the need to obtain an appropriate solution leads to a substantial programme of research and development. The creation of new knowledge, however, is only one component of an interactive process that also involves the utilization of knowledge.

(d) *Enlightenment approach.* Probably the most common way in which knowledge derived from educational research is used for policy making or practice is through the cumulative effects from a substantial number of research studies each of which contributes to a change in thinking about certain educational questions. In this approach there is no assumption that decision makers or practitioners seek out research-based knowledge to assist them, but rather they are influenced by an enlightenment that has come to them as a result of the cumulative findings derived from research, often without an awareness of the origins of the knowledge.

(e) *Political approach.* Recognition that policy and practice are influenced by an accumulated body of research findings has led many educational policy makers and practitioners to resolve to make certain changes, and then to seek legitimation from research. This can occur through a search in the research literature to find support for the proposed change; a task that is not as difficult as would seem at first because of the often contradictory nature of the results of research studies in the same area. Alternatively, it can occur through the commissioning of research, particularly of an evaluative kind, to find evidence to legitimate a decision that has already been made but perhaps not been publicly or explicitly stated. Some of the research in recent years into open-plan schooling was of this kind.

(f) *Tactical approach.* Related to the political approach is a tactical approach where certain decisions which were made have subsequently come under challenge. In these circumstances it is a common ploy to commission research as a delaying action to enable the new policy or practice to become more thoroughly established. The implications of the findings of the research may have to be faced at a later stage.

(g) *Research-oriented approach.* Underlying this approach to the utilization of research-based knowledge is the view that the process of inquiry is of value in itself. It is assumed that if policy makers and practitioners are directly engaged in the research enterprise they will not only facilitate the utilization of research findings but they will also promote wider diffusion and acceptance of research-based knowledge. This approach emphasizes the unity of the three components of creation, diffusion, and utilization of knowledge rather than the distinctiveness of each component process. In part this is an underlying theme in action research and in the teachers as researchers or the teachers as evaluators movements that were advocated in the early twentieth century and which have gained acceptance once more in recent years.

3. The Diffusion Process

The theoretical framework that has helped to guide much of the thinking about the diffusion process in education, although of relatively recent development, has come to be called the "classical diffusion model". A detailed statement of this model is provided by Rogers and Shoemaker (1971). The four main elements of this model are: (a) an innovation defined as an idea perceived as new by an individual, (b) is communicated through certain channels, (c) over a sustained period of time, (d) among the members of a social system. This classical model in one form or another is still the most popular for the study of diffusion or for an understanding and use of the diffusion process. There are many other models that differ in their degree of comprehensiveness, such as the suggestion made by Hood (1973) that there are three models for the study of change in education: the organizational improvement model, the extension network model, and the research, development, and marketing model. However, the most extensive treatment of models of the diffusion process has been undertaken by Havelock and his colleagues and their models provide a sound basis for the consideration of the transmission or dissemination of knowledge in education. In this article the models developed by Havelock will be described in some detail, because with these models it is possible to investigate the diffusion process in education in a coherent way. In addition, it is possible to consider the planning of a range of services for the transmission of knowledge in education in terms of various combinations of the Havelock models. It is also important to note the interrelations between the

Havelock models and the various categories of knowledge creation and utilization considered in the previous sections of this article.

4. The Havelock Models

In the mid-1960s, Havelock undertook a major review of the literature in the diverse fields of medicine, agriculture, industrial technology, and education and, in 1970, a national survey of school districts in the United States, to learn what research workers and practitioners said about the processes of dissemination and utilization of knowledge from research. From the review he concluded that there were three existing perspectives or models which described the transmission of knowledge from the research centres to the user.

4.1 Research, Development, and Diffusion Model

In this model it was assumed that there was a rational and orderly sequence from basic research, to applied research, to the development and testing of a prototype, the preparation and packaging of a product, and the planned dissemination to the user (Havelock 1971). This model is presented diagrammatically in Fig. 1. In it, the user is seen to play a relatively passive role. While this model gained wide acceptance in the 1960s, experience would appear to indicate that it involves a gross oversimplification of the manner in which knowledge about education and the products of research actually spread. It should be noted that the model relates directly to one of the approaches to utilization of knowledge advanced by Weiss (1979).

4.2 Social Interaction Model

This second perspective is seen to apply widely in the spread of knowledge both in agriculture and in medicine. In this model individuals are seen as interacting with colleagues within a reference group or through membership of an association, and these colleagues influence whether or not the individuals accept the research findings and the practices advocated, or adopt particular products. Informal personal contacts within the reference group provide the opportunity for the transmission of ideas. This model is portrayed in Fig. 2. Some educational innovations spread in this way, but the operation is dependent on the leaders of the reference groups and associations gaining access to the necessary information from research sources.

4.3 Problem-solving Model

A third approach, that is widely accepted as applying in education, is the problem-solving model. Again it relates to one of the categories of knowledge utilization advanced by Weiss (1979). In this model each user identifies a need, diagnoses a problem, undertakes a search for a solution, and tries possible alternative solutions to the problem. In education, this model would appear to be particularly applicable to the solving of organizational problems. Consultation with a research worker or person outside the system engaged in solving a problem

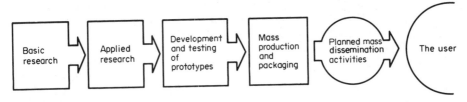

Figure 1
The research, development, and diffusion model

Source: Havelock R G 1971

is not necessarily part of the process, and when one is consulted it is customary for a nondirective or advisory role to be adopted. This approach involves an emphasis on a local initiative and the development of a local solution that in all probability would not apply in another setting. The nature of this problem-solving model is shown in Fig. 3.

4.4 Linkage Model

Subsequently, Havelock (1973) attempted to combine the best documented features of each of the previous models in order to account for a two-way flow of information between the source and the user. This led to the development of a fourth model, which is presented in simplified form in Fig. 4. The user and the resource system are involved in a reciprocal and collaborative interaction, and each reacts to assimilate the ideas that the other can provide. Thus there is a linkage established between the two systems and the model is known as the linkage model. An important component of the linkage model is the presence of a linkage medium, since direct face-to-face contact is rarely possible in educational work between the users and the resource system. It should be noted that the linkage model has three major components; the resource system, the linkage medium, and the user system. Within the user system are the schools, their teachers and students, the parents of the students, the regional and state education boards or authorities, and the administrative staff serving those boards or authorities. The linkage medium comprises

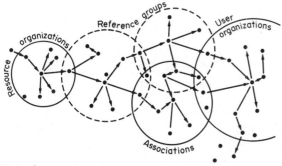

Figure 2
The social interaction model

Source: Havelock R G 1971

the linkage agents, linkage instruments, and linkage institutions. The linkage institutions include the colleges of education and teachers' colleges, curriculum centres, inservice education centres, teachers' centres and resource centres, and the regional offices or district offices as these institutions are variously called in different parts of the world. The linkage agents are, in the main, the persons who work within the linkage institutions, and include college lecturers, education officers, advisory officers, school district officers, supervisory and inspectorial officers, and curriculum consultants. The linkage instruments consist of published reports, journals, video programmes, pamphlets, and the like. All three components are used in one way or another for the two-way communication between the two systems. There remains the resource system which necessarily includes the research institutions, the universities, and their research centres, curriculum development centres, and other research and development centres. It is important to recognize that in the linkage model there is not just a one-way transmission of information from the resource system to the user system. There is in addition a necessary transmission of information from the user system to the resource system. Without this communication of issues and needs for research and development, the resource system would be operating largely in a vacuum. Huberman et al. (1981) have examined the operation of the linkage model in terms of knowledge transfer theory and organizational theories. They have emphasized that very few real-world knowledge transfer situations involve only one resource system and only one user, and the linkage paradigm presented above must be enlarged to provide for these complexities. In addition they suggest that the term "network" must be employed to refer to relations among individuals, and the term "interorganizational arrangements" to refer to the more formal relations that must necessarily be established between organizations or institutions. Not only are networks and interorganizational arrangements built up among the members of a resource system and among the members of a user system, but they must also be built up between the user system, the linkage agents and linkage organizations, and between these agents and organizations and the resource system. Huberman et al. (1981) have begun to explore the nature of the transactions that occur between and within these systems.

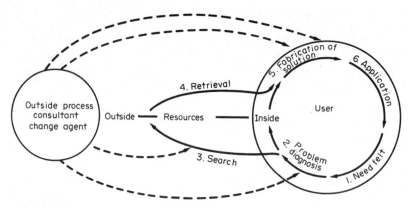

Figure 3
The problem-solver model

Source: Havelock R G 1971

4.5 A Study of the Linkage Model

Owen (1979) has carried out a significant study to investigate the applicability of the linkage model to the adoption and implementation of the Australian Science Education Project materials by Australian secondary schools. The research undertaken by Owen has found that elements of all three models: the research, development, and diffusion model; the problem-solving model; and the social interaction model operate in a complex way within the linkage model in a manner that is consistent with the perspective advanced by Havelock (1973). The contribution made by Owen has been not only to identify in the Australian setting the characteristics of the user system but also to investigate the dimensions of the linkage medium. The user system was viewed by Owen in terms of five characteristics: knowledge of research findings; openness to innovation and change; interaction with other users, and with the linkage medium; organization within the user unit, so that resources available are effectively displayed; and cooperation within the user unit, so that individual users share

with each other experiences gained during the introduction of the innovation. In addition, Owen identified four linkage mechanisms which were associated with a high level of adoption and maintenance of an innovation. These were: participation within the research and development enterprise; contact with the charge agent; engagement in relevant teacher education programmes; and the examination of appropriate dissemination material. Adoption and effective utilization of innovative practices in the Australian setting appeared to require not only possession of a high degree of several of the user characteristics, but also the effective operation of several of the linkage mechanisms. Possession of one characteristic alone by a user, or the operation of one mechanism alone within the linkage medium was not enough.

Owen did not investigate directly how the resource system could act most effectively in the diffusion and dissemination of its research findings and products. However, the account that he has provided of the way in which and the degree to which one innovation spread across Australia gives some picture of how a resource

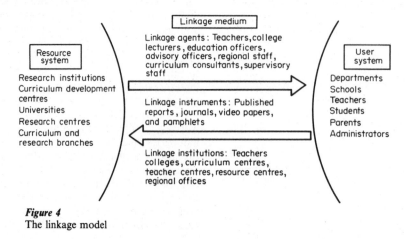

Figure 4
The linkage model

system should operate to ensure that maximum gains are made in the use of findings and products of educational research and development. Nevertheless, it is clear that a one-way flow from the resource system to the user system is not considered an appropriate or effective account of the processes of dissemination or diffusion of the products of research and development in education. Furthermore, the chance interactions within a social network or interorganizational arrangement as envisaged within the social interaction model, or the passive wait for the users to identify a need as envisaged in the problem-solving model are clearly not efficient approaches to the diffusion and utilization of knowledge in education. Nevertheless, there are situations operating in practice in which Owen and his colleagues have been able to show that one of the three component models is operating largely in isolation and without interplay with either of the other two models as is envisaged within the linkage model. Hence all four models are required to give a complete account of the real-world situation.

5. Approaches to Planned Diffusion

There is no single method or procedure which alone can be recommended to carry out the effective transmission of useful knowledge in education. Rather there would seem to be many approaches that should be used when and where they are considered appropriate. It is clearly necessary to identify different approaches and promote and develop their use in ways judged to be most effective. Nevertheless, it is important to recognize that not only should the resource system be planning to ensure

Figure 5
The diffusion continuum

that the maximum benefits flow from its research and development work, but the user system should also be planning to ensure that it receives maximum benefit from the research and development work that is carried out. This latter is accomplished both by ensuring that knowledge is disseminated in appropriate ways as well as by ensuring that the research being undertaken takes cognizance of the perceived needs of the users.

Thompson (1981) in an account of the programmes sponsored by the National Institute of Education in the United States, saw these dissemination programmes lying along a continuum from the Educational Resources Information Centre (ERIC) at one end to local problem-solving work at the other. This view of dissemination may be extended to suggest that most dissemination activities in education may be considered to lie along a similar continuum ranging from a research, development, and diffusion orientation at one end to an orientation towards problem solving at the school and classroom levels at the other. While this view is perhaps an oversimplified one, the two orientations do take cognizance of the perspectives of the resource system and the user system respectively. Thus to consider diffusion programmes and activities as lying along a continuum is helpful in ordering thinking about such programmes. This framework, the diffusion continuum, which is represented in Fig. 5, may be used to give a brief account of the major types of formal programmes or planned activities that are operating in the transmission of knowledge about education. It must be recognized that there are informal activities which occur as well to assist in the diffusion of knowledge. These are covered, in the main, by the social interaction model where it operates at an informal level. This model can, however, be used in a more deliberate way through the establishment of networks among individuals.

5.1 Programmes of Publication

Perhaps the most obvious form of dissemination of information is through planned programmes of publication in the form of books, research monographs, journals, microfiche documents, summary reports, and newsletters. The major problems encountered are associated with the need to write for different audiences. Reports providing full technical detail are necessary in order for an assessment to be made of the quality of the research, but such reports are largely incomprehensible to practising teachers and administrators. On the other hand, summary reports can receive widespread publicity, but be based on poor quality work that is effectively concealed by skilful writing and lack of detail. It is important to note that while some of the costs of production of publications can be reduced through the increased use of technology in typesetting and preparation, the overall costs of printing and distribution might be expected to rise to such an extent that much important material may become lost or buried through lack of resources for publication.

5.2 *Indexing and Abstracting Services*

A second approach to dissemination is the systematic compilation of an index and the provision of an abstracting service in the field of education. In the late 1970s and early 1980s significant steps were taken through the introduction of new technology to improve both the quality of such services and their accessibility. Access can now be provided to indexing and abstracting services by means of computer-based systems across countries linked by satellite, through microfiche copies of reports, and through videographic procedures. It must be recognized, however, that such systems based on advanced technology are costly to install.

5.3 *Research and Development Information Exchanges*

Both the profusion and diffuseness of much of the reporting in the field of educational research makes it difficult for individual users to select directly from the publications available, or through an abstracting service, the more general ideas that could influence their thinking on specific issues, or that could assist with the solving of particular problems. However, there are increasing numbers of newsletters and similar publications which provide both summaries of research that is reported more fully elsewhere, as well as discussions of current problems and issues. At the present time the programmes and activities in this area and the information available are perhaps too far towards the research, development, and diffusion end of the continuum in Fig. 5. They do not present as fully information on the problems being encountered by schools that would be helpful to the research system in its thinking about research studies which might be planned and conducted. Moreover, there is a need for such exchanges to promote the widespread adoption of validated innovations as opposed to simply disseminating information from research or from the evaluation of particular programmes.

5.4 *Research and Development Networks*

The establishment of research and development networks is based on the assumption that the exchange of information can take place in ways other than those provided by printed documents. In the main, networks rely on social interaction between individuals, and operate at an informal level. The functions of the networks are: (a) to select, synthesize, and interpret the findings of educational research for practitioners in the schools and for policy makers, (b) to identify validated innovations and to spread information about such practices, (c) to provide information to consumers on products together with evidence of their effectiveness, (d) through discussion and debate to communicate the needs of practitioners and policy makers to research workers, and (e) to collect information on the experiences of practitioners and to add this information to the accumulated body of knowledge about education. In general, networks are loosely structured and rely on informal contacts and the social interaction between members of the network to achieve the goals set within the network, rather than through the adoption of clearly defined policies and programmes. It is, however, possible for change agents to be appointed to develop such networks and so to fulfil a mission to effect the widespread adoption of particular innovations or products rather than to merely supply information regarding new practices and policies.

5.5 *Research and Development Utilization Centres*

From the time of the setting up of the Schools Council in the United Kingdom in the mid-1960s there has been an increase in the establishment and growth of a range of centres and units, both in that country and more recently elsewhere, whose activities are directed towards: (a) the enhancement of problem-solving capabilities, (b) the supply of appropriate research and development resources, (c) the promotion of an awareness of the existence and nature of problems, and (d) the stimulation and motivation of personnel within schools and districts to meet the conditions necessary for change and innovation. In general, the centres which have been established are of two types, differing in the extent to which they focus on more specific but widely occurring problems, or on more general issues relating to the common problems of schools and teachers in an area. The former more specific problems are catered for in resource centres, which commonly provide services and facilities to assist with the resolution and treatment of particular problems. The latter more general problems are catered for in teachers' centres that have far greater flexibility of operation in order to meet the specific needs of the teachers and school administrators served by the centres. Since many of the centres that have been established are self-governing, there has been marked variation in their stated aims and the ways in which they function. As a consequence, the impression is often gained of an amorphous collection of small centres and units serving many different purposes. Nevertheless, since such centres are located more at the problem-solving end of the continuum presented in Fig. 5 than at the research, development, and diffusion end it is not surprising that such differences in purpose and function should appear since, in the main, these research and development utilization centres have been set up to help solve the problems of a specific group of educational practitioners, rather than to fulfil a highly specified role or to promote a highly specific programme or product.

5.6 *School-based Problem-solving Programmes*

During the 1970s there was an increased emphasis and a widespread acceptance in many parts of the world of school-based evaluation programmes. Stemming from this work the practice has developed of examining specific problems of a curricular or organizational kind within schools without conducting a full-scale evaluation exercise. There is clearly a growing interest in the identification and analysis of specific problems in schools, together with attempts to find solutions to those problems. The effectiveness of such programmes may, in part, depend on their capacity to draw on the knowledge and expertise available from research and development enterprises. While there may be little cause to doubt that a great deal of value is being achieved by such programmes, there would sometimes appear to be a lack of appropriate structures and strategies by which guidance and assistance could be obtained from resource systems to provide the knowledge and understanding which can be derived from research and development in education.

6. Some Issues in Dissemination in Education

The models of the diffusion process advanced above expose some of the weaknesses in current dissemination programmes. The research, development, and diffusion approach is deficient in so far as it assumes relatively passive consumers and a linear sequence of activities. The problem-solving perspective has limitations as a strategy in so far as it involves responding only to local initiatives, and makes no provision for the planning and promotion of change through the dissemination of knowledge about improved practice. The social interaction approach pays little attention to the nature of the knowledge or innovation to be diffused or to how implementation takes place after adoption. The linkage perspective, in so far as it combines the most appropriate features of the three earlier models is the most useful. It permits a diagnosis of need and a planned organization of the resources whether in the form of knowledge or innovatory practice and product, to ensure their relevance to the user. However, as Raizen (1979) has pointed out, unless those responsible for the implementation of proposed changes are involved at an early stage in the process of identification of the problem, and in the consideration of alternative strategies for its solution, it is unlikely that effective implementation will occur after the adoption of a proposed improvement. It is clear that future research in the field of diffusion needs to focus on the implementation process and the subsequent history of an innovation once it has been introduced. In the planning of strategies for widespread programmes of diffusion it would appear important to give full consideration to the range of alternatives that lie along the continuum extending from research, development, and diffusion at one extreme to specific problem-solving programmes at the other. However, it is necessary to recognize the need for full cooperation between the individuals and agencies involved, rather than to depend on programmes originating solely from the resource system or from a centralized bureaucracy.

Furthermore, recognition must also be given to the need to provide information in forms that are appropriate to the specific audience receiving the information. In addition, it is necessary to acknowledge both the difficulty and the importance of combining and condensing the information available so that a coherent and consistent message is presented. Following a decade or more of intensive research and development in the field of education during the 1970s, the major task in the diffusion of knowledge is the finding of ways of synthesizing the evidence that is available and presenting the findings in a manner that is meaningful to audiences who conduct school systems and who implement change in systems, schools, and classrooms. Following the synthesis of the evidence available, the next major development would appear to be the formation of dissemination centres in which linkage agents would work to promote educational policies and practices that would incorporate the best of what is known from research about the educational process.

See also: Dissemination of Educational Research; Knowledge Utilization

Bibliography

Fullan M 1980 An R & D prospectus for educational reform. In: Mack D P, Ellis W E (eds.) 1980 *Interorganizational Arrangements for Collaborative Efforts: Commissioned Papers.* Northwest Regional Educational Laboratory, Portland, Oregon, pp. 29–48
Havelock R G 1971 The utilisation of educational research and development. *Br. J. Educ. Technol.* 2: 84–98
Havelock R G (ed.) 1973 *Planning for Innovation through Dissemination and Utilization of Knowledge.* Center for Research and Utilization of Scientific Knowledge, Ann Arbor, Michigan
Hood P D 1973 How research and development on educational roles and institutional structures can facilitate communication. *J. Res. Dev. Educ.* 6(4): 96–113
Huberman A M, Levinson N S, Havelock R G, Cox P L 1981 Interorganizational arrangements: An approach to educational practice improvement. *Knowledge: Creation, Diffusion, Utilization* 3: 5–22
Husén T, Kogan M (eds.) 1984 *Educational Research and Policy: How do they Relate?* Pergamon, Oxford
Kosse G B (ed.) 1982 *Social Science Research and Public Policy Making.* National Foundation for Educational Research, Slough; Nelson, Windsor
Owen J M 1979 The Australian Science Education Project: A study of factors affecting its adoption and implementation in schools. Doctoral Thesis, Monash University, Monash
Raizen S A 1979 Dissemination programs at the National Institute of Education: 1974–1979. *Knowledge: Creation, Diffusion, Utilization* 1: 259–92
Rich R F 1977 Uses of social science information by federal bureaucrats: Knowledge for action versus knowledge for understanding. In: Weiss C H (ed.) 1977 *Using Social Research in Public Policy Making.* Heath, Lexington, Massachusetts, pp. 199–211
Rogers E M, Shoemaker F F 1971 *Communication of Innovations: A Cross-cultural Approach,* 2nd edn. Free Press, New York
Suppes P (ed.) 1978 *Impact of Research on Education: Some Case Studies.* National Academy of Education, Washington, DC
Thompson C L 1981 Dissemination at the National Institute of Education: Contending ideas about research, practice and the federal role. Paper presented at the 1981 Annual Meeting of the American Educational Research Association, Los Angeles, California
Weiss C H 1979 The many meanings of research utilization. *Public Admin. Rev.* 39: 426–31

Knowledge Utilization

W. Dunn, B. Holzner, and G. Zaltman

The study of knowledge utilization is concerned with understanding and improving the utilization of scientific and professional knowledge in settings of public policy and professional practice. The field itself is a product of the historic rise in reflective awareness of the importance of knowledge in contemporary societies and has been accompanied by the emergence of professional roles and practices for knowledge utilization in such fields as agriculture, mental health, and education (Cernada 1982, Lehming and Kane 1981). This article describes the major research traditions on which contemporary work draws and describes available conceptual frameworks, methodology, and practice.

1. The Research Traditions

The field of knowledge utilization has emerged from several different research traditions, including the history and philosophy of science (Laudan 1977) and the sociology of knowledge (Remmling 1967). There has been a call for a sociology of knowledge applications, a classic sociology of knowledge "turned upside down" (Holzner 1978). A convergent program has emerged in the psychology and economics of knowledge applications in the major efforts of Campbell (1977) and Machlup (1980, 1982).

Another origin of present perspectives is the research tradition of applied social science, as exemplified by the Bureau of Applied Social Research at Columbia University under Lazarsfeld. Late in his career Lazarsfeld turned explicitly to the study of the social and intellectual processes of knowledge application, culminating in his conceptualization of the "utilization cycle" (Lazarsfeld et al. 1975). An even earlier source stemmed from the work of Lewin in the style of "action research" (Marrow 1969), which became influential as one model for the interlinking of research and practical action.

Most empirical studies of knowledge utilization were not based on these conceptual perspectives. They tended to be practice-oriented investigations, often responsive to urgent administrative information needs. Investigators drew on conceptual resources from research on planned social change, marketing, and the communication of innovations. Much of this work has been oriented to the translation of social science knowledge into guidelines for the improvement of practice. There has been a lag in developing the needed empirical base for a better understanding of knowledge-use processes.

Since the early 1960s there has been a great increase in applied and practice-oriented studies of this kind. Glaser (1976) estimates that there are as many as 20,000 items in the research literature on knowledge use and planned change. This figure may well double by the mid-1980s. The field has its own scholarly journal, *Knowledge: Creation, Diffusion, Utilization*, established in 1979. Since the early 1970s many investigations were

carried out in such domains as education, mental health, criminal justice, community development, information management, program evaluation, policy analysis (Glaser 1976, Weiss 1977, Rich 1981, Ciarlo 1981), and technology assessment.

Some of the more active centers of current research in North America are the Knowledge Transfer Institute at American University, the Center for Research on Utilization of Scientific Knowledge at the University of Michigan, and the Program for the Study of Knowledge Use at the University of Pittsburgh. Major research programs on knowledge utilization have been sponsored by several national and international agencies, including the Mental Health Services Branch of the National Institute of Mental Health, the Research and Educational Practices Unit of the National Institute of Education, and the Organisation for Economic Co-operation and Development.

2. Conceptual Frameworks

A prominent metaphor for knowledge utilization as a cognitive process is the image of the "two cultures" drawn from Snow's *The Two Cultures and the Scientific Revolution* (1959) and his recommendations for bridging the gap. This notion of "gaps" has brought forth ideas about bridging them, as in the new roles of "linkers" (Havelock 1969), "translators" (Lazarsfeld et al. 1975), and "brokers" (Sundquist 1978). It also focuses attention on knowledge transformations, as in Lazarsfeld's idea of the gap between the formulation of a practical problem and the structure of a research problem, or the gap between research findings and policy recommendations.

A methodological and conceptual review of the extant literature on knowledge utilization with a focus on education (Dunn and Holzner 1982) concludes that the following four propositions provide an integrative framework:

(a) Knowledge use is interpretive. This means that potentially transferable knowledge products, whether research based or experiential, do not "speak for themselves." They are, rather, interpreted by the various stake holders in terms of their own frames of reference.

(b) Knowledge use is socially constrained. The interpretive processes of knowledge utilization themselves are located in social structure and are constrained by role responsibilities, networks, and other institutional arrangements and the "situated rationalities" they engender.

(c) Knowledge use is systemic. Problems of knowledge utilization are rarely decomposable into discrete parts, since knowledge utilization involves typically a whole system of problems in the production, organization, storage, retrieval, transfer, and utilization of knowledge (Holzner and Marx 1979).

(d) Knowledge use is transactive. Knowledge cannot really be said to be "exchanged," "marketed," or "transferred"—terms which suggest a one-directional process of moving discrete pieces of information among parties who share an a priori common definition of what constitutes "knowledge." On the contrary, knowledge is in fact transacted among parties engaged in symbolic or communicative acts of negotiating the adequacy, relevance, and cogency of knowledge claims (Dunn 1982).

Given this framework, an array of conceptual tools for the analysis of knowledge utilization becomes necessary (Holzner and Salmon-Cox 1982). These concepts permit the analysis of social knowledge systems, of the construction of knowledge and practice, and the identification of strategic foci in the analysis of knowledge utilization processes.

Knowledge-related activities are differentially distributed in society and often occur in highly specialized social frameworks (Gurvitch 1972). As the economist Machlup (1962, 1963, 1969) has shown, it is fruitful to view a society from the point of view of the structured distribution of knowledge-related activity. This aspect of a social system is called the social-knowledge system. It encompasses a complex array of institutions and organizations as well as social roles and positions. The social structure of knowledge systems is in complex ways related to the creation and use of knowledge, but it is also limited to a society's moral culture and sense of identity (Robertson and Holzner 1980). Processes of knowledge creation and utilization now can be seen in their interdependence. It should be emphasized that such interdependence is not always beneficial—as illustrated by the vigorous utilization of Lysenko's "findings" by the Communist Party of the Soviet Union and the resulting constraints for Soviet biology at the time.

The diffuse (that is, nonspecialized) knowledge systems of simple societies have long since been replaced in the advanced industrial countries by highly specialized and often formally institutionalized structures. In complex modern knowledge systems, the scientific community and the science-based professions, while they constitute the core, do not exhaust the system (Mendelsohn et al. 1977, Knorr et al. 1980, Elias et al. 1982, Mendelsohn and Elkana 1981, Agassi 1981, Merton 1968, 1973).

Knowledge systems can be analyzed in terms of knowledge functions, institutional domains, and frameworks for knowledge, as well as in terms of the centrality or peripherality of system components or "regions." The major knowledge functions can be described under the following five headings:

(a) producing knowledge, for example, in scientific research and scholarship;

(b) organizing and structuring knowledge as in the construction of theories, but also of texts, curricula, and the like;

(c) distributing knowledge, for example, through journals or through linkage agents;

(d) storing knowledge in archives as well as in the memory of individuals and collectivities; and

(e) using knowledge, with varying kinds of feedback relations to any of the other functions.

The analytical distinctiveness but empirical interpenetration of activities and structures serving these functions is emphasized in the third section of this article.

Major institutional domains, such as agriculture, education, medicine, or other domains of public policy may evolve into specialized social knowledge systems of their own. The established professions are good examples of this (Freidson 1970).

Finally, the distinction between center and periphery (Shils 1975) points to the fact that these systems are not only differentiated, but also ordered along a dimension of higher and lower degrees of prestige, influence, and, in some instances, formal authority. Further, the regions of the knowledge system are variously limited or peripheral to the center of political power.

The knowledge system constitutes a society's most important resource for a collective learning capacity. Societies, like individuals, live in a reality which is often harsh and dangerous, but they can only come to terms with their realities by what they learn about them, that is with the manner in which they socially construct what is taken to be real.

This raises the question of the definition of knowledge. It is undeniably true that different societies, regions within one knowledge system, and different historical epochs exhibit vast differences in what is taken to be valid knowledge. Is the student of knowledge utilization therefore to conclude that "knowledge" is whatever is socially taken to be knowledge? The answer is no. There needs to be a critical assessment of knowledge. Throughout history there has been a quest for valid knowledge, recently vastly accelerated. Such validity was at times established on the basis of traditional authority, or religious revelation, or the dictates of conscience, or rationally guided empirical inquiry, or formal, logical, or mathematical calculation, or in still other ways. It is quite clear that not all such modes of validation of knowledge claims are of equal merit. Indeed, we are living in the context of an historical process striving for ever more "adequate" knowledge claims.

Yet there is not now and will never be a single algorithm for the determination of ultimate knowledge. This position, which is that of a constructivist and evolutionary epistemology, accentuates the importance of certain conceptual tools for the analysis of processes within and across regions of the knowledge system. They are the concepts' frame of reference, reality tests, theories-in-use, and situated rationality.

A frame of reference is the structure of assumptions and implicit or explicit decision rules in inquiry which provides the framework for the construction of meanings. It provides a perspective that focuses attention, but it also sets boundaries for what is to be considered the field of relevant information (Holzner et al. 1977, Weiss and Bucuvalas 1980, Holzner et al. 1976).

Reality tests are important components of frames of reference. In knowledge-use studies and practice, it is of crucial importance to discover empirically in what ways knowledge claims are scrutinized and on what grounds they are accepted or rejected.

The concept of theories-in-use will be dealt with especially in the section on knowledge-utilization practice. It refers to the working theories of practitioners that, embedded in their frames of reference, actually guide their actions. The surfacing of these often tacit theories and their formalization and critique is an important tool in knowledge-utilization practice.

Situated rationality refers to the fact that actors often attempt to proceed rationally within their frames of reference, even as they are tied into situations which pose for them certain more or less inescapable predicaments.

3. Methodology

Empirical research on knowledge utilization has been variously criticized by the research community itself (Weiss 1977, Dunn 1983a, Dunn and Holzner 1982). This section of this article is primarily a description of the methodology employed in a large sample of knowledge-utilization studies scrutinized in a multiyear project supported by the United States National Institute of Education (Dunn and Holzner 1982, Dunn 1983a, 1983b).

A key decision in knowledge-utilization research is the selection of an appropriate unit of analysis. In studying the impact of knowledge use on collective decisions it is often essential to obtain data about a respondent's relationship with other individuals. Aggregations of individual responses may provide an inaccurate or actually misleading picture. However, in the actual set of empirical studies almost all dealt with individuals as units of analysis. For example, questionnaires are often used to assess the concerns of individual users and nonusers about the implementation of particular educational innovations.

Available studies reflect a diversity of research designs ranging from case studies and cross-sectional analyses to quasi-experiments conducted in representative contexts of practice. Some case studies are based on prior theory, while others are not. A few knowledge-use studies are based on quasi-experimental designs, including real-time field experiments where research-based ideas, suggestions, or recommendations are actively introduced into practice settings. Cross-sectional or longitudinal studies exploring factors affecting the utilization of research include research on the sources of information used by congressional staff members and studies of the uses of social science research by federal, state, and local policy makers.

The prevailing method for obtaining data in knowledge-use studies is the self-administered questionnaire. The use of content analysis, naturalistic observation, and interview schedules is relatively rare, while few studies are qualitative in the specific sense that they seek to capture the underlying contextual meanings attached to knowledge and its uses. Knowledge-use studies, while they can be based heavily on the use of questionnaires whose reliability may be readily assessed, are frequently based on procedures with unknown or unreported reliability and validity. Given that knowledge-use studies are intimately related to the assessment of cognitive (subjective) properties of many kinds, the absence of information about the reliability of procedures and the validity of constructs represents a serious unresolved problem of most research in the field.

A central problem of knowledge-use studies is defining what is meant by use. The most widely used definition in the field is one that distinguishes between conceptual and instrumental uses of knowledge (Rich 1975, Caplan et al. 1975, Weiss 1977). Generally, conceptual use refers to changes in the way the users think about problems, while instrumental use refers to changes in behavior, especially changes that are relevant to decision making. While many unresolved difficulties continue to plague this two fold distinction (Dunn 1983a), many knowledge-use studies continue to employ it. Instrumental use, for example, tends to imply that respondents are single decision makers, notwithstanding the collective or systemic nature of organizational decision making. Given these and related difficulties it is striking that most studies define use in primarily instrumental terms, with the remainder stressing uses that are conceptual (Weiss and Bucuvalas 1980), symbolic, or affective (Anderson et al. 1981).

Available research yields little consistent empirical support for claims that particular classes of factors —economic, political, social, organizational, behavioral, attitudinal—affect the creation, diffusion, and utilization of knowledge in decisive and practically significant ways. There are many reasons for the inconsistency or instability of research findings, many of which stem from conceptual and methodological problems documented by Downs and Mohr (1976), Weiss (1977), Berman (1981), Miles (1981), Larsen (1981), Dunn and Holzner (1982), and Huberman and Miles (1982). The most important of these problems are reviewed below.

3.1 The Problem of Criteria

In terms of what criteria should knowledge use be defined? Answers to this basic question assume a variety of forms. Knowledge use may be viewed as principally conceptual, defined and measured in terms of mental processes of various kinds, and it may be represented and measured in terms of overt behavior. The distinction between conceptual and instrumental use, while it provided an initial focus for early studies, conceals a number of important dimensions according to which knowledge and its uses may be classified and measured. Instrumentally focused definitions of use, for example, generally neglect properties related to the expected benefits, purposes, and underlying assumptions of knowledge and its uses. Even those studies based on a conceptual definition of use often focus on surface properties of knowledge, taking for granted the meaning of knowledge, research, or information.

3.2 The Multiattribute Problem

Why does knowledge vary in perceived relevance, adequacy, and cogency? This question calls attention to the fundamentally interpretive character of processes of knowledge use. Processes of knowledge use are structured by the ways that policy makers, practitioners, and social scientists anticipate or predict events, such anticipation being a function of collective and individual reference frames and of the coordinative social contexts in which they are established, maintained, and changed. The specification of these subjectively meaningful contexts is frequently a product of the meanings of researchers, and not of those to whom such categories are applied. What is needed are procedures for identifying criteria actually employed to assess knowledge, as distinguished from criteria that are imposed on research contexts by investigators.

3.3 The Transactional Problem

How can knowledge transactions be conceptualized and measured? Research on individual frames of reference, while important for mapping the meanings surrounding processes of knowledge use, does not necessarily deal with the distribution of various reality tests or with changes in the structure of individual and collective frames of reference over time. A recognition of the contextual, relational, and generative properties of knowledge use has prompted many researchers to discard the terms interaction, exchange and transfer, replacing these with the concept of transaction. While research on communication networks recognizes the importance of distinguishing contextual and referential meanings (Rogers and Kincaid 1981), it has been difficult to preserve subjectively meaningful dimensions of knowledge transactions.

4. Knowledge Practice

Practice refers to processes whereby data are given meanings that pass certain reality tests and are incorporated into a frame of reference, consequently reinforcing or changing existing beliefs and/or behaviors. For example, at an individual level a set of research results may be interpreted as supporting court-mandated school busing. Reality tests applied by the individual may certify this meaning as being both socially and technically valid. This may reinforce the individual's assumptions and decision rules about the merits of court-ordered school busing. Such reinforcement may be expressed through more vigorous social actions on the part of the individual whose sociopolitical beliefs have now been heightened.

4.1 Knowledge Application in Relation to Production and Dissemination

Traditionally social processes related to knowledge production have been studied relatively independently of the social processes of dissemination and knowledge application. More recent thinking is taking a somewhat different perspective (Zaltman 1983). This perspective suggests that knowledge production, dissemination, and application are interactive in nature or, more accurately, that they are not separable constructs. Knowledge production occurs during application and dissemination. Similarly knowledge dissemination may occur during its production and application. To borrow a metaphor from statistics, rather than focusing on so-called "main" effects it may be more helpful to concentrate on so-called "interaction" effects. A kind of dialectic may also characterize the three processes. That is, while substantial pressures encourage the production of knowledge, equally powerful, though less well-understood, pressures "forbid" the production and dissemination of knowledge, keeping significant social events "hidden" and hence difficult to study or inform others about (Nelkin 1982, Westrum 1982, Peters and Ceci 1982). Also, while there is significant motivation to apply knowledge there are equally significant and prevalent motivations to prevent knowledge application or to even disavow the presence of knowledge. Thus, while it is conceptually convenient to separate the different knowledge functions, it is also necessary to remember that they comingle to the degree that one process may contain the others.

4.2 Theories-in-use and Frames of Reference

The assumptions, expectations, and decision rules which constitute frames of reference set the context for ideas guiding action. Such sets of ideas represent theories which individuals as well as complex social units such as government bureaucracies use in dealing with their internal and external environments. These causal maps or theories have been labelled theories-in-use (Argyris and Schön 1974). This concept has developed in the context of knowledge applications (Zaltman 1979, 1983).

Research findings concerning the impact of theories-in-use on knowledge practice include the well-documented finding that knowledge developed without consideration of theories-in-use among practitioners is unlikely to pass their reality tests (Rogers and Shoemaker 1971). Research about the value of prevention in mental health, if conducted with an understanding of the dominant curative orientation of mental health practitioners, is more likely to be accepted than the same research ideas developed without this sensitivity to practitioner theories-in-use. Moreover, when practitioners are actively involved in the development of knowledge as reverse consultants the resulting research is generally judged by all parties to be of higher technical quality and greater relevance to practice. Finally, the more that practitioners share researcher frames of reference about the conduct of research, the more likely that research will be accepted independently of the researcher's sensitivity to practitioner concerns. Thus, shared frames of reference with respect to knowledge-production issues affect knowledge applications.

The more consonant a set of research findings are with practitioners' theories-in-use the more likely their acceptance and application. The more divergent these findings are the more likely they are to be rejected or to be adapted in a way the originators of the research would themselves reject. These processes of knowledge rejection and knowledge adaptation have received considerable attention. They pertain not only to practitioners' behaviors but to the behaviors of agents active in knowledge production and dissemination systems. Knowledge which is perceived as surprising—as contrary to expectations—is likely to be rejected even if the surprise is in a positive direction. Frames of reference establish a kind of intellectual and social "comfort zone" and an item of information whose meaning could cause an agency to operate outside this comfort zone will tend to be rejected. This is partially described by the notion of group think (Boje and Murningham 1982). Group dynamics often present evidence which runs contrary to an existing or emerging consensus. Individuals and groups will often stop short of the point in their information-acquisition activities at which they might encounter information falling outside their comfort zones and which might require a major alteration in their theories-in-use. This is reflected by the term "half-knowledge" (Lazarsfeld cited in Marin 1981): enough is known about a situation that the organization realizes that there is a possibility that if more were known a difficult decision or action may be required. The notion of hidden events is also relevant here (Westrum 1982). A hidden event is a social phenomenon whose existence is either seriously doubted or simply not known about at all. Events may be hidden for several reasons: fear of ridicule keeps individuals from reporting phenomena and hence multiple experiences of the event go uncorrelated; arrogance with respect to evidence, for example, "If it existed I'd know about it"; misclassification (Greaves 1980); the absence of and/or the inability of accepted methodology to study the event (Charman 1979); restricted or "forbidden" access to information collection and application opportunities (Nelkin 1982); and so forth.

The meanings assigned to data by those who orignate or create them may not be congruent with the meanings assigned or developed by those who disseminate and apply the data. More precisely, the meanings which are enacted by users of a research report may be at substantial variance with the meanings disseminators felt they were conveying. Moreover, both disseminators and users may have interpretations which are not shared by knowledge producers. Data are assimilated into frames of reference in ways which are biased toward reinforcing existing theories-in-use (Ross and Lepper 1980, Nisbett and Ross 1980). These tendencies have been observed

not only at the level of the individual but among informal groups and formal organizations as well. The mechanisms whereby this occurs cannot be treated here. The important point is that a given set of statistics or a given verbal reporting of an event can give rise to very different "productions" of knowledge. These productions may be so divergent that the stake-holder group originating the data, when observing practitioners' behaviors based on the latter group's assigned meaning of these data, would conclude that a very different set of data were being acted upon. Of course practitioners often do agree with meanings assigned by producers and disseminators. However, the social realities of the context of application might require giving greater or lesser emphasis to certain concepts or sets and omitting some concepts altogether while adding yet others. In effect, a somewhat different theory is required and hence developed even if unwittingly by practitioners as a result of the realities of the implementation context.

4.3 Planned Social Change

A second major approach for viewing knowledge-use practices utilizes planned social-change concepts (Havelock 1969, Zaltman 1979, Rich and Zaltman 1978, Rothman 1980, Cernada 1982, Glaser 1981). This approach argues that new information may result in new social constructions or interpretations which are innovations. These innovations may exist only as ideas or as practices and products. If these innovations pass the reality tests applied by key stake holders and are adopted they may result in changes in the structure and functioning of social systems. Thus the application of knowledge may result in social change.

If knowledge "products" can be regarded as innovations resulting in social change then strategies for promoting product innovations such as medical drugs, solar energy technology, and instructional tools might be usefully applied to achieve more complete dissemination and use of other types of innovations such as scientific research intended for use by research scientists or practice innovations intended for other practitioners (Fine 1981, Larsen 1981, 1982). This is consistent with the view of knowledge practice as transactional and knowledge as a social construct. That is, the field of planned social change considers the diffusion of innovations as exchange processes between different communities which may have different frames of reference. Thus there is an emphasis on researcher understanding of the needs and requirements of potential users prior to the production of knowledge and in the design of knowledge products. The communication behaviors of potential users as well as their adoption decision processes are considered in the design of dissemination strategies. The role of linking agents (Havelock et al. 1973) and linking systems (Holzner and Salmon-Cox 1982) become central concepts when knowledge use is viewed as planned social change. Moreover, formal management information systems assume greater prominence as user-initiated linking systems within this view of knowledge applications.

4.4 Conclusions

As a field of inquiry and professional practice, knowledge use is a distinctively modern enterprise. Until recently the field has not been consciously shaped by theory and research in the sociology, economics, and psychology of knowledge applications or, more broadly, by a basic interdisciplinary social science that seeks to examine the practical consequences of applying scientific and professional knowledge. Instead, the field of knowledge use has been mainly oriented towards the translation of social science knowledge into guidelines for the improvement of practice. While this applied research orientation has created greater sensitivity to the costs and benefits of the social sciences, this same orientation has contributed less to the resolution of basic theoretical, conceptual, and methodological issues. A basic social science of knowledge utilization still needs to be constructed.

See also: Dissemination of Educational Research; Knowledge Diffusion in Education; Educational Research and Policy Making; Research Paradigms in Education; Action Research

Bibliography

Agassi J 1981 *Science and Society: Studies in the Sociology of Science.* Reidel, Dordrecht

Anderson C, Ciarlo J A, Brodie S 1981 Measuring evaluation: Induced change in mental health programs. In: Ciarlo J A (ed.) 1981 pp. 97–123

Argyris C, Schön D 1974 *Theory in Practice: Increasing Professional Effectiveness.* Jossey-Bass, San Francisco, California

Berman P 1981 Educational change: An implementation paradigm. In: Lehming M, Kane M T (eds.) 1981 pp. 253–86

Boje C, Murningham C 1982 Group confidence pressures in interactive decisions. *Manage. Sci.* 28(10): 1187–96

Campbell D T 1977 *Descriptive Epistemology: Psychological, Sociological and Evolutionary.* Preliminary Draft of the William James Lectures. Harvard University, Cambridge, Massachusetts

Caplan N S, Morrison A, Stambaugh R J 1975 *The Use of Social Science Knowledge in Policy Decisions at the National Level: A Report to Respondents.* University of Michigan Institute for Social Research, Ann Arbor, Michigan

Cernada G P 1982 *Knowledge into Action: A Guide to Research Utilization.* Baywood, Farmingdale, New York

Charman W N 1979 Ball lightening. *Physics Reports* 54: 261–306

Ciarlo J A (ed.) 1981 *Utilizing Evaluation: Concepts and Measurement Techniques.* Sage, Beverly Hills, California

Downs C W, Mohr L B 1976 Conceptual issues in the study of innovation. *Admin. Sci. Q.* 21: 700–13

Dunn W N 1980 The two-communities metaphor and models of knowledge use: An exploratory case survey. *Knowledge: Creation, Diffusion, Utilization* 1(4): 515–36

Dunn W N 1981 If knowledge utilization is the problem, what is the solution? Working Paper KU-109. Program for the Study of Knowledge Use, University of Pittsburgh, Pittsburgh, Pennsylvania

Dunn W N 1982 Reforms as arguments. *Knowledge: Creation, Diffusion, Utilization* 3(3): 293–326

Dunn W N 1983a Measuring knowledge use. *Knowledge: Creation, Diffusion, Utilization* 1(5): 120–33

Dunn W N 1983b Qualitative methodology. *Knowledge, Creation, Diffusion, Utilization* 4(4): 590-97

Dunn W N, Holzner B 1982 *Methodological Research on Knowledge Use and School Improvement.* Final Report. US Department of Education, Washington, DC

Elias N, Martins H, Whitley R (eds.) 1982 *Scientific Establishments and Hierarchies.* Sociology of the Sciences Yearbook, Vol. 6. Reidel, Dordrecht

Fine S H 1981 *The Marketing of Ideas and Social Issues.* Praeger, New York

Freidson E 1970 *Profession of Medicine: A Study of the Sociology of Applied Knowledge.* Dodd, Meade, New York

Glaser E 1976 *Putting Knowledge to Use: A Distillation of the Literature Regarding Knowledge Transfer and Change.* Human Interaction Research Institute, National Institutes for Mental Health, Los Angeles, California

Glaser E 1981 Knowledge transfer strategies. Paper presented at Conference on Knowledge Use. University of Pittsburgh, Pittsburgh, Pennsylvania

Greaves G B 1980 Multiple personality, 165 years after Mary Reynolds. *J. Nervous and Ment. Disease* 168: 577–96

Gurvitch G 1972 *The Social Frameworks of Knowledge.* Harper and Row, New York

Havelock R G 1969 *Planning for Innovation Through Dissemination and Utilization of Knowledge.* Center for Research on Utilization of Scientific Knowledge, University of Michigan, Ann Arbor, Michigan

Havelock R G, Havelock M C, Markowitz E A 1973 *Educational Innovation in the US,* Vol. 1: *The National Survey: The Substance and the Process.* Center for Research on Utilization of Scientific Knowledge, University of Michigan, Ann Arbor, Michigan

Holzner B 1978 The sociology of applied knowledge. *Sociol. Symposium* 21: 8–19

Holzner B, Marx J 1979 *Knowledge Application: The Knowledge System in Society.* Allyn and Bacon, Boston, Massachusetts

Holzner B, Salmon-Cox L 1982 Knowledge systems and the role of knowledge synthesis in linkages for knowledge use. In: Beal G M, Dissayanake W, Konoshima S (eds.) 1982 *Knowledge Generation, Exchange and Utilization.* East-West Center, University of Hawaii, Honolulu, Hawaii

Holzner B, Fisher E, Marx J 1977 Paul Lazarsfeld and the study of knowledge applications. *Sociol. Focus* 10(2): 97–116

Holzner B, Mitroff I, Fisher E 1976 An empirical investigation of frames of reference, case studies in the sociology of knowledge. Unpublished working paper. University of Pittsburgh, Pittsburgh, Pennsylvania

Huberman M, Miles M 1982 Drawing valid meaning from qualitative data: Some techniques of data reduction and display. Paper prepared for a symposium on Advances in the Analysis of Qualitative Data. Annual Meeting of the American Educational Research Association, New York, March 1982. American Educational Research Association, Washington, DC

Knorr K D, Krohn R, Whitley R (eds.) 1980 *The Social Process of Scientific Investigation.* Sociology of the Sciences Yearbook. Reidel, Dordrecht

Larsen J 1981 Knowledge utilization: Current issues. In: Rich R F(ed.) 1981 *The Knowledge Cycle.* Sage, Beverly Hills, California

Larsen J 1982 *Information Utilization and Nonutilization.* American Institutes for Research in the Behavioral Sciences, Washington, DC

Laudan L 1977 *Progress and Its Problems: Toward a Theory of*

Scientific Growth. University of California Press, Berkeley, California

Lazarsfeld P, Reitz J, Weiss C 1975 *An Introduction to Applied Sociology.* Elsevier, New York

Lehming R, Kane M (eds.) 1981 *Improving Schools: Using What We Know.* Sage, Beverly Hills, California

Machlup F 1962 *The Production and Distribution of Knowledge in the United States.* Princeton University Press, Princeton, New Jersey

Machlup F 1963 *Essays on Economic Semantics.* Prentice-Hall, Englewood Cliffs, New Jersey

Machlup F 1969 If matter could talk. In: Morgenbesser S, Suppes P, White M (eds.) 1969 *Philosophy, Science and Method: Essays in Honor of Ernest Nagel.* St. Martin's Press, New York, pp. 286–305

Machlup F 1980 *Knowledge: Its Creation, Distribution, and Economic Significance,* Vol. 1: *Knowledge and Knowledge Production.* Princeton University Press, Princeton, New Jersey

Machlup F 1982 *Knowledge: Its Creation, Distribution, and Economic Significance,* Vol. 2: *The Branches of Learning.* Princeton University Press, Princeton, New Jersey

Marin B 1981 *Knowledge: Creation, Diffusion, Utilization.* Sage, Beverly Hills, California

Marrow A J 1969 *The Practical Theorist: The Life and Work of Kurt Lewin.* Basic Books, New York

Mendelsohn E, Elkhana Y (eds.) 1981 *Sciences and Cultures: Anthropological and Historical Studies of the Sciences.* Reidel, Dordrecht

Mendelsohn E, Weingart P, Whitley R (eds.) 1977 *The Social Production of Scientific Knowledge.* Reidel, Dordrecht

Merton R K 1968 *Social Theory and Social Structure.* Free Press, New York

Merton R K 1973 *The Sociology of Science: Theoretical and Empirical Investigations.* University of Chicago Press, Chicago, Illinois

Miles M B 1981 Mapping the common properties of schools. In: Lehming R (ed.) 1981 *What We Know.* Sage, Beverly Hills, California, pp. 42–114

National Institute of Education 1973 *Building Capacity for Renewal and Reform.* National Institute of Education, Washington, DC

Nelkin D 1982 Forbidden research: Limits to inquiry in the social sciences. In: Beecham T L, Faden R (eds.) 1982 *Ethical Issues in Social Science Research.* Johns Hopkins University Press, Baltimore, Maryland

Nisbett R E, Ross L 1980 *Human Inference: Strategies and Shortcomings of Social Judgment.* Prentice-Hall, Englewood Cliffs, New Jersey

Peters D P, Ceci S J 1982 Peer review practices of psychological journals: The fate of published articles submitted again. *Behav. and Brain Sci.* 5: 187–95

Remmling G W 1967 *Road to Suspicion: A Study of Modern Mentality and the Sociology of Knowledge.* Appleton-Century-Crofts, New York

Rich R F 1975 Selective utilization of social science related information by federal policymakers. *Inquiry* 13(3): 239–45

Rich R F 1981 *Social Science Information and Public Policymaking: The Interaction Between Bureaucratic Politics and the Use of Survey Data.* Jossey-Bass, San Francisco, California

Rich F, Zaltman G 1978 Toward a theory of planned social change: Alternative perspectives and ideas. *Evaluation* (Special issue)

Robertson R, Holzner B (eds.) 1980 *Identity and Authority: Explorations in the Theory of Society.* St. Martin's Press, New York

Rogers E M, Kincaid D L 1981 *Communication Networks: Toward a New Paradigm for Research.* Free Press, New York

Rogers E M, Shoemaker F F 1971 *The Communication of Innovation: A Cross-cultural Approach,* 2nd edn. Free Press, New York

Ross L, Lepper M 1980 The perseverance of beliefs: Empirical and normative conclusions. *New Directions for Methodology of Social and Behavioral Sciences* 4: 17

Rothman J 1980 *Using Research in Organizations: A Guide to Successful Application.* Sage, Beverly Hills, California

Shils E A 1975 *Center and Periphery: Essays in Macrosociology.* University of Chicago Press, Chicago, Illinois

Snow C P 1959 *The Two Cultures and the Scientific Revolution.* Cambridge University Press, New York

Sundquist J 1978 Research brokerage: The weak link. In: Lynn L (ed.) 1978 *Knowledge and Policy: The Uncertain Connection.* National Academy of Science, Washington, DC, pp. 126–44

Weiss C H (ed.) 1977 *Using Social Research in Public Policy Making.* Heath, Lexington, Massachusetts

Weiss C H, Bucuvalas M 1980 Truth-tests and utility tests: Decision makers' frames of reference for social science. *Am. Sociol. Rev.* 45(2): 302–12

Westrum R 1982 Social intelligence about hidden events. *Knowledge: Creation, Diffusion, Utilization* 3(3): 381

Zaltman G 1979 Knowledge utilization as planned social change. *Knowledge: Creation, Diffusion, Utilization* 1(1): 82–105

Zaltman G 1983 Theory-in-use among change agents. In: Seidman E (ed.) 1983 *Handbook of Social and Community Intervention.* Sage, Beverly Hills, California, pp. 289–312

Data Banks and Data Archives

J. Anderson and M. J. Rosier

Research data are arranged in data sets, defined as organized collections of related data. The term data bank is commonly used to refer to a collection of related data sets, often associated with a single research project or survey. The quantity of data in most data sets or data banks usually necessitates the use of computerized retrieval systems with data stored in machine-readable form. Data archives are places where machine-readable data, such as those contained in data sets, are stored, preserved, and catalogued for access and use by others. Increasingly, educational researchers are making use of data held in data archives to answer questions, for example, about the achievement, attitudes, or attributes of students and schools, or to compare their data with other data collected at a different time or in a different place.

1. Data Banks in the Social Sciences

Although the concept of an educational data bank may conjure up visions of vast amounts of information being kept on file about schools, teachers, and students and thus may be thought of as depersonalizing education, there are reasons that may be advanced for maintaining such data banks.

The collection of research data, particularly large longitudinal studies or studies conducted nationwide or across countries, is expensive. The possibility that such data may be used by other research workers, for secondary analysis or for providing benchmarks to enable comparisons at some time in the future, helps to justify the expenditure. There is also a certain obligation on the part of researchers to ensure that collections of data, especially if funded by public monies, are made available as soon as possible to colleagues in the wider research community. This represents an extension of the current practice of the evaluation of the quality of scientific work by means of peer review and thus may lead to better educational research. The analysis of a data set by secondary analysts asking different questions and using a variety of models and statistical techniques should lead to a more robust interpretation of the data, particularly where initial analyses were conducted under severe time constraints imposed by the sponsoring agencies.

The archiving of data and their use by others may also reduce the need to interrupt schools and other educational institutions, which may in turn enhance the response by institutions on occasions when data are collected in the future. This applies particularly to the use of archived data sets for the training of research workers who wish to concentrate their efforts on developing a repertoire of statistical techniques rather than on data collection. Part of the justification for establishing the Social Science Research Council (SSRC) Survey Archive in the United Kingdom was that survey data are "a valuable resource in terms of both human effort and cash funds, and ought, therefore, to be protected and utilized so that the gain in knowledge that each individual effort represents is not needlessly dissipated, nor needlessly replicated".

One of the pioneering data banks in education was prepared for Project TALENT (Tiedeman 1972). Other well-known data banks have been associated with the cross-national studies conducted by the International Association for the Evaluation of Educational Achievement (IEA): the IEA Mathematics Data Bank (Wolf 1967) and the IEA Six-subject Data Bank (Schwille and Marshall 1975, Walker 1976). The IEA Six-subject Data Bank, for instance, holds data collected from approximately 250,000 students, 50,000 teachers, and 10,000 schools in 21 countries as part of six international surveys of achievement in science, reading comprehension, literature, civic education, and French and English as foreign languages. In each of the surveys, student achievement data, as well as information about students' home and socioeconomic backgrounds, attitudes, and interests, together with information from teachers and schools, were gathered by testing students age 10 years, 14 years, or in the last year or pre-university year of schooling. The data bank is lodged in data archives in Sweden (Institute of International Education, University of Stockholm) and in the United States (Inter-University Consortium for Political and Social Research, Ann Arbor, Michigan), as well as in other repositories at research centres and universities in Australia, the United Kingdom, Canada, Japan, and New Zealand. The rich IEA data banks have been accessed by research workers from many countries (Postlethwaite and Lewy 1979).

For preparing data for lodgment in a data bank as well as for accessing them once there, the computer is a vital research tool. However, even though physically smaller and ever more powerful computers are constantly being developed, not even today's largest computer could store in its central processing unit (CPU) more than a small fraction of, say, an IEA data bank. A data bank must usually be held in supplementary storage, such as on magnetic disc or tape. Data arranged in data files are stored as small magnetized dots on the iron oxide surface of the disc or tape. Reading heads, reading across the surfaces of a disc (random access) or sequentially through a tape (sequential access), are able to retrieve particular data as requested by users and return these to the CPU. In this way computers permit the storing of vast quantities of data in compact form for subsequent analysis by the research workers who gathered the data originally or by other researchers engaged in secondary analysis of the data.

The establishment of data banks in the social sciences has been paralleled by the development of refined statistical software packages which facilitate the researcher's task of accessing and analysing data. Most computer installations have integrated packages of programs for the management and analyses of social science data: for example, the Statistical Package for the Social Sciences, commonly known as SPSS (Nie et al. 1975), and OSIRIS (Institute for Social Research 1981). The major packages usually have the facility to access data sets prepared by the use of other packages.

2. Data Documentation

Before any use can be made of a particular data set, such as, say, the science survey data set for 10-year-olds in Italy held in the IEA Data Bank, it is necessary to have adequate documentation to enable the data to be interpreted.

The documentation requirements are of two kinds. First, there is general documentation providing information about the study for which the data were collected; and, second, there is specific documentation describing the format or layout of the machine-readable data. The central requirement is the adequacy of the documentation rather than the particular conventions adopted. The total documentation for any data set would normally contain:

(a) identifying information (e.g. title of study, investigator(s), abstract, related publications);

(b) background information (e.g. describing the context within which the study was conducted);

(c) details of design and sampling (of which greater detail may be included in a report cited in the bibliography);

(d) data gathering information (including test instruments and how these were administered); and

(e) information about data organization (e.g. coding of responses and how the response data are stored in the data set).

All or part of this documentation may be located with the data on the computer in machine-readable form. Again, the crucial issue is the availability of this information, rather than how it is stored.

3. Data Organization

In educational research a data set typically comprises measures obtained for a sample of cases. The case, which is the basic unit of analysis, may be some larger unit such as a class of students or a school. Measures might include, for instance, personal characteristics, demographic data, and achievement scores, in which event each case would contain these groups of variables, and the ordering of the variables would be exactly the same for all cases.

When data are being prepared in a form ready for analysis, all variables for each case are organized into a data file. Three steps are involved: coding, entering data, and file building. At the same time a codebook is usually prepared, containing information about the coding scheme adopted for all variables and their location on the data file.

3.1 Coding the Data

In entering data into the computer it is usual to code the information collected for each case by assigning symbols to each item on the completed instrument(s). Alphabetic and special characters are generally to be avoided in coding the data, since the computer is able to process numerical data more efficiently. The practice of using multiple codes for a single item, which would involve making several punches in a single column of a card, should also be avoided since many statistical software packages cannot handle this format.

To illustrate the assigning of symbols to items, respondents' names are often coded 001, 002, 003 . . . while sex might be coded as 1 (male), 2 (female). Coding is thus seen to result in compact storage and, in the case of personal data, helps to preserve confidentiality. Accompanying documentation must clearly indicate the meaning of all assigned codes (though names of respondents or schools are not displayed) and this information is commonly included in a codebook.

For open-ended questionnaire items coding must frequently follow the data collection. An example of an item involving both pre- and post-coding is illustrated in the following:

> Do you speak a language other than English?
> Yes? No?
> If so, which main one? . . . .

Upon examination of responses, a decision may be made to group the languages elicited in the second question: for example, as North European, South European, and Other. Consequently, a single digit could be used to code responses to both questions as follows:

1—English only
2—English and North European
3—English and South European
4—English and other

There are several good texts (e.g. Johnson 1977) that provide details of coding schemes.

Where possible, the coding of the data should preserve the information contained in the original responses, provided that the requirements of anonymity are observed. For example, a variable measuring school size should be coded in terms of the actual enrolments, allowing the investigator or secondary analyst to group the numbers as desired (e.g. less than 600, 601–800, 801–1,000, more than 1,000). Similarly, if the study includes a test, the responses to each test item should be individually coded. Optionally, the data set may contain in addition certain derived scores, such as totals or subscores for groups of items, provided the accompanying documentation details how the derived scores were obtained.

Where respondents fail to answer, or respond "inapplicable" or "don't know", such responses should also be given specific code values. Many of the statistical software packages allow up to three values to be designated as missing and thus it is possible to distinguish between these particular instances of missing data and yet at the same time to process them similarly in any analysis (for example, by excluding all such cases in analyses). If, for instance, two digits have been used to code a given variable, then the following codes could be reserved as missing value codes:

97—Inapplicable
98—Don't know
99—Omitted (or not ascertained)

For some analysis packages, problems may occur if missing responses are represented by blanks or spaces on the data file, instead of by alphanumeric symbols.

3.2 Data Entry and File Building

Once the data are coded, they may then be entered into the computer. This is commonly accomplished by

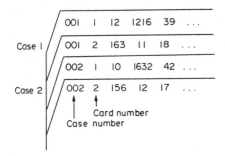

Figure 1
Arrangement for identifying records where each case extends
over two cards

punching the data on to 80-column cards, or by using
response formats that can be optically scanned by a
computer-linked device, or by keying directly via a terminal (key-to-disc). Where there is more than one card
per respondent (or case), it is usual to identify each
record with the case and card number, a useful precau-
tion with cards in the event of dropping them. Suppos-
ing each case extended over two cards, an arrangement
such as that illustrated in Fig. 1 might be used.

The first stage in building a data file is to merge these
cards into a single record, which means that the identification data on each card need to be included once only
on each record. As the cards are merged, a "sort-and-
merge" check is usually made to ensure that the number
of cases in the data file corresponds to the number of
cases in the study and that for each case there is the
same number of cards. Other kinds of checks attempt to
identify the presence of "wild" code values (values
outside the range specified for the variable), resulting
from miskeying or mispunching.

When the originally coded data on the data file are
assembled, and corrected as necessary, a common practice is to create a range of secondary variables from
particular original or primary variables. For example, a
variable to measure socioeconomic level may be a composite formed from variables measuring occupation,
education, and income. The procedures adopted in
forming such secondary variables always need to be
fully documented.

3.3 Preparing the Codebook

The preparation of a codebook is an essential part of
preparing the data file, since the codebook contains
details about the characteristics of each variable and its
location on the file. The following features are included
for each variable in most codebooks:

(a) Variable identification: Each variable is identified
by a number or a set of alphanumeric characters.
For example, the SPSS system uses a set of alphanumeric characters with a maximum length of eight
characters.

(b) Variable name: In general, the variable identification is linked to a variable name or label. Variables
to be used in an analysis are usually selected by

means of the variable identification, while the
printout may give both the variable identification
and the variable name in order to improve
readability.

(c) Location: The location of each variable within a
given record on a data file must be specified in
terms of the numbers of the columns it spans,
which is equivalent to giving the number of the first
column of the entry for the variable and the width
of the entry (the number of columns occupied by
the entry).

(d) Format: The format of the variables should be
specified in terms of the number of decimal places
present or implicit in the data for the variable.

(e) Missing data code(s): Where code values have been
assigned to missing responses, these should be
specified.

(f) Item text: It is also useful to include with each item
the actual text of the item used to solicit the data
for each variable, even if such information is available in accompanying documentation.

(g) Code values: For each variable with a defined set of
code values, the values should be given together
with the responses to which they are assigned.

(h) Notes: It is often useful to add notes providing further information about a variable, especially for
warnings about problems associated with the data
for a given variable.

If the codebook is prepared in machine-readable
form, access to data in a data file and statistical analyses
of the data are greatly facilitated. Computer software is
available for preparing and generating codebooks at
most data archives. Software (written in FORTRAN) is
also available (Anderson 1981) for reading machine-
readable codebooks. This program extracts the information that defines and describes the full data set or any
desired subset of the data, and then, in conjunction with
SPSS, it generates SPSS data-definition control cards.
Output from the program simply requires the insertion
of SPSS task-definition or procedure cards and data
analysis can immediately commence. Because the
codebook is accessed directly, accuracy is ensured in
locating all variables, variable labels, format specifications, missing data values, and value labels. This procedure avoids both the tediousness and susceptibility to
error of the manual assembly of control cards.

*4. Documenting Data Sets for Lodgment in Data
Archives*

The following description of a national study exemplifies the type of documentation necessary for a data set
to be lodged in a data archive. The document was prepared under the kind of cost and time constraints which
normally apply in research studies.

The Second IEA Mathematics Study (Rosier 1980a)
collected information in Australia in 1978 from large

samples of students in two target populations: 13-year-old students and Year 12 mathematics students. Information was also collected from mathematics teachers and school principals. The main report of the study made comparisons between the 1978 data and those collected in 1964 for the First IEA Mathematics Study (Husén 1967, Keeves 1968).

The data files from the IEA data bank for the First IEA Mathematics Study were reorganized to bring them into a form compatible with the files for the Second IEA Mathematics Study. Thus the second study included secondary analysis on the data from the first study. The data from the second study and the reorganized data from the first study were both set up using the OSIRIS system, which includes a machine-readable dictionary linked to the set of data. There were 12 data files altogether: separate files for students, teachers, and schools, for the two population levels, and for the two studies (1964 and 1978).

It was decided to present the documentation describing the data for the second study as a technical report in a microfiche format that could be reproduced by photocopying rather than in a machine-readable format (Rosier 1980b). The microfiche format was more economical in terms of the resources available for the study, and had the additional advantage that copies of administrative documents and the testing instruments could be included in the same volume. In particular, the mathematics test items for this study included diagrams, and so could not have been included in a normal machine-readable format.

The same technical document also included the codebooks for the reorganized data files from the first study, but excluded details of sampling and administration which had been reported earlier. The technical document contained the following sections:

(a) Section 1: Introduction, including reference to the main publications of the study and acknowledgment of the persons associated with its conduct.

(b) Section 2: Sampling of schools and students for each of the two populations.

(c) Section 3: Administrative procedures involved in liaison with education departments, and school coordinators, and in the conduct of the testing in schools.

(d) Section 4: Preparation of data for analysis including coding and punching procedures, and details of the stages following in building the data files for the second study and in reorganizing the data files from the first study.

(e) Appendix 1: Copies of the main administrative documents used in contacting schools and conducting the testing in schools.

(f) Appendix 2: Copies of the testing instruments, including the responses of the first case in each file and the code values assigned to these responses.

(g) Codebooks: The codebook for each of the 12 files contained:
    (i) description of variable types and names,
    (ii) variable list containing coding details for each variable,
    (iii) variable location, and
    (iv) sample data, giving the value for each variable for the first five cases on each file.

5. Access to Data Archives

Major data archives have already been established for the social sciences. The archives collect data sets, often reorganizing the data files and documentation before making them available to other users. The archives also provide a range of services to distribute information about the nature and availability of the data sets, and to assist researchers in accessing them.

Two major archives are the SSRC (Social Science Research Council) Survey Archive, and the Interuniversity Consortium for Political and Social Research (ICPSR). The former is the national repository of social science data in the United Kingdom. Established in 1967, its brief is "to collect and preserve machine-readable data relating to social and economic affairs from academic, commercial, and governmental sources and to make that data available for secondary analysis". This archive is located at the University of Essex, Colchester, Essex CO4 3SQ, England.

The latter archive, the ICPSR, is based at the University of Michigan, and is a major source of archived data sets for universities and other institutions in the United States. The ICPSR also maintains links with universities and national bodies in other countries, such as the SSRC Survey Archive in the United Kingdom, and provides reciprocal borrowing rights. It is located at the Institute for Social Research, University of Michigan, Ann Arbor, Michigan 48106, United States.

The archives produce catalogues describing the data sets that may be borrowed. Researchers normally gain access to the data sets by using the formal channels that have been established between the archives and the institutions participating in the system. Data sets are usually supplied on magnetic tapes according to specified technical formats. Documentation in the form of codebooks and test instruments is usually supplied at a nominal cost.

Two international bodies have been established to promote the development and use of data archives. The International Association of Social Science Information Services and Technology (IASSIST) was established in 1976. The International Federation of Data Organizations (IFDO) was started in 1977.

6. Some Issues

Although much progress has been made in establishing good data archives, more work is needed before the level of data archiving can be regarded as satisfactory. Three issues affect future developments.

6.1 Obtaining Data Sets

One of the major problems faced by archives is the difficulty in obtaining data sets. Even where data sets are identified and located, there may be problems in obtaining them for inclusion in the archives. Some researchers are still wary of releasing their data for examination by other persons. Progress in this area will depend largely on a spirit of cooperation between the original researchers and the secondary analysts. One avenue is to encourage the joint authorship by the primary and secondary researchers of publications arising from secondary analysis. At the least, the original researchers should be offered the opportunity to make rejoinders in publications which include the results of secondary analysis.

Frequently, there are certain conditions governing access to particular data sets. The SSRC Survey Archive, for instance, has three access categories: (a) unconditional access, (b) access conditional on the depositor being informed of the request, and (c) access conditional on the prior consent of the depositor being obtained. The researcher requesting access to archived data is usually required to sign an undertaking to protect the anonymity of individuals and of institutions supplying the data, to acknowledge indebtedness to the original data collectors and to the archive, and to furnish to the archive any publications resulting from use of the data.

Some funding agencies are now making it a condition of their grants that any data collected under the grant should be lodged in appropriate data archives. However, the grants should also be large enough so that the researcher has sufficient resources to build good data sets supported by adequate documentation.

6.2 Adequate Documentation

The usefulness of a data set depends largely on the adequacy of the documentation which describes details of the collection of the data and characteristics of the data. Good documentation is necessary if for no other reason than that it reduces the costs of secondary analysis by increasing the efficiency with which data can be accessed.

For example, good documentation may include a listing of the data for the first few cases on each file. When the secondary analyst first reads an archived file, it is then possible to compare the results from the archived file with the documented listing to ensure that all the data are present, and that the data files correspond to those submitted by the original researcher. In the same way, the codebook entries for each variable should contain a statement about the number of cases (frequency) associated with each code value. The secondary analyst should be able to reproduce these frequencies from the archived data set. As further assistance to the secondary analyst, the set of data collection instruments could be reproduced with the original responses and the associated coding for one case—say, the first case.

6.3 Level of Aggregation of Data

Data are most useful to secondary analysts when they are stored at a minimal level of aggregation (the microlevel). This means that the original responses to questionnaire or test items are retained in a coded form on the data file. The secondary analyst then has the option of changing the level of aggregation, for example by deriving total test scores from a set of test items, or by deriving a mean school score from the data for students in a given school. If only the aggregated data (total or mean scores) are provided, the option of conducting analyses at the individual level is no longer available. Of course, steps must be taken to ensure that access to microlevel data does not enable conditions of anonymity or confidentiality to be breached.

Bibliography

Anderson J 1981 *Machine-readable Codebooks*. Flinders University of South Australia, Adelaide

Husén T (ed.) 1967 *International Study of Achievement in Mathematics: A Comparison of Twelve Countries*. Almqvist and Wiksell, Stockholm

Institute for Social Research 1981 OSIRIS *IV User's Manual*, 7th edn. Institute for Social Research, University of Michigan, Ann Arbor, Michigan

Johnson M C 1977 *A Review of Research Methods in Education*. Rand McNally, Chicago, Illinois

Keeves J P 1968 *Variation in Mathematics Education in Australia*. Australian Council for Educational Research, Hawthorn, Victoria

Nie N H, Hull C H, Jenkins J G, Steinbrenner K, Bent D H 1975 SPSS *Statistical Package for the Social Sciences*, 2nd edn. McGraw-Hill, New York

Postlethwaite T N, Lewy A 1979 *Annotated Bibliography of IEA Publications (1962–1978)*. International Association for the Evaluation of Educational Achievement (IEA), University of Stockholm, Stockholm, Sweden

Rosier M J 1980a *Changes in Secondary School Mathematics in Australia 1964 to 1978*. Australian Council for Educational Research, Hawthorn, Victoria

Rosier M J 1980b *Sampling, Administration and Data Preparation for the Second IEA Mathematics Study in Australia*. Australian Council for Educational Research, Hawthorn, Victoria

Schwille J, Marshall S 1975 *The IEA Six-subject Data Bank: A General Introduction*. University of Stockholm, Stockholm

Tiedeman D V 1972 *Project TALENT Data Bank: A Handbook*. American Institutes for Research, Project TALENT, Palo Alto, California

Walker D A 1976 *The IEA Six-subject Survey: An Empirical Study of Education in Twenty-one Countries*. Almqvist and Wiksell, Stockholm

Wolf R M 1967 *Data Bank Manual: International Project for the Evaluation of Educational Achievement, Phase I: International Study of Achievement in Mathematics: A Comparison of Twelve Countries*. Almqvist and Wiksell, Uppsala

Training of Research Workers in Education

K. Härnqvist

Research training, both generally and in the field of education, has been a minor topic in educational research itself. Most sources of information are of a descriptive or normative kind and little empirical research has explicitly dealt with this advanced level of higher education. This article will focus on training for educational research workers but will try to place it in the broader context of graduate education in general.

An interest in promoting educational research training developed during the 1960s. It was a consequence of the rapid growth of educational research as an instrument for guiding educational policy and practice. Before that, educational research was an activity of largely academic interest and a by-product of the regular system of degree requirements and academic promotions within universities and schools of education. The need for professional educational research workers grew, arising from the establishment of large funds for contract research, specialized research institutes, and research and development centers for various fields of education. In the United States, for instance, the Office of Education supported research training and the American Educational Research Association (AERA) took on a responsibility for promoting training. In Europe, several national education authorities had similar ambitions and the Council of Europe through its Committee for Educational Research worked out recommendations for research training. A background paper for the Council of Europe Committee (Härnqvist 1974) as well as some of the recommendations of a working party form the basis of this article. Where specific references are not given in the following text the reader is referred to that paper for documentation.

The major part of this article deals with research training within the system of advanced academic degrees. In addition, specialized programs for updating or broadening of research skills, and for introducing trained researchers from other fields into the field of education, will be discussed.

1. Graduate Education in General

The main instrument for research training in most countries is the program leading up to a Ph.D. or similar academic degree. This degree usually serves two purposes: the preparation of teachers for higher education and the training of researchers. These two aims may conflict with each other—the former requiring a rather broad coverage of a discipline, the latter requiring specialization and research expertise. In most fields, however, limitations in teaching facilities and labor market prospects make a combination necessary. Already in 1960, Berelson, in an American setting, discussed this conflict and recommended a rather specialized training

in research and scholarship, providing the skilled specialist with a greater depth of knowledge and understanding.

Another trend observed by Berelson (1960) was the growing professionalization at the doctorate level, that is, using the Ph.D. program for increasing and specializing competence in professions outside research and teaching. This meant a trend toward skills and technical expertise at the expense of traditional academic values. At the same time the basic disciplines seemed to have strengthened their impact on professional degrees, such as engineering and medicine.

A third major issue in Berelson's discussion was the place and purpose of the dissertation in the doctoral program. Traditionally the dissertation was supposed to be "an original and significant contribution to knowledge," bearing witness to the student's competence to do independent research. With team research, individual originality had become difficult to evaluate, and the contributions to knowledge had so often been just additions of marginal interest that the fruitfulness of this aim could be questioned. Instead the dissertation could be seen as a training instrument—a start in research and not, as so often had been the case, both the first and the last contribution to knowledge.

These trends and issues in graduate education appeared first on the North-American scene but later on they have, at least in the natural and social sciences, spread to other countries as well. One example is found in the Swedish reforms of doctoral programs implemented in the early 1970s, where graduate courses stressing research methods, and increased guidance for the dissertation, were recommended.

2. Graduate Education in Education

The target groups for doctoral programs in education and related disciplines are the same as those mentioned above: teachers (especially for teacher training), researchers, and professionals in, for instance, educational planning, administration, and evaluation. It is not possible here to give a representative survey of existing programs, but some distinctions of a more principal nature will be made.

The focus of educational research is the educational process which is studied in its different stages: from the goals and systems set by society and the input characteristics of the students, through the teaching–learning situation, to the evaluation of outcomes. The different stages are studied at different levels of complexity or aggregation, and from the perspectives of different disciplines. At a macro level, the stress is laid upon education's role in society and upon the structure and functioning of the educational system in relation to the goals set for it and the resources allocated to it. At a micro level, research deals with the development and characteristics of the individual student as well as the basic conditions of learning. At an intermediate level, the teaching situation is emphasized: curriculum, methods of instruction, social interaction in the teaching–learning situation.

Research at these three levels, which roughly correspond to the operations of planning, learning, and teaching, need to be based on theory, concepts, and methods from several disciplines. At the macro level, for instance, economics, sociology, and systems theory as well as history and philosophy have important contributions to make. At the micro level the main scientific support comes from different branches of psychology. At both these levels it is important that the contributions of the disciplines be integrated within the context of the study of education. At the intermediate level, educational research is building up its own conceptual and methodological framework within a theory of curriculum and teaching. In a way this is the most characteristic contribution proper of educational research and one through which a better integration between macro and micro levels could be achieved.

The multidisciplinary character of educational research and the need for integration within an educational frame-work manifest themselves in different organizational structures in different systems of higher education. In many European countries, education, or pedagogy, is taught as a separate subject both at undergraduate and graduate level, alongside, for instance, psychology and sociology—drawing heavily from these disciplines, from philosophy and history as well, but trying to integrate different kinds of knowledge relevant for education. In American schools of education the disciplines just mentioned, as well as economics, administration, and curriculum, are taught as educational specialities with their own graduate programs and probably with less stress on integration between disciplines than in the European setting. To some extent this difference is a reflection of differences in resources for graduate education—a European professor of education often being expected to teach within a broader field than his or her American colleague—but it may also reflect historical and philosophical differences in outlook. This is not the place to evaluate the merits of one system against the other, but just to make explicit that training for educational research can be found within the degree programs of several disciplines: education (in its integrated approach) as well as educational psychology, educational sociology, and so on.

Also the term research can be given different meanings. A basic line of demarcation exists between different philosophies of science. The dominating tradition, at least in the English-speaking and Scandinavian countries, is an empirical–analytical approach founded on the philosophy of logical empiricism. In fact it has dominated to such an extent that many researchers only recently have become aware of their affiliation. In the countries on the European continent, different

approaches to educational research compete (Malmquist and Grundin 1973). Phenomenology, existentialism, hermeneutics, and Marxism are strong alternatives that have a deep influence both upon "knowledge interests" and methodology. These alternative approaches also seem to be gaining some ground in the "empiricist" countries.

Even within the empirical–analytical tradition, the term research is used with different degrees of strictness—from controlled experimentation and quantitative measurement to naturalistic observations and qualitative analysis of data. This article largely remains within the empirical–analytical tradition but without any special methodological restrictions as regards "hard" or "soft" procedures. The research ideals adhered to correspond to those of "disciplined inquiry" as defined by Cronbach and Suppes (1969). Such inquiry not only comprises empirical studies within the continuum just indicated but also logical and philosophical analyses and historical studies, provided that they display "the raw materials entering the argument and the logical processes by which they are compressed and rearranged to make the conclusion credible" (p. 15).

Finally, before going into more specific questions, it should be stated that the term research as used here refers to both fundamental and applied research, and both conclusion- and decision-oriented research. A research student in education needs preparation for both, and often the distinction is not very clear when it comes to procedures or results even though there is a difference as to where the initiative comes from in a specific study.

3. Two Sets of Recommendations

Writing on behalf of a committee of the United States National Academy of Education, Cronbach and Suppes (1969 pp. 212–13) make the following recommendations for a training program for educational researchers:

(a) full-time study for three consecutive years, preferably at an early age;

(b) training as part of a student group individually and collectively dedicated to research careers;

(c) participation in research, at a steadily advancing level of responsibility, starting in the first year of graduate school if not earlier;

(d) a thorough grounding in at least one academic discipline, together with solid training in whatever technical skills that discipline employs; and

(e) study of the educational process and educational institutions, bringing into a single perspective the social goals of education, the bases on which policy decisions are made, the historical development of the curriculum, the nature of the learners, and other factors.

Another set of recommendations is found in the Council of Europe Committee report (1974 pp. 6–7) where the working party states that the goals of regular research training for education should include:

(a) a thorough knowledge of a discipline, usually one of the social or behavioral sciences;

(b) an integrated understanding of the educational process and of educational institutions, based on historical, philosophical, and comparative considerations;

(c) an understanding of the functions of educational research, acquired against the background of theory and the history of science, and an awareness of alternative methodological approaches;

(d) technical research skills of relevance to education and in line with the research style chosen;

(e) direct experience of carrying out and reporting empirical research within a particular area of the educational sciences; and

(f) skills in communicating with specialists in other disciplines and with educational practitioners.

Many of these goals can be traced back to the Cronbach–Suppes recommendations but there are some interesting additions too. Most important of these is the explicit reference to alternative methodological approaches and research styles—an emphasis that is probably attributable to the fact that six European countries were represented in the working party.

The two sets of recommendations can be compared with the conclusions from an analysis made by Krathwohl (1965) where he distinguished between three different orientations among existing empirically oriented training programs:

(a) a professional education orientation with emphasis on curriculum and teaching and minor importance attached to research methods and own research experience;

(b) a social science orientation with emphasis on a discipline and its research methods as well as on the dissertation research;

(c) a methodology orientation with emphasis on design and mathematical statistics, and research experience in addition to the dissertation.

It seems that both sets of recommendations correspond best with the social science orientation. The intermediate location of this orientation lays stress on the skills of communicating with specialists on both sides as well as with other disciplines and educational practice.

4. Recruitment of Students

Candidates for training in educational research are traditionally recruited from two main groups—those who hold a certificate to teach at primary or secondary level, and those who have acquired a first level university education in the social and behavioral sciences. Some candidates meet both requirements. The proportion coming

to research training from each of these groups varies from country to country. In some countries the teacher intake dominates, and may even be the only one permitted, in other countries the intake from the social and behavioral sciences forms the majority.

The type of recruitment has to do with the organizational structure and the location of resources for doctoral programs. Where the graduate programs in education are located in schools of education and similar institutions, a teacher's certificate and a period of teaching practice often have been a formal requirement for entry to the doctoral program. Where education, or pedagogy, is taught as a social science discipline the intake has been more varied—sometimes even with a predominance of those who have a combination of behavioral science courses and no training or experience in teaching.

In empirical studies in the United States (e.g., Buswell et al. 1966, Sieber and Lazarsfeld 1966) it was observed that the research productivity of postdoctoral researchers coming from schools of education was low. In Buswell's study, the average age on completion of the doctoral studies was 39 years. The average age was nearly 10 years less in many science disciplines. Both the low research productivity and the high age were related to the predominance of experienced teachers in the programs—teachers who started their doctoral studies late and completed them in a situation where family and alternative professional aspirations competed for their time and involvement. Sieber and Lazarsfeld (1966 p. 349) ended up recommending that "the requirement of professional experience or of the teaching certificate for admission to doctoral candidacy in education should be eliminated for students who wish to specialize in empirical research." Such a recommendation is also implicit in the list of Cronbach and Suppes (see Sect. 3).

In the late 1960s, the low research productivity resulting from existing degree programs in education, and the lack of qualified research personnel in spite of great numbers of people with Ph.D.s, led to the establishment under the United States Office of Education of a support program for graduate research training. Selected graduate institutions received extra funds and the graduate students special stipends. Those recruited during the first years of the program differed strongly from the intake in ordinary doctoral programs in education and were more similar to doctoral students in the sciences. Long-term follow-ups of their research productivity will become of great interest.

A development in the opposite direction can be observed in Sweden. During the 1960s, young persons with first degrees in education, psychology, and sociology dominated the intake to graduate programs in education, and many of those now active as professors and researchers in education have this type of background. The introduction of a special degree for professional psychologists during the 1970s, however, led to a decrease in the recruitment from the behavioral sciences. At the same time the possibilities increased for teachers to return to universities for further courses in education.

Now the teacher intake to doctoral programs in education tends to dominate and the age at entry has increased very considerably.

These examples have been reported in order to show how sensitive the recruitment situation is not only to formal entry requirements but also to factors over which the graduate institutions have very little control. Since youth and experience are difficult to combine in one person, it seems that the institutions should strive for a varied intake and adapt their programs individually in order to get the most out of the years of research training. Another conclusion is that those funding educational research must share with the graduate institutions the responsibility for building up the research competence in the field, for instance, through supporting graduate students in their dissertation research and creating positions for postdoctoral research. Otherwise it is not possible for the graduate institutions to compete for competent students, and for research to compete with alternative professional careers.

Economic incentives, however, are not a sufficient means of attracting students to research training. Firstly, for a person not involved in research it is difficult to know what research is like and whether one's own interests and capabilities meet the demands made by graduate studies and dissertation work. Preferably the prospective research students should have some experience of research already at undergraduate level. This may function both as a recruitment incentive and as an instrument for self-selection. In addition, undergraduate research performances would be one of the best selection instruments for admission to graduate school. It is likely that such early research experience is a more normal part of a first degree in social sciences than in teacher education, and therefore it is desirable to introduce such components in teacher education or arrange an intermediate step of this kind between the teacher certificate and admission to doctoral studies. Such intermediate courses are now being built up in Swedish higher education for professional educators who do not have traditional research experience.

Another aspect of the recruitment problem is to make educational research visible among competing fields of research. These opportunities vary with institutional factors. Where education is studied at undergraduate level only in schools of education and teacher training colleges, reaching social science students is a difficult task since it will be highly dependent on the interest for educational matters among teachers and researchers in social science disciplines. In this case it seems necessary to establish organized links between education faculties and undergraduate departments in the social sciences. The situation may look easier where education is studied as a social science subject, but then it has to compete with other disciplines, and the lack of familiarity among the students with the situation in schools and teaching practice may be a hindrance. Therefore research-oriented departments of education need organized contacts with schools and practical teacher education.

5. Degree Programs

The highest university degree in most countries, the doctorate, normally includes research. The programs for this degree vary considerably in length and organization. In many countries there exist intermediate research degrees requiring from one to three years of full-time study after the first university degree. Examples of such intermediate degrees are Masters in English-speaking countries, "*Maitrise*" in France, and "Candidate" in the Soviet Union. Germany has doctorates at two levels, Dr.Phil. and "*Habilitation.*" Where the intermediate degree requires several years of study, for instance in the Soviet Union (three years), course work is often concentrated at this level (in addition to a short thesis), and the only further requirement for the doctorate is research reported in a dissertation. This was the case also in the earlier system in Sweden with a "Licentiate" followed by a doctorate—a system which around 1970 was succeeded by a new doctoral program including both course work and dissertation.

The Soviet "Candidate" degree is regarded as the normal research degree and a rather small proportion of the candidates continue to the doctor's degree. In general, however, the shorter programs are less prestigious and particularly so when the intermediate degree gets a reputation for being used as a "consolation prize" for interrupted doctoral studies. In the American system of graduate education the Master's degree exists but seems to have no independent function in a research career. Most researchers take a four-year program for the doctor's degree. On the other hand, in the field of education there exist two doctor's degrees—the doctor of philosophy (Ph.D.) in education or subdisciplines, and the doctor of education (Ed.D.). In general the Ph.D. is more research oriented and the Ed.D. more professionally oriented but the variation between graduate schools is great.

Ideally, research training covers the three to five years that follow upon the successful completion of a first university degree, but since a great proportion of the doctoral candidates do not start directly after their first degree, and often teach or do professional work during their studies, the time lapse between the degrees tends to become at least twice as long as the ideal. Attempts have been made to reduce this interval and to produce postdoctoral researchers at an earlier age. This is important not least for their future research productivity. Five main remedies have been tried: organizing graduate studies in courses, providing more research supervision, cutting down the size of the dissertations, simplifying the procedures of publication, and providing economic support in order to get more full-time graduate students. In the Swedish reform just mentioned, all these measures were tried but so far with only moderate success.

The regular university programs in education have been criticized not only for producing graduates who are too old and not very research productive, but also for not having adapted themselves to the needs of large-scale research efforts, particularly of an inter-disciplinary character. It is maintained that admission and degree requirements tend to be too rigid and too much influenced by intradisciplinary value systems. Minor research problems with high security are preferred to those that are socially important but involve a high risk. The training takes place in isolation from other disciplines and the field of application.

There is certainly a good deal of truth in this criticism. The stress on regular university programs in this article, on the other hand, stems from two convictions. One is that educational research is such a difficult and expensive enterprise that it must be based on a thorough grounding in basic disciplines and methodology, which cannot be achieved just through a few research courses or through apprenticeship without the guidance of a basic training program. The other conviction is that unversities, in general, are flexible organizations with great potentials for adaptation and change in contents and methods, even if their freedom and flexibility now and then seem to be used for rigid decisions. This risk follows from the autonomy with which they have been granted and which is good for other purposes. According to these convictions it is better to adjust the regular programs to forthcoming needs than to set up basic training programs outside a degree system—a situation which is common to most disciplines and professional fields. Not least the competition for good graduate students calls for such a strategy.

The recommendations quoted in Sect. 3 outlined the main components of a program for research training. More specific requirements have been formulated by an AERA Task Force on Research Training and synthesized by Worthen (1975) in a list of 25 general tasks which researchers and/or evaluators frequently must perform. For most of the tasks, competencies necessary to perform the task were also identified. It would take too much space to list the tasks and competencies in this article, but a few remarks on their general character will be made.

The tasks are listed in a sequence from the search for information on earlier research and formulation of a research problem, through design, instrumentation, and data collection, to analysis, interpretation, and reporting. The competencies involved are important especially for empirical behavioral science research of a quantitative and statistical type although some of them, especially in the beginning and the end of the sequence, are of a more general nature. One could see the list as a syllabus for a rather extensive methodology course in the logical empirical tradition within a social science oriented doctoral program. It is, on the other hand, weak on alternative methodological approaches and metascientific background. By definition it does not cover the substantive content of a discipline, nor the broader educational context of the research.

In addition to typical research tasks, the list also comprises tasks that are specific for educational evaluation. This is in line with the fact that evaluation is one of the most important professional specializations for persons with a research training in education. It also fits the training recommendations in a recent book on program evaluation (Cronbach et al. 1980). The authors prefer the doctoral preparation in a social science discipline to specialized programs for evaluation without a disciplinary base.

> Doctoral training in a discipline can be counted on to emphasize competence in research design, data analysis, procedures for collecting data, and tough-minded interpretation. Whatever coloration a particular discipline gives to these topics, thorough training gives a critical perspective that is invaluable in looking at plans and results of evaluations. (Cronbach et al. 1980 p. 344)

The specialization in evaluation then comes through interdisciplinary evaluation seminars, apprenticeship to practicing evaluators, and internship in an agency where policy is formulated.

A specialization which is more difficult to achieve within a social science oriented program is that of curriculum and teaching methods in nonelementary subject matter areas, for instance, natural sciences and foreign languages. Research with such orientations requires rather advanced subject matter competence in addition to training for empirical educational research. It is not very likely that a social science oriented postdoctoral researcher will continue with graduate studies in a subject matter area. It may be easier for a subject matter teacher to go in the other direction but this also tends to take too much time to be attractive. A program that comprises about one year of graduate courses in a subject matter discipline, for example, physics, one year of methodology- and education-oriented courses, and two years of dissertation research is being tried in Sweden, but it is still too early to evaluate its contributions to research on curriculum and teaching in special subjects.

6. Methods and Institutional Arrangements

The trend in the direction of more organized course work at graduate level should not mean substituting conventional lecturing for the independent study that has predominated. But the expectations put on the candidates may become more clearly defined and their studies organized in such a way that they can complete the degree requirements within more reasonable time limits. The methods of instruction, on the other hand, must vary with the goals and contents. In some technical parts, lecturing in combination with exercises would be well-adapted to the situation. In others, independent reading followed by seminars or small-group discussions are more appropriate.

The examination procedures, too, should be adjusted to the level of the candidates. Written reports based on the literature can be substituted for conventional questioning. These reports could also be used as exercises in concise writing which is a skill that seems to be lacking even among high-level students in many countries. Then it is important that the candidates receive feedback not only on content but also on format and style.

The main instrument for research training is active participation in research in all its phases. Even when regarded as a training instrument, the dissertation still is the central and most exacting requirement for a research degree. The facetious American expression A.B.D. (all but dissertation) indicates a threatening reality for many doctoral candidates. Very often a failure is generated already in the initial phase of the dissertation work where much time and attention must be given to the finding and formulation of the research problem.

Research supervision involves a delicate balance between support from the side of the supervisor and freedom on the side of the research candidate. The optimal relation varies from case to case but in general a nonauthoritarian and nonpatriarchal relation is preferable where the candidate is treated as a fellow researcher and not as a student. Sometimes emotional support can be as important as intellectual. Under favorable circumstances, the research supervisor may continue to function as a mentor for the new doctoral researcher—become a role model, giving academic advice and assistance in gaining access to the profession (Blackburn et al. 1981).

One of the most relevant influences in research training is to have the candidates work in a research-oriented setting—that is, in an institution where good research is done and a favorable research climate created—with fellow students also dedicated to research. Learning from models cannot be replaced by methodology courses. An ideal setting would be an apprenticeship in a research group under the guidance of an experienced researcher and working side by side with fellow students—this in turn would be complemented by courses and seminars where methodological and substantive problems can be treated in a more systematic way than with apprenticeship only. The institution within which the research group is located should preferably be big and varied enough to afford communication with groups in other specializations so that the perspective does not become too narrow (Kaplan 1964 p. 865).

7. Specialized Courses

So far, this article has focused on the regular degree system. Research training, however, is a continual process which does not end with a doctorate. Most of the postdoctoral training is integrated into continued research, but is has to be supplemented now and then with specialized courses.

The AERA Task Force on Research Training identified four objectives for a future inservice training program (Sanders et al. 1970):

(a) upgrade the skills of researchers who are now poorly trained;

(b) maintain the high level of competence of researchers now entering the field;

(c) teach new skills made necessary by innovations in educational techniques and products; and

(d) broaden the base of personnel engaged in activities calling for the application of educational research skills.

The group also mentioned several "vehicles" for an expanding training program, for instance, courses arranged in connection with the AERA annual conventions (presession courses), summer institutes, conferences and workshops, and development of instructional materials. Some examples from the presession programs of the last few years are given below.

(a) Cost analysis in educational evaluation

(b) Item response theory: concepts, tools, and applications

(c) Recent advances in criterion-referenced measurement

(d) Quality control of instruction and instructional development

(e) Meta-analysis of empirical research

(f) Cumulating results across studies

(g) Discriminant analysis in behavioral research

(h) Information technology and the educational researcher

(i) Educational criticism: naturalistic, qualitative, and related modes of inquiry

(j) The analysis of qualitative data: an introduction to log-linear analysis

(k) Statistical quality control: a research and evaluation tool

(l) The study of educational policy and politics

Another instrument is a series of tape recordings and study guides assembled under the title "Alternative methodologies in educational research."

In Europe several summer Seminars on Learning and the Educational Process (SOLEP), partly staffed with American researchers, were given around 1970, with support from UNESCO and different national foundations. Young researchers from many different countries spent several weeks together discussing research problems and methods. In addition to upgrading research competence, the seminars contributed to the formation of personal contacts among the present generation of researchers—"invisible colleges" which are so important for the infrastructure of a discipline. On the international level also, research projects like the comparative studies organized by the International Association for the Evaluation of Educational Achievement (IEA) have had most important functions in research training and the development of networks among educational researchers.

The Council of Europe Committee on Educational Research arranged during the 1970s symposia for researchers and practitioners in specialized fields, for instance, preschool education, teacher education, innovation and change in higher education. Similar activities have been initiated by UNESCO, the Organisation for Economic Co-operation and Development (OECD), and other international organizations. Education has been represented also in the postdoctoral program of research courses run by the Nordic countries in cooperation. In general, however, it seems that the international arrangements decreased during the late 1970s, perhaps as a consequence of a less affluent situation for educational research than a decade earlier.

Another target group for specialized courses are trained researchers from other fields that enter research in the field of education as partners in interdisciplinary projects or subject-matter experts. Some of them may come from the behavioral sciences, having completed their doctorates in areas within their own disciplines not related to education, for example, psychologists, sociologists, anthropologists, and child psychiatrists. Others may come from linguistics, statistics, economics, political science, philosophy, history, and so on. In all these cases they bring the methodology of their disciplines with them to be used for educational problems, but they need an introduction to the special perspectives of educational study, and they are in need of courses in empirical social science methodology.

See also: Research Needs and Priorities

Bibliography

Berelson B 1960 *Graduate Education in the United States.* McGraw Hill, New York

Blackburn R T, Chapman D W, Cameron S M 1981 Cloning in academe: Mentorship and academic careers. *Res. Higher Educ.* 15: 315–27

Buswell G T, McConnell T R, Heiss A M, Knoell D M 1966 *Training for Educational Research.* Center for Research and Development in Higher Education, Berkeley, California

Council of Europe 1974 *Report on the Training and Career Structures of Educational Researchers.* Council of Europe, Strasbourg

Cronbach L J, Suppes P (eds.) 1969 *Research for Tomorrows' Schools: Disciplined Inquiry for Education: Report.* Macmillan, London

Cronbach L J et al. 1980 *Toward Reform of Program Evaluation.* Jossey-Bass, San Francisco, California

Härnqvist K 1974 The training and career structures of educational researchers. In: Council of Europe 1974

Kaplan N 1964 Sociology of science. In: Faris A E L (ed.) 1964 *Handbook of Modern Sociology.* Rand McNally, Chicago, Illinois, pp. 852–81

Krathwohl D R 1965 Current formal patterns of educating empirically oriented researchers and methodologists. In: Guba E G, Elam S (eds.) 1965 *The Training and Nurture of Educational Researchers.* 6th Annual Phi Delta Kappa symposium on educational research. Phi Delta Kappa, Bloomington, Indiana

Malmquist E, Grundin H U 1973 *Educational Research in Europe Today and Tomorrow.* Gleerup, Lund

Sanders J R, Byers M L, Hanna G E 1970 A survey of training programs of selected professional organizations. *AERA Task Force on Training.* Technical Paper no. 11. AERA, Washington, DC

Sieber S D, Lazarsfeld P F 1966 *The Organization of Educational Research in the United States.* Bureau of Applied Research, Columbia University, New York

Worthen B R 1975 Competencies for educational research and evaluation. *Educ. Res. AERA.* 4: 13–6

Section 3

Measurement
for
Educational Research

Section 3

Measurement
for
Educational Research

Introduction

The Improvement of Measurement
for Educational Research

The issues confronting educational research commonly involve the investigation of constancy and change in the characteristics of individuals and social groups. From the early years of educational research, marked by studies and systematic investigation in the field of education in the late nineteenth century by Sir Francis Galton in his *Inquiry into Human Faculty and its Development* (1883) and by Stanley Hall in *The Study of Children* (1883), there has been interest in questions of growth and development. It was perhaps inevitable that the initial work in the area of psychometrics and educational measurement which was carried out during the first decade of the twentieth century should take a relatively static view of the study of individual differences. However, at a later stage the behaviourist approach developed and there was greater interest in the processes of learning. As studies were undertaken into the problems of the measurement of change, which was essential if the extent of learning was to be recorded with accuracy and if development was to be described with precision, the difficulties associated with measuring change were gradually appreciated. Two major problems were encountered. First, there was the question of defining a scale with properties that would enable measurements to be recorded across the range of development or the extent of learning, so that the differences between the two values on different sections of the scale that were necessary to measure change were equivalent. Second, there were problems associated with the presence of sizeable errors of measurement.

1. The Three Theories of Measurement

In 1905, Binet and Simon published the report of their initial scale for the assessment of intelligence. At approximately the same time Spearman published his model for test scores that laid the foundations of classical test theory. This theory, with its concepts of "true score", "measurement error", and an index of "test reliability" dominated the field of educational and psychological measurement for approximately 50 years. In time, a substantial body of statistical theory and related computational techniques was assembled and articles on *True-score Models, Scaling Methods, Reliability,* and *Validity* give an account of current knowledge and understanding of educational measurement from this perspective. Nonetheless, two major issues emerge as significant problems. The first involved the estimation of the contributions of different sources of error to the total error variance associated with the use of a test. The second was related to the selection of items that were included in a particular version of a test. Although parallel forms were developed for many tests, in general the selection of items was left to the judgment of the research workers who developed a particular instrument.

Gradually, two other competing theoretical approaches to educational and psychological measurement have evolved. These measurement models have become known as the *random sampling model* and the *latent trait model.* Bejar (1983) has compared the random sampling and the latent trait approaches to measurement. The random sampling model is clearly oriented towards the obtaining of a total score, whereas the latent trait model is more concerned with assessing level of performance on particular items. This leads to differences in definition of the content being tested. In the former case there is assumed to be a pool of homogeneous items from which a sample can be drawn. Alternatively, it is possible to stratify items by type or content into a hierarchy of levels of difficulty from which sampling can occur. In the latter case, it is necessary to assume that the items occupy a place along the latent trait continuum that is invariate across the groups of students to whom an instrument is given.

A further important difference between random sampling models and latent trait models is that in the former the estimates of errors of measurement and the reliability of a test apply to the instrument as a whole. However, in latent trait measurement it is possible to assign an estimate of error at each level of the continuum. One adjustment for error, which involves a correction for guessing, is applied in norm-referenced assessment, but this correction underestimates the extent to which an allowance might be made for guessing. In random sampling theory and criterion-referenced assessment an adjustment can be employed both for guessing and for carelessness using Bayesian procedures, but necessarily this applies to the test as a whole and not to individual items (Morgan 1979). However, in latent trait measurement models an allowance is made for guessing with respect to each individual item, if the three parameter logistic model is employed.

2. Towards Improving Measurement

There are three major advantages that the use of latent trait measurement models has over the use of classical test theory and random sampling models. First, latent trait models record the performance of a student in a group on a continuum that has the properties of an interval scale. Using such a scale with a well-defined metric there is the potential to measure growth and change or stability in performance in a way that has not previously been possible. Since the magnitude of the errors of measurement are obtained in latent trait measurement at each point on the scale, it is possible to calculate with accuracy the errors associated with each score. Furthermore, the effects of a threshold or a ceiling which commonly contaminate measurement with norm-referenced or criterion-referenced tests are eliminated by the nature of the latent trait scale, provided that this scale has been accurately calibrated across the range over which it is employed. Certain problems are encountered if the latent trait scale does not remain invariate over the populations being investigated. However, the capability exists to define scales that have properties of invariance as well as to use multiple criteria. Insufficient work has been carried out into the use of such scales to determine the limitations imposed on the research questions that can meaningfully be investigated, such as the robustness of scales measuring educational achievement in contrast to tightly defined cognitive abilities, and the validity of the results obtained under different circumstances.

The second advantage of latent trait measurement models is the capacity to apply these models to the measurement along an interval scale of attitudes, to essay marking, and in open-ended testing situations where partial credit can be assigned to a response. These approaches to measurement have not been extensively applied in major research studies and the strength of the procedures has again not been fully assessed. A third advantage of latent trait measurement procedures lies in the proven ability to use them effectively and efficiently in tailoring a test to assess the performance of an individual person without depending on a reference group. The article on *Adaptive Testing* discusses this important application of latent trait measurement.

It is becoming apparent that these new approaches to educational and psychological measurement, namely the random sampling model and the latent trait model, have the potential to improve and possibly to transform educational research and the assessment of educational outcomes. The random sampling model has been described in articles on *Generalizability Theory* and *Criterion-referenced Measurement*. The latent trait model is presented in a series of articles, namely, *Item Response Theory*, *Latent Trait Measurement Models*, *Rasch Measurement Models*, *Partial Credit Model*, *Rating Scale Analysis* and *Sufficient Statistics in Educational Measurement*. The historical development of educational and psychological measurement is provided by the articles on *Measurement in Educational Research*, *History of Mental Testing*, *Scaling of Nominal Data*, and *Thurstone Scales*.

3. Achievement Testing and Attitude Measurement

In this *International Handbook* consideration is given to the application of the three theories to the tasks of achievement testing and attitude measurement. The use of the principles of educational measurement occurs most extensively in the area of achievement testing, and it has been the success of work in this area that has supported, in the main, the recent advances in educational measurement. Many of the articles concerned with achievement testing relate to all three models, namely, *Taxonomies of Educational Objectives*, *Objective Tests*, *Item Writing Techniques*, *Test Bias*, *Item Bias*, and *Scaling of Achievement Test Scores*. The articles on *Norm-referenced Assessment*, *Item Analysis*, and *Reliability of Test Results* are related more specifically to classical test theory. The articles on *Criterion-referenced Tests*, and *Domain-referenced Tests* are linked more closely to random sampling theory, while the article on *Adaptive Testing* is associated with developments in latent trait theory.

The measurement of attitudes is of growing importance both in educational research and practice and several articles provide accounts of different approaches to attitude measurement. Following a general introductory article on *Attitudes and their Measurement* there are articles on more specific aspects of this area, namely, *Likert Scales*, *Guttman Scales*, *Semantic Differential*, and *Projective Testing Techniques*.

4. Other Applications of Educational Measurement

In the fourth collection of articles in this section a wide variety of applications of measurement principles are considered in a range of practical situations. Several articles are concerned with the measurement of both classroom climate and classroom behaviour, namely, *Environmental Measures*, *Classroom Observation Techniques*, *Structured Observation Techniques*, and *Video Recording in Educational Research*. Two articles consider in detail the measurement of characteristics of the home, *Measurement of Social Background* and *Environmental Measures*. Articles are provided on some different procedures that are widely used in educational research, namely, *Interviews in Sample Surveys*, *Questionnaires*, *Rating Scales*, and the *Repertory Grid Technique*. Information on *Census Data and Statistics* and *Educational Indicators* is presented in articles under these titles. In addition, consideration is given to three important issues in educational and psychological measurement in articles on *Models of Intelligence*, *Sex Differences in Ability and Achievement*, and *Unintended Effects in Educational Research*.

5. Assessment, Evaluation, and Measurement

The three topics of assessment, evaluation, and measurement are treated in numerous articles throughout this *International Handbook*. It is important to recognize that, in the main, these topics are interpreted separately and differently. As a consequence it is necessary to draw as clear distinctions as possible between the three different terms and to provide some guidance as to where to look for a treatment of a particular problem or issue.

In the minds of many educational practitioners the words *assessment, evaluation, measurement*, and *testing* appear to be used interchangeably. What assessment, evaluation, and measurement have in common is testing. Each frequently, but not always, makes use of tests. Nevertheless, none of these three terms is synonymous with testing, and the types of tests required for each of the three processes may be very different. The three processes are considered in turn below in reverse order.

5.1 Measurement

The regular dictionary definition of "assigning a numerical quantity to..." will serve in most applications of educational measurement. While instruments such as rulers and stopwatches can be used directly to determine height and speed, many characteristics of educational interest must be measured indirectly. Thus ability tests are typically used to measure such characteristics as intelligence, and achievement tests are used to measure the amount of material learned or forgotten. It will be apparent that measurement is not undertaken for its own sake; it is a useful operation in the process of evaluation, or for a research study, or as part of the tasks of assessment.

5.2 Evaluation

In general, the use of the term *educational evaluation* is reserved for application to abstract entities such as programmes, curricula, and organizational situations. Its use implies a general weighing of the value or worth of something. Evaluation commonly involves making comparisons with a standard, or against criteria derived from stated objectives, or with other programmes, curricula, or organizational schemes. Evaluation is primarily an activity involved in research and development. It may require the measurement of educational outcomes, and it may involve the testing of both individuals and groups. Its potential importance in the improvement of educational practice is widely recognized, but fierce controversy surrounds the issue of the methods which should be used.

5.3 Assessment

As far as is possible, the term *assessment* should be reserved for application to people. It may include the use of testing procedures, or it may simply involve activities of grading or classifying according to some specified criteria. Student achievement on a particular course may be assessed, or students' attitudes towards particular aspects of their schooling may be assessed. Such assessments are commonly based on an informal synthesis of a wide variety of evidence, although they may include the use of test results, or responses to attitude scales and questionnaires. Attention is being given increasingly to improving the quality of assessment and with this end in view the principles of educational measurement theory are increasingly being applied to achievement testing and attitude measurement. Articles listed under the headings of *Achievement Testing* and *Attitude Measurement* in this section of the *International Handbook* provide an account of these developments. However, it is unfortunate that the term *student evaluation* is now being widely used as a consequence of the growing emphasis on evaluation of educational programmes, and the financial assistance available for such work.

6. Future Developments

The advent of the electronic computer has greatly increased the use that can be made of quantified information and has led directly to the development of both the random sampling and the latent trait models. In addition, it has provided a means by which the use of classical test theory can be greatly extended in practice. As a consequence there has been remarkable progress in the field of educational measurement during the 25-year period from 1960 to 1985. Moreover, there is little sign that these developments will cease, as powerful microcomputers become readily accessible not only in the research institute but also in the school and classroom.

Carroll in the leading article of this section of the *International Handbook* on *Future Developments in Educational Measurement* states that: "Educational measurement is concerned basically with the devising and construction of *variables* that may be useful in education—in educational research and/or in practical actions such as selection and guidance of students and the diagnosis and appraisal of student learning."

The ready availability of microcomputers will greatly facilitate the use of the processes of educational measurement in practice, and will almost certainly make such processes more personalized and more flexible. These opportunities for innovation and change are likely to provide a stimulus for the development of new theories as well as the development of new procedures. Carroll's article provides important perspectives on the developments that are likely to emerge in the future. Several articles that address these issues can also be found in issue 21(4) of the *Journal of Educational Measurement* that appeared in late 1984 (pp. 313–406).

The impact of future developments in educational measurement for educational research has also been addressed by Carroll, and it is evident that many problems that have in the past proved to be intractable are likely to yield valuable findings with improved measurement procedures where data are recorded on an interval scale. The opportunities that lie ahead appear to be concerned with the use of the measurement models that are available for studies of learning and the development of human characteristics. Latent trait models, in particular, seem to have the potential to advance inquiry where measures of change are needed. The study by Wilson (1985) is an excellent example of such possibilities, and the years ahead should be both challenging and exciting in this respect.

Bibliography

Bejar I I 1983 *Achievement Testing: Recent Advances*, Sage University Paper series on Quantitative Applications in the Social Sciences, series No. 07-036. Sage Publications, Beverly Hills, California and London

Morgan G 1979 *A Criterion-referenced Measurement Model with Corrections for Guessing and Carelessness*. Australian Council for Educational Research (ACER), Hawthorn, Victoria

Wilson M 1985 *Measuring Stages of Growth: A Psychometric Model of Hierarchical Development*. Australian Council for Educational Research (ACER), Hawthorn, Victoria

Measurement Theory

Future Developments in Educational Measurement

J. B. Carroll

It would be presumptuous to try to predict the precise way in which the field of educational measurement will evolve over the next few decades. This article attempts only to comment on likely developments, and to indicate what developments might be most desirable, in view of advances that have occurred in the last decade.

Educational measurement is concerned basically with the devising and construction of variables that may be useful in education—in educational research and/or in practical actions such as selection and guidance of students and the diagnosis and appraisal of student learning. The scientific aspects of educational measurement pertain to assessing the characteristics of those variables in respect to their accuracy and faithfulness to the intentions of their creators or, in somewhat more technical terms, in respect to their reliability and validity. Examples of variables are scores of psychological and educational tests; ratings of behavior, performance, or learning by teachers or observers; measures of socioeconomic status or home background; and quantitative evaluations of schools or social settings. Over the years, educational measurement science has progressed toward ever more precise ways of establishing and assessing such variables. The trend has been toward better linking variables with appropriate statistical, mathematical, and psychological theories to support them. The future will probably see further strengthening of these linkages.

Educational measurement comprises a number of relatively separate and, in some cases, highly specialized fields. This article will survey these fields chiefly from the standpoint of their possible future development. It will not go into much detail or cite many references, since details and references are covered in separate articles in this volume.

1. Constructing Variables

A broad distinction can be made between variables that arise from single observations or judgments and variables that arise from some kind of compositing of multiple observations or judgments that are not necessarily equivalent. Examples of the former are ratings, such as teacher's grades or observers' ratings of learning ability, and measurements of single attributes like height and weight. Examples of the latter are test scores that are a weighted sum of scores assigned to single items or tasks that compose a test, the single items being not necessarily equivalent in difficulty, reliability, or validity. Note, however, that *after* a variable of the second type has been established through appropriate techniques, it becomes a variable of the first kind, amenable to study by various techniques of classical test theory. The distinction is made in order to contrast applications of classical test theory with applications of item response theory.

Many aspects of classical test theory will continue to pertain to the former type of measurement. Concepts of reliability and validity, true and error scores, and parallelism of equivalent measure will continue to be applicable to these types of variables. It would be a mistake to abandon the fundamental principles and techniques of classical test theory, because they are the only principles and techniques that are applicable to variables that arise from single observations or judgments. Note that a single variable can be of this kind, even though it can be matched by other variables of the same kind. For example, even though the measurement of height comes from a single observation, one could be concerned with the reliability of such measurements by obtaining similar measures on multiple occasions and performing appropriate statistical procedures on them.

In this realm, one can foresee the further development and application of generalizability theory, concerned with the degree to which measurement errors can be identified as attributable to different sources (Brennan 1983). For example, the reliability of teachers' ratings of essays can be studied as a function of teacher, student, essay, subject matter, etc. A difficulty is that multifaceted studies of this type tend to become large and unwieldy if conducted according to presently available procedures. Whether it would be possible to overcome these difficulties is unclear, but it would in any case be desirable to conduct generalizability studies on many types of variables.

Issues concerning reliability and construct validity can now easily be addressed with linear structural relationships analysis (LISREL) modeling applied to multitrait–multimethod data, in order to determine the relative variances due to traits and to particular methods of measuring those traits (Marsh and Hocevar 1983,

Schmitt and Stults 1986). This procedure should be applied to a wide variety of educationally important variables.

2. Item Response Theory

Undoubtedly the most striking development of the past several decades in educational measurement has been the establishment and elaboration of what has become known as "item response theory" (IRT), closely related to latent trait measurement models. It is important to notice that these theories and models apply to variables of the second kind noted above, that is, to variables that arise from multiple measurements that are not necessarily equivalent. In the usual case, these measurements are responses to a series of test items or tasks that are not necessarily equivalent in difficulty or validity in measuring the presumed underlying trait or traits. The basic idea of these theories and models is that from a set of observed responses to a set of items it is possible to derive measures or estimates of the underlying trait or traits that have superior measurement and interpretive properties as compared to, say, an unweighted sum of the item scores. Item response theory is essentially a theory of the relation between item response and an underlying trait. Usually, the underlying trait is assumed to be an "ability" of some kind, that is, a property of the person such that there is a systematic relation between the ability levels of different individuals and their probabilities of "passing" or correctly responding to different items.

Actually, such a theory was assumed from the earliest days of the history of educational measurement (Carroll 1987). In the 1930s and 1940s, it was generally assumed that the relation between ability and item response could be well-described by a normal ogive model; the implications of this model were not fully followed up in detail because of the apparent intractability of the mathematics required by this model. Present-day item response theory has been developed mainly on the basis of a more mathematically tractable model, namely the logistic function, which gives results closely similar to those from the normal ogive model. IRT admits several alternative models based on the logistic function, differing mainly in the number of parameters that are required to describe the function. In frequent use are the one-parameter "Rasch" model, that specifies only the position of an item on a difficulty scale, and the three-parameter model that specifies position, slope, and "guessing" parameters for each item.

Item response theory can be successfully applied only for what has been called "serious testing," that is, to multi-item tests and examinations that are intended to be, or have been, applied to hundreds or even many thousands of examinees. For example, Educational Testing Service has used IRT in an interesting way to develop a so-called Reading Proficiency Scale on the basis of matrix-sampled test responses from thousands of persons tested at various ages in a national assessment of reading comprehension ability (National Assessment of Educational Progress/Educational Testing Service 1985). Educational Testing Service, like many other testing organizations, regularly uses IRT in compositing and equating various types of aptitude and achievement examinations. Undoubtedly the future will see many more uses of IRT for these purposes.

A further motive for the development and use of IRT has been the need and possibility of so-called "adaptive testing", also called "tailored testing", that is, testing that is conducted in such a way that items or tasks administered at any point in the testing can depend upon the individual's responses to previous items. Adaptive testing is nothing new in educational measurement; a simple form of it occurs in the administration of individual tests like the Stanford–Binet, where the particular tasks administered to the individual depend upon the examiner's initial impression of the subject's ability and upon the individual's success in passing progressively more difficult items. IRT makes it possible, however, to select items for presentation that, in the light of the individual's total pattern of responses up to any given point, will maximize the reliability of the score and at the same time minimize the number of items that have to be presented to arrive at a sufficiently reliable score. Such use of IRT normally requires extensive computations throughout the testing, but with the increasing availability of computer terminals and personal microcomputers, it is certain that adaptive testing will make its way into many testing situations. For example, the United States armed forces are presently making serious studies of the possibilities of using computerized adaptive testing in a wide variety of selection and training functions (Green et al. 1984).

Nevertheless, there are many difficult and worrisome aspects of IRT and related theories. The state of the art has not reached anything like a completely satisfactory condition, although there is now a tremendous amount of activity and research. The chief difficulty centers in problems of estimating item and ability parameters. Classical maximum likelihood procedures require large data sets and extensive computations, with results that are sometimes unreliable or even meaningless. Various other procedures and algorithms are being investigated; Bock (1985) proposes that Bayesian estimation procedures are likely to give the best results. A related difficulty concerns the choice of IRT models. Generally, the more parameters in the model (e.g., three as opposed to two or even just one), the more difficult the problems of estimation and computation become. A particular problem has to do with models that assume a "guessing" parameter, i.e., a parameter that specifies the probability of correct response from an individual with (theoretically) infinitely low ability, who can often make a correct response by "guessing." It seems that this parameter is critically necessary for analyzing sets of multiple-choice items such as are very often employed in tests. There is a further problem connected with this, incidentally, namely that some item response curves show "valleys" or "troughs," there being some individuals who are likely to respond less correctly than they would by chance, since they are unduly attracted to incorrect alternatives. Researchers are now working on models to take care of this problem (Thissen 1986). It would seem important to do this because multiple-choice distractors are often written with the deliberate purpose of misleading persons of low ability.

There is a set of further problems with IRT that urgently call for solutions. Simple item response theory assumes that there is a single dimension of "ability" that underlies performance on a test. This assumption may be reasonable enough in the case of certain kinds of tests, for example, tests of verbal ability, reading comprehension ability, or spatial ability. (One application of IRT is to determine which items best measure the single underlying ability, and to eliminate the items that measure it poorly or not at all, thus reducing the dimensionality of the test.) Unidimensionality may not be a reasonable assumption in the case of certain types of achievement tests, where in a sense each item may measure a separate ability—an ability unique or specific to itself. IRT procedures tend not to work well in such cases. There is need for alternative procedures to deal with these cases, or at least a need for procedures to indicate when all is not well.

Dimensionality is a multifaceted problem. It has long been known that factor-analytic procedures, often employed to investigate dimensionality, are at best problematic when they are applied to binary or dichotomous data. Test items scored either 0 or 1 depending on correctness of response are perfect examples of such data, and cause difficulties in factor analysis, particularly if there is a chance guessing factor, as is usually the case with multiple-choice items, or if there are many "omit" responses. Recent developments, under the heading of what is called "full-information factor analysis" (Muraki and Engelhard 1985), appear to have surmounted many of these difficulties, but further exploration and testing of these procedures in a variety of situations should command a high priority.

Another aspect of dimensionality is this: in using the common factor model with binary data, one has to assume that each item score is a function of one or more dimensions of ability; regression weights or factor loadings would indicate the extent to which each ability affects item response, for every individual. But this model ignores at least two possibilities: (a) that the weights are different for different individuals, depending upon their strategies of item solution, and (b) that the ways in which abilities affect item response cannot be described by a linear model. (The first of these possibilities, of course, represents a limitation of factor analysis even when applied to nonbinary variables.) For example, it could be that in order to be successful in passing an item, an examinee would have to be above a certain critical point on each of two or more abilities. Solutions to these difficulties are much to be sought; possibly, they will arise from current work on multicomponent latent trait models (Fischer 1983, Embretson 1985a). This work also has implications that will be discussed later

when we look at substantive issues about how ability and content are relevant to test construction.

Problems of dimensionality also arise in connection with the equating of tests, either horizontally or vertically. It has been shown that test equating can be inaccurate when the unidimensional assumptions of normal item response theory are violated (Holland and Rubin 1982). This problem becomes exacerbated if attempts are made to equate achievement tests that do not have an underlying ability of the usual kind. Under these conditions it may be desirable to investigate the applicability of more classical methods of test equating.

Despite all the problems mentioned, item response theory makes possible highly sophisticated analyses of test data in the case of large data sets, that is, where the number of examinees is at least 200, and preferably many more, and where the number of items is within the range of usual test lengths. The standard version of LOGIST, a program distributed by Educational Testing Service, permits use of $N = 15,000$ examinees and $n = 400$ items, but this test length would probably be only rarely encountered and would entail excessive computational costs. Use of LOGIST frequently runs into problems that are due to violations of assumptions. Researchers will probably continue to explore the problems of this and other computing algorithms.

Full use of item response theory with classroom tests is generally impractical, but certain principles and simplifications may be applicable (Harnisch 1983, Izard and White 1982, Yen 1984). Conventional item analysis procedures are certainly in order and incorporate some of the principal notions of item response theory.

There has been interest in the concept of "appropriateness," that is, the extent to which an individual's pattern of responses is consistent with the general pattern found in a large sample of examinees (Drasgow and Levine 1986, Trabin and Weiss 1983). An extreme case of an "inappropriate" pattern would be one where an individual fails easy items but passes difficult items. One purpose of appropriateness measurement would be to identify examinees who misunderstand directions, cheat, or otherwise fail to respond to the test on the basis of ability alone. An excessive number of inappropriate patterns might also reveal an underlying multidimensionality of the test. There is need for investigations of these possibilities.

Closely related to this is the concept of the person characteristic curve, obtained by plotting probabilities of passing, for individuals, or for groups of individuals with closely similar abilities, as a function of item difficulties. If the test is essentially unidimensional, person characteristic curves will form a family of generally parallel curves and will be useful in interpreting patterns of ability. Carroll (1985) has proposed that this technique is useful in defining abilities as a function of item or task difficulty; his work needs to be extended over a wide range of abilities. The concept of the person characteristic curve can easily be applied to classroom tests with small N and relatively small numbers of items.

3. Ability Theory

We now consider a number of substantive issues with which educational measurement has been, and will continue to be, concerned.

One dominant issue has been the nature, variety, and organization of human abilities and their potential relevance to students' educational progress. The last decade has seen the introduction of a surprising variety of new theories and theoretical standpoints.

As summaries or reconceptualizations of more or less traditional views, mainly based on factor-analytic work, we can mention: Humphreys' (1985) discussion of general intelligence (*g*); Jensen's (1984) defense of *g* against a "specificity doctrine" according to which intelligence is broken down into many separate abilities; Horn's (1985) reformulation of the Cattell hierarchical model of intelligence; Gustafsson's (1984) validation of a hierarchical model through confirmatory factor analysis; Royce and Powell's (1983) new structural model of intellectual abilities; Jäger's (1984) "Berlin model of intelligence"—an interesting reformulation based in part on Guilford's "Structure-of-Intellect model"; and Snow et al.'s (1984) presentation of a radex model of abilities. There are basic similarities in all these viewpoints, along with differences that will have to be resolved by further consideration and empirical research. Snow and Lohman (1984) have presented a promising theory of the relevance of aptitude to learning and instruction.

In the category of new theories of intelligence we can mention: Sternberg's (1985a) "triarchic" theory of intelligence that features a theory of information-processing components of intellectual activity; and Gardner's (1983) theory of "multiple intelligences," proposing that intellectual abilities can be classified as linguistic, musical, logical–mathematical, spatial, bodily–kinesthetic, and personal relations. At the same time, these and other writers propose that more attention be devoted to the measurement of "social" intelligence (Frederiksen et al. 1984, Sternberg and Smith 1985), and "practical intelligence" (Sperber et al. 1985, Wagner and Sternberg 1985). How all these proposals can be actualized and interrelated could be a major concern of future research in the nature and variety of cognitive abilities.

Much of the impetus for these new research directions has come out of recent developments in cognitive psychology. Carroll (1976) pointed out that most psychometric tests of abilities can be viewed as cognitive tasks. Much of the research in the past decade has centered on detailed examinations of cognitive abilities in terms of their information-processing components. Examples of such studies can be found in several volumes edited by Sternberg (1982a, 1982b, 1984, 1985b) and by Dillon (1985) and Dillon and Schmeck (1983). The essential idea behind this work is that cognitive tasks can often be subdivided into components, each of which may represent a distinct ability or personal characteristic; further, that the difficulties, response-time latencies, and other measurable aspects of performance on these tasks can be related to particular features of the stimuli and of the response requirements of the tasks. By studying these relations, it is possible to attain better understanding of the nature of abilities and to find foundations for them in theories of cognitive psychology. Thus far, this idea has been implemented on only a small number of abilities—certain kinds of verbal, reasoning, and spatial abilities, and the available studies raise numerous questions still to be answered. There is need to extend this type of investigation to still other abilities.

Recent studies have reopened the question of whether there is some kind of intrinsic relation between general intelligence and mental processing speed as measured by reaction time (Barrett et al. 1986, Jensen 1985, Vernon and Jensen 1984). This research has been highly controversial, with alternative interpretations and counterclaims proposed by Longstreth (1984) and Smith and Stanley (1983), among others. Further, British research cited by Eysenck and Barrett (1985) suggests that general intelligence is related to physiological measures as obtained by the average evoked potential and the electroencephalogram. There is need further to confirm these findings and to resolve the differences of interpretation that have arisen.

Some of these developments have an interesting relation to what Embretson (1985b p. 3) calls "test design": "specifying the aspects of individual differences that a test measures by constructing and/or selecting items according to their substantive properties." The collection of papers edited by Embretson presents useful examples of test design studies that could be emulated in future research, as well as appropriate mathematical techniques for implementing such studies.

Given the present state of the art, it should be possible to develop a scientific theory of cognitive abilities that would consistently identify and describe all the major and minor cognitive abilities and provide unquestioned methods of measuring them and stating how they enter into different types of cognitive behavior, learning, and performance. More large, well-designed factorial studies are needed to specify the status of various factors or latent traits of ability in the hierarchy of abilities.

Throughout the history of factor analysis, there has been the tantalizing hope that it would eventually be possible to construct so-called "pure factor" tests of abilities. In general, this hope has proved elusive, but that may have been because the theory and technology used were not adequate. Theories of cognitive abilities and the technology of test construction are now adequate to justify mounting a new program of constructing tests of separate cognitive abilities, with alternate forms appropriate for different age ranges, that would be demonstrably unidimensional. One important aspect of such a program would be the careful control of level of mastery and speed effects.

Sternberg (1986) provides a good summary of some current trends and activities in intelligence testing.

4. Measurement and Analysis of Learning and Educational Achievement

Cognitive psychology has had a considerable influence on the measurement and analysis of learning and educational achievements, or more generally, on what has been called instructional psychology. Discussions of this point can be found in volumes edited by Plake (1984) and Ronning et al. (1987). As in the case of abilities, viewpoints from cognitive psychology stress the importance of analyzing tasks—in this case, learning tasks—in terms of the types of perceptions, understanding, declarative and procedural knowledge, and response capabilities that the student must possess or acquire in order to achieve learning success. In the past, constructors of achievement tests have tried to apprehend these matters on an intuitive basis and incorporate them in these tests. Insights from cognitive psychology may enable test constructors to approach these problems more systematically (Resnick 1983).

Recent studies of the learning of reading comprehension, science, and mathematics confirm the idea, long held by many teachers, that students' errors come about not so much from carelessness or lack of memory but because they have constructed incorrect rules or algorithms for solving the problems presented. This fact has given rise to measurement procedures designed to diagnose student's "bugs" or incorrect rules (Tatsuoka and Tatsuoka 1983). On the other hand, Resnick (1984) has argued that detailed diagnosis of incorrect rules is less important than trying to understand the incorrect mental representations that lead students to make errors. Resnick's work was in the area of elementary mathematics teaching. In any event, achievement tests must be better oriented to assist teachers in diagnosing incorrect mental representations and erroneous procedural rules, and one can expect further refinements and applications along these lines.

A pronounced trend of the last two decades has been increased recognition of a distinction between *norm-referenced* and *criterion-referenced* tests, with an effort to construct better tests of the latter kind (Berk 1984). It is not often realized, however, that in many cases, one and the same test can be treated either as a norm-referenced or a criterion-referenced test, depending upon how scores are interpreted. Many tests originally constructed as norm-referenced tests could readily be criterion referenced by analyzing, in concrete terms, the levels of performance or achievement that their scores indicate. A recent example of this process has been the criterion referencing of the Reading Proficiency Scale developed by NAEP/ETS (1985) by specifying types of reading performances characteristic of five discrete score levels. This criterion-referencing information helps in interpreting the normative information that is also provided.

Writing items for achievement tests has always been regarded as almost an arcane art possessed by very few people. Recently, however, there have been renewed attempts to reduce this art to a system accessible to ordinary mortals (Roid and Haladyna 1982), and it is proposed that computers can be programmed to construct items and tests (Bejar 1985). Computer generation of items may indeed be possible in some limited domains, and this possibility deserves to be further explored. However, it is likely that most domains of educational achievement will continue to require item construction by the creative effort of subject-matter experts in collaboration with experts in testing.

In the meantime, teachers and test constructors will continue to be aided by the increasing availability of large banks of items at appropriate locations throughout the world (Millman and Arter 1984). Items in such banks can be indexed not only in terms of subject matter but also in terms of their item difficulty and discrimination parameters derived from item response theory. It will continue to be the case, despite possible claims to the contrary, that these item parameters must be evaluated in terms of the kinds of samples from which they are derived. It is not yet clear whether ways of circumventing this difficulty can be devised.

The use of computers in testing has already been mentioned in several connections. There will also be increasing use of computers in instruction, offering the possibility of what Baker (1984) has called "nonintrusive testing," that is, testing that occurs automatically in the course of instruction. Special attention should be given to the problem of separating level of mastery and speed dimensions of ability and/or achievement; acquisition of data by computers should facilitate this work because the computer can separately record speed and accuracy aspects of performance.

5. Some Final Remarks

Educational measurement should not be concerned only with the construction of variables; it must also participate in the investigation of causal and associative relations among variables. For example, there needs to be further concern with models of cognitive growth over the life-span and in a variety of mental functions (Bock 1983, Keats 1983). The structural modeling of important educational variables such as home background, cognitive ability, personality, motivation, type of instruction, duration of learning, and education achievement is a topic that should continue to receive devoted and sophisticated attention.

Educational measurement will undoubtedly continue to become more professionalized and specialized. The construction and publication of measurements used in education will be held to increasingly high standards (AERA, APA, and NCME 1985, Levy and Goldstein 1984, Mitchell 1985). It is difficult indeed to keep abreast of the many books, monographs, and journals that are now being published in this field in many countries. Volumes such as the present one, however, may enable educational measurement specialists to take the long view and retain a modicum of sanity amidst the profusion.

Bibliography

American Educational Research Association (AERA), American Psychological Association (APA), National Council on Measurement in Education (NCME) 1985 *Standards for Educational and Psychological Testing*. American Psychological Association, Washington, DC

Baker F B 1984 Technology and testing: State of the art and trends for the future. *J. Educ. Meas.* 21: 399–406

Barrett P, Eysenck H J, Lucking S 1986 Reaction time and intelligence: A replicated study. *Intelligence* 10:9–40

Bejar I I 1985 Speculations on the future of test design. In: Embretson S E (ed.) 1985 pp. 279–94

Berk R A (ed.) 1984 *A Guide to Criterion-Referenced Test Construction*. Johns Hopkins University Press, Baltimore, Maryland

Bock R D 1983 The mental growth curve reexamined. In: Weiss D J (ed.) 1983 *New Horizons in Testing: Latent Trait Test Theory and Computerized Adaptive Testing*. Academic Press, New York, pp. 205–19

Bock R D 1985 Contributions of empirical Bayes and marginal maximum likelihood methods to the measurement of individual differences. In: Roskam E E (ed.) 1985 *Measurement and Personality Assessment*. North Holland, Amsterdam, pp. 75–99

Brennan R L 1983 *Elements of Generalizability Theory*. American College Testing Program, Iowa City, Iowa

Carroll J B 1976 Psychometric tests as cognitive tasks: A new "Structure of Intellect." In: Resnick L (ed.) 1976 *The Nature of Intelligence*. Erlbaum, Hillsdale, New Jersey, pp. 27–56

Carroll J B 1985 Defining abilities through the person characteristic function. In: Roskam E E (ed.) 1985 *Measurement and Personality Assessment*. North Holland, Amsterdam, pp. 121–31

Carroll J B 1987 Measurement and educational psychology: Beginnings and repercussions. In: Glover J, Ronning R R (eds.) 1987 *Historical Foundations of Educational Psychology*. Plenum, New York

Dillon R F (ed.) 1985 *Individual Differences in Cognition*, Vol. 2. Academic Press, Orlando, Florida

Dillon R F, Schmeck R R (eds.) 1983 *Individual Differences in Cognition*, Vol. 1. Academic Press, New York

Drasgow F, Levine M V 1986 Optimal detection of certain forms of inappropriate test scores. *Appl. Psychol. Meas.* 10: 59–67

Embretson S 1985a Component latent trait models for test design. In: Weiss D J (ed.) 1985 *Proceedings of the 1982 Item Response Theory and Computerized Adaptive Testing Conference*. Department of Psychology, University of Minnesota, Minneapolis, Minnesota, pp. 295–316

Embretson S E (ed.) 1985b *Test Design: Developments in Psychology and Psychometrics*. Academic Press, Orlando, Florida

Eysenck H J, Barrett P 1985 Psychophysiology and the measurement of intelligence. In: Reynolds C R, Willson V L (eds.) 1985 *Methodological and Statistical Advances in the Study of Individual Differences*. Plenum, New York, pp. 1–49

Fischer G H 1983 Logistic latent trait models with linear constraints. *Psychometrika* 48:3–26

Frederiksen N, Carlson S, Ward W 1984 The place of social intelligence in a taxonomy of cognitive abilities. *Intelligence* 8:315–37

Gardner H 1983 *Frames of Mind: The Theory of Multiple Intelligences*. Basic Books, New York

Green B F, Bock R D, Humphreys L G, Linn R L, Reckase M D 1984 Technical guidelines for assessing computerized adaptive tests. *J. Educ. Meas.* 21:347–60

Gustafsson J-E 1984 A unifying model for the structure of intellectual abilities. *Intelligence* 8:179–203

Harnisch D L 1983 Item response patterns: Applications for educational practice. *J. Educ. Meas.* 20:191–206

Holland R W, Rubin D B (eds.) 1982 *Test Equating*. Academic Press, New York

Horn J L 1985 Remodeling old models of intelligence. In: Wolman B B (ed.) 1985 *Handbook of Intelligence: Theories, Measurements, and Applications*. Wiley, New York, pp. 267–300

Humphreys L G 1985 General intelligence: An integration of factor, test, and simplex theory. In: Wolman B B (ed.) 1985 *Handbook of Intelligence: Theories, Measurements, and Applications*. Wiley, New York, pp. 201–24

Izard J F, White J D 1982 The use of latent trait models in the development and analysis of classroom tests. In: Spearritt D (ed.) *The Improvement of Measurement in Education and Psychology: Contributions of Latent Trait Theories*. Australian Council for Educational Research, Hawthorn, Victoria, pp. 161–88

Jäger A O 1984 Intelligenzstrukturforschung: Konkurrierende Modelle, neue Entwicklungen, Perspektiven. *Psychol. Rundsch.* 35:21–35

Jensen A R 1984 Test validity: g versus the specificity doctrine. *J. Soc. Biol. Struct.* 7:93–118

Jensen A R 1985 Methodological and statistical techniques for the chronometric study of mental abilities. In: Reynolds C R, Willson V L (eds.) 1985 *Methodological and Statistical Advances in the Study of Individual Differences*. Plenum, New York, pp. 51–116

Keats J A 1983 Ability measures and theories of cognitive development. In: Wainer H, Messick S (eds.) 1983 *Principals of Modern Psychological Measurement: A Festschrift for Frederic M. Lord*. Erlbaum, Hillsdale, New Jersey, pp. 81–101

Levy P, Goldstein H (eds.) 1984 *Tests in Education: A Book of Critical Reviews*. Academic Press, London

Longstreth L E 1984 Jensen's reaction-time investigations of intelligence: A critique. *Intelligence* 8:139–60

Marsh H W, Hocevar D 1983 Confirmatory factor analysis of multitrait multimethod matrices. *J. Educ. Meas.* 20:231–48

Millman J, Arter J A 1984 Issues in item banking. *J. Educ. Meas.* 21:315–30

Mitchell J V Jr (ed.) 1985 *The Ninth Mental Measurements Yearbook*, 2 vols. Buros Institute of Mental Measurements, University of Nebraska, Lincoln, Nebraska

Muraki E, Engelhard G Jr 1985 Full-information item factor analysis: Application of EAP scores. *Appl. Psychol. Meas.* 9:417–30

National Assessment of Educational Progress/Educational Testing Services (NAEP/ETS) 1985 *The Reading Report Card: Progress Toward Excellence in Our Schools; Trends in Reading over Four National Assessments. 1971–1984*. Educational Testing Service, Princeton, New Jersey

Plake B S (ed.) 1984 *Social and Technical Issues in Testing: Implications for Test Construction and Usage*. Erlbaum, Hillsdale, New Jersey

Resnick L B 1983 Toward a cognitive theory of instruction. In: Paris S G, Olson G M, Stevenson H W (eds.) 1983 *Learning and Motivation in the Classroom*. Erlbaum, Hillsdale, New Jersey, pp. 5–38

Resnick L B 1984 Beyond error analysis: The role of understanding in elementary school arithmetic. In: Cheek H N (ed.) 1984 *Diagnostic and Prescriptive Mathematics: Issues, Ideas, and Insights*. Research Council for Diagnostic and Prescriptive Mathematics, Kent, Ohio, pp. 2–14

Roid G H, Haladyna T M 1982 *A Technology for Test-Item Writing*. Academic Press, New York

Ronning R R, Glover J, Conoley J C, Witt J C (eds.) 1987 *The Influence of Cognitive Psychology in Testing.* Erlbaum, Hillsdale, New Jersey

Royce J R, Powell A 1983 *Theory of Personality and Individual Differences: Factors, Systems, and Processes.* Prentice-Hall, Englewood Cliffs, New Jersey

Schmitt N, Stults D M 1986 Methodology review: Analysis of multitrait-multimethod matrices. *Appl. Psychol. Meas.* 10:1–22

Smith G A, Stanley G 1983 Clocking *g*: Relating intelligence and measures of timed performance. *Intelligence* 7:353–68

Snow R E, Kyllonen P C, Marshalek B 1984 The topography of ability and learning correlations. In: Sternberg R J (ed.) 1984 pp. 47–103

Snow R E, Lohman D F 1984 Toward a theory of cognitive aptitude for learning from instruction. *J. Educ. Psychol.* 76:347–76

Sperber W, Wörpel S, Jäger A O, Pfister R 1985 *Praktische Intelligenz: Untersuchungsbericht und erste Ergebnisse.* Freie Universität, Berlin

Sternberg R J (ed.) 1982a *Advances in the Psychology of Human Intelligence,* Vol. 1. Erlbaum, Hillsdale, New Jersey

Sternberg R J (ed.) 1982b *Handbook of Intelligence.* Cambridge University Press, Cambridge

Sternberg R J (ed.) 1984 *Advances in the Psychology of Human Intelligence,* Vol. 2. Erlbaum, Hillsdale, New Jersey

Sternberg R J 1985a *Beyond IQ: A Triarchic Theory of Human Intelligence.* Cambridge University Press, Cambridge

Sternberg R J (ed.) 1985b *Human Abilities: An Information-Processing Approach.* Freeman, New York

Sternberg R J 1986 The future of intelligence testing. *Educ. Meas. Iss. Prac.* 5(3):19–22

Sternberg R J, Smith C 1985 Social intelligence and decoding skills in nonverbal communication. *Soc. Cognit.* 3:168–92

Tatsuoka K K, Tatsuoka M M 1983 Spotting erroneous rules of operation by the individual consistency index. *J. Educ. Meas.* 20:221–30

Thissen D 1986 The formulation and representation of item response models for multidimensional ability tests with guessing. Paper presented at the meeting of the Psychometric Society, Toronto, Canada.

Trabin T E, Weiss D J 1983 The person response curve: Fit of individuals to item response theory models. In: Weiss D J (ed.) 1983 *New Horizons in Testing: Latent Trait Test Theory and Computerized Adaptive Testing.* Academic Press, New York, pp. 83–108

Vernon P A, Jensen A R 1984 Individual and group differences in intelligence and speed of information processing. *Pers. Indiv. Diff.* 5:411–23

Wagner R K, Sternberg R J 1985 Practical intelligence in real-world pursuits: The role of tacit knowledge. *J. Pers. Soc. Psychol.* 49:436–58

Yen W M 1984 Obtaining maximum likelihood trait estimates from number-correct scores for the three-parameter logistic model. *J. Educ. Meas.* 21:93–111

Measurement in Educational Research

J. A. Keats

In describing the application of measurement principles to educational research, it is impossible to separate the contributions which have come from the disciplines of education, psychology, sociology, physical sciences, and mathematical statistics. There is little to be gained from making such separations but certain approaches tend to be known by the name of their principal protagonist and this reference tends to imply that a particular person's discipline is the one making the contribution. No such implication is intended in the present account when techniques are referred to by their customary name.

Measurement in education has been practiced for more than a millenium in China and for centuries elsewhere. However it was not until the beginning of the twentieth century that research workers studying educational problems became self-conscious about measurement methods. This situation also existed in the physical sciences where Campbell's (1917) account of physical measurement was the first to be widely recognized and adopted. It was not until educational measurement methods had developed considerably that it was possible to compare them with physical measurement and this was done by a committee of the British Association for the Advancement of Science in 1938 (Ferguson et al. 1940).

In the first four decades of the twentieth century two quite different educational measurement techniques were developed for quantifying individual differences.

The first of these was developed by Binet in the context of an educational problem associated with compulsory education. Binet not only constructed an instrument for deciding whether or not a child could benefit from formal education as it was in those days, but also established the criteria of item difficulty and discriminating power which are still currently used for the selection of items, tasks, and so on to be used in educational and psychological tests.

While Binet was constructing a psychological instrument to solve an educational problem, others, such as Sir Francis Galton and Spearman (1904), were developing and applying statistical methods suitable for the study of individual differences. Binet's criteria of difficulty and discriminating power which he defined graphically were soon converted to statistical indices which in the case of discriminating power was sometimes associated with a test of statistical significance. However, Binet's developmental measure, the mental age, was severely criticized by those with a more statistical approach as being ambiguous in definition and lacking generality (Thurstone 1926). Thurstone recommended measures based on the standard score at particular age levels.

It has only recently been pointed out (Keats 1982a) that the differences between the approaches of Binet and Thurstone were not only those of the convenience of one measure as opposed to another but went much deeper. Both approaches implied that cognitive growth could be described by a single number. However Binet's approach implied that individual differences at any age level could be accounted for by differences in rate of growth whereas Thurstone's approach implied that individual differences at all ages arose from differences in the value approached at intellectual maturity, but that rate of approach to the ultimate level is the same in percentage terms. According to Thurstone's implicit assumption everyone reaches a given fraction, for example one-half of his or her ultimate level at a particular age level. In the case of physical height this assumption is very nearly correct. With Binet's assumption, all human beings are approaching the same ultimate level but at quite different rates. Both Binet's and Thurstone's implicit assumptions have been shown to be seriously in error (Keats 1982a).

While these arguments were proceeding, a third criterion for selecting items, that of item homogeneity, was being ignored. Spearman (1904) had established conditions which would lead to the conclusion that the relationships between a given set of measures could be accounted for by a single variable or factor. Spearman used these techniques to try to establish a single general ability underlying all tests of cognitive performance (the techniques are known as factor analysis). While Spearman's thesis was proved incorrect empirically, his methods could have been used to establish criteria for concluding that a given set of cognitive tasks or items all measured the same underlying variable, that is were homogeneous. This condition for educational and psychological measurement was not stressed until the middle of this century. Thus the three criteria for incorporating cognitive tasks into a single instrument with a single score are difficulty, discriminating power, and homogeneity.

1. The Relationship Between Educational Measurement and Physical Measurement

The conditions for physical measurement stated by Campbell (Campbell 1917) involved two basic operations each requiring a condition to be satisfied. The first of these is an operation of ordering whereby two objects can be compared with respect to (say) weight and a decision made as to which is heavier. In this case the condition to be met is that of transitivity so that if object A is judged heavier than object B and object B heavier than object C then object A *must* be judged heavier than object C. Failure to meet this condition could be due to unreliability in the comparing instrument or to a confusion in the dimensionality on which the objects are being compared.

Given that the ordering condition can be met with consistency, a second operation, that of combining must be possible, that is, two or more objects can be combined with respect to the dimension being measured in such a way that the combination can be compared on that dimension with any other object or combination of objects. With a consistent ordering operation and a

combining operation it is possible to associate a number with any object by combining standard units and subunits. The combining or additivity condition is that the number associated with object A plus that associated with object B must equal the number associated with the combination of A and B. If the additivity condition holds for all pairs of objects then the set of numbers associated with these operations and objects is unique apart from a multiplying constant to convert, for example pounds to kilograms.

With the development of educational measurement using objective testing methods, rating scales, attitude scales, and soon, the question of the extent to which these methods can be made to satisfy Campbell's conditions naturally arose. A Committee of the British Association for the Advancement of Science (BAAS) in 1938 examined this question in the context of psychological applications of these techniques and concluded that they did not do so completely (Ferguson et al. 1940). The ordering operation and condition could be met by a number of methods with allowance for unreliability of comparisons but a suitable combining operation could not be identified and so the additivity condition could not be checked.

Following the BAAS report, Gulliksen (1946) has pointed out that in the case of the method of paired comparisons a combining of differences operation was in fact defined and additivity of differences could be checked. This observation led naturally to the definition of interval scales, that is, scales for which differences between objects could be measured but for which no zero point could be defined from the data obtained by the method of measurement used. Stevens (1951) proposed a fourfold classification of measurement methods:

(a) Nominal scales which are really unordered classifications of objects.

(b) Ordinal scales which have an operation of ordering which exhibits transitivity.

(c) Interval scales which have ordering and combining operations for *differences* and these meet the consistency conditions of transitivity and additivity.

(d) Ratio scales which satisfy Campbell's criteria for fundamental measurement of individual objects.

Stevens' classification has been widely adopted in the literature reporting educational and psychological research since the early 1950s. However his conclusion that certain types of statistical procedures are applicable or inapplicable to one or more types of scale has caused considerable controversy. This conclusion has not been substantiated in terms of the assumptions underlying the various statistical techniques and so should not be taken seriously.

2. Conjoint Measurement

The general lack of a combining operation in educational and psychological research was finally overcome by research workers in Denmark and the United States, apparently independently, developing conjoint measurement at approximately the same time. Technical accounts of this theory are contained in Luce and Tukey (1964) and Ross (1964). The latter account is marred by a general "theorem" which is not only incorrectly proved but is in fact untrue. Rasch (1960) working at the Danish Institute for Educational Research published what amounts to an application of conjoint measurement to the preparation of objective tests and analysis of data obtained from their application. His method has been developed and widely applied in recent years (see *Rasch Measurement Models*).

The simple account given here follows Coombs et al. (1970) using objective testing as an example. The measurement method is based on a matrix or table in which rows correspond to groups of subjects who have each attempted all of the items which define the columns. The entries in the cells of the table, for example P_{gi}, are the proportions of subjects in group g who give the correct response to item i. Table 1 displays such a table. If the letters a, b, c denote the measures corresponding to any three of the groups of subjects and p, q, and r to the measures corresponding to any three of the items then it must be possible to define three functions, ϕ, f, and h such that:

(a) $\phi (a, p) = f (a) + h (p)$, that is, the function ϕ is decomposible into two additive components which separately are functions of a and p.

(b) $\phi (a, p) \geqslant \phi (b, q)$ if and only if $P_{ap} \geqslant P_{bq}$.

The following axioms are sufficient for the existence of functions satisfying the above conditions:

(a) The cancellation axiom: if $P_{ap} \geqslant P_{bq}$ and $P_{br} \geqslant P_{cq}$ then $P_{ar} \geqslant P_{cp}$.

(b) The solvability axiom: if $P_{ap} \geqslant t \geqslant P_{ap''}$ for some real t then there exists a p such that $P_{ap} = t$ and the corresponding condition for the individual differences subscripts.

Table 1
Proportions of subjects in groups giving the "correct" responses to items

		Items								
		1	2	3	$\cdots$	i	$\cdots$	j	$\cdots$	N
Groups	1	P_{11}	P_{12}	P_{13}	$\cdots$	P_{1i}	$\cdots$	P_{1j}	$\cdots$	P_{1N}
of	2	P_{21}	P_{22}	P_{22}	$\cdots$	P_{2i}	$\cdots$	P_{2j}	$\cdots$	P_{2N}
subjects		.	.	.		.		.		.
		.	.	.		.		.		.
		.	.	.		.		.		.
	g	P_{g1}	P_{g2}	P_{g2}	$\cdots$	P_{gi}	$\cdots$	P_{gj}	$\cdots$	P_{gN}
		.	.	.		.		.		.
		.	.	.		.		.		.
	n	P_{n1}	P_{n2}	P_{n3}	$\cdots$	P_{ni}	$\cdots$	P_{nj}	$\cdots$	P_{nN}

All measures of the type a, b, c and p, q, r satisfy the conditions for an interval scale which may under certain circumstances be transformed to a ratio scale.

Rasch (1960) proposed a transformation of the proportions obtained in tables such as those in Table 1. He observed that if

$$\frac{P_{gi}}{1 - P_{gi}} = \frac{A_g}{D_i} \tag{1}$$

where A_g is now used to denote the ability of group g and D_i the difficulty of item i then:

$$\text{Logit } (P_{gi}) = \log \frac{P_{gi}}{1 - P_{gi}} = \log A_g - \log D_i \tag{2}$$

which meets the order preserving and additivity conditions. The values of $\log A_g$ satisfy interval-scale conditions and the values of A_g thus satisfy ratio-scale conditions. Similarly the values of D_i satisfy the conditions for a ratio scale. Rasch presents examples of test data which satisfy the conditions of this model and some which do not. Other workers have made empirical investigations of the applicability of the model to tests which were not constructed in accordance with the model and often report satisfactory fits of the data by the model.

Many years before Rasch's publication, Lord (1952) had developed the theory of the normal ogive latent ability model. The methods of estimating ability values for the normal model are very complex and certainly require computer assistance. It is thus not surprising that latent ability models and measures were not used in educational and psychological research until after Rasch's logit model had appeared with its much greater simplicity.

From the time that advances in electronic computers made the normal ogive model a viable alternative to the logit model (sometimes called the "one parameter logistic model", a title which is somewhat misleading) there has been considerable discussion as to which model should be used. Before summarizing the points made in this controversy it is as well to remember that the advantages of using latent ability measures are not questioned. The most efficient way of obtaining estimates of these measures however, is the subject of considerable current debate.

One of the reasons for the greater simplicity of the Rasch logit model lies in the fact that the model assumes that although the test items have different difficulties, they all have the same discriminating power. This restriction places an added restraint on selecting items for a test: they must not only have significant discriminating power but also, at least approximately *equal* discriminating power. The advantage claimed for such instruments is that the simple, number correct score is a sufficient statistic for estimating ability. There are other consequential advantages related to chaining or equating tests.

The disadvantages of the logit model are argued in terms of the fact that, given (say) 200 trial items, a test of 80 items chosen with tight restriction on discriminating power will in general have lower reliability than one, also of 80 items, in which the highly discriminating as well as the moderately discriminating items are included. However, to utilize this greater reliability for the estimation of latent ability, it would not be possible to use the simple, number correct score as the basis of estimation. Some kind of weighted score would be required. These matters are demonstrated by Birnbaum (1968).

Birnbaum suggested what is usually taken to be the inclusion of an item discrimination parameter in the logit model but what is really a different model—the two- (or more correctly three-) parameter logistic model. In terms of the logit model, Birnbaum's model would be

$$\frac{P_{gi}}{1 - P_{gi}} = \left(\frac{A_g}{D_i}\right)^{C_i} \tag{3}$$

where C_i is the index of discriminating power of the item. In terms of dimensional analysis this equation is unbalanced unless C_i is dimensionless for all items which it is not. Thus the Rasch form is the only logit model which is dimensionally balanced.

However, Birnbaum and others write the alternative model by transforming A_g and D_i into a_g and d_i where $A_g = e^{a_g}$ and $D_i = e^{d_i}$ from which

$$\frac{P_{gi}}{1 - P_{gi}} = \frac{e^{c_i a_g}}{e^{c_i d_i}} \quad \text{or} \quad \text{logit} (P_{gi}) = c_i(a_g - d_i) \tag{4}$$

or

$$P_{gi} = \frac{e^{c_i a_g}}{e^{c_i a_g} + e^{c_i d_i}} \quad \text{or} \quad \frac{e^{c_i (a_g - d_i)}}{e^{c_i(a_g - d_i)} + 1} \tag{5}$$

This logistic model is dimensionally balanced if C^i is taken to be of dimensionality (ability)$^{-1}$ which is defensible. Similar definitions are used in the normal ogive model (Lord 1952). The sacrifices made for this additional parameter are firstly that the number correct score is no longer a sufficient statistic for the estimate of ability and the ability estimates obtained are not on a ratio scale. However, the additional care needed to construct tests to meet the conjoint measurement conditions in the way Rasch suggests is worthwhile. The further application of latent ability measures to the measurement of cognitive growth will be discussed later.

3. Frequency Distributions of Educational and Psychological Measurements

A further problem associated with measurement of individual differences relates to the frequency distribution of scores on objective tests obtained from administration to large random samples. This problem has practical significance because of the use of percentile ranks and normalized percentile scores as derived scores. Keats (1951) was the first to suggest on general theoretical grounds that the negative hypergeometric distribution

should give a reasonable representation of score distributions. Because of computational problems he followed Karl Pearson (1930) in using the Beta function to estimate the theoretical frequencies. Keats demonstrated that this method gave good representations of most frequency distributions found in practice and was useful not only in providing stable estimates of percentile points but also in revealing bias in samples.

At approximately the same time Mollenkopf (1949) showed that the error variance of an objective test was greatest for the middle range of scores and least for extreme scores. Keats (1957) showed that a binomial error distribution accounted for this phenomenon and Lord (1965) gave a general account of the binomial error model. Keats and Lord (1962) showed that the binomial error model together with linear regression of true score on raw score leads to a derivation of the negative hypergeometric distribution. This finding stimulated considerable further research into representations of data obtained from objective tests. Lord (1965) looked into possible additional forms of the distribution of true scores while Keats examined some of the effects of nonlinear regressions of true scores on raw scores. Many of these results and some additional ones were brought together in Lord and Novick (1968).

The practical usefulness of theoretically based frequency distributions in defining percentile values on objective tests for carefully defined populations has seldom been applied in practice despite the obvious advantages in standardizing and equating tests. More recently Huynh (1976) has confirmed the robustness of the negative hypergeometric distribution and suggests its use when criterion-referenced as opposed to normatively based tests are being developed (see below).

4. Parameters of Persons

Gulliksen (1950) based his theory of mental tests essentially on the notion that a raw score on the test could be thought of as consisting of a true score and an error score which were additive and uncorrelated. He showed that much of the existing test theory could be derived in these terms. There were, however, problems of strict definition and of estimation which were not developed. Lord and Novick (1968) attempted to solve these problems by means of axioms they claim to be not inconsistent with conjoint measurement. However Lumsden (1976) severely criticized true score theory on the grounds that any set of axioms which had been proposed for the definition of true score was unlikely to be satisfied in any domain so far explored.

Rasch (1960) also implicitly criticized true score theory when he complained that as a student he was always being assessed on an arbitrarily difficult set of tasks and relative to an undefined population. He argued strongly for ability measures which did not have these relativities associated with them but were "person parameters" in an absolute sense. Criticism of a similar kind was being expressed by Bayley (1955) who pointed out that it was impossible to develop a quantitative theory of cognitive development unless such an absolute measure could be developed. She did not seem to accept the notion that latent trait measures of the Rasch type could meet these requirements. Subsequently two extensive longitudinal studies, those reported by McCall et al. (1973) and by Hindley and Owen (1979), have been carried out without using such measures.

More recently Lumsden (1978) has proposed that, in addition to a level parameter of the latent trait kind, one could also distinguish between subjects in terms of the extent to which their performance varies with the difficulty of the task. Some subjects obtain most of their score on what are usually called "easy" items and fail on "difficult" items whereas others perform almost as well on the difficult items as they do on the easy ones. This concept is the person's equivalent of the concept of discriminating power of an item, that is, the extent to which a low-scoring subject gives the right answer much less often on more difficult items than less difficult items. Attempts to establish this as a reliable and valid dimension for persons have not so far been very successful. A possibly related measure of a subject's tendency to guess (Miles 1973) has also not been developed to a stage where it can be regarded as an established dimension.

Keats (1982a) criticized the term "person parameter" which has been commonly used following Rasch (1960) on the grounds that in the cognitive area subjects continue to develop up to an age of approximately 20 years. Thus an estimate of this parameter at age 10 years will be consistently different from one at 15 years. Such a variable quantity hardly deserves to be called a parameter. He proposed a more basic parameter which determines the greatest level the subject will approach with age and raised the question as to whether this was the basic person parameter or whether a rate of development parameter might be required as well as, or even instead of, a greatest level parameter.

By assuming that cognitive development could be represented in terms of a latent ability being projectively related to time, Keats (1982a) showed that Binet's mental-age measure was only a consistent measure if all subjects were approaching the same adult value at quite different rates. The deviation measure advocated by Thurstone (1926) and Wechsler (1939) among others is, on this assumption, stable only if the rate of development is approximately the same for each subject but the adult value approached varies from person to person. Using longitudinal data reported by Skodak and Skeels (1949), Keats was able to show that both a rate parameter and an adult level parameter seemed to be important. In a subsequent paper Keats (1982b) considered mechanisms which could be thought of as underlying cognitive development and thus gave these parameters a theoretical significance independent of their mensurational significance.

Even though current evidence suggests that in the quantification of general ability an independent rate and asymptote parameter are required to represent development, this must not be taken to mean that purely rate of development models are not applicable in educational research. If one considers minimal skills in reading and number work which almost all can master, it is still significant to measure how quickly they are mastered by subjects of different ability and in different settings. There is much more research to be done investigating personal parameters in these areas.

5. Criterion-referenced Testing

This form of educational measurement arose in part as a reaction to normative testing which relates a person's performance to that of a particular norming group, for example an age group or a grade group. The objective of this form of testing is to relate the person's performance to some kind of standard or level of mastery but the problem arises of attempting to define such a standard in terms of a test performance. This problem exists whether or not the score on the test has been converted to some kind of derived score such as a standard score or even to an estimate of some underlying latent trait.

Various ways of solving the basic problem of setting a mastery level in terms of a test score have been suggested. These range from the exercising of a value judgment by curriculum experts through decision theory approaches which assume knowledge of a true mastery score to utilizing the ratio of the two costs of misclassification, that is false positives and false negatives and alternatively the use of an independent criterion such as degree of success in a referral task. Huynh (1976) suggests that mastery classification should imply a high probability of success in training to which only persons classed as masters at the lower level are admitted. He explores the statistical implications of this approach in terms of the beta–binomial model (Keats and Lord 1962) with constant losses and pass–fail referral performance.

There are very few areas of knowledge for which content criteria can be specified precisely. One could consider mechanical arithmetic as one such and require a criterion of (say) 90 percent accuracy in adding and/or multiplying two digit numbers by two digit numbers. However such criterion referencing ignores the fact that some combinations are more likely to produce errors than others and also the fact that some students make systematic errors due to inappropriate strategies. Thus the problems of developing criterion-referenced instruments touch on the very core of the educational process. Until more of the theoretical problems of education are solved the possibility of developing useful criterion-referenced instruments seems to be unattainable.

In this context the development of computer-administered tests is proceeding rapidly. The further goal of adapting items to the level of performance of the student is also being approached in some areas. It should also be possible to develop programmes to explore the patterns of errors made by a particular student to determine deficient strategies that can be corrected. The interaction between measurement and diagnosis and treatment of weaknesses in performance must be studied in detail before criterion referencing can be successful and the wide use of computers should facilitate this work.

6. *Measurement of Attitudes*

Attitude measurement began as a result of Thurstone's development of scale values for stimuli on dimensions for which there is no corresponding physical measure. Using the method of paired comparisons Thurstone and Chave (1929) showed that it was possible to find scale values for statements reflecting positive and negative attitudes and that subjects could be measured in terms of the scale values for statements they agreed with. Shortly after Thurstone's contribution, Likert (1932) suggested that the methods which had been developed for constructing objective tests of cognitive abilities could be applied to the construction and use of scales for measuring attitudes. Later still, Guttman (1947) proposed criteria that could be used to select statements which formed a scale.

A valuable collection of scales for the quantification of attitudes has been provided by Shaw and Wright (1967). Their publication corresponds in many ways to the Mental Measurements Yearbooks published by Buros (1978) in the field of psychological testing but is more immediately useful because the scales are presented in full along with the evaluative material. As a means of organizing their material, Shaw and Wright classify scales according to the quantified attitudes. The classes of attitudes that are distinguished are attitudes towards social practices, social issues and problems, international issues, abstract concepts, political and religious issues, ethnic and national groups, "significant others", and social institutions. A revised edition of this volume is urgently needed.

The three methods, Thurstone's, Likert's, and Guttman's, use different models as the basis of their quantification methods and all have some current use. Allport and Vernon (1931), among others, have used essentially ranking methods to obtain measures which are then interpreted as if they corresponded to Likert's scales. This confusion of models by Allport and Vernon is quite unscientific as it can lead to unjustified interpretations of data and the neglect of other possible interpretations. Models for ordinal data are relatively recent.

The Likert method of constructing and applying attitude scales is by far the most common as it resembles most nearly the objective test approach. The major difference arises from the fact that whereas items in cognitive tests are usually scored as either $+1$ (correct) or zero (incorrect), the Likert items often have alternatives of the kind "strongly agree, agree, undecided, disagree, strongly disagree" which are scored 2, 1, 0, -1, and -2 respectively. However the inclusion of the alternative "undecided" has been shown to lead to anomalous results and so should not be used.

There was little practical or theoretical development of this method from the 1930s until quite recently. Andrich (1978) applied the Rasch approach to model building to the analysis of attitudinal data collected by either the Likert or the Thurstone method. In particular he indicated ways in which data could be collected and analysed to test the assumptions of these two methods. Andrich also quotes some results from empirical studies which tend to support the use of integral values allocated to the possible categories in the Likert method.

The Thurstone method depends on the possibility of reliably scaling statements in terms of the attitude level of persons who would endorse the statement. He suggested the method of paired comparisons as a way of determining these scale values but because of the experimental time required by this method he developed other, quicker procedures. Thurstone emphasized that the scale values obtained by one of these methods should be independent (up to a linear transformation) of the attitudes of the judges scaling the statements. This condition has rarely been checked in practice and is similar to the requirement of the Rasch model that the estimates of the difficulties of items should be independent of the abilities of the subjects used to obtain them.

Given that sufficient numbers of appropriately scaled statements are available, a subject's attitude can be measured by averaging the scale values of those items he or she endorses. Again, the second requirement for the Rasch model should apply in that the measurement obtained for a subject should not depend on the particular set of statements with which the subject is presented. This condition is harder to check because Thurstone scales currently available tend to have a relatively small number of items so that any sampling of these statements would tend to give unreliable as well as coarse measures.

Guttman scales can best be thought of as Likert scales with items of infinite discriminability. If the Likert scale items meet the requirements of the Rasch model then the Guttman scale property that a person's score indicates precisely which items he or she endorsed is weakened to the extent that, for each score, the probability of its being obtained with each of the possible patterns can be calculated. If the items in the scale have a wide range of item parameter values and high discrimination there will be a most probable pattern for each score. In the rarely obtained case of a perfect Guttman scale these most probable patterns will, of course, have a probability of unity.

The unifying effect of applying the Rasch model to methods of measuring attitudes should be clear from the above discussion. Only with the restrictions of this model is it possible to justify giving a unique interpretation to the usual raw score whether from an ability test, an attainment test, or an attitude scale. If more general models which allow for variation in the discriminating power of items are used then the value of the measure differs from one pattern of responding to another. Even for an instrument of only 20 items, there are at least one million patterns of responding but only 21 possible raw scores. Thus the data reduction possibilities obtained by using the Rasch model are enormous.

7. Multivariate Approaches to Measurement in Education

Spearman (1904) proposed that measures of cognitive achievement, including sensory judgments could be accounted for by an underlying single factor or general ability. Much of the data he used came from school achievement measures and the balance from the psychophysical laboratory. This approach was developed and explored for almost 30 years before Thurstone (1931) proposed multivariate factor analysis.

Both methods were directed towards the problem of representing human cognitive performance in terms of a relatively small number of cognitive factors. The technical problems of factor analysis have been actively investigated for more than 50 years and although they cannot be said to have been solved many least squares and maximum likelihood methods are now available for exploring and testing data. Most, if not all, are available in the form of computer programs. However, there is still debate as to which method is the most appropriate in a given situation and the various methods do not produce the same results.

On the substantive side many attempts have been made to define the significant factors by means of which individual differences in cognitive behaviour can be represented. Thurstone proposed a set of primary mental abilities and provided research instruments to measure these. More recently groups working with French (Ekstrom et al. 1976) have after a great deal of empirical research proposed 23 cognitive ability factors and provided at least three tests measuring each of these. The tests are referred to as cognitive factor reference tests and are intended for use in identifying factors rather than for direct use in assessment or selection situations.

The predominant tendency today is to use a large number of group factors rather than to retain Spearman's concept of a general factor and supplement this with well-established group factors. However this practice tends to obscure the one most pervasive and substantiated result from cognitive achievement studies, namely that measures of cognitive performance with quite different content are almost always positively related. It is probably true to assert that if the general plus group factor approach were adopted the number of cognitive factors to be referenced would be reduced from 23 to perhaps as few as 15 uncorrelated measures.

In the case of personality or temperament factors the group led by French (Dermen et al. 1978) have had a much more difficult task as there is far less agreement about which factors have been clearly and reliably defined. The manual of reference tests for temperament factors reflects this uncertainty by the fact that only 18 of the 28 factors listed could be confirmed by the group, the remainder, however, have often been reported in the literature. A further problem with temperament scales is that they are far more susceptible to the effects of response styles than are cognitive tests.

While the French group has provided a valuable service to educational research by investigating both cognitive and personality factors in this almost exhaustive fashion, it should be noted that almost all of their work has been carried out on adults. There is still the task of determining to what extent they also apply to children of primary and secondary schools. For at least some factors this question has some urgency for educators who wish to obtain a concise way of recording children's cognitive performance.

Factor analytic methods can also be regarded as ways of accounting for patterns or structures in correlations between variables by postulating more fundamental variables underlying the manifest observations. Two other ways of accounting for such patterns in correlation are also of concern when considering measurement in educational research. The first concerns the special patterns that arise in developmental studies when measures are administered on several different occasions to the same group of subjects. The second seeks to interpret patterns in terms of causal relationships and is called path analysis.

Anderson (1940) was the first to propose an explanation for the particular pattern of correlations obtained in developmental studies when performance on a particular measure, at a given age level, is correlated with performance on the same measure at other age levels. When all such correlations are tabulated the table obtained usually exhibits a distinctive pattern sometimes called a simplex pattern (Anderson 1940). Anderson demonstrated that such a pattern could be generated by means of cumulations of random numbers. Thus the first measure would be a random number and the second measure would consist of the first measure plus a second random number and so on. In due course there would be considerable overlap between one measure in the series and the next and so high correlation. Thus development could be thought of as random cumulations of the products of experience without any individual differences parameters.

This possible explanation of development was repeated by many writers without any great amplification until Drösler (1978) demonstrated, using time series methods, that it was possible to distinguish graphically between simplex patterns which could have arisen in this fashion and those which could not. From published data Drösler showed that educational achievement tests provided correlation patterns which were *not* inconsistent with Anderson's proposed explanation over most of the compulsory education period. However, general ability or aptitude tests reject the Anderson proposal for age levels above approximately 5 years. This finding has been confirmed for other sets of published data. Thus educational measures can be classified into those that do and those that do not conform to the random cumulation model. Factor analysis is not an appropriate method in the case of developmental data.

A second situation in which the factor analytic model is not an appropriate one for analysing tables of correlations between measures obtained in educational research, is one in which relationships are asymmetric in that A can influence B but B cannot influence A. An example would be where a social class measure is related to school achievement. It is most unlikely that a child's school achievement could affect his or her parents' social class whereas social class could influence school achievement. A method which accounts for patterns of correlations under these circumstances is path analysis and both least squares and maximum likelihood programmes are available for estimating the weightings of causal paths. With present knowledge of causal paths in education it is probably desirable to use the least squares method which makes fewer assumptions and so is much more influenced by the data than maximum likelihood methods.

A related form of studying correlations between educational measures is the method of Herbst (1970) which he termed cyclic network analysis. In that publication Herbst illustrates application of this method using measures of pupil's work effort, boredom, and anxiety in relation to work expected by the teacher as perceived by the pupil. However, as Herbst notes, path analysis applied at the group level will often yield different results from those obtained by cyclic network analysis at the group or individual level.

See also: Research Paradigms in Education

Bibliography

Allport G W, Vernon P E 1931 *A Study of Values: A Scale for Measuring the Dominant Interests in Personality: Manual of Directions*. Houghton Mifflin, Boston, Massachusetts

Anderson J E 1940 *The Prediction of Terminal Intelligence from Infant and Pre-school Tests*. Thirty-ninth Yearbook, National Society for the Study of Education. American Educational Research Association, Chicago, Illinois, pp. 385–403

Andrich D 1978 A rating formulation for ordered response categories. *Psychometrika* 43: 561–73

Bayley N 1955 On the growth of intelligence. *Am. Psychol.* 10: 805–18

Birnbaum A 1968 Some latent trait models and their use in inferring an examinee's ability. In: Lord F M, Novick M R (eds.) 1968 *Statistical Theories of Mental Test Scores*. Addison Wesley, Reading, Massachusetts, pp. 395–479

Buros O K (ed.) 1978 *The Eighth Mental Measurements Yearbook*. Gryphon Press, Highland Park, New Jersey

Campbell N R 1917 *Foundation of Science: The Philosophy of Theory and Experiment*. Dover Publications, New York

Coombs C H, Dawes R M, Tversky A 1970 *Mathematical Psychology: An Elementary Introduction*. Prentice Hall, Englewood Cliffs, New Jersey

Dermen D, French J W, Harman H H 1978 *Guide to Factor Referenced Temperament Scales 1978*. Educational Testing Service, Princeton, New Jersey

Drösler J 1978 Extending the temporal range of psychometric prediction by optimal linear filtering of mental test scores. *Psychometrika* 43: 533–49

Ekstrom R B, French J W, Harman H H 1976 *Manual for Kit of Factor-referenced Cognitive Tests, 1976*. Educational Testing Service, Princeton, New Jersey

Ferguson A, Meyers C S, Bartlett R J et al. 1940 Quantitative estimation of sensory events. Final report. *Advancement of Science* 2: 331–49

Gulliksen H 1946 Paired comparisons and the logic of measurement. *Psychol. Rev.* 53: 199–213

Gulliksen H 1950 *Theory of Mental Tests*. Wiley, New York

Guttman L 1947 The Cornell technique for scale and intensity analysis. *Educ. Psychol. Meas.* 7: 247–79

Herbst P G 1970 *Behavioural Worlds: The Study of Single Cases*. Tavistock, London

Hindley C B, Owen C F 1979 An analysis of individual patterns of DQ and IQ curves from 6 months to 17 years. *Br. J. Psychol.* 70: 273–93

Humphreys L G 1960 Investigations of the simplex. *Psychometrika* 25: 313–23

Huynh H 1976 Statistical consideration of mastery scores. *Psychometrika* 41: 65–78

Keats J A 1951 *A Statistical Theory of Objective Test Scores*. Australian Council for Educational Research, Hawthorn, Victoria

Keats J A 1957 Estimation of error variances of test scores. *Psychometrika* 22: 29–41

Keats J A 1982a Comparing latent trait with classical measurement models in the practice of educational and psychological measurement. In: Spearritt D S (ed.) 1982 *The Improvement of Measurement in Education and Psychology: Contributions of Latent Trait Theories*. Australian Council for Educational Research, Hawthorn, Victoria, pp. 61–72

Keats J A 1982b Ability measures and theories of cognitive development. In: Messick S (ed.) 1982 *Festschrift for F. M. Lord*. Educational Testing Service, Princeton, New Jersey

Keats J A, Lord F M 1962 A theoretical distribution of mental test scores. *Psychometrika* 27: 59–72

Likert R 1932 A technique for the measurement of attitudes. *Arch. Psychol.* 140

Lord F M 1952 A theory of test scores. *Psychometric Monogr.* 7

Lord F M 1965 A strong true-score theory, with applications. *Psychometrika* 30: 239–70

Lord F M, Novick M R 1968 *Statistical Theories of Mental Test Scores*. Addison-Wesley, Reading, Massachusetts

Luce R D, Tukey J W 1964 Simultaneous conjoint measurement: A new type of fundamental measurement. *J. Math. Psychol.* 1: 1–27

Lumsden J 1976 Test theory. *Ann. Rev. Psychol.* 27: 251–80

Lumsden J 1978 Tests are perfectly reliable. *Br. J. Math. Stat. Psychol.* 31: 19–26

McCall R B, Appelbaum M I, Hogarty P S 1973 Developmental changes in mental performance. *Monogr. Soc. Res. Child Dev.* 38 (3, Serial No. 150)

Miles J 1973 Eliminating the guessing factor in the multiple choice test. *Educ. Psychol. Meas.* 33: 637–51

Mollenkopf W G 1949 Variation of the standard error of measurement. *Psychometrika* 14: 189–230

Pearson K (ed.) 1930 *Tables for Statisticians and Biometricians*, 3rd edn. Cambridge University Press, Cambridge

Rasch G 1960 *Probabilistic Models for some Intelligence and Attainment Tests*. Danish Institute for Educational Research, Copenhagen

Ross S 1964 *Logical Foundations of Psychological Measurement: A Study in the Philosophy of Science*. Munksgaard, Copenhagen

Shaw M E, Wright J M 1967 *Scales for the Measurement of Attitudes*. McGraw-Hill, New York

Skodak M, Skeels H M 1949 A final follow-up study of one hundred adopted children. *J. Genet. Psychol.* 75: 85–125

Spearman C 1904 "General intelligence," objectively determined and measured. *Am. J. Psychol.* 15: 201–93

Stevens S S (ed.) 1951 *Handbook of Experimental Psychology.* Wiley, New York

Thorndike, R L (ed.) 1971 *Educational Measurement*, 2nd edn. American Council on Education, Washington, DC

Thurstone L L 1926 The mental age concept. *Psychol. Rev.* 33: 268–78

Thurstone L L 1931 Multiple-factor analysis. *Psychol. Rev.* 38: 406–27

Thurstone L L, Chave E J 1929 *The Measurement of Attitude: A Psycho-physical Method and Some Experiments with a Scale for Measuring Attitude toward the Church.* University of Chicago Press, Chicago, Illinois

Wechsler D 1939 *The Measurement of Adult Intelligence.* Williams and Williams, Baltimore, Maryland

History of Mental Testing

G. O. B. Thomson and S. Sharp

The history of mental testing and its influence on psychology and education is of special interest and value because it can be studied from so many different points of view and because it throws light on the interaction of widely differing developments, not only academic and theoretical but also social, political, and economic. There is no better case study of the common ground between social history and the history of ideas than the emergence of the mental-testing movement and its applications in society. The forces which determine how favourably academic developments are received by policy makers, the effects which those developments are intended to have and the effects they actually do have, the economic and political constraints to which they are subject, and many other relevant themes are illustrated by the history of psychological testing. This article seeks to illustrate these issues by selectively referring to key individuals and events in the United States and the United Kingdom. Carroll (1978) has referred to the development of mental testing in Europe.

The applications of educational assessment may be placed into two seemingly distinct categories, namely the examination of normal children as a part of the process of selection within the educational ladder and of streaming within schools, and the detection of subnormality in the context of removing children unable to benefit from orthodox education and assigning them to special schools. This second theme was chronologically the first to appear and has been far less controversial; the developments of the two have been affected by different social forces and have been in the jurisdiction of different policy makers, so from this aspect they may be considered separately. But the same academics were often involved and the same advances in educational psychology were relevant to both so it is misleading to regard them as completely divorced.

It is generally recognized that the first intelligence scale of the type which was to become so widespread was published in 1905 by the French psychologist Alfred Binet. Binet's work was not without foreshadows—psychologists had for some years been trying to arrive at an acceptable formulation of the essence of intelligence. Francis Galton and his pupil J. M. Cattell had used the term mental test as early as 1890 and believed that the essential constituent of intelligence was

"power of discrimination". They had made attempts to construct intelligence tests based on sensory acuity and speed but the results had proved disappointing. Similarly, Binet himself had made previous attempts to construct a method of measuring intelligence but had been able to arrive at nothing more robust than a comprehensive assessment of all aspects of performance by means of interviews, case notes, and so on.

In contrast, the achievement of the Binet scales was twofold. First, the questions asked and tasks set were such as to give the results the appearance of testing intelligence as opposed to attainment in scholastic subjects. This property was to be seized on vigorously by the proponents of educational testing in subsequent debates over the susceptibility of the results to environmental influences and the extent of their determination by heredity. The second innovation was the concept of mental age. A child's mental age was said to be 8 years if his or her performance was equal to that of the average 8-year-old child. By this method it was possible for the first time to compare children on an ostensibly objective basis and to draw quantitive standards for the assessment of children's intelligence and their assignment to appropriate educational channels. Shortly afterwards, William Stern suggested dividing mental age by chronological age and multiplying by 100 to derive the intelligence quotient or IQ, a term still used today although it is now a misnomer.

The timing of Binet's work could not have been better, for in the previous year, 1904, Charles Spearman had published his seminal paper on general intelligence. This concept was an obvious candidate to fill the gap which was, from the psychologist's point of view, the major defect in Binet's work, which was a lack of any theoretical basis. Spearman had been motivated to experiment on intelligence by reading Galton's work mentioned above. Using children's marks on a variety of subjects taught in a local school, Spearman was able to use the then newly developed techniques of correlation theory to investigate the pattern of covariances between them. He showed that the pattern approximated to that which would be expected if ability in each subject consisted of a general component which was fixed for each child but varied in the extent of its influence in each subject, and a specific component whose size represented the child's relative strengths and weaknesses across subjects. The general component could then be identified with the results of the Binet scale.

The appearance of these two works so close together appears to have been something of a coincidence. Certainly each was done in ignorance of the other. In fact Binet was critical of Spearman's work, distrusting its relatively heavy emphasis on statistics, while Spearman for his part considered Binet's work to be a case of serendipity in that he had found a way of measuring general intelligence almost without realizing it. Be that as it may, this combination of theoretical and methodological advance served to impart considerable appeal to the idea of intelligence in the eyes of those responsible for the efficient functioning of the education system.

The problems inherent in ensuring this efficiency had been attracting attention for some time. Primary education in England and Wales had been compulsory since the 1870s. Although the letter of the law had not always been fully observed, the extension of the educational franchise to encompass compulsorily greater numbers of children brought to greater prominence the increasing number of children near the borderline of subnormality. This forced on educators the need to diagnose, categorize, and provide for their differing educational needs. Thus, as early as 1912, George Auden, school medical officer for Birmingham called for more experimental research on the standardization of tests so that they might be used to sample the whole population and sift the "feebleminded". In this the origins of the development of group tests by Thomson, Burt, and Spearman in the 1920s can be seen.

Accordingly, the advantages of standardized testing were recognized first in the arrangements for the treatment of the educationally subnormal. The concept of subnormality was finally emerging as distinct from that of lunacy, with which it had long been legally associated, but although there was general agreement on the need to supply separate and adequate provision for the subnormal, implementation was dogged by the lack of a reliable, accurate method of identifying the condition. The problem was more than educational—although it was agreed that subnormal children should go to special schools, there were also good grounds for ensuring that less affected children were not so assigned. Attendance at a special school inevitably carried a certain stigma which parents were unwilling to incur unless it was clearly in the child's interest. But uppermost was the question of economy. Staff–pupil ratios were much higher in special than ordinary schools and expenditure per pupil was correspondingly greater. With restrictions on public funds and the need for value for money being as important as ever, officials had good reason (though not the same one) to join parents in wishing to make identification as accurate as possible.

In such a receptive climate, the Binet tests quickly became noticed. They began to be mentioned in official reports advocating their use, such as those of the chief medical officer of health to the board of education in London. Shortly before the First World War, the advantages of incorporating the tests in the diagnostic procedure were given institutional recognition. In this they were helped by another development in the psychology of the time, a rapidly expanding trend of classroom experimentation. This work, and the journals then being founded to promote its dissemination, had gained enough influence to motivate the London County Council to establish a half-time post of psychologist to help in that part of the work of the education committee which concerned subnormal children.

The significance of this post is that it marked the beginning of the professionalization of psychology as an independent discipline and the recognition of its members as possessing an expertise of their own and an aura of scientific respectability. Equally significantly, the post was not established without opposition, particularly from the medical profession who, while they did not resent the encroachment of psychology into their work, did resent the encroachment of psychologists, arguing instead that the post should be given to a medic with training in psychology. In this they were unsuccessful. The appointee was Cyril Burt.

The first foothold gained by mental testing in education may be seen therefore to have been concerned with the diagnosis of and provision for subnormality. In the next few years, however, the major developments were not only in a very different area of application but in a very different part of the world. The entry of the United States into the First World War gave the army authorities a problem for which there was no precedent: the processing, evaluation, and classification of more conscripts than anyone had ever had to deal with before. However, the means were at hand: following Binet's death in 1911, Lewis Terman at Stanford University had started work on an American version of the scale. Because of the changes made to the original items, the result became known as the Stanford–Binet Revision. This work was in progress anyway, but the sudden need for evaluating such numbers of recruits obviously gave it a new importance.

In characteristic North American fashion, the problem was tackled by the United States Government establishing a "think tank" of specialists—test makers, statisticians, and measurement experts—charged with solving the psychological problems posed by the military emergency. In this way Thorndike, Goddard, Yerkes, and Terman amongst these specialists collaborated on the rapid classification of Army conscripts. The resultant test technology which they developed was the Army Alpha and Beta Tests. The immediacy of the need for these tests gave them obvious impact—any reservations about the meaning of test results tended to be swept aside by the fait accompli of having administered them to 1,700,000 recruits. The sheer mass of this achievement seemed to imbue the tests with an authority they may not otherwise have possessed. Their widespread use continued after the war ended, and in such numbers that they inevitably had great influence on thinking at that time about the definition and measurement of intelligence. However, while reservations about the use of mental testing had been temporarily submerged by the practicalities of the army testing programme, they reappeared in the 1920s when the results were used for research purposes. The opportunities thus presented opened a veritable "Pandora's box" of claims, alleged findings, criticisms, and arguments which may have lost their freshness, but certainly not their impetus, in the intervening 65 years.

A digest of this mass of data was published in 1921 and was immediately used to advance a series of highly controversial claims. Apart from the famous result that the average American has a mental age of 14, comparisons were drawn between the average performances of various cultural, ethnic, and racial groups with a view to making inferences about differences in their respective intellectual capacities. In view of the effects of such obvious confounding influences as variations in the length of time members of the respective groups had been in the country, it is no great surprise that large differences were found. Yet the assumption that mental tests invariably measured innate capacity carried sufficient authority to enable the inferences to be made and widely publicized. Opposition was immediate and vociferous and many of the major criticisms of the incautious use of IQ test data were rehearsed in some form or other during the 1920s. Despite this, the views of the growing psychometric movement were taken sufficiently seriously in positions of influence for legislation to be passed which was informed by their claims and which reflected the importance which they attached to racial differences. For instance, H. H. Goddard, who had conducted screening tests for the "feebleminded" at the Ellis Island immigrant receiving station is reported by Kamin (1977 p. 31) as stating that:

> the test results established that 83 percent of the Jews, 80 percent of the Hungarians, 79 percent of the Italians and 87 percent of the Russians were feebleminded.

It is arguable that Goddard's work on screening immigrants together with Yerkes' and Brigham's later work in screening army recruits directly contributed to Congress passing the Johnson-Lodge Immigration Act of 1924 which effectively established national origin quotas as permanent immigration policy discriminating against southern and eastern Europeans. There is thus considerable evidence to indicate that in America, eugenic concerns received sufficient prominence from these social changes to have a marked impact on attitudes and policy making at the highest level.

In the United Kingdom there had not been the immigration which America experienced in the nineteenth century and the debate was rather more muted. Certainly, claims were made concerning the heritability of intelligence and its implications for social-class differences which were later to attract trenchant criticism but at the time of the First World War and its aftermath, few thought it necessary to speak out against the hereditarian assumption.

There was, however, one development which was to have considerable implications for the future status of mental testing. It has already been seen that the contribution of Charles Spearman was to supply a theoretical rationale for intelligence by introducing his concept of general ability and investigating its properties by studying patterns of intertest correlations. In 1916 Godfrey Thomson demonstrated that the correlation pattern compatible with the theory of general ability was also compatible with a theory of group abilities, each of which played a part in determining proficiency in several tests but none of which was involved in all tests. This opposition between general and group factor theories of intelligence came to form, as it does today, the major distinction between factorial models of the intellect. At first it was thought that they were competing alternatives with a possibility of discriminating in favour of one or the other, but subsequent mathematical developments showed that they are alternative ways of factor analysing the same data.

This critical stance by Thomson attracted the attention of E. L. Thorndike, regarded as the founding father of psychometrics in the United States. His position and influence within American psychometrics is well-documented, especially his association with Terman, Goddard, and Yerkes in the development of the Army Alpha test. The link across the Atlantic is provided by Teachers College at Columbia University where Thorndike remained a professor throughout this period and beyond, and where Thomson was invited to be a visiting professor in 1923–1924. It is possible that this association played a significant part in the thrust and direction of the mental–testing movement in America along multifactorial lines. Certainly, the group-factor view advocated by Thomson was espoused later by Thurstone and has come to be very much more characteristic of the American psychology of individual differences than of its European counterpart (Thurstone 1938).

Thurstone's model proposed that intelligence was not a unitary ability but a collection of a number of independent, primary abilities—seven in number, namely, verbal, numerical, spatial, perceptual, memory, reasoning, and word fluency—and that an individual could be "plotted" as a profile across these seven primary mental abilities. Such a view contrasts markedly with that of Spearman, making fundamentally different assumptions about the relationship between intelligence and the various skills which it subsumes. The analogy has been made by Butcher (1968) that Spearman viewed intelligence as being comparable with playing bridge, that is, anticipating and coordinating a variety of subordinate skills towards a superordinate goal, whereas Thurstone's interpretation was akin to competence at events such as the decathlon—a measure of all-round athletic ability with no evidence that the subskills are related.

Such a difference may, as already noted, be regarded statistically as a choice between alternative factor-analytic models. Nevertheless, they clearly have widely differing implications for education and here again there is a contrast between the United Kingdom and the United States. The American concept of the high school is compatible with the idea of mixed-ability education and a reluctance to segregate children of different ability levels into different schools. While it is very difficult to establish causal relationships between the views of psychometrists and those of educational policy makers, it is certainly true that the preference for this type of organization was also compatible with the prevailing group-factor view: an emphasis on maximizing differences between factors rather than their common element naturally goes with a distrust of segregation based on one general measure of educational proficiency or potential. It is significant in this context that Thomson, one of the few British advocates of group factors, approved warmly of the idea behind the high school.

In the United Kingdom, however, while it is still difficult to ascribe causal connections, it is again true that policy and psychometrics went together, this time inclining towards a single-factor view of intelligence and a greater emphasis on educational selection. Inevitably, it was not long before the existence of the job to be done (efficient overall educational assessment) found the technology to do it—standardized group tests of general intelligence.

The first case of an education authority in England using a group test as part of the assessment of normal children in ordinary schools was in 1920. The authority was Northumberland and their motives were impeccably egalitarian. The area for which they were responsible contained both rural and urban areas and they were aware of a trend for schools in more remote districts to submit few or no candidates for the scholarship examination at age 11. Anxious to know whether this was due to a lack of ability on the part of the children or of resources on the part of the schools, they asked Godfrey Thomson (ironically in the light of his other views) who was then living in Northumberland, to devise an appropriate test to help resolve the problem.

This initial case is of interest because it is typical in many respects of the motivation behind the use of tests—the most efficient use of educational resources and the aim of ensuring that, when those resources are limited, they are directed towards those children best able to profit from them. Of course the authorities were aware that the performance of a given child would be influenced by its background and that children from better homes would be at an advantage. The reason for switching to standardized tests was that this advantage would manifest itself anyway and that its extent was likely to be greater if the new methods were not implemented.

The problems were certainly not local to Northumberland. At national level, there was a growing move towards the provision of secondary-school places which did not involve the parents in the payment of any fees. Regulations implemented in 1907 stipulated that one-quarter of secondary-school places should be of this type before the full government grant could be given. The regulations also stipulated that applicants should be required to pass an "entrance test of attainments and proficiency". Initially, this test was intended merely to safeguard standards and to ensure that the free places

did not go to children whose previous education was insufficient to enable them to profit fully from attendance at a secondary school. Inevitably, however, demand for the places far exceeded supply and the entrance examination rapidly became seen not as a safeguard but as a competitive arena, success in which assumed great importance not only for individual children but also for primary-school teachers who recognized the need to give children every chance of doing well. This in turn led to the problem of the curriculum being oriented towards the examination rather than the examination being tailored to fit the curriculum, a topic which has been the concern of educationists ever since.

The appeal of standardized tests for use in the assessment of normal children continued to be reinforced in the period between the wars. The report of the wordily but significantly titled Board of Education Consultative Committee on Psychological Tests of Educable Capacity, published in 1924, had taken evidence from Thomson and was in large part written by Burt. It stressed the potential value of intelligence tests in selecting children for different forms of education and, significantly, drew attention to the distinction between intelligence tests and tests of scholastic attainment and vocational aptitude. This has clear affinities with the distinction between inborn ability and acquired skills. Although it was never spelled out explicitly in official circles, the implied claim of intelligence tests to separate out talent inherent in the child from knowledge dependent on upbringing was not the least of its attractions to those concerned with the equitable and efficient use of resources.

Nevertheless, despite prodding from the centre, intelligence tests were not universally accepted by English local authorities; just over half of them used an intelligence test of some description in their scholarship selection procedure prior to 1940. Even so, this proportion indicates that intelligence testing was becoming respectable in the United Kingdom in the interwar period and, coupled with continued encouragement at the Board, culminated in a report of 1938, the Spens Report, which was as sympathetic to the notion of educational selection based on standardized testing as any government report was ever to be. Along with the Norwood Report of 1943, it laid the foundation for accepting the principle of segregation which was to be enshrined in the Education Act of 1944. This implemented the principle of primary and secondary education being provided in different schools with the break being at age 11 plus: inevitably this name was attached to the selective examination itself. Although the Act did not place any restrictions on how secondary education was to be organized, the placing of the critical selection as early as age 11 owes something to the confidence which had been won by mental tests as accurate and powerful predictors of intellectual potential. It is certainly also true that this age choice was determined in part by administrative reasons, concerned for example with the school-leaving age and the duration of secondary schooling. Nevertheless, it is unlikely that this choice would have been as acceptable if the mental-testing movement had not lent its support to the meaningfulness and justifiability of decisive assessment at this stage of the child's school career.

In the postwar period in the United Kingdom, economic restrictions—which were much more influential before 1940 than this account has had space to convey—have in part given way to political forces. The move towards comprehensive education and the introduction of a system of organization much closer to that advocated by Thomson (some 40 years after he advocated it) have inevitably altered the role played by mental tests. They are certainly still used for streaming, screening, and selection but they no longer have that aura of authority and validity which attached to them in the first half of this century. This reduction in the status of psychometric testing both in the United States and the United Kingdom reflects a growing scepticism amongst applied psychologists of the value of IQ scores. In the United States particularly, there has been strong reaction to IQ testing for selection and screening purposes, partly as a consequence of a series of legal actions and partly as a result of a growing awareness of the presumed "cultural bias" of most testing procedures in favour of white, Anglo-Saxon populations. In the United Kingdom, the decline in testing, in particular screening for secondary education, dates from the mid-1950s when the effects of coaching and practice on tests were reported. When taken with the knowledge that in England and Wales the provision of grammar-school places was so unequal and that differing authorities used tests in ways varying from one authority to another, public concern could not go unheeded. (The position in Scotland was different, with an established pattern of comprehensive education which contrasted with that in England and Wales.) As with the United States, awareness of the importance of wider sociocultural factors on test performance came to be appreciated and accepted. Furthermore in both the United States and the United Kingdom, applied psychologists came to recognize that in addition to dealing with technology, psychologists dealt with people and as a professional group have begun to articulate roles and practices that, superficially at least, appear to reject assessment and testing in favour of intervention, support, therapy, and so on.

There have also been significant postwar developments in the area of theoretical formulations of intelligence and the construction of tests based on them. With the emergence of a large literature on factor analysis, statistics have played an increasingly central role. In particular, general and group abilities have been incorporated into a single model. One such case is that of Vernon (1950) for whom general ability or "g" does exist but it subsumes two major group factors—v:ed (verbal–educational) and k:m (spatial–mechanical), with each of these major group factors in turn subsuming specific factors. Thus, Vernon proposed an hierarchical model of the structure of the intellect recognizing "g" but at the same time supporting the Thurstone view of a

number of independent so-called "primary mental abilities". This hierarchical model apparently reconciles the opposing stances adopted by Spearman and Thurstone and leads Eysenck (1979 p. 49) to state

Summarizing the factor-analytic evidence on validity of the Spearman–Thurstone theory of intelligence, we find that on the whole there is strong support for the following conclusions: (a) the data are in agreement with the proposition that all cognitive behaviour is determined to varying degree by a general ability underlying all special manifestations; (b) different persons possess this ability to varying degrees; (c) tests similar in item content (verbal, numerical, etc.) or mental processing requirement (memory, reasoning) may require additional special abilities; (d) a hierarchical model best encompasses these various facts.

It is relevant to indicate that in Vernon's model there exists the theoretical basis upon which Wechsler (1949) developed his scales for the measurement of intelligence, with the distinction between verbal and performance scales being analogous to Vernon's v:ed and k:m factors. These Wechsler scales remain to date amongst the most widely used of individual tests and are part of the technology of psychometrics that has developed apace since the infancy of the "science".

Another prominent name in the multifactorial tradition of American psychometry is that of J. P. Guilford. His 1956 "Structure of the Intellect" model does not include the idea of general ability but argues instead that intellectual functioning is the outcome of the interaction of a number of dimensions. It is a theoretical formulation which supposes that any account of intelligence must consider the kind of mental operation engaged; the content upon which such mental operations are performed; and also the product that results. To complete the theory, Guilford suggests the existence of five kinds of mental operation, four types of content, and six types of product. In this theory, intellectual abilities comprise an hypothetical $6 \times 5 \times 4$ matrix producing 120 separate abilities. This in essence is what is referred to as Guilford's SI model and the research activity which it has generated continues with the literature indicating that 98 of these "elements" in the matrix have been demonstrated empirically and are amenable to testing (Guilford and Hoepfner 1971). Debate continues as to the efficiency of this model as well as to its utility value for applied psychologists as an advance in the technology of psychometrics.

The emergence of Guilford's SI model and the related research activity which it has generated coincide with a period during which psychometrists have focused increasingly upon the assessment of discrete factors contributing to intellectual functioning rather than eliciting global measures. The reason for this lies partly in the continuity of the mainstream tradition in psychometrics initiated by Binet—the identification of the feeble-minded—although nowadays the euphemistic terminology "those with special (educational) needs" is more acceptable. Another trend has resulted in an apparent diminution in testing activity which results from applied psychologists' recognizing the importance of wider socio-cultural factors affecting test performance and, in their professional identities, seeking more therapeutic and less assessment-oriented roles.

It cannot be argued that this is a comprehensive or even representative outline of the history of mental testing in Western Europe and the United States. The best that can be claimed is that the prominent events and processes mentioned serve to illustrate some of the major recurrent themes which emerge from its study.

Possibly the most important of these has been the motivation of the proponents of testing. They have been subject to sustained and powerful criticism on both sides of the Atlantic ranging from complaints that their practices have undesirable effects on the process of education through to accusations that they are tools of a repressive social control whose work serves to buttress the status quo and preserve social inequality. But of course the testers themselves have never seen it this way. No evidence has been produced to refute the view that the testers believed, at the time they did it, that what they did was genuinely in the best interests of society. Sometimes they recanted—C. C. Brigham, who spent much of the 1920s disseminating racial eugenic views, spent much of the 1930s refuting them, while it is well-known that, towards the end of his life, Lewis Terman came to have great doubts about the hereditarian position. Indeed, some testers worked in spite of their other views about education, such as Thomson whose Moray House Tests were highly influential in the United Kingdom between the wars and which helped to lead to the very system of segregative schools which in his other writings on education he argued against.

Such paradoxes can only be resolved by referring to the perceived advantages and disadvantages of alternatives to test use. Testers have never denied the element of truth in the argument that home background influences test performance and that tracking or streaming then leads to differential educational provision which preserves inequalities to the disadvantage of those children from poorer homes. On the other hand, psychologists and policy makers who favour testing have been aware that if resources are limited—and for most of this century they have been limited even more than they are now—then not all children can be given as good an education as might be wished and the most important aim becomes to allocate available resources as fairly and efficiently as possible. It is when the debate has been restricted to this relatively narrow consideration that the arguments of the testers have been strongest and, in the long run, most influential, which is why much of the material in this article has concentrated on it.

Another point to have emerged from the many applications made of tests is that they have played a reinforcing rather than an innovative role in the development of social policy. They have provided means whereby aims could be pursued more effectively and with greater speed, but they have not acted to bring those aims into existence. Thus, for example, there was growing concern about provision for subnormal children in the United

Kingdom before 1905, though legislative progress was slow due to the difficulties of definition. The Binet scales thus acted to accelerate and facilitate a process which predated their appearance. It remains possible, therefore, that most major educational initiatives would have occurred in some form or other in the absence of the testing movement.

A third feature worthy of comment, this time relevant to psychometrics as an applied science, concerns the apparently static nature of the controversy. Most of the major theoretical and technical distinctions and most of the principle points of dispute were in existence by 1925. The differences between individual and group testing and between general and group factor models of intelligence were established and the relative influences on intelligence of heredity and the environment and the implications for social and educational policy were provoking heated debate. Since then, the argument has not been at a constant level, but has flared up from time to time after interest has apparently lagged. The most recent instance of this was Arthur Jensen's 1969 article in the *Harvard Educational Review*. But although new data are brought forward and statistical models become ever more elaborate, philosophers of science are beginning to notice the lack of new substantive argument and are relating it to Kuhn's (1962) concept of a preparadigmatic science. It is possible that future work in this direction will offer more understanding than the debate itself.

There are many other themes touched upon but too numerous to mention in detail. The effect of testing in helping to establish psychometrics first as an independent profession with its own expertise and later as a burgeoning industry controlling entry to an ever increasing range of social positions both inside and outside education; the relationship between testing as a research activity and testing as a policy instrument and the influences on this relationship of a range of pressures ranging from limitations in government spending through to the vested interests of large commercial corporations; the unending controversy about whether test results can be used not only to manage society but also to investigate its nature and to demonstrate the possibility, inevitability or current existence of a meritocracy; these and many other strands of social science are relevant to the study of the history of mental testing. The rich and varied potential of the topic make it certain, therefore, that it will continue to attract attention and to generate both understanding and controversy as its study continues to develop.

See also: History of Educational Research; Factor Analysis

Bibliography

Butcher H 1968 *Human Intelligence: Its Nature and Assessment.* Methuen, London

Carroll J B 1978 On the theory–practice interface in the measurement of intellectual abilities. In: Suppes P (ed.) 1978 *Impact of Research on Education: Some Case Studies.* National Academy of Education, Washington, DC

Evans B, Waites B 1981 *IQ and Mental Testing: An Unnatural Science and its Social History*. Macmillan, London

Eysenck H J 1979 *The Structure and Measurement of Intelligence*. Springer, Berlin

Guilford J P 1956 The structure of intellect. *Psychol. Bull.* 53: 267–93

Guilford J P, Hoepfner R 1971 *The Analysis of Intelligence*. McGraw-Hill, New York

Jensen A 1969 How much can we boost IQ and scholastic achievement? *Harvard Educ. Rev.* 39: 1–123

Kamin L J 1977 *The Science and Politics of IQ*. Wiley, New York

Karier C J 1972 Testing for order and control in the corporate liberal state. *Educ. Theory* 22(2): 154–80

Kuhn T S 1962 *The Structure of Scientific Revolutions*. University of Chicago Press, Chicago, Illinois

Sharp S 1980 Godfrey Thomson and the concept of intelligence. In: Smith J V, Hamilton D (eds.) 1980 *The Meritocratic Intellect: Studies in the History of Educational Research*. Aberdeen University Press, Aberdeen

Spearman C 1904 "General intelligence": Objectively determined and measured. *Am. J. Psychol.* 115: 201–92

Sutherland G 1977 The magic of measurement: Mental testing and English education 1900–1940. *Transactions of the Royal Historical Society*, 5th series. 29: 135–53

Terman L M 1916 *Measuring Intelligence*. Houghton Mifflin, New York

Thomson G H 1916 A hierarchy without a general factor. *Brit. J. Psychol.* 8: 271

Thurstone L L 1938 *Primary Mental Abilities*. University of Chicago Press, Chicago, Illinois

Vernon P E 1950 *The Structure of Human Abilities*. Methuen, London

Wechsler D 1949 *The Wechsler Intelligence Scale for Children*. Psychological Corporation, New York

True-score Models

R. R. Wilcox

Suppose N examinees take an n-item test. A frequent goal in mental test theory is making inferences about the examinees, or items, that go beyond the observed test scores. For example, the items on a test might represent some larger item domain, and the goal might be to estimate the proportion of items an examinee would get correct if he/she answers every item in the item pool. Another goal might be to determine how well an examinee would perform if he/she were to take the same n items at another point in time. There are many related problems as well. For example, if examinees either pass or fail a test, how can observed scores be used to characterize how well a test is performing? How many items should be used on a test?

True-score models are essentially probability models that yield solutions to the problems described above. The term "true score" refers to some unknown parameter that represents an examinee's ability level. However, there are several notions of true score which represent different conceptualizations of ability. The true score used in a particular situation will depend on the goals of the test constructor, the related measurement problems, and the assumptions that are reasonable in a given situation. Thus, it is important to have a precise description of the different true scores, and to understand how they relate to one another. The remaining sections outline these differences.

1. Classical Test Theory

Consider a single examinee responding to a specific item that is scored either right or wrong. Suppose the item is repeatedly administered to the same examinee, and that the examinee's responses are independent of one another. If a 1 indicates a correct response, and a 0 an incorrect response, then an examinee's responses can be represented by a sequence of 1's and 0's. The distribution of the 1's and 0's is called a propensity distribution.

The examinee's expected score, μ, where the expectation is taken with respect to the propensity distribution, is the examinee's true score. That is, μ is the average value of the 1's and 0's over the independent and repeated responses to an item.

In this particular situation, the examinee's true score is just the probability of a correct response, where the probability μ is defined in terms of the repeated, independent, and identically distributed trials. However, this notion of true score is easily extended to any measuring instrument. In particular, let x be an examinee's score on some test. Then the examinee's true score is defined to be $E(x)$, that is, the expected value of x, where the expectation is taken with respect to the propensity distribution of x.

In order to make inferences about μ, classical test theory makes some additional assumptions about the observed scores of examinees. Measurement journals are replete with articles on characterizing tests under these assumptions, and the work continues. Here the important point is the interpretation of μ. For a summary of the basic ideas in classical test theory, see Lord and Novick (1968).

2. Latent Trait Models

A class of true-score models that grew out of classical test theory are known as latent trait models. These models consist of a mathematical equation that proposes how an examinee's "ability" level combines with certain item characteristics to yield the probability that an examinee will produce the correct response. An appealing feature of these models is that once an examinee's ability level has been estimated, it is possible to determine the probability of a correct response to an item the examinee has never taken, assuming that certain item parameters have already been determined.

267

Let $p_i(\theta)$ be the probability that a specific examinee with ability θ, $-\infty < \theta < \infty$, answers the ith item correctly on an n-item test. Several mathematical forms for $p_i(\theta)$ have been proposed (Lord 1980).

For present purposes, the important point is how these probabilities are interpreted. It might seem that the term "probability" is a precise description of $p_i(\theta)$, and in a certain sense it is; however, probabilities are frequently interpreted in terms of some process. In classical test theory, the process is repeatedly administering the same item to the same examinee which leads to the true score μ. A similar interpretation is sometimes given to $p_i(\theta)$. That is, $p_i(\theta)$ is the examinee's expected score (assuming dichotomously scored items) where the expectation is taken with respect to a propensity distribution. However, Lord (1980 Chap. 15) objects to this interpretation, and suggests that one of two alternative interpretations be used instead. The first imagines a pool of items that have the same item parameters. For a randomly sampled item, $p_i(\theta)$ is the probability of a correct response from an examinee having ability level θ. The second interpretation is that $p_i(\theta)$ is the probability of a correct answer from a randomly sampled examinee who has ability level θ.

3. Item Sampling Models

A third class of true-score models is known as item sampling models. Again consider a single examinee responding to an n-item test. This time items are viewed as being randomly sampled from some item domain. In some cases the item domain exists de facto, and tests do indeed consist of randomly sampled items. In other situations, sampling items from an item domain is just a convenient conceptualization.

The binomial error model is the most commonly used item sampling model. This means that if ξ is the proportion of items an examinee would get correct if he/she were to respond to every item in the item pool, the probability of getting y correct on an n-item test is:

$$f(y\,|\,\xi) = \left[\frac{n}{y}\right]\xi^y(1-\xi)^{n-y}$$

Note that ξ is different from μ, θ, and $p_i(\theta)$; ξ does not, for example, involve a propensity distribution—examinees are assumed to respond only once to an item in the definition of ξ. Also, latent trait models are usually assumed to be unidimensional (e.g., Lord 1980) while item sampling models do not require this assumption. This is not necessarily a criticism of latent trait models since it has been argued that tests should be homogeneous in some sense. A disadvantage of the binomial model is that it implies that all the items on a test have the same level of difficulty when every examinee takes the same items. However, this problem can be avoided (Lord and Novick 1968 Chap. 23), and it appears that it is not a serious problem in practice (Wilcox 1981).

It might be surmised that Lord's first interpretation of $p_i(\theta)$ is the same as ξ, and this conclusion might be reinforced by observing that when latent trait models are assumed, the probability of y correct responses to an n-item test reduces to a binomial probability function in certain special cases (Lord and Novick 1968 p. 385). The quantities $p_i(\theta)$ and ξ are related, but they are not necessarily the same. To see this, note that under a latent trait model each item in a domain of items has some set of item parameters a, b, and c; and the value of these parameters will presumably vary over the items. If $g(a,b,c)$ is the joint probability function of a, b, and c for the item domain, then the probability of a correct response to a randomly sampled item is:

$$\xi = \iiint p(\theta, a, b, c)\,g(a, b, c)\,da\,db\,dc$$

Of course, if Lord's second interpretation is used, ξ and $p(\theta,a,b,c)$ again represent different quantities.

4. Latent State Models

A fourth class of true-score models assumes examinees responding to an item belong to one of finitely many states. The most common situation is a two-state model where examinees are assumed to either know or not know the correct response. Other models include the possibility of having misinformation. That is, an examinee eliminates the correct response on a multiple-choice item in the belief that it is indeed incorrect. The problem is that an examinee's response might not reflect his/her true state. If, for example, an examinee does not know the answer to a multiple-choice item, he/she might choose the correct response by chance.

Numerous latent structure models have been proposed for measuring and correcting errors at the item level such as guessing. As a simple illustration, one of these models is described below.

Suppose randomly sampled examinees respond to an answer-until-correct test. That is, examinees choose an alternative on a multiple-choice test item, and they are told immediately whether they are correct. This can be accomplished by having examinees erase a shield on an especially designed answer sheet. If the symbol underneath the shield reveals that the examinee is incorrect, he/she chooses another alternative. This process continues until the correct response is identified.

Among the population of examinees, let p_i be the proportion of examinees who would choose the correct response on the ith attempt of a particular item. Let ζ be the proportion of examinees who would know, and suppose ζ_i is the proportion who can eliminate i distractors ($i = 1,\ldots, t-2$) where t is the number of alternatives. The idea is that some examinees might be able to eliminate certain responses from consideration via partial information without knowing the correct response. If after eliminating as many distractors as possible, a testee chooses at random from among those that remain, then:

$$\zeta = p_1 - p_2$$

(Wilcox 1982). Thus, if among N examinees, y_1 is the number who get an item right on the first try, and if y_2 get it correct on the second try, the estimate of ζ, the proportion of examinees who know the correct response, is just $\zeta = (y_1 - y_2)/N$. A similar model can be used to estimate the proportion of skills among a domain if skills that an examinee has acquired, and a modification of the model can be used to measure misinformation. Many other measurement problems can be solved including an exact test for random guessing, and an empirical method of determining how many distractors are needed on multiple-choice items. For results on related models, see Macready and Dayton (1980) and the references therein.

Bibliography

Lord F M 1980 *Applications of Item Response Theory to Practical Testing Problems*. Erlbaum, Hillsdale, New Jersey

Lord F M, Novick M R 1968 *Statistical Theories of Mental Test Scores*. Addison-Wesley, Reading, Massachusetts

Macready G B, Dayton C M 1980 The nature and use of state mastery models. *Appl. Psychol. Meas.* 4: 493–516

Wilcox R R 1981 A review of the beta-binomial model and its extensions. *J. Educ. Stat.* 6: 3–32

Wilcox R R 1982 Some empirical and theoretical results on an answer-until-correct scoring procedure. *Br. J. Math. Stat. Psychol.* 35: 57–70

Item Response Theory

F. M. Lord and M. L. Stocking

Item response theory (IRT) models the relationship between a person's level on the trait being measured by a test and the person's response to a test item or question (Lord 1980). Because trait levels are inherently unobservable, item response theory falls into the general class of latent trait models.

In contrast to classical test theory, item response theory makes strong assumptions about a person's behavior when responding to items. Many advantages accrue from these strong assumptions: (a) it is possible to characterize or describe an item, independently of any sample of people who might respond to the item; (b) it is possible to characterize a person independently of any sample of items administered to the person; (c) it is possible to predict properties of a test in advance of test administration.

Item response theory has some disadvantages. It is currently not possible to completely check the accuracy with which the assumptions are met by the data. For data that appear to meet the assumptions, however, it is reassuring that predictions made from item response theory can often be independently verified. Applications of item response theory are generally more expensive than similar applications of classical test theory, and many applications of item response theory require the use of a computer.

1. Basic Concepts of Item Response Theory

1.1 Assumptions

Most item response theory models assume that only a single latent trait underlies performance on an item. This is often a reasonable assumption: most tests are constructed to measure a single trait, for example, verbal ability. Models that incorporate more than one latent trait are currently beyond the state of the art.

All of item response theory assumes that it is possible to describe mathematically the relationship between a person's trait level and performance on an item. This mathematical description is called an item response function, an item characteristic curve, or a trace line.

1.2 Item Response Functions

For dichotomously scored items (items that are scored right or wrong), the item response function (IRF) states mathematically the probability of a correct response for a given level of trait. This conditional probability is a function of the item characteristics or parameters. Usually, the mathematical function chosen to represent this conditional probability is from the logistic ogive family or the normal ogive family of functions. There is little difference between the two. More practical work has been done using the logistic family, because of its mathematical simplicity.

If u_i stands for a response to item i (0 for incorrect and 1 for correct) and θ stands for the trait being measured, then the logistic item response function is:

$$P(u_i = 1 | \theta) = c_i + (1 - c_i)/(1 + e^{-1.702 a_i (\theta - b_i)}) \tag{1}$$

The normal ogive item response function is:

$$P(u_i = 1 | \theta) = c_i + (1 - c_i)\Phi[a_i(\theta - b_i)] \tag{2}$$

where $\Phi[\ ]$ is the normal cumulative distribution function. In these equations a_i, b_i, and c_i, are parameters that describe characteristics of item i. Figure 1 displays a typical item response function and the meaning of the three item parameters. The pseudo-guessing parameter c_i is the probability that an examinee with very low θ will respond correctly to the item. The item discrimination parameter a_i is related to the steepness of the curve at the point of inflection. The item difficulty b_i is the θ-level at the point of inflection.

Not all items require three parameters to characterize them adequately. Some work has been done with two-parameter models ($c_i = 0$). A great deal of work has been done with one-parameter models in which the items vary only in difficulty ($a_i = $ constant, $c_i = 0$). If this latter model is logistic, it is called the Rasch model.

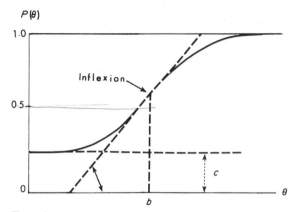

Figure 1
Meaning of item parameters[a]

a Source: Lord (1980), reprinted by permission

Note that the three-parameter model in Eqn. (1) and Eqn. (2) subsumes models with fewer parameters.

Item response models have also been developed for items with more complex scoring procedures. Consider a multiple-choice item for which it is informative to know which incorrect option was selected by a person. Item response theory applicable to this type of scoring has been developed by Bock (1972) and Samejima (1969).

1.3 Information Functions

Information functions (Birnbaum 1968) are used to describe the measurement effectiveness of a test or an item at each level of the trait being measured. In contrast, classical test theory usually provides only one measure of effectiveness, which is applied to all people regardless of their θ.

The test information function for a particular scoring method has two equivalent definitions, both of which are useful. By the first definition, the information function for test score y, $I(\theta, y)$, is inversely proportional to the square of the length of the asymptotic confidence interval for estimating trait θ from score y. A high level of information at a particular θ means that this θ can be more precisely estimated from score y than a θ for which the level of information is relatively low.

The second definition states that the information function for test score y is the square of the ratio of (the slope of the regression of y on θ) to (the standard error of measurement of y for fixed θ). In this context, $I(\theta, y)$ can be viewed as a signal-to-noise ratio. The signal is the change in mean y due to a change in θ. The noise is measured by the standard error of measurement of y for fixed θ.

An item information function $I(\theta, u_i)$ is defined as $I(\theta, u_i) \equiv [P_i'(\theta)]^2 / [P_i(\theta)Q_i(\theta)]$, where $p_i(\theta) \equiv P(u_i = 1|\theta)$ is the item response function, $Q_i(\theta) = 1 - P_i(\theta)$; and $P_i'(\theta)$ is the derivative of the item response function with respect to θ. The test information function $I(\theta)$ is

defined as the maximum information available from a test, regardless of the scoring method. The test information function is the simple sum of the item information functions: $I(\theta) = \Sigma_{i=1}^{n} I(\theta, u_i)$, where n is the number of items in the test. For conventional tests $I(\theta)$ is typically a bell-shaped curve. Each item contributes to $I(\theta)$ independently of all other items in the test. In classical item and test analysis, the contribution of each item to test reliability and test validity depends upon what other items are in the test.

Information functions are useful when the metric established for measuring θ is not subject to challenge. However, slight changes in this metric can drastically alter the shape of an information function and therefore the conclusions drawn.

1.4 Relative Efficiency Functions

Suppose there are two tests, x and y, both measuring the same trait θ. The relative efficiency (R.E.) function of test y versus test x, R.E. (y, x), is the ratio of their information functions at corresponding values of θ: R.E. $(y, x) = I(\theta, y)/I(\theta, x)$ (Birnbaum 1968). Most practical applications of item response theory will rely on relative efficiency functions since, unlike information functions, relative efficiency is invariant under any monotonic transformation of the metric used to measure θ.

If R.E.$(y, x) > 1$ for a particular θ, then test y gives more information than test x at that θ. Relative efficiency functions are useful tools for redesigning existing tests and for investigating novel tests, without actually administering them.

2. Illustrative Applications

The first steps in any application of item response theory to practical problems are to choose a model for the item response function and to obtain estimates of item parameters and θ's. The process of obtaining these estimates (frequently referred to as calibration) is generally accomplished by one of the many available computer programs (see Wingersky 1983). The following sections describe some applications.

2.1 Test Construction

Tests with prespecified measurement properties can be constructed from a pool of calibrated items. The first step is to specify a target information function for the new test. The shape of this target indicates the θ levels at which the test should provide the most precise measurement. Next select items for the new test that will fill in areas under the target that might be difficult to fill, for example, areas where relatively few items are available. Compute the test information function for this part test. Then add items that contribute information in areas that are far from meeting the target. Continue to choose items, always comparing the information function of the part test to the target, until a satisfactory approximation to the target has been reached.

2.2 Redesigning an Existing Test

Relative efficiency functions provide a convenient way of investigating various design changes in a test and comparing them with the original test. Figure 2 illustrates this.

The curves in Fig. 2 are relative efficiency functions for three different tests designed from an original 50-item test. Curve 1 is a test containing only the 25 harder items. This half-length test is less efficient for all test scores. The loss of efficiency is small, however, for high scores. Curve 2 is a test containing only the 25 easier items. This half-length test is less efficient at high scores but is actually more efficient than the full-length test at low scores. This is true because guessing on hard items by low-scoring people destroys information. Better measurement is obtained for these people by discarding the harder items. Curve 3 is a 50-item test with all b_i changed to a middle value. This "peaked" test measures very much better for the middle range of scores.

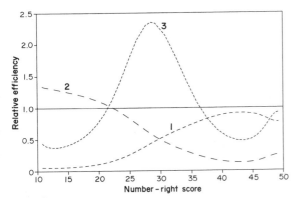

Figure 2
Relative efficiency functions of three modified tests

2.3 Equating

Equating is a measurement topic of interest to test publishers who produce many different forms of a test but wish to report scores on a single scale. The process of finding corresponding scores on different forms of a test is called equating. In general, observed scores on two different forms of a test cannot be equated except under conditions that make the equating unnecessary (Lord 1980). However, true scores can be equated under a wide variety of conditions, and item response theory facilitates true-score equating.

Suppose there are two tests, x and y, both measuring the same trait. The items in both tests are calibrated on the same scale. A person's (number-right) true score T_x on test x is a transformation of the person's θ: $T_x = \sum_{i=1}^{n} P_i(\theta)$, where $P_i(\theta)$ is the item response function for item i evaluated at θ, and n is the number of items in test x. Similarly, the true score on test y is $T_y = \sum_{i=1}^{m} P_i(\theta)$, where the sum is taken over the m items in test y. These two expressions imply that for any particular θ, a true score on test x and a corresponding true score on test y can be computed. These two true scores are equated because they represent the same trait level on two different measuring scales.

In practice, estimated item parameters are substituted into the two expressions and equated pairs of true scores are computed for arbitrary values of θ. Even though only observed scores are known, the process continues as if the true-score equating holds for observed scores as well.

2.4 Item Bias

Items in a test that measures a single trait must measure the same trait in all subgroups of the population to which the test is administered. Items that fail to do so are biased for or against a particular subgroup. Since item response functions in theory do not depend upon the group used for item calibration, item response theory provides a natural method for detecting item bias.

Suppose a test is administered to two different groups and the item response functions are estimated separately for each group. If, for a particular item, the item response function for one group is uniformly higher than for the other group, then a person in the first group has a higher probability of a correct response for the same θ. This item is clearly biased in favor of the first group. Typical instances of item bias are not this clear. Usually item response functions will cross, rather than lie all above or all below each other. This means that the item is differentially biased at different θ levels.

2.5 Mastery Testing

Mastery tests are designed to determine if a person has reached a specified level of achievement, in which case the person is a "master." Item response theory can be used to construct optimal mastery tests.

Suppose there is a pool of calibrated items, and subject matter experts have defined the mastery level. The test construction specialist then selects items from the pool that have the highest item information functions at that level. The test constructed in this way will measure most precisely at the mastery level, thus minimizing errors in classifying people. In addition, item response theory can aid in the determination of the optimal item difficulty, item weights, and cutting score, also the necessary test length. Various test designs may be compared in relative efficiency.

2.6 Tailored Testing

Conventional tests are usually designed to measure best near the middle of the θ range for some group. A tailored test is one in which every person is administered items that measure that person's θ best. The general testing algorithm is as follows: (a) obtain an estimate of a person's θ; (b) from a pool of calibrated items, select an item that measures best at that θ; (c) administer and score the item, revise the estimated θ; (d) if the estimate is precise enough, stop, otherwise, return to step (b). Many tailored testing designs are possible, most of which require a computer for item administration.

Information functions for tailored tests are generally higher than for conventional tests over a broad range of

271

θ. Much work has been recently done in this field, investigating and implementing various designs (McBride 1979).

Item response theory is essential for many aspects of tailored testing. For example, conventional scoring does not apply, since every person may take a different test. In contrast, item response theory provides estimates of θ that are independent of the particular items administered. With item response theory, many different designs can be examined and evaluated using relative efficiency functions.

See also: Adaptive Testing

Bibliography

Birnbaum A 1968 Some latent trait models and their use in inferring an examinee's ability. In: Lord F M, Novick M R (eds.) 1968 *Statistical Theories of Mental Test Scores.* Addison-Wesley, New York

Bock R D 1972 Estimating item parameters and latent ability when responses are scored in two or more nominal categories. *Psychometrika* 37: 29–51

Hambleton R K, Swaminathan H, Cook L L, Eignor D R, Gifford J A 1978 Developments in latent trait theory: Models, technical issues, and applications. *Rev. Educ. Res.* 48: 467–510

Lord F M 1980 *Applications of Item Response Theory to Practical Testing Problems.* Erlbaum, Hillsdale, New Jersey

McBride J R 1979 Adaptive mental testing: The state of the art, TR No. 423. United States Army Research Institute for the Behavioral and Social Sciences, Alexandria, Virginia

Samejima F 1969 Estimation of ability using a response pattern of graded scores. *Psychometr. Monogr.* No. 17, Psychometric Society

Wingersky M S 1983 LOGIST: A program for computing maximum likelihood procedures for logistic test models. In: Hambleton R K (ed.) 1983 *Applications of Item Response Theory.* Educational Research Institute of British Columbia, Vancouver, British Columbia

Generalizability Theory

L. Allal

Generalizability theory provides a conceptual framework for estimating the reliability of behavioral measurements obtained by a wide range of procedures—tests, rating scales, observation forms, attitude scales—used in educational research and decision making. The statistical techniques of generalizability analysis can be applied to virtually any set of data collected by means of a factorial design which includes persons (or other objects of measurement) as well as one or several factors formed by the random sampling of conditions of measurement (for instance, items, examiners, moments of test administration).

Historically, within the context of classical test theory, a variety of procedures were developed for estimating different aspects of reliability: calculation of test–retest correlations to estimate the stability of measurements over different testing occasions; correlation of scores obtained from parallel forms of a test to estimate the equivalence of measurements based on different sets of items; application of various formulas to estimate the internal consistency, or homogeneity, of a pool of test items. Generalizability theory offers a comprehensive set of concepts and estimation procedures for treating any one or, simultaneously, all of these aspects of reliability. It is applicable, moreover, to designs which include other sources of fixed or random sampling variations than those typically considered by the classical procedures. In conducting a generalizability analysis, the effects of multiple sources of potential error can be assessed. It is then possible to determine the improvements of design that are needed to reduce error and increase precision of measurement.

This article will present the basic concepts of generalizability theory, as developed by Cronbach et al. (1972).

Several of the more recent extensions of the model will be briefly discussed. An example will be used to illustrate the types of analyses that can be carried out using generalizability theory. Finally, several areas of application of the theory will be indicated.

1. Basic Concepts

Behavioral measurements used in educational research and decision making are almost always based on procedures involving one or more sources of potential error due to fluctuations in the conditions of measurement. In generalizability theory, the design of a measurement procedure implies the specification of the admissible variations that can occur along one or several facets, for instance, items, occasions, correctors, observers. The universe of admissible observations is defined by all possible combinations of the conditions corresponding to the levels of the facets. Any given observed score is thus a sample from the universe of scores that would exist if measurements were obtained under all admissible conditions. The classical concept of "true" score is replaced in generalizability theory by the concept of universe score, which Cronbach and co-workers (1972 p. 15) define as follows:

> The ideal datum on which to base the decision would be something like the person's mean score over all acceptable observations, which we shall call his "universe score." The investigator uses the observed score or some function of it as if it were the universe score. That is, he generalizes from sample to universe. *The question of "reliability" thus resolves into a question of accuracy of generalization, or generalizability.*

In conducting a generalizability study, it is necessary to include all relevant facets of the universe of admissible observations in the design used for data collection. The design must include at least one facet formed by the random sampling of measurement conditions. It may include, however, any number of other facets constituted by random or fixed modes of sampling. For example, if data are collected by a design in which persons are crossed with a random sample of items, the facet "items" could be nested within the levels of a fixed facet such as "instructional objectives," or it could be crossed with levels of a random facet such as "occasions." It would also be possible to construct a design in which items are nested within objectives and crossed with occasions.

Once the data have been collected, the standard procedures of analysis of variance are applied to determine the mean square for each source of variation present in the design. By successively inserting the numerical values of the observed mean squares into the equations for the expected mean squares, estimates are obtained for the variance components corresponding to all sources of variation. The choice of the analysis of variance estimation model (that is, use of the random effects model or the appropriate mixed effects model) is determined by the mode of sampling (random, finite random, fixed) of the levels of the facets.

For a simple design in which persons are crossed with items, variance components can be estimated by the random effects model for three sources of variation: persons ($\hat{\sigma}_p^2$), items ($\hat{\sigma}_i^2$), and error ($\hat{\sigma}_{pi,e}^2$). For a more complex design in which items are nested in fixed objectives, the appropriate mixed effects model would be used to estimate the variance components for five sources of variation: persons (P), items $(I:O)$, objects (O) and the interactions $P \times (I:O)$ and $P \times O$. If items were crossed with the facet occasions, variance components could be estimated by the random effects model for seven sources of variation: persons (P), items (I), occasions (O) and the interactions $P \times I$, $P \times O$, $I \times O$, $P \times I \times O$.

Once the variance components have been estimated, the principles of generalizability theory are used to determine the allocation of the components for the estimation of three major parameters. After a general definition of each parameter, the formula will be given for the estimate corresponding to the $p \times i$ design in which the objects of measurement are persons crossed with a random sample of items.

(a) *Universe-score variance*. This parameter, symbolized by $\sigma^2(\mu)$, is defined as the variance of the expected values of the scores belonging to the universe of admissible observations. It reflects the systematic variations due to differences among the objects of measurement. For the $p \times i$ design described above, it is estimated by the variance component estimate due to persons: $\hat{\sigma}_p^2$.

(b) *Relative error variance*. Observed scores are frequently interpreted by comparing the relative positions of the objects of measurement within the score distribution. In this case, the sources of error are limited to the interactions of the objects of measurement with the facet(s) formed by random sampling of the conditions of measurement. The relative error variance, symbolized by $\sigma^2(\delta)$, is estimated by the sum of the weighted variance component estimates corresponding to the sources of relative error. Each component is weighted inversely to the number of times its effect is sampled when calculating the average score of one of the objects of measurement. For the $p \times i$ design, the estimate of relative error variance is based on a single variance component estimate: $\hat{\sigma}^2(\delta) = 1/n_i \hat{\sigma}_{pi,e}^2$ where n_i is the number of levels of the facet items.

(c) *Absolute error variance*. For some situations, particularly in the areas of criterion-referenced and domain-referenced measurement, the observed scores are used as estimates of universe scores. In crossed designs, if decisions are based on the absolute rather than the relative values of the observed scores, additional sources of error must be considered. The absolute error variance, symbolized by $\sigma^2(\Delta)$, includes the components of relative error plus the components that are due specifically to the facet(s) formed by random sampling of the conditions of measurement. Thus, for the $p \times i$ design, the estimate of absolute error variance is based on two variance component estimates: $\hat{\sigma}^2(\Delta) = 1/n_i \hat{\sigma}_{pi,e}^2 + 1/n_i \hat{\sigma}_i^2$.

The precision of measurement provided by a given design is assessed by a generalizability coefficient, defined as the ratio of the universe-score variance to the expected observed-score variance. For the case of relative comparisons of observed scores, the expected observed-score variance is composed of the universe-score variance plus the relative error variance. The corresponding generalizability coefficient for the $p \times i$ design would be estimated as follows:

$$\frac{\hat{\sigma}_p^2}{\hat{\sigma}_p^2 + \hat{\sigma}^2(\delta)}$$

In crossed designs, if decisions are based on the absolute rather than the relative values of the observed scores, the estimate of absolute error variance, $\hat{\sigma}^2(\Delta)$, would be used in place of $\hat{\sigma}^2(\delta)$, and the corresponding coefficient estimated as follows:

$$\frac{\hat{\sigma}_p^2}{\hat{\sigma}_p^2 + \hat{\sigma}^2(\Delta)}$$

The interpretation of these coefficients is analogous to that of classical reliability coefficients. Values approaching 1.0 indicate that the scores of the persons can be differentiated with a high degree of accuracy while generalizing over random variations in the sampling of items.

Cronbach and co-workers (1972) distinguish two stages in the application of generalizability theory. The first is the generalizability (G) study carried out by the developer of the measurement procedure. Its aim is to provide future users of the procedure with the information they will need to assess the adequacy of the design, or of various modified versions of the design, with respect to the purposes of their investigations. A generalizability study is therefore designed to furnish estimates of the variance components for all sources of variation of potential interest to future users. It may also provide estimates of generalizability parameters for one or more versions of the basic design.

On the basis of this information, a variety of decision (D) studies may then be conducted by the persons planning to use the procedure. In carrying out a decision study, various modifications of the initial generalizability-study design may be considered. Certain modifications may be required because of practical constraints affecting the application of the procedure. For example, due to limitations on the availability of training supervisors, the number of observations of each trainee may be reduced in the decision-study design as compared to the frequency of observation in the generalizability study. Other design modifications may be considered in order to improve the precision of measurement. The most obvious example is the reduction of measurement error by increasing the sample of the levels of the random facets which, as shown in the generalizability study, make the largest contributions to the error variance. For example, in the case of the $p \times i$ design, an increase of the number of items (n_i) would lead to a decrease of the estimates of both relative and absolute error, as defined by the formulas presented above. Once an appropriate decision-study design has been defined, the corresponding generalizability parameters can be estimated using the data already collected in the generalizability study.

2. Extensions of Generalizability Theory

An article by Shavelson and Webb (1981) offers a detailed review of the contributions to generalizability theory since the 1972 publication by Cronbach and co-workers. Two areas of development will be mentioned here.

The first is the work by a number of researchers on problems associated with the underlying statistical models used in generalizability analysis. A paper by Brennan et al. (1980) deals with several important aspects of the estimation and interpretation of variance components for balanced and unbalanced designs used in generalizability studies. Their paper offers useful clarifications with respect to the definition and estimation of generalizability parameters based on variance components estimated by mixed models. It also points out the limitations of many existing statistical approaches and computer programs as far as their application in the context of a generalizability study is concerned. Continued work in this area is needed since unbalanced designs and designs involving fixed facets are relatively frequent in the field of educational measurement.

The work on underlying statistical models also includes efforts to develop multivariate extensions of the basic univariate procedures for generalizability analysis. In addition to the proposals of Cronbach et al. (1972) for the generalizability analysis of profiles of scores,

some work has been carried out on multivariate methods for estimating the components of variance and covariance associated with composite scores defined by canonical coefficients or other weighting schemes. Much of the work in this area involves issues of statistical estimation that are far broader than the specific concerns of generalizability theory.

A second area of development is based on the principle of symmetry, which as proposed by Cardinet et al. (1981 p. 184), affirms "that each factor of a design can be selected as an object of study, and generalizability theory operations defined for one factor can be transposed in the study of other factors." This principle has led Cardinet and his colleagues to develop a framework for generalizability analysis that is applicable to a very wide range of situations in educational measurement. The procedures proposed in this framework can be used not only in the classical situations focused on the measurement of individual differences, but also in a variety of other situations where the objects of measurement are factors other than persons. In addition, these procedures can be applied to designs in which the objects of measurement (whether persons or other factors) are defined by the crossing and/or nesting of the levels of several fixed or random factors. Generalizability theory is thus extended to the analysis of the sources of error and of bias that occur when multifaceted measurement procedures are applied to multifaceted populations.

A further advantage of the proposed framework is its usefulness in situations where data are collected in order to carry out comparisons along each of several facets which are of interest to educational decision makers. In multipurpose educational surveys, for example, school administrators may wish to compare achievement levels of classes or of school districts, whereas curriculum developers may be interested in comparisons of achievement levels for different items or sets of items. To deal with these multiple measurement aims, Cardinet and co-workers (1981) propose a clear separation between the initial phases of analysis based on analysis of variance (that is, computation of mean squares and estimation of variance components) and the subsequent phases of analysis based on the principles of generalizability theory. This separation implies that variance components are estimated without reference to any particular aim of measurement. Subsequently, several alternative measurement designs can be defined by distinguishing, in each case, two types of facets: the facets of differentiation (corresponding to the objects of measurement) and the facets of instrumentation (corresponding to the conditions or instruments of measurement). It is then possible to determine the allocation of the variance component estimates for the estimation of the variance of differentiation (universe-score variance) and the error variances associated with each design. In the final phase of the framework, various modifications of the initial design are considered in order to optimize the measurements needed for different decision-making or research purposes.

3. An Illustration of Generalizability Analysis

In this illustration, the principles of generalizability analysis will be applied to a relatively complex design that typifies several aspects of data collection in the field of education measurement. In many instances, rather than simple random sampling of persons from a homogeneous population, persons are randomly sampled within levels of one or more fixed stratification variables. The data collection design thus entails the nesting of the facet persons within other facets. For example, pupils may be nested within facets such as age, sex, grade, instructional treatment, or in the case of a study of teaching behavior, teachers may be nested within facets such as type of training, years of experience, sector of employment. In a similar manner, measurement procedures (tests, rating scales, and so on) are often constructed by the generation of randomly equivalent items nested within levels of one or more fixed classification variables (for example, objectives, content chapters, tasks) corresponding to the dimensions of a predetermined table of specifications. In addition, designs often include one or more sources of random sampling fluctuations due to facets such as examiners (observers, correctors) or occasions (moments of observation or of test administration).

To illustrate the application of generalizability theory for designs of this type, the following example will be used: A 30-item multiple-choice test has been administered on two occasions to a sample of 100 eighth grade pupils, 50 boys and 50 girls. The test has been constructed to measure pupil achievement with respect to three instructional objectives, and is composed of 10 items per objective.

The data collection design for this example is formed by five facets. The random facet pupils (P) is nested within the fixed facet sex (S). Items (I) constitute a second random facet nested within the fixed facet objectives (O). The facets $P:S$ and S are crossed with the facets $I:O$ and O. In addition, the random facet moments of testing (M) is crossed with the other four facets.

For this design, variance components can be estimated for 17 sources of variation, the five sources corresponding to the main effects of the facets (S, $P:S$, $I:O$, O, M), and the 12 sources corresponding to the interactions among facets: $S \times O$, $S \times (I:O)$, $S \times M$, $(P:S) \times O$, $(P:S) \times (I:O)$, $(P:S) \times M$, $O \times M$, $(I:O) \times M$, $S \times O \times M$, $S \times (I:O) \times M$, $(P:S) \times O \times M$, $(P:S) \times (I:O) \times M$. Since two facets of the design, S and O, are fixed, the variance components would be estimated using the appropriate mixed model of analysis of variance.

Once the variance components have been estimated, several directions of generalizability analysis could be considered, depending on the aim of measurement. For illustrative purposes, two contrasting cases will be described using the terminology proposed by Cardinet and co-workers (1981). The description of each case will be limited to the definition of the measurement design

and the corresponding allocation of the variance component estimates for the estimation of the generalizability parameters.

The first, and more conventional, case is the use of the test scores to compare pupil achievement levels in the context of school certification or placement decisions. In this situation, the aim of measurement is to differentiate pupils while generalizing over testing moments and over items based on a fixed set of objectives (see Table 1). If decisions pertain to individual pupil scores regardless of sex, the measurement design is defined by two facets of differentiation ($P:S$ and S) and three facets of instrumentation ($I:O$, O, and M).

The estimation of the differentiation (that is, universe-score) variance is based on the variance component estimates for the two facets of differentiation, $P:S$ and S. The relative error variance is estimated on the basis of the variance component estimates due to the interactions of the differentiation facets with the random instrumentation facets. For this design, the sources of relative error correspond to the following interactions: $(P:S) \times (I:O)$, $(P:S) \times (I:O) \times M$, $(P:S) \times M$, $S \times (I:O)$, $S \times (I:O) \times M$, $S \times M$. The estimate of absolute error variance includes the above interaction components plus the variance component estimates due to the effects of the random instrumentation facets and the interactions among these facets: in this case, $I:O$, M, and $(I:O) \times M$.

The second case to be considered is the comparison of the achievement levels attained for different instructional objectives, as might be required in the context of curriculum evaluation or in a survey monitoring educational outcomes of the school system. In this case, the aim of measurement is to differentiate objectives, while generalizing over random variations in items, moments, and pupils nested within sex. The measurement design therefore includes a single differentiation facet (O) and four instrumentation facets ($I:O$, M, $P:S$, S).

The corresponding allocation of the variance component estimates differs in several respects from that of the previous design (see Table 1). The estimation of the differentiation variance is based on the variance component estimate for the facet O. The estimate of the relative error variance includes the estimated variance component for the random facet $I:O$, and the components for the interactions of O and $I:O$ with the remaining random instrumentation facets $P:S$ and M, that is, a total of seven components, as shown in Table 1. The absolute error variance is estimated on the basis of the above components plus the components due to the random instrumentation facets and their interactions: $P:S$, M, and $(P:S) \times M$.

In examining the indications in Table 1, it can be seen that the allocation of the variance components is quite different depending on the aim of measurement. Only two sources of relative error, $(P:S) \times (I:O)$ and $(P:S) \times (I:O) \times M$, and one additional source of absolute error, M, remain the same in the two cases under consideration. It should be noted, moreover, that further differences would arise in computing the estimates of the generalizability parameters for these designs. Adjustments of certain components would be required in each case due to the presence of fixed differentiation facets (compare with Brennan et al. 1980), and different coefficients would be used for the weighting of the components entering into the formulas for the estimated error variances.

4. Areas of Application

In addition to the application of generalizability theory in the classical area of norm-referenced test construction for the measurement of individual differences, a number of other areas of application have been developed over recent years (see *Norm-referenced Assessment*). In the brief description that follows, several selected references are given for four areas. Further indications can be found in the review article by Shavelson and Webb (1981).

4.1 Criterion-referenced and Domain-referenced Measurement

For some of the specific problems of criterion-referenced mastery testing, such as the fixing of the criterion score so as to minimize false positive and false negative decision errors, Bayesian methods are likely to provide the most adequate approach. However, when dealing with the broader aspects of domain-referenced interpretation of test scores, several basic concepts of generalizability theory can be applied to estimate levels of competency within a multifaceted domain and the error associated with absolute decisions. Brennan and Kane (1977) have developed an "index of dependability" for domain-referenced testing in which observed scores are used to estimate the positions of universe scores with respect to a specified criterion.

4.2 Surveys of Educational Attainments

The flexibility of generalizability theory, as enlarged by the principle of symmetry, is particularly useful for dealing with multiple problems of reliability in large-scale surveys involving multifaceted measurement procedures applied to multifaceted populations. An example of multidirectional generalizability analysis based on data from a survey of mathematics achievement is briefly described in Cardinet et al. (1981). An article by Tourneur and Cardinet (1981) provides a more detailed presentation of the analyses carried out for a complex design involving content domains crossed with pupils, nested in age and class, and with test forms in which item series and classes are nested.

4.3 Observational Studies

Generalizability theory provides an appropriate framework for dealing with the multiple aspects of reliability (time and event sampling, interobserver agreement) that must be considered in designing observation procedures for the measurement of student or teacher behaviors. Proposals for the design and analysis of generalizability and decision studies based on observational data are provided by Mitchell (1979). At present, however, solutions have not been found for problems arising from the degree of correlations that may exist among observations collected within various time spans (class period, day, week, etc.).

4.4 Ratings of Occupational Skills and Instruction

Both univariate and multivariate generalizability procedures were applied in a study by Webb and Shavelson (1981) of ratings of educational skills required for different types of occupations. This study considered multiple facets of error (occasions × centers × raters nested in

Table 1
Allocation of the variance component estimates for the estimation of generalizability parameters associated with two contrasting aims of measurement

| Generalizability parameters | Aim of measurement | |
	Differentiation of pupils	Differentiation of objects
Differentiation variance	$P:S$ S	O
Relative error variance	$(P:S) \times (I:O)$ $(P:S) \times (I:O) \times M$ $(P:S) \times M$ $S \times (S:O)$ $S \times (I:O) \times M$ $S \times M$	$I:O$ $(P:S) \times (I:O)$ $(P:S) \times (I:O) \times M$ $(I:O) \times M$ $O \times (P:S)$ $O \times (P:S) \times M$ $O \times M$
Absolute error variance	Components of relative error plus: $I:O$ M $(I:O) \times M$	Components of relative error plus: $P:S$ M $(P:O) \times M$

centers) associated with the ratings of three skills (reasoning, mathematics, language) needed in various jobs (jobs being the objects of measurement). An example of generalizability analysis applied to student ratings of instruction can be found in Gillmore et al. (1978).

See also: Reliability of Test Results; Analysis of Variance and Covariance; Criterion-referenced Measurement; Domain-referenced Tests

Bibliography

Brennan R L, Kane M T 1977 An index of dependability for mastery tests. *J. Educ. Meas.* 14: 277–89

Brennan R L, Jarjoura D, Deaton E L 1980 Some issues concerning the estimation and interpretation of variance components in generalizability theory. ACT *Technical Bulletin* No. 36. American College Testing Program, Iowa City, Iowa

Cardinet J, Tourneur Y, Allal L 1981 Extension of generalizability theory and its applications in educational measurement. *J. Educ. Meas.* 18: 183–204

Cronbach L J, Gleser G C, Nanda H, Rajaratnam N 1972 *The Dependability of Behavioral Measurements: Theory of Generalizability for Scores and Profiles.* Wiley, New York

Gillmore G M, Kane M T, Naccarato R W 1978 The generalizability of student ratings of instruction: Estimation of the teacher and the course components. *J. Educ. Meas.* 15: 1–15

Mitchell S K 1979 Interobserver agreement, reliability and generalizability of data collected in observational studies. *Psychol. Bull.* 86: 376–90

Shavelson R J, Webb N M 1981 Generalizability theory: 1973–1980. *Br. J. Math. Stat. Psychol.* 34: 133–66

Tourneur Y, Cardinet J 1981 L'étude de la généralisabilité d'un survey. *Educ. et recherche* 3(1): 33–50

Webb N M, Shavelson R J 1981 Multivariant generalizability of general education development ratings. *J. Educ. Meas.* 18: 13–22

Criterion-referenced Measurement

R. K. Hambleton

Criterion-referenced tests are constructed to permit the interpretation of examinee test performance in relation to a set of well-defined competencies (Popham 1978). In relation to the competencies, there are three common uses for criterion-referenced test scores: (a) to describe examinee performance, (b) to assign examinees to mastery states (e.g., "masters" and "nonmasters"), and (c) to describe the performance of specified groups of examinees in program evaluation studies. Criterion-referenced tests are presently receiving extensive use in schools, industry, and the military in the United States because they provide information which is valued by test users and different from the information provided by norm-referenced tests. This article will introduce basic criterion-referenced testing concepts, compare these tests to norm-referenced tests, consider some aspects of criterion-referenced test development, and describe several promising applications.

1. Basic Concepts

One of the first articles on the topic of criterion-referenced testing appeared in the *American Psychologist* (Glaser 1963). Over 700 papers on the topic have been published since then, and the scope and direction of educational testing has been changed dramatically. Glaser was interested in assessment methods that would provide necessary information for making a number of individual and programmatic decisions arising in connection with specific objectives or competencies. Norm-referenced tests were seen as limited in terms of providing the desired kinds of information.

At least 57 definitions of criterion-referenced measurement have been offered in the literature. Popham's definition which was introduced earlier in this article is probably the one which is most widely used. Several points about the definition deserve comment. First,

terms such as objectives, competencies, and skills are used interchangeably in the field. Second, the competencies measured by a criterion-referenced test must be well-defined. Well-defined competencies make the process of item writing easier and more valid, and improve the quality of test score interpretations. The quality of score interpretations is improved because of the clarity of the content or behavior domains to which test scores are referenced. There is no limit on the breadth and complexity of a domain of content or behaviors defining a competency. The intended purpose of a test will influence the appropriate breadth and complexity of domains. Diagnostic tests are typically organized around narrowly defined competencies. End-of-year assessments will normally be carried out with more broadly defined competencies. Third, when more than one competency is measured in a test it is common to report examinee performance on each competency. Fourth, Popham's criterion-referenced test definition does not include a reference to a cutoff score or standard. It is common to set a minimum standard of performance for each competency measured in a criterion-referenced test and interpret examinee performance in relation to it. But, the use of test scores for describing examinee performance is common (e.g., the best estimate of student A's performance in relation to the domain of content defined by the competency is 70 percent) and standards are not needed for this type of score use. That a standard (or standards) may not be needed with a criterion-referenced test will come as a surprise to persons who have assumed (mistakenly) that the word "criterion" in "criterion-referenced test" refers to a "standard" or "cutoff score." In fact, the word "criterion" was used by Glaser (1963) and Popham and Husek (1969) to refer to a domain of content or behavior to which test scores are referenced.

Three additional points about criterion-referenced tests deserve mention: (a) the number of competencies measured by a criterion-referenced test will (in general) vary from one test to the next, (b) the number of test items measuring each competency and the value of the minimum standard will (in general) vary from one competency to the next, and (c) a common method for making mastery–nonmastery decisions involves the comparison of examinee percent (or proportion-correct) scores on competencies to the corresponding minimum standards. With respect to (c), when an examinee's percent score is equal to or greater than the standard, the examinee is assumed to be a "master" (M), otherwise the examinee is assumed to be a "nonmaster" (NM). There are however more complex decision-making models (for a review, see van der Linden 1980).

It is common to see terms like criterion-referenced tests, domain-referenced tests, and objectives-referenced tests in the psychometric literature. Popham's definition for a criterion-referenced test is similar to one Millman and others proposed for a domain-referenced test. There are no essential differences between the two if Popham's definition for a criterion-referenced test is adopted. The term "domain-referenced test" is a descriptive one and therefore it is less likely to be misunderstood than the term, "criterion-referenced test." One reason for continuing to use the term, "criterion-referenced test," even though it is less descriptive and its definition has become muddled in the psychometric literature, is that there is considerable public support in the United States for "criterion-referenced tests." It would seem to be a waste of valuable time to mount a campaign for a new term.

Objectives-referenced tests consist of items that are matched to objectives. The principal difference between criterion-referenced tests and objectives-referenced tests is that in a criterion-referenced test, items are organized into clusters with each cluster serving (usually) as a representative set of items from a clearly defined content domain measuring an objective, while with an objectives-referenced test, no clear domain of content is specified for an objective, and items are not considered to be representative of any content domain. Therefore, interpretations of examinee performance on objectives-referenced tests should be limited to the particular items on the test.

2. Norm-referenced and Criterion-referenced Tests

Proponents of norm-referenced and criterion-referenced tests in the United States waged a battle in the 1970s for supremacy of the achievement testing world. A third group argued that there was only one kind of achievement test from which both criterion-referenced and norm-referenced score interpretations could be made when needed. It is now clear that there was no winner although in the 10-year period the uses of criterion-referenced tests did increase substantially in the United States. Also, there was a reduction in the amount of norm-referenced testing taking place. There was no winner because it is clear that it is meaningful to distinguish between two kinds of achievement tests and both kinds of tests have important roles to play in providing information for test users. Norm-referenced achievement tests are needed to provide reliable and valid normative scores for comparing examinees. Criterion-referenced achievement tests are needed to facilitate the interpretation of examinee performance in relation to well-defined competencies.

Although the differences between norm-referenced tests and criterion-referenced tests are substantial, the two kinds of tests share many features. In fact, it would be a rare individual who could distinguish between them from looking at the test booklets alone. They use the same item formats; test directions are similar; and both kinds of tests can be standardized.

There are a number of important differences, however, between them. The first difference is test purpose. A norm-referenced test is constructed specifically to facilitate comparisons among examinees in the content area measured by the test. It is common to use age-, percentile-, and standard-score norms to accomplish the test's purpose. Since test items are (or can be) referenced to competencies, criterion-referenced score interpretations (or, more correctly, objectives-referenced score interpretations) are possible but are typically limited in value because of the (usually) small number of test items measuring any competency in the test. Criterion-referenced tests, on the other hand, are constructed to assess examinee performance in relation to a set of competencies. Scores may be used (a) to describe examinee performance, (b) to make mastery–nonmastery decisions, and (c) to evaluate program effectiveness. Scores can be used to compare examinees but comparisons may have relatively low reliability if score distributions are homogeneous.

The second difference is in the area of content specificity. It is common for designers of both test types to prepare test blueprints or tables of specifications. It is even possible that norm-referenced test designers will prepare behavioral objectives. But, criterion-referenced test designers must (typically) prepare considerably more detailed content specifications than provided by behavioral objectives to ensure that criterion-referenced test scores can be interpreted in the intended way. This point will be considered further in the next section. Thus, with respect to content specifications, the difference between the two types is in the degree to which test content must be specified.

The third difference is in the area of test development. With norm-referenced tests, item statistics (difficulty and discrimination indices) serve an important role in item selection. In general, items of moderate difficulty (p-values in the range 0.30 to 0.70) and high discriminating power (point biserial correlations over 0.30) are most likely to be selected for a test because they contribute substantially to test score variance. Test reliability and validity will, generally, be higher when test score variance is increased. In contrast, criterion-referenced test items are only deleted from the pools of test items measuring competencies when it is determined that they violate the content specifications or standard principles of item writing, or if the available item statistics reveal serious noncorrectable flaws. Item statistics can be used to construct parallel forms of a criterion-referenced test or to produce a test to discriminate optimally between masters and nonmasters in the region of a minimum standard of performance on the test score scale.

The fourth and final major area of difference between criterion-referenced tests and norm-referenced tests is test score generalizability. Seldom is there interest in making generalizations from norm-referenced achievement test scores. The basis for score interpretations is the performance of some reference group. In contrast, score generalizability is usually of interest with criterion-referenced tests. Seldom is there interest in the performance of examinees on specific sets of test items. When clearly specified competency statements are available and assuming test items are representative of the content domains from which they are drawn, examinee test performance can be generalized to performance in the larger domains of content defining the competencies. It is this type of interpretation which is (usually) of interest to criterion-referenced test users.

3. Content Specifications

Behavioral objectives had a highly significant impact on instruction and testing in the 1960s and 1970s. But, while behavioral objectives are relatively easy to write and have contributed substantially to the specification of curricula, they do not usually lead to clearly defined content descriptions defining competencies. Popham (1974) described tests built from behavioral objectives as "cloud-referenced tests." Several suggestions have been made for addressing the deficiency in behavioral objectives and thereby making it possible to construct valid criterion-referenced tests. These suggestions include the use of item transformations, item forms, algorithms, and structural facet theory. Possibly the most versatile and practical of the suggestions was introduced by Popham (1978) and is called domain specifications, item specifications, or expanded objectives. Domain specifications serve four purposes: (a) they provide item writers with content and technical guidelines for preparing test items, (b) they provide content and measurement specialists with a clear description of the content and/or behaviors which are to be covered by each competency so that they can assess whether items are valid measures of the intended competencies, (c) they aid in interpreting examinee competency performance, and (d) they provide users with clear specifications of the breadth and scope of competencies. Some educational measurement specialists have even gone so far as to suggest that the emphasis on content specification has been the most important contribution of criterion-referenced testing to measurement practice (Berk 1980).

Using as a basis the work of Popham (1978), Hambleton (1982) suggested that a domain specification might be divided into four parts:

(a) Description—a short, concise statement of the content and/or behaviors covered by the competency.

(b) Sample directions and test item—an example of the test directions and a model test item to measure the competency.

(c) Content limits—a detailed description of both the content and/or behaviors measured by the competency, as well as the structure and content of the item pool. (This section should be so clear that items may be divided by reviewers into those items that meet the specifications and those items that do not.) Sometimes clarity is enhanced by also specifying areas which are not included in the content domain description.

(d) Response limits—a description of the kind of incorrect answer choices which must be prepared. The structure and content of the incorrect answers should be stated in as much detail as possible.

An example of a domain specification is shown in Fig. 1. Once properly prepared domain specifications are available, the remaining steps in the test development process can be carried out.

Description

The student will identify the tones or emotions expressed in paragraphs.

Sample directions and test item

Directions: Read the paragraph below. Then answer the question and circle the letter beside your answer.

> Jimmy had been playing and swimming at the beach all day. Now it was time to go home. Jimmy sat down in the back seat of his father's car. He could hardly keep his eyes open.

How did Jimmy feel?

A. Afraid   B. Friendly   C. Tired   D. Kind

Content limits

1. Paragraphs will describe situations which are familiar to grade 3 students.

2. Paragraphs should contain between three and six sentences. Readability levels should be at the third grade (using the Dale-Chall formula).

3. Tones or emotions expressed in the passages should be selected from the list below:

sad	mad	angry	kind
tired	scared	friendly	excited
happy	lucky	smart	proud

Response limits

1. Answer choices should be one word in length.

2. Four answer choices should be used with each test item.

3. Incorrect answer choices may be selected from the list above.

4. Incorrect answer choices should be tones or emotions which are familiar to students in grade 3 and which are commonly confused with the correct answer.

Figure 1
A typical domain specification in the reading area

Table 1
Steps for constructing criterion-referenced tests

Steps	Comments
1. Preliminary considerations (a) Specify test purposes. (b) Specify groups to be measured and (any) special testing requirements (due to examinee age, race, sex, socioeconomic status, handicaps, etc.). (c) Determine the time and money available to produce the test. (d) Identify qualified staff. (e) Specify an initial estimate of test length.	This step is essential to ensure that a test development project is well-organized and important factors which might have an impact on test quality are identified early.
2. Review of competency statements (a) Review the descriptions of the competencies to determine their acceptability. (b) Make necessary competency statement revisions to improve their clarity.	Domain specifications are invaluable to item writers when they are well-done. Considerable time and money can be saved later in revising test items if item writers are clear on what it is that is expected of them.
3. Item writing (a) Draft a sufficient number of items for pilot-testing. (b) Carry out item editing.	Some training of item writers in the importance and use of domain specifications, and in the principles of item writing is often desirable.
4. Assessment of content validity (a) Identify a sufficient pool of judges and measurement specialists. (b) Review the test items to determine their match to the competencies, their representativeness, and their freedom from bias and stereotyping. (c) Review the test items to determine their technical adequacy.	This step is essential. Items are evaluated by reviewers to assess their match to the competencies, their technical quality, and their freedom from bias and stereotyping.
5. Revisions to test items (a) Based upon data from 4(b) and 4(c), revise test items (when possible) or delete them. (b) Write additional test items (if needed) and repeat step 4.	Any necessary revisions to test items should be made at this step and when additional test items are needed, they should be written, and step 4 carried out again.
6. Field test administration (a) Organize the test items into forms for pilot testing. (b) Administer the test forms to appropriately chosen groups of examinees. (c) Conduct item analyses, and item validity and item bias studies.	The test items are organized into booklets and administered to appropriate numbers of examinees. That number should reflect the importance of the test under construction. Appropriate revisions to test items can be made here. Item statistics are used to identify items which may be in need of revision: (a) items which may be substantially easier or harder than other items measuring the same competencies, (b) items with negative or low positive discriminating power, and (c) items with distractors which were selected by small percentages of examinees.
7. Revisions to test items (a) Revise test items when necessary or delete them using the results from 6(c).	Whenever possible, malfunctioning test items should be revised and added to the pools of acceptable test items. When revisions to test items are substantial they should be returned to step 4.
8. Test assembly (a) Determine the test length, and the number of forms needed and the number of items per objective. (b) Select test items from the available pool of valid test items. (c) Prepare test directions, practice questions, test booklet layout, scoring keys, answer sheets, etc.	Test booklets are compiled at this step. When parallel-forms are required, and especially if the tests are short, item statistics should be used to ensure matched forms are produced.
9. Selection of a standard (a) Initiate a process to determine the standard to separate "masters" and "nonmasters."	A standard-setting procedure must be selected and implemented. Care should be taken to document the selection process.

Table 1 *Continued*

Steps	Comments

10. Pilot test administration
  (a) Design the administration to collect score reliability and validity information.
  (b) Administer the test form(s) to appropriately chosen groups of examinees.
  (c) Evaluate the test administration procedures, test items, and score reliability and validity.
  (d) Make final revisions based on data from 10(c).
	At this step, test directions can be evaluated, scoring keys can be checked, and reliability and validity of scores and decisions can be assessed.

11. Preparation of manuals
  (a) Prepare a test administrator's manual.
  (b) Prepare a technical manual.
	For important tests, a test administration manual and a technical manual should be prepared.

12. Additional technical data collection (a) Conduct reliability and validity investigations.	No matter how carefully a test is constructed or evaluated, reliability and validity studies should be carried out on an ongoing basis.

4. Criterion-referenced Test Development

It is essential to specify in as clear a form as possible the domain of content or behaviors defining each competency which is to be measured in the test being constructed. The mechanism through which the competencies are identified will vary from one situation to the next. For high-school graduation exams, the process might involve district educational leaders meeting to review school curricula and identifying a relatively small set of important broad competencies (e.g., reading comprehension, mathematics computations). When criterion-referenced tests are needed in an objectives-based instructional program, it is common to define a curriculum in broad areas (and, sometimes into a two-dimensional grid). Then, within the cells of the grid the sets of relevant objectives, often stated in behavioral form, are specified, reviewed, revised, and finalized. With certification exams, it is common to first conduct a "role delineation study" with individuals working in the area to identify the responsibilities, subresponsibilities, and activities which serve to define a role. Next, the knowledge and skills which are needed to carry out the role are identified.

A set of 12 steps for preparing criterion-referenced tests adapted from Hambleton (1982) is suggested in Table 1.

5. Applications of Criterion-referenced Tests

Criterion-referenced tests (or domain-referenced tests, mastery tests, competency tests, basic skills tests, or certification exams as they are alternately called) are being used in a large number of settings in the United States to address many problem areas. Criterion-referenced tests are finding substantial use in American schools. Classroom teachers use criterion-referenced test score results to locate students correctly in school programs, to monitor student progress, and to identify student deficiencies. Special education teachers are finding criterion-referenced test scores especially helpful in diagnosing student learning deficiencies and monitoring the progress of their students. Criterion-referenced test results are also being used to evaluate various school programs. While it is less common, criterion-referenced tests are finding some use in higher educational programs as well (e.g., those programs based upon the mastery learning concept). Also, criterion-referenced tests are in common use in military and industrial training programs.

In recent years, it has become common for state departments of education and (sometimes) school districts to define sets of skills (or competencies) which students must achieve in order to be promoted from one grade to the next, or in some states, to receive high-school diplomas. The nature of these criterion-referenced testing programs varies dramatically from one place to another. For example, in some places, students are held responsible for mastering a specified set of skills at each grade level, in other states, skills which must be acquired are specified at selected grade levels, and in still other states, only a set of skills which must be mastered for high-school graduation is specified.

One of the most important applications of criterion-referenced tests is to the areas of professional certification and licensure. It is now common in the United States, for example, for professional organizations to establish entry-level examinations which must be passed by candidates before they are allowed to practice in their chosen professions. In fact, many of these professional organizations have also established recertification exams. A typical examination will measure the competencies which define the professional role and candidate test performance is interpreted in relation to minimum standards which are established. There are now hundreds of professional organizations, including most groups in the medical and allied health fields, which have instituted certification and recertification exams.

Bibliography

Berk R A (ed.) 1980 *Criterion-Referenced Measurement: The State of the Art*. Johns Hopkins University Press, Baltimore, Maryland

Glaser R 1963 Instructional technology and the measurement of learning outcomes. *Am. Psychol.* 18: 519–21

Hambleton R K 1982 Advances in criterion referenced testing technology. In: Reynolds C, Gutkin T (eds.) 1982 *Handbook of School Psychology*. Wiley, New York

Hambleton R K, Swaminathan H, Algina J, Coulson D B 1978 Criterion-referenced testing and measurement: A review of technical issues and developments. *Rev. Educ. Res.* 48: 1–47

Popham W J 1974 An approaching peril: Cloud referenced tests. *Phi Delta Kappan* 55: 614–15

Popham W J 1978 *Criterion-Referenced Measurement*. Prentice-Hall, Englewood Cliffs, New Jersey

Popham W J, Husek T R 1969 Implications of criterion-referenced measurement. *J. Educ. Meas.* 6: 1–9

van der Linden W J 1980 Decision models for use with criterion-referenced tests. *Appl. Psychol. Meas.* 4: 469–92

Latent Trait Measurement Models

G. Douglas

The theory and practice of educational and psychological measurement, whereby society's educational intentions are evaluated through achievements, abilities, aptitudes, and attitudes, has for most of the twentieth century been founded on a model which views the score, X, that a person receives on a test, as the sum of two unobservable components, τ and ε, which form the relationship $X = \tau + \varepsilon$, where X is the total observed score, τ is the "true score", and ε is the "error score". This true-score model produces units for both the estimated true score and the estimated standard deviation of error scores (the standard error of measurement, SE_{meas}), which are necessarily on the same scale as are the units for the observed score X. This means that for tests composed of items scored 0 for incorrect and 1 for correct, τ is bounded by 0 and L where L is the maximum possible score on the test. The random part of this model, which allows conventional statistical confidence statements, is embodied in the assumption that

$$\varepsilon \sim NID[0, \sigma_\varepsilon^2]$$

that is, errors are normally and independently distributed with expectation 0 and variance σ_ε^2, where σ_ε and SE_{meas} are alternative notations for the precision of measurement.

An understanding of the basics of a latent trait approach to measurement can be gained by identifying those aspects and axioms of true-score theory which have been too restrictive, unsubstantiated, or of inadequate scope for the measurement required in many educational and psychological circumstances. In view of its inadequacies, it may appear puzzling that true-score theory was ever useful; however, the differences between true-score and latent trait approaches, when translated into practice, are more ones of enhanced understanding of the latter approach rather than of theoretical conflict between the two.

The core of the problem in the true-score model is that the units of X (and of τ), do not lie on an interval scale. The increase in ability arising from one more item correct on test A is not necessarily the same as that from one more item correct on test B (even when A and B are designed to measure the same ability and have the same number of items). The very use of the word "ability" presupposes the existence of an underlying scale (a latent trait), with some equal-interval units. The symbol

θ will be used for this ability. Whether the latent variable θ has an equal-interval scale is axiomatic and can never be proved "correct" or "incorrect". However since equal intervals and the corresponding linearity are crucial in most, if not all other types of measurement, there is some precedent for demanding these concepts in mental measurement. It is also axiomatic that θ is continuous, admitting of all possible values within its range. Hence there is a sense in which τ, the true score, and θ, the latent trait measure, represent the same ability but on different scales with $0 < \tau < L$ and $-\infty < \theta < \infty$.

A plot of one against the other is necessarily monotonic and nonlinear and demonstrates the nonintervality of the true scores. This point and others are illustrated in Fig. 1.

In order to make a meaningful comparison in which the number of items, L, does not play a role, the true score τ has been converted to a relative true score, ζ, where $\zeta = \tau/L$ and $0 < \zeta < 1$.

In Fig. 1, relative true score ζ is plotted against latent trait value θ for tests A and B of the same trait. For test A of 20 items, 19 points may be plotted, of which 14 are shown on the figure. For test B of 10 items, 9 points may be plotted and all 9 are shown on Fig. 1. The incompatibility of the ζ-scores is demonstrated by two observations:

(a) the latent trait value corresponding to a ζ of 0.6 depends directly on which test is used—this disparity is a function of the differing difficulty levels of the items within the two tests. Since a lower θ value

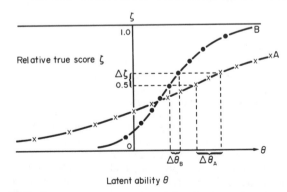

Figure 1
Latent ability versus relative true score for two tests A and B

is obtained for a ζ of 0.6 on test **B**, it would be argued that test **B** is "harder" than test **A**;

(b) a given increment in ζ for test **A** (changing from a ζ of 0.5 to a ζ of 0.6, for example), results in a change in trait θ_A which is not of the same magnitude as the corresponding change in trait θ_B.

Associated with both true-score and latent trait models are certain item characteristics, such as difficulty, discrimination, and intercorrelations. A limiting factor in the applicability of true scores has been the sample dependence of the indices used to describe these characteristics. The proportion of persons in a calibrating sample who get an item incorrect (item difficulty) changes when a shift is made from a sample whose mean ability is low to one whose mean ability is high. Item indices which remain "invariant" from one sample to another have been viewed as the desideratum of any well-formulated psychometric theory since the earliest writings of Thurstone. The discovery of these invariant indices has eluded many psychometricians along the way, although the call for their use has been frequent.

On the other hand, few calls have been heard for person ability indices (raw score, true scores, etc.), which are "invariant" from one test to another (see Fig. 1); the usual way to handle this problem has been through "test equating" via parallel forms. A methodology in which unrestricted selection of different numbers of precalibrated, valid, and relevant items from a pool can lead to ability measures freed from the characteristics of the particular items, has been even more elusive.

Any limitations which arise from using true scores instead of ability measures carry over to the concept of measurement error. Without the concept of a latent ability, it is not possible to give expression to the fact that, other things being equal, a person with a score of 48 out of 50 is not measured with the same precision as is one whose score is 25 out of 50. The standard error of true-score measurement is in the metric of the raw scores and actually decreases as ζ tends to the extremes of 0 and 1. But, as can be seen from Fig. 1 again, it is just at these extreme scores where one increment in ζ produces a large θ-increment, that there is most uncertainty about the actual location of θ. This paradox is resolved if the errors of measurement are expressed in the metric of θ. When θ tends to its extremes, the error variance increases. The score of 48 out of 50 transforms to a θ estimate with a larger error of measurement than that arising from the transformation of the score of 25. This sensible arrangement of measurement error follows automatically if θ is estimated by powerful statistical procedures (maximum likelihood) in which formulas for standard errors follow directly from the theory. A useful theory of mental measurement must address the question of precision of ability indices with respect to the problems outlined above.

Perhaps the most fundamentally important aspect which serves to illustrate the restrictive nature of the traditional methodology revolves around what latent trait theorists call "fit of data to the model". If items are ordered according to increasing difficulty from easy to hard and simultaneously order people from least able to most able and arrange the observed data matrix accordingly, the observed patterns in the data may be compared with expected patterns, the expectations being governed by the choice of latent trait model.

Figure 2 shows a hypothetical data matrix of three persons' responses to five items, and conveys the essence of fit. Persons are ordered by their raw scores and items by the count of the number of persons who had each item correct, although some latent trait models would use different criteria for ordering.

In Fig. 2, the items and persons are still ordered according to the previous criteria; however, there are no inversions to the "triangular" pattern which the model dictates. This particular set of patterns is known as a "Guttman scale". Its defining characteristic is that knowledge of a person's raw score tells everything about the person's behaviour on every item or, in other words, all it is necessary to know about the person's ability. Some years prior to the development of probabilistic latent trait models, Guttman presented this deterministic scale and the associated concept of reproducibility. Guttman postulated an underlying unidimensional latent trait, but the nonprobabilistic nature of his model prevented a satisfactory analysis of fit. Only in the context of probabilities of response patterns does a truly sensible concept of fit emerge. The degree to which modelled patterns depart from those of real data, and the implications of ignoring varying amounts of departure, is of fundamental importance to latent trait theory. This is because the predictions from, and utility of, any model are of value only to the extent that the data conform in some specified way with that model.

The contrasts between true scores and latent traits lead into a more formal definition; a latent trait is a psychological dimension (construct) whose existence is postulated to account for replicable variation in observations of behaviour in certain well-articulated situations. There is no question of physical existence for psychological traits; the value of any "trait" lies wholly in its utility as a tool for understanding experience through behaviour. Since a trait is an abstraction, it may be manipulated, restricted, varied, and otherwise transformed according to whatever purpose is to be served.

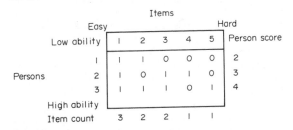

Figure 2
Guttman pattern of response

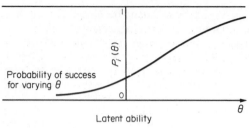

Figure 3
Item characteristic curve—item *i* and varying θ

Latent trait models are probabilistic models which describe the probability relationship between observations (and their summaries), and unknown parameters (representing the trait). The probabilistic aspect insures that the mathematical form of the model provides just the probability and not the certainty of occurrence of prescribed events. These models contain three sets of elements: an enumeration of the possible events (the "sample space"), an identification of the latent parameter(s) deemed necessary to account for systematic item "behaviour", and an identification of the latent parameter(s) deemed necessary to account for systematic person behaviour. In the discussion which follows, some limits are placed on these elements to keep to fundamentals:

(a) There are only three sets of elements (some models have more).

(b) The sample space consists of the numbers 0 and 1 (multiple-choice items need not be stipulated for this sample space to be operative). Some models have other sample spaces.

(c) There is only one parameter θ to account for person behaviour.

(d) The mathematical form of the model is a monotonically increasing function of θ, that is, the probability of success on an item increases with increasing θ. This orderliness requirement has particular appeal for the practice of measurement.

The use of the term "systematic" to describe behaviour of either persons or items is deliberate. There is a need for assurance that the parameters identified as necessary, relate to characteristics which are persistent, replicable, and invariant within a well-defined frame of reference. The existence is not denied of other characteristics which might influence responses (since there must surely be an infinity of them), but there can be no legitimate reason to parameterize them unless they display the above characteristics. This point is crucial to understanding the difference among competing latent trait models.

Since knowledge of traits can only arise from responses to items, it has been customary to formulate the mathematical equations in terms of "item characteristic curves" (ICCs), that is, in terms of the probability of

success on an item as a function of θ. One such formulation is plotted in Fig. 3. $P_i(\theta)$ is the notation used to convey the fact that the item characteristic curve is for item *i* (and that its shape, location along the abscissa, and other characteristics depend on item parameters), and that θ is an independent variable.

Some psychometricians use the label "item response theory" (IRT) for this formulation. Others find this alternative detracts from understanding persons' behaviour through traits. This latter group writes the probability statement connecting observed data and latent parameters as $P(\lambda_{vi})$, where λ_{vi} is a suitable function of item and person parameters, and the identification of θ as a type of "independent variable" is little more than a convenience for plotting curves like Fig. 3. With this latter orientation it makes equal sense to describe the "person characteristic curve" (PCC) in Fig. 4.

Figure 4 describes the probability of success for person *v* according to encounters with items whose latent characteristic (for example, difficulty level), is increasing. Upon justification of a particular shape for the item characteristic curve (or person characteristic curve), θ may be related monotonically to the probability of success.

The identification of θ and δ with a line running from $-\infty$ to $+\infty$ is an important aid in understanding latent trait theory since it relates items to people directly in the same metric. Furthermore, since the models are probabilistic, it is sensible to show $P_i(\theta)$ [or $P(\lambda_{vi})$], reaching its limits asymptotically. The shape of the curve depends on the choice of mathematical function; this choice is governed, in turn, by the number, nature, and arithmetic arrangement of item and person parameters and these are ultimately governed by the philosophy of what it means to make useful psychological measures of people.

A selection of the best-known models is now described. The "normal ogive" model, used by Thurstone from psychophysics, is now mainly of historical interest since other forms of the probability distribution pose less problems for parameter estimation and yet still retain the essential characteristics of a measurement model.

Birnbaum (1968) borrowed ideas from bioassay to justify his logistic model of mental measurement:

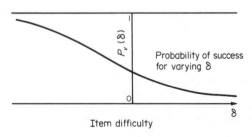

Figure 4
Person characteristic curve—persons *v* and varying δ

$$P_i(\theta) = p(x_i = 1; \theta, \alpha_i, \delta_i)$$

$$= \frac{\exp[\alpha_i(\theta - \delta_i)]}{1 + \exp[\alpha_i(\theta - \delta_i)]}$$

The alternative notation for $P_i(\theta)$ has been chosen to emphasize that, from one point of view, all latent trait measurement models are genuine probability distributions relying on discrete random variables and one or more parameters. According to the logistic model, the probability of success on an item is governed by the logistic distribution in which:

(a) $\alpha_i(\theta - \delta_i)$ is the "logit";

(b) δ_i is an item parameter called the item difficulty;

(c) α_i is an item parameter called the item discrimination; and

(d) θ is the (latent) independent variable of ability.

The arbitrary inclusion of additional parameters beyond one for person and one for item leads, however, to an irreconcilable disparity between assumed sophistication and the actual practice of measurement. On the other hand, this model (and its extension to one with three item parameters) is in use, particularly in the United States, so some further comments are pertinent.

One claim to the validity of these models is that the item characteristic curve has a shape which closely parallels those shapes which arise when unrestricted and unedited real data are plotted. These empirical plots are usually of raw score (on the abscissa) versus proportion of correct answers (on the ordinate). Although the abscissa has finite bounds, it is argued that a suitable transformation of this scale to an ability scale would produce curves like the logistic. Therefore, for example, if curves actually do differ in slope, this is taken as evidence of the necessity for the inclusion of the item discrimination parameter, and hence α_i has to be modelled. In this sense there are no a priori grounds for this model—"it must be justified on the basis of the results obtained, not on a priori grounds" (Lord 1980 p. 14).

There are at least four problems with this approach to modelling data (apart from the serious practical ones of parameter estimation with real and realistic data sets). In the first instance, the intersection of the item characteristic curves leads to a counterintuitive and complex description of the concepts of "easiness of an item" and "ability of a person". That is, the simplicity of equating "easiness" directly with chances of success (the easier the item, the greater the chance of success), and the corresponding simplicity of equating "ability of the person" directly with number of items correct is lost. This loss of simplicity is a result of the absence of sufficient statistics for the parameters.

Secondly, if the sole criterion for model choice is a closer and closer fit to observed data, then there is theoretically no limit to the number and nature of item and person parameters (already four item parameters have been proposed by some writers). Complexities of this nature do not occur in physical science measurements and they do retard the development of social science measurement since the clear interpretation of data in the presence of many parameters is a difficult exercise.

The third point relates to practice. The unrealistic nature of models with more than one parameter per person and/or per item, is well-appreciated by those working daily with tests and measurements. Even though classroom teachers, for example, may not acquire a full knowledge of latent trait theory, the underlying principles of the simplest and recommended model have been known and adopted for many decades. Working with this model, for example, the analysis of person response patterns (across a set of items) is made conceptually and operationally very simple whereas with the two- and three-parameter models the exercise is exceedingly complex and unlikely to gain acceptance.

Fourthly, it is unclear how to carry out successfully a number of central measurement tasks with two- and three-parameter models: equating, linking, test design, and person measurement are some examples of exercises which present little difficulty under the one-parameter model. For those whose job it is to make measurements, evaluate them and report results, one dominant criterion for the adoption of new procedures is: does it make an appreciable difference? It is suggested that the answer to this, from the point of view of latent trait theory in general, is positive, but that the additional benefit from the complexities of two- and three-parameter models is not forthcoming.

Latent trait models which go under the name of "Rasch" models were derived by the Danish mathematician, Georg Rasch, and have been promoted in the United States by B. D. Wright in Chicago and in Europe by G. Fischer in Vienna, and by their respective colleagues. For binary-scored data, the Rasch model has the form:

$$p(X_{vi} = 1; \theta_v, \delta_i) = \frac{\exp(\theta_v - \delta_i)}{1 + \exp(\theta_v - \delta_i)}$$

At first impression it would appear that this model may be made equivalent to Birnbaum's by setting all discriminations equal to the value 1.0. However, despite the algebraic identity between them, it should be noted that two fundamental differences exist between the Rasch model and the equal-discrimination version of the Birnbaum model. In the first case, Rasch arrived at the shape of his item characteristic curve by an a priori argument about what he believed to be the essential nature of measurement and hence the class of models which must follow from his measurement axioms of invariance. Secondly, the double subscripting of the random variable X_{vi}, and the consequent subscripting of θ gives a status to θ_v equivalent to that of δ_i. This means that attention may be focused on an individual person v to the same extent and in the same way that attention is paid to an individual item i. Thus realistic study of individual differences arises in which person v may be studied in his or her own right, and not just as a representative number of the population of persons. In other words, both θ_v and δ_i are seen as "fixed" effects rather than "random and fixed" effects. This makes possible the extension of this model to other facets (person and items represent two facets), since all that is required is a suitable subscripting of X and the inclusion of extra parameters, provided the logit combines all parameters additively.

Thus a Rasch model for measuring written composition, in which the decision concerning the numerical value to attach to a given response is possibly made by different graders for different person's essays, might require the random variable X_{vig} with the logit $\theta_v - \delta_i - \gamma_g$ where the parameter γ_g is identified as "grader harshness". The inclusion of extra facets, and the extension to other polychotomous scoring systems, takes place within the framework of a single, undimensional latent trait.

Historically, the different orientations to latent trait theory exposed here arise from an uncritical adaptation from a similar theory in biological assay. The fundamental difference between the bioassay models and the psychometric models is that the former operate with known values of the independent variable (for example, drug dosage), whereas θ remains an unknown parameter and must always be estimated in the psychometric models.

In a discussion of the theory of latent traits not much attention need be paid to peripheral aspects such as estimation; however, since this topic and "tests of fit" really have no counterpart in true-score theory, some comment is warranted. When psychometricians advance from the linearity of the true-score model and its simplistic distributional assumptions to the nonlinearity of logistic distributions with explicit parameters, they are able to take advantage of a range of powerful parameter estimation techniques. In particular, the method of maximum likelihood has been well-developed and used by statisticians working with a wide variety of probability models. A considerable literature has evolved around estimation in latent trait models and someone wishing to make use of latent trait theory would be advised to consult this literature.

Somewhat later on the scene, but proposed with equal enthusiasm, have been the various tests of fit. Most of these have been associated with the Rasch model and encompass "person" fit as well as the more conventional "item" fit. The relationship between fit of data to the Rasch model and such topics as unidimensionality, local independence, and varying discriminations occupy a large part of the recent literature on Rasch models. It is sufficient here to point out that the use of a formal probability model and all its contingent framework of estimation and fit strategies, has given to modern psychometrics a status that is not only of theoretical soundness but one which permits ready adoption to the practical realm of educational and psychological measurement.

See also: True-score Models; Rasch Measurement Models; Item Response Theory; Guttman Scales

Bibliography

Andrich D 1973 Latent trait psychometric theory in the measurement and evaluation of essay writing ability. Doctoral dissertation, University of Chicago

Birnbaum A 1968 Some latent trait models and their use in inferring an examinee's ability. In: Lord F M, Novick M R (eds.) 1968 *Statistical Theories of Mental Test Scores*. Addison-Wesley, Reading, Massachusetts

Fischer G H 1973 The linear logistic test model as an instrument in educational research. *Acta Psychol.* 37: 359–74

Guttman L 1954 The principle components of scalable attitudes. In: Lazarsfeld P F (ed.) 1954 *Mathematical Thinking in the Social Sciences*. Free Press, Glencoe, Illinois

Lord F M 1980 *Applications of Item Response Theory to Practical Testing Problems*. Erlbaum, Hillsdale, New Jersey

Rasch G 1980 *Probabilistic Models for Some Intelligence and Attainment Tests*. University of Chicago Press, Chicago, Illinois

Thurstone L L 1929 Theory of attitude measurement. *Psychol. Rev.* 36: 222–41

Wright B D 1971 Solving measurement problems with the Rasch model. *J. Educ. Meas.* 14: 97–116

Wright B D, Stone M H 1979 *Best Test Design*. MESA Press, Chicago, Illinois

Rasch Measurement Models

B. D. Wright

The "Rasch measurement" models developed by Danish mathematician Georg Rasch between 1951 and 1959 and explained in his 1960 book, *Probabilistic Models for Some Intelligence and Attainment Tests*, are the most important advance in psychometrics since Thurstone's 1927 *Law of Comparative Judgment*. Objective measurement depends on measuring instruments which function independently of the objects measured. This requires a response model for calibrating their functioning which can separate the effects of instrument and object. Rasch was the first psychometrician to realize the necessity and sufficiency for objectivity of logistic response models

with no interaction terms. The methods introduced in his book go far beyond measurement in education or psychology. They exemplify the principles of measurement on which all scientific objectivity is based.

Rasch models are practical realizations of "fundamental measurement." When data can be selected and organized to fit a Rasch model, the cancellation axiom of additive conjoint measurement is satisfied, a perfect Guttman order of response probabilities and hence of item and person parameters is established, and items are calibrated and persons measured on a common interval scale.

The nuclear element from which all Rasch models are built is

$$P(x; \beta, \delta) = \exp(\beta - \delta)/[1 + \exp(\beta - \delta)] \qquad (1)$$

with raw-score statistics r for person parameter β, and s for item parameter δ. The linear relation between β and δ in the exponent enables $P(x; \delta|r)$ to be noninformative concerning β, and $P(x; \beta|s)$ to be noninformative concerning δ. It follows that r is sufficient for x concerning β and ancillary concerning δ, while s is sufficient for x concerning δ and ancillary concerning β. Margining to r and s estimates β and δ sufficiently while conditioning on s and r enables their inferential separation.

1. Rasch Models

The Poisson and item analysis models introduced in Rasch's 1960 book belong to the family of measurement models described by him in his 1961 article "On general laws and the meaning of measurement in psychology." Four models from this family have come into use.

The general unidimensional Rasch model can be written

$$P[k; \beta, \delta, (k),(\phi)] = \exp[\phi_x(\beta - \delta) - k_x]/\gamma \qquad (2)$$

where the available response categories are labeled 0, 1, 2,..., m, a response in the xth category by a person to an item is denoted by x, the parameters β and δ are the metric positions of the person and the item on their common variable, (k) is a vector of $m + 1$ response category parameters, (ϕ) is a vector of $m + 1$ nonparametric category coefficients and

$$\gamma = \sum_{j=0}^{m} \exp[\phi_j(\beta - \delta) - K_j] \qquad (3)$$

is the sum of all possible numerators.

1.1 Rating Scale Model

When m is finite and the $m + 1$ response categories are ordered, two simplifications occur. Andersen (1977) shows that the nonparametric category coefficients (ϕ) must be equidistant and may as well be successive integers. Andrich (1978) shows that the category parameters (k_j, $j = 0$, m) can be interpreted in terms of thresholds (τ_j, $j = 1$, m) that govern the transitions across adjacent categories. With these interpretations

$$\phi_x = x = 0, 1, 2, \ldots, m \qquad (4)$$

$$k_0 = 0 \qquad (5)$$

$$k_x = \sum_{j=1}^{x} \tau_j \qquad (6)$$

$$\gamma = 1 + \sum_{k=1}^{m} \exp\left[x(\beta - \delta) - \sum_{j=1}^{k} \tau_j \right] \qquad (7)$$

and Rasch's general unidimensional model becomes the rating scale model studied by Andrich (1978) and Wright and Masters (1982)

$$P[x; \beta, \delta, (\tau)] = \exp\left[x(\beta - \delta) - \sum_{j=1}^{x} \tau_j \right]\bigg/\gamma \qquad (8)$$

1.2 Poisson Model

When the response process allows x to take any positive integer so that $m = \infty$, and individual contributions to x occur independently, then $k_x = \log (x!)$, $\gamma = \exp[\exp(\beta - \delta)]$ and the rating scale model becomes the Poisson model Rasch used for the analysis of oral misreadings and reading speeds

$$P[x; \beta, \delta] = \exp[x(\beta - \delta)]/x! \exp[\exp(\beta - \delta)] \qquad (9)$$

1.3 Partial Credit Model

When the thresholds τ_j are individualized to the item difficulties δ to form $\delta_j = \delta + \tau_j$ so that each item has its own set of internal step difficulties and $\delta_0 = 0$, the model becomes:

$$P[x; \beta, (\delta_j)] = \exp \sum_{j=0}^{x} (\beta - \delta_j)\bigg/ \sum_{k=0}^{m} \exp \sum_{j=0}^{k} (\beta - \delta_j) \qquad (10)$$

which is useful for the analysis of graded performance and partial credit data (Wright and Masters 1982).

1.4 Item Analysis Model

When there are only two alternatives so that $m = 1$, the model becomes

$$P(x; \beta, \delta) = \exp[x(\beta - \delta)]/[1 + \exp(\beta - \delta)] \qquad (11)$$

which is the simple logistic "Rasch Model" so widely used for the sample-free calibration of educational test items and the test-free measurement of individual attainment (Wright and Stone 1979).

These four models, and a fifth for finite numbers of independent trials, can be expressed in the partial credit form as in Eqn. (10) by specifying

$$\delta_j = \delta_j \ldots\ldots\ldots\ldots\ldots\ldots\ldots\ldots \text{partial credit}$$
$$\delta_j = \delta \ldots\ldots\ldots\ldots\ldots\ldots\ldots\ldots \text{item analysis}$$
$$\delta_j = \delta + \tau_j \ldots\ldots\ldots\ldots\ldots\ldots\ldots \text{rating scale}$$
$$\delta_j = \delta + \log (j) \ldots\ldots\ldots\ldots\ldots\ldots \text{Poisson counts}$$
$$\delta_j = \delta + \log (j) - \log(m + 1 - j) \ldots\ldots \text{binomial trials}$$

2. Methods of Estimation

Measurement models require methods for estimating their parameters. The LOG method Rasch used for item calibration in 1953 is easy to follow and brings out the necessity of additivity in the construction of a measuring system.

Rasch also describes a pairwise calibration in which the ability parameters of persons scoring one on two-item tests cancel when estimating the difficulty difference between the two items. This leads to a PAIR method of item calibration in which items are tabulated against one another in all possible pairs and the responses of persons attempting each pair but succeeding on only one item provide the item calibrations.

The PAIR method can also be used for person measurement because the difficulty parameters of items attempted by both of a pair of persons but succeeded on by only one of them cancel when estimating the ability difference between the two persons. In this case the persons are tabulated against one another in all possible pairs and responses to items attempted by each pair of persons, but succeeded on by only one of them, provide the person measures. This method is useful when one has too few persons to establish a useful item calibration and is sufficiently satisfied that the items work together to define a useful variable to get along without verifying this by trying to calibrate them.

LOG uses ability estimates when the ability parameters could have been removed by conditioning. PAIR does not use information based on item relationships more complex than pairwise comparisons. To improve on this, Rasch outlines a conditional method of estimation, FCON, in which all person parameters are explicitly removed by conditioning and all data are used for item calibration. Simulations done in 1965 and 1974 (Wright and Douglas 1977a), however, show that tests exceeding 30 or 40 items can encounter round-off errors which spoil FCON estimates. This provoked the development of an unconditional counterpart UCON (Wright and Panchapakesan 1969). In FCON, the person parameters are replaced by a term indexed to items as well as person scores, and calculated from symmetric functions of item estimates. In UCON this term is indexed to person scores only and its variation over items averaged out.

Rasch (1960 p. 182) shows why UCON works. The symmetric functions σ_{ri} in FCON can be written $\beta_{ri} = \log(\sigma_{r-1,i}/\sigma_{ri})$ so that the conditional probability of a person with score r succeeding on item i becomes

$$\exp(\beta_{ri} - \delta_i)/[1 + \exp(\beta_{ri} - \delta_i)] \qquad (12)$$

The item parameter β_{ri}, which replaces person parameter β_r, is calculated from the set of item difficulties with δ_i removed. But removing the current estimates d_i one at a time has little effect on the matrix of estimates (b_{ri}). As a result person parameter conditioning is well-approximated by reducing each vector of (b_{ri}) to b_r so that the working probability of a person with score r succeeding on item i becomes

$$\exp(b_r - d_i)/[1 + \exp(b_r - d_i)] \qquad (13)$$

Wright and Douglas (1977b) show that the average effect of using b_r, the estimated ability of any person with score r, instead of calculating the symmetric functions of the item difficulty estimates, can be removed by multiplying centered UCON item difficulties by $(L-1)/L$, where L is the number of items.

If items and persons are more or less normally distributed, an even simpler method of estimation, PROX, can be used (Wright and Douglas 1977a; Wright and Stone 1979 pp. 30–45). The PROX equation for estimating item difficulty d from item score s in a sample of N persons normally distributed in ability with mean M and standard deviation S is

$$d = M + [1 + (S/1.7)^2]^{1/2}\log[(N-s)/s] \qquad (14)$$

The divisor 1.7 scales the standard deviation of item difficulty from logits to probits. When persons and items are symmetrically distributed around one mode and targeted on one another, PROX produces item estimates equivalent to those of UCON or FCON.

Once an item bank is calibrated, a person can be measured with any suitable selection of items. An especially reasonable choice is a sequence of items evenly spaced over the region where the person is thought to be. This motivates an interest in how to estimate measures from tests of evenly spaced items.

The UFORM method for estimating person ability b from relative score $f = r/L$ on a uniform test of L items with average difficulty H and difficulty range W is

$$b = H + (f - 0.5)W + \log(A/B) \qquad (15)$$

where

$$A = 1 - \exp(-fW), \text{ and}$$

$$B = 1 - \exp[-(1-f)W]$$

This makes the transformation of test scores into measures simple. The ability measure implied by $f = r/L$, a proportion correct on a particular uniform test, is determined by adding H, the average difficulty of the test items and the easily tabled increment based on f and W given above. A standard error for this measure can be calculated by looking up an error coefficient in a corresponding table and dividing it by the square root of L (Wright and Stone 1979 pp. 143–151).

3. The Analysis of Fit

Before estimates are used as calibrations and measurements, it is necessary to verify that the data from which they came are suitable for measuring. The requirements for measuring are specified by the model. If the data cannot be managed by the model, then they cannot be used to calibrate items or measure persons. To evaluate the fit between data and model, the validity of item response patterns must be examined during item calibration, and the validity of person response patterns examined during measurement.

The fit analysis Rasch (1960 pp. 88–105) applies to his LOG method of estimating parameters for the item analysis model is simple and elegant. Its graphical form brings out the essential part additivity plays in the construction of measures. A useful alternative for the item analysis model is to compare each response of each person to each item with its estimated expectation $p = \exp(b - d)/[1 + \exp(b - d)]$ in which b and d are the current estimates of person ability and item difficulty. When this comparison is summarized over persons for an item, it indicates the overall validity of that item. When it is summarized over items for a person, it indicates the overall validity of that person's responses (Wright and Stone 1979 pp. 66–80). More detailed and more sensitive analyses of fit can be implemented by partitioning these comparisons into relevant classes of items and/or persons and analyzing the variance structure of these partitions.

If the observed response $x = 0$ or 1 has an expectation E estimated by

$$Ex \simeq \exp(b - d)/[1 + \exp(b - d)] = p \qquad (16)$$

in which b and d are used exactly as they come from the estimation procedure (*before* unbiasing by $(L - 1)/L$ in the case of UCON) and a variance estimated by

$$Vx \simeq p(1 - p) = w \qquad (17)$$

then the BIAS statistic

$$g = \Sigma(x - p)/(wL)^{1/2} \qquad (18)$$

and the NOISE statistics

$$v_1 = \Sigma[(x - p)^2/w]/L$$
$$v_2 = \Sigma(x - p)^2/\Sigma w \qquad (19)$$

with expectations

$$Eg = 0$$
$$Ev = 1 \qquad (20)$$

and variances

$$Vg = 1$$
$$Vv_1 = \Sigma[(1/w) - 4]/L^2$$
$$Vv_2 = (\Sigma w - 4\Sigma w^2)/(\Sigma w)^2 \qquad (21)$$

test the fit of responses (x) to their corresponding expectations (p). The average restriction in the mean squares caused by replacing the unknown probabilities by estimates based on N persons taking L items can be corrected by multiplying v by $[NL/(N - 1)(L - 1)]$. The development and use of fit statistics for the other models are discussed and illustrated in detail by Wright and Masters (1982 pp. 90–117).

4. Applications of Rasch Measurement

4.1 Item Banking

When a family of test items are constructed so they calibrate along a single dimension, and when they are used so they retain these calibrations over a useful realm of application, then a scientific tool of great simplicity and far-reaching potential becomes available. The resulting "bank" of calibrated items defines the variable in exquisite detail. Its item contents serve the composition of an infinite variety of pre-equated tests: short or long, easy or hard, wide in scope or sharp in focus. Neither the difficulty nor shape of these tests need have any effect on their equating. All possible scores on all possible tests are automatically equated in the measures they imply through the common calibrations of their bank items. Whatever the test, its measures are expressed on the common variable defined by the bank. Furthermore the validity of these calibrations and of each measure made with bank items can be verified at every step.

4.2 Test Design

The positioning of items along the dimension they define makes test design easy. Tests can be targeted on any region along the variable represented by calibrated items. The items chosen for a particular test can be spread over the target region in whatever way is most informative. The best designs are obtained by bunching items at decision points to maximize decision information and by spreading them evenly over targets to maximize target information.

4.3 Tailored Testing

The basic recipe for turning $f = r/L$, the proportion of correct answers on a test of average item difficulty H, into b, its corresponding measure in logits, is:

$$b = H + \log[f/(1 - f)] \qquad (22)$$

A simple formula for optimal sequential testing follows. If each succeeding item is chosen on the basis of prior performance, the logit difficulty of the best next item can be estimated from h, the average logit difficulty of preceding items, and f, the proportion of these items answered correctly,

$$d = h + \log[f/(1 - f)] \qquad (23)$$

The final measure equals the last difficulty chosen. Response validity can be checked by periodic administrations of off-target items for which the expected response is all but certain. Should invalidity emerge it can be used to revise or terminate the session.

4.4 Self-tailoring

Persons can also make their own choice of item difficulty as they go along. The items in their test can be arranged to increase in difficulty. People may choose their own starting point. If they feel strong, they may work ahead into harder items until they reach their limit. If they feel weak, they may stay with easy items. Capitalization on opportunity can be controlled by scoring persons on all items contained in the item segment their easiest and hardest item selections embrace, whether they attempt them all or not.

4.5 Response Validation

The analysis of fit enables the validity of each response to be examined. This is an important step in estimating a measure from test performance. The items used will vary in their positions along the variable. This will happen when items are spread to cover the target. It will also be forced by limitations in item resources. As the simplicity and necessity of verifying response pattern validity are appreciated, items for measuring will be selected which spread out enough to facilitate the evaluation of the response patterns they stimulate.

When items vary in their difficulty, persons are expected to do better on easier items than on harder ones. Because the response model is explicit in this regard, this expectation can be formulated into an analysis of fit for any response pattern. This enables the validity of each and every test performance to be examined before any measures estimated from it are reported.

4.6 Item Bias

The analysis of response pattern fit allows each person's item responses to be diagnosed in detail. If any theory is possessed that classifies items by response format, page layout, booklet location, item text, topic, or approach, then it is possible to calculate how much each person's responses are disturbed by these categories.

When a disturbance is found, it is possible to estimate the extent to which the unusual category is biased for each person. There is no other objective basis for the analysis of item or test bias. Bias estimated from groups can never satisfy the right of each individual to be fairly treated regardless of membership.

4.7 Individual Diagnosis

More important is the identification of each test taker's strengths and weaknesses and the use of this diagnosis to find what he or she needs next. Most test takers are associated with programs dedicated to improving them. The justification for testing is the intention to use tests to help test takers. For this, an item content diagnosis of each test taker's response pattern is essential. Since the response residuals from the measurement model manifest all the diagnostic information the test contains, their analysis is also all that can be done statistically.

5. Connections with Traditional Test Statistics

The person and item statistics of a Rasch analysis do not correspond directly to the indices of item difficulty, test reliability, and test validity of traditional test theory. Nevertheless, Rasch item difficulties and person abilities are closely related to traditional *p*-values and test scores, and the Rasch model provides valuable insight into traditional concerns for test reliability and validity.

5.1 Item p-values

The traditional approach to item difficulties uses a "*p*-value" or "proportion of persons attempting the item who are successful". These *p*-values have two shortcomings. First, they are dependent upon the abilities of the persons who took the test: the more able the persons, the higher the proportion of persons succeeding on each item. This makes it awkward to compare the difficulties of items taken by different groups of persons. Second, because they are bounded by zero and one, *p*-values cannot form an interval or linear scale: equal differences in *p*-values cannot represent equal differences in item difficulties.

Rasch item difficulty estimates are freed from both of these shortcomings. The way in which this is done can be illustrated for the particular case in which person abilities are assumed to be normally distributed. In this case, sample-free item difficulties can be approximated from item *p*-values using the formula

$$D = M + Y[\log(1 - p)/p]$$

where $Y = (1 + S^2/2.89)^{1/2}$, D is the Rasch item difficulty, M is the mean ability for the sample of persons, S is the standard deviation of these abilities, and p is the traditional item *p*-value. The values of D, M and S are in logits on the linear scale shared by item calibrations and person measures and the factor $2.89 = 1.7^2$ rescales the normal distribution to follow the logistic.

This formula removes the two shortcomings of *p*-values. First, the *p*-values are transformed onto a linear scale by the logit function $\log[(1 - p)/p]$. Second, this transformed *p*-value is rescaled so that the influence of the sample standard deviation S and sample mean M are removed. If the person abilities are more or less normally distributed, the resulting item calibration D is sample free. This means that the difficulties of items can be compared even though they might come from quite different samples of persons.

5.2 Test Scores

A Rasch ability estimate is reported for each person taking a test, provided that the test is not so easy that the person answers all items correctly or so difficult that they are able to answer none. The traditional approach to reporting a person's ability is to count the number of correct answers made and to report either this raw test score or some norm-based transformation of it. But like *p*-values, these raw scores have two shortcomings. First, they are dependent upon the difficulties of the items in the test. If the items are easy, raw scores will be high. This makes it awkward to compare the abilities of persons taking tests of different difficulty. The second disadvantage is that, because they are bounded by zero and the maximum possible score, raw scores are also not on an interval scale. The result is that a difference of one score point does not represent the same difference in ability from one end of the score range to the other.

Rasch ability estimates are freed of these disadvantages. Under the assumption that items are normally distributed, ability estimates can be approximated from raw scores with the formula:

$$B = H + X\{\log[r/(L - r)]\}$$

where $X = (1 + W^2/2.89)^{1/2}$, B is the person's ability measure, H is the mean difficulty of the test items, W is the standard deviation of these item difficulties, all in logits, r is the person's raw score, and L is the number of items in the test. Once again, the disadvantages of the raw scores are removed in two steps: First by transforming the scores onto an interval scale using the transformation $\log[r/(L - r)]$ and second by removing the influence of the mean and standard deviation of the test item difficulties. If the item difficulties are more or less normally distributed, then the resulting person measures are test free. This means that they can be compared even though persons take quite different sets of items. The general formula which can be used for any distribution of item difficulties is slightly more complicated. For details, see Wright and Stone (1979).

5.3 Reliability

The reliability of a test is intended to specify the accuracy with which the test measures the variable it is designed to measure. The traditional formulation of test reliability can be derived from a "true score" model which assumes that the observed test score of each person can be resolved into two components: an unknowable true score and a random error. The reliability of a test is defined as the proportion of a sample's observed score variance SD^2, which is due to the sample's true-score variance ST^2

$$R = ST^2 / SD^2 = 1 - (SE^2/SD^2)$$

where $SD^2 = ST^2 + SE^2$, and SE^2 is the error variance of the test, averaged over that sample.

The size of this traditional reliability coefficient, however, depends not only upon the test-error variance SE^2 which describes how precisely the test measures (i.e., for a given ST^2, the greater the precision of measurement, the smaller SE^2, and so, the larger R), but also on the sample true-score variance ST^2 which describes the ability dispersion of the sample (i.e., for a given SE^2, the greater the sample true-score variance ST^2, the larger R). Rather than combining ST^2 and SE^2 into one compound statistic which is easily mistaken for a sample-free index of how accurately a test measures, it is more useful to distinguish between these two components of variance in the traditional reliability expression and to examine ST^2 and SE^2 separately.

The observed sample variance SD^2 can be calculated directly from the observed measures, but the test error variance SE^2 must be derived from a model describing how each score occurs. The traditional approach to estimating this error variance is to estimate the reliability first. This is done in various ways, for example, by calculating the correlation between repeated measurements under similar conditions, or by correlating split halves, or by combining item point biserials. An average error variance for the test with this particular sample is then estimated from $SD^2(1 - R')$ where R' is the estimate of R.

The magnitude of the estimated reliability R', however, also depends upon a third factor, namely the extent to which the items in the test actually work together to define one variable. The traditional estimate of R can be expressed as a function of an observed sample variance SD^2 and an "actual" test-error variance SA^2:

$$R' = 1 - (SA^2/SD^2)$$

This actual error variance has two parts. The modeled test error variance SE^2 is its theoretical basis. But it is also influenced by the extent to which the items actually fit together, and are thus internally consistent. When item inconsistency is estimated by a fit mean square V for the test as a whole, then the actual error variance is

$$SA^2 = V.SE^2$$

so that the estimated reliability becomes

$$R' = 1 - (V.SE^2)/SD^2$$

The Rasch analysis resolves these complications by dealing separately with each of the three components V, SE and SD which are submerged in the traditional test reliability coefficient.

First, the model provides a direct estimate of the modeled error variance SE^2. This modeled error indicates how precisely each person's ability can be estimated when the test items are internally consistent. Unlike the traditional reliability coefficient, this estimate is not influenced by any sample variance or fit and is not sample specific. It is a sample-free test characteristic which estimates how precisely any person's ability can be estimated from their particular score, regardless of any sample to which they may belong. Also unlike the traditional reliability coefficient, this estimate is not an average for the entire test, but is particular to whatever test score is actually obtained.

Under a Rasch analysis, the term "reliable" is best reserved for this single score-specific, sample-free aspect of traditional reliability. Rather than referring to the reliability of a whole test with respect to some sample, the term is used to describe the precision of each person's measure. Analogously, the estimate of the standard error for each item makes it possible to refer to the "reliability" of each item's calibration.

Once values for the test measurement error SE^2 of each person observed are available, an estimate of the true-sample variance ST^2 can be obtained:

$$ST^2 = SD^2 - MSE$$

where MSE is the sample mean of the individual error variances:

$$MSE = \left(\sum_{n=1}^{N} SE^2 \right) \Big/ N$$

The third factor influencing estimates of traditional test reliability, namely the internal consistency among items, is treated as the "internal validity" of the instrument.

5.4 Validity

In traditional test theory, a distinction is made between internal and external validity. The usual statistics employed to assess the internal validity of a test are the item point biserials and their accumulation into the test reliability estimate. Since the magnitude of this item statistic depends on the ability distribution of the sample, in particular, on the relationship between the item p-value and the sample ability spread, it has the disadvantage of being sample dependent. When an explicit measurement model is used, the internal validity of a test can be analyzed in terms of the statistical fit of each item to the model in a way that is independent of the sample ability distribution. A mean-square test of fit can be used to estimate the extent to which the data on each item are consistent with the latent variable implied by the collection of items in the test. The evaluation of this fit is a check on internal validity. If the fit statistic of an item is acceptable, then the item is "valid".

The pattern of each person's performances can be analyzed in the same way and, if the fit statistic for a person's performance is acceptable, then that person's test performances are interpreted as a "valid" basis for inferring a measure of that person's ability. To the extent that a person's test performances do not approximate the model (e.g., if the person tends to get easy items wrong and hard items right), the validity of that person's ability estimate is in doubt.

6. Conclusion

Rasch has devised a truly new approach to psychometric problems. . . . He makes use of none of the classical psychometrics, but rather applies algebra anew to a probabilistic model. The probability that a person will answer an item correctly is assumed to be the product of an ability parameter pertaining only to the person and a difficulty parameter pertaining only to the item. . . the ability assigned to an individual is independent of that of other members of the group and of the particular items with which he is tested; similarly for the item difficulty. . . . Thus Rasch must be credited with an outstanding contribution to one of the two central psychometric problems, the achievement of nonarbitrary measures. Rasch is concerned with a different and more rigorous kind of generalization than Cronbach, Rajaratnam, and Gleser. When his model fits, the results are independent of the sample of persons and of the particular items within some broad limits. Within these limits, generality is, one might say, complete. (Loevinger 1965 p. 151)

Bibliography

Andersen E B 1977 Sufficient statistics and latent trait models. *Psychometrika* 42: 69–81
Andrich D 1978 A rating formulation for ordered response categories. *Psychometrika* 43: 561–73
Loevinger J 1965 Person and population as psychometric concepts. *Psychol. Rev.* 72: 143–55
Rasch G 1960 *Probabilistic Models for Some Intelligence and Attainment Tests.* Danmarks Paedogogiske Institut, Copenhagen. (Reprinted 1980 University of Chicago Press, Chicago)
Rasch G 1961 On general laws and meaning of measurement in psychology. *Proceedings of the Fourth Berkeley Symposium on Mathematical Statistics and Probability.* pp. 312–33
Rasch G 1977 On specific objectivity: An attempt at formalizing the request for generality and validity of scientific statements. *Danish Yearbook of Philosophy* 14: 58–94
Wright B D, Douglas G A 1977a Best procedures for sample-free item analysis. *Appl. Psychol. Meas.* 1: 281–95
Wright B D, Douglas G A 1977b Conditional versus unconditional procedures for sample-free item analysis. *Educ. Psychol. Meas.* 37: 47–60
Wright B D, Masters G N 1982 *Rating Scale Analysis.* MESA Press, Chicago, Illinois
Wright B D, Panchapakesan N 1969 A procedure for sample-free item analysis. *Educ. Psychol. Meas.* 29: 23–48
Wright B D, Stone M H 1979 *Best Test Design.* MESA Press, Chicago, Illinois

Partial Credit Model

G. N. Masters

The partial credit model is an extension of the Rasch model for dichotomously scored test data to outcomes recorded in more than two ordered response categories. One approach to the analysis of polychotomously scored data is to group the ordered response categories and to carry out multiple dichotomous analyses. A preferable approach is to implement a model for ordered response categories directly. The partial credit model is a general polychotomous item response model belonging to the Rasch family of measurement models.

1. An Illustration of Use of the Model

There are many situations in educational research in which students' attempts at a task can be categorized into several ordered levels of outcome. The use of multiple outcome categories is common practice when scoring performances on complex tasks like essay writing and problem solving. But even in situations in which it is usual to score students' performances dichotomously (right/wrong), it is often possible to identify among students' "incorrect" answers varying degrees of partial understanding, and so to define more than two levels of outcome on an item. This can be illustrated with the following item from a test of basic mathematics: "A calculator shows the figure 25.634817. Express this correct to two decimal places". Students give a variety of answers to this item, but by far the most common are 25.63, 25.64, 2563.4817, and .25634817.

The usual dichotomous scoring of this item would give full credit for the first of these answers and no credit for any other. However, the second answer, 25.64, shows partial understanding: students who give this answer understand that correcting a number to two decimal places involves reducing to two the number of digits after the decimal point. These students appear to believe that because the original number is greater than 25.63 it must be rounded *up* to 25.64. The last two answers indicate no understanding of rounding and result from moving the decimal point two places (as in multiplication and division by 100). The most that can be said for these two answers is that they show some understanding of "two decimal places". This is more than can be said for the other answers that students give to this item (e.g., 25.634.817).

The answers given to this mathematics item by a group of 570 ninth grade students are summarized in Fig. 1. Students' answers have been grouped to form four ordered outcome categories: (a) 25.63, (b) 25.64,

(c) either 2563.4817 or .25634817, (d) some other answer. The 570 students have been divided into 10 equal-sized groups on the basis of their total mathematics test scores. Students with the lowest test scores are at the bottom of Fig. 1, and those with the highest test scores are at the top. Figure 1 shows the proportion of students in each test score group in each of the four outcome categories.

Among the lowest-scoring group of students (at the bottom of Fig. 1), only about 20 percent of students gave the correct answer, 25.63, to this item. The most common answer given by this group was either 2563.4817 or .25634817. More than 60 percent of incorrect answers given by this low-scoring group were of this type. Among the highest-scoring group (at the top of Fig. 1), about 80 percent of students gave the correct answer. Ninety percent of high-scoring students who gave incorrect answers to this item gave the answer 25.64.

Figure 1 shows that the types of errors made on this item change with increasing mathematics test score. Very few of the incorrect answers given by students with low test scores show any understanding of rounding. In fact, about 20 percent of low-scoring students give "other" answers like 25.634.817, suggesting that these students may not even understand "two decimal places". In contrast, the incorrect answers given by high-scoring students display some understanding of rounding but reveal confusion about when to round up or down. In an instructional setting, it would be inappropriate to treat every student giving an "incorrect" answer to this mathematics item in the same way. The type of instruction in rounding decimal numbers required by most low-scoring students in Fig. 1 is likely

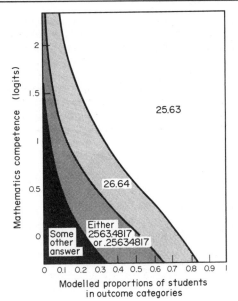

Figure 2
Modelled outcome map

to be very different from the instruction required by most high-scoring students.

The partial credit model is a statistical model for the analysis of test and questionnaire items for which two or more ordered levels of outcome are defined. Its purpose is to model changes in the distribution of students' answers over the available outcome categories with increasing competence. For the mathematics item described above, the four outcome regions as modelled by the partial credit model are shown in Fig. 2. The four regions of this map correspond to the four regions in Fig. 1. The difference is that these regions no longer show the observed proportions of students in each category, but show *modelled* proportions. The basic shapes of the smooth curves in Fig. 2 are fixed by the algebra of the partial credit model. The locations of these curves were estimated from the answers this group of 570 students gave to this item.

When students' answers to an item approximate the partial credit model (i.e., Fig. 1 resembles Fig. 2), that item can be used to help estimate students' locations on the path of developing competence that runs up the left edge of these figures. It is in this sense that the partial credit model is a "measurement" model: it provides a probabilistic connection between the categories of observed outcome on an item and locations on a latent path of developing competence. This probabilistic connection provides a basis for constructing measures of competence from students' performances on a set of items with multiple outcome categories.

2. The Algebra of the Model

In common with all latent trait models, the partial credit model represents each student's level of competence or

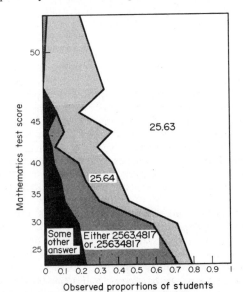

Figure 1
Observed outcome map

achievement as a location on a *continuum* of increasing competence. In Figs. 1 and 2, this continuum runs up the left edge of the figure. The location β_n of student n on this continuum is estimated from that student's answers to a set of appropriate items. Answers to each item are classified into a set of ordered outcome categories labelled $0, 1, 2, \ldots, m_i$ for that item. Under the partial credit model, the probability of student n's answer being in outcome category x of item i is given by

$$P_{nix} = \begin{cases} \dfrac{1}{1 + \displaystyle\sum_{k=1}^{m_i} \exp \sum_{j=1}^{k} (\beta_n - \delta_{ij})} & \text{for } x = 0 \\[2em] \dfrac{\exp \displaystyle\sum_{j=1}^{x} (\beta_n - \delta_{ij})}{1 + \displaystyle\sum_{k=1}^{m_i} \exp \sum_{j=1}^{k} (\beta_n - \delta_{ij})} & \text{for } x = 1, 2, \ldots, m_i \end{cases} \quad (1)$$

where the parameters $\delta_{i1}, \delta_{i2}, \ldots, \delta_{im_i}$ are a set of parameters associated with item i which jointly locate the model probability curves for that item (see Fig. 2). There are m_i item parameters for an item with $m_i + 1$ outcome categories.

For the mathematics item described above, four outcome categories were defined, meaning that $4 - 1 = 3$ parameters δ_{i1}, δ_{i2}, and δ_{i3} were estimated for this item. These three estimates and the algebra of the model provide the modelled outcome regions in Fig. 2. At any estimated level of competence β_n, the partial credit model provides the widths P_{ni0}, P_{ni1}, P_{ni2} and P_{ni3} of the four outcome regions at that level. These widths can be interpreted either as the estimated probabilities of a student at that level of competence responding in outcome categories 0, 1, 2, and 3, or as the expected proportions of students at that level of competence responding in these four categories. For values of β_n near the bottom of Fig. 2, P_{ni0} and P_{ni1} are larger than P_{ni2} and P_{ni3}. For values of β_n near the top of Fig. 2, P_{ni3} is large, and all other probabilities are small. A more complete discussion of the algebra of the partial credit model is provided by Masters (1980, 1982), Wright and Masters (1982), and Masters and Wright (1984).

3. Ordered Outcome Categories

The partial credit model could be applied to any set of test or questionnaire data collected for the purposes of measuring students' abilities, achievements or attitudes provided that responses to each test or questionnaire item are scored in two or more ordered categories. There are many different ways in which a set of ordered outcome categories might be defined for a task. Some of these are considered below.

3.1 Levels of Partial Understanding

The four outcome categories defined for the mathematics item above were the product of a careful study of all answers given by students to this item. This approach to developing a set of outcome categories is described in some detail by Dahlgren (1984). For some tasks, the types of misconceptions and errors that are likely to occur will be well understood, making it possible to construct a set of outcome categories before the task is given to a group of students. For most tasks, however, the construction of a set of categories which capture levels of partial understanding will probably require a close study of students' responses. These might then be grouped according to the levels of understanding that they reflect: "Starting with a comparatively large number of categories the researcher will gradually refine these, arriving at a smaller set of categories that may finally be difficult or impossible to collapse further" (Dahlgren 1984 p. 26). Dahlgren describes this approach to constructing a set of outcome categories as the partitioning of the "outcome space" associated with a task. The final set of categories is then used in future applications of the task.

3.2 Multistep Problems

For complex problems which require the completion of a number of steps, it is usual to identify several intermediate stages in the solution of each problem and to award partial credit on the basis of the number of steps a student completes. This scoring procedure is common in subject areas like mathematics and the physical sciences where students must first identify the problem type, select an appropriate solution strategy, and then apply this strategy which may itself involve a number of steps. By awarding credit for the steps a student has successfully completed, a set of ordered outcome categories can be defined for each multistep problem.

3.3 Rating Scales

Another common method for recording performances on an item is to rate students' attempts at the item on a scale (e.g., 1 to 5). This scoring procedure is popular for recording performances on tasks like building a model, assembling a piece of apparatus, carrying out a procedure, and writing an essay. To ensure a degree of comparability across raters and over time, the criteria to be applied in rating performances on a task might be made explicit and accompanied by samples of student attempts at that task to illustrate the available score points.

Rating scales are also common methods of measuring attitudes and personalities. In these contexts, respondents are usually provided with a fixed set of response alternatives like "never," "sometimes," "often," "always," or "strongly disagree," "disagree," "agree," "strongly agree" to be used with all items on the questionnaire. Questionnaires of this form can be analyzed with the partial credit model. However, the fact that the response alternatives are defined in the same way for all items introduces the possibility of simplifying the partial credit model by assuming that, in questionnaires of this type, the pattern of modelled outcome regions (Fig. 2) will be the same for all items on the questionnaire and that the only difference between items will be a difference in location on the measurement variable (e.g., difficulty of endorsement). This assumption yields the rating scale model.

3.4 Question Clusters

Occasionally, test and questionnaire items come in clusters with all items in a cluster relating to the same piece of introductory text. Each item in a cluster could be treated as an independent item to be scored "right" or "wrong." However, if items of this type are to be treated as independent dichotomously scored items, then the assumption of local independence must be made. Each student's response to any one item must be assumed to be uninfluenced by his or her responses to the other items in that cluster. In most dichotomously scored tests, this is a reasonable assumption. But in an item cluster, items have a shared dependence on a common stem and so are less likely to be locally independent. In this context, it is often more appropriate to treat a cluster as a single "item" on which students' scores are counts of the questions in that cluster answered correctly and take values between 0 and m_i (where m_i is the number of questions in the cluster). In this way, $m_i + 1$ ordered levels of outcome are defined for each cluster (Andrich 1982, Masters and Evans 1986).

3.5 Interactive Items

Finally, ordered outcome categories can be constructed from students' performances on computer-administered items which provide feedback to students during a test. The feedback given during a test may simply inform students of their success or failure on an item and offer a second attempt if the item is failed. Failure on a second attempt might be followed by a third or fourth attempt and credit awarded on the basis of the number of attempts required to provide the correct answer. This procedure usually is referred to as "answer-until-correct" scoring. Alternatively, students failing on their first attempt at an item might be given a "hint" and offered an opportunity to try again (Trismen 1981). Failure after a hint might be followed by further assistance and each student's score based on the number of hints required to arrive at the correct answer. This format not only defines several ordered levels of outcome for each item but also, through the careful construction of hints, might be used to trace students' misunderstandings to their source.

4. Related Models

The partial credit model is a latent trait (or item response) model and, in particular, is a member of the Rasch family of latent trait models. The relationship of the partial credit model to a number of other members

of this family (e.g., Poisson counts model, binomial trials model) is described by Masters and Wright (1984). Several of these related models are described briefly here.

4.1 Dichotomous Rasch Model

The dichotomous model is designed for the analysis of test items for which only *two* levels of outcome are defined ($x = 0$ and $x = 1$). The dichotomous model is obtained by setting $m_i = 1$ in Eqn. (1). This provides the model probabilities.

$$P_{nix} = \begin{cases} \dfrac{1}{1 + \exp(\beta_n - \delta_{i1})} & \text{for } x = 0 \\[2ex] \dfrac{\exp(\beta_n - \delta_{i1})}{1 + \exp(\beta_n - \delta_{i1})} & \text{for } x = 1 \end{cases} \qquad (2)$$

The resulting outcome map (compare with Fig. 2) contains only two regions (fail and pass) and the single parameter estimate δ_{i1} locates the modelled boundary between these two regions. This model is the best known of the item response models and is widely used for the analysis of educational tests.

4.2 Rating Scale Model

The rating scale model can be used to analyze questionnaires in which a fixed set of response alternatives like "strongly disagree," "disagree," "agree," "strongly agree" is used with every item on the questionnaire. The rating scale model is obtained by resolving the general item parameter δ_{ij} in Eqn. (1) into two components: one for item i, and one associated with the transition between response alternatives $j - 1$ and j:

$$\delta_{ij} = \delta_i + \tau_j$$

The rating scale model is obtained by substituting $(\delta_i + \tau_j)$ for δ_{ij} in Eqn. (1):

$$P_{nix} = \begin{cases} \dfrac{1}{1 + \sum\limits_{k=1}^{m} \exp \sum\limits_{j=1}^{k} (\beta_n - \delta_i - \tau_j)} \\[1ex] \text{for } x = 0 \\[3ex] \dfrac{\exp \sum\limits_{j=1}^{x} (\beta_n - \delta_i - \tau_j)}{1 + \sum\limits_{k=1}^{m} \exp \sum\limits_{j=1}^{k} (\beta_n - \delta_i - \tau_j)} \\[1ex] \text{for } x = 1, 2, \ldots, m \end{cases} \qquad (3)$$

When this model is applied, a single location δ_i is estimated for each item and m parameters $\tau_1, \tau_2, \ldots, \tau_m$ are estimated for the $m + 1$ response alternatives provided with the questionnaire.

4.3 Other Constraints

Other cases of the partial credit model can be generated by imposing constraints on the values of the item parameters $\delta_{i1}, \delta_{i2}, \ldots, \delta_{im_i}$ for each item. One simple constraint is to restrict these parameters to a *uniform* spacing such that $(\delta_{i2} - \delta_{i1}) = (\delta_{i3} - \delta_{i2}) = \ldots = (\delta_{im} - \delta_{im-1}) = \sigma_i$. Under this constraint (Andrich 1982), only the mean item parameter δ_i and the uniform spacing σ_i are estimated for each item i. If there is a reason to expect that the outcome categories for every item on a test will be uniformly spaced, and the data conform to this expectation, this case of the partial credit model offers a more parsimonious representation than the full-rank model in that it requires the estimation of fewer parameters. This constrained version of the model also may be useful with small data sets which provide insufficient data to reliably estimate all parameters for an item.

Further cases of the partial credit model have been proposed by introducing other constraints on the item parameters (e.g., steadily increasing or steadily decreasing differences $(\delta_{i2} - \delta_{i1}) < (\delta_{i3} - \delta_{i2}) < \ldots < (\delta_{im} - \delta_{im-1})$. In general, constraints such as these are only likely to be of value if they have a basis in theory (i.e., if they follow from the way in which the ordered categories have been defined).

5. Applications

Estimation algorithms for the partial credit model are described by Masters (1982) and Wright and Masters (1982). Computer programs to implement these algorithms have been developed by Wright et al. (1981), and Andrich (1982). Since the development of these programs, the partial credit model has been applied to a variety of measurement problems. Some of these are summarized briefly here.

5.1 Variable Definition

Figures 1 and 2 illustrate how, by classifying "incorrect" answers to an item into a number of ordered levels of understanding or completion, it is possible to build a more detailed picture of how competence in a subject area develops. This is an important general application of the partial credit model. The probabilistic connection between categories of observed outcome on an item and the latent continuum that these items are constructed to measure, enables each level of competence on the measurement variable to be interpreted in terms of the types of misconceptions or processing errors that are likely to be found among students at that level. Students with estimated locations near the top of Fig. 2, for example, are likely to have very different misunderstandings from students with estimated locations near the bottom of this figure.

Adams et al. (1987) have used this method to build a detailed picture of a path of developing competence in second language learning. The items in their instrument were questions posed to second language learners in face-to-face interviews. Each learner's response to each question was rated using a set of ordered outcome categories specific to that question.

The Education Department of Western Australia has taken a similar approach to analyzing students' performances on written expression tasks. They have identified a number of aspects of writing competence and have developed a set of rating points for each of these aspects of writing. Each set of ordered rating points is illustrated using samples of student writing. In this way, a number of "ladders" of developing competence corresponding to different aspects of writing ability have been constructed and calibrated. These are used as a framework for scoring students' performances on writing tasks and provide a detailed picture of the development of writing competence.

5.2 Item Banking

Calibrated item banks usually are limited to dichotomously-scored test items. This is a serious limitation if the bank is to be used as part of a program of educational assessment. A large proportion of what is taught in schools is not adequately assessed with items that can be scored either right or wrong. If an item bank is to be useful as an assessment resource, it must be capable of incorporating calibrated tasks like essay writing, problem solving, and model building.

The partial credit model provides a basis for the calibration of a range of tasks which cannot adequately be scored dichotomously. If these tasks are to be calibrated and included in an item bank, then it will usually be necessary to provide explicit guides to the scoring of individual tasks, possibly with samples of student responses to illustrate the score points to be used with each task. Some experimental work on the construction of banks of non-dichotomously scored items is described by Masters (1984) and Masters and Evans (1986).

5.3 Computer Adaptive Testing

The availability of a bank of calibrated items introduces the possibility of selecting items to suit an individual's current level of competence. If items are administered by computer, then the items to be presented to a student can be selected automatically during the course of a test. After each item is answered, the student's level of competence is reestimated and the bank is searched for the most appropriate remaining item. (This is the item that provides most information at the student's current estimate.)

Computer adaptive testing can be generalized to items which use systems of partial credit scoring, thereby enabling the construction of tailored tests based on more complex outcome spaces than right and wrong answers. The simplest adaptive testing algorithm for the partial credit model uses the statistical "information" I_{ni} available from bank item i at competence level β_n. This can be calculated as

$$I_{ni} = \sum_{k=1}^{m_i} (k^2 P_{nik}) - \left(\sum_{k=1}^{m_i} P_{nik} \right)^2 \qquad (4)$$

where P_{nik} $(k = 1, 2, \ldots, m_i)$ is the model probability of person n with an estimated level of competence β_n giving an answer in outcome category k of item i. The value of this information might be calculated for each item in a bank, given student n's current estimate, and the item with the largest value of I_{ni} chosen as the next item to be administered to person n.

Important foundational work on the extension of computer adaptive testing procedures to items which use systems of partial credit scoring has been done by Koch and Dodd (1985, 1986) and Dodd and Koch (1985, 1986). They describe a number of potential applications of this methodology, including the possibility of constructing computer adaptive questionnaires in which items designed to measure attitudes or opinions might be calibrated and selected to maximize the information available from a questionnaire. Another very promising application of this method is the construction of computer adaptive tests in which feedback is provided and multiple attempts are permitted at individual computer-administered test items.

Bibliography

Adams R J, Griffin P E, Martin L 1987 A latent trait method for measuring a dimension in second language proficiency. *Lang. Test.* 4: 9–27

Andrich D 1982 An extension of the Rasch model for ratings providing both location and dispersion parameters. *Psychometrika* 47: 105–13

Dahlgren L O 1984 Outcomes of learning. In: Marton F, Hounsell D, Entwistle N (eds.) *The Experience of Learning.* Scottish Academic Press, Edinburgh

Dodd B G, Koch W R 1985 Item and scale information functions for the partial credit model. Paper presented at the annual meeting of the American Educational Research Association, Chicago, Illinois

Dodd B G, Koch W R 1986 Relative efficiency analyses for the partial credit model. Paper presented at the annual meeting of the American Educational Research Association, San Francisco, California

Koch W R, Dodd B G 1985 Computerized adaptive attitude measurement. Paper presented at the annual meeting of the American Educational Research Association, Chicago, Illinois

Koch W R, Dodd B G 1986 Operational characteristics of adaptive testing procedures using partial credit scoring. Paper presented at the annual meeting of the American Educational Research Association, San Francisco, California

Masters G N 1980 A Rasch model for rating scales. Doctoral dissertation, University of Chicago, Illinois

Masters G N 1982 A Rasch model for partial credit scoring. *Psychometrika* 47: 149–74

Masters G N 1984 Constructing an item bank using partial credit scoring. *J. Educ. Meas.* 21: 19–37

Masters G N, Evans J 1986 Banking non-dichotomously scored items. *Appl. Psychol. Meas.* 10: 355–67

Masters G N, Wright B D 1984 The essential process in a family of measurement models. *Psychometrika* 49: 529–44

Trismen D M 1981 The development and administration of a set of mathematics items with hints. ETS-RB-81-5, Educational Testing Service, Princeton, New Jersey

Wright B D, Masters G N 1982 *Rating Scale Analysis.* MESA Press, Chicago, Illinois

Wright B D, Masters G N, Ludlow L H 1981 CREDIT: A Rasch program for ordered response categories. MESA Psychometrics Laboratory, University of Chicago, Illinois

Rating Scale Analysis

D. Andrich and G. N. Masters

Rating scales are used to help identify the degrees of a property, or in modern terms trait, an object or person may have when no instrument for measuring the trait directly is available. One common example of rating scales in education is in attitude questionnaires where responses to statements on an issue are expressed using alternatives like: strongly disagree; disagree; neutral or undecided; agree; and strongly agree. Another is in performance ratings where judges classify performances on tasks in categories like: poor; fair; good; excellent. The former, with a neutral category, are said to be bipolar scales, while the latter are said to be unipolar.

Many variants on the above formats for rating scales have been suggested. In some cases, the only cues given are descriptions of the two extreme categories, with the remaining categories simply being cut-off points on a line segment. In others, such as in judgment of essay-writing ability, examples of specimens at each level are provided. In each case the trait rated needs to be made as clear as possible with the examples or cues clarifying the way it is operationalized.

Because direct measurements of variables in the social sciences are difficult, rating scales are extremely common. Dawes (1972) points out that some 60 percent of studies have rated variables as the only form of dependent variable.

1. Contingency Table Contexts

In many contexts individuals who belong to well-defined classes or populations may be asked to rate their opinions with respect to some issue. For example, educators identified and involved with different aspects of education may be asked to provide an opinion on, for example, public examinations or minimum competency testing. Table 1 shows the kind of format in which responses may be collected and presented. A topic such as public examinations may prompt more than one statement being considered. Then results are often reported statement by statement and inferences are drawn regarding the level of support enjoyed by each issue.

Table 1
Format for ratings in contingency tables

Response score		Strongly disagree (0)	Disagree (1)	Agree (2)	Strongly agree (3)	Total number
		Please respond to the following statement in one of the categories provided: There should be publicly defined standards which all students should pass before leaving high school				
Teaching level	Elementary	$f_{10}{}^a$	f_{11}	f_{12}	f_{13}	N_1
	Secondary	f_{20}	f_{21}	f_{22}	f_{23}	N_2
	Tertiary	f_{30}	f_{31}	f_{32}	f_{33}	N_3

a f denotes frequency

2. Individual Classification Contexts

Often more refined classifications than those provided by contingency tables are required. First, the performance of each person rated, or providing an opinion, may need to be considered individually rather than as a member of some population. Secondly, it may be necessary to obtain more precise information about that person than that which can be obtained from one statement or rating. Therefore, either more than one statement on a related topic is presented, or more than one task is required to conduct the rating, or sometimes both. In situations with two or more statements or two or more tasks, the information is collapsed into a single value for each person. Table 2 shows the kind of format in which the responses may be collected and presented.

With respect to the case where many statements or tasks are provided, whether in opinion, attitude, performance, or achievement ratings, the statements or tasks have the same role as they do in Thurstone scales to which dichotomous responses rather than ratings are required. That is, they serve to define a continuum, and the ratings can be seen as extensions and refinements to dichotomous responses such as disagree or agree, and correct or incorrect. Viewed from this perspective, the increase in the number of categories beyond two helps increase the precision. The greater the number of

categories, and to the degree that the categories can be used meaningfully, the greater the precision.

Unlike performance ratings, where a rater rates a performance explicitly, the rater in attitude testing is the person whose attitude is to be assessed. Attitude questionnaires requiring such ratings are said to be of the Likert style following the work by Likert (1932) on attitude measurement.

3. Scoring the Response Categories

Whether in contingency table or individual testing contexts, the issue which has received a great deal of attention is the scoring of the ordered response categories. The most elementary approach follows closely the measurement analogy.

With a formalized measuring instrument, any object can be placed between the two cut-off points or thresholds on a continuum mapped onto a real line. On a typical measuring instrument the thresholds are represented by line segments of equal width which cut the real line at equal intervals. The measure then is the number of thresholds which the object is seen to pass and this measure may be refined by having smaller intervals between thresholds and by having thresholds represented by finer lines. Often, measurement errors are considered sufficiently small relative to the variation of the

Table 2
Format for ratings of individuals

Person (ratee)	Rating score x	Statements of tasks					
		1	2	$\cdots$	i	$\cdots$	I
		0 1 2	0 1 2		0 1 2		0 1 2
1		x_{11}	x_{12}	$\cdots$	x_{1i}	$\cdots$	x_{1I}
2		x_{21}	x_{22}	$\cdots$	x_{2i}	$\cdots$	x_{2I}
3		x_{31}	x_{32}	$\cdots$	x_{3i}	$\cdots$	x_{3I}
.		.	.		.		.
.		.	.		.		.
.		.	.		.		.
n		x_{n1}	x_{n2}	$\cdots$	x_{ni}	$\cdots$	x_{nI}
.		.	.		.		.
.		.	.		.		.
.		.	.		.		.
N		x_{N1}	x_{N2}	$\cdots$	x_{Ni}	$\cdots$	x_{NI}

measured property that they may be ignored and the measures are then treated as continuous variables.

By analogy, in the rating scale the thresholds are placed so that they indicate equal spacing, and the raters are supposed to place their response between two thresholds. Elementary quantification and analysis extends this measurement analogy. Thus the successive categories are scored with successive integers, and the resultant numbers are again treated as continuous variables. The integers may start with either 0 or 1. For convenience here, they will be taken to commence with 0 and to have a maximum of m, where there are m thresholds and therefore $m + 1$ categories.

In the contingency table context, the relative status of each group g is calculated then simply by

$$r_g = \sum_{x=0}^{m} x f_{gx}$$

while in the assessment of individuals on statements or tasks i, $i = 1, \ldots, k$, the status of each individual n is calculated simply by

$$r_n = \sum_i x_{ni}.$$

That is, the integer ratings are simply summed.

Standard analyses based on these summary statistics, and following the true score model of traditional test theory, have been developed. Guilford (1954 Chap. 11) provides a comprehensive discussion on the construction of rating scales and on the analyses using the above scoring.

However, the assumption of equality of intervals, on which the integer scoring is supposed to be based, has often been questioned. This has led to more formal representations of the rating process.

4. Mathematical Response Models

In the analysis of ratings which is more sophisticated, two qualifications to the elementary analogy of the measuring instrument are made. First, the error in classification is recognized explicitly by formulating a continuous random variable d for a response process when a rater makes a rating according to $d = \mu + \varepsilon$ where μ is the true location or true value of the rating, and ε is the error with mean 0 and variance σ^2. This simple additive equation may be subscripted in different ways depending on the context. Thus with contingency tables and ratings on a single statement or task, it may take the form $d_g = \mu_g + \varepsilon$ for every person in group g. In the rating of a person n on more than one statement or task i, it may take the form $d_{ni} = \mu_{ni} + \varepsilon_i$ in which case the error variance σ_i^2 depends only on the statement or task. The true value μ_{ni} of the rating may then be taken to depend on both the location value β_n of person n and the location value δ_i of task i. This value is then usually resolved according to $\mu_{ni} = \beta_n - \delta_i$. In performance rating, β_n is an ability of person n and δ_i is the difficulty of task i, while in attitude ratings the formulation may be

identical, with β_n representing the attitude of person n and δ_i the affective value of statement i.

Whatever the context, the rating is then supposedly determined by the interval in which the value of the random variable d falls. This formulation leads to the second qualification to the measurement analogy: instead of distances between thresholds simply being presumed to be equal, they are estimated.

4.1 The Traditional Threshold Model

The traditional model, which has its origins in the work of Thurstone (1927), assumes either a normal or a logistic distribution for the random response process. After a simple linear scaling, the two are indistinguishable numerically. Therefore, the latter is usually preferred because it is more tractable. Then the probability of a response above each threshold is the area beyond the threshold in the cumulative normal or the cumulative logistic, whichever is used. Figure 1 shows the process formalised for the logistic distribution, in which the probability p_x^* of a response *above* threshold τ_x, $x = 1, m$, is given by:

$$p_x^* = \frac{1}{\gamma} \exp[(\mu - \tau_x)/\sigma] \qquad (1)$$

$$= \frac{1}{\gamma} \exp[\alpha(\mu - \tau_x)]$$

where (a) $\alpha = 1/\sigma$ is termed the discrimination and (b) $\gamma = 1 + \exp[\alpha(\mu - \tau_x)]$ which ensures that p_x^* and its complement, the probability of a response below threshold x, sum to 1. The probability p_x of a response in category x, $x = 0, 1, 2, \ldots, m$ is then given simply by the difference between successive cumulative probabilities as $p_x = p_x^* - p_{x+1}^*$ with $p_0 = 1$ and $p_{m+1} = 0$. It is worthwhile noting that the ratio of p_x^* and $1 - p_x^*$ gives:

$$\frac{p_x^*}{1 - p_x^*} = \exp[\alpha(\mu - \tau_x)]$$

of which the natural logarithm

$$\ln\left(\frac{p_x^*}{1 - p_x^*}\right) = \alpha(\mu - \tau_x)$$

is called the logit.

Just as μ may be qualified depending on the context, so may the threshold values τ_x. For example, in the contingency table context, the exponent of Eqn. (1) may take the form $\alpha_g(\mu_g - \tau_x)$ or the same discrimination

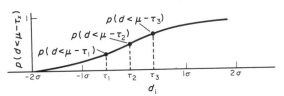

Figure 1
Probability that d is less than $\mu - \tau_x$ for each τ_x in the traditional threshold model

may be retained for all groups, giving simply $(\mu_g - \tau_x)$, where the discrimination is absorbed into the location parameters. Alternatively, not only may the discrimination be different from group to group, but so may the threshold values. The exponent would appear then as $\alpha_g(\mu_g - \tau_{xg})$.

In the case for the assessment of individual n and across more than one task or statement i, μ again is resolved according to $\mu_{ni} = \beta_n - \delta_i$. Then if each task or statement is assumed to have the same discrimination and equal thresholds, the exponent in Eqn. (1) may take the form $(\beta_n - \delta_i - \tau_x)$. If each task or statement has a different discrimination and different threshold values, this exponent may be written as $\alpha_i(\beta_n - \delta_i - \tau_{xi})$.

The estimation of the parameters may be carried out in various ways. In the early work, and in the case where ratings are associated with a group or population, the proportions of responses in the respective categories were taken as a direct estimate $\hat{p}_x$ of the corresponding probabilities p_x. Then the estimates of $\mu - \tau_x$ were given simply by either the corresponding standard normal deviate, or the logit given by $\ln(\hat{p}_x^*/(1 - \hat{p}_x^*))$ for each group. More recent techniques usually involve so-called maximum likelihood estimation (MLE) procedures. This requires identifying the values of the parameters of the chosen model which maximize the probability of obtaining the data observed.

It is interesting to note that Likert originally investigated the possibility of deriving weights for categories in the manner described above. Thus he considered that as far as the calculation of weights was concerned, the persons to be assessed for attitude belonged to some general population. Then with his emphasis on the subsequent assessment of individuals, he used as his criterion for the quality of the weightings the correlation between scores obtained by summing simply the integers and by summing the empirically derived weights. These correlations were generally almost the maximum. As a result, and for the obvious reason of simplicity, Likert and the majority of users of rating scales since then have used the simple integer scoring followed by simple summing. That is, in their statistical work, they have continued with the measurement analogy.

While the simple characterization or measurement of individuals is often the main criterion, understanding and controlling the rating mechanism is also important for researchers. Therefore, researchers have continued to show concern about the assumption of equal intervals on the rating scales. The traditional threshold model and its mathematical formulation described above is one attempt to accommodate these concerns, for which Bock (1975 Chap. 8) provides the mathematics for contingency tables and Samejima (1969) for the assessment of individuals.

4.2 The Rasch Rating Model

A more recent formulation of a mathematical model for ratings (Andrich 1978) accommodates not only the features of a random response process and the estimation

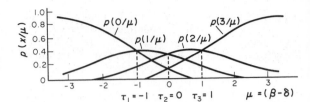

Figure 2
Probability of response x for a value of μ in the Rasch rating model

of thresholds but also the simple integer scoring of the successive categories and the simple summing among tasks or statements (see *Rasch Measurement Models*). If p_x is again the probability that a rating, governed by a true value μ, is in category x, the model takes the form:

$$p_x = \frac{1}{\gamma} \exp\left(x\mu - \sum_{k=1}^{x} \tau_k \right) \qquad (2)$$

where

$$\gamma = \sum_{k=0}^{m} \exp\left(k\mu - \sum_{j=1}^{k} \tau_j \right)$$

is a normalizing factor ensuring that

$$\sum_{x=0}^{m} p_x = 1$$

and where τ_x, $x = 1, 2, \ldots, m$ are again m thresholds on the continuum. This model has been called the Rasch rating model because it has all the distinguishing properties of the Rasch model for dichotomously scored responses. Figure 2 shows the response probability curves for three ordered categories. As with Eqn. (1), the exponent of Eqn. (2) can be modified to suit the particular data collection format. Thus for contingency tables, the exponent may take the form

$$\left(x\mu_g - \sum_{k=1}^{x} \tau_k \right)$$

Alternatively, if the thresholds are considered differently spaced from group to group, it may be modified to

$$\left(x\mu_g - \sum_{k=1}^{x} \tau_{kg} \right)$$

It is important to note an essential similarity and three essential differences between Eqn. (1) and Eqn. (2). The similarity is that they both take the logistic form. One difference, however, is how the logistic response process is formalized. As has been seen, in Eqn. (1) there is one process across *all* thresholds and the logit is identified by forming the ratio of the cumulative probabilities on either side of each threshold. In Eqn. (2) there is a process at *each* threshold and the logit is identified by forming the ratio of probabilities of adjacent categories, that is, by p_{x+1}/p_x giving

$$(p_x/p_{x-1}) = \exp(\mu - \tau_x)$$

from which:

$$\ln(p_x/p_{x-1}) = \mu - \tau_x$$

The second difference is that the exponent in Eqn. (2) has parameters which are additive. That is, there is no general discrimination α as in the exponent of Eqn. (1). The third difference is that even though the same term "threshold" is used in both models, because they are defined differently, they have different values.

In the case where the ratings pertain to members of a population or group, the proportion of responses in each category can be used to estimate the probability p_x. The simple logistic transform given above can be used to estimate the parameters in the exponent. This technique, however, is not elegant or efficient when some categories have small response frequencies. Therefore, the maximum likelihood estimation approach to estimation is again usually preferred.

When the maximum likelihood estimation is used, it becomes evident that the sufficient statistic for the estimate of μ_g is $r_g = \Sigma_x x f_{gx}$. and that the sufficient statistic for the estimate of τ_x is $t_x = \Sigma_x f_{gx}$. Further, the solution equations for μ_g and τ_x respectively are

$$r_g = \frac{1}{\gamma} N_g \sum_x \exp\left(x\hat{\mu}_g - \sum_{k=1}^{x} \hat{\tau}_k \right) \quad g = 1, G$$

$$t_x = \frac{1}{\gamma} \sum_g \exp\left(x\hat{\mu}_g - \sum_{k=1}^{x} \hat{\tau}_k \right) \quad x = 1, m$$

These equations with the imposed constraints $\Sigma_g \hat{\mu}_g = 0$ and $\Sigma_x \hat{\tau}_x = 0$ must be solved iteratively because they are implicit, and not explicit, equations in the parameters.

The existence of sufficient statistics is particularly important because it indicates that these statistics contain all the information about the parameters which is available in the responses. But it is equally important that these statistics, containing all the information, are the simple sums of the integers. That is, the statistic r_g is exactly the one used in the elementary measurement analogy. The probabilistic model [Eqn. (2)] and its form serves to rescale the constrained qualitative responses onto an additive or linear scale, and in the process also scales the thresholds. The simple total score r_g is then not seen as the sum of equally spaced thresholds as in the full measurement analogy, but as a count of the number of thresholds which have been passed. The actual weighting of the thresholds, obtained as estimates, is taken account of separately. Andrich (1979) discusses the application of the rating model to contingency table contexts.

In the case of assessment of individuals, the location μ in the exponent of Eqn. (2) is again modified to include a person parameter β_n and a difficulty or affective value parameter δ_i so that $\mu_{ni} = \beta_n - \delta_i$ giving the exponent

$$(\beta_n - \delta_i) - \sum_{k=1}^{x} \tau_k$$

In this case, the sufficient statistic for the person parameter β_n is $r_n = \Sigma_i x_{ni}$, for the task or statement parameter δ_i it is $s_i = \Sigma_n x_{ni}$ and for the threshold parameter τ_x it is $t_x = \Sigma_n \Sigma_i I_{nix}$ where $I_{nix} = 1$ if the response is in category x, and 0 otherwise. That is, t_x is simply the total number of responses in category x across all tasks or statements and across all persons. The solution equations for β, δ_i, and τ_x respectively, are given by

$$r_n = \frac{1}{\gamma} \sum_i \exp\left[x(\hat{\beta}_n - \hat{\delta}_i) - \sum_{k=1}^{x} \hat{\tau}_k \right] \quad n = 1, N$$

$$s_i = \frac{1}{\gamma} \sum_n \exp\left[x(\hat{\beta}_n - \hat{\delta}_i) - \sum_{k=1}^{x} \hat{\tau}_k \right] \quad i = 1, I$$

and

$$t_x = \frac{1}{\gamma} \sum_n \sum_i \exp\left[x(\hat{\beta}_n - \hat{\delta}_i) - \sum_{k=1}^{x} \hat{\tau}_k \right] \quad x = 1, m$$

with the constraints $\Sigma_i \delta_i = 0$ and $\Sigma_k \hat{\tau}_k = 0$.

Again, the statistic r_n for estimating the person parameter is identical to that used in the elementary measurement analogy and shown by Likert to be satisfactory for the measurement of persons. In fact, because β_n and r_n are monotonically related, their correlation is nearly perfect. The transformation of r_n to $\hat{\beta}_n$ again maps or transforms the qualitative responses onto a linear scale.

If it is assumed that the threshold spacings, whatever they are, are not equal across tasks or statements, then the exponent of Eqn. (2) may be qualified further to: $x\beta_n - \Sigma^x_{k=1} \tau_{ki}$. Wright and Masters (1982) provide a comprehensive treatment of the Rasch model for rating and the various qualifications in the exponent of Eqn. (2). In all these models, the total score $r_n = \Sigma_i x_{ni}$ continues to be the sufficient statistic in relation to the person parameter β_n, thus indicating the appropriateness of scoring successive categories with successive integers while taking account of variations in spacing between the thresholds.

5. Connecting Ratings to Measurements

Because the Rasch rating model does not require that the distances between thresholds are equal, the integer score on each rating is not itself a measure. However, the parameter estimates are on a linear scale and are measures up to an interval level. With respect to a conformable set of statements or tasks, the only difference between usual measures and those estimated through the Rasch model for ratings is one of degree. And the precision can be increased by increasing the number of tasks or statements. Thus the Rasch rating model formally completes the measurement analogy.

A related aspect of the Rasch rating model is that it formalizes the popular and simple, yet theoretically weak, Likert approach to the attitude measurement of individuals. Likert had originally proposed his approach to circumvent the time-consuming requirement of scaling statements required by the approaches of Thurstone. The formalization permits the Likert approach to subscribe to all the rigorous requirements of Thurstone for scales including the scaling of tasks or statements. In particular, and with respect to a conformable set of tasks or statements, any subset will lead to the same measure of a person. Similarly, the scale values of the statements and thresholds will be invariant across the abilities or attitudes of the persons measured. The linearity and this form of invariance are key aspects of Thurstone Scales. Andrich (1982) presents a full discussion of the way the Rasch rating model unifies the Thurstone and Likert approaches to scaling and measurement.

6. Quality Control

It should be appreciated that these invariance properties hold in observed responses only if they conform with the Thurstone or Rasch models. Thus the Rating model will connect ratings to measurements only if these ratings conform to the model, and whether or not they do so conform, is an empirical question.

There are two related advantages with the above explicit measurement model to which the ratings may be expected to conform. The obvious one is that the measures, not simply ratings, are available. The second, and equally important, is that in the very process of attempting to obtain formal measurements, a greater understanding of the variable or trait in question should follow. A close examination of response patterns which do not conform to the rating model may be as informative in understanding the variable as when they do conform, and the Rasch rating model permits a refined analysis which detects lack of conformity in various ways. These issues are discussed in detail in Wright and Masters (1982).

6.1 The Response Pattern

One important and necessary feature for measurement, which can be checked, is whether the response pattern is internally consistent. According to the rating model, every person is expected to score higher on an easier question in achievement testing, or a smaller affective value in attitude measurement. If the ratings do not conform satisfactorily to this pattern, then a single measure to represent the responses cannot be justified.

6.2 The "Halo" Effect

There can be many sources of inconsistency, as in all measurement data. When judges rate performances, a judge may gain an overall impression which affects all his ratings of the performance, even if these ratings are supposed to reflect different criteria. This is called the "halo" effect. The ratings in this case are "too consistent" as a result of the artificial dependence among them.

6.3 Rater Leniency

In performance ratings, some raters may be more lenient or more harsh than others. If more than one rater rates with respect to a single task, then the Rating Model accounts for this effect. In particular, when δ is made to characterize the rater, it represents rater harshness. Alternatively, if more than one rater and more than one task is involved, then the exponent in Eqn. (2) may be further modified to include the rater effect. For example, it may take the form $x(\beta_n - \delta_i - \eta_j) - \Sigma_{k=1} \tau_k$ where η_j is the harshness of rater j. Other qualifications are also possible.

6.4 Response Sets

Another possible systematic source of inconsistency occurs when different individuals use the categories differently. For example, some raters may use the extreme categories, while others may use the central categories, relatively too often. Both types of response patterns, reflecting what are known as response sets, can threaten valid measurement.

6.5 Number of Categories and the Neutral Category

In constructing rating response formats which will minimize the above problems, two further issues need to be considered. Firstly, the number of categories should be large enough to take advantage of the judge's capacity to discriminate, but not greater. Guilford (1954 Chap. 11) gives empirical evidence to guide the choice of the number of categories. Usually four or five are used for unipolar scales and five to nine for bipolar scales.

Secondly, in bipolar scales, the "neutral" or "undecided" category has been the subject of much study. It seems to not attract responses consistent with those found on either side of it, it being a "catch all" category in which people who do not understand the question, as well as people who are genuinely undecided, or neutral, respond. It seems best to construct statements which would attract few responses in this category, and then to exclude the category when the statements are used to obtain measures.

See also: Partial Credit Model

Bibliography

Andrich D 1978 A rating formulation for ordered response categories. *Psychometrika* 43: 561–73
Andrich D 1979 A model for contingency tables having an ordered response classification. *Biometrics* 35: 403–15
Andrich D 1982 Using latent trait measurement models to analyse attitudinal data: A synthesis of viewpoints. In: Spearritt D (ed.) 1982 *The Improvement of Measurement in Education and Psychology*. Australian Council for Educational Research, Hawthorn, Victoria
Bock R D 1975 *Multivariate Statistical Methods in Behavioral Research*. McGraw-Hill, New York
Dawes R M 1972 *Fundamentals of Attitude Measurement*. Wiley, New York
Guilford J P 1954 *Psychometric Methods*, 2nd edn. McGraw-Hill, New York

Likert R 1932 A technique for the measurement of attitudes. *Archives of Psychology*, No. 140

Samejima F 1969 Estimation of latent ability using a response pattern of graded scores. *Psychometric Monogr.* Supplement 13(4)

Thurstone L L 1927 Psychological Analysis. *Am. J. Psychol.* 38: 368–89

Wright B D, Masters G N 1982 *Rating Scale Analysis*. MESA Press, Chicago, Illinois

Thurstone Scales

D. Andrich

Thurstone's extensive work on the construction of scales for understanding and measuring educational, psychological, and sociological variables, shows great care in formalizing the fundamentals of measurement. Such care, exemplified in the following remarks which preceded an analysis of opinion data, reflect a concern in the very foundations of scientific enquiry.

> We shall avoid mere correlational procedures since it is possible to do better than merely to correlate the attributes. When a problem is so involved that no rational formulation is available, then some quantification is still possible by the coefficients of correlation of contingency and the like. But such statistical procedures constitute an acknowledgement of failure to rationalize the problem and to establish the functions that underlie the data. We want to measure the separation between the two opinions on the attitude continuum and we want to test the validity of the assumed continuum by means of its internal consistency. (Thurstone 1959 p. 267)

For Thurstone, the rationalizing principle was that of linearity, which means that if the value of object A is greater than that of object B by an amount a_1, and if the value of object B is greater than that of object C by an amount of a_2, then the value of object A should be greater than that of object C by an amount close to the sum $a_1 + a_2$.

Many of Thurstone's papers on scaling, written in the 1920s and 1930s as the one from which the above quote has been drawn, are republished in Thurstone (1959).

1. Unidimensionality

Preceding the formalization of linearity is the notion of a single continuum or unidimensionality. Unidimensionality is a relative concept and is constructed either to understand complex phenomena or to facilitate decision making. Attitudes of people are clear examples of complex phenomena; yet Thurstone argued convincingly that there was a sense to placing them on a single continuum.

> When we discuss opinions, about prohibition for example, we quickly find that these opinions are multidimensional, that they cannot all be represented in a linear continuum. The various opinions cannot be completely described merely as "more" or "less". They scatter in many dimensions, but the very idea of measurement implies a linear continuum of some sort, such as length, price, volume, weight, age. When the idea of measurement is applied to scholastic achievement, for example, it is necessary to force the qualitative variations into a scholastic linear scale of some kind. And so it is also

with attitudes. We do not hesitate to compare them by the "more or less" type of judgment. We say about a man, for example, that he is more in favour of prohibition than some other, and the judgment conveys its meaning very well with the implications of a linear scale along which people or opinions might be allocated. (Thurstone 1959 pp. 218–19)

2. Defining a Continuum

Whatever the property, or in modern terminology, trait, for which a scale is to be constructed, it is necessary to operationalize and formalize the continuum. In the case of mental tests, such as intelligence, aptitude, or achievement, this is done by formalizing the notion of the difficulty of a question, and by spacing the questions on the continuum according to their relative difficulties.

> We shall, therefore, locate these test questions on the scale as landmarks of different levels of intellectual growth. (Thurstone 1925 p. 434)

The continuum identifying a particular attitude, and termed by Thurstone generally as the "affective continuum" (Thurstone 1959 p. 292), is characterized in the same way. Statements such as "I feel the church services give me inspiration and help to live up to my best during the following week", and "I think the church seeks to impose a lot of worn-out dogmas and medieval superstitions" (Thurstone 1959 p. 267), are scaled so that they have affective values which locate them on the particular continuum.

3. Statistical Formulations

Thurstone's mathematical–statistical formulations for his scales arise from the psychophysical methods and models of Fechner and Weber in which the basic data collection design is that of pair comparisons. In such a design, each of a group of persons compares objects with respect to some physical property, such as weight or brightness, and declares which of the pair has more of the property. Thurstone contributed to the logic of psychophysics, and in the process, liberated the construction of scales for subjective values from the need of any physical continuum.

3.1 The Law of Comparative Judgment

The basis for this liberation was Thurstone's law of comparative judgment (Thurstone 1959 p. 39), which may be summarized as follows:

(a) When person n reacts to object i, the person perceives a value d_{ni} of the property in question. This value is assumed to be a continuous random variable defined by

$$d_{ni} = \alpha_i + \varepsilon_{ni} \qquad (1)$$

where α_i is the subjective scale value of object i and is constant with respect to all persons in a specified population, and ε_{ni} is the error component associated with person n. Over the population of persons, d_{ni} is defined to be normally distributed with mean α_i and variance σ_i^2.

(b) When person n compares two objects i and j then the person judges that object i has more of the property if the difference $d_{ni} - d_{nj} > 0$. In the population, this difference:

$$d_{ij} = d_{ni} - d_{nj} = (\alpha_i - \alpha_j) + (\varepsilon_i - \varepsilon_j) \qquad (2)$$

is a continuous random variable normally distributed with mean value $\alpha_{ij} = \alpha_i - \alpha_j$ and variance $\sigma_{ij}^2 = \sigma_i^2 + \sigma_j^2 - 2\rho_{ij}\sigma_i\sigma_j$.

This difference process for a fixed α_{ij}, is shown in Fig. 1 in which the shaded region represents the probability that $d_{ij} > 0$.

In empirical data, the proportion of persons who judge that object i has more of the property than object j is an estimate of this probability. The associated estimate of $\alpha_i - \alpha_j$ then is the corresponding normal deviate. The step of transforming a proportion, taken as an estimate of a probability in a normal distribution, was, in fact, the key step in Thurstone's linearization of his scales.

The expression for σ_{ij}^2 was further modified by Thurstone (1959 p. 39) into special cases. One special case is to assume that the correlation ρ_{ij} is zero. A further specialization is to let $\sigma_i^2 = \sigma_j^2 = \sigma^2$. This produces Thurstone's Case V of the law of comparative judgment, and is the easiest case to apply. Torgerson (1958) and Bock and Jones (1968) elaborate on the law of comparative judgment and develop more advanced techniques for estimating the scale values. Edwards (1957) provides an excellent elementary treatment.

Figure 1
Probability that $d_{ij} > 0$ for fixed $(\delta_i - \delta_j)$ in a pair comparison design

3.2 Attitude Testing—Subjective Values

Thurstone stressed that comparisons need not be constrained to physical objects:

One of the main requirements of a truly subjective metric is that it shall be entirely independent of all physical measurement. In freeing ourselves completely from physical measurement, we are also free to experiment with aesthetic objects and with many other types of stimuli to which there does not correspond any known physical measurement. (Thurstone 1959 pp. 182–83)

For constructing attitude scales, statements reflecting different intensities of attitude may be scaled through the pair comparison design.

3.3 Mental Testing

Thurstone applied the principles of the law of comparative judgment to mental testing by a simple redefinition of one of the variables. Effectively, the ability of each person replaced the value of one of the two entities which were compared. Thus, the ability of a person was compared with the difficulty of a question.

A common classification of persons taken by Thurstone was an age group. Then the proportion of any age group which succeeded on any question was transformed to a normal deviate and used as a basis for scaling. This principle is described in detail in Thurstone (1925).

3.4 The Absolute Zero of Scales

Armed with the law of comparative judgment, and its various modifications which gave him scales with equal intervals, Thurstone pushed rational measurement even further. He sought to find natural origins for scales both in the measurement of intelligence (Thurstone 1928) and in the measurement of subjective values.

With respect to the former, Thurstone established that, when measured on an interval scale, the variance of intelligence at any age group was proportional to the mean of the age group. Accordingly, he extrapolated the relationship to the age level at which the variance was zero, and concluded that this was a reasonable estimate of the natural origin of intelligence scales.

With respect to the natural origin of subjective values, the principle used was to first scale single objects using the pair comparison design, and then to scale objects in combinations. The values of the objects were relative to a natural origin when the sum of the values of two single objects was the same as the value assigned to the objects as a combination.

This work on a rational origin has not had much impact on psychometric research, but it is exemplary methodologically, and may yet prove to be important, particularly in understanding intellectual growth and development.

3.5 The Methods of Equal Appearing Intervals and Successive Intervals

Two disadvantages of the pair comparison design are that it is time consuming and taxing on judges. As a result of these disadvantages, the much simpler method of rank ordering was adapted to the law of comparative judgment (Thurstone 1959) and models for incomplete pair comparison designs have been developed (Bock and Jones 1968).

Another adaptation of the law of comparative judgment was with respect to the design of *equal appearing intervals* and its extension to the method of successive intervals. This design was specifically considered in relation to the construction of an attitude scale as an instrument for measuring attitudes of persons. After creating a list of some 100 statements, based on a literature search of the topic in question and opinions of experts, the statements are placed by 200 or 300 judges into 11 intervals. These intervals are to be considered equally spaced in intensity on the affective continuum.

Scale values for the statements are then computed on the assumption that the equal appearing intervals actually operate as if they were equal. For the method of successive intervals, the data collection design is essentially the same, but instead of assuming that equality of intervals prevails, estimates of scale values of intervals are calculated.

The model for computing the scale values is a direct extension of the model in Fig. 1. As in the derivation of the law of comparative judgment, it is assumed that a continuous random variable d_i is induced when the person encounters and reacts to a statement. Then if there are m boundaries or thresholds between the $m + 1$ successive intervals on the affective continuum designated by $\tau_1, \tau_2, \ldots, \tau_k, \ldots, \tau_m$, the response corresponds to the interval in which the value of the random variable falls.

The estimate of the appropriate model probabilities is again given by a proportion; this time by the proportion of persons who classify the statement to be in or below a given category. By transforming these probability estimates to corresponding normal deviates, the scale values of both the statements and the category boundaries can be estimated.

The approach and modelling associated with the method of successive intervals has been used as a basis for the analysis of qualitative data in which three or more categories have some order, and the mathematical statistical and computing techniques have been advanced considerably (Bock 1975). A contrasting approach to dealing with ordered categories is presented in Andrich (1978).

4. Checks on the Scales

Once a set of statements or questions has been placed on a continuum, various checks or controls on the scales must be made. Because Thurstone was concerned that measurement be scientifically defensible, he stressed that the scales must be checked for validity, and that it must be possible for the data not to accord with the theory underlying the scale construction. The first check is that the ordering and spacing of the questions or statements is consistent with an informal appreciation of the continuum. If the observed ordering or spacing violates this informal understanding, then a closer examination of the scale construction should follow. Perhaps only some questions or statements need to be eliminated. Alternatively, it may be that the effects of dimensions other

than the one intended have played too great a role. Finally, it may be that the scale construction is sound, and that a new understanding about the continuum, not appreciated before the construction of the scale, has been revealed.

4.1 Statistical Tests

More formal statistical checks are also usually applied. Many of these checks take advantage of the feature that the estimates of the scale values of questions are a summary of the data. From this summary, and the particular mathematical model, an attempt is then made to "recover" the observed details of the data, usually the relevant proportions. To the degree that the detail is recovered, to that degree the scale is confirmed to be internally consistent. Such statistical checks on the model are generally called tests of fit: they test the fit between the data and the model.

Finally, it is possible to test directly the degree to which the differences among scale values of questions, taken in threes, satisfy the requirement of additivity mentioned in Sect. 1. It should be appreciated that no test of fit is necessary and sufficient for the models, and the results of the different tests of fit are not mutually exclusive. Bock and Jones (1968) elaborate on the statistical tests of fit.

4.2 Principles of Invariance

Another fundamental requirement which can be applied in checking the validity of a scale is that of invariance of scale values of statements across populations of persons who may have different attitudes.

> If the scale is to be regarded as valid, the scale values of the statements should not be affected by the opinions of the people who help to construct it. This may turn out to be a severe test in practice, but the scaling method must stand such a test before it can be accepted as being more than a description of the people who construct the scale. (Thurstone 1959 p. 228)

To the degree that the invariance is demonstrated across different groups of persons, including those with known differences on the trait under investigation, to that degree the scale is applicable across those groups. The scale is deliberately constructed both to capture the trait in questions and to exhibit the desired properties of a measuring instrument.

4.3 Person Measurement

Thurstone also appreciated the complementary requirement that a person's measure should not depend on the actual questions used in a scale. In the context of constructing a mental test, among the requirements he listed is the following:

> It should be possible to omit several test questions at different levels of the scale without affecting the individual score. (Thurstone 1926 p. 446)

Interestingly, however, Thurstone never seemed to formalize a person parameter in his mathematical statistical models. And despite the specifications of invariance, both in the scaling of questions or statements and in the measurement of persons, he seemed to be constrained by considering persons always to be sampled from some specified population. Possibly it was this constraint which prevented his formalizing a person parameter in his models.

The procedure for attitude measurement of individuals, though based on a set of scaled statements and though eminently plausible, is essentially ad hoc. A person responds to an attitude scale, which consists of statements approximately equally spaced on the continuum, by either agreeing or disagreeing with each statement. Then the person's measure of attitude is taken as the median of the scale values of the statements endorsed.

It seems that a further reason why Thurstone did not formalize the person parameter in attitude scales was that he dealt with only one of the two types of scales, and in particular, the one in which it is more difficult to formalize a person parameter. The type of scale with which he dealt implies that a person would tend to endorse the statements in a given range on the scale which represented his or her attitude, and would tend not to endorse statements more extreme in either direction. The other type of scale, subsequently elaborated by Guttman (1950), implies that if a person endorses a statement of a particular scale value, then the person will tend to endorse all statements with smaller scale values and tend not to endorse all statements with greater scale values.

In a small 1929 monograph I described two types of attitude scales. . . . These were called the *maximum probability type* and the *increasing probability type*. All our work was with the first type. Recently, there has been interest in the second type of scaling, which lends itself to certain types of attitude problems. The scaling of attitude statements can be accomplished directly from the records of acceptance and rejection for a group of subjects without the sorting procedure that we used, but, as far as I know, such a scaling procedure has not yet been developed. (Thurstone 1959 p. 214)

The model which (a) is a probabilistic version of the Guttman-type scale; (b) permits measurement of persons and the scaling of statements from the direct endorsement or otherwise of the persons; and (c) which also captures all the properties of linearity articulated by Thurstone, is the simple logistic model known as the Rasch model (Rasch 1960, 1980). The scales produced are those of the increasing probability type.

See also: Latent Trait Measurement Models; Guttman Scales; Likert Scales; Scaling Methods; Attitudes and their Measurement

Bibliography

Andrich D 1978 A rating formulation for ordered response categories. *Psychometrika* 43: 561–73
Bock R D 1975 *Multivariate Statistical Methods in Behavioral Research.* McGraw-Hill, New York
Bock R D, Jones L V 1968 *The Measurement and Prediction of Judgment and Choice.* Holden-Day, San Francisco, California
Edwards A L 1957 *Techniques of Attitude Scale Construction.* Appleton-Century-Crofts, New York
Guttman L 1950 The problem of attitude and opinion measurement. In: Stouffer A et al. (eds.) 1950 *Measurement and Prediction.* Wiley, New York
Rasch G 1960 *Probabilistic Models for Some Intelligence and Attainment Tests.* University of Chicago Press, Chicago, Illinois, repr. 1980
Thurstone L L 1925 A method of scaling psychological and educational tests. *J. Educ. Psychol.* 16: 433–51
Thurstone L L 1926 The scoring of individual performance. *J. Educ. Psychol.* 17: 446–57
Thurstone L L 1928 The absolute zero in intelligence measurement. *Psychol. Rev.* 35: 175–97
Thurstone L L 1959 *The Measurement of Values.* University of Chicago Press, Chicago, Illinois
Torgerson W S 1958 *Theory and Methods of Scaling.* Wiley, New York

Scaling Methods

P. Dunn-Rankin

Since the early 1960s relative measurement (scaling) in the social sciences has surged forward on the crest of the enumerative speed and accuracy available from modern computers. In education, where almost all measures are value based and relative to a specific population, the sophisticated measurement of attitudes and perceptions about education in general and learning in particular are just now beginning to emerge. Subkoviak (1975) has described possible ways in which multidimensional scaling methods may have relevance in educational use and Dunn-Rankin (1983) has indicated how both unidimensional and multidimensional methods are utilized in educational research.

Kruskal and Wish (1978) provide a good introduction to multidimensional scaling and Napier in Shepard et al. (1972) provides an effective presentation of the use of nonmetric techniques in the analysis of summated ratings.

Cliff (1973) and Carroll and Arabie (1980) provide extensive reviews related to the development of scaling algorithms since the early 1960s. The educational researcher should be aware of the extensive number and diversity of such methods and should become familiar with the source programs (the software) to carry on analyses in the affective domain. This article is not exhaustive but attempts to outline several of the most useful methods of scaling as they relate to the field of education. For specific methods and computer programs the reader should consult the references provided. Today all scaling methods are made tractable by the use of high-speed computers.

1. Psychological Objects

Psychological objects can be tangible, such as chairs and postcards, but they can also be almost anything which is perceived by the senses and which results in some cognitive affect. Psychological objects can be colors, words, tones, and sentences as well as houses, gold stars, and movie stars. Psychological objects are most often sentences or statements, such as "There will always be wars" or "I hate war." With young children the objects are often pictures. In marketing analysis, psychological objects are the products of industry: cars, soap, televisions, and toothpaste.

Rensis Likert's suggestion that statements (psychological objects) should be chosen so that people with different points of view will respond to each statement differently is still valuable. He suggests that statements may vary widely in emphasis although their content remains similar. Thus the statements: "I would recommend this course to a friend," and "This is the worst course I have ever taken" should evoke different responses but remain generally evaluative in nature or dimensionality. Specifically social scientists should use statements that:

(a) refer to the present rather than the past;

(b) have only one interpretation;

(c) are related to the continuum under consideration;

(d) will have varied endorsement;

(e) cover the range;

(f) are clear and direct;

(g) are short (rarely over 20 words);

(h) contain a complete thought;

(i) are nonuniversal;

(j) are positive; and

(k) contain simple words.

Scaling is concerned with classes of objects about which people can manifest some attitude. Usually the experimenter wishes to know the relationship among the objects; that is, how far apart they are and in what relative directions the objects may lie. Generally, the familiar Euclidean space provides a framework within which numbers can be assigned to objects in a relative but meaningful way.

This use of Euclidean space in one dimension is demonstrated by the scaling of lower case letters of the English alphabet. Letters are the psychological objects placed on a linear scale in terms of their similarity to specific target letters (Dunn-Rankin 1978). Note that when the letter *a* is used as a target the other letters are scaled in their perceived similarity to *a* as follows:

In this scale the letter *l* is seen as least similar to the target letter *a* while *o*, *e*, and *c* are judged much closer to *a*.

Distances are not a necessary requisite for a scale. A set of objects could be selected for which order is the scale. If, for example, the following mathematics problems were presented to a group of school children they would be well-ordered in difficulty:

(a) $2 + 2 =$

(b) $24 - 16 =$

(c) $375.5 \div 4 =$

(d) $4!/2!(4 - 2)! =$

(e) $d(3x^2 + 4)/dx =$

Each succeeding problem is more difficult than the one before it. The questions or psychological objects constitute a scale based on difficulty and the numbers (the ranks) have been assigned in a meaningful way. If a 1 is scored for each correct answer and 0 for an incorrect answer, the pattern of ones and zeros over the five questions will indicate where the student is on this mathematics difficulty scale. Thus a person who has the pattern 11110 is farther along on the scale than the student scored responses of 11000.

2. Judgments or Choices

The measurement objectives of a particular study or experiment must be decided prior to commencement. If a psychological scale is to be constructed then the responses to the objects should initially be judgments of similarity. Subjective preference between objects is used when a description of the data from a sample is desired instead of a scale, or when it is felt that the sample is an accurate representation of some population, or both. Thus the two main kinds of responses that subjects can make are (a) judgments and (b) choices (preferences).

Figure 1 presents a diagrammatic outline for attitudinal measurement. First the psychological objects are chosen. The selection is dictated by the interests of the experimenter. Once the objects have been obtained or formulated they are presented in a task. If the task requires judgments, unidimensional or multidimensional methods are used to scale the objects. From this analysis a subset of the objects may be chosen and the objects formulated into a psychological scaling instrument. These instruments can then be presented to the target group(s) and their responses scored. Should judgments of similarity between tangible objects, such as letters, odors, sounds, and so on be obtained in several dimensions, the distance between the objects can be used in future studies as specific measures of similarity. Should preferences instead of judgments be obtained, a descriptive analysis occurs directly. Such analyses can generate or test hypotheses.

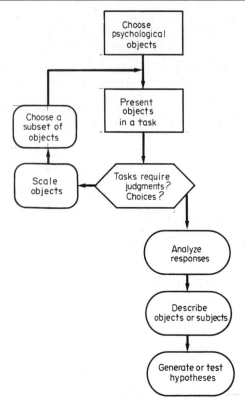

Figure 1
Diagrammatic representation of attitudinal measurement

3. Tasks Used in Assessing Subjective Perception

Psychological objects can be any object about which subjects have some perception or attitude. A taxonomy of tasks for assessing people's judgments or choices about psychological objects is provided in Table 1. See Dunn-Rankin (1983) for a fuller description of tasks.

Table 1
Taxonomy of tasks for assessing people's judgments or choices about psychological objects

Types of tasks	Examples
Placing or grouping	Clustering: "Put the similar ones together."
Naming or categorizing	Opinion polls: "Do you agree or disagree?"
Ordering	Judging a contest: "Who is the best?"
Quantifying	Fixing a price: "I say it's worth $20."
Combinations	Ordered categories: *onions* × Good – – – – Bad

4. Data Types and Associated Procedures

The data that are collected after the presentation of different kinds of tasks can be identified as consisting of four major forms. (See Shepard et al. 1972 for a more complete discussion.) These forms of data are dominance, profile, proximity, and conjoint.

4.1 Dominance Data

One subject, object, or group is chosen, preferred, or judged over another, that is it dominates. The data may be directly ranked. Pairs may be formed and indirectly ranked by judgment or preference for one object of each pair. Pairs of pairs may be formed and indirectly ranked.

4.2 Profile Data

Subjects respond to or are evaluated by a set of variables or stimuli. Objects or variables may also be scored. The variables can be quantitative, binary, or qualitative. Ordered categories fit this data type. By interrelating the columns or rows of this basic data matrix (subjects by variables) a proximity data set can be formed between objects or subjects.

4.3 Proximity Data

The data are some form of similarity, confusion, association, correlation, or distance measures between pairs of objects or subjects. The data can be drawn from profile information or by methods of direct appraisal and assessment.

4.4 Conjoint Data

The position of a point in a matrix is represented by its value in two or more simple dimensions. Thus a point could represent a person with regard to health, sociability, and intelligence at the same time.

5. Measures of Proximity

Proximities are numbers which tell how similar or different objects are. A great number of proximity measures are available that relate to the tasks and types of data that can be collected. These can be categorized as measures of (a) correlation, (b) distance, (c) direct estimates of similarity, and (d) association. In order to analyze a set of objects by clustering or multidimensional scaling, some measure of similarity or dissimilarity between all the pairs of the objects is needed.

Some specific representative measures of proximity are: Pearson's r; Kendall's tau; Gamma; scalar product; direct estimation; association (percent overlap); and Gower's similarity measure.

6. Unidimensional Scaling Methods

Four major unidimensional methods are presented. Despite recent advances in multidimensional scaling, unidimensional methods have value because of their simplicity and versatility, and because they are amenable to hand-calculated solutions. It is theoretically just as advantageous to create three separate unidimensional scales as it is to derive three dimensions from one multidimensional analysis. In fact, one methodology can serve as a check on the other. (Judgments rather than preferences are more frequently used in unidimensional methods.)

Each of four methods presented offers something unique to scaling analysis. With rank scaling it is simplicity and tests of significance. In comparative judgment it is meeting normality assumptions about attitude. Scalogram analysis provides an "order" definition of scaling. In ordinal categories, profile data is handled instead of paired data. Popular "Likert" scaling is a form of ordered-category scaling.

6.1 Rank Scaling

(a) *Scale values proportional to rank sums.* The variance stable rank method of scaling (Dunn-Rankin 1983) is an adaptation of a two-way analysis of variance by ranks. In other words it is a nonparametric subject by treatment analysis in which the treatments are the psychological objects which are scaled. The basic assumption of the method is that the scale values are proportional to the sum of the ranks assigned by the judges to each of the objects. In this method the maximum and minimum possible rank totals, for a given number of judges and objects, act as a convenient and interpretive frame of reference within which the objects are scaled. A linear transformation of these two extreme rank totals into 100 and zero respectively defines the limits of the scale.

(b) *Variance stable rank sums.* The psychological objects can be ranked directly or the ranks can be determined from the votes given to the objects when they are arranged in all possible pairs and a choice made of the most preferred of each pair. A group of second grade children were asked what they most preferred as a reward after a job was well-done; an A grade, a score of 100, a gold star (GS), or the word excellent (Ex). For these children the objects were formed in all $(K(K-1)/n)$ possible pairs. The circled objects in Fig. 2 indicate

Reward pairings

(Circled object was preferred in each pairing)

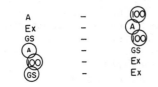

Sum of the choices

Figure 2
Subject 1's preference for the objects is shown and the rank values obtained by counting the choices for each object

the preferred choice in each pairing for subject 1. The figure also shows the preference values for subject 1. These values are found by summing the votes for each different object. In this case three choices or votes were made for a 100, two votes for an A, 1 vote for the gold star, and no preference for the word Excellent. The 3, 2, 1, and 0 rank values are the reverse of the rank order of the objects but are utilized in this position so that the value associated with most preferred object has the largest magnitude.

Table 2 shows the rank values obtained for 24 subjects over the same objects. After obtaining the rank totals (R_k), the scale values (SV) are obtained by dividing each rank total by the maximum rank possible and multiplying by 100. These values and a unidimensional graph are presented in Fig. 3.

The scale scores obtained by this simplified rank method can be utilized in traditional ways and are strikingly isomorphic with values obtained under Thurstone's Case V model.

6.2 Comparative Judgment

L. L. Thurstone provided a rationale for ordering objects on a psychological continuum. Psychological objects are stimuli for which some reaction takes place within the sensory system of the individual. The objects could be a beautiful girl, a telephone's ring, sandpaper, sugar water, or nitrous oxide. They could also include visual statements, such as, "stop," "I hate school," "patriot," and so on.

Table 2
Calculation of scale values (SV) from sum of the rank values

Subjects	Min	Ex	GS	A	100	Max
1	0	0	1	2	3	3
2	0	0	1	3	2	3
3	0	0	1	2	3	3
4	0	1	1	1	3	3
5	0	3	2	0	1	3
6	0	0	1	2	3	3
7	0	1	0	3	2	3
8	0	0	3	2	1	3
9	0	0	1	3	2	3
10	0	2	0	2	2	3
11	0	1	0	2	3	3
12	0	1	0	3	2	3
13	0	0	1	3	2	3
14	0	3	2	0	1	3
15	0	1	0	2	3	3
16	0	0	1	3	2	3
17	0	3	0	2	1	3
18	0	0	1	2	3	3
19	0	0	3	2	1	3
20	0	0	3	1	2	3
21	0	2	0	2	2	3
22	0	0	1	3	2	3
23	0	0	1	2	3	3
24	0	0	1	2	3	3
Sums (R_k)	0	18	25	49	52	72[$N(K-1)$]
SV (100 R_k/R_{max})	0	25	34.7	68.1	72.2	100

Figure 3
Graph of reward preference scale values

(a) *Reactions are normally distributed.* Thurstone postulated for any psychological object, (i) reactions to such stimuli were subjective and (ii) judgment or preference for an object may vary from one instance to another. Thurstone suggested that, while a person may have more or less favorable reactions to a particular psychological object, there was a most frequent reaction to any object or stimulus. The most frequent reaction is called the modal reaction. The mode can be based on repeated reactions of a single individual or the frequency of the reactions of many subjects.

Thurstone assumed that reactions to various stimuli were normally distributed. Because the normal curve is bell shaped and symmetrical the most frequent reaction (the mode) occupies the same scale position as the mean. Thus the mean can represent the scale value for the particular psychological object.

Scale values can only be acquired, however, within a relative frame. Thus it is necessary to have at least two objects so that a comparison can be made. In this case Thurstone assumed that the reactions to each object would be normally distributed and additionally that the variance of the reactions around each mean would be the same for both objects. Figure 4 illustrates this case.

Suppose i and j are two psychological objects which are to be judged on a continuum of positive affect toward school. Suppose i is "I hate school," and j is "Sometimes school is dull." A group of subjects might be asked to judge which statement is more favorable toward school attendance. If 80 percent of the subjects choose j as more favorable than i and therefore 20 percent choose i as more favorable than j, it might be argued that the average reaction to j should be higher on a scale than the average reaction to i, or $\bar{s}_j > \bar{s}_i$. The separation between $\bar{s}_j$ and $\bar{s}_i$ is a function of the number of times j is rated over i. Using paired comparisons the votes can be counted and proportions of preference obtained. If, with 50 subjects, j (sometimes school is dull) is chosen 40 times over i (I hate school) then the proportion is 40/50 or 0.80.

The proportions in this method, however, can be expressed as normal deviates, that is, (z) standard scores can be obtained for proportions. In this case the normal deviate $(z_{ij}) = 0.84$ (for $p = 0.80$). The scale separation

Figure 4
Theoretical distribution of responses about two different psychological objects

between two reactions can be made in terms of this normal deviate, that is $z_{ij} = \bar{s}_j - \bar{s}_i$. Diagrammatically it can be said that somewhere on the continuum of "attitude toward school attendance" j and i are separated by a distance of 0.84 as shown in Fig. 5.

(b) *Thurstone's Case V.* Thurstone's procedure for finding scale separations starts with the votes derived from some paired comparison schedule of objects. The votes can be accumulated in a square array by placing a 1 in each row and column intersection in which the column object is judged or preferred over the row object.

One matrix can accumulate a large number of different subjects' responses to the objects.

Initially the column sums of the frequency matrix are found and if the sums are not in order the rows and columns of the matrix are rearranged so that the column sums are ordered from smallest to largest. Under the variances table or simplified rank method the sum of the votes could be used directly as scale scores. But, under Thurstone's rationale, the individual frequencies are first converted to proportions.

A proportion of 0.50 is placed on the diagonal of this matrix under the assumption that any object judged against itself would receive a random number of votes. The expectation is that 50 percent of the time the subject would choose the column object and 50 percent of the time the row object. Next the proportions are converted to normal deviates by reference to the normal distribution. Finally the differences between column stimuli are found. If the data are complete, the differences between the column sums of the normal deviates are equal to the sums of the column differences.

Knowing the differences between the objects, scale values can be assigned to each by accumulating the differences or distances between them. Should proportions greater than 0.98 occur in the data they are reduced to 0.98. This is similarly true for proportions less than 0.02 which are made equal to 0.02. The reason for this restriction is that normal deviations for extreme proportions usually result in an extreme distortion of the scale values. If data are missing, the entries are left blank and no column differences are found for the blank entries. Averages of column differences are then found by dividing by an n reduced by the number of incomplete entries. The Case V method requires assumptions of equal dispersion of reactions and uncorrelatedness between judgments of different objects. If these assumptions cannot be met, some other method or case may have to be used. The Case V is the simplest of the various cases that Thurstone explored.

6.3 Ordered Categories

When the number of objects becomes increasingly large, greater than 20, for example, the number of pairs necessary for rank or paired-comparison methods becomes unwieldy (for 20 objects it would equal 20(19)/2 = 190 pairs). While some experimenters have asked subjects to compare 50 (1,225 pairs) and 70 (3,660 pairs) items, such studies are atypical and usually involve single items in the comparison rather than statements.

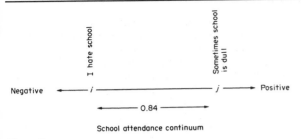

Figure 5
"Attitude toward school attendance" continuum

The most popular unidimensional method of attitude measurement involves ordered categories. In this method the judges are asked to place items in a fixed number of categories usually 2, 3, 4, 5, 7, 9, or 11. A typical example of this format is given in Table 3.

In this case a unidimensional scale of attitude toward reading is proposed for these eight statements. Judges are asked to indicate the degree of positive affect toward reading for each statement by marking appropriately. It is clear that the format can accommodate a great many statements since it calls for only one action per statement by each judge. It is the accumulation of the responses of a number of judges that provides the data for creating the scale.

The scaling method of successive intervals is an attempt to accommodate more items than other unidimensional techniques and in addition to estimate the distance or interval between the ordered categories.

When a number of judges have marked the items, a distribution of judgments for each item is created. In this method the average of the normal deviates assigned to the cumulative proportions of responses in each category represents the scale score of the item but only after each deviate is subtracted from the category boundary. As in the Case V model, variances around scale values are assumed to be equal.

The boundaries of the intervals are located under the assumption that the judgments for each item are distributed normally. In order to analyze the items under the cumulative normal distribution, the categories are numbered from least to most favorable and the cumulative frequency distributions are found.

These frequencies are converted to cumulative probabilities. Any probabilities greater than 0.98 or less than 0.02 are rejected and the cumulative proportions are converted into normal deviates by referring to areas of normal distributions.

The differences between the categories for each item are found and the average of the differences is equal to the boundary between the two columns. For missing entries no differences are found and the average is found for those items for which a difference is available.

Initial item selection for ordered category scaling can be aided by the guidelines prescribed. "Foldback" analysis should be carefully avoided in which a selection of discriminating items is used to predict differences in the sample from which the items were originally selected.

The steps used in creating an ordered category scale are as follows:

(a) Decide on the number of dimensions. (If more than one use multidimensional methods.)

(b) Collect objects. (Make pilot instrument.)

(c) Make a semantic description and exclude semantic outliers.

(d) Present instrument to judges, obtain their judgments.

(e) Find item statistics [mean (proportion passing), SD, r with total test score].

(f) Analyze using successive intervals.

(g) Revise scales.

In the finished scale the category continuum is changed to one of agreement–disagreement instead of judgment.

Table 3
Example of ordered category rating scale

	Positive					Negative	
	7	6	5	4	3	2	1
1 I try reading anything I can get my hands on.	—	—	—	—	—	—	—
3 When I become interested in something I read a book about it.	—	—	—	—	—	—	—
2 I read when there is nothing else to do.	—	—	—	—	—	—	—
7 I don't read unless I have to.	—	—	—	—	—	—	—
4 I have never read an entire book.	—	—	—	—	—	—	—
5 I seldom read anything.	—	—	—	—	—	—	—
6 I almost always have something I can read.	—	—	—	—	—	—	—
8 I only read things that are easy.	—	—	—	—	—	—	—

If an ordered category instrument contained a large number of items and many are eliminated, it may be expected that the instrument contains more than one unidimensional scale. If this is the case the multidimensional methods of clustering, factor analysis, or multidimensional scaling methodologies may be used (see *Cluster Analysis*; *Factor Analysis*).

6.4 Summated Ratings

Likert argues that (a) the intervals between categories are generally equal, (b) preference categories should be established immediately, and (c) the judgment phase of creating a scale should be replaced by item analysis techniques. These three arguments mean that in Likert scaling a person's reaction to or preference about all the psychological objects replaces the direction and intensity of specifically rated objects, that is a respondent's judgments. Surprisingly, both successive intervals and Likert scaling, when carefully applied, yield similar results. Since Likert scaling is easier it is more popular.

The methodology of Likert scaling is as follows: the objects are chosen by the experimenter and unit values are assigned to each ordered category; for example, the integers 1 through 5. After subjects respond by checking or marking one of the categories for each item, an $N \times K$ (subject by item) matrix of information is generated. Each subject's categorical value is provided in the body of the table.

Next, item analyses are performed on the data. The mean (item difficulty) and standard deviation of each item are calculated and the Pearson's r correlation of each item with the total score on all items is found. This correlation acts as a discrimination index for each item. That is, if the item correlates highly with the total score it is internally consistent and should be retained. Finally, a split-half reliability is found or Cronbach's alpha reliability coefficient. Items are eliminated on the basis of poor internal consistency, very high or low endorsement, or lack of variability.

6.5 Guttman Scaling

Louis Guttman described a unidimensional scale as one in which the subject's responses to the objects would place individuals in perfect order. Ideally persons who answer several questions favorably all have higher ability than persons who answer the same questions unfavorably. Arithmetic questions make good examples of this type of scale.

Suppose elementary-school children are given the following addition problems:

(a)	2	(b)	12	(c)	28	(d)	86	(e)	228
	+3		+15		+24		+88		+894

It is probable that if subject A responds correctly to item (e) that he or she would also respond correctly to items (a), (b), (c), and (d). If subject B can answer item (b) and not item (c), it is probable that he or she can

answer item (a) correctly but would be unable to answer item (d) and (e). By scoring 1 for each correct answer and 0 otherwise a profile of responses can be obtained. If the arithmetic questions form a perfect scale then the sum of the correct responses to the five items can be used to reveal a person's scale type in terms of a series of ones and zeros. In this example:

	Items						Sum
	1	2	3	4	5		
Subject A has scale type	1	1	1	1	1	=	5
While Subject B has scale type	1	1	0	0	0	=	2

Given a perfect scale the single summed score reveals the scale type. Thus a single digit can be used to recreate all of the responses of a subject to a set of items that constitute a perfect scale.

With five questions, and scoring the item as correct or incorrect there are only six possible scale types. These are:

	Scale type					Score
1	1	1	1	1	1	5
2	1	1	1	1	0	4
3	1	1	1	0	0	3
4	1	1	0	0	0	2
5	1	0	0	0	0	1
6	0	0	0	0	0	0

While there exist 32 possible arrangements of five ones and zeros, only six of these form scale types. In general the number of scale types for dichotomously scored data is $(K + 1)$ where K is the number of objects. While the perfect Guttman scale is unlikely to be found in practice, approximations to it can be obtained by a careful choice of items and careful analysis of a set of pilot subjects' responses to a larger number of items than are to be used in the final scale.

7. Multidimensional Scaling Methods

The technique of factor analysis, traditionally developed and utilized with tests of ability and achievement, has also been applied extensively to the reduction of matrices of proximities. Restrictive assumptions of linearity between variables and homogeneity of variance as well as the multiplicity of factors generated, however, allow the simpler assumptions underlying multidimensional scaling to be utilized in a different and generally more parsimonious description of a data matrix. Preference mapping and individual differences scaling are extensions of factor and multidimensional scaling analyses which provide insights into how individuals differ with regard to the same psychological objects.

7.1 Factor Analysis

Factor analysis attempts to simplify a large body of data by identifying or discovering categories of variables. These categories are called structures, dimensions, or more commonly factors. It is, statistically, an analysis of the interdependence between variables and can be used to (a) describe, (b) fulfill hypotheses, or (c) discover new relationships.

Factor analysis starts with a correlation matrix (R) derived from a set of responses of N subjects to K variables or stimuli. (A matrix is a rectangular or square arrangement of data.) All the columns of the raw data matrix are intercorrelated by pairs to produce the square matrix of correlations. The standard or Z score representing the raw score is equal to the raw score minus the mean divided by the standard deviation or

$$Z_i = \frac{X_i - \bar{X}}{S} \tag{1}$$

Pearson's correlation is defined as the average cross-product of the standardized scores:

$$r_{ij} = \frac{\sum Z_i Z_j}{N} \tag{2}$$

Each entry of the correlation matrix (R) is a measure of the relationship between two stimuli as perceived by the subjects. Because science is constantly trying to simplify a complex array of data, it is one purpose of factor analysis to present the information contained in a correlation matrix in more concise terms, that is, a smaller matrix called a factor matrix.

Once the factor matrix [for example, (F)] has been determined, its elements can be plotted and analyzed spatially as shown in Fig. 6.

If it was known, for example, that tests C and D were tests of arithmetic and A, B, and E were tests of reading, then psychological meaning could probably be attached to this two-dimensional representation. As has been suggested, what is meant by factors is nothing more than the dimensions of the space required to contain a certain set of correlations. It is therefore the central problem in factor analysis to find a dimensional (factor) matrix which is the simplest and most meaningful explanation of a larger matrix of correlations.

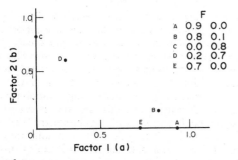

Figure 6
Plot of variables of the factor matrix

Multidimensional scaling is the name for a number of methods which attempt to spatially represent the proximities between a set of stimuli. The methods can determine metric Euclidian distances between objects with only ordinal assumptions about the data. The method is applicable to a wide number of measures of similarity or dissimilarity and unlike factor analysis can be used on data derived from a small number of subjects and with few assumptions about the data. Its primary purpose is a parsimonious spatial representation of the objects.

7.2 Shepard and Kruskal's Nonmetric Monotonic

Multidimensional scaling proceeds as follows:

(a) There is a given set of n objects.

(b) For every two objects (i and j) some measure or function of proximity $f(\int_{ij})$ is obtained. (These measures may be correlations, similarities, associations, distances, etc.) If similarities are obtained ($\int_{ij}$), they are usually converted to theoretical distances ($\hat{d}_{ij}$) by subtracting from a constant.

(c) A number of dimensions *(t)* are selected which may fit the data. The n objects are then placed (randomly or selectively) in the dimensional space.

(d) Multidimensional scaling MDS searches for a replotting of the n objects so that physical distances ($\hat{d}_{ij}$) between pairs of objects in the plot are related to their measures of proximity $f(\int_{ij}) = (\hat{d}_{ij})$. The relation is such that if the distance between two objects is large the expectation is that their original similarity measure will be small, that is, distances and similarity measures are related inversely but monotonically (in regular order). If, for example, the similarity between the words "war" and "peace" is estimated to be small then the two words should be a relatively "large" distance apart, farther apart than the words "lady" and "mother," for example. If d is a measure of distance then its relation to similarity (s) can be stated as $d_{ij} < d_{kl}$ when $s_{ij} > s_{kl}$, that is, the distance is greater when the similarity is smaller or specifically: $d_{\text{lady–mother}} < d_{\text{war–peace}}$ when $s_{\text{lady–mother}} > s_{\text{war–peace}}$.

The process of arriving at the best spatial configuration to represent the original similarities has been presented most effectively by Kruskal (1964). In this method a resolution of the spatial configuration is made by steps (iterations). At each step the objects are moved from their initial placement in the dimensional space and the physical distances between all pairs of objects are calculated. The distances (d_{ij}) between pairs of objects in the new placement are ordered and then compared with the original proximities ($\hat{d}_{ij}$) between the same pairs of objects, which have also been ordered. If the relationship is increasingly monotonic, that is, if the order of the new distances is similar to the order of the original distances, the objects continue to move in the same direction at the next step. If the relationship is not monotonic, changes in direction and step length are made. It is clear that a measure of monotonicity is primary in nonmetric scaling. This measure is provided by ordering the proximity measures ($\hat{d}_{ij}$) on the x axis and measuring horizontal deviations of the newly obtained distances in the plot (d_{ij}) from the original distances ($\hat{d}_{ij}$). The deviations are squared so they can be summed. The object is to make the sum of the squared deviations as small as possible. That is, to make

$$\sum_{i<j} (d_{ij} - \hat{d}_{ij})^2 \tag{3}$$

a minimum.

Kruskal averages the raw stress sum of squares by dividing by $\Sigma \, d_{ij}^2$. He then gets the formula back into the original linear units by taking the square root. He calls this index stress (S):

$$S = \left(\frac{\sum (d_{ij} - \hat{d}_{ij})^2}{\sum d_{ij}^2} \right)^{1/2} \tag{4}$$

In general, minimum stress means better fit.

Stress is a numerical value which denotes the degree of departure of the observed or calculated similarity from the true or judged similarity among objects taken two at a time. More precisely, stress is analogous to the standard error of estimate in bivariate regression. Note that in linear regression, the best line location is fitted to points while in Kruskal's nonmetric the points are best arranged to fit a line. Stress is a normalized sum of squared deviations about a monotonic line fit to the scatter plot of corresponding distances and proximity values. Because of normalization, stress can be expressed as a proportion or a percentage, and the smaller the stress, the better (Subkoviak 1975).

Distances can be calculated in n dimensions and three or four dimensions may make better fits to the data than one or two dimensions. One way to determine the dimensional space is to plot the stress values for each dimensional solution against the evenly spaced number of dimensions and test the configuration using Cattell's scree test. Since the spatial configuration in multidimensional scaling is arbitrary with regard to the coordinate axes around which they have been assigned, rotation of these axes is often used to make the spatial representation more clearly recognizable.

8. Preference Mapping

For almost any entity, grape jelly, University of Florida, Enrico Valdes, and so on, a directional identification can be made. That is, given two or more psychological objects the subject (almost automatically) prefers one of the elements of the set.

Individual differences in preference are of interest to the behavioral scientist because the interaction between attitude and treatment has not been fully explored. Different people may react differently to the same stimulus. Some people prefer spinach, others dislike it. Some children prefer teacher approval as a reward; others prefer freedom, competitive success, peer approval, or consumable rewards. Children vary in their preferences for reinforcers.

The methods previously discussed have looked at psychological objects from the view of the average subject. A unidimensional scale may be thought of as a single axis or vector that represents this average. When all subject's responses are consistently similar such scaling is reasonable. A multidimensional mapping of objects (like a unidimensional scale) is also represented as the average subject's judgment or preference between the pairs of objects. It is important, however, to look at the specific individual's preference.

8.1 Inclusion of the Ideal Point

A simple way to measure individual preference is to include an "ideal" stimulus among the authentic stimuli and obtain similarity estimates among all the $n + 1$ pairs of stimuli. If, for example, the "ideal professor" is included among the names of the graduate faculty and similarity estimates between faculty members are obtained from each graduate student in a department, it is assumed that those professors scaled closest to their ideal are most preferred. The scaling is done using multidimensional methods for each subject.

Configuration of stimuli obtained in this manner, however, are not always meaningful or stable since they are based on the responses of a single subject. It is also questionable whether similarities between the "ideal" and other stimuli are interpretable as preferences. Nevertheless preference mapping in this manner can yield important results and is thus included.

8.2 Carroll's Multidimensional Vector Model

The vector model of preference mapping is analogous to scoring a subject's preference on a unidimensional scale in multidimensional space. The process usually starts with a two- or three-dimensional configuration of objects whose interpoint distances have been derived from judgments of their similarity and then the subject's preference mapping is included on that configuration. The results from a multidimensional scaling by an appropriate sample are often used as a starting point.

Suppose, for example, the similarity between four desserts (chocolate cake, chocolate ice cream, pound cake, and vanilla ice cream) was judged by a panel of householders and the resulting configuration from multidimensional scaling was as shown in Fig. 7.

It is easy to label the dimensions as (a) chocolate versus nonchocolate and (b) cake versus ice cream. Next, suppose two children were asked to rank order their preference for the four desserts and these results were as shown in Table 4.

Surprisingly, the direction and scale scores for each subject can be estimated by the constraints imposed by the initial configuration on the subjects' rank order of preference. In Fig. 8 the two vectors are taken as scales upon which the desserts have been projected. In order to accommodate the rank order in each subject's preference the vectors can only be drawn as shown in Fig. 8.

Notice that the closest (perpendicular) projection of the stimuli on each vector preserves each subject's preference values (rank order). The direction of the vectors is of particular interest since it reveals individual differences in preference with regard to these desserts. A large number of different vectors may be accommodated in a two-dimensional space. When there are several objects and their configuration has been well-defined (as by the householders in this case), the direction of each subject's preference vector is uniquely determined. The case in which the object configuration is determined in advance of the preference mapping has been called external analysis.

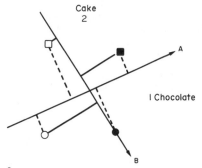

Figure 8
Subject vectors drawn to accommodate configuration and rank order of preference

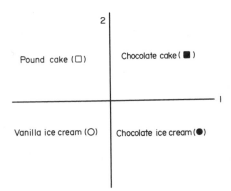

Figure 7
Householder panel configuration of four desserts

9. Individual Differences Scaling

The recent development of methodologies which relate differences between individuals to the dimensional aspects of the objects promises to have wide application in the behavioral sciences. In factor analysis and multidimensional scaling a description of the objects was the primary purpose. In those methods, an average measure of similarity between pairs of objects is used as the primary data. The subject's individual emphasis is lost in the average.

In order to measure individual differences, similarity or preference information between the objects must be obtained for each subject. Each subject responds to the same set of stimuli, for example, "color names" paired in all possible ways. Estimates of the similarity between colors represented by the names are obtained from each subject. Each subject has therefore a matrix of similarity

representing all pairs of stimuli. The data can be displayed in a redundant square array or in a lower (or upper) triangular matrix as shown in Fig. 9.

The most useful and popular representation of individual differences is a model of a weighted Euclidean space elucidated by Carroll and Chang (1970). Their procedure is called INDSCAL for *In*dividual *Di*fferences *Scal*ing. This model assumes that different subjects perceive stimuli on common sets of dimensions. The authors assume that some dimensions may be more important for one individual than another. It seems clear that a color-blind individual might weight the red–green dimension differently than subjects with normal vision. The importance of a dimension for an individual, however, can be zero. (A weight of zero can occur for an individual who fails to use a dimension in making decisions of similarity, for example.)

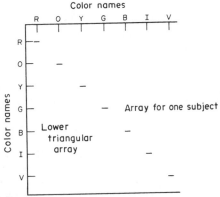

Figure 9
Lower triangle matrix for data on subject response to "color names"

Individual differences scaling is similar to factor analysis since it seeks to represent a large body of information in a more parsimonious way. The analysis seeks a small-dimensional solution for the objects and an individual weighting for each subject of these few (*t*) dimensions.

Once a solution (a set of weights or loadings for each object and subject) is determined, calculated distances

Table 4
Rank order preference for four desserts judged by two children

| | Preference scale values | | | |
| | Chocolate cake | Chocolate ice cream | Pound cake | Vanilla ice cream |
Child	■	●	□	○
A	1	2	3	4
B	3	1	4	2

(d_{ij}) between the objects are compared with the original or theoretical distances $(\hat{d}_{ij})$ between the objects provided by the proximity data. Pearson's r is used as a criterion in the comparison.

See also: Scaling of Nominal Data; Guttman Scales; Thurstone Scales; Likert Scales; Factor Analysis

Bibliography

Carroll J D, Arabie P 1980 Multidimensional scaling. *Annu. Rev. Psychol.* 31: 607–49
Carroll J D, Chang J J 1970 Analysis of individual differences in multi-dimensional scaling via an n-way generalization of "Eckart-Young" decomposition. *Psychometrika* 35: 283–319
Cliff N 1973 Scaling. *Annu. Rev. Psychol.* 24: 473–506
Dunn-Rankin P 1978 The visual characteristics of words. *Sci. Am.* 238(1): 122–30
Dunn-Rankin P 1983 *Scaling Methods.* Erlbaum, Hillsdale, New Jersey
Kruskal J B 1964 Multidimensional scaling by optimizing goodness of fit to a nonmetric hypothesis. *Psychometrika* 29: 1–27
Kruskal J B, Wish M 1978 *Multidimensional Scaling.* Sage, Beverly Hills, California
Shepard R N, Romney A K, Nerlove S B (eds.) 1972 *Multidimensional Scaling: Theory and Applications in the Behavioral Sciences*, Vol. 1: *Theory.* Seminars Press, New York
Subkoviak M J 1975 The use of multidimensional scaling in educational research. *Rev. Educ. Res.* 45: 387–423

Scaling of Nominal Data

D. Defays

Scaling is defined as establishing a correspondence between a set of data, with observed relations, and a set of numbers. In a wider sense, a mathematical geometric model is usually used to represent the set of data as points in a multidimensional space, graph-theoretical structure, or a more complex geometric model. Different scaling methods may be distinguished according to type of data being scaled. Educational researchers and social and behavioural scientists often have to contend with data like race, sex, marital status, success or failure in a task, presence or absence of some characteristic which are all, in fact, nominal or categorical or qualitative variables. Unlike quantitative or ordinal variables, their different values or levels are categories (e.g., male or female), that is to say, they are neither numeric nor ordered. For nominal data the level of measurement of the different observations is nominal; their scaling is called "scaling of nominal data".

The problems of scaling of nominal data may be demonstrated by the following simple, but typical, example, namely: the case of a teacher who is interested in the study of the dependencies between different mathematical tasks. The data could, for instance, be the results obtained by a group of students tested on a set of relevant items. For the sake of simplicity let it be assumed that each response for each subject is coded 0 (incorrect) or 1 (correct), thus, it is in the form of binary-coded data. Binary data are, in fact, the lowest possible form of nominal data, there being only two categories. One of the simplest assumptions the teacher could make about the data is the following. The different items can be ordered on a one-dimensional continuum with regard to the level of cognitive development needed to solve them. The basic idea is that the items are not measuring within more than one dimension. Such an assumption about the organization of the data is always necessary in order to make scaling possible. It can in fact be formalized by a fairly simple model called a Guttman scale, in which both the subjects and the items are represented by points on a line, each subject being supposed to have solved all the items which are represented by points situated to the left of his or her representative point and none of the items to the right of that point. Assigning points to subjects and items is called scaling the subjects and the items. This model, namely the points on the straight line which represent the data, is called a scale. The model can be shown to impose severe restrictions on the data. If the items and the subjects can both be ordered on a one-dimensional continuum, as has been assumed, some patterns of response are obviously impossible. The way in which different types of scales impose different types of restrictions on data is the subject of the theory of measurement. Scaling theory can be viewed as a branch of measurement theory that focuses on rationales and mathematical techniques for fitting models to actual data, typically in multidimensional spaces. On the other hand, it is easy to see that different configurations of the points on the scaling line are compatible with the data and the model. The type of transformation that will maintain the scale's representation of the property or the relations being measured, defines the type of the scale. In addition, the type of scale will determine the operations that can be carried out with the scale values of the objects. If the different conditions imposed on the data are fulfilled or, at least, if the number of violations is not too great the model can be fitted in different ways according to the type of representation needed and to the type of method used. These involve the different algorithms which are available to fit fallible data. However, if the structure imposed by the model is obviously incompatible with the data, alternative approaches are required. For instance, the violations can be dealt with as the result of random events (guessing for instance) and a probabilistic variant of the model may then be considered applicable. Other models, in which points occur in a plane or in a higher dimensional space, are also conceivable. A third solution could be to reject the first line of thought and fit another, weaker, model like a network representation, which imposes less restriction on the data.

Some further general comments can be made from the consideration of the above example. First of all, it must be noticed that the specificity of the scaling of nominal data lies in the lack of metric properties in the data and not in the representation which almost always has metric properties. The purpose of scaling is then to recover the metric information presumed to underlie the data. Secondly, the way the data are scaled will obviously depend on both the kind of model used and the structure of the data. The scaling of nominal data comprises a family of mathematical models for the representation of different kinds of data and a corresponding set of methods for fitting such models to actual data. Thirdly, it should be noted that the development of computing facilities and the increased use of computers has made it possible in recent years to apply many new statistical methods for fitting models. The increasing number of algorithms and related computer programs can make the choice of an appropriate method, and the interpretation of the results, a fairly difficult task. The scope of applications of this field is relatively large. All the phenomena which are not subject to direct numerical measurement must be studied either by indirect observations on a set of indicators, which are often nominal variables, or, more generally, by the observation of some relations associated with the set of entities to be scaled. Many different disciplines are concerned with the problems of scaling nominal data, for example, sociology, psychology, education, history, and marketing.

A taxonomy of the field is possible from different points of view. After a short description of the type of data being scaled and of the type of model being used for their representation, a brief review of the most popular methods will be given.

1. The Starting Point of Scaling

Historically, most developments in scaling have dealt with scaling of stimuli, such as attitudes or psychological stimuli. Scaling methods deal usually with different ways of observing and analysing behaviour. Data can be derived from a great number of very different empirical situations. The researcher can be faced, for instance, with dichotomous judgments made by different subjects on simple stimuli, or on pairs of stimuli, or on pairs of pairs of stimuli. But the data can also be concerned with observations characterized by polychotomous nominal variables, or subjects characterized by their choices of different subsets of objects, and so on. Different ways of organizing the data have been proposed by different authors (Coombs 1964, Shepard et al. 1972, Carroll and Arabie 1980).

The nominal data can generally be defined, at first, as relational systems, that is to say, by sets of entities (subjects, stimuli, items, tasks, or schools) and relations associated with those sets (choice or rejection of stimuli, successful or unsuccessful results in a set of tasks, or preferences). For instance, if the interest is in different stages of child development, the data could be a set of children, a set of stages, and a relation from the set of children to the set of stages which makes it possible to associate with each child one or more stages of development. Relational systems may be distinguished with regard to the type and the number of sets with which relationships are associated, as well as with regard to the number and type of relations. In most cases, to make scaling possible either a fairly skilful collection of the data or a mathematical transformation of the original data is required. The most widely used scaling methods need data sets in the form of an $(n \times n)$ similarity matrix. In many cases the measures of similarity, or more generally measures of association, are not observed directly but are obtained from an $(n \times p)$ data matrix. Given observations on p nominal variables for each of n individuals or objects, there are many ways of constructing an $(n \times n)$ matrix, showing their similarities. A number of different quantities have been proposed. For instance, the so-called simple matching coefficient is the proportion of variables for which two individuals have the same value. Various other measures are discussed by Jardine and Sibson (1971) among others.

2. Type of Models Used to Represent the Data

Two classes of models for scaling data can be identified: spatial and nonspatial models. The spatial models represent each object as a point in a coordinate space in such a way that the significant features of the data about these objects are revealed in the geometrical relations between the points. The nonspatial models represent each object as a node in a graph so that the relations between the nodes in the graph reflect the observed relations within the data.

The first class is well-known. In the analysis of numerical data, factor analysis and principal component analysis can be viewed as attempts to map data into models which belong to this class. Such analyses have proved their effectiveness for a large range of applications and they seem particularly suited to the study of factorial structure. Multidimensional scaling and correspondence analysis are examples of techniques which make it possible to map similarity matrices or contingency tables within this class of models.

The second class of models is more recent. It leans heavily upon graph theory and algebra. All the techniques of hierarchical cluster analysis, for instance, aim at representing data by some particular graphs which are called ultrametric trees. Some generalizations of Guttman scalogram analysis, too, are essentially devoted to the representation of data by some special graphs, called in French "*Tresses de Guttman*". Tree and graph representations have been shown to be useful in the study of hierarchical and evolutionary processes.

A very popular and useful model which can be seen as either a particular spatial model or as a particular nonspatial model is the real line. The one-dimensional scaling of a set of objects is called seriation. This model is widely used in archeology, where the concern often lies with a chronological ordering of a set of objects.

A rather extensive review of the two classes of models can be found in Carroll and Arabie (1980).

Another distinction can also be made between deterministic and probabilistic models. Probabilistic models are, generally, variants of corresponding deterministic models. In deterministic models, the representation is constructed in spite of the possible discrepancies between the model and the data. If those discrepancies must be taken into account by the model, it is necessary to employ probabilistic methods. These last models are generally more complex and often need replications of the data.

3. Techniques Used to Map the Data into the Models

The techniques used to map data into models involve both the structure of the data and the type of representation. Furthermore, any criterion of the goodness of fit between the model and the data will define a method. Their number is therefore too great to permit an exhaustive review to be undertaken. Consequently only some of the most popular methods will be outlined.

3.1 Guttman Scales

The general strategy which underlies the fitting of a Guttman scale has already been introduced by the first example. The model was invented by Guttman in 1944 and has been widely used in many different contexts. Its main purpose is to test the assumption that the characteristics being studied involve only one single dimension. Multidimensional extensions of the model have been proposed.

It should be recalled that the starting point of the analysis is generally a 0–1 data matrix in which the rows represent subjects and the columns represent items, tasks, or specific properties. If a subject has passed (failed) an item, a 1 (0) is assigned to the corresponding elements in the matrix. Polychotomously scored items can be dealt with by an extension of the model. To make the presentation of the method clearer, this discussion will be restricted to a (3×4) input data matrix, recorded in Table 1. The basic assumption on which the model is built is as follows: the subjects and the items can all be ranked on a line, in ascending order of competence and difficulty, in such a way that any subject will pass all the items which are represented on the left (i.e., of difficulty smaller than his or her competence)

Table 1
Results to a test represented in a data matrix

		Items			
		A	B	C	D
Subjects	a	0	1	0	0
	b	1	1	0	0
	c	1	1	0	1

and will fail the other ones. Such a representation is given in Fig. 1.

From this example, different comments can be made. First, the representation can be shown to be unique as a monotonic transformation of the scale, that is, a transformation that does not alter the relative order of the scale values. This scale is called an ordinal scale. Secondly, if a subject fails item A and passes item B, it means that item A is more difficult than item B. To fail B and pass A would be incompatible with the assumed model. The model is, in fact, a very restrictive one which puts strong limitations on the data. Thirdly, even if the size of the data matrix is great, the appropriate representation of subjects and items can be quickly obtained. They have only to be ranked according to the number of ones in their corresponding rows and columns, each subject being put between an item he or she has failed and an item he or she has passed. Finally, if the number of violations of the model is too great, different extensions of the Guttman scale are available to deal with these discrepancies. An introductory text on the subject can be found in Degenne (1972).

3.2 Rasch Model

One of the most popular probabilistic extensions of the Guttman scale is the so-called Rasch model. The Rasch model is in fact one of the simplest of a class of models known as latent trait models. In these models, the behaviour of a subject on a task is accounted for, ignoring a random component, by certain human characteristics, called traits, and certain task characteristics; the relationship between the response of a subject, his or her traits, and the characteristics of the task varies according to the type of model employed. If the Rasch model is used, the probability of a successful result by a given subject on a given task is a function of only two parameters: a task parameter which can be thought of as a measure of difficulty, and a subject parameter which can be regarded as a measure of ability. If a is the ability parameter of the subject, and d is the difficulty parameter of the task, the probability of success in the task is given by the following logistic function:

$$\text{pr (successful result)} = [\exp(a - d)/(1 + \exp(a - d)] \quad (1)$$

The responses given by a specific subject to different tasks are assumed to be independent. As in a Guttman scale, subjects and tasks can be represented on a straight line, their coordinates being their relevant ability or difficulty parameters. However, in this last representation, it is possible for a subject to be represented on the right of a task which he or she has failed. This situation is not possible with a perfect Guttman scale. A Guttman scale can, in fact, be thought of as a very particular latent trait model, the probability of a correct answer being always 0 or 1 and depending only on the relative order of the relevant ability and difficulty parameters. The principal advantage of the Rasch model is that it makes possible the scaling of subjects (or tasks) independently

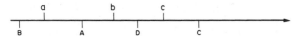

Figure 1
Representation of subjects (lower case) and items (capitals)

of an actual set of tasks (or subjects). This model is widely employed in different fields: research in education, evaluation, and psychology. Many variants have been developed by different authors. The interested reader will find in Lord and Novick (1968) a useful introduction to the latent trait class of models. Another interesting class of models which also makes use of latent variables to explain the behaviour of a subject is the latent structure model developed by Lazarsfeld (Lazarsfeld and Henry 1968). In this type of model, the latent variables are not required to be quantitative variables as in the preceding ones. The existence of a latent space in which the subjects are located is assumed, and a relationship between their location and the probability of a favourable response is defined. These models have been used, for instance, in the description and analysis of achievement tests and achievement tests items.

3.3 Multidimensional Scaling

The starting point in multidimensional scaling is usually some index (numerical, ordinal, or even nominal) of the degree of association between any couple of the objects being scaled. It is assumed that the objects can be embedded in a multidimensional space model in such a way that the measure of association is represented by the distance between the respective points. Multidimensional scaling which is closely associated with the works of Torgerson, Shepard, and Kruskal, is interesting for several reasons. Its results are generally presented as readily visualizable pictures; the identification of the axes of the spatial representation can give interpretations of the data; the spatial configuration of the data can lead to meaningful general interpretations: for example, points clustered in homogeneous groups or the location of some points on a line or on a circle. A drawback is, perhaps, the lack of control in evaluating the adequacy of the representation. Indeed, multidimensional models impose fewer restrictions on the data than unidimensional or more simple models do, especially if the number of dimensions is great. Only a measure of the goodness of fit makes it possible to evaluate the model used. A variety of methods are available, depending on the structure of the data, the measure of the discrepancy between the model and the data, and the type of distance used in the model. A fairly extensive review of the present state of the art of multidimensional scaling can be found in Carroll and Arabie (1980).

3.4 Correspondence Analysis

Correspondence analysis is a technique for interpreting contingency tables, and it has several links with principal-component analysis. This technique, widely used in

the social sciences, makes it possible to represent nominal data by points in a multidimensional space. The starting point of the analysis, the type of distance measure used, the dimensionality of the space, the methodology used, and the factorial feature of the approach distinguish it from the methods of multidimensional scaling. Among the leading contributors to its development are Hirschfeld (1935) and Fisher (1940) and more recently Benzécri (1980). Correspondence analysis has the known advantages and disadvantages of classical factorial analysis. Moreover, it can be shown to be a special case of canonical analysis. Furthermore, it allows representation in the same diagram of different sets of points, and possesses some interesting properties of invariance, for example, some categories of nominal variables can be clustered without altering the results. The main features of correspondence analysis may be highlighted through a simple example. Take, for instance, a researcher who studies the verbal interactions between children and their teacher in a certain grade in an elementary school. The researcher might record for each child (i), and each type of interaction to be distinguished (j), the number of interactions between the child and the teacher ($k_{i,j}$). The interactions can easily be represented as a rectangular array. The rows correspond to the children, and the columns to the different types of interaction recorded. In a correspondence analysis, the proximity between two children (or types of interaction) will not depend on the absolute value of the $k_{i,j}$ in the corresponding two rows (or columns) but on their relative values. This means that two children will be considered similar if their corresponding numbers for the particular interactions are proportional, but not necessarily equal. More formally, the squared distance between two children i and i' is defined by

$$d^2(i, i') = \sum_j (1/k_{\bullet j})(k_{i,j}/k_{i\bullet} - k_{i',j}/k_{i'\bullet})^2 \qquad (2)$$

with

$$k_{i\bullet} = \sum_j k_{i,j}, \ k_{\bullet j} = \sum_i k_{i,j} \qquad (3)$$

Thus, two subjects, i and i', will be represented by the same point if, for all j, one has

$$k_{i,j}/k_{i\bullet} = k_{i',j}/k_{i'\bullet} \qquad (4)$$

The children can be, a priori, represented in a multidimensional space, with the number of dimensions required being the number of types of interactions considered. As in component analysis, the aim of the method is to represent the set of children in a space with fewer dimensions in such a way that, to an acceptable degree of approximation, the resulting interpoint distances do not differ greatly from the original distances between children. In correspondence analysis, rows and columns are processed in the same way. It can be shown that both data sets can be represented in a single space. Correspondence analysis is, in fact, an eigenvalue problem; the computational procedure is similar to the one used in principal components analysis.

3.5 Representation of Data by Graph-theoretical Structures

Complementing the multidimensional-scaling approach, there has arisen recently an interest in representing data by graph-theoretical structures. It should be recalled that a graph is a set of nodes linked by edges. The mathematical problem that has been most extensively studied can be stated as follows: given a set of objects and a measure of association between pairs of objects, find a graph, typically a tree, in which the objects are represented as nodes so that some measure of distance on the set of nodes reflects the measure of association. One of the best-known representations of data by a graph is the Linnaean classification of living species. Representation of data by this type of graph (called an ultrametric tree) is the field of hierarchical cluster analysis. More simple structures have been explored by various authors (Hubert 1974, Sattah and Tversky 1977). These methods have not yet been applied to any great extent in the field of education.

4. Conclusions

Attention has been focused in this article on only some of the most popular scaling models which are applicable to nominal data. Some well-known methods have either been omitted or merely noted; for example, representation by semiorders, latent structure analysis, Thurstone scales, and unfolding theory. The interested reader will find a more extensive introduction to the subject in Coombs (1964), Coombs et al. (1970), Van der Ven (1980).

Scaling has been defined as a mapping of data into mathematical models, not only into uni- or multi-dimensional space. When such a general definition is adopted, the topic is sometimes referred to as the modelling of data. What is essential to scaling is, in fact, the representation of the total underlying pattern of interrelations in the data by the geometrical structure of the model. From this point of view, there is no reason other than historical, to restrict the models to a uni- or multi-dimensional continuum.

It is of little value to have a quantitative theory if feasible methods of measurement cannot be developed. On the other hand, scaling of data without any interpretation of the results and without any reference to a model or a theory, seems to serve little purpose. Scaling should be thought of as a first step in the analysis of data and in model building. It should make it possible to assess the actual level of measurement of the data and to justify their use in subsequent analysis. When used in connection with psychological and pedagogical theories, scaling should help to give substantive explanations of the data.

See also: Scaling Methods; Rasch Measurement Models; Guttman Scales; Thurstone Scales

Bibliography

Benzécri J P (ed.) 1980 *L'Analyse des données: Leçons sur l'analyse factorielle et la reconnaissance des formes et bravaux du Laboratoire de Statistique de l'Université de Paris VI*, 3rd edn. Vol. 2. *L'Analyse des correspondances*. Dunod, Paris

Carroll J D, Arabie P 1980 Multidimensional scaling. *Annu. Rev. Psychol.* 31: 607–49

Coombs C H 1964 *A Theory of Data*. Wiley, New York

Coombs C H, Dawes R M, Tversky A 1970 *Mathematical Psychology: An Elementary Introduction*. Wiley, New York

Degenne A 1972 *Techniques ordinales en analyse des données*, Vol. 2: *Statistique*. Hachette Université, Paris

Fisher R A 1940 The precision of discrimination functions. *Annu. Eugen. Lond.* 10: 422–29

Hirschfeld H O 1935 A connection between correlation and contingency. *Proc. Camb. Phil. Soc.* 31: 520–24

Hubert L J 1974 Some applications of graph theory and related non metric techniques to problems of approximate seriation: The case of symmetric proximity measures. *Br. J. Math. Stat. Psychol.* 27: 133–53

Jardine N, Sibson R 1971 *Mathematical Taxonomy*. Wiley, London

Lazarsfeld P F, Henry N W 1968 *Latent Structure Analysis*. Houghton Mifflin, Boston, Massachusetts

Lord F M, Novick M R 1968 *Statistical Theories of Mental Scores*. Addison-Wesley, Reading, Massachusetts

Sattah S, Tversky A 1977 Additive similarity trees. *Psychometrika* 42: 319–45

Shepard R N, Romney A K, Nerlove S B (ed.) 1972 *Multidimensional Scaling: Theory and Applications in the Behavioral Sciences*. Seminars Press, New York

Van Der Ven A H 1980 *Introduction to Scaling*. Wiley, New York

Sufficient Statistics in Educational Measurement

E. B. Andersen

In social science (including educational) research, a sufficient statistic is a function of a given set of observations which extracts the available information about a given parameter. Under certain regularity conditions the statistical model must belong to a so-called exponential family to allow for a nontrivial sufficient statistic. In educational measurement sufficient statistics are found in the form of the raw score for a set of binary items, but also other scoring formulas are sufficient statistics. The article surveys these formulas.

1. Sufficient Statistics

A sufficient statistic for an unknown parameter θ was defined by Fisher (1922) as a function $t(x_1, \ldots, x_n)$ for which the conditional distribution of any other statistic

$t^*(x_1, \ldots, x_n)$ given $t(x_1, \ldots, x_n) = t$ is independent of θ. This is the most direct way to express that t extracts all the available information in the sample $(x_1, \ldots, x_n)$ about θ. When the value of t is known no other statistic t^* can provide further information about θ.

An equivalent definition is that the conditional distribution of $x_1, \ldots, x_n$ given the value of $t(x_1, \ldots, x_n)$ does not depend on θ. This can also be expressed as

$$f(x_1, \ldots, x_n | \theta) = h(x_1, \ldots, x_n | t) g(t | \theta) \qquad (1)$$

where f is the joint density or probability of $x_1, \ldots, x_n$, h is the conditional density or probability given $t(x_1, \ldots, x_n) = t$ and g is marginal density or probability of t. The converse of Eqn. (1) is known as Neyman's criterion: If $f(x_1, \ldots, x_n | \theta)$ can be written as in Eqn. 1, where h does not depend on θ and g only depends on the x's through t, then t is sufficient for θ.

A statistic t_1 is called minimal sufficient if for any other sufficient statistic t, t_1 is a function of t.

2. Distributions Admitting Sufficient Statistics

In the mid-1930s it was shown by Darmois (1935), Pitman (1936), and Koopman (1936) that under certain regularity conditions only so-called exponential families admitted nontrivial sufficient statistics. These regularity conditions were primarily of two types:

(a) $f(x_i | \theta)$ is twice differentiable in x_i

(b) The range of x_i, that is, those x_i for which $f(x_i | \theta) > 0$, does not depend on θ.

Under (a) and (b) it can be shown, that the density $f(x_i | \theta)$ has the form

$$f(x_i | \theta) = c(\theta) \exp[v(x_i) \phi(\theta)] h(x_i) \qquad (2)$$

and that the minimal sufficient statistic is

$$t = \sum_{i=1}^n v(x_i) \qquad (3)$$

$\tau = \phi(\theta)$ is called the canonical parameter. For further references the reader should consult Brown (1964).

When the x's are discrete random variables assumption (a) of course does not hold and must be replaced by other assumptions, essentially to ensure that t represents a true data reduction. This is a critical assumption as the observations themselves are sufficient. Papers by Andersen (1970) and Denny (1972) give more details.

But also for the discrete case, where $f(x_i | \theta)$ is the probability of getting the observation x_i, the expression in Eqn. (2) defines an exponential family, where t, given by Eqn. (3), is a minimal sufficient statistic.

In the case of the vector valued parameter $(\theta_1, \ldots, \theta_n)$ an exponential family takes the form

$$f(x_i | \theta_1, \ldots, \theta_k) = c(\theta_1, \ldots, \theta_k)$$
$$\times \exp\left[\sum_{j=1}^m v_j(x_i) \phi_j(\theta_1, \ldots, \theta_k)\right] h(x_i) \qquad (4)$$

with m sufficient statistics

$$t_j = \sum_{i=1}^n v_j(x_i), \quad j = 1, \ldots, m \qquad (5)$$

for the canonical parameters $\phi_1, \ldots, \phi_m$. Note that m can be and often is less than k, which means that only m parameters can be estimated in a minimal sufficient way.

3. Sufficient Statistics for Latent Trait Models

In educational research binary responses to n items, that is, $x_i = 0$ or 1, are considered, and the latent trait $p_i(\theta)$ of item i is defined by:

$$f(x_i | \theta) = \begin{cases} p_i(\theta) & \text{for } x_i = 1 \\ 1 - p_i(\theta) & \text{for } x_i = 0 \end{cases}$$

The latent trait is thus the probability of $x_i = 1$ for latent parameter θ. The latent parameter is often an individual parameter, for example the ability of a given individual. When θ goes from $-\infty$ to $+\infty$ it is usually assumed that $p_i(\theta)$ goes from 0 to 1. It is not assumed that the x_i's are identically distributed, but rather that $p_i(\theta)$ depends on certain item parameters (α_i, β_i). In Andersen (1977) it was proved that if there exists a minimal sufficient statistic $t(x_1, \ldots, x_n)$ for θ, which does not depend on the item parameters, then $p_i(\theta)$ has the form

$$p_i(\theta) = \exp(\theta - \alpha_i)/[1 + \exp(\theta - \alpha_i)] \qquad (6)$$

or what is known as the Rasch model. In this case the minimal sufficient statistic is the so-called raw score

$$t = \sum_{i=1}^n x_i \qquad (7)$$

If t is allowed to depend on the item parameters, no results are available on the general form of $p_i(\theta)$, but the two-parameter logistic model

$$p_i(\theta) = \exp[(\theta - \alpha_i) \beta_i]/\{1 + \exp[(\theta - \alpha_i) \beta_i]\}$$

introduced by Birnbaum (Lord and Novick 1968 Chap. 18) has the property that the weighted score

$$t = \sum_{i=1}^n \beta_i x_i \qquad (8)$$

is sufficient for θ.

The concept of sufficiency is essential when working with latent trait models. When the statistic t is sufficient for θ, the inference concerning θ can be based on the frequency distribution of t in the population without losing information about θ. It is also essential that t represents a real data reduction as is the case for the raw score, Eqn. (7). For the weighted score, Eqn. (8), with odd parameter values $\beta_1, \ldots, \beta_n$, there may only exist one response pattern $x_1, \ldots, x_n$ for a specific value of t and the scoring does not represent a data reduction.

4. The Polychotomous Case

Andersen (1977) also discusses the case, where x_i is a categorical variable with $m > 2$ possible values. For this case, it can be shown that the score vector $(t_1, \ldots, t_m)$, where t_j = number of responses in answer category J, is a sufficient statistic, but not necessarily minimal sufficient. If θ is a one-dimensional latent parameter, it is thus of importance to find a real-valued statistic t to estimate θ with. As the vector $(t_1, \ldots, t_m)$ is sufficient t will be a function of $(t_1, \ldots, t_m)$. Under certain assumptions on the kind of data reduction provided by t, it was shown by Andersen (1977) that t must have the form

$$t = \delta_1 t_1 + \ldots + \delta_m t_m$$

where $\delta_1 - \delta_2 = \delta_2 - \delta_3 = \ldots = \delta_{m-1} - \delta_m$. Such δ's are known as equidistant scorings of the response categories.

Bibliography

Andersen E B 1970 Sufficiency and exponential families for discrete sample spaces. *J. Am. Statist. Assoc.* 65: 1248–55
Andersen E B 1977 Sufficient statistics and latent trait models. *Psychometrika* 42: 69–81
Brown L 1964 Sufficient statistics in the case of independent random variables. *Ann. Math. Statist.* 35: 1456–74
Darmois G 1935 Sur les lois de probabilité à estimation exhaustive. *C.R. Acad. Sci. Paris* 200: 1265–66
Denny J L 1972 Sufficient statistics and discrete exponential families. *Ann. Math. Statist.* 43: 1320–22
Fisher R A 1922 On the mathematical foundations of theoretical statistics. *Phil. Trans. Royal Soc. A* 222: 309–68
Koopman B O 1936 On distributions admitting a sufficient statistic. *Trans. Amer. Math. Soc.* 39: 399–409
Lord F M, Novick M R 1968 *Statistical Theories of Mental Test Scores.* Addison-Wesley, Reading, Massachusetts
Pitman E J G 1936 Sufficient statistics and intrinsic accuracy. *Proc. Camb. Phil. Soc.* 32: 567–79

Validity

R. A. Zeller

That valid measurement is essential to successful scientific activity is widely accepted among science methodologists, theoreticians, researchers, and philosophers. Nonetheless, this importance has not led, until quite recently, to a systematic, focused approach to the problem of evaluating the validity of particular measurement procedures. Indeed, the reaction of most scientists to the question of validity has been one of the recitation of abstract ritualistic dogma of validity's importance, rather than a serious investigation of the place of validity in scientific research. In this discussion, validity will be defined and contrasted with its companion concept in the measurement process, reliability. Then the types of validity will be described and the procedures used to evaluate each type of validity will be developed and illustrated.

1. The Definition of Validity

A measure is valid if it does what it is intended to do. Alternatively stated, an indicator of some abstract concept is valid to the extent that it measures what it purports to measure. In science, indicators "purport" to measure concepts. To the extent that the indicators provide accurate empirical representations of their respective concepts, theoretical statements about the relationships among concepts based upon an analysis of their respective indicators can proceed in an orderly fashion. However, when indicators do not represent their respective concepts (i.e., when indicators are invalid), scientific statements about the relationships among concepts become distorted.

There is virtual agreement on the importance of valid measurement to the success of scientific endeavors. For example, Hauser (1969 pp. 127–29) stated: "I should

like to venture the judgment that it is inadequate measurement, more than inadequate concept or hypothesis, that has plagued social researchers and prevented fuller explanations of the variances with which they are confounded." In a similar vein, Greer (1969 p. 160) stated:

> The link between observation and formulation is one of the most difficult and crucial of the scientific enterprises. It is the process of interpreting our theory or, as some say, of "operationalizing our concepts." Our creations in the world of possibility must be fitted in the world of probability; in Kant's epigram, "Concepts without percepts are empty." It is also the process of relating our observations to theory; to finish the epigram, "Percepts without concepts are blind."

But why, when it is so crucial to the success of scientific endeavors, does valid measurement receive ritualistic recitations instead of serious investigation? There are two important interrelated answers to this question. First, theoretical considerations (and hence, considerations of validity) were excluded from an early, important definition of "measurement." Second, as shall be seen, it is immensely difficult to provide compelling evidence of the validity of measurements. Each of these impediments to a vigorous and rigorous investigation of validity will be discussed.

1.1 An Inadequate Definition of Measurement

Stevens (1951 p. 22) defined measurement as ". . . the assignment of numbers to objects or events according to rules." While this definition takes into account the empirical activities associated with the measurement process, it ignores the theoretical ones. For example, suppose that a researcher wanted to measure the concept "self-esteem." According to Stevens, the researcher would have accomplished that task by constructing a set of rules for the assignment of a number to each individual. Presumably, that number would empirically represent that individual's level of self-esteem. One possible "rule for assigning numbers of objects" is: father's weight (in pounds) divided by mother's height (in inches). Thus, if a respondent's father weighed 200 pounds and mother was 50 inches tall, the number "4" (i.e., 200/50) would be assigned to that respondent. If the father weighed 120 pounds while the mother was 60 inches tall, the number "2" (120/60) would be assigned.

However, as is obvious from this example father's weight and mother's height do not give a valid representation of an individual's self-esteem. The problem is that this "rule" fully satisfies Stevens' definition of measurement. Any definition of measurement that considers only the world of sense experience and omits consideration of abstract theoretical concepts is an inadequate definition of measurement. Widespread use of Stevens' exclusively empirical definition of measurement may have impeded efforts to come to grips with the problem of validity in social research.

While Stevens allegedly defined "measurement," he actually provided the context for assessing reliability. Reliability focuses on the extent to which a measurement procedure consistently yields the same result on repeated observations. Alternatively stated, reliability is the degree of repeatability or consistency of empirical measurements. In scientific discourse, when indicators are unreliable, scientific statements about the relationships among the variables become obscured. Thus, an appropriate epigram concerning reliability and validity is: unreliability obscures; invalidity distorts.

Stevens' definition of measurement establishes the context for reliability because it lays the empirical groundwork but does not lay the theoretical groundwork for the measurement process. Correspondingly, reliability focuses upon the empirical aspects, but ignores the theoretical aspects, of the measurement process. Validity, on the other hand, focuses on the theoretical aspects of the measurement process and seeks to interweave these concerns with the empirical ones. In this sense, it is much easier to assess reliability than it is to assess validity, for the assessment of reliability requires no more than manipulation of empirical observations while the assessment of validity requires the manipulation of both empirical observations and theoretical concepts simultaneously.

1.2 An Adequate Definition of Measurement

In this regard, Blalock (1968 p. 12) has observed that "...theorists often use concepts that are formulated at rather high levels of abstraction. These are quite different from the variables that are the stock-in-trade of empirical sociologists." In this tradition, measurement can be defined as the process of linking abstract concepts to empirical indicants. To illustrate the measurement process, the situation where a researcher wants to measure the concept "self-esteem" can again be used. According to Blalock, the research must engage in a variety of tasks to provide a valid empirical measure of

this concept. These tasks include: (a) defining the concept "self-esteem"; (b) selecting indicants that will provide empirical representations of the concept "self-esteem"; (c) obtaining empirical information for those indicants; and (d) evaluating the degree to which those indicants did, in fact, provide a valid representation of the concept "self-esteem." These four tasks will briefly be carried out in the attempt to establish the validity of a measure of self-esteem.

(a) *Defining the concept "self-esteem."* Rosenberg (1979 p. 54) defines self-esteem as a positive or negative orientation towards oneself. An individual of low self-esteem "...lacks respect for himself, considers himself unworthy, inadequate, or otherwise seriously deficient as a person." On the other hand, a person of high self-esteem considers himself or herself to be a person of worth. High self-esteem carries no connotations of "...feelings of superiority, arrogance, conceit, contempt for others, [or] overweening pride." This, then constitutes a widely used theoretical definition of the concept "self-esteem."

(b) *Selecting measures of self-esteem.* Having defined "self-esteem" theoretically, Rosenberg then constructed indicants that he thought would measure the concept (Rosenberg 1979 p. 291). The indicants are statements about oneself; subjects respond to these indicants by expressing strong agreement, agreement, disagreement, or strong disagreement. Some indicants are written with a positive description of self; examples include: "On the whole, I am satisfied with myself," and "I feel that I'm a person of worth, at least on an equal plane with others." Other indicants are written with a negative description of self; examples include: "I feel I do not have much to be proud of," and "I wish I could have more respect for myself." Rosenberg constructed 10 such indicants; five were positive statements while the other five were negative statements.

(c) *Obtaining empirical information for indicants.* Rosenberg then obtained empirical information for these indicants by asking adolescents to respond to each indicant in terms of the response categories.

(d) *Evaluating the validity of the indicants.* Having completed the first three steps in the measurement process, it is then possible to examine the validity of the indicants as empirical representations of the concept. The question being asked at this stage in the research process is: "To what degree do the indicants represent the concept 'self-esteem' empirically?" The answer to this question is a major challenge in scientific discourse. There are a variety of approaches to this problem. Section 2 describes these different types of validity.

2. Types of Validity

Validity refers to the extent to which an empirical indicant measures what it purports to measure. Such activity does not go on inside a vacuum. Instead, it occurs within the context of a measurement situation, as described above. Thus, it is not the indicant itself that is being validated, but rather, it is the purpose for which the indicant is being used that is submitted to validation procedures. In Cronbach's words (1971 p. 447): "One validates, not a test, but an *interpretation of data arising from a specified procedure.*"

There are a variety of approaches that social researchers have taken in order to establish the validity of their measures. These different approaches to the assessment of validity will now be considered; for each, their different meanings, uses, and limitations will be described and illustrated.

2.1 Content Validity

Fundamentally, content validity focuses upon the extent to which the content of an indicant corresponds to the content of the theoretical concept it is designed to measure. For example, the self-esteem indicants focused upon the same content as the conceptual definition of self-esteem. Thus, Rosenberg's self-esteem measure could be judged as a content valid measure of the concept "self-esteem" because the content of the indicants corresponded to the content of the concept.

Establishing content validity, therefore, involves specifying the domain of content for the concept and constructing and selecting indicants that represent that domain of content. Neither of these tasks can be done unequivocally. Self-esteem can again be used as an example. One question concerns the theoretical development of the concept. Does Rosenberg's definition include all relevant aspects of the concept? Does his definition exclude any relevant aspects of the concept? Neither of these questions can be answered with certainty because of the fundamental openness of meaning that is characteristic of concepts. As Kaplan (1964 p. 63) asserts: "As the theory is used—for scientific as well as practical purposes—its meaning is progressively more fixed; but some degree of openness always remains." Thus, in content validation, "acceptance of the universe of content as defining the variable to be measured is essential" (Cronbach and Meehl 1955 p. 282). Obtaining this acceptance has proved to be exceedingly difficult for many of the concepts in the social and behavioral sciences.

The second question concerns the construction and/or selection of indicants designed to represent a domain of content. Do Rosenberg's indicants include all relevant aspects of his definition of self-esteem? Do his indicants exclude any relevant aspects of this definition? Neither of these questions can be answered with certainty either, because of the fundamental nature of indicants. Specifically, empirical indicants are designed to be as specific, as exact, and as bounded as the conceptual definitions and the research settings will allow. Hence, indicants never duplicate nor fully exhaust the meaning of the respective concept. While Rosenberg chose to represent the concept "self-esteem" by 10 indicants, he could have used 100 or 1,000. Even if he had done this, he would not have established the content validity beyond doubt. This is so because there is no agreed-upon criteria for evaluating whether content validity has or has not been established. Thus, while it is important to make a reasonable effort to establish the content validity of a set of indicants, these two liabilities prevent content validation from being sufficient for establishing the validity of indicants as measures of their respective concepts.

2.2 Criterion-related Validity

Criterion-related validity focuses upon the correlation between an indicant and some criterion variable of interest. Within this context, the criterion-related validity of college board exam scores is established by the degree to which they are correlated with performance in college. Frequently, the criterion-related validity of coaching effectiveness is established by the won–lost record of the team. Thus, criterion-related validity is the degree of correspondence between the indicant and the criterion. If this correlation is high, the indicant is considered to be criterion-related valid *for that criterion.*

There are two types of criterion-related validity: concurrent validity and predictive validity. Concurrent validity describes a criterion-related validity situation where the criterion variable exists in the present. For example, a researcher might wish to establish the awareness of students about their performance in school during the past year. In this situation, each student could be asked the question: "What was your grade point average last year?" This response could then be concurrent criterion validated by correlating it with the grade point average obtained from the school's record office.

Predictive validity describes a criterion-related validity situation where the criterion variable will not exist until a later point in time. For example, a researcher might wish to have students anticipate their performance in school during the next year. In this situation, each student could be asked the question: "What do you think your grade point average will be next year?" This response could then be predictive criterion validated by correlating it with the grade point average obtained from the school's records office after the elapse of a year's time.

Most tests used to screen applicants for various occupational and educational opportunities are, by nature, concerned with predictive validity. In each case, the purpose of the test is to differentiate between those who will be successful in the position in the future and those who will not. Ordinarily, one cannot fully establish the predictive validity of such an instrument. This is because the instrument is actually used to choose who will and who will not be allowed into the respective positions. For example, suppose that a university entrance examination is administered to 2,400 applicants to a particular university. The university then establishes a minimum score for admission. The university then wishes to discover whether the entrance examination is effective in predicting who will and who will not succeed in the program. It embarks upon "an evaluation research project" to assess the predictive validity of the entrance examination. The following is a discussion of the practical and conceptual difficulties that such a research team would face.

In order to explore this situation, some reasonable assumptions should be made about the nature of the situation faced by "the research team." First, there is a positive and relatively strong correlation between score on the entrance examination and performance in the program. Second, the university can only admit half of the applicants. Third, the university uses performance on the entrance examination as the criterion for admission. Fourth, only those students who exhibit a certain level of performance or better "succeed" at the program. Figure 1 provides a scatterplot of the behavior that would occur if these assumptions were, in fact, the case. In Fig. 1, the horizontal axis represents score on the entrance examination, where 1 represents the lowest score and 6 represents the highest. The vertical axis represents performance in the program, where 1 represents the lowest performance and 6 represents the highest. In this contrived situation, there are 100 observations at each of the 24 locations designated by the letters, A, B, C, and D; these represent the 2,400 applicants to the program. An examination of this scatterplot reveals that it is consistent with the assumption that there is a positive and relatively strong correlation between score on the entrance examination and performance in the program. This product moment correlation coefficient is 0.64; thus, 41 percent of the variance in performance in the program is associated with entrance examination score. By social science standards, this is a relatively strong association.

Recall, however, that the university can only admit half of the applicants to the program, and that it uses the entrance examination scores as the criterion for admission. Since half of the applicants have entrance examination scores of 4 or higher, these individuals are admitted to the program; applicants whose entrance examination scores are 3 or less are not admitted. Thus, only those applicants designated in Fig. 1 by the letters A and C are admitted into the program; applicants designated by the letters B and D are not admitted. Moreover, the university requires a minimum level of performance of 4 in order for that individual to "succeed" in the program; those whose program performance is 3

or less fail in the program. Hence, A's are admitted and succeed in the program; B's are not admitted to the program, but they would have succeeded if they had been admitted; C's are admitted to but fail in the program; and D's are not admitted to the program, and would have failed in the program if they had been admitted.

The university thus admits the A's and the C's; it rejects the admission requests of the B's and the D's. The A's and the C's participate in the program; the A's succeed in the program; the C's fail. At the end of this time, the evaluation research team is commissioned to investigate the effectiveness of the entrance examination in predicting success in the program. This research team compiles the data on entrance examination scores and performance in program ratings. They then calculate the product moment correlation between these two variables. However, they discover that they only have information on both variables for the 1,200 A's and C's who were admitted into the program; they have no information on "performance in program" for those B's and D's who were not admitted. Hence, instead of the 0.64 correlation that was conjectured from Fig. 1, their observed correlation is a mere 0.32; thus, from their observations, only 10 percent of the variance in performance in the program is associated with entrance examination score. By social science standards, and much to the delight of critics of the entrance exam, this is a relatively weak association. Hence, critics charge, the entrance examination provides little useful information about the potential for success in the program, and the entrance examination should therefore be scrapped forthwith.

A more sober look at the research situation, however, reveals that the critics were guilty of making an *ad hominem* argument; they were appealing to prejudices about entrance tests rather than to the believability of the evidence. A reexamination of Fig. 1 shows that 75 percent of those admitted to the program succeeded at it, while only 25 percent of those who were not admitted would have succeeded if they had been admitted. Any admissions officer will testify to the fact that an admissions criterion that has a 75 percent predictive success rate (above the 50 percent success rate if applicants were admitted randomly) is a valuable tool in deciding which applicants are most likely to succeed in the program.

This example illustrates one fundamental difficulty in the use of predictive validity in social research. This difficulty is that when a predictor is used to choose which subset of applicants from a larger pool of applicants will be provided an opportunity to succeed in a program, later attempts to assess the effectiveness of that indicator are inextricably intertwined with the operation of that predictor as an admissions criterion. The result is that the predictor may appear to be only marginally correlated with success in the program when it may well be strongly correlated with success in that program.

A second fundamental difficulty in the use of criterion-related validity in social research settings is that there simply do not exist appropriate criterion variables for many of the concepts that social researchers wish to

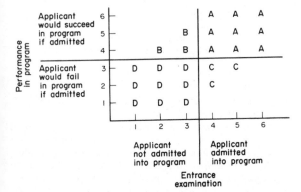

Figure 1
Relationship between entrance examination and performance in program

investigate. For example, no appropriate criterion variable is known for a measure of self-esteem. That is, there is no group in society that has a clear and undeniably high (or low) self-esteem such that this group could be used as a criterion variable to validate a measure of self-esteem. Moreover, the more abstract the concept, the more difficult it is to establish the viability of appropriate criterion variables for use in criterion-related validity analysis. Thus, while criterion-related validity would appear to be an attractive method for establishing the degree to which a measure represents what it purports to measure, its value is primarily by and large an illusion, for it is extremely difficult to satisfy the theoretical demands of validity in its empiricist character.

2.3 Construct Validity

Construct validity focuses on the assessment of whether a particular measure relates to other measures consistent with theoretically derived hypotheses concerning the relationships among the concepts. As Cronbach and Meehl (1955 p. 290) observe: "Construct validation takes place when an investigator believes his instrument reflects a particular construct, to which are attached certain meanings. The proposed interpretation generates specific testable hypotheses, which are a means of confirming or disconfirming the claim." Thus, of necessity, construct validity is assessed within a given theoretical context.

Establishing construct validity, therefore, involves the following steps:

(a) construction of a theory by defining concepts and anticipating relationships among them;

(b) selecting indicants that represent each concept contained within the theory;

(c) establishing the dimensional nature of these indicants;

(d) constructing scales for each of the respective sets of indicants;

(e) calculating the correlations among these scales; and

(f) comparing these empirical correlations with the theoretically anticipated relationships among the concepts.

The problems and opportunities inherent in the assessment of construct validity (and hence, each of the above steps) can be illustrated by again examining the concept of self-esteem.

Step 1 involves construction of a theory by defining concepts and anticipating relationships among them. Consistent with Rosenberg (1979), the theory will assert the theoretical relationships among (A) social background factors, (B) self-esteem, and (C) social and political knowledge, attitudes and behavior as follows:

A	+	B	+	C
Social background	→	Self-esteem	→	Social and political knowledge, attitudes, and behavior

In words, social background factors cause self-esteem which, in turn, causes social and political knowledge, attitudes, and behavior. The plus signs (+) in the above theoretical digraph represent the anticipation that the relationship between the cause and the effect will be positive. Thus, the theoretical digraph suggests that a more positive social background will cause a more positive self-esteem and that a more positive self-esteem will cause greater social and political knowledge and more positive social and political attitudes and behaviors.

Step 2 involves selection of indicants that represent each concept contained within the theory. For the purpose of this example, the following are the indicants selected to represent each concept:

(A) Social background is represented by:

+ a_1 is years of father's formal education
+ a_2 is years of mother's formal education
+ a_3 is father's occupational prestige

(B) Self-esteem is represented by the following 10 Likert attitude indicants:

+ b_1 is "I feel that I have a number of good qualities"
− b_2 is "I wish I could have more respect for myself"
+ b_3 is "I feel that I'm a person of worth, at least on an equal plane with others"
− b_4 is "I feel I do not have much to be proud of"
+ b_5 is "I take a positive attitude toward myself"
− b_6 is "I certainly feel useless at times"
− b_7 is "All in all, I'm inclined to feel that I am a failure"
+ b_8 is "I am able to do things as well as most other people"
− b_9 is "At times I think I am no good at all"
+ b_{10} is "On the whole, I am satisfied with myself" (Rosenberg 1979 p. 291)

(C) Social and political knowledge, attitudes, and behavior is represented by:

+ c_1 is understanding of democratic principles
+ c_2 is knowledge of government services
+ c_3 is knowledge of political authorities
− c_4 is political cynicism
+ c_5 is political efficacy
+ c_6 is participation in community activities
+ c_7 is participation in school activities

The positive (+) and negative (−) signs to the left represent whether the specific indicant is a positive or negative measure of its respective concept. For instance, agreement with the statement b_6, "I certainly feel useless at times" indicates less self-esteem than disagreement with that statement. Moreover, there are many ways to measure each of these concepts other than those illustrated. For example, social background could have been measured by marital status of parents, degree of parental disagreement, disciplinary consistency, disciplinary extremes, and so on; such measurement would be consistent with much theory in child development.

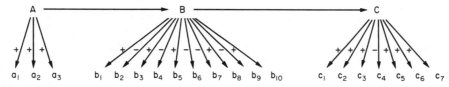

Figure 2
Theoretical measurement model

The theoretical model can now be reformulated to include the anticipated measurement properties and using the symbolic representations as presented in Fig. 2. Again, the arrows represent a causal linkage from the cause to the effect. Also, the algebraic sign represents the nature of the relationship. Moreover, the arrows between capital letters represent a causal relationship among the concepts. The arrows from the capital letters to the lower case letters represent the causal effect of the concept on its respective indicant. These arrows, called "epistemic correlations," are the major structural building blocks on which the assessment of validity proceeds. Thus, the indicants have been selected and have been represented within the theoretical model.

Step 3 involves establishing the dimensional nature of the indicants designed to measure their respective concepts. The illustration of step 3 will focus on the indicants of self-esteem, as an attempt is being made to establish the construct validity of the concept, self-esteem. Similar analyses can and should be carried out for measures of all concepts within the theory. The data to be used in this analysis come from a study of 340 high-school students (Carmines 1978). Each respondent was asked to respond to each of the 20 indicants illustrated in step 2. A principal components factor analysis of the 10 self-esteem indicants was performed and is presented in Table 1. For an excellent, extensive discussion of the use of factor analysis in this context, see Marradi (1981).

An examination of Table 1 reveals two possible interpretations for the indicants of self-esteem. One interpretation is represented by the extracted factor loadings on the left; the other is represented by the rotated factor loadings on the right. The two possible interpretations will be discussed in turn.

The extracted factor loadings in Table 1 reveal one factor of great strength and a second factor of moderate strength. Since the negative indicants were reflected such that higher scores indicate higher self-esteem, a reasonable interpretation is that the first factor represents the concept "self-esteem" empirically; within this context, factor I will be called the "self-esteem" factor. That is, the higher a respondent's answer to each item, the higher his or her self-esteem is inferred to be. The second factor has positive factor loadings for the positively phrased indicants and has negative factor loadings for the negatively phrased indicants. A reasonable interpretation of factor II is that it represents a method artifact known as "response set," the general tendency to respond to interview or questionnaire items in a particular manner, irrespective of their content. In this context,

response set would occur if the respondent would agree (or disagree) with all 10 indicants. The theoretical inference to be made from this extractional scheme is that the conceptualization of self-esteem was correct. Specifically, there is only one conceptual dimension of self-esteem that operates in the theoretical arrangement of things; thus, only one such concept is included in the theoretical model. This assertion has been made repeatedly by Rosenberg (1979). This analysis also identifies the method artifact "response set" as reliably but invalidly influencing the indicants.

An alternative interpretation of the factor analysis would occur by examining the rotated factor loadings in Table 1. This set of factor loadings reveals two distinct factors. Factor I is defined by strong loadings for items 1, 3, 5, 8, and 10; factor II is defined by strong loadings for items 2, 4, 6, 7, and 9. The common content that defines the former set of items is that each is a positive statement of self-esteem; the common content that defines the latter set of items is that each is a negative statement of self-esteem. Hence, in this interpretation, factor I is named "positive self-esteem" while factor II is named "negative self-esteem." The theoretical inference to be made from this rotational scheme is that the conceptualization of self-esteem was erroneous. Specifically, two different conceptual dimensions of self-esteem, one positive and the other negative, operate in the theoretical arrangement of things and, thus, should be included in the theoretical model.

Since these two interpretations are contradictory, both cannot apply to the situation. More precisely, factor analysis cannot resolve this issue, because both interpretational structures are consistent with accepted factor analytic practice. Moreover, the most common

Table 1
Factor analysis of self-esteem indicants[a]

Items	Extracted			Rotated		
	I	II	h^2	I	II	h^2
1	0.590	0.109	0.360	0.493	0.339	0.360
2	0.328	−0.176	0.138	0.109	0.356	0.138
3	0.581	0.314	0.436	0.633	0.187	0.436
4	0.600	−0.085	0.367	0.365	0.483	0.367
5	0.669	0.198	0.487	0.614	0.332	0.487
6	0.577	−0.346	0.453	0.165	0.653	0.453
7	0.731	−0.202	0.575	0.376	0.659	0.575
8	0.549	0.387	0.451	0.662	0.113	0.451
9	0.640	−0.359	0.539	0.200	0.706	0.539
10	0.480	0.196	0.269	0.478	0.200	0.269

a Items 2, 4, 6, 7, and 9 have been reflected such that higher scores indicate higher self-esteem "default" interpretation, the rotated factor structure, will be the erroneous interpretation, as will be shown. However, a construct validational approach to the problem can provide evidence consistent with one interpretation and inconsistent with the other. This evidence focuses on the relationship of the self-esteem indicants to the indicants of the other concepts contained within the theoretical model. In this case, self-esteem is theoretically anticipated to be related both to social background factors and the social and political knowledge, attitudes, and behavior. If the positive and negative self-esteem factors measure different theoretical components of the self-image, they should relate differentially to indicants of these theoretically relevant concepts. If, on the other hand, the factors measure a single dimension of self-esteem with the bifactorial structure being due to a method artifact, the two factors should relate similarly to these theoretically relevant variables. Thus, the dimensional nature on these indicants cannot be unequivocally established until the remaining steps in the process of establishing construct validity take place. This process will now be looked at.

Step 4 involves the construction of scales for each of the respective sets of indicants. Because the interpretational contradiction described above is unresolved, new scales must be created in such a way so as to resolve the contradiction. Thus, one scale will be created out of the positive self-esteem indicants (1, 3, 5, 8, and 10) and a second scale out of the negative self-esteem indicants (2, 4, 6, 7, and 9). These will be called the "positive self-esteem" and the "negative self-esteem" scales respectively. The scales were created by the simple expedient of summing the scores of each respondent on each scale.

Step 5 involves the calculation of correlations among the scales. Step 6 involves the comparison of these empirical correlations with the theoretically anticipated relationships among the concepts. While the theoretical anticipations of the nature of the relationship were presented in Fig. 2, the appropriate empirical correlations for the construct validity analysis are presented in Table 2. Specifically, the correlations of the "positive self-esteem" and the "negative self-esteem" scales with the social background indicants and with the social and political knowledge, attitudes, and behavior indicants are presented. Most of these correlations are statistically significant (at the 0.05 level) with the anticipated algebraic sign. Thus, the positive and negative self-esteem scales appear to capture an important dimension of adolescent self-esteem. Moreover, the two scales appear to measure the same, rather than different, dimensions of self-esteem, for their correlation with these theoretically relevant indicants are almost identical to one another in terms of direction strength, and consistency. Indeed, the average difference between correlations across all 10 indicants is approximately 0.03, with the highest difference being 0.05. None of these differences is statistically significant (at even the 0.25 level), and there is no compelling theoretical interpretation of such differences.

Thus, a construct validity analysis supports the theoretical unidimensionality of self-esteem as asserted by Rosenberg (1979) rather than theoretical bidimensionality. The two-factor (rotated) solution, thus, offers only spurious evidence for the dual theoretical dimensionality of self-esteem. The more appropriate interpretation

Table 2
Correlations between positive and negative self-esteem scales and indicants of theoretically relevant concepts

Comparison indicant	Positive self-esteem scale	Negative self-esteem scale	Difference between correlations	N
Socioeconomic background factor				
Father's education	0.17[b]	0.15[b]	0.02	198
Mother's education	0.11[a]	0.08	0.03	208
Father's occupation	0.12[a]	0.08	0.04	198
Social and political knowledge, attitudes, and behavior				
Understanding of democratic principles	0.16[b]	0.13[b]	0.03	334
Knowledge of government services	0.12[a]	0.10[a]	0.02	333
Knowledge of political authorities	0.14[b]	0.09[a]	0.05	331
Political cynicism	−0.09[a]	−0.13[b]	0.04	331
Political efficacy	0.18[c]	0.22[c]	−0.04	334
Participation in community activities	0.05	0.02	0.03	228
Participation in school activities	0.14[b]	0.11[a]	0.03	338

a $p < 0.05$ b $p < 0.01$ c $p < 0.001$

is that the bifactorial structure of the indicants is a function of a single theoretical dimension of self-esteem that is contaminated by a method artifact response set.

This example graphically illustrates a key point that this article has attempted to make: that in spite of the usefulness of factor analysis, it does not always lead to unambiguous inferences about the theoretical dimensionality of concepts. Therefore, factor analysis cannot be used as the sole criterion for establishing the adequacy of the concept–indicant linkage. On the contrary, naive and simplistic interpretation of factor structures (such as the automatic use of the default varimax rotation) can be misleading in terms of the theoretical nature of the empirical indicants. It has been shown how response set can artificially produce an inference of two underlying dimensions when in fact there is only one. Any method artifact that can systematically alter the correlations among the indicants may produce this kind of faulty inference.

From the above discussion, it should be clear that the process of construct validation is, by necessity, theory laden. Indeed, strictly speaking, it is impossible to "validate" a measure of a concept unless there exists a theoretical network that surrounds the concept. Without such a network, it is impossible to generate theoretical predictions, which, in turn, lead directly to empirical tests involving measures of the concept. This should not lead to the erroneous conclusion that only formal fully developed theories are relevant to construct validation. On the contrary, Cronbach and Meehl (1955 p. 284) note: "The logic of construct validation is involved whether the construct is highly systematized or loose, used in ramified theory or a few simple propositions, used in absolute propositions or probability statements." What is required is only that one be able to state several theoretically derived hypotheses involving the particular concept.

In the self-esteem example described above, the construct validity evidence was positive. That is, the self-esteem scale correlated as theoretically anticipated with the indicants of the theoretically relevant concepts. Moreover, it is possible to have relatively strong confidence in this construct validation because positive construct validational evidence was found for multiple measures of more than one theoretically relevant concept. For a more complete discussion of the procedures for handling external associations with sets of indicants, see Curtis and Jackson (1962), and Sullivan and Feldman (1979).

But what would the appropriate inference have been if the construct validity evidence had been negative? That is, what should a researcher conclude if the empirically observed relationships are inconsistent with those that were theoretically anticipated? Four different interpretations are possible (Cronbach and Meehl 1955 p. 295). One possible interpretation is that the indicant of the concept lacks construct validity; that is, that the indicants do not measure the concept that they purport to measure. Unfortunately, negative construct validity evidence is also consistent with three other interpretations:

(a) the theoretical arrangement of the concepts was incorrect; and/or

(b) the procedures for deriving empirical hypotheses from the theory were incorrect; and/or

(c) the indicants of the other concepts in the theory lack construct validity.

There is no foolproof procedure for determining which of these interpretations of negative evidence is correct in any given instance. Bits of evidence can be accrued from additional data analysis that suggests one or more of these interpretations. However, it is important to acknowledge that the process of construct validation is more analogous to a detective searching for clues than it is analogous to an accountant proving out a balance. A researcher does not establish validity once and for all; instead, a researcher obtains bits of information that are consistent or inconsistent with a construct validity interpretation. The more systematic the pattern of such bits of information that are consistent with construct validity, the more confidence one has in that interpretation.

3. Conclusion

In this article, validity has been considered. An indicator is valid to the degree that it empirically represents the concept it purports to measure. As such, valid measurement becomes the *sine qua non* of science. There are several strategies for establishing valid measurement including content, criterion-related, and construct validity. It has been argued that construct validity is most appropriate for most questions in social research. Construct validity not only has generalized applicability for assessing validity of social science measures, but it can also be used to differentiate between theoretically relevant and theoretically meaningless empirical factors. This is a crucially important contribution to measurement, because reliability assessment in general and factor analysis in particular are insensitive to this problem. Heise (1974 p. 12) comments: "The meaningfulness of a factor does not depend on the statistical characteristics of its indicators but on their theoretical content, and in ordinary analytic procedures these considerations are not entered as constraints on the numerical analysis." Thus, however useful factor analysis may be for assessing the reliability of a measure, it is not directly relevant to assessing its validity. Viewed from this perspective, efforts to assess validity within a strictly factor-analytic approach—as with Heise and Bohrnstedt's (1970) validity coefficient and with Jöreskog's (1973) linear structural equation system—have the important limitation that they *assume* what a researcher wants to test in validity assessment— whether the set of items measure what they are intended to measure. Thus, "...there should be no question that an internal index of validity is not a complete substitute for an external check on the validity of a composite scale" (Smith 1974 p. 177). Specifically, it is believed that analysis of a set of indicants designed to measure a concept can never be an adequate substitute for a theoretically oriented assessment of a measure's validity.

Moreover, the key question underlying validity—inferring the dimensional nature of the posited theoretical concepts—is not a question that lends itself to a solely statistical solution. On the contrary, in order to properly decide which of the empirical factors represents the respective concept, it is necessary to go beyond the statistical criteria used in factor analysis to the more explicit theoretically relevant criteria used in construct validation. Only in this way can the social researcher ensure that his or her measures are valid.

See also: Reliability; Measurement in Educational Research

Bibliography

Blalock H M 1968 The measurement problem. In: Blalock H M, Blalock A B (eds.) 1968 *Methodology in Social Research*. McGraw-Hill, New York, pp. 5–27

Carmines E G 1978 Psychological origins of adolescent political attitudes. *Am. Pol. Q.* 6: 167–86

Carmines E G, Zeller R A 1979 *Reliability and Validity Assessment*. Sage, Beverly Hills, California

Cronbach L J 1971 Test validation. In: Thorndike R L (ed.) 1971 *Educational Measurement*, 2nd edn. American Council on Education, Washington, DC, pp. 443–507

Cronbach L J, Meehl P E 1955 Construct validity in psychological tests. *Psychol. Bull.* 52: 281–302

Curtis R F, Jackson E F 1962 Multiple indicators in survey research. *Am. J. Sociol.* 68: 195–204

Greer S 1969 *The Logic of Social Inquiry*. Aldine, Chicago, Illinois

Hauser P 1969 Comments on Coleman's paper. In: Bierstedt R (ed.) 1969 *A Design for Sociology: Scope, Objectives, and Methods*. American Academy of Political and Social Science, Philadelphia, Pennsylvania, pp. 122–36

Heise D R 1974 Some issues in sociological measurement. In: Costner H L (ed.) 1974 *Sociological Methodology 1973–1974*. Jossey-Bass, San Francisco, California

Heise D R, Bohrnstedt G W 1970 Validity, invalidity, and reliability. In: Borgatta E F, Bohrnstedt G W (eds.) 1970 *Sociological Methodology 1970*. Jossey-Bass, San Francisco, California

Jöreskog K G 1973 A general method for estimating a linear structural equation system. In: Goldberger A S, Duncan O D (eds.) 1973 *Structural Equation Models in the Social Sciences*. Seminar Press, New York, pp. 85–132

Kaplan A 1964 *The Conduct of Inquiry: Methodology for Behavioral Science*. Chandler, San Francisco

Marradi A 1981 Factor analysis as an aid in the formation and refinement of empirically useful concepts. In: Jackson D J, Borgatta E F (eds.) 1981 *Factor Analysis and Measurement in Sociological Research: A Multi-dimensional Perspective*. Sage, Beverly Hills, California, pp. 11–49

Rosenberg M 1979 *Conceiving the Self*. Basic Books, New York

Smith K W 1974 Forming composite scales and estimating their validity through factor analysis. *Social Forces* 53: 168–80

Stevens S S 1951 Mathematics, measurement and psychophysics. In: Stevens S S (ed.) 1951 *Handbook of Experimental Psychology*. Wiley, New York, pp. 1–49

Sullivan J A, Feldman S 1979 *Multiple Indicators: An Introduction*. Sage, Beverly Hills, California

Reliability [1]

R. L. Thorndike

Any test presents a set of tasks that sample from some universe of responses by the examinee. The universe corresponds, it is hoped, to the latent attribute in which one is interested. In evaluating a test two broad questions are encountered that are different but overlapping. A first question is how accurately the test sample represents the broader universe of responses from which it is drawn; a second is how faithfully that universe corresponds to the latent attribute in which one is interested. The first relates to what is commonly called the "reliability" of the test, the second to its "validity." Collectively, they have been spoken of by Cronbach et al. (1972) as the generalizability of the test score—the range of inferences that can be made from it.

There are typically three sides to the issue of reliability: the basic rationale, the procedures for data collection, and the statistical procedures for data analysis. These facets interact, in that certain empirical data sets are appropriate for certain conceptions of the universe to which inference is desired, and the possible types of statistical analysis depend on the data at hand. Ideally, one would feel that the rational analysis of the universe to which generalization was desired should be primary and that data collection and statistical treatment should flow from this analysis. Realistically, however, practical considerations may limit the data that it is possible to collect, and these limitations may set boundaries on the universe to which inferences can logically be made and on the statistical analyses that can be carried out.

This article starts with a consideration of "classical" reliability theory. This is the true-score-and-error model of a test score that was presented by Spearman in 1904 and that provided the accepted theoretical model for discussions of reliability for the next 50 years. There follows an analysis of the multifacet model of reliability presented by Lindquist (1953) and elaborated by

1   This article is an edited version of material by R L Thorndike which first appeared in *Applied Psychometrics* (1982), Chap. 6 pp. 143-83. It appears here by permission of Houghton Mifflin, Boston.

Cronbach and his associates (1972). Then the discussion returns to the practical issues involved in data collection and analysis. Finally, the meaning of reliability in the context of domain mastery or criterion-referenced testing is briefly considered.

1. The Classical Reliability Model

The classical reliability model views a test score as having two additive components, the "true" score and a random "error." The error is defined as unrelated to the true score and as unrelated to the error that would occur in another measurement of the same attribute. The true score is defined as the value that the average of repeated measurements with the identical measure approaches as the number of measurements is increased without limit. The term "identical" implies that it is possible to measure an individual repeatedly without changing that individual—a condition that obviously cannot be achieved in the real world. Though the model is in this respect and some others, an oversimplification and not a representation of reality, development of the model brings out a number of relationships that are instructive and useful in the design and construction of tests and in the evaluation of test scores.

1.1 Basic Assumptions and Resulting Relationships
The basic assumptions of the model are as follows:

(a) The obtained score is the sum of true score plus error; that is, $X_{obt} = X_{true} + X_{error}$. The subscripts o, t, and e will be used for observed score, true score, and error, respectively. The subscript x is used for the variance (s_x^2) of x_o.

(b) Over the population, error is independent of true score; that is, $r_{te} = 0$.

(c) In pairs of measures, the error in one measure is independent of the error in the other; that is, $r_{ee'} = 0$.

Given these assumptions, it can be concluded that, as the number of persons or the number of measurements increases, the mean error approaches 0 as a limit. That is, $\bar{X}_e \cong 0$ when the number of measures increases without limit. This follows from the definition of errors as *random* deviations from the true score that are equally likely to be positive or negative. Any consistent direction to "error" would be indistinguishable from, and hence assimilated as part of, the operational "true" score.

It follows that, in the limit, the mean of observed scores is equal to the mean of true scores; that is:

$$\bar{X}_o \cong \bar{X}_t \tag{1}$$

This relationship holds both for repeated measures of an individual and for the mean of a group. That is, as the number of observations increases, the observed mean approaches the mean of true scores and is an unbiased estimate of the true-score mean.

It is shown next that the variance of observed scores equals the true-score variance plus the error variance. Most of the development from here on will work with scores that are expressed as deviations from the mean; that is, $x = X - \bar{X}$.

$$s_x^2 = \frac{1}{N} \sum (x_t + x_e)^2$$

$$= \frac{1}{N} \sum (x_t^2 + x_e^2 + 2x_t x_e)$$

$$= \frac{1}{N} \sum x_t^2 + \frac{1}{N} \sum x_e^2 + \frac{2}{N} \sum x_t x_e$$

$$= s_t^2 + s_e^2 + 2 s_t s_e r_{te}$$

But by definition, $r_{te} = 0$, so

$$s_x^2 = s_t^2 + s_e^2 \tag{2}$$

It can also be shown that the correlation between two equivalent test forms is equal to the true-score variance divided by the observed variance; that is:

$$r_{xx'} = \frac{s_t^2}{s_x^2} \tag{3}$$

Thus the alternate-forms reliability of a test equals true-score variance divided by observed variance. From this it follows that $s_t^2 = s_x^2 r_{xx'}$ and $s_t = s_x \sqrt{[r_{xx'}]}$. The standard deviation of true scores can be estimated by multiplying the observed standard deviation by the square root of the reliability coefficient.

Returning to Eqn. (2) and transposing, gives $s_e^2 = s_x^2 - s_t^2$. But it has been seen that $s_t^2 = s_x^2 r_{xx'}$, so therefore $s_e^2 = s_x^2 - s_x^2 r_{xx'}$, or:

$$s_e = s_x \sqrt{1 - r_{xx'}} \tag{4}$$

Thus the standard error of measurement is estimated from the observed standard deviation and the alternate-forms reliability coefficient.

Next the correlation between observed score and true score, and the correlation between observed score and measurement error can be derived. Remembering that $x_o = x_t + x_e$,

$$r_{x_0 x_t} = \frac{\frac{1}{N} \sum (x_t + x_e) x_t}{s_x s_t}$$

$$= \frac{\frac{1}{N} \sum x_t^2 + \frac{1}{N} \sum x_t x_e}{s_x s_t}$$

But the second term in the numerator approaches zero because of the independence of true score and error. Hence

$$r_{x_0 x_t} = \frac{s_t^2}{s_x s_t} = \frac{s_t}{s_x} \tag{5}$$

Referring to Eqn. (3), it was found that $r_{xx'} = s_t^2 / s_x^2$ so $r_{x_0 x_t} = \sqrt{[r_{xx'}]}$. The correlation of an observed measure with the underlying true score is equal to the square root of the alternate-forms reliability coefficient.

Turning to observed score and error,

$$r_{x_0 x_e} = \frac{\dfrac{1}{N} \sum (x_t + x_e) x_e}{s_x s_e}$$

$$= \frac{\dfrac{1}{N} \sum x_t x_e + \dfrac{1}{N} \sum x_e^2}{s_x s_e}$$

Once again referring to the independence of true score and error, it can be seen that the first term of the numerator approaches 0, and

$$r_{x_0 x_e} = \frac{s_e^2}{s_x s_e} = \frac{s_e}{s_x}$$

But it can be seen from Eqn. (4) that $s_e/s_x = \sqrt{[1 - r_{xx'}]}$ and therefore $r_{x_e x_e} = \sqrt{[1 - r_{xx'}]}$. This correlation of observed score with error is a specific example of the more general expression $\sqrt{[1 - r_{xy'}]}$ which has been called the coefficient of alienation when predicting y from x.

1.2 Effects of Increasing or Decreasing Test Length

The discussion turns now to the effects of increasing (or decreasing) the length of a test, considering enroute the general expressions for the correlations of sums (and differences; a difference is, algebraically speaking, still a sum).

The equation for the mean of the unweighted sum of two or more variables is simply:

$$\text{Mean}_{(X_1 + X_2 + \cdots + X_k)} = \bar{X}_1 + \bar{X}_2 + \cdots + \bar{X}_k$$

Illustrating with the case of two variables, gives

$$\bar{X}_{(1+2)} = \frac{1}{N} \sum (X_1 + X_2)$$

$$= \frac{1}{N} \sum X_1 + \frac{1}{N} \sum X_2$$

$$= \bar{X}_1 + \bar{X}_2$$

If X_1 and X_2 are equivalent forms of the same test, each will have the same mean, because in each case the observed mean will equal the true-score mean, and one can write:

$$\text{Mean}_{2X} = 2(\text{Mean } X)$$

When the length of a test is doubled by adding equivalent items, the mean can be expected to double. More generally:

$$\text{Mean}_{kX} = k(\text{Mean } X)$$

If the variables are combined with different weights, we then get

$$\text{Mean}_{\text{wtd sum}} = \sum W_i \bar{X}_i \tag{6}$$

Turning now to the variance of a sum, gives:

$$s_{(x_1 + x_2)}^2 = \frac{1}{N} \sum (x_1 + x_2)^2$$

$$= \frac{1}{N} \sum x_1^2 + \frac{1}{N} \sum x_2^2 + \frac{2}{N} \sum x_1 x_2$$

$$= s_1^2 + s_2^2 + 2 s_1 s_2 r_{12}$$

Coming back to the situation of dealing with equivalent forms of the same test, the effect of doubling the length of the test will be investigated. One then has:

$$s_{(x + x')}^2 = s_x^2 + s_{x'}^2 + 2 r_{xx'} s_x s_{x'}$$

But because the test forms are equivalent, and so have the same standard deviation, this can be expressed as:

$$s_{(2x)}^2 = 2 s_x^2 + 2 r_{xx'} s_x^2$$

$$= s_x^2 (2 + 2 r_{xx'})$$

and

$$s_{2x} = s_x \sqrt{2 + 2 r_{xx'}} \tag{7}$$

In general terms, when the length of a test is increased by a factor of k, the variance can be expected to increase by a factor of $k + k(k - 1) r_{xx'}$, in which case $s_{kx} = s_x \sqrt{[k + k(k - 1) r_{xx'}]}$. The rate at which the standard deviation increases as the length is increased depends on the correlation between unit-length tests. At one limit, as the correlation approaches 0.00, the increase is proportional to $\sqrt{[k]}$. At the other, as the correlation approaches 1.00, the increase is proportional to k.

Though covariance and correlation between tests has been applied here, average interitem covariance or correlation could also be applied. The relationships developed between unit-length tests and longer tests also apply at the limit where the unit is a single item, and the k-length test is a test composed of k items.

What happens to the variance of true scores and to the variance of errors when the length of the test is doubled? Using Eqn. (7) and remembering that the correlation of true scores on alternate forms is 1.00, it can be seen that:

$$s_{(2t)}^2 = 2 s_t^2 + 2 r_{tt} s_t^2 = 4 s_t^2$$

$$s_{(2t)} = 2 s_t$$

For the variance of errors, remembering that the correlation of errors on alternate forms is by definition 0, one has:

$$s_{(2e)}^2 = 2 s_e^2 + 2 r_{ee'} s_e^2 = 2 s_e^2$$

$$s_{(2e)} = s_e \sqrt{2}$$

In the general case of increasing test length by a factor k,

$$s_{kt}^2 = k^2 s_t^2, \qquad s_{kt} = k s_t$$

and

$$s_{ke}^2 = k s_e^2, \qquad s_{ke} = s_e \sqrt{k}$$

Thus it can be seen that true-score variance increases as the square of test length, whereas error variance increases only as a linear function of test length. This relationship accounts for the progressively greater reliability of a test as its length is increased.

A variety of interesting relationships can be derived when the sum of variables $x_1 + x_2 + \cdots + x_m$ is correlated with the sum of variables $y_1 + y_2 + \cdots + y_n$. Consider first the case in which there is the same number of elements in each sum and in which all of both the x's and the y's represent equivalent forms of the same test. Then, if the tests are in fact equivalent, all the covariances will be equal, except for sampling fluctuations, and the same will be true of all the variances. It can be shown that:

$$r_{(1 \text{ to } m)(1 \text{ to } m)} = \frac{m\bar{r}_{ii'}}{1 + (m-1)\bar{r}_{ii'}} \tag{8}$$

This is the general form of the Spearman–Brown Prophecy Formula to estimate the reliability of a test the length of which has been increased by a factor of m. When $m = 2$, then

$$r_{2x} = \frac{2r_{xx'}}{1 + r_{xx'}} \tag{9}$$

This is the specific form for a double length test. It is most frequently encountered in adjusting a split-half reliability coefficient obtained by correlating score on odd-numbered items with score on even-numbered items to give the reliability of the complete test.

When all the x's are to be considered equivalent forms of one test and all the y's equivalent forms of another test, the correlation when one or both of the two tests are lengthened can be estimated. If both are lengthened, it can be shown that:

$$r_{(x_1 + \cdots + x_m)(y_1 + \cdots + y_n)}$$
$$= \frac{\bar{r}_{xy}}{\sqrt{\frac{1}{m} + \left(\frac{m-1}{m}\right)\bar{r}_{xx'}}\sqrt{\frac{1}{n} + \left(\frac{n-1}{n}\right)\bar{r}_{yy'}}} \tag{10}$$

For proofs of these relationships see Thorndike (1982).

This equation makes it possible to estimate what the effect would be on the correlation between any two variables, say a predictor test and some type of criterion measure, if more (or less) data were gathered for either or both. Suppose, for example, it had been found that the correlation between two forms of an aptitude test was 0.80, the correlation between two independently obtained supervisory ratings was 0.60, and the correlation of a single test with a single rating was 0.25. One might ask what the correlation would be between a test twice as long and the average of 5 ratings. As an estimate it would be found that:

$$r_{2x \cdot 5y} = \frac{0.25}{\sqrt{\frac{1}{2} + \frac{1}{2}(0.80)}\sqrt{\frac{1}{5} + \frac{4}{5}(0.60)}}$$
$$= \frac{0.25}{\sqrt{(0.90)(0.68)}} = \frac{0.25}{0.78}$$
$$= 0.32$$

If one of the tests, say x, remains of unit length while the length of the other is changed, then:

$$r_{x(y_1 + \cdots + y_n)} = \frac{\bar{r}_{xy}}{\sqrt{\frac{1}{n} + \frac{n-1}{n}r_{yy'}}}$$

If the length of y is now increased without limit, giving in effect the correlation between x and y_t, the true score on y, then:

$$r_{xy_\infty} = r_{xy_t} = \frac{r_{xy}}{\sqrt{r_{yy'}}}$$

Furthermore, if the length of both tests is allowed to increase without limit then:

$$r_{x_\infty y_\infty} = r_{x_t y_t} = \frac{r_{xy}}{\sqrt{(r_{xx'})(r_{yy'})}} \tag{11}$$

This is the general form of the correction for attenuation. It provides an estimate of the correlation between true scores on x and y, or measures that are of such a length that measurement errors are negligible. Taking the values from our previous illustration would give:

$$r_{x_t y_t} = \frac{0.25}{\sqrt{(0.80)(0.60)}} = \frac{0.25}{0.693} = 0.36$$

1.3 Problems in Defining True Score and Error

True score and error, of course, are not observables. Behavior samples are observed, and from these observations inferences about the constructs of "true score" and "error" are made. And the inferences that can legitimately be made depend on the nature of the samples of behavior that are observed.

The key point is that a universe has a dimension of *content* as well as one of trials or occasions and/or one of judges or appraisers, and variable performance arises in part from the extent of variation in the specific content in terms of which the universe is assessed. Content may be defined quite narrowly, as when all the words in a vocabulary test are drawn from a single area of knowledge such as biology, or broadly to cover the whole of a field. The universe may be defined solely in terms of content, or it may also be limited in terms of format—as when the measure of vocabulary consists only of words out of context presented in pairs, with the examinee to judge whether the members are synonyms or antonyms. As the definition of the universe is broadened, any single task or narrow sampling of tasks becomes less adequate to represent that universe. Thus any estimate of reliability for a testing procedure appropriately refers to its

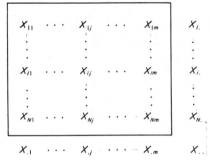

Figure 1
Two-dimensional matrix representing N examinees answering m questions.

precision as estimating some *particular* universe score, and it will depend as much on the definition of the universe as on the instrument.

2. Reliability Estimates and Variance Components

2.1 Error Variance

The classical definition of reliability was framed in terms of true score and error variance and took the form:

$$r_{xx'} = \frac{\sigma_t^2}{\sigma_t^2 + \sigma_e^2}$$

What is included under the heading "error variance" depends on how the universe that the test score is presumed to represent is defined, with certain sources of variance being treated as error under one definition of the universe and as true score under another. In theory, at least, an ideal set of data and an ideal analysis would be those that made it possible to estimate the magnitude of each possible component of variance, so that estimates could be made of the reliability of an instrument as representing universes defined in various ways, and so that the effectiveness of various alternative strategies for increasing the reliability of generalization to a particular universe score could be compared.

If the different facets that are likely to be sources of variation in the resulting score have been identified, the theoretically ideal data-gathering and data-analysis design for getting information about the sources of error in an instrument or procedure would seem to be that of a completely crossed multidimensional analysis of variance.

A two-dimensional illustration is shown in Fig. 1. Suppose that each of N examinees has written answers to m test questions. Each answer has been evaluated by the same single reader. One then has an $N \times m$ data matrix that can be represented by the entries in the box The border entries represent summations, where a subscript of a dot ($\cdot$) indicates summation over that facet. In this matrix, each row represents a person and $X_{i.}$ is the sum over questions for person i, whereas each column represents a question and $X_{.j}$ represents the sum

over all persons for question j. The usual computations for analysis of variance (see Winer 1971, for example) is:

$$\text{Total sum of squares} = \sum_1^N \sum_1^m (X_{ij})^2 - (X_{..})^2/mN$$

$$\text{Persons sum of squares} = \frac{1}{m}\sum_1^N (X_{i.})^2 - (X_{..})^2/mN$$

$$\text{Questions sum of squares} = \frac{1}{N}\sum_1^m (X_{.j})^2 - (X_{..})^2/mN$$

$$\text{Residual sum of squares} =$$
$$\text{(Total SS} - \text{persons SS} - \text{questions SS)} \quad (12)$$

and then

$$\text{Persons mean square} = \frac{\text{(persons sum of squares)}}{(N-1)}$$

$$\text{Questions mean square} = \frac{\text{(questions sum of squares)}}{(m-1)}$$

$$\text{Residual mean square} = \frac{\text{(residual sum of squares)}}{[(N-1)(m-1)]} \quad (13)$$

A numerical illustration is shown in Table 1, in which each of a group of six examinees responded to the same set of four questions. All were evaluated by one exam reader.

The precision of the scores that result from a test composed of a set of m questions can now be investigated. Note that the only facet of the domain that can be studied is that of questions rated by a single rater. There is no evidence on the variability that would be introduced if the examinees were tested on different occasions or if the questions were rated by different judges. To obtain evidence on these facets, they would have to be systematically introduced into the data-gathering and data-analysis design.

Table 1
A numerical illustration of six examinees responding to a set of four questions

Examinees	Questions 1	2	3	4	Sum
1	9	6	6	2	23
2	9	5	4	0	18
3	8	9	5	8	30
4	7	6	5	4	22
5	7	3	2	3	15
6	10	8	7	7	32
Sum	50	37	29	24	140

$\Sigma(X_{ij})^2 = 972$ $\Sigma(X_{i.})^2 = 3486$
$\Sigma(X_{.j})^2 = 5286$ $(X_{..})^2 = 19{,}600$

Total SS = $972 - 19{,}600/24 = 155.3$
Examinees SS = $3486/4 - 19{,}600/24 = 54.8$
Questions SS = $5286/6 - 19{,}600/24 = 64.3$
Residual SS = $155.3 - 54.8 - 64.3 = 36.2$
Examinees MS = $54.8/5 = 10.96$
Questions MS = $64.3/3 = 21.43$
Residual MS = $36.2/(3 \times 5) = 2.41$

In this context, the usual situation is that all examinees respond to the same questions. When that is the case, "questions" becomes a fixed condition, does not vary, and consequently introduces no variance. Then the only source of error variance is the residual term: the interaction between persons and questions—that is, the fact that each examinee does better on some questions and worse on others than would be expected in light of that person's average performance and the difficulty of a given question for all examinees. The *observed* variance among persons includes both "true" between-persons variance and error, so we must subtract the error, to get an estimate of σ_t^2. Thus, $\sigma_t^2 =$ examinees MS $-$ residual MS, and hence:

$$\text{Reliability} = \frac{\text{examinees MS} - \text{residual MS}}{\text{examinees MS}} \quad (14)$$

In the illustrative example presented in Table 1, this becomes:

$$\text{Reliability} = \frac{10.96 - 2.41}{10.96} = 0.78$$

and the standard error of measurement is $\sqrt{2.41} = 1.55$.

The foregoing estimate applies to the total score, in this example the score based on four questions. It is also possible to estimate the average error variance and the average reliability of a single element, in this illustration the response to a single question. The relationships are as follows:

$$\sigma_E^2 = \frac{\text{residual MS}}{m}$$

Reliability =

$$\frac{\text{examinees MS} - \text{residual MS}}{\text{examinees MS} + (m-1) \text{ residual MS}} \quad (15)$$

For the illustrative example being considered, the values come out:

$$\sigma_E^2 = \frac{2.41}{4} = 0.60$$

$$\text{Reliability} = \frac{10.96 - 2.41}{10.96 + 3(2.41)} = 0.47$$

and the standard error of measurement equals $\sqrt{[0.60]} = 0.77$. Naturally, a score based on just a single question provides a much less accurate estimate of the universe score than one based on the pooling of a number of questions.

It is possible, of course, that questions are not uniform across examinees, and that it is not known which, from a pool of possible questions, a given examinee is going to encounter. If that is so, and the questions vary from examinee to examinee, "questions" variance becomes part of error and must be so treated. There are then only two distinguishable components, examinees and residual, in which case:

$$\text{Total SS} = \sum\sum (X_{ij})^2 - (X_{..})^2/mN$$

$$\text{Persons SS} = \frac{1}{m}\sum (X_{i.})^2 - (X_{..})^2/mN$$

$$\text{Residual SS} = \text{total SS} - \text{persons SS}$$

$$\text{Persons MS} = \frac{\text{persons SS}}{N-1}$$

$$\text{Residual MS} = \frac{\text{residual SS}}{N(m-1)}$$

Applying these relationships to the illustrative example considered here, gives

$$\text{Examinees SS} = 54.8$$

$$\text{Residual SS} = 100.5$$

$$\text{Examinees MS} = \frac{54.8}{5} = 10.96$$

$$\text{Residual MS} = \frac{100.5}{18} = 5.58$$

$$\text{Reliability of total score} = \frac{10.96 - 5.58}{10.96} = 0.49$$

$$\text{Reliability of single item} = \frac{10.96 - 5.58}{10.96 + 3(5.58)} = 0.19$$

The reduction in reliability is quite dramatic in this example—and rightly so, because the questions obviously differed widely in their mean score for this group of examinees.

The approach to reliability through analysis of the facets of variance can be quite instructive, as the example brings out. It indicates in this case that a great deal of precision will be lost if different examinees are given different questions. However, for this conclusion to be dependable, it is important that the sample of questions be representative of the universe of admissible questions. Of course, if the estimate of examinee variance is to be meaningful, it is also important that the sample of examinees be representative of the population of examinees to which one wants to generalize. However, research workers in general and test makers in particular are used to worrying about their sample of persons. The point is that if estimates are to be made about the size of effects from varying any other facet of the situation, *equal attention must be devoted to sampling from the other facet*. It may be desirable to have as large a sample from the facet of questions, or of raters or of observation periods, as from the facet of persons.

2.2 The General Multifacet Model

In the illustration considered so far only one facet of the domain was varied—the facet represented by questions. Table 2 illustrates a two-facet problem. Suppose that each of the questions had also been read by a second reader and that this reader had assigned scores as shown on the right below. (The scores assigned by the first reader are repeated on the left.)

Table 2
A two-facet problem representing six examinees responding
to a set of four questions evaluated by two readers

	First reader				Second reader				Sum		
Question	1	2	3	4	1	2	3	4				
Examinee									First reader	Second reader	Both readers
1	9	6	6	2	8	2	8	1	23	19	42
2	9	5	4	0	7	5	9	5	18	26	44
3	8	9	5	8	10	6	9	10	30	35	65
4	7	6	5	4	9	8	9	4	22	30	52
5	7	3	2	3	7	4	5	1	15	17	32
6	10	8	7	7	7	7	10	9	32	33	65
Sum	50	37	29	24	48	32	50	30	140	160	300

Item sum for both readers 98 69 79 54

The actual scores on single questions are enclosed in
the two boxes. The sums over questions and over questions and readers are shown at the right. The sums over
examinees and over examinees and readers are shown at
the foot of the table.

The raw material is now available for a three-way
analysis of variance allowing the possibility of obtaining
estimates of seven distinct components of variance. If
the facet that is represented by raters is designated k, the
sums are as follows:

$$\sum_i \sum_j \sum_k (X_{ijk})^2 = 2{,}214 \quad \text{squares of single observations}$$

$$\sum_j \sum_k (X_{.jk})^2 = 12{,}014 \quad \text{squares of sums over persons}$$

$$\sum_i \sum_k (X_{i.k})^2 = 8{,}026 \quad \text{squares of sums over questions}$$

$$\sum_i \sum_j (X_{ij.})^2 = 4{,}258 \quad \text{squares of sums over readers}$$

$$\sum_j (X_{.j.})^2 = 23{,}522 \quad \text{squares of sums over both persons and readers}$$

$$\sum_k (X_{..k})^2 = 45{,}200 \quad \text{squares of sums over both persons and questions}$$

$$\sum_i (X_{i..})^2 = 15{,}878 \quad \text{squares of sums over both questions and readers}$$

$$(X_{...})^2 = 90{,}000 \quad \text{square of grand sum}$$

From these sums, the sum of squares associated with
each component can be derived.

$$\text{Total sum of squares} = 2214 - \frac{90{,}000}{48} = 339.0$$

$$\text{Persons sum of squares} = \frac{15{,}878}{8} - \frac{90{,}000}{48} = 109.8$$

$$\text{Questions sum of squares} = \frac{23{,}522}{12} - \frac{90{,}000}{48} = 85.2$$

$$\text{Readers sum of squares} = \frac{45{,}200}{24} - \frac{90{,}000}{48} = 8.3$$

$$P \times Q = \frac{4258}{2} - \frac{90{,}000}{48} - 109.8 - 85.2 = 59.0$$

$$P \times R = \frac{8026}{4} - \frac{90{,}000}{48} - 109.8 - 8.3 = 13.4$$

$$Q \times R = \frac{12{,}014}{6} - \frac{90{,}000}{48} - 85.2 - 8.3 = 33.8$$

$$P \times Q \times R = 339.0 - (109.8 + 85.2 + 8.3 + 59.0$$
$$+ 13.4 + 33.8) = 29.5$$

The mean squares for each of the seven components,
can now be derived by dividing by the number of
degrees of freedom, as shown in Table 3.

It is now possible to estimate the seven variance components. To do this, it must be noted that each mean
square at a given level already includes, within itself,
variance represented in the higher levels of interaction.
That is, the persons-by-questions mean square includes
a contribution from persons × questions × readers, and
the persons mean square includes contributions from
persons × questions and from persons × readers. It
must also be noted that the mean squares represent the
values that attach to a sum of several observations. For
example, the mean square for persons is a sum over four
questions each read by two readers. If the variance component for a single observation is wanted, the given
value must be divided by the number of observations on
which it is based.

Taking these two points into account gives the following set of equations from which the variance components can be determined:

Table 3
Data matrix of mean squares

Source	Sum of squares	Degrees of freedom	Mean square
Persons	109.8	5	21.96
Questions	85.2	3	28.40
Readers	8.3	1	8.30
$P \times Q$	59.0	15	3.93
$P \times R$	13.4	5	2.68
$Q \times R$	33.8	3	11.27
$P \times Q \times R$	29.5	15	1.97

$$\sigma_{pqr}^2 = \mathrm{MS}_{pqr}$$

$$\sigma_{pq}^2 = \frac{1}{n_r}(\mathrm{MS}_{pq} - \mathrm{MS}_{pqr})$$

$$\sigma_{pr}^2 = \frac{1}{n_q}(\mathrm{MS}_{pr} - \mathrm{MS}_{pqr})$$

$$\sigma_{qr}^2 = \frac{1}{n_p}(\mathrm{MS}_{qr} - \mathrm{MS}_{pqr})$$

$$\sigma_p^2 = \frac{1}{n_q n_r}(\mathrm{MS}_p - \mathrm{MS}_{pq} - \mathrm{MS}_{pr} + \mathrm{MS}_{pqr})$$

$$\sigma_q^2 = \frac{1}{n_p n_r}(\mathrm{MS}_q - \mathrm{MS}_{pq} - \mathrm{MS}_{qr} + \mathrm{MS}_{pqr})$$

$$\sigma_r^2 = \frac{1}{n_p n_q}(\mathrm{MS}_r - \mathrm{MS}_{pr} - \mathrm{MS}_{qr} + \mathrm{MS}_{pqr}) \qquad (16)$$

In this problem the values become:

$$\sigma_{pqr}^2 = 1.97$$

$$\sigma_{pq}^2 = \tfrac{1}{2}(3.93 - 1.97) = 0.98$$

$$\sigma_{pr}^2 = \tfrac{1}{4}(2.68 - 1.97) = 0.18$$

$$\sigma_{qr}^2 = \tfrac{1}{6}(11.27 - 1.97) = 1.55$$

$$\sigma_p^2 = \tfrac{1}{8}(21.96 - 3.93 - 2.68 + 1.97) = 2.16$$

$$\sigma_q^2 = \tfrac{1}{12}(28.40 - 3.93 - 11.27 + 1.97) = 1.26$$

$$\sigma_r^2 = \tfrac{1}{24}(8.30 - 2.68 - 11.27 + 1.97) < 0$$

The values for the seven components of variance provide estimates of how important the various facets will be in producing variation in the estimates of a given examinee's ability. These values are worth examining with some care.

First, note that the estimate for readers is less than zero. Of course, variation less than zero is meaningless. What this value points out is that it is, after all, *estimates* that are being dealt with. These estimates may in some cases fall above the universe value and in some cases below. Furthermore, the estimates are often (and certainly in our data) based on a small number of degrees of freedom and are correspondingly unstable. There were only two readers. It happened that these two were similar in the overall severity of their grading standards (though they differed rather markedly in their severity on *specific* questions), and when account was taken of the interactions of readers with questions and with examinees, the residual contribution of readers per se appeared to be nil.

The result on readers points out the need, in studies of the importance of different variance components, to sample adequately from each of the facets—in this case examinees, questions, and readers. Practical realities often make it difficult to get as large or as well-designed a sample from such facets as test tasks, evaluators, and occasions as the sample of examinees, but the need is as great in the one case as in the other.

Returning to the list of variance components, it should be noted with satisfaction that the largest single component is that for persons (or examinees). This is the component that represents "true score" or "universe score" and is of primary interest in this assessment. The next largest component is that designated σ_{pqr}^2. This should more accurately be labeled $\sigma_{pqr}^2 + \sigma_\epsilon^2$, because it incorporates both the second-order interaction of person × question × reader and the random "error" in its purest form. With only one observation in each $p \times q \times r$ cell of Table 3, it is impossible to separate these two elements. In most instances it will happen that at the highest level of interaction there *will* be only a single observation, so that "error" and this highest interaction will be confounded.

The next three components, in order of size, are question-by-reader interaction (1.55), questions (1.26), and person-by-question interaction (0.98). All these involve the sampling of questions, and collectively they indicate that the particular set of questions included in the test is a very potent determiner of the score that a given examinee will achieve. From the viewpoint of a strategy for accurate measurement, the size of these components indicates that it will be important (a) for all examinees to answer the same questions and (b) for the number of questions to be large.

The importance of the different variance components can be seen more clearly if the "coefficient of reproducibility," (the ratio of expected true score or universe variance to expected observed variance) is calculated. Universe variance for score that is the sum of observations on n_q questions, each rated by n_r readers, is given by:

$$\sigma_{\mathrm{true}}^2 = (n_q n_r)^2 \sigma_p^2$$

where σ_p^2 is the estimate of the *persons* variance component. This follows from the formula given in Sect. 1.2, because to add questions and readers is in effect to increase the length of the behavior sample. The expected observed variance is given by:

$$\sigma_{\mathrm{obs}}^2 - (n_q n_r)(n_q n_r \sigma_p^2 + n_q \sigma_r^2 + n_r \sigma_q^2 + n_q \sigma_{pr}^2$$
$$+ n_r \sigma_{pq}^2 + \sigma_{qr}^2 + \sigma_{pqr}^2) \qquad (17)$$

With appropriate divisions in both numerator and denominator, the coefficient of generalizability becomes:

$$\frac{\sigma_{\mathrm{true}}^2}{\sigma_{\mathrm{obs}}^2} = \frac{\sigma_p^2}{\sigma_p^2 + \dfrac{\sigma_q^2}{n_q} + \dfrac{\sigma_r^2}{n_r} + \dfrac{\sigma_{pq}^2}{n_q} + \dfrac{\sigma_{pr}^2}{n_r} + \dfrac{\sigma_{qr}^2}{n_q n_r} + \dfrac{\sigma_{pqr}^2}{n_q n_r}} \qquad (18)$$

Using the data derived from Table 3, this gives:

$$\frac{\sigma_{\mathrm{true}}^2}{\sigma_{\mathrm{obs}}^2} = \frac{2.16}{2.16 + \dfrac{1.26}{4} + \dfrac{0}{2} + \dfrac{0.98}{4} + \dfrac{0.18}{2} + \dfrac{1.55}{8} + \dfrac{1.97}{8}}$$

$$r_{xx'} = \frac{2.16}{3.25} = 0.66$$

This coefficient is an estimate of the correlation that would be obtained between two sets of scores for a group of examinees, when each examinee is tested with a random set of four questions chosen independently for that examinee and rated by a random two readers also chosen independently for each examinee.

Looking only at the denominator, the source of most of the "error variance" becomes evident. Thus:

$$\sigma^2_{\text{obs}} = 2.16 + \left(\underset{p}{\frac{0.32}{}} + \underset{q}{0} + \underset{r}{\frac{0.24}{}} + \underset{pq}{\frac{0.09}{}} + \underset{pr}{\frac{0.19}{}} + \underset{qr}{\frac{0.25}{}}\right)$$

It can be seen that the largest components of the error variance, in order of size, are questions (0.32); the interaction of persons, questions, and readers (0.25); and the interaction of persons and questions (0.24). The strategy for reducing all these would be to increase the number of questions. This would increase the divisors in the largest terms of the denominator of Eqn. (18)—and hence would reduce those largest terms and increase the precision of the resulting score. If the number of questions were doubled, this would give

$$\sigma^2_{\text{obs}} = 2.16 + (0.16 + 0 + 0.12 + 0.09 + 0.10 + 0.12)$$

$$= 2.75$$

$$r_{xx'} = \frac{2.16}{2.75} = 0.79$$

By contrast, if the number of readers were doubled without any change in the number of questions, this would give:

$$\sigma^2_{\text{obs}} = 2.16 + (0.32 + 0 + 0.24 + 0.04 + 0.10 + 0.12)$$

$$= 2.98$$

$$r_{xx'} = \frac{2.16}{2.98} = 0.72$$

and the gain in precision would be a good deal less.

2.3 Nonrandom Questions and Readers

Up to this point, it has been assumed that both the questions facet and the readers facet have been sampled at random, such that a given examinee could have any four questions drawn from the universe of admissible questions rated by any two readers drawn from the universe of admissible readers. It is a good deal more common for the set of questions (and possibly the readers) to be the same for all examinees. If the set of questions will be uniform for all examinees, the variance component associated with questions (σ^2_q) disappears, which gives:

$$\sigma^2_{\text{obs}} = 2.16 + (0.24 + 0.09 + 0.19 + 0.25) = 2.93$$

$$r_{xx'} = \frac{2.16}{2.93} = 0.74$$

Naturally enough, an estimate of a person's standing in the group is appreciably more precise when it is known that all members of the group will take the same test. If it is *also* known that the readers will be the same for all examinees, two other variance components (σ^2_r and σ^2_{qr}) drop out of the observed variance, leaving:

$$\sigma^2_{\text{obs}} = \sigma^2_p + \frac{\sigma^2_{pq}}{n_q} + \frac{\sigma^2_{pr}}{n_r} + \frac{\sigma^2_{pqr}}{n_q n_r}. \tag{19}$$

For the data given this becomes:

$$\sigma^2_{\text{obs}} = 2.16 + (0.24 + 0.09 + 0.25) = 2.74$$

$$r_{xx'} = \frac{2.16}{2.74} = 0.79$$

Thus, in the illustrative example considered here, keeping the questions and readers uniform for all examinees raises the true-score variance, as a percentage of the total, from 66 to 79.

It is also possible that one may be interested only in a *specific set* of test questions, considering these to be the universe to which it is wished to generalize. The questions facet then becomes a *fixed* facet, rather than one that is sampled randomly from some larger universe. Considering a certain facet to be fixed has two effects: (a) the interaction between persons and that fixed facet, σ^2_{pq} in the illustration under consideration, is treated as a component of true score rather than error; (b) the component associated with that fixed facet (σ^2_q) disappears. Thus

$$\sigma^2_{\text{true}} = \sigma^2_p + \frac{\sigma^2_{pq}}{n_q}$$

$$\sigma^2_{\text{obs}} = \left(\sigma^2_p + \frac{\sigma^2_{pq}}{n_q}\right) + \left(\frac{\sigma^2_r}{n_r} + \frac{\sigma^2_{pr}}{n_r} + \frac{\sigma^2_{qr}}{n_q n_r} + \frac{\sigma^2_{pqr}}{n_q n_r}\right)$$

$$\sigma^2_{\text{true}} = 2.16 + 0.24 = 2.40$$

$$\sigma^2_{\text{obs}} = 2.40 + (0 + 0.09 + 0.19 + 0.25) = 2.93$$

$$r_{xx'} = 0.82$$

If there were interest in generalizing only to this set of questions as appraised by these specific readers, this could be shown by:

$$\sigma^2_{\text{true}} = 2.16 + 0.24 + 0.09 = 2.49$$

$$\sigma^2_{\text{obs}} = 2.49 + 0.25 = 2.74$$

$$r_{xx'} = 0.91$$

2.4 Confounding of Variance Components

In all of these analyses, the situation has been one in which the design for *collection* of the original data was completely "crossed"—that is, every examinee answered every question and every response was evaluated by every rater. Collection of the original data in this format has very real advantages in that it allows for the generation of estimates (though somewhat fragile ones because of small *n*'s for some of the facets) of *all* the variance components. However, it may not always be possible to gather such data. Thus the readers might vary from one examinee to another and it might not be known which reader had read a particular examinee's paper. It might only be known that two from a sizable universe of readers had read a given paper. In this case, the reader is said to be "nested within persons." When it is not known which readers have read a given examinee's paper, certain of the variance components become confounded and cannot be separated from one another.

Table 4
Analysis of confounded variance components

Component	Sum of squares	Number of degrees of freedom	Mean square
P	109.8	5	21.96
Q	85.2	3	28.40
$(R, P \times R)$	$8.3 + 13.4$	6	3.62
$P \times Q$	59.0	15	3.93
$(Q \times R, P \times Q \times R)$	$33.8 + 29.5$	18	3.52

Specifically, reader variance (σ_r^2) cannot be separated from the interaction between reader and examinee (σ_{pr}^2), because information for a particular pair of readers can be identified only within the data for a single examinee. Similarly, σ_{qr}^2 and σ_{pqr}^2 cannot be separated. Thus the only identifiable variance components are, σ_p^2, σ_q^2, σ_{pq}^2, $(\sigma_r^2, \sigma_{pr}^2)$, and $(\sigma_{qr}^2, \sigma_{pqr}^2)$. Table 4 shows how the data for our illustrative problem are analyzed.

It should be noted that both the sum of squares and the number of degrees of freedom collapse for the two components that are confounded and cannot be separated.

The analysis of variance components also reduces to just the five that can be isolated. Thus:

$$\sigma_{qr, pqr}^2 = \mathrm{MS}(Q \times R, P \times Q \times R)$$

$$\sigma_{pq}^2 = \frac{1}{n_r}[\mathrm{MS}(P \times Q) - \mathrm{MS}(Q \times R, P \times Q \times R)]$$

$$\sigma_{r, pr}^2 = \frac{1}{n_q}[\mathrm{MS}(R, P \times R)$$
$$- \mathrm{MS}(Q \times R, P \times Q \times R)]$$

$$\sigma_q^2 = \frac{1}{n_p n_r}[\mathrm{MS}(Q) - \mathrm{MS}(P \times Q)]$$

$$\sigma_p^2 = \frac{1}{n_q n_r}[\mathrm{MS}(P) - \mathrm{MS}(P \times Q) - \mathrm{MS}(R, P \times R)$$
$$+ \mathrm{MS}(Q \times R, P \times Q \times R)] \tag{20}$$

For the data of the example shown in Table 4, this becomes:

$$\sigma_{qr, pqr}^2 = 3.52$$
$$\sigma_{pq}^2 = \tfrac{1}{2}(3.93 - 3.52) = 0.20$$
$$\sigma_{r, qr}^2 = \tfrac{1}{4}(3.62 - 3.52) = 0.02$$
$$\sigma_q^2 = \tfrac{1}{12}(28.40 - 3.93) = 2.04$$
$$\sigma_p^2 = \tfrac{1}{8}(21.96 - 3.93 - 3.62 + 3.52) = 2.24$$

The analyses of true score and observed variances parallel the development previously given, except that the confounding prevents the testing of some of the models. Thus, for generalization to a situation in which each examinee is tested with a random set of four questions drawn from the universe of admissible questions:

$$\sigma_{\text{true}}^2 = 2.24$$
$$\sigma_{\text{obs}}^2 = 2.24 + \left(\frac{2.04}{4} + \frac{0.02}{2} + \frac{0.20}{4} + \frac{3.52}{8}\right)$$
$$= 2.24 + (0.51 + 0.01 + 0.05 + 0.44) = 3.25$$
$$r_{xx'} = \frac{2.24}{3.25} = 0.69$$

If it were known that all examinees would have the same questions, then:

$$\sigma_{\text{obs}}^2 = 2.24 + (0.01 + 0.05 + 0.44) = 2.74$$
$$r_{xx'} = \frac{2.24}{2.74} = 0.82$$

If, however, there were interest only in generalizing to a universe of scores on these specific questions, then the following could be derived:

$$\sigma_{\text{true}}^2 = 2.24 + 0.05 = 2.29$$
$$r_{xx'} = \frac{2.29}{2.74} = 0.84$$

The effects of uniform readers or a universe of only specified readers cannot be analyzed because the required variance components involving readers are confounded.

It is even conceivable that both questions and readers could be confounded with persons (though it is unlikely that data would be gathered in this form). This would occur if all that was known was that, in the original analysis of the test, each examinee had taken *some* form of a test composed of four questions and that each person's paper had been read by *some* pair of readers. Confounding then becomes complete, and all that can be isolated are between-persons and within-persons components of variance, as shown in Table 5.

Table 5
Analysis of completely confounded variance components

Component	Sum of squares	Number of degrees of freedom	Mean square
p	109.8	5	21.96
Within p	229.2	42	5.46

$$\sigma_p^2 = \frac{1}{m_q n_r} [MS(p) - MS(\text{within})]$$

$$= \tfrac{1}{8}(16.50) = 2.06$$

$$\sigma_{\text{obs}}^2 = 2.06 + \frac{5.46}{8} = 2.06 + 0.68 = 2.74$$

$$r_{xx'} = \frac{2.06}{2.74} = 0.74$$

The estimate is that, for a randomly chosen four-question test read by two randomly chosen readers, 74% of the variance is true-score or universe variance of persons and the other 26% is contributed by the composite of all other components. No further analysis of the situation is possible. This value may be compared with the 66% found in Sect. 2.2, which results from the variance components of the completely crossed data. That the agreement is not better than this must be attributed to the small number of degrees of freedom underlying several of the specific variance components.

This two-facet illustration of the variance-components approach to analysis of reliability and the precision of measurement has been discussed in some detail, because it serves to exhibit both the logic and the empirical possibilities of the method. The same type of approach is possible with three or more varied facets, but the number of variance components approximately doubles each time a facet is added. In such multifacet studies, obtaining the full set of completely crossed data becomes quite an undertaking. Furthermore, obtaining samples of adequate size and of suitable randomness for each facet can present serious practical difficulties.

The variance-components model is one into which practically all the conventional procedures for gathering data on reliability can be fitted, and understanding any procedure is enhanced by seeing how it handles the several components of variance. The simplest procedure is to test each examinee with two forms of a test, giving everyone form A followed by form B—either immediately or at some later date. It has then been the usual procedure to compute the correlation between form A and form B. This is a single-facet problem, but the facet is a compound one that could be designated test-form-confounded-with-order. Thus there are three variance components: (a) persons, (b) test-form-and-order, and (c) the interaction of components (a) and (b). Component (b) shows up as a difference between mean scores on the two forms and does not influence the correlation, because product-moment correlations are based on deviations from the respective group means. Thus,

$$r_{AB} = \frac{\sigma_{\text{persons}}^2}{\sigma_{\text{persons}}^2 + [\sigma_{(\text{persons} \times \text{forms})}^2]/2]}$$

(One divides by 2 because the persons-by-forms components is based on two forms.)

Coefficient alpha (α) (Cronbach 1951) and its special case, Kuder–Richardson Formula 20, are also single-facet approaches in which analysis is carried out at the item level. Thus, in the case under consideration there is:

(a) a between-persons variance component, (b) a between-items component, and (c) an interaction-of-persons-with-items component. Once again, items are thought of as a fixed effect. The results from this analysis can be shown to be algebraically equivalent to coefficient alpha, computed by the equation:

$$\alpha = \frac{n}{n-1} \left(1 - \frac{\sum_{i=1}^{m} s_i^2}{s_x^2} \right) \tag{21}$$

where s_i^2 is the variance of item i and s_x^2 is the variance of test x.

If a test is appreciably speeded and there are a number of students who do not have time to attempt a number of items then coefficient alpha tends to become meaningless. Furthermore, in the persons-by-items data matrix, there are a number of empty cells. In effect one assigns a value of zero to each of these empty cells, but it is done in the absence of data. The series of zeros for a given examinee produces a kind of spurious consistency in his or her scores on the later items and consequently inflates to some degree the estimate of the reliability coefficient.

3. Reliability with Conventional Data-collection Strategies

Carrying out a systematic analysis of variance components is the most instructive way to obtain a complete understanding of the sources of error in a measurement procedure. However, collecting the data for such a complete analysis is rarely practical and perhaps not really necessary. The circumstances of life usually *do* make it possible (a) to give two presumably equivalent forms of a test and study the correlation between the resulting two sets of scores, (b) to give the same test form on two separate occasions and study the correlation between the results from the two testings, or (c) to give a single test form consisting of several sections or a number of items and study the consistency of performance over the sections or items. Much of the evidence on test reliability stems from one or another of these procedures.

The foregoing procedures permit the allocation to error of only certain components of variance. Consequently each provides a somewhat different and a somewhat limited definition of the universe being sampled by the test. However, each offers some information about the generalizability from a testing procedure.

3.1 Reliability Estimated from Equivalent Forms

If two equivalent forms of a test are administered (forms that are measures of the same latent attribute and that can both be expected to measure it with the same precision), the correlation between them serves as an estimate of the reliability coefficient. That is, it can be shown that, if the foregoing conditions hold,

$$r_{12} = \frac{\sigma_{\text{true}}^2}{\sigma_{\text{observed}}^2} = \frac{\sigma_{\text{true}}^2}{\sigma_{\text{true}}^2 + \sigma_{\text{error}}^2}$$

The value obtained for this coefficient is critically dependent on the heterogeneity of the group to which the two forms are administered—that is, on the size of σ^2_{true}. For this reason, an estimate of the error variance or of its square root, called the standard error of measurement, is often a more serviceable statistic. It is a good deal less sensitive to the range of talent in the sample on which the reliability estimate is based. This standard error of measurement is given by $\sigma_{\text{meas}} = \sigma_{\text{obs}}\sqrt{[1 - r_{xx'}]}$.

So far the error variance has been treated as though it kept the same value at all levels of the latent attribute. Of course, this is not necessarily the case. A test often measures more accurately within certain limits on the latent attribute than it does at other points; the location of higher accuracy depends on the way in which the items that compose the final test were chosen. The standard error of measurement, estimated from the correlation between two forms of a test, is a kind of pooled overall estimate of precision, an estimate that is often better replaced by estimates at each of a number of different score levels. A procedure for obtaining those estimates is provided by Thorndike (1982).

3.2 Reliability Estimated from Retesting

As indicated above, an alternative data-gathering strategy is to use one specific measure of a latent attribute and to repeat the identical measure after an interval. This is a reasonable strategy if (a) all test exercises are so similar in content or function that any one sample of exercises is equivalent to any other and (b) the exercises are so numerous and/or nondescript that, at the second testing, there will be little or no memory of the responses given on the initial testing. Specific memory will, of course, become less and less of a problem as the interval between the two testings is lengthened. However, as the time interval is lengthened, the variation from one testing to the other reflects in increasing proportion the impact of intervening experiences or of differential rates of growth. The variation then becomes, in increasing proportion, an indicator of instability of the underlying attribute over a time span, rather than of lack of precision in the measuring instrument.

The standard error of measurement at each score level can appropriately be obtained from retesting with the identical test. It now provides information about the consistency with which persons at different ability levels respond to the test tasks. The difference in mean score between the first and second testing constitutes a variance component reflecting some mixture of practice effect and growth between the two testings. The two are not separable, but the relative importance of each can be inferred at least crudely from the length of the interval between testings.

3.3 Reliability Estimated from Internal Consistency

The third data-collecting strategy relies on the internal analysis of a single test administration. This has very great practical advantages, because (a) it requires development of only a single form of the test and (b) cooperation of examinees is required for only a single period of testing. These practical advantages have led test makers and research workers to use procedures of internal analysis frequently, in spite of their fairly severe theoretical limitations. One limitation is, of course, that all testing is done within a single brief period, so that no evidence can be obtained on diurnal variability—changes in individual performance from one occasion to the next. Another limitation is that the estimates of reliability become more and more inflated as the test is speeded. This issue will be discussed further after the basic procedures have been set forth.

The early procedure for extracting reliability estimates from a single administration of a test form was to divide the test items into equivalent fractions, usually two equivalent halves, and obtain two separate scores—one for each fraction. The correlations between the sets of scores were then obtained and were corrected by the Spearman–Brown Prophecy Formula to give an estimate of the reliability coefficient for the full-length test. As indicated in Sect. 1.2, when the test is divided into halves, the correction formula becomes:

$$r_{11} = \frac{2r_{1/2\,1/2}}{1 + r_{1/2\,1/2}}$$

When items are numerous and arranged either by subarea or in order of gradually increasing difficulty (or by increasing difficulty within subareas), putting alternate items into alternate test forms has often seemed a sound strategy for achieving equivalence: hence the odd–even correlations often reported. An investigator or test maker must decide in each case whether this or some other procedure is the most reasonable way to define equivalent halves for the instrument she or he is studying.

In recent years, those extracting reliability estimates from a single test administration have tended increasingly to base the estimates on analysis of variance approaches, in which single items constitute the units on which the analysis is based. The analysis is built on the assumption that all items are measures of the same underlying attribute—that is, that the test is homogeneous in content. For this reason, when a test is composed of two or more diverse subtests, it is usually necessary to apply the analysis to each subtest separately and then to use a formula for the correlation of sums to estimate the reliability of the total. Analysis of variance procedures do not depend on any particular choice in subdividing the items, and they approximate an average of all the possible correlations that might have been obtained by different ways of assigning items to alternate forms. When the assumption of homogeneity of function measured is justified, this would appear to be the most objective way to determine consistency across the items of the test.

The most general form of the analysis of item variance is provided by Cronbach's coefficient alpha

(Cronbach 1951), the formula for which is:

$$\alpha = \frac{n}{n-1}\left(1 - \frac{\sum s_i^2}{s_t^2}\right) \tag{22}$$

where n is the number of items in the test, s_i^2 is the variance of item i, and s_t^2 is the variance of the total test. This expression is quite general in its application. It will handle test exercises in which score can take a range of values, as in essay tests or in inventories that provide multiple levels of response. It can even be applied when the "items" are themselves groups of test exercises.

When all the items are scored either 0 or 1, coefficient alpha reduces to the form reported earlier by Kuder and Richardson (1937) and known as Kuder–Richardson Formula 20. It is:

$$\text{Reliability} = \frac{n}{n-1}\left(1 - \frac{\sum p_i q_i}{s_t^2}\right) \tag{23}$$

A lower-bounds estimate of this value, which is exact if all items are of the same difficulty, is provided by Kuder–Richardson Formula 21, which takes the form:

$$\text{Reliability} = \frac{n}{n-1}\left(1 - \frac{\sum n\bar{p}\bar{q}}{s_t^2}\right)$$

where $\bar{p}$ is the mean percent of correct responses, and $\bar{q}$ the mean percent of incorrect responses. K.R. 21 can also be expressed as:

$$\text{Reliability} = \frac{n}{n-1}\left\{1 - \frac{\bar{X} - [(\bar{X})^2/n]}{s_t^2}\right\} \tag{24}$$

This formula provides a convenient way to get a quick, conservative estimate of coefficient alpha, because it requires information only on the mean, standard deviation, and number of items in the test. It differs from the full formula by the amount ns_p^2/s_t^2 where s_p^2 is the variance of the item difficulty indices, p. For a test of 50 or more items, this element is likely to be no greater than 0.02 or 0.03. For example, if the items have a range of p-values from 0.30 to 0.90 with a standard deviation of 0.10, and the test's standard deviation is 6 points (a realistic figure), for a 50-item test, this gives:

$$\frac{50(0.10)^2}{6^2} = \frac{0.50}{36} = 0.014$$

Thus, with tests of a length commonly encountered in practice, Eqn. (24) provides a very serviceable approximation.

It was indicated earlier that coefficient alpha in its standard form is applicable only to homogeneous tests in which all items are designed to measure the same common latent attribute. When test items are not designed to be measures of a single homogeneous attribute, a test may often be divided into subtests each of which is designed to be homogeneous in what it measures. Then Eqns. (22), (23), or (24) can be applied to each subtest separately to estimate the reliability (in the internal-consistency sense) of the subtest.

4. Reliability of Domain Mastery or Criterion-referenced Tests

In discussing reliability up to this point, the main concern has been the precision with which an individual can be located on the scale of a latent attribute through the administration of a test. Within limits, this conception can still be applied to a domain mastery test. The adaptation that may be required is to think of the attribute as having a limited range, because the tasks that fall within a precisely defined domain may have a limited range of difficulty. Within that range, correlations may be attenuated because of the presence of substantial numbers of perfect (or zero) scores. Such scores indicate individuals who fall at the boundaries of the difficulty range of the domain and who are in a sense not fully measured. The presence of such scores acts to attenuate correlation coefficients. The location of these extreme cases on a continuous scale representing the domain is in a sense indeterminate, so it is difficult to estimate a meaningful standard error of measurement for them.

Within the domain mastery model, interest usually focuses on some one level of performance—often 80% or 90% of correct answers—that has been defined as constituting "mastery" of the domain. When this is the case, the critical issue so far as reproducibility of results is concerned would appear to be whether another sample from the domain would lead to the same decision (mastery or nonmastery, as the case may be) for each individual.

The most direct approach to answering the question of consistency in the critical decision is to obtain two test scores for each individual by administering two equivalent test forms—equivalent in that each sampled by the same rules from the defined domain. The two could be given concurrently or with a lapse of time, depending on the nature of the universe to which one wished to generalize. From the test results, one could produce a 2×2 table such as the one shown in Table 6. Table 6 would present the basic data on consistency, but finding a statistic that adequately evaluates the test is not easy. The simple percentage of cases with consistent decisions depends on the range and level of talent in the group. In the extreme case, if one is dealing with a group for whom the domain is completely new and untaught (no one approaches mastery), we will get an appearance of a very accurate test, because all cases will

Table 6
Results of mastery domain tests

		Form A	
		Nonmastery	Mastery
Form B	Nonmastery		
	Mastery		

fall in the upper left-hand cell. Of course, consistency of performance could also appear if the test were extremely easy for all members of the group. Furthermore, if the group were extremely varied in competence (including a number for whom the test was very hard, a number of others for whom it was very easy, and very few who were just about at the threshold of mastery), high consistency of placement would be the rule. In all of these cases, consistency in placement reflects properties of the groups tested rather than excellence of the test. Furthermore, in the intermediate range of excellence of examinees, both percentage of agreement and the point correlation represented in the phi-coefficient are sensitive to the proportional split between the two groups.

If the two forms of the test have been equated for difficulty and if it is reasonable to assume that, within the domain as defined, competence shows a normal distribution, then one can postulate a normal bivariate distribution of competence underlying the score distribution on the tests, and one can appropriately calculate a tetrachoric correlation for the fourfold table. This should be relatively independent of the average *level* of ability in the group tested, though it would be sensitive to the variability in the ability being studied and would be higher for a group that is more heterogeneous in ability. However, the tetrachoric correlation coefficient will not be sensitive to differences in the proportion achieving the criterion score level on form A and form B. If these differences appear to be due to something in the forms themselves, rather than to the sequence of testing, the tetrachoric correlation will yield an overestimate of the test's reliability.

Various measures that have been proposed for use with criterion-referenced tests depend in some way on the average of squared deviations of test scores from the established "mastery" level, developed as formulas analogous to those for error variance. However, these formulas are substantially (perhaps even primarily) dependent on level of competence within the group of examinees, and they reveal little about the properties of the test as a testing instrument. They seem to be going off in an unproductive direction.

If one is dissatisfied with the conventional reliability coefficient when a test is being used for mastery decisions, perhaps the best alternative is the standard error of measurement for scores within a range of a few percentage points above and below the critical percentage that is defined as "mastery." This is one index that does *not* depend to any substantial degree on the range or level of talent within the group, but solely on consistency of performance from trial to trial. Though this statistic might be difficult to interpret in terms of proportion of cases receiving the same decision on two testings (that *does* depend on the nature of the group), the standard error would permit comparison of one test with another.

The procedures for calculating a standard error of measurement are described in Thorndike (1982), and these procedures can be applied in the present case. The form that the results might take can be illustrated for a triad of tests (unfortunately not designed to be mastery tests) for which standard errors by score level happen to be available. Consider the Cognitive Ability Tests at Level A. Standard errors of measurement based on a sample of 500 and expressed as percentage of items got right were as follows for examinees with an *average* score of from approximately 70% to 90% of correct answers:

(a) verbal test, 3.96%;

(b) quantitative test, 3.99%;

(c) non-verbal test, 3.15%.

Within the limits of the data, these results would be interpreted as showing that the verbal test and the quantitative test are quite comparable in the precision with which a judgment can be made that a person has achieved "mastery" of their domain, but that the non-verbal test permits this decision to be made with appreciably greater precision.

Bibliography

Cronbach L J 1951 Coefficient alpha and the internal structure of tests. *Psychometrika* 16: 297–324

Cronbach L J, Gleser G, Nanda H, Rajaratnam N 1972 *The Dependability of Behavioral Measurements*. Wiley, New York

Kuder G F, Richardson M W 1937 The theory of estimation of test reliability. *Psychometrika* 2: 151–60

Lindquist E F 1953 *Design and Analysis of Experiments in Psychology and Education*. Houghton Mifflin, Boston, Massachusetts

Thorndike R L 1982 *Applied Psychometrics*. Houghton Mifflin, Boston, Massachusetts

Winer B J 1971 *Statistical Principles in Experimental Design*, 2nd edn. McGraw-Hill, New York

Achievement Testing

Taxonomies of Educational Objectives

V. De Landsheere

Originally, the term taxonomy (or systematics) was understood as the science of the classification laws of life forms. By extension, the word taxonomy means the science of classification in general and any specific classification respecting its rules, that is, the taxonomy of educational objectives.

A taxonomy related to the social sciences cannot have the rigour or the perfect branching structure of taxonomies in the natural sciences. In education, a taxonomy is a classification constructed according to one or several explicit principles.

The term "taxonomy of educational objectives" is closely associated with the name of B. S. Bloom. This is explained by the extraordinary worldwide impact of the *Taxonomy of Educational Objectives* first edited by Bloom in 1956. This taxonomy was enthusiastically received by teachers, educationists, and test developers because it offered easily understandable guidelines for systematic evaluation covering the whole range of cognitive processes (and not only the lower mental processes, as was too often the case in the past). This taxonomy had also a definite influence on curriculum development and teaching methods for the same reason: it emphasized processes rather than content matter, and helped determine a proper balance between lower and higher cognitive processes.

Bloom's Taxonomy of cognitive objectives was soon followed by taxonomies for the affective and psychomotor domains. Within two decades, several taxonomies were developed by other authors and a great number of philosophical and empirical studies appeared on this topic.

A presentation of the main taxonomies so far published follows.

1. The Cognitive Domain

1.1 Bloom's Taxonomy

This taxonomy, which has inspired the majority of the other taxonomies, uses four basic principles: (a) the major distinction should reflect the ways teachers state educational objectives (methodological principle); (b) the taxonomy should be consistent with our present understanding of psychological phenomena (psychological principle); (c) the taxonomy should be logically

developed and internally consistent (logical principle); and (d) the hierarchy of objectives does not correspond to a hierarchy of values (objective principle).

The taxonomy itself comprises six cognitive levels:

(a) Knowledge: recall or recognition of specific elements in a subject area. The information possessed by the individual consists of specifics (terminology, facts), ways and means of dealing with specifics (conventions, trends, sequences, classifications, categories, criteria, universals), and abstractions in a field (principles, generalizations, theories, and structures).

(b) Comprehension:
  (i) Translation: the known concept or message is put in different words or changed from one kind of symbol to another.
  (ii) Interpretation: a student can go beyond recognizing the separate parts of a communication and see the interrelations among the parts.
  (iii) Extrapolation: the receiver of a communication is expected to go beyond the literal communication itself and make inferences about consequences or perceptibly extend the time dimensions, the sample, or the topic.

(c) Application: use of abstractions in particular and concrete situations. The abstractions may be in the form of general ideas, rules of procedure, or generalized methods. The abstractions may also be technical principles, ideas, and theories which must be remembered and applied.

(d) Analysis: breakdown of a communication into its constituent elements or parts such that the relative hierarchy of ideas is made clear and/or the relations between the ideas expressed are made explicit. One can analyse elements, relationships, organizational principles.

(e) Synthesis: the putting together of elements and parts so as to form a whole. This involves arranging and combining in such a way as to constitute a pattern of structure not clearly there before.

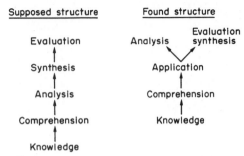

Supposed structure   Found structure

Figure 1
Schematic representation of an hypothesized perfect hierarchy and of the hierarchical structure found by Madaus et al. 1973

(f) Evaluation: evaluation is defined as the making of judgments about the value of ideas, works, solutions, methods, material, and so on. Judgments can be in terms of internal evidence (logical accuracy and consistency) or external criteria (comparison with standards, rules...).

The content validity of the taxonomy is not considered as perfect by any author but, in general, they are satisfied with it: taken as a whole, it allows nearly all the cognitive objectives of education to be classified. Nevertheless, the taxonomical hierarchy is questionable and the category system is heterogeneous. De Corte (1973) has pointed out that the subcategories used are not always based on the same classification principle. He writes: "For knowledge, analysis and synthesis, the subcategories correspond to a difficulty scale of products resulting from cognitive operations. For comprehension, the subdivisions are specifications of operations and not of their products. For evaluation, the subcategories depend on the nature of the criteria chosen to formulate a judgment."

Gagné (1964) has also pointed out that some categories or subcategories only differ in their content and not by formal characteristics which affect their conditions of learning.

According to Cox (De Corte 1973), the agreement on classification among the users of the taxonomy ranges from 0.63 to 0.85. The lack of reliability must come from the vagueness of the concepts for which the authors of the taxonomy propose essential rather than operational definitions.

The taxonomy has been elaborated for evaluation purposes. It has also been very useful in developing blueprints for curriculum development. It helped in identifying and formulating objectives, and, as a consequence, in structuring the material and specifying assessment procedures.

When developing a test for a particular curriculum, the curriculum often only presents a theme (Bacher 1973). No indication is given about which behaviours of the theme are to be tested. The test constructor is left to

guess about which behaviours are to be tested. Furthermore, the taxonomy of objectives movement could signal a renaissance of nineteenth-century faculty psychology. Instead of training separate mental faculties such as memory, imagination, etc., one could artificially cultivate memory (knowledge in Bloom), application, analysis, synthesis, judgment, aptitudes.

Several authors are of the opinion that the taxonomy pays too much attention to knowledge, and not enough to higher mental processes.

It is not possible to use the taxonomy without reference to the behavioural background of the individual. There is an obvious difference between the individual who solves a specific problem for the first time and the individual who has met the same problem before. In both cases, however, the answer can be the same.

To test the validity of the hierarchical structure of the taxonomy, Madaus and his associates developed a quantitative causal model (see Fig. 1) to reveal not only the proportion of variance at each level explained directly by the preceding adjacent level, but also any proportion of variance explained indirectly by nonadjacent levels. The statistical techniques used were principal components analysis to identify the role of a factor of general ability *g,* and multiple regression analysis to measure the links between taxonomic levels. Hill (1984) has employed maximum likelihood estimation procedures, using LISREL, to list the hierarchical assumptions of the Bloom taxonomy, and has provided important evidence to support a hierarchical structure between the five higher-order categories.

In a pure hierarchy, there must be a direct link between adjacent levels and only between these two. As one proceeds from the lower to the higher levels in Bloom's taxonomy, the strength of the direct links between adjacent levels decreases and many links between nonadjacent levels appear. Knowledge, comprehension, and application are well-hierarchized. Higher up in the hierarchy, a branching takes place. On one side, analysis is found (even if the *g* factor is taken into account, analysis entertains an indirect link with comprehension). It is what Ebel (1973) calls the stage of content mastery. On the other side, synthesis and evaluation are found; they are differentiated clearly from the rest in that they are highly saturated in the *g* factor. This dependence increases if the material is not well-known to the students, or is very difficult, or if the lower processes have not been sufficiently mastered to contribute significantly to the production of higher level behaviours.

Horn (1972) suggested an algorithm to classify objectives along Bloom's taxonomy. He notes that in lower mental processes, objectives content and problem cannot be separated. For instance, for the objective: "The student will be able to list the parts of a plant", there is no problem. The answer will be possible only if the student has it "ready made" in his or her memory. For higher mental processes, the problem is general, and can be formulated without reference to a specific content.

To quasioperationalize Bloom's taxonomy, Horn takes the level of complexity of the problem posed as a classification criterion. At each level, he considers the formal aspect and the content. Figure 2 presents Horn's algorithm.

Using Horn's algorithm, well-trained judges can reach a high interreliability in their classification of objectives.

Bloom's taxonomy is formulated in an abstract way. To help the users apply the taxonomy properly, Metfessel et al. (1970) suggested a list of verbs and a list of objects which, appropriately combined, give the framework for an operational objective at the different taxonomic levels.

Bloom is aware of the limits of the instrument to whose development he has contributed. What really matters to Bloom is that educators question as often as possible whether they have varied the cognitive level of the tasks, exercises, and examinations they propose, whether they stimulate their students sufficiently, and whether they really help them develop.

1.2 Guilford's Structure of Intellect Model

To organize intellectual factors, identified by factor analysis or simply hypothesized, Guilford (1967) designed a structure of intellect (SI) model (see Fig. 3). This model was essentially conceived to serve the heuristic function of generating hypotheses regarding new factors of intelligence. The placement of any intellectual factor within this nonhierarchical model is determined by its three unique properties: its operation, its content, and its product.

Content categories are:

(a) Figural: figural information covers visual, auditive, and kinesthesic sense.

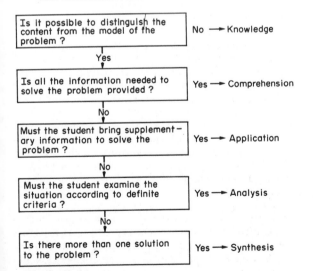

Figure 2
Horn's algorithm

(b) Symbolic: signs that can be used to stand for something else.

(c) Semantic: the verbal factor.

(d) Behavioural: behavioural content is defined as information, essentially nonverbal, involved in human interactions, where awareness or attention, perceptions, thoughts, desires, feelings, moods, emotions, intentions, and actions of other persons and of ourselves are important.

Operation categories are:

(a) Cognition: awareness, immediate discovery or rediscovery, or recognition of information in various forms; comprehension or understanding.

(b) Memory: retention or storage, with some degree of availability, of information in the same form in which it was committed to storage, and in connection with the same cues with which it was learned.

(c) Divergent production: the generation of information from given information where the emphasis is upon variety and quantity of output from the same source; this category is likely to involve transfer.

(d) Convergent production: the area of logical productions or at least the area of compelling inferences. The input information is sufficient to determine a unique answer.

(e) Evaluation: the process of comparing a product of information with known information according to logical criteria, and reaching a decision concerning criterion satisfaction.

Product categories are:

(a) Units: relatively segregated or circumscribed items of information having "thing" character.

(b) Classes: recognized sets of items grouped by virtue of their common properties.

(c) Relations: recognized connections between two items of information based upon variables or upon points of contact that apply to them.

(d) Systems: organized or structured aggregates of items of information, a complex of interrelated or interacting parts.

(e) Transformations: changes of various kinds, of existing or known information in its attributes, meaning, role, or use.

(f) Implications: expectancies, anticipations, and predictions, the fact that one item of information leads naturally to another.

Each cell of Guilford's model represents a factor that is a unique combination of operation, content, and product. For instance, cell 1 (see Fig. 3) represents cognition of figural units.

Can Guilford's model be utilized to formulate or at least to generate objectives? First of all, it can be noted

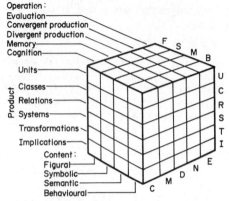

Figure 3
Guilford's Structure of Intellect Model

that the three dimensions of the model are hierarchical at least to a certain extent. Furthermore, Guilford has discussed the implications of his model for education. He thinks that it indicates clearly the kinds of exercises that must be applied to develop intellectual abilities. He remarks, in particular, that school, in general, overemphasizes cognition and the memorization of semantic units. It is important, says Guilford, to apply oneself much more to the exercise of the other products: classes, relations, systems, transformations, and implications.

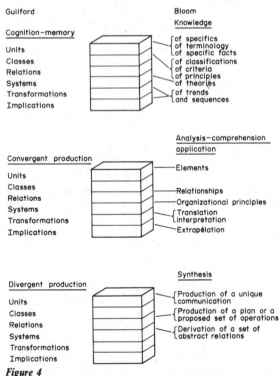

Figure 4
Parallelism between Guilford's model and Bloom's cognitive taxonomy

The fact that Guilford compares his model to Bloom's taxonomy and acknowledges important similarities between both of them seems to confirm that Guilford does not exclude the possibility that his model may be used to generate and classify objectives.

Guilford's model can absorb Bloom's whole cognitive taxonomy (see Fig. 4). By its greater precision, the SI model may allow easier operationalization and, more generally, may offer greater taxonomic possibilities.

De Corte (1973) has adapted and transformed Guilford's model. The four dimensions of De Corte's general model of classification are: (a) the subject matter of specific content of a given universe of objectives; (b) the domain of information to which the subject matter belongs (content in Guilford's model); (c) the product: the objectives are classified with respect to the formal aspect of the information they produce (products in Guilford's model); (d) the operation is defined as in Guilford's model.

De Corte focuses on this fourth category and develops Guilford's five operations into a seven category system. Cognition comprises receiving–reproducing operations: (a) perception of information; (b) recall of information; (c) reproduction of information and productive operations; (d) interpretative production of information; (e) convergent production of information; (f) evaluative production of information; (g) divergent production of information.

De Corte's system is of interest in that it develops Guilford's model in such a manner that it becomes a practical tool for the definition of the cognitive objectives of education. It seems to indicate how Bloom and Guilford's contributions could be integrated and be of use to education.

1.3 The Gagné–Merrill Taxonomy

Gagné proposes a hierarchy of processes needed to achieve the learning tasks assigned by objectives. Merrill designates the behaviour and psychological condition under which learning can be observed.

With Gagné's learning conditions, the push-down principle constitutes the basis of the Gagné–Merrill taxonomy. In the process of development, a person acquires behaviour at the lower levels before acquiring behaviour at the higher levels. Later, the conscious cognitive demand on the learner increases. Learners have an innate tendency to reduce the cognitive load as much as possible; consequently, a learner will attempt to perform a given response at the lowest possible level. The push-down principle states that a behaviour acquired at one level will be pushed down to a lower level as soon as conditions have changed sufficiently so that the learner is able to respond to the stimulus using lower level behaviour. It is rather surprising that this important principle is often neglected or even ignored in the literature related to the taxonomies of educational objectives.

The Gagné–Merrill taxonomy is an original formulation, integrating the affective, psychomotor, and cognitive domains.

The following is a condensed version of Merrill's presentation:

(a) *Emotional behaviour (signal learning)*. In the presence of every stimulus situation, students involuntarily react with physiological changes which they perceive as feelings. The direction (positive or negative) and the relative magnitude of this emotional behaviour can be inferred by observing the students' approach/avoidance responses in unrestrained choice situations.

(b) *Psychomotor behaviour*. A student is able to execute rapidly, without external prompting, a specified neuromuscular reaction in the presence of a specific stimulus situation. The observable behaviour is an overt skeletal–muscular response which occurs in entirety without hesitation. Psychological conditions of importance are the presence of a specific cue and the absence of prompts. Psychomotor behaviour may be further broken down into three constituent behaviours.

First, topographic behaviour (stimulus response) is where a student is able to execute rapidly without external prompting, a single new neuromuscular reaction in the presence of a particular stimulus cue. This can be observed as a muscular movement or combination of movements not previously in the student's repertoire. The important psychological conditions are the presence of a specific cue and the absence of prompts.

Secondly, chaining behaviour, where a student is able to execute, without external prompting, a coordinated series of reactions which occur in rapid succession in the presence of a particular stimulus cue, is observed as a series of responses, and occurs in the presence of a specified cue and in the absence of prompts.

Thirdly, skilled behaviour is where a student is able to execute sequentially, without external prompting, complex combinations of coordinated psychomotor chains, each initiated in the presence of a particular cue when a large set of such cues are presented. In some skills, cue presentation is externally paced while in other skills cue presentation is self-paced. This is seen as a set of coordinated chains, and occurs when there is a paced or unpaced presentation of a set of cues and an absence of prompts prior to or during the performance.

(c) *Memorization behaviour*. A student immediately reproduces or recognizes, without prompting, a specific symbolic response when presented with a specific stimulus situation. The observable behaviour always involves either reproduction or recognition of a symbolic response, and occurs under psychological conditions similar to those of psychomotor behaviour. Memorization behaviour can be broken into naming behaviour where a student reproduces or recognizes, without prompts, a single symbolic response in the presence of a particular stimulus cue; serial memorization behaviour (verbal association) which occurs in the presence of a particular stimulus cue, so that a student reproduces, without prompting, a series of symbolic responses in a prespecified sequence; and discrete element memorization behaviour (multiple discrimination) where a student reproduces or recognizes, without prompting, a

unique symbolic response to each of a set of stimulus cues.

(d) *Complex cognitive behaviour*. The student makes an appropriate response to a previously unencountered instance of some class of stimulus objects, events, or situations. This can further be broken into classification behaviour, analysis behaviour, and problem-solving behaviour.

Classification behaviour (concept learning) is where a student is able to identify correctly the class membership of a previously unencountered object or event, or a previously unencountered representation of some object or event. It occurs when the student must make some kind of class identification, the important psychological conditions being the presentation of unencountered instances or non-instances.

Analysis behaviour (principle learning) is when a student is able to show the relationship between the component concepts of an unencountered situation in which a given principle is specified as relevant. The student must first identify the instances of the several classes involved in the situation and then show the relationship between these classes. The psychological condition of importance is presentation of a situation which the student has not previously analysed or seen analysed.

Problem-solving behaviour is when a student is able to select relevant principles and sequence them into an effective solution strategy when presented with an unencountered problem situation for which the relevant principles are not specified. Creativity and/or divergent thinking occurs when some of the relevant principles are unknown to the student and the strategy developed represents a new higher order principle. It can be observed when the student must synthesize a product which results from analysing several principles in some appropriate sequence and generalize new relationships not previously learned or analysed. The psychological conditions of importance are: an unencountered problem for which the relevant principles are not specified, and which in some cases may require principles not previously analysed by the student or perhaps even by the instructor.

Without any doubt, Gagné–Merrill's taxonomy provides some order in the field of fundamental learning processes. However, it does not claim exhaustivity, and certain categories such as "process learning" and "problem solving" are rather vague.

D'Hainaut (1970) believes that Gagné does not give enough emphasis to the creative processes. Divergent thinking can be categorized under the heading "problem solving", but this category is perhaps too large.

Merrill and Gagné have made two important contributions to the definition of objectives. Their categories are expressed in terms of definite behaviour and the psychological conditions are considered, although these conditions are still to be integrated into an operational definition of objectives.

1.4 Gerlach and Sullivan's Taxonomy

Sullivan in association with Gerlach (1967) attempted to replace a description of mental processes in general terms (as in Bloom's taxonomy) by classes of observable learner behaviours which could be used in task description and analysis. Their model is empirical. After listing hundreds of learning behaviours, Sullivan has progressively grouped them into six categories, each headed by a typical verb. The six categories are ordered according to the increasing complexity of behaviours they represent, but the whole does not constitute a rigorous hierarchy and, for that reason, cannot be considered as a true taxonomy.

(a) Identify: the learner indicates membership or non-membership of specified objects or events in a class when the name of the class is given.

(b) Name: the learner supplies the correct verbal label (in speech or writing) for a referent or set of referents when the name of the referent is not given.

(c) Describe: the learner reports the necessary categories of object properties, events, event properties, and/or relationships relevant to a designated referent.

(d) Construct: the learner produces a product which meets specifications given either in class or in the test item itself.

(e) Order: the learner arranges two or more referents in a specified order.

(f) Demonstrate: the learner performs the behaviours essential to the accomplishment of a designated task according to pre-established or given specifications.

Gerlach and Sullivan consider their "taxonomy" as a check list helping to ensure that no important behaviour is forgotten when planning school activities. This may succeed, as long as "mastery objectives" (i.e., objectives concerning a fully defined behaviour universe) are kept in sight. However, the six categories suggested do not cover creative productions and do not even make a clear place for transfer.

1.5 De Block's Taxonomy

De Block (1975) suggests a model of teaching objectives (see Fig. 5). He thinks that teaching pursues objectives in three directions: (a) from partial to more integral learning. Comprehension seems more desirable than rote learning (knowledge); in this perspective, mastery and integration are final objectives; (b) from limited to fundamental learning. Facts gradually become background data; concepts and methods come to the fore; (c) from special to general learning. The objective is thinking in a productive rather than in a reproductive way, taking initiatives, and being able to adapt oneself to a great variety of situations.

The combination of all subcategories yields 72 classes of objectives. De Block's system does not deal sufficiently with the criteria by which it is recognized whether an objective has been achieved or not. However, it can certainly help teachers to reconsider their activities, and to make their students work at higher cognitive or affective levels.

1.6 Conclusion to the Cognitive Domain

Not one of these taxonomies can be considered as entirely satisfying. Looking at highly nuanced classifications, only moderate reliability can be hoped for. If the system is reduced to a few operationalized categories, content validity decreases.

The taxonomy of Bloom and his associates has already been used successfully by hundreds of curriculum and test developers throughout the world. Furthermore, it has stimulated fruitful discussion and reflection on the problem of objectives. The several taxonomies that appeared after Bloom are useful to curriculum developers, to test constructors, and to teachers planning their next lesson and preparing mastery tests for their pupils.

2. The Affective Domain

According to Bloom, the affective domain includes objectives which describe changes in interest, attitudes, and values, and the development of appreciations and adequate adjustment.

What are the main difficulties in the pursuit of affective objectives? Imprecision of concepts, overlap of the affective and the cognitive domains, cultural bias (Western culture still tends to consider feelings as the most secret part of personality), ignorance about affective learning processes, and poor evaluation instruments.

So far, the only significant taxonomy for the affective domain is the one published by Krathwohl et al. (1964), hence the brevity of this section when compared to the first.

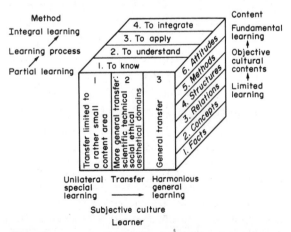

Figure 5
De Block's model of instruction

2.1 Krathwohl's Taxonomy

The main organizing principles for the cognitive domain were "from simple to complex" and "from concrete to abstract". It soon appeared that these could not be used for the affective domain which dealt with attitudes, interests, values, and so on. After a long search, the authors discovered an ordering principle that was precisely characteristic of affective development: the degree of internalization, that is, the degree of incorporation of the affects within the personality. When the process of internalization is completed, the person feels as if the interests, values, attitudes, etc. were his or her own and lives by them. In Krathwohl's taxonomic terms, the continuum goes from merely being aware that a given phenomenon exists, and giving it a minimum attention, to its becoming one's basic outlook on life. The main organizing principles in Krathwohl's taxonomy are receiving, responding, valuing, organization, and characteristics.

(a) Receiving: "Sensitivity to the existence of certain phenomena and stimuli, that is, the willingness to receive or attend to them." Receiving consists of three subcategories that represent a continuum: (i) awareness; (ii) willingness to receive; and (iii) controlled or selected attention.

(b) Responding: "Behaviour which goes beyond merely attending to the phenomena; it implies active attending, doing something with or about the phenomena, and not merely perceiving them." Subcategories of responding are: (i) acquiescence in responding; (ii) willingness to respond; and (iii) satisfaction in response.

(c) Valuing: "It implies perceiving phenomena as having worth and consequently revealing consistency in behaviour related to these phenomena." The individual is motivated to behave in the line of definite values. Subcategories are: (i) acceptance of a value; (ii) preference for a value; and (iii) commitment.

(d) Organization: "For situations where more than one value is relevant, the necessity arises for (i) the organization of the values into a system; (ii) the determination of the interrelationships among them; and (iii) the establishment of the dominant and pervasive one." Subcategories are: (i) conceptualization of a value and (ii) organization of a value system.

(e) Characteristics by a value or value complex: "The values already have a place in the individual's value hierarchy, are organized into some kind of internally consistent system, have controlled the behaviour of the individual for a sufficient time that he has adapted to behaving in this way." Subcategories are: (i) generalized set and (ii) characterization.

The most striking feature of this taxonomy is its abstract, general character. Krathwohl is aware of the problem. The taxonomy deals with objectives at the curriculum construction level. This means that objectives as defined in the taxonomy are approximately midway between very broad and very general objectives of education and the specific ones which provide guidance for the development of step-by-step learning experiences.

For a short presentation of Krathwohl's taxonomy, G. De Landsheere (1982) tried to find a classification principle that would be easier to formulate in behavioural terms than internalization. He suggested a continuum of activity, or of personal engagement. De Landsheere's frame of reference was developmental psychology. He wrote: "An individual has really reached the adult stage if his behaviour has found its coherence, its logic and stability; he has developed at the same time a sound tolerance to change, contradiction, frustration; he is cognitively and affectively independent; he is, at the same time, able to abide by his engagement and feelings." Education is a long process leading to this ultimate balance.

De Landsheere suggests the following taxonomy:

(a) *The individual responds to external stimulation.*

(i) The individual receives: this is a rather amorphous stage. The individual encounters, for instance, beauty or ugliness without any reaction, like a mirror that would not reflect any image. This behaviour is hard to distinguish from the cognition (in Guilford's sense) that takes place before memorization. Only some manifestation of attention is observable.

(ii) The individual receives and responds to the stimulus: an observable reaction takes place. The individual obeys, manifests pleasure by his or her words or attitudes. At this stage, there is not yet explicit acceptance or rejection that would reflect a deliberate choice.

(iii) The individual receives and reacts by accepting or refusing: now the individual knows what he or she wants or likes, provided things or events are presented.

(b) *The individual takes initiatives.* The individual tries spontaneously to understand, to feel, and then act according to the options available. Here the adult stage is reached. For instance, the individual lives a life in accordance with his or her values, feelings, beliefs, likings, but is also able to change his or her mind if convincing proofs or arguments are offered. This stage is parallel to evaluation in the cognitive domain.

The classification suggested by De Landsheere seems clearer than Krathwohl's taxonomy, but more limited. Objectives can be more easily operationalized, but the criticism of Krathwohl's work also applies here.

2.2 Conclusion to the Affective Domain

The situation in the affective domain remains unsatisfactory. Why does it appear that so much work is still to be undertaken in the field? Krathwohl has not succeeded in filling completely the gap in the theoretical framework and the methodology of educational evaluation in the affective domain. A more systematic attack on the problem of affective objectives is required, and, in particular, an inventory of existing studies, experiments, and evaluation instruments in the field should be undertaken. Indubitably, the affective domain will constitute a priority area in the field of educational research in the decades to come.

3. The Psychomotor Domain

Why is the psychomotor domain important? First of all, motion is a necessary condition of survival and of independence. Life sometimes depends on physical strength correctly applied, on agility, and on rapidity. Locomotor behaviour is needed to explore the environment and sensory-motor activities are essential for the development of intelligence. Some psychomotor behaviours such as walking and grasping, are also necessary for physical and mental health to be maintained. Dexterity is crucial for the worker, and also in civilizations giving a lot of time to leisure, corporal ability plays a considerable role in artistic and athletic activities.

Numerous taxonomies have been developed for the psychomotor domain. Some of them tend to be comprehensive, in strict parallelism with the taxonomies inspired by Bloom and Krathwohl for the cognitive and affective domains. Others have been developed for specialized fields and have, in many cases, a very technical character. Only six taxonomies which fall in the first category are presented in this article.

Ragsdale, Guilford, Dave, and Kibler's taxonomies are summarized very briefly for they are mainly of historical interest.

3.1 Ragsdale's Taxonomy

As early as in 1950, Ragsdale published a classification for "motor types of activities" learned by children. He worked with three categories only: (a) object motor activities (speed, precision): manipulation or acting with direct reference to an object; (b) language motor activities: movement of speech, sight, handwriting; (c) feeling motor activities: movements communicating feelings and attitudes.

These categories are so general that they are of little help in the definition of educational objectives.

3.2 Guilford's Taxonomy

Guilford (1958) suggested a simple classification in seven categories that is not hierarchical, and also does not seem of great utility for generating objectives. The seven categories are: power, pressure, speed, static precision, dynamic precision, coordination, and flexibility.

3.3 Dave's Taxonomy

Dave's classification (1969), although also rather schematic, can be considered as an embryo of a taxonomy. The categories are: initiation, manipulation, precision,

articulation, naturalization (mechanization and internalization). The meaning of the first three categories is clear. Articulation emphasizes the coordination of a series of acts which are performed with appropriate articulation in terms of time, speed, and other relevant variables. As for naturalization, it refers to the highest level of proficiency of an act that has become routine.

3.4 Kibler's Classification

Kibler and his associates suggest a classification (1970) more developed than that of previous authors. The main frame of reference is developmental child psychology.

(a) Gross bodily movements: movements of entire limbs in isolation or in conjunction with other parts of the body (movements involving the upper limbs, the lower limbs, two or more bodily units).

(b) Finely coordinated movements: coordinated movements of the extremities, used in conjunction with the eye or ear (hand–finger movements, hand–eye coordination, hand–ear coordination, hand–eye–foot coordination, other combinations of hand–foot–eye–ear movements).

(c) Nonverbal communication behaviours: facial expression, gestures (use of hands and arms to communicate specific messages), bodily movements (total bodily movements whose primary purposes are the communication of a message or series of messages).

(d) Speech behaviours: sound production (ability to produce meaningful sounds), sound–word formation (ability to coordinate sounds in meaningful words and messages), sound projection (ability to project sounds across the air waves at a level adequate for reception and decoding by the listener), sound–gesture coordination (ability to coordinate facial expression, movement, and gestures with verbal messages).

3.5 Simpson's Taxonomy (1966)

Simpson's taxonomy can be divided into five main categories.

(a) *Perception.* This is the process of becoming aware of objects, qualities, or relations by way of the sense organs.

(i) Sensory stimulation: impingement of a stimulus upon one or more of the sense organs (auditory, visual, tactile, taste, smell, kinesthesic).

(ii) Cue-selection: deciding to what cues one must respond in order to satisfy the particular requirements of task performance, for example, recognition of operating difficulties with machinery through the sound of the machine in operation.

(iii) Translation: relation of perception of action in performing a motor act. This is the mental process of determining the meaning of the cues received for action, for example, the ability to relate music to dance form.

(b) *Set.* Preparatory adjustment of readiness for a particular kind of action or experience.

(i) Mental set: readiness, in the mental sense, to perform a certain motor act.

(ii) Physical set: readiness in the sense of having made the anatomical adjustments necessary for a motor act to be performed.

(iii) Emotional set: readiness in terms of attitudes favourable to the motor act's taking place.

(c) *Guided response.* Overt behavioural act of an individual under the guidance of the instructor (imitation, trial and error).

(d) *Mechanism.* Learned response has become habitual.

(e) *Complex overt response.* The individual can perform a motor act that is considered complex because of the movement pattern required. A high degree of skill has been attained. The act can be carried out smoothly and efficiently.

(i) Resolution of uncertainty: the act is performed without hesitation.

(ii) Automatic performance: the individual can perform a finely coordinated motor skill with a great deal of ease and muscle control.

Simpson suggests that there is perhaps a sixth major category: adapting and originating. "At this level, the individual might originate new patterns of actions in solving a specific problem."

The weakness of this taxonomy is to be found again in its very abstract and general formulation.

3.6 Harrow's Taxonomy

As operationally defined by Harrow (1972), the term "psychomotor" covers any human voluntary observable movement that belongs to the domain of learning. Harrow's taxonomy is the best available for the psychomotor domain, although some of the category descriptives are unsatisfactory:

(a) Reflex movements: segmental, intersegmental, suprasegmental reflexes.

(b) Basic–fundamental movements: locomotor, nonlocomotor, manipulative movements.

(c) Perceptual abilities:
Kinesthetic discrimination: body awareness (bilaterality, laterality, sidedness, balance), body image, body relationship of surrounding objects in space.
Visual discrimination: visual acuity, visual tracking, visual memory, figure–ground differentiation, perceptual consistency.
Auditory discrimination: auditory acuity, tracking, memory.

Tactile discrimination.
Coordinated abilities: eye–hand and eye–foot coordination.

(d) Physical abilities: endurance (muscular and cardio-vascular endurance), strength, flexibility, agility (change direction, stops and starts, reaction–response time, dexterity).

(e) Skilled movements: simple adaptive skill (beginner, intermediate, advanced, highly skilled), compound adaptive skill (beginner, intermediate, advanced, highly skilled), complex adaptive skill (beginner, intermediate, advanced, highly skilled).

(f) Nondiscursive communication: expressive movement (posture and carriage, gestures, facial expression), interpretative movement (aesthetic movement, creative movement).

In fact, Harrow does not describe her model in relation to a general, unique criterion (i.e., coordination), but simply looks for a critical order; mastery at an inferior level is absolutely necessary to achieve the immediate higher level in the hierarchy of movements.

This taxonomy has great qualities. First, it seems complete, not only in its description of the major categories of psychomotor behaviour, but also in terms of the subcategories within the different taxonomic levels. Furthermore, the author defines the different levels clearly. For each subcategory, she proposes a clear definition of the concept and indicates, where necessary, the differences from other authors who have written in this field. She also presents concrete examples.

Harrow's taxonomy seems to be of direct use to teachers in physical education. Level (c) is specially interesting for preschool and for elementary-school teachers. It contains a good example of a battery for testing the perceptive abilities of pupils, diagnosing difficulties, and proposing appropriate remedial exercises. The author underlines the dependence between the cognitive and psychomotor domains at the level of perceptual abilities. Several examples also show the great interrelation between the three domains. However, Harrow's hierarchy is not governed by a specified criterion, such as internalization or coordination. Moreover, the subcategories are not mutually exclusive.

3.7 Conclusion to the Psychomotor Domain

It seems that taxonomies in the psychomotor domain have not yet been given the attention they deserve. They should be tried in many varied situations and their relations with the other two domains should be carefully investigated.

4. Conclusion

The cognitive domain is the best developed. First, it is by nature favourable to the construction of logical models. Secondly, schools have traditionally been interested in cognitive learning, especially in the acquisition of factual knowledge which in turn leads to easy evaluation.

Compared with the cognitive domain, the affective domain is less developed. Only since about 1970 has the educational world been trying to change the situation (in the past, affectivity has sometimes been intensively cultivated, but nearly always in terms of indoctrination processes). Affects seem less observable than cognitive activities and in most cases are less susceptible to rigorous measurement.

One would think that the psychomotor domain would present fewer difficulties, but little systematic work has been undertaken. In most Western educational systems, physical and artistic education is comparatively neglected in the curriculum.

Despite certain weaknesses, the two taxonomies with which Bloom is associated, and Harrow's taxonomy dominate the field. The others should, however, not be neglected, since they supply further clarifications and suggestions.

At present, the taxonomy movement in education is of great value. Even though the instruments are so far imperfect, they stimulate educators to fruitful reflection. Half-way between the great ideological options and the micro-objectives, the taxonomies seem to relate philosophy and educational technology and practice. It is one of their great merits.

Bibliography

Bacher F 1973 La docimologie. In: Reuchlin M (ed.) 1973 *Traité de psychologie appliquée*. Presses Universitaires de France (PUF), Paris

Bloom B S (ed.) 1956 *Taxonomy of Educational Objectives: The Classification of Educational Goals*, Handbook 1: *Cognitive Domain*. McKay, New York

Dave R H 1969 *Taxonomy of Educational Objectives and Achievement Testing. Developments in Educational Testing*, Vol. 1. University of London Press, London

De Block A 1975 *Taxonomie van Leerdoelen*. Standard Wetenschappelijke Uitgererij, Amsterdam

De Corte E 1973 *Onderwijsdoelstellingen*. Universitaire Pers, Louvain

De Landsheere G 1982 *Introduction à la recherche en éducation*. Thone, Liège; Armand Colin, Paris

De Landsheere V, De Landsheere G 1984 *Définir les objectifs de l'éducation*. Presses Universitaires de France (PUF), Paris

D'Hainaut L 1970 Un modèle pour la détermination et la sélection des objectifs pédagogiques du domaine cognitif. *Enseignement Programmé* 11: 21–38

Ebel R L 1973 Evaluation and educational objectives. *J. Educ. Meas.* 10: 273–79

Gagné R M 1964 The implications of instructional objectives for learning. In: Lindvall C M (ed.) 1964 *Defining Educational Objectives*. University of Pittsburgh Press, Pittsburgh, Pennsylvania

Gerlach V, Sullivan A 1967 *Constructing Statements of Outcomes*. Southwest Regional Laboratory for Educational Research and Development, Inglewood, California

Guilford J P 1958 A system of psychomotor abilities. *Am. J. Psychol.* 71: 164–74

Guilford J P 1967 *The Nature of Human Intelligence*. McKay, New York

Harrow A J 1972 *A Taxonomy of the Psychomotor Domain: A Guide for Developing Behavioral Objectives*. McKay, New York

Hill P W 1984 Testing hierarchy in educational taxonomies: A theoretical and empirical investigation. *Eval. Educ.* 8: 181–278

Horn R 1972 *Lernziele und Schülerleistung: Die Evaluation von den Lernzielen im kognitiven Bereich*, 2nd edn. Beltz, Weinheim

Kibler R J, Barker L L, Miles D T 1970 *Behavioral Objectives and Instruction*. Allyn and Bacon, Boston, Massachusetts

Krathwohl D R, Bloom B S, Masia B B 1964 *Taxonomy of Educational Objectives: The Classification of Educational Goals*, Handbook 2: *Affective Domain*. McKay, New York

Madaus G F, Woods E N, Nuttal R L 1973 A causal model analysis of Bloom's taxonomy. *Am. Educ. Res. J.* 10: 253–62

Merrill M D 1971 Necessary psychological conditions for defining instructional outcomes. In: M D Merrill (ed.) 1971 *Instructional Design: Readings*. Prentice-Hall, Englewood Cliffs, New Jersey

Metfessel N S, Michael W B, Kirsner D A 1970 Instrumentation of Bloom's and Krathwohl's taxonomies for the writing of educational objectives. In: Kibler R J, Barker L L, Miles D J (eds.) 1970

Ragsdale C E 1950 How children learn motor types of activities. *Learning and Instruction*. 49th Yearbook of the National Society for the Study of Education, Washington, DC

Simpson E J 1966 *The Classification of Educational Objectives, Psychomotor Domain*. University of Illinois, Urbana, Illinois

Objective Tests

B. H. Choppin

Objective methods of observation are those in which any observer who follows the prescribed rules will assign the same values or categories to the events being observed as would another observer. Similarly, an objective test is one for which the rules for scoring it are so specific and comprehensive that anyone who marks a test script in accordance with these rules will arrive at the same test score. Most objective tests used in education are composed of a sequence of individual "objective" test items (sometimes called structured-response items) in which the testees must choose their answers from a specified list of alternatives rather than by creating them for themselves. It is important to remember, however, that the definition relates to the method of scoring the test and not to the format of its constituent items as such. Not all objective tests require the student to select from a presented list. Items which require the student to write down a phrase, a word, or a number, and in the scoring of which there are clear and unequivocal rules for deciding whether the response is right or wrong, also qualify as "objective."

Objective tests stand in clear contrast to essay examinations and other forms of open-ended tests in which few constraints are put on the testee. Such tests are characterized by the very great variation in the responses that are produced even among students of similar ability or attainment, and their scoring requires the examiner to weigh a variety of evidence, a task which calls for substantial amounts of personal judgment. As a result, different examiners usually arrive at different scores for the same essay, and hence this type of assessment is not regarded as objective.

Objective tests may also be distinguished from short-answer (or restricted-response) tests in which, although the testee must produce his or her own answers, the constraints imposed by the formulation of the question are such as to make the scoring more objective. For example, students might be asked to draw a diagram of a terrestrial telescope paying particular attention to the characteristics and positioning of the lenses. The scoring instructions might dictate that the student's response be accepted as correct if and only if the objective lens has a longer focal length than the eye-piece. Tests of this last type are sometimes referred to as semiobjective tests.

1. Areas of Application

Objective tests are widely used to measure intelligence, aptitude, and achievement (or attainment). Almost all tests of aptitude and intelligence are of the objective type because of the uses to which such measures are put. Raw scores of intelligence or aptitude have little meaning in themselves, and need to be translated to well-established scales before they can be used. In consequence, reliability of the scores is a major consideration and using objective test formats is one way to maximize this.

However, the appropriateness of objective tests for the measurement of achievement is much more controversial. Essay tests are still preferred to objective tests for most educational purposes in many countries. Where the teacher scores the tests for a single class, objectivity as such is less important, and the advantages of getting the students to express themselves fully and openly tend to outweigh the demands for a reliable score. For example, although the typical American high-school teacher will use objective tests (self-developed) for routine assessment of students on a weekly or monthly basis, the teacher in England or Wales will almost always prefer to use nonobjective tests for this purpose. The system of public examinations in England and Wales, which certify levels of attainment for secondary-school leavers, are largely nonobjective despite the need for reliability (given the importance of the results to the future careers of individual students). However, it

should be noted that the proportion of objective test material in these examinations has been increasing in recent years.

2. Item Formats

Most objective test items appear in one of four alternative formats. These will be considered in turn below, and examples of each type appear in Fig. 1.

2.1 Supply Items

Unlike the other types in which the student is selecting from a list of alternative responses presented to him or her, the supply type of item requires a student to construct a response. However, the question is so structured as to limit the scope of the student's response so that (ideally) there will be one, and only one, acceptable answer. Demanding that the student construct rather than recognize the response avoids some of the common criticisms of objective tests described below. However, it does give up some of the convenience (such as automated scoring) that selection-type items offer. The format's most frequent area of application is in mathematics on questions which call for a specific quantitative answer. However, Fig. 1 demonstrates that it can be used effectively in other areas.

Specification of the acceptable answers is an essential part of the item construction process, but there is always the danger that certain students will invent unforeseen answers that could arguably be accepted as correct. For example, on item 1(b) in Fig. 1 the student might respond "N_2." It is advisable with supply items to compile a comprehensive list of answers that give appropriate evidence of achievement before scoring begins. Note that the criterion is not grammatical correctness nor even truth. The answer "invisible" to question 1(b) makes the statement true, but does not demonstrate that the student has achieved the objective being tested.

2.2 The True/False Item Format

The true/false item presents a declarative statement and requires the examinee to indicate whether he or she judges it to be true or false. (Some generally similar items have other dichotomous response options such as yes/no or appropriate/inappropriate.) Although such items are easy to construct, this is not a format to be generally recommended. Tests composed of true/false items tend to be rather unreliable, and are particularly susceptible to contamination by guessing. Ebel (1970) argues that this is not serious and that true/false tests may be very efficient, but few other writers support this view. True/false items can be quite effective for assessing factual knowledge (especially if great precision is not required), but are usually inappropriate for testing more complex skills.

2.3 Multiple-choice Item Format

The multiple-choice item is by far the most frequently used in educational achievement testing. The number of alternative answers offered varies but is usually four or

1. *Supply-type items*

   (a) A new school building has 12 classrooms. The school ordered 30 desks for each classroom. Only 280 desks were delivered. How many more are needed?

   _____
   (Scoring key: 80)

   (b) The gas which is most abundant in the atmosphere is:

   _____
   (Scoring key: Nitrogen)

   (c) Through which country does the canal that links the Mediterranean Sea to the Red Sea pass?

   _____
   (Scoring key: Egypt or UAR)

   (d) A solid element X forms two oxides which contain respectively 71.1% and 62.3% of X. Calculate the equivalent weight of X in each oxide. The specific heat of X is 0.084. Given that the product of the atomic weight and specific heat of a solid element is approximately 6.4, write down the formulae for the two oxides of X.

   _____ and _____
   (Scoring key: XO_2 and XO_3)

2. *True/false items*

   (e) The capital city of Sweden is Stockholm   True : False

   (f) The rate of juvenile delinquency is usually higher in the older parts of a city   True : False

   (g) The oceans are deepest at the center and shallowest near the edges   True : False

   (h) Light rays always travel in straight lines   True : False

3. *Multiple-choice items*

   (i) The amount of heat required to raise the temperature of one gram of a substance by one degree ($^\circ$C) is called:
     (i)   its thermal conductivity
     (ii) its specific heat
     (iii) its thermal capacity
     (iv) its thermal expansion

   (j) John brought the skull of an animal to school. His teacher said she did not know what the animal was but she was sure that it was one that preyed on other animals for its food. Which clue, do you think, led her to this conclusion?
     (i)   The eye sockets faced sideways
     (ii) The skull was much longer than it was wide
     (iii) There was a projecting ridge along the top of the skull
     (iv) Four of the teeth were long and pointed
     (v) The jaws could work sideways as well as up and down

4. *Matching item format*

   For each piece of apparatus listed below, identify the scientist who invented it, and enter the appropriate code letter on the answer sheet.

	Apparatus		*Inventor*
(k)	X-ray spectrometer	(i)	Angstrom
(l)	Reflection grating	(ii)	Bragg
(m)	Interferometer	(iii)	Helmholtz
(n)	Ophthalmoscope	(iv)	Michelson
		(v)	Newton
		(vi)	Rowland
		(vii)	Thomson

Figure 1
Examples of objective test items

five. As a rule only one of the alternatives is correct, the others (the distractors) being constructed so as to provide plausible examples of common errors. If the distractors are carefully written a wrong-answer analysis can yield valuable diagnostic information about the types of error being made by students. Many variations of the basic format have been developed (Wood 1977) mainly to increase the amount of information elicited by an item or to improve its applicability to the testing of higher mental processes.

The chief difficulty in constructing good multiple-choice questions is to find appropriate distractors. To be effective they must be plausible at least to a substantial minority of students, yet they must be clear and unambiguously wrong in the judgment of experts. Distractors should not give inadvertent clues which permit test-wise students to eliminate them irrespective of their ability to correctly solve the question. The multiple-choice questions given in Fig. 1 may be regarded as exemplars of the type.

Although they too may effectively be used to assess specific knowledge, multiple-choice items are readily adaptable to measure more complex skills involving reasoning and analysis. It has been found to be relatively straightforward to construct an achievement test, all of whose items are in the multiple-choice format which assesses student performance on a wide range of objectives involving different skill levels.

2.4 Matching Items

The fourth widely used item format to be considered is the matching exercise. This is a logical extension of the multiple-choice item in which the same list of alternative responses is used for several items in sequence. An example of this format is included in Fig. 1.

The most obvious advantage of the matching item format is one of economy. More responses are obtained from the student for the same amount of reading. The format can be effectively employed to test knowledge of specific facts, but is generally unsuitable for more complex objectives. However, it has been suggested (Thorndike and Hagen 1969) that a variation of the format, the classification task, can be used to appraise comprehension and application type objectives.

3. Disadvantages of Objective Tests

Many critics of the multiple-choice format have pointed out that it required students only to recognize the correct answer rather than to recall and/or construct it for themselves. It is suggested that recognition is a fundamentally lower form of behavior, and that many students who are able to recognize the correct answers on a test are unable to apply what they have learned in practice. In general, the research evidence does not support this. Students who are good recallers of knowledge are also good recognizers. Several studies (e.g. Godshalk et al. 1966, Choppin and Purves 1969) which compared objective tests with free-response essays written by the same students showed that the objective tests predicted

overall performance on the essay about as well as the limited reliability of the essay scoring would permit.

Associated with this criticism is the complaint that objective tests place an undue emphasis on reading rather than writing skills, so that the latter tend to become devalued. Wood (1977) comments that although this may have some validity in the United States, elsewhere (in the United Kingdom for example) traditional testing practices have paid entirely too much regard to the ability of the testees to express themselves in writing.

A third form of criticism is that the multiple-choice test item typically presents the student with three or four times as many false answers as correct ones. As a rule the distractors are written so as to be quite plausible, and thus the opportunities for the student to "learn" incorrect information during the test session are substantial. Thorndike and Hagen (1969) note that little research had been done on this point.

Two other disadvantages of objective tests deserve mention. The first is that it is in general much easier to write objective test questions to test comparatively low-level skills (e.g., factual knowledge) rather than the more complex skills of analysis and synthesis. As a result, many existing objective tests are overloaded with items focusing on pieces of specific knowledge. Objective test items (particularly in the multiple-choice format) can be constructed to assess higher mental processes, but in general this is rather more difficult to do, and too often professional test constructors have not paid sufficient attention to this problem.

The other criticism is that objective tests encourage guessing behavior. Although a minority of critics (e.g., Hoffmann 1962) appear to regard guessing itself as an immoral activity on a par with betting on horses or using illegal drugs, most feel it is an appropriate behavior for the student, in a restricted choice situation, who lacks sufficient information to solve the test item directly. The problem arises from the number of correct guesses that occur. They can lead to an overestimate of an individual student's level of achievement, and tend to lower the measurement reliability for a whole group. Various countermeasures have been proposed (see *Correction for Guessing*).

4. Advantages of Objective Tests

Against these real or imagined disadvantages, there are clearly a number of benefits ensuing from the use of objective tests of achievement. The first is that by focusing the attention of the student, it is possible to gather information rapidly on particular parts of his or her learning—a feature especially important in diagnostic work and in formative evaluation. This focusing of individual items allows the test maker to control the scope of what is being assessed by the complete test, so that items may be sampled from across a very broad domain or from only a very narrow part of it. In contrast, responses on an essay-type examination are less subject to control by the examiner, and it is often difficult to persuade all students to provide evidence about their mastery of particular skills.

Minute by minute, an objective test is probably the most efficient basis for obtaining information about an individual's learning. Because of its structure, the instrument is relatively easy to score, is reliable, and its data are amenable to a wide range of statistical analyses. Automated scoring procedures have played a major part in making the multiple-choice item format so popular. These have ranged from a simple template (which when placed over a test or answer sheet allows the scorer to quickly observe how many correct responses have been selected), to computer-controlled electronic scanning machines which can "read" the pattern of pencil marks made on an answer sheet very rapidly. The use of such methods whether on a large or small scale substantially reduces the time and cost of achievement testing. However, it should be noted that some of the time saved in scoring may be used up by the additional time required for test preparation. Constructing clear, unambiguous, and valid objective test items is not an easy task.

Since each objective test item is usually short, many of them can be included in a single test, and this contributes to the higher reliability that is usually achieved. The items can be spread more evenly over the topics to be covered, so that a more representative sampling of performance is obtained. Another way of stating this is to note that the score from a well-made objective test is likely to be more accurate than that from a comparable essay test. Two separate objective tests, based on the same content area, will rank an individual at more nearly the same place in his or her group, than would two free-response measures.

5. Summary

Objective tests have been found to be efficient and effective instruments for obtaining measures of learning as well as of general mental ability and aptitude. They yield scores that are more dependable than those from comparable open-ended tests, and their quality can be readily assessed through statistical item analysis.

Nevertheless, their full advantages are only realized when considerable care is exercised in their construction. Writers of objective items for achievement tests have an unfortunate tendency to concentrate on factual, and often trivial, information, and to produce tests which seem to distort the full range of educational goals. It is possible, however, to create objective test items which assess abilities to comprehend, interpret, and apply knowledge, to analyze and to synthesize ideas. The extra effort needed to write such items is justified when valid and reliable measures of achievement are desired.

See also: Item Analysis; Item Writing Techniques; History of Mental Testing

Bibliography

Choppin B H, Purves A C 1969 Comparison of open-ended and multiple-choice items dealing with literary understanding. *Res. Teach. Eng.* 3: 15–24
Ebel R L 1970 The case for true–false test items. *Sch. Rev.* 78: 373–89
Ebel R L 1979 *Essentials of Educational Measurement*, 3rd edn. Prentice-Hall, Englewood Cliffs, New Jersey
Godshalk F I, Swineford F, Coffman W E 1966 *The Measurement of Writing Ability*. College Entrance Examinations Board, New York
Hoffmann B 1962 *The Tyranny of Testing*. Collier Macmillan, New York
Roid G H, Haladyna T M 1982 *A Technology for Test-item Writing*. Academic Press, New York
Thorndike R L, Hagen E 1969 *Measurement and Evaluation in Psychology and Education*, 3rd edn. Wiley, New York
Wood R 1977 Multiple-choice: A state of the art report. *Eval. Educ.* 1: 191–280

Item Writing Techniques

J. L. Herman

Item writing techniques provide rules and prescriptions for constructing sound test items, items that measure what they are intended to measure. Until relatively recently, these rules have incorporated the conventional wisdom of test writers and have provided only general guidance on how to devise test items that do not clue or unnecessarily confuse an examinee's response. Since the 1960s, however, in tandem with the growth of criterion-referenced testing, item writing techniques increasingly have focused attention on the nature and structure of test content and ways to define and operationalize what is being measured. The match between the intended content of a test and that of test items is no longer left to the implicit understanding of the item writer; rather, newer item writing technologies provide explicit, specific rules to help insure that test items measure particular domains of knowledge, skills, and/or abilities. This article provides an overview to a range of current item writing techniques. It is limited to techniques for measuring academic achievement and focuses principally on selected response or "objective" measures.

1. Conventional Guidelines

Conventional item construction guidelines help inhibit the inclusion of extraneous factors in test items that confound an examinee's response. They concentrate on factors such as linguistic, semantic, and grammatical features that may enable an unknowing examinee to give a correct response or that may prevent a knowing examinee from responding correctly. Typical rules for multiple-choice items, short answer and completion

Typical rules for multiple-choice items:
1. The stem of the item should be meaningful by itself and should present a clear problem.
2. The stem should be free from irrelevant material.
3. The stem should include as much of the item as possible except where an inclusion would clue. Repetitive phrases should be included in the stem rather than being restated in each alternative.
4. All alternatives should be grammatically consistent with the item stem and of similar length, so as not to provide a clue to the answer.
5. An item should include only one correct or clearly best answer.
6. Items used to measure understanding should contain some novelty and not merely repeat verbatim materials or problems presented in instruction.
7. All distractors should be plausible and related to the body of knowledge and learning experiences measured.
8. Verbal associations between the stem and correct answer or stereotyped phrases should be avoided.
9. The correct answer should appear in each of the alternative positions with approximately equal frequency and in random order.
10. Special alternatives such as "none," "all of the above" should be used sparingly.
11. Avoid items that contain inclusive terms (e.g., "never," "always," "all") in the wrong answer.
12. Negatively stated item stems should be used sparingly.
13. Avoid alternatives that are opposite in meaning or that are paraphrases of each other.
14. Avoid items which ask for opinions.
15. Avoid items that contain irrelevant sources of difficulty, such as vocabulary, or sentence structure.
16. Avoid interlocking items, items whose answers clue responses to subsequent items.
17. Don't use multiple choice items where other item formats are more appropriate.

Typical rules for short answer and completion items:
1. A direct question is generally better than an incomplete statement.
2. Word the item so that the required answer is both brief and unambiguous.
3. Where an answer is to be expressed in numerical units, indicate the type of units wanted.
4. Blanks for answers should be equal in length. Scoring is facilitated if the blanks are provided in a column to the right of the question.
5. Where completion items are used, do not leave many blanks.
6. For completion items, leave blank only those things that are important to remember.
7. In composing items, don't take statements verbatim from students' textbook or instruction.

Typical rules for true–false or alternative response items:
1. Avoid broad general statements for true–false items.
2. Avoid trivial statements.
3. Avoid negative statements and especially double negatives.
4. Avoid long complex sentences.
5. Avoid including two ideas in a single statement unless cause–effect relationships are being measured.
6. Include opinion statements only if they are attributed to particular sources.
7. True statements and false statements should be approximately the same length.
8. The number of true statements and of false statements should be approximately equal.
9. Avoid taking statements verbatim from students' text or instruction.

Figure 1
General guidelines for item writing

items, and true–false response items are given in Fig. 1 (Gronlund 1971, Conoley and O'Neil 1979).

2. Techniques for Constructing Replicable Test Items

While general guidelines of the sort listed in Fig. 1 are useful for constructing sound test items, they represent necessary but not sufficient criteria. Left open is the issue of how to construct items that capture and validly reflect intended test content. A number of approaches to this problem have evolved over the years; these approaches differ in the degree of specificity, amount of discretion left in the hands of the item writer, and replicability of the items generated.

Content–process matrices represent the loosely structured end of the continuum, where item writers are accorded a great deal of discretion in devising individual items. Derived from a curriculum general scheme described by the work of Tyler and Bloom et al., broad subject domains are partitioned into two dimensions of content and process. Content includes the key concepts of the subject field and process the levels of reasoning specified by Bloom's taxonomy. Subject area experts write items they consider appropriate for each cell of the matrix, guided only by the simple content–process designation.

Criterion-referenced approaches, exemplified first by objectives-based techniques and later by domain referencing, provide more direction for item writers' efforts. Objectives specify observable stimulus and response conditions that describe the nature of the task that is expected of the learner and conditions under which the task is to be performed. The objective becomes the target of assessment, and test items are generated to match the conditions specified, for example, "Given a short story, the student will select, from among four given alternatives, the main idea."

The probability that items produced by two writers will be parallel is higher for objectives-based approaches than for content–process schemes; however significant discretion and areas of item writer variability still exist. For example, different writers may vary in their definitions of "short story," in the extent to which main ideas are stated or implied, in the amount of supporting detail, and so on.

More fine-grained specifications of the intended test content have been developed to control this variability and to more precisely define the domain of behavior to be assessed—descriptions that serve to prescribe test item development. The goal of these more elaborate specifications is to define a pool of items that represents an important universe of knowledge or skill domain—such that student performance on one set of items drawn from the domain would generalize to a second set of items and to the entire defined domain. In its most highly prescribed form, domain specifications provide an exhaustive set of rules for generating a set of related test items. For example, item forms developed by Hively et al. (1973) include:

(a) general description of what the item form is about;

(b) item form shell, which provides a sample item as it would be administered to examinees and the common unvarying elements of each item generated;

(c) stimulus and response characteristics, which describe the theoretical characteristics of the item generation scheme and the dimensions which are varied to comprise the replacement sets;

(d) replacement schemes and replacement sets, which detail the exact mechanics of generating item pools for the given domain;

(e) scoring specifications, which describe the properties to be used to distinguish between a correct and an incorrect response (see Fig. 2).

Similarly, Osburn has described item forms which (a) generate items with a fixed syntactical structure; (b) contain one or more variable elements; (c) define a class of item sentences by specifying the replacement sets for the variable elements. Facet design, originated by Guttman, likewise specifies a universe of content in terms of a mapping sentence that contains variable facets—the latter operates like replacement sets in Hively's item forms.

The most highly specific item forms and mapping sentence approaches permit computerized test item writing. Using author languages such as COURSEWRITER, PLANIT, and TUTOR, a series of computer commands define the wording of an item form and the way the variable elements are chosen or computed.

Producing a number satisfying a given order relation to specified numbers(s) (spoken form).

General description

The child is asked to say the name of a number that bears a specified order relation ("greater than" or "less than") to a given number or numbers in the range 0 through 20. Given numbers are presented in spoken form and response is spoken.

Stimulus and response characteristics

Constant for All Cells

The presentation is completely spoken; a spoken response is required.

Distinguishing Among Cells

Three scripts are used asking respectively for a number greater than a given number, for a number less than a given number, and for a number greater than one given number and less then another

Within the third script, three conditions are allowed: (1) first given numeral greater than second with required number possibly an integer; (2) first given numeral greater than second with required number necessarily not an integer; and (3) first given numeral less than second so that the solution to the problem is the empty set.

Varying Within Cells.

Within each cell, the given numbers are integers from the range 0 through 20 chosen so that the correct response (when it is not the empty set) can be a real number from the range 0 through 20.

Cell matrix

Script (a)	"greater than b_1"	"less than b_1"	"greater than b_1" but less than b_2"		
Numerals (b)	$0 \leqq b_1 \leqq 19$	$1 \leqq b_1 \leqq 20$	$0 \leqq b_1 \leqq 18$ $b_1 + 2 \leqq b_2 \leqq 20$	$0 \leqq b_1 \leqq 19$ $b_2 = b_1 + 1$	$1 \leqq b_1 \leqq 20$ $0 \leqq b_2 < b_1$
	(1)	(2)	(3)	(4)	(5)

Item form shell

Materials None	
Directions to examiner Read script to child. Write down child's exact words.	Script Tell me a number that is ________

Replacement scheme

(a) Script
Cell 1: "less than b_1" "greater than b_1"
Cells 3,4,5: "greater than b_1 but less than b_2"

(b) Numerals within Script
Cell 1: Choose b_1 from R.S. 9.1
Cell 2: Choose b_1 from R.S. 9.2
Cell 3: Choose two numbers from R.S. 9.3
Cell 3: Choose two numbers from R.S. 9.3
Let b_1 = smaller number; b_2 = larger number
Reject if $b_2 - b_1 \leqq 1$
Cell 4: Choose b_1 from R.S. 9.3
Let $b_2 = b_1 + 1$
Cell 5: Choose two numbers from R.S. 9.3
Let b_1 = larger number; b_2 = smaller number
Reject if $b_1 = b_2$

Replacement sets

R.S. 9.1: Whole numbers 0,1,2,...,19.
R.S. 9.2: Whole numbers 1,2,3,...,20.
R.S. 9.3: Whole numbers 0,1,2,...,20.

Scoring specifications

Cell 1: Any real number X where $X > b_1$
Cell 2: Any real number X where $X < b_1$
Cell 3: Any real number X where $b_1 < X < b_2$
Cell 4: Any real number X where $b_1 < X < b_2$
Cell 5: Any response equivalent to saying that there are no numbers which can fulfill the conditions.

Figure 2
Sample item form

The applicability of highly specific item forms has been questioned for content areas which are not highly structured; their cost feasibility and widespread practical utility are also a concern. Popham and Baker have both suggested a compromise strategy to optimize descriptive rigor and feasibility. Derived from Hively's work, their approach features an expanded objective which delimits the nature of the intended content and response and provides explicit rules for generating test items. First known as amplified objectives and in their more recent refinement, domain specifications, these statements detail (a) a general description of the knowledge, skill, or attitude being measured; (b) content limits, which describe the range of eligible content for constructing the item stem; (c) response limits, which describe the nature of the correct response, including specific criteria for

judging the adequacy of a constructed response, or rules for generating distractors for multiple-choice items; and (d) sample items and directions for administration. Figure 3 provides a sample domain specification.

3. Item Writing Algorithms

Domain specifications provide rules for generating test items, and the source of such rules has received modest attention. Hively has indicated the curriculum as a source, and has described inductive and deductive approaches to generating item generation rules and schemes. Others have attempted to describe rules for item generation which are applicable across curricula and content areas, for instance, assessing prose learning and comprehension and concept learning.

Grade level:	Grade 3
Subject:	Reading comprehension
Domain description:	Students will select from among written alternatives the stated main idea of a given short paragraph.
Content limits:	1. For each item, student will be presented with a 4–5 sentence expository paragraph. Each paragraph will have a stated main idea and 3–4 supporting statements.
	2. The main idea will be stated in either the first or the last sentence of the paragraph. The main idea will associate the subject of the paragraph (person, object, action) with a general statement of action, or general descriptive statement. For example, "Smoking is dangerous to your health," "Kenny worked hard to become a doctor," "There are many kinds of seals."
	3. Supporting statements will give details, examples, or evidence supporting the main idea.
	4. Paragraphs will be written at no higher than a third grade reading level.
Response limits:	1. Students will select an answer from among four written alternatives. Each alternative will be a complete sentence.
	2. The correct answer will consist of a paraphrase of the stated main idea. Paraphrased sentences may be accomplished by employing synonyms and/or by changing the word order.
	3. Distractors will be constructed from the following:

(a) One distractor will be a paraphrase of one supporting statement given in the paragraph (e.g., alternative "a" in the sample item).

(b) One or two distractors will be generalizations that can be drawn from two of the supporting statements, but do not include the entire main idea (e.g., alternative "d" in the sample item).

(c) One distractor may be a statement about the subject of the paragraph that is more general than the main idea (e.g., alternative "b" in the sample item).

Format:	Each question will be multiple choice with four possible responses.
Directions:	Read each paragraph. Circle the letter that tells the main idea.
Sample item:	Indians had many kinds of homes. Plains Indians lived in teepees which were made from skins. The Hopi Indians used bushes to make round houses, called hogans. The Mohawks made longhouses out of wood. Some Northeast Indians built smaller wooden cabins.

What is the main idea of this story?

  a. Some Indians used skins to make houses.
  b. There were different Indian tribes.
  c. Indians built different types of houses.
  d. Indian houses were made of wood.

Figure 3
Sample domain specifications

3.1 Linguistic-based Approaches to Item Writing

Bormuth was among the first to stress the need for an item writing technology, and pioneered linguistic-based approaches to assess prose learning and assure a logical connection between test items and instructional materials. Bormuth proposed a detailed set of rules for transforming segments of prose instruction into test items, using his "wh-transformation." He described transformations for two types of items: those derived from a single sentence, and those derived from the relationship between sentences. For example, a sentence is selected from the instructional materials, a substantive word is deleted and replaced with the appropriate *wh* word (*who, what, when, where*, etc.), and the item is constructed by transforming the sentence into a question.

Anderson emphasized the use of paraphrasing in constructing such test items. He pointed out that verbatim questions do not require comprehension, but merely recall. To assess whether an examinee has comprehended the original information, it must be paraphrased and then transformed. He outlined two requirements for paraphrased statements: (a) they have no substantive words in common; (b) they are equivalent in meaning. In addition to assessing comprehension of prose materials, Anderson also outlined a method for testing concepts and principles by substituting particular terms for superordinate ones and replacing with synonyms all remaining substantive words, a process further operationalized by Conoley and O'Neil.

Bormuth's transformational approaches were further refined by Finn who used case grammar to develop an 82-step algorithm for selecting sentences and for transforming them into questions. Finn's procedures were subsequently streamlined into three major steps:

(a) Analyzing the text and selecting the sentences, including procedures for screening tests and selecting the most instructionally relevant and significant sentences, for writing summary sentences, and for using word frequency analyses to identify keywords.

(b) Transformation of sentences into questions, by clarifying referents and simplifying the selected sentences, replacing the keyword noun, and rewriting the sentences and a question.

(c) Construction of distractors, from learner-free responses, from a fixed list of keywords, or from other similar function words in the instructional passage.

3.2 Concept Learning Approaches to Item Writing

Tiemann and Markle's research on concept learning provides guidance on how to circumscribe and define valid domains for teaching and assessment. A concept represents a class of objects, events, ideas, or relations which vary among themselves, but are nonetheless classified as the same. For example, the concept "dog" includes dobermans, spaniels, poodles, mutts; "democracy" subsumes parliamentary and congressional varieties; "reinforcer" includes endless specific instances. Concept testing basically involves assessing generalization to *new* examples and discrimination of nonexamples of a particular concept.

Systematic analyses of the critical and variable attributes of a concept are central to both teaching and testing. Critical attributes are those which are common to all members of the class, while variable attributes are those which may differ among members; these attributes define and differentiate the concept domain. For example, all dogs have four legs and a tail, but vary in size, color, length of hair, and so on. Examples and nonexamples of the concept, embodying the presence and/or absence of these various attributes, are constructed for teaching, and new, previously unencountered examples of both types are used to test students' understanding. Novel examples are essential—otherwise simple recall rather than higher levels of thinking are being assessed. Further, examples and nonexamples representing systematic variation of critical and variable attributes can heighten the diagnostic value of resultant test items.

3.3 Other Approaches to Higher Levels of Learning

Williams and Haladyna's typology is also concerned with constructing higher level test items and provides rules for matching syntactical forms with objectives at various cognitive levels. They define a three-dimensional matrix for classifying objectives and test items: content (including facts, concepts, and principles); task (including reiteration, summarization, illustration, prediction, evaluation, application); and response mode (selected and constructed). Generic objectives for each cell describe the type of situation to which the examinee must respond, the nature of the information or stimulus presented, and the type of response required, for instance, "name," "identify," "define." After selecting the content and task to be tested, the item writer can then use the matrix to determine how to construct an appropriate test item. The Instructional Quality Inventory, developed for use in United States military training, relies on a similar content by task matrix and is particularly concerned with objective/test consistency and adequacy.

4. Summary and Conclusions

In summary, a range of item writing strategies has been advanced since the 1970s. These strategies have been aimed predominantly at defining a universe or domain of knowledge to be tested and at assuring a match between test items and significant instructional content; they seek to maximize instructional and content validity.

Unfortunately, however, there appears to be conflict between features which maximize such validity and those which affect feasibility. For example, the approaches which offer the greatest descriptive rigor are least likely to be implemented by teachers because of time, cost, and technical sophistication requirements. These more elaborate approaches may be more feasible for large-scale national, state, and province assessments, and for creating item banks which are maximally useful for instructional planning and certification—situations where greater resources are available, and resultant items are intended for widespread use.

Item writing is but one step in the test development process. Sound procedures must be used at all steps to assure test validity.

See also: Item Analysis; Item Response Theory

Bibliography

Anderson R C 1972 How to construct achievement tests to assess comprehension. *Rev. Educ. Res.* 42: 145–70

Bormuth J R 1970 *On the Theory of Achievement Test Items.* University of Chicago Press, Chicago, Illinois

Conoley J, O'Neil H F 1979 A primer for developing tests items. In: O'Neil H F(ed.) 1979 *Procedures for Instructional Systems Development.* Academic Press, New York

Finn P J 1975 A question-writing algorithm. *J. Read. Behav.* 4: 341–67

Gronlund N E 1971 *Measurement and Evaluation in Teaching,* 2nd edn. Macmillan, New York

Hively W, Maxwell G, Rabehl G, Sension D, Lundin S 1973 *Domain-referenced Curriculum Evaluation: A Technical Handbook and a Case Study from the Minnemast Project,* CSE Monograph Series in Evaluation No. 1. Center for the Study of Evaluation, University of California, Los Angeles, California

Millman J 1980 Computer-based item generation. In: Berk R (ed.) 1980 *Criterion-referenced Measurement.* Johns Hopkins University Press, Baltimore, Maryland

Roid G, Haladyna T 1980 The emergence of an item writing technology. *Rev. Educ. Res.* 50: 293–314

Roid G, Haladyna T 1982 *A Technology for Test–item Writing.* Academic Press, New York

Tiemann P W, Markle S M 1978 *Analyzing Instructional Content: A Guide to Instruction and Evaluation.* Stipes, Champaign, Illinois

Williams R G, Haladyna T 1982 Logical operations for generating intended questions (LOGIQ): A typology for higher level test items. In: Roid G, Haladyna T (eds.) 1982

Norm-referenced Assessment

D. Vincent

Educational assessment is said to be norm referenced, or normative, when it compares performance amongst those assessed. "Performance" is used to include a wide variety of cognitive and noncognitive processes which may be assessed for educational purposes. Most characteristic of these are learning outcomes, or achievements, measured by objective tests. However, nonobjective assessment of attainment and performance in the form of response to affective measures are both often entirely amenable to norm-referenced treatment. The following account of the main principles of norm referencing thus applies to these also, although many published accounts of the topic refer primarily to the measurement of achievement in the academic or cognitive sense. The process of comparison takes two forms. First, it may be based simply on the relative performance of individuals within a specified group, for example, candidates in a competitive entrance test for college or university. Secondly, and more generally, norm-referenced assessment involves the estimation of individual or group performance in relation to a level which is in some sense typical or average; the "norm", for a specified population. Thus, the two definitive features of a norm-referenced assessment "instrument"—typically a standardized test—are the capacity to spread out those assessed so that variations in performance can be clearly identified, and the availability of norms of performance, usually estimated population means and associated indices of dispersion. It is this that is meant by the "standardization" of a test.

The more effectively a test discriminates amongst testees of different abilities, the more accurate will be the normative interpretations made subsequently. A number of scaling systems are in use to express individual performance in normative terms. The majority of these express performance relative to the mean of a definitive group, either a population or, more commonly, a "standardization" sample representative of the population. It follows that the more sensitive an instrument is to fine differences of performance in the standardization sample, the more precisely individuals or subgroups can be compared subsequently with the norm.

The history of educational assessment—and of a large part of mental measurement—has been, effectively, a history of norm-referenced assessment. The expression "norm referenced" became current in the 1960s to contrast this established model of educational assessment with emerging alternatives, particularly criterion-referenced assessment of achievement. A review of the contrasts between criterion- and norm-referenced assessment is given in Mehrens and Lehmann (1969).

Norm-referenced assessment deals with rankings and relative performance amongst individuals. This has a primarily statistical rather than curricular meaning. Norms are thus essentially contingent and neutral indices. They convey little in absolute terms about the quality or content of learning or attainment. The content of a normative attainment test may, of course, be selected to reflect desirable outcomes of learning. However, the norms for a test do not necessarily constitute a desirable standard, only a typical one. Norms describe, they do not prescribe.

In the assessment of skills and achievements a distinction can be made between performance and progress. In practice, education is as much concerned with the latter as the former. Many programmes involving norm-referenced assessment regularly monitor and record progress throughout a school or college career, going beyond once-only appraisals of performance. Published norm-referenced instruments are thus usually designed to take account of progress by provision of equivalent forms of a test, incorporation of appropriate age or grade level adjustments in the scaling system and by adjustments for retesting and, occasionally, time of testing. Such technical refinements eliminate or hold constant influences which may distort evidence of apparent progress or improvement. They provide evidence of progress by default: elimination of extraneous or spurious sources of variation makes it more likely that whatever remains can be attributed to genuine progress. This may provide sufficient precision for many practical applications of norm-referenced assessment. However, it should be noted that the majority of such procedures rely upon data derived from cross-sectional studies. In the case of adjustments for age and grade, linear increases in raw-score levels across age or grade samples are used to infer the extent to which progress can be attributed to developmental, maturational or temporal factors and, thus, to normal progress. Such procedures cannot be as authoritative as direct study of progress through longitudinal monitoring of the same, or equivalent, groups of learners. Strictly speaking, therefore, true norms for progress are rarely available.

1. Construction

Two main sets of principles govern the construction of norm-referenced measures: those concerning content and format and those concerning psychometric properties. Matters of content are determined according to the type of process to be assessed. For example, measures of general intellectual ability would be based, ideally, on fully developed theories or models of intelligence. Contrastingly, an attitude scale might develop atheoretically, commencing simply with a pool of statements people have made of their own attitudes to a subject. Most standard texts on achievement tests recommend an initial curriculum analysis be made. This takes the form of a rationale or blueprint which specifies, often as a cross-tabulated grid, processes and content to be assessed. Such an analysis may already exist as a result of systematic specifications of learning objectives at some prior curriculum planning stage. In either case, items are thereafter drafted to accord with the categories of behaviour and content specified. Exact numbers and balance of items will be selected to reflect the relative importance attached to different categories. At this stage it is customary for draft items to be reviewed by subject specialists. This may assist in weeding out poor items and ensuring general content validity of the test. These content planning and review procedures also perform an important consultative function where a large-scale or potentially controversial testing programme is proposed.

Many techniques and formats exist for the presentation of items, but objective formats, particularly multiple choice, are consistently popular, being more economical while no less valid than other methods.

The psychometric characteristics of norm-referenced assessment are fully treated in many textbooks, both introductory and advanced. These show how a sophisticated technology can be brought to bear in evaluating and controlling statistical features of items and tests. However, most judicious authors would accept that technical considerations should not apply to the exclusion of cognate and curricular issues.

The apparent extent of the statistical dimension to normative measurement need not entirely deter teachers who are not test specialists from application of these principles in devising their own tests. For example, use of even simple item analysis procedures would help ensure a school-made test provided the required spread and discrimination amongst testees. In this respect, at least, the teacher-made instrument can approach the efficiency of the published product of the test specialist. Estimations of reliability and error of measurement also enhance the clarity with which teachers might interpret results on their own tests. However, establishing meaningful norms is a task which, perhaps by definition, lies outside the scope of individual institutions. It is also debatable whether studies exploring underlying dimensions or latent trait structure would be appropriate, although these are of great theoretical interest to the researcher. They are also subject to more academic controversy than routine aspects of item analysis and reliability. Published guides for the nonspecialist in basic principles of normative test construction are certainly available (e.g., Marshall and Hales 1971, Nuttall and Skurnik 1969) although the extent of their actual use has not been widely researched.

2. Applications

Norm-referenced assessment is used extensively throughout many education systems in administration and teaching, clinical and guidance work, research, and evaluation. The practical and conceptual basis for applying and interpreting normative measurement in such fields is dealt with in established texts such as Cronbach (1970), and Thorndike and Hagen (1977).

The wisdom of this great reliance upon testing has been questioned (e.g., Broadfoot 1979), particularly where it has been an instrument of administrative policy. Certainly, for national or regional administrators, the potential of norm-referenced measurement to differentiate between students of differing abilities, has proved particularly attractive. Problems of screening and selection can be conveniently tackled by use of instruments with the requisite measuring powers. For example, numerous published tests have been produced to identify children who have difficulty in learning to read English as a first language. These are selected, or devised, to contain a sufficient number of relatively easy items to enable the test to distinguish between poor and average readers and to make fine distinctions and rankings within the former group. Such tests are widely used on an administrative regional scale to identify children who may require specialist remedial instruction. At the other extreme, it is the practice in some countries to employ general ability and scholastic aptitude tests to select candidates for advanced or higher education. Here the emphasis may well be upon above-average difficulty for the relevant population. This will allow the maximum discrimination amongst high performers and thus assist, or indeed determine, the process of selection. Use of norm-referenced instruments for selection and placement in education has aroused criticism in some countries. However, the most telling of these criticisms tend to concern the psychological theories on which such tests are based rather than their psychometric properties. In some countries, concern for accountability in education has brought pressure for greater use of system-wide monitoring and evaluation. This may include a strong component of normative measurement. Indeed the need for comprehensive curriculum coverage and longitudinal continuity in such programmes, has acted as a stimulus for innovations in methods of assessment, notably in the field of item banking.

The social impact of accountability-related assessment programmes can be considerable, particularly where results for individual institutions are published. Here the use of norm-referenced assessment cannot avoid close scrutiny. Even where criticisms of technical adequacy can be answered, a more fundamental question remains. This concerns the capacity of normative measurement to fully express or encapsulate school achievement. In this respect assessment of what is learned (criterion-referenced assessment), as opposed to measurement of normative relationships, is of considerable interest. There are also more radical alternatives, such as those proposed in Burgess and Adams (1980) for assessment in British secondary education.

The purposes served by norm-referenced assessment at national or regional level have close counterparts at the level of school or college administration. Screening, selection, placement, and monitoring of standards are perennial concerns of school administration. There are also some additional purposes, notably the keeping of individual student records, where information from normative assessment may feature as a matter of routine. The extent to which a distinction can be made between the use of norm-referenced assessment as an administrative rather than pedagogic device, depends largely upon local circumstances. Ideally, there would be continuity between the two purposes. In practice, the extent to which the normative assessments made in an institution contribute constructively to the work of individual teachers varies greatly. Much of this is probably determined by the approach and emphasis of national and local policy. Where this has aroused resentment because of its extent, or suspicion over the way results will be used, it may seem ironic to suggest normative measurement has any genuine pedagogic value. Defenders of norm-referenced assessment would, nevertheless, point to intrinsic capacity to clarify and add perspective, if not objectivity, to teachers' judgments of individual and group achievement. Applied at class or group level, it can be illuminative of range and differences in achievement and the effects of changes and innovations in teaching method. It can also dispel conjecture concerning standards of achievement in relation to relevant population norms and elucidate strengths and weaknesses in different skill or subject areas. All this presupposes appropriate training, expertise, and availability of a suitable choice of instruments. In these respects the resources available at school level rarely match those at other levels.

See also: Criterion-referenced Measurement; Criterion-referenced Tests

Bibliography

Broadfoot P 1979 *Assessment, Schools and Society*. Methuen, London

Burgess T, Adams E 1980 *Outcomes of Education*. Macmillan, Basingstoke

Cronbach L J 1970 *Essentials of Psychological Testing*. Harper and Row, New York

Marshall J C, Hales L W 1971 *Classroom Test Construction*. Addison-Wesley, Reading, Massachusetts

Mehrens W A, Lehmann I J 1969 *Standardized Tests in Education*. Holt, Rinehart and Winston, New York

Mehrens W A, Lehmann I J 1975 *Measurement and Evaluation in Education and Psychology*. Holt, Rinehart and Winston, New York

Nuttall D L, Skurnik L S 1969 *Examination and Item Analysis Manual*. National Foundation for Educational Research, Slough

Thorndike R L, Hagen E P 1977 *Measurement and Evaluation in Psychology and Education*, 4th edn. Wiley, New York

Criterion-referenced Tests

R. A. Berk

A criterion-referenced test is deliberately constructed to assess an individual's performance level with respect to a well-defined domain of behaviors. The principal concern in its development is obtaining rigorous and precise domain specifications to maximize the interpretability of an individual's domain score. This emphasis on the domain has prompted some measurement experts to refer to the test as domain-referenced. Such a distinction is meaningful inasmuch as another type of criterion-referenced test has also emerged in practice. This alternative conceptualization, derived from mastery learning theory and popularized by many of the recent technical articles on item statistics and reliability, is represented by the mastery test. It is used to classify students as masters and nonmasters of an objective in order to expedite individualized instruction. Empirical item analysis procedures are recommended to determine whether the items are instructionally sensitive or discriminate between instructed and uninstructed groups. Methods for setting performance standards for mastery, the estimation of classification errors, and the determination of mastery–nonmastery decision consistency are particularly important elements in its development.

To date there have been four books (Berk 1980c, Berk 1984, Brown 1980, Popham 1978) and one issue of a journal (*Applied Psychological Measurement* 1980 Vol. 4 No. 4) devoted exclusively to the topic of criterion-referenced tests. They describe the procedures for test construction, score use, and interpretation. Very often the technical characteristics are compared to those of norm-referenced tests. For purposes of clarification, the specific differences between norm-referenced tests and the two types of criterion-referenced tests defined above are summarized in Table 1. A brief explanation of the characteristics of mastery and domain-referenced tests is given next.

1. Domain Specification

The mastery test is built on a set of instructional and behavioral objectives. While the objectives-based definition is relatively less precise and "ambiguous" compared to the strategies used to construct a domain-referenced test, it is extremely practicable. In addition, it is possible to improve upon this definition by using amplified objectives, instructional objectives exchange (IOX) test specifications, or mapping sentences.

The primary emphasis in the development of a domain-referenced test is at this first stage. The "unambiguous" definition of a behavioral domain and the generation of an item domain from that definition have been recommended to provide the most useful interpretation of an individual's domain score. These goals are difficult to achieve even with the technologies currently available (Roid and Haladyna 1981). Among the various domain specification strategies, only item transformations, item forms, and algorithms come close to attaining unambiguous definitions via sophisticated rule structures (Berk 1980a).

2. Item Construction

The objectives-based strategies associated with the mastery test necessitate a heavy reliance upon traditional item construction rules. The use of mapping sentences (facet theory) in conjunction with objectives holds considerable promise for refining this process so that it is more systematic and mechanical.

The domain-referenced approach requires detailed, explicit rules for generating the test items. The unambiguous specification strategies noted previously provide objective, computer-based technologies for producing item domains.

3. Item Domain

Until recently, the distinction between infinite and finite item domains was rarely considered in the test development process. The technological advances since the early 1970s in the specification of behavioral domains, however, have made it possible to actually generate "all possible items" in a domain. The level of precision in the specifications necessary to produce a finite domain is quite unlike that of the objectives-based schemes. There are at least two advantages to the exact specification and enumeration of the items in a domain: (a) the items that comprise one test form or alternate forms can be drawn from the domain using a random or stratified sampling plan, and (b) the characteristics of the domain can be identified and, consequently, can be incorporated into the sampling design (for example, stratification by difficulty level), and other stages of test construction and score analysis (for example, parallel forms assumption, selection of an appropriate reliability index).

The objectives employed to define the content domain for a mastery test may suggest either a finite or an infinite domain. Typically, such a distinction is theoretical except in the case of very specific behavioral objectives; for example, the student will be able to multiply all combinations of single digit numbers. The items written to be included on a given test are usually not sampled from any domain. Rather, those items viewed collectively are assumed to constitute a sample from the domain of "all possible items" that could have been written from the objectives. Since the distinction between item domains makes little practical difference in the context of mastery test construction, the concept of "all possible items" is often associated with the assumption of an infinite item domain.

4. Test Length

The problem of determining how many items should be written for each objective on a mastery test has been approached from both practical and statistical perspectives. The former considers a multiplicity of factors, including importance and type of decision making, importance and emphases assigned to objectives, number of objectives, and practical constraints; the latter deals with the relationship between number of items and decision validity and decision reliability indices.

For the domain-referenced test, the analogous test length issue is translated into how many items should be sampled from the domain. It has been studied from the same perspectives. The statistical methods, however, have focused on the relationship between number of items and the reliability of the domain score estimate.

5. Item Analysis

An item analysis is desirable for mastery test items due to the intended uses of the test scores for mastery–nonmastery decisions and to the traditional, relatively subjective procedures employed in writing the items. The items must be scrutinized to appraise whether or not they measure their respective objectives, are unbiased in relation to women and minority groups, and differentiate between groups of masters and nonmasters of the objectives (item discrimination). In addition, they must be free of structural flaws that could cue or confuse the students.

This type of item analysis is unnecessary and, in fact, undesirable for domain-referenced test items. The use of item statistics for refining and selecting the items would theoretically destroy the defining character of the test, thereby weakening the interpretability of the domain score. Furthermore, given the precision of most of the strategies that are used to generate the item domain, the need to assess item–objective congruence or search for flaws in the items seems questionable.

6. Item Selection

Mastery test items are selected nonrandomly based on their congruence with the objectives and their sensitivity

Table 1
Technical characteristics of norm-referenced tests and criterion-referenced tests

Characteristic	Norm referenced	Criterion referenced Mastery	Domain referenced
Domain specification	Content outline Table of specifications	Instructional and behavioral objectives	Possible strategies: (a) Amplified objectives (b) IOX test specifications (c) Mapping sentences (d) Item transformations (e) Item forms (f) Algorithms
Item construction	M–C, T–F, matching Short answer Essay	Traditional rules used to produce traditional formats	Generation rules used to produce traditional formats
Item domain	Infinite (or finite)	Infinite (or finite)	Infinite (or finite)
Test length	Based on reliability	Based on decision validity and decision reliability	Based on estimate of domain score
Item analysis	Difficulty Discrimination (item-total score r) Choice response analysis to revise faulty items	Item-objective congruence Difficulty (mastery group) Difficulty (nonmastery group) Discrimination (between mastery and nonmastery group performance) Choice response analysis to revise faulty items	
Item selection	Nonrandom	Nonrandom	Random
Parallel forms assumption	Classically parallel	Classically parallel	Randomly parallel
Standard setting	Optional	Judgmental or judgmental–empirical method (state or continuum model)	Optional
Validity	Content Criterion related Construct	Content Criterion related Construct (Decision)	Content Construct
Reliability	Possible approaches: (a) Parallel forms (b) Test–retest (c) Internal consistency	Possible approaches: (a) Threshold loss estimate of p_o or κ (b) Squared-error loss estimate of $k^2(X, T_X)$	Possible approaches: (a) Squared-error loss estimate of $\phi(\lambda)$ or ϕ (b) Point estimate of domain score (individual specific or group specific standard error of measurement)

to instructional treatments. The item selection criteria recently proffered by Berk (1980c) emphasize clearly the primary importance of congruence and the secondary importance of statistical item properties.

As indicated previously, the items in a domain-referenced test are sampled randomly from an item domain. This assures that they are representative and congruent with the domain.

7. Parallel Forms Assumption

The assumption about parallel forms of a criterion-referenced test is related to (a) how the item sample that comprises one test form and the samples that comprise alternate forms are generated, and (b) the characteristics of the item domain from which those samples are generated.

When items are written from objectives-based specifications, it is possible to develop two or more item samples for the same objectives and domain. Frequently, those samples are constructed systematically to contain content and to yield means, variances, and item intercorrelations identical to the first sample. Item samples or alternate test forms with those properties are said to be classically parallel or equivalent to the first form. This statistical equivalence imposes restrictions on the domain; it requires that the content or set of behaviors being measured by the items be relatively homogeneous and, therefore, that the items in the domain possess similar difficulty levels.

Since domain-referenced item samples can be drawn randomly from an item domain, they are said to be randomly parallel. No specific statistical properties apply to these test forms nor is there any condition imposed that limits the variability of item difficulty levels in the domain. When the test maker cannot actually build test forms by randomly sampling from the domain, these forms and their characteristics can be "assumed."

8. Standard Setting

More than 20 different methods for setting performance standards have been recommended in the literature. Despite several extensive reviews of these methods, standard setting is still the stickiest technical topic. Perhaps the simplest framework for understanding the various methods is a bilevel classification (Berk 1980d). The first level partitions the methods into two major categories based on their assumptions about the acquisition of the underlying trait or ability: state models and continuum models. The second level classifies the methods according to whether they are based purely on judgment or incorporate both judgmental and empirical information: judgmental methods and judgmental–empirical methods/models.

8.1 State Models

State models assume that mastery or true-score performance is an all-or-nothing state; the standard is set at 100 percent. Deviations from this true state are presumed attributable to "intrusion" (false mastery) and/or "omission" (false nonmastery) errors. After a consideration of these errors, the standard is adjusted to values less than 100 percent. The judgmental–empirical models employ decision rules to identify the cutoff score that minimizes expected loss due to classification errors. These rules require judgments in designating the loss ratio.

8.2 Continuum Models

Continuum models assume that mastery is a continuously distributed ability that can be viewed as an interval on a continuum, that is, an area at the upper end of the continuum circumscribes the boundaries for mastery. This conceptualization appears to fit the design and intent of most criterion-referenced tests. It is therefore not surprising that the bulk of the research has concentrated on continuum models.

Although it was inevitable that the experts on criterion-referenced testing would not agree on a "best method" for setting standards, there is consensus on one issue—all of the methods involve some form of human judgment. A completely objective, scientifically precise method does not exist. Regardless of how complex and technically sophisticated a method might be, judgment plays a role in the determination of the cutoff score and/ or in the estimation of classification error rates.

8.3 Judgmental Methods

These are based on judgments of the probability that competent persons would select particular distractors in each item or would answer each item correctly. The subjectivity of these item content decisions used to arrive at an overall cutoff score has been expressed succinctly as "pulling the probabilities from thin air." This problem is reflected in the variability among judgments within a single method and also across methods.

8.4 Judgmental–Empirical Methods

These are based on some type of judgment and actual or simulated data, judgmental data, and/or distribution assumptions. The role of judgment should not be underestimated. That is, the judgmental component usually supplies the foundation for much of the statistical estimation of probabilities of correct classification decisions and false mastery/false nonmastery decision errors.

The judgmental–empirical methods differ according to other characteristics as well: (a) their overall purpose; (b) the definition of the criterion variable; (c) a consideration of utilities; (d) the statistical sophistication; and (e) their practicability. Perhaps the most important initial distinction pertains to their purpose. Only the criterion groups and contrasting groups approaches are intended to select a cutoff score. All of the remaining methods presume that a standard already exists on a criterion or latent variable. Subsequently, this standard is translated into a cutoff score for the test, and decision error rates based on various assumptions are estimated. In some cases, those rates can be used to adjust the cutoff. The decision–theoretic models are not techniques for setting standards or optimizing mastery decisions; they are techniques for minimizing the consequences of measurement and sampling errors once the true cutoff has already been chosen.

8.5 Application of the Methods

Although a domain-referenced test is not designed expressly for mastery–nonmastery decision making, a cutting score may be set. The choice of a single approach appears to be dependent on the specific test application and several factors related to that application, including political considerations, decision consequences, practical constraints, statistical expertise and resources, and the types of mastery decisions to be made.

A standard *must* be set for the mastery test. The number of cutting scores that need to be selected for a test will differ with the structure of the test and the types of decisions. For objectives-based tests used for individual decisions at the classroom level, cutting scores should be chosen for each item cluster or subtest keyed to an instructional objective. There is nothing implicit in any of the approaches that dictates that the cutting score has to be identical for all subtests. The customary use of one "blanket mastery standard" for all objectives seems inadvisable for the following reasons. First, objectives vary in level of complexity and, therefore, applying the same standard to different objectives will be insensitive to that variability. Second, the difficulty and discrimination indices of items measuring one objective may be quite different from the indices of items measuring other objectives; consequently, it is unrealistic to expect a high proportion of students to obtain the same standard for each objective. Third, since the instruction associated with different objectives is rarely given the same time allotment and attention, performance on some objectives might be noticeably better than the performance on others. Again, this is inconsistent with setting the same standard for all objectives.

If the mastery test happens to be developed as a "minimum competency test" to be used for individual certification decisions at the school level, a single cutting score may be set for the total test rather than for each objective. Decisions regarding graduation and grade-to-grade promotion ordinarily do not require objective-by-objective analysis, although it is possible to specify a certain number of objectives that must be mastered in order to "pass." The information on objective mastery might be employed for follow-up diagnostic purposes along with instructional prescriptions for students who "fail."

9. Validity

While the assessment of content validity, criterion-related validity, and construct validity is applicable to both test conceptualizations, the emphases differ markedly. Given the objectives-based specifications of the mastery test, a special review process is necessary in order to determine content validity. This involves an examination of the technical quality and representativeness of the items. Procedures for evaluating item-objective congruence using rating scales and matching tasks have been suggested. It is significant to note that the judgmental and empirical procedures used to establish content validity for the mastery test are quite different from the domain specification strategies used to build in content validity for the domain-referenced test.

In addition to the steps required to ensure content validity, it is also essential to investigate the criterion-related validity and construct validity of the test. The mastery decision framework provides a specific focus for such investigations. The most complex and problematic aspect of this line of inquiry pertains to the definition of the success or mastery criterion. An operational definition must be specified and criterion success and nonsuccess groups of persons need to be identified. The criterion-related validity studies may be concurrent or predictive depending upon how success is defined, for example, success in the current program, or success in the next unit of instruction.

Furthermore, a particular type of construct validity for mastery test scores that deserves special attention is decision validity. It relates to the evidence gathered on the accuracy of mastery–nonmastery classification decisions. That evidence is often expressed as probabilities of correct and incorrect (false mastery and false nonmastery) classifications. Such evidence is crucial in the attempt to justify the selection of the cutting score. When decision validity evidence is not available, it seems pointless even to compute a reliability index. A high reliability index based on an "invalid" or "unjustified" standard, for example, might mean that the mastery test can consistently classify students into the wrong groups. Consistent decision making without accurate decision making has questionable value in criterion-referenced evaluation.

For the domain-referenced test, the tasks employed in developing the test concentrate, for the most part, on building in content validity. The rigor of the domain specifications and their direct link with the test items are the principal features. The effort devoted in the initial stages is designed to pay off with the dividends of descriptive clarity and precise score interpretations.

Another important concern is the construct validity of the scores. Empirically based construct validity studies that employ factor analysis or Guttman scalogram analysis should be conducted. Unfortunately, few such studies have been executed by test makers at the district or state levels.

10. Reliability

Similar to the topic of standard setting, the literature is replete with studies and reviews of reliability methods, with more than a dozen methods proposed to date. The types of reliability that are appropriate for mastery and domain-referenced tests are contingent upon the parallel forms assumption, cutting score selection, and the intended uses of the test scores.

Several different approaches to mastery test reliability are indicated according to the usual though not essential assumption of classically parallel test forms, the selection of a cutting score, and the use of the scores for mastery–nonmastery decisions. The classification consistency estimates of p_o or κ based on a threshold loss function have been highly recommended. The recent comparisons of various one- and two-administration estimates suggest that Hambleton and Novick's method for estimating p_o and Huynh's method for estimating p_o and κ may be especially useful (Berk 1980b). When distinctions among degrees of mastery and nonmastery along the score continuum are desirable, not just the qualitative master–nonmaster classification assumed by the threshold loss function, Livingston's k^2 (X, T_X) squared-error loss index should be considered.

Since the major purpose of the domain-referenced test is to estimate and to clearly interpret an individual's domain score in terms of a well-defined behavioral domain, point and interval estimation approaches would seem to be most appropriate. When that purpose is viewed in conjunction with the randomly parallel test forms assumption, there appear to be at least two point estimates and two standard errors of measurement for interval estimates that a test maker should consider (see Berk 1980b). In addition, two indices of "dependability" derived from generalizability theory have been proposed which also merit serious attention. One of those indices, $\phi(\lambda)$, is a function of the cutting score (λ). When it is desirable to make mastery–nonmastery decisions with a domain-referenced test, a cutting score should be selected and the $\phi(\lambda)$ index could be used as a measure of test score dependability relative to λ.

11. Conclusions

This review of the most salient characteristics of the mastery and domain-referenced approaches to criterion-referenced measurement indicates that each type of test is designed systematicaly to yield scores for particular uses. As in norm-referenced test construction (see *Norm-referenced Assessment*), the selection and estimation of the technical characteristics are governed primarily by the intended interpretation(s) of the test scores and the subsequent decisions based on them. Therefore, the technical aspects of the development process must be addressed in order to assure meaningful results. The procedures outlined in Table 1 and described in the accompanying text should facilitate the choice of appropriate methodologies in specific applications.

Bibliography

Berk R A 1980a A comparison of six content domain specification strategies for criterion-referenced tests. *Educ. Technol.* 20: 49–52

Berk R A 1980b A consumers' guide to criterion-referenced test reliability. *J. Educ. Meas.* 17: 323–49

Berk R A (ed.) 1980c *Criterion-Referenced Measurement: The State of the Art*. Johns Hopkins University Press, Baltimore, Maryland

Berk R A 1980d A framework for methodological advances in criterion-referenced testing. *Appl. Psychol. Meas.* 4: 563–73

Berk R A (ed.) 1984 *A Guide to Criterion-Referenced Test Construction and Use*. Johns Hopkins University Press, Baltimore, Maryland

Brown S 1980 *What Do They Know? A Review of Criterion-Referenced Assessment*. Scottish Education Department, Edinburgh

Popham W J 1978 *Criterion-Referenced Measurement*. Prentice-Hall, Englewood Cliffs, New Jersey

Roid G H, Haladyna T M 1981 *A Technology for Test-Item Writing*. Academic Press, New York

Domain-referenced Tests

E. L. Baker

A domain-referenced test attempts to provide clear specifications about the nature of the tested performance in order to clarify what is being measured and to provide a basis for assessing the representativeness of the items with regard to the competency in question.

Domain-referenced testing is a special case of criterion-referenced testing. Criterion-referenced testing focuses upon assessing the respondent's performance with respect to a well-defined level or body of knowledge. When the test designer wishes to describe well the content and skills sampled by the test, the use of domain-referenced testing is suggested. The domain that is referred to in this context does not correspond to the term domain as used by Bloom et al. (1956) in describing broad areas of competency in their well-known taxonomies of objectives. Rather, domain refers to the specifically circumscribed universe from which performance

is sampled and to which performance is expected to generalize. Thus, in domain-referenced testing, part of the problem is devising or describing the parameters of the domain and another is devising a rule of algorithm to permit sampling.

1. Specifications for Domains

All tests have certain specifications, describing the broad range of content and skills to be assessed. Domain-referenced tests present specifications that attempt to reduce successively the uncertainty first of the test item writer in creating comparable items, that is, items which represent the same universe of skills and content, and secondly, of the test user who is attempting to understand what a test score means. Because criterion-referenced testing emphasizes measuring what or how much the learner knows, the first problem is to describe that general area. Various writers have attacked this problem using their own special language. More generally, however, the problem consists of describing what content the respondent will be faced with under what conditions, in what form the response is expected, and what criteria will be used to judge the adequacy of performance. Because of the history of criterion-referenced testing in general and domain-referenced testing in particular, a common starting point is in the description of the objectives of the instructional program that the tests purport to measure. The point of entry derives from objectives because the entire movement of criterion-referenced tests and domain-referenced tests grew out of a preoccupation with assessing instruction (Glaser 1963). A common way for educators to think about domains is in terms of clarifying the objectives that they want to assess, [e.g., the "amplified objectives" of Popham (1981)].

At a practical level, it is necessary to assure that items used to assess a particular area conform in some regularized way to specifications. Although at the outset of this movement, in the late 1960s in the United States, much emphasis was given to the behavior that was to be elicited by the test, further effort pointed to the major problem of clarifying the content in the objective. The content limits of the domain are its most critical feature. How may content be circumscribed? One approach, taken by Hively et al. (1973) depends upon the use of an item shell into which specific content may be inserted according to an algorithm, for example, $a + b = \text{-----}$, where a equals any two-digit number and b equals any three-digit number. Given such a shell, and the rule "any," comparable items may be developed and an estimate may be made of the performance in respect to the entire universe of two-digit and three-digit sums. Because of the relative simplicity of using an algebraic form for a mathematical task, it is not surprising that the earliest efforts in domain-referenced testing came from mathematics and science problems that involved quantity (Hively et al. 1973). Naturally, the problem of content becomes unwieldly as a move is made from content that has a clear structure to content with arbitrary arrangements. For that reason, domain-referenced tests are easier to prepare in those fields where either there exists a complete list of content itself (e.g., English consonants), rather a vast set of information, or creative works that differ in more ways than they are similar, for example, French novels. Nonetheless, domain-referenced testing has developed some approaches to describing and limiting content for testing. One procedure involves describing features of the content thought to be critical to an assessment of competency. For example, in the assessment of reading comprehension, children may need to be presented with both fiction and nonfiction as stimuli, but because the cognitive processes for understanding may differ, such content domains might be separated and further specified in a domain-referenced test. Therefore, the content limits might specify not only the genre, (fiction or nonfiction,) but also the length of passage, the complexity of the

writing, and the novelty of the information. Clearly such limits exclude certain passages from consideration, but permit enormous variation in those selected, raising the question of what is comparable content. Another approach to the problem of content limits in fields such as social studies or literature has been to enumerate the concepts or works to which students will be expected to generalize, for example, mercantilism, capitalism, economic socialism, or *The Duinio Elegies* by Rilke and *Four Quartets* by Eliot. In this approach, there is no attempt to equate the concepts or pieces to which the student is supposed to respond. Instead, the list is simply to assure that the test items (and, as well, the preceding instruction) take the enumerated content explicitly to heart.

Thus, content established by enumeration communicates content on a practical and concrete level rather than an abstract, rule level. Another type of enumeration occurs when all of a particular set of information represents the universe. The rule is simply "go to" a reference or resource and use it as a base for content. For example, to be able to read aloud any passage from the *London Times*. An effective universe of discourse has been circumscribed and clearly what is fair game for testing is any sort of article or advertising in the periodical named. Operationally, such a limit communicates a good deal to test writer, teacher, and perhaps to the learner (should the specifications be made available to students).

Another example is to refer to a particular text, for example, any anthropological concept from Beals and Hoijer, *Introduction to Anthropology*. The table of contents provides the functional content limits. However, the topics included in the book itself may be arbitrary and reflect the biases of the authors rather than some more generally applicable structure of the field. So in the same way that specifying particular concepts such as mercantilism is arbitrary, so is the reference to a particular work a weakened form of domain-referenced testing. Whereas the student may demonstrate competency with respect to the defined limits, the validity of those limits still needs demonstration.

A second feature of content limits relates to the determination of the adequacy of the students' responses. For constructed responses, the typical approach is to provide scoring criteria, and training regimens for their application. Thus, in the domain of expository writing, scoring criteria include (a) mechanical, (e.g., grammatical) errors, (b) topic-related criteria (e.g., correct information), and (c) stylistic criteria (e.g., support provided for assertions). When the explication of criteria is too complex, some examples of domain-referenced testing have used excellent, average, and poor samples of student effort to assist the scorer in classifying responses. To the extent such criteria can be identified into components, the domain-referenced test takes on more utility as a diagnostic or placement tool, for on the basis of poor performance on specific criteria, instruction can be developed or revised. The source of these performance criteria may be at best arbitrary, for example, no more than three spelling errors, thereby opening the test developer to the charge of casual curriculum design. It is probably best to include as criteria those features of performance that are expected to be subtasks of the major goal, for example, the inclusion of a thesis statement in an expository essay, or else those known to be prerequisites to a next course or unit in the same instructional sequence (e.g., past tense of Spanish verbs).

When the student is asked to make a selection from a set of options rather than to produce a response, the criteria of adequate performance are used as the basis for constructing the response options. For instance, if a student is to set the proper modifier for a given sentence, it may be critical that the test provide options that are modifiers but which differ according to semantic (does it make good sense?), and syntactic (adjective or adverb) features. Perhaps the greatest contribution of domain-referenced tests will be to regularize the manner in which response options are generated so that a right answer means some mastery over a comparable set of options, and a wrong answer has direct diagnostic value.

The next major feature of domain-referenced test specifications is the description specifically of the item format, the directions, and the conditions under which the response is observed. Although more properly the focus of the item writing article (see *Item Writing Techniques*), format decisions have strong implications for assessing the validity of the domains.

2. Problems in Domain-referenced Testing

A number of theoretical and practical problems remain in domain-referenced test generation and validation. One problem relates to the relative broadness and narrowness of the domain and whether it is practical to use specific domains in the large-scale assessment of a performance developed under a variety of conditions. Some efforts have been made to use domain-referenced testing in regional assessments and evaluations in the United States, but as yet no specific analysis of this problem has been undertaken. In addition, questions have been raised about the sampling rules, including the number of items necessary to get reasonable estimates of a domain. This problem has a tautological component since number of items, or test length, depends upon the cut score used, which may very well be a function of the quality of instruction. A third major question involves the addition of components explicitly addressed to the linguistic features of the test rather than to its content or response features. Of interest is the extent to which variation can be attributed to language rather than to more traditional characteristics of tests and instruction.

A fourth issue involves the match between items and the domain specifications to which they presumably relate. Present procedures are particularly weak, in that simple on–off judgments are usually made about a match. Clearly, the level of detail of the specifications will interact with the quality of judgment, for with very broad specifications almost any item will fit. However, some application of set theory appears promising.

See also: Criterion-referenced Tests; Criterion-referenced Measurement

Bibliography

Baker E L 1974 Beyond objectives: Domain referenced achievement. In: Hively W (ed.) 1974 *Domain Referenced Testing*. Educational Technology Publications, Englewood Cliffs, New Jersey

Bloom B S (ed.) 1956 *Taxonomy of Educational Objectives: The Classification of Educational Goals: Handbook 1. Cognitive Domain*. McKay, New York

Glaser R 1963 Instructional technology and the measurement of learning outcomes: Some questions. *Am. Psychol.* 18: 515–21

Hively W, Maxwell G, Rabehl G, Sension D, Lundin S 1973 *Domain Referenced Curriculum Evaluation*, CSE Monograph Series No. 1. Center for the Study of Evaluation, University of California at Los Angeles, Los Angeles, California

Popham W J 1981 *Modern Educational Measurement*. Prentice Hall, New Jersey

Adaptive Testing

D. J. Weiss

An adaptive test is one in which different sets of test questions (items) are administered to different individuals depending on each individual's status on the trait being measured. Adaptive tests contrast with conventional tests in which all examinees are administered the same fixed set of items (e.g., a typical paper-and-pencil test). Adaptive testing has also been referred to as tailored, response-contingent, programmed, computerized, automated, individualized, branched, and sequential testing.

In an adaptive test, one or more items are administered to an examinee and scored correct or incorrect. Based on the responses of the examinee, additional items are selected from an item bank (pool) with items of known difficulties and discriminations. The items selected for administration to the examinee during the process of testing are selected to be those in the item bank which are most appropriate for measuring that individual, primarily in terms of their difficulties. In this way, the items are adapted to the characteristics of the examinee during the process of testing. The items administered to each individual are those that are neither too easy nor too difficult for the individual.

Some adaptive tests are designed for individual administration by a trained psychometrist. Others are amenable to paper-and-pencil administration. Still others require that test items be administered by an interactive computer. The latter approach takes full advantage of the capabilities of adaptive testing. While most adaptive tests have been developed for measuring ability or achievement variables, the technology of adaptive testing can be fruitfully applied to the measurement of homogeneous personality and attitudinal variables.

Adaptive tests have demonstrated substantial advantages over conventional tests. A major advantage is that of efficiency. Adaptive tests yield measurements of comparable or superior quality to those of conventional tests with considerably fewer items administered to each individual. These increases in testing efficiency are reflected in savings in test administration time, making it possible to measure two or more traits using adaptive tests in the same amount of time that would be required to measure a single trait using conventional tests. Along with the increases in measurement efficiency, adaptive tests provide improved measurement characteristics in terms of greater precision of the measurements for all or most trait levels, which translate into higher degrees of reliability and potentially higher levels of validity. Even with a set of items that constitute a conventional test, computer-administered adaptive tests can improve measurement efficiency with no loss in the psychometric characteristics of the measurements. Adaptive testing can also result in efficient and more accurate mastery classifications, and provides an efficient and practical approach to the measurement of individual change.

1. The Test Constructor's Bandwidth–Fidelity Dilemma

Given the requirement of administering a fixed set of items to a group of examinees, a test constructor can construct a "peaked" conventional test or a "rectangular" conventional test, with possible variations in between these two extremes. The peaked conventional test has all of its items concentrated at one level of difficulty. It will measure very well for individuals whose trait levels are at or near that level of difficulty, but as the trait levels of individuals deviate from the point at which the test is peaked, the precision of the measurements obtained by the conventional test decreases very rapidly since items peaked at an average level of difficulty will be too difficult for individuals with lower trait levels or too easy for individuals with higher trait levels. A rectangular conventional test includes several very easy items which will be appropriate for individuals with very low trait levels, several moderate difficulty items which will be appropriate for individuals at moderate trait levels, and several items at each of a number of levels of higher difficulty which will be appropriate for individuals with higher trait levels. However, only a few of the items in each test will be appropriate for individuals at any trait level. As a consequence, while a rectangular conventional test will provide measurements of relatively equal precision at most trait levels, the overall

magnitude of precision of these measurements will be relatively low.

Thus the constructor of a conventional test is caught in a "bandwidth–fidelity" dilemma: a peaked conventional test provides measurements of high fidelity (precision) at the point at which it is peaked, but it has little bandwidth, that is it has little capability of differentiating examinees at other trait levels. By contrast, a rectangular conventional test has good bandwidth—it is capable of differentiating trait levels all along the trait continuum; but it has low overall fidelity—the differentiations it can make are of relatively low precision.

Since a test peaked in difficulty at an individual's trait level provides the best measurements for that individual, adaptive testing solves the bandwidth–fidelity dilemma by selecting from an item bank for each individual a test designed of items which are appropriate in difficulty level for each examinee. The result of a good adaptive testing procedure is a set of items selected for each examinee which have 0.5 probability of a correct response (assuming no guessing) for that individual. This test is the test that is designed to differentiate each individual's trait levels from contiguous trait levels with maximum precision.

2. Principles of Adaptive Testing

2.1 Adaptive Testing Using Prestructured Item Banks

The general principles of adaptive testing were first applied by Alfred Binet in the Binet intelligence test, developed in France in the early 1900s and later made available as the Stanford–Binet Intelligence Test in the English-speaking countries. In the language of adaptive testing, Binet's intelligence test, which used an item pool prestructured by age (difficulty) levels, is a mechanical branching strategy using a fixed branching rule, a variable entry point, and a variable termination criterion. The entry point for Binet's adaptive test is the level at which the individual is assumed to be functioning. Items are administered and scored immediately.

If all items are answered correctly at a given age (difficulty) level, items at a higher level are administered until an age level is identified at which all items are answered incorrectly (ceiling level). If all items are answered incorrectly at a given age level, items at lower age levels are administered until an age level is identified at which the individual answers all items correctly (basal level). The termination criterion is to stop testing when both a ceiling level and a basal level have been identified. In between the ceiling and basal levels, the examinee will have answered some items correctly and some items incorrectly, providing a set of items approximately adapted to the individual's ability level. The variable termination criterion usually results in different numbers of items administered to different individuals.

Other adaptive tests developed beginning in the late 1950s used paper-and-pencil administration but did not use variable entry and variable termination (Weiss 1974). The two-stage adaptive test (Lord 1980) has minimal adaptive capability. All examinees take a short test, called a routing test, which is typically a test of average difficulty. Based on their scores on the routing test, examinees are branched to a second stage "measurement" test which is roughly adapted to their trait level. The pyramidal adaptive test consists of a set of items prestructured by difficulty into a structure resembling a pyramid. At the top of the pyramid is an item of average difficulty which is the first item administered to an examinee. At the next stage of the test are two items whose difficulties are slightly above and below the difficulty of the first item. At subsequent stages, each item leads to two additional items—a slightly more difficult item, or a slightly easier item. The slightly more difficult item is administered following a correct response to any item, and the slightly easier item is administered following an incorrect response to an item.

The flexilevel test (Lord 1980) consists of a series of items with one item at each of a number of equally spaced difficulties varying from very easy to very difficult items. Individuals begin the test with the item of average difficulty; a correct response leads to the next more difficult item not previously administered, and an incorrect response leads to the next less difficult item not previously administered. A person with a high level on the trait will receive the highest difficulty items, and an individual with a low trait level will receive the 50 percent of the lower difficulty items, while examinees in between will receive a subset of items that span their trait level.

The stratified adaptive (stradaptive) test, like the Binet test, operates from an item bank stratified into item subsets of different difficulty levels (Weiss 1979). Testing can begin at any difficulty level, and a new item is selected after each item is administered. A correct response to an item leads to the most discriminating unadministered item in the next higher level of difficulty. An incorrect response leads to the most discriminating unadministered item at the next lower level of difficulty. Similar to the Binet test, testing continues until a "ceiling" stratum has been identified—a level of difficulty at which the individual answers none of the items correctly (or in the case of multiple-choice items, answers at or below the chance level). The fixed-branching strategies are useful if adaptive tests are to be administered by paper and pencil or by simple testing machines.

2.2 Adaptive Testing Using Item Response Theory and Unstructured Item Banks

The full power of adaptive testing is made available through variable-branching strategies based on item response theory (latent trait test theory or item characteristic curve theory), and using computerized item administration. The item response theory item information curve, which combines information on an item's difficulty, discrimination, and "guessing" parameters, describes how precisely an item measures at various points along the continuum or how well an item differentiates between contiguous trait levels. In addition, item response theory-based methods of scoring tests permit estimation of individuals' trait levels based on

their responses to one or more items and provide an error of measurement associated with the trait level estimate (Lord 1980) (see *Item Response Theory*).

The maximum information adaptive testing strategy selects items which provide maximum levels of item information at an individual's currently estimated trait level. An item is administered, an estimate made of the individual's trait level based on the responses to one item (using Bayesian estimation procedures) or two or more items (using maximum likelihood estimation procedures). The new trait level estimate is then used to select the next item to be administered to that examinee. This process—selecting the item that provides maximum information at the current estimated level of the trait and reestimating trait level—is repeated until a termination criterion is reached. Adaptive tests of this type can be terminated when the current trait level estimate has a given standard error of measurement (or its reciprocal, precision of information) derived from maximum likelihood scoring or, using Bayesian scoring, a given Bayesian posterior variance of the trait level estimate (squared standard error of estimate).

A Bayesian-based variation of the maximum information item selection procedure (Owen 1975) uses Bayes's theorem to select the one item from all the unadministered items that will minimize the Bayesian posterior variance of the trait level estimate after it is answered. The trait level is then reestimated using Bayesian estimation procedures, and the item pool is again searched to identify the single item as yet unadministered that minimizes the posterior variance. The procedure is repeated until some predetermined level of the Bayesian posterior variance is reached. This procedure permits more explicit use of prior information to determine starting points than does the maximum information item selection procedure. However, the use of prior information introduces biases into the scoring procedure which reduce levels of measurement precision for individuals whose trait levels are not near the prior estimate, at least in relatively short adaptive tests.

3. Applications of Adaptive Testing

3.1 Adaptive Testing to Improve Measurement Efficiency and Measurement Precision

These tests, comprising most of the adaptive testing literature, are those that are designed to solve the tester's bandwidth–fidelity dilemma. Adaptive tests of this type approximate "equiprecise" measurement at all trait levels, that is, measurements that measure all trait levels equally well. The successful implementation of adaptive tests for this purpose requires: (a) an adequate item bank, (b) an efficient item selection routine and scoring method, and (c) an appropriate termination criterion.

In order to have enough good items at all possible trait levels so that each individual will be administered a test peaked at his or her trait level, there must be a reasonably large number of items spanning a wide range of difficulties. Good results have been achieved with item banks ranging from 100 to 200 items, with banks of

116 to 150 items providing excellent results. Regardless of the size of the item bank, however, there must be a relatively equal number of items throughout the range of item difficulties. The adaptive testing item bank designed for equiprecise and efficient measurement will function best with items of high discrimination. The higher the discriminations, assuming an adequate distribution of difficulties, the more efficient will be the adaptive test.

Different adaptive testing strategies have differential efficiency. The most efficient strategy in terms of providing equiprecise measurement is the maximum information strategy combined with maximum likelihood scoring. Second is the Bayesian strategy with Bayesian scoring, although its efficiency tends to decrease for trait level estimates that are discrepant from the prior estimate, at least for relatively short adaptive tests. The stradaptive strategy also yields relatively equiprecise measurement.

Equiprecise measurement is best achieved by using a variable termination criterion. In this way, testing can continue until a specified degree of measurement precision is reached for each examinee. If the item pool permits, this will guarantee equiprecise measurement across all trait levels.

Research on adaptive tests designed to improve both measurement efficiency and measurement precision supports the theoretical expectations (Weiss 1982, 1983). Adaptive tests can solve the bandwidth–fidelity dilemma, resulting in tests of high precision and equal levels of precision across all trait levels measured. Adaptive tests also generally show higher reliabilities at very short test lengths, with reliabilities equal to those of peaked conventional tests with two or more times the number of items. In addition, adaptive tests have shown equal or higher validities with substantially fewer items, in comparison to conventional tests.

3.2 Adaptive Testing to Improve Efficiency of Measurement

While adaptive tests can be designed to improve both measurement efficiency and provide equiprecise measurement by using.an appropriately designed item bank, adaptive testing can also be used to improve test efficiency with the kinds of item pools typically found in conventional tests (Weiss 1979). In this case, the objective is to select from a fixed subset of items (which might comprise a conventional test) only those items that are necessary to measure a given individual. Adaptive tests of this type can result in substantially shorter tests, and therefore more efficient tests, without any loss in the measurement characteristics of the test. Test length reductions may range up to 80 percent of the items in a conventional test, with typical reductions of about 50 percent.

To improve measurement efficiency with a fixed and relatively small item bank (e.g., 20 or 30 items), adaptive tests can use a maximum information item selection strategy. As indicated, this strategy selects at each stage

in the adaptive test the single item providing most information at the individual's current estimated trait level. Testing continues until there are no items left in the bank that provide more than some predetermined minimum amount of information. If the minimum information cut-off value is very low (e.g., 0.01 or 0.05), the adaptive test administered will have captured from all of the items available all potential psychometric information in the item subset. Any remaining items will be items that provide no capability of differentiating between contiguous trait levels at the individual's final trait level estimate.

When more than one trait is to be measured (e.g., in the case of a multiple aptitude battery) this intra-subtest adaptive testing procedure can be combined with information on the intercorrelations of the subtests, in order to further improve testing efficiency. Based on the known intercorrelations of the subtests in some reference group, predictions of probable trait levels on subsequent subtests can be made from the trait level estimates for tests already completed and the known regression of the current test on previous tests. These starting points can then be used for the administration of subsequent adaptive tests within each subtest. Ability estimates at the end of each subtest then are combined in later regression equations to predict starting points for other subtests in the battery. When combined with intrasubtest adaptive item selection, additional savings in items administered will be realized, depending upon the values of the intercorrelations among the subtests.

3.3 Adaptive Testing for Classification and Mastery Decisions

All of the adaptive testing strategies described thus far have been concerned with measuring trait level status on an assumed continuous underlying variable. Frequently, however, the problem in testing is one of classification, that is determining whether an individual is below or above a specified cut-off value. This problem is characteristic of the use of tests in personnel selection, where it is desired to know whether an individual possesses the minimum qualifications for a job, or in mastery (criterion-referenced) testing where the objective is to determine whether an individual has mastered at a sufficient level the material in a course of instruction. The classification problem can also be a polychotomous one, for instance, whether an individual is above some minimum cut-off value and below some maximum cut-off value, or a multicategory mastery decision analogous to the grade classification of assigning grades A, B, or C.

Adaptive testing can be used to improve measurement efficiency for making dichotomous or polychotomous classification decisions by selecting only those items from a fixed small item bank that are necessary for any particular individual in order to make the desired classifications. In this context, adaptive testing can be contrasted with sequential classification procedures. In a sequential classification procedure, a fixed sequence of items is determined a priori for everyone to be classified.

Items are administered one at a time, and a classification decision is attempted after each item has been administered. If a classification can be made within predetermined error rates, the item administration procedure is terminated. Otherwise, item administration continues until a classification can be made for each individual, or until all of the items available have been administered.

Adaptive classification procedures do not require a fixed item sequence for all individuals. Although both the adaptive and sequential procedures may use a fixed item bank, the adaptive procedure selects at each stage of the testing process the item from the entire available item bank that provides the most capability of differentiating the individual from the predetermined cut-off criterion level. As a consequence, different individuals may be administered different sequences of items. Similar to the sequential procedure, however, the adaptive procedure would administer tests of different lengths to different individuals, terminating the classification process when an appropriate decision or classification can be made.

An adaptive classification or mastery testing procedure based on item response theory first converts the cut-off value(s) to the item response theory trait metric by the test characteristic curve. Items are then selected by a maximum information procedure and scored by a Bayesian scoring procedure. The first item to be selected, and the Bayesian prior distribution used, assumes that the individual is at the cut-off value. This serves to draw all trait level estimates toward the cut-off value, permitting maximum discrimination around the cut-off level. After an item is administered, a Bayesian trait level estimate and its confidence interval (based on its standard error) are computed. If the confidence interval includes the cut-off value, no decision is made as to whether the individual is reliably above or below the cut-off value, and testing continues. Once the confidence interval no longer includes the trait level, a classification decision is made depending on whether the individual's trait level is above or below the cut-off level.

An advantage of this procedure is that, assuming an adequate item bank, the confidence level of the decision will be at the same minimum level for all individuals tested. This leads to the capability of controlling decision accuracy for each individual and for the group as a whole.

This adaptive testing approach has resulted in better classifications (i.e., more accurate classifications) with fewer items than a "best conventional test," which is one designed with all items peaked at the cut-off level.

The adaptive testing strategy also performed better than a sequential test, particularly when the items used were realistic multiple-choice items which differed in their item response theory item parameters (Weiss 1982) (see *Item Response Theory*).

3.4 Other Potential Applications

Adaptive testing also has potential for the measurement of individual change. In the adaptive testing approach to the measurement of individual change, each individual can be measured to a prespecified degree of precision at a given point in time. Later, when it is desired to determine whether change has occurred, testing can begin at the trait level associated with the upper limit of the error of measurement of the individual's trait level estimate at the first testing. Testing can proceed by administering and scoring items one at a time, and determining the measurement error associated with each new trait level estimate. Termination of the test at a second point in time can result when the new trait level estimate lies significantly outside of the trait level estimate observed at the first point in time, or when an indication of no change can be confidently made. This procedure can continue at subsequent testings utilizing the same item pool (since all the items will be on the same metric), but ensuring that no items previously administered will be administered. This approach can also incorporate mastery classifications, terminating testing when change has occurred and/or when a specified level of mastery has been reached.

See also: Latent Trait Measurement Models; Criterion-referenced Tests

Bibliography

Lord F M 1980 *Applications of Item Response Theory to Practical Testing Problems.* Erlbaum, Hillsdale, New Jersey

Owen R J 1975 A Bayesian sequential procedure for quantal response in the context of adaptive mental testing. *J. Am. Stat. Ass.* 70: 351–56

Weiss D J 1974 *Strategies of Adaptive Ability Measurement.* Research Report 74–5, University of Minnesota, Department of Psychology, Psychometric Methods Program, Minneapolis, Minnesota

Weiss D J 1979 Computerized adaptive achievement testing. In: O'Neil H F (ed.) 1979 *Procedures for Instructional Systems Development.* Academic Press, New York

Weiss D J 1982 Improving measurement quality and efficiency with adaptive testing. *Appl. Psychol. Meas.* 6(4): 473–93

Weiss D J 1983 *New Horizons in Testing: Latent Trait Test Theory and Computerized Adaptive Testing.* Academic Press, New York

Item Analysis

R. Wood

The case for preferring item analysis procedures based on item characteristic curve theory (ICC) is made elsewhere. Here it is sufficient to observe that for a good

deal of practical work in test construction, direct use of the basic sample statistics on which ICC theory builds, and of the original item response data themselves, can take the user a long way. Paradoxically, perhaps, these conventional or classical item analysis procedures gain more value as the connections with modern methods are better understood. A transformation of item difficulty like Δ, and a coefficient like the biserial correlation, no longer seem ad hoc when it is realized how they fit into ICC theory (Thorndike 1982). And, of course, an appreciation of the limitations of the classical statistics must act as a curb on any tendency to over-interpret results. It might be added that the virtue of placing ICC theory in the hands of neophyte users is not at all obvious. An apprenticeship with the classical methods, even if a short one, seems obligatory.

1. Item Difficulty

For any item, the raw response data consist of frequency counts of the numbers of individuals choosing each option, together with the number not answering the item at all, known as the "omits". From this information, it is immediately possible to calculate the proportion or percentage of individuals choosing the right answer. This statistic is known as the item difficulty or facility, depending on which nomenclature is preferred. Facility is perhaps the more felicitous term, since the greater the percentage correct, the easier the item.

Item difficulty or facility—usually termed p—suffers, like all percentages, from the drawback that the scale implied cannot be regarded as calibrated in equal intervals. The difference (in intensity of difficulty) between items with facilities of 0.40 and 0.50 is not the same as, rather it is somewhat smaller than, the difference between items with facilities of 0.10 and 0.20. This elasticity in the scale makes for misjudgments in comparing facilities and rules out simple statistical manipulations of p, except for summation which results in an estimate of the total test mean (see Sect. 5.1).

A solution to this problem which, incidentally, gives a direct measure of item difficulty, is to transform p to an ostensibly equal interval scale according to the following rationale (Henrysson 1971). A very common assumption made in test theory is that the ability to answer a particular item varies from very low ability to very high ability in a population of subjects. It is assumed that the subjects are distributed on this item continuum according to the normal distribution as illustrated in Fig. 1.

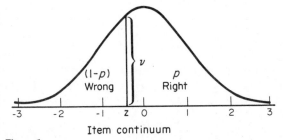

Figure 1
Normal distribution of subjects on the item continuum

The item continuum is a hypothetical construct specific to each item, that is, a scale measuring the ability to solve the item in question. In practice, however, it is dichotomized into only the two categories, right and wrong, in proportions p and $1 - p$. This is illustrated in Fig. 1. The value z expresses this point of categorization in standard score form. A table of normal probability curve values is used to find z corresponding to p and gives the level of ability (as measured in standard scores z on the item continuum) necessary to answer the item correctly.

For the item analysed in Table 1, the item proportion is $p = 0.46$. From a normal curve table it is found that the standard score that divides this distribution in proportions 0.54 and 0.46 is $z = 0.10$ (entering with area equal to 0.04). This is the difficulty index of the item. Because z can run from -3 to $+3$, there is merit in transforming it to a scale of all positive values. The standard score z with mean equal to 0 and standard deviation equal to 1 can be transformed into scores Δ with mean equal to 13 and standard deviation equal to 4 by the linear transformation equation $\Delta = 13 + 4z$. Δ will in practice take values from about 6 to 20, a high value indicating a difficult item. In the example, with z equal to 0.1, Δ equals 13.4. This indicates that the item is of a little more than average difficulty.

Other transformations of z are possible; this one merely happens to have been used over the years by the Educational Testing Service. An alternative would be $50 + 10z$, which gives difficulty measures with a mean of 50.

It is not imperative that p be transformed. It can be left as it is providing its limitations are observed. Note that Δ does not have, as p has, a direct relationship with a test statistic like the mean, but this is easily remedied by transforming the total score so that it has the same mean and standard deviation as Δ. The same applies to other transformations.

2. Item Discrimination

A discrimination index is meant to communicate the power of an item in separating the more from the less capable on some latent attribute. Operationally, the usual procedure is to compute a correlation, either biserial or point biserial, between success and failure on the item and score on a measure that is considered to represent the latent attribute. This is typically and conveniently the total score on the test to which the item belongs, but other measures will do. The idea is that the higher the correlation between candidates' scores on an item and their scores on the test, the more effective the item is in separating them. Naturally, this relationship is a relative one; when included in one test, an item could have a higher item–test correlation than when included in another, yet produce poorer discrimination. Those who are uncomfortable with an internal criterion because the reasoning behind the choice seems to be circular, are advised to seek an external criterion.

Choice of correlation lies between two forms, although there are some outsiders which will be considered briefly. The point biserial correlation is a special case of the general Pearson product–moment correlation, where one of the variables (test score) is regarded as continuous and the other (item score) can take one or other of two discrete values, typically 1 for correct and 0 for incorrect. The biserial correlation is based on the assumption that both variables are continuous but that one has been divided at some point into two groups, those who pass the item and those who fail it. The passers are thought to differ from the failers only in having more of whatever the item measures—that is, as having enough to get over the threshold and get the item right (Thorndike 1982 p. 71). The two variables are each assumed to follow a normal Gaussian distribution in the population of persons from whom the sample is drawn. That assumption was already made for the dichotomized scale (item continuum) when p was transformed to z and Δ. Note that the biserial is *not* a form of product–moment correlation; rather it should be thought of as a measure of association.

2.1 Point Biserial Correlation

The standard form for the sample point biserial correlation is

$$r_{pbis} = \frac{M_R - M_W}{S_T} [p(1-p)]^{\frac{1}{2}} \qquad (1)$$

but it may be more convenient to use the equivalent form

$$r_{pbis} = \frac{M_R - M_T}{S_T} \left(\frac{p}{1-p}\right)^{\frac{1}{2}} \qquad (2)$$

where

M_R = mean score on continuous variable for those getting item right

M_W = mean score on continuous variable for those getting item wrong

M_T = mean score on the continuous variable for the whole sample

S_T = standard deviation of scores on the continuous variable for the whole sample

p = percentage getting the item right or item facility. $(1 - p)$ is often written as q.

Evidently r_{pbis} serves as a measure of separation through the action of the term

$$\frac{M_R - M_T}{S_T}$$

It is also a function of item facility and the effect of this will be looked at presently.

To calculate r_{pbis} for the item in Table 1, the values of M_R and M_T can be found in the row directly underneath the body of the table labelled, "mean criterion", where "criterion" means test score. These mean test scores provide useful supplementary information. Thus, the mean score on the test obtained by those choosing A, the correct answer, was 30.79. This is M_R. Similarly, the 13 candidates choosing B scored an average of 18.77 on the test, which made them the lowest scoring of the four distractor groups. The mean score on the test for the entire group, M_T, is given at the right end of the "mean criterion" row, and is 26.02. The value of the standard deviation, S_T, which is not given in the table, was 8.96. The calculation for r_{pbis} is therefore

$$\frac{30.79 - 26.02}{8.96} \cdot \left(\frac{0.46}{0.54}\right)^{\frac{1}{2}}$$

which turns out to be 0.49.

The question immediately arises, "Is a value of 0.49 good, bad, or indifferent?" This is a fair question to ask of any correlation taking this value. If it were an ordinary product moment correlation, one might interpret the value within the limits -1 to $+1$ but with the point biserial that will not work because it has a curtailed range. If the distribution of scores in the total group is normal, the point biserial can never go beyond ± 0.8 (Thorndike 1982). Furthermore the range of possible values depends on the percentages of passers and failers, contracting as the split becomes more uneven. The maximum values of r_{pbis} for $p = 0.10$ and $p = 0.25$ when the total score distribution is normal are 0.58 and 0.73 respectively, (0.80 when $p = 0.50$). In these circumstances a value of 0.49 signifies quite powerful discrimination.

Table 1
Example of the analysis of one item

Score	Options						Item reached
	A	B	C	D	E	O	
	146	13	54	22	82	2	319
	0.46	0.04	0.17	0.07	0.26	0.01	1.00
0–18	9	6	18	7	21	2	63
18–22	16	5	16	8	19	0	64
22–29	30	1	7	7	19	0	64
29–35	42	1	8	0	13	0	64
35–47	49	0	5	0	10	0	64
Mean criterion	30.79	18.77	22.02	19.18	23.45	12.50	26.02

2.2 Biserial Correlation

The formula for calculating the sample biserial correlation coefficient resembles that for the point biserial quite closely, being

$$r_{bis} = \frac{M_R - M_T}{S_T} \cdot \frac{p}{y} \tag{3}$$

where the terms are as before, except for y, which stands for the ordinate or elevation of the normal curve at the point where it cuts off a proportion p of the area under the curve (see Fig. 1). y enters into the formula because of the assumption about the normally distributed underlying variable. It will usually be found in the same statistical tables as z.

In theory, the biserial can take any value between -1 and $+1$. Negative values usually indicate that the wrong answer has been keyed. Values greater than 0.75 are rare, although, in exceptional circumstances, the biserial can exceed 1, usually due to some peculiarity in the test score or criterion distribution. For the item in Table 1, the biserial estimate was 0.62, about which it is possible to say the same as about the point biserial value, that it signifies quite powerful discrimination.

2.3 Biserial and Point Biserial Correlations Compared

The point biserial r is always lower than the biserial r as can be seen from the relationship

$$r_{pbis} = r_{bis} \cdot \frac{y}{[p(1-p)]^{\frac{1}{2}}} \tag{4}$$

It follows from this formula that $r_{pbis} = 0.82 r_{bis}$ when $p = 0.50$ and that r_{pbis} shrinks with respect to r_{bis} the further p gets from 0.50, although the effect is only dramatic when p becomes very high or very low. While it is always a simple matter to convert from one coefficient or index to the other, their respective strengths and weaknesses need to be understood. Where the point biserial r is used, there are considered to be only two distinct positions on the item continuum, right or wrong. But passers would seem to differ from failers more in degree than in kind, which makes the assumption of continuity underlying the biserial correlation more plausible, although the requirement that it should take a particular distributional form (normal) is harder to believe.

It has been seen that the point biserial is confounded by item difficulty. This is not necessarily a bad thing; in fact, it may be argued that the point biserial value is rather more informative about the item's contribution to the functioning of the test, because very easy or very difficult items make relatively few differentiations between more and less capable examinees. Even so there is no hiding the fact that the point biserial is effectively a combined index of difficulty and discrimination. Those who believe that the two concepts should not be muddled up in a single index (Thorndike 1982) will incline towards the biserial. Because it is less influenced by item difficulty, it has been thought that the biserial might prove to be invariant, or at least reasonably stable, from one examinee group to another. This is necessarily a matter for empirical investigation (Lord and Novick 1968) and the results are still not available. For what it is worth, personal experience indicates that even with ostensibly parallel groups of candidates, biserial estimates for the same item can "bounce" around beyond what would be expected from a "guestimated" margin of error, guestimated because no really good estimate of precision is available for this statistic—a mark against it.

The biserial plays a part in item characteristic curve theory (in the equation for estimating the steepness parameter of the curve); the point biserial does not. Against that, and importantly, the point biserial fits directly into the algebra of multivariate analysis (Thorndike 1982). When it comes to estimating test parameters from item parameters (see below) it is the point biserial which is needed. For the sort of bread and butter item analysis with which this article is concerned, this is an important plus. Indeed, it may be stated quite generally that any item statistic which does not bear a definite (preferably a clear and simple) relationship to some interesting total test score parameter (Lord and Novick 1968) is of limited value for practical test construction purposes.

Evidently both biserial and point biserial have shortcomings, serious enough to rule either out if the objections were to be pressed. The practical user will find that as long as a markedly nonnormal distribution of ability is not anticipated, substantially the same items will be selected or rejected, whichever index is used to evaluate discrimination. It is when item selection is linked to the engineering of test score distributions with desirable properties, as it ought to be for conventional group testing situations grounded in more or less norm-referenced contexts, that the point biserial has the edge. Otherwise the best advice is to fasten on to one or other statistic, learn about its behaviour (for available information about sampling error is not impressive), and stick with it. Switching from one to the other, or trying to interpret both simultaneously, is likely to be futile.

2.4 Other Discrimination Indices

Of all the discrimination indices which have been proposed, the simplest is undoubtedly D, or net D, as it is sometimes called. If, for any item, P_h is the proportion of correct answers achieved by the 27 percent highest scorers, and P_l is the corresponding figure for the 27 percent lowest scorers, then $D = P_h - P_l$. It may seem odd that just as good results can be obtained by discarding middle scores of the score distribution as by using the whole distribution, but providing the ability being measured is normally distributed, and that is a big proviso, this is the case. Incidentally, it has been shown that the correct percentage is more like 21 percent, but, even so, 27 percent, or more conveniently 25 percent, cannot be far from optimal.

It is important to remember that the D statistic was invented to fill a need at the time for a shortcut manual method of estimating the discriminating power of an item. For those who want or need to carry out an item analysis by hand—and it is still a good way of getting the "feel" of item performance—it can be said that D agrees quite closely with biserial correlation estimates, even when the underlying distribution is non-normal. Like the point biserial and even the biserial, the D index is dependent on item facility. In particular, it decreases sharply as the facility approaches 0 or 1, when it must be interpreted with caution but then, as already noted, the test constructor will probably not be interested in these items anyway. (Thorndike 1982 provides tables for calculating D.)

Those who prefer a discrimination index which is independent of item difficulty might be interested in the rank biserial correlation coefficient (Henrysson 1971). However, there are problems with this index when frequent ties among test scores occur, and it is, therefore, not recommended for large groups ($n > 50$). Many other discrimination indices have been proposed. A recent Monte Carlo study of 10 such indices (Beuchert and Mendoza 1979) concluded that selection of an index should be based solely on ease of computation or the need for statistical tests of significance. Such advice ignores the need for linkage with test parameters and should be viewed circumspectly, but it may be regarded as a judgment on the utility of "fringe" indices.

2.5 Correcting Estimates for Spuriousness

It is argued (Henrysson 1971 p. 150) that the point biserial between item score and total test score is spuriously high because the item score enters in both variables. It is further argued that the obvious correction, removing the item score from the test score and correlating with the sum of the remaining $n - 1$ items, is misconceived because the criterion changes each time a new item is analysed, and the construct validities for each dimension may shift subtly. To overcome this objection it has been argued that what is required is the correlation of each item with the common factor (the latent attribute measured by the whole set of items), freeing it of any specific variance of the item in question (Thorndike 1982).

The amount of correction for spuriousness is in inverse proportion to n, the number of items entering into the total score with which the item is correlated. When n is large—say 40 to 50—the correlation is too small to be of any practical significance. Furthermore, the correction will rarely alter noticeably the relative size of the correlations themselves. Thus decisions about which items to include in the final form of a test are not often likely to be changed as a result of applying the correction (Thorndike 1982). It is said that if a computer program is used routinely for item analysis, there is good reason to include the correction formula in the programme but that is debatable.

3. Fractile Tables

Whatever item statistics are concocted, being of a summary nature they are bound to be less informative than

we would like. Evidently an infinite number of items can have different response patterns, yet possess the same discrimination index, or the same difficulty. The message is that it is a mistake to rely too heavily on item statistics; in particular they cannot describe how persons of different levels of achievement or ability respond to specific items. By defining fractiles of the distribution of test scores, and classifying item responses according to membership of these fractiles, the user can observe the behaviour of items across the ability range and also keep an eye open for malfunctioning distractors, something which will not be revealed by plots (see below). It is a matter of doing informally what item characteristic curve theory does more formally, although usually only for the correct response.

Items may

(a) fail to differentiate between persons in the lower, and sometimes the middle fractile bands;

(b) be useful over lower fractiles but give little or no information about persons in the higher fractiles;

(c) discriminate in a way which fluctuates wildly over fractiles.

By way of illustration, consider Table 1. The item generating data belonged to a 50-item chemistry test taken by 319 candidates. The correct (starred) answer was option A, chosen by 146 candidates, which, as the number underneath indicates, was 0.46 of the entry. The facility of this item was, therefore, 0.46, and the difficulty (Δ) 13.42. As already noted, the point biserial correlation was 0.49. Of the distractors, E was most popular (endorsed by 82 candidates, or 0.26 of the entry), followed by C, D, and B. Only two candidates omitted the item.

The five ability bands—and five is a good number to use, although three would do—have been constructed so as to contain equal numbers of candidates, or as nearly equal as possible, which means that, unless the distribution of scores is rectangular, the score intervals will always be unequal. However, there is no reason why the bands should not be defined in terms of equal score intervals or according to some assumption about the underlying distribution scores. If, for instance, a person wanted to believe that the underlying score distribution was normal, the bands could be constructed so as to have greatest numbers in the middle bands and smallest in the outer bands. The problem then is that, given small numbers, any untoward behaviour in the tails of the distribution would be amplified or distorted. Also, interpretation of the table would be more prone to error because of the varying numbers in the bands.

Turning to the body of the table, a pattern will be evident. Whereas under the correct answer A the count increases as the ability level rises, under the distractors (excepting D, where the trend is unclear), the gradient runs in the opposite direction. This is just as it should be if we want the item to discriminate in terms of total test score. The pattern we should *not* want to see would be one where the counts under A were equal to those under another distractor or, worse, where the count in each cell of the table was the same. As it is, the distribution of answers tells us quite a lot. Relatively speaking, options B and C were much more popular in the bottom ability band than in the rest, and in the bottom band the correct answer was barely more popular than B and D, which were almost totally rejected by the top two bands. Taken as a whole, the table underlines the observation that wrong answers are seldom, if ever, distributed equally across the distractors, either viewing the candidates as a whole, or in bands. Nor is there any evidence of blind guessing, the sign of which would be an inflated number in the top left hand cell of the table—the one containing a "9"—causing the gradient to flatten out at the bottom, or even go in the other direction. (The writer takes the view that most guessing is informed and that the best instructions are those which exhort examinees to answer as many questions as possible; see Wood 1977.)

The question arises as to whether there is some percentage below which a distractor score should not fall if it is to be regarded as "working" satisfactorily. There is not, if only because the percentage of wrong responses to be shared among the distractors depends on the percentage correct. That said, anything of the order of 5 percent or less should be looked at askance. Such distractors are clearly wrong to nearly everybody and a search should be made for more plausible wrong answers.

It will be seen that "omits" have been treated as incorrect responses in computing a difficulty index. This is a strictly pragmatic decision. Theoretical work has properly sought to treat omits as a conceptually distinct category of response and there is still much to be learned about omitting behaviour. It should be obvious that displaying response data in fractile table form enables the user to keep an eye on omit levels and on who is omitting (via the mean criterion score).

4. Generalized Item Statistics

It is always desirable to inspect fractile tables, but it may still be asked whether there is any way of summarizing all response patterns simultaneously. The appropriate statistics would be generalizations of the point biserial and biserial coefficients, and these have, in fact, been developed. To calculate the point multiserial, each response option, including the right answer, is treated as a separate nominal category, as if each represented a character such as eye colour. With the polyserial, on the other hand, being a generalization of the biserial, it is necessary that the distractors can be ordered or graded in terms of degree of "wrongness" or "rightness", so that the assumption of an underlying normally distributed trait can be better met. It is doubtful whether items often lend themselves to this kind of ordering, at least not on a large scale. The polyserial coefficient will generally find a more suitable application when the polychotomized variable is something like an examination grade or a rating, where there is a natural order of

measurement. The point multiserial is the more suitable statistic, but it is rather cumbersome to calculate (although not once it is programmed). Whether it is any more informative than the ordinary point biserial is another matter. The feeling is that these generalized statistics are not of much value in regular item analysis. The user would be just as well off with point biserial estimates calculated for each distractor, and some item analysis programmes do provide this information.

5. Estimating Test Parameters from Item Statistics

There are three aspects to this. Firstly, there are the algebraic relationships between test parameters and item statistics; secondly, there is the utilization of these relationships in the choice of items to produce (hopefully) desired test score distributions; and thirdly there is the practical business of selecting items to meet the test specification.

5.1 Estimating the Mean, Standard Deviation, Average Intercorrelation, and Reliability

As with any comparable estimation procedure, it is necessary, or certainly preferable, for the sample on which the estimates are based to have the same characteristics as the population with which the final test will be used.

The relationship between item difficulties and mean test score is very simple. If $\bar{x}$ is the mean test score and p_i is the difficulty of item i, then for an n item test

$$\bar{x}_T = \sum_{i=1}^{n} p_i \tag{5}$$

This relationship can be checked out easily by drawing up a person-by-item response matrix composed of entries of 0 or 1, and summing the item and person scores in the borders.

The standard deviation of test scores is estimated by the expression

$$s_T = \sum_{i=1}^{n} (p_i q_i)^{\frac{1}{2}} \cdot r_{it} \tag{6}$$

where $q_i = (1 - p_i)$ and r_{it} is the point biserial correlation of item i with the total test. There are certain grounds for believing that estimates of discrimination gained from tryouts will be lower than in the test proper, for example, poorer quality criteria, and more casual responses from examinees and this should be allowed for when using Eqn. (6).

Once a trustworthy estimate of the standard deviation is to hand, an estimate of the internal consistency of the test in the form of Kuder–Richardson 20 can be obtained using the following formula

$$r_{TT} = \frac{n}{n-1} \left(1 - \frac{\sum_{i=1}^{n} p_i q_i}{S_T^2} \right) \tag{7}$$

Item intercorrelation is not a statistic that pertains to any one item and in that sense fails to satisfy the Lord and Novick test of a useful item parameter. However, in other respects, it (or rather the average item intercorrelation) is a most useful statistic, especially when it comes to engineering or forecasting the shape of test distributions. The relationships between item intercorrelations, item–test correlations, and test reliability are shown in Eqn. (7). It can be seen that reliability depends entirely on item intercorrelations.

$$r_{TT} = \frac{\bar{r}_{ij}}{\bar{r}_{it}^2} = \frac{n\bar{r}_{ij}}{1 + (n-1)\bar{r}_{ij}} = \frac{n\bar{r}_{it}^2 - 1}{(n-1)\bar{r}_{it}^2}$$

$$\text{or } \frac{n}{n-1}\left(1 - \frac{1}{n\bar{r}_{it}^2}\right) \tag{8}$$

where $\bar{r}_{ij}$ is the average item intercorrelation. (Silverstein 1980 shows how these statistics can be related through mean squares if item analysis is treated as an ANOVA problem, as it can be.)

The last expression is handy for back-of-the-envelope calculations where the test constructor has a good idea of what the average point biserial is likely to be. Likewise, if a "guestimate" of the average item difficulty, $\bar{p}$, is available, the mean score can be estimated as $n\bar{p}$, and the standard deviation as $n(\bar{p}\bar{q}\bar{r}_{ii})^{1/2}$. Note that because $n(\bar{p}\bar{q})^{1/2}$ is always greater than $\Sigma(pq)^{1/2}$, the foregoing expression tends to overestimate slightly the standard deviation that will result (Thorndike 1982).

5.2 Engineering Test Score Distributions

The influence of item difficulty and discrimination on the properties of the total test is a rather complicated matter, especially if multiple-choice items are involved (Henrysson 1971). A full account of the subject is still awaited, and those who have studied it in the past have not always agreed on the effects of various selection strategies. It used to be said that there was no consensus concerning the best method of obtaining a rectangular score distribution (Scott 1972), but authorities now seem to be agreeing that what is wanted are intercorrelations of 0.33 and difficulties of 0.50 (Stanley 1971 shows that it must be necessary but not sufficient to have this degree of item intercorrelation if a person wishes to obtain a rectangular distribution from 50 percent difficulty items.) Above the item intercorrelation of 0.33, the total scores tend to become more frequent at the extremes and less frequent in the middle, until for the perfect intercorrelation situation only the extreme two scores have any frequencies. Test constructors prevent this by varying the item difficulty from easy to difficult, rather than setting it at approximately 0.50 for each item, so that even with high intercorrelations, thinning out in the middle does not occur (Stanley 1971). In fact, few if any achievement tests have average item intercorrelations approaching 0.33; they are more often of the order of 0.10 to 0.20, and even 0.20 would be high. Thus the test constructor who wishes to discriminate maximally among candidates is always liable to be frustrated.

The optimum strategy in these circumstances of item heterogeneity is to choose items in the difficulty range 0.60 ($\Delta = 12$) to 0.40 ($\Delta = 14$), the departure from the theoretically desirable figure of 0.50 being necessary to ring the changes on content (Henrysson 1971). In other words, one acts as if rectangular distributions were realizable.

Experience indicates that many people think intuitively that item difficulties should be widely distributed. The argument goes something like this. If all items are of the same difficulty, they can only measure efficiently those whose ability level corresponds to the difficulty level. Only if items are distributed across the difficulty range so that everyone has something they can tackle, can everyone be measured reasonably efficiently. This argument is impeccable—as far as it goes. The fact is that neither item selection policy will give the best results, the first because it neglects the most and least able candidates, and the second because, unless the test is to be grotesquely long, there are too few items at each point of the difficulty/ability range to provide effective measurement. The equal difficulty strategy is simply the better of two poor alternatives for large candidate populations. If candidates at the extremities are to be measured efficiently, what is needed are tests tailored to their abilities. Therein lies the motivation for developing individualized testing procedures.

Naturally, there are specialized measurement needs which require special treatment; an example would be a severe selection situation where, say, only 5 percent of candidates are to be selected. In these circumstances, items should all be of a difficulty level commensurate with the cut-off point and discriminations (and therefore intercorrelations) should be as high as possible.

5.3 Selecting Items in Practice

When selecting items in practice, a handy way of displaying the available items in terms of their statistical characteristics is to plot values of facility or difficulty against values of the discrimination index, whatever that is. It is conventional to plot difficulty along the horizontal axis and discrimination up the vertical axis, with the position of items being signified by the item number, and also, perhaps, by some coding, like a box or a circle or a colour, to indicate different item types or content areas. On top of the plot can be superimposed horizontal and vertical lines indicating the region within which "acceptable" items are to be found depending on the specifications (Wood 1977). A similar effect is obtained by using the Shewart control chart.

6. Item Analysis For Criterion-referenced Tests

The writer counts himself among those who wish to de-emphasize the distinction between norm-referenced and criterion-referenced testing but when it comes to item analysis there are undeniable differences.

Item analysis has always been a source of ambivalence among advocates of criterion-referenced testing. Doctrine requires belief in perfect congruence between objectives, item generators and items, so that items which function less than satisfactorily are not supposed to occur. Experience, however, indicates that there will always be subjective and uncertain elements in the formulation of objectives and therefore in the production of items, suggesting that there is room for some kind of item analysis.

This empirical view is generally accepted nowadays but in the beginning, ambivalence led to some gratuitous inversions. It was argued that items with facilities as near as possible to 100 percent should be favoured above all others, when a moment's thought would have shown that such items can provide no evidence on the effectiveness of instruction, or on progress towards mastery. What was wanted, it was said, were items with nonsignificant item-test correlations; items that discriminate positively usually indicate a need for revision. This, of course, was simply to misuse norm-referenced item statistics. If the idea is to find items which are sensitive to changes within individuals, then it is necessary to test items out on groups before and after they have received instruction. Items showing little or no difference, indicating insensitivity to learning, would then be discarded. The best items, in this view, are those which have p values approaching 0 prior to instruction, and p values approaching 1 subsequent to instruction.

Various refinements of the simple difference measure have been proposed. There is no point mentioning them all here because no two writers seem to be able to agree on the superiority of any one statistic. Besides, there now seems good reason to view them all with suspicion (Van der Linden 1981). Noting that all the item analysis statistics (or validity coefficients, as he calls them) are based on the same idea of instructional sensitivity, require pretest–posttest administration, and entail gain scoring, Van der Linden acknowledges that such features are welcomed in many papers as being typically criterion-referenced but argues that these coefficients have many disadvantages and serious interpretation problems. When the validity of instruction is not established, low pretest–posttest differences may be due to poor instruction rather than to weak items. Two items with the same difference between pretest and posttest p values may cover different intervals of the mastery continuum with different degrees of discrimination. Complicating everything are the threats to internal validity—history, maturational effects, scaling effects—which are inherent in all quasi-experimentation, of which criterion-referenced item validation is clearly an instance. The pretest–posttest method mixes up two sources of information—the characteristics of the item and the differences between the pretest and posttest mastery distributions—and blames the former for the peculiarities of the latter. By doing so, it is not surprising to find that it weeds out items of high quality (van der Linden 1981). A latent trait analysis, with prominence given to the "information function"—which does not mix up the two sources of information—is recommended. The critique is persuasive and those who wish to persist with simple difference measures will have to deal with it.

7. Choosing Items to Discriminate Between Groups

Not only may items be chosen to discriminate between and within individuals, but also between groups of individuals. The principal importance of such a measure lies in the evaluation of teaching programmes or instructional success. Suppose a number of classes within a school have been taught the same material, and it is desired to set all class members a test to find out which class has learnt the most. The items which differentiate within classes will not necessarily register differences between classes (Lewy 1973). This is what would be expected, given that the basic units of observation—the individual score and the class average—are so different. For item selection to differentiate between classes, the appropriate discrimination index is the intraclass correlation. Using indices like the biserial will most likely result in tests which are not sensitive to differences between class performance. (Critics of the American studies which claimed that school makes little or no difference to achievement, make much of this point.)

It will be evident that there are other possibilities once the distinction between unit of observation and unit of analysis is observed. Interest may lie in maximizing discrimination among students within particular classes or, more generally, in differentiating between individuals within their respective subgroups rather than among all of them (Lewy 1973). The current lively interest in the unit of analysis problem is bound to touch item analysis. Personal experience with intraclass correlation on item response data from achievement tests has been that the highest values occur with items on topics that are either new to the syllabus or are controversial. If, as seems likely, these topics are taken up by only some teachers, the effect will be to create a possibly spurious impression of greater between-school variability than really exists.

Bibliography

Beuchert A K, Mendoza J L 1979 A Monte Carlo comparison of 10 item discrimination indices. *J. Educ. Meas.* 16: 109–17

Henrysson S 1971 Gathering, analyzing and using data on test items. In: Thorndike R L (ed.) 1971 *Educational Measurement*. American Council on Education, Washington, DC

Lewy A 1973 Discrimination among individuals vs. discrimination among groups. *J. Educ. Meas.* 10: 19–24

Lord F M, Novick M R 1968 *Statistical Theories of Mental Test Scores*. Addison-Wesley, New York

Scott W A 1972 The distribution of test scores. *Educ. Psychol. Meas.* 32: 725–35

Silverstein A B 1980 Item intercorrelations, item-test correlations and test reliability. *Educ. Psych. Meas.* 40: 353–55

Stanley J C 1971 Reliability. In: Thorndike R L (ed.) 1971 *Educational Measurement*. American Council on Education, Washington, DC

Thorndike R L 1982 *Applied Psychometrics*. Houghton Mifflin, Boston, Massachusetts

van der Linden W J 1981 A latent trait look at pretest–posttest validation of criterion-referenced test items. *Rev. Educ. Res.* 51: 379–402

Wood R 1977 Multiple choice: A state of the art report. *Eval. Educ.* 1: 191–280

Correction for Guessing

B. H. Choppin

Guessing on tests includes both the apparently random selection of an answer to a question without consideration of the alternatives, and the selection of an answer on criteria unrelated to the trait being assessed (e.g., the strategy of "always choosing option C"). It is a problem on mental tests to the extent that it can affect total scores in a way not directly related to the trait being assessed. This means that in practice it is important only for multiple-choice tests. Three separate effects give rise to concern:

(a) Guessing introduces an apparently random factor into test scores which lowers reliability and validity.

(b) Lucky guesses inflate the score of the candidate leading to the possible overestimation of his or her level of achievement.

(c) This inflation of scores gives an unfair advantage to candidates who guess frequently as opposed to those who do not.

1. The Standard Correction

Since multiple-choice tests came into widespread use in the 1920s, there has been a steady stream of research studies aimed at finding ways to ameliorate the effects of guessing. Many of the early papers were based on a simple model that said if a candidate knew the correct answer to a question he or she would choose it; if not, he or she would omit the item or would select at random from among all the alternatives presented. This permits an estimate of the number of items on which guesses have been made;

$$G = \frac{m}{(m-1)} W$$

where W is the number of incorrect alternatives selected and m is the number of alternative choices per question. Assuming that $1/m$ of the guessed responses are correct, this suggests that the subtraction of $W/(m-1)$ from the raw score R would remove the inflation caused by guessing. This, the so-called "standard correction" for guessing, has come into widespread use. (It should be noted that the same principle can be applied to items rather than to persons in order to estimate the number of testees who can really solve an item.)

The standard correction has been criticized ever since it was first introduced. Its assumptions are too simple to be credible. In general students who do not know the right answer may still know enough to be able to eliminate one or more of the distractors so that, when they come to guess, their probability of success would be greater than $1/m$. This would suggest a higher proportion of correct guesses so that, in general, the standard guessing correction would be too small. However, a number of empirical studies (e.g., Brownless and Keats 1958) have shown that even the standard formula leads to too many negative corrected scores (i.e., the correction is too large). Other research, using score reliability and validity as criteria, confirms this result (Diamond and Evans 1973, Choppin 1974). Optimal gains in reliability and validity were achieved with corrections only one-third to one-half as large as those produced by the standard formula. Other important studies based on the "standard correction" were reported by Ziller (1957) and Traub et al. (1969).

2. Other Models and Formulas

Chernoff (1962) proposed that different weights should be accorded to items depending on how much guessing was estimated to have occurred *on that item*. Thus more credit would be earned for a correct answer on an item where there were few incorrect responses, than on one in which the responses were evenly distributed across all the alternatives. This model treats guessing as a phenomenon associated with particular items rather than particular people, and does not enjoy empirical support.

Coombs et al. (1956) suggested that students be directed to cross out each alternative answer that could be definitely identified as incorrect. The special scoring formula they proposed is claimed to minimize the effects of guessing by overconfident testees. De Finetti (1965) tackles guessing by asking students to assign probabilities of correctness to all the different alternatives on each question.

Wainer and Wright (1980) treat the regular one/zero persons-by-items response matrix that occurs with conventional response and scoring modes. They propose a jackknife technique applied to scaled estimates of ability, and report that, for simulated data at least, the method appears to work very well.

3. Latent Trait Theories

Latent trait theories represent a different approach to the problem of guessing on multiple-choice tests. They attempt to examine guessing by plotting relative rates of success on the item for examinees of different abilities to produce item characteristic curves (ICCs). The simplest of the latent trait models in common use, the Rasch model, assumes that no random guessing is taking place. Indeed, Rasch pointed out that the presence of guessed correct responses in a data set violated the requirements for objective measurement.

However, the three-parameter latent trait model developed by Lord (see *Item Response Theory*) includes an item parameter representing the asymptotic probability of success on an item for a person of very low ability. A weakness of this approach is that it regards "guessing" as a property of a particular item rather than a behavior exhibited by a particular person on a specific occasion. The parameter, usually represented by c_i (and misleadingly described as the guessing parameter), is estimated from considering the pattern of responses for *all* the people who attempted the item under consideration rather than modeling guessing behavior for any individual and it actually describes the shape of the item characteristic curve for the group as a whole. Item response theory does offer a way of estimating ability on a multiple-choice test that allows for the possibility of guessing—by giving less credit than normal for correct responses to difficult questions—but some uncertainties about the validity of this approach remain.

Several research studies (e.g., Choppin 1982) have demonstrated that item characteristic curves for multiple-choice items intended to measure achievement have a shape similar to the solid curve shown in Fig. 1, so that neither the Rasch model nor item response theory can be expected to provide a satisfactory account of test-taking behavior for students of low ability. The trough in the item characteristic curve appears to result from students with fairly low achievement levels tending to act on the basis of misinformation so as to systematically choose one or the other of the distractors in the item, and hence to choose the correct response much less often than chance would suggest. The location and depth of the trough varies considerably from item to item. This is an area where more research is needed.

4. The Avoidance of the Guessing Problem

In multiple-choice testing situations where the existence of guessing poses a serious problem to the interpretation of the results, several alternative strategies to minimize

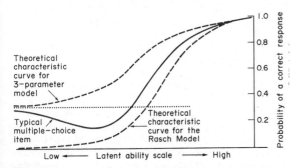

Figure 1
Empirically established characteristic curve for a typical multiple-choice item compared to curves for two latent trait theories

the effects are available. The major alternatives are discussed below with the most effective being considered first and the least effective last.

4.1 Choose Item Formats that Minimize the Problems Associated with Guessing

Although students lacking needed information to solve a problem directly may frequently guess on open-ended items, the chances of success in most cases are too small for the behavior to spoil the measurement. The problem becomes serious when the student has to select the correct response from only a limited number of alternatives (only two in the extreme case of "true/false" tests). One way to handle the problem is, therefore, to avoid the multiple-choice format altogether, and to use item formats which require constructed responses. Alternatively, if multiple-choice items have a relatively large number of distractors (say five or more), and they are reasonably plausible so that the typical low-achieving student will not be able to rule out many of them, then the success rate on guessing is likely to be quite low and the problem will not be serious.

4.2 Prepare Appropriate Instructions to the Test-taking Student

Here two quite different strategies may be followed depending on whether the test is intended for ranking the students (norm referenced), or for measuring as accurately as possible what each student knows (criterion referenced). In the first case, a guessing problem arises if some students are more inclined than others to guess, rather than to omit an item when they do not know enough to be able to solve it directly. In this case, the appropriate instruction to the students is to tell them to guess if they are not sure of the answer, and *not to omit any items* at all. In the second case, the problem arises from correctly guessed responses by individual students which could lead to inappropriate deductions about the student's level of achievement. In these circumstances the opposite type of instruction is appropriate. The students should be told *not to guess*, and to omit items to which they do not know the correct answer. It may be appropriate to warn of a heavy penalty being imposed for incorrect responses. Unfortunately, experience shows that both sets of instructions are of only limited effectiveness. In practice some students still omit items even though they were told to attempt all of them, and other students still guess when they are not sure even though they are warned of the penalties.

4.3 Use a Latent Trait Model to Adjust for Guessing Behavior

If it is not possible to arrange the test session so as to minimize the guessing problem by one of the methods outlined above, then it is suggested that a latent trait model be employed to analyze the results. Where aggregated results for a group of individuals are of interest, the three-parameter model may be appropriate.

Alternatively, if individual estimates of achievement are the goal, then the procedure for editing the observation matrix and applying the Rasch model proposed by Choppin (1982) is suggested.

4.4 Use the Standard Correction for Guessing

Although there is little reason for believing that this procedure is fair to all students, or that it improves the psychometric quality of the measures, this procedure is simple to apply and appears to be a small step in the appropriate direction. Where large variations in the frequency of guessing between testees exist, then the standard correction can remove a substantial proportion of the bias in the ranking of raw scores.

See also: Future Developments in Educational Measurement

Bibliography

Brownless V T, Keats J A 1958 A retest method of studying partial knowledge and other factors influencing item response. *Psychometrika* 23: 67–73

Chernoff H 1962 The scoring of multiple choice questionnaires. *Ann. Math. Stat.* 33: 375–93

Choppin B H 1974 *The Correction for Guessing in Objective Tests* (IEA Monograph Series No. 4). International Association for the Evaluation of Educational Achievement (IEA), Stockholm

Choppin B H 1982 *A Two-parameter Latent Trait Model* (CSE Technical Report). Center for the Study of Evaluation, UCLA, Los Angeles, California

Coombs C H, Milholland J E, Womer F B 1956 The assessment of partial knowledge. *Educ. Psychol. Meas.* 16: 13–37

De Finetti B 1965 Methods for discriminating levels of partial knowledge concerning a test item. *Br. J. Math. Stat. Psychol.* 18: 87–123

Diamond J, Evans W 1973 The correction for guessing. *Rev. Educ. Res.* 43: 181–91

Traub R E, Hambleton R K, Singh B 1969 Effects of promised reward and threatened penalty on performance on a multiple choice vocabulary test. *Educ. Psychol. Meas.* 29: 847–61

Wainer H, Wright B D 1980 Robust estimation of ability in the Rasch model. *Psychometrika* 45: 373–91

Ziller R C 1957 A measure of the gambling response-set in objective tests. *Psychometrika* 22: 289–92

Reliability of Test Results

S. A. Livingston

A student's score on a test is a highly specific piece of information. It refers to a particular set of questions, administered at a particular time under a particular set of circumstances, and scored by a particular scorer. Yet, the test results are useful only to the extent that they can be generalized beyond these specific conditions. A good testing procedure would be expected to produce results that do not depend heavily on the particular set of questions used, or the time at which the test was given, or the person who scored the test. Factors such as these can cause students who are equal in the ability the test is intended to measure to receive different scores on the test. The influence of these factors is referred to as "measurement error." Notice that the term "measurement error" does not mean that someone has made a mistake in constructing, administering, or scoring the test. It means only that the student's test score is affected to some extent by factors the test is not intended to measure. Reliability is the level of agreement between test results that would be the same if there were no measurement error.

1. Sources of Measurement Error

Because there are several sources of measurement error, there are several types of reliability. Each type of reliability refers to a particular source of measurement error (or a particular combination of sources of measurement error). It is meaningless to talk about the reliability of a test without specifying the sources of measurement error that are being considered.

One important source of measurement error is the selection of specific questions to test a more general ability. The term "ability" is used here to mean the characteristic of the students that the test is intended to measure. It includes factual knowledge and specific skills as well as more general abilities. For example, a researcher might want to test the student's ability to remember the meanings of certain words, or to solve a particular type of arithmetic problem, or to choose a sentence that summarizes the main idea of a written paragraph, and so on. For almost any such ability to be tested, the questions or problems on the test are only a small sample of all the questions or problems that could have been used. A test score based on this sample of questions or problems will be only an approximate indicator of the student's ability.

There are three common ways to determine the influence of this source of measurement error. One way is to give the same students two different versions of the test, each containing different specific questions written to measure the same more general abilities. These different versions of the same test are called "alternate forms," and this type of reliability is called "alternate-forms reliability." Another way is to split the test into two similar half-tests. The half-test scores can then be used to determine what the agreement between two full-length tests would have been. This type of reliability is called "split-halves reliability." A third way is to analyze the data from the individual test questions, under the assumption that all the questions on the test are intended to measure the same ability. This type of reliability is called "internal consistency." A test that measures many different abilities may have little internal consistency even though its alternate-forms reliability is quite good.

A second important source of measurement error is the time of testing. This source of measurement error includes short-term, temporary changes in the students' ability, and changes in the conditions of testing. To determine the influence of this source of measurement error, it is necessary to give the test to the same students at two or more different times. The agreement between the test results for the same students tested at different times is called "stability."

A third important source of measurement error in some kinds of tests is the person who grades or scores the tests. This source of measurement error is not present in multiple-choice tests, but it can be a serious problem in essay tests, oral tests, and performance (practical) tests. To determine the influence of this source of measurement error, it is necessary to have two or more graders grade the same test papers (or oral responses, or samples of the students' performance). The agreement between the results obtained from different graders is called "interrater reliability."

Table 1 lists the three major sources of measurement error and the corresponding types of reliability. The results of a test may show good interrater reliability but poor alternate-forms reliability (or vice versa). They may show good alternate-forms reliability but little stability over time. No type of reliability is a substitute for any other type unless they both refer to the same sources of measurement error.

It is possible to determine the combined influence of two or more sources of measurement error at the same time. For example, one might compare the results of a test given to the same students at two different times, each time using a different form of the test, with each form scored by a different scorer. This comparison would include all three major sources of measurement error. The more sources of measurement error included, the lower the agreement between the test results (i.e., the reliability) can be expected to be.

It is important to remember that the concepts of measurement error and reliability apply not only to test scores, but also to other types of information about students. For example, a researcher might well be concerned about the interrater reliability of teachers'

Table 1
Types of reliability

Source of measurement error	Type of reliability
1. Selection of specific questions to test a more general ability	1. (a) "alternate forms reliability" (b) "split-halves reliability" (c) "internal consistency"
2. Time of testing (including short-term changes in the student's ability)	2. "stability"
3. Scorer (grader, observer, rater, etc.)	3. "interrater reliability"

recommendations: do different teachers agree in their evaluations of the same students? If a teacher's recommendation depends heavily on which teacher is making the recommendation, it may not be a very useful piece of information.

There are two ways to reduce the effects of measurement error in testing. One way is to remove the source of measurement error by standardizing the testing conditions. The other way is to increase the number of separate pieces of information that make up the test score, so that irrelevant factors will tend to "average out." In practice, both ways are used. Measurement error that might be caused by differences in the time limits or in the instructions to the students is prevented by holding these factors constant. Measurement error caused by the selection of specific questions is reduced by increasing the number of questions testing each of the abilities.

Standardizing the testing conditions actually limits the extent to which the student's test score can be generalized to nonstandard conditions. For example, if an essay test is always scored by the same scorer, it is not possible to be sure another scorer would score it the same way. On the other hand, having several scorers score each essay allows generalization beyond those particular scorers, if the agreement between them is good. The reasoning is that if the scorers who actually scored the test tend to agree, other scorers probably would also agree with them.

Testing experts often believe that "a longer test is a more reliable test." This statement is true, but it is not the whole truth. Increasing the number of questions reduces the measurement error caused by the selection of specific questions. It does not reduce the measurement error caused by day-to-day changes in the student's ability, or by differences between scorers. To improve day-to-day stability, the test would have to be given on several different days and the results averaged. To improve interrater reliability, several different scorers would have to score each test paper and average the results.

2. Reliability of What?

Although test makers and test users often talk about "the reliability of a test," this phrase is not very precise. Reliability is a characteristic of the results of the test—the information that is produced when a group of students takes the test. The reliability of the test results will depend on what group of students takes the test. It will also depend on what type of results the test user is concerned about. The test user may be interested in a student's relative standing in the group, or in the percentage of the test questions that the student answered correctly, or only in whether the student's score is above or below some specified level.

For example, test scores are often used to classify students into a higher scoring group and a lower scoring group. In this case, the reliability of the classification will depend not only on how reliable the students' scores are, but also on how close their scores are to the dividing line between the two groups (the "passing score"). If a student's test score is close to this dividing line, a small change in the student's score may change the student's classification. Therefore, if most of the students have scores close to the dividing line, even a test that produces reliable scores may not produce reliable classifications. On the other hand, if very few students have scores close to the dividing line, a test that produces only moderately reliable scores may produce highly reliable classifications. The second case—very few students with scores near the dividing line—is most likely to occur when the test measures a single specific skill. In this case even a small sample of each student's performance may be adequate for deciding which students have learned the skill adequately and which have not.

3. The Reliability Coefficient

Suppose a researcher wants to determine the reliability of the scores of a particular group of students on a particular test. The researcher must first decide which sources of measurement error should be included—for example, the selection of specific questions and the time of testing. The same students are given two different forms of the test, a week apart—a week in which the students did not receive any instruction in the ability the test measures. Therefore, for each student, there are two test scores that would be the same if there were no measurement error. How can the level of agreement between these scores be described?

The most common way to describe the level of agreement between scores on two tests given to the same group of students is to compute the correlation coefficient. When the correlation coefficient is used to measure agreement between test scores that differ only because of measurement error, it is called a reliability coefficient. For example, the correlation coefficient of scores on two forms of the same test is called an "alternate-forms reliability coefficient."

The reliability coefficient indicates the extent to which the differences between students, as reflected in their test scores, are due to factors that were the same on both occasions of testing. For example, suppose the students took two forms of a test, a week apart. The reliability coefficient would indicate the extent to which the test-score differences between students (on either form of the test) are due to factors that were the same on both forms of the test and both days of testing—presumably, to genuine differences in the ability the test is intended to measure. Similarly, an internal-consistency reliability coefficient indicates the extent to which the differences between students, as reflected in their total scores, are due to factors that are common to all the questions on the test. Again, one would hope that the main factor common to all the test questions would be the general ability they are intended to measure.

This interpretation of the reliability coefficient suggests two possible reasons why a reliability coefficient could be low. One possibility is that the test scores might be heavily influenced by the sources of measurement error that were taken into consideration. The other possibility is that there might be very little variation between the students in the ability the test is intended to measure. If all the students were exactly equal in the ability the test is intended to measure, any test score differences between students would be entirely the result of measurement error, and the reliability coefficient would be zero.

The reliability coefficient for a nationally standardized test will usually be lower for the students in a particular school than for the nationwide sample of students on which the test was standardized. The reason is that the students in a single school tend to be more similar in ability than students from many different schools. Because the students are more similar, the test will be less effective at distinguishing reliably among them.

4. The Standard Error of Measurement

Suppose a researcher wants to describe the extent to which a group of students' test scores are influenced by measurement error, in a way that does not depend on the amount of variation between individual students. The statistic commonly used for this purpose is called the standard error of measurement. Although the standard error of measurement may vary from one group of students to another, it will tend to vary much less than the reliability coefficient.

To understand the standard error of measurement, it is necessary to understand the concept of a student's "true score." Suppose it were possible to test each student over and over again without affecting the student's ability (that is with no improvement as a result of practice, no boredom or fatigue, etc.). Now suppose each student were tested many, many times, with changes each time in such "measurement error" factors as the specific questions or problems on the test, the grader, and so on. Finally, suppose each student's long-term average were computed over all the different occasions of testing that might be of interest: all possible versions of the test, all possible graders, and so on. This long-term average is called the student's "true score." Because the student's true score is an average, it may be a score that is not actually possible to get by taking the test once. For example, if the test score is the number of questions the student answers correctly, the only possible scores are whole numbers: 9, 10, 11, and so on. But a student's true score, which is an average over all possible occasions of testing, could be a fractional number, such as 10.33.

The difference between a student's "true score" and the student's score on any one testing is called the "error of measurement." When a large number of students take a test, it can be expected that about half the students will have positive errors of measurement. That is, their test scores on that occasion will be higher than their true scores. The other half will have negative errors of measurement; their test scores will be below their true scores. The mean of the errors of measurement for the whole group will be close to zero, since the positive and negative errors of measurement will tend to balance each other out. To get an idea of the average size of the errors of measurement, the standard deviation of the errors of measurement can be estimated. This statistic is the standard error of measurement.

To put it another way, suppose the average size of the "errors of measurement" could be computed for all the students in the group—not in the usual way, but by using a type of average called the "root mean square," in which each number is squared, then the average is found, and then the square root taken. If this method is used to average the errors of measurement for all the students in the group, the standard error of measurement would be obtained.

In practice it is never possible to find out how large the error of measurement in an individual student's test score is, but it is possible to estimate the standard error of measurement for a group of students. The standard error of measurement (SEM) is computed from the reliability coefficient (r) and the standard deviation (s) of the scores, by the formula:

$$\text{SEM} = s(1 - r)^{1/2} \tag{1}$$

The standard error of measurement computed in this way will include those sources of measurement error that were taken into account in computing the reliability coefficient.

The standard error of measurement is expressed in the same units as the test score itself. If the scores are expressed in terms of the number of questions answered correctly, so is the standard error of measurement. If the scores are percentages of the total possible score, the standard error of measurement is expressed in terms of percentage points. If the scores are "T-scores," then the standard error of measurement is expressed in terms of T-score units.

The standard error of measurement given by the above formula is an average figure that applies to a group of students. It does not necessarily apply to any particular student in the group. The standard error of measurement for an individual student will depend on the student's true score. If the student's true score is in the range of 40 to 60 percent correct, the standard error of measurement will be relatively large. If the student's true score is very high or very low, the standard error of measurement is much smaller. For a student with a true score of 100 percent correct, the standard error of measurement would be zero. (That is, the student would always answer every question correctly, so the student's score would always be the same—100 percent correct.)

If one is concerned about only one source of measurement error—the selection of specific test questions—it is possible to estimate the standard error of measurement for students with a particular true score (t) from the number of questions on the test (m) by the formula

$$\text{SEM}|t = (t(m - t)/m)^{1/2} \tag{2}$$

This formula assumes that the test is scored by awarding one point for each correct answer. It is especially useful for tests that are used to make pass/fail decisions. In this situation, the overall standard error of measurement may be quite different from the standard error of measurement for students with true scores near the passing score. For example, suppose the passing score is in the range of 50 to 70 percent correct, while most of the students have true scores in the range of 80 to 90 percent correct. In this case, the standard error of measurement for students with true scores near the passing score will be considerably larger than the overall standard error of measurement.

5. Test Length and Reliability

Often the reliability coefficient and the standard error of measurement are computed so as to take into account only one source of measurement error: the selection of test questions. In this case, there are formulas for estimating these statistics for a lengthened or shortened version of the test. For the standard error of measurement, the formula is quite simple. When the number of questions on the test is multiplied by k, the standard error of measurement for the raw scores (number of correct answers) is multiplied, not by k, but by the square root of k. Therefore, the standard error of measurement for the percentage-correct scores is divided by the square root of k. For example, if the number of questions on the test is doubled, the standard error of measurement of the raw scores will be multiplied by 1.4 (the square root of 2), while the standard error of measurement of the percentage-correct scores will be divided by 1.4.

The formula for predicting the change in the reliability coefficient is somewhat more complicated. It is called the Spearman–Brown formula. Let r_o represent the reliability coefficient for the original test. Then the reliability coefficient for a test k times as long as the original test can be estimated from the formula

$$r_k = \frac{kr_o}{1 + (k - 1)r_o} \tag{3}$$

6. Alternate Forms, Split Halves, and Internal Consistency

The source of measurement error that is usually of greatest concern to test makers is the selection of specific questions to test a more general ability. There are three types of reliability associated with this source of measurement error: alternate-forms reliability, split-halves reliability, and internal consistency. Can they be used interchangeably? Sometimes, and sometimes not.

Usually, the test maker's main reliability concern is with the similarity of results on alternate forms of the test, that is, versions of the test using different questions or problems to test the same abilities. To what extent would the use of a different form of the test lead to different conclusions about the students? This question can be answered directly by having the students take two forms of the test. The correlation between the two forms of the test will be the alternate-forms reliability coefficient. But what if it is impossible or impractical to test the students twice? One alternative is to split the test into two half-tests that are as similar as possible to each other. The two half-tests will then be alternate forms of a test like the full test, but half as long. The correlation between the two half-tests will be the reliability coefficient for a half-test. The Spearman–Brown formula with $k = 2$ can then be used to find the reliability coefficient for a test twice as long as the half-test, that is, for the full test. A reliability coefficient computed in this way is called a split-halves reliability coefficient.

Another way to compute the split-halves reliability coefficient is by using Guttman's formula "L4." Let V_1 and V_2 represent the variances of scores on the two half-tests, and let V_{total} represent the variance of scores on the full test. Then the split-halves reliability of the full test is given by

$$r = 2\left(1 - \frac{V_1 + V_2}{V_{\text{total}}}\right) \tag{4}$$

When V_1 and V_2 are equal, formula L4 is equivalent to the Spearman–Brown formula with $k = 2$.

As a practical matter, the splitting of the test into two half-tests can usually be done as part of the scoring process. In most cases it is not necessary that the two halves of the test be given separately. However, if speed is an important factor affecting the students' scores, then the two halves of the test must be separately timed.

One problem with the split-halves method is that there are many ways to split a test into two half-tests. For example, if the test contains 20 questions, there are 92,378 ways to split it into two 10-question tests. Of course, some of these ways may be better than others for producing two half-tests that are similar in content and difficulty. Still, there may be many satisfactory ways to split the test. These different "splits" may produce differing estimates of reliability, and each of these estimates can be considered correct. Therefore, if it is important to have an accurate estimate of the alternate-forms reliability, it may be wise to use several different ways of splitting the test into halves and average the resulting split-half reliability coefficients. Carrying this approach to its logical extreme, it might be interesting to compute the average of all possible split-half reliability coefficients. This quantity is called "coefficient alpha." It can be computed from the students' scores on the individual test questions and on the total test by the formula

$$\text{alpha} = \frac{m}{m - 1}\left(1 - \frac{\sum V_i}{V_{\text{total}}}\right) \tag{5}$$

where m is the number of questions, $\sum V_i$ is the sum of the variances of scores on the individual questions, and V_{total} is the variance of total scores. (This formula is similar to Guttman's formula L4, but instead of the sum of the variances of scores on two half-tests, it uses the sum of the variances of scores on the individual questions.)

If the scores on the individual questions are uncorrelated with each other, coefficient alpha will be zero. The more highly the individual test questions correlate with each other, the larger coefficient alpha will be. If all the questions are perfectly correlated with each other, coefficient alpha will be 1.00. For this reason, coefficient alpha is usually described as a measure of internal consistency—the extent to which the questions on the test are consistent with each other in what they indicate about the students' abilities.

If a test is scored by simply counting the number of questions answered correctly (with no penalty for guessing, no partial credit, etc.), then the formula for coefficient alpha can be expressed in terms of the proportion of students answering each question correctly. In this form it is referred to as "Kuder–Richardson Formula 20," or "KR20." The formula is

$$\text{KR20} = \frac{m}{m - 1}\left[1 - \frac{\sum p_i(1 - p_i)}{V_{\text{total}}}\right] \tag{6}$$

where p_i is the proportion of students answering a question correctly.

The reliability coefficient computed from formula KR20 or coefficient alpha can be interpreted as "an estimate of the correlation expected between two tests drawn at random from a pool of items (questions or problems) like the items in the test" (Cronbach 1951). If the proportion of correct answers does not vary greatly from one question to another, a simpler formula, called "Kuder–Richardson Formula 21" or "KR21" may be adequate:

$$\text{KR21} = \frac{m}{m - 1}\left[1 - \frac{m p_{\text{avg}}(1 - p_{\text{avg}})}{V_{\text{total}}}\right] \tag{7}$$

where p_{avg} represents the average proportion of correct answers for all questions on the test. Since p_{avg} is simply the mean score divided by the number of questions, KR21 is simple to compute, especially if the mean and the variance (or the standard deviation) of the students' scores have already been computed.

6.1 Stratified Tests

Under most conditions, coefficient alpha or KR20 will provide a good estimate of the alternate-forms reliability coefficient. However, there are some important exceptions. Many tests are "stratified"; that is, they are made up of two or more clusters of questions, each cluster testing a different ability. A student may be stronger in some abilities and weaker in others. Different students may have very different patterns of strengths and weaknesses. In this case, coefficient alpha or KR20 will not provide a good estimate of the alternate-forms reliability coefficient. An example may help to explain why not. Suppose the test is a test of general knowledge of the physical sciences. And suppose that the group of students tested includes many students who know more chemistry than physics and many others who know more physics than chemistry. If the test were split into halves in such a way as to put most of the chemistry questions in one half of the test and most of the physics questions in the other half, many students would do much better on one half of the test than the other. A split-halves reliability coefficient based on this kind of split would be lower than the alternate-forms reliability coefficient. Of course, such a split would not intentionally be used in computing a split-halves reliability coefficient. But coefficient alpha is the average of all possible split-halves reliability coefficients, including such obviously wrong splits as the one in the example. The best possible splits—those that result in very similar half-tests—will give an accurate estimate of alternate-forms reliability, but coefficient alpha or KR20 will average these in with other splits that give systematically low estimates. As a result, coefficient alpha or KR20 will tend to underestimate the reliability of a stratified test.

How, then, should the alternate-forms reliability of a stratified test be estimated, if the same students cannot actually take two forms of the test? One way is to use the split-halves method, making sure that the two halves of the test are as similar as possible in content. This way is best when the test is made up of many small clusters of questions. However, if the test contains only two or three large clusters of questions, it may be better to compute coefficient alpha separately for each cluster. To estimate the alternate-forms reliability coefficient for the whole test, calculate the variance of errors of measurement—the squared standard error of measurement—for each cluster of questions. Then apply the formula:

$$r = 1 - \frac{\sum \text{SEM}^2_{\text{cluster}}}{V_{\text{total}}} \tag{8}$$

where $\Sigma\text{SEM}^2_{\text{cluster}}$ is the sum of the variances of errors of measurement for all the clusters of questions and V_{total} is the variance of scores on the test. The estimated alternate-forms standard error of measurement for the full test is simply:

$$\text{SEM}_{\text{total}} = \Sigma\text{SEM}^2_{\text{cluster}} \tag{9}$$

6.2 Speeded Tests

A "speeded" test is one on which the time limit causes some students to earn lower scores than they would have earned if there were no time limit. The greater this effect, the more highly speeded the test. A speeded test measures the students' ability to answer the questions or solve the problems quickly. In estimating the alternate-forms reliability of a speeded test, it is important to remember that the difference between a student's scores on the two forms of the test is likely to reflect a difference in speed. Some students may be able to solve the problems on Form A faster than those on form B; others may work faster on Form B than on form A. Any estimate of alternate-forms reliability must take account of these differences in speed.

Internal-consistency methods such as coefficient alpha will not give a valid estimate of the alternate-forms reliability of a highly speeded test. These methods all consider each problem as an independent measure of the student's ability. But if speed is part of the ability being measured, each problem cannot provide an independent measure (unless each problem is separately timed). A student who works quickly on one problem will have more time left for the next problem. A student who works slowly on the earlier problems may have no time left for the later problems.

There are two ways to estimate the alternate-forms reliability of a speeded test: (a) administer two or more forms of the test; (b) use the split-halves method with each half of the test separately timed. The full test consists of a specified number of problems to be solved (or questions to be answered) in a specified amount of time. To split the test into halves, it is necessary to split both the number of questions or problems and the amount of time allowed. Then the reliability of the full test can be estimated by using either the Spearman–Brown formula or Guttman's formula L4.

7. Interrater Reliability

Estimating interrater reliability involves a complication that is not present in estimating alternate- forms reliability: the problem of systematic differences between raters. Some raters tend to give higher ratings than others. Should this systematic variation between raters be considered as measurement error? In most practical cases, it should. The exceptions are (a) the case in which the students' scores are adjusted to compensate for the raters' strictness or leniency, and (b) the case in which a student's score will be compared only with the scores of other students rated by the same rater (or raters). In all other cases, any systematic differences between raters will influence the results of the test and should be considered as measurement error.

One of the most commonly used methods of estimating interrater reliability is to compute the correlation between scores assigned to the same students by two raters (or the average correlation between scores assigned by several pairs of raters). This correlation is then entered into the Spearman–Brown formula, with k equal to the number of raters rating each student. This method of estimating interrater reliability does not include systematic variation between raters as a source of measurement error. As a result, it may give a misleading picture of the interrater reliability of the test scores.

To compute a measure of interrater reliability that includes the systematic variation between raters as a source of measurement error, one can use a statistical technique called "analysis of variance." This technique provides estimates of the variance between students rated by the same raters (V_{students}) and between raters rating the same students (V_{raters}). It also estimates an "interaction" variance that indicates the effect of disagreements between raters about the relative ratings of different students ($V_{\text{raters} \times \text{students}}$). The interrater reliability coefficient can then be estimated by:

$$r_{\text{interrater}} = \frac{V_{\text{students}}}{V_{\text{students}} + V_{\text{raters}} + V_{\text{raters} \times \text{students}}} \qquad (10)$$

and the interrater standard error of measurement by:

$$\text{SEM}_{\text{interrater}} = (V_{\text{raters}} + V_{\text{raters} \times \text{students}})^{1/2} \qquad (11)$$

8. Stability over Time

The estimation of the stability of test results over time involves a type of measurement error that is not a part of the measurement process: the tendency of students' abilities to change from hour to hour, day to day, and so on. The usual method of investigating the stability of test results over time is called "test–retest." The students take the same test twice, with a specified time interval between. One problem with this method is that the students' memory of the specific questions or problems on the test may affect their scores. The only solution is to use different questions or problems at the different times of testing, which introduces an additional source of measurement error. Even if different questions or problems are used, the experience of taking the test may change the way the students respond. These practical problems make it very difficult to estimate stability over time for tests of knowledge. For tests of skills, however, it is often practical and useful to estimate stability over time.

Estimating stability over time involves a problem similar to that of interrater reliability. There may be a general tendency for students to score higher if tested at some particular times and lower if tested at other times. For example, students may tend to perform better in the morning than in the middle of the day. Should this kind of difference be considered as measurement error? In general, it should. The exceptions are (a) when a student's test score will be compared only with the scores of other students tested at the same time and (b) when the scores are adjusted to compensate for the effects of the different times of testing.

The statistical procedures for estimating stability over time correspond to those for estimating interrater reliability. The same students are tested at two or more different times and analysis of variance is used to estimate variances for students, for times, and for the interaction of students with times. The stability coefficient and the standard error of measurement over time are then estimated by formulas that correspond exactly to those used for interrater reliability:

$$r_{\text{stability}} = \frac{V_{\text{students}}}{V_{\text{students}} + V_{\text{times}} + V_{\text{times} \times \text{students}}} \qquad (12)$$

$$\text{SEM}_{\text{stability}} = (V_{\text{times}} + V_{\text{times} \times \text{students}})^{1/2} \qquad (13)$$

See also: Validity; Sufficient Statistics in Educational Measurement; Measurement in Educational Research; True-score Models; Reliability

Bibliography

Cronbach L J 1951 Coefficient alpha and the internal structure of tests. *Psychometrika* 16: 297–334

Cureton E E 1958 The definition and estimation of test reliability. *Educ. Psychol. Meas.* 18: 715–38

Guilford J P, Fruchter B 1978 *Fundamental Statistics in Psychology and Education*, 6th edn. McGraw-Hill, New York

Gulliksen H 1950 *Theory of Mental Tests*. Wiley, New York

Guttman L 1945 A basis for analyzing test-retest reliability. *Psychometrika* 10: 255–82

Kuder G F, Richardson M W 1937 The theory of the estimation of test reliability. *Psychometrika* 2: 151–60

Lord F M 1957 Do tests of the same length have the same standard error of measurement? *Educ. Psychol. Meas.* 17: 510–21

Lord F M, Novick M R 1968 *Statistical Theories of Mental Test Scores*. Addison-Wesley, Reading, Massachusetts

Nunnally J C 1967 *Psychometric Theory*. McGraw-Hill, New York

Stanley J C 1971 Reliability. In: Thorndike R L (ed.) 1971 *Educational Measurement*, 2nd edn. American Council on Education, Washington, DC

Test Bias

C. K. Tittle

Bias is defined as prejudice or having a particular bent or direction. To say a test is biased is to charge that it is prejudiced or unfair to groups or individuals characterized as different from the majority of test takers. In the United States these groups have included ethnic minorities, women, individuals whose first language is not English, and persons with handicapping conditions. Charges of test bias have been based on examination of individual test items, group differences in average performance, and the use of tests. Test bias has been examined for tests used in the selection of students for admission to institutions of postsecondary education, placement of students in special education classes, certification of minimum competencies or standards of achievement in secondary education, evaluation of educational programs, and career counseling.

Test bias, from a broader, construct-oriented perspective, has been examined in studies of tests used in cross-cultural research and in earlier attempts to develop tests which are culture free or culture fair. Early research in the 1900s on intelligence measures recognized the problems of testing children in different groups, for instance, those whose native language was not English. With the development of group mental tests and the first large-scale use of tests, the Army Alpha in the First World War, these measures came into wider use and to the attention of the public. By the 1920s cross-cultural test results were being used to counter deterministic interpretations of mental test scores. In the 1930s there were studies of the effect of language and culture on test scores. During the 1940s and early 1950s, there were again studies of racial differences in intelligence measures. Havighurst and Davis studied the relation of social class and test performance, and Eells, with others, attempted to develop culture fair mental tests.

No one now would claim that a test can be culture free or culture fair, nor is there consensus on a set of procedures which would establish that a test measures the same construct for groups with different cultural environments. Thus the tensions between professional testing practices and public concerns that arise in court cases and legislation in the United States, such as federal regulations for assessment practices for employment selection and educational placement of the handicapped, have been fruitful. The result has been a series of studies since the early 1970s, studies resulting in renewed attention to the theory underlying tests, the test development process, and a broader view of the validity evidence appropriate for the justification of tests used in educational settings. The issues that have arisen in each test-use setting are described first, followed by a summary of the major methodological approaches in studies used to detect item bias in the absence of criteria external to the test. This is the usual situation in educational achievement testing. Brief mention is made of experimental and correlational studies which can be used to provide further evidence that tests are measuring the same constructs in different groups.

Detailed reviews of methods and related studies can be found in Berk (1982), Cole (1981), Jensen (1980), and Weiss and Davison (1981).

1. Settings for Test Use

The fundamental role of validity in questions of test bias is made clear in describing the settings for test use. Validity of a test, or more accurately, the validity of inferences based on test scores has been established typically through one of three strategies: (a) criterion-related or predictive studies of validity; (b) content analyses for validity; and (c) construct studies of validity. Criterion-related studies examine the accuracy with which a test predicts a criterion, such as the use of a test of developed abilities to predict a criterion of college grades in an admissions setting. Content validity depends upon the definition of a domain of achievement to be sampled, the classification of test items in terms of this domain of reference, and expert judgment that the content of the test samples or represents accurately the achievement domain. An example is the knowledge and application of facts, concepts, and principles in a measure of science achievement. The construct strategy is

used to determine how well a score represents a construct, such as achievement motivation, anxiety, or literacy and requires logical and empirical bases in studies testing hypotheses about the relationship of scores on the construct measure to other variables.

The view which suggests that a particular type of validity is appropriate for different types of tests has been challenged by public concerns over the use of tests and the issues raised in studies of test bias. Several authors have suggested a more unified view of validity in which it is argued that the role of construct validity is fundamental. The accuracy of an inference that a pupil cannot read based on the results of a single test score labeled as a measure of reading comprehension is dependent on more than expert judgment or classification of the test items in relation to objectives of instruction. The inference that an individual child cannot read assumes that motivation in the testing situation is optimal, that anxiety or unfamiliarity with the testing format does not interfere with performance, that questions can be answered only within the context of the reading passage, that the vocabulary is appropriate, that is, within the child's experience or readily inferred from the context, and so on. Variables such as motivation and anxiety are extraneous to the construct of reading comprehension which the test purports to measure. There are, therefore, questions of an educational and psychological nature that should be examined when group differences in average test performance are observed. One facet of construct validity is to examine alternative explanations for differences in test performance.

Test bias in educational settings has another dimension. If evidence on the accuracy of interpretations is provided and it is satisfactory, there remains the question of the logical and empirical consequences of test use in a particular instance. If in admissions testing, proportionally fewer (in terms of the applicant pool) minority students are selected at elite institutions, what is the social value of this outcome? Similarly, if a career interest inventory used in counseling suggests fewer science and technological occupations to women for exploration than to men, what is the social value of this outcome? Whether one incorporates the social value questions within an expanded conception of validity or considers values as a matter for public policy and hence separate from a technical definition of validity, social values are a part of the study of test bias in educational settings.

1.1 Admissions Testing

In the use of tests for admission to postsecondary education an issue has been whether the tests are fair to particular groups of students. Although there have been studies of individual test items for bias, bias in this setting has focused on the use of tests in the selection process. In the selection situation a test is assumed to have predictive validity to the extent that students scoring well on the test also do well on a criterion. When there are differences between test scores, on the average, for groups such as blacks and whites or men and women, the question arises as to whether the group differences are also reflected in criterion differences or whether they represent bias. The criterion is typically limited to college grades and little study has been made of possible criterion bias. Similarly, the majority of studies have compared data for blacks and whites; fewer analyses have examined data for females and males (Wild and Dwyer 1980).

In defining bias in the selection setting, initially the relationship of the test (the predictor) to college grades (the criterion) was examined for differential validity: for situations in which the correlations expressing the relationship between the test and criterion were different for minority group and majority (white) groups or between women and men. Within-group regression equations used to estimate criterion scores were also studied. There were several ways in which group differences could occur in the correlations, predictor reliabilities, and differences in slopes, intercepts, or standard errors of estimate. In general, however, the comparison of these statistics for black and white groups of students has shown little evidence of differential validity to date.

There has been a shift from the criterion orientation expressed in the search for differential validities, to a decision orientation found in the study of the use of test results under different models proposed for fairness in selection. Several models or approaches have been proposed as fair procedures for selecting students for an educational institution. In these models a criterion score (grades) and a predictor (test score) are available and a cut score on the test needs to be found for each group such that the definition of fair selection in a particular model is satisfied. As an example, the standard regression approach has been used and a test defined as unfair if use of the common regression line systematically over- or under-predicts criterion scores for members of a particular group. If the regression equations are identical within each group, the use of the common regression line to select students with the highest criterion scores is considered fair. Selection is fair (to individuals) if it is optimal, based on the best prediction available.

An alternative model suggested that if the effect on groups was examined, a smaller proportion of one group than another might be selected with the regression model, even though the potential rates of success (if all applicants were admitted) of individuals in both groups would be similar. A possible decision or policy alternative, then, would be to select from the two groups in proportion to past rates of success for the groups (a constant-ratio model). Other models have been suggested, with variants on the idea of bringing values or utilities for particular outcomes for majority and minority individuals or groups explicitly into consideration. The models of fairness in selection that have been proposed have different outcomes when there are group differences in predictor and/or criterion scores. Decisions about the use of the test scores can place explicit utilities (values) on the possible outcomes for the educational institution and individual or groups of students affected

by the decision. Recognition of the social value of different outcomes has also led to the application of statistical decision theory. The general view at present is that the models of fairness in selection will not resolve questions of fairness and bias. Rather, the explicit consideration of values (utilities) placed upon outcomes for the institution, the individual, groups of concern, and the larger social body will further discussions of equity in educational opportunity and outcomes.

Another facet to the fairness discussion has been proposed by Novick (1980), in suggesting a move from defining groups for special consideration on the basis of ethnicity, race, or sex. An alternative is to define disadvantage operationally (e.g., family income). A measure of disadvantage could thus be made for each individual rather than using the group membership as a proxy for the disadvantage for which compensation or equalization is sought. A further refinement of this approach would be to identify the educational and psychological variables for which "disadvantage" is proxy, and link these to educational selection and placement within the university setting. Paradoxically, as the issue of test bias in selection has been clarified into its technical and social components, there is a trend toward less selectivity on the part of many postsecondary institutions in the United States. This trend should reinforce the placement and instructional use of tests, resulting in less reliance on traditional predictors such as aptitude (developed ability) measures.

1.2 Special Education Placement

The use of educational and psychological tests in placing students into special classes, as for the mildly retarded, has been the subject of controversy and court litigation. There are two main issues here—overrepresentation of minorities in special education classes and charges of bias in the IQ tests that are often the basis of placements. The assessment process leading to classification and placement typically involves standardized tests, and is most important for the mildly handicapped classifications of learning disability, educable or mild mental retardation, and emotional disturbance/behavior disorders. More severe handicaps occur with lower frequency, standardized tests are less important in classification, and no significant disproportionality by race, social status, or gender exists with the more severe handicaps in the United States.

Questions of test bias have arisen when items on individual measures of intelligence are examined, and when evidence of predictive validity has been used. In two court cases in the United States, *Larry P. versus Riles* and *Parents in Action on Special Education* (PASE) *versus Hannon*, judges reached opposite conclusions on the issue of bias in the test items. In *Larry P.*, the opinion remarks that the cultural bias of the tests was hardly disputed in litigation. In PASE the judge examined test items and found nine items should not be used because of bias.

In relation to validation, which in the employment or admissions settings has meant predicting a criterion, the judge in *Larry P.* defined validity as showing the appropriateness of the test and placement decision to the specific educational needs of the child. Evidence of high correlations between intelligence test scores and school performance in general did not justify placing a child in an environment in which the attempt at academic education would, for all practical purposes, cease (Sherman and Robinson 1981).

Studies of bias or fairness in special-education placement includes issues related to tests and other assessment procedures, among them the question of cultural bias in items (see Sect. 2 for methodology), the potential adverse impact of test use (disproportionate classification of groups into special classes), and studies of effects—evidence that the classification into "treatments" is of educational benefit to children. Special issues in the testing of linguistic minorities are also relevant (Olmedo 1981), such as language dominance and test translation procedures.

1.3 Competency Testing

In the United States minimum competency testing (MCT) programs have been started by local school districts and more than 30 states to assess basic academic skills students are expected to master in order to graduate with a diploma from secondary schools. In many minimum competency testing programs the tests are typically objective in form and measure reading and mathematics, sometimes language and writing skills. A passing score or standard for acceptable levels of student performance is established and the main uses of the test results are to certify students for grade promotion, graduation, or a diploma and to classify or place students in remedial or other special service programs.

Test or item bias issues have been raised in a major court case, *Debra P. versus Turlington*, in the state of Florida (US). The plaintiffs charged that the test was racially biased, that inadequate preparation time had been given, and that use of the test to classify and group students for remediation reinstituted segregation in the public schools. Initially the test was judged not racially biased, although analyses of individual items judged or statistically identified as biased against blacks found differential effects on the pass rate. However, another form of "bias" can be found in lack of opportunity to learn test content. In 1981 the Appeals Court remanded the case for further findings because the state had not made any effort to make certain whether the test covered material actually studied in the classrooms of the state.

In addition to issues of racially biased items, and the match between curriculum, instruction, and minimum competency tests, other questions of bias involve testing special groups, such as those for whom English is a second language, and the handicapped. Can skills included in minimum competency tests be the same for handicapped and nonhandicapped students?.

1.4 Evaluating Educational Programs

Issues of test bias in evaluation have been raised primarily in studies of compensatory education programs.

The debates over the standardized achievement tests used in evaluation focus on group differences in test scores and individual items which are identified as biased—items that may represent life styles or experiences more typical of middle socioeconomic white groups in United States culture. A second focus is on the interpretation of scores and use of the tests. Criticisms of the interpretation and use of the tests are based on the inference which is sometimes made that students cannot learn what the tests measure. Bias or lack of fairness in this context has included claims that items are set in contexts unfamiliar to urban students and also that tests do not measure the skills being taught in compensatory programs. These issues, as with the issues in minimum competency test programs, require a variety of methods to provide evidence of the fairness or lack of bias in a test.

1.5 Career Counseling

Issues of test bias in career counseling have centered on whether career interest inventories are biased against women. Earlier versions of a well-known United States interest inventory had separate forms for men (blue in color) and for women (pink). Fewer occupational scales were developed for women, thus limiting the occupations suggested for consideration by women students. In 1974 the National Institute of Education sponsored the development of *Guidelines for Assessment of Sex Bias and Sex Fairness in Career Interest Inventories*. Several aspects of interest measurement, the inventory itself, technical information and interpretive information, are considered in the *Guidelines*. Sex bias was examined in stereotyping of female and male roles, in the development of new scales, and in providing the same range of occupations for men and women. Gender-neutral language—firefighter, letter carrier, and flight attendant—was recommended. One issue is not readily resolved, the issue of whether the test is sex biased if it results in different distributions of basic interest areas or occupational groups suggested for men and women. This issue, and others that require technical data, as well as the value judgments that are made when particular interest measures are used with women, are discussed in a series of papers edited by Diamond (1975) and Tittle and Zytowski (1978).

What little evidence is available suggests that the validity of interest inventories may be the same for minority and white groups. Because interest measures are frequently used within a program of career guidance in schools, studies of the effects or outcomes of using interest measures have been carried out. Outcome measures can also provide evidence on bias or lack of fairness in the use of interest inventories by using student ratings, the number of occupations considered by females and males, and number of nontraditional occupations considered.

2. Item-bias Methodology

The study of test bias in the absence of an external criterion is an active area of research. For the most widely used tests in education—achievement, developed abilities, and basic interest measures—there are no external standards by which judgments of bias or fairness can be made. The statistical methods, which are the main area of research, all make the assumption that the test, over all items, is not biased. The methods rely upon detecting items which are by some definition aberrant from the majority of items in the test.

However, the statistical definition is not the only definition of bias. Critics have examined test content from several perspectives, making judgments as to whether portrayals of minorities and women are stereotyped or are broadly representative of all the roles—occupational, educational, familial, recreational—that persons in a particular culture can occupy. And, as mentioned earlier, another form of bias detection lies in analyses of the overlap of the opportunity to learn provided by curriculum materials and instruction with the items in standardized tests.

Each of these areas of item-bias detection is examined below. In the development of major standardized tests many test publishers in the United States now conduct judgmental reviews of test material for stereotyping, representativeness and familiarity of content to particular groups, as well as statistical item-bias analyses. The judgments or analyses of overlap among test items, curriculum, and instruction have been examined in research studies but are rarely done routinely and systematically by schools. Together these methods begin to define and document the use of a set of procedures that permit decisions that a test is fair or unbiased for particular groups of students.

2.1 Judgmental Reviews

The use of judgmental reviews in the test development process is described by Tittle (in Berk 1982). Test planning, item writing and review, item tryout, selection of final items, and development of norms and scaling are all stages in the test development process where judgments are made that affect perceptions of test bias. Procedures used to judge item bias include review forms and directions to judges that focus on identifying stereotyping of women, minorities, and the handicapped. Judges are asked to identify items that may be more or less familiar to particular groups. Tallies are made of the representativeness of item content and art work in tests for portraying women, men, and minorities in a positive manner (rather than omitting them, as is sometimes the case). Analyses may use categories such as the following for tallies: adult and child characters, female and male, main or secondary character, types of environment, behavior exhibited, and types of consequences of behavior.

Although judges are now being used more consistently in test development, there is little research that answers questions such as, who is an "expert" judge?

And, how much agreement exists between judges? Or, should agreement be important? The statistical item-bias approaches described below do not substitute for these judgmental reviews. Also, there is no expectation that judges and statistical procedures will identify the same items as "biased." Both approaches are necessary, although neither may be the final criterion for accepting or rejecting items in a particular measure.

There are more data available on the categories for classification and agreement between judges in the judgments of items, curricula, and opportunity to learn. Although this is a fundamental aspect of examining test validity and establishing the program sensitivity of tests used in evaluation, the types of classification schemes used have varied widely. A series of studies at Michigan State University provide a model for future analyses. A detailed set of categories was developed for analyzing fourth-grade tests of mathematics and curriculum materials. The main dimensions were: mode of presentation, nature of material, and operations. The opportunity to learn judgments are made by using teacher, student or external ratings of the opportunity to learn each item during the instructional process. Little is known about the characteristics of these ratings in terms of reliability and relationship to other variables.

2.2 Statistical Methods

Statistical methods of examining items for possible bias are being developed and studied. Research on the results of using different methods has begun, using both computer simulations and empirical data. The item-bias methods have been used when there is no criterion external to the test which can serve as the basis of estimating bias. The methods are intended to be used in the process of test development, to assist in building an unbiased test. Their development was stimulated by findings of group differences in test scores such as those for disadvantaged and advantaged groups.

All methods start by assuming the test as a whole is less biased than the individual items in the test. Thus the test questions designed to measure the same construct are studied together and bias is discovered when an item does not fit the pattern of the majority of items. Bias, as assessed by these methods, is the finding that an item is deviant from others in the test. Thus the definition of item bias is circular—it is possible to detect relative but not constant bias across all items in the test. Recognizing this limitation to the studies, an item can be defined as biased if equally able individuals from different groups do not have the same probability of success on the item.

Although a number of statistical procedures have been proposed, only four general types are mentioned here: (a) transformed item difficulty (TID); (b) item discrimination; (c) item characteristic curve methods; and (d) chi square.

The transformed item difficulty approach has been used since the 1960s. Using Angoff's procedures (see Berk 1982), the item difficulty (p) value or proportion getting the item right, is computed for each group. Each *p* value is transformed to the normal deviate (*z*) that would cut off that proportion of the area under the unit normal curve. The normal deviates may have a second transformation, to a delta value (delta = $4z + 13$). Deltas are plotted, one pair for each item. Items falling away from the principal or major axis of the ellipse are examined for the perpendicular or shortest distance of each point from the line, and the distance is taken as a measure of the degree of item bias. A limitation of the method is that the *p* values reflect group differences in ability as well as item difficulties.

The item discrimination method uses the difference between point biserial correlations (correlation of the item and the total test score) as a measure of item discrimination. A weakness of this technique is that mean differences in groups will give false indications of biased items. This method does not correlate well with other methods, and it is not frequently used in practice.

Item characteristic curve (latent trait or item response theory) methods are theoretically more satisfying because the characteristics of an item are described in terms of a function with parameters that are invariant over samples. The item characteristic curve describes the probability that a student with a given ability answers a test item correctly in terms of three parameters: the *a* parameter, the slope of the curve at the inflection point (point at which the slope of the curve changes direction), which reflects item discrimination; the *b* parameter, the inflection point, which reflects item difficulty; and the *c* parameter, the lower asymptote, which is the probability of guessing correctly for students of low ability.

For an item to be unbiased, the item characteristic curves must be the same for each group being compared. That is, the item has equal probabilities of success for students of the same ability regardless of group membership. Item characteristic curves may be based on one, two, or three parameters. The one parameter model, called the Rasch model, is a special case of the three parameter model (see *Rasch Measurement Models*). It assumes that there is no guessing on the test (no *c* parameter) and that all items discriminate equally (no *a* parameter). Various indices of item bias have been proposed for the three and one parameter models. The three parameter model requires large sample sizes (1,000) and numbers of items (40) for good estimates, as well as a complex computer analysis. The one parameter model has assumptions that are difficult to meet in practice. Both methods essentially require unidimensionality in the item set.

An application of chi square was proposed by Scheuneman. This approach approximates the latent-trait method by establishing categories of ability on the basis of total test score. The correct responses for groups are compared within ability levels. The total score range on the test is usually divided into five categories. Observed and expected proportions are calculated and compared using chi square. Generally these

approaches appear to be useful and practical, if imperfect, approximations to the three-parameter item characteristic curve. Smaller sample sizes are tolerable and large-scale computer facilities are not required.

2.3 Experimental Design Studies

Another approach to the study of item bias has been to vary the type of content on which groups might be expected to respond differently. For example, content thought to "favor" black or white students is selected and used in test development. Students of each group are randomly assigned to treatments in which type of item context or content is varied, and scores are compared in an analysis-of-variance design. This approach, although not as extensively applied as the statistical item-bias techniques, has potential for providing an understanding of why items may function differently for groups of students.

2.4 Correlational Studies

Correlational methods have also been used both to study the underlying dimensions or constructs in a set of items and to examine the patterns of relationships between a test and other measures. The emphasis is again on whether the dimensions or patterns of correlations are the same for different groups. These studies fit within the usual view of construct validity. Comparisons of factor structures have been made, using statistical tests of the comparability of factor patterns in two or more populations (confirmatory factory analysis). Correlational methods are also part of examining the functional equivalence of tests.

3. Summary

Examining a test and test use for bias or fairness to groups and individuals is a many-sided problem and there is no one method which will substantiate the claim that a test is fair. The variety of procedures currently being applied has not resulted in a clear consensus on a single set of procedures. However, research on the relationship between methods as well as their technical adequacy is being conducted. Researchers have argued that there is a conflict between the use of judgments, reviews of test content, and the statistical methods, since there is often little overlap between the items identified as "biased" by these methods. In practice, however, two points can be made. The first is that the judgments and content reviews provide information that the statistical methods cannot, while the reverse is also true. Second, the published test remains the outcome of a series of decisions made by each test developer, not the result of rote application of any bias procedures. This practice is unlikely to change in the near future.

Studies that may provide additional insight into group differences in test performance are, for example, those examining psychological variables such as test anxiety and responses to changes in item types, formats, and familiarity of context material. Similarly, studies of coaching and test-taking skills may also lead to educational practices that reduce the influence of extraneous variables on test performance. Renewed attention to problems of test bias holds the promise of bringing testing closer to educational practice and to psychological theory.

See also: Validity

Bibliography

Berk R (ed.) 1982 *Handbook of Methods for Detecting Test Bias.* Johns Hopkins University Press, Baltimore, Maryland

Cole N S 1981 Bias in testing. *Am. Psychol.* 36: 1067–77

Diamond E E (ed.) 1975 *Issues of Sex Bias and Sex Fairness in Career Interest Measurement.* National Institute of Education, Washington, DC

Jensen A R 1980 *Bias in Mental Testing.* Free Press, New York

Novick M R 1980 Policy issues of fairness in testing. In: van der Kamp L J T et al. (eds.) 1980 *Psychometrics for Educational Debates.* Wiley, New York

Olmedo E L 1981 Testing linguistic minorities. *Am. Psychol.* 36: 1078–85

Sherman S W, Robinson N M (eds.) 1981 *Ability testing of Handicapped People: Dilemma for Government, Science, and the Public.* National Academy Press, Washington, DC

Tittle C K, Zytowski D G (eds.) 1978 *Sex-fair Interest Measurement: Research and Implications.* National Institute of Education, Washington, DC

Weiss D J, Davison M L 1981 Test theory and methods. *Annu. Rev. Psychol.* 32: 647–51

Wild C L, Dwyer C A 1980 Sex bias in selection. In: van der Kamp L J T et al. (eds.) 1980 *Psychometrics for Educational Debates.* Wiley, New York

Item Bias

R. J. Adams and K. J. Rowe

Despite an already large and growing literature on the subject of item bias in educational and psychological tests, it seems that no universally accepted definition yet exists. However, in the case of ability tests, Shepard et al. (1981) are helpful: "an item is biased if two individuals with equal ability but from different groups do not have the same probability of success on an item" (p. 316). The detection of test item bias is an active area of psychometric research that has grown in response to concerns with the possibility of bias in educational and psychological testing for evaluation, selection, and placement purposes. These concerns have primarily grown out of a broader social interest in the equitable treatment of socio-political and ethnic minority groups.

One important distinction which is often made is between bias that is *external* to a test and bias which is *internal* to the test instrument itself. According to Osterlind (1983), "external bias is the degree to which test scores may manifest a correlational relationship with variables independent of the test" (p. 9). External bias issues include the social consequences of test use as well as fairness in tests and procedures for selection. These issues are usually treated under the general heading of "test bias" which focuses interest on the construct and predictive validity of a whole test, rather than on individual test items per se. Alternatively, internal bias is primarily concerned with the psychometric properties of the test items themselves; the focus of interest being the relationship between the construct validity of individual items and that of the total test. In much of the literature, internal bias is known as "item bias".

The major concern of item bias detection procedures involves examinations of whether individual test items behave in a similar manner (i.e. have similar measurement properties) for different subgroups drawn from the same population, without reference to an external criterion. In this context, a test item is said to be biased when there is evidence of interaction between group membership and item performance, when ability or psychological differences between the groups have been controlled.

The identification of item bias is important, even for tests that are mainly dependent on predictive validity (e.g. selection tests), since internal indications of bias make it increasingly likely that the test will also show predictive bias. Hence, techniques for identifying test item bias are useful in test construction, since potentially biased items, in the predictive sense, can be rejected during the initial item-selection process and prior to any attempts to evaluate a test's predictive validity in populations.

The emotive and somewhat pejorative connotations associated with the word "bias", have prompted some psychometricians to adopt the terms "differential item performance" or "differential item functioning" rather than item bias. This alternative nomenclature reflects the aim of item bias detection methods in identifying those items that function differently for different groups of testees. In this article, however, for the sake of consistency with most of the research literature, we use the term "item bias".

1. Statistical Techniques for Measuring Item Bias

In recent years there has been a proliferation of statistical techniques for measuring item bias, particularly in tests of educational attainment. Since the large number of existing techniques and their related literature makes it impossible for them to be fully discussed here, the reader is referred to reviews and handbooks such as Berk (1982) and Osterlind (1983) for more detailed discussions and technical formulations of item bias detection methods, as well as for references to original sources.

Briefly, methods for identifying item bias include: factor analysis, examinations of item discrimination through point-biserial and partial correlations, the examination of item difficulty through various transformations, ANOVA methods, item response theory or latent trait methods, a variety of chi-square approaches, and methods of using log-linear models and the Mantel–Haenszel statistic. From the numerous techniques which have been developed, however, findings from comparative studies suggest that only a few of them are of sufficient value for their use to be encouraged. While, in this article, we focus on methods which have been developed primarily for the detection of item bias in educational and psychological tests of attainment or ability, these methods may also be applied to sets of test items designed to measure any latent trait of interest. First, we outline those methods that provide some indication of bias and are easy to apply, despite their known inadequacies, and then discuss a couple of the more recently proposed, albeit more complex, methods. The application of alternative techniques to the study of a practical problem concerned with sex bias in aptitude testing is found in such studies as Adams (1983).

1.1 Quick but Incomplete Methods

A set of methods have been developed which, although incomplete and often misleading, may serve as initial indicators of items that behave differently for separate groups. The first of these requires the calculation of the item difficulties (*p*-values) for each group. The items are then ranked within groups according to the *p*-values, and the rank orders for each group are compared. Any item that notably deviates in its comparative ranking for the groups may be indicative of bias. Nevertheless, like all incomplete methods, the comparison of rank orders can be misleading. For example, if the groups have different ability distributions, the items will not have the same *p*-value ranking unless all of the items have the same discrimination (see Ironson 1983).

A second possibility involves the comparison of the item discrimination indices for each of the groups. These are usually represented as the point-biserial correlations between the item and total test scores. While differences between the point-biserial coefficients for the group can be useful indicators of bias, they are sensitive to differences in the score distributions for each group. Since the point-biserial correlation coefficient is a function of the *p*-value of an item, if the two groups have different ability distributions, a nonbiased item will be more discriminating in the group for which the *p*-value is closest to 0.5.

Factor analysis has also been used for detecting item bias. If the factor structure of the test is computed separately for each group and then compared, any item which does not produce comparable loadings may be regarded as biased. Factor analysis of biserial correlation matrices has considerable conceptual appeal since it allows for a comparison of underlying constructs in the test for each group. Unfortunately, however, even with tests that are known to contain bias, factor analytic methods often produce the same underlying structure for the groups. Furthermore, it is widely recognized that

factor analysis is inappropriate when used with dichotomous data of the type that normally appear in educational and psychological tests of ability. Given these limitations, it may also be considered as an incomplete method for detecting item bias.

Another widely applied method involves the use of ANOVA. If two or more groups, sampled from the same population, are given a common test, the occurrence of a significant Items × Group interaction is used to indicate differential item behaviour, suggesting that the items may not have the same meaning for the different groups in terms of construct validity. Nevertheless, such interpretations are potentially misleading since significant Items × Groups interactions are often observed as a function of either differing ability levels among testees or differences in overall group performance.

Each of these incomplete methods relies on traditional item analyses that produce statistics dependent on the ability distributions obtained from the respondent samples. Consequently, when the distribution of ability in the groups under investigation varies, unpredictable influences on bias indicators invariably occur, thus confounding the identification of item bias.

1.2 Transformed Item Difficulty (TID)

The transformed item difficulty (TID) strategy is essentially an extension of the ANOVA approach which seeks to identify the extent to which particular items contribute to the Items × Groups interaction. While the TID approach, like the incomplete methods, is also based on traditional item analyses, its ease of use and strong performance in comparative studies support its utility with small samples and/or short tests.

In the TID method, the *p*-values for each item are calculated separately for each group and are transformed to a scale that is more likely to be interval than the *p*-value scale. The usual method of transformation involves converting the *p*-values to *z*-values, where *z* is the (1-*p*)th percentile in a normal distribution, and then producing a delta (Δ) scale, where for item *i* of group *j*,

$$\Delta_{ij} = 4z_{ij} + 13$$

The transformation of *z* to the Δ scale is favoured because it removes negative values and adequate precision can be shown using only one decimal place.

When the pairs of Δ values are shown in a scatter plot, they form an ellipse with major axes given by $y = bx + a$. *a* and *b* are given by Angoff and Ford (1973) as:

$$a = M_x - bM_y$$
$$b = (s_y^2 - s_x^2) \pm [(s_y^2 - s_x^2)^2 + 4r_{xy}^2 s_x^2 s_y^2]^{1/2}/2r_{xy}s_x s_y$$

where s_x^2 is the variance of the Δ values for the group plotted on the horizontal axis, s_y^2 is the variance of the delta values plotted on the vertical axis, M_x and M_y are the respective means, and r_{xy} is the correlation between the two sets of Δ's.

The perpendicular distance between the plotted delta pair for each item *i*, and the major axis is given by:

$$d_i = (bx_i + a - y_i)/(b^2 + 1)^{1/2}$$

where x_i and y_i are the pair of Δ scores for item i. The magnitude of this distance is used to indicate the amount of bias in the item. However, there is some conjecture about the magnitude of the distance that should be used to indicate bias.

In many instances, the TID method is adequate for identifying item bias. It is conceptually simple, easy to compute and provides a visual indication of the amount of bias. Comparative studies of item bias detection techniques have shown that the TID method performs well as an approximation to more sophisticated methods, especially when short tests are being analysed or sample sizes are small. Unfortunately, when using the TID method, like most of the incomplete methods, differences in the group score distributions can unjustifiably make items appear to be biased because of a lack of statistical control over ability differences between the groups. Moreover, the fact that the focus of attention for both the ANOVA and TID approaches is solely on item difficulty gives rise to several problems, not the least of which is that Items × Groups interactions have been shown to occur in any test regardless of item bias.

1.3 Chi-Square Methods

In an attempt to avoid these problems, a chi-square goodness-of-fit approach has been used, by examining differences in proportions of groups responding correctly to an item across total test score categories. The score distribution is broken into a number of arbitrary levels and the probabilities of test takers from different groups with the same ability level responding correctly to an item are compared. When the proportions are similar for all groups, an item is said to be unbiased. While the chi-square approach is comparatively simple to compute, it has the disadvantage of being particularly sensitive to within-groups item discriminations, as well as being constrained by the arbitrary selection of ability levels. For a review of chi-square methods, see Marascuilo and Slaughter (1981).

1.4 Latent Trait Models

Latent trait theory, sometimes called item response theory (IRT), provides statistical models for describing the relationship of an index of a testee's ability to the probability of a correct response to an item. Under such models, item responses can be described in the form of an item characteristic curve (ICC), which relates the probability of success on an item to a function of the testee's ability position on the latent trait being measured by the test, and the characteristics of the item. For item bias detection, the most frequently used IRT models include the three-parameter logistic model and the Rasch model.

The mathematical form of the three parameter ICC is given by:

$$P_i(\theta) = c_i + (1 - c_i)/[1 + e^{-Da_i(\theta - b_i)}] \quad (i = 1, \ldots, n)$$

where $P_i(\theta)$ is the probability of a correct response for a testee of ability θ; a_i, b_i and c_i are parameters characterizing item i, and $D = 1.7$ is a constant scaling factor. Figure 1 shows two possible item characteristic curves. Parameter b_i is a location parameter for the ICC on the underlying continuum and it is generally called the item difficulty. Parameter a_i corresponds to the slope of the ICC at $\theta = b_i$ and is generally regarded as the discrimination index, while c_i gives the lower asymptote for the curve. This parameter is regarded as a pseudo-guessing parameter because it corresponds to the probability of a correct answer for an individual with very low ability.

Thus, under an IRT model, an item would be regarded as unbiased if all individuals having the same underlying ability have an equal probability of getting the item correct, regardless of subgroup membership. In such circumstances there would be no significant differences in group item-characteristic curves.

In the attempt to identify biased items, group ICC's generated by the three-parameter logistic model are compared. This is achieved by first estimating the parameters for items, and placing the obtained values on the same scale. Bias is estimated for an item by observing the differences in ICC's for two groups when θ is equated (i.e. both groups are placed on the same ability scale), and it is evident that different probabilities of success result for each group. For example, from Fig. 1, it is evident that the probability of a correct response is greater for group A than for group B at all levels of ability, except for group B testees of high θ values. Moreover, the effects of bias are confounded by both discrimination and difficulty. Since the ICC's for the two groups are demonstrably different, the item does not discriminate equally between the two groups and the presence of bias is thus inferred.

A range of methods has been advocated for accurately examining the differences between the ICC's for different groups. The reader is referred to Shepard et al. (1984), where eight of these methods are briefly described as part of a comparative study of item bias detection methods using the three-parameter logistic

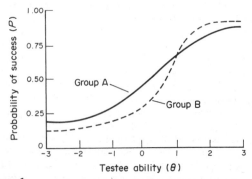

Figure 1
Hypothetical equated item characteristic curves for two groups different in discrimination, difficulty and pseudochance. Adapted from Osterlind (1983 p. 64)

model. As a result of their study, they recommend the use of a weighted sum of squares calculated as:

$$\text{SOS}_i = \frac{1}{N_A + N_B} \sum_{j=1}^{N_A + N_B} \frac{[\hat{P}_{iA}(\theta_j) - \hat{P}_{iB}(\theta_j)]^2}{s^2_{\hat{P}_{iA} - \hat{P}_{iB}}}$$

where $\hat{P}_{iA}$ is the estimated probability of an individual with ability θ_j responding correctly to item i, N_A and N_B are the number of individuals in groups A and B respectively, $s^2_{\hat{P}_{iA} - \hat{P}_{iB}}$ is the standard error of the difference in estimated probabilities, and the summation is performed over all values of θ_j that occur in the analyses.

While the three-parameter logistic model allows items to differ in difficulty, discrimination and guessing, the Rasch model includes only a single parameter for each item, namely, a difficulty parameter. Essentially, the model provides a common measurement scale on which testee ability and item difficulty are simultaneously calibrated. Although derived independently, the Rasch model is functionally equivalent to the three-parameter logistic model with $c_i = 0$ and $Da_i = 1$.

Despite their similarity, the Rasch and three parameter logistic models were developed on very different philosophies. Advocates of the three parameter model claim that its three parameters more closely describe, in psychometric terms, the tests and test data that are most widely used, while Rasch model advocates argue that it is deductively derived from the requirements of valid measurement. If a test or item does not conform to the Rasch model, it is argued that the test or the item must contain some form of bias. This may not be item bias in terms of bias against a minority, but may be indicative of a number of possible threats to valid measurement. For example, Masters (1988) has shown that differences in item discrimination may be due to bias against a minority group.

In comparative studies, however, the three parameter model has generally received more favourable attention for item bias detection. This is mainly due to its feature of more closely describing, in psychometric terms, multiple choice tests as they are currently constructed. In simulation studies it could well be an outcome of the fact that most simulated data are generated by the model in the first place.

Among the claimed advantages of IRT or latent trait approaches to item bias detection, perhaps the most important is the "sample-invariant" property of the models' parameters, which implies that differences in ability should not create artifactual instances of bias. This theoretical property of the models means that the item parameters are independent of the distributional characteristics of the sample and are therefore not subject to the distortions described for the incomplete and TID methods. Hence, under any latent trait model, parameters from different samples should be equal. Items whose parameters are notably unequal violate the assumptions of the model, and in consequence are said to be biased because they may be measuring something different for a particular group.

Despite the widespread acceptance of IRT technology, it is subject to some fundamental difficulties. For example, it has been shown in practice that the a_i and c_i parameters of the three parameter model do not exhibit the strong invariance required by the model. Similarly, the ICC's are not entirely independent of the distribution of ability since possibly biased items cannot be excluded from the initial ability estimate. Moreover, the analyses are complex, expensive and require large samples (i.e. preferably $n > 1,000$). Further, IRT models do not only assume that the average item is unbiased, but are incapable of detecting the presence of constant bias across all items.

Of more crucial importance perhaps, is that the applicability of any IRT model in a given testing situation is conditional on the validity of its underlying assumptions. These assumptions, namely, unidimensionality, local independence, and logistic model adequacy, can be debilitatingly stringent, since even the choice of items may be governed a priori by the models, regardless of their substantive educational or psychological appropriateness. In the context of test item selection, Novick (1980) emphasizes that when the particular requirement of a unidimensional latent trait is not satisfied, it is "impossible to differentiate between additional traits which are meaningful in the testing situation and those which are reflective of bias" (p. 132).

2. The Future

While item bias detection is among the most active of all areas of psychometric research, much remains to be done before a satisfactory battery of procedures with known properties is available. For example, further work needs to be done in explicating the currently available procedures, developing new procedures and extending item bias technology beyond dichotomously scored tests. In terms of current techniques, the distributional properties of many of the bias detection indices need to be investigated such that the power of the detection methods can be determined.

Future developments will undoubtedly involve the extension of item bias procedures beyond dichotomous items to polychotomous items that result from measurement instruments employing partial credit scoring, graded scoring, or rating scales. Since instruments of this type have widespread application in educational and psychosocial research, the possibility of bias in such instruments is equally important as that for dichotomous tests. A number of latent trait measurement models now exist for the modelling of data of this type and their use in the detection of item bias for data of this type may become an important area of research.

Currently, the most active area of item bias research is concerned with the development of new techniques based on log-linear or logit models, and the Mantel–Haenszel approach to contingency table analysis. These approaches are essentially modifications to chi-square methods and also employ elements of item response theory.

2.1 Mantel–Haenszel Statistic

The use of the Mantel–Haenszel statistic (see Holland and Thayer 1986) is a relatively new method for the detection of item bias that is gaining considerable support.

The Mantel–Haenszel approach is a chi-square technique with a number of distinct advantages over its predecessors. To apply the Mantel–Haenszel approach, the two groups being examined are divided into matched subgroups. The simplest method of matching is to use the total test score (research is still required on refining the methods for establishing appropriate groups) and for each matched group a table is calculated, as in Table 1. Using the notation of Holland and Thayer, T_j is the total number of students in the matched group j; n_{R_j} is the number from group R, and A_j is the number from group R who got the item correct, and so on. Then, for the item being examined for bias, the p-values for each group P_{R_j} and P_{F_j} are calculated. The null hypothesis, $H_0 : P_{R_j} = P_{F_j}$ is then tested. In most chi-square approaches, the H_0 is tested against the simple negation of H_1 (i.e. $H_1 : P_{R_j} \neq P_{F_j}$) and they are not powerful against any specific violations to H_0. In contrast, the Mantel–Haenszel approach reduces the alternatives to H_0, to $H_1 : P_{R_j}/Q_{R_j} = \alpha \, P_{R_j}/Q_{F_j}$ (where $Q = 1-P$). The Mantel–Haenszel statistic for testing the null hypothesis against H_1 (after correction for continuity) is given by Holland and Thayer as:

$$\text{MH-CHISQ} = \left[\left| \sum_j A_j - \sum_j \text{E}(A_j) \right| - \frac{1}{2} \right]^2 \Big/ \sum_j \text{var}(A_j)$$

where

$$\text{E}(A_j) = n_{R_j} M_{1_j}/T_j$$
$$\text{var}(A_j) = n_{R_j} n_{F_j} M_{1_j} M_{0_j} / T_j^2 (T_j - 1)$$

MH-CHISQ is distributed as chi square with one degree of freedom.

In addition to having greater power than other chi-square methods, the Mantel–Haenszel approach allows the calculation of a measure of the degree of bias in the item. This measure of bias is given through the odds ratio alpha (α_{MH}). The estimate of α_{MH} is given by:

$$\hat{\alpha}_{\text{MH}} = \left(\sum_j A_j D_j / T_j \right) \Big/ \left(\sum_j B_j C_j / T_j \right)$$

Table 1
Contingency table for the calculation of the Mantel–Haenszel statistic (MH-CHISQ)

Group	Score on Test Item		
	1	0	Total
R	A_j	B_j	n_{R_j}
F	C_j	D_j	n_{F_j}
Total	M_{1_j}	M_{0_j}	T_j

Holland and Thayer have provided the following interpretation of $\hat{\alpha}_{\text{MH}}$:

> The value of $\hat{\alpha}_{\text{MH}}$ is the average factor by which the odds that a member of R is correct on the studied item exceeds the corresponding odds for a *comparable* member of F. The values of $\hat{\alpha}_{\text{MH}}$ that exceed 1 correspond to items on which the reference group performed better on average than did comparable members of the focal group. (1986 p. 9)

Preliminary studies of the Mantel–Haenszel approach to item bias detection are still in progress and the results are not yet sufficiently clear to make any strong conclusion in respect of its utility. Although its usefulness is yet to be fully determined, early evaluation work indicates that it could be a cheap and effective alternative to the more complex latent trait methods.

2.2 Log-linear and Logit Models

Log-linear and logit models are beginning to have an impact on new directions in item bias research. Recent work by Kelderman (1984), who formulates the Rasch model as a quasi log-linear model, and van der Flier et al. (1984) who use an iterative logit model, provide the groundwork for future developments in item bias detection technology.

Kelderman provides a method for formulating the Rasch model as a quasi log-linear model and uses the log linear formulation to test specific violations to the Rasch model's assumptions. Although not directly concerned with item bias, Kelderman shows how various tests of independence on a group × score × item 1 × item 2 ×,..., × item k contingency table may be undertaken. Many of these tests can be used to identify specific forms of item bias. While the log-linear Rasch approach requires further development, the theoretical formulations of the approach to date indicate some promise.

Van der Flier et al. also use a contingency table approach where a score × group × item response table is set up for each item. If the score categories are denoted by $i = 1,2,\ldots,s$, the groups are denoted by $j = 1,2,\ldots,g$ and the item response categories by $k = 1,2$ say, then the expected cell frequency in the table is denoted F_{ijk}. The logit is then defined as the natural logarithm of the ratio of the correct and incorrect responses. This is very similar to the formulation of the odds ratio in the Mantel–Haenszel and is also closely related to the basic steps in the formulation of the Rasch model.

The saturated logit model is therefore denoted as:

$$\log(F_{ij_1}/F_{ij_2}) = C + S_i + G_j + (SG)_{ij}$$

with constraints:

$$\sum_i S_i = \sum_j G_j = \sum_i (SG)_{ij} = \sum_j (SG)_{ij} = 0$$

where C is the item difficulty parameter, S_i is the score effect, G_j is the group effect, and $(SG)_{ij}$ is the score by group interaction. This model, by definition, fits the data perfectly.

If the restricted model, log $(F_{ij_1}/F_{ij_2}) = C + S_i$ fits the data, there is no group effect, so the item is not biased against any group. If the model log $(F_{ij_1}/F_{ij_2}) = C + S_i + G_i$ is required to fit the data, then uniform bias is detected; that is, there is bias against one of the groups which is uniform over score levels. If the saturated model is required to fit the data, then nonuniform bias has been detected; that is, bias that varies over the score levels. Note that it is possible, however, for an item to have bias that changes in direction over ability levels.

In most of the item bias detection procedures, the total test score (or some transformation of it) is used as the criterion against which to judge bias. In other words, a testee's ability is defined by the items being investigated for bias. To avoid this kind of circularity, van der Flier et al. used the logit model iteratively, with biased items being used successively from the calculation of the group score. Iterative methods can be employed with any of the chi-square or item response theory approaches, but they have not been extensively explored. One possible problem with iterative methods is that they are likely to be order-dependent so that the final set of unbiased items may depend on which item is chosen to be deleted first. In many instances, this choice could be somewhat arbitrary. In their comparative study, van der Flier et al. found that the iterative logit method performed favourably when compared to ANOVA and TID methods. Comparisons with IRT approaches have yet to be reported.

3. Concluding Comments

Prospects for the further development of item bias detection procedures, the explication of their properties and their relative usefulness, are indeed promising. Nevertheless, there is need for such optimism to be tempered with caution.

In recent years, the issue of bias in educational and psychological tests has received intense public and technical scrutiny, stimulating both public debate and psychometric research. However, despite advances in item bias detection technology, some of which have been reviewed here, it is important to note that apart from statistical criteria, none of the proposed methods for the detection of item bias is able to indicate *why* an item identified as "biased" is biased, or *what* constitutes an item being biased. Clearly, in the absence of substantive theoretical criteria, no amount of statistical manipulation of test data can provide the *what* and *why* of "item bias", nor facilitate the drawing of valid inferences about its presence or absence. While psychometric research continues to yield notable improvements in test quality, much of this work cannot be said to have significantly clarified the public controversies, or to have resolved some of the more pressing substantive problems related to the issues of test and item bias. This state of affairs is primarily due to the fact that the efforts directed toward "improvements" have addressed technical rather than the substantive issues of item bias associated with its psychoeducational cognitive correlates.

Bibliography

Adams R J 1983 *Sex Bias in ASAT?* Australian Council for Educational Research, Hawthorn, Victoria

Angoff W H, Ford S F 1973 Item–race interaction on a test of scholastic aptitude. *J. Educ. Meas.* 10: 95–106

Berk R A (ed.) 1982 *Handbook of Methods for Detecting Test Bias.* John Hopkins University Press, Baltimore, Maryland

Holland P W, Thayer D T 1986 Differential item performance and the Mantel–Haenszel procedure. Paper presented at the Annual Meeting of the American Educational Research Association, San Francisco, California

Ironson G H 1983 Using item response theory to measure bias. In: Hambleton R K (ed.) 1983 *Applications of Item Response Theory.* Educational Research Institute of British Columbia, Vancouver, pp. 155–74

Kelderman H 1984 Loglinear Rasch model tests. *Psychometrika.* 49: 223–45

Marascuilo L A, Slaughter R E 1981 Statistical procedures for identifying possible sources of item bias based on χ^2 statistics. *J. Educ. Meas.* 18: 229–48

Masters G N 1988 Item discrimination: When more is worse. *J. Educ. Meas.* 25(1)

Novick M R 1980 Policy issues of fairness in testing. In: van der Kamp J T, Langerak W F, de Gruitjer P N M (eds.) 1980 *Psychometrics for Educational Debates.* Wiley, New York, pp. 123–37

Osterlind S J 1983 *Test Item Bias.* Sage University Paper series on Quantitative Applications in the Social Sciences, Series No. 070-030. Sage Publications, Beverly Hills, California, and London

Shepard L, Camilli G, Averill M 1981 Comparisons of procedures for detecting test-item bias with both external and internal ability criteria. *J. Educ. Stat.* 6: 317–75

Shepard L, Camilli G, Williams D M 1984 Accounting for statistical artifacts on item bias research. *J. Educ. Stat.* 9: 93–128

van der Flier H, Mellenbergh G J, Ader H J, Wijn M 1984 An iterative item bias detection method. *J. Educ. Meas.* 21: 131–45

Scaling Achievement Test Scores

J. P. Keeves

This article is concerned with the scaling procedures that are employed in the field of education, not only to make the scores on achievement tests more readily interpretable in a variety of practical situations but also, and more importantly, to strengthen the scores resulting from the assessment of educational achievement so that more effective and meaningful analyses can be carried out on the data, and more valid conclusions can be obtained. The article considers the types of scales used in the assessment of performance on achievement tests, the classes of scaling models used, the alternative approaches to scaling available for the obtaining of achievement test scores, the scaling procedures used for converting achievement test scores to measures on specific scales, the equating of different test forms, and the moderation of scores obtained using different scales. There is growing recognition that latent trait procedures will in the future perform an important function in scaling, equating, and moderation and that there is a need for research in this field of educational measurement. Consideration is limited to the scaling of achievement test data. Other aspects of scaling are examined in other articles (see *Scaling of Nominal Data*; *Scaling Methods*).

1. Preliminary Steps to Scaling Students' Responses

Prior to undertaking scaling it is necessary to carry out one or more of the necessary preliminary steps of (a) classifying, (b) ordering, and (c) measuring. These processes are defined as follows:

(a) Classifying is the process of assigning students' responses to qualitatively different classes or categories.

(b) Ordering is the process of ranking students' responses to qualitatively different classes or categories.

(c) Measuring is the process of estimating the location of the students' responses (or ordered categories) on an underlying trait. Locations are expressed in terms of some unit that retains a consistent meaning across all locations.

1.1 Types of Scales

The assessment of students' responses involves the assigning of numbers to the individual students for their responses according to some defined rule. The rule specifies a quantitative aspect of a response with respect to the categories of an attribute, and thus defines the scale which is used for obtaining the associated measures. In this operation, four types of data exist. The four types of data involve four properties which the data may or may not possess. These properties are:

(a) identity: the responses that are classified together into one category are identical in nature;

(b) transitivity or order: the responses may be ranked in order from least to greatest or greatest to least;

(c) metric: the responses can be quantitatively distinguished from each other in terms of a fixed or constant sized unit of measurement;

(d) functional zero: the underlying scale of measurement has a known functional zero point and the measurements made are related to this functional zero point.

The types of scales and related data arise from these four properties.

(a) *Categorical or nominal data.* These possess identity only. For example, students may be classed into categories according to whether they answered a multiple-choice test item correctly or incorrectly, indicated that they guessed the answer, or omitted the item. These four types of response are essentially categorical in nature. Nevertheless, the presence of a response could be scored $+1$ and the absence of a response scored 0, and a very crude scale could be formed. More elaborate procedures have been developed for the scaling of such data.

(b) *Ordinal scales and data.* These possess both identity and transitivity properties. For example, students' essays may be classified into one of five ordered classes in which placement in a higher class is associated with superior performance than for those essays placed in a lower class. Much of the data collected in educational research studies is essentially ordinal in nature, and a wide range of procedures has been developed in order to scale these data.

(c) *Interval scales and data.* These possess the properties of identity, transitivity and metric. In the measurement of educational achievement, for example, in assessing the number of correct responses to a sample of 50 items on a test of a limited domain of knowledge such as knowledge of the basic number facts, an interval scale is frequently assumed. However, achievement measured in this way does not involve the use of a truly interval scale. Latent trait measurement procedures seek ways of converting such data into measures on a scale that approximates more closely to an interval scale. These measurement procedures are discussed more extensively below.

(d) *Ratio scales and data.* These possess all four properties of identity, transitivity, metric, and a functional zero. For example, a student may take 5 minutes 25 seconds to solve a specified problem. Here time is measured on a ratio scale. The functional zero is that time at which the student commenced work on the problem.

Togerson (1958) has drawn attention to a fifth type of scale, namely an ordinal scale with a natural origin, rather than a functional zero. Such scales include bipolar attitude scales, where the uncertain category provides a natural origin. A simple ordinal scale of achievement associated with number of books read during a semester would have a natural origin that also had the characteristics of a functional zero.

In order to investigate relationships between variables in educational research, it is desirable to obtain measures on a scale which permits the data to hold as many of the four properties as possible. By employing an interval scale instead of an ordinal scale to make observations in the investigation of an educational problem, it is possible to add and subtract measures, and by using a ratio scale instead of an interval scale multiplication and division may also be applied to the measures.

Thus the strength of such scales and the data they provide may range from strong ratio scales and the associated measures to relatively weak ordinal scales and measures.

In the analysis of data different statistical procedures have been developed for data possessing different properties, and since the power of these analytical techniques increases with the strength of the scales employed, considerable effort is directed towards increasing the strength of the scales used in educational research and practice. These attempts to improve the strength of the scales, and the data they yield, must be seen to be different from the efforts made to increase the accuracy of the data by more careful measurement or by more effective sampling. Scaling as a procedure in educational measurement is directed towards upgrading the data by the use of operations that will change the properties of the data with respect to transitivity and metric. For example, the rankings of essay markers are subject to error as a consequence of both within-judge errors (which arise when a judge fails to discriminate consistently) and between-judge errors (when judges differ in the rankings they assign). These rankings form at least an ordinal scale. Through the multiple marking of the essays by two or more judges, and through the use of an average ranking, the strength of the scale can be increased. Similarly, the percentage of passes achieved by a class group on an examination scored 1 and failures on the examination scored 0, are at least quasi-interval data and the strength of the scale concerned with the proportion passing can be increased through the use of the logit transformation (Snedecor and Cochran 1967) prior to analysis. The use of logits transforms the data to a normal distribution that has many properties that facilitate the analysis of the data.

2. Achievement Test Scores and Scales

The strategies employed in the measurement of educational achievement are, in general, based upon samples of student behaviours that are responses to requests for the student to perform clearly identified tasks. Commonly, achievement tests employ multiple-choice test items which are questions with alternative answers provided, from which the student must choose the most appropriate answer. This answer must be indicated by a pencil mark on a printed paper booklet or separate paper answer sheet. Tightly specified instructions are provided by the examiner. If the student is well-motivated to perform in this test situation, and if the student has understood correctly the examiner's instructions, it is assumed that the pencil and paper record will provide an accurate measure of the student's level of achievement on the field of tasks under survey. Other types of behaviour can be assessed in a similar way by, for example, constructing a response, writing an extended answer, pressing an identified key on a keyboard of a computer terminal, or by an observer observing behaviour and making a record of the type of behaviour observed. For the simplest types of test items, and using

the simplest scoring procedure, a student is assigned a score of $+1$ for each response that is classed as correct, and 0 for each response that is classed as incorrect. Because of the complex structures associated with the organization of knowledge in the mind of each student, the responses made on one question are not completely independent of answers to other questions. However, it is generally assumed that each question answered, and each score $+1$ or 0, has provided an independent sample of student behaviour.

2.1 Sources of Error

It is also assumed that the number of correct responses made by a student has a rough one-to-one relation to the amount of knowledge possessed by the student in the area under investigation or to the student's ability to perform the skill being measured. Likewise, it is assumed that there is a strong one-to-one relation between the response made by the student and the score assigned in the scoring process. However, each response made by the student or each score assigned has a component of error associated with it, which arises from several sources.

(a) The response made by a student may exhibit random fluctuations associated with factors such as carelessness that are not related to the extent of knowledge held by the student.

(b) Since it is rarely possible to require students to respond to a complete population of tasks associated with an area of knowledge or performance it is necessary, in general, to sample behaviour by requiring a limited number of tasks to be answered. Consequently, there are errors associated with the sampling of tasks from the total population of such tasks.

(c) Although it is common to develop procedures that are standardized and objective, errors can occur in the scoring process. It is assumed that such errors are the result of random fluctuations in the scoring process and are not related to the extent of knowledge held by the student.

(d) There is a further source of error associated with the appropriateness of the rule involved in defining the scale which is used in the measurement process for the type of performance being assessed. If the errors associated with this source are systematic they can be detected and adjustments made. However, commonly such errors are not systematic and, like the other three types of error, can be considered to be random fluctuations which have arisen in the measurement process. The existence of such errors is common in all types of measurement.

2.2 Scaling Methods

The problems confronting research workers engaged in educational measurement are those of constructing a scale that has the properties of transitivity, metric, and if possible a functional zero, as well as the property of identity, so that the separate scores on individual items or tasks can be used to indicate extent of achievement on a defined scale. The functions of theory and practice in educational measurement are to upgrade the procedures involved in the measurement process, so that the measures obtained possess as fully as possible these four properties. The use of an appropriate scaling procedure is an important step in the measurement process, and much of the work of scaling involves transforming data that are essentially ordinal in nature to interval data with metric properties.

There are three broad classes of scaling models that can be employed with educational achievement tests. First, there are those scaling models that are concerned with attributes of the stimulus tasks to which the student is asked to respond. Second, there are those scaling models that are concerned with the attributes of the responder in relation to a defined population of responders. In these models there is dependence on differences between individuals in their attributes or characterisitics and in their observed behaviour in order to establish an appropriate scale. However, since it is rarely possible to administer a test to a complete population of students, it is necessary to employ an appropriate sample of students and, as a consequence, errors of sampling are introduced into the measurement process in order to establish the scale of measurement. Third, there are those scaling models in which both the stimulus tasks and the responders are assigned scale values. In these scaling models the purpose of the scale is to assign scale values to both the stimulus tasks and to the responders. This third model assumes specifically that there is an underlying latent trait of performance that is common to both individuals and tasks and that the items or tasks employed assess performance of the individuals with respect to that latent trait.

2.3 Approaches to Measurement

There are also two broad approaches to measurement in education and psychology that are employed to convert the scores on individual tasks to measures on a defined scale. In the first approach to measurement it is assumed that extent of knowledge or level of performance in the area under investigation is in some sense cumulative along a linear dimension. In addition, it is assumed that there is an identity relationship, with allowance made for the types of errors considered above, between the amount of knowledge that each individual possesses, or the level of performance of each individual, and the algebraic sum of the scores assigned for individual items. These assumptions have led to two separate theories of measurement — classical test theory (see *True-score Models*) and random sampling theory (see *Generalizability Theory*). The difference between these two theories lies in the emphasis placed in the latter on the random sampling of items or tasks from a specified population of tasks. These models are essentially deterministic models. Using these theories of measurement the scales developed are at best quasi-interval scales.

Nevertheless, there are significant problems with this class of theories, particularly within classical test theory. Suppose that an 80-item test has been developed comprising multiple-choice items, with four distractors, which are arranged in order of difficulty from the easiest to the hardest items. Suppose one student answers correctly the first 40 items and a random one-quarter of the remainder. With a simple scoring procedure, in which each item answered correctly is scored $+1$, each item answered incorrectly is scored 0, and the scores on individual items are added together, this student would obtain a total score of 50. Then suppose a second student answers correctly the 40 odd-numbered items, and a random one-quarter of the even-numbered items. Under the same scoring procedure this student would also obtain a total score of 50. These two students exhibit extreme and perhaps artificially different patterns of response. However, there are likely to be significant differences in the levels of achievement of the two students, because the latter student was able to answer correctly more hard items, even though missing many easy items, while the former student obtained the same score largely by getting more easy items right. In general, this approach to measurement takes no cognizance of attributes of the responders to the test items. It considers only the characteristics of the items. However, some work has been undertaken to investigate the problem typified by the patterns of responses of the two students (Harnisch and Linn 1981).

In order to overcome this problem between the two different types of attribute involved in the calculation of scores, namely, the characteristics of the responders and the charateristics of the stimulus tasks, it is necessary to assume the existence of an underlying latent trait that is common both to all responders as well as to all the stimulus tasks or test items which are used. Both stimulus tasks and individual responders are located at levels along a scale defined by the latent trait. The level of performance of an individual responder on this latent trait scale is that level at which the responder would answer correctly with a specified degree of probability a stimulus task located at that level. Commonly, a probability of 0.50 is employed. Thus it might be expected that an individual responder would answer correctly more than 50 percent of the tasks below this level and answer incorrectly more than 50 percent of the tasks above this level. In a similar manner the location of a stimulus task or test item on this scale is identified in terms of the probability that a specified proportion, commonly 50 percent of responders located at that level, would answer correctly the item associated with the task. Whereas the first approaches to measurement described above were deterministic in nature with a regard to the location of items or individuals on a scale, this second approach to measurement, namely latent trait theory, is essentially probabilistic in nature.

In latent trait measurement the stimulus task or achievement test item must be designed in such a way that responders depend on the latent attribute which the examiner is seeking to measure in order to answer it

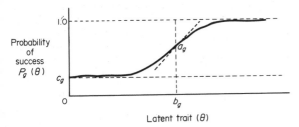

Figure 1
Item characteristic curve

correctly. Consequently, for an item to be acceptable, the probability of a responder answering correctly the item must increase regularly as the level of standing of the responder on the latent trait increases. In Fig. 1 the probability $P_g(\theta)$, of a responder with ability θ scoring 1 on an item g is plotted against θ. This relationship between probability of success and the latent trait is known as the item characteristic curve.

In general, an item characteristic curve can be described by three parameters:

(a) a_g, the steepness of the curve, or the discrimination index;

(b) b_g, the difficulty of the item;

(c) c_g, chance level of success on the item.

Two mathematical models are available for theoretical work on test items and the tests that are produced using the latent trait approach. The first uses the normal curve function of the form:

$$P_g(\theta) = \int (b_g - \theta)\,\theta(t)\,\mathrm{d}t$$

where the symbols in the formula are defined above.

The second model is the logistic function of the form:

$$P_g(\theta) = C_g + \frac{1 - C_g}{1 + e^{-Da_g(\theta - b_g)}}$$

where the symbols have been defined above, and D is a constant of scale, according to the units in which θ is recorded, so that the scale units for the logistic function are equivalent to those for the normal curve function.

These two functions, the logistic function and the normal curve function yield very similar results. The advantage of one over the other lies largely in the mathematics of subsequent analytical and computational work in which the functions are employed.

Independently of the development and use of these two functions in educational measurement Rasch proposed the use of the logistic function, in a form in which the parameter a_g for the slope of the item characteristic curve is considered uniform across all items, and the chance level of success c_g, is considered to be zero.

We may wish to calculate an expected score on a set of items which are located at different levels on the latent trait continuum and so to plot a test characteristic

curve between test scores and scores on the latent attribute. The expected number of correct responses for a given value of θ can be found by obtaining the probability of success on each item separately ($P_g\theta$) and then summing the P values over items to give the expected score. Using the logistic function form we obtain

$$\mathrm{E}(x\,|\,\theta) = \sum_{g=1}^{n} P_g(\theta) = \sum_{g=1}^{n} C_g + \frac{1 - C_g}{1 + e^{-Da_g(\theta - b_g)}}$$

A typical test characteristic curve for an 80-item multiple choice test with four alternatives is shown in Fig. 2.

The test characteristic curve shows the correspondence between expected scores of responders and the scale defined on the latent attribute. It is clear that equal increments in raw scores do not correspond with equal increments in θ across the range of the latent attribute scale. Thus the scaling procedure has provided an equal interval scale which has considerable advantages in analytical work. However, it should be noted that while the raw score scale appears to have a functional zero, the existence of this zero point is artificial insofar as guessing on items with four alternatives is likely to take place. Consequently the lowest score with a very high level of probability for a correct response commonly lies between 0 and 20. Moreover, it will be noted that the latent attribute scale clearly does not have a functional zero, and as a consequence this scale is not a ratio scale but an interval scale.

3. Scaling

Thorndike (1982) has identified four types of procedures that are used for converting achievement test scores to measures on specific scales. They can employ one or other of the three scaling models, namely, attributes of the stimulus task, attributes of the responder, or the latent trait model in which both stimulus tasks and responders are considered. The converted score values are assumed to have the properties of an interval scale, although the raw data are clearly not interval data. However, the extent to which an interval scale is

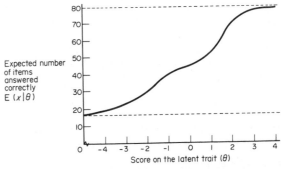

Figure 2
Test characteristic curve

achieved varies considerably. In addition, in the conversion of scores to a new scale consideration is customarily given to the meaning that can be attached to the scale values employed, and care is often taken to avoid conversion scales that have similar values to the percentile scales and the IQ scales.

3.1 Linear Score Conversions

Linear score conversions, in general, simply transform the raw score scale to a more convenient scale. It is assumed that the raw score distribution obtained by adding together scores on individual items indicates, in at least an adequate way, the distribution of the attribute assessed by the set of items. As a consequence no attempt is made to change the shape of the distribution of raw scores. The linear conversion formula is

$$Z(x) = X_s = S_s \frac{(X_r - \bar{X}_r)}{S_r} + \bar{X}_s$$

where X refers to score values, $\bar{X}$ refers to score mean values, S refers to standard deviations, r refers to the raw score values, and s refers to the standard score values.

Scores which have been converted in this way to a standard score scale are generally referred to as standard scores. Commonly occurring scales are 50 – 10 scores ($\bar{X} = 50$, $S = 10$); Z scores ($\bar{X} = 0$, $S = 1$); College Board scores ($\bar{X} = 500$, $S = 100$).

Figure 3 shows an example of a raw score frequency distribution expressed as Z scores in standard deviation units.

3.2 Area Conversions

Area conversions are, in general, employed when the shape of the raw score distribution is considered inappropriate. It must be assumed that the distribution of the attribute in the population under survey can be characterized by a known frequency distribution, or that the statistical and analytical procedures being employed in the examination of the data require a particular type of distribution. Under these circumstances it is appropriate to convert the raw scores to a scale with the defined distribution. In this scale conversion, equal areas associated with the cumulative frequency distributions of the raw scores and the scores which are associated with a defined scale are equated.

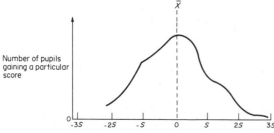

Figure 3
Example of raw score frequency distribution expressed in standard deviation units

In situations where it is desired to obtain a maximum spread of scores, the *rectangular distribution* is defined to be the underlying score distribution. Such a spread of scores arises in practice where all items are at the 50 percent difficulty level. However, where maximum spread is required and the items do not have a common difficulty level of 50 percent, the rectangular distribution is employed. This conversion is readily applied in the case of percentile ranks to yield centile scores, and decile ranks to yield decile scores.

In situations where multivariate analyses are carried out, the statistical tests are based on the multivariate *normal distribution*. There are also cases where the analytical procedures being used assume the multivariate normal distribution. For example, in linear structural relations analysis (LISREL), the shape of the distribution of the criterion measures must be known, and commonly a normal distribution is selected. While it is unlikely that proof can be obtained to support the assumption of a normal distribution, several sources of evidence recommend the choice of this distribution in practice. First where raw scores are added together and averaged, the central limit theorem indicates that averaged scores tend quite rapidly to a normal distribution. Second, where in nature an attribute is generated by many small, independent causes, a normal distribution of that attribute in a population might be expected. This assumption requires that a large probability sample has been drawn from the population, so that the score distribution in the sample will approximate to that occurring in the population. Third, where a test is comprised of a large number of independent items scored $+1$ and 0, the negative hypergeometric distribution provides the theoretical underlying score distribution, but with a large number of items this can be approximated to by the normal distribution.

Conversion of raw scores to a normal distribution is undertaken by means of the probit transformation (Fisher and Yates 1963). With this score conversion procedure the cumulative frequency distribution of the raw scores is calculated and scores associated with that distribution are converted to normal standard scores in order to correspond with equal areas under the normal curve whose equation is given by

$$P(X) = \int_{-\infty}^{\infty} \frac{1}{\sqrt{2\pi}} \exp\left(\frac{-x^2}{2}\right) dx$$

Commonly occurring scales are normal standard scores ($\bar{X} = 0$, $S = 1$), and IQ deviation scores ($\bar{X} = 100$, $S = 15$).

Figure 4 illustrates the conversion of a skewed raw score distribution to a normal standard score distribution. It should be noted that the phrases "normalized, standard" scores or "normal standardized" scores have not been used. "Standardized" score is a term that has generally been reserved for other somewhat arbitrary conversion systems, while the term "standard" score is

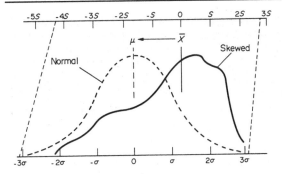

Figure 4
Skewed, transformed to normal distribution

reserved for *Z* scores, and closely related scales. Likewise, to a mathematician "normalizing" involves producing scores each equal to *Z* with the sum of squares (instead of the standard deviation) set at *N* or unity; a procedure that does not involve the normal distribution.

A commonly used scale is the stanine scale, which also involves an equal area conversion procedure. In Table 1, details of the stanine scale and its relation to the *Z* score range and the centile range, together with the proportion of the population in each stanine score category are recorded.

A similar scale is the sten scale that has a mean value of 5.5 and 10 score categories. Figure 5 shows the normal distribution score equivalents for the *Z* scale, the IQ deviation scale, centiles, stens, and stanines.

3.3 Age and Grade Conversions

Age and grade scaling involves the making of the assumption that a year of growth in the attribute being measured represents an equal unit whether there is concern for years of schooling as provided by the grade index or years of natural development as provided by the age index. The two aspects are necessarily related, but there seems little basis for the supposition that for individuals, development or schooling occur uniformly; although for populations, individual fluctuations will probably average out. Nevertheless, both age and grade norms are widely employed as indexes of growth and learning with respect to such attributes as intelligence,

verbal ability, reading, vocabulary, numerical ability, arithmetic achievement, and spatial ability (Lindquist 1951).

Since the construction of age and grade scales is dependent on attributes of the students who responded to the tests in the particular areas of educational achievement, it is essential that high quality representative samples from the specified age and grade populations should be drawn in order to establish standards of performance at the age and grade levels under investigation. While in general the evidence obtained by those engaged in norming studies to develop appropriate scales indicates that marked fluctuations do not occur, and that sampling irregularities can be smoothed by the careful drawing of norming curves, the errors associated with the construction of such scales have commonly been underestimated. Particular problems arise through sampling errors associated with nonresponse bias and the clustering of students in schools, to the extent that the effective numbers of students in samples are commonly many times smaller than the numbers of students who were tested. Further problems arise for both age and grade norming from the fact that reading and arithmetic performance is dependent on the time of the school year at which testing was undertaken. However, the procedures of interpolation assume that growth in the attribute being measured occurs uniformly across a school grade or a year of life.

Thorndike (1982 p. 109) has summarized the basic steps involved in constructing age and grade scales:

1. Obtain large and representative probability samples of students from the target populations, so that stable estimates with known errors of sampling can be calculated.

2. Administer the tests to the samples at appropriate age and grade levels.

3. Determine the average raw score for each age or grade grouping. Where possible with age samples subdivide each year sample into three month subgroups. These scores are then assigned to the specific age and grade values.

4. Interpolate between successive age and grade levels to determine an age and grade equivalent for each raw score on the tests.

Table 1
Details of stanine scale

Stanine	*Z* score range	Centile score range	Population percentage in stanine
9	+1.75 and over	96–99	4
8	+1.25 to +1.75	89–95	7
7	+0.75 to +1.25	77–88	12
6	+0.25 to +0.75	60–76	17
5	−0.25 to +0.25	41–59	20
4	−0.75 to −0.25	24–40	17
3	−1.25 to −0.75	12–23	12
2	−1.75 to −1.25	5–11	7
1	−1.75 and below	1–4	4

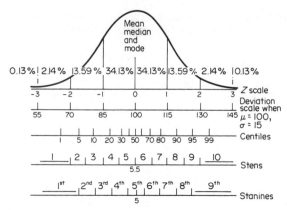

Figure 5
Some normal distribution scale equivalents

5. Extrapolate beyond the lowest and highest age and grade levels at which testing occurred in order to locate scale values at the tails of the raw score distribution.

6. Construct a table showing age and grade equivalents for each raw score value.

Interpolation and extrapolation can be carried out graphically where straight lines do not appear appropriate. However, where straight lines can be drawn, numerical estimates can be readily calculated. Sometimes theoretical score distributions such as the negative hypergeometric distribution or the normal distribution are employed, with these distributions being fitted to the data. With the increased availability of computers some attempts have been made to fit empirical curves to age and grade data in order to improve the accuracy with which the age and grade norms are estimated. For a more detailed account of norming procedures Angoff (1971) should be consulted.

Since the early 1970s there has been some criticism of the use of tests that have been normed by procedures of age and grade conversion, or standardized, as the scaling process is commonly called. However, normed tests continue to be extensively used in such countries as the United States and the United Kingdom.

3.4 Latent Trait Scaling

Latent trait scaling is a technique that is being used increasingly for the scaling of ability and achievement tests in both educational and psychological research and practice. Different methods of latent trait scaling have been developed using variations of the statistical model involving the logistic function given above. The simplest and most widely used model is the one parameter or Rasch model which employs the location parameter only. Use is also being made of a variation of the three-parameter model, which employs the difficulty parameter and the guessing parameter, but because of problems in obtaining convergence in the estimates of the three parameters, the third parameter — the discrimination parameter—is sometimes set at a fixed value for all items (see *Item Response Theory*). The two-parameter model

which involves the difficulty and the discrimination parameters does not appear to have been widely used in practical applications. In addition, variations of the general logistic function have been developed for use with attitude scales and rating scales and for use with polychotomous responses where partial credit is given for a less than complete answer. In the paragraphs that follow only the use of the Rasch model for scaling will be extensively discussed.

The use of a latent trait approach requires the assumption of a clearly defined underlying trait associated with a specific dimension of knowledge or skill, together with the assumption that individual respondents can be located at specific positions along the defined continuum. This approach does not demand a hypothetical universe of items from which random samples of items can be drawn, although it could work within such a situation. However, it does postulate that the response of a student to a given item is a function of the responder's position on the continuum associated with the latent trait, together with random error. For a set of items, the error terms associated with each item in the set must be uncorrelated with each other and with the latent trait. This assumption is referred to as one of local independence of the items and implies a unidimensional trait. If the items have been chosen in such a way that they are related to a highly specific educational achievement objective or with a specific ability, experience has established that the statistical procedures employed work well. Nonetheless, as Bejar has pointed out:

> ...unidimensionality does not imply that performance on the items is due to a single psychological process. In fact, a variety of psychological processes are involved in the act of responding to a set of items. However, as long as they function in unison — that is, the performance on each item is affected by the same processes and in the same form — unidimensionality will hold. As a violation of this principle, consider an achievement test, some of the items in which call for numerical computation, whereas the rest of the items call for the recall of factual material. If within the populations being tested with this instrument there is variability with respect to numerical ability, then the performance on the test as a whole will depend on that ability and achievement. (Bejar 1983 p. 31)

In the illustration of the Rasch model on the following pages a primary-school mathematics test associated in the main with numerical computation has been chosen as an appropriate application of the use of these procedures. All questions are constructed response items and not multiple-choice items, so that a guessing parameter is not required in the model. Furthermore, the items in the test do not have widely discrepant discrimination indexes, so that the discrimination parameter need not be included in the model.

The Rasch model uses the logistic function to relate the position of the items on the scale associated with the latent attribute to the probability of success on the item. According to this model, when the difficulty of an item and the ability level of the group of students just match,

50 percent of the students will get the item right and 50 percent will get it wrong, or the odds are even, or one to one.

The odds of getting an item right can be stated as:

$$\frac{P_i}{N - P_i}$$

where N is the total number of students in the group and P_i is the number of persons in the group getting the item right.

Using the logistic function, with the natural logarithm this ratio can be restated as follows:

$$b - d_i = \log\left(\frac{P_i}{N - P_i}\right)$$

where b is the ability or achievement level of the group, and d_i is difficulty parameter of item i when

$$b = d_i, \quad \log\left(\frac{P_i}{N - P_i}\right) = 0 \quad \text{and} \quad \frac{P_i}{N - P_i} = 1$$

so that the proportion of correct responses P_i is 0.50. In Table 2 the proportion of correct responses corresponding to integral scale values of $b - d_i$ are recorded.

The nature of the relationship specified for an item, with respect to the scale associated with the latent attribute, is assumed to remain unchanged with changes in mean level of performance and the spread in performance of the group of responders. Thus the analysis is considered to be largely sample-free. A systematic investigation of sampling errors associated with different sample sizes and different sample types by Farish (1984), has shown that small sampling errors can be expected. The effects of sampling will be greatest where the students responding have been subjected to different curricula, and where there is not a perfect fit of the data with the latent attribute. Thus the analyses will only be sample-free where perfect fit occurs, and the items are in agreement with the specified relationship (Douglas 1982).

Once a reference point for locating the scale of the latent attribute has been chosen, the zero point for the scale determined by analysis for a set of items and persons can be referred to this reference point. Likewise, an appropriate spread of scores can be chosen and can be related to the scale units found from the analysis of the data. Thus while the zero point and spread of scores remains arbitrary, it is possible to define an appropriate and meaningful scale. A variety of procedures are available for the analysis of the data in order to estimate the scale values and with large sample sizes, where there is concern for maximum precision, the use of a maximum likelihood procedure would seem to be the most satisfactory. Wright and Stone (1979) should be consulted for a more detailed account of appropriate procedures.

In Fig. 6, a kid-map for a student is presented in the form of a mathematics report to students, parents, and teachers. A scale has been defined with a mean score of 250 and a scale unit of 20 score points. It is evident from the figure that both the students and the items can be located on the same scale through the use of the Rasch scaling procedure. The student whose performance is recorded in Fig. 6 has a mean score of 280 on this scale with a relatively small error as indicated by the upper and lower boundaries of the box in the kid-map. An error in responding to the item ($5 \times 18 = ?$) is unexpected since the difficulty of the item is marginally below the expected level of performance on the scale. However, the remaining items that have not been mastered are above the expected performance level. The kid-map provides not only information on level of achievement and reports the type of test items that have and have not been mastered but it also provides information of a diagnostic nature for teachers. It is possible that the incorrect response to the item ($5 \times 18 = ?$) was the result of a careless error. However it is also possible that the skill of carrying in multiplication had not been mastered. It would seem appropriate for a teacher to select multiplication items at the level between 270 and 290. These items should then be used to diagnose further the problems experienced by the student in calculating answers to items which were appropriate to the expected level of performance and were equivalent in difficulty to the item that the student might have been expected to answer correctly but had not mastered. Maps of student performance, class group performance, and levels of difficulty of individual items provide information of both a mastery and diagnostic nature by combining student performance and item difficulty on a single scale.

A scale developed by latent trait scaling procedures can be likened to a ladder of achievement. The student is able to climb this achievement ladder, and at an appropriate rung a diagnostic test can be used to identify accurately particular weaknesses in the student's performance, as well as to identify curricular areas where the student is ready for further instruction. The principles of student assessment which have been discussed with respect to the performance of an individual student can be extended to yield evidence on the performance of class groups, and thus to provide information on which a teacher could base classroom instruction.

Table 2
Proportion of correct responses for integral scale values

$b - d_i$	percentage correct
+3.0	95
+2.0	88
+1.0	73
0	50
−1.0	27
−2.0	12
−3.0	5

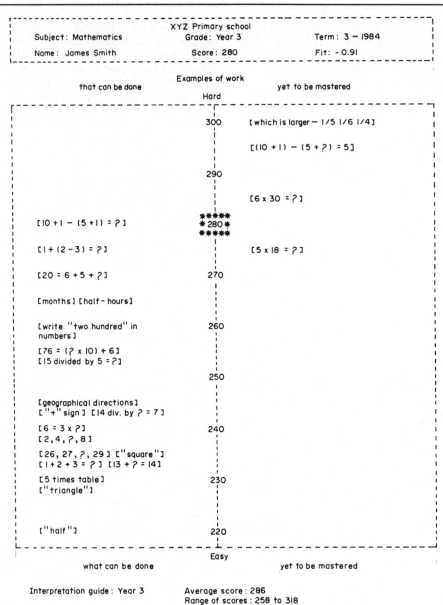

Figure 6
Kid-map

4. Equating Test Forms

Where test items are sampled at random from a universe of test items, or where test items are constructed to specification or to match existing items, it is possible to generate what are known as parallel forms of a test. Such parallel forms of a test do not, in general, have identical mean values or standard deviations. However, it is assumed that the parallel forms of a test are strongly correlated, and that the associated correlation coefficient does not differ significantly from 1.0. Under these circumstances it is possible to equate the parallel forms

of a test so that equivalence can be maintained. Further problems are encountered in measuring achievement outcomes in longitudinal studies in so far as it is clearly inappropriate to use the identical test instruments at different age levels, and it is commonly necessary to make changes to the test items between occasions. Nonetheless, it is possible to construct tests that have common items across adjacent age or grade levels, and that have common items at the same level between occasions. The equating of tests using common items between age or grade levels is referred to as vertical equating, while the equating of tests administered at the same level between occasions is referred to as horizontal equating. In theory the same procedure could be used for vertical equating as for horizontal equating. Nevertheless, it must be recognized that in practice, because of ceiling and floor effects in vertical equating, and because of substantial curriculum change effects in horizontal equating, significant problems may be encountered in maintaining a high level of equivalence between the tests employed in longitudinal studies.

Three general procedures are available for use to bring achievement test scores to a common scale. These procedures correspond in kind to those described above in the discussion of scaling, namely linear score conversion, equal area score conversion, and latent trait scaling. The further approach referred to above — of age and grade conversion — involved setting up a scale that had an external frame of reference, and the equating of parallel forms of tests would become redundant if each parallel form had been scaled by conversion to an age or grade scale. It is of course possible to equate parallel forms before carrying out the conversion of one of the forms to an age or grade scale. However, it should be noted that age and grade scales are rarely constructed with sufficient accuracy to permit their use in longitudinal research studies.

This article will only consider the general issues associated with the equating of tests. A general introduction is provided by Angoff (1971) and by Thorndike (1982). A comprehensive technical discussion of the problems of test equating is given in the volume edited by Holland and Rubin (1982).

4.1 Linear Equating

The procedure of linear equating is appropriately used whenever the shapes of the two raw score distributions being equated are the same, or when it can be assumed that both the test items and the persons tested represent appropriate samples for the measurement of an attribute that has a specified distribution with respect to both test items and persons. The scores are converted to standard scores, commonly to a mean of zero and a standard deviation of one, and the line of equivalence is used to equate one set of scores with the other (see Angoff 1971 p. 569). This procedure was used in the First IEA Science Study to bring scores on the science tests, which were administered across countries and across three age levels, to a common scale. The data available on common items were used to establish two lines of equivalence for the 10-year-old to the 14-year-old age levels, and for the 14-year-old to the terminal secondary-school levels respectively, by pooling data to obtain three grand mean values and the corresponding grand standard deviations. National mean values were set along these lines of equivalence through the use of all items in the tests at each age level (see Comber and Keeves 1973).

4.2 Equal Area or Equipercentile Equating

In this procedure it is similarly assumed that both the test items and the persons tested represent appropriate samples for the measurement of a specific attribute. In the use of this procedure cumulative frequency distributions are calculated, the scores are obtained at equal percentile points for each test, and a line of equivalence is plotted (see Angoff 1971 p. 571). This method of equating allows for differences in the shapes of the score distributions. As a consequence there is a more accurate location of equivalent scores in the tails of the tests, which is of some consequence if one or both of the score distributions are highly skewed. This procedure may prove to be more accurate and effective in vertical equating, but experience suggests that with large samples the procedure has few advantages in horizontal equating where the tests measure an attribute that is normally distributed in the population under survey. The equipercentile equating technique has been used in the equating of College Board Achievement Test scores over time in the United States. However, linear equating was used in the equating of Scholastic Aptitude Test Scores until 1981; since 1982, latent trait procedures have been used (Donlon 1984).

4.3 Latent Trait Equating

It is also possible to employ models based on the assumption of an unobservable, but underlying, latent trait which exhibits a relationship that can be represented by a logistic function. Morgan (1982) has illustrated the use of Rasch scaling procedures with the Australian Scholastic Aptitude Test. In addition, Cowell (1982) has employed the three parameter model with a language test (TOEFL). Goldstein (1980) has challenged the use of latent trait procedures in the development of a scale for horizontal equating which involves a common scale of measurement over time, particularly for educational achievement, because of the alleged problems of finding sensible interpretations of any results from such models for other than narrowly defined psychological attributes. Nevertheless, experience is being gained in the use of latent trait procedures for the equating of achievement tests in educational research, which seems to indicate that the procedures are both robust and meaningful.

Sontag (1984) has provided evidence to support the use of the one-parameter model for the logistic function in the vertical scaling of the data collected in the IEA Six Subject Study across the 10-year-old, the 14-year-old, and terminal secondary-school levels in the areas of science, reading comprehension, and word knowledge. The one-parameter model was found to yield more stable results than the two- and three-parameter models. Sontag concluded that:

These results may be due to several factors. The first is the overfitting of the model to the data. In a cross-comparison design, a complicated model can overfit to a specific sample. Thus the analysis may be unique to a given group and not reproducible because of the idiosyncrasies specific to that group. The second factor is that a model with few parameters will be most consistent due to small variance alone. Lastly, this particular data set might not fit the item response theory models. On several occasions the three parameter

413

model was unable to converge due to misfits of the items. (Sontag 1984)

Beaton (1987) has reported that the National Assessment of Educational Progress (NAEP) used latent trait scaling procedures for the vertical equating of tests across the 9-year-old, 13-year-old, and 17-year-old age levels in the development of a combined reading scale. Instead of identifying the reading scale employed in a particular NAEP testing program as the standard for past and future assessments, the research workers, who were engaged in the task of scaling the reading tests, advanced the idea of a hypothetical reading proficiency test with idealized properties. The key properties of this hypothetical test were:

(a) it contained 500 items, so that scores ranged from 0 to 500,

(b) all item characteristic curves were logistic in shape,

(c) correct answers to items could not be achieved by guessing,

(d) an average level of discrimination was assumed to apply to all items,

(e) item difficulties were evenly distributed along the θ scale of difficulty from -4.99 to 4.99,

(f) the function used to transform scores from the θ scale to the reading proficiency scale was linear and of the form $RP_s = 250.5 + 50\ (\theta)$, where RP_s was the score for subjects on the reading proficiency scale. This reading proficiency scale then had a mean over all age groups of 250.5 and a standard deviation of 50.

This scale is a latent trait scale and is not norm-referenced. In order to give meaning to this scale, it was decided to anchor scale points and identify items that discriminated between each pair of adjacent points. For the NAEP reading scale a decision was made to anchor the following points: 150, 200, 250, 300, and 350, since these points spanned the range in which most students scored. The results were presented on a Reading Report Card and the five levels of proficiency were described as rudimentary (150), basic (200), intermediate (250), adept (300), and advanced (350). Two sample items were provided to indicate the standards achieved with a probability of a correct response of 0.8 on the chosen items by the students located at those score levels with which the items were associated. Expressed in other words, 80 percent of the students performing at each of the specified score levels could be expected to answer correctly the items associated with each level. The findings of the four NAEP reading surveys conducted so far have shown that practically no 13-year-old students and a small proportion of the 17-year-old students could read at the advanced level. Less than 20 percent of the 13-year-olds and about 40 percent of the 17-year-olds could read at or above the adept level. Over 60 percent of the 13-year-olds and 80 percent of the 17-year-olds could read at the intermediate level, and practically all

students of both ages could read at the rudimentary and basic levels. While the anchoring process was not a necessary consequence of the use of latent trait theory, this theory was used to establish the scale, equate the tests at the 9-year-old, 13-year-old, and 17-year-old levels, and identify the scale points at which anchoring would occur (Beaton 1987). This work has made highly significant advances towards the development of a meaningful and valid scale of reading achievement that could endure over a substantial period of time.

4.4 Models of Data Collection

Angoff (1971) and Thorndike (1982) have identified three basic data collection models from which equating could be carried out that (a) would be free from bias, and (b) would, for a given cost of both effort and money, be as accurate as possible. These three methods are: (a) equivalent random samples of students, (b) double cross-tested samples of students, and (c) anchor or core test procedures.

(a) *Equivalent random samples.* In this procedure the total sample of students is divided into the required number of random balanced subsamples and a different form of a test is administered to each subsample of students. While this procedure has the advantage that the students are only required to take one form of the test, it is a necessary requirement that the different parallel forms of the test should be rotated in an appropriate way and randomly distributed within each primary sampling unit, for example, each classroom. Equating can be undertaken using either linear or equipercentile procedures. However, this strategy is a relatively inefficient one since the standard errors of equating under this model are large.

(b) *Double cross-tested samples.* In this model all students are required to take two forms of the tests which are being equated, but the total sample of students must be divided into two matched subsamples, and the order in which each subsample takes the forms should be crossed. This approach yields markedly increased precision in the standard errors of equating. In general, this model is four times as precise as the equivalent random sample model, but precision is obtained at a cost of twice the total time of testing. It should be noted, moreover, that 16 times as many students would need to be tested in the equivalent random sample model to achieve the same level of precision as would be obtained for the double cross-tested sample model. There is, however, the problem of reduced motivation during the second testing in this second model, and the need to make an appropriate adjustment for practice to the results of both groups.

(c) *Core test procedures.* In the third model, all students in the total sample take a common core test, or anchor test, as well as one or more of the parallel forms. The core test may be conceived of as a separate relatively short test or as a common set of test items. In either case the core test should be given at similar locations in the testing program so that any effects of practice or fatigue apply equally to the different test forms.

The capacity for the core test to provide a bridge with the different forms of the test depends on its correlation with each of the parallel forms being equated. In addition, the core test should have adequate reliability so that its correlations with the tests being equated are not markedly reduced. The advantage of this procedure is that it is not essential for the different forms of the test to be administered at the same time.

If linear equating of two or more different forms is being carried out, then a mean value on each test must be estimated for the total group, by using the data from the bridging test. This estimate is calculated as the sum of a subgroup's score on one form of the test together with the regression of the score of that test on the bridging test. In a similar way the standard deviations for the total group on that form can be estimated. Once these estimated values have been calculated for the different forms they can be used in the standard equation for linear scaling, since the mean and standard deviation for each form have been estimated for the total group of students. With only moderate correlations between the core test and the different forms there is a substantial loss in precision for this third model compared to the second model but a considerable advance on the precision provided by the equivalent random sample model.

Equipercentile scaling can also be carried out when a core test has been employed to bridge two or more different forms. Details of these procedures are given in Thorndike (1982). Rock et al. (1985) have used a modified three-parameter latent trait model to score and equate with core test procedures two tests in mathematics each comprising 25 items, of which 12 items were identical and 6 had minor editorial and format changes. The two forms of this mathematics test were administered to large samples in 1972 and 1980 respectively in a study of factors associated with decline in test scores of high school seniors between the two occasions.

5. Moderation

Moderation is a procedure that was first employed at Oxford University to compare and equate levels of performance in the examinations conducted within the colleges of the university. The statistical procedures that have been developed to serve the purposes of equating levels of achievement on different examination papers have also come to be known as "moderation". The main advantage of using these procedures in examining is that they provide greater scope for flexibility of syllabus and teaching methods, and greater opportunities for matching the examinations with individual and local needs. Thus teachers are less restricted by an examination conducted internally or within a school or group of schools and externally moderated than by any other methods of examining. The function of moderation in this situation is to establish and maintain comparable standards between different examinations in the same subject area that are conducted on different syllabuses or in different settings. A further use of moderation occurs when a total score must be calculated from examination marks in different subject areas. The procedures employed for the equating of marks in different subject areas is sometimes referred to as "standardization". However, this term should not be confused with the calculation of standard scores, a procedure that has been discussed above.

Howard (alias used by Sir Cyril Burt) (1958) identified the key requirements of moderation procedures. They are that candidates should not be disadvantaged by the marking patterns of examiners nor by the candidatures with whom they compete. In practice these requirements demand that the same mark on different examinations should imply the same level of performance relative to a common population. Moderation, in its different forms, of the scores awarded within schools either by examinations or by the systematic assessment of student class work, is required on four counts. First, there are differences between subjects in the quality of the candidatures they attract. Second, there are differences between schools in the characteristics of the students who attend them. Third, there are differences between markers, both between and within schools, in the mean level of scores awarded, the spread of scores, and the shapes of the distributions of scores that they give to students. Fourth, there are differences between the courses of instruction that the students have studied and as a consequence in the assessment procedures employed. Moderation procedures are needed to provide effectively for these differences in a way that satisfies equitably the key requirements advanced by Burt.

It is necessary to recognize that in situations where moderation is applied, for example, between two sets of scores, the correlations between those scores may differ significantly from 1.0. If the correlation did not differ from 1.0 then equating procedures could be employed. As a consequence distinctions can be drawn between the procedures of rescaling, equating, and moderation, although the three procedures have much in common. In rescaling, the mean values may be changed; the spread of scores changed; and the shape of the score distributions may or may not be changed; but the relative location of the component scores do not change with respect to one another. A conversion or transformation procedure is applied to achieve the rescaling of scores. In equating, two or more tests essentially similar in kind that correlate strongly are brought to a common scale. A special case of test equating is where the same essay examination is marked by two or more markers and the scores assigned by the different markers are brought to a common scale. This is sometimes erroneously referred to as moderation. However, in true moderation it is not assumed that the examinations or tests are identical in kind, since they do not correlate perfectly, and an external scale of reference is required to bring the scores to a common scale. Thus moderation has some features in common with the procedure of scaling. However, where scaling involves the conversion of only one set of scores, moderation commonly involves the bringing of two or more disparate sets of scores to a single scale which must be defined.

As with scaling, there are three broad classes of procedures that can be employed in the moderation of examinations. First, there are procedures for moderation that involve attributes of a common stimulus task to which the groups of students are required to respond. Second, there are those procedures used for moderation that are concerned with the attributes of the groups of students with respect to a larger population of students. Third, there are moderation procedures that are concerned with both common stimulus tasks and the attributes of students. This third set of moderation procedures involve essentially predictive methods, and a prediction equation is developed for separate groups of students whose performance is measured on a set of tasks to provide a criterion measure. The statistical procedures that are employed in moderation also draw upon the different theories of educational measurement, and the different types of scaling procedures, namely, linear, equal area, or latent trait procedures as discussed above.

The different procedures described below are employed in the different circumstances that arise in the conduct of examinations, particularly those associated with entry into higher education.

5.1 Use of a Moderator Test

In its simplest form this type of moderation procedure involves the moderation of scores on the ith achievement test Y_i using a moderator test X. Cooney (1975) has considered in some detail the issues associated with the procedures of moderation. If two assumptions are made, namely, (a) the joint distribution of the moderator test and the achievement test scores is bivariate normal, and the marginal distributions are normal, and (b) the moderator test has a significant correlation r with the achievement test, then the following linear equation can be employed in the process of moderation.

$$T_{ij} = Y_{i.} + \frac{rS_{y_i}}{S_x}(X_j - X_.) \qquad (1)$$

where T_{ij} is the moderated score for student j on achievement test i, $Y_{i.}$ is the mean score on the achievement test i, X_j is the score of student j on the moderator test, $X_.$ is the mean score on the moderator test, S_{y_i} is the standard deviation of the achievement measure Y_i, and S_x is the standard deviation on the moderator test X.

An extension of this procedure is employed in the United States for the scaling of College Board subject examination scores using the two moderator tests of verbal scholastic aptitude (SAT$_V$) and mathematical scholastic aptitude (SAT$_M$). In formulating the linear equation for moderation, the partial regression coefficients for predicting achievement using SAT$_V$ and holding SAT$_M$ constant, and using SAT$_M$, holding SAT$_V$ constant, are used. The major problem is that performances in different subject areas do not correlate equally with the Scholastic Aptitude Tests. The greater the correla-

tions between the achievement test scores and the moderator variables the greater the values of the adjustments made in moderation (Donlon 1984). Equipercentile scaling could also be used if the evidence suggested that the assumption of a bivariate normal distribution did not hold and either the achievement test scores or the moderator test score departed markedly from a normal distribution. These approaches to moderation have been rejected in Australia because the scores obtained in different subject examinations do not correlate equally with scores on the moderator variables available.

5.2 Use of Characteristics of Candidatures

Two approaches have been developed to use characteristics of the candidatures in the process of moderation of examinations at the terminal secondary-school level.

The first approach uses achievement characteristics. The most obvious achievement characteristic that is available for adjusting the level of performance of a student group to allow for differences in the quality of the candidatures is the performance of the students on the other subjects that they sat on the same occasion. This procedure involves the calculation of an aggregate score on a specific number of other subjects which were taken by the students. For each subject group these aggregate scores can be averaged for the group, and the mean score and standard deviation for the group on a particular examination can be rescaled using these values of the mean and standard deviations of the averaged aggregate scores for the group. This is a simple linear rescaling operation. This operation can be expressed symbolically as follows:

$$T_{ij} = \sum_{i=1}^{m} \sum_{j=1}^{n_i} \frac{X_{ij}}{mn_i} + \frac{(Y_{ij} - Y_{i.})}{S_{y_i}} S_x \qquad (2)$$

Where the symbols are similar to those in Eqn. (1), except that X_{ij} is the score for student j on achievement test i, and where there are n_i students in each subject group, and a maximum of m subjects are used in the aggregate. S_x is the standard deviation of the averaged aggregated achievement test scores.

The moderated score T_{ij} replaces X_{ij} for each subject in turn and the process can be repeated iteratively until the values of T_{ij} converge. With a large number of students taking each subject and with considerable overlap in the candidatures between subjects this iterative procedure gives stable estimates. However, because of the high intercorrelations between certain achievement test scores, those groups of students taking subjects that correlate highly, such as the mathematics and sciences subjects, have a greater spread of scores (S_x) than are estimated for those groups of students taking subjects that do not correlate highly with each other (Keeves and Parkyn 1979). As a consequence this procedure may be seen to be biased in favour of certain student groups.

An alternative procedure using aptitude characteristics employs the characteristics of a student group given by the average performance of the group on a scholastic aptitude test. In this procedure the quality of the candidature is assessed by the average level of scholastic aptitude of the group of students. This operation is expressed symbolically by:

$$T_{ijk} = X_{i..} + \frac{(Y_{ijk} - Y_{i..})}{S_{y_i}} S_{x_i} \qquad (3)$$

where the symbols employed correspond to those in Eqns. (1) and (2) above except for the addition of terms to include consideration of k schools (Keeves et al. 1977).

Superficially this procedure is similar to that associated with the use of a moderator test, and the similarity arises from the fact that for all examination subjects the correlation between the subject and the moderator variable is set at unity, to account for the differences in the magnitudes of the correlations which were seen to pose particular problems for that method. In a similar way this procedure overcomes some of the problems which arise from the differences in the intercorrelations between subjects when achievement characteristics of student groups are used. In practice this procedure described above establishes a scholastic aptitude test scale on which the qualities of the candidatures of the different school and subject groups are measured. The performances of the groups as groups are moderated using measured ability on this scale. The shortcomings of this approach are that it gives little recognition to the quality of instruction in a school and it depends heavily on the meaningfulness and consistency of the scholastic aptitude test that is used as the basis for the scaling of the student groups. Where student groups differ significantly in their performance on this reference test, for example where male and female students and ethnic groups differ in their performance on this test, problems become obvious, whereas similar problems while present in the other procedures described above, are not so obvious. Some research has been undertaken into these problems (Adams 1984, Masters and Beswick 1986).

5.3 Prediction Methods

Prediction methods of moderation that incorporate both the characteristics of the achievement-based examinations and those of student groups are available for use in moderation. Their use is implied when external moderators from a higher level of education undertake moderation programs to compare both scripts and the quality of the candidatures who come from different institutions and with different academic backgrounds. These judgmental approaches to moderation suffer from the high level of subjectivity of the decisions required (Goldstein 1986). In addition, difficulties are encountered in showing publicly that the methods employed are fair and just, as is necessary when large numbers of candidates from different social backgrounds are involved.

Research studies that examine the predictive powers of different selection procedures are not uncommon and

the investigations by Parkyn (1959), Choppin and Orr (1976), and Donlon (1984) are important studies. However, examples where these principles and the findings of predictive studies have been applied to the process of moderation have not been found. The development of a profile of information might be proposed for use in such situations. The components of the profile would be combined into a prediction equation using weights that sought to optimize student success at a later stage in education. The weights could be calculated as regression weights obtained from prior predictive studies. This approach would merely formalize and quantify what has previously been carried out by moderators using their judgments based on experience.

5.4 Item Banking

Choppin (1985) has discussed the concept of an item bank and the ideas presented below are drawn largely from that source. An item bank is a collection of test items organized, classified, and catalogued in order to facilitate the construction of a variety of achievement and other types of test. The item bank can be seen as a replacement for tests that have been converted to a specific scale, such as the age and grade scales described above. The key characteristic that changes a pool of test items from one in which random sampling can occur into a potential item bank is a comprehensive procedure for deriving the properties (reliability, precision, difficulty, etc.) of the tests constructed in this way using the statistical properties of the items with which the tests are built. Inasmuch as item banks are not mere collections of test items, but are organized and scaled in order to provide a basis for generalized measurement, they must rely on some underlying theory or model of the test-taking process. An approach to the construction of an item bank which is steadily increasing in influence stems from a proposal by Choppin (1968) to use latent trait theory, and specifically the Rasch model, for this purpose. A good example of the use of this approach is to be found in Cornish and Wines (1977).

The availability of large banks of items would permit their employment as a source of tests which were scaled in advance of use. An examiner in a school or school district in a particular curriculum area would be able to select either at random, or to a specified plan, a set of items that would form a test from the bank of items in that curriculum area. Since the characteristics of the items were already known, the characteristics of the test formed from the set of items would also be known with respect to an underlying scale. Consequently, the performance of individual students and school or classroom groups could be mapped within a specified curriculum area. However, the major advantage of the latent trait scaling of the items in a bank is the possibility of comparing scores on different tests administered at different points in time. Nevertheless, this leads to a new problem, namely, the changing validity of an item bank as changes in the school curriculum occur. It is too early to say whether regular updating and rescaling of the items in an item bank can successfully maintain its validity over substantial periods of time. Even if this problem cannot be completely solved, the item bank should provide a sound basis for quantitative description of curriculum change that is more powerful than has previously been available.

It will be seen from this brief discussion of item banks and their use that they involve the application of latent trait measurement procedures to develop a generalized scale associated with the field of knowledge represented by the items in the bank. Any test which employs a set of items drawn from the bank is automatically equated to other tests that can be drawn from the bank. The benefits of setting up such a bank of test items are that the bank can be used to moderate student performance between schools in the field of knowledge associated with the bank. The performance of students in a particular school can be compared with the performance of students in any other school, provided that it can be assumed that the differences in curricula between the two schools are not so great as to invalidate the scaling of items in the bank and their use. A more flexible approach to the use of item banks has been explored by Palmer (1980) who sought not to compare performance between schools directly, but to use the information obtained from the administration of tests based on items drawn from a bank to establish levels of performance and tolerance limits outside of which measured performance would not be expected to occur. This approach applied the ideas of quality control to school performance.

6. Conclusion

With a growing emphasis on standards of achievement in school at the same time as there is movement towards universal secondary education and the completion of 12 years of schooling by each age cohort, it seems likely that increased attention will be given to the moderation of examinations and achievement tests at the terminal secondary-school level. The advantage of the use of moderation procedures is that it will allow teachers to have greater flexibility in the design and development of appropriate curricula for particular groups of students. Moderation procedures will permit the standards of achievement of different groups to be compared. Moreover, it seems probable that latent trait procedures that have the capability to scale accurately sets of achievement test items, provided the items assess performance on a clearly specified trait, will be used increasingly in the future. Furthermore, there is a need for research and developmental work in the field of item banking, which involves the application of latent trait theory to a range of practical problems.

Bibliography

Adams R J 1984 *Sex Bias in ASAT?* Australian Council for Educational Research (ACER), Hawthorn, Victoria
Angoff W H 1971 Scales, norms and equivalent scores. In:
Thorndike R L (ed.) 1971 *Educational Measurement*, 2nd edn. American Council on Education, Washington, DC
Beaton A E 1987 Implementing the new design: The NAEP 1983–84 technical report. National Assessment of Educational Progress/Educational Testing Service, Princeton, New Jersey
Bejar I I 1983 *Achievement Testing: Recent Advances*, Sage University Paper Series on Quantitative Applications in the Social Sciences Series No. 07-036. Sage Publications, Beverly Hills, California
Choppin B H 1968 Item bank using sample-free calibration. *Nature* 219:870–72
Choppin B H 1985 Item bank. In: Husén T, Postlethwaite T N (eds.) 1985 *International Encyclopedia of Education*. Pergamon, Oxford, pp. 2742–45
Choppin B H, Orr L 1976 *Aptitude Testing at Eighteen Plus*. National Foundation for Educational Research (NFER), Slough
Comber L C, Keeves J P 1973 *Science Education in Nineteen Countries*. Almqvist and Wiksell, Stockholm
Cooney G H 1975 Standardization procedures involving moderator variables. *Aust. J. Educ.* 19(1): 50–63
Cornish H G, Wines R 1977 *ACER Mathematics Profile Series*. Australian Council for Educational Research (ACER), Hawthorn, Victoria
Cowell W R 1982 Item-response-theory pre-equating in the TOEFL testing program. In: Holland P W, Rubin D B (eds.) (1982)
Donlon T F (ed.) 1984 *The College Board Technical Handbook for the Scholastic Aptitude Test and Achievement Tests*. College Entrance Examination Board, New York
Douglas G A 1982 Conditional inference on a generic Rasch model. In: Spearritt D (ed.) 1982 *The Improvement of Measurement in Education and Psychology*. Australian Council for Educational Research (ACER), Hawthorn, Victoria
Farish S J 1984 *Investigating Item Stability*. Australian Council for Educational Research (ACER), Hawthorn, Victoria
Fisher R A, Yates A 1963 *Statistical Tables for Biological, Agricultural and Medical Research*, 6th edn. Oliver and Boyd, Edinburgh
Goldstein H 1980 Dimensionality bias independence and measurement scale problems in latent trait test score models. *Br. J. Math. Stat. Psychol.* 33: 234–46
Goldstein H 1986 Models for equating test scores and for studying the comparability of public examinations. In: Nuttall D L (ed.) 1986 *Assessing Educational Achievement*. Falmer Press, London
Harnisch D L, Linn R L 1981 Analysis of item response patterns: Questionable test data and dissimilar curriculum practices. *J. Educ. Meas.* 18(3): 133–46
Holland P W, Rubin D B (eds.) 1982 *Test Equating*. Academic Press, New York
Howard M 1958 The conversion of scores to a uniform scale. *Br. J. Stat. Psychol.* 11(2): 199–207
Keeves J P, Parkyn G W 1980 *The Higher School Certificate Examination in New South Wales*. New South Wales Board of Senior School Studies, Sydney
Keeves J P, McBryde B, Bennett L A 1977 The validity of alternative methods of scaling school assessments at the HSC level for the colleges and high schools of the Australian Capital Territory. In: Australian Association for Research in Education (AARE) 1977 *Curriculum Evaluation: Conference Papers*. AARE, Canberra
Lindquist E F (ed.) 1951 *Educational Measurement*. American Council on Education, Washington, DC
Masters G N, Beswick D G 1986 *The Construction of Tertiary*

Entrance Scores: Principles and Issues. Centre for the Study of Higher Education, University of Melbourne, Melbourne

Morgan G N 1982 The use of the latent trait measurement model in equating of scholastic aptitude tests. In: Spearritt D (ed.) 1982 *The Improvement of Measurement in Education and Psychology*. Australian Council for Educational Research (ACER), Hawthorn, Victoria

Palmer D G 1980 Item banking. *Educ. through Technol.* 1(3): 17–24

Parkyn G W 1959 *Success and Failure at the University*. New Zealand Council for Educational Research (NZCER), Wellington

Rock D A, Ekstrom R B, Goertz M E, Hilton T L, Pollack J 1985 *Factors Associated with Decline in Test Scores of High School Seniors, 1972 to 1980*. Center for Statistics, US Department of Education, Washington, DC

Snedecor G W, Cochran W G 1967 *Statistical Methods*, 6th edn. Iowa State University Press, Ames, Iowa

Sontag L M 1984 Vertical equating methods: A comparative study of their efficacy. Ph.D. thesis, Teachers College, Columbia University, New York

Thorndike R L 1982 *Applied Psychometrics*. Houghton Mifflin, Boston, Massachusetts

Togerson W S 1958 *Theory and Methods of Scaling*. Wiley, New York

Wright B D, Stone M H 1979 *Best Test Design*. Mesa Press, Chicago, Illinois

Attitude Measurement

Attitudes and their Measurement

L. W. Anderson

Allport referred to attitude as "the most distinctive and indispensable concept in contemporary American social psychology." Thurstone boldly asserted that "attitude can be measured." In view of these two quotes it is no surprise that attitude has become an important concept within the field of education. At the same time, however, attitude has been a misunderstood concept. In the introduction to their book Fishbein and Ajzen (1975) suggest that attitude is "characterized by an embarrassing degree of ambiguity and confusion." The purpose of this article is to clarify the meaning of attitude and to suggest ways in which attitude can be measured.

1. Definitions of Attitude

Attitude has been defined in many different ways over the years. Allport (1935) cites some 16 definitions of attitude that were formulated prior to the preparation of his manuscript. He attempted to glean from the various definitions the common elements or what he referred to as the essential features of attitude. He arrived at three such features: (a) preparation or readiness for favorable or unfavorable responses, (b) which is organized through experience, and (c) which is activated in the presence of all objects and situations with which the attitude is related.

Fishbein and Ajzen (1975) also identify three essential features of attitude. "Attitude is learned, . . . it predisposes action, and such actions are consistently favorable or unfavorable toward the object." The similarity of the essential features is striking. Over a period of some 40 years, then, a certain degree of agreement as to the nature of attitude has been achieved.

In an effort to understand attitude in relationship to other elements of the affective domain, Anderson (1981) began by delineating the essential features of affective characteristics in general. He identified five such characteristics: (a) emotion, (b) consistency, (c) target, (d) direction, and (e) intensity. Each of these features will be described briefly below and their relationship with attitude will be described where appropriate.

(a) *Emotion.* Affective characteristics involve primarily the feelings and emotions of persons. Affective characteristics typically are contrasted with cognitive characteristics (which primarily involve knowing and thinking)

and psychomotor characteristics (which primarily involve acting and behaving). Since an attitude is an affective characteristic it also involves a person's feelings and emotions. Quite likely, then, the preparedness or readiness mentioned by Allport is emotional (in contrast with intellectual or behavioral preparedness or readiness). In fact, Chave had defined attitude as a complex of feelings, desires, fears, convictions, prejudices, or other tendencies that have given a set or readiness to act to a person because of varied experiences. In Chave's definition feelings are directly mentioned; desires, fears, convictions, and prejudices are quite clearly emotions.

(b) *Consistency.* Consistency differentiates affective characteristics from affective reactions induced by particular situations or settings. A reasonable degree of consistency of responses is necessary before it can be inferred that a person possesses a particular affective characteristic. If a great deal of inconsistency of responses is noted, it may be suggested that the person does not possess the particular affective characteristic being sought. Rather the responses are determined more by factors external to the person than factors internal to the person (i.e., characteristics of the person). Both Allport, and Fishbein and Ajzen cite consistency as an essential feature of attitudes. While Fishbein and Ajzen explicitly mention consistency ("such actions are consistently favorable or unfavorable"), Allport implies consistency in his third essential feature. If preparedness or readiness is activated in the presence of all related objects and situations, consistency of activation is clearly implied.

(c) *Target.* As is indicated in Allport's third essential feature and in the above discussion, affective characteristics are related to particular objects, situations, ideas, and experiences. These objects, situations, ideas, and experiences can be subsumed under the general label "target." All emotions and feelings, including attitude, are directed toward (or away from) some target. While Allport identifies these targets as objects and situations, Fishbein and Ajzen limit the targets to objects.

(d) *Direction.* Given a target, affective characteristics prepare people to approach or avoid it. Hence, direction (or in Allport's terms "directedness") is an essential feature of affective characteristics. Direction is concerned with the positive or negative orientation of the emotions or feelings toward the target. Differences in orientation are typically expressed in terms of bipolar adjectives which indicate the opposite directions. Both Allport, and Fishbein and Ajzen suggest the appropriate bipolar adjectives for attitude are favorable and unfavorable.

(e) *Intensity*. Intensity refers to the degree or strength of the emotions or feelings. Intensity is an essential feature of affective characteristics; some people experience more intense emotions than other people. Similarly, some emotions are more intense than other emotions. "Hate," for example, is a more intense emotion than "dislike." Intensity per se is not addressed in the definitions of Allport, or Fishbein and Ajzen. It seems likely, however, that intensity is related to the level of preparedness (Allport) and the extent to which attitude predisposes action (Fishbein and Ajzen).

As has been mentioned, Anderson (1981) identified his five essential features so that attitude could be differentiated from other affective characteristics. Interestingly enough, the first two features (emotion and consistency) do not permit such differentiation. Rather, all affective characteristics possess these two features. Likewise, that attitude is learned (Fishbein and Ajzen) or organized through experience (Allport) does not allow the differentiation of attitude from other affective characteristics.

The differentiation of attitude from other affective characteristics is possible only if the last three essential characteristics identified by Anderson are considered: target, direction, and intensity. Anderson was able to differentiate some of the more common affective characteristics discussed in the field of education from attitude on the basis of these three essential features.

As has been indicated above, the most common target of attitude is an object; frequently a social object. In contrast, the most common target of interest is an activity. That is, people develop interest in doing things. The most common target of value is an idea or abstraction. Rokeach refers to a value as a standard. Unlike the targets of attitude which are fairly concrete, the targets of values are largely abstract. Consider the "study of values" for example. This instrument was designed to measure six value types: aesthetic, economic, political, religious, social, and theoretical. As can be seen, these types are clearly abstract in nature.

The measurement of preferences requires the specification of two or more targets since preferences involve a choice to be made between or among alternatives. On the *Kuder Preference Record, Vocational*, for example, students are presented with three alternative activities. The targets of the preferences measured by the KPR-V correspond with 10 vocational areas, including outdoor, mechanical, artistic, and literary.

Self-esteem is an affective characteristic gaining in popularity in the field of education. Quite clearly, the target of self-esteem is the persons themselves. Often more specific aspects of self-esteem are examined. One such component is termed academic self-esteem. Here the target is the persons as students in academic settings.

As can be seen, then, attitude differs from other affective characteristics in terms of target. While targets of other related affective characteristics include activities, abstractions, and perceptions of self, the targets of attitude are most likely fairly concrete, social objects.

Attitude also can be differentiated from other affective characteristics in terms of direction. As has been noted the directional indicators of attitude are favorable and unfavorable. Other affective characteristics are associated with other directional indicators. For interest these indicators are disinterested and interested. Several directional indicators are appropriate for defining value depending on the definition being used: undesirable and desirable, unimportant and important, and unacceptable and acceptable.

The directional indicators for preference are in fact the targets themselves. That is, the directions indicated by preferences are toward one target and, by definition, away from another target. For self-esteem the directional indicators for self-esteem are negative and positive, or worthless and worthy.

Finally, attitude can be differentiated from other affective characteristics in terms of intensity. From the definition of attitude it can be inferred that attitude is an emotion of moderate intensity. An attitude is more or less a reactive emotion. That is, when an object is encountered by an individual, attitude is activated. Several affective characteristics are more intense than attitude.

Interest is a more intense emotion. According to Getzels an interest "*impels* an individual to *seek out* particular objects, activities, understandings, skills, or goals for attention or acquisition" (emphasis added). In contrast with attitude, then, interest is a proactive emotion. Interest impels a person to action; either covert action (attention) or overt action (acquisition).

Similarly, value is a more intense emotion than attitude. Each of the definitions referred to earlier include words and phrases that indicate quite clearly the high intensity nature of value. Getzels suggests that a value influences the selection of behavior. Rokeach defines a value as a standard that guides and determines action, attitudes toward objects and situations, ideology, presentations of self to others, evaluations, judgments, justifications, comparisons of self with others, and attempts to influence others. That a value "guides and determines" suggests that it is a highly intense emotion. Tyler indicates that the educational significance of value stems from its role in "directing. . .interests, attitudes, and satisfactions." The inclusion of the verb "directing" again suggests a fairly high intensity level.

Self-esteem also tends to be a more intense emotion than attitude largely because the target of the emotion is the self. Virtually all emotions related to the self tend to be of high intensity. Finally, preference tends to be a fairly low intensity emotion. A preference demands a choice between or among targets. Since the choice is "forced" on the individual, a great deal of emotion may not accompany the choice. If, of course, the targets are all related to a great deal of interest or value, the intensity level may rise greatly. This increase in intensity, however, is associated more with interest and value than with preference per se.

In summary, then, attitude can be considered a moderately intense emotion that prepares or predisposes an individual to respond consistently in a favorable or unfavorable manner when confronted with a particular object. This definition contains all five of the essential features of affective characteristics identified by Anderson (1981). In addition, this definition is consistent with the composite definitions offered by Allport (1935) and Fishbein and Ajzen (1975). Furthermore, this definition permits the differentiation of attitude from other related affective characteristics such as interest, value, preference, and self-esteem. Such a differentiation is based primarily on (a) the nature of the targets toward which the emotion is directed, (b) the directionality of the emotion, and (c) the intensity of the emotion. As can be seen, then, attitude is a fairly specific affective characteristic. It has unique features and should not be equated with the general concept, affect. Unfortunately one of Thurstone's later definitions virtually equates attitude with affect. Failure to consider the unique features of attitude, and failure to differentiate attitude from other related, yet distinct affective characteristics have led in part to the embarrassing degree of ambiguity and confusion identified by Fishbein and Ajzen.

2. Measurement of Attitude

Attempts to measure attitude fall into one of three categories. All such attempts require the making of inferences about attitude from some observable indicator. The categories can be formed on the basis of the type of indicator on which the inference is made. The first category contains those methods that enable inferences to be made based on individuals' responses to a series of sentences or adjectives. Methods falling into this category are called scaling techniques and the instruments developed are called scales.

The second category contains those methods that permit inferences to be made from individuals' overt behaviors. These methods require the gathering of observational data and the establishment of sufficiently strong attitude–behavior relationships. The third category includes those methods that allow inferences to be made based on individuals' physiological responses. Each of these methods will be discussed in one of the following sections.

2.1 Inferences made from Responses to a Set of Statements or Adjectives

The most prevalent means of measuring attitudes is providing individuals with a list of sentences or adjectives and asking them to respond to each sentence or adjective in accordance with their true feelings. As has been mentioned previously these lists are called scales. The most frequently used scales are Thurstone scales, Likert scales, Guttman scales, and semantic differential scales.

Although other scaling techniques have been developed since 1952, these four types of scales continue to enjoy the greatest popularity .

Several key differences exist among the four aforementioned types of scales. Semantic differential scales can be differentiated from the other three types in terms of format. A semantic differential scale consists of a set of bipolar, evaluative adjectives (e.g., good–bad, nice–awful, relaxed–tense). Thurstone, Likert, and Guttman scales contain sentences, not adjectives.

Differences among Thurstone, Likert, and Guttman scales can be seen by viewing attitude as existing along an underlying continuum. Such a view is consistent with the definition of attitude presented in an earlier section. The target is indicated above the continuum. The midpoint of the continuum indicates change in direction. The distance from the midpoint in either direction indicates intensity.

The placement of the sentences along the continuum differentiates Likert scales from Thurstone and Guttman scales. Sentences included on Likert scales are written only at (or near) the two ends of the continuum. In fact, sentences that may be interpreted as representing points around the midpoint are excluded from Likert scales by judges. In contrast, sentences included on Thurstone and Guttman scales are written to represent points all along the continuum.

The extent to which the scale is cumulative distinguishes Guttman scales from Thurstone scales. Guttman scales are cumulative. That is, a positive response to a sentence positioned somewhere along the continuum implies a positive response to all statements to the left of that statement on the continuum. Thurstone scales are noncumulative. While sentences are written to reflect feelings at approximately equal intervals along the continuum, there is no assumption that the responses are cumulative. Rather the assumption is that positive responses should cluster around a particular point on the continuum. Sentences to the left of that cluster represent overly negative feelings given the attitude of the individual being measured. Similarly, sentences to the right represent overly positive feelings given the attitude.

In summary, three features distinguish the four most frequently used types of attitude scales. These features and the relevant differentiations are presented in Table 1.

Once the type of scale has been identified, it is then necessary to either select adjectives or write statements. Two sources are available for the selection of adjectives for inclusion on a semantic differential scale. The first source is Osgood, Suci, and Tannebaum (1957). This volume contains lists of bipolar adjectives that have been examined empirically as part of the field testing of the semantic differential technique. The second source is Allport and Odbert (1936). This manuscript contains a list of 17,953 adjectives that seem appropriate for use in designing attitude scales. Either these adjectives can be combined to form bipolar adjectives for use on semantic differential scales, or they can form the basis for generating appropriate sentences for use on Thurstone, Likert, or Guttman scales.

Edwards (1957 pp. 13–14) has identified 14 "informal criteria" for writing statements for inclusion on attitude scales. These 14 criteria are as follows:

(a) Avoid statements that refer to the past rather than the present.

(b) Avoid statements that are factual or capable of being interpreted as factual.

(c) Avoid statements that may be interpreted in more than one way.

(d) Avoid statements that are irrelevant to the psychological object under consideration.

(e) Avoid statements that are likely to be endorsed by almost everyone or almost no one.

(f) Select statements that are believed to cover the entire range of the affective scale of interest.

(g) Keep the language of the statements simple, clear, and direct.

(h) Statements should be short, rarely exceeding 20 words.

(i) Each statement should contain only one complete thought.

(j) Statements containing universals such as *all*, *always*, *none*, and *never* often introduce ambiguity and should be avoided.

(k) Words such as *only, just, merely*, and others of a similar nature should be used with care and moderation in writing statements.

(l) Whenever possible, statements should be in the form of simple sentences rather than in the form of compound or complex sentences.

(m) Avoid the use of words that may not be understood by those who are to be given the scale.

(n) Avoid the use of double negatives.

Fiske (1971) has proposed what may be termed a more formal approach to the generation of attitude statements appropriate for inclusion on affective scales. Kifer (1977) has operationalized the approach as a series of steps to be followed. The first step involves the identification of the specific affective characteristic and appropriate target (e.g., attitude toward school). The second step involves the delineation on the kinds of actions or opinions that would be exhibited or expressed by people possessing a positive attitude toward school. Such people may (a) discuss school matters with parents and friends, (b) participate in school-related activities and functions, (c) volunteer to talk to incoming students about the school, (d) enjoy the vast majority of their classes, (e) volunteer to participate in school-improvement projects, and (f) enjoy friendships with a large number of students in their class(es).

The third step requires the identification of facets and elements of attitude toward school. Kifer suggests two general facets. The first is the behavior to be exhibited or the opinion to be expressed if a positive attitude is to be inferred. The second facet is the settings or situations in which the behavior is likely to be exhibited or the opinion is meant to be elicited. The elements of each facet are identified by examining and categorizing the actions and opinions resulting from the second step of the approach. Continuing with the attitude toward school example, the following elements of the two facets may be identified. The elements of the situation facet may be, for example: (a) at home; (b) outside of school; (c) in school; (d) in the classroom; (e) after school. The elements of the behavior/opinion facet may be, for example: (a) enjoys friends, classes; (b) participates in activities; (c) volunteers services; (d) discusses school.

The fourth step involves the formation of sentences by selecting one element from the situation facet and one element from the behavior/opinion facet. These elements are then combined into a grammatically correct sentence. For example, "*After school*, I frequently *participate in* extracurricular *activities*." Or, "I *enjoy the friends* I've made *in school*." Quite clearly, Edwards' (1957) "informal criteria" could serve a useful editing function at this point in the process.

One final topic must be addressed prior to moving on to the next category of instruments. That topic is the technical adequacy (i.e., objectivity, reliability, and validity) of the data gathered by means of attitude scales.

The nature of Thurstone, Likert, Guttman, and semantic differential scales ensures a high degree of objectivity. All responses can be scored with the aid of a scoring key or template. Computer scoring of responses is also possible.

Table 1
Features differentiating Thurstone, Likert, Guttman, and semantic differential scales

Feature	Type of scale			
	Thurstone	Guttman	Likert	Semantic differential
Format	Sentence	Sentence	Sentence	Adjective
Position on continuum	Points along	Points along	Endpoints only	
Nature of continuum	Noncumulative	Cumulative		

Two types of reliability estimates are appropriate for attitude scales: internal consistency and stability. Internal consistency estimates for well-developed attitude scales containing as few as 10 items can approach 0.80 (Anderson 1981). For well-designed scales of 20 items the internal consistency estimates can approach 0.90. Thus attitude scales of sufficient internal consistency can be developed.

Estimates of the stability of attitudes have been computed less frequently than estimates of internal consistency. One possible reason is the issue of interpretation of such estimates. Quite clearly, the degree of stability of attitude scores should approximate the degree of stability of attitude as a construct. Put simply, before stability estimates are interpreted, it is necessary to know the degree of stability expected from the construct over the time period between administrations of the attitude scale.

The little available evidence that does exist suggests that reasonable stability can be expected over periods as long as four to five weeks. Stability coefficients over this time period can approach 0.90 with the majority falling between 0.85 and 0.90 (Anderson 1981).

Two of the scaling techniques have reliability estimates included in the technique itself. The Guttman technique requires the computation of two coefficients: the coefficient of reproducibility and the coefficient of scalability. Combined, these two coefficients estimate the degree to which a cumulative scale is present. As such, these coefficients provide information about the internal consistency of the responses.

In the Thurstone technique reliability can be computed separately for each person. In fact, traditional indicators of internal consistency (e.g., split-half, alpha) do not provide accurate internal consistency estimates. Each sentence on a Thurstone scale is associated with a scale value ranging from 1 to 11. The extent to which a person is responding consistently can be estimated by examining the range of scale values associated with the sentences endorsed by the person. The larger the range of scale values, the more inconsistent the responses.

The major problems of attitude scales lie in the area of validity. Several threats to validity are commonly cited. The most common threat is social desirability. Socially desirable responses are those that are inconsistent with the true feelings of the person; rather the responses are consistent with what the person believes to be expected or acceptable responses. A second common threat is acquiescence. Acquiescence refers to the tendency for persons to agree with sentences when they are unsure or ambivalent. Despite these problems validity of attitude scales can be enhanced by using appropriate hypotheses in order to empirically test the construct validity of the scales.

2.2 Inferences made from Overt Behaviors

Sechrest (1969) argues that inferences about attitude should be made based on people's behavior. Part of Sechrest's advocacy of this position stems from the concerns for validity of attitude scales mentioned in the previous section. In order to enhance the validity of the inferences made from behavior Sechrest suggests that the observations of the behavior be naturalistic. He defines naturalistic measures as those that "(a) do not require the cooperation of the subject, (b) do not permit the subject's awareness that he is being measured or treated in any special way, and (c) do not change the phenomenon being measured" (p. 152). Sechrest questions the almost total reliance on attitude scales for the measurement of attitudes and recommends that such observations of behavior be used to supplement these traditional measures.

To what extent can attitudes be inferred from overt behaviors? This is an interesting question in view of the extremely low correlation between attitude scale scores and behavioral indicators that have continuously been reported in the literature. Wicker (1969) summarizes his review of relevant studies as follows:

> Taken as a whole, these studies suggest that it is considerably more likely that attitudes will be unrelated or only slightly related to overt behaviors than that attitudes will be closely related to actions. Product–moment correlation coefficients relating the two kinds of responses are rarely above .30, and often are near zero. Only rarely can as much as 10% of the variance in overt behavioral measures be accounted for by attitudinal data. (p. 65)

Much of the lack of relationship can be attributed to the use of single behavioral indicators in the research. That is, typically the presence or absence of a single behavior is correlated with the scores on an attitude scale. Examples of such behaviors include whether a person signed a petition for fair employment and whether a person cheated on a self-graded examination. Given the unreliability of single-item measures, in general, the lack of relationship cited above should come as no surprise. Thus while the inclusion of behavioral data may have the potential of increasing the validity of the inferences made about attitude, more reliable measures of behavior must be made if this potential is to be realized. Reliability of such measures can be enhanced in several ways. It can be increased by identifying a variety of behaviors that can reasonably be associated with a given attitude. Reliability also can be enhanced by increasing the number of observations of such behaviors. Both of these ways of increasing reliability are similar to increasing internal consistency of tests by increasing the number of items.

As can be seen, increasing the reliability of the observation of behaviors is necessary before sound inferences about attitude can be made from overt behavior. Some such attempts have been made in a related area, namely, the measurement of self-esteem of students (Coopersmith 1967). Both of these attempts involve the preparation of a checklist of behaviors. The checklist includes a variety of behaviors believed to be related to the self-esteem of students. Once the checklist has been prepared it is to be completed by the student's teacher. The assumption is that teachers will base their responses to the checklist items on multiple observations of, and experiences with, the students. The reported reliabilities of these measures are quite reasonable (e.g., internal consistency estimates from 0.70 to 0.80).

2.3 Inferences made from Physiological Responses

Many of Sechrest's (1969) concerns could be alleviated if an appropriate physiological measure of attitude could be found. To date a number of such measures have been proposed; the galvanic skin response (GSR), pupillary dilation and constriction, respiration, and heart rate are among them. While such measures do detect arousal (i.e., intensity), the information they provide is not specific enough for the measure of attitude. Specifically, the direction and target of the arousal remains unknown and probably unknowable. As Fishbein and Ajzen (1975) conclude in their discussion of physiological measures, "it would definitely be desirable to have a non-verbal measure of attitude not under the subject's control, but it appears unlikely that any known physiological reaction will serve this purpose" (p. 94).

3. Interpretation of Attitude Measures

Even with sufficiently objective, reliable, and valid measures of attitude, problems of interpretation will likely remain. Norm-referenced interpretations, common to cognitive measures, are of limited utility when interpreting data obtained from attitude measures. That one fifth-grade student has a more positive attitude towards mathematics than 99 percent of all fifth-grade students provides very limited information. Anderson (1981) discusses two other approaches to interpretation that will likely result in improved interpretation.

The first approach is to identify groups of people who are known or suspected to possess varying degrees of attitude toward the target. Each group is described in terms of the relevant characteristics that define group membership (e.g., highly motivated, eager learners). The mean scores for each group are computed. As a check on the validity of the data the differences among the group means can be subjected to a statistical test such as the analysis of variance. If the mean scores of the groups do in fact differ in the expected direction, then a person's score can be interpreted by describing the characteristics of the group whose mean score is most similar to the person's score.

Anderson's (1981) second approach involves an understanding of the underlying attitude continuum. As has been mentioned the attitude continuum contains a point at which the direction changes from negative to positive. For interpretive purposes this point may be referred to as a neutral point. For Thurstone scales the neutral point corresponds with statements having a scale value of six. For Likert and semantic differential scales the neutral point can be computed by multiplying the value assigned to the middle response option for each statement or adjective by the total number of statements or adjectives. For Guttman scales the neutral

point must be estimated by considering the position of the statements on the attitude continuum.

Based on the estimate of the internal consistency of the measure, the standard error of measure for the score corresponding to the neutral point can be computed. Two standard errors of measure can be added to and subtracted from the neutral point score. Scores falling within the band of scores formed by the neutral point plus or minus two standard errors of measure are interpreted as indicating a neutral attitude toward the target. Scores to the right and left of this band are interpreted as indicating a positive or negative attitude respectively. Anderson suggests that the use of both approaches (combined with the norm-referenced approach as needed) will provide a more complete interpretation of the data.

4. The Future of Attitudes and their Measurement

If the future of attitudes is to be bright, several conditions must exist. First, the importance of attitudes in relation to school learning must be realized. In certain conditions, attitudes are important as entry characteristics, as outcomes, and as consequences (i.e., unplanned outcomes).

Second, the precision with which people talk and write about attitude must be increased. Vagueness in the meaning attached to attitude serves no useful purpose. Third, attitude measures of sufficient technical quality must be developed and used. Such measures are necessary if the nature of attitude in the field of education is to be better understood.

Bibliography

Allport G W 1935 Attitudes. In:Murchison C A (ed.) 1935 *Handbook of Social Psychology*. Russell and Russell, New York, pp. 798–844

Allport G W, Odbert H 1936 Trait names: A psycho-lexical study. *Psychol. Monogr.* 211

Anderson L W 1981 *Assessing Affective Characteristics in the Schools*. Allyn and Bacon, Boston, Massachusetts

Coopersmith S 1967 *The Antecedents of Self-esteem*. Freeman, San Francisco, California

Edwards A L 1957 *Techniques of Attitude Scale Construction*. Appleton-Century-Crofts, New York

Fishbein M, Ajzen I 1975 *Belief, Attitude, Intention, and Behavior: An Introduction to Theory and Research*. Addison-Wesley, Reading, Massachusetts

Fiske D W 1971 *Measuring the Concepts of Personality*. Aldine, Chicago, Illinois

Kifer E 1977 An approach to the construction of affective evaluation instruments. *J. Youth Adolescence* 6: 205–14

Osgood C E, Suci G, Tannebaum P 1957 *The Measurement of Meaning*. University of Illinois Press, Urbana, Illinois

Sechrest L 1969 Nonreactive assessment of attitudes. In: Willems E P, Raush H L (eds.) 1969 *Naturalistic Viewpoints in Psychological Research*. Holt, Rinehart and Winston, New York

Wicker A W 1969 Attitudes vs. actions: The relationship of verbal and overt behavioral responses to attitude objects. *J. Soc. Issues* 25: 41–78

Likert Scales

L. W. Anderson

Likert scales (Likert 1932) consist of a series of statements all of which are related to a person's attitude toward a single object (for instance, attitude toward teachers). Two types of statements appear on Likert scales. The first type includes statements whose endorsement indicates a positive or favorable attitude toward the object of interest (to be called "favorable statements"). The statement "I like the teachers in this school" is an example of a favorable statement. The second type includes statements whose endorsement indicates a negative or unfavorable attitude toward the object (to be called "unfavorable statments"). The statement "Most teachers make life in school miserable" is an example of an unfavorable statement. An approximately equal number of favorable and unfavorable statements typically are included on a Likert scale.

People to whom a Lickert scale is administered are directed to indicate the extent to which they endorse each statement. Typical response options are strongly agree, agree, not sure, disagree, and strongly disagree. A numerical value is assigned to each response option. For a favorable statement five points can be assigned to a "strongly agree" response, four points to an "agree" response, and so on. For an unfavorable statement the scoring is reversed (that is, five points are assigned to a "strongly disagree" response). After a numerical value has been assigned to each response made by a particular individual, the numerical values are summed to produce a total score. For this reason, Likert scales are sometimes referred to as summated scales.

According to Anderson (1981), satisfactory Likert scales can be developed if a series of eight steps are followed by the designer. These steps are described below:

(a) Statements must be written that are favorable or unfavorable with respect to the attitude object.

(b) Judges are called in to examine the statements that have been written. The judges should be selected from the population for whom the scale is designed. They are asked to examine each statement and classify it either as favorable, unfavorable, or neither.

(c) Any statement not classified as favorable or unfavorable by the vast majority of the judges is eliminated.

(d) The remaining statements are placed on a piece of paper in a random order. Appropriate directions and response options are added. The directions typically indicate that the respondents should indicate how they feel about each statement by marking SA if they strongly agree, A if they agree, NS if they are not sure of their feelings, D if they disagree, and SD if they strongly disagree. The directions also may indicate the purpose of the scale and suggest that there are no right or wrong answers. At this point an initial version of a Likert scale has been prepared.

(e) The initial version of the Likert scale is administered to a sample of the population for whom the scale is intended. In order to gather meaningful, reliable data on statements individually and collectively, a sample that is several times larger than the number of statements should be used.

(f) The correlation between the responses made to each statement and the total scale scores is computed.

(g) Each statement whose correlation with the total score is not statistically significant is eliminated. The fact that each statement must be correlated with the total scale score if it is to be included on the final form of the scale is referred to as Likert's Criterion of Internal Consistency.

(h) The final form of the scale is prepared.

Following these eight steps will produce a traditional Likert scale.

Over the years various modifications have been made by developers and users of Likert scales. These modifications fall into one of two categories: (a) modification of the response options, and (b) modification of the statement format.

Original Likert scales contained five response options ranging from strongly agree to strongly disagree as indicated earlier. Two-, three-, four-, six-, and seven-response options have been used on subsequent scales. The use of even number of response options reflects the concern on the part of scale designers that respondents might use the "not sure" response option to avoid making a real choice. With an even number of response options the respondents are "forced" to choose between favorable and unfavorable responses to the attitude object.

The use of a larger number of response options reflects the attempt to increase the internal consistency of the scale by increasing the number of total response opportunities given to the respondents. Increasing the number of response options on a Likert scale is similar in this regard to increasing the number of items on dichotomously scored cognitive tests. The use of a smaller number of response options, on the other hand, reflects the attempt to make the scale more appropriate for younger or less well-educated respondents. These types of respondents typically are able to make fewer reliable differentiations. Fewer response options require fewer differentiations.

In addition to modifications in the number of response options, alterations have been made in the statement format. Incomplete statements rather than complete statements have been used. When incomplete statements have been used, appropriate modifications in the response options also have been made. The following illustrates these modifications.

When school is cancelled because of bad weather, I am:

(a) very happy

(b) happy

(c) sad

(d) very sad

In this example, an unfavorable incomplete statement has been written. The response options suggest different degrees of attitude, as do the more traditional response options. At the same time, however, these response options are more appropriate given the nature of the incomplete statement.

The advantages of Likert scales include ease of construction (relative to Guttman and Thurstone scales); adaptability to a wide variety of attitude objects, situations, and settings; and ability to assess both directions and intensity of attitude. The major disadvantage is that different response patterns can produce the same total score. Likert scales therefore are not as sensitive to assessing attitude change as are Guttman and Thurstone scales.

In summary, then, Likert scales consist of statements possessing two characteristics. First, the statements represent either favorable or unfavorable attitudes as determined by judges. Second, the responses to each statement are significantly correlated with the sum total of responses to the entire set of statements. Statements not possessing these characteristics are eliminated from the final form of the scale. For this reason designers of Likert scales are encouraged to write more statements than will ultimately be needed.

See also: Guttman Scales; Thurstone Scales

Bibliography

Anderson L W 1981 *Assessing Affective Characteristics in the Schools.* Allyn and Bacon, Boston, Massachusetts
Edwards A L 1957 *Techniques of Attitude Scale Construction.* Appleton-Century-Crofts, New York
Likert R 1932 A technique for the measurement of attitudes. *Arch. Psychol.* No. 140 (whole issue)

Guttman Scales

L. W. Anderson

Guttman scales (Guttman 1944) contain a set of statements which all relate to a person's attitude toward a single object (e.g., attitude toward school). Guttman scales possess two characteristics. First, the statements included on such scales represent increasingly positive feelings with respect to the attitude object. This characteristic differentiates Guttman scales from Likert scales. Second, the endorsement of any statement implies the endorsement of each less positive statement. Scales possessing this second characteristic can be referred to as cumulative scales (Anderson 1981). This latter characteristic differentiates Guttman scales from Thurstone scales.

When a Guttman scale is administered the respondents are directed to indicate whether they agree with (endorse) or disagree with (do not endorse) each statement. Each respondent's score is simply the number of statements endorsed. Because of the cumulative nature of Guttman scales this total score provides information about the particular statements that were and were not endorsed. If, for example, a person received a score of five on an eight-statement Guttman scale, he or she would have most likely agreed with the five least positive statements on the scale. Furthermore, he or she would have most likely disagreed with the three most positive statements.

The reasonableness of inferring the pattern of responses from the total score depends on whether a scale is, in fact, a Guttman scale. Unlike Thurstone and Likert scales, judges are not used to examine the appropriateness of the statements to be included on Guttman scales. Rather, the determination that a scale is a Guttman scale is made solely on the basis of two empirical criteria: the coefficient of reproducibility and the coefficient of scalability. In order to compute these two coefficients the tentative Guttman scale must be administered to a fairly large sample of the population for whom the scale is intended. The responses are submitted to a Guttman scale analysis, typically performed by a standard computer program.

The Guttman scale analysis begins with an examination of the number of inappropriate response patterns. Based on the two characteristics of Guttman scales mentioned earlier, certain response patterns are appropriate while others are inappropriate. Consider, for example, a scale in which five statements are ordered from least positive to most positive. Suppose that responses of agree are designated by the number "1" and responses of disagree are designated by the number "0." A response pattern of 1 1 1 0 0 is appropriate since the three least positive statements were endorsed while the two most positive statements were not endorsed. On the other hand, a response pattern such as 1 1 0 1 0 is inappropriate since the fourth most positive statement was endorsed while the third most positive statement (that is, a less positive statement) was not. As a rule, any response pattern in which a "1" appears to the right of a "0" is an inappropriate response pattern. Furthermore, for each inappropriate response pattern an error is counted every time a "1" appears to the right of a "0." In the example above one error is present in the inappropriate response pattern.

The total number of errors is computed by summing across all of the response patterns of the sample of respondents. The total number of responses is found by multiplying the number of statements appearing on the scale by the number of respondents in the sample. The percent of errors is calculated by dividing the total number of errors by the total number of responses. Finally, this percent of errors is subtracted from 100 percent to yield what Guttman refers to as the coefficient of reproducibility (CR). Guttman suggests that this coefficient should be larger than 90 (that is, the percent of errors does not exceed 10 percent) if the scale is to be considered a Guttman scale.

That the coefficient of reproducibility is greater than 90 is a necessary but not sufficient condition for a Guttman scale. A second empirical criterion must be met if a scale is a Guttman scale. This second criterion is based on Guttman's coefficient of scalability (CS). According to Anderson (1981), "Guttman believed that it was impossible to interpret the magnitude of the coefficient of reproducibility without some knowledge of the minimum value that this coefficient can assume. He also was aware that the minimum value of the coefficient of reproducibility (which he called the minimum marginal reproducibility, or MMR) would be computed for the scale" (p. 256). In common terms, the minimum marginal reproducibility index represents a chance score. That is, the minimum marginal reproducibility index is the percent of appropriate response patterns that would occur "by chance" given the number of respondents receiving the various total scores and the number of respondents endorsing each statement.

Several computations are needed to produce the coefficient of scalability from the index of minimum marginal reproducibility. The first involves the subtraction of the minimum marginal reproducibility from the coefficient of reproducibility. This computation yields what Guttman referred to as the percent improvement (PI), the difference between the actual and minimal coefficient of reproducibility. The second computation involves the subtraction of the minimum marginal reproducibility from 100 percent. This computation yields the possible percent improvement (PPI), the difference between the maximal and minimal coefficient of reproducibility. The third computation requires dividing percent improvement by possible percent improvement and results in the coefficient of scalability. This coefficient, then, represents the extent to which the coefficient of reproducibility is substantially beyond that which could be expected by chance. Guttman suggested that the coefficient of scalability should exceed 60.

These dual criteria of 90 and 60 are used to determine a Guttman scale. If both criteria are met, then a Guttman scale has been developed. If not, then a Guttman scale is not present. As can be seen, then, a scale either is or is not a Guttman scale; there is no room for close approximations. Proctor (1970) expressed some concern about this dichotomous nature of Guttman scales. As a consequence, he developed a probabilistic formulation of the Guttman scale model. Interested readers are referred to the Proctor formulation for additional information. Sato (1975) has also extended the model in order to analyze and evaluate achievement tests.

Guttman scales are difficult to construct. Statements may appear to be cumulative in nature, but the results of the Guttman scale analysis may fail to support this appearance. If either the coefficient of reproducibility or the coefficient of scalability is too low, the assumptions underlying Guttman scales are not met. If this is the case several alternatives are possible. First, modifications in statements can be made based on the evidence obtained from the initial administration of the scale. These modifications may result in legitimate Guttman scales. Second, the Proctor reformulation can be used to transform Guttman's original deterministic model into a probabilistic model. Such a transformation may be especially beneficial for scales closely approximating Guttman scales.

Despite the difficulty in developing Guttman scales, such scales do have several advantages over Thurstone and Likert scales. First, as has been mentioned, it is possible to determine the entire pattern of responses to the statements from a single total score. Thus, more specific information about the nature of the respondent's attitude is possible. Second, the cumulative nature of Guttman scales makes it feasible to assess change in attitude. An increase of one point on the total score means that the respondent has moved up the attitude continuum by one statement. Change then becomes additive.

In summary, then, Guttman scales are difficult to construct but extremely useful as measures of attitude. In general, the benefits of achieving a Guttman scale far outweigh the difficulties in achieving one.

Bibliography

Anderson L W 1981 *Assessing Affective Characteristics in the Schools.* Allyn and Bacon, Boston, Massachusetts

Guttman L 1944 A basis for scaling qualitative data. *Am. Sociol. Rev.* 9: 139–50

Proctor C H 1970 A probabilistic formulation and statistical analysis of Guttman scaling. *Psychometrika* 35: 73–78

Sato T 1975 *The Construction and Interpretation of S–P Tables.* Meiji Tosho, Tokyo (in Japanese)

Semantic Differential

J. L. Phillips

The semantic differential is a method for measuring aspects of the meaning of various concepts. In addition, it is widely used as an attitude measurement technique. It was developed to tap connotative meaning by Charles Osgood and his associates at the University of Illinois during the 1950s. Used in its original form and in various transformations, it is attractive for its simplicity and its versatility, but is not without controversy.

1. Description

The semantic differential consists of a set of seven-point bipolar scales and a set of concepts. Each concept (a word, short phrase, picture, etc.) is rated on each scale (for instance, good–bad, loud–quiet, old–young). A typical format presents a concept at the top of a printed page with the set of scales below, but there are variations. Single concept–scale pairs are often isolated. Subjects are instructed to mark towards the extremes of each scale if a concept is closely related to one of the bipolar adjectives and toward the middle if a concept is only slightly related. The midpoint of the scale means that the concept is neutral on the scale, ambivalent on the scale, or the scale is irrelevant to the concept.

2. Results and Applications

The simplicity of the format provides an unusual economy in data collection. For example, a semantic differential instrument consisting of 30 concepts and 12 scales administered to 50 subjects generates, in an hour, $30 \times 12 \times 50 = 18,000$ data points. While such economy has value, it creates a need for data reduction. An advantage of the semantic differential is that data reduction techniques are available. It has been shown that when concepts are sampled representatively, data subjected to factor analysis will allow a partition of scales into three categories or factors. These factors are evaluation (E), potency (P), and activity (A). These factors accounted for over 47 percent of the variance in the original (Thesaurus) study and 58 percent or more in a recent study (Mann et al. 1979). This EPA structure is robust and replicable. Reduction of semantic differential data into evaluative, potency, and activity scores is empirically warranted.

Evidence for robustness has been summarized by Osgood et al. (1975). These writers have claimed that EPA is independent of specific scales, age, sex, political orientation, and pathology of subject, as well as specific concepts. They have reported evidence for this trifactorial pattern across 21 different language communities. Invariance has been shown by Mann et al. (1979) over procedural and analytic variations. A study by Chapman et al. (1980) identified EPA using evoked brain potentials.

The semantic differential has been adapted for many uses. Recently, articles using the semantic differential to measure attitudes have been approximately four times as frequent as those directed to semantic concerns. It has been applied to such domains as sports, health, familial issues, industrial/organizational considerations, and to ecological concepts. The semantic differential has been geographically widespread. From 1977 through 1981, articles about the semantic differential have appeared in at least eight countries. By a conservative estimate, approximately 15 articles about the semantic differential appear each year.

In most applications, the concepts were determined by the objectives of the study. They were not selected through any sampling process or else were sampled from the limited domain of interest. This presents no problem for the semantic differential methodology. Assuming an appropriate selection of scales, these concepts can be scaled on each of the three factors. Investigators often report using "semantic differential-type" scales, by which they mean bipolar scales chosen to be appropriate to the concepts to be rated. The investigator should be aware that using such ad hoc scales may preclude the scaling of concepts using EPA. If such scale values are desired, then semantic differential scales with known relationships to EPA should be used. Frequently, however, the study may have objectives for which the EPA-structure is neither of practical nor theoretical significance. Adaptations (for instance, Alexander and Husek 1962, Guttentag and Bray 1976) have proven useful despite this lack of correspondence.

3. Criticisms of the Semantic Differential

In most applications the procedures associated with the semantic differential can be used as if they were theoretically neutral. Indeed, measures of evaluation, potency, and activity can be treated as stable descriptions of the concepts. While criticisms of the semantic differential have detracted from this utility (for instance, does the semantic differential have equal scale intervals?) there is no convincing evidence that such defects have any practical significance, nor is there evidence that alternatives to the semantic differential do not have similar problems.

Nevertheless, the semantic differential has received criticism. Of the articles about this technique, nearly one-third have addressed methodological or theoretical criticisms. Criticisms may be classified into three major categories. One group has directed itself to a set of scaling assumptions fundamental to the semantic differential methodology. Criticisms concerning the bipolarity of semantic differential scales and the integrity of the midpoint fall into this category. A second group deals with the interpretation of semantic differential data in terms of EPA. These criticisms include concept–scale interaction, and concept domain differences. A third group relates to the choice of the analytic model used to transform semantic differential data into the EPA structure. While this third group is important, its discussion is beyond the present scope. Readers should refer to such sources as Maguire (1973) or Murakami (1977).

3.1 Criticisms of Scaling Assumptions

Previously it was noted that the midpoint had the meanings of neutrality, ambivalence, and irrelevance. The semantic differential has been criticized for this confound (Forthman 1973). Mann et al. (1979) found that variations in the meaning of the midpoint have only a minimal effect on the data, but did recommend separating out the irrelevance meaning.

Efforts to deal with the midpoint issue have focused on scale irrelevance as the point of contention. The fact, however, that the midpoint can stand for ambivalence points up a conceptual difficulty. If a concept is simultaneously "good" and "bad" for example, and if this holds for many concepts, then "good" and "bad" would not represent the polar opposition required. This view of concepts as imbued with both properties suggests something other than the perfect negative correlation assumed by semantic differential scales.

Concepts can be constructed for which a scale would lack bipolarity in some phenomenological sense. The bipolar scale "hot–cold" seems other than bipolar when applied to concepts like "frozen enchilada" or "laid-back nymphomaniac." Green and Goldfreid (1965) showed that unipolar variations of semantic differential scales did not manifest perfect negative correlations over a range of ordinary concepts. The correlation between the polar anchors varied across concepts. Such lack of bipolarity is damaging to the semantic differential and challenges the well-established EPA structure. It would not be expected, however, that unipolar scales exhibit perfect negative correlations. Given that neither of the unipolar scales have perfect reliability, their actual correlation would be constrained by their reliabilities. Mann et al. (1979) corrected unipolar scale correlations for unreliability and found that the median correlation, over 15 scales, was approximately -0.97. While this correlation is not perfect, it suggests that concerns about bipolarity have been exaggerated.

3.2 Criticisms of the EPA Structure

Despite the ubiquity of the EPA structure, not all data will generate EPA. Data that fail to reflect EPA can be obtained easily. If a list of things valued by some group are used as concepts to be rated by that group, the EPA structure will not emerge because there will be no evaluative factor. This is so because all concepts will be rated positively on all evaluative scales. A set of data based upon arbitrarily chosen concepts may thus not yield the EPA structure and this failure does not discredit the generality of EPA.

Despite this, many studies have "failed to find" EPA and have claimed that some alternative to EPA is the appropriate structure for their domain of interest. Because EPA has been proposed, not for a specific domain of concepts, but for the universe of concepts, it is not clear how this issue of universality versus domain specificity is to be resolved. While it may be the case that certain domains may have unique scale organizations, the demonstration of a divergent factor structure does not tarnish the universalistic claim of EPA. The issue is more complicated. From the standpoint of the semantic differential, the universal domain is nothing less than those concepts uniformly distributed through a "semantic space" defined by the dimensions of E, P, and A. A sample of concepts that reflect this uniformity is likely to display the EPA structure. A sample that does not may show a different organization, but such a sample would be rejected as nonrepresentative by the prior logic. If this issue is resolvable at all, then the focus of resolution would be on the methods of random sampling from some hypothetical "universal domain of concepts."

Of promise in this regard is empirical work dealing with an issue raised originally by Osgood et al. This is the issue of concept–scale interaction. Concept–scale interaction occurs whenever "the meanings of scales and their relation to other scales vary considerably with the concept being judged." For example, the scales good–bad, beautiful–ugly, valuable–worthless, and wise–foolish are evaluative in nature, and positively evaluated concepts are highly rated on all. Such a positively evaluated concept is "puppies." Indeed, "puppies" is seen as good, beautiful, and valuable, but also as foolish. In the context of "puppies," "foolish" most likely functions as a positive attribute, roughly synonymous with "cute."

Osgood et al. noted a high degree of such concept–scale interaction but also observed that this interaction does not obscure the EPA structure. Mann et al. (1979) showed that concept–scale interaction accounted for 10–15 percent of the variance, under typical conditions of administration, and that it did not alter the factor structure.

What has not been widely appreciated is that concept–scale interaction may be evidence for concept domain differences. If semantic differential scales have a different meaning for one set of concepts than for another, a research strategy would be to treat them as separate groups. The argument for EPA would be the demonstration of this structure for each group of concepts, rather than the demonstration of EPA for the total sample.

See also: Attitudes and their Measurement

Bibliography

Alexander S, Husek T R 1962 The anxiety differential: Initial steps in the development of a measure of situational anxiety. *Educ. Psychol. Meas.* 22: 325–48

Chapman R M, McCrary J W, Chapman J A, Martin J K 1980 Behavioral and neutral analyses of connotative meaning: Word classes and rating scales. *Brain and Lang.* 11: 319–39

Forthman J H 1973 The effects of a zero interval on semantic differential rotated factor loadings. *J. Psychol.* 84: 23–32

Green R F, Goldfried M R 1965 On the bipolarity of semantic space. *Psychol. Monogr.* 79 (6)

Guttentag M, Bray H 1976 *Undoing Sex Stereotypes: Research and Resources for Educators.* McGraw-Hill, New York

Maguire T O 1973 Semantic differential methodology for the structuring of attitudes. *Am. Educ. Res. J.* 10: 295–306

Mann I T, Phillips J L, Thompson E G 1979 An examination of methodological issues relevant to the use and interpretation of the semantic differential. *Appl. Psychol. Meas.* 3: 213–29

Murakami Y 1977 On stratum factor structure: Containing the critics and theorizing of semantic differential method. *Psychologia* 20: 98–106

Osgood C E, May W H, Miron M S 1975 *Cross Cultural Universals of Affective Meaning.* University of Illinois Press, Urbana, Illinois

Osgood C E, Suci G J, Tannenbaum P H 1971 *The Measurement of Meaning.* University of Illinois Press, Chicago, Illinois

Projective Testing Techniques

J. J. Walsh

Projective techniques, while not generally considered as psychometric instruments, are widely used principally in clinical settings for descriptive and diagnostic purposes in the study of personality and adjustment. They make use of a wide variety of symbolic, pictorial, verbal, and expressive stimuli to elicit responses which are scored and interpreted by specially trained examiners. These responses are considered to be indicators of covert, latent, or unconscious aspects of personality which are not revealed by answers to self-report inventories.

The concept of projection which is inherent in these techniques refers to the process of unwittingly attributing one's own drives, needs, perceptions, attitudes, and style to others, or of giving meaning to relatively ambiguous or unstructured stimuli by drawing upon one's private desires, traits, fears, and experience. Most projective techniques are disguised tests in which the examinee is seldom aware of the psychological interpretation which will be attached to the responses.

Since the subject does not perceive the responses as revelatory of self they can be relatively free of distortion or personal censorship, and can provide data about personality dynamics of which the respondent may be unaware. Central in the theory underlying these techniques is the belief that when someone is required to interpret an unstructured or ambiguous stimulus the person draws upon those impulses, needs, conflicts, and other psychological characteristics which are dominant in that personality, and that the quality of those variables can be determined from the responses by a competent projective tester. Most of these techniques utilize psychoanalytic and organismic concepts in developing a description of the whole personality and of the interrelationships among its various aspects.

Several bases for classifying the wide array of techniques which are subsumed under the rubric of "projectives" have been proposed. One scheme (Frank 1948) differentiated the techniques on the basis of "what they require or seek to evoke from the subject." The five categories identified are: (a) constitutive, which require the imposition of a structure on some relatively unstructured material such as ink blots, modeling clay, or finger painting supplies; (b) constructive, which require the arrangement of materials such as blocks or tiles into some pattern, or which require the drawing of some specified form; (c) interpretive, which require the subject to find personal meaning in stimuli such as pictures or words; (d) cathartic which require an acting out of expressive and emotional reactions in fantasy situations such as playing with dolls; and (e) refractive, which evoke idiosyncratic variation in tasks such as handwriting. Another fivefold categorization (Lindzey 1961) utilizes the following classifications with some typical examples included: (a) association techniques—Rorschach or word association; (b) construction techniques—Thematic Apperception Test; (c) completion techniques—sentence completion, Rosenzweig Picture Frustration; (d) choice or ordering techniques—Szondi, Picture Arrangement Test; and (e) expressive techniques—psychodrama, painting.

The most widely used and best-known projective technique was developed by a Swiss psychiatrist, Hermann Rorschach, who published an account of his method in 1921. In this technique the subject is asked to tell what is seen in each of 10 inkblots printed on $5\frac{1}{2} \times 9\frac{1}{2}$-inch white cards and presented in a prescribed sequence. The blots, which vary in shape and color (black, gray, red, and pastels), elicit a vast range of responses. There are no time limits, and no definite number of responses to each card is required. In current clinical practice the Rorschach is used with subjects from nursery-school age to adults. Verbatim records of responses, as well as notations for reaction time, total time per card, positions in which cards are held, emotional reactions and behavior, are made by the examiner. Following the presentation of the 10 cards the examiner conducts an inquiry in order to ascertain what elements or aspects of the blots were utilized by the subject in making responses, and to allow for clarification of or additions to the original responses.

As the purpose of Rorschach testing shifted from diagnostic classification of subjects to an understanding of their psychodynamics, many modifications in the scoring system were introduced. Two of these (Klopfer and Kelly 1942) and (Beck 1949) are the most frequently used.

The first step in the interpretation of Rorschach responses is the calculation of the subject's scores in three categories which are referred to as location, determinants, and content. Location scores are based on the area of the blot (whole or part) which was used in formulating the response. In this category responses are classified as whole, cut-off whole, or confabulatory whole, and responses to parts of the blots are sorted into categories such as large usual, small usual, and unusual detail, or space, when a response is based on the white area of a card. Scores for the determinants category reflect the extent to which responses are based on the form, color, or perceived movement in the blots. Color responses are subdivided to allow for differentiation of responses based on shading, texture, achromatic color, and chiaroscuro responses. The content category aspects which are generally scored include human, animal, object, and abstract responses. Content responses are also frequently classified as popular or original responses, based on the relative frequency of the response in various tabulations. Additional analysis involves a comparative study of the number of responses in the various scoring categories, of the ratios of combinations of categories, and of rather complex interrelationships among categories.

While the scoring procedure is relatively systematic and objective, the interpretation of the scores and the development of the global description of the subject is necessarily qualitative and clinical. Typically, for example, emphasis on wholes is interpreted as being a characteristic of subjects with a high level of ability for conceptualization and abstraction, while responses emphasizing details are regarded as indicative of plodding, unoriginal mental processes. A preponderance of form–color responses perceived as wholes is considered as evidence of emotional control and social adaptability, while pure color responses are seen as evidence of emotional impulsiveness. Responses involving movement when combined with responses to color are viewed as evidence of creativity and a rich imaginative life, while movement responses without color reference suggest internal emotional control with a low level of affect in interpersonal relations. In developing the description of the subject's personality structure the examiner is required to integrate all the information yielded by the Rorschach protocol with all the data which are available from other sources, such as personal history, other test scores, and clinical interviews.

Many researchers have raised serious questions about the validity and the reliability of the Rorschach technique and the hypotheses which underlie its interpretation. One of the best evaluations of available evidence (Goldfried et al. 1971) concludes that this technique has its greatest validity when used as a measure of cognitive and perceptual modes, and is least satisfactory when responses are treated as fantasy productions amenable to psychoanalytic interpretation.

Some modifications of the standard Rorschach technique have substituted group administration for individual testing, and multiple-choice format instead of open-ended response. In these procedures the blots may be shown on a slide projector, standard sets of cards may be given to all subjects, or special booklets containing reproductions of the blots and the listing of choices from which responses are to be selected may be used. These modifications have not been widely adopted principally because of the loss of spontaneity in response due to the forced choice format and the impossibility of carrying out the inquiry phase of the standard Rorschach procedure.

The Holtzman Inkblot Technique (HIT), which was published in 1961, is an effort to use blots in an approach which conforms to the technical standards for psychometric instruments. Two parallel sets of 45 cards are available for use, with a single response given to each, and scoring is completely objective. Scores on 22 variables are interpreted in terms of percentile norms which are provided for various age and clinical groups. Machine scoring and computer-generated interpretation are available options.

The Thematic Apperception Test (TAT), developed by Murray and the staff of the Harvard Psychological Clinic, is a different type of widely used projective technique. The test material consists of 30 picture cards and one blank card. Some of the pictures are appropriate for use with all subjects, but others are used with only particular age or sex groups. In the original description of the technique the use of 20 pictures administered in two sessions was recommended, but in recent practice only 10 to 14 cards are generally used. The subject is instructed to make up a story about each picture by telling what led up to the depicted scene, what is happening, what are the thoughts and feelings of the people involved, and what is the outcome of the situation. No time limits are imposed, and verbatim record of the story and of time gaps, gestures, irrelevant remarks, questions, and so on is made by the examiner.

The interpretation of the stories rests on content analysis, with the nature of the analysis varying as a function of the purpose of the testing and the psychological orientation of the examiner. Murray's scheme emphasized the identification of "needs"—forces emanating from the "hero", the character with whom the subject has identified, and of "press"—forces deriving from the environment. Examples of needs are achievement, affiliation, aggression. Danger, criticism, and deprivation are illustrations of press. In another scheme areas such as mental approach, imaginative processes, family dynamics, emotional reaction, and sexual adjustment may be employed as the framework for the content analysis. Sometimes the analysis may be limited to a single dimension, as in studies of achievement motivation. Regardless of whether the clinician's purpose in administering the Thematic Apperception Test is broad or limited, the material elicited by this technique is more useful for acquiring knowledge of the content of the subject's thoughts and fantasies than for understanding the personality structure or problem-solving style.

Because only two of the cards in the Thematic Apperception Test material were specifically intended for use with children, a number of additional thematic techniques have been developed for use with subjects who may be as young as 3 years of age. The most commonly used test for children between the ages of 3 and 10 is Bellak's Children's Apperception Test (CAT). The test material consists of 10 cards with animal figures in various situations, with the representation of the animals ranging from complete naturalness to total anthropomorphism. The procedures for administration are similar to those of the Thematic Apperception Test. The pictures are intended to arouse fantasies which will be useful in understanding a child's relation to important life figures, and the dynamics of the youngster's approach to such childhood experiences as feeding, oral problems generally, sibling rivalry, toilet training, aggression, and fear of loneliness. An analysis sheet which provides space for a summary of the responses in terms of 11 variables which are considered important is normally completed as an aid in preparing the interpretive report.

Bellak's assumption that children identify more readily with animals than with people was challenged by a number of researchers whose findings indicated that children's responses to human figures yielded more and richer clinical material. In 1966 the Bellaks published a modification known as CAT-H, in which human figures replaced the animal drawings, and which was recommended for use with children whose mental age is at least 10 years.

Another Thematic Apperception Test derivative which makes use of animal figures is known as the Blacky Pictures. The material consists of 11 cartoon-type drawings of Blacky—a small dog described as either male or female to agree with the sex of the subject—Blacky's parents, and a sibling named Tippy who is of unspecified sex. While the use of dogs might suggest that the test is intended for use only with children, it was developed with adults and is used with subjects from 5 years to adulthood. The content of each of the 11 cards is derived from the psychoanalytic theory of psychosexual development. Subjects respond to the cards in three ways: by telling a spontaneous story, by responding to six multiple-choice (open-ended for children) questions for each card, and by sorting the cards into "like" and "dislike" piles, with the best liked and most disliked cards being identified. The 11 variables which are of primary concern in this technique are: oral eroticism, oral sadism, anal sadism, oedipal intensity, masturbation guilt, castration anxiety (males) or penis envy (females), positive identification, sibling rivalry, guilt feelings, positive ego ideal, and love object.

Two projective techniques which make use of verbal stimuli are word association tests and sentence completion tests. Free association to words has been used by psychologists since at least 1879, when Galton reported on its use in some of his studies. Jung made use of the technique in studies designed to test Freud's theory of repression beginning about 1906. His list consisted of 100 words selected as representative of common emotional problems. It was administered by saying each word, and asking the subject to reply promptly with the first word that came to mind. The reply to each stimulus word was recorded and note was made of all unusual verbal or behavioral reactions which accompanied any response. The responses and their accompanying characteristics were then analyzed in order to identify emotional problems which were inferred from the types of stimulus words that triggered psychologically significant responses.

The first formal word association list (Kent and Rosanoff 1910) consisted of 100 stimulus words which are neutral in character and which tend to evoke similar responses from normal subjects. The Kent–Rosanoff Free Association Test is scored objectively and is interpreted on the basis of norms for the proportion of common or individual responses for various subgroups. It is used primarily as a psychiatric screening procedure. The 60-word list developed by Rapaport (Rapaport et al. 1946) consists only of nouns, many of which have significance in the psychosexual area. The purpose of the Rapaport technique is twofold: to discover impairment of thought processes, and to identify significant conflict areas.

Sentence completion tests require the subject to add words, usually in writing, to a sentence stem in order to produce a complete sentence, which is often indicative of a belief, attitude, or some other residual of one's experience. Examples of such stems are: I get nervous when..., I would be much better if..., My mother.... While the systematic use of this technique for personality assessment dates from the late 1920s and early 1930s, the experience of American military psychologists during the Second World War served to thrust it forward as a useful clinical and research instrument in the postwar years. The technique possesses very great flexibility, and the content and structure of the stems can be varied in order to maximize the possibility of eliciting responses which are relevant to whatever particular aspect of personality is of interest. Many applications of this technique involve the construction by the researcher or clinician of stems which are germane to some immediate purpose. But a number of standardized instruments have been developed and they are the most frequently used. The prototypical sentence completion test is generally considered to be the one developed by Rohde and Hildreth in 1940, and many of their items have been incorporated in subsequently developed instruments.

The Rotter Incomplete Sentences Blank was designed for use with college students. It consists of 40 stems to be completed in such a way as to express the subject's "real feelings." Responses are rated on a 7-point scale depending on the level of adjustment suggested by the completion, and a composite score is recommended for screening purposes. Quite a different use of the technique is exemplified by the Washington University Sentence Completion Test. This, used primarily with adult women, is designed to provide a measure of ego development based upon a conceptualization of a 7-stage process. The scoring procedure is elaborate and formalized and requires extensive practice.

One important methodological issue in the use of sentence completion tests involves the person reference, that is, first or third person, which is used in the stem. Some research has been reported showing that stems which include first person pronouns have little value as projective techniques since they are essentially self-report items, but that responses to stems containing third-person references can tap covert or latent reactions (Getzels and Walsh 1958), qualifying them as projective instruments.

A wide variety of projective techniques provide the subject with an opportunity for relatively free nonverbal self-expression. Drawing and finger painting tasks are prominent examples. While originally used as an indicator of children's intellectual capacity, the task of drawing a person has evolved into a projective technique because emotional and nonintellectual factors are reflected in the drawings. In Machover's Draw-a-person Test the subject is given paper and pencil and is asked to draw a person. When that task is completed the examinee is instructed to draw another person, this time of the opposite sex of that represented in the first drawing. The examiner notes the subject's comments and procedures while drawing, and then conducts an inquiry in which the subject is asked to make up a story about each person drawn. The analysis of the drawings takes into account such characteristics as relative size of male and female figures, placement on the page, midline emphasis, front or side view, proportions, and erasures. Significance is attached to the qualities of major parts of the body. A global personality description is developed from the analysis of the elements of the drawings. A similar technique requires the subject to draw a house, tree, and person, in that order (Buck 1948). The analysis focuses on characteristics of the drawing of the person, with the other two drawings serving principally as bench marks.

The projective hypothesis, that significant aspects of personality and important attributes of an individual's private world can be discovered by analyzing the responses the person makes to ambiguous or affect-oriented stimuli, has spawned the development of a very wide variety of assessment techniques. The diversity in the nature of the tasks, in the purposes for which they are used and in the types of inferences which are drawn from the responses makes it impossible to reach any firm generalizations about the validity of these techniques as a class. They are the source of much controversy; they have enthusiastic users and supporters, but also caustic and unrelenting critics. They will continue to be used by clinicians who find them useful, but the projective hypothesis and the techniques associated with it are still being tested.

See also: Attitudes and their Measurement

Bibliography

Beck S J 1949 *Rorschach's Test: Basic Processes*, Vol. 1, 2nd edn. Grune and Stratton, New York

Bell J E 1948 *Projective Techniques*. Longmans Green, New York

Buck J N 1948 The H-T-P technique: A qualitative and quantitative scoring method. *J. Clin. Psychol. Monogr.* 5

Frank L K 1948 *Projective Methods*. Thomas, Springfield, Illinois

Getzels J W, Walsh J J 1958 The method of paired direct and projective questionnaires in the study of attitude structure and socialization. *Psychol. Monogr.* 72(1) (whole no. 454)

Goldfried M R, Stricker G, Weiner I B 1971 *Rorschach Handbook of Clinical and Research Application*. Prentice-Hall, Englewood Cliffs, New Jersey

Holtzman W H, Thorpe J S, Swartz J D, Heron E W 1961 *Inkblot Perception and Personality: Holtzman Inkblot Technique*. University of Texas Press, Austin, Texas

Kent G H, Rosanoff A J 1910 A study of association in insanity. *Am. J. Insanity* 67: 37–96, 317–90

Klopfer B, Kelly D M 1942 *The Rorschach Technique: A Manual for Projective Method of Personality Diagnosis*. World Book, New York

Lindzey G 1961 *Projective Techniques and Cross-cultural Research*. Appleton-Century-Crofts, New York

Murstein B I 1963 *Theory and Research in Projective Techniques, Emphasizing the TAT*. Wiley, New York

Rabin A I 1968 *Projective Techniques in Personality Assessment: A Modern Introduction*. Springer, New York

Rapaport D, Gill M, Schafer R 1946 *Diagnostic Psychological Testing: The Theory, Statistical Evaluation and Diagnostic Application of a Battery of Tests*. Yearbook, Chicago, Illinois

Rorschach H 1932 *Psychodiagnostik: Methodik und Ergebuisse eines Wahrnehmungsdiagnostischen Experiments*, 2nd edn. Huber, Bern

Semeonoff B 1976 *Projective Techniques*. Wiley, London

Applications of Measurement in Other Fields

Models of Intelligence

J. E. Gustafsson

Research on the structure of intelligence has sought to determine the answers to two basic questions, namely: (a) how many dimensions are needed to describe individual differences in cognitive abilities? and (b) what are the interrelationships among the dimensions of ability? During the first six decades of the twentieth century these questions were investigated by several groups of researchers, each presenting competing models of the structure of intelligence. Among these, one line of distinction goes between models which postulate a general factor of intelligence (e.g., Burt 1949, Spearman 1904, Vernon, 1950), and models which do not allow for a general factor (e.g., Cattell 1971, Guilford 1967, Thurstone 1938). Another line of distinction goes between hierarchical models (e.g., Burt 1949, Horn and Cattell 1966, Vernon 1950) and models in which all dimensions are ascribed equal generality (e.g., Guilford 1967, Thurstone 1938).

It has proved difficult to secure evidence that firmly establishes one of these models as the superior one. This led Sternberg (1981 p. 143) to conclude that the factor analytic approach has "...failed because it has been too successful in supporting, or at least in failing to disconfirm, too many alternative models of intelligence". However, one purpose of this article is to present some research which provides at least a tentative resolution of the problems of choice of model.

In parallel with the research on the structure of intelligence an entire industry has developed which specializes in producing and using psychological tests of cognitive abilities for purposes of diagnosis, classification, and selection of individuals within a vast array of institutions, such as schools, hospitals, the armed forces, and industry. The relationship between research and application is not simple, however, and another purpose of the present article is to discuss some of the relationships between the more theoretically oriented work on models of intelligence on the one hand, and the more practically oriented work aiming to develop instruments to measure intelligence on the other.

1. One or Many Dimensions of Intelligence?

Building upon work conducted by Galton and Pearson in the late nineteenth century, Spearman (1904) suggested the first, rather crude, analytical techniques for investigating the rank of a matrix of correlations and, on the basis of empirical studies of several sets of variables, he concluded that "all branches of intellectual activity have in common one fundamental function (or group of functions), whereas the remaining or specific elements of the activity seem in every case to be wholly different from that in all the others" (Spearman 1904 p. 284). These results were formalized in the two-factor theory of intelligence, which states that performance on a task is affected by two factors only, the g-factor, which is common to all tasks, and the s-factor which is unique to each task.

In his empirical work Spearman used small samples of variables and subjects and often he did find a very good fit between the observational data and the model. But there were also deviations. For one thing it was in some cases found that the s-factors were correlated, thus giving rise to group-factors. For another thing it was found that the model broke down when tests that were "too similar" were included in a battery of tests, again because of a correlation between the s-factors. These facts were readily admitted by Spearman, but they came to cause great problems for his theory when other researchers tested and rejected it (e.g., Kelley 1928).

At about the same time that Spearman published his first results on the two-factor theory, Binet and Simon (1905) published the first intelligence test. As is well-known, this test differed from previous mental tests in that it contained quite complex items, and in that it used a very varied set of items. This test proved to be most useful in practical applications, and it set a model for several generations of tests of general mental ability.

The contributions of Spearman and Binet appeared close in time so it might be thought that the Spearman model provided a theoretical basis for the Binet and Simon test. However, in spite of the fact that for both these researchers a single, general, mental ability was the focus of interest, the simultaneous appearance of their work seems to be a coincidence. They were in fact highly critical of one another: Binet did not approve of the statistical nature of Spearman's work, and Spearman argued that Binet's conception of the total score on the test as an average of several abilities was theoretically indefensible. Spearman sympathized, however, with the basic idea of "throwing many miscellaneous tests into a single pool" (Spearman 1927 p. 84) and he admitted that "Our *g* is, in fact, really obtained by this practice, with rough — much too rough — approximation" (Spearman 1927 p. 84).

The fundamental difference between the positions of Spearman and Binet is that while Spearman thought of *g* as a dimension of individual differences in its own right, Binet regarded general intelligence as being composed of several partly independent characteristics. Thus, Binet saw the test score as reflecting a mean of several different abilities, while Spearman saw the test score as reflecting a unitary dimension. These two basic positions concerning the nature of general intelligence can be identified in many controversies within the field of intelligence.

Binet's work had the strongest impact on practice (Carroll 1982), however, and during the first decades of the twentieth century a large number of tests were developed. In parallel, statistical methods for test and item analysis were developed and the testing technique was accommodated to allow group testing as well. As Carroll pointed out, these early tests "employed a rather wide array and variety of tasks involving the understanding and manipulation of verbal and nonverbal materials and problems" (Carroll 1982 p. 36) but during the 1920s tests started to appear that purported to measure somewhat independent dimensions of ability (Carroll 1982 p. 35).

However, it was not until improved factor-analytic techniques were available that viable multidimensional alternatives to Spearman's theory could be formulated. Through a generalization of the Spearman method, Thurstone (1931, 1935) extended factor analysis to encompass multiple common factors, and developed computational techniques which made it feasible to apply the method with large numbers of tests.

Thurstone (1938) applied multiple factor analysis to a test battery of 38 tests, many of which were newly developed, and found about a dozen factors, each of which accounted for performance on a subset of the factors in the battery. There was no sign of a general factor.

Most factors identified by Thurstone (1938) were replicated several times by Thurstone and his colleagues (e.g., Thurstone and Thurstone 1941) and it was possible to set up a list of six or seven easily replicable primary mental abilities (PMAs), such as: Verbal Comprehension (*V*), involved in understanding of language and frequently found in tests such as reading, verbal analogies, and vocabulary; Word Fluency (*W*), affecting the fluent production of language, and measurable by tests such as rhyming or naming words in a given category; Induction (*I*), measured by tests requiring the subjects to find a rule in complex material; Space (*S*), found in manipulation of geometric or spatial relations; Perceptual Speed (*P*), reflected in quick and accurate grasping of visual details; and Number (*N*), involved in quick and accurate arithmetic computations.

In further studies conducted during the 1940s and 1950s by Thurstone and others the list of factorially identified primary abilities was considerably extended, partly by demonstrations that several of the original PMAs were differentiable into more narrow factors, and partly by extensions into new domains, such as perception (Thurstone 1944), language (Carroll 1941) and number (Coombs 1941).

The influence of the multiple factor approach on test construction and test use is clearly seen from about 1940 onwards, in that a considerable number of "multi-factor" batteries were published [e.g., the SRA Primary Mental Abilities (PMA) battery by Thurstone and Thurstone (1949–1965) and the Differential Aptitude Test (DAT) by Bennett et al. (1947–1975)]. These batteries contain homogeneous subtests to measure different specific abilities, and they yield profiles of scores, which may be used for purposes of diagnosis, guidance, and counselling, as well as for purposes of prediction and selection. Frequently, however, the subtest scores are also aggregated into subtotal and total scores, to represent broader areas of competence.

It would seem, however, that the multifactor batteries have not fared very well in evaluations of their ability to provide differential prediction of achievements in areas that should require different profiles of abilities (e.g., Thorndike 1986). On the basis of analyses of validity coefficients for the Differential Aptitude Test and six other multitest batteries, McNemar (1964) concluded: "Aside from tests of numerical ability having differential value for predicting school grades in math, it seems safe to conclude that the worth of the multitest batteries as differential predictors of achievement in school has not been demonstrated." In a similar vein, Carroll speculated ". . . that a large part of whatever predictive validity the DAT and other multiple aptitude batteries have is attributable to an underlying general factor that enters into the various subtests . . ." (Carroll 1982 pp. 83-84).

The rapid proliferation of mental abilities produced by Thurstone and his followers made it necessary to bring order to the multitude of factors and from the 1950s onwards much effort has been devoted to this task. An example of this is the work by French and his colleagues (French 1951, French et al. 1963, Ekstrom et al. 1976) who reviewed the research, trying to determine which factors were distinct and cross-identified in several studies.

The Guilford (1967) "Structure of Intellect" (SI) model may be seen as another attempt to organize the factor-analytic findings, and to develop guidelines for further test development and research. In the SI model each test and factor is uniquely identified as a combination of levels on three facets (operations, content, and products). Guilford argued that each of the PMAs could be mapped onto the SI model, and that the model provides the guidelines necessary for constructing tests so that the other cells in the model may be factorially identified. However, as a consequence of the assumption that the factors are orthogonal the levels on all three facets must be identified, and a very large number of abilities must be assumed. Thus, instead of solving the problem of achieving a parsimonious description of abilities it would seem that the SI model has contributed further to the problem of proliferation of abilities.

2. *The Hierarchical Approach*

Ever since multiple factor analysis was invented by Thurstone it has been the dominating form of factor analysis, and it may be argued that this particular kind of factor analysis bears a large part of the responsibility for the proliferation of factors (Undheim 1981). However, still another way to solve the problem of the multitude of factors is to allow the factors to be correlated, and then analyse the correlations among the factors with factor-analytic methods to obtain higher-order factors. Such higher-order analyses yield hierarchical models, in which factors at lower levels are subsumed under factors at higher levels. Thurstone and Thurstone (1941) conducted such an analysis of the intercorrelation among six PMAs and they did, indeed, find a general factor in the second-order analysis, which factor was most highly loaded by the *I*-factor.

A more elaborate hierarchical model has been developed by Cattell and Horn (e.g., Cattell 1963, Horn 1968, Horn and Cattell 1966). The two dimensions of most central importance in this model are fluid intelligence (*Gf*) and crystallized intelligence (*Gc*), and the whole theory is often referred to as *Gc–Gf* theory. Both these dimensions reflect the capacity for abstraction, concept formation, and perception and eduction of relations. The *Gc* dimension, however, is thought to reflect individual differences associated with systematic cultural influences, and is central in tasks of a verbal–conceptual nature. The *Gf* dimension in contrast reflects effects of biological and neurological factors, and factors such as incidental learning, and this dimension is most strongly shown in tasks that are either new or very familiar to the examinees.

In the early formulation of *Gc–Gf* theory Horn and Cattell (1966) identified some three or four additional second-order factors, such as General Speediness (*Gs*), General Fluency (*Gr*), and General Visualization (*Gv*). In later research reported by Horn and collaborators (e.g., Horn 1980, Horn 1986, Horn and Stankov 1982, Stankov and Horn 1980) the list of second-order factors has, however, been considerably expanded, and a hierarchical model based on levels of functions has been proposed. Cattell (1971) likewise has proposed an elaborate theory in hierarchical terms of the organization of abilities.

While hierarchical models are of relatively recent origin in American research, such models have had a strong position in the British research following Spearman. One contributor of such a model is Burt (e.g., 1949), who also made contributions to the development of factor analysis. The most influential model was, however, proposed by Vernon (1950, 1961) "... as a hypothetical integration of all the factorial investigations that have been carried out" (Vernon 1961 p. 26).

In the Vernon model, factors of at least three degrees of generality are identified: the general factor, major group-factors and minor group-factors. Among the major group-factors Vernon distinguishes between verbal–numerical–educational (*v:ed*) and spatial–practical–mechanical–physical (*k:m*) ability. The *v:ed*

factor subdivides into minor group-factors, such as verbal and number factors and reading, spelling, linguistic and clerical abilities, and also into fluency and divergent thinking abilities. The *k:m* factor subdivides too and this complex includes minor group-factors such as perceptual, physical, psychomotor, spatial and mechanical factors. At the level below the minor group-factors the tests would be found but "...there is ample evidence to support the view that group-factors are almost infinitely subdivisible, depending only on the degree of detail to which the analysis is carried" (Vernon 1961 p. 26.)

The Vernon model thus represents the most influential hierarchical model from the British tradition of research while the Cattell–Horn model represents the most elaborate and influential of the hierarchical models developed within American research. There are obvious similarities between these models, but there are also differences: The Cattell–Horn model lacks the *g* factor which has such a prominent place in the Vernon model, and there are only two broad group-factors in the Vernon model, while there are several broad abilities in addition to *Gf* and *Gc* in the Cattell–Horn model.

3. *Studies Comparing Hierarchical Models*

In a series of recently conducted studies these competing hierarchical models have been compared empirically (Gustafsson 1984, in press, Undheim 1981, Undheim and Gustafsson 1987). In these studies confirmatory higher-order factor-analytic techniques (LISREL, Jöreskog and Sörbom 1981) were used to test hypotheses about the arrangement of factors at different levels within a hierarchical model. In brief summary the results were as follows:

(a) At the first-order level very good support was obtained for the primary factors (e.g., *V, I, S, P, N,*...) in the Thurstone and Guilford traditions, and it seems that these are easily identifiable as soon as a sufficient number of tests measuring the factor is included in the battery.

(b) At the second-order level very good support was obtained for the broad factors proposed within the framework of the Cattell–Horn model, and in two or more studies the factors *Gf, Gc, Gv, Gs* and *Gr* have clearly been identified.

(c) At the third-order level a general factor has been obtained. What is most interesting, however, is the fact that all the studies have shown that there is a loading of unity of *Gf* in the *g*-factor, which implies that *Gf* is equivalent with the *g*-factor.

This latter result implies that *Gf* for reasons of parsimony should be lifted above, as it were, the other broad factors identified by Cattell and Horn, and that these other factors should be purged of their *g*-variance. This would leave a *Gc*-residual (*Gc'*) which seems to be more or less identical with the major group-factor that Vernon labels *v:ed*; and it would leave a *Gv*-residual (*Gv'*) that is very similar indeed to the *k:m* factor in the

Vernon model. Thus, the fact that *Gf* is identical with *g* in a sense resolves the conflict between the hierarchical models proposed by Vernon and by Cattell–Horn. Since the hierarchical model includes the primary abilities identified in the Thurstone tradition as well, it does in a sense unify several previous models that have been viewed as being quite incompatible. It must be stressed, though, that the *g*-factor identified within this model is quite different from what is obtained by most current measures of general mental ability. While the former would be derived mainly from nonverbal reasoning tests, many IQ tests have such a strong verbal bias that they should probably best be considered measures of *Gc*.

It is interesting to consider the implications of this hierarchical model for the measurement of intelligence. It has already been concluded that throughout the history of mental testing, measures have been obtained of a rather loosely defined general mental ability, either through use of IQ tests of the Binet type, or through creation of composites of scores on homogeneous tests. Throughout most of the history of mental testing specific abilities have been measured as well, as is done with the multifactor batteries. The hierarchical model includes both broad and narrow abilities so both these practices would, in a general sense, be compatible with such a model of the structure of abilities. However, it would seem that the hierarchical model of abilities also carries much more far-reaching implications for the measurement of general and specific abilities, and in the remainder of this article these implications will be described in general and nontechnical terms.

4. Measurement of General and Specific Abilities

With the exception of Spearman very few researchers seem to have regarded general ability as anything but an aggregate of those quite different abilities that are important for school achievement. Horn (1986), for example, argued strongly against the concept of general intelligence on the ground that the conglomerate measures used to identify it cannot represent a functional unity. However, the fact that *g* and *Gf* have been shown to be equivalent implies that the *g*-factor may be identified "not only as the first, unrotated centroid or principal factor axis factor or as the inevitable summit factor after successive higher order analyses — but as a general dimension uniquely identified through simple structure" (Undheim 1981 pp. 251-52). Since dimensions identified under the criterion of simple structure fulfil rather stringent criteria of invariance, this implies that the general factor of intelligence can be "objectively determined and measured". How best to measure *g* and other abilities still remains to be determined however.

From the hierarchical model it follows that the observed variance obtained on any test is due to a set of orthogonal factors of varying breadth. For example, of the variance in the scores on a spatial visualization (*Vz*) test 35 percent may be due to the *g*-factor; 15 percent to *Gv'* (the residual in *Gv* which remains after *g* has been partialled out), 15 percent to *Vz'* (the residual visualization primary after *g* and *Gv'* have been partialled out), 15 percent to a test specific factor, and the remainder random error variance.

While the relative size of the contributions from these sources of variance may be influenced to a certain extent, it is quite inconceivable that any one of them could be brought up to 100 percent within a homogeneous test. This illustrates the fundamental principle that "no test measures a single factor" (Vernon 1961, p. 133); each and every intellectual performance measure is affected by several sources of influence of different degrees of generality, and it is even theoretically impossible to achieve a truly "univocal" measure of a single specific ability.

From this line of reasoning it also follows that when the aim is to obtain measures of the broader abilities (i.e., *g* and the second-order abilities in the Cattell–Horn model) a single homogeneous test is unlikely to suffice, since the scores to a rather large extent will be influenced by narrow factors. The Raven Progressive Matrices Test is frequently cited as a good measure of the *g*-factor, and upon the suggestion of Spearman it was indeed constructed to be such a measure. However, studies (for example Gustafsson, in press) indicate that only some 55 percent of the variance in this test is due to the *g*-factor. This implies that the test measures the *g*-factor with a reliability of 0.55, which for most theoretical and practical purposes is too low to be acceptable.

It would thus seem that the only way to estimate broad abilities is to combine information from several tests. Optimally this is done through an estimation procedure which takes into account the differential relationships between the tests and the broad abilities. Simple versions of such procedures were developed a long time ago (Spearman 1927), but they have only rarely been used in practical applications, and there is a need to develop new procedures which take advantage of the advances within the statistical and computational fields.

From the fact that any observed measure represents a composite of abilities it also follows that to identify uniquely a specific ability it is necessary to partial out the effects of the more general abilities. This in turn implies that even if only a certain specific ability is in the focus of interest it is necessary to administer several tests, in order to allow estimation of the general and specific dimensions of ability.

5. Conclusion

The hierarchical model of ability supports the measurement of general mental ability as well as identification of specific abilities. However, in previous psychometric work it seems that general mental ability has been conceived of as a conglomerate or as an average of several more narrowly defined abilities, while in the hierarchical model the general factor is uniquely identified through the principle of simple structure as an ability in its own right.

From the hierarchical model it also follows that in all those measurement situations where the purpose is to identify any particular ability, it is necessary to use multiple measures, and to adopt a multivariate psychometric model. At present multivariate models of measurement (Wittman in press) are only at a crude stage of development. It may be noted, however, that throughout the history of psychometrics "many of the advances, even in 'pure' statistics, were occasioned by the technological requirements of the mental ability testing movement" (Carroll 1982 p. 43). It may be hoped, therefore, that the progress in the description of the hierarchical structure of ability will cause a rapid development of multivariate psychometric models.

See also: Models and Model Building; History of Mental Testing; Factor Analysis; Multitrait–Multimethod Analysis

Bibliography

Bennett G K, Seashore H G, Wesman A G 1947-1975 *Differential Aptitude Tests*. Psychological Corporation, New York
Binet A, Simon T 1905 Méthodes nouvelles pour le diagnostic du niveau intellectuel des anormaux. *L'Année Psychol.* 11: 191-244
Burt C L 1949 The structure of the mind: A review of the results of factor analysis. *Br. J. Educ. Psychol.* 19: 100-11, 176-99.
Carroll J B 1941 A factor analysis of verbal abilities. *Psychometrika* 6: 279-307
Carroll J B 1982 The measurement of intelligence. In: Sternberg R J (ed.) 1982 *Handbook of Human Intelligence*. Cambridge University Press, Cambridge, pp. 29-120
Cattell R B 1963 Theory of fluid and crystallized intelligence: A critical experiment. *J. Educ. Psychol.* 54: 1-22
Cattell R B 1971 *Abilities: Their Structure, Growth and Action*. Houghton-Mifflin, Boston, Massachusetts
Coombs C H 1941 A factorial study of number ability. *Psychometrika* 6: 161-89
Ekstrom R B, French J W, Harman H H 1976 *Kit of Factor-Referenced Cognitive Tests*. Educational Testing Service, Princeton, New Jersey
French J W 1951 The description of aptitude and achievement tests in terms of rotated factors. *Psychometric Monogr.* No. 5
French J W, Ekstrom R B, Price L A 1963 *Kit of Reference Tests for Cognitive Factors*. Educational Testing Service, Princeton, New Jersey
Guilford J P 1967 *The Nature of Human Intelligence*. McGraw-Hill, New York
Gustafsson J E 1984 A unifying model for the structure of intellectual abilities. *Intelligence* 8: 179-203
Gustafsson J E Hierarchical models of individual differences in cognitive abilities. In: Sternberg R J (ed.) *Advances in the Psychology of Human Intelligence*, Vol. 4. Erlbaum, Hillsdale, New Jersey, in press
Horn J L 1968 Organization of abilities and the development of intelligence. *Psychol. Rev.* 79: 242-59
Horn J L 1980 Concepts of intellect in relation to learning and adult development. *Intelligence* 4: 285-317
Horn J L 1986 Intellectual ability concepts. In: Sternberg R J (ed.) 1986 *Advances in the Psychology of Human Intelligence*, Vol. 3. Erlbaum, Hillsdale, New Jersey, pp. 35-78
Horn J L, Cattell R B 1966 Refinement and test of the theory of fluid and crystallized intelligence. *J. Educ. Psychol.* 57: 253-70
Horn J L, Stankov L 1982 Auditory and visual factors of intelligence. *Intelligence* 6: 165-85
Jöreskog K G, Sörbom D 1981 LISREL V: *Analysis of Linear Structural Relationships by Maximum Likelihood and Least Squares Methods*. Research report 81-8 Department of Statistics, University of Uppsala, Uppsala
Kelley T L 1928 *Crossroads in the Mind of Man: A Study of Differentiable Mental Abilities*. World Book, Yonkers-on-Hudson, New York
McNemar Q 1964 Lost: Our intelligence. Why? *Am. Psychol.* 19: 871-82
Spearman C 1904 General intelligence objectively determined and measured. *Am. J. Psychol.* 15: 210-93
Spearman C 1927 *The Abilities of Man*. Macmillan, London
Stankov L, Horn J L 1980 Human abilities revealed through auditory tests. *J. Educ. Psychol.* 72: 21-44
Sternberg R J 1981 Nothing fails like success: The search for an intelligent paradigm for studying intelligence. *J. Educ. Psychol.* 73: 142-55
Thorndike R L 1986 After 80 years of *G* is testing going to *H*? Paper presented at the annual meeting of the American Educational Research Association, San Fransisco
Thurstone L L 1931 Multiple factor analysis. *Psychol. Rev.* 38: 406-27
Thurstone L L 1935 *The Vectors of the Mind*. Chicago University Press, Chicago, Illinois
Thurstone L L 1938 Primary mental abilities. *Psychometric Monogr.* No. 1
Thurstone L L 1944 *A Factorial Study of Perception*. Chicago University Press, Chicago, Illinois
Thurstone L L, Thurstone T G 1941 Factorial studies of intelligence. *Psychometric Monogr.* No. 2
Thurstone L L, Thurstone T G 1949-1965 *Primary Mental Abilities*. Science Research Associates (SRA), Chicago, Illinois
Undheim J O 1981 On intelligence IV: Toward a restoration of general intelligence. *Scand. J. Psychol.* 22: 251-65
Undheim J O, Gustafsson J E 1987 The hierarchical organization of cognitive abilities: Restoring general intelligence through the use of linear structural relations. *Multivariate Behav. Res.* 22: 149-71
Vernon P E 1950 *The Structure of Human Abilities*. Methuen, London
Vernon P E 1961 *The Structure of Human Abilities*, 2nd edn. Methuen, London
Wittman W W Multivariate reliability theory: Principles of symmetry and successful validation strategies. In: Cattell R B, Nesselroade J R (eds.) *Handbook of Multivariate Experimental Psychology* 2nd edn. Plenum Press, New York, in press

Census Data and Statistics

J. N. Johnstone

Statistics compiled from the data collected during a census are becoming increasingly important in all spheres of endeavour. They provide scenarios of populations of any kind at various points in time. These scenarios can be used for planning, to pose or refute arguments, or simply to understand the character of a particular population at a given time. To be truly useful, census data must be properly collected, processed, and disseminated. Without adequate safeguards at all stages of their formation and presentation, data can lose their reliability and validity. The application of such safeguards to the enormous tasks of data collection and data processing entailed in conducting a census is, however, extremely involved. Consequently, censuses—especially those of populations of nations—cannot be held frequently. The human, material, and financial costs are too great. Census data must therefore sometimes be supplemented and even updated with data from sample surveys.

1. The Concept of a Census

A census is generally regarded as being a count or tally, especially one conducted by a government to enumerate a particular population. The word has the same form as in the original Latin where it meant the registration of citizens. As used now, the connotation implies a counting rather than a listing of all people in a country, and it is in this context that the United Nations provides the following definition of a population census: "A census of a population may be defined as the total process of collecting, compiling, and publishing demographic, economic, and social data pertaining, at a specified time or times, to all persons in a country or delimited territory" (1958 p. 4).

Although the term census usually implies a census of the entire population of a country, it can also be used to mean the enumeration of any defined or delimited set of entities whether they be special kinds of people, all schools administered by a particular ministry, private organizations in a single industrial sector, animals or organisms in a defined area, and so on. Censuses of entities such as these are conducted at various times and for different purposes. What they have in common is the attempt to collect, compile, and publish information about certain characteristics aggregated from each and every member of a defined population. In the education system context, the usual referent of the term census is the periodic (mostly annual) collection of data from all schools under the responsibility of a particular ministry or department of education. The data collected in these school censuses describe the number and characteristics of such aspects as pupils, teachers, finance, equipment, and space.

It is not possible to identify when the first population census might have been conducted. Governments have always been concerned with knowing how many people were under their jurisdiction. Originally a census was conducted to compile lists either of households so that taxes might be levied or of men so as to estimate potential military strength. It is known that detailed censuses of population, agriculture, and produce were taken in Babylon before 2,000 BC. Documents relating to most of the ancient civilizations—Egypt, Persia, Japan, and China—refer to censuses being conducted during those

times. The Old Testament records the numbering of the tribes at the time of the Exodus and then again under David. The Romans conducted a census every five years and Augustus extended this from Italy to the whole Roman Empire about 5 BC. In the more modern era, censuses were conducted in Switzerland in the fifteenth and sixteenth centuries. During the second half of the seventeenth century and the first half of the eighteenth century, censuses of the kind conducted now were becoming widespread in Europe, America, and India.

The census in the United States provides the longest periodic series. It has been conducted every 10 years since 1790. Almost as long is the census of the United Kingdom which began in 1801 and has been conducted every 10 years since except on one occasion (in 1941).

2. The Purpose of Collecting Census Data

There is no single purpose motivating the collection of data through a census. As noted previously, the original purposes envisaged for a census centred on taxation and military concerns. Present-day censuses relating to any defined population attempt to fulfil at least three distinct purposes.

A first purpose for collecting data through a census is to provide a guide for policy formation and planning. Data from a complete enumeration of a population reveal the ways and extent to which certain quantities, characteristics, skills, and so on are distributed throughout that population. On the basis of these distributions, social and economic policies can be formulated to fulfil certain political objectives. Programmes can also be identified to bring about changes in the existing conditions in accordance with these policies. These programmes might, for example, encourage people to live in certain areas, promote higher progression and/or retention rates in schools, further develop certain resources or commodities, and so on. Without a complete and adequate database, proper planning and policy formulation cannot be undertaken. To guide policy therefore, the range of information collected in a census must be sufficiently diverse to enable adequate analysis of a range of actual or possible government undertakings.

A second purpose envisaged for census data is the formation of a base to guide financial and other kinds of allocations. This purpose is not so important for a national or population census but it can be of critical importance to censuses of schools or education systems. Some programmes may, for example, allocate finance on a per pupil, per teacher, or per classroom basis. Before the level of an allocation per unit can be decided, it is often important to know or to estimate the numbers of likely receiving units in various categories.

A third purpose underlying the collection of census data—but one which is a consequence rather than a motivating reason—is that census data provide a very extensive data bank facilitating a considerable research effort often having direct consequences for government understanding and activity. Patterns of distributions of people, skills, and property can be examined by researchers who would not otherwise have access to such data except perhaps through expensive and independently conducted sample surveys—if indeed the data could be collected at all. For example, researchers wishing to investigate the relationship between level of education and level of income or category of occupation would need a very large sample size to obtain stability in their estimates. Obtaining this large sample would be both difficult and costly. In addition, the results would apply only to one point in time. Incorporating questions on education level, income, and occupation into a population census not only allows the relationship to be determined exactly in a given context but it also allows the level of the relationship to be monitored over time as data from successive censuses become available. The results of research using census data frequently have important implications for governments and ministries as well as for private, commercial, or industrial organizations and pressure groups. Unfortunately, from an educational research perspective, data banks from a population census are generally much more accessible to researchers than are data banks from a school census. Hence education researchers have only limited opportunities to analyse many of the critical issues surrounding school provision and operation (see *Legitimatory Research*).

3. The Time to Conduct a Census

Although a census can be conducted at any time a government chooses, the data and statistics should be collected at a time which maximizes the benefits to be gained from them. As policy making, planning, and programme implementation are continuous processes of government, census data need to be relatively recent if they are to maintain their relevance. Hence a government cannot plan to conduct just one census to provide all the data it requires. Instead, it must plan to conduct a series of censuses with a fairly regular interval of time separating successive censuses. In determining what might be an appropriate interval, a government must balance the desire for up-to-date information against the costs and time involved in planning the census, collecting the data, and then processing them. Most countries attempt to conduct a population census every 5 or 10 years, although frequencies of less than 10 years are becoming increasingly difficult to implement due to costs and processing time problems. Indeed, due partly to United Nations coordination, a pattern has emerged for nations to conduct their population censuses at the beginning of each decade or one year after (viz. in 1980 or 1981 and then in 1990 or 1991, etc.). For example, as stated in Sect. 1, the United States conducts its census at the beginning of each decade while the United Kingdom conducts its census in the following year.

For education systems, censuses are generally conducted on an annual basis. A one-year interval between successive school censuses provides statistics which are up-to-date, relevant, and integral to the process of policy formation and planning. Further, the one-year

period does not involve inordinate costs for collecting and processing, nor does it generate too much data and so prevent proper processing, analysis, and publication of the data. In some education systems, attempts are made to conduct three or four censuses during each school year. Attempts of this kind generally provide a surfeit of information, most of which is never used and certainly never processed to a stage where publication of the data is routinely possible.

Regularly conducted censuses having a reasonable time period between successive data collection stages can, by their regularity, facilitate the entire process of preparation, administration, and processing. Those charged with responsibility for conducting the census are given the opportunity to organize all activities within a known time frame. Respondents become accustomed to anticipating that the data collection exercise will be held at a given, regularly occurring point in time and therefore are less likely to ascribe to it purposes which are not in accord with the real intention of the exercise. They are also more likely to be willing to participate.

In addition to the desirability of establishing a regular time period between successive censuses, it is important for a census to be conducted at an appropriate and regular time during that year. For a population census to collect data about each individual in a country or territory, for example, it is desirable not to plan to collect data during holiday months when many people would be away from their place of residence or engaged in activities outside the house. Censuses held during harvest time encounter similar problems. For school censuses, it is not desirable to collect data at the beginning or the end of a school year. Enrolments at these times tend to be respectively higher and lower than the numbers enroled about the middle of the school year and which, because of greater stability, provide a better estimate of the numbers of students in a school system.

The selection of a time to conduct a census is partly guided by the comparisons intended for the statistics produced. For population censuses of a nation, comparisons with previous censuses of that nation would be envisaged and hence data should be collected in months corresponding to those used previously. This similarity would help maximize data comparability with the past. Another consideration for population censuses is the increasing need for many policies to reflect international structures and distributions. Similarity in the years in which censuses are conducted in different nations is therefore essential to allow the production of comparable national statistics. United Nations efforts in this regard have been most successful in encouraging many nations to standardize the timing of their data collection periods. For school censuses, the stability of enrolment estimates noted above is one aspect which can lead to a comparability of education statistics across systems. Another action enhancing comparability, especially in countries having decentralized education structures, is for school censuses to be conducted in each of the subsystems at or about the same time. For example, in countries like Australia, the Federal Republic of Germany, and the United States which have education systems in each state independent of systems in the other states, data collection from schools should be comparable especially through the use of a month for data collection which is common across all states in that country. This commonality then allows the aggregation of statistics from each state system to form a valid national estimate of particular education system characteristics.

4. A Census or a Sample Survey

An important distinction is that between a census and a sample survey. The former attempts to attain a complete enumeration of a population whereas the latter aims to provide estimates of the characteristics of that population derived from a subset of the entire population. Surveys are well-known and commonly used in all spheres of government, research, economic, and social activity. They can require relatively few respondents and consequently are much easier to organize, implement, and process than a census. For most information, estimates of population characteristics derived from surveys are sufficiently accurate to result in surveys being frequently used to collect important information—including some of that used by governments for policy making and planning. This information can then be used to supplement census data. At times survey data are even used to cross check the reliability and/or validity of statistics derived from a census. Data obtained through each of the two different approaches are really required. A census is essential for governments because of the completeness with which the data cover a population. All areas throughout a country, all people, all kinds of households, and so on are included in a census, and hence detailed analyses can be undertaken in a way not possible with a sample survey. A survey does, however, offer a most proper alternative, especially because it is easier and cheaper to conduct. Data from a survey can be used to monitor, at least to some extent, changes in selected characteristics of a population between successive censuses.

5. The Method of Conducting a Census

The method of conducting a census varies depending on the kind of census it is. For a census of schools or even organizations in a given economic sector, a questionnaire seeking the relevant information would be sent to every school (organization, etc.) in a given system or area. Each institution would then supply the required data and return the questionnaire to the appropriate ministry or to a nominated regional office. Nonresponding institutions would be contacted and possibly assisted to complete the questionnaire. Checks could therefore be made to ensure every appropriate institution responded and did so within a reasonable time.

Population censuses have a variety of ways in which they might be conducted. In some situations, specially trained interviewers visit every person in a defined area

and ask the questions contained in the census form. The interviewer records each response as accurately as possible. This method introduces the necessity for the interviewer to interpret the respondent correctly—a requirement not necessarily met (Gibril 1979). In other situations a questionnaire is delivered to every place of residence by a government official who has been designated with the responsibility to collect the census data from all residences in a defined census tract. Such a tract might contain up to 100 residences. This official would deliver the questionnaire on the appropriate day and collect it a few days later. All questions in the census form could then be checked at the residence to ensure that all had been completed. If some questions had not been answered, the official could attempt to obtain the appropriate information either by interviewing the head of the household at that residence or by observation. In both of these approaches, it is necessary to develop procedures to ensure that every individual, no matter how remote in a country, is included in one but only one census form. Duplication and omission of individuals must be avoided. It is also important for the procedures to ensure that every completed census form is processed. Some errors of omission and double counting probably occur in every census despite the safeguards that are incorporated into the data collection and processing procedures. These errors would be particularly likely to occur in many developing countries and in areas of developed countries where there is a lack of appreciation of the purpose of the census and of the statistics to be produced. The impact these errors have on the final statistical distributions must be minimized. In most developed countries, the effects appear to be negligible.

6. The Construction of the Census Form

To maximize the levels of reliability and validity of the data collected, the census form must embody all of the basic principles for constructing good questionnaires and interview schedules. These principles need not be elaborated here beyond noting that all questions must be clearly worded, that all terms must be easily understood, and that the format should be simple to facilitate all sections being answered easily, especially by people who have almost no cause to complete questionnaires and/or forms during their everyday lives. These requirements alone pose sufficient problems for people having the responsibility of preparing for a census (Gibril 1979 pp. 32–48).

Only questions which are appropriate and easy for an individual to answer should be asked in a census. Thus three types of question must be avoided. One type covers questions which are too personal in nature. Information of this kind is not usually integral to a government's planning. Also, when it is essential to have that information, it can be collected more easily by using a sample survey. Questions an individual may find offensive must also be avoided.

A second type of question to be avoided is that seeking information not directly related to the individual who is responding. Questions of this kind might relate to other people, to attitudes, skills, and knowledge or to characteristics of a nonpersonal nature. For information of these kinds, data collected through a sample survey can be used to estimate the required statistics.

A third type of question to be avoided is that imposing a considerable effort on the part of the respondent. If complexities are involved or records need to be checked, an individual is likely to provide only an estimate of the quantity, to omit that question, or to refuse to participate at all. With many kinds of censuses, particularly those of schools or private organizations, records do often need to be checked before the required data can be provided. If these checks are too involved or extensive and beyond normal usage, a respondent might not bother to check completely and will simply enter estimates of the quantity being referenced in a question. For example, many a busy school principal, when required to complete a school census questionnaire on the last day of a school term, has had time only to guess how many students were enrolled in that school in various age, grade, and other categories. Busy officials in all spheres, when completing official census questionnaires, often take the view "if the numbers look approximately correct and the totals agree, that is sufficient". A view like this threatens the reliability and validity of the data collected but is, at least in part, a consequence of the imposition of considerable extra effort to answer a questionnaire of unknown or at least unappreciated purpose.

Obtaining valid and reliable data from individuals, even about matters concerning them personally, can be a very difficult task. Restricting questions only to those an individual can supposedly answer easily does not mean that no difficulties will be encountered. Personal age presents an example of the kinds of problems involved. It is a statistic collected in the censuses conducted in most, if not all, countries. In developed countries, common problems include:

(a) people giving their age to the nearest decade or 5 years, for example, 40 or 45 not 43;

(b) middle-aged people underestimating their age so as to appear younger, for example, 35 not 40;

(c) older people overestimating their age so as to appear even older, for example, 85 not 81.

Errors of these kinds show up very clearly when distributions of the number of people by age are prepared. Ta-Ngoc-Châu (1969 p. 21) is one source reporting an age distribution (in his study for Turkey) to highlight the errors resulting when individuals estimate their own ages.

In developing countries, the difficulties of reporting an individual's age are compounded partly through age not being an important personal statistic for many people. To estimate a respondent's age, it is sometimes necessary to relate date of birth to some known major (in the local context) historical event. Events of this kind include major floods, wars, and visits by important local

people. This historical calendar method can often provide reasonable estimates of an individual's age but, as the Gibril (1979) study shows, it needs to be implemented by properly trained interviewers.

Formats used for present-day population censuses have the advantage of being prepared on the basis of an understanding developed through considerable research effort. Consequently most population census forms provide excellent examples of good questionnaire preparation practice. Unfortunately school census forms do not generally rely on such research. They are often prepared by statistical officers or clerks with little appreciation of good questionnaire practice. Such forms sometimes lead to confusion when they are completed, with a subsequent lowering of the response rate and of the reliability and validity of the data collected.

A questionnaire for a census can be completed either for the household, institution, or organization as an entity by itself or for the individual within one of these settings. It is important to identify which is the more appropriate level of response for a particular census. The differences between the two possibilities in terms of type and orientation of questions, analyses, and kind of conclusions to be drawn about the population being reviewed are generally quite marked.

A government must decide in advance, therefore, what kind of information is required from a census, and for what purpose it will be used. Corresponding analyses performed on different levels of unit can provide significantly different implications (see *Units of Analysis*). With population censuses, the individual within the household is now normally used as the respondent level and this level has been used for quite some time. The United Kingdom census, for example, changed its emphasis from households and families to individuals in 1841. Data in population censuses in almost all countries and territories in the world now pertain to the individual. This orientation is despite the fact that census questionnaires are generally distributed to places of residence. Questions to be completed thus relate to individuals within each residence. With school censuses and certain industrial/commercial censuses, the level is the organizational unit rather than the individual within that unit. Hence, data are collected on the school and its characteristics. This restriction can mean that the interrelationships between certain variables might not be able to be estimated. The purpose for conducting a particular kind of census and the use envisaged for the results and analyses must therefore be determined precisely in advance. The appropriate response level can then be identified and the required distributions obtained.

In some situations, a special questionnaire would not have to be constructed before a census was conducted. This need would have been removed by the prior establishment of a data bank containing up-to-date information on every individual or institution (depending on requirements) in a nominated population. All essential data required for policy making, planning, research, and so on would then be routinely collected and simply updated once a basic record had been established. For example, many education systems presently have computer records on every student enrolled and every teacher employed in that system. To conduct a census for such a system, it is necessary only to prepare the required statistical tables from data pertaining to a nominated date. It is not necessary to approach either an individual or an institution for additional data. When a central data bank of this kind can be developed, the importance of censuses and the demands that accompany them diminish. It is of course imperative to evaluate whether a system of this kind is required and can be economically maintained given the use to which it would be put. For example, centrally operated data banks based on each individual in a nation's population would be difficult to maintain, would be a threat to individual privacy, and would be expensive to operate and to analyse.

7. Processing of the Census Data

Contained in the United Nations definition of a population census cited in Sect. 1, was the insistence that data collected in a census should be fully processed, published, and disseminated. Without these actions occurring, census data and the consequent statistics would not fulfil the purposes envisaged for them. Usually government departments charged with the responsibility of conducting a census prepare a publication containing basic cross-tabulations summarizing the main data, particularly those of general interest. No information is ever published or assessed on individuals nor are data published which may allow a particular person to be identified.

The task of census data processing usually entails the use of extensive computer facilities. Each questionnaire must be coded, the data entered into the appropriate record then checked before any processing can commence. With such a large quantity of data, errors do occur and attempts are made to eliminate them. Despite all efforts, errors can still be present in some records. Generally these errors in no way affect the distributions nor the interpretations of general social or economic conditions. They are, however, sometimes detectable. Coale and Stephan (1970), for example, examined the data from the 1950 Census of the United States population and "found a surprising number of widowed fourteen-year-old boys, and equally surprising, a decrease in the number of widowed teenage males at older ages...male divorcees also decrease in number as age increases from 1320 at age 14 to 575 at age 17" (1970 p. 426). The two researchers hypothesized that perhaps

these and certain other anomalies might be due to errors made in punching the data onto computer cards. "If occasionally cards were erroneously punched one column to the right, teenagers would appear to be males aged 40 to 80 years. Heads of households would be the source of erroneous white teenagers, while all other relationships to the head would produce erroneous non white teenagers. Persons aged 42 would be listed as widowed 14-year-olds, 52 as widowed 15-year-olds etc., while persons aged 43, 53, 63, 73, and 83 would be listed as 14-, 15-, 16-, 17-, and 18-year-old divorcees" (1970 p. 430). This study is one of the few examples reporting the kind of errors which can be made in processing census data and evaluating their effects. According to Coale and Stephan, at least for the 1950 United States census, the impact of errors introduced by processing is insignificant.

With some censuses, especially those of school systems, processing of questionnaires can be undertaken by regional, district, or state offices of the relevant ministry. Partly such decentralization can speed up the processing of returns because of the essentially simultaneous operations which then occur throughout a country. Another advantage is also gained however. It is that regional offices become more involved in the whole operation and hence develop vested interests to ensure high quality data and complete enumeration. The statistics collected are also better appreciated and likely to be used more widely in local planning and policy formation. After processing to some degree at least, regional census data can then be returned to the central office for preparation of the national aggregate. Unfortunately, this option of regional processing is presently used in few school systems despite the very considerable benefits it can confer.

Bibliography

Coale A J, Stephan F F 1970 The case of the Indians and the teenage widows. In: Tufte E R (ed.) 1970 *The Quantitative Analysis of Social Problems*. Addison-Wesley, Reading, Massachusetts, pp. 426–36

Gibril M A 1979 *Evaluating Census Response Errors: A Case Study for the Gambia*. Organisation for Economic Co-operation and Development (OECD), Paris

Stone R 1971 *Demographic Accounting and Model-building*. Organisation for Economic Co-operation and Development (OECD), Paris

Ta-Ngoc-Châu 1969 *Demographic Aspects of Educational Planning*. UNESCO, International Institute for Educational Planning, Paris

United Nations 1958 *Handbook of Population Census Methods*. United Nations, New York

Environmental Measures

K. M. Marjoribanks

Families and classrooms are two of the most significant learning environments that influence students' school

outcomes. In this article, methods that have been used in educational research to measure those two environments are examined. The methods have been classified as involving either an environmental press approach or an interpretive mode of investigation.

1. Environmental Press Approach

Perhaps the most influential theoretical framework for generating environmental press measures has been Murray's theory of personality. Murray (1938 p. 16) suggests that if the behaviour of individuals is to be understood then it is necessary to devise a method of analysis that "will lead to satisfactory dynamical formulations of external environments". He proposes that an environment should be defined by the kinds of benefits or harms that it provides. If the environment has a potentially harmful effect then Murray claims that individuals attempt to prevent the harmful occurrence by avoiding the context or by defending themselves against it. In contrast, if the environment has a potentially beneficial effect, then it is assumed that individuals will attempt to interact with it.

The directional tendency implied in Murray's framework is designated as the press of the environment. Each press is defined as having a qualitative aspect which is the kind of effect that the environment has or might have upon an individual. Each press also has a quantitative element, which is assessed by the variation in power that an environment has for either harming or benefiting different individuals or the same individual at different times. In his framework, Murray (1938 p. 122) distinguishes between the *alpha press* "which is the press that actually exists, as far as scientific discovery can determine it", and an environment's *beta press* "which is the subject's own interpretation of the phenomena that is perceived". Studies that have used measures to assess the press of family and classroom environments are considered in the following section.

1.1 The Press of Family Environments

It was not until Bloom (1964) and a number of his doctoral students examined the environmental correlates of children's affective and cognitive characteristics, that a school of research emerged to assess the alpha press of family environments. Bloom defined the environment as the conditions, forces, and external stimuli that impinge on individuals. It is proposed that these forces, which may be physical or social as well as intellectual, provide a network which surrounds, engulfs, and plays on the individual. As Bloom (1964 p. 187) suggests, "such a view of the environment reduces it for analytical purposes to those aspects of the environment which are related to a particular characteristic or set of characteristics". That is, the total context surrounding an individual may be defined as being composed of a number of subenvironments. If the development of a particular characteristic is to be understood, then it becomes necessary to identify that subenvironment of press variables which potentially is related to the characteristic.

In the initial subenvironment studies, Dave (1963) and Wolf (1964) examined relations between the family environment and measures of academic achievement and intelligence, respectively. Dave defined six press variables as constituting the family learning environment and they were labelled as achievement press, language models, academic guidance, activeness of the family, intellectuality in the home and work habits in the family. These variables were defined further by process characteristics such as parental aspirations for their children, the quality of parents' language use and the use of television and other media. A semistructured home interview schedule was designed to assess the variables and their associated process characteristics. Scores on the total environment measure were related to approximately 50 percent of the variance in arithmetic problem solving, reading, and the word knowledge performance of 11-year-olds. Wolf proposed that the intellectual environment of the home could be defined by three press variables that were categorized as press for achievement motivation, press for language development and provisions for general learning. When combined into a predictor set, the measures were associated with nearly 49 percent of the variation in children's intelligence test scores.

In a penetrating study of the press of family environments, Keeves (1972) collected data on Australian children when they were in the final year of elementary school and in their first year of secondary school. Family contexts were assessed by three dimensions that were categorized as structural, attitudinal and process. The structural dimension included variables such as sibsize, birth order, parents' occupation, education and income, parents' ages and linguistic background. In the attitude dimension there were measures of parents' attitudes towards their child's present education, their ambitions for the child's future education and occupation, and the parents' hopes and aspirations for themselves. Educational practices in the family such as the use of books and library facilities, provision of help with formal schoolwork, and arrangements made for undertaking home assignments were used to gauge the process dimension. The three dimensions had moderate to strong associations with mathematics and science achievement and low to modest concurrent validities with the children's attitudes to mathematics and science.

In a further example of the environmental press approach, Marjoribanks (1986) investigated the impact of family environments and individual characteristics at 11 years of age on the aspirations of 16-year-olds, in different social status groups. A typology devised by Merton (1968, 1976) was used to construct a family environment measure. The typology suggests that individual behaviour can be related to the goals that are set for individuals and to the means that are used to achieve those goals. In the environment measure, parents' goals for their children were assessed by questions such as: "How much education would you like your child to receive if at all possible?" and "What kind of job would you really like your child to have?" Procedures adopted by parents to support their aspirations were assessed by scales that measured parent–child learning interactions and the family press for independence. In the interaction scale there were items of the form: "When your child was small, how often did you read to her or him?" and "How often would you help your child now with reading?" Press for independence was measured by items in which parents indicated the age at which they would allow their child to undertake certain activities. Also included in the scale were statements similar to those used by Strodtbeck (1961) to measure independence of the family, such as: "Even when children get married their main loyalty still belongs to their family", and "When the time comes for children to take jobs, they should try and stay near their parents even if it means giving up good opportunities". Scores on the items for each dimension were factor analysed to generate factor scales that had reliability estimates greater than 0.75.

In the follow-up survey, a structured questionnaire consisting of 5-point items was used to gather information about the adolescents' perceptions of their parents' educational and occupational aspirations for them, the encouragement they had received from their parents in relation to schooling, and their parents' general interest in their education. From the responses, two scales were constructed and they were labelled as adolescents' perceptions of father support and mother support for learning. The findings from the investigation indicated that in different social status groups, adolescents' aspirations are influenced strongly by the interaction between ability, attitudes to school, and the situational variables of parents' early aspirations for their children and the adolescents' later perceptions of their parents' support.

These illustrative studies indicate that by defining family learning environments by proximal social-psychological dimensions, it is possible to measure potentially alterable variables that make significant unique contributions to variations in students' school outcomes. Bloom (1980 p. 16) claims that:

> If we are convinced that a good education is necessary for all who live in modern society, then we must search for the alterable variables which can make a difference in the learning of children...Our basic research task is to understand further how much alterable variables can be altered and their consequent effect on students, teachers and learning.

What is required now in educational research are investigations that define the alpha press with even more elegance and then relate those press variables to a more complex set of affective and cognitive characteristics. McCall (1983 p. 408) suggests, for example, that most of the family variables which have been investigated are "characteristics that distinguish the general environment of one family from another, and they might be expected to influence all children within a family to approximately the same extent. As a result they are called 'between-family environmental factors'."

He goes on to suggest, however, that while between-family environmental factors are influential, they are not the only kind of environmental circumstances and that within-family factors should be investigated. Such factors are those not typically shared by siblings and thus they tend to make them different from one another. The variables might include sibling interactions, birth order and spacing, differential treatment of siblings by parents, illness and separation, cohort differences and nonfamily effects specific to individual children. McCall (1983 p. 408) also suggests that

> One might add to this list, environmental events that impinge on all family members (e.g., relocation, divorce, neighbors, death of relatives) but they have different effects on individual members because of differences in their ages, personalities, genetic dispositions, and other factors.

It is proposed further that nonshared within-family influences may be of two types. First, there are those factors that exert a continuing influence over one child versus another. There may be, for example, differential patterns of consistent parental support for siblings in a family. Second, there are discontinuous nonshared within-family environmental factors such as moving into a new neighbourhood or the death of a sibling or another family member. As McCall (1983 p. 414) observes, to study such within-family factors we must "abandon our arm's length approach and get closer to our subjects and their families and friends".

In part, getting closer to families may be achieved by combining alpha and beta family measures in studies. There are now many investigations that have included students' perceptions of significant others in analyses of outcome measures. Increasingly, the studies have used adaptations of what has become labelled as the Wisconsin model of status attainment (e.g., Carpenter and Hayden 1985, Davis 1985, Natriello and McDill 1986). In the model, students' perceptions of parent, teacher, and peer group influences are typically included as mediating variables between social background measures and the students' aspirations and eventual educational and occupational attainment. Unfortunately, in much of the research, family influences are assessed by limited measures. Typically, parent effects are gauged by single items that require respondents to answer questions such as "How much encouragement have you received from your parents to stay at school, or to go on to university?"

In a review of such investigations, Campbell (1983 p. 53) claims that "there is a need to go into the sources of family effects more deeply". He proposes, for example, that "if one could show, by whatever means, that family background affects the aspiration formation process in terms of timing, clarity and focus, and the ways in which that occurs, he or she would make a significant contribution (Campbell 1983 p. 60; also see Alwin and Thornton 1984, Jencks et al. 1983, Schulenberg et al. 1984 for other criticisms of measurement in analyses using students' perceptions of family influences). In a later section of this article, studies that have used ethnographic approaches to examine family learning environments are reviewed.

1.2 The Press of School Environments

In a comprehensive review, Fraser (1986) provides an assessment of 20 years of research that has used perceptual measures to gauge the press of classroom and school learning environments. He suggests that classroom environment measures have typically been used:

> to assess student perceptions of what a classroom is actually like. But especially in more recent studies, classroom environment instruments have been used to assess (a) student perceptions of preferred environment, (b) teacher perceptions of actual environment, and (c) teacher perceptions of preferred environment. (Fraser 1986 p. 21)

In contrast to methods which rely on observers, the perceptual approach defines classroom environments by the shared perceptions of students and sometimes by teachers' perceptions. The schedules are often referred to as high inference measures, as opposed to low inference techniques that assess specific explicit phenomena such as the number of questions asked by students in a certain section of a lesson. It is suggested that perceptual measures of classroom and school environments have the advantages that they:

> are more economical than classroom observation techniques which involve the expense of trained outside observers...they are based on students' experiences over many lessons, while observational data usually are restricted to a very small number of lessons...they involve the pooled judgments of all students in a class, whereas observation techniques typically involve only a single observer...students' perceptions, because they are determinants of student behaviour more so than the real situation, can be more important than observed behaviours...perceptual measures of classroom environment typically have been found to account for considerably more variance in student learning outcomes than have directly observed variables. (Fraser 1986 p. 3)

Four of the most commonly used perceptual measures of classrooms are the Learning Environment Inventory (LEI) (Fraser et al. 1982), the Classroom Environment Scale (CES) (Moos 1979), the Individualized Classroom Environment Scale (ICEQ) (Fraser 1986), and the My Class Inventory (MCI) (Fraser et al. 1982).

The Learning Environment Inventory, for example, consists of 15 scales that are labelled as cohesiveness, diversity, formality, speed, environment, friction, goal direction, favouritism, cliqueness, satisfaction, disorganization, difficulty, apathy, democraticness and competitiveness. Each scale is assessed by seven Likert-type items. Typical items are "All students know each other very well" (cohesiveness), "Certain students in this class are responsible for petty quarrels" (friction), "Students do not have to hurry to finish their work" (speed), and "The class is well organized and efficient" (disorganization). The MCI is a simplification of the LEI, designed for children between 8 and 12 years of age. It differs, however, from the LEI in a number of ways. First, to minimize fatigue among younger children it contains only five of the original LEI scales (cohesiveness, friction, satisfaction, difficulty and competitiveness). Also, item wording has been simplified and the LEI's 4-point response format has been reduced to a Yes–No answer choice.

The Classroom Environment Scale assesses three general categories that are labelled as the relationship dimension, the personal development dimension, and the system maintenance and system change dimension. In the latest version of the schedule there are nine scales, each with 10 items using True–False responses. It has been designed to measure the actual (or real) classroom environment and the preferred (or ideal) environment. Fraser suggests, however, that:

> despite the wide application and proven usefulness of the LEI and CES, these instruments exclude some of the aspects of classroom environment which are particularly relevant in classroom settings commonly referred to as individualized, open or inquiry-based. Consequently, the ICEQ was developed to measure those dimensions which differentiate conventional classrooms from individualized ones involving either open or inquiry-based approaches. (Fraser 1986 p. 27)

In the ICEQ there are 50 items that are assessed by 5-point scales. It has four separate forms which assess, respectively, student perceptions of actual environment, student perceptions of preferred environment, teacher perceptions of actual environment, and teacher perceptions of preferred environment.

From an analysis of research findings from studies that have used such perceptual measures, Walberg (1985 p. 754) concludes that:

> student perceptions of the social environment of learning accounted for a median of 30 percent (range = 13 percent to 46 percent; all significant) of the variance in cognitive, affective, and behavioral postcourse measures beyond that accounted for by parallel precourse measures. Efforts at generalizing these results suggest consistency across different school subjects and different languages and cultures (also see Haertel et al. 1981 for a meta-analysis of classroom perception studies).

Many educators will argue that classrooms and schools need to be examined with a greater sensitivity than can be generated from perception schedules. Researchers using such perceptual scales, however, generally suggest that the measures provide a portrayal of learning environments that may be enhanced by adopting other investigative methodologies. In the following section of the article, interpretative models of investigating classrooms are examined.

2. Interpretative Models of Investigation

Increasingly, in family and classroom environment research, concepts and methodologies are being adopted from a number of theoretical orientations such as social phenomenology, cognitive sociology, ethnomethodology, symbolic interactionism, dramaturgical sociology, and ethogenic theories of human behaviour. Although there are significant conceptual differences in the orientations, Bernstein (1977) suggests that they share common features such as an opposition to structural functionalism, a view of individuals as creators of meanings, a focus on the assumptions underlying social order together with the treatment of social categories as themselves problematic, a distrust of quantification and the use of objective categories, and a focus on the transmission and acquisition of interpretative procedures.

In learning environment research these interpretative perspectives have emphasized the need to investigate the processes by which individual members of families and classrooms define and manage their everyday lives. Studies typically adopt variations of ethnographic methods to obtain accounts of why students perform certain acts and what social meanings they give to the actions of themselves and of others. Taft suggests that one of the main advantages of the ethnographic approach is that:

> ...in the course of becoming involved in the group, the investigator becomes acculturated to it. This means that he or she develops personal knowledge about the rules of the group and begins to perceive the same meanings in events as do the members of the group. The investigator learns what behaviour is expected when, where, and in response to what situations. (Taft 1985 p. 1731)

Fensham et al. (1986), for example, used case study techniques to investigate alienation in three high schools. In relation to family–school influences it is suggested of one of the schools, that:

> Another aspect of home background was that (as always) the staff as a whole lacked knowledge of what went on in the homes in general, and the lives of individual pupils in particular. This is the inevitable result of teaching being a middle-class profession, but is accentuated by teachers living outside the area in which they teach. This lack of knowledge makes it difficult for teachers either to relate school knowledge to their pupils' out-of-school experience, or to understand pupils' problems, academic and social. (Tripp 1986 p. 141)

In another investigation using case study techniques, Hatton (1985) examined the relations between parental control and teaching practices within an elementary school that was in an established and prestigious suburb of an Australian city. From interviews with teachers, Hatton concludes that their autonomy was limited by the power of parents.

Although such interpretative studies have provided fresh insights into students' learning contexts, Rist (1980) has been critical of much ethnographic research. He claims that:

> Ethnography is becoming a mantle to legitimate much work that is shoddy, poorly conducted, and ill-conceived. And when such work is questioned, the response is to turn to the terminology for defence. The logic of the method becomes inverted. Rather than make the uncommon and unknown comprehendible, the defense becomes one of privatizing what ought to have been open to scrutiny. (Rist 1980 p. 8)

Rist is extremely critical of "qualitative researchers" who adopt "hit-and-run" forays rather than spending considerable time in schools or families. He proposes that:

> Just as educational research has accrued some heavy costs from an overreliance on quantitative methods when they

were inappropriate and unable to answer the questions at hand, so also qualitative research faces growing costs. The more the reliance on the method as an end in itself, the less it is a meaningful research tool. (Rist 1980 p. 9)

Hammersley (1985) suggests that although the interpretative approach has provided a sensitive awareness of some previously underestimated problems in educational research, its orientation has been primarily descriptive. Karabel and Halsey (1977) express a further concern of interpretative studies of learning environments. They suggest, for example, that while:

> stress on the fact that relations in educational institutions are humanly constructed products is a welcome antidote to the deterministic and reifying tendencies of some of the "old" sociology of education ...emphasis on "man the creator" often fails to take adequate account of the social constraints on human actors in every day life. There is, to be sure, a considerable latitude available to those engaged in struggles over the "definition of the situation", but the question of whose definition will ultimately prevail is preeminently one of power. Battles between students and teachers as to who will define the situation, for example, clearly illustrate this point...there is, without doubt, an important element of creativity in student–teacher interaction; but there are also limits to the extent to which "definitions of the situation" may be negotiated. (Karabel and Halsey 1977 p. 58)

They propose further that "if empirical work is confined to observation of classroom interaction, it may miss the process by which political and economic power sets sharp bounds to what is negotiable" (Karabel and Halsey 1977 p. 58).

Similar conceptual concerns are expressed by Scott-Jones (1984) who observes, for example, that the contexts in which parents and children live are important in understanding the family's influence on children's school outcomes. It is suggested that the family is an important context but that it is embedded in other contexts. She claims that there is a need to study "children who develop normally or excel under conditions such as low-income status. The family may be able to cope with adverse conditions in a manner that prevents the expected effects on the child". (Scott-Jones 1984 p. 262)

This would mean that for a more refined analysis of families and schools, ethnographic studies of families and schools need to be complemented by measures of the social constraints that surround parents and their children.

3. Some Future Research Orientations

If learning environment research is to advance significantly then measures adopted in the environmental press approach and the interpretative model of analysis need perhaps to be brought together. Studies are required that analyse with greater discrimination the interactions within families and classrooms, and the relations of those interactions to the position of students' learning contexts in different social settings. As well as examining between-context variation, more attention needs to be directed at differences that operate within families and classrooms. By using such a combination of alpha press measures and ethnographic environment studies we may generate a more complete understanding of the relations between students' learning contexts and their outcomes, and hopefully develop a more appropriate social theory of children's learning outcomes.

Bibliography

Alwin D F, Thornton A 1984 Family origins and the schooling process: Early versus late influences of parental characteristics. *Am. Sociol. Rev.* 49: 784-802

Bernstein B B 1977 *Class, Codes and Control*, 2nd edn. Vol. 3: *Towards a Theory of Educational Transmissions*. Routledge and Kegan Paul, London

Bloom B S 1964 *Stability and Change in Human Characteristics*. Wiley, New York

Bloom B S 1980 The new directions in educational research: Alterable variables. In: Sloane K D, O'Brien M L (eds.) 1980 *The State of Research on Selected Alterable Variables in Education*. Department of Education, University of Chicago, Chicago, Illinois

Campbell R T 1983 Status attainment research: End of the beginning or beginning of the end? *Sociol. Educ.* 56: 47-62

Carpenter P G, Hayden M 1985 Academic achievement among Australian youth. *Aust. J. Educ.* 29: 199-220

Dave R 1963 The identification and measurement of home environmental process variables related to educational achievement. Unpublished doctoral dissertation, University of Chicago, Chicago, Illinois

Davis R A 1985 Social Structure, belief, attitude, intention and behaviour: A partial test of Liska's revisions. *Soc. Psychol. Q.* 48: 89-93

Fensham P, Power C, Tripp D, Kemmis S 1986 *Alienation from Schooling*. Routledge and Kegan Paul, London

Fraser B J 1986 *Classroom Environment*. Croom Helm, London

Fraser B J, Anderson G J, Walberg H J 1982 *Assessment of Learning Environments: Manual for Learning Environment Inventory (LEI) and My Class Inventory (MCI), (third version)* Western Australian Institute of Technology, Perth, Western Australia

Haertel G D, Walberg H J, Haertel E H 1981 Socio-psychological environments and learning: A quantitative synthesis. *Br. Educ. Res. J.* 7: 27-36

Hammersley M 1985 From ethnography to theory: A programme and paradigm in the sociology of education. *Sociology* 19: 244-59

Hatton E J 1985 Equality, class and power: A case study. *Br. J. Sociol. Educ.* 6: 255-72

Jencks C, Crouse J, Mueser P 1983 The Wisconsin model of status attainment: A national replication with improved measures of ability and aspiration. *Sociol. Educ.* 56: 3-19

Karabel J, Halsey A H (eds.) 1977 *Power and Ideology in Education*. Oxford University Press, New York

Keeves J P 1972 *Educational Environment and Student Achievement*. Australian Council for Educational Research, Hawthorn, Victoria

Marjoribanks K 1986 A longitudinal study of adolescents' aspirations as assessed by Seginer's model. *Merrill-Palmer Q.* 32: 211-30

McCall R B 1983 Environmental effects on intelligence: The forgotten realm of discontinuous nonshared within-family factors. *Child Dev.* 54: 408-15

Merton R K 1968 *Social Theory and Social Structure*. Free Press, New York

Merton R K 1976 *Sociological Ambivalence and Other Essays*. Free Press, New York

Moos R H 1979 *Evaluating Educational Environments*. Jossey-Bass, San Francisco, California

Murray H 1938 *Explorations in Personality*. Oxford University Press, Oxford

Natriello G, McDill E L 1986 Performance standards, student effort on homework, and academic achievement. *Sociol. Educ.* 59: 18-31

Rist R C 1980 Blitzkrieg ethnography: On the transformation of a method into a movement. *Educ. Res.* 9(2): 8-10

Schulenberg J E, Vondracek F W, Crouter A C 1984 The influence of the family on vocational development. *J. Marriage Fam.* 46: 129-43

Scott-Jones D 1984 Family influences on cognitive development and school achievement. In: Gordon E W (ed.) 1984 *Review of Research in Education*. American Educational Research Association, Washington, pp. 259-304

Strodtbeck F L 1961 Family integration, values and achievement. In: Halsey A H, Floud J, Anderson C A (eds.) 1961 *Education, Economy and Society*. Free Press, New York, pp. 315-47

Taft R 1985 Ethnographic research methods. In: Husén T, Postlethwaite T N (eds.) 1985 *The International Encyclopedia of Education*. Pergamon, Oxford, Vol. 3, pp. 1729-33

Tripp D H 1986 Greenfield: A case study of schooling, alienation and employment. In: Fensham et al. (1986), p. 141

Walberg H J 1985 Classroom psychological environment. In: Husén T, Postlethwaite T N (eds.) 1985 *The International Encyclopedia of Education*. Pergamon, Oxford, Vol. 2, pp. 750-55

Wolf R M 1964 The identification and measurement of home environmental process variables that are related to intelligence. Unpublished doctoral dissertation, University of Chicago, Chicago, Illinois

Educational Indicators

J. N. Johnstone

In the context of research in education, an indicator can be described as being the way in which a basic unit in a proposition, description, or schema can be operationalized for empirical purposes. For example, if a researcher wishes to test a proposition of the form "If A then B", the basic units A and B must be defined in such a way as to facilitate the production of values for those units from some measurement operation. An indicator does just this. It describes what is intended by the entities or characteristics A and B and, as a consequence of that definition, establishes both procedures for determining how values for A and B will be formed and criteria for interpreting those values. Particular features of an indicator implied in this definition are elucidated and discussed in the next section.

Despite the somewhat antithetical views held, especially by researchers of a scientific or a symbolic interactionist philosophy, the discipline of educational research must develop a language with which to discuss the phenomena of direct concern to education. Like natural phenomena, education characteristics can be diffuse. Hence any language developed for or leading towards educational theory in any area must be flexible and encompass overall or general descriptions to accommodate the diffuseness. Through such flexibility, the scientific usefulness of the "educational language" developed is enhanced. An indicator as described could therefore be regarded in some ways as being a research tool having some degree of acceptance by researchers holding any one of a variety of research convictions. The nature of an indicator admittedly embodies elements of the scientific approach. It explicitly acknowledges also the diversity of characteristics which can exist within any single concept or unit. By attempting to combine diverse aspects or at least to account for the separate dimensions underlying a concept or unit, an indicator develops a degree of generalizability, allowing researchers holding other convictions to use it as a sensitizing agent.

Indicators are used in all kinds of educational research. Researchers interested in psychology, sociology, policy analysis and development—to list just a few areas—can all have recourse to indicators. One unfortunate aspect of indicator use has, however, been confusion over what the term "indicator" really represents. During the 1970s, it became fashionable to relabel almost any observation as being an indicator. The confusion arising from this labelling of different types of measurements as indicators has now begun to impede proper developments in the indicator field. Some views of what is regarded as an indicator are now outlined.

1. Concepts of Indicators

In the educational research literature, the term indicator has at least four different connotations. Although these differences cannot be resolved simply, a description of each of these uses might at least clarify some of the issues and misinterpretations surrounding the term.

One connotation of indicator is inseparable from that for variable. It implies an indicator is something observable or measurable. Each observation or degree of the characteristic being considered can be classified into one of a number of mutually exclusive categories. Under this view, the terms indicator, variable, and statistic are interdependent. Such a view as this is held by researchers who take a global view of classes of objects. Such people perhaps focus more on the methods of analysis than on the kind of entity to be analysed. To some extent at least, such a view can be quite proper. It does, however, fail to differentiate among degrees of generalizability or specificity of a measurement. Certainly a number of researchers adhere to this view. Jaeger (1978)

is one such person. He admits that a very large literature has been published about indicators and that "perhaps because of it, indicators are not clearly distinguished from statistics" (1978 p. 276). Indeed, after reviewing a number of the main definitions of social indicators, Jaeger concludes that opinions "of what an indicator is are anything but clear and consistent...perhaps some variables should be termed indicators while others should not—for if all variables were called indicators, there would be no need for an additional term" (1978 p. 285). Jaeger is correct in asserting that the term indicator should have a different connotation to that of a variable or a statistic. Such a required difference thus implies that this first view of an indicator as being synonymous with a variable must be regarded as being too wide.

The second connotation of an indicator is that it is a quantity measuring or estimating the level of a single characteristic of a population but in such a way as to remove the effect of the potential of the population to contribute directly to the value calculated. Generally this objective can be achieved simply by ratioing the quantity measured to the total people, time, money, and so on, which could have contributed to the observation. This view of an indicator is perhaps the most common of all four views. It underlines, for example, the whole of the social indicators movement (Sheldon 1975). A typical example of a measurement classified as a (simple ratio) indicator under this view is "higher education enrolments per 10,000 population". Here the characteristic being measured is higher education enrolments. If only the enrolment figure is reported, however, populous countries would (almost automatically) have higher values than less populous countries. The division by population value and the subsequent multiplication to a scale of 10,000 removes any influence on the value due to the population size of a country. The variable of higher education enrolments is thus transformed into an indicator. Other examples of simple ratio indicators are the pupil–teacher ratio, percentage of a community who are of a given ethnic or racial origin, and the difficulty index of a test item.

This view of an indicator is widely accepted. Most of the measurements termed social indicators are of this kind. Documents like *Toward a Social Report* (US Department of Health, Education and Welfare 1969) base their discussion on such ratio measures. International agencies often publish tables whose title includes the term indicator to imply this type of approach to measurement (see, for example, World Bank 1981). Arithmetic averages are another form embodying this view of an indicator. So, for example, average achievement score for a group, average satisfaction level for a class or faculty, and average expenditure on books can be regarded as being simple ratio indicators. Measurements made especially in classroom interaction or special education studies of the number or proportion of specified behaviours manifest per time period can also be classified under this review. Examples of these measurements are the number of questions per minute and the percentage of total observed time spent in initiation behaviour.

Such measures can be properly termed indicators although they are only slightly more general than the term variable. They can be so classified because they possess two of the essential qualities of an indicator: they relate to a definable population and their values do not depend on the size of the contexts of their measurement. They do not, however, possess another vital quality of proper indicators—that of proffering general rather than specific comment.

The third connotation of the term indicator extends the second by demanding that an indicator makes a general or global comment about a characteristic of a population in addition to having the property of providing a value which is independent of the size of the population being measured. This requirement of generality is also implied in the entries for indicator in the main dictionaries. Webster's, for example, defines the word as "something which points out or points to with more or less exactness".

The contrast between requiring an indicator to make a global comment and the specificity of comment imbedded in both of the first two connotations is reflected in a comment allegedly made by President Franklin D. Roosevelt. In the second draft of his second inaugural address, many specific comments were made about the number of million people who earned so much, the number of million who were unemployed, or who were housed in quarters of various conditions, and so on. Roosevelt then wrote onto the draft his summary of all of these statistics—"I see one third of a nation ill-housed, ill-clad, and ill-nourished" (cited by Cohen 1975 p. 59).

What Roosevelt did was precisely what an indicator is intended to do—summarize a large amount of data in a succinct way so as to form a general, overall comment. Indeed, an indicator might combine 10 or more variables to provide its comment. Certainly such a summary is not as precise as the specific description provided by each component variable of an indicator. The summary conveyed by an indicator—and by Roosevelt's comment—does, however, convey the essence of what an overall situation is like.

The demand that indicators have this property of generality of comment is not commonly voiced in the literature. Land (1975) and Johnstone (1981) are two of the few researchers who require it as a property. If indicators are not required to make general comment, they can become indistinguishable from variables especially in the way they are referenced. Jaeger's view as cited earlier then becomes more valid.

The fourth connotation of the term indicator which is occasionally encountered in the research literature is in the sense of a "dummy variable". Here a nonordinal characteristic is described in terms of one of two categories. Each category is answerable as "yes" or "no" depending on whether the characteristic is or is not possessed. Treatment group, nationality, and occupation are typical characteristics which can be categorized into

dummy variables. Such a procedure is common in educational research especially when regression analysis techniques are being applied. Researchers using this connotation refer to indicator variables. In terms of the above discussion, such a description complicates the establishment of a valid concept for the term indicator. The term dummy variable is, however, more common and better understood than the term indicator variable. For this reason, this relatively infrequent use of the term indicator is not analysed further here in terms of its features and possible properties.

In summary, only the second and the third of the above connotations of the term indicator are correct and acceptable although really these two uses are very closely related. Both require an indicator to be a composite of at least two variables and to remove the potential of the size of an entity to affect the value calculated. Both require an indicator value to refer—either directly or indirectly—to the characteristic of a population. The distinction between the two acceptable connotations lies in the degree of generality of comment demanded of the measurement. When possible, an indicator should make a general rather than a specific comment and the best way to do this from a measurement viewpoint is to combine a number of variables. In the remainder of this article, discussion is confined to only these two kinds of composite indicators.

2. Methods of Indicator Formation

There are many mathematical models with which indicator values may be calculated. As with all research and planning analyses however, the choice of the appropriate model depends on the purpose for which an indicator is to be used. For the simple ratio indicator, no major problem exists as to choice of model. Two variables are combined through the process of arithmetic division. The only safeguard needing to be observed concerns the quantities measured by the two variables being combined. Although the two variables could—and often do—measure quite different kinds of quantities (e.g., area and people or money and people, etc.), they must be chosen so that they have a logical and educationally meaningful relationship. A commonly used social indicator, for example, is the "number of telephones per 10,000 population". These two quantities are logically and meaningfully interrelated because telephones are distributed throughout a population both inside and outside homes. Such an indicator does therefore measure one aspect of the communication network in a population.

Not all quantities which might be combined are so logically and meaningfully interrelated. One such indicator, occasionally referenced in the social development literature is "enrolments in primary education per 10,000 population". With this indicator, the two component variables—primary level enrolment and population—are not meaningfully interrelated. Not all members of a population are really able to enrol in primary schools. Hence differences in the age structure of a population can alone create differences in the value computed for an indicator like this. A much more preferable indicator (net enrolment ratio) would limit the totals in both the numerator and denominator of the model to those children of an age equivalent to the formal limits of the primary school in a given country. In a different context the indicator "average number of questions asked by a young child per day" has a similar weakness. It does not allow for variations between young children, for example, in their sleeping patterns. A more appropriate indicator of inquisitiveness might be "average number of questions per hour the child is awake".

To model the composite form of an indicator, one of two ways can be used to combine a defined set of variables or measurements across separate entities. Either it can be done empirically or it can be done theoretically and literally. Which of these two approaches is adopted to form a particular indicator depends on the context of its development and, as noted previously, the purpose intended.

An empirical approach is where an indicator uses some kind of analytical process to define a unit. The most common form of such analysis is factor analysis. With this method, a defined set of variables measured across a sample of people, groups, countries, and so on, is analysed so that the basic characteristics underlying that set are identified. These characteristics, which can be generalized to a population, then become the indicators. Scores can be calculated for each member of the sample for each indicator. Typical studies explicitly forming education indicators through factor analysis are Brandis (1970) in the field of educational sociology and Johnstone (1977) in comparative education. This approach to indicator formation depends very heavily both on the sample from which the observations derived and on the variables included. To be strictly correct, empirically defined indicators should only be used in the context in which they are formed. In practice, however, they are often generalized to situations similar to that originally analysed. Mostly this extension is quite appropriate. The indicator formed by Brandis, for example, can be easily generalized and one way to do this is demonstrated in the study. Other methods of empirically forming indicators include Guttman scale analysis and hierarchical cluster analysis. Both of these techniques are less commonly applied than factor analysis and are not elaborated here.

A theoretical or literal approach is a more usual procedure for defining composite indicators in educational research. The essence of this method of formation is that the researcher nominates those variables considered to be most appropriate to the description of the unit being considered and, as well, selects a method of combination for those variables. This literal approach to definition is thus a translation made by the researcher from the unit of concern used in a postulate or statement to the indicator on which values are to be calculated. Perhaps this translation might be viewed as pure

operationism of the style of Bridgman (1927). It certainly implies—as both Bridgman and especially his disciples advocated—that the only legitimate scientific models are those in which the units can be operationalized. This view is perhaps too extreme but, as the present article is not the appropriate place to explore this view of the philosophy of scientific measurement, the issues cannot be pursued further here.

In selecting variables for combination, a researcher must attempt to ensure that each aspect defined as being part of the general characteristic being measured is included in the proportion in which it is contained in the characteristic. It is inappropriate for example, to define an indicator only through those aspects which are easy to measure and to ignore aspects which are difficult. If only the easy aspects are included, a bias is built into the value for the indicator and this could result in incorrect representations—and thus interpretations—of the characteristic being studied.

In selecting a method of combination for the selected variables, a researcher can select from one of three general models. These models are the additive model, the multiplicative model, and the formula model, using existing formulas.

The additive model simply requires that values for the selected variables be combined according to the following equation:

$$I = a_1 V_1 + a_2 V_2 + a_3 V_3 + \cdots + a_n V_n \tag{1}$$

where I is the indicator for nominated unit or characteristic; V_i is the ith component variable defined to represent one aspect of the characteristic; a_i is the defined weight for variable V_i; and n is the number of variables covering defined characteristic.

When comparability in value across a number of indicators is required, an average can be calculated by dividing the value resulting from Eqn. (1) by the number of component variables (n). Such an additive model assumes that variations in one variable can be counterbalanced either: (a) by equal variations in another variable, or, (b) by adding to or subtracting from another variable an amount equal to a_i/a_j (where a_i is the weight of the variable which changed in value and a_j is the weight of the counterbalancing variable).

In educational research, particularly in analyses of questionnaire, survey, and test data, this assumption is often justifiable. In other education contexts—for example some system characteristics measured in comparative education studies—the assumption is not valid and an alternative model must be used. Naturally in any additive model, the weights (a_i) would have to reflect not only the desired relativities in the importance of the component variables (V_i) but they would also have to account for variations in the variability in values for each variable across the entities being measured. For example, if indicator I was to measure the general ability of an individual and the component variables (V_i) were test results in specific areas, all those test results would require equal standard deviations (or at least be standardized so as to be equal) before the desired weights (a_i) were applied.

The multiplicative model requires that values for the selected variables be combined according to the equation:

$$I = a_1 V_1 \cdot a_2 V_2 \cdot a_3 V_3 \cdots a_n V_n \tag{2}$$

where the symbols are as before. Again an average can be calculated to make values for different indicators comparable by taking the nth root of the value estimated by Eqn. (2). Using the multiplicative model, simple differences (even weighted) between variables do not compensate to produce the same value. Instead a corresponding proportional increase in a variable must occur to counteract a lower value and this is generally much more difficult to record than a simple additive change. For example, if, for one individual, two ratings of ability are given as 4 (very good) and 2 (satisfactory), and for another individual, both ratings are 3 (good), then the first individual has a (multiplicative) indicator value of 8 while the second has 9. Under an additive model, both individuals would be equal with an indicator value of 6.

In educational research studies, many situations really require a multiplicative model to be used to calculate a composite indicator value. Unfortunately, as the additive model is very much better known, it is the one used with the consequence that there is generally a reduction in the total variance analysed and a consequent reduction in the significance of results.

The third model for combining selected variables to compute values for an indicator uses one of a number of existing formulas. Such formulas as are intended are available to suit many purposes. For educational research purposes, four common measurements relate to inequality, cost changes, degrees of concentration, and implications of varying promotion and repetition rates. Details of specific formulas appropriate to these and other purposes are available elsewhere (e.g., Johnstone 1981) and hence need not be restated here in detail. An example must suffice to demonstrate the principle of using existing formulas where possible to compute indicator values.

Researchers often encounter situations in which it is desirable to measure the degree of inequitable provision or possession of a property. Sociologists, for example, often need to measure differences in particular features across social classes or between males and females; economists wish to measure income distribution across defined subgroups in a population; educational planners wish to measure effects of schooling across population subgroups and the distribution of education participation rates across regions. For all of these purposes, a variety of formulas are available including, in particular, the coefficient of variation and the Gini coefficient. The former has been used by sociologists like Jencks et al. (1972) to demonstrate the degree of inequality amongst different groups of American society (e.g., males and females, blacks and whites, etc.) in variables such as income, test scores, and the number of years of schooling. The latter formula has been used by planners like Alker (1965) and Bezeau (1979) to assess respectively how the distributions of enrolments across schools and per pupil expenditures reveal inequalities in education provision.

There are many formulas which can be used to estimate indicator values measuring problems and features of concern to educational researchers. For any given purpose, a researcher must select from the available formulas and apply the chosen indicator to the nominated problem.

3. Advantages of Indicator Use

Although many specific advantages have been claimed for the use of indicators, perhaps the single greatest advantage of the composite or aggregative kind of indicator is that a more general comment can be made about an entity. Such a comment avoids the specificity of detail which can accompany a description provided by the use of a number of single variables. For example, in the Alker study cited above, 10 variables would need to have been interpreted and their interrelationships inferred. As an indicator, the Gini coefficient used by Alker makes a general comment through its single value about the overall level of equality of enrolment. The generality conferred by an indicator conveys a clearer concept as to the status of what is being measured.

A second advantage of using indicators is that the reliability and validity with which a concept is measured can mostly be maintained at a high level. When a concept is defined in an educational research study, it is normally shown to involve a number of separate aspects. The concept of satisfaction with the operation of an institution, for example, might be disaggregated into such diverse aspects as satisfaction with each of the formal communication methods, the frequency of staff meetings, the balance between administrators and professional staff, and the degree of involvement in decision making. Because of these very diverse aspects, any attempt to measure the concept with just a single measurement of one aspect must result in both low reliability due to the dilemma in which a respondent would be placed and low construct validity due to an insufficient mapping of the defined domain. If each aspect of a concept is entered into analyses separately, the original concept is destroyed even though the separate measures may individually have high reliability and validity. However the use of a composite indicator, through the combination of all the component aspects into a single value, preserves the concept itself and as well retains the high levels of reliability and validity of the components. In so many applications in education, whether they be in planning, policy formation, research, or some other area, the use of general concepts is both common and important. The potential for indicator development is thus very large.

One advantage which is claimed for indicators by some of their proponents is that indicators can make normative comment on a concept. This alleged advantage is not considered to be either true or appropriate. Indicators should only be developed in such a way as to make a neutral comment on that which is being measured. It is then left to the interpreter to conclude what the measurement is showing about a particular situation. An interpretation would, of course, have to be made in relation to the particular objectives stated for that characteristic and entity being measured. An example demonstrates this assertion. The degree of decentralization of decision making in a single school or in an entire national education system could be measured in a most basic way on a three point scale from 1 = centralized, to 3 = decentralized. Some educationalists might interpret a rating of 1 to be very good while others would seek a situation with a rating of 3. Such differences in opinions are most proper because they reflect the objectives of the individuals concerned. There is nothing inherent in the value of the (simple) indicator of decentralization which per se comments on a desirable or undesirable situation.

4. Problems of Indicator Use

Despite the distinct advantages, particularly of operationalization and measurement, which are conferred on a research study by using properly developed indicators, three major problems are associated with indicator use in educational research projects.

A first problem is that confusion surrounds the use of the term indicators. This problem has already been described in Sect. 1. Some researchers use the term loosely with the consequence that their results have specificity rather than the intended generalizability to a broad concept.

A second problem is that there can be a high degree of interchangeability among indicators. This degree needs to be identified or assessed so that uniqueness of operationalization is not claimed unnecessarily. It may be, for example, that two indicators are defined so that each measures a different general characteristic. On computing values for each indicator across a group of individuals, classrooms, schools, and so on, the correlation between the two indicators might be estimated to be 0.9. Such a high degree of interrelationship indicates either that the two alleged definitions are really measuring only slightly different aspects of the same trait or that both characteristics are so heavily influenced by a third or underlying characteristic that it might be better to abandon both definitions and identify the third. Whatever the situation, when two or more indicators are identified as having a high degree of interchangeability, there is little point in continuing to use both.

A final major problem with indicator usage in educational research is that the method of construction must reflect the intended manner of interpretation. The essential aspect of this problem is demonstrated by the proposition that indicator values based on means and standard deviations can almost never be interpreted in a way that comments on education standards. Specifically, with the interpretation of test scores, there can be norm-referenced, criterion-referenced, and self-referenced measurements. Although a high value based on a computing formula incorporating means and standard deviations might be interpretable as reflecting an acceptable level of performance (e.g., above some defined criterion value), this does not necessarily follow in all situations. For example, an indicator of general teacher behaviour might be computed by combining standardized scores of the degree of questioning, explaining, reacting, and structuring. A high value on such an indicator does not, however, identify a teacher as being good (if that would be the interpretation). Instead it reflects that the teacher has demonstrated a greater number of those four behaviours than other teachers who have been observed. In contrast, an indicator such as the Gini coefficient (where it can be calculated) can be interpreted in any of the three possible ways. Researchers must therefore be particularly careful in their interpretations to avoid any possible confusion, especially between the norm-referenced and the criterion-referenced alternatives.

Bibliography

Alker H R 1965 *Mathematics and Politics*. Macmillan, New York

Bezeau L M 1979 Measures of inequality of per pupil expenditure: Application to Ontario. *J. Educ. Fin.* 5: 133–48

Brandis W 1970 An index of social class. In: Brandis W, Henderson D (eds.) 1970 *Social Class, Language, and Communication*. Routledge and Kegan Paul, London

Bridgman P W 1927 *The Logic of Modern Physics*. Macmillan, New York

Cohen W J 1975 Educational indicators and social policy. *Educational Indicators: Monitoring the State of Education*, Proceedings of the 1975 ETS Invitational Conference. Educational Testing Service, Princeton, New Jersey

Jaeger R M 1978 About educational indicators: Statistics on the conditions and trends in education. In: Shulman L S (ed.) 1978 *Review of Research in Education 1978*. Peacock, Itasca, Illinois

Jencks C, Smith M, Acland H, Bane M J, Cohen D, Gintis H, Heyns B, Michelson H 1972 *Inequality: A Reassessment of the Effectiveness of Family and Schooling in America*. Basic Books, New York

Johnstone J N 1977 Dimensions of educational systems. *Comp. Educ. Rev.* 21: 51–68

Johnstone J N 1981 *Indicators of Education Systems*. Kogan Page, London

Land K C 1975 Theories, models and indicators of social change. *Int. Soc. Sci. J.* 27: 7–37

Sheldon E B 1975 The social indicators movement in ETS. *Educational Indicators: Monitoring the State of Education*, Proceedings of the 36th ETS Invitational Conference, New York, Nov. 1, 1975. Educational Testing Service, Princeton, New Jersey, pp. 3–10

United States Department of Health, Education and Welfare 1969 *Toward a Social Report*. United States Government Printing Office, Washington, DC

World Bank 1981 *World Development Report*. World Bank, Washington, DC

Interviews in Sample Surveys

P. V. Miller and C. F. Cannell

A sample survey is a measurement technique. It consists of a set of interrelated components, each of which is important for the achievement of measurement objectives, and includes conceptualization of the research problem, sample design, questionnaire construction, interviewing, coding, data processing, and analysis. Random and nonrandom errors can intrude on the measurement process at any of these stages. This article focuses on procedures for reducing error in two important survey phases—questionnaire construction and interviewing.

The fact that much is learnt in everyday life by asking people questions leads to the conclusion that framing questions and asking them in surveys are simple tasks. Certainly, the gift of language permits information to be gathered from fellow humans by asking questions in surveys, and it is conceivable to believe that their answers reflect the actual conditions of their lives. At the same time, the vagaries of experience and language and the peculiar characteristics of formal interview "conversations" refute the idea of unproblematic data gathering. Writing questions and conducting survey interviews present truly complex problems. The following model of the question–answering process illustrates the issues involved in communication in the interview.

1. Model of the Response Process

The objective of questionnaire construction and interviewing can be seen largely as the creation of "shared meaning" between respondent and interviewer. Simply put, respondents will give accurate information in survey interviews if they are able and willing to do so. Data collection procedures should be designed to increase respondents' ability to meet response objectives and to increase their willingness to expend the necessary effort for response tasks. This can be accomplished by explicit and precise communication of question objectives and of the process which respondents should undertake in formulating their responses.

To exemplify, consider the diagram of the response process in Fig. 1 which begins with comprehending the question (step 1). Comprehension includes issues of vocabulary level, clarity of concept, complexity of sentence structure, and other familiar issues of question wording. In this article, however, the interest lies in broader issues of question interpretation: the respondent's orientation in contemplating a question. When more than one plausible interpretation exists, the respondent needs to consider the various possibilities and must often think up and answer an internal questionnaire to help decide which interpretation to accept. Take, for example, the question: "How many times have you talked to a doctor about your health during the past month?" The respondent may wonder whether to

include telephone consultation, whether visits to chiropractors should be included, whether immunizations are part of health, or whether "past month" refers to the past four weeks or to a calendar month. Whether or not the respondent goes through this process explicitly, he or she must proceed on the basis of assumptions concerning the intended meaning of the question.

Step 2 is the stage of information processing that includes the respondent's assessment of what information he or she needs in order to respond accurately and what cues or frames of reference are relevant. Usually this stage involves searching the memory for relevant information and organizing the material to formulate a response.

For step 3 the respondent must evaluate whether the formulated response fulfills the objectives of the question. If the potential response is judged inadequate, the respondent loops back to repeat some or all of the preceding activities (step 2).

At step 4, a second kind of evaluation occurs as the respondent evaluates the psychological meaning of the response in relation to personal goals extraneous to the survey. Some respondents, however well-intentioned, will probably evaluate an intended answer in terms of its potential threat to their personal goals—for instance, self-esteem—in addition to the goal of giving accurate responses. If the potential response is evaluated as nonthreatening, the respondent states the response (step 5).

This brief description of the question–answering process, when it is proceeding ideally, illustrates the demands placed on respondents and the potential complexity of responding to questions. Carrying out this process can be difficult, especially when the question requires considerable effort to produce an accurate response or when the respondent regards the accurate response as embarrassing or otherwise personally uncomfortable. Undoubtedly, there are respondents who accept this task only provisionally; they will attempt to produce accurate responses as long as this does not require much effort on their part and does not embarrass them.

Figure 1 also suggests ways in which the responding process may go awry. While the ideal respondent follows steps 1 through 4 and eventually produces an adequate response (step 5), at any step he or she may deviate to other response modes (step 6) and produce a response (step 7) that is, to some degree, inadequate.

For the respondent who has not understood the question or is not sufficiently skilled or motivated to go through the retrieval and organizational processes, the extraneous situational cues suggested in step 6 are more likely to be the basis for response selection. Even respondents who proceed adequately through step 3 (that is, who formulate a response they judge to be adequate) will undoubtedly evaluate the response further to

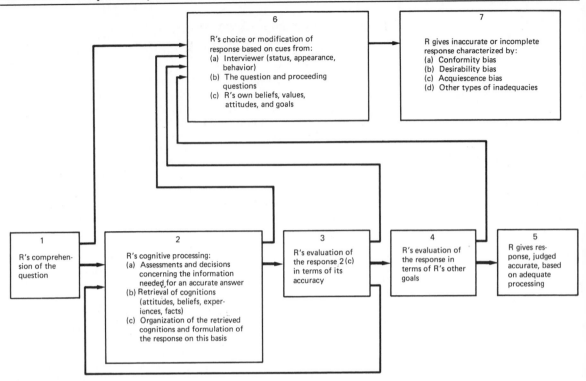

Figure 1
Diagram of the respondent's (R's) question–answering process[a]

a Source: Cannell et al. 1981 p. 393

determine whether it threatens or is incompatible with some other personal goal (step 4). If a threat emerges at this step, the respondent may deviate (steps 6 and 7) and modify his or her potential response or substitute another.

Once the respondent departs from the appropriate answering process (steps 1 to 5) and relies on other situational cues (steps 6 and 7), the response will exhibit some kind of invalidity (step 7). Researchers have labeled the effects on responses of such situational cues as social desirability bias, acquiescence bias, and the like. It is sometimes argued that these biases result from the respondent's personality characteristics—such as an "acquiescence trait," a "social desirability trait," or a need for approval—but it must be assumed that the response process is most likely to be shaped by situational cues in the interview itself: from the interviewer, the questionnaire, or the organization for which the research is being conducted. While it may be possible to differentiate people by their willingness to agree to give a socially appropriate response, for the purposes of this article agreeing responses and socially desirable responses are best understood in terms of their perceived appropriateness in the immediate interview situation.

Cognitive and motivational difficulties in answering questions are more common and more serious than is generally realized. Questions are often ambiguous in

ways that can have important implications for interpreting research data. Questions may make excessive demands on the cognitive skills of respondents by making unrealistic demands on the respondent's memory or ability to process and integrate retrieved information. Finally, the psychological implication of providing responses that truly reflect the respondent's beliefs or experience may lead to suppressing the information or distorting it into a more acceptable response.

The mechanisms of the responses when adequate processing fails are identified in step 7. Their effect is to distort survey data. That is, the reported information varies from truth in some predictable direction. Perhaps the most common distortion is a failure to report information—that is, making "false negative" reports—because of a failure of retrieval and processing (step 2), which may reflect true memory lapse or carelessness and unwillingness to make the effort necessary to retrieve the information. This form of inadequate response is probably the most frequent in report of past events and behavior.

Another common distortion involves making "false positive" reports—that is, falsely reporting events, behavior, or other information. This distortion may occur frequently when a time reference is specified in the question. For example, in answering a question about events occurring within the past month, the respondent may report things that occurred before that month

Such false reports may reflect faulty recall or may be more purposeful. (The respondent may falsely report information that seems to reflect to his or her credit, for example, or seems to meet some other goal.)

Response problems associated with one or another of these stages have been the focus of a number of methodological studies. For example, consider the problem of the respondent's comprehension of the question (box 1 in Fig. 1). In an investigation of the accuracy with which medical data are reported, the following question was asked: "Last week or the week before, did anyone in the family talk to a doctor or go to a doctor's office or clinic?" The question was intended not only to include routine office visits, but also telephone calls for medical advice and visits for inoculations or other treatments given by a nurse or technician in a doctor's office, and calls and visits by any member of the family whether on his or her behalf or for another. The mother's call to ask the doctor about her child was to be included, whether or not the child was present. From the researcher's viewpoint this single question included all these situations, and an analysis of the words supports the claim in a literal sense. The respondents' frame of reference, however, often produced very different interpretations. Many understood the question to include only personal visits, and then only when the physician was seen. The subsequent inclusion of probe questions asking specifically about these other events resulted in a sizable increase in the number of calls and visits reported (Cannell and Fowler 1965).

Similar problems occur in other content areas, when the researcher fails to take account of the respondent's frame of reference. Mauldin and Marks (1950) described efforts to obtain accurate data on education level. For many years the Bureau of the Census interviewers asked the education question in this form: "What is the highest grade of school you have completed?" Interpreted literally, this question should offer no difficulty for the vast majority of people. However, many people heard the phrase "highest grade of school" and immediately thought in terms of the highest grade of the school they "went to." Some people did not even hear the final word in the question, that is, the word "completed." When interviewers obtained answers to the above question and then said, "Did you complete that grade?" a substantial number of respondents answered "No."

In the same study the authors told of asking farmers whether they had any fruit or nut trees or grapevines. Those who answered that they did not were then asked if they had even one or two trees or vines, or whether they had any not now producing fruit. To those probe questions over half the farmers who originally said they had no trees or vines now said that they did. Mauldin and Marks concluded that the farmers took it for granted the census enumerators would not be interested in one or two trees, especially if they were not producing, and were trying to be helpful rather than deceptive.

Bancroft and Welch (1946) showed that respondents answer questions about their labor force status in terms of what they consider to be their major activity, rather than in terms of the actual wording of the question. Even if they were working part time, people who considered themselves primarily students or housewives answered "No" to the question, "Did you do any work last week for pay or profit?" A substantial improvement in the validity of employment estimates was attained by accepting the respondents' frame of reference and building a sequence of questions which first asked for their major activity and then asked students and housewives whether they were also doing any paid work.

These illustrate common comprehension problems for survey respondents. Other investigations demonstrate cognitive processing difficulties in answering survey questions (boxes 2 and 3 in Fig. 1), and offer these generalizations: (a) as the time between the event being investigated and the interview increases, reporting of the event becomes worse; (b) events which are psychologically unimportant to respondents are poorly reported.

The problem caused by time lapse between the event and the interview is exemplified in a study of reported visits to physicians. Failure to report the visit increased over a two-week period from 15 percent in interviews one week after the visit to 30 percent in interviews two weeks after (Cannell and Fowler 1963). Similarly, invalid reporting of hospitalizations increases as the time between the event and the interview increases, from 3 percent for events within 10 weeks of the interview to over 20 percent for episodes which occurred nearly a year prior. Other studies have shown similar findings for reporting of personal finances, household repairs, and household appliance purchases.

The psychological importance (or salience) of the event, as indexed in these studies by the gravity of the illness or the costliness of household goods and repairs, appears to have a marked effect on reporting accuracy, that is, hospitalizations which involved longer stays for respondents were better reported, as were episodes involving surgery (Cannell and Fowler 1963). Major household repairs and purchases were also more apt to be reported than less costly ones.

An adequate job of information retrieval from memory requires effort from the respondent, but many survey tasks ask for greater effort than respondents may be willing to make. Response errors often appear to be the result of the failure of cognitive processing outlined in boxes 2 and 3 of Fig. 1.

Boxes 4 and 5 signal a different reporting problem. Methodologists agree that the respondents' motivation or willingness to report is the most important issue in accuracy of interview data, and that the content of the material sought has a major effect on respondent motivation. The data from methodological research can be interpreted as a postulated need on the respondent's part to maintain self-esteem, to be perceived by the interviewer as a person who does not violate important social norms in thought or act, and to present an image of consistency and worthiness.

Clark and Wallin (1964) describe an example of response bias stemming from a different respondent need. They compared the individual reporting of husbands and wives on the frequency of sexual intercourse and found that the agreement was close for partners who expressed satisfaction with their sexual relations. Those who expressed dissatisfaction showed a greater discrepancy in report. Those who wanted more frequent sexual contacts tended also to report a lower frequency of marital coitus.

Conversely, voting or being registered to vote was found in several studies to be overreported (Bradburn et al. 1979). Wenar (1963) reported that mothers distort facts of their children's developmental history, and that they do so in ways that make the children appear precocious. Similarly, the reports of mothers regarding their own child-training practices tend to conform more closely to the advice of pediatricians than is justified by data from other sources.

These examples highlight the problem of question threat in survey reporting. As shown in boxes 4 and 5, respondents will often evaluate their answers according to the criterion of whether an answer will make them "look good." Reporting embarrassing events or properties presents considerable difficulty for many respondents, and not being able to report normatively valued characteristics can also cause some psychological discomfort. Therefore, respondents are often apt to censor response intentions which do not meet their preceived standards of social propriety.

2. Some Principles of Question Design and Interviewing

From a model of the question–answering process and data on response errors illustrating how responses can go awry, the practical implications of these observations for survey practice can now be considered.

2.1 Question Design

The elemental unit of a survey interview is the question. Over the years there has been a good deal of writing on question design, and some general principles have been enunciated (Payne 1951, Kahn and Cannell 1957, Warwick and Lininger 1975). More recently, Schuman and Presser (1981) report experiments on the effects of various question formats. (The various "rules" or folklore of question wording and structure will not be discussed here; they can be found in the sources mentioned above.) The more abstract principles of relating question design to the response process will be discussed.

Survey respondents may be seen as administering an "internal" questionnaire to themselves in order to arrive at a response to a survey question (see Fig. 1). They must decide what sorts of information and experiences are relevant to answering the question and must consider how to organize this material for presentation to the interviewer. They must decide how much effort to put into this process in order to arrive at an adequate answer.

In the ideal case, the survey question should provide the structure needed for the respondent to answer his or her own internal questionnaire. Each question should be specific enough to allow respondents to review thoroughly their own relevant experience and to arrive at an accurate and complete response.

Additionally, the question should communicate some rules about the process of question answering. For example, to find out whether respondents have been the victims of crime in the recent past, it is necessary to ask specifically about the range of incidents which are classified as "crimes" in the survey. If the question were "Have you been a victim of crime in the last six months?" the respondents' "internal questionnaire" would be very complex indeed. They will have to decide what "crime" is, and what it means to be a "victim." Each respondent will use his or her own definition, and what is included in an answer to the question will vary markedly from one respondent to another. Specific cues will help respondents share a common concept and definition. For example, respondents might be asked if they have had things stolen from their mailboxes, whether someone cheated them in a business deal, or whether their automobiles were vandalized. Each specific question, in turn, can be further refined. Respondents could be directed to think about particular kinds of goods which might be stolen or damaged. Specifically, researchers might want crime questions to inform respondents they should mention even incidents which may seem trivial to them. The importance can be stressed of reporting embarrassing or painful events. Each of these cues can help to reduce the complexities of the respondent's "internal questionnaire," and come closer to a shared definition between the interviewer and the respondent.

Questions also can communicate a suggested process for respondents to use in reviewing their experience for relevant material, and for evaluating the adequacy of their intended response. Queries can be prefaced with suggestions that respondents take their time and think carefully before answering or, alternatively, that their first general impressions are all that is required. An exact number can be requested or respondents can be asked to tell in detail about their feelings on a particular issue. These messages about the process of response are intended to answer the questions which people ask themselves when they try to respond to survey items.

In summary, the ideal survey question should clearly communicate a single and common objective for information retrieval. It should also inform respondents on how to produce a response—how much and what kind of effort to invest in answering. Naturally, every questionnaire compromises on the number of questions which can be devoted to a single variable since employing detailed and specific questioning inevitably lengthens the total questionnaire and increases survey cost. The researcher must constrict the scope of the survey so that the areas explored can be investigated thoroughly.

3. Interviewing

The process of interviewing—whether face-to-face or over the telephone—involves issues related to question design. Ideally, the information requested in the question would spring from the respondent's psyche directly to the computer input. But since the data collection process has an intervening interviewer, the effects of interpersonal relationship between interviewer and respondent must be a concern. Some rather different models of the interview are described which seek to control "interviewer effects" on responses.

3.1 Rapport

A common belief among survey researchers is that in order to obtain valid information the interviewer must gain the trust (and perhaps affection) of the respondent. Despite much lip-service paid to this concept (termed "rapport"), it is not entirely clear what is meant. However, the manifestations of rapport seeking in interviewer behavior can be identified. Using a clinical approach to interviewing, the survey interviewer seeks to establish rapport and takes a friendly, empathic attitude, he or she is nondirective—giving the respondent no cues about "correct" answers—and certainly does not express his or her own opinions. A combination of the nondirective approach and a friendly attitude is supposed to decrease response error by relieving the respondent of the pressure to maintain a totally positive self-presentation and by motivating the respondent to reveal him/herself accurately.

The problem is that the neutral or nondirective interviewer style frequently does not sufficiently motivate or inform respondents. A survey interview is a rare experience for most people, and they need guidance to appropriate response behavior. Cues to the respondent for deciding when an adequate response has been rendered are obscure, and they are likely to remain so if the interviewer conforms to the simple rules of being nondirective and friendly. In many studies, respondents may be ignorant of the most simple facts—the purpose of the investigation and the auspices under which the survey is conducted. Following their participation in a National Health Survey interview (Cannell et al. 1968) 45 percent (of 412 respondents) said they did not know what agency was doing the survey or the agency for which it was done; although each respondent had been informed that the survey was being conducted for the United States Public Health Service by the Bureau of the Census; only 11 percent identified the Census Bureau. Other identifications were even more vague—"some government agency," "a state agency." When asked why they thought the information was being collected, more than half said they had no idea. Of those who did report something, most responses were quite general—"for statistical purposes."

The study also examined respondents' perceptions of the interviewers' expectations and goals. Although the questionnaire had been set up to obtain specific and complete reports on specific health conditions (illnesses,

days of disability, medication taken, chronic conditions) and health events (physician visits and hospitalizations), only about one-half of the respondents thought the interviewer wanted a detailed report; the rest thought that general ideas were adequate. Three-quarters of the respondents thought the interviewer wanted a report of everything; the rest thought only the important things were to be mentioned. These findings suggest that respondents do not know what is expected of them. They understand neither the general goals of the survey nor what they are supposed to do on a particular question. Apparently "rapport" itself is not sufficient for achieving good interview communication. Moreover, since rapport seeking is an ad hoc procedure, there is considerable variance among interviewers in their approaches to the interview and this introduces error into the data-collection process.

4. Task Orientation and Standardization

A newer model of the interview has been developed which stresses teaching respondents to perform response tasks adequately and motivating them to undertake the effort to answer accurately. More effort also has been spent in attempting to standardize interviewer behavior. While these approaches do not deny the importance of gaining the respondent's cooperation on an affective level, they place considerably more emphasis on "taking care of business" in the interview. They entail a more active role on the part of the study director to specify interviewer behavior. As in question writing, according to this model the investigator must design interview techniques which are scripted in the questionnaire and administered in a standardized manner by all interviewers. As discussed above, such efforts are based on the premise that to achieve accurate measurement, a clear, standard communication environment must be established for the respondent. The specific techniques involved in this approach are elaborated below in discussing commitment, instructions, and feedback.

4.1 Components of Interviewing

The four main components of the interviewer's job are: (a) to introduce the interview to the person and convince him/her to accept it and to apply him/herself diligently to the responding role, (b) to administer the questions using standardized procedures, (c) to follow up those responses which are inadequate—those which fail to fulfill the objectives of the question—using acceptable, nonbiasing techniques, and (d) to record the response accurately and completely. These require the following techniques.

(a) *Introductions.* The purposes of the introduction are to encourage the prospective respondent to agree to be interviewed and to accept the respondent role wholeheartedly. Essentially this means the interview must be perceived as worthwhile, the interviewer as legitimate, and the undertaking as sufficiently valuable to make an effort to respond diligently.

First the interviewer identifies himself or herself, the research agency or university from which he or she comes, and the general topic of the research. He or she explains something of the method by which respondents have been selected and a reference to the amount of time required. How the introduction should be elaborated will depend upon the expressed needs of the respondent or the interviewer's hunches about them, and upon the interviewer's knowledge of the nature and the demands of the interview which is to come. The introduction and any early enlargements on it should make the rest of the interview plausible.

The legitimacy of the research is established by official documents, letters on appropriate stationery, use of the university name, and the like. The interviewer should be able to refer the respondent to a telephone number at which confirming information can be obtained. Sending advance letters or using mass media to announce large-scale data collection is helpful and is increasingly common. The interviewer should be prepared to be explicit as to the uses of the data, the sponsoring agencies, and the kinds of reports to be issued. Reports of similar studies, journal articles, or books can be shown as useful and reassuring evidence of good faith. It is important to disassociate the interview from nonresearch contexts encountered by respondents. Bill collectors and credit investigators ask questions as do welfare officers, police officers, and a whole array of civil servants and private employees, and all are perceived differently by people of different socioeconomic classes. Usually the respondent wants only the assurance that he/she is not being sought for some special and personal reason; a brief description of random and anonymous selection is enough. But, the interviewer should be able to offer an accurate and non-technical account of the sampling process if necessary.

Some studies follow the introduction with a commitment procedure which is often a signed agreement by respondents that they will make an effort to respond carefully and accurately. This shows evidence of improving response quality (Cannell et al. 1981).

(b) *Administering the questionnaire.* Questions often are accompanied by instructions providing cues on the exact kind of information desired and how to be efficient in responding. Including instructions in the questionnaire helps to standardize techniques and is more effective in getting valid reporting than ad hoc instructions or cues devised by the interviewer. Thus, the survey instrument becomes not simply a series of questions but a programmed measurement device including the questions, instructions, and probes. Questions are to be asked exactly as written and, if misunderstood, to be repeated without change. Clarifications or explanations are to be used only when specifically permitted.

(c) *Follow-up of inadequate responses.* If the respondent has performed his or her role properly, the interviewer's task is simply to record the response. At times, however, even after use of probes incorporated into the questionnaire, the response is in some way inadequate. It may be incomplete, irrelevant to the objective, or unintelligible. The interviewer needs techniques which

will stimulate further response activity or redirect the communication into relevant channels. Such techniques, designed to accomplish this without influencing the content of the response, are referred to as "nondirective" probes. To request further information they might be: "How do you mean?" "Is there anything else?" "Please tell me more about that." To request specific details, they may include: "Why do you think that is so?" or "When was that?" Training manuals can specify lists of acceptable nondirective probes (Survey Research Center *Interviewer's Manual*, rev. edn. 1976).

Probes (both those incorporated into the question design and those used at the option of the interviewer) are intended to steer the communication and also to motivate respondents to reply adequately. Feedback can both teach respondents what is expected of them and motivate them in task performance. Feedback is used naturally in social communication and serves to inform the other person that the message is being received, attended to, and accepted. Both verbal and nonverbal communication is used in face-to-face interviews; nonverbal is of course absent in telephone interviews. As used in teaching, feedback provides an evaluation to the learner of his/her performance and as reinforcement it rewards good performance and tends to motivate behavior. Feedback may be a simple statement of understanding and interest: "I see, Um-hmm." "I understand." Or it may be more positive in evaluation: "Thanks, that's the kind of information we need." "That will help us in this research." "That's useful." Because of these evaluative and reinforcing properties, feedback can be effective in improving reporting performance. If improperly used, however, respondents will either not learn or will learn the wrong lessons. Consider the following exchange:

Q: How often do you get a dental check-up?
R: Every six months.
Feedback: That's good.

"That's good" is likely to be interpreted as approving of the answer content rather than to give positive support to adequate response behavior. Such misinterpretation by the respondent makes it ineffective in teaching acceptable behavior and may lead to response bias. Therefore, feedback statements must focus on reinforcing hard work by respondents and must avoid expressing approval of the particular response. As survey researchers become more aware of the power and dangers of feedback, they are beginning to include major feedback statements in the questionnaire. They also focus attention on acceptable and unacceptable feedback during interviewer training.

(d) *Recording responses.* Accurate recording of the response is the last component of the interviewing task. For closed questions this usually consists simply of checking the appropriate response category or recording the reply if no box can be checked. The task is more demanding for open questions. This requires recording the respondent's own words and a complete description of the response. Paraphrasing is usually unacceptable since it may miss significant segments—perhaps those of interest to the researcher. Experienced interviewers find that responses can be recorded during the course of the conversation with only minor editing required after the interview. The record should also include any spontaneous probes used by the interviewer, extraneous conversation which occurs during the interview, comments by respondents on questions, and observations about respondents' difficulty in answering questions. All of this information can be coded and used to contextualize the responses to questions in the interview.

4.2 Training and Selection

Research directed at reducing response errors has not been matched with research on procedures to select interviewers or effective techniques for training, supervising, and administering interviews. For example, there are few objective criteria or procedures for selecting competent interviewers. While some selection measures have been tried experimentally, none have demonstrated significant relationships to successful interviewing. Those which are used focus largely on the clerical nature of the interview task. Those studies which have been conducted suggest that interviewing skills can be communicated to a large proportion of the population and that the emphasis needs to be on training rather than on selection of the ideal interviewer type.

This is not to suggest that an interviewer will be equally successful in communicating with all respondents or that all interviewers will attain optimal interviewing skills. Respondent and interviewer differences in age, voice, sex, socioeconomic or cultural background may interfere with accurate reporting when the demographic characteristic is related to the subject of the survey (e.g., when a white interviewer interviews a black respondent about racial attitudes; Schuman and Converse 1971).

The major source of variability in interviewers is, however, probably not in their selection but in variations in techniques from interviewer to interviewer. While there is no training program which is accepted by all survey practitioners, here are some general principles: (a) new interviewers should be provided with the principles of measurement; they should be given an intellectual grasp of the data-collecting function and a basis for evaluating interviewing behavior; (b) they should be taught the techniques of interviewing; (c) they should be provided with the opportunity for practice and evaluation by actually conducting interviews under controlled conditions; (d) they should be offered careful evaluation of interviews, especially at the beginning of actual data collection. Such evaluation should include review of interview protocols.

Steps (a) and (b) are intended to provide the interviewers with a concept of the goals of interviewing, including the principles of measurement and the exposition of techniques which meet these criteria. Most of the time and attention in training is spent on steps (c) and (d). The assumption underlying technique training is

that while it is important to communicate the goals and principles of the research, most of the time needs to be spent in developing the appropriate skills. Simply reading an essay about how to interview will not produce a skilled interviewer. Effective instructional materials must actively involve the trainee in the learning process. The nature of the task dictates the nature of the instruction. Interviewing requires listening, speaking, reading, and writing skills. Therefore, training must incorporate all these modes.

Trainees begin by observing a model of the task they are to learn—they listen to and read along with the tape recording of a skilled interviewer taking an interview. Skills necessary for total task mastery are introduced sequentially throughout a five-day training session. At each skill level, trainees must first recognize appropriate behaviors, then produce them accurately. Providing a model of the desired behavior along with a model of the behavior in which one feature is incorrect highlights the aspect of the behavior to be taught. Standards are gradually built into the head of the learner and self-modification can occur.

Concepts are introduced in self-instructional written materials. Trainees then listen to the tape recording accompanying each section and evaluate the interviewer behaviors which are demonstrated. Role play follows. Lastly, each trainee tape records a sample interview. Then self-evaluation allows the trainee to improve his or her interviewing skills. Practicing those skills in front of the group gives the trainee an opportunity to listen to model behavior, ask questions, and get further feedback on individual performance. Monitoring interviews is an ongoing part of interviewer evaluation.

4.3 Monitoring

Learning and becoming proficient in the skills of interviewing can be enhanced by monitoring of interviewer performance and then using immediate feedback to correct errors. Telephone interviewing from a central location provides opportunity for monitoring and feedback which is more difficult and expensive in field survey. To be most effective, monitoring should consist of the objective coding of interviewer behavior which can identify both good and poor use of techniques based on the principles of interviewing included in the original training. This serves to reinforce training since it can identify the principles which are violated. One system identifies the major categories of interviewer behavior, with the monitor listening to the interview and coding each behavior, identifying it as correct or incorrect. For example, several codes assess the interviewer's delivery of a question: Was it read exactly as written? Read with minor changes without changing the intent of the question? Read with major changes? and so on. Other codes are directed at evaluating the probes used, the feedback, clarifications, the pace with which the interview was conducted, and so on. This results in a sequence of numeric codes for each interviewer behavior for each question. This record is reviewed with the interviewer after the interview to provide immediate feedback and retraining, if needed. Monitoring interviewers in field settings is more cumbersome and expensive. The most efficient procedure has been to make tape recordings of interviews and code behaviors in the office while listening to the tapes. Such monitoring enhances the original training by reinforcing acceptable procedures and correcting poor ones.

5. Issues in Telephone Interviewing

Recent years have seen a growing use of the telephone for survey research. Reduction in survey costs is a primary motivation for the shift from face-to-face contacts to the telephone, and increased household coverage by telephone and techniques for sampling phone numbers through probability methods have made telephone results more comparable to personal interview surveys.

When a survey interviewer makes contact with a respondent by telephone, he or she faces some particular problem of establishing legitimacy and communicating response tasks. Telephone solicitation done under the guise of "doing a survey" hampers the efforts of legitimate survey enterprises to an unknown degree. Survey organizations try to reassure potential respondents by offering toll-free numbers to verify the legitimacy of the contact, and by contacting local police to provide them with information on the survey which can be passed on to inquisitive citizens. "Refusal conversions" are also standard in telephone surveys. An accomplished interviewer calls a respondent who has initially refused to be interviewed and attempts to convince him or her to participate. Such techniques are common in personal interview surveys as well, but they pay off more highly in telephone studies since there are many initial, "soft" refusals in that mode of contact.

5.1 Communication Issues in Telephone Interviews

Some factors which differentiate the style of communication in telephone and face-to-face interviews are obvious. Use of visual cues such as "show cards" is impossible in telephone contacts (unless the materials have been mailed to respondents before the interview and they agree to use them). Therefore, investigators have been concerned about the comprehensibility to respondents of some response tasks when they are presented over the phone. How many scale points can be presented to respondents verbally for their consideration and judgment? Are questions involving a reference period for recall possible to ask effectively without showing the respondent a calendar? The "channel capacity" of the telephone is limited.

Other differences in communication between telephone and face-to-face modes are more subtle, and involve not only perceptual mechanisms but also social custom. Communication by telephone is somewhat less intimate than in-person dialogue. The inability to see conversational partners (facial expressions, gestures, and so forth) may lead to heightened uncertainty about the meaning behind words and about people's ability to understand what is being conveyed. In addition, the

pace of dialogue, which is often regulated by nonverbal cues in face-to-face interaction, has to be maintained by verbal or paralinguistic utterances in telephone conversations. Since the household telephone is normally used for speaking with friends and family, and for self-initiated business communication, any call from a stranger is likely to be treated with suspicion. Thus, custom dictates what sorts of telephone contacts are "appropriate," and some people may view any call which does not fall in these categories as an unwarranted intrusion.

In research on mediated communication, investigators have found support for hypotheses that the visual channel is important for conveying affect and evaluation to others (Ekman 1965; Mehrabian 1968) and for regulating conversational flow (Kendon 1967; Duncan 1972). Tasks involving transmission of factual information and cooperative problem solving appear relatively unaffected by whether the participants can see each other or not (Williams 1977). But there is a consistent tendency for subjects to be less confident of their judgments in no-vision conditions, and to express a preference for face-to-face contact (Williams 1977, National Research Council 1979).

The implications of these findings for telephone interviewing are several. In personal interviews, visual communication plus the preinterview acquaintance period allow the interviewer easily and naturally to establish both the legitimacy of the interview and the image of herself/himself as a pleasant, understanding, and safe person with whom to interact. The interviewer's physical presence permits the communication of attention to, interest in, and acceptance of what the respondent has to say, through nonverbal as well as verbal indicators. By contrast, telephone interviews, which may surprise and disturb respondents, lack the sense of legitimacy of the personal contact, and the phone interview may seem somewhat mechanical. The pace of interaction—unregulated by nonverbal cues—may be faster on the telephone, leading to hurried and perhaps less thoughtful responses (Groves and Kahn 1979).

These comparisons imply that the telephone may produce data of lower quality than those collected in person. But it is also possible that the limited channel capacity of the telephone may eliminate distracting or biasing cues from the interviewer, and that phone communication's lack of intimacy may be a boon when the interview questions cover very sensitive matters. Several comparative studies have involved such hypotheses (Colombotos 1969, Hochstim 1967, Bradburn et al. 1979).

In summary, interviewing by telephone has both advantages and disadvantages. In any case, the nature of communication in the interview will be affected by the medium through which it takes place. While research comparing telephone and face-to-face interviews suggests that the differences in data collected via the two modes are generally small (Groves and Kahn 1979), inferences from the research are tentative because most of the studies were not carefully designed to assess the effect of the mode of communication. Interpretation of findings is confounded by the fact that sampling procedures and interviewing styles were not standardized across modes. Miller and Cannell (1982) have reported an experimental study of interviewing procedures for telephone interviews, but more research is needed to develop optimal techniques.

Bibliography

Bancroft G, Welch E 1946 Recent experience with problems of labor force measurement. *J. Am. Stat. Ass.* 41: 303–12

Bradburn N M, Sudman S et al. 1979 *Improving Interview Method and Questionnaire Design.* Jossey-Bass, San Francisco, California

Cannell C F, Fowler F J 1963 A study of the reporting of visits to doctors in the National Health Survey. Survey Research Center, University of Michigan, Ann Arbor, Michigan

Cannell C F, Fowler F J 1965 *Comparison of Hospitalization Reporting in Three Survey Procedures. Vital and Health Statistics*, Series 2, No. 8. Public Health Service, Washington, DC

Cannell C F, Fowler F J, Marquis K H 1968 *The Influence of Interviewer and Respondent Psychological and Behavioral Variables on the Reporting in Household Interviews. Vital and Health Statistics*, Series 2, No. 26. Public Health Service, Washington, DC

Cannell C F, Miller P, Oksenberg L 1981 Research in interviewing techniques. In: Leinhardt S (ed.) 1981 *Sociological Methodology, 1981.* Jossey-Bass, San Francisco, California, pp. 389–437

Clark A L, Wallin P 1964 The accuracy of husbands' and wives' reports of the frequency of marital coitus. *Pop. Stud.* 18: 165–73

Colombotos J 1969 Personal versus telephone interviews: Effect on responses. *Public Health Reports* 84: 773–82

Duncan S 1972 Some signals and rules for taking speaking turns in conversations. *J. Pers. Soc. Psychol.* 23: 283–92

Ekman P 1965 Differential communication of affect by head and body cues. *J. Pers. Soc. Psychol* 2: 726–35

Groves R M, Kahn R L 1979 *Surveys by Telephone: A National Comparison with Personal Interviews.* Academic Press, New York

Hochstim J A 1967 A critical comparison of three strategies of collecting data from households. *J. Amer. Stat. Ass.* 62: 976–82

Kahn R, Cannell C F 1957 *The Dynamics of Interviewing.* Wiley, New York

Kendon A 1967 Some functions of gaze-direction in social interaction. *Acta Psychol.* 26: 22–63

Mauldin W P, Marks E S 1950 Problems of response in enumerative surveys. *Am. Sociol. Rev.* 15: 649–57

Mehrabian A 1968 Inference of attitudes from the posture, orientation, and distance of a communicator. *J. Consult. Clin. Psychol.* 32: 296–308

Miller P, Cannell C F 1982 A study of experimental techniques for telephone interviewing. *Public Opinion Q.* 46: 250–69

National Research Council 1979 *Privacy and Confidentiality as Factors in Survey Response.* National Academy of Sciences, Washington, DC

Payne S 1951 *The Art of Asking Questions.* Princeton University Press, Princeton, New Jersey

Schuman H, Converse J M 1971 The effects of black and white interviewers on black responses in 1968. *Public Opinion Q.* 35: 44–68

Schuman H, Presser S 1981 *Questions and Answers in Attitude Surveys: Experiments on Question Form, Wording, and Context.* Academic Press, New York

Survey Research Center 1976 *Interviewer's Manual*, rev. edn. Survey Research Center, University of Michigan, Ann Arbor, Michigan

Warwick D P, Lininger C 1975 *The Sample Survey: Theory and Practice.* McGraw-Hill, New York, pp. 182–202

Wenar C 1963 The reliability of developmental histories. Summary and evaluation of evidence. University of Pennsylvania School of Medicine, Philadelphia, Pennsylvania

Williams E 1977 Experimental comparisons of face-to-face and mediated communication: A review. *Psychol. Bull.* 84: 963–76

Measurement of Social Background

J. P. Keeves

Since the early 1930s it has been increasingly recognized that in most countries differences in social background are strongly related to educational outcomes. In recognition of this relationship many countries have introduced compensatory programmes to assist with the provision of educational services to those who are seen to be socially and economically disadvantaged. Underlying these developments has been the work undertaken primarily in the disciplinary area of sociology concerned with the study of social stratification and social mobility and the measurement of social status. This article is concerned with the measurement of social background and social status and the problems encountered in the development of more consistent and valid scales.

Meaningful measurement requires that the properties being measured have a sound conceptual basis within an established theory and that the operational definitions linking the theory and the scaling techniques employed yield both valid and reliable measures. Social stratification and social mobility are fields in which there is considerable controversy. Haug (1977) has pointed out that there are at least two types of characteristics which are used to cluster persons into strata or groups that are hierarchically ordered. First, there are biologically based characteristics such as age, sex, race, and ethnic origin. Secondly, there are acquired characteristics such as power, wealth, and social prestige. Societies differ in the emphasis given to particular characteristics in the processes of stratification within them, and even within a given society the characteristics change over time. There is little consensus regarding which characteristics should form the basis of a general theory of social stratification. Nevertheless, the theories of Marx, that class categories are derived from the relation of a group to the means of production and thus are based on differences between ownership of property and the provision of labour, have greatly influenced thinking in this area. Another prominent view advanced by Weber is that position in society is built around the three concepts of status, power, and class, with status being related to prestige ascribed by the community, power being associated with a political context, and class having an economic basis. These three dimensions of status, power, and class are conceptually interrelated and might be expected to be highly correlated with one another. As a consequence they have provided the main foundation on which the measurement of social stratification has proceeded, particularly in industrial societies.

Two broad approaches have been employed in the investigation and measurement of social background and social status. Warner et al. (1949) have identified these two approaches distinguishing between the approach in which an assessment is made of social standing by the observed and evaluated participation of an individual in the social system of a community, and the approach in which indices of the status level of the individual in the community are developed using information obtained directly from the individual by either objective or subjective responses.

As a result, in undertaking the task of measuring social status it is necessary not only to consider the theoretical basis of the concepts to be employed but also how information related to an individual with respect to those concepts might be obtained. The most commonly used single indicator of a person's relative standing with respect to the concepts of status, power, and class is that of occupation. Information on the standing of an occupation can be obtained by the use of the perceptions of members of the community, or by the use of concomitant characteristics of the occupation associated with the level of skill required, the level of education necessary to engage in the occupation, and the income received from regular employment in the occupation. These three characteristics are interrelated in so far as economic return is determined, in part, by both level of skill and level of education.

1. Measurement of Occupations

In the main, the starting point for the measurement of occupations involves the setting up of a classification of the full range of occupations which exist in a society. Since such a large number of classified occupations exists, it is then usually necessary to group them into categories. Once occupational categories have been formed they must be assigned to a rank order. The simplest grouping in industrialized societies is into two categories of "white-collar workers" and "blue-collar workers". White-collar occupations typically require a high proportion of the work to be carried out within an office. Blue-collar occupations involve a high proportion of the work being undertaken out-of-doors or away from an office desk. In most societies white-collar occupations are perceived to require a higher level of education and skill. In the main, they are more highly

rewarded and are thus accorded higher status than blue-collar occupations. A more extensive categorization, again based essentially on levels of education, skill, and income, involves six categories of occupation; professional, managerial, clerical, skilled, semiskilled, and unskilled. The first three named are white-collar occupations, the last three are blue-collar occupations.

Broom et al. (1977) have identified five main approaches which have been involved in the measurement of occupations beyond the simple categorizations referred to above. First, it is possible to develop a more extensive set of occupational categories using level of education, skill, and income and to assign integer scores to the hierarchically ordered occupational categories (Jones 1971). A second approach has been to derive socioeconomic scores for each occupation by combining average years of education and average income associated with each occupation, customarily with equal weight [for example: for Canada—Blishen (1958), for New Zealand—Elley and Irving (1972), and for the United States—Nam and Powers (1968)]. A third strategy has been to carry out an auxiliary study of occupational prestige, and using regression analysis, to estimate the weights for such characteristics as years of education and income in order to predict the prestige score for major occupations. Scores for those occupations not estimated directly may be obtained by interpolation (Duncan 1961, Pineo and Porter 1967). A fourth approach is to make direct estimates of social standing or prestige using information obtained from a single study which provides data for all occupations, or to use previous rating studies to provide some of the necessary data (Siegel 1971). A fifth procedure that has been employed is to assign scores to occupational categories from the analysis of measures obtained on several separate characteristics using the interactions between the measures to generate the scores. The statistical techniques of principal components analysis, factor analysis, and canonical analysis have been employed to this end (Keeves 1972).

In the section that follows the procedures which have been employed in selected countries have been briefly described.

1.1 Australia

The starting point of the work of Broom et al. (1965) was the classified list of occupations which had been developed for use in national censuses. As a first step, Broom and colleagues grouped the 342 occupational titles into 100 clusters on the basis of interrelations between occupations and then into 16 broad categories using as the main criterion that each group should contain jobs involving the same level of skill or skill type. These 16 categories were ordered to form a prestige scale broadly in agreement with the findings of an earlier study into occupational prestige by Congalton (1963) that had produced an occupational prestige scale. More recently, Broom et al. (1977) have extended this work using the third strategy described above, namely that of fitting an equation to prestige scores for measures of age, sex, birthplace, schooling and qualifications, housing and vehicle ownership, and interpolating for a wider set of occupations.

1.2 The United Kingdom

The first attempt in the United Kingdom to form an occupational classification was carried out for the census in 1911 when five occupational categories were defined. This classification was revised in 1971 to six classes which are: I—professional; II—intermediate occupations; III N—skilled occupations (nonmanual); III M—skilled occupations (manual); IV—partly skilled occupations; V—unskilled occupations. In addition, a stratification measure was developed by Hall and Caradog Jones (1950) based on community perceptions of occupational prestige. Initially a scale was constructed for 30 occupational categories, and was later extended to include approximately 650 occupations (Oppenheim 1966). Subsequently, Goldthorpe and Hope (1974) grouped all the occupations in the United Kingdom census classification into 125 categories which were as homogeneous as possible with respect to both intrinsic and extrinsic rewards. They then selected a representative sample of occupational titles from each category, and in a single study obtained rankings of the prestige of each of the occupational groups. From these rankings a single scale was formed, but no attempt was made to group the final 124 categories into a smaller number of classes or strata.

1.3 The United States

In the United States, the major system of classifying occupations developed by the Bureau of the Census has been used as the basis for setting up measures of stratification. Edwards (1938) developed the first scale; using education and income as criteria he grouped together all occupations into 10 hierarchically ordered classes. Such a scale, employing income in the formation of socioeconomic groups, has become known as a scale of socioeconomic status (SES). This term is now widely used even where the measures employed do not strictly involve income. For the 1971 United States Census a 12-category scale was developed from Edward's scale, but whether it retains the socioeconomic groupings of the earlier scale is open to question.

Perhaps the most frequently used measure of social stratification in the United States is the Duncan Socio-Economic Index (SEI) (Duncan 1961) which is based on occupational prestige as evaluated by public opinion, using the third strategy outlined above. However, the estimated prestige scores showed many shortcomings and Siegel (1971) sought to obtain a more secure empirical basis for the prestige ratings from a public opinion survey for as many of the major census occupations as possible.

1.4 Canada

The construction of measures of stratification in Canada has followed closely the work carried out in the United States. Blishen (1958) developed an occupational scale for combining the mean standard scores for both education and income for members of occupational groups using Canadian census classifications and data from a national census. Subsequently, Pineo and Porter (1967) sought to obtain information on occupational prestige through a national survey. Blishen (1967) then followed the procedures used by Duncan (1961) to obtain regression weights for education and income measures in the prediction of prestige scores. The weights obtained by Blishen for education exceeded that for income, where Duncan had obtained approximately equal weights.

2. The Standard International Occupation Prestige Scale

Husén (1967) used an occupational scale developed at the University of Chicago with considerable success in the mathematics study for the International Association for the Evaluation of Educational Achievement in 1964, although there are major societal and cultural differences between nations. More recently, Treiman (1977) has sought to combine the many diverse scales of prestige into a single scheme that could be used in cross-cultural research and other comparative studies. Treiman obtained information from prestige studies in 55 countries and recoded the occupational titles according to the appropriate categories employed in the International Standard Classification of Occupations (ISCO) published by the International Labour Office in 1969. After conversion to a common standard metric, the scores obtained from the 55 countries for each occupational group were averaged across countries to obtain the international scale. Treiman claimed that the concurrent validity of the scale was high because the average coefficient obtained by correlating each country's occupational scale scores with those for the international scale with that country removed was 0.89. In addition, with the exclusion of a few developing countries and some socialist countries, the correlations between scales were unrelated to level of industrialization as measured by gross national product. In common with most of the scales in current use there are shortcomings in the scales with respect to the positions of farm and rural workers. Thus for a country with a high percentage of the labour force engaged in primary industry it must be anticipated that some problems will be encountered.

3. Some Special Problems

As noted above, occupational scales have shortcomings in relation to workers engaged in agriculture and primary industry. Furthermore, many of the scales currently used have been constructed primarily using male members of the workforce. Thus with an increasing proportion of the workforce of many countries being made up of women, and with an increasing proportion of women now engaged in occupations that were formerly the preserve of males, it must be recognized that occupational scales are not equally appropriate for use with both male and female members of a population. Likewise, within many countries a marked change in the composition of the workforce has resulted from crossnational migration, and with certain occupations increasingly being taken by persons from particular ethnic groups, who for a variety of reasons are assigned a lower status, the scales that were constructed for a more homogeneous population within a particular country are no longer as meaningful as they were formerly. Such scales may still be valid in the sense that the prestige assigned to the occupations remains the same. However, for females, ethnic, and other groups the scale scores cannot be predicted as well as formerly from education and income because of discrimination. As a consequence, in educational research alternative measures of the social background of the home are being employed increasingly in preference to the use of measures based on an occupational or socioeconomic status scale, since the latter type of scale was not designed for use as a predictor or as an explanatory variable in educational research.

4. The Sociocultural Level of the Home

Floud (1961) has pointed out that the French use a phrase "*la famille éducogène*" to describe families who provide an educative environment that reinforces the intellectual pressures exerted by the school. It is widely recognized that the educative climate of the home not only influences the intellectual development of the child during the years of schooling, but more particularly during the early years of childhood (Bloom 1964). Recognition of this led to the International Association for the Evaluation of Educational Achievement (IEA) in the Six Subject Study to develop an index of social background for each country taking part in the study based upon six measures: father's occupation, father's education, mother's education, use of the dictionary, number of books in the home, and family size. These six variables were weighted by criterion-scaling procedures using achievement on tests of science, reading, and word knowledge as criteria to form a composite measure assessing the sociocultural level of the home (Comber and Keeves 1973). Keeves (1972) had previously developed a similar index using five measures: family size, father's occupation, father's education, mother's occupation before marriage, and religious affiliation, combining the variables by principal components analysis. The incorporation of a scaled measure of religious affiliation led to the acceptance that the index developed involved a cultural rather than an economic emphasis. Likewise the inclusion of mother's occupation before marriage was seen to be associated with the competence of the mother rather than being related to the contribution that she made to the total family income.

It should be noted that indexes of occupational status and socioeconomic status correlate positively and significantly with the educational outcomes of both

achievement and attainment in cases where the school population has not been truncated by the removal of less able students. Even where the school population has been reduced in this way these indexes are, in the main, positively related to educational outcomes. Recent research shows a clear tendency for indexes of sociocultural level to be more strongly related to educational outcomes than are indexes of occupational and socioeconomic status, and thus they have greater explanatory power. The evidence available strongly supports the contention that it is not the occupational status of the home per se that influences educational outcomes but rather the related sociocultural level of the home with its emphasis on reading and the use of language.

Bibliography

Blishen B R 1958 The construction and use of an occupational scale. *Canadian J. Econ. Polit. Sci.* 24: 519–31
Blishen B R 1967 A socioeconomic index for occupations in Canada. *Canadian Rev. Soc. Anthropol.* 4: 41–53
Bloom B S 1964 *Stability and Change in Human Characteristics.* Wiley, New York
Broom L, Duncan-Jones P, Jones F L, McDonnell P 1977 *Investigating Social Mobility.* Australian National University Press, Canberra
Broom L, Jones F L, Zubrzycki J 1965 An occupational classification of the Australian workforce. *Aus. N.Z. J. Sociol.* 1. (supplement)
Comber L C, Keeves J P 1973 *Science Education in Nineteen Countries: An Empirical Study.* Almqvist and Wiksell, Stockholm
Congalton A A 1963 *Occupational Status in Australia.* University of New South Wales, School of Sociology, Kensington
Duncan O D 1961 A socioeconomic index for all occupations. In: Reiss A J (ed.) 1961 *Occupations and Social Status.* Free Press, New York, pp. 109–38
Edwards A 1938 *A Social–Economic Grouping of the Gainful Workers of United States, Gainful Workers of 1930 in Social–Economic Groups, by Color, Nativity, Age, and Sex, and by Industry, with Comparative Statistics for 1920 and 1910.* GPO, Washington, DC
Elley W B, Irving J C 1972 A socioeconomic index for New Zealand based on levels of education and income from the 1966 Census. *N.Z. J. Educ. Stud.* 7: 153–67
Floud J 1961 Social class factors in educational achievement. In: Halsey A H (ed.) 1961 *Ability and Educational Opportunity.* Conf., Kungälv, 11–16 June 1961. Organisation for Economic Co-operation and Development, Paris, pp. 91–109
Goldthorpe J H, Hope K 1974 *The Social Grading of Occupations: A New Approach and Scale.* Clarendon, Oxford
Hall J, Caradog Jones D 1950 Social grading of occupations. *Br. J. Sociol.* 1: 31–55
Haug M R 1977 Measurement in social stratification. *Ann. Rev. Sociol.* 3: 51–78
Husén T (ed.) 1967 *International Study of Achievement in Mathematics: A Comparison of Twelve Countries.* Almqvist and Wiksell, Stockholm
Husén T 1975 *Social Influences on Educational Attainment.* Organisation for Economic Development and Co-operation, Paris
Jones F L 1971 Occupational achievement in Australia and the

United States: A comparative path analysis. *Am. J. Sociol.* 77: 527–39

Keeves J P 1972 *Educational Environment and Student Achievement.* Almqvist and Wiksell, Stockholm

Nam C B, Powers M G 1968 Changes in relative status of workers in the United States, 1950–60. *Social Forces* 47: 158–70

Oppenheim A N 1966 *Questionnaire Design and Attitude Measurement.* Basic Books, New York

Pineo P, Porter J 1967 Occupational prestige in Canada. *Canadian Rev. Sociol. Anthropol.* 4: 24–40

Siegel P M 1971 Prestige in the American occupational structure. PhD. Thesis, University of Chicago, Chicago, Illinois

Treiman D J 1977 *Occupational Prestige in Comparative Perspective.* Academic Press, New York

Warner W L, Meeker M, Eells K 1949 *Social Class in America: A Manual of Procedure for the Measurement of Social Status.* Science Research Associates, Chicago, Illinois

Classroom Observation Techniques

J. A. Stallings and G. G. Mohlman

There are many techniques used to observe and record human behavior and physical environments. These include checklists, rating scales, narrative descriptions, and interactive coding systems. Each of these techniques is appropriate for specific kinds of data to be collected. Each has some advantages and some disadvantages.

1. Common Elements

Although the observational techniques differ, there are several elements that all observation systems have:

(a) *A purpose.* The purpose of the observation will guide the selection of the technique to be used. Observations may be used for research on effective teaching; to evaluate teachers' performance; to evaluate a child's social, physical, or cognitive development; or to examine program implementation.

(b) *A set of operational definitions.* Operational definitions guide the observers so that by following the prescribed rules, each observer will assign the same value or category to the event being observed. For example, what must a student be doing to be recorded as "off task?" (Staring? Sleeping? Chatting? Doodling? Waiting?) The operational definition must state explicitly which behaviors are included in being "off task."

(c) *A means to train observers.* To collect reliable observation data, training for observers must be provided. Observers must learn the operational definitions and specific procedures for recording data. Depending upon the complexity of the observation technique, the training period may be a few hours, several days, or several weeks. Observers should be checked for accuracy before they begin collecting data. There are several means to measure observer accuracy. The most often used is to have paired observers record the same event in the natural situation and calculate their interrater agreement or the interrater reliability of observation. Another method is to show observers a precoded videotaped event and compare their recordings to the criterion.

(d) *A focus of observation.* Each observation has a focus phenomenon to be looked at or listened to. This might be a teacher, an aide, a child, materials, activities, or physical facilities.

(e) *A setting.* All observations have a setting. They may be conducted in classrooms, school grounds, hallways, lunch rooms, students' homes, or staff rooms. The observer will go where it is necessary to obtain the data required for the study.

(f) *A unit of time.* Each observation has a specified length: seconds, minutes, hours, or days. Observation data can be collected according to a time sample or a real-time method. To illustrate the difference, consider the coding of interactions between a teacher and a child. Under the time sample method, the observer uses a time piece and only records an interaction, for example, every 10 seconds. The only interaction coded is the one occurring when exactly 10 seconds have passed. Thus, the interactions that occur between the time intervals are not recorded. In a real-time method, every interaction is coded. Another real-time method is the narrative description—everything that is relevant to the purpose is recorded. The issue here is one of interpretation. Do the data collected during the selected coding intervals (for example, one code every five minutes) accurately represent what went on between the coding intervals? Are the intervals spaced so far apart that some important events were not coded by the observer? This issue usually arises when using checklist category systems. If one is counting behaviors only during certain equally spaced intervals, then the target behaviors should be relatively stable ones. In any other case, real-time data are likely to provide a more accurate picture.

(g) *Observation schedule.* All observations need a schedule for gathering the data. This might be a fall pretest and a spring posttest for research purposes. For staff development, weekly or monthly observations may be required, whereas staff evaluation might only occur on a yearly basis.

The time of day for observations must also be established. End-of-the-day teacher and student behavior is likely to appear different from early morning behavior. Monday activities may be different from Tuesday and Wednesday activities. Therefore, to obtain a more stable sample of behavior, the schedule should allow for the same period of time to be observed on several consecutive days at each period of observation. All members of the sample should be observed during a similar time period. For example, if some teachers and students are

Classroom Snapshot

Material → Activity ↓		01 Textbook	02 Workbook/ Worksheet	03 Test	04 Game/ Manipulative material	05 Machine	06 Chalkboard	07 Noncurricular reading	08 No material
01 Reading silently	T	I S L E	I S L E	I S L E	I S L E	I S L E	I S L E	I S L E	I S L E
	A	I S L E	I S L E	I S L E	I S L E	I S L E	I S L E	I S L E	I S L E
	O	I S L E	I S L E	I S L E	I S L E	I S L E	I S L E	I S L E	I S L E
	i	I S L E	I S L E	I S L E	I S L E	I S L E	I S L E	I S L E	I S L E
02 Reading aloud	T	I S L E	I S L E	I S L E	I S L E	I S L E	I S L E	I S L E	I S L E
	A	I S L E	I S L E	I S L E	I S L E	I S L E	I S L E	I S L E	I S L E
	O	I S L E	I S L E	I S L E	I S L E	I S L E	I S L E	I S L E	I S L E
	i	I S L E	I S L E	I S L E	I S L E	I S L E	I S L E	I S L E	I S L E
03 Marking assignments	T	I S L E	I S L E	I S L E	I S L E	I S L E	I S L E	I S L E	I S L E
	A	I S L E	I S L E	I S L E	I S L E	I S L E	I S L E	I S L E	I S L E
	O	I S L E	I S L E	I S L E	I S L E	I S L E	I S L E	I S L E	I S L E
	i	I S L E	I S L E	I S L E	I S L E	I S L E	I S L E	I S L E	I S L E
04 Instruction/ explanation	T	I S L E	● S L E	I S L E	I S L E	I S L E	I S L E	I S L E	I S L E
	A	I S L E	I S L E	I S L E	I S L E	I S L E	I S L E	I S L E	I S L E
	O	I S L E	I S L E	I S L E	I S L E	I S L E	I S L E	I S L E	I S L E
	i	I S L E	I S L E	I S L E	I S L E	I S L E	I S L E	I S L E	I S L E
05 Discussion/ Reviewing assignments	T	I S L E	I S L E	I S L E	I S L E	I S L E	I S L E	I S L E	I S L E
	A	I S L E	I S L E	I S L E	I S L E	I S L E	I S L E	I S L E	I S L E
	O	I S L E	I S L E	I S L E	I S L E	I S L E	I S L E	I S L E	I S L E
	i	I S L E	I S L E	I S L E	I S L E	I S L E	I S L E	I S L E	I S L E
06 Practice drill	T	I S L E	I S L E	I S L E	I S L E	I S L E	I S L E	I S L E	I S L E
	A	I S L E	I S L E	I S L E	I S L E	I S L E	I S L E	I S L E	I S L E
	O	I S L E	I S L E	I S L E	I S L E	I S L E	I S L E	I S L E	I S L E
	i	I S L E	I S L E	I S L E	I S L E	I S L E	I S L E	I S L E	I S L E
07 Written assignments	T	I S L E	I S L E	I S L E	I S L E	I S L E	I S L E	I S L E	I S L E
	A	I S L E	I S L E	I S L E	I S L E	I S L E	I S L E	I S L E	I S L E
	O	I S L E	I S L E	I S L E	I S L E	I S L E	I S L E	I S L E	I S L E
	i	I S L E	I S ● E	I S L E	I S L E	I S L E	I S L E	I S L E	I S L E
08 Taking test quiz	T	I S L E	I S L E	I S L E	I S L E	I S L E	I S L E	I S L E	I S L E
	A	I S L E	I S L E	I S L E	I S L E	I S L E	I S L E	I S L E	I S L E
	O	I S L E	I S L E	I S L E	I S L E	I S L E	I S L E	I S L E	I S L E
	i	I S L E	I S L E	I S L E	I S L E	I S L E	I S L E	I S L E	I S L E
09 Nonmath or nonreading instruction	T	I S L E	I S L E	I S L E	I S L E	I S L E	I S L E	I S L E	I S L E
	A	I S L E	I S L E	I S L E	I S L E	I S L E	I S L E	I S L E	I S L E
	O	I S L E	I S L E	I S L E	I S L E	I S L E	I S L E	I S L E	I S L E
	i	I S L E	I S L E	I S L E	I S L E	I S L E	I S L E	I S L E	I S L E
10 Social inter- action (TAAO)	T	I S L E	I S L E	I S L E	I S L E	I S L E	I S L E	I S L E	I S L E
	A	I S L E	I S L E	I S L E	I S L E	I S L E	I S L E	I S L E	I S L E
	O	I S L E	I S L E	I S L E	I S L E	I S L E	I S L E	I S L E	I S L E
	i	I S L E	I S L E	I S L E	I S L E	I S L E	I S L E	I S L E	I S L E
11 Student uninvolved	T	I S L E	I S L E	I S L E	I S L E	I S L E	I S L E	I S L E	I S L E
	A	I S L E	I S L E	I S L E	I S L E	I S L E	I S L E	I S L E	I S L E
	O	I S L E	I S L E	I S L E	I S L E	I S L E	I S L E	I S L E	I S L E
	i	I S L E	I S L E	I S L E	I S L E	I S L E	I S L E	I S L E	I S L E
12 Being disciplined	T	I S L E	I S L E	I S L E	I S L E	I S L E	I S L E	I S L E	I S L E
	A	I S L E	I S L E	I S L E	I S L E	I S L E	I S L E	I S L E	I S L E
	O	I S L E	I S L E	I S L E	I S L E	I S L E	I S L E	I S L E	I S L E
	i	I S L E	I S L E	I S L E	I S L E	I S L E	I S L E	I S L E	I S L E
13 Classroom ● manage- ment (AO)	T	I S L E	I S L E	I S L E	I S L E	I S L E	I S L E	I S L E	I S L E
	A	I S L E	I S L E	I S L E	I S L E	I S L E	I S L E	I S L E	I S L E
	O	I S L E	I S L E	I S L E	I S L E	I S L E	I S L E	I S L E	I S L E
	i	I S L E	I S L E	I S L E	I S L E	I S L E	I S L E	I S L E	I S L E

Figure 1
The Snapshot, a comprehensive classroom observation system[a]

a Source: Stallings and Needels M 1978

observed in early September, and others are observed in October, the data will not be comparable since those observed in October will be more acclimatized to school.

(h) *A method to record data.* Observations may be recorded with audiotapes, videotapes, minicomputers, optical scan forms, or paper and pencil. The method of recording will affect how the data are processed.

(i) *A method to process and analyze data.* The events recorded must be processed and categorized systematically in order to draw conclusions from the data. Processing can take several forms. Observation data can be optically scanned, key punched directly from the records, or hand sorted for key words and concepts in narratives. Analysis of observation data usually takes the form of frequency counts, percent of occurrences, scores on rating scales, presence or absence of events, and quality statements.

2. Types of Observational Techniques

The following sections will describe some of the purposes, advantages, and disadvantages of several observational techniques.

2.1 Checklists

A list of expected behaviors is prepared and every time the behavior occurs during the specified observation time unit, the observer enters a tally mark next to the appropriate category. The time unit is usually in terms of seconds; for example scan the room for 30 seconds and record it; five minutes later, scan the room and record again. Checklists are particularly useful in showing the presence or absence of specific teacher or student behaviors.

Another type of checklist is the seating chart. One way this is used is to code each student by name who is off-task at the time the observation is made. An "S" under the student's name on the chart indicates socializing. "W" indicates waiting, and "U" indicates uninvolved. A check of off-task students is usually made every five minutes throughout the period.

A more sophisticated checklist is the "Snapshot." One mark indicates the activity occurring, the material being used, and with whom the teacher is working.

As shown in Fig. 1, the Snapshot, the classroom activities are listed down the left side of the page, and the materials are listed across the top. The observer records the information in each appropriate space, recording each unique grouping occurring in the classroom. A completed Snapshot documents the number and kind of groupings, the activity and materials of each group, and whether an adult is present.

The letters at the beginning of each row indicate the placement of each category of participants in the classroom: T = teacher; A = aide; O = other adult; I = independent student.

If it is a team-teaching arrangement, both teachers are shown in the activity with the student or students they are working with when the Snapshot is recorded. The 1, S, L, and E in the rows relate to the number of students

with whom the teacher is working: 1 = one student; S = 2–8 students; L = 9 to one less than the total group, and E = everyone.

The letters marked in Fig. 1 indicate that the teacher is giving instruction to one student in a workbook. The other students are working alone in workbooks. An aide is doing some classroom management task. Five grids are completed each 45-minute period and each class period is observed three days in a row.

The advantage of the checklist is that observers can be trained to use it rather easily if categories to be checked are discrete and if the operational definitions are clear and not overlapping. The event either is or is not occurring at the time the record is made. Another advantage is that the data can be easily keypunched directly from the records and frequency counts are easily produced. This makes processing and analyzing the data relatively inexpensive.

A disadvantage of the checklist is that only a limited number of preselected events can be recorded. If the list becomes too long (over 20) the observer has a difficult time scanning the list to see whether the event occurred during the specified time frame. The data collected will not provide information about interactions, continuous behavior, or the quality of the events.

2.2 Rating Scales

Rating scales require the observer to watch the focus of the observation for a specified period of time. The period of time to observe may vary from five minutes to 60 minutes. At the end of the time, the observer rates the prevalence of certain behaviors during the period on a scale (see Fig. 2).

A good use of the rating scale is to assess high-inference variables such as teacher enthusiasm or student initiative. These types of variables can be evaluated better over a period of continuous time rather than from frequency counts made during short time samples. Similar to the checklists, the rating scales have the advantage of being easily processed and quantified.

A disadvantage of rating scales is the inherent subjectivity of ratings. A summary of the observer's opinion is produced rather than actual observed events. In order to produce usable data, very specific definitions must be made of the attributes of each point of the scales. What one observer rates as high teacher enthusiasm may be rated as moderate enthusiasm by another observer. Therefore, the scale must define how frequent the teacher seems to be enthusiastic as well as what an enthusiastic teacher looks like and sounds like. The training of observers to develop acceptable interrater reliability is likely to require several days of practice in the classrooms and frequent checking of interrater agreement.

2.3 Interactive Coding Systems

An interactive coding system allows an observer to record everything a teacher or a student says or does during a given time span. The time is usually several

Example questions:
(a) Circle the rating which best described the teacher's attitude towards the class:

Highly positive	Positive most of the time	Neither positive nor negative	Negative occasionally	Highly negative
5	4	3	2	1

For example, if you felt the teacher's attitude towards the class was *extremely* positive, you would rate this question "5."

(b) Circle the rating that best describes the students in this class:

Class appears extremely happy and/or satisfied	Most students appear happy and/or satisfied much of the time	About half appear happy and/or satisfied much of the time	Occasionally pupils appear happy and/ or satisfied	Class appears extremely unhappy and/ or dissatisfied
5	4	3	2	1

For example, if you felt the class was satisfied most of the time, but not always, you would rate this question "4."

Figure 2
Overall emotional-attitudinal climate: Affective categories and Florida Climate Control System (FLACCS) classroom global ratings[a]

a Source: Soar 1975

five-minute intervals spaced evenly throughout a class period.

An interaction system developed by Ned Flanders has been widely used in research. The categories are nonjudgmental and the system is particularly useful in evaluating teacher-led group discussions. The level of the group's involvement, as well as the teacher's questioning and feedback strategies, can be assessed. Statements made by the teacher and students are entered on a matrix. The Flanders categories and codes are well-defined and reasonably easy to memorize and use (see Fig. 3). Seven codes show whether the student is responding to the teacher's question, or initiating a new idea. For example, a T-4 followed by an S-8 and then a T-2 indicates that the teacher asked a question, a student responded, and the teacher praised the student. This kind of information can help teachers see how often they accept, praise, or categorize students. The system can be particularly useful to teachers if they analyze audiotapes or videotapes made while they are instructing a class.

An elaboration of the Flanders system has been widely used to identify effective classroom teaching processes and to guide teacher training. Profiles prepared of each teacher's classroom behavior are based upon approximately 900 interactions taken over a three-day period. Recommendations are made to increase or decrease specific behaviors to a criterion level. A second set of observations at the end of a semester will show the teachers how much they have changed behaviors.

Interaction systems have the advantage of being very objective. The variables are understandable and acceptable to teachers and administrators. Each code is defined so that it is unique. A frequency count is provided for each type of question asked, response given, praise offered, correction given, and instruction provided. Counts are made of organizing statements and behavioral control statements. Specific positive and negative affect statements or actions are also recorded. The frequency counts can then be transformed to percentages of total interactions.

Teacher talk:
Response
    (a) Accepts feelings
    (b) Praises or encourages
    (c) Accepts or uses ideas of student
    (d) Asks questions
Initiation
    (e) Lectures
    (f) Gives directions
    (g) Criticizes or justifies authority
Student talk:
Response
    (h) Responds
Initiation
    (i) Initiates conversation
Other
    (j) Silence or confusion

Figure 3
Flanders categories for interaction analysis[a]

a Source: Flanders 1970

The disadvantage of an interaction coding system is that some of the quality of the interaction is lost. For example, a very good thought-provoking question will be coded as "2" which equals an "open-ended/thought-provoking" question. The data will not show that the level of questioning was truly excellent. Another disadvantage is that the content of the lesson is lost. The data will only show that the appropriate academic subject is being pursued, for example, reading aloud is occurring, but the data will not reveal what is being read. A final disadvantage is that comprehensive interaction systems, such as Stallings', require a five- to seven-day training session to collect data reliably. The data require complicated programming to process. Once the program is developed, however, an advantage is that the optical scan processing is available and is quite efficient in saving time and money.

2.4 Narrative Description

This technique involves writing in narrative form everything observed that is relevant to the focus and purpose of the observation. Although some technical terms may be useful and desirable, for the most part, the terms used to describe the observed phenomena are the observer's natural words.

Narrative descriptions can be used for clinical supervision, for individual child observation, or for case studies of individuals or schools. In most cases, the observer is guided to look for specific events. For example, in a beginning-of-the-year classroom management study conducted by Evertson and Emmer (1980), observers were instructed to record teacher statements about rules for behavior penalties, and expectations for quality and quantity of work. They were also asked to record teachers' consistency of carrying out rules and procedures. The narrative descriptions had a clear focus which was guided by the hypotheses and interests of the investigators.

Narratives may also take the form of anecdotal records that describe an episode in specific detail. For example, the episode might be a heated discussion between teachers in a staff meeting or between children in the playground.

Specimen records are another form of narrative description. In this case, all of the behavior of a single individual is recorded over a specified period of time. The purpose is to record everything the person says or does during that period of time. It is not interpreted or summarized by the observer. Such records kept on a daily or weekly basis help develop case study material. Over time, patterns of behavior are likely to emerge.

Narrative descriptions have several advantages. The context of the observation can be described in a rich and holistic manner. The natural sequence of events is preserved. Unpredicted events can be reported. Qualitative statements can be made, for example, "The teacher is very warm and loving to the children as she strokes them and sings softly during rest time." None of the quantitative observation instruments could adequately record that kind of incident.

Another advantage is the short training period. Observers do not have to learn complicated coding systems or the definitions for points on rating scales. Their records are usually kept in notebooks or on forms with wide margins and with space left for coding at a later date.

Evertson et al. (1980) have described the process of building a good research team for classroom observation. Observers must practice writing what they see, keeping the purpose of the observations clearly in mind. There may be some difficulty in getting two observers to describe the same event in the same way. The activities in classrooms often happen simultaneously and the phenomena selected to record may be different for different observers. Developing consistency in gathering the original narrative data may require considerable paired practice in classrooms.

A major disadvantage lies in the processing of narrative data. Many pages of handwritten text must be read, categories selected, and narratives coded for key words and concepts before the data can be summarized. This can be a time-consuming and costly process if the sample is very large. Narrative descriptions that are well-focused such as those collected by Evertson and Emmer are less difficult to code because many categories are preselected. This still allows for other categories to emerge from the data.

3. Selecting an Observation Instrument

The purpose of the observation must guide the selection of the instrument. What are the questions? If a teacher is to be evaluated for carrying out a specific lesson plan, then a clinical narrative description approach is most likely required. If a researcher is trying to learn about a large array of effective teaching strategies in a large sample, a comprehensive coding system may be required. If the teachers wish to learn more about which students are off-task during specific activities, a checklist may be most appropriate.

Any observation system used must be checked for validity to see whether it is indeed collecting the data it expects to collect, for example, the variable "students show initiative and are self-motivated." How do students look? What do they do or say that indicates self-motivation? Does the operational definition of this variable have good face validity?

Another important point to consider is whether observers can be trained to gather the data accurately. Here, it is helpful to have a criterion for correctness as well as reports of interrater agreement.

The stability of the behavior must also be considered. Teachers may be consistent in their manner of asking questions and providing feedback from one day to another in the same subject. However, they may alter this approach in a different subject. Or, the teacher may use a very dictatorial approach to classroom management in September and a more democratic one in November. The observation system should be sensitive enough to reflect these differences.

See also: Participant Observation; Rating Scales; Structured Observation Techniques; Videotape Recording in Educational Research; Ethnographic Research Methods

Bibliography

Borich G D, Madden S K 1977 *Evaluating Classroom Instruction: A Sourcebook of Instruments*. Addison-Wesley, Reading, Massachusetts
Boyer E G, Simon A, Karafin G R (eds.) 1973 *Measures of Maturation: An Anthology of Early Childhood Observation Instruments*. Research for Better Schools, Philadelphia, Pennsylvania
Brandt R M 1972 *Studying Behavior in Natural Settings*. Holt, Rinehart and Winston, New York
Evertson C, Emmer E 1980 *Effective Management at the Beginning of the School Year in Junior High Classes*. Research and Development Center for Teacher Education, University of Texas, Austin, Texas
Evertson C, Emmer E, Clements B 1980 *Report of the Methodology, Rationale, and Instrumentation of the Junior High*

Classrooms Organization Study. Research and Development Center for Teacher Education, University of Texas, Austin, Texas
Flanders N A 1970 *Analyzing Teacher Behavior*. Addison-Wesley, Reading, Massachusetts
Kowalski J P S 1978 *Evaluating Teacher Performance*. Educational Research Service, Arlington, Virginia
Simon A, Boyer E G 1967 *Mirrors for Behavior: An Anthology of Classroom Observation Instruments*. Research for Better Schools, Philadelphia, Pennsylvania
Soar R S 1975 Follow through classroom process measurement and pupil growth (1970–71). Final Report. Educational Research Service, Arlington, Virginia. ERIC Document No. ED 106 297
Stallings J A 1977 *Learning to Look: A Handbook on Classroom Observation and Teaching Methods*. Wadsworth, Belmont, California
Stallings J A, Needels M 1978 *Secondary Observation Instrument*. SRI International, Menlo Park, California

Structured Observation Techniques

M. Galton

Structured observation, as used to monitor classroom events, requires an observer to assign such events into previously defined categories. These events may be either recorded by mechanical means such as film, audiotape, or videotape and subsequently coded, or the observer can record and code the events simultaneously while present in the classroom. The three stages of the process therefore involve (a) the recording of events in a systematic manner as they happen, (b) the coding of these events into prespecified categories, and (c) subsequent analysis of the events to give descriptions of teacher–pupil interaction. Structured observation is also referred to as systematic observation or more particularly as interaction analysis, although the latter term is more usually applied to observation systems derived from the Flanders (1964) Interaction Analysis Category System (FIAC). According to Flanders, interaction analysis is a "specialized research procedure that provides information about only a few of the many aspects of teaching and which analyses the content-free characteristics of verbal communication" (Flanders 1964 p. 198). Structured observation techniques have, however, also been used to monitor nonverbal behaviours so that Flanders' definition of the methodology is now seen to be too restrictive.

1. The Origins of Structured Observation

The origin of these observational techniques arose, in part, from the creation of the committee of child development by the American National Research Council at the beginning of the 1920s. This committee sponsored research into teaching methods at nursery and kindergarten stages and the researchers found it necessary to observe these infants and record their behaviour "as it

happened". The first attempts to do this consisted of diaries or narrative logs of the activities observed, but the sheer volume of descriptive material collected made the task a very arduous one. Olson (1929) introduced the notion of time sampling whereby certain categories of behaviours were recorded at specified fixed intervals of time. Although other approaches existed (Barr 1935), an essential distinction used to classify behaviours by workers in the child development movement was that between direct teaching where pupils were told what to do and indirect teaching where pupils were consulted and decisions reached by means of discussion and consensus. By the early 1970s, an anthology of American observation systems listed 92 instruments (Simon and Boyer 1970) of which the majority appear to be derived from FIAC (Rosenshine and Furst 1973). This system of Flanders' has been widely criticized, however, for its limited applicability in that it was originally designed for relatively static classrooms where teachers stood in front of pupils who were arranged before them in rows while working on the same subject matter (Silberman 1970, Hamilton and Delamont 1974). More recently, with the increase of "open" or informal approaches to classroom organization, a greater variety of observational methods have been developed. In the United Kingdom, for example, a review of observation studies (Galton 1979) identified only two systems derived from FIAC and showed that most of the research has been carried out at the primary stage of schooling where informal approaches are more likely to be found.

2. Characteristics of Structured Observation

Structured observation involves low-inference measurement (Rosenshine 1970). This requires the development of unambiguous criteria for assigning the various events into categories. Provided that the criteria are sufficiently explicit to be shared by different people, then different observers should arrive at identical descriptions of the same events. Thus an important requirement of a successful systematic observation system is high interobserver agreement. Although the choice of categories and the definition of the criteria may be highly subjective, reflecting the values of those who construct the system, the technique is objective in the sense that the criteria used to describe classroom life are clearly defined so that when the system is used correctly it is unaffected by the personal biases of individual observers. This is in sharp contrast to ethnographic methods where the researcher, although sometimes claiming to take a total view of the classroom before gradually focusing on the more meaningful features (Hamilton and Delamont 1974), in practice, can only offer a partial view in which the criteria governing the selection are rarely available for consideration by others (see *Ethnographic Research Methods*).

Low-inference measurement may be contrasted with high-inference measurement where the criteria are less specific. Rating systems are the most common example of high inference measures, where an observer has to integrate his or her impressions into some global assessment of a teacher's or a pupil's performance on such dimensions as warmth, application, or sociability. Such rating systems do not give a direct record of classroom events so that no analysis of teacher and pupil behaviour is possible.

Low-inference observation schedules may be described as either category or sign systems. An observer, using a sign system of observation, is provided with a list of specific behaviours and records the occurrence of these behaviours during a given time period. Certain events are therefore ignored. The alternative approach is to use a category system of observation where the observer is provided with a list of more generalized categories and within a given unit of time classifies every behaviour which occurs into the category that is best thought to represent that behaviour. An early example of a sign system was the OSCAR observation system (Medley and Mitzel 1958) while Flanders' FIAC is an example of a category one. In practice, most modern observation schedules are combinations of category and sign systems. For example, the Pupil Record (Boydell 1975) uses a category system to code the pupils' activities but a sign system to code teacher–pupil and pupil–pupil interactions. The selection of behaviours for use in a sign system is dependent upon those which are thought to be most useful for the particular research purpose. In classroom research, such variables are selected because they are thought to be related to learning outcomes or to systematic differences between teachers and their pupils.

3. Data Collection

At first sight, the use of mechanical means of recording classroom behaviour would appear to have several advantages over the use of an observer recording and coding events as they happen. When the observer carries out direct observation in the classroom there is no permanent record of the interaction available for re-examination. Mechanical recording, using either audiotape or videotape, allows for repeated observation thereby increasing the likelihood of interobserver agreement. However, the observer in the classroom enjoys certain advantages when attempting to code more complex behaviours. After a certain amount of time the observer will come to appreciate something of the shared meanings which exist between pupils and the teacher and so will be able to interpret certain behaviours in the light of this experience. Permanent records also tend to be highly selective, focusing on the pupil or the teacher so that the listener or viewer does not know what is going on in the remainder of the classroom. A category such as "target pupil is interested in another pupil's work" might not be coded from videotape because the camera focuses directly on the target pupil and a viewer is uncertain whether the target is looking at someone elsewhere in the classroom or simply staring into space. To try to overcome this latter difficulty, two cameras are used, one focused on the teacher and one providing a general view of the classroom. Another method of producing visual cues is the use of stop-frame photography with synchronized sound (Adelman and Walker 1974). The flexibility of such systems has been greatly increased by the development of hand-held television cameras and by the use of radio microphones which, because they do not have leads, allow the teacher to move freely around the classroom and lessen the problem of background noise.

The process of transcribing the permanent record from a recording is, however, very tedious and time consuming. It is estimated that to transcribe one hour's audiotape takes nearly a week of an efficient typist's time. Research involving a large number of teachers will therefore tend to favour direct observation methods because of the costs involved in transcribing and processing the data. In practice, studies which seek to examine the nature of the language used by teachers and pupils tend to require a permanent record, while researchers who investigate such matters as teacher–pupil contacts, the nature of the pupil's task, and the proportion of time that is spent on it favour direct observation.

4. Training Observers

According to Flanders, one of the main problems of training observers in the use of systematic observation is "converting men into machines" (Flanders 1967 p. 158). The usual training technique is to concentrate on a few categories at a time using a teach–test and feedback–reteach cycle. Usually audiotape and videotape recording are used to introduce the observer to the problems of classifying particular categories and at the end of a training session another tape can be used to test if the observers can achieve acceptable levels of agreement. It is important to provide simple examples initially with the guarantee that most observers will obtain total mastery. Observers who fail to identify behaviours correctly during training can often develop hostile reactions to the observation instrument. It is also useful to provide observers with experience of coding under classroom conditions as soon as possible. As stated earlier, it is often difficult to identify the context in which a behaviour takes place on videotape which in turn means that the decision about the use of a particular category is not as clear cut as the trainer might wish. Once the initial training has been completed, it is important to build into any observation study refresher periods in which the observers go over the categories and check on their reliability. This is to protect against what is termed "observer drift" where observers who have come to accept criteria which do not conform to their own view of a particular behaviour gradually modify the category definitions over time to fit in with their own view.

5. Reliability and Validity

Reliability serves to indicate how free a particular measurement is of error. Two major potential sources of error in the classroom concern the extent to which two or more observers can agree in their coding of the same event—the interobserver agreement coefficient, and the degree to which the observed variation in classroom behaviour is consistent from occasion to occasion—the teacher stability coefficient. Since the total amount of time spent observing is usually only a small fraction of the total time spent teaching, it is important to be able to demonstrate that the sample of teacher and pupil behaviour is representative.

Most studies, however, record only the observer agreement reliability. The simplest measure is the percentage of occasions on which a pair of observers agree but this does not allow for the fact that even two observers who were coding categories at random would still code the same categories on certain occasions by chance. The Scott (1955) coefficient corrects for this chance effect and is a more rigorous test of reliability. A weakness of this method, however, is that it does not permit study of observer agreement using a number of teachers. Medley and Mitzel (1963) offer a number of designs, based upon analysis of variance in which each teacher is visited on one occasion by a pair of observers such that different observers are paired on each visit. Such a design also allows the teacher stability coefficient to be estimated.

If an observation instrument is to be used by researchers other than the authors then the question of interinvestigator agreement arises, since each group may achieve high levels of observer agreement but interpret the categories differently (Rosenshine and Furst 1973). Some authors of observation systems therefore provide videotape examples already coded so that new users can check their degree of agreement with the authors on a trial tape (Eggleston et al. 1975).

Most researchers concern themselves only with the face validity of the observation instrument, assuming that the definition of the categories is so clear cut that validity may be assumed, providing observer agreement is high. The more complex the observation instrument, however, the less advisable it is to take this face validity for granted. A number of alternative procedures then suggest themselves. Where cluster analysis is used to create a typology of teaching styles or pupil types then observers can be asked to write descriptive accounts (mini case studies) of the teachers and the appropriate pupils. These accounts can then be cross-referenced with the descriptions derived from the clusters. Such descriptions can also be fed back to the observed teachers who can be asked to identify their own particular style or recognize particular types of pupil present in their class. Where two different observation systems exist having a similar focus then they can be used in the same classroom to compare and contrast results. This type of cross-validation is recommended by Rosenshine and Furst (1973) but few studies have attempted this task. In the ORACLE study, however, both the teacher and the pupils were observed using two instruments and the asymmetry of classroom behaviour from both the teachers' and the pupils' perspective was contrasted (Galton et al. 1980). The same study also made it possible to compare and contrast the "real curriculum" as perceived through both the teachers' and the pupils' activity.

6. Coding and Analysis

In any observation system, discrete analytic units must be used in order to code the behaviours. The simplest division is based on some form of time sampling where the time unit may vary from three seconds, as used by Flanders, to five minutes as used in Medley and Mitzel's OSCAR schedule. Every system has its own ground rules which differentiate between the beginning and the end of successive time units and which deal with the problem of behaviours which overlap from one unit to the next. It is important to choose time units so that observed behaviours do not regularly overlap into the next unit since when this happens it is found that the degree of agreement between observers decreases rapidly. Observer agreement is also improved when a steady rhythm of recording can be maintained.

Researchers using time sampling methods tend to proceed in one of two ways. Some use point sampling whereby behaviours occurring at regular time intervals are recorded. The extent to which the sample of behaviour recorded is representative of the total behaviour during the lesson is clearly dependent on the length of the interval between recordings. If the period is too short, the observers are likely to make mistakes while if the time interval is too long it may record the behaviour accurately but underestimate its overall frequency.

When difficult and complex decisions have to be made by the observer, many researchers prefer a one–zero time sampling procedure. Here the observer is required to record a behaviour only once when it occurs within a given time unit. As the time interval of a one–zero time sampling method decreases it begins to approximate to a continuous recording of classroom activity. With longer time intervals—and some researchers have used five minute units (Eggleston et al. 1975)—then only the minimum frequency of occurrence is recorded and the data cannot be used to estimate the overall occurrence of individual categories within the classroom.

The above sampling methods are generally used with sign systems. Where time sampling is used with a category system it is usual to employ a ground rule where only one category is recorded, either because it is the dominant one occurring or because it is infrequently used. If the time interval is very short, then the observer is in effect recording a change of category rather than sampling behaviour within a defined period. Recording a new behaviour every time a different category is used employs the use of what are termed naturalistic units. The problem for the researcher is to define a set of rules which will identify the unit of classroom transaction which will then be coded under a particular category. Smith and Meux (1962) defined these natural units as episodes and monologues where an episode involved more than one speaker and a monologue identified a solo performance. The ground rules for identifying the nature of the transaction, however, make it difficult, if not impossible, for an observer to use such a system live in a classroom. For this reason the use of naturalistic units is most frequently used for analysis based upon transcribed recordings. Observers can play and replay recordings until general agreement is obtained on the classification of the transaction.

When naturalistic units are used, the total number of episodes represents the total recorded behaviour, since one tally only is made for each episode. In such a case, some record of the sequence of events can be obtained but the most usual practice is to sum the number of recorded tallies for each category and to divide this sum by the total number of analytic units observed. With naturalistic units, this ratio closely represents the proportion of the total behaviour occurring in a particular category. With longer time units, when a point-time sampling procedure is used, the ratio of the sum of tallies in a particular category compared to the total number of tallies recorded can again be interpreted as a proportion of total behaviour. One–zero time sampling methods in which frequently occurring events may only be coded once during a time unit can give no absolute value for the frequency of the particular behaviour. Instead, an estimate of the minimum frequency of occurrence is obtained by dividing the total number of tallies obtained for a category by the total number of observation units.

Much criticism has recently been directed at the use of one–zero time sampling procedures and it is claimed that they seriously underestimate the total frequency by as much as 85 percent (Dunkerton 1981). Properly used, however, such systems fulfil an important function. Their main purpose is not to chart the frequency with which particular behaviours occur but to discriminate between different teachers according to their use of certain categories of behaviour. Behaviours which serve to discriminate between teachers are usually the very infrequent ones. For example, in the analysis of the Science Teacher Observation Schedule (Eggleston et al. 1976), the schedule clearly underestimates the degree to which teachers made statements of fact but even with a five-minute time sampling interval it was rare for a teacher to make problem-solving statements, to hypothesize, or to make statements concerned with the design of experimental procedure. Yet it was the latter categories which served to discriminate most sharply between teachers. Categories involving more common behaviours such as making factual statements, were retained in the schedule because they helped observer reliability. It was found that unless observers were able to code continuously they tended to become anxious and their concentration and reliability decreased. The advantage of a one–zero time sampling procedure was that the observers quickly coded the more frequently occurring categories and were then able to concentrate on the more difficult ones. Systems using this procedure are therefore able to include a greater variety of behaviours in the observation instrument because they give the observer time to reach decisions in the more difficult coding areas.

In theory, time sampling systems where the recorded behaviours provide a representative sample of the overall pattern of classroom interaction can be used to determine the sequence of events. Most attempts to do this have used probabilistic models based on Markov chains. A one-stage model tries to predict the behaviour at $T + X$ seconds given a knowledge of the behaviour at T seconds where X is the length of time unit. A two-stage model will attempt to predict the behaviour at $T + X$ seconds from a knowledge of the behaviours at both T and $T - X$ seconds respectively. In theory, higher order models can also be developed. In practice, however, a two-stage model involving upwards of a dozen categories of behaviour offers so many different combinations of possible behaviours that the total number of observations recorded would need to be impossibly high to test the model.

With transcribed accounts of lessons, either from videotape or audiotape, greater attention can be paid to the sequential character of exchanges between teachers and pupils. Once suitable units of transcript have been identified, then different patterns in the sequence of these units can be identified. Unfortunately, successive researchers have tended to use different units for analysis. Thus the episode developed by Smith and Meux (1962) became the incident in Nuthall and Lawrence's (1965) study. Others have defined pedagogical moves (Bellack et al. 1966) and thought units within teaching modules (Taba 1966). Comparison between different studies is therefore difficult and although it is attractive to believe that effective teaching will eventually be explained in terms of sequential behaviour rather than simple frequency units, there has been little progress in this direction since the early 1970s.

7. General Conclusions

In spite of these difficulties, there remains a continued interest in the collection of systematic data. Recent reviews of research on teaching in the United States list a large number of studies which have been carried out since the publication of Rosenshine's review (Rosenshine and Furst 1973). According to Brophy (1979), studies since the early 1970s have provided firm evidence to suggest what teachers should do in order to improve their pupils' performance on basic skills. Central to these ideas is the provision of warm, highly structured teaching designed to ensure that pupils remain actively engaged on their task and are provided with the maximum amount of feedback. However, some recent studies have suggested that such conditions apply only in the case of fairly low-level cognitive outcomes (Galton and Willcocks 1982) and more emphasis should be placed on increasing the degree of teacher–pupil interaction both in individual and group settings. There is also a conspicuous lack of evidence about the nature of the learning strategies adopted by children. It may be expected that the next generation of classroom studies will turn its attention to these key issues.

See also: Classroom Observation Techniques; Participant Observation; Videotape Recording in Educational Research; Naturalistic and Rationalistic Enquiry

Bibliography

Adelman C, Walker R 1974 Stop-frame cinematography with synchronized sound: A technique for recording in school classrooms. *J. Soc. Motion and Picture and Television Engineers* 83: 189–91

Barr A S 1935 The validity of certain instruments employed in the measurement of teaching ability. In: Walker H (ed.) 1935 *The Measurement of Teaching Efficiency*. Macmillan, New York, pp. 73–141

Bellack A A, Hyman R T, Smith F L, Kliebard H M 1966 *The Language of the Classroom*. Teachers College Press, Columbia University, New York

Boydell D 1975 Pupil behaviour in junior classrooms. *Br. J. Educ. Psychol.* 45: 122–29

Brophy J E 1979 Teacher behaviour and its effects. *J. Educ. Psychol.* 71: 733–50

Dunkerton J 1981 Should classroom observation be quantitative? *Educ. Res.* 23: 144–51

Eggleston J F, Galton M J, Jones M E 1975 *A Science Teaching Observation Schedule*. Macmillan, London

Eggleston J F, Galton M J, Jones M E 1976 *Processes and Products of Science Teaching*. Macmillan, London

Flanders N A 1964 Some relationships among teacher influence, pupil attitudes and achievement. In: Biddle B J, Ellena W J (eds.) 1964 *Contemporary Research on Teacher Effectiveness*. Holt, Rinehart and Winston, New York, pp. 196–231

Flanders N A 1967 Problems of observer training and reliability. In: Amidon E J, Hough J B (eds.) 1967 *Interaction Analysis: Theory, Research, and Applications*. Addison-Wesley, Reading, Massachusetts, pp. 158–66

Galton M 1979 Systematic classroom observation: British research. *Educ. Res.* 21: 109–15

Galton M, Simon B, Croll P 1980 *Inside the Primary Classroom*. Routledge and Kegan Paul, London

Galton M J, Willcocks J 1982 *Moving from the Primary Classroom*. Routledge and Kegan Paul, London

Hamilton D, Delamont S 1974 Classroom research: A cautionary tale. *Res. Educ.* 11: 1–15

Medley D M, Mitzel H E 1958 A technique for measuring classroom behaviour. *J. Educ. Psychol.* 49: 86–93

Medley D M, Mitzel H E 1963 Measuring classroom behavior by systematic observation. In: Gage N L (ed.) 1963 *Handbook of Research on Research on Teaching: A Project of the American Educational Research Association*. Rand McNally, Chicago, Illinois, pp. 247–328

Nuthall G A, Lawrence P J 1965 *Thinking in the Classroom: The Development of a Method of Analysis*. New Zealand Council for Educational Research, Wellington

Olson W C 1929 *The Measurement of Nervous Habits in Normal Children*. University of Minnesota Press, Minneapolis, Minnesota

Rosenshine B 1970 Evaluation of classroom instruction. *Rev. Educ. Res.* 40: 279–300

Rosenshine B, Furst N 1973 The use of direct observation to study teaching. In: Travers R M W (ed.) 1973 *Second Handbook of Research on Teaching: A Project of the American Educational Research Association*. Rand McNally, Chicago, Illinois, pp. 122–83

Scott W A 1955 Reliability of content analysis: The case of nominal coding. *Public Opinion Q.* 19: 321–25

Silberman C E 1970 *Crisis in the Classroom: The Remaking of American Education*. Random House, New York

Simon A, Boyer E G (eds.) 1970 *Mirrors for Behavior: An Anthology of Classroom Observation Instruments*. Research for Better Schools, Philadelphia, Pennsylvania

Smith B O, Meux M 1962 *A Study of the Logic of Teaching*. Bureau of Educational Research, University of Illinois, Urbana, Illinois

Taba H 1966 *Teaching Strategies and Cognitive Functioning in Elementary School Children*. San Francisco State College, San Francisco, California

Questionnaires

R. M. Wolf

A questionnaire is a self-report instrument used for gathering information about variables of interest to an investigator. It consists of a number of questions or items on paper that a respondent reads and answers.

The questions or items can be structured or unstructured. That is, the categories of response may be specified or left unspecified. A structured item such as sex would have the two categories, male and female, and the respondent is asked to check the one that describes him/her. An unstructured item, on the other hand, may ask the respondent to describe how he/she spent his/her last vacation.

A questionnaire, as a self-report instrument, is based on three assumptions. These are:

(a) the respondent can read and understand the questions or items;

(b) the respondent possesses the information to answer the questions or items; and

(c) the respondent is willing to answer the questions or items honestly.

These assumptions may or may not be warranted for a particular questionnaire in a particular study. Accordingly, the assumptions often have to be tested through adequate developmental work before a questionnaire can be used with confidence. Such developmental work often includes interviewing, piloting, and pretesting.

The variables of interest for which information is sought in a questionnaire can be quite varied. They can include factual questions about the respondent such as age, sex, and occupation, attitudes, opinions, interests, beliefs, aspirations, expectations, past, present, and planned activities in particular areas, memberships in various groups, and perceptions of various things. The list of what can be included in a questionnaire is almost without limit. What is included in a questionnaire will obviously be limited by the interests of an investigator, what can reasonably be asked in a questionnaire, and time constraints.

An investigator should limit the questions or items in a questionnaire to variables of primary interest. Each question or item should be explicitly or implicitly related to a particular research question or hypothesis. Even when investigators so restrict themselves, they often find it difficult to fully investigate all variables of interest without making the questionnaire so long as to substantially reduce the likelihood that respondents will answer it. Consequently, even when investigators restrict themselves to variables of interest, decisions will still need to be made about what can and should be included in a particular questionnaire.

The second constraint on what will be included in a questionnaire involves the sensitivity or delicacy of the content of particular questions or items. Matters of a personal nature such as sexual behavior and attitudes are a case in point. Many individuals do not wish to reveal their attitudes and behavior in an area that they consider to be a matter of privacy. Respondents may simply refuse to answer such questions, give what they believe to be socially desirable responses or, perhaps even worse, consign the questionnaire to the nearest wastebasket.

It is clear that asking highly personal questions can produce problems in a questionnaire. It is less obvious that apparently straightforward and objective questions can also create problems for a respondent. For example, a question regarding the amount of schooling may pose a problem for a respondent. If the residents of a community have, by and large, earned a university degree, an individual with only a high-school diploma may feel threatened by a question regarding the amount of schooling. Similarly, divorced people may feel reluctant to report their true marital status if they view divorce as containing some social stigma. Sensitivity on the part of the individual developing a questionnaire is needed along with considerable developmental work if such problems are to be fully identified and provisions made to deal with them.

The third constraint as to what will be included in a questionnaire is time. Respondents cannot be expected to spend a great deal of time answering a questionnaire. Experience with adults suggests that 30 minutes is the upper limit that can be expected in the way of answering time when questionnaires are administered in a group setting. When questionnaires are mailed to respondents, about 15 minutes appears to be the limit of respondent time. Questionnaires that are administered to students would need to be shorter and require less time. There are two issues involved here. The first is respondent fatigue. Simply stated, answering questionnaire items requires effort. After a while, respondents will tire and this can lead to careless or inaccurate responses. How much questionnaire material can be presented to a respondent is an issue to be addressed in development work. The second issue is more serious. It is the issue of respondent cooperation. A lengthy, time-consuming questionnaire may cause a respondent to cease to cooperate after a period of answering questions. At best one will receive an incomplete questionnaire and, at worst, the questionnaire will not be returned. Again, careful developmental work is needed to establish how much questionnaire material can be presented to a particular target group.

A well-made questionnaire is highly deceptive. It appears to be well-organized, the questions are clear, response options are well-drawn and exhaustive, and there is a natural ordering or flow to the questions that keeps the respondent moving towards completion of the questionnaire. These desirable attributes and the deceptive simplicity of a well-made questionnaire do not spring naturally out of the process of questionnaire construction but are the result of a great deal of painstaking developmental work. The remainder of this article will describe the steps that are needed to achieve such a result along with some attention to the problems that arise and decisions that are required at each step.

The first step in developing a questionnaire is the identification of variables to be studied. Such identification will depend on the nature of the research problem to be studied and the specific hypotheses and questions to be investigated. Theory and previous research will be a major guide in this area as well as conversations with knowledgeable individuals. It is also at this initial stage that the population of interest that will be studied needs to be identified.

Once the list of relevant variables has been identified, it is necessary to decide how data will be collected. A questionnaire is only one means of data gathering. Interviews, tests, and observational procedures are some of the other ways in which information can be gathered. A decision about an appropriate method of data collection will depend on: (a) the nature of the variables to be studied, (b) the nature of the target population that is to be studied, and (c) the amount of resources available for the investigation. Kinsey, for example, decided that the nature of the variables he wished to study, that is, sexual behaviors, were of such a delicate nature that only a carefully structured and sensitively conducted interview could elicit the information he needed. Other examples can be cited. The point is that the use of a questionnaire as a method of data gathering is neither automatic nor obvious.

Assuming that a decision has been made to use a questionnaire to gather data as a result of a conscious, deliberate process, it is then necessary to translate the variables into questions that can elicit the desired information. At this early stage it is generally recommended that the questions or items be unstructured. That is, no attempt be made to provide a set of response categories for the items. The items should then be organized into an order that appears reasonable to the investigator for tryout in an interview format. The investigator and one or two co-workers would then try out the questions in an interview with a few, for example, four or five, respondents from the population that will be studied. The aim of such an exercise is to obtain some information on the comprehensibility of the questions and whether they appear to elicit the desired information. Such an exercise is important in helping to provide a reality base for further development work and to furnish some feedback on how the questions and items are being received and interpreted as well as some idea as to the range of responses.

On the basis of such small tryout work it should be possible to revise the initial set of questions so that both their clarity and the likelihood of eliciting the desired information are increased. While it is expected that the wording of the initial questions will be modified and that additional questions may have to be added, it is possible that other questions will be eliminated. In the case of the tryout of several alternative ways of asking a particular question, it should be possible to decide which of the alternatives is most suitable. Also, it may be found that particular questions fail to elicit the information that is needed with regard to a variable of interest and, consequently, may need to be eliminated.

While considerable revision can and will take place on the basis of an initial tryout in an interview format, it is premature to structure the items by providing a set of response categories for each item. The information to structure items at this point in the developmental work is too limited. What is recommended rather is that the items and questions be organized into a pilot questionnaire that is reproduced for administration to a group of respondents from the target population. Such a pilot questionnaire would require some introductory statement informing the respondent of the nature of the study being undertaken, why the requested information will be important, a request for cooperation, and a pledge of anonymity and confidentiality in the treatment and use of information supplied by the respondent. This last requirement is the easiest to honor since the information supplied by the respondent will be used solely for further developmental work. Not having the respondent supply his or her name at this stage will usually enhance cooperation. Whether respondents do or do not supply their names in the main collection of data is an ethical issue (see *Ethical Considerations in Research*).

At the pilot stage there are still likely to be many more questions than will be included in a final questionnaire. This is to be expected since many decisions about the selection of a final set of questions or items will require additional information. Since the tryout questionnaire is apt to contain considerably more questions than a final questionnaire and since questions will be asked in an unstructured or open-ended form, the amount of time that would be required to complete the questionnaire might be considerable. If this is so, the questionnaire could be fractionated into two, three, or even more parts for the tryout. This would reduce the amount of time required for answering since the respondent would be answering only a fraction of the questions. Since the object of the tryout is to find out how individual items or, at most, groups of items are being answered, such fractionation is not only permissible but probably even desirable. Generally, when fractionating a questionnaire one tries to develop several forms of about equal length or, more important, of equal answering time. In administering the tryout questionnaire(s), one seeks to have roughly equivalent groups take each of the several forms. The desired number of respondents for each form should be at least 30 with a goal of about 50 people who are fully representative of the target population.

The results of the tryout will yield a wealth of information. Since this is the first set of results of the questions and items administered in written form, it will be interesting to determine whether the questions provided the desired type of response data or whether further work on the wording of questions is needed. Examination of the response data will also provide a basis for structuring many of the questions or items. For example, if one question asks respondents to indicate the number of books in their home, it will be possible to produce a frequency distribution of the number of books in the home, and, on the basis of that frequency distribution, produce a set of categories that will encompass the distribution and have sufficient variability for later analysis. Other variables that yield quantitative responses can be handled similarly. For qualitative variables, the data should permit the identification of a number of response categories and a frequency count for each category. In this way, it should be possible to structure or "close" many of the items. This will considerably facilitate later coding and analysis in the main study.

It may not be possible to structure all the items in a questionnaire although this remains a goal. For example, items about occupation, either the respondent's or his or her father's and mother's, may require unstructured items in order to obtain sufficient descriptive material to permit classification into an occupational categorization scheme. In such a case, a closed-ended item will not suffice. In addition, unstructured questionnaire items can be a source of rich and spontaneous response material that can enhance the interpretation of results. On the other hand, unstructured items place an additional burden on the respondent that can result in a reduction of the level of cooperation. Consequently, an investigator needs to achieve a delicate balance between the number of structured versus unstructured items. Information from the next phase of developmental work, pretesting, should furnish some guidance on the appropriate balance between the two types of items.

The results of the questionnaire in tryout form should enable an investigator to produce a penultimate version of the questionnaire. This version should consist largely of items in a structured form. However, since one cannot be sure that the response categories for all structured items are exhaustive, it is common practice to provide an extra category labeled "Other (please specify)" for many items and to allow ample space for the respondent to supply the needed information.

There are a number of other considerations that are necessary at this stage of the developmental work. A short statement of the purpose of the questionnaire needs to be placed at the beginning of the questionnaire along with the specific directions for answering. The material from the tryout version, with appropriate modification, should be used. It is also customary to begin the body of the questionnaire with an item asking the respondent to note the time he or she started to answer the questionnaire, requesting that the questionnaire be answered in a single sitting and, at the end of the questionnaire, requesting that the ending time be noted. In this way, it will be possible to estimate the time required to complete the questionnaire. This is important for two reasons. First, it will enable an investigator to decide whether to further shorten the questionnaire or not. Second, it will furnish a basis for scheduling the administration of the final questionnaire. The last task in the assembly of the questionnaire for pretesting is to affix a short statement at the end of the questionnaire instructing the respondent how to return the questionnaire to the investigator and to thank the respondent for his or her cooperation. Instructions regarding the return of the questionnaire are critical if the questionnaire is to be mailed.

One variable that is critical at this stage of development is the layout of the questionnaire. A good deal of work is required to produce a draft of the questionnaire in which the items are presented in a format that is attractive and will assist the respondent to complete the instrument. Consideration needs to be given to the size of type, sequencing of items, provision of adequate space to answer unstructured items, and other details of presentation. Unfortunately, there are few detailed guides for such work. Experimentation with different layouts and review by a few people from the population on whom the questionnaire will eventually be used are often undertaken for guidance on such matters. It is not necessary that the questionnaire actually be administered at this time, merely that it be reviewed on the basis of layout.

One area in which there has been research and where there is a fair degree of agreement is with regard to classificatory items such as sex, age, race, and the like. It is generally recommended that such items be placed at the end of a questionnaire and be preceded by a short introductory statement that such items are supplementary and will be used for classificatory purposes. The reason for this recommendation is that if the questionnaire began with such items and the stated purpose of the questionnaire was to survey, say, television viewing, a respondent might be put off by the apparent irrelevance of the items and, consequently, not answer the questionnaire. It is better to begin with items that are clearly related to the stated purpose of the questionnaire.

The draft questionnaire, reproduced in bulk, should be administered to a sample of individuals from the target population. A sample size of 50 to 100 respondents should be sufficient. Postadministration analysis should focus on producing frequency distributions of responses for each variable. Additional "closing-up" of items should take place, if warranted. The investigator will also need to pay attention to items in which the rate of nonresponse, or of "don't know" responses, exceeds 5 percent of the respondent sample (see *Missing Data and Nonresponse*). Such high rates are usually indicative of ambiguities that are still inherent in items or inadequacies in the response categories. Such problems will need to be dealt with in one way or another. If the variable that the item is measuring is central to the study, further developmental work might be needed. Finally, an analysis of the data on time to complete the questionnaire will have to be made to determine whether the questionnaire will have to be shortened or not. Even if the time data indicate that the time needed to answer the questionnaire is reasonable, a suggested time limit needs to be established for purposes of administration. It is generally recommended that a time limit be set at the time corresponding to the 90th percentile in the distribution of time data. This will ensure that virtually everyone will have sufficient time to answer the questionnaire.

At this point, a final questionnaire should be ready for use in a study. It should be attractive and present no problems for a respondent. If so, it is the fruit of a long and often painstaking process of development. The questionnaire should consist largely of structured items in which the respondent can easily find and check an appropriate response category. The number of items in which the respondent has to supply an answer in his or her own words should be small. The full questionnaire should require certainly less than 30 minutes to complete and, preferably, less than 15 or 20. It should also be possible to develop a codebook for easy postadministration coding and analysis.

The above presentation is intended to describe the process of questionnaire development. It is by no means exhaustive. Further information about each step can be found in the references. Particular attention will also need to be given to question wording so that subtle or not so subtle cues are not supplied, that suggest responding in a particular way. For example, consider the following questions:

(a) Do you approve of school prayer?

(b) You *do* approve of school prayer, don't you?

(c) Don't you disapprove of school prayer?

(d) You don't approve of school prayer, do you?

While the above four questions appear to be asking the same question, they are not. Questions (c) and (d) are highly suggestive and question (b) is rather suggestive. It should not be surprising that if each question was given to an independent random sample from the same population, results would differ. The point is that sensitivity and care are required in question wording if unbiased results are to be obtained.

A final note should be made about the use of questionnaires with students, especially those aged 12 and lower. It is obvious that great care needs to be taken in the development and use of questionnaires with children. Subtleties of language and complexity of wording must be avoided at all costs. Vocabulary must be at the simplest level. In addition, certain kinds of questions need to be avoided. Questions that deal with past experiences or actions as well as future intentions should not be asked since children's memories are apt to be faulty on past matters and future intentions are usually unclear. Thus, an investigator who is soliciting information from children is best advised to restrict questions to the present. Within the domain of the present, however, it is possible to inquire about actions and present circumstances as well as attitudes, opinions, and beliefs.

See also: Interviews in Sample Surveys; Survey Studies, Cross-sectional; Attitudes and their Measurement

Bibliography

Berdie D R, Anderson J F 1974 *Questionnaires: Design and Use.* Scarecrow, Metuchen, New Jersey
Jacobs T O 1974 *Developing Questionnaire Items: How to Do It Well.* Human Resources Research Organization, Alexandria, Virginia
Labaw P J 1980 *Advanced Questionnaire Design.* Abt, Cambridge, Massachusetts
Oppenheim A N 1966 *Questionnaire Design and Attitude Measurement.* Basic Books, New York
Payne S L 1951 *The Art of Asking Questions.* Princeton University Press, Princeton, New Jersey

Sex Differences in Ability and Achievement

J. P. Keeves

For nearly a century there has been continuing research into the nature and origins of sex differences in ability and achievement. This research has both led and supported the marked change in views towards the education of girls that has occurred during this period. In turn, however, the nature of the research being undertaken has changed several times in response to changing societal views and concerns. Perhaps more studies concerning sex differences have been undertaken and reported in the fields of education, psychology, and sociology than on any other single topic during this time, and as a consequence it is not possible to review all the studies that have examined and reported on sex differences. The research carried out in the United States into sex differences in ability and achievement has been surveyed successively by Tyler (1956), Anastasi (1958), and Maccoby (1966). They have reported that in the United States boys generally show stronger numerical and spatial abilities and perform better on tests of mathematical reasoning than girls, but girls usually do better in verbal and linguistic studies. However, Tyler (1969) has emphasized that the differences between the sexes in these areas are, in general, not large when compared with differences within each sex group. Nevertheless, there remains the major question for investigation of why marked differences between the sexes are observed in the patterns of education and career paths which are followed by the two groups. This article seeks to review the developments that have taken place in the research into this issue and to summarize the current state of knowledge and understanding.

1. Historical Overview

In 1873, Herbert Spencer in an article "Psychology of the Sexes" argued in terms of the theories of Charles Darwin that the intellectual attributes of women developed differently in the course of evolution. Women were thus deficient in the powers of abstract reasoning and in the most abstract of the emotions, the sentiment of justice. The prevalent views in Germany were even less favourable to women, who were considered to have developed differently in the course of evolution. Women were thus deficient in the powers essential for the survival of the race (Sherman 1978). In 1906 E. L. Thorndike rejected the view that the differences between the sexes which he had observed could be inherent, since such differences were too small to be of practical significance. Hollingworth, a student and colleague of Thorndike's at Teachers College, Columbia University, contended that the small differences observed were due to social influences and not to biological causes, and that the true intellectual potential of women would only be revealed when women received a similar education and had the right to choose equivalent careers. Such views supported the claims of the feminist movement and generated interest in research that sought evidence for the equality of the sexes. Nevertheless, the question remained: why were there apparently so few women of genius and more male mental defectives as had been pointed out by Havelock Ellis in his book *Men and Women* in 1894? He argued that there was social significance in the hypothesis of greater male variability for the development of civilization. However Karl Pearson, in 1897, challenged Ellis on both empirical and conceptual grounds, and concluded that the male variability hypothesis remained unproven. The reasons for such a low perceived proportion of women among the famous and eminent even today remains unclear.

During the 1920s and 1930s the techniques for the measurement of aspects of personality were developed, and research into sex differences was primarily concerned with the study of differences in attitudes and emotional needs, including the use of scales of masculinity and femininity in attempts to differentiate more accurately the characteristics of persons within the same sex group. Many of the studies undertaken were related to psychoanalytic theories which hypothesized that emotional differences arose from biological rather than sociological sources. However, during the 1950s the emphasis in research shifted once again to the study of sex roles in order to account for differences in personality development.

The very comprehensive review by Maccoby (1966) has proved to be a further turning point in the study of sex differences in so far as it focused on sex differences as an identifiable field of psychological and sociological inquiry. The subsequent emergence of the women's liberation movement led to new strands of research which sought to understand the implications of measured sex differences for female psychology and development. Recent research has sought to examine issues without using the male group as the reference group for the study of both differences and similarities. New approaches include the investigation of the processes operating within sex groups that are associated with biological, psychological, social, and cognitive development (Petersen et al. 1982).

It should be noted that a distinction is sometimes drawn between those differences which have their origins in genetic or biologically based factors, referred to as sex differences, and those that have their origins in environmental or sociocultural factors, referred to as gender differences. Since the latter group are malleable, the investigation of these so-called gender differences is attracting increased attention.

2. Sex Differences in Achievement

The basic issue in the examination of sex differences in achievement is concerned with the cognitive factors that lead boys and girls to study different subjects during the years of secondary schooling and thus to prepare themselves for different types of occupations and different careers. The rapid growth of the women's liberation movement and the increasing recognition of equal pay for women and men have led to some change in the patterns of subjects studied at school and in the courses taken at tertiary level, and thus to changes in career paths for women. As a consequence it is of relevance to examine not only sex differences in achievement across countries but also across time to determine whether different relationships are observable in different parts of the world, and at different points in time. It is unfortunate that the published findings of research have to date been dominated by work carried out in the United States. Clearly consideration of sex differences in educational achievement in only one country has severe limitations.

Tyler (1956) in a review of research in the United States reported that in all studies girls achieved consistently higher grades than did boys, were less frequently retarded, and were more frequently accelerated through the years of schooling than boys. When batteries of achievement tests were used to assess achievement rather than using school grades for this purpose, girls continued to exceed boys in performance in language studies, and boys tended to perform better in mathematics and science. However, the differences between the sexes were small and frequently inconsistent within the same subject area; for example, boys performed better on problem solving in mathematics, while girls frequently performed better on computation. Tyler contended that the magnitude of the sex differences reported afforded no justification for the setting up of different schools to provide different teaching for boys and girls.

Keeves (1973) reported from the International Association for the Evaluation of Educational Achievement (IEA) studies of mathematics and science that while the general pattern of results was one of superior performance by male students in both these subjects, there was considerable variation between countries in the extent to which boys exceeded girls in performance. Furthermore, while the differences between the sexes in achievement in science increased markedly from primary to secondary schooling and to the terminal years of schooling (Comber and Keeves 1973), with a similar relationship being observed in mathematics from the lower-secondary to the upper-secondary-school levels, the relationships were confounded by sex differences in retentivity or holding power, both in the particular subject and the particular school. Consequently, it is important when reporting sex differences in achievement to do so for an age level where attendance at school and the study of the subject under review are compulsory to ensure that the findings are not confounded by selection, differences in retentivity, or patterns of subject choice. Alternatively, where such differences in selection or retentivity occur, some adjustment must be made before effective comparisons can be carried out. It is evident from the data recorded that the differences across countries are too great for simple explanations, for example, in terms of sampling variations, to be advanced as to why such sex differences should have been observed. The differences recorded could well be related, in part, to differences in the time given to the study of the subjects of mathematics and science, and thus to differences in opportunity to learn or to the patterns of provision in single-sex schools and coeducational schools which would appear to reflect different expectations for the roles of men and women in society. An index of enrolment at single sex and coeducational schools has, for example, been found to correlate (0.70) with differences between the sexes in achievement in mathematics at the lower-secondary-school level across 12 countries. Whatever the origins of these sex differences in achievement, it is clear that, primarily as a consequence of effects operating at the secondary-school level, girls are less well-prepared to enter occupations and careers that require a prior knowledge of mathematics and science.

Walker (1976) has reported from the IEA Six Subject Study on sex differences in other subject areas. On reading comprehension tests, boys showed lower performance than girls in a majority of countries, but the differences between the sexes were, in general, slight. In the cognitive literature tests, at both the 14-year-old and the preuniversity levels and in all countries the boys did less well, and they also showed less interest in literature. Again, in the study of the teaching of English as a foreign language, the boys scored below the girls on both the reading and the listening tests, but the differences were small. In the study of the teaching of French as a foreign language, it should be noted that fewer boys had chosen to study French, and showed inferior achievement in some countries. In the main, the statistically significant differences between the sexes in the learning of French were recorded in the English-speaking countries. When other factors were taken into consideration, it was only for the preuniversity students in the English-speaking countries that the sex of the student was important.

In the civic education achievement tests, the boys at the 14-year-old age level generally recorded higher scores than the girls, and in all countries taking part in the study the boys showed greater superiority at the preuniversity level.

That these differences in both achievement and participation between the sexes were found in the several different subjects examined at the secondary-school level and that the patterns of differences varied across countries, suggests that these differences are related to the sex-role expectations of the societies in which these young people are undertaking their secondary schooling.

Moss (1982) reported on sex differences in achievement in mathematics in Australia across an interval of 14 years from 1964 to 1978, during which period the women's liberation movement started to have a significant influence on employment opportunities and on the participation by girls in education at the upper-secondary and tertiary levels. The findings from this study, which involved the use of the same tests on the two occasions and across seven autonomous state educational systems within Australia, indicated at the lower-secondary-school level a slightly higher level of performance by girls on subtests involving elementary arithmetic and algebra, and a higher level of performance by boys on subtests involving advanced arithmetic and geometry. There was little evidence of change in the patterns of sex differences associated with the learning of mathematics over the 14-year interval, and recognizable and consistent sex differences in achievement were recorded over this time period for the different state systems. When sex was the only variable taken into account at the preuniversity level, this study reported not only the superior average level of achievement of boys on both occasions, but also an increase in the sex difference in achievement between 1964 and 1978. On the surface, this change in average level of achievement appears contrary to expectations. That the change is only superficial becomes apparent when variables other than achievement are considered as well. Over the 14-year period there were marked increases in the retention of girls at school and in their participation in mathematics courses at this level. In terms of the yield associated with the learning of mathematics at the upper-secondary level, then, while the average achievement and participation of girls did not equal that of boys, greater gains in yield (achievement × participation) were made by girls over the period from 1964 to 1978. Furthermore, after adjustments were made statistically for time given to the study of mathematics, the sex differences in achievement in all but one of the seven systems showed a tendency to reverse, with girls showing a superior level of adjusted performance in a majority of systems on the later occasion.

The recorded evidence appears to suggest that sex differences in educational achievement, at the upper-secondary-school level, while influential in determining courses undertaken at the postsecondary level and in determining employment and career opportunities available on the completion of study, show different patterns across countries and some differences over time. This seems to indicate that such sex differences in achievement arise at least, in part, from societal and cultural factors.

3. Sex Differences in Abilities

It is of course possible that the sex differences recorded above have their origins not in societal and cultural factors but in differences in abilities between the sexes.

3.1 Intelligence

Many research workers have from time to time reported differences between the sexes in performance on intelligence tests. However, some tests have given boys a slight advantage and other tests would appear to have favoured girls. Where such results have shown a consistent result favouring one sex rather than the other, the tests have been revised to remove what is considered to be a sex bias, by the deletion of items from a test that shows substantial sex differences. Tyler (1956) has noted that in an extensive and well-executed study carried out by the Scottish Council for Research in Education in 1937, using the Stanford–Binet intelligence test with children aged approximately 11 years, there was a difference in IQ in favour of boys of less than one point. However, when the study was repeated in 1947 using the Terman–Merrill revision of the Stanford–Binet, with a large, carefully drawn, and equivalent sample, a difference of four points of IQ in favour of girls was recorded. This difference, while of statistical significance, does not appear to be of marked practical significance. Nevertheless, the problem remains as to whether the differences recorded between the two occasions were a consequence of the sampling and the execution of the two studies, changes in the characteristics of male and female student populations, or differences resulting from the revision of the test that was employed.

3.2 Verbal, Quantitative, and Spatial Abilities

In the context of the achievement differences discussed above it is more relevant to consider whether the sexes differ with respect to specific abilities rather than whether they differ in general intelligence. Female students would appear to perform better on tests of verbal ability than do male students, although the results supporting this conclusion show some inconsistencies. There is greater consistency in the results for all areas of verbal function, but generally the differences are relatively small. Maccoby and Jacklin (1974) describe the female advantage in the verbal area as about 0.25 of a student standard deviation. Moreover, Maccoby and Jacklin (1974) give little credence to the long-held view that girls gain the advantage in verbal skills during the early years, before the age of 3 years. They suggest that, if girls have an early advantage boys catch up by about age 3, and both sexes perform similarly until about 10 or 11 years of age.

Males generally score higher than females on tests of quantitative ability, when this is assessed in terms of quantitative reasoning or problem solving rather than in terms of computational skill. Again there are inconsistencies in the results obtained up to the age of about 12 or 13 years, when the quantitative ability of boys appears to develop at a faster rate.

There are, generally, significant sex differences associated with the superior performance of boys recorded with respect to spatial abilities (Petersen et al. 1982). Sherman (1978), however, emphasizes that the size of the differences reported is very small, certainly much

smaller than has been suggested in some of the writing on the subject. Moreover, the age at which differentiation between the sexes becomes clear is, as Maccoby and Jacklin (1974) suggest, during the years of early adolescence.

It seems possible that the apparent superiority of females on verbal ability tests and of males on spatial and quantitative ability tests could account for the differences reported above with respect to achievement test performance. In the main, sex differences in achievement test scores in mathematics are substantially reduced or eliminated when spatial ability has been partialled out. However, it is not possible to conclude from this that the sex differences in spatial ability cause the differences in mathematics achievement which have been observed, although the results obtained are consistent with this hypothesis. Fennema and Sherman (1977) have shown that it is possible to eliminate sex differences by controlling for time spent in learning mathematics or attitudes towards mathematics, variables which are associated with distinct differences between the sexes. The effects of differences in ability on achievement test scores would be more soundly based if the origins of the differences in ability could be identified, and the possibility thus examined that the differences in both ability and achievement have related origins. It is evident that at the secondary-school level substantial differences in achievement do emerge in some situations. However, differences in verbal, quantitative, and spatial abilities which might be seen to be causes of these achievement differences are harder to establish, particularly since sex differences in these abilities do not become clear until adolescence, and would not appear, in general, to be large.

4. The Origins of Sex Differences in Abilities

The origins of sex differences in abilities and achievement, under the assumption that effects of the factors on achievement are mediated through their effects on abilities, or that identified factors will influence conjointly both abilities and achievement, lie in several possible areas: biological factors include genetic, maturational, hormonal, and brain lateralization influences; socialization factors including effects which are transmitted by parents, teachers, or the peer group and are related to sex roles in society; and affective factors including expectancy of success, attitudes, and values.

4.1 Biological Differences

For detailed discussions of the evidence available from research carried out in a range of disciplines and of the many theoretical and methodological issues associated with research into the biological basis of sex-related differences in cognitive performance both Sherman (1978) and Wittig and Petersen (1979) should be consulted.

(a) *Genetic differences.* Perhaps the most basic difference between the sexes is the chromosomal difference, and the evidence of a relationship between parent–child scores on spatial ability tests has led to the suggestion of a possible sex-linked genetic factor. However, the hypothesis that spatial visualization is sex limited has not been supported by later findings.

(b) *Maturational differences.* It has been suggested that the observed accelerated female physical development is paralleled mentally. Ljung (1965) has shown using group data that there was general agreement between the physical growth pattern and the mental growth pattern at adolescence, and that the mental growth of girls occurred sooner than that of boys. However, psychologists have not been successful in linking maturation to cognitive ability, although this possibility cannot be overlooked.

(c) *Hormonal differences.* Since differences in abilities begin to emerge at adolescence, when hormonal differences between the sexes are increased, the possibility of a relationship between hormones and the development of cognitive abilities cannot be ignored. However, very few effects have been demonstrated although some relations have been shown between androgen levels and cognitive performance.

(d) *Brain lateralization differences.* Studies of sex differences in brain organization have been carried out in recent years. While there are sex-related differences in bilaterality, in so far as females use the left hemisphere for spatial function more than males do, such differences have not as yet been related to sex differences in cognition or more importantly in space perception.

4.2 Socialization Differences

There is a growing body of evidence to support the theory that sex-role socialization both directly and indirectly influences sex-related cognitive differences. Moreover, the effects of sex-role socialization differences start to emerge at the beginning of secondary schooling and continue throughout the years of adolescence. A study by Keeves (1972) has shown that parental attitudes and home practices, student–teacher interpersonal relationships, and peer group attitudes and practices had small but recognizable effects on achievement in mathematics and science at the lower-secondary-school level in Australian high schools. It was also evident that there were relationships of significance between such factors, achievement, and the sex of the student. In Wittig and Petersen (1979) the effects of sex role as a mediator of intellectual functioning, together with relationships between sex-role socialization and achievement in mathematics are reviewed. Further work is required to clarify the relationships seen to exist and trace in full the effects of sex role on cognitive functioning. Nevertheless, it is evident that differences in the patterns of socialization of male and female students, both across countries and across time, as well as between students within a particular country at a particular time, are likely to be the most powerful factors influencing the development of the sex differences in abilities and achievements reported in this article.

Meece and Parsons (1982) have argued with respect to the development of sex differences in achievement in mathematics that socializers are likely to contribute in three important ways: (a) male and female socializers create differences through their power as role models; (b) socializers convey through a variety of direct and indirect means different expectations and goals for boys and girls; and (c) socializers promote the development of different activities for male and female children. The studies reviewed by Meece and Parsons (1982), particularly the studies by Parsons et al. (1982a, 1982b), strongly endorse the hypothesis that socializers treat girls and boys differently in a variety of ways that would seem to be related to course selection. Some of the studies reviewed assessed directly the causal relationships between these socialization experiences and both achievement and academic choices. Such factors as parental encouragement and parental perceptions and expectations were related to the children's plans to continue to take mathematics courses. However, the direction of causality has been difficult to determine. In addition, factors associated with the behaviours of students in classrooms which their teachers foster may also contribute to the development of sex differences in performance.

4.3 Affective Differences

It seems likely that the effects of socializers would be most marked on the attitudes and values held by students which act as mediating influences between the socializers and ability and achievement outcomes. Many affective factors have been studied in relation to the learning of mathematics. In particular, girls have been found to be more likely to be less confident about their ability to solve mathematical problems, and to be less likely to believe that mathematics would be personally useful to them.

(a) *Expectancy of success.* It is often hypothesized as a partial explanation of the apparently poorer achievement of girls in mathematics and science that there is a motive to avoid success that is stronger in girls than in boys. There is a growing body of evidence that girls are higher on measures of fear of success than boys and that this attitude acts more strongly towards quantitative studies, perceived to be a male preserve, than towards verbal and language studies. If this were a significant factor influencing performance on both ability and achievement tests, there is some hope that it would be a malleable factor and gains could be effected in the performance of girls through programmes to change attitudes. A study which examines the factors to which girls attribute their ability or inability to learn mathematics and their persistence or lack of persistence in the study of mathematics has been reported by Wolleat et al. (1980). A related intervention study to increase participation by both male and female students in the learning of mathematics has been reported by Fennema et al. (1981).

(b) *Attitudinal and value differences.* All the available evidence from studies of sex differences in personality leads to the conclusion that the sexes differ far more in the values they hold and in their general orientation to life than they do in measured abilities. In so far as girls have different interests, express different attitudes to learning, and hold different values with regard to learning that is of importance to them, such differences can be expected to influence their achievement in different subjects at school, and possibly through cumulative experience and the development of cognitive skills, influence their measured verbal, quantitative, and spatial abilities (Maccoby and Jacklin 1974).

5. Problems in Sex Difference Research

In concluding this article on sex differences in ability and achievement, it is necessary to draw attention to some of the problems of research that have no doubt led to the confounding of relationships and the contamination of results. First, the complexities of sex identification when anomalous chromosomal arrangements occur cannot be ignored, particularly when dealing with subgroups such as the retarded. Secondly, the development of tests of intelligence in such a way as to eliminate items with apparent sex bias poses problems for establishing what the tests measure. Likewise there is a tendency in research into general and specific abilities to label a particular test in terms of a specific ability. However, this test may have markedly different item types and properties when compared with other tests purporting to measure the same ability. Thirdly, it is not possible to conduct an experimental study involving sex characteristics, because subjects cannot be randomly allocated to a sex group; from birth subjects have been treated in ways considered appropriate to their sex. Fourthly, many studies involving large numbers of cases have reported differences which are statistically significant as a consequence of the large sample sizes, but which are associated with effects of such a size as to be of little practical significance. These are some of the concerns associated with research in this area. For further discussion of these issues the reader should consult Fairweather (1976) and Sherman (1978).

Bibliography

Anastasi A 1958 *Differential Psychology: Individual and Group Differences in Behavior*. Macmillan, New York
Comber L C, Keeves J P 1973 *Science Education in Nineteen Countries: An Empirical Study*. Almqvist and Wiksell, Stockholm
Fairweather H 1976 Sex differences in cognition. *Cognition* 4: 231–80
Fennema E, Sherman J A 1977 Sex-related differences in mathematics achievement, spatial visualization and affective factors. *Am. Educ. Res. J.* 47: 51–71
Fennema E et al. 1981 Increasing women's participation in mathematics: An intervention study. *J. Res. Math. Educ.* 12: 3–14
Keeves J P 1972 *Educational Environment and Student Achievement*. Almqvist and Wiksell, Stockholm
Keeves J P 1973 Differences between the sexes in mathematics and science courses. *Int. Rev. Educ.* 19: 47–63
Ljung B O 1965 *The Adolescent Spurt in Mental Growth*. Almqvist and Wiksell, Stockholm
Maccoby E E (ed.) 1966 *The Development of Sex Differences*. Stanford University Press, Stanford, California
Maccoby E E, Jacklin C N 1974 *The Psychology of Sex Differences*. Stanford University Press, Stanford, California
Meece J L, Parsons J E 1982 Sex differences in math achievement: Toward a model of academic choice. *Psychol. Bull.* 91: 324–48
Moss J D 1982 *Towards Equality: Progress by Girls in Mathematics in Australian Secondary Schools*. Australian Council for Educational Research, Hawthorn, Victoria
Parsons J E, Alder T F, Kaczala C M 1982a Socialization of achievement attitudes and beliefs: Parental influences. *Child Dev.* 53: 310–21
Parsons J E, Kaczala C M, Meece J L 1982b Socialization of achievement attitudes and beliefs: Classroom influences. *Child Dev.* 53: 322–39
Petersen A C et al. 1982 Sex differences. In: Mitzel H E (ed.) 1982 *Encyclopedia of Educational Research*, 5th edn. Free Press, New York, pp. 1696–712
Sherman J A 1978 *Sex-related Cognitive Differences: An Essay on Theory and Evidence*. Thomas, Springfield, Illinois
Tyler L E 1956 *The Psychology of Human Differences*, 2nd edn. Appleton–Century–Crofts, New York
Tyler L E 1969 Sex differences. In: Ebel R L (ed.) 1969 *Encyclopedia of Educational Research*, 4th edn. Macmillan, Toronto, pp. 1217–21
Walker D A 1976 *The IEA Six Subject Survey: An Empirical Study of Education in Twenty-one Countries*. Almqvist and Wiksell, Stockholm
Wittig M A, Petersen A C (eds.) 1979 *Sex-related Differences in Cognitive Functioning: Development Issues*. Academic Press, New York
Wolleat P E et al. 1980 Sex differences in high school students' causal attributions of performance in mathematics. *J. Res. Math. Educ.* 11: 356–66

Repertory Grid Technique

R. J. Alban-Metcalfe

Repertory grid (repgrid) technique was devised by George Kelly within the context of his "personal construct theory", but has come to be used as a technique in its own right. In essence, it is an approach designed to carry out effectively the everyday process of trying to find out how people view the world from their own perspectives. For this reason, in its simpler forms, repertory grid technique has been compared to a well-structured interview. It can, however, be modified in a wide variety of ways, and can be augmented by sophisticated statistical and other mathematical procedures.

In repertory grid technique, the term element is used to denote the persons (including self), things, and events that together constitute an individual's environment.

The term construct denotes the dimensions or reference axes used by the individual to discriminate between elements. According to Kelly, each person characteristically builds up an internal representation of the world in terms of a finite number of constructs. Constructs are conceived of as being bipolar, for example, "nice to know, versus not nice to know", "interesting, versus boring". Each person's constructs, which are based on the unique way that he or she perceives the world, are themselves unique, though individuals living in the same culture tend to have similar constructs. Unique also is the way that constructs are interrelated to form that person's construct system. Repertory grid technique can be used specifically to determine (a) which constructs an individual uses, (b) how those constructs are used, and (c) the interrelationships between the constructs.

The commonest ways of eliciting constructs are verbal, for example, by an interviewer asking people to indicate what similarities and what differences they see between specified groups of elements, though nonverbal approaches have also been developed. It is important to recognize, however, that a construct is a dimension; it is not a verbal label. Thus, different individuals are likely to have subtly (or in some cases fundamentally) different constructs to which the same verbal label is attached. As an example, the verbal label "funny, versus not funny" may be used to indicate two very different constructs used by a pupil and a teacher. Conversely, though, in the vast majority of instances, people from the same culture use mutually agreed verbal labels to indicate similar constructs. The particular constructs that given individuals use can be determined directly by asking them to verbalize discriminations they make between elements with which they are familiar. How they used these constructs, and the meaning of the constructs, can be inferred by asking the individuals to apply the same constructs to other elements, or exploring the implications of each discrimination. The interrelationships between constructs, and more information about their meaning, can be inferred either by eliciting a series of constructs that the individual sees as being causally related (i.e., laddering), or by recourse to mathematical techniques.

In eliciting constructs from individuals, a number of procedures can be adopted. Of these, the simplest involves presenting the person with combinations of three elements at a time (triads), with the name of each element written on a separate card, and asking for some important way in which two of the elements are similar to each other, and different from the third. The way in which two of the elements are similar is referred as the emergent pole of the construct. The other pole can either be the way in which the third element was different, or be the logical opposite of the emergent pole. As an alternative, the elements can all be presented at the same time, written in a row across the top of a piece of paper marked out into squares, and the constructs elicited by the interviewer directing attention to specified triads (or dyads) (see Fig. 1). After a specified number of constructs has been elicited, and written in columns at each side of the sheet of paper, the person can be asked to construe each of the elements in relation to each of the constructs. Indication of which pole applies to each element can be made either by dichotomous or rated responses, or by rank ordering the elements. A third approach to eliciting constructs is through "free" description, oral or written. "Self-characterization" grids, for example, can be devised by extracting bipolar constructs from individuals' descriptions of themselves. Such descriptions are usually given in the third person, as if they were descriptions of the principal character in a play or film.

Two major developments of the repertory grid have been laddering and pyramid construction. In the first of these, a construct is chosen by the interviewer, and the person asked which pole applies to a given element, say, for example, the element "me as I am now", and why. For example, a teacher might say that the construct pole "like to work in a large school, versus don't like to work in a large school" best describes "me as I am now". In response to a series of "Why?" questions, the sequence of constructs elicited might be—"like to have lots of

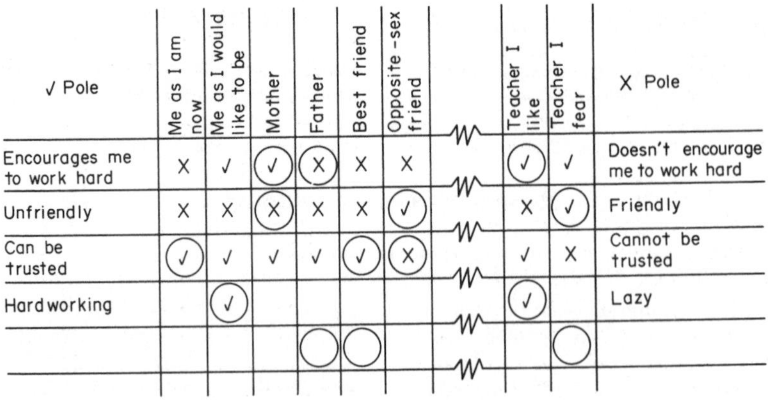

√ Pole	Me as I am now	Me as I would like to be	Mother	Father	Best friend	Opposite-sex friend		Teacher I like	Teacher I fear	X Pole
Encourages me to work hard	X	√	Ⓥ	Ⓧ	X	X		Ⓥ	√	Doesn't encourage me to work hard
Unfriendly	X	X	Ⓧ	X	X	Ⓥ		X	Ⓥ	Friendly
Can be trusted	Ⓥ	√	√	√	Ⓥ	Ⓧ		√	X	Cannot be trusted
Hard working		Ⓥ						Ⓥ		Lazy
			Ⓞ		Ⓞ				Ⓞ	

Figure 1
A partially completed repertory grid. Constructs elicited with reference to the triads of elements indicated by the circles

other teachers around me" (versus the opposite), "like to have other adults to talk to" (versus the opposite), "like to have my mind stimulated by intelligent conversation" (versus the opposite), and "keeps me sane" (versus the opposite). Note (a) that the constructs elicited are related logically to one another (at least from the individual's point of view), and (b) that the sequence of constructs can be thought of as being arranged in an hierarchical manner. Thus, "like to work in a large school" is a relatively subordinate construct, whereas "like to have my mind stimulated by intelligent conversation" is relatively superordinate. Note also, that the teacher could not be expected to give a reasoned answer to the question "Why do you want to remain sane?" "Keeping sane" is a core construct, that is, a construct that is essential to that person's very being as a person.

The elicitation process just described is known as laddering up a construct system. The opposite process of laddering down can be achieved by asking questions of the type, "How do you know that construct pole X applies to element A?", or "What evidence is there that X is true of element A?" In this way, subordinate constructs can be elicited.

In pyramid construction, individuals are asked, first of all, to think of some other element, say, a teacher or a pupil, with whom they feel most relaxed, and to specify an attribute which is characteristic of that element. Secondly, the request is made to state the kind of element (in this case a person) that would represent the opposite of the selected attribute. Having elicited two poles of a construct, the interviewer inquires what kind of a person the first element is. The third stage involves laddering down each of the opposite poles of the construct, so identifying a "pyramid" of relationships between constructs.

Two principles should govern the choice of elements in the repertory grid technique: (a) the relevance of the elements to the part of the construct system to be investigated, and (b) the representativeness of the chosen elements. Thus, if intimate personal relationships are the focus of interest, then the elements should include persons who correspond to role titles such as, "me as I am now" (and perhaps also "me as I would like to be", "me as my best friend/mother/wife sees me", and so on), members of close family and friends, and "significant" others, such as teachers, and older friends and acquaintances who are loved, admired, or feared. Similarly, if the focus of interest is relationships at school or work, or school subjects, hobbies and interests, careers, or clothes, then representative elements from these areas should be chosen. Relevance of elements selected is important because constructs have only limited ranges of convenience, or appropriateness: thus, the construct "printed, versus not printed" is relevant to construing books and syllabi, and also dresses and skirts, but it cannot be used meaningfully in relation to people, school subjects, or careers. Further, it is likely that a complete range of relevant constructs will be elicited only if the elements constitute a fully representative sample. The number of elements used commonly varies from around 10 to 25. The greater the number of elements, the more likelihood of representativeness being achieved, though in some circumstances, the subject matter may mean that fewer elements are available, or the nature of the sample (e.g., less able pupils) may mean that fewer are desirable.

Just as with elements, the greater the number of relevant constructs that are elicited, the greater their likelihood of being representative. Again, optimal numbers range from around 10 to 25, though most people appear to use fewer than 20 different constructs in relation to people, and some use as few as one or two. Constructs can be classified in a number of ways, such as into physical, for example, "tall" (versus the opposite), situational, for example, "is a pupil from this school?" (versus the opposite), behavioural, for example, "writes quickly" (versus the opposite), and psychological, for example, "is likely to do badly under exam pressure", (versus the opposite); or into vague, for example, "is OK" (versus the opposite), and excessively precise, for example, "is a medical student" (versus the opposite).

Repertory grid data can be analysed in a wide variety of ways, and manipulated using a wide range of procedures. Thus, the interviewer may simply be concerned to note which constructs a given individual uses, and in the case of laddering or pyramid construction, also to infer relationships between constructs. Alternatively, elicited constructs can be used in idiographic or nomothetic instruments, relevant to a particular individual or group of individuals, or to particular elements. In some forms, repertory grid data can be subjected to statistical or other mathematical procedures, or used as the basis for devising interactive computer programs.

Mathematical analyses of repertory grids have been used to calculate a number of "structural" indices concerned with relationships between elements and constructs. Notable among these are cognitive complexity, cognitive differentiation, and articulation, which are measures of tendency to construe elements in multidimensional ways, identification and assimilative projection, which are concerned with perceived similarity between self and others, and constellatoriness and the coefficient of convergence, which measure similarities in the use of constructs. Mathematical techniques commonly applied to repertory grid data include cluster and factor analysis, and on the bases of these, diagrammatic representations of element and construct relationships have been devised.

The applications of repertory grid technique fall into two principal groups, "static" and "dynamic". In both groups, repertory grids can either be idiographic, in which case the individual's own constructs (or a mixture of own and provided constructs) are used, or nomothetic, in which case, for purposes of comparison, provided constructs are used commonly (though not exclusively). Examples of the "static" use of repgrid data are determination of a student's (or teacher's) perceptions of, say, self, family, and peers, or perceptions of self in relation to career opportunities in vocational guidance. "Dynamic" use of the repertory grid can involve completion of a comparable grid on two or more occasions, in order to give a measure of the extent to which an individual's construct system changes over time. This can be useful, for example, in studying the development of self-awareness, or friendship development. Alternatively, repertory grid data can form the basis of interactive computer programs, for example, in decision-making exercises.

Bibliography

Fransella F, Bannister D 1977 *A Manual for Repertory Grid Technique*. Academic Press, London
Pope M L, Keen T R 1981 *Personal Construct Psychology and Education*. Academic Press, London
Shaw M L G (ed.) 1981 *Recent Advances in Personal Construct Technology*. Academic Press, London

Unintended Effects in Educational Research

S. Ball

An unintended effect is an outcome that is peripherally related to, and *not* the reason for the implementation of an experimental program or treatment. This article will consider (a) not only side effects, but also other unintended effects that have been observed in research and evaluation; (b) reactive effects; (c) after effects; (d) the Hawthorne effect; (e) the John Henry effect; (f) the Pygmalion effect; and (g) the Golem effect.

1. Side Effects

Side effects are usually unintended outcomes, but it is not uncommon for program developers to recognize the possibility of a side effect and plan to have it happen.

An example of an unintended side effect is a foreign-language teaching program that is so heavily structured that the students dislike learning the foreign language. The intended main effect was the learning of the foreign language. The unintended side effect was the development of a distaste for further learning of the language. Certainly the program developers would not want that to happen. Note, then, that in this instance the unintended side effect was negative. It could have been positive. For example, a children's television show might have as an intended main goal that the viewers learn about children in other countries. An unintended positive side effect might be that viewers take out relevant books from the school library and their reading comprehension and vocabulary are thereby improved.

Intended side effects are hoped-for outcomes that usually are outside the domain of the intended main effects. Thus, if the intended main effects are achievement and cognitively oriented, then the intended side effects will usually be attitudinally affectively oriented. If the major goal is to improve the students' knowledge and skill in mathematics, the intended side effect might be to enhance the students' self-confidence in and liking of mathematics.

Some side effects may be so important that they outweigh the main intended outcomes. A tragic illustration of this occurred in the drug evaluation field with the tranquilizer, thalidomide. It was found to be effective in its intended role but it was not until it had gone into general use in Europe that it was found to have tragic consequences on the fetuses of pregnant women.

Because side effects can be vitally important in evaluating educational programs, Scriven (1972) proposed a goal-free model of program evaluation. He argued that an evaluator who knows the program goals will be too prone to assess only those goal areas ignoring the unintended side effects. With a goal-free evaluation, however, the evaluator according to Scriven is more likely to assess the impact of a program whether intended or not.

Evaluators should be aware that sometimes the intended main effects fail to appear yet positive side effects do occur. For example, innovative educational program A is not superior to traditional program B, but program A does have the positive side effect that students are more motivated to stay on in school. This side effect may itself become the rationale for recommending the substitution of program A for program B.

A difficult question is who decides what side effects to look for. In general, program developers do not want evaluators to search for negative side effects. There should be clarity in the contract or the work order specifying the degree of autonomy given the evaluator in making decisions on what side effects to look for. Ideally this decision should be arrived at only after full consultation among the program developers, funders, clients, staff and evaluators.

2. Reactive Effects

Reactive effect is a term used in research and evaluation when the measurement procedures or research/evaluation design distort the data obtained and the conclusions reached.

Reactive effects in measurement occur when the behavior elicited by the measurement procedures is not characteristic of the behavior that would have occurred in the absence of the measurement procedure. For example, suppose a researcher wishes to know the impact of a new teaching technique on student behavior, and suppose further that the measurement procedure involves an observer in a classroom using a behavior checklist as the teacher works with the students. The presence of the observer may cause the students to behave differently in comparison to how they would behave with no observer in the classroom. The observer, in this case, has a reactive effect on the evidence obtained.

Distortions due to reactive effects in measurement may be the result of subjects trying to make a good impression on the data gatherer, of personal interactions between interviewer and interviewee (in this case the sex, race, age, and ethnicity of the interviewer can affect the responses obtained), of response sets (for example young children tend to answer "yes" to questions posed by authority figures), of initial questions in a test leading to changes in understanding or to a new appreciation by the test taker of what is considered important and so affecting the way the test taker answers the later questions, and of changes in the environment created by the measurer (for example the placing of a videotape machine in a library might affect the way students behave during a library period).

In general, the less obtrusive the measurement procedure, the less reactive it is likely to be. Webb et al. (1966) provide an excellent presentation of unobtrusive measures in their book: *Unobtrusive Measures: Nonreactive Research in the Social Sciences*. A more extensive discussion of response sets, reactive effects, and unobtrusive measures is presented by Anderson et al. (1975).

Reactive effects (distortions) due to research/evaluation design deficiencies may also lead to erroneous conclusions.

3. After Effects

An after effect, as the term implies, is an impact that occurs some time after a treatment has been implemented. The term "sleeper effect" has also been used instead of after effect. Sometimes an after effect is noted years after the treatment has ended. Most research and evaluation studies fail to test for the long-delayed after effects because the final posttest occurs too soon after a treatment is ended. If there is a possibility of an after effect occurring, the evaluation design should include both an immediate posttest (at the end of the treatment) and at least one delayed posttest.

An example of after effect is provided by Kersh and Wittrock (1962) in their review of research on teaching techniques. They found that "direct" teaching techniques seemed to show a stronger impact than "discovery learning" techniques when the groups were tested immediately after the respective treatment. However, a delayed posttest (some six weeks after the treatment was over) showed the reverse to be true. The discovery learning group had shown little fade out of results and now performed better than the direct teaching group. Presumably an after effect of discovery learning was motivational, causing the students to continue to rehearse and learn to a degree not matched by the direct teaching group.

A controversial but potentially important example of after effect has been noted in the evaluative research on Head Start, a program for disadvantaged preschoolers. In the first decade of Head Start research it was noted that the program had an initial impact on children but that this impact did not seem to provide a permanent aid. That is, although the impact was observable when the children started regular school at the age of 5 or 6, it seemed to lessen so that there was little or no difference between the erstwhile Head Start participants and their comparable non-Head Start peers by third grade (age 8–9). However, an after effect (sleeper effect) was noted. Children who had been in Head Start seemed to forge ahead of their controls in the middle-school years (grades 6 and 7).

An after effect should not be confused with a side effect. The side effect happens concurrently with the main, intended effects but the after effect, if it occurs, happens at a time after the main and side effects.

4. The Hawthorne Effect

The Hawthorne effect is a reactive effect and it refers to the change in behavior that occurs when the subjects in an evaluation or experiment are aware that they are being studied. This awareness is confounded with the independent variable being studied; so any positive impact noted in the research can be causally ascribed either to the independent variable or to the awareness of the subjects.

The Hawthorne effect is well-illustrated by the series of experiments (Pennock 1929) which took place at the United States Western Electric Company factory from 1924 to 1927 at Hawthorne, Illinois. The label "Hawthorne effect" was coined by Pennock to describe the unexpected findings noted by him and his colleagues (Snow 1927). Many independent variables were systematically manipulated (e.g., illumination, rest pauses, pay incentives) and the employees were informed of what was happening. The enigma was that productivity tended to increase irrespective of the experimental manipulation. It became clear that the employees' awareness that they were being studied, itself had a positive impact on their productivity.

A number of researchers have studied the impact of the Hawthorne effect in educational settings (Cook 1962) and some have questioned its strength (Bauernfeind and Olson 1973). Nonetheless there is general agreement among educational researchers that the Hawthorne effect is a potential threat to the validity of educational experiments. Researchers are cautioned to guard against it (Sax 1979).

Consider, for example, a situation where a new kind of textbook is being tested in a random sample of classrooms, while another random sample of control classrooms is also being studied for comparison. If the experimenters had no regard for the Hawthorne effect, the experimental classrooms would receive the new kind of textbook, the teachers and students would be allowed to know they were the mediating variables in a textbook experiment, and observers might even spend time in the experimental, but not the control, classrooms. As a result the teachers and students might work harder; and the positive impact thus seen might then be wrongly ascribed to the new textbook (Trow 1971).

To avoid the contamination by the Hawthorne effect, care should be taken with the teachers and students *not* to emphasize the experiment. The control classrooms should be observed as much as the experimental classrooms, and since the experimental classes are receiving new books, the control classes might at least receive new copies of the old text, a "placebo".

The presence of the Hawthorne effect helps to explain the fads of educational practice. A new idea (e.g., the initial teaching alphabet or i.t.a. approach to reading, or the "open" classroom) is implemented with enthusiasm and with considerable apparent success. Over the following years the fad dies off. It could well be that much of the early success was a manifestation of the Hawthorne effect. As the new treatment becomes routine, the Hawthorne effect and positive impacts accruing therefrom are lost.

The obverse side of the Hawthorne effect is the John Henry effect.

5. The John Henry Effect

The John Henry effect is a type of reactive effect in which members of the control group perform better than they typically would perform. The reason why the control group outperform themselves is presumably because they feel competitive about the experimental group thereby creating enhanced enthusiasm to do well. The John Henry effect is to the control group as the Hawthorne effect is to the experimental group.

The term John Henry is taken from a folk hero of the United States, a black railroad worker who was told that the steam drill would replace human labor in laying railroad tracks. By amazing effort he did better than the machine but the exertion eventually killed him.

The John Henry effect was associated with educational research by Saretsky (1972). He pointed out a peculiar phenomenon with respect to the evaluative research that had taken place on performance contracting. Control groups and experimental groups in 18 sites had been studied: the control groups had made much greater than anticipated gains though they were presumably receiving no new or different treatment. It seemed, however, that the teachers of the control classes were definitely trying harder than they would normally have worked.

The John Henry effect (improved control group performance), may lead to the wrong conclusion that the experimental treatment, whatever it may be, is ineffective. Frequently the researcher looks at differences between the mean performance of the experimental group and the control group to see if the experimental treatment is effective. The researcher should also ensure there is no unusual change in the untreated control group. Perhaps the most appropriate evaluation (research) design to employ when the John Henry effect is thought likely to occur is a time series design in which measures are taken to provide baseline data before the experiment is introduced. Measurement should also occur after the treatment (experiment) is over. If the John Henry effect has occurred, the control group performance should be enhanced during the duration of the experiment and should return to baseline afterwards. If the treatment is effective the experimental group, of course, will also show enhanced performance during the experiment. The comparison might then be made with the experimental group's performance and the baseline or projected baseline performance of the control group, thereby discounting the John Henry effect.

Preferably the John Henry effect should not be allowed to occur. Control groups should not be made to feel threatened or in competition with the treatment group just as the experimental group should not be made to feel special and different.

6. The Pygmalion Effect

The Pygmalion effect was given emphasis when Rosenthal and Jacobson (1968) published *Pygmalion in the Classroom*. The term Pygmalion comes from the Greek myth in which life was infused into an inanimate object by the power of positive thinking. In the Rosenthal studies (Rosenthal and Rubin 1978), expectancies of the experimenter (or teacher) lead to improved performance by the subjects (or students). Thus, if a teacher believes a student will do better in the coming year, there is a stronger than chance possibility that this belief will be fulfilled.

7. The Golem Effect

Babad et al. (1982) also coined the less used term "Golem effect" after a Jewish myth in which a mechanical creature runs amok and becomes destructive. The Golem effect is a negative expectancy effect (in contrast to the positive expectancy effect called Pygmalion) and it is used to explain in part why students about whom teachers have low expectations often perform more poorly than would be likely given their previous school record.

Because reactive effects can be misleading, it is most important in developing and administering measures and in developing research and evaluation designs to guard against them. Being aware of their potential mischief is a first step.

See also: Research Methodology: Scientific Methods

Bibliography

Anderson S B, Ball S, Murphy R T 1975 *Encyclopedia of Educational Evaluation.* Jossey-Bass, San Francisco, California
Babad E Y, Inbar J, Rosenthal R 1982 Pygmalion, Galatea, and the Golem: Investigations of biased and unbiased teachers. *J. Educ. Psychol.* 74: 459–74
Bauernfeind R, Olson C 1973 Is the Hawthorne effect in educational experiments a chimera? *Phil Delta Kappan* 55: 271–73
Cook D L 1962 The Hawthorne effect in educational research. *Phil Delta Kappan* 44: 116–22
Kersh B Y, Wittrock M C 1962 Learning by discovery: An interpretation of recent research. *J. Teach. Educ.* 13: 461–68

Pennock G 1929 Industrial research at Hawthorne: An experimental investigation of rest periods, working conditions and other influences. *Personnel J.* 8: 296–313

Rosenthal R, Jacobson L 1968 *Pygmalion in the Classroom: Teacher Expectation and Pupils' Intellectual Development.* Holt, Rinehart and Winston, New York

Rosenthal R, Rubin D B 1978 Interpersonal expectancy effects: The first 345 studies. *Behav. Brain Sci.* 377–415

Saretsky G 1972 The OEO P.C. experiment and the John Henry effect. *Phil Delta Kappan* 53: 579–81

Sax G 1979 *Foundations of Educational Research*, 2nd edn. Prentice Hall, Englewood Cliffs, New Jersey

Scriven M 1972 Pros and cons about goal-free evaluation. *Eval. Comment* 3(4): 1–4

Snow C E 1927 Research on industrial illumination. *The Tech Engineering News* 8(6): 257–82

Trow M 1971 Methodological problems in the evaluation of innovation. In: Caro F G (ed.) 1971 *Readings in Evaluation Research.* Russell Sage, Rensselaer, New York

Webb E J, Campbell D T, Schwartz R D, Sechrest L 1966 *Unobtrusive Measures: Nonreactive Research in the Social Sciences.* Rand McNally, Chicago, Illinois

Zdep S M, Irvine S H 1970 Reverse Hawthorne effect in educational evaluation. *J. Sch. Psychol.* 8(2): 89–95

Videotape Recording in Educational Research

G. Leinhardt

Since the early 1960s, videotape has been a popular tool in educational research and training. This article covers one aspect of videotape use, that of its role in research. Videotape, as it is used in training, will be only briefly mentioned. The article covers the following: equipment, historical uses, summary of current use and techniques, examples of use in current research, and issues of intrusion, reliability, and validity.

1. Equipment

Before describing the uses of videotape in educational research, videotape itself must be described. Videotape refers to a large number of manufactured magnetic instant replay tape systems. There are different sizes of tape—one-quarter inch, half-inch, three-quarter inch, and different winding mechanisms—cassette and reel-to-reel. There are several types of cassette reading systems and sizes. Usually these consist of a recording unit, a camera, and a monitor to watch the action that is being recorded. The entire system is powered by electrical line current or by portable rechargeable battery current which lasts from one to two hours. These three pieces of equipment can be used in a variety of configurations. For example, cameras can be visible or hidden, recording units can be near to the camera or in a console-type control room.

The camera can have a built-in, wireless, or a wired microphone. The equipment is, in some situations, permanently mounted in experimental classrooms, or settings where there is frequent videotaping; and in other cases it is more portable and can be brought to specific sites.

2. Historical Use

The most prominent early use of videotape was in the development of teacher-training materials. Essentially there were two basic approaches. Tape was used to model appropriate behaviors by developing microlessons on such topics as tutorials, questioning, topic introducing, and so on. Staged instructional packets with a small number of students served as the model. Tape was also used as a feedback device for teachers who self-critiqued or worked with a supervisor in watching their own performance in the classroom. These techniques are most successful when the trainee has his/her attention focused on a few specific behaviors (Biberstine 1971).

3. Current Use

By 1982, videotape was no longer an exotic gimmick in research, but an integral part of many studies. This is because the equipment has become commonplace, relatively lightweight, highly portable, and robust. Videotape provides a semipermanent, very complete, audiovisual record of events. The instant replay permits it to be used as a stimulus for recall, as well as an artifact of an action sequence that can be coded from multiple perspectives. The tape can be scored and rescored, so observer reliability and training is greatly simplified.

Videotape is used most frequently in the following types of studies: process–product or evaluation research as an audiovisual data source of teacher–student interactions (Cooley and Leinhardt 1980, Leinhardt et al. 1981); research on the cognitive processes and decision making of teachers (Peterson and Clark 1978); ethnographic microlevel studies of student and teacher behaviors (McDermott 1977); and laboratory studies of situational interactions, such as task persistence. In the first type of research, videotape is used instead of an in-class observer. Information is used in real time, but a permanent record is constructed. In the second type of research, the tape is the stimulus that prompts the production of the data to be actually used, as well as providing a validity check on action. In the third type of research, tape is used to document a short event that is representative of a larger system of actions. A small segment of videotape is intensely analyzed and studied in slow motion so that the implications of the microlevel actions for macroevents can be explored. In the last type of research, the tape is used as an unobtrusive recorder of events. Examples of each of the types of studies will be briefly described.

Videotape is used in process–product studies by sampling a small portion of instructional time (one to six hours), and coding the videotape with respect to teacher–student interactions. The purpose of process–product research is to explain or predict student outcomes using student inputs and instructional processes as predictors. Videotape is used to help capture important characteristics of the instructional process.

Literally thousands of codes can be used. However, some basic elements seem to permeate the majority of the literature: teacher affect, instructional content, managerial content, questioning style, initiation, interruption, and feedback. These codes can be estimated by time or even sampling procedures. The codes may be used singly or collapsed and used to form a core measure of teacher instructional behaviors (Cooley and Leinhardt 1980). Information obtained in this way should be no different from that which would have been obtained if in-class observers had been used. The advantage is increased precision and reliability due to recoding potential.

Videotape is used in a quite different way in research on teachers' thinking. In this type of research the videotape serves the role of an unbiased record and acts as a stimulus to produce data for future analysis. The purpose of such research is to understand the nature of teachers' information processing, decision making, problem solving, or execution of plans. The teacher is taped for some period of time (usually one class). The tapes are analyzed by the researcher for key points, either regarding decisions, lesson objectives, or alterations in routines. The tape is played back, in part or in whole, to the teacher fairly soon after the occurrence and the teacher is questioned with respect to his or her thoughts during activity sequences. It is the responses to these questions that are analyzed. Versions of this work have been carried out in Australia, the United Kingdom, the United States, Canada, France, the Federal Republic of Germany, and Belgium. It is a relatively new field and has not yet produced major results. However, it is an interesting convergence of process–product studies and studies of teacher attitude and background. In this research videotaping makes the work possible and plays a significant role (Bennett 1978, Calderhead 1981, Clark and Joyce 1981).

Ethnographic work that examines the context and content of classroom actions uses videotape in a third way. In these studies, videotaping is done over many months and an exemplary slice is taken and analyzed in tremendous detail. In the work of McDermott (1977), for example, a very small piece of a teacher-directed reading lesson is analyzed. The tape is slowed down and many aspects are studied: the body position of all actors, the changes in those positions, voice inflection,

eye contact, culturally consistent and clashing behaviors. This microlevel analysis is used to support the description of a more global reality. The tape is a vehicle for showing the consistency of that reality from life success or failure at one end, all the way to unconscious eye contact or aversion at the other. Here again, the videotape plays an especially significant role because it is possible to replay any part or to observe any section in slow motion. It should be noted that film has better resolution (at much greater cost) in extreme slow motion (McDermott 1977).

Videotaping has largely replaced filming in laboratory settings. In these situations the subjects are usually unaware of the fact that they are being taped. The tape is analyzed by examining their behaviors while interacting with people or things, or responding to unexpected situations. One of the more common types of studies involves motivational or task persistence research. Another type of laboratory usage involves constructing scenarios that show confederates engaging in a scripted behavior. The tape is then used as a stimulus.

4. Techniques of Use

This article now turns to techniques of use of videotape. Four issues will be discussed: the entrance into the setting; the time frame of the videotape segment; the audio and visual point of focus; and orientation. For simplicity it will be assumed that lightweight portable cassettes are in use.

Whenever possible, entrance should be gradual. Ideally, observers should be in the classroom for a week prior to taping, and several days before taping the observer should bring the equipment to the classroom and briefly explain it (15 to 20 minutes). Finally, two to three tapings should be made (or one long one), in order to minimize the effects of the taping process. In large-scale studies it is sometimes too costly to spend very much time on the entrance process. Often as little as half a day, or even one hour of preparatory time is given, in which the children and adults can see the equipment—the recorders and the teacher wired up for the various sound devices. In these cases the effects of entrance are felt or seen on tape, and estimates will have to be made of the degree to which the teacher and the students are responding artificially.

The observer/taper role must be clearly defined, regardless of setting. The role can range from no communication at all to almost the participant observer level. There are advantages to each approach. No communication assures a minimum of camera stares and sneaked looks. However, because it looks natural does not mean it is. A more complete involvement of the observer/taper assures more sincere cooperation of students and teacher.

The second issue is time frame. Videotape reels are either 40 or 60 minutes long; cassettes are as long as six hours. Most classroom lessons last either 40 or 60 minutes. There is a question as to when the tape should be started. Should it start with the class bell? In this case some of the tape may be taken up with the children coming in, settling down, and getting started. Or should the tape start with the beginning of the lesson? If the tape starts with the beginning of the lesson, or the main instructional segment, then the density with which this activity seems to take place is inflated because extraneous material has been deleted from the estimate. It is essentially a sampling problem. If a researcher's interest lies in taping a particular lesson, a certain amount of time prior to and after the lesson should be taped as well. If the researcher is interested in getting a feel for the dynamics of the classroom and naturally occurring activity structures, then the tape should run on a randomly sampled time basis, not limited by period boundaries.

The third issue is audiovisual focus. Present technology does not easily permit multiple audio sources, although these will soon be available. The best system currently available is to wire the main actor (teacher) with a small wireless mike, and to film using a camera which has a mounted directional mike with a wireless override. When the teacher is giving a lesson, the camera mike can be used; when the teacher is interacting, the wireless mike will pick up both teacher and student. Switching from one to the other only involves plugging and unplugging a camera mounted jack.

Similarly, there are few devices for multiple visual focuses. It is possible to insert the overlay of the class in a frame that is primarily focused on the teacher, by using several cameras, and it is possible to use multiple audio pickups. However, this type of work is best done in a laboratory setting. Multiple cameras are more intrusive. It seems that one camera and one audio system is optimal. The camera operator should be focusing on either a geographic area, following individual children; or following the teacher, and then catching people as they come into the view of the individual on target. There is no way the camera can capture the whole class all of the time. It must focus on one element or another which restricts the information available to coders and to analyzers later on. Some tapes focus exclusively on a group of children, and other tapes focus exclusively on a teacher. Some tapes focus on a teacher and then scan the children at regular intervals, which is a reasonable system for understanding what is going on in the classroom (Cooley and Leinhardt 1980).

The last issue is orientation. This is related to visual focus, but refers to the point of reference rather than what is on the tape. The camera can act as the eyes of an actor in the class; for example, if the camera is to take the position of a child, it can be shot over the shoulder of a child. The audio focus would be on the individual that the child was looking at, probably the teacher. For other types of research, such as stimulated recall, the camera can focus from the perspective of the teacher.

5. Reliability and Validity of Videotaping

Regardless of the positioning, or the care taken in familiarizing the subjects with the equipment, videotaping is intrusive. The question is, is the taping process so disruptive that the record produced is neither reliable nor valid? Taping is an event that teachers and children prepare for (even if they don't know when it will happen); however, a teacher that is punitive and loud cannot suddenly change for the camera because the students will not follow. What has been seen to happen is that major elements in the normal routine are accidentally left out because of nervousness. Such changes in behavior are rare and do not usually happen on the second or third taping. Taping can and does produce changes, but these changes are not likely to reverse the basic ordering of teachers along a single dimension. Good teachers tend to look a little better than usual—poor teachers look a little worse. Thus, the representativeness of taping can be questioned to some extent, but it is an area in which little research has been carried out.

The coding of videotape is far easier than in-class coding. Thus, interobserver reliability can be raised to very high levels and can be maintained by systematic checks of coders' tapes (Cooley and Leinhardt 1980) and recoding when necessary. The potential for validity is raised by having reliable coding and frequent taping. Videotaping is, in some cases, the only way to carry out a study; in such cases, issues of whether taping is more or less obtrusive are moot. As taping becomes more popular, it is likely that more rigorous techniques for studying the effects of taping will be forthcoming.

See also: Ethnographic Research Methods; Classroom Observation Techniques; Structured Observation Techniques; Naturalistic and Rationalistic Enquiry

Bibliography

Adams R S, Biddle B J 1970 *Realities of Teaching: Exploration with Video Tape.* Holt, Rinehart and Winston, New York
Bennett S N 1978 Recent research on teaching: A dream, a belief, and a model. *Br. J. Educ. Psychol.* 48: 127–47
Biberstine R D 1971 The utilization of videotape equipment in teacher education. *Contemp. Educ.* 42: 217–21
Calderhead J 1981 Stimulated recall: A method for research on teaching. *Br. J. Educ. Psychol.* 51: 211–17
Clark C, Joyce B 1981 Teacher decision making and teaching effectiveness. In: Joyce B R, Brown C C, Peck L (eds.) 1981 *Flexibility in Teaching: An Excursion into the Nature of Teaching and Training.* Longman, New York
Cooley W W, Leinhardt G 1980 The instructional dimensions study. *Educ. Eval. Policy Anal.* 2: 7–25
Leinhardt G, Zigmond N, Cooley W W 1981 Reading instruction and its effects. *Am. Educ. Res. J.* 18: 343–61
McDermott R P 1977 Social relations as contexts for learning in school. *Harvard Educ. Rev.* 47: 198–213
Peterson P L, Clark C M 1978 Teachers' reports of their cognitive processes during teaching. *Am. Educ. Res.* 15: 555–65

Rating Scales

R. M. Wolf

Rating scales are paper and pencil devices that are used to describe and/or appraise human performances or products. They are widely used in education, psychology, business, and industry for a variety of purposes. While no accurate usage figures are available, it is believed that rating scales may be the second most widely used measurement procedure, exceeded only by teacher-made achievement tests. A typical rating scale consists of a number of trait names, perhaps somewhat further defined, and a number of categories that are used to represent varying degrees of the traits. A rater is called upon to rate one or more persons or objects on the trait or traits by assigning the number, letter, adjective, or description that is judged to best fit. An example of one rating scale is presented in Fig. 1.

Rating scales were developed initially to overcome the extreme subjectivity of the unstructured statement evident in letters of recommendation, interviews, and other forms of testimonials where there was a lack of a common core of content or standard of reference from person to person. People also faced extraordinary difficulties in quantifying information produced by subjective and unstructured procedures. Rating scales attempt to overcome these deficiencies by obtaining descriptions on a common set of attributes for all raters and ratees and to have these expressed on a common quantitative scale.

While rating scales were developed to obtain systematic descriptions and appraisals of performances and products, they often fail in this respect. There are several reasons for this. The first has to do with a rater's willingness to rate conscientiously. In some cases raters are unwilling to take the necessary steps to obtain sound ratings. At best, ratings are a bother. If a rater does not take the task seriously, then the ratings that are obtained are apt to be worthless. Also, raters may identify with the person being rated. If, for example, a school principal is asked to rate the performance of one of the teachers in the school, he or she may have developed such a close working relationship with the teacher that it is impossible for that principal to stand back and objectively rate that person. A second major reason for failure to obtain sound ratings is inherent in the rater's inability to rate accurately. Specific factors that limit the validity of ratings include: the opportunity to observe the person or product to be rated, covertness of the trait or performance to be rated, ambiguity of the quality to be observed, lack of a uniform standard or reference, and specific rater biases and idiosyncracies. The consequences of these factors are a number of distortions in ratings, relatively low reliabilities and doubtful validity of ratings. Some specific influences that have been identified are: the generosity error or tendency to rate individuals at a higher level than is warranted, the halo error or the tendency for a rater's general impression of

a ratee to influence the ratings of specific traits, the central tendency error or the inclination to rate others in the middle of a scale and avoid the extremes, and the logical error or the tendency to give similar ratings on traits that the rater thinks go together but may not.

While much of the research involving rating scales has been disappointing in terms of the validity and reliability, there is sufficient evidence to indicate that rating scales that have been properly developed and used can yield sound and useful information (Jason 1962). For rating scales to work well, two essential conditions must be met. First, the rating scales need to be as clear and as usable as possible. This can be accomplished in two ways: (a) refining the presentation of the stimulus variables or attributes to be rated, and (b) refining the form of the response variables. Refinements in the presentation of the stimulus variables can be achieved by defining the traits to be rated, supplementing or replacing trait names with concrete definitions of the trait, and elaborating traits with specific descriptions of the behaviors to be observed and rated. Improvements in the form of the response categories can be made by defining categories in terms of percentage of a group falling in each category, by defining categories in terms of behavioral descriptions, or by defining categories in terms of known individuals.

The second major way of improving the usefulness of rating scales is through a training program for individuals who will serve as raters. Rating scales depend heavily on the abilities of the individuals who use them. Thus, a systematic program to train raters, even of relatively short duration, can yield large dividends in terms of the

Leadership:

Consider his or her ability to inspire confidence. How much respect does he/she command as an individual, not merely because of his/her position? Do people look to him/her for decisions? Is he/she "afraid to stick his neck out" for what he/she believes? Does he/she have teamwork?

(a) Completely lacking. Definitely a follower with equals. Does not try to convince others that his/her way is best

(b) Tries to lead with some success, but has never achieved a strong position. Is passive in directing his/her subordinates

(c) Good leader. People wait to hear what he/she has to say. Respected by colleagues. People call for his/her opinion

(d) Exceptional leader. Able to take over and pull things into shape. People seem to enjoy going along on his/her side. Is respected by subordinates and colleagues

Figure 1
Rating scale for leadership[a]

a Source: Thorndike and Hagen 1977

reliability and validity of ratings. A typical training program would involve discussion of the rating scale with all prospective raters and a set of scheduled observations in which the prospective raters observe and rate the same ratee or product and meet to discuss and resolve differences in their ratings. Three or four such observations can result in marked improvement in inter-rater reliability. In one study (Jason 1962), an extensive training program for raters resulted in rating scale reliabilities ranging from 0.86 to 0.93.

The picture obtained of the current status of rating scales is rather mixed. Generally, rating scales have yielded rather disappointing results. Clearly, there are hazards and pitfalls in their development and use. There have, however, been some successes. Despite their limitations, there is a host of situations in which human judgments will be needed. Rating scales remain one of the best means of securing these judgments.

Bibliography

Anastasi A 1982 *Psychological Testing*, 5th edn. Macmillan, New York

Guilford J P 1954 *Psychometric Methods*, 2nd edn. McGraw-Hill, New York

Jason H 1962 A study of medical teaching practices. *J. Medical Educ.* 37: 1258–84

Thorndike R L, Hagen E P 1977 *Measurement and Evaluation in Psychology and Education*, 4th edn. Wiley, New York

Research Techniques
and Statistical Analysis

Section 4

Research Techniques and Statistical Analysis

Introduction

Increasing the Strength of Inference from Evidence

The articles in this section have been grouped under three headings, namely: humanistic approach procedures, scientific approach procedures, and statistical analysis procedures. There are very few articles within the first category concerned with procedures relating to the humanistic approach. Furthermore, it must be noted that the articles on procedures of statistical analysis are concerned exclusively with servicing the scientific approach. Although the humanistic approach has a substantial and, in many parts of the world, a rapidly growing number of adherents, this does not appear to have led to the development and formulation of a wide range of techniques and procedures that strengthen the conduct of research in this area.

Clearly there is considerably less concern for methodology among the proponents of the humanistic approach than among those who employ the scientific approach. In part, this may be due to the commitment of many research workers within the humanistic approach to the implementation of change, and the assessment of the value of their research in terms of the extent of change that is generated. In part, it may be due to a denial of a "social reality" in the world of education for which an explanation is sought. For some of these research workers each case is unique and a description with an interpretation of events must suffice. Consequently, some workers undertaking humanistic research would challenge the meaningfulness of generalization or of replication in another situation. However, the issue remains of whether investigations conducted within the humanistic approach and the interpretations or conclusions that are drawn could be verified. Unless research workers who adopt this perspective report in detail on the methodology which they employ in order to observe accurately, to describe consistently, and to develop a valid interpretation of the events observed and described, then reviewers of their research have no basis on which to assess the quality of the research. Consequently, in order to ensure the usefulness of any account of the methods of research employed in an investigation undertaken with a humanistic approach, both to the interested reader and the critical reviewer of research, it would seem essential that the methodology of this approach should be formulated and conventions established for the conduct of research using these methods. It is unsatisfactory in the field of scholarly research to rely solely on the novelty of the ideas presented, the vividness or clarity of presentation, the appeal of the incidents described, or the interest generated by the stories reported. The paucity of the articles in this *International Handbook* that are concerned with the procedures of research methodology associated with the humanistic approach reflects accurately the current state of the art in this area of educational research.

The article on *Analysis of Evidence in Humanistic Studies* is presented as a contribution based on the work of Miles and Huberman (1984) which aims to remedy the situation that has been observed in the assembling of articles for this *International Handbook*. Miles and Huberman summarize their position in the following terms:

> In brief, the field of qualitative research badly needs explicit, systematic methods for drawing conclusions, and for testing them carefully—methods that can be used for replication by other researchers, just as correlations and significance tests can be used by quantitative researchers. (Miles and Huberman 1984 p. 16)

1. Humanistic Research Procedures

The four articles on research procedures that are employed in investigations conducted within the humanistic approach indicate a recent concern by research workers in this area to strengthen the inferences that can be drawn from evidence collected in humanistic studies. The first article is concerned with *Participant Observation*, where the research worker enters the situation under examination in order to undertake a more valid and more detailed investigation than would be possible from outside. Under these circumstances the research worker is in a face-to-face relationship with those being observed, and generally without their knowledge, while evidence is being gathered. In the second article on *Participant Verification Procedures* the research worker completes the first phase of an investigation and, having assembled and interpreted the evidence, returns to the social situation in which the research was conducted to confront the participants in that situation with both the evidence and the emerging findings and, where appropriate, the theoretical perspectives that are being derived from the investigation. The aim of the procedure is to validate the evidence, the conclusions drawn, and the theory being developed.

The third article examines the procedure of *Triangulation* which is the combination and use of several different research methodologies in the study of the same phenomenon. There are four basic types of triangulation: data triangulation, which involves replication in time, space, and with different persons; investigator triangulation, which involves the employment of several rather than one observer; theory triangulation, which consists of using more than one theoretical perspective in the collection of evidence and the interpretation of the phenomenon being investigated; and methodological triangulation, which involves the use of two or more different methods of investigation. Multiple triangulation occurs when more than one of the four basic types of triangulation is used. The final article is concerned with procedures associated with humanistic studies. As commented on above, it is derived from the work of Miles and Huberman (1984) and is titled *Analysis of Evidence in Humanistic Studies*. This article places into a broader context the procedures of *Participant Verification* and *Triangulation*, and presents tactics for deriving the findings of humanistic research studies, based on empirical evidence, through systematic analysis of the available data.

2. Scientific Research Procedures

The articles grouped under this heading are concerned with the broad strategies of investigation within the scientific approach rather than the more specific techniques and procedures of statistical analysis. The first two articles are concerned with *Sampling* and *Sampling Errors*. These are particularly valuable contributions to this *International Handbook*, because they provide an account of the procedures employed in sampling and the calculation of sampling error in the situations commonly encountered in educational research where samples of schools are chosen, and then students within schools are sampled at a second stage. There are relatively few reference books that provide a clear account of the problems associated with cluster samples and the drawing of sound inferences from data in which a cluster sample rather than a simple random sample has been employed. The next four articles are concerned with approaches to the drawing of inferences from quantitative data, namely, *Bayesian Statistics*, *Decision Theory in Educational Research*, *Hypothesis Testing* and *The Bootstrap*. While inferential procedures concerned with the rejection of the null hypothesis are widely used in research studies in education and psychology, the use of decision theory or Bayesian perspectives must be regarded as rare in educational research. Nevertheless, much of educational practice demands the making of a decision to implement the findings of research and then to make changes, as further evidence subsequently becomes available. The potentially important contributions of decision theory and Bayesian statistics to educational research must be recognized.

Two articles, *Status Attainment Models* and *Models and Model Building* are concerned with approaches to the examination of data that link theory with the testing of evidence. Likewise the article on *Prediction in Research* describes an important step in the validation of theory. Furthermore, the article on *Multitrait–Multimethod Analysis* is concerned with establishing the validity of different measures of a set of related characteristics which have been obtained in a particular research situation. The concluding article is *Single-Subject Research* which presents the tactics employed when an intensive study of a single subject is carried out. In such studies the changes that occur within the single subject are investigated, rather than examining changes within a group of subjects sampled from a defined population. To date intensive research studies conducted with a single subject are rare in the field of education, although more common in psychological research.

3. Statistical Analysis Procedures

The presentation of a substantial number of procedures for the statistical analysis of data in educational research is clearly a consequence of the ready availability of computers for undertaking data analysis since the 1960s. Moreover, as computers have become more powerful, the range of analytical procedures which are readily available has greatly increased. It might be expected that the use of such procedures is likely to increase as powerful microcomputers are introduced into the office and the home. However, there are dangers always present that with the growing complexity in the statistical techniques available, adequate awareness of the assumptions associated with the use of particular techniques, and sound understanding of the meaning of the operations employed and the results produced, will not always be maintained.

In the collection of articles in the final section of this *International Handbook* concerned with statistical analysis procedures, the articles have been listed in alphabetical order because any attempt to classify the topics is likely to be, at least to some extent, misleading. However, in discussing the articles presented in this section an attempt has been made to group together the articles which are similar in purpose. The first set of articles is concerned with general and introductory statistical procedures. *Exploratory Data Analysis* is described in an article which provides an excellent introduction to techniques that are very useful, but too new to have been presented in the commonly available reference books. The article on *Statistical Analysis in Educational Research* provides a clear and nontechnical account of the major procedures available for the analysis of data collected in school and classroom research studies. The brief article on *Profile Analysis* examines a technique that is not only useful for the presentation of results, but also permits the performance of groups of students to be compared. The more technical article on *Meta-analysis* describes a procedure that is being employed increasingly in the synthesis of the results from large numbers of equivalent or similar investigations.

A substantial battery of techniques has been developed for the examination of categorical and nonmetric data. The simpler procedures associated with the analysis of *Contingency Tables* and *Expectancy Tables* have been available for many years, but the relatively new technique of *Configural Frequency Analysis* facilitates the more accurate estimation of factors contributing to significance and the presentation of patterns in the findings observed in a matrix of tables. In addition, the article on *Log-linear Models* introduces an approach that permits the detailed examination of complex contingency tables as well as the testing of causal relationships contained in such data. The article on *Nonparametric Statistics* describes the wide range of simple tests that are available for detecting significance in nominal and ordinal data, while the article on *Correspondence Analysis* provides an account of a technique that enables more complex patterns of relationships in such data to be detected. *Partial Order Scalogram Analysis* is one of the newer multivariate data analytic techniques that is available for examining nonmetric data and presenting the relationships detected. Likewise, the use of *Galois Lattices* serves a similar function with complex sets of dichotomous data.

Several important techniques have been developed for the clustering of individuals and variables in order to summarize large sets of data and to identify patterns existing within the data. The article on *Cluster Analysis* describes a range of clustering procedures, while the article on *Factor Analysis* provides a clear account of this widely used technique in the search for relationships between variables. *Smallest Space Analysis* is another data analytic procedure for representing geometrically the pair-wise similarities that exist within a set of observations. The articles on *Sociometric Methods* and *Q-Methodology* describe how analytical techniques can be reoriented to cluster persons instead of variables.

The most rigorous inferences can be drawn and the most efficient procedures of analysis can be applied to experimental studies in which subjects have been assigned randomly to experimental and treatment groups. The article on *Analysis of Variance and Covariance* gives an account of the statistical techniques available that can be used to examine the data collected in such studies. The technique of *Regression Discontinuity Analysis* is a procedure for the analysis of data collected in quasi-experimental design investigations where it has not been possible to employ a true and more rigorous experimental design.

The most commonly used statistical procedures which are employed in educational research are those that involve bivariate and multivariate correlational analysis. The article on *Correlational Procedures* provides an introduction to this class of statistical techniques. Detailed accounts are presented of a range of multivariate analysis procedures in articles on *Canonical Analysis, Discriminant Analysis, Factorial Modeling, Path Analysis, Partial Least Squares Path Analysis, Regression Analysis*, and *Structural Equation Models*. This set of articles is brought together in an overview article on *Multivariate Analysis*, and one of the problems in this area that has caused concern is examined in an article on *Suppressor Variables*.

There is, in addition, a collection of articles that considers the wide range of problems which arise in the analysis of data. The collection contains articles on *Change Assessment, Units of Analysis, Multilevel Analysis, Interaction Effects, Detection of Interaction,* and *Reciprocal Effects, Analysis of.*

Finally, there is an article that examines the problems which arise as a result of *Missing Data and Nonresponse.* This problem, which occurs to markedly different degrees in different countries, unless controlled by an adequate level of careful planning, leads to invalidity in the findings of otherwise valuable and meaningful studies. Little can be done to rectify a situation where the extent of nonresponse and the amount of missing data exceed certain critical levels.

The statistical procedures described and discussed in the collection of articles in this section are by no means exhaustive or complete. Indeed, this is a field where new techniques are being developed all the time in order to increase the strength of the inferences which can be drawn from quantitative and qualitative data.

Bibliography

Miles M B, Huberman A M 1984 *Qualitative Data Analysis.* Sage, Beverly Hills, California

Humanistic Research Procedures

Participant Observation

S. J. Ball

Participant observation as a research method is a technical and theoretical, as well as a social process which employs the researcher as the main tool of investigation. It is a form of research which raises difficult ethical issues. The idea of participant observation is open to a variety of interpretations and definitions but in clear and concise terms it is defined by Becker et al. (1968):

> as a process in which the observer's presence in a social situation is maintained for the purpose of scientific investigation. The observer is in a face-to-face relationship with the observed, and, by participating with them in their natural life setting, he gathers data.

1. Theory and Technique

The participant observer's task is that of attempting to share, and thus understand, the social world of the actors in the setting under study; to come to know the actors' social world as they know it themselves. The participant observer's primary strategy is being there. But this does not specify a particular set of procedures, relationships, and pattern of contacts in every case. One of the basic assumptions upon which participant observation rests is that social settings are to a greater or lesser extent idiosyncratic and novel. Thus the researcher embarking upon a participant observation study must arrive at a creatively and responsively constructed research role, relevant to, and sensitive to, the nature of and demands of the social setting being studied. An appropriate, worked out, and successful research role in a factory or a hospital is unlikely to be useful or acceptable in a school or in involvement with an adolescent gang. Nonetheless, whatever the setting, the participant observer's concerns remain the same—by following those under study through their daily round of life, watching what they do, under what circumstances, when and with whom, by questioning them about the meaning of their activities, the researcher accumulates data. These data consist, in the main, of field notes and interview materials. The participant observer's stock-in-trade is the notebook, which in written-up form constitutes a research diary. However, as a research strategy, participant observation can encompass a whole range of subsidiary data collection techniques.

A classic work, employing participant observation in an educational setting, Lacey's (1970) *Hightown Grammar* will serve to illustrate the collection and handling of different categories of data—observation data, enumeration data, and informant interview data. Observation data are presented from classroom and staffroom settings; reference is also made to material collected from involvement with the second-year cricket team, from Lacey's own teaching experiences in the school, and from involvement in the social problems of individual students, which included, in some cases, visits to the students' homes. Lacey was also "camped" in the Hightown community with his family and met with and observed the boys being studied outside of the school. Enumeration data collected in the study included various questionnaire responses concerning students' estimates of their school-leaving age; teachers' estimates of students' likely examination performance; and ratings of students' behaviour. In addition, Lacey collected sociometric data based on the students' friendship choices. He also gathered a variety of "naturalistic" indices, of student absences, lateness, and detentions. In this category Lacey collected historical materials which allowed him to plot changes in school-leaving ages; the social composition of the school; job attainment; and school certificate passes. Lastly, there are some enumeration data on the staff. Lacey gathered informant interview data from teachers and students, and some students completed diaries for him.

Here the extent can be seen to which the participant observer can, in certain circumstances, collect and employ a whole range of types of data. But this is not simply a matter of eclecticism; these data collection techniques are subsumed within the overall strategy of participant observation and the data they yield are related to a single, coherent methodological position. That is, that an understanding of social activities cannot be achieved without reference to social meanings, and that these social meanings are derived from and embedded in the culture or perspectives of specific social groups.

The orientation of participant observation research is toward discovery. As far as possible the researchers' normal preconceptions should be suspended on entry into "the field" and left open to challenge. Every piece of research begins with a research problem of some kind, but in the case of participant observation the researcher is concerned to allow the social meanings and lived experiences of his or her subjects to determine the primary focus and significant empirical referents of the study. The participant observer begins only with "foreshadowed problems" (Malinowski 1922). The initial focus is wide and often changing until the actors' "contours of relevance" are identified and plotted. The object is to generate analytical categories from "the field", rather than defining them in advance. Fieldwork and the analysis of data proceed (these are not distinct phases in participant observation) by the constant comparison of categories in order to throw up properties and thus modify and extend emergent hypotheses and refine analytical concepts. This is done in two ways. First, the researcher collects a wide variety of data relating to a particular issue or concept that is generated by involvement in the field, in order to maximize the differences between categories or groups. This often provides deviant cases. Secondly, the researcher seeks to collect the greatest possible amount of data of all kinds on a particular group or limited set of phenomena in order to "test" or refine specific propositions. This can involve the detailed examination of deviant cases. Emergent ideas and explanations are continually ploughed back into fieldwork to guide the choice of particular groups or categories for further examination. The emphasis here is upon the process of analytic induction whereby the negative case and exceptional instance assume particular importance in the rejection or revision of generalizations.

1.1 Reliability and Verification

One of the common criticisms levelled against participant observation research is that it lacks methodological rigour. It is labelled by its critics as "impressionistic" and thus unreliable. As Fairbrother (1977) suggests, participant observation research is surrounded by a climate of distrust. This climate of distrust possibly has two bases; one being the comparison made between participant observation and the statistically verified techniques of positivist research; the other undoubtedly being the cavalier reporting and poor empirical basis of some studies claiming to be participant observation. Clearly, participant observation research cannot be justified and verified in exactly the same ways as positivist research and still retain its theoretical concern with the primacy of the social meanings of participants. There are however techniques of verification, for establishing the reliability of data, which are consonant with the methodological procedures of participant observation. The two most often used are (a) respondent validation and (b) triangulation. Respondent validation rests on the notion that the truth of the researchers' analyses, their validity, can be ascertained by establishing some sort of correspondence between the researchers' and the actors' views of the setting under study. This is done by

feeding back to the actors, and seeking their assent to, the researchers' judgments and interpretations. At face value this is an attractive possibility. Not only does it provide intrinsic support for the researchers' accounts (if the actors recognize it as valid), but in addition the technique generates further data.

Unfortunately there are problems in translating respondent validation into practice, especially in complex institutional settings like schools and colleges. First, the multifacetedness of such organizations ensures that no single account is likely to be recognized and accepted by all of their members. Different actors with different statuses and positions, different biographical experiences and ideological commitments will make sense of the structure and process of institutional life in different ways. Indeed, participant observation assumes this to be the case. Secondly, there is an irreducible conflict between the social scientist and those who are studied, since the social scientist's view of the world may be very different from that of the actors under study. Despite these problems the careful use of forms of respondent validation—employing key informants for example—can serve to check upon the accuracy of data and the viability of analytic schemes. Whyte (1955) made valuable use of his key informant "Doc" in this way, in his classic study of "corner boys" in an American city.

The idea of triangulation is founded upon an analogy with navigation, the idea of fixing a concept in logical space, and it can take a number of forms in participant observation research. In the case of data triangulation, the notion is that every form of data is potentially biased and that the use of a variety of different forms of data collection (e.g., observation, interview, and questionnaires, as in Lacey's study referred to above) can either eliminate or highlight these biases by convergence. In collaborative research involving several field workers, investigator triangulation becomes a possibility. Becker et al. (1961) took full advantage of this in their study of the college experience of medical students. In some circumstances respondent triangulation may be necessary, for instance the recollections and observations of different respondents may be employed to reconstruct an historical account of events in an institution, although again it must be recognized that the use of multiple sources will throw up differences between actors that are the product of differences in interpretation.

Another rather different strategy employed by participant observers for overcoming sources of invalidity in their research is the presentation, alongside data and analysis, of a research biography. The research biography represents what Denzin (1971) calls "sophisticated rigour". That is, a commitment to making data, data elicitation, and explanatory schemes as visible as possible, thus opening up the possibility of replication or the generation of alternative interpretations of data.

2. The Social Dimension

The social process of participant observation research, the "moral career" of the fieldworker, directly underpins the technical and theoretical issues outlined above. The participant observer is, unlike other researchers, directly involved in the setting under study. Indeed the participant observer's social relationships in "the field" are the basis for the collection and elicitation of data. In part at least, the interactions with and reactions to the researcher by the participants are in themselves data. The use of participant observation methods thus requires any researcher to take account of a whole range of social problems including confrontation with oneself as a research instrument. This personal dimension demands an awareness by researchers of the ways in which they are perceived by the researched. The role adopted by or assigned to the participant observer shapes the circumstances within which the research is done (Vidich 1955). This shaping begins as soon as the researcher begins to negotiate entry into "the field", if, that is, such negotiation is undertaken. Types of participant observation research vary from those which are based upon principles of "informed consent" and the signing of legally executed and binding contracts (Smith and Dwyer 1979), to those which are undertaken totally in covert form.

Entry itself may have significant implications for the conduct of the research. The permission obtained from formal institutional "gatekeepers", the principal or headteacher in the case of educational institutions, may carry little weight with teachers and students. Indeed, certain kinds of entry can lead to a "tainting" effect whereby the researcher is identified by others with a particular host or host group (e.g., Bain 1960). In reality the process of participant observation research frequently requires that access is constantly negotiated and renegotiated, as the research itself evolves and new participants are approached or encountered. Participant observation thus demands particular human relations skills from its exponents. This includes the sublimation of the researcher's personality and the ability to be all things to all men and women. To be able to establish working relationships with a whole range of actors in the social setting, whatever their status, position, age, sex, race, personality, or personal ideologies. In other words, the participant observer is engaged in "impression management".

Central to the process of participant observation is the tension which exists in the researcher's social position of marginality, a tension between being a stranger and being a friend (Powdermaker 1966). On the one hand, participant observation demands the establishment of "rapport" with the researched and requires the researcher to attempt to use a developing knowledge and understanding of those being studied in order to act in their world. But on the other, it demands that the researcher maintain a social distance, which allows the taken-for-granted realities of those being studied to be treated as problematic. Marginality is both uncomfort-

able and productive. If social distance is lost there is always a danger that the fieldworker becomes more of a participant than a researcher. "Overrapport" with participants may lead to a loss of confidence in or belief in the worthwhileness of the research project and can end in the researcher "going native".

3. The Ethical Dimension

The focus of concern in considering the ethics of participant observation is exactly that quality which differentiates participant observation from all other research strategies. That is, direct intervention in the social world, and thus the social lives, of ordinary participants. But the nature and extent of that intervention varies from case to case. In educational research it is usual to find that access for the participant observer is openly negotiated and relies on the consent and cooperation of those being studied (at least in the case of adults). Controversy arises when the participant observer attempts to "pass" as an ordinary actor for the purpose of collecting data secretly. Covert observation is employed, for the most part, in those circumstances where an overt research role would have been impossible.

Nonetheless, the attention attracted by the rather dramatic examples of covert research also serves to highlight the more routine ethical problems faced by any participant observer. The boundaries between covert and open research are rarely as clearcut as suggested in the discussion of controversial cases. In open research, researchers are not faced with the problem of disguising their intentions but rather how much of their intentions they should reveal. The more "open" the research, the greater are the possibilities of the researcher disturbing or distorting those practices under study. In addition, the researcher must decide who to tell. While formal access is negotiated via "gatekeepers" or "sponsors", the actual focus of research may be upon groups of "lower participants" who may not be consulted or who, in some instances, may be unaware of the researcher's real purposes.

And the ethical problems of participant observation do not end when fieldwork is completed. The researcher still has decisions to make about the use, handling, and possible publication of data. Whether to include data that are potentially damaging to the group or institution under study? What lengths to go to to anonymize or otherwise protect respondents? In some cases, where a formal research contract is entered into, these issues may be clarified before fieldwork is begun. For example, the Centre for Applied Research in Education at the University of East Anglia practice and advocate an approach to educational research and evaluation which gives ultimate control over data to the respondents concerned. This is expressed most strongly in Macdonald's "Democratic Model" (Macdonald and Walker 1974) which stresses the rights of participants. The central issue identified by Macdonald is the participants' rights to privacy over and against the public rights to know.

See also: Classroom Observation Techniques; Ethnographic Research Methods; Structured Observation Techniques; Analysis of Evidence in Humanistic Studies

Bibliography

Bain R K 1960 The researcher's role: A case study. In: Adams R N, Preiss J J (eds.) 1960 *Human Organization Research: Field Relations and Techniques.* Dorsey Press, Homewood, Illinois

Becker H S, Geer B, Hughes E C, Strauss A L 1961 *Boys in White: Student Culture in Medical School.* University of Chicago Press, Chicago, Illinois

Becker H S, Geer B, Hughes E C 1968 *Making the Grade: The Academic Side of College Life.* Wiley, New York

Denzin N K 1971 The logic of naturalistic enquiry. *Social Forces* 50: 166–82

Fairbrother P 1977 Experience and trust in sociological work. *Sociology* 11: 359–68

Lacey C 1970 *Hightown Grammar: The School as a Social System.* Manchester University Press, Manchester

Macdonald B, Walker R (eds.) 1974 *Innovation, Evaluation, Research and the Problems of Control.* SAFARI Interim Papers 1. CARE, University of East Anglia, Norwich

Malinowski B 1922 *The Argonauts of the Western Pacific: An Account of Native Enterprise and Adventure in the Archipelagoes of Melanesian New Guinea.* Routledge, London

Powdermaker H 1966 *Stranger and Friend: The Way of an Anthropologist.* Norton, New York

Smith L, Dwyer D 1979 Educational policy analysis: Methodological and procedural issues. *Federal Policy in Action Project.* Washington University, St Louis, Missouri

Vidich A J 1955 Participant observation and the collection and interpretation of data. *Am. J. Sociol.* 60: 354–60

Whyte W F 1955 *Street Corner Society: The Social Structure of an Italian Slum.* University of Chicago Press, Chicago, Illinois

Participant Verification Procedures

L. Sharpe

The term participant verification refers broadly to the research practice of confronting participants with an emerging theoretical explanation of their actions and inviting them to respond to its status with respect to reality, and then using these responses to refine that explanation. Its purpose as a methodological tool is to explore the links between first order, participants' accounts, and second order, theoretical accounts, as a definite state in the generation of theory (Weber 1949, Schutz 1970).

The investigation in which this method was used was a study of 80 parent couples at a boys' comprehensive school in Greater London (Sharpe 1980). Its intention was to generate a new model of parent–school relations which would remedy weaknesses in existing research, principally by respecting the authenticity of parents' views. To this end a heavy emphasis was placed on interpretive research procedures, especially open-ended interviews, participant observation, and the use of ideal-type constructs. As the research progressed, there was an emerging concern with structural dimensions of parent–school relations and this led to the use of a range of other research techniques and a broadening of the sample to include teachers and pupils. The final model aimed to bring together both action and structural dimensions of parent–school relations to produce an account which though respecting members' definitions went beyond them in certain significant respects.

The first stage in the research involved open-ended interviews with the sample parents in their own homes. These interviews, which were tape-recorded and later transcribed, gave parents an opportunity to talk freely and in an unprompted way about their own understandings of the school and their relationships to it. They produced a wealth of sensitizing data that demonstrated clearly that there were marked differences in the way

that parents viewed the school and that these differences in meaning had different consequences for their relationship with the school. Three ideal-type parent figures were constructed to emphasize these differences and to act as heuristic devices for furthering the research. The first was the "agent". This parent figure was constructed so as to hold a view of the school that led to the strategy of lobbying the teachers on behalf of the student, or of engaging in various public relations exercises, at a range of school meetings, all with the intention of marking out the student for special attention by the teachers. The second was the "touchliner" whose view of the school led to the student being encouraged within the home rather than being closely involved with the school. Thirdly, the "absentee" type was constructed whose disillusionment with the school led to the strategy of staying away and encouraging the student to pursue other, nonschool forms of education. These were, in broad outline, the three types constructed to deal with the vast quantity of qualitative material yielded by the interviews. As types, of course, they were not intended as descriptions of particular parents, though the next stage of the research involved using them as classifications.

By the time that the first interviews were completed and the types constructed, the outlines of a new model of parent–school relations were becoming clear. It was apparent that much previous research and policy statements could be grouped together under the heading "hidden-hand" models of parent–school relations: these emphasized that parents' influence on their children's education and schooling occured in the home and not in the school. Theirs was a hidden-hand at work in the home, providing children with latent culture, such as language skills, encouragement, and appropriate attitudes—a hidden-hand that had to be grasped in a partnership between teacher and pupils. In contrast, the interviews were suggesting that parents could take a direct hand in school affairs and that the hidden-hand model fitted at best just one type of parent—the touchliner.

The technique of participant verification was used during the next stage of the research which involved subjecting the types to tests of meaning and causal adequacy. Though the tests of meaning adequacy are the major focus here, a brief comment on the tests of causal adequacy will be useful. One test involved hypothesizing that parents provisionally classified as agents attended school more regularly than other parents, visits being the lowest common denominator of the agent strategy. Another test sought to establish whether there was any relation between the various strategies and the recognition of parents and students by teachers. These tests generally confirmed the agent and touchliner types, but raised serious doubts about the adequacy of the absentee type, as did the participant verification test. This involved subjecting the parents to a brief description of the emerging model and of the types and inviting them to comment on their validity. For this purpose a second set of interviews was held with a proportion of the original sample, and as before the interviews were tape recorded and later transcribed. The model invited parents to view the school as primarily a differentiating institution, with the process of differentiation giving rise to changes in the official school identities of students as students were moved from band to band in their earlier years at the school before being finally allocated to examination bands. Such changes could give rise to discrepancies between parents' and teachers' definitions of the students' identities, as well as to a concensus of views. The parent–school relations model was essentially a process of negotiation of students' identities occasioned by the process of differentiation, with the types representing distinct ways of dealing with this process.

Participant verification proved to be an important methodological tool in generating theory. Allowing parents an opportunity to verify the emerging theoretical account in terms of their own understandings did much to cast doubt on the adequacy of conventional views of parent–school relations. However, somewhat paradoxically, the process also raised serious doubts about the validity of parents' understandings of parent–school relations. The exercise demonstrated that the social context in which parental strategies are carried out is in many respects beyond the comprehension of the individual parent, whose definition may be a partial one and may even be incorrect in certain respects. So that, although a knowledge of parental meanings and intentions is indispensible, it is necessary to study these as part of a social situation which is defined by others as well, and which has certain nonnegotiable features. Thus, parents' actions can be interpreted by teachers in a way quite unintended by parents. Students can create for their parents a distorted view of the school by selectively delivering information to them. Teachers may only be conscious of a need to encourage, or even contemplate, meetings with parents under certain circumstances, such as when they experience problems with difficult children. Each party may have a vested interest in parent–school relations, and emphasize the aspect which is central to them. Thus there are manifold definitions of parent–school relations, complexly related to each other. The sociological problem for the researcher was to explain how these different definitions were interrelated to form the orderly and unremarkable pattern of parent–school relations found at the school. The final explanation was that the differentiation process at the school was a nonnegotiable fact which gave rise to a common problem for teachers, parents, and students, thus providing a common focus for their interaction. This was the problem of continuity and change in student identities. Whether this explanation is valid is ultimately a matter which rests with sociologists rather than with the parents.

See also: Research Methodology: Scientific Methods; Validity; Analysis of Evidence in Humanistic Studies

Bibliography

Schutz A 1970 *On Phenomenology and Social Relations: Selected Writings.* Chicago University Press, Chicago, Illinois

Sharpe L 1980 Parent–school relations: A reconceptualization. Unpublished D.Phil Thesis, University of Sussex, Sussex

Weber M 1949 *The Methodology of the Social Sciences.* Free Press, New York

Triangulation

N. K. Denzin

Triangulation is the application and combination of several research methodologies in the study of the same phenomenon. The diverse methods and measures which are combined should relate in some specified way to the theoretical constructs under examination. The use of multiple methods in an investigation so as to overcome the weaknesses or biases of a single method taken by itself is sometimes called multiple operationalism. The insistence on a multiple operational orientation in the social sciences is commonly associated in the field of psychology with the work of Donald T. Campbell and his associates (Brewer and Collins 1981).

Two outgrowths of Campbell's works have included the multitrait–multimethod matrix technique (Campbell and Fiske 1959) and the invention of the cross-lagged panel correlational technique (Pelz and Andrews 1964). The use of multiple measures and methods so as to overcome the inherent weaknesses of single measurement instruments, has, however, a long history in the physical sciences. The concept of triangulation, as in the action of making a triangle, may be traced to the Greeks and the origins of modern mathematics.

1. The Need for Triangulation

The social sciences rely, in varying degrees, on the following research methods: social surveys, experiments and quasiexperiments, participant observation, interviewing, case study and life history constructions, and unobtrusive methods (Denzin 1978). Each of these methods have built-in weaknesses which range from an inability to enter realistically the subject's life-world in experiments and surveys, to the problems of reflecting change and process in unobtrusive methods, the controlling of rival interpretive factors in participant observation and life histories, or an excessive reliance on paper and pencil techniques in surveys and interviewing.

The realities to which sociological methods are fitted are not fixed. The social world is socially constructed, and its meanings, to the observer and those observed, is constantly changing. As a consequence, no single research method will ever capture all of the changing features of the social world under study. Each research method implies a different interpretation of the world and suggests different lines of action the observer may take towards the research process. The meanings of methods are constantly changing, and each investigator brings different interpretations to bear upon the very research methods that are utilized.

For those reasons, the most fruitful search for sound interpretations of the real world must rely upon triangulation strategies. Interpretations which are built upon triangulation are certain to be stronger than those which rest on the more constricted framework of a single method.

2. The Hermeneutics of Interpretation

What is sought in triangulation is an interpretation of the phenomenon at hand that illuminates and reveals the subject matter in a thickly contextualized manner. A triangulated interpretation reflects the phenomenon as a process that is relational and interactive. The interpretation engulfs the subject matter, incorporating all of the understandings the researcher's diverse methods reveal about the phenomenon.

A hermeneutic interpretation does not remove the investigators from the subject matter of study but rather places them directly in the circle of interpretation.

While it is commonplace in the social sciences to place the investigator outside the interpretive process, hence asking the research methods to produce the interpretation that is sought, the hermeneutic interpretation dictates that "what is decisive is not to get out of the circle [of interpretation] but to come into it the right way" (Heidegger 1962 p. 195). Triangulation is the appropriate way of entering the circle of interpretation. The researcher is part of the interpretation.

3. Types of Triangulation

While it is commonly assumed that triangulation is the use of multiple methods in the study of the same phenomenon, this is only one form of the strategy. There are four basic types of triangulation. Data triangulation, involving time, space, and persons is the first type. Investigator triangulation consists of the use of multiple, rather than single observers. Theory triangulation consists of using more than one theoretical scheme in the interpretation of the phenomenon. Methodological triangulation, using more than one method, may consist of within-method or between-method strategies. Multiple triangulation exists when the researcher combines in one investigation multiple observers, theoretical perspectives, sources of data, and methodologies (Denzin 1978 p. 304).

4. A Case of Multiple Triangulation

The social sciences must move beyond investigations that triangulate only by data source, or by research method. Multiple triangulation must become the goal and aim of these disciplines. There are, however, few outstanding illustrations of this commitment. Perhaps Thomas and Znaniecki's publication, *The Polish Peasant in Europe and America* (1918, 1919, 1920) remains the classic in the social sciences.

This five-volume work, which sought to build a social psychology within the nascent field of sociology, utilized personal, historical, religious, and economic documents from and about Polish society, as it was disintegrating and undergoing transition prior to the First World War. The work consists of five documentary volumes which offer a study of the social organization and evolution of the peasant primary groups (family and community) under the influence of industrialization and immigration to America and Germany. Volumes 1 and 2 study the peasant family, the Polish marriage and class system, economic life, religious attitudes, and include correspondence between members of six family groups. Volume 3 is the autobiography of a peasant immigrant. Volume 4 examines the dissolution of primary groups in Poland and Volume 5 is based on studies of the Polish immigrant in America.

Thomas and Znaniecki's investigation used triangulated data, investigators, theories, and methods. Life histories, autobiographies, and family letters were at the core of their study, yet, in an unparalleled fashion, the research utilized participant observation, interviews, quasicomparative experiments on a grand scale, unobtrusive methods (letters), and surveys. Theoretically, the work wove its way (often implicitly) through the theories of Freud, James, Marx, Spencer, Durkheim, Mauss, Weber, Tonnies, Simmel, Hegel, Mead, Cooley, and Comte.

This study, still a classic and in need of reinterpretation, illustrates the scope and volume that multiple triangulation may assume. Smaller in size, but illustrative and pivotal in importance, stands Geertz's (1972) study on the "Balinese Cockfight." This investigation, based on description and interpretation, also triangulated data, investigators, theory, and methods.

5. Problems in Designing Multiple-triangulated Investigations

There are at least four basic problems to be confronted in such research. These are: (a) locating a common subject of analysis to which multiple methods, observers, and theories can be applied; (b) reconciling discrepant findings and interpretations; (c) novelty, or the location of a problem that has not been investigated before; (d) restrictions of time and money.

The location of a common subject of analysis can only be resolved through a clear understanding of the question the investigator wishes to answer. Divergent and discrepant findings are to be expected, for each inspection of the phenomenon is likely to yield different pictures, images, and findings.

These differences are not to be ignored, but should be reported so that future investigators can build upon such observations. Novel or new problems are often, upon inspection, not new, but merely manifestations of familiar topics previously examined from different perspectives and questions. Restrictions of time and money are the least problematic, for if investigators are thoroughly committed to understanding a problem area they will persist in examining it, even under difficult circumstances.

Triangulation is the preferred line of research in the social sciences. By combining multiple observers, theories, methods, and data sources, social scientists can begin to overcome the intrinsic bias that is bound to come from single-method, single-observer, single-theory investigations.

See also: Research Paradigms in Education; Research Methodology: Scientific Methods; Analysis of Evidence in Humanistic Studies

Bibliography

Brewer M B, Collins B E 1981 *Scientific Inquiry and the Social Sciences: A Volume in Honor of Donald T. Campbell.* Jossey-Bass, San Francisco, California
Campbell D T, Fiske D W 1959 Convergent and discriminant validation by the multitrait–multimethod matrix. *Psychol. Bull.* 56: 81–105
Denzin N K 1978 *The Research Act: A Theoretical Introduction to Sociological Methods*, 2nd edn. McGraw-Hill, New York
Geertz C 1972 Deep play: Notes on the Balinese cockfight. *Daedalus* 101: 1–37
Heidegger M 1962 *Being and Time.* Harper, New York
Pelz D C, Andrews F M 1964 Detecting causal priorities in panel study data. *Am. Sociol. Rev.* 29: 836–48
Thomas W I, Znaniecki F 1918, 1919, 1920 *The Polish Peasant in Europe and America: Monograph of an Immigrant Group.* Gorham Press, Boston, Massachusetts

Analysis of Evidence in Humanistic Studies

S. Sowden and J. P. Keeves

Much of the evidence available about educational processes is collected in the form of published documents, transcripts of interviews, observations of practice, field notes, tape recordings of oral presentations, and written statements. Such data that are qualitative in nature are of considerable value. They are rich, personal, close to the real world, and contain a depth of meaning that more abstract forms of evidence lack. Nevertheless, substantial difficulties arise in educational research in the collection and use of data in this form. While bodies of evidence of this kind can provide an understanding of educational phenomena and enable individuals to develop their own personal interpretations of the educational situations in which they work, there are significant problems involved in the assimilation of the evidence into the corpus of knowledge about education and its processes. The collection of such data is labour intensive, lasting sometimes many years. Furthermore, the analysis of the data is time consuming and sometimes very difficult because the evidence has been collected without a recognizable structure. Commonly, sampling has not been employed, and if representative or random sampling were attempted it has been abandoned as rich data became available from other sources.

As a consequence the important question of the generalizability of the findings cannot be considered. Furthermore, in general, the procedures by which the evidence has been analysed have not been reported or discussed.

Miles and Huberman (1984) have addressed these issues in an important publication titled *Qualitative Data Analysis: A Sourcebook of New Methods.* They are specifically concerned with the generalizability of the findings derived from qualitative research and with the replicability of analyses of qualitative data. They have advanced canons for the examination of evidence collected in naturalistic research investigations that increase the consistency and robustness of the findings. Their proposals cut across the several areas of knowledge that contribute to humanistic research in education, namely the disciplines of sociology, history, law, political science, linguistics, psychology, and anthropology.

Miles and Huberman advance systematic procedures for the drawing of conclusions, testing the conclusions for consistency and coherence, and indeed simplifying the tasks of analysing large bodies of qualitative data. They argue that in the reporting of research it is essential for the researcher to accept the responsibility of being accountable, and to present clearly a statement on the analytical procedures employed. However, such a strategy demands that there should be consensus about the appropriateness and strength of the particular procedures which have been used. Their practical sourcebook is a highly significant contribution of educational research. This article draws extensively on their work and illustrates their strategy through the discussion of an application to a research study in education concerned with some factors influencing the conduct of evaluation studies.

The philosophical and epistemological foundations of Miles and Huberman's work have been subjected to criticism by Donmoyer (1985, 1986), to which Huberman and Miles (1986) have replied. It is not necessary to address these issues in this article. However, this article endorses the view that neither the scientific nor the humanistic research perspectives have a unique advantage and that there is an epistemological unity in educational research. Furthermore, we recognize that the hardline distinctions that are commonly made between quantitative and qualitative research methods are largely artificial. The difference between quantitative and qualitative data lies in the level of abstraction and the extent of simplification since, as Kaplan (1964 p. 207) has argued, "quantities are of qualities", and the claim that one method is antithetical or alternative to the other is misconceived. In addition, it is necessary to consider the view that all inquiry into educational questions is at least to some extent value-laden. Kaplan (1964 pp. 374-86) has examined the several ways in which values play a part in inquiry. There are implications for the replicability of the results of inquiry where another investigator with different values conducts a similar inquiry. Kaplan (1964 p. 387) has also suggested that the only way to avoid subjective relativism in inquiry is to "face the valuations and to introduce them as explicitly stated, specific and sufficiently concretized value premises". The problem is not whether values are involved in inquiry and whether it is possible to gain access to "reality" independently of values, but "how they are to be empirically grounded". This article presents procedures for building the findings of humanistic research studies on empirical evidence through the systematic analysis of qualitative data.

1. Strategies of Analysis

The approach to data analysis using these procedures is characterized by strategies that employ both deduction and induction. These procedures are deductive insofar as some orientating constructs — informed by the prior knowledge, the experience, and the values of the investigator — have been put forward and operationalized and matched to a body of field data. This has the advantage of focusing and reducing the data that could be collected. Induction is employed insofar as the gathered data are used to modify and rebuild the original constructs. While deduction and induction are distinct and separate concepts, the difference between the deductive

process and the inductive process becomes blurred when it is recognized that the conception of the orientating constructs which were used in the process of deduction were themselves a product of induction (Miles and Huberman 1984 p. 134). The interaction between deductive and inductive processes in the strategy of research where investigation is grounded in empirical evidence and the real world, is a key characteristic of the procedures proposed by Miles and Huberman (1984).

There are four major stages in this strategy of research into educational problems, namely: (a) design of investigation, (b) collection of data, (c) analysis of data, and (d) summarizing and integrating the findings. This article is primarily concerned with the third of these stages, the analysis of data. However, insofar as analysis is dependent on design, collection, and integration, an account must be provided of these three other stages and of their influence and dependence on the analysis of data. Miles and Huberman (1984 pp. 21–23) have identified three key components of data analysis, namely: (a) data reduction, (b) matrix display and examination, and (c) conclusion drawing and verification. This article will explore in some depth these three components of data analysis. Following Miles and Huberman (1984 p. 23), an interactive model is presented of the way in which the four stages of a research strategy interact with the three key components of data analysis listed above. In Fig. 1 the four stages and the three key components of data analysis form an interactive and cyclical process. As the research worker progresses through the four stages it is necessary for consideration to be given continuously to the analysis of the data and to the reduction, display, and conclusion drawing and verification components. The whole process is iterative as well as being interactive in a way that only successive iterations permit.

It is important to recognize that this model does not differ greatly from a model that could be constructed to represent the strategy employed in quantitative research in education. The major difference is that quantitative research commonly starts with a stronger knowledge base, and tends to proceed sequentially in well-defined stages, rather than in the interactive or iterative way that is characteristic of qualitative research, which is more fluid and has a weaker knowledge base. This article seeks to elucidate the components of the model being advanced for the analysis of qualitative evidence, so that studies conducted within this context can be more effectively audited.

2. A Research Example

The research study employed in this article to illustrate the use of the procedures advanced by Miles and Huberman (1984) was associated with an investigation into the influence of research workers' views of evaluation (e.g., their views of the politics of evaluation and their philosophical orientations) and the influence of factors in the research situation on the types of evaluation studies that the evaluators undertook and the manner in which they

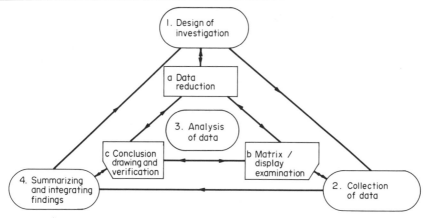

Figure 1
An interactive model of qualitative data analysis

conducted an evaluation. While much has been written about educational evaluation and many different models and approaches to evaluation have been advanced, at the time the study was planned, no previous research was known that examined the factors influencing the way particular evaluators conducted their evaluation studies.

Thus the investigation had little on which it could draw in opening up this area of inquiry. A qualitative exploratory study appeared to be the desirable design, although if the scope of investigation had been restricted a more quantitative approach might have been attempted, particularly if an already existing instrument to measure views of evaluation had been employed. Fifteen evaluators were selected as a representative sample of research workers and other persons engaged in evaluation studies. Each evaluator was asked to identify two evaluation studies that he or she had conducted, for which research reports were available and for which the clients would be willing to be interviewed regarding the conduct of the evaluation study. Thus the raw data comprised 30 reports of evaluation studies, the tape recordings of 30 interviews with the clients who had commissioned each of the 30 reports, and tape recordings with each of the 15 evaluators on two occasions. In addition, the research worker accumulated field notes associated with each evaluator and with each evaluation study. Moreover, since reports on both the views of each evaluator and the conduct of each evaluation were prepared and sent to each evaluator for confirmation, correspondence with each evaluator was assembled. This investigation can be seen to have involved case studies of 15 evaluators, each of whom had undertaken two evaluation studies. Thus the research investigation was one that involved a multisite case study strategy.

This strategy of investigation, the multisite case study approach, is being used increasingly in the field of educational research. Sometimes such an investigation is conducted together with a quantitative study, and the

qualitative multisite case studies are carried out to complement the more quantitative work. However, sometimes in educational research only one case is investigated, and where this occurs it is common to examine the changes that occur over time and the two or more occasions provide replications of the initial case. Thus a research situation is developed that is akin to the multisite case study approach, with each occasion being considered equivalent to a separate site for the case study. This present investigation through the use of two occasions for each evaluator included certain features of this alternative strategy.

3. The Design of Investigations

The conventional views of both quantitative and qualitative investigations in education are that the former, the quantitative investigation, involves a highly structured approach while the latter, the qualitative investigation, involves a minimal amount of prestructuring and a very loose design. On the one hand, quantitative research is seen to involve an identified theoretical perspective, the use of standardized instruments, the testing of prespecified aspects of a conceptual framework, and a high degree of abstraction from the real world. On the other hand, qualitative research is seen to be building theory from observations of the real world, to be loosely structured, and to be very open-ended with respect to the collection of data. It is not surprising that neither description is appropriate. Most quantitative research workers in education are more flexible than is suggested above. Likewise most investigators engaged in qualitative research now work somewhere between these two extremes. Qualitative research workers also recognize that a conceptual framework, at least in rudimentary form, has commonly been employed to guide an investigation, and that with little effort previous research could be found that would account conceptually for the phenomenon under investigation, even if it could not be classed as an established theory. It is this conceptual

515

framework that serves to focus and restrict the collection of data as well as to guide the reduction and analysis of the evidence collected.

A conceptual framework serves to describe and explain the major facets of an investigation. It identifies the key factors and the assumed relationships between them. It is not essential that such relationships should be causal. They may simply involve sequences which occur over time, or alternatively there may merely be a pattern in the events or between the factors being observed. If such patterns or time sequences in relationships or causal connections are not assumed to be present, then it is unlikely that the factors being investigated will hold much interest for the research worker. The conceptual framework commonly attempts to state in graphical or narrative form these factors and the relationships between them. Use is made of this conceptual framework in the design of the study. First, it identifies who and what will be examined. Second, it postulates relationships between the persons and the factors being investigated. Such presumed relationships can influence the order in which information is assembled and the type of information collected, as well as the extent of detail obtained.

The conceptual framework also provides a map for the research worker of the field being investigated. Miles and Huberman (1984 p. 33) have made several suggestions with regard to developing a conceptual framework:

(a) use a graphical rather than a narrative format;

(b) expect to revise successively the framework;

(c) encourage each research worker in a team to develop a separate framework, and compare the different versions;

(d) avoid a global level of generality that is not specific enough to provide focus and identify bounds, and is not so general that it cannot be proved wrong; and

(e) use prior theorizing and previous empirical research to test the framework.

Once the framework has been developed it can be used for formulating specific research questions. The process of deduction is commonly involved. Many research workers engaged in qualitative studies reject this step. However, the development of their ideas, while latent and implicit, commonly uses similar processes. Such investigators should be challenged to make as explicit as possible their thought processes. The research questions advanced for a study will require successive refinements. Priorities will need to be proposed, and the number of questions to which answers are being sought will need to be reduced to a manageable size. It is important to ensure that all field workers in a multisite study are familiar with the research questions being investigated, and that during an extended study both the chief investigator and the field workers keep the research questions under review.

Once the research questions have been identified, the collection of data must be influenced by identifying cases to be studied. Some form of sampling is generally involved. One of the great dangers in qualitative research is to sample too many cases. The number of cases is limited both by the amount of data that can be processed and by the costs involved. It would seem from experience that 15–20 cases is the maximum amount of evidence that one person can work with for a detailed qualitative analysis. Where more cases have been involved in studies, it is not unusual for much of the available information to be cast aside and only evidence from up to 15–20 cases to be used, at least in the detailed reporting of the study. Furthermore, with more than 15–20 cases quantitative methods can be readily employed, through the use of contingency table analysis and the Fisher Exact Test. Other quantitative statistical procedures can be used with numbers of cases in excess of 30.

Even with up to 15 cases some basis for sampling of cases must be employed, whether the cases are typical, exemplar, random, extreme, innovative, or simply the most accessible. The extent to which the findings can be generalized beyond the single case depends on the basis upon which the cases were selected and the relationship between the selected cases and a wider population. It is important to recognize that sampling can occur of settings, events, and processes as well as of people. In the long term the major constraints on the number of cases to be studied are those of time and cost. Balance must be achieved between the research questions, time, cost, the complexity of the investigation, the number of research workers available to assist, and the number of cases selected.

The extent to which instrumentation is employed likewise depends on the research questions being asked, the number of research workers engaged in the data collection phase, and the level of clarity of the conceptual framework. Arguments can be advanced for both little or no prior instrumentation and for detailed instrumentation. However, failure to develop a conceptual framework or to identify appropriate research questions or to construct suitable instruments should not be justified on the grounds of lack of time or lack of effort. Advanced planning usually pays.

4. The Conceptual Framework: An Example

A conceptual framework for the investigation is shown in Fig. 2. The key actors in this situation under investigation are the evaluator and the client. Of primary importance to the investigation are the evaluator's views of evaluation. These include the evaluator's research perspectives, views about the politics of evaluation, and views of the role of evaluation in relation to policy. In addition, there are research situation factors, which subdivide into external factors and internal factors. The external factors in the research situation involve the nature of the programme being evaluated, the political climate, and the concerns of the different stakeholders in

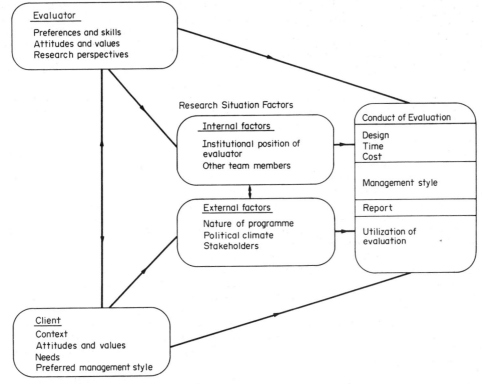

Figure 2
Conceptual framework for investigation

the evaluation. The internal factors in the research situation include those factors directly related to the evaluator, such as the institutional position of the evaluator and of the team members with whom the evaluator works. These two sets of factors — namely the evaluator's views of evaluation and the research situation factors — influence not only each other but, more importantly, the conduct of the evaluation. Likewise, the views of the client interact with those of the evaluator to influence the conduct of the evaluation.

The conduct of evaluation includes the design of the study, how the study is managed, (e.g., who controls the direction of the evaluation and the strategies used by the evaluator to share this control), as well as the nature of the report. A further important element in the conduct of the evaluation is the likely utilization of the evaluation. The nature and extent of utilization of the findings of the evaluation arise from a complex interaction between the characteristics of the evaluator, the internal and external research situation factors, and the characteristics of the client.

In this study the key research question was concerned with the influence of the evaluators' views of evaluation and the research situation factors on the conduct of the evaluation. However, there were a substantial number of subsidiary questions, the answers to which were considered to assist with an understanding of the key ques-

tion. The employment of arrows in Fig. 2 indicates not only time sequences in events which take place during the course of an evaluation, but also causal influences between the different factors in the conceptual framework. There were, in addition, certain patterns or relationships which were likely to be revealed by the study, such as those between the research perspective preferences of the client and the evaluator. It was agreed that an evaluator with particular characteristics was likely to attract work from a particular client, and a client was likely to choose an evaluator where their research perspectives were consistent with each other. These different possible relationships gave rise to a series of research questions that were assigned a lower level of priority in the investigation.

The number of evaluators to be investigated was set at 15. A representative sample of evaluators was chosen from persons in different geographical locations who were known to have different research perspectives, and who were employed in different contexts, namely academic research situations, independent research organizations, governmental authorities, and commercial organizations. The selection of evaluators also sought to ensure that scientific, humanistic, and critical social science perspectives, as well as both male and female perspectives were represented. In addition, the evaluators were encouraged to select evaluation studies that were typical of their work, but which at the same time covered a range of different types of evaluations that they had conducted.

5. Data Collection

Miles and Huberman (1984) have argued that the preliminary analysis of data should proceed concurrently with the collection of data so that the phase of data collection merges with that of data analysis. There are two important reasons for this. First, there is the very real danger, in a study in which qualitative data are collected, of assembling such a huge amount of evidence that the analysis becomes an overwhelming task which not only jeopardizes the completion of the work associated with the analysis phase of the investigation, and in some cases has been known to lead to the termination of a study, but more commonly reduces the quality of the work carried out. A second advantage of undertaking the analysis concurrently with the collection of data is both that gaps in the data become apparent, and new hypotheses and relationships emerge before it is too late to collect relevant data. In addition, an understanding of the evidence, which commonly takes time to grow, benefits from the longer period available. Sometimes ongoing analysis permits the preparation of an interim report that is reassuring for the client and facilitates the flow of funding for the study.

It is of value to prepare an overall tabular plan for the collection of data to show which items of data are going to be obtained through each particular stage in the inquiry. To some extent such a table serves also as a checklist to ensure that each item of information required for the investigation will be collected in the most appropriate way.

It is also important to maintain detailed documentary records of the data collected and Miles and Huberman (1984 pp. 50–51) suggest the use of the following forms:

(a) *A contact summary form*. This should be used to record the information associated with each contact made in the collection of data, such as an interview with an evaluator or client. In addition, this form would also record memoranda and information of importance to the study which should be noted as they arise.

(b) *A document summary form*. This should be employed to maintain a concise record of all documents which are obtained such as newspaper articles, correspondence, agendas and minutes of meetings that provide background information of relevance to the investigation. The documents are often bulky and must be filed separately. However, a file summary which indicates clearly the relevance of the document to the investigation as well as the location of the document is of considerable assistance as the volume of such material grows during the course of the study.

(c) *Field notes*. These should be compiled daily, if possible, on a standard form and inserted in a looseleaf folder to record information of relevance to the investigation. Such notes are additional to an interview schedule, observation schedule, or tape recording of an interview and serve to record key items of information that are obtained or observed independently of the interview or observation period. Commonly these field notes can contain reflective remarks that arise from watching a situation or talking to people linked to the evaluator or the client. A distinction must be made between the raw field notes, which are rough scribblings and jottings, and the permanent notes that could be read by any reviewer of the work. The permanent notes are more than a sum of the raw notes. They contain reflections and commentary on issues that emerge from a consideration of the raw notes.

(d) *Memos*. These are an important additional source of ideas. Field work and coding are absorbing tasks. However, the very intensity of these stages of an investigation frequently gives rise to new and original ideas, which if not recorded in some way as they occur are lost. The most effective procedure is to have available a standard memorandum form on which these ideas can be recorded as they arise. Probably some sifting of such memoranda is required at a later stage, if a large number are produced. Of particular importance among the memos that are written are ones relating to propositions or relationships to be examined in the course of the investigation.

(e) *Data accounting sheets*. These are an essential documentary record of progress on a particular question. If possible the data collected should be related as closely as possible to the major research questions, or if this is not possible, to the areas of the investigation linked to the research questions. On the data accounting sheet a record should be maintained of whether or not a particular source of data relevant to a research question or an area of inquiry has been collected.

6. Analysis of Data

The analysis of the data collected in a study passes through three interrelated stages, namely, data reduction, data display, and conclusion drawing and verification. As already mentioned in an earlier section of this article, in qualitative research these stages are not sequential, but form part of an iterative process. Nevertheless, unless the stages are seen as separate there is the danger that they can merge to such an extent that the tasks associated with each are not examined or adequately planned. Each of these three stages will be considered in turn.

6.1 Data Reduction

The primary task in data reduction is that of coding the interview record, the observation record or the document. To code evidence obtained by these data collection procedures two approaches are available: the use of key words, or a numerical classification system, which may or may not involve a taxonomy. The development of a taxonomy requires considerable effort in advance of the coding, as well as a detailed understanding of the field. The use of key words has greater flexibility on the surface, but is likely to become complex and confusing unless careful initial planning has occurred. A pilot run through a reduced sample of the evidence, or preferably a pilot study with perhaps three to six cases, should be carried out in order to develop the key words or the taxonomy. The major danger in the development of a numerical coding system or a key word system is that the system will lack the structure necessary to use it systematically in the detailed examination of data. A further relevant aspect is the identification of important quotes that could be used in the reporting of the study. It is common in presenting the findings of an investigation based on the use of qualitative data to rely on telling quotes to make an important point and to convince the reader of the report. The process of data reduction should include a starring of codes or key words so that appropriate quotes related to a particular idea or relationship can be readily identified.

One of the most difficult items of evidence to summarize, that arises in the processing of qualitative data, is the taped interview. The use of a tape recording of an interview permits the interviewer to conduct the interview in a relatively relaxed way, without concern that key points will be lost. There is, however, always the danger that the interviewee will withhold comment because a permanent record is being made. In addition to this, the reduction of the data held on a tape recording poses substantial problems. At one time when taped interview records were less commonly used, it was possible to recommend that each interview record should be typed and hard copy obtained. Today this involves a prohibitive cost for most investigations and procedures have to be employed that will minimize cost and yet achieve effective coding of the available evidence. The procedures adopted in the research study being used to illustrate this approach to the analysis of qualitative data are described below.

In this study, taped interviews with evaluators and clients were coded using the following method.

(a) While listening to a tape, a summary of each point made by the interviewee was recorded. These summaries involved paraphrasing responses and were sometimes accompanied by transcriptions of relevant quotations.

(b) A set of key words was developed from the first six interviews that could be used to summarize and reduce further the evidence held. The structure for the key word system was built around the structure of the interview, which had been planned in advance.

(c) In order to access the information held both on tape and in the point-to-point summaries, a key word was placed in the left-hand margin of the pages of the summary to provide a reference to the content of each point made in the interview.

(d) In order to access quickly the source material on a tape, the tape counter numbers giving that section of the tape within which each point was made were recorded in a second column adjacent to each key word.

(e) Once an interview was coded in the above way, a summary of the themes occurring in the interview was made. The summary was built around the planned structure of the interview. Separate summaries were prepared for each of the two interviews with the evaluators and for each of the interviews with the clients.

(f) The four interview summaries associated with each evaluator were examined for inconsistencies, and systematic checks with the tape recording were made to confirm or resolve the inconsistencies.

(g) A summary of the views and perspectives of each evaluator was prepared and returned to the evaluator with a request to confirm the record that had been obtained and where necessary to resolve observed inconsistencies. In this way each evaluator was provided with an opportunity to verify information that was being carried forward to the next stage in the process of analysis. This sequence of steps, while time consuming and laborious, ensured that the research worker had assimilated thoroughly the views of each evaluator, and in the processes of condensation and assimilation had not, in an unwarranted way, distorted the evidence provided by an evaluator or a client.

It is important to note that the research worker was not limited to using the information contained in the summary that had been verified by the evaluator. However, the confirmation given by the evaluator, or in rare cases the correction provided, was further evidence that in summarizing the tape recordings significant distortion of the data had not occurred.

In addition, to provide a further check on the reliability of the coding procedures employed, a second person coded a sample of 12 taped interviews with evaluators and clients using the methods outlined above. Ten-minute sections of the taped interviews for each of the two interviews with four evaluators, and for one interview with a client of each of the four evaluators, were used. This involved the recoding of 120 minutes of taped interviews. The reliability of the coding procedures was estimated using the following formula.

$$\text{Reliability} = \frac{\text{Number of agreements}}{\text{Total number of agreements and disagreements}}$$

A level of intercoder reliability of 80 percent was sought. The criteria for agreement were that each of the following three conditions had to be met: (a) the same section of a taped interview was considered to represent a point; (b) for each point summarized, the same key word, selected from the final listing of key words was used by both coders; and (c) the two summaries of each point had the same meaning.

6.2 Matrix Display and Examination

The use of a matrix display is a valuable procedure for summarizing information so that patterns are evident in a form that can subsequently be used in the presentation of results. Success in the use of a matrix display lies not in whether a "true" or "correct" matrix has been developed, but in whether the use of a matrix display has served the function of providing answers to a research question being asked. Miles and Huberman (1984 pp. 211-12) have listed the key features of a matrix display as well as a set of rules for matrix construction.

The key features of a matrix display are concerned with choices made during the design of a matrix that are associated with ways of partitioning the data.

(a) The first feature relates to whether the matrix has a descriptive or explanatory purpose, and whether an attempt is being made to lay out the data in a manner that might reveal a pattern in the data, or in a way that shows why things happen.

(b) The matrix can be constructed to show relationships within a single case or across cases involved in a study.

(c) The matrix consists of rows and columns and can be constructed in such a way that the categories employed in the rows and columns are ordered or nonordered. Once the development of a matrix has proceeded beyond the initial stages of describing the evidence, it would seem likely that some ordering of categories would be required.

(d) A special case of ordering the information contained in the rows and columns is associated with time ordering. Time sequences are involved in temporal flow, causal chains, or cycles of events.

(e) Sometimes a matrix is constructed with the categories of a particular variable along one axis, or with social units along an axis as is common in educational investigations, where the units commonly used are: students, classrooms, schools, school districts, state systems, and a national system.

(f) The most commonly used matrix is the two-way grid. However, it is sometimes necessary to construct a three-way or four-way matrix, although they are hard to use and present. A three-way matrix can be shown diagrammatically by subdividing each column in a parallel fashion, and a four-way matrix can also be shown diagrammatically by subdividing each row in a similar manner. The pattern involved in the data is usually lost, by using more than a four-way matrix. Greater clarity can be gained by breaking the data down into submatrices.

(g) Furthermore, a choice is available with respect to what is recorded in each cell. Commonly an identifying code is recorded that refers to each case, but sometimes direct quotes or extracts from field notes can be recorded.

(h) Finally, if the set of key words has been carefully developed or if the taxonomy associated with numerical coding is appropriate, then these coding systems are naturally associated with the categories that are employed in matrix displays.

Miles and Huberman (1984, p. 212) advanced nine rules of thumb for the building of matrix displays:

(a) keep each display on one large sheet;

(b) restrict the number of categories used in each row or column to the range 5 to 15;

(c) plan to use a preliminary form of a matrix display and to revise it several times before constructing a final form;

(d) encourage members of the research team to develop alternative ways of displaying data in a matrix;

(e) transpose rows and columns where appropriate;

(f) collapse the categories of a complex matrix, since a reduced form will sometimes reveal clearer patterns;

(g) be prepared to add new rows and new columns at all times;

(h) maintain fine-grained rows and columns so that important differences in the data can be shown; and

(i) remember that a particular research question may require a series of matrix displays and be ready to try additional forms.

The development of appropriate matrix displays is an art in research that is acquired with practice and with increased depth of understanding of the issues involved. Miles and Huberman (1984 pp. 212–13) also suggest certain rules of thumb for recording entries in a matrix display so that detail is not lost and yet patterns that exist in the data emerge. In addition, they propose rules for examining a matrix display. It is important to recognize that the tasks of summarizing and of entry of data into a matrix display serve to make the investigator thoroughly familiar with the data, so that some interrelationships between factors operating in the data are held in mind and new relationships emerge. The development of a matrix display thus serves several purposes of familiarization, testing of relationships, providing a basis for speculation on new relationships, and a form of presentation of findings to the reader of a report. Ultimately the purpose of matrix display is the identification of a pattern and the provision of an explanation.

6.3 A Research Example of Matrix Display

In the study of evaluators described above there were four sources of data, which included two interviews with each evaluator, one interview with each client, and the evaluation reports. In this research the analysis was divided into three parts. The first part was concerned with the evaluator's views of evaluation; the second was concerned with the conduct of evaluation and the factors influencing conduct, and considered both research situation factors and the views held by an evaluator; while the third part involved cross-case comparisons. In relation to the second and third parts of the analysis the data from each of the above four sources had to be initially analysed together for each evaluator so that relevant information could be combined from the different sources. As a consequence one set of matrix displays involved each evaluator as a separate case, and another set of matrix displays involved cross-case comparisons. It was not desirable to develop a display that kept each source of information in a separate cell, although it was possible that the views of clients would differ in systematic ways from the views of evaluators, or that reports would consistently reveal different perspectives from those advanced by evaluators at interviews. Thus a letter code could be used to indicate the source of an item of information, and a number to indicate the evaluator involved.

The first part of the analysis was concerned with each evaluator's views of evaluation which included views on the nature of educational research. As a consequence, a series of two-way matrix displays was developed, one for each evaluator to examine evidence concerned with the evaluators' views of evaluation and the epistemologies that they endorsed. In Fig. 3 the structure of a matrix display which was used to examine evidence of the epistemologies endorsed by the 15 evaluators is given. The vertical entries in this display indicate the source of evidence that could be used to classify or type each evaluator according to his or her epistemological

approach. The horizontal entries in the matrix display include three salient and distinguishing features of both the scientific and naturalistic epistemological approaches to evaluation. Other approaches, such as a critical social science approach, had to be allowed for. Entries for each evaluator can be placed under the appropriate column headings. The completed matrix displays permitted the researcher to classify or type the epistemological approaches preferred by evaluators. The matrix display was started after the first of the two interviews with the evaluators in order to check whether an adequate representation of the different views of educational research was being obtained. If gross imbalances had been observed, it might have been necessary to add further evaluators to the study so that an adequate range of views had been sampled.

Figure 4 records the matrix display that was constructed for evaluators so that evidence could be examined on the consistency of the views of each evaluator with respect to epistemology and evaluation models. In this matrix display, the horizontal axis provides for the classification of epistemological approaches preferred by evaluators, while the vertical axis classifies the views evaluators expressed about evaluation models. The categories used on this latter axis emerged from an analysis of the previous matrix displays of evaluators' views of evaluation models. The categories of epistemological preferences used on the horizontal axis were developed from the analyses considered in the matrix display in Fig. 3. In Fig. 4, the evaluators were located in appropriate cells, with notes on justifications given by evaluators for what might seem to be inconsistent positions on the two axes. In studying the consistency

Epistemology	Scientific			Interpretative / Naturalistic			Other
Evaluator and source of information	Value-free inquiry	Explanation by inquiry	Empirical general-ization	Value-laden inquiry	Under-stand-ing by inquiry	Interpre-tative inquiry in context	Critical social science approach
A Interview 1 Interview 2 Report							
B Interview 1 Interview 2 Report							
C Interview 1 Interview 2 Report							
D Interview 1 Interview 2 Report							

Figure 3
Matrix display of epistemological views of evaluators

521

Epistemology	Scientific			Interpretative / Naturalistic			Other
Evaluation models	Quasi–experi–mental	Non–experi–mental	Inter–vention	Non–inter–vention	Ethno–graphic	Partic–ipatory	Critical social science
Goal based							
Eclectic							
Utility focused							
Interpretative							
Participatory							
Critical self–reflection							

Figure 4
Matrix display of relationship between epistemology and evaluation models

between the views evaluators expressed about evaluation and the way evaluators conducted their studies, it was possible to locate the evaluation studies conducted by the evaluators in these cells. This provided an indication as to whether the views expressed by evaluators had an influence on the design of the studies they undertook.

Information on the views of each evaluator came primarily from the first of the two interviews with each evaluator. The other two sources, namely the second of the two interviews with the evaluator, and the evaluation reports, were sometimes used. Information from these different sources did not necessarily provide consistent evidence. Consequently, a report was sent to each evaluator on the researcher's interpretations of the evaluator's views to obtain confirmation that the researcher had recorded the dominant views of each evaluator.

It will be apparent to the reader that the preferred epistemological approach expressed by an evaluator may not be that underlying a methodological approach adopted by that evaluator in a particular evaluation study. In such cases, it was of interest to investigate factors in the research situation which were influential in the choice of the approach. In the conceptual framework informing the research, one external factor in the research situation postulated as influencing the conduct of an evaluation was the client's preference. This preference might account for the situation where an evaluator employed a methodological approach at variance with the epistemological preference expressed by the evaluator. However, it is also reasonable to assume that a client would be attracted to, and in turn attract, an

evaluator with similar preferences. Consequently, on research question in this investigation was the extent t which the preferences of the evaluator interacted wit the preferences of the client and were subsequentl related to the nature of the evaluation conducted. A examination of this question would require three matri displays. One matrix display would examine the rela tionship between the epistemological preferences of th 15 evaluators and the preferred approaches of the 3 clients. A second would investigate the relationshi between the epistemological preferences of the 15 evalu ators and the methodological approaches adopted b the evaluators in the 30 studies, while the third woul investigate the relationship between the approach pre ferred by each of the 30 clients and the approac adopted in each of the 30 studies. These three matri displays involved cross-case analyses along the thr dimensions: epistemological preferences of evaluator preferred approaches of clients, and the actu approaches adopted in the studies. Some of the cas illustrated interesting interactions, and where no met odological preference was expressed by a client, th evaluator was found to adopt a methodological app oach that was consistent with that evaluator's preferre epistemological stance.

6.4 Conclusion Drawing and Verifying
The crucial stage in the analysis of the data is the dra ing of conclusions and the verification of the concl sions. Miles and Huberman (1984 pp. 215-31) ha identified 12 tactics for deriving meaning from evidenc The important issue at this stage in the analysis of th

data is not one of whether meaning can be found in the evidence available, however chaotic the evidence might seem, but rather whether or not the conclusion is soundly drawn from the evidence available. The checks that can be applied in the drawing of conclusions are whether the results can be presented in a meaningful way to the reader of a research report and whether another person analysing the same body of evidence would draw the same conclusions. In addition, there is the important question as to whether the research worker is entitled to claim generality for the conclusions beyond the particular body of data that was collected. While the tactics for the deriving of conclusions differ from those of verifying meaning, eliminating possible bias, and confirming the generality of the findings, it is evident that the processes of derivation and verification are interrelated.

6.5 Tactics for Deriving Meaning

(a) *Counting*. In qualitative research there is a tendency to reject counting the number of instances for which a relationship is observed or an event occurs. However, to ignore a count is to overlook the most obvious data. Whether so simple a test should be applied to verify that a pattern was unlikely to occur by chance could become more controversial, particularly if little could be said about the nature and quality of the sample.

(b) *Noting patterns and themes*. Commonly in textual reports or matrix displays recurring patterns of results are quickly seen. A real danger is that of not remaining open to evidence that disconfirms the pattern.

(c) *Imputing plausibility*. Once a particular result or a specific pattern of results has been observed, there is commonly a need on the part of the investigator to consider the plausibility of the result or pattern. The question is asked as to whether the result "makes good sense". There is a very real danger that once a result has been observed, justification will be found and plausibility will be imputed, and the finding will be accepted without further checking.

(d) *Clustering*. Qualitative research lends itself to classifying and clustering events and people into groups. The use of matrix displays greatly facilitates simple clustering. It should be recognized that the outlier or exceptional case can help to provide an understanding of the manner in which a naturally occurring cluster is formed. As a consequence both the outliers and the typical cases should be studied in detail.

(e) *Using metaphors*. At the analysis stage of an investigation and prior to the reporting of results it can be of considerable value for the qualitative researcher to think about the available evidence in terms of metaphors. The use of analogies and metaphorical thinking provides not only a means for writing a report in an interesting and lively way, but also provides a valuable tactic for seeing through a morass of detail in order to detect new and different perspectives. There is of course the danger for the research worker of developing an analogue ahead of the evidence and failing to test the underlying idea or

relationship adequately against the data, and "premature closure" of this kind should be avoided. The wisest approach is to seek opportunities to discuss ideas both formally and informally in order to test out such ideas with both colleagues and critics.

(f) *Splitting categories*. In the planning of the coding and the analysis of the data, categories can be formed that collect a very high proportion of the cases. Classification schemes that fail to discriminate between cases serve little useful purpose. Efforts should be made in such circumstances to use the available evidence, as well as further data that might be obtained to subdivide the category and the associated cases into groups that could add meaning to the analyses and lead to the detection of an important relationship.

(g) *Combining categories*. The converse to splitting categories is also important. Where there are too few cases in certain categories, these categories serve little purpose in the task of cross-classification. If categories can be combined so that the distribution of cases across categories is more balanced, then it is more likely that meaningful patterns and relationships will be observed.

(h) *Compositing*. It is common to include in a study factors that are either conditionally related or have elements in common. There is a danger that the use of too many factors that have fine distinctions between them will lead to loss of meaning. The solution is to combine factors and the categories within those factors by procedures of union of sets of elements or the intersection of sets of elements in order to form new factors that have greater meaning.

(i) *Noting relations*. An important step in the analysis of evidence is to examine factors that vary directly (i.e., both increase) or indirectly (i.e., one increases while the other decreases) together. The large amount of evidence which is collected in a qualitative study makes the identification of such relationships extremely difficult. Nevertheless, if the number of likely relationships could be restricted on logical grounds then a systematic search is likely to yield valuable results.

(j) *Finding mediating factors*. It is not uncommon for factors at the beginning and the end of a chain to be found to be related, such as the preference an evaluator has for a particular methodological approach, and the type of approach used in an evaluation. This particular relationship, while of interest, provides little understanding of the influence of factors that mediate between the two linked concepts. The search for mediating factors might lead to an examination of preferences of the client which could be shown to provide the link in a chain of evidence.

(k) *Building a logical chain of evidence*. The preceding tactic was concerned with searching for a factor that mediated within a logical chain, and this tactic began the development of a related chain of factors such that the prior members of the chain were related in a logical way to the subsequent members of the chain. For example, to extend the chain which was commenced above where it was suggested that the preferences of the client operated as a mediating factor, could lead to the inclusion of external factors, such as the type of program being evaluated, the political climate, and the interests of the stakeholders, as further possible links in a logical chain.

(l) *Constructing a causal chain.* A causal chain of factors should not only involve a logical sequence as was sought in the preceding two tactics, but should also involve a temporal sequence. Since earlier events influence later events and not vice versa, the construction of a causal chain must of necessity be governed by a strict time sequence between the operation of the factors in the chain. The evidence collected in a qualitative study might provide tentative support for the existence of mediating factors, logical chains, and causal chains and indicate whether a link between adjacent factors is present. However, to proceed beyond a tentative link requires the employment of related theory, rather than the observation of evidence collected from a natural setting and linked in a meaningful way in the concluding stages of an investigation. The approach advanced here is that of induction from the evidence, rather than deduction from theory, although as suggested earlier these processes may not be formally distinguishable in the search for meaning within a study that makes extensive use of qualitative data.

7. Confirming Findings

The dangers associated with the pondering over large bodies of qualitative data are that while striking relationships may be suggested which are strong in analogy and clearly presented using metaphor, they run the risk of being incomplete, inadequate, and possibly wrong. Another investigator examining the same body of evidence, but without perhaps the same extent of total immersion in the data, may be unable to detect the relationships reported. Alternatively, a research worker investigating the same or similar cases may advance radically different findings. Similar problems arise in studies that employ quantitative methods. However, researchers using qualitative methods have, in general, not addressed the question of how to ensure that their findings are replicable and robust, and how to convince other researchers that the tactics they have employed are sound in these respects. Miles and Huberman (1984 p. 230) have identified some of the common sources of error in developing conclusions from qualitative data. They include:

(a)   the holistic fallacy, which involves ignoring the outlier cases and erratic strands so that events are interpreted as more patterned and with greater congruence than they actually possess;

(b)   elite bias, which involves giving greater credence to the opinions of high status, articulate respondents than to lower status, less articulate ones; and

(c)   "going native", which involves accepting the perceptions and explanations of events advanced by the respondents being studied without bringing scholarship and experience in investigation to bear on the work of inquiry.

Miles and Huberman (1984 p. 231–43) have advanced 12 tactics that are useful in qualitative research for confirming findings.

(a) *Checking the investigation for representativeness.* This tactic seeks to avoid the pitfalls of sampling nonrepresentative respondents, observing nonrepresentative events, and drawing inference from nonrepresentative processes. Nonetheless, it must be recognized that the exceptional case can sometimes reveal more than can be seen from the uniformity of all the representative cases. These dangers are overcome by: searching deliberately for contrasting cases, sorting the cases into categories in a systematic way, sampling randomly from within a total universe, and increasing the number of cases being studied.

(b) *Checking for researcher effects.* This tactic seeks to diminish in every way possible the influence that the intrusion of an investigator into the situation being studied may have. It is important to recognize that not only may the researcher influence the situation being investigated, but the situation may also have an effect on the perceptions of the researcher in ways that may introduce bias. These problems may be avoided by: spending more time at the site of the investigation, using unobtrusive observation procedures, coopting the assistance of an informant to report on the effects of the researcher on the situation being studied, making sure that misinformation about the investigation does not contaminate the research, undertaking interviews off the site in order to examine the effects the place of interview may have, reducing emphasis on the role of the investigator, guarding against identifiable sources of bias (e.g., the holistic fallacy, elite bias, and going native), avoiding undue concern for individuals by thinking conceptually, trying to sense if deliberate attempts are being made to mislead, keeping research questions in mind, discussing field notes with an experienced researcher, and avoiding the effects on the respondent of knowledge about the issues being investigated.

(c) *Triangulation.* This involves a range of procedures that the research worker can use to increase the strength of observation. There are four types of triangulation: methodological triangulation which involves the use of more than one method to obtain evidence; theory triangulation which involves the use of more than one theoretical perspective in the interpretation of phenomena; investigator triangulation which involves the use of more than one observer; and data triangulation which involves replication of the investigation in time, in location, or with another sample of persons. The use of more than one method of triangulation is both costly and time consuming. However, if the issues under investigation are of sufficient importance then the costs of time and money are no doubt worth the increased strength of the findings provided by extensive triangulation.

(d) *Weighting the evidence*. This is a tactic that can be employed to make allowance for the fact that some data are stronger and other data are more suspect. In order to employ differential weighting of evidence, it is necessary to identify clearly the assessed strength of the data, preferably at the time of collection. This would involve the keeping of a running log on data quality issues and the preparation of a clear summary of information on the relative quality of different items of evidence. There are significant dangers involved in the weighting of data unless it is undertaken on well-argued and rational grounds.

(e) *Making contrasts and comparisons*. This is a sound tactic for drawing conclusions and presenting results. In qualitative research contrasts can be made between persons, cases, groups, roles, activities, and sites. However, it is important that the units being compared or contrasted should be identified in some way that is not directly related to the data to be used in the comparisons. Moreover, it is necessary to recognize in advance the extent of a difference that is worthy of consideration.

(f) *Examining the outlier case*. This is a tactic that can reveal information which would otherwise remain hidden. The temptation is to ignore the outlier and seek uniformity, yet understanding can result from the search for reasons as to why the extreme case has occurred. Outlier cases are not just exceptional people, but can include atypical situations, unique treatments, uncommon events, and unusual sites. Once these exceptional cases have been identified, the characteristics that make them exceptional should be investigated and an explanation as to why the exception has arisen should be sought.

(g) *Using the exceptional case to account for regularity*. This is the complementary side of identifying, examining, and explaining the outlier. The exceptional case should be seen as not only telling much about itself but also telling something about the group from which it was drawn.

(h) *Searching for a spurious relationship*. This tactic is often rewarding. While two factors might be seen to be related in a way that could be interpreted as causal, establishing the existence of a third factor which influenced both commonly leads to a rejection of the causal nature of the observed relationship.

(i) *Replicating a finding*. Conducting a further separate study or providing an opportunity for an independent investigator to re-examine the available evidence is an important tactic in research, where generality is sought. As indicated above, the exceptional case or the outlier can be of considerable value. However, it is also important to distinguish between those cases where regularities are present and where a nomothetic dimension exists, and those cases which are unique and where an idiographic dimension is involved.

(j) *Checking out rival explanations*. This is an important step in developing full understanding. While it is important to search for a reasoned explanation of an event or problematic situation, it is also necessary to advance alternative explanations and if possible to resolve between the two or more explanations that have been proposed. Evidence that would help determine which of two alternative explanations was more coherent must be considered to be critical. A greater contribution to understanding is achieved by a resolution between two rival explanations than by merely confirming a well-held explanation or established result. However, confirmation is in itself of consequence.

(k) *Looking for negative evidence*. This is a useful tactic since it extends the approaches of examining outlier cases, and testing out a rival explanation. The search for evidence that could disconfirm an established result can provide opportunities for the development of understanding, whether or not the pursuit of negative evidence is successful. The failure to find negative evidence after a deliberate search does not and cannot establish the "truth" of a result. However, it does increase the probability that the original result is sound.

(l) *Getting feedback from respondents*. This can provide understanding of both the events being studied and the interpretation or explanation provided for the events. This tactic involves confronting respondents with emerging theoretical explanations of events and inviting them to report on the validity of the explanations with respect to their knowledge and understanding. The purpose is not one of counting heads to indicate support or rejection of a particular explanation, but rather to obtain additional evidence, to provide new insights, and to learn more about the problematic situation under investigation. Only if the procedures of participant verification are carefully and deliberately planned, with key findings clearly presented, together with coherent interpretations of the findings will the participants be able to contribute in a meaningful way.

8. Summarizing and Integrating the Findings

Whereas standard procedures have been developed for the writing of theses, research reports, and journal articles that record the conduct and present the findings of quantitative research conducted from a scientific perspective, in the reporting of qualitative or naturalistic research appropriate procedures have not been developed. The dangers are that while an increasing amount of empirical research using qualitative data is being carried out, either it is not being reported or it is being reported in such a way that the research cannot be audited and the conclusions cannot be verified (see, for example, the influential Australian report by Connell et al. 1982). This gives rise to the anomalous situation that while in research using qualitative data the evidence is rich and detailed, the very richness and detail of the data collected prevent presentation in a coherent form that would lead to acceptance of the findings as a contribution to scholarly inquiry.

There are few agreed-upon procedures or established conventions for the reporting of research based on qualitative data. As a consequence, the quality of such research cannot be verified, because information on the methods employed is lacking. Furthermore, because of the detail in the data, the reports that are prepared are lengthy and time consuming to read, and as a result the findings from such studies are quickly lost in the growing volume of published research.

There are two important aspects of reporting research which is based on qualitative data. The first involves the presentation of the findings of the research, the second involves reporting on the methods that were employed in the conduct of the research. Research in education, irrespective of the nature of the data collected, is part of the ongoing work of contributing to and building a body of knowledge about educational processes as well as providing guidance for policy making and practice. Thus any specific piece of research will make contributions, first to theory about educational processes, second to educational practice, and third to the planning of further investigatory activity. It would seem important that, if possible, each of these three aspects should be addressed in the preparation of a report. Nonetheless, the reader of a research report is initially interested in grasping the key findings of the investigation, before examining other aspects relating to theory, practice, and further inquiry.

Two tactics can be suggested to assist in the presentation of the findings of research based on qualitative data. After the development of a logical sequence or alternatively a causal chain of factors, it can be of value to present this information in diagrammatic form where a path diagram is used to portray the relationships. The path diagram possesses the characteristics of a model in a form that assists comprehension of both the known constructs and their interrelations, and gives rise to the generation of further constructs and relationships that might be examined. A second tactic that is of value in the presentation of results is the formulation of propositions. These propositions can enter into a report in two ways. First, in the opening chapters where a conceptual framework is discussed, propositions can be advanced that can guide the collection of data and the analysis of data, in a similar way to research questions. Furthermore, in the drawing of conclusions attention can again turn to the propositions stated at the beginning of a study and they can be examined or tested with the evidence available. An alternative approach involves the developing of a set of propositions using inductive processes and based upon the conclusions that are drawn from the analysis of evidence. In this use the propositions serve to summarize the findings in a form that can be readily comprehended by the reader and tested in subsequent investigations. They provide a clear and concise focus for both the reporter and the reader to use in identifying what a particular investigation has shown.

A second important task involved in the reporting of an investigation that makes use of qualitative data is the provision of a clear and concise account of how the data

were analysed. Guba and Lincoln (1981) refer to the provision of this type of information as an "audit trail". The idea is that another investigator should be able to follow step by step the audit trail to verify the procedures employed in the analysis of the data. Miles and Huberman (1984 pp. 244–45) have developed a documentation form for use by research workers in education who are working with qualitative data to record the procedures used to analyse the data. A separate form is employed for each specific research question. The researcher is required to summarize on the form "what the analysis of the research question was designed to do". The researcher also records on the form the procedural steps taken, the decision rules employed, and the operations of analysis involved in the examination of data with respect to the specific research questions. The form requires at the end a summary of what the analysis found. The amount of detail included on a form will be determined by the nature of the analyses carried out. Miles and Huberman (1984 p. 247) indicate that for the detailed examination of a research question, commonly seven or eight steps are involved and each step or episode requires approximately a page in order to summarize the information. They also suggest that the forms should be completed concurrently with the conduct of the analyses. The use of the documentation form will also indicate to the research worker the extent and manner in which the analytical techniques are employed on a specific analytical task. Where too great a reliance is made on a very limited number of analytical techniques the researcher should deliberately seek to increase the range of procedures employed. Miles and Huberman indicate that the completion of the standard form requires something of the order of 20 percent of the time necessary to analyse the data with respect to a particular research question. While these audit procedures are time consuming, they form part of a deliberate attempt to develop standard procedures for the analysis of qualitative data on which consensus might be achieved.

Bibliography

Connell R W, Ashenden D J, Kessler S, Dowsett G W 1982 *Making the Difference*. Allen and Unwin, Sydney
Donmoyer R 1985 The rescue from relativism: Two failed attempts and an alternative strategy. *Educ. Res.* 14(10): 13–20
Donmoyer R 1986 The problem of language in empirical research: A rejoinder to Miles and Huberman. *Educ. Res.* 15(3): 26–27
Guba E G, Lincoln Y S 1981 *Effectiveness Evaluation*. Jossey Bass, San Francisco, California
Huberman A M, Miles M B 1986 Concepts and methods in qualitative research: A reply to Donmoyer. *Educ. Res.* 15(3): 25–26
Kaplan A 1964 *The Conduct of Inquiry*. Chandler, San Francisco, California
Miles M B, Huberman A M 1984 *Qualitative Data Analysis: A Sourcebook of New Methods*. Sage, Beverly Hills, California

Scientific Research Procedures

Sampling

K. N. Ross

Social science research is aimed at developing useful generalizations about society and the ways in which individuals behave in society. However, due to practical constraints on research resources, the social scientist is usually limited to the study of a sample rather than a complete coverage of the population for which these generalizations are appropriate. Provided that scientific sampling procedures are employed the use of a sample often provides many advantages compared with a complete coverage: reduced costs associated with obtaining and analyzing the data, reduced requirements for specialized personnel to conduct the fieldwork, greater speed in most aspects of data manipulation and summarization, and greater accuracy due to the possibility of closer supervision of fieldwork and data preparation.

Kish (1965) has divided the social science research situations in which samples are used into three broad categories: (a) experiments—in which the treatment variables are deliberately introduced and all extraneous variables are either controlled or randomized; (b) surveys—in which all members of a defined population have a known nonzero probability of selection into the sample; and (c) investigations—in which data are collected without either the randomization of experiments or the probability sampling of surveys. Experiments are strong with respect to internal validity because they are concerned with the question of whether a true measure of the effect of a treatment variable has been obtained for the subjects in the experiment. In contrast, surveys are strong with respect to external validity because they are concerned with the question of whether the findings obtained for the subjects in the survey may be generalized to a wider population. Investigations are weak on both types of validity and their use is due frequently to convenience or low cost.

In educational research, the survey and experimental approaches have often been portrayed as quite separate methodologies. The perceived differences between these approaches have not been a consequence of statistical theory but rather would appear to be associated with the degree of control which the researcher may exert over the educational environment. Educational researchers have rarely been placed in the enviable situation of being able to introduce experimental treatments in an independent fashion, with appropriate allowances

for extraneous variables, into randomly selected portions of a large and dispersed population. Consequently, the practical difficulties involved in the design of educational research experiments so as to investigate causal relationships within specific populations have often resulted in questions of sample design being largely ignored.

The following discussion of sample design for educational research has focused on some aspects of the survey approach and its application to large-scale educational studies. However, the issues which have been raised have a direct bearing on the conduct of experimental studies because the distributions of relationships between characteristics in causal systems, like the distributions of these characteristics taken alone, exist only with reference to particular populations.

1. Populations

The populations which are of interest to educational researchers are generally finite populations that may be defined jointly with the elements that they contain. A population in educational research is therefore, usually, the aggregate of a finite number of elements, and these elements are the basic units that comprise and define the population.

Kish (1965) stated that a population should be described in terms of (a) content, (b) units, (c) extent, and (d) time. For example, in a study of the characteristics of Australian secondary-school students, it may be desirable to specify the populations as: (a) all 14-year-old students, (b) in secondary schools, (c) in Australia, (d) in 1985.

In order to prepare a description of a population to be considered in an educational research study it is important to distinguish between the population for which the results are desired, the desired target population, and the population actually covered, the survey population. In an ideal situation these two populations would be the same. However, differences may arise due to noncoverage: for example, for the population described above, a list may be compiled of schools during early 1985 which accidentally omits some new schools which begin operating later in the year. Alternatively, differences may occur because of nonresponse at the data collection stage. For example, a number of schools having large concentrations of educationally retarded students might be unwilling to participate in the study.

Strictly speaking, only the survey population is represented by the sample, but this population may be difficult to describe exactly and therefore it is often easier to write about the defined target population (Kish 1965). The defined target population description provides an operational definition which is used to guide the construction of a list of population elements, or sampling frame, from which the sample may be drawn. The elements that are excluded from the desired target population in order to form the defined target population are referred to as the excluded population.

For example, during a cross-national study of science achievement carried out in 1970 by the International Association for the Evaluation of Educational Achievement (IEA), one of the desired Australian target populations for the study was described as:

> All students aged 14.0–14.11 years at the time of testing. This was the last point in most of the school systems in IEA where 100 percent of an age group were still in compulsory schooling. (Comber and Keeves 1973 p. 10)

In Australia it was decided that, for certain administrative reasons, the study would be conducted only within six states of Australia and not within the smaller Australian territories. It was also decided that only students in those school grade levels which contained the majority of 14-year-old students would be tested.

The desired Australian target population was therefore reformulated in order to obtain the defined Australian target population:

> All students aged 14.0–14.11 years on 1 August 1970 in the following Australian states and secondary-school grades:

New South Wales	Forms I, II, and III
Victoria	Forms I, II, III, and IV
Queensland	Grades 8, 9, and 10
South Australia	1st year, 2nd year, and 3rd year
West Australia	Years 1, 2, and 3
Tasmania	Years I, II, III, and IV.

The majority of students in the excluded population were 14-year-olds who were in grade levels which were outside the ranges specified in the description of the defined target population. The students in the "other territories" of Australia (Australian Capital Territory and Northern Territory) were excluded because of certain administrative and cost constraints which were placed on the study.

2. Sampling Frames

Before selecting the sample, the elements of the defined target population must be assembled into a sampling frame. The sampling frame usually takes the form of a physical list of the elements, and is the means by which the researcher is able to "take hold" of the defined target population. The entries in the sampling frame may refer to the individual elements (for example, students) or groups of these elements (for example, schools).

In practice, the sampling frame is more than just a list because the entries are normally arranged in an order which corresponds to their membership of certain strata. For example, in a series of large-scale studies of educational achievement carried out in 21 countries during the early 1970s (Peaker 1975), sampling frames were constructed which listed schools according to their size (number of students), type (for example, comprehensive or selective), region (for example, urban or rural), and sex composition (single sex or coeducational). The use of strata during the preparation of a sampling frame is often undertaken in order to ensure that data are obtained which will permit the researcher to study, and more accurately assess, the characteristics of both individual and combined strata.

3. Probability Samples and Nonprobability Samples

There are usually two main aims involved in the conduct of sample surveys in educational research: (a) the estimation of the values of population attributes (parameters) from the values of sample attributes (statistics), and (b) the testing of statistical hypotheses about population characteristics. These two aims require that the researcher has some knowledge of the accuracy of the values of the sample statistics as estimates of the population parameters. Knowledge of the accuracy of these estimates may generally be derived from statistical theory provided that probability sampling has been employed. Probability sampling requires that each member of the defined target population has a known, and nonzero, chance of being selected into the sample. The accuracy of samples selected without using probability sampling methods cannot be discovered from the internal evidence of a single sample.

Nonprobability sampling in educational research has mostly taken the form of judgment sampling in which expert choice is used to guide the selection of typical or representative samples. These samples may be better than probability samples, or they may not. Their quality cannot be determined without knowledge of the relevant population parameters and if these parameters were known then there would be no need to select a sample.

The use of judgment samples in educational research is sometimes carried out with the (usually implied) justification that the sample represents a hypothetical universe rather than a real population. This justification may lead to research results which are not meaningful if the gap between this hypothetical universe and any real population is too large. Since nonprobability samples are not appropriate for dealing objectively with the aims of estimation and hypothesis testing, they will not be examined in the following discussion.

4. Accuracy, Bias, and Precision

The sample estimate derived from any one sample is inaccurate to the extent that it differs from the population parameter. Generally, the value of the population parameter is not known and therefore the actual accuracy of an individual sample estimate cannot be assessed. Instead, through a knowledge of the behaviour of estimates derived from all possible samples which can be drawn from the population by using the same sample design it is sometimes possible to assess the probable accuracy of the obtained sample estimate.

For example, consider a random sample of n elements which is used to calculate the sample mean, $\bar{x}$, as an estimate of the value of the population mean, μ. If an infinite set of independent samples of size n were drawn from this population and the sample mean calculated for each sample then the average of the sampling distribution of sample means, the expected value, could be denoted by $E(\bar{x})$.

The accuracy of the sample statistic, $\bar{x}$, as an estimator of the population parameter, μ, may be summarized in terms of the mean square error (MSE). The MSE is defined as the average of the squares of the deviations of all possible sample estimates from the value being estimated (Hansen et al. 1953).

$$\text{MSE}[\bar{x}] = E[\bar{x} - \mu]^2$$

$$= E[\bar{x} - E(\bar{x})]^2 + [E(\bar{x}) - \mu]^2$$

$$= \text{Variance of } \bar{x} + [\text{Bias of } \bar{x}]^2 \qquad (1)$$

A sample design is unbiased if $E(\bar{x}) = \mu$. It is important to remember that "bias" is not a property of a single sample, but of the entire sampling distribution, and that it belongs neither to the selection nor the estimation procedure alone, but to both jointly.

The reciprocal of the variance of a sample estimate is commonly referred to as the precision, whereas the reciprocal of the mean square error is referred to as the accuracy.

For most well-designed samples in educational survey research, the sampling bias is either zero or small—tending towards zero with increasing sample size. The accuracy of sample estimates is therefore generally assessed in terms of the sampling variation of the values of $\bar{x}$ around their expected value $E(\bar{x})$.

4.1 The Accuracy of Individual Sample Estimates

The educational researcher is usually dealing with a single sample of data and not with all possible samples from a population. The variance of a sample estimate as a measure of sampling accuracy cannot therefore be calculated exactly. Fortunately, statisticians have derived some formulas which provide estimates of the variance based on the internal evidence of a single sample of data.

For a simple random sample of n elements drawn without replacement from a population of N elements, the variance of the sample mean may be estimated from a single sample of data by using the following formula (Kish 1965 p. 41):

$$\text{var}(\bar{x}) = \frac{N - n}{N} \frac{s^2}{n} \qquad (2)$$

where $s^2 = \Sigma(x_i - \bar{x})^2/(n - 1)$ is an unbiased estimate of the variance of the element values, x_i, in the population.

Note that for sufficiently large values of N, the variance of the sample mean may be estimated by s^2/n because the finite population correction, $(N - n)/N$, tends to unity.

In many practical survey research situations, the sampling distribution of the estimated mean is approximately normally distributed. The approximation improves with increasing sample size even though the distribution of elements in the parent population may be far from normal. This characteristic of the sampling distribution of the sample mean is associated with the "central limit theorem" and it occurs not only for the mean but for most estimators commonly used to describe survey research results (Kish 1965).

From a knowledge of the properties of the normal distribution, it is possible to be "68 percent confident" that the range $\bar{x} \pm \sqrt{[V(\bar{x})]}$ includes the population mean, where $\bar{x}$ is the sample mean obtained from one sample from the population. The quantity $\sqrt{[V(\bar{x})]}$ is called the standard error, $\text{SE}(\bar{x})$, of the sample mean, $\bar{x}$. Similarly, it is known that the range $\bar{x} \pm 1.96 \, \text{SE}(\bar{x})$ will include the population mean with 95 percent confidence. The calculation of confidence limits for estimates allows researchers to satisfy the estimation aim of survey research. Also, through the construction of difference scores $d = \bar{x}_1 - \bar{x}_2$, and using a knowledge of the standard errors $\text{SE}(\bar{x}_1)$ and $\text{SE}(\bar{x}_2)$, the statistical hypothesis aim may be satisfied.

It should be remembered that, although this discussion has focused on sample means, confidence limits could also be set up for many other population values, which, for example, are estimated by $\bar{v}$, in the form $\bar{v} \pm t\sqrt{[V(\bar{v})]}$. The quantity t represents an appropriate constant which is usually obtained from the normal distribution or under certain conditions from the t distribution. For most sample estimates encountered in practical survey research, assumptions of normality lead to errors that are small compared to other sources of inaccuracy.

5. Multistage Sampling

A population of elements can usually be described in terms of a hierarchy of sampling units of different sizes and types. For example, a population of school students may be seen as being composed of a number of classes each of which is composed of a number of students. Further, the classes may be grouped into a number of schools.

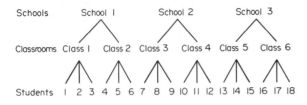

Figure 1
Hypothetical population of eighteen students grouped into six classrooms and three schools

The hypothetical population of school students in Fig. 1 shows 18 students distributed among six classrooms (with three students per class) and three schools (with two classes per school).

From this population a multistage sample could be drawn by randomly selecting two schools at the first stage, followed by randomly selecting one classroom from each of the selected schools at the second stage, and then randomly selecting two students from each selected classroom at the third stage. This three-stage sample design would provide a sample of four students. It would also provide a sample which is an epsem sample (equal probability of selection method) (Hansen et al. 1953). That is, the probability of selecting any student in the population would be the same for all students $(2/3 \times 1/2 \times 2/3 = 4/18)$. Similarly, a simple random sample of four students from the population of 18 students would also provide an epsem sample in which the probability of selection would be the same for all students (4/18). Epsem sampling is widely used in survey research because it usually results in self-weighting samples. In these samples an unbiased estimate of the population mean may be obtained by taking the simple average of the sample cases.

It is important to remember that the use of probability sampling does not automatically lead to an epsem sample. Probability sampling requires that each element in the population has a known and nonzero chance of selection which may or may not be equal for all elements. There are many examples in the literature which demonstrate that educational researchers often overlook this point, For example, one popular sample design in educational research has been to select a simple random sample of, say, a schools from a list of A schools, and then select a simple random sample of b students from each selected school.

The probability of selecting a student by using this design is ab/AB_i, where B_i is the size of the ith school in the population. Consequently, students from large schools have less chance of selection and the simple average of sample cases may result in biased estimates of the population mean—especially if the magnitudes of the B_i values vary a great deal and the survey variable is correlated with school size.

6. Stratification

The technique of stratification is often employed in the preparation of sample designs for educational survey research because it generally provides increased precision in sample estimates without leading to substantial increases in costs. Stratification does not imply any departure from probability sampling—it simply requires that the population be divided into subpopulations called strata and that the random sampling be conducted independently within each of these strata. The sample estimates of population parameters are then obtained by combining the information from each stratum.

Stratification may be used in survey research for reasons other than obtaining gains in sampling precision. Strata may be formed in order to employ different sample designs within strata, or because the subpopulations defined by the strata are designated as separate domains of study. Some typical variables used to stratify populations in educational research are: school location (metropolitan/rural), type of school (government/ nongovernment), school size (large/medium/small), and sex of pupils in school (males only/females only/ coeducational).

Stratification does not necessarily require that the same sampling fraction is used within each stratum. If a uniform sampling fraction is used then the sample design is known as a proportionate stratified sample because the sample size from any stratum is proportional to the population size of the stratum. If the sampling fractions vary between strata then the obtained sample is a disproportionate stratified sample. The simple random sample design is called a self-weighting design because each element has the same probability of selection equal to n/N. For this design, each element has a weight of $1/n$ in the mean, 1 in the sample total, and $F = 1/f$ in the population total, where $f = n/N$ is the uniform sampling rate for all population elements (Kish 1965 p. 424).

In a stratified sample design of elements, different sampling fractions may be employed in the defined strata of the population. The chance of an element appearing in the sample is specified by the sampling fraction associated with the stratum in which that element is located. The reciprocals of the sampling fractions, which are sometimes called the raising factors, describe how many elements in the population are represented by an element in the sample. At the data analysis stage either the raising factors, or any set of numbers proportional to them, may be used to assign weights to the elements. The constant of proportionality makes no difference to the sample estimates. However, in order to avoid confusion for the readers of survey research reports, the constant is usually selected so that the sum of the weights is equal to the sample size.

For example, consider a stratified sample design of n elements which is applied to a population of N elements by selecting a simple random sample of n_h elements from the hth stratum containing N_h elements. In the hth stratum the probability of selecting an element is n_h/N_h, and therefore the raising factor for this stratum is N_h/n_h. That is, each selected element represents N_h/n_h elements in the population.

The sum of the raising factors over all n sample elements is equal to the population size. If there are two strata for the sample design then:

$$\left(\frac{N_1}{n_1} + \frac{N_1}{n_1} + \ldots \text{ for } n_1 \text{ elements}\right)$$
$$+ \left(\frac{N_2}{n_2} + \frac{N_2}{n_2} + \ldots \text{ for } n_2 \text{ elements}\right) = N \quad (3)$$

In order to make the sum of the weights equal to the sample size, n, both sides of the above equation will have to be multiplied by a constant factor of n/N. That is:

$$\left(\frac{N_1}{n_1} \cdot \frac{n}{N} + \ldots \text{ for } n_1 \text{ elements}\right)$$
$$+ \left(\frac{N_2}{n_2} \cdot \frac{n}{N} + \ldots \text{ for } n_2 \text{ elements}\right) = n \quad (4)$$

Therefore the weight for an element in the hth stratum is $N_h/n_h \cdot n/N$.

An estimate of the variance of the sample mean, $\bar{x}_{st}$, for the stratified random sample design described above may be obtained from the following formula (Kish 1965 p. 81):

$$\text{var}(\bar{x}_{st}) = \sum_h \frac{N_h^2}{N^2} \frac{N_h - n_h}{N_h} \frac{s_h^2}{n_h} \quad (5)$$

where

$$s_h^2 = \sum_i (x_{hi} - \bar{x}_h)^2/(n_h - 1)$$

is the variance of the simple random sample of n_h elements in the hth stratum.

Note that for fixed values of n, n_h, N, and N_h, the precision depends upon the sum of the s_h^2 values across strata. If the stratification procedures are extremely successful then element values within strata will be very similar and consequently the magnitude of $\text{var}(\bar{x}_{st})$ will be small. For the special case of proportionate stratified random sampling of elements, the values of n_h/N_h are equal to n/N for all strata. The element weight in this special case is 1 for all sample elements.

Kish (1965 p. 88) has listed several aspects of a research study which benefit from using proportionate random sampling of elements from the strata: (a) sampling precision—the variance of the sample estimate of the mean cannot be greater than for an unstratified sample of the same size; (b) administration—proportionate allocation can typically be done simply and easily; and (c) analysis—proportionate allocation generally leads to self-weighting designs.

7. The Comparison of Sample Designs

In a previous section it was shown that, for the hypothetical population in Fig. 1, either a three-stage sample design or a simple random sample design could be used to select epsem samples of the same size. However, equality of selection probabilities in the two designs provides no guarantee that the variances of sample estimates obtained from each design will be the same.

Fisher (1922) suggested that sample designs could be described and compared in terms of their efficiency. For example, one sample design, denoted i, may be compared to another sample design, denoted j, by considering the inverse of the variance of sample estimates for the same sample size. Using E to represent the efficiency of a sample design for the sample mean, and n to represent the sample size, the efficiency of these two sample designs can be compared by constructing the following ratio:

$$\frac{E_i}{E_j} = \frac{\text{Var}(\bar{x}_j)}{\text{Var}(\bar{x}_i)} \quad (n_i = n_j). \quad (6)$$

More recently, Kish (1965) recommended that the simple random sample design should be used as a standard for quantifying the efficiency of other types of more complex sample designs. Kish introduced the term Deff (design effect) to describe the ratio of the variance of the sample mean for a complex sample design, denoted c, to the variance of a simple random sample, denoted srs, of the same size:

$$\text{Deff} = \frac{\text{Var}(\bar{x}_c)}{\text{Var}(\bar{x}_{srs})} \quad (n_c = n_{srs}) \quad (7)$$

The values of Deff for sample means and multivariate statistics, such as correlation coefficients and regression coefficients, have been found to be greater than unity for many sample designs which are commonly used in educational survey research (Peaker 1975, Ross 1978).

8. The Effective Sample Size

Complex sample designs may also be compared to simple random sample designs by calculating the value of the effective sample size (Kish 1965 p. 259) or the simple equivalent sample (Peaker 1967 p. 149). For a given complex sample, the effective sample size is, for the variable under consideration, the size of the simple random sample which would have the same variance as the complex sample. For example, consider a population of N students. If a complex sample design is used to select an epsem sample of n_c students, then the variance of the sample mean, $\text{Var}(\bar{x}_c)$ may be written as:

$$\text{Var}(\bar{x}_c) = \text{Deff} . \text{Var}(\bar{x}_{srs})(n_c = n_{srs}) \quad (8)$$

Or, alternatively, since $n_c = n_{srs}$, this expression may be written in the form presented by Kish (1965 p. 258):

$$\text{Var}(\bar{x}_c) = \text{Deff} \cdot \frac{N - n_c}{N} \cdot \frac{S^2}{n_c} \quad (9)$$

where S^2 is the population variance.

Now consider a simple random sample design which is used to select a sample of n^* elements from the same population of students. Let the variance of the sample mean for this sample, $\text{Var}^*(x_{srs})$, be equal to the variance of the sample mean for the complex sample design, $\text{Var}(\bar{x}_c)$. That is, $\text{Var}(\bar{x}_c) = \text{Var}^*(\bar{x}_{srs})$.

Substituting on both sides gives the following:

$$\text{Deff}\,\frac{N-n_c}{N}\cdot\frac{S^2}{n_c}=\frac{N-n^*}{N}\cdot\frac{S^2}{n^*} \tag{10}$$

If N is large compared to n_c or n^*, then $n^* \simeq n_c/\text{Deff}$ is the effective sample size for the complex sample design.

It is important to recognize that in complex sample designs the sampling precision is a function of the whole sample design and not just the total sample size. In order to make meaningful comparisons of the sampling precision of complex sample designs, the design effects must be compared in association with the total sizes of the complex samples.

9. Simple Two-stage Cluster Sampling

In educational research, a complex sample design is often employed rather than a simple random sample design because of cost constraints. For example, a two-stage sample consisting of the selection of 10 schools followed by the selection of clusters of 20 students within each of these schools would generally lead to smaller data collection costs compared with a simple random sample of 200 students. The reduced costs occur because the simple random sample may require the researcher to collect data from as many as 200 schools. However, the reduction in costs associated with the complex sample design must be balanced against the potential for an increase in the variance of sample estimates. The selection of groups of students at the first stage in a two-stage sample design is referred to as cluster sampling. Cluster sampling involves the division of the population into clusters which serve as the initial units of selection.

The variance of the sample mean for the simple two-stage cluster sample design depends, for a given number of clusters and a given ultimate cluster size, on the value of the intraclass correlation coefficient. This coefficient is a measure of the degree of homogeneity within clusters. In educational research, student characteristics are generally more homogeneous within schools than would be the case if students were grouped at random. The homogeneity of individuals within sampling units may be due to common selective factors, or to joint exposure to the same influence, or to mutual interaction, or to some combination of these. It is important to remember that the coefficient of intraclass correlation may take different values for different populations, different clustering units, and different variables.

Consider a population of elements divided into equal-sized clusters. Firstly, a simple random sample can be drawn of size n from the population. Secondly, a two-stage sample of the same size can be drawn from the population by using simple random sampling to select m clusters, and then for each of the selected clusters by using simple random sampling to select $\bar{n}$ elements, so that the total sample size n is given by: $n = m\cdot\bar{n}$. The relationship between the variances of the sampling distributions of sample means for these two designs is (Kish 1965 p. 162):

$$\text{Var}(\bar{x}_c) = \text{Var}(\bar{x}_{srs})[1 + (\bar{n} - 1)\cdot roh] \tag{11}$$

where $\text{Var}(\bar{x}_c)$ is the variance of the sampling distribution of sample means for the simple two-stage cluster design; $\text{Var}(\bar{x}_{srs})$ is the variance of the sampling distribution of sample means for the simple random sample design; $\bar{n}$ is the ultimate cluster size; and roh is the coefficient of intraclass correlation.

By transposing the above equation, the value of the design effect for the simple two-stage cluster sample design may be written as a function of the ultimate cluster size and the coefficient of intraclass correlation:

$$\text{Deff} = \frac{\text{Var}(\bar{x}_c)}{\text{Var}(\bar{x}_{srs})} = 1 + (\bar{n} - 1)roh \tag{12}$$

Since roh is generally positive (for students within schools and students within classrooms) the precision of the simple two-stage cluster sample design (which uses either schools or classrooms as primary sampling units) will generally result in sample means which have larger variance than for a simple random sample design of the same size. The losses in sampling precision associated with the two-stage design must therefore be weighed against the "gains" associated with reduced costs due to the selection and measurement of smaller numbers of primary sampling units.

Experience gained from large-scale evaluation studies carried out in many countries (Peaker 1967, 1975) has shown that roh values of around 0.2 provide reasonably accurate estimates of student homogeneity for achievement variables within schools. Higher values of roh for achievement variables have been noted in Australia when considering student homogeneity within classrooms (Ross 1978). These higher values for students within classrooms are sometimes due to administrative arrangements in school systems. For example, students could be allocated to classrooms by using ability streaming within schools, or there may be substantial differences between classroom learning environments within schools.

10. Estimation of the Coefficient of Intraclass Correlation

The coefficient of intraclass correlation was developed in connection with studies carried out to estimate degrees of fraternal resemblance, as in the calculation of the correlation between the heights of brothers. To establish this correlation there is generally no reason for ordering pairs of measurements obtained from any two brothers. The initial approach to this problem was the calculation of a product–moment correlation coefficient from a symmetrical table of measures consisting of two interchanged entries for each pair of measures. This method is suitable for small numbers of entries—however the number of entries in the table rises rapidly as the number of pairs increases.

Some computationally simpler methods for calculating estimates of this coefficient have been described by Haggard (1958). The most commonly used method appears to have been based on using one-way analysis of variance where the clusters which define the first-stage sampling units, for example schools or classrooms, are regarded as the "treatments". The between clusters mean square, BCMS, and the within clusters mean square, WCMS, are then combined with the number of elements per cluster, $\bar{n}$, to obtain the estimate of *roh*:

$$\text{estimated } roh = \frac{\text{BCMS} - \text{WCMS}}{\text{BCMS} + (\bar{n} - 1) \text{WCMS}} \quad (13)$$

An alternative formula, which is based upon variance estimates for elements and cluster means has been presented by Ross (1983):

$$\text{estimated } roh = \frac{\bar{n}s_c^2 - s^2}{(\bar{n} - 1)s^2} \quad (14)$$

where s_c^2 is the variance of the cluster means; s^2 is the variance of the elements; and $\bar{n}$ is the ultimate cluster size.

Both of these formulas assume that the data have been collected by using simple two-stage cluster sampling, and also that both the number of elements and the number of clusters in the population are large.

11. Sample Design Tables for Simple Two-stage Cluster Sample Designs

The two-stage cluster sample design is probably the most often used sample design in educational research. Generally this design is employed by selecting either schools or classes at the first stage of sampling, followed by the selection of either students within schools or students within classes at the second stage. In many research situations these sample designs will be less expensive than simple random sample designs of the same size. Also, they offer an opportunity for the researcher to conduct analyses at higher levels of data aggregation. For example, the selection of clusters of students according to their membership of classes would allow the researcher, provided there were sufficient numbers of classes and sufficient numbers of students per class in the sample, to create a data file based on class mean scores and then to conduct analyses at the "between-class" level.

The previous discussion showed that the precision of the simple two-stage cluster design relative to a simple random sample design of the same size was a function of $\bar{n}$, the ultimate cluster size, and *roh*, the coefficient of intraclass correlation. With a knowledge of both of these statistics, in combination with the required level of sampling precision, it is possible to establish a planning equation which may be used to guide decisions concerning the appropriate numbers of first- and second-stage sampling units.

For example, consider an educational research study in which test items are administered to a sample of students with the aim of estimating the item difficulty values and mean test scores for the population. If a simple random sample of n^* students is selected from the population in order to calculate the proportion p who have obtained the correct answer on an item, the variance of p as an estimate of the population difficulty value may be estimated from the following formula (Kish 1965 p. 46):

$$\text{var}(p) = \frac{p(1 - p)}{n^* - 1} \quad (15)$$

This formula ignores the finite population correction factor because it is assumed that the population is large compared to the sample size.

If it is specified that the standard error of p, expressed as a percentage, should not exceed 2.5 percent, then by assuming normality this would give $p \pm 5$ percent as 95 percent confidence limits for the population value. The maximum value of $p(1 - p)$ occurs for $p = 50$. Therefore in order to ensure that these error requirements could be satisfied for all items, it is necessary to require that

$$(2.5)^2 \geqslant \frac{50(100 - 50)}{n^* - 1} \quad (16)$$

That is, n^* would have to be greater than or (approximately) equal to 400 in order to obtain 95 percent confidence limits of $p \pm 5$ percent.

The variance of a sample mean obtained from a simple random sample which is greater than or equal to 400 in size would be less than or equal to $s^2/400$. Also, the standard error of the sample mean would be less than or equal to $s/20$. Assuming normality, this would give a 95 percent confidence band of ± 10 percent of a student standard deviation score when the sample mean is used as an estimate of the population mean.

Now consider the size of a simple two-stage sample design which would provide equivalent sampling accuracy to a simple random sample of 400 students. That is, it is necessary to discover the numbers of primary sampling units (for example, schools or classes) and the numbers of secondary sampling units (students) which would be required in order to obtain 95 percent confidence bands of ± 5 percent for item difficulty estimates, and ± 10 percent of a student standard deviation score for test mean estimates.

From previous discussion, the relationship between the size of a complex sample, n_c, which has the same accuracy as a simple random sample of size $n^* = 400$ may be written as:

$$n^* = \frac{n_c}{\text{Deff}} = 400 \quad (17)$$

Since the complex sample is a simple two-stage cluster sample design, the value of Deff may be replaced by

$1 + (\bar{n} - 1)roh$ in the above expression to obtain the planning equation:

$$n_c = 400[1 + (\bar{n} - 1)roh] = m\bar{n} \qquad (18)$$

where roh is the coefficient of intraclass correlation for the student measure which is being considered; m is the number of primary selections; and $\bar{n}$ is the number of secondary selections within each primary selection.

It is important to remember that the planning equation is derived with the assumption that the two-stage sample design fits the model of a simple two-stage cluster sample design. In practical educational research studies sample designs may depart from this model by incorporating such complexities as the use of stratification prior to sample selection, and/or the use of varying probabilities of selection at each of the two stages of sampling. Consequently the planning equation must be seen as a tool which assists with the selection of a sample design, rather than a precise technique for predicting sampling errors. The actual sampling accuracy of a sample design must be determined after the sample data become available for analysis.

As an example, consider $roh = 0.2$ and $\bar{n} = 10$. Then,

$$\begin{aligned} m &= \frac{400}{\bar{n}} [1 + (\bar{n} - 1)roh] \\ &= \frac{400}{10} [1 + (10 - 1)0.2] \\ &= 112. \end{aligned} \qquad (19)$$

That is, for $roh = 0.2$, a simple two-stage cluster design of 1,120 students consisting of 112 primary selections followed by the selection of 10 students per primary selection would be required to obtain accuracy which is equivalent to a simple random sample of 400 students.

In Table 1, the planning equation has been employed to list sets of values for $\bar{n}$, m, and n_c which describe a group of simple two-stage cluster sample designs that have equivalent sampling accuracy to a simple random sample of 400 students. Two sets of sample designs have been listed in the table corresponding to roh values of 0.2 and 0.4.

Table 1
Sample design table for simple two-stage cluster samples having an equivalent sample size of 400[a]

Students per cluster $\bar{n}$	roh = 0.2			roh = 0.4		
	Deff	n_c	m	Deff	n_c	m
1 (*srs*)	1.0	400	400	1.0	400	400
2	1.2	480	240	1.4	560	280
5	1.8	720	144	2.6	1,040	208
10	2.8	1,120	112	4.6	1,840	184
15	3.8	1,520	102	6.6	2,640	176
20	4.8	1,920	96	8.6	3,440	172
30	6.8	2,720	91	12.6	5,040	168
40	8.8	3,520	88	16.6	6,640	166
50	10.8	4,320	87	20.6	8,240	165

a Note: The values of m, the number of clusters selected, have been rounded upwards to the nearest integer value

The most striking feature of Table 1 is the rapidly diminishing effect that increasing $\bar{n}$, the cluster size, has on m, the number of clusters which must be selected. This is particularly noticeable for both values of roh when the cluster size reaches 10 to 15 students. For example, when $roh = 0.4$, the selection of 15 students per cluster from 176 clusters would have equivalent sampling accuracy to a design in which 50 students per cluster were selected from 165 clusters. The total sample size in these two cases differs by a factor of over three—from 2,640 to 8,240.

The selection of an appropriate cluster size for an educational research study usually requires the researcher to reconcile the demands of a set of often competing requirements. A number of authors (for example, Hansen et al. 1953, Kish 1965, Sudman 1976) have presented descriptions of the use of cost functions to calculate the optimal or most economical cluster size for certain fixed costs associated with various aspects of sampling and data collection. These approaches provide useful guidelines but they must be considered in combination with the need for high validity in the collection of data. For example, achievement tests which are to be administered in schools should preferably be given at one point of time in order to prevent the possibility of those students who have completed the test being able to discuss the answers with students who will be given the test at some later time. Educational researchers generally cope with this problem by limiting the cluster size to the number of students who can be tested under standardized conditions in one test administration. In most education systems this would represent cluster sizes of around 20 to 30 students when tests can be given by group administration. Much smaller cluster sizes may be necessary for tests which require individualized administration unless a large number of test administrators can be assigned at the same time to a particular school.

A further constraint on the choice of the cluster size may occur when analyses are planned for the between-student level of analysis and also at some higher level of data aggregation—for example, at the between-school level of analysis. In order to conduct analyses at the between-school level, data from students are usually aggregated to obtain data files consisting of school records based on student mean scores. If the number of students selected per school is too small then estimates of school characteristics may be subject to large within-school sampling errors.

12. PPS Two-stage Cluster Sample Designs

The preceding discussion of the simple two-stage cluster sample design was based on the assumption that the primary sampling units were of equal size. In educational research the most commonly used primary sampling units, schools and classes, are rarely equal in size. If the sizes of the primary sampling units vary a great deal then problems often arise in controlling the total sample size when the researcher aims to select a two-stage epsem sample.

For example, consider a two-stage sample design in which *a* schools are selected from a list of *A* schools, and then a fixed fraction of students, say $1/k$, is selected from each of the *a* schools. This design would provide an epsem sample of students because the probability of selecting a student is a/Ak which is constant for all students in the population. However, the actual size of the sample would depend directly upon the size of the schools which were selected into the sample.

One method of obtaining greater control over the sample size would be to stratify the schools according to size and then select samples of schools within each stratum. A more widely applied alternative is to employ probability proportional to size (PPS) sampling of the primary sampling units followed by simple random sampling of a fixed number of elements within these units. An exact execution of the PPS method provides complete control over the sample size and yet ensures epsem sampling of elements.

For example, consider a sample of *m* schools selected with PPS from a population of *M* schools followed by the selection of a simple random sample of *n̄* students from each of the *m* schools. Consider student *i* who attends school *j* which has n_j members from the total of *N* students in the defined target population.

The probability of selecting student *i*, p_{ij}, into this sample may be expressed as:

$$p_{ij} = m \times \frac{n_j}{N} \times \frac{\bar{n}}{n_j} = \frac{m\bar{n}}{N} \tag{20}$$

Since *m*, *n̄*, and *N* are constants then all students in the defined target population have the same chance of selection. That is, this PPS sample design would lead to epsem sampling, and at the same time fix the total sample size as *mn̄* students.

An estimate of the variance of the sample mean, $\bar{x}_{pps}$, obtained from the PPS sample design described above may be obtained from the following formula (Yamane 1967 p. 255):

$$\text{var}(\bar{x}_{pps}) = \frac{1}{m(m-1)} \sum_j (\bar{x}_j - \bar{x}_{pps})^2 \tag{21}$$

where $\bar{x}_j = 1/\bar{n}\Sigma_i x_{ij}$, is the mean score for students in the *j*th ultimate cluster, and $\bar{x}_{pps} = 1/m\bar{n}\Sigma_j \Sigma_i x_{ij} = 1/m\Sigma_j \bar{x}_j$, is the mean score for students in the total sample.

This formula emphasizes two important points which emerged from the discussion of the simple two-stage cluster sample design. First, the variance of the sample mean may be reduced (for a given population of clusters) by increasing the number of primary selections. Second, the variance of the sample mean may be reduced (for a given number of primary selections) by allocating the elements to clusters in a fashion which reduces the variation between cluster means.

When accurate information concerning the size of each primary sampling unit is not available, then PPS sampling is often conducted by using "measures of size"

rather than true sizes. That is, at the first stage of sampling, the clusters are selected with probability proportional to their measure of size. The difference between the actual size of a cluster and its measure of size is compensated for at the second state of sampling in order to achieve an epsem sample design. Kish (1965 pp. 222–23) has presented formulas which demonstrate how to calculate the appropriate second-stage sampling fractions for these situations.

12.1 The Lottery Method of PPS Selection

An often-used technique for selecting a PPS sample of, say, schools from a sampling frame is to employ a lottery method of sampling. Each school is allocated a number of tickets which is equal to the number of students in the defined target population.

For example, consider the hypothetical population described in Table 2. Only the first seven and final three schools have been listed. However the total number of schools and students are assumed to be 26 and 4,000, respectively.

If five schools are to be selected then five winning tickets are required. The ratio of number of tickets to the number of winning tickets is $4,000/5 = 800$. That is, each ticket should have a 1 in 800 chance of being drawn as a winning ticket.

The winning tickets are selected by using a random start-constant interval procedure. A random number in the interval 1 to 800 is selected from a table of random numbers and a list of five winning ticket numbers is created by adding increments of 800. For example with a random start of 520 the winning ticket numbers would be 520, 1320, 2120, 2920, and 3720. The schools which are selected into the sample have been marked in Table 2. School D corresponds to winning ticket number 520, and so on to school X which corresponds to winning ticket number 3,720. The chance of selecting a particular school is proportional to the number of tickets associated with that school. Consequently each of the five schools is selected with probability proportional to the number of students in the defined target population.

Table 2
Hypothetical population of schools and students

School	Number of students in target population	Cumulative tally of students	Ticket numbers
A	50	50	1–50
B	200	250	51–250
C	50	300	251–300
D[a]	300	600	301–600
E	150	750	601–750
F	450	1,200	751–1,200
G[a]	250	1,450	1,201–1,450
.	.	.	.
.	.	.	.
.	.	.	.
X[a]	100	3,750	3,651–3,750
Y	50	3,800	3,751–3,800
Z	200	4,000	3,801–4,000

a Schools selected into final sample

535

13. The Problem of Nonresponse

In most educational research studies there is usually some loss of data due, for example, to the nonparticipation of schools, or the nonresponse of sample members within selected schools. The resulting missing data give rise to differences between the designed sample and the achieved sample.

One of the most frequently asked questions in educational research is: "How much missing data can be accepted before there is a danger of bias in the sample estimates?" The only realistic answer is that there is no general rule which defines a safe limit for nonresponse. The nonresponse bias may be large even if there are small amounts of missing data, and vice versa.

There are two broad categories of nonresponse: total nonresponse and item nonresponse. Total nonresponse refers to a complete loss of data for particular sample members, and is often dealt with by employing weights in order to adjust for differential loss of data among certain important subgroups of the sample. Item nonresponse refers to the loss of a few items of information for particular sample members, and is usually dealt with by the assignment of values which replace the missing data.

It is important to remember that the level of bias in sample estimates which may occur through nonresponse generally cannot be overcome by increasing the sample size. The common approach of using random replacement of nonresponders usually provides additional sample members who resemble responders rather than nonresponders. The level of bias which actually occurs in these situations depends upon the variables which are being examined and their relationships with the nature of the nonresponding subgroup of the defined target population.

The problem of nonresponse in educational research appears to have received limited research attention. This is unfortunate because even doing nothing about nonresponse is an implicit adjustment scheme in itself which is based upon the assumption that loss of data is equivalent to random loss of data.

In studies where only a few items of information are missing for a small number of sample members, the procedure of value assignment is often used. This approach requires that the researcher, working from information which is available from the achieved sample, provides the values which replace the missing data. Lansing and Morgan (1971) recommend that the use of assignment procedures should be restricted either to situations where there are very few missing values associated with an important explanatory variable, or to situations where a limited amount of missing data appears for a variable that forms one component of a variable made up of many components.

The simplest form of assignment, sometimes referred to as matching, involves the direct copying of items of information from another sample member who is matched with the nonrespondent on the basis of their similarity across a set of key variables. An extended form of this approach occurs when the nonrespondent is assigned a value which is equal to the mean or the median for a group of respondents having similar characteristics.

The hot deck assignment procedure, developed by the United States Bureau of the Census, also employs a form of matching. Initially the data available from the sample members are partitioned into homogeneous subgroups based on a set of key variables. A cold deck of information derived from past survey data is then stored in the computer. If the first record to be processed has complete information then it replaces the cold deck; if information is missing from this record then the cold deck data is assigned. The process continues with the hot deck being continually updated to reflect the most recently processed sample cases. All sample records, after the first record with computer information, for which information is missing are consequently assigned the values recorded for the last record processed in the subgroup. It is thus possible for the same record to be used to assign values to many different records in which data are missing.

Assignment may also be carried out by using regression estimates of missing data. This approach capitalizes on the correlational associations between items for the responders. For example, a group of student home background variables may be used to prepare a regression equation with family income as the dependent variable. The sample members who do not respond to the family income question are then assigned a predicted value obtained from a regression equation estimate based on the home background information which they have provided.

See also: Sampling Errors; Interviews in Sample Surveys; Experimental Studies; Survey Research Methods; Statistical Analysis in Educational Research; Research Methodology: Scientific Methods

Bibliography

Comber L C, Keeves J P 1973 *Science Education in Nineteen Countries: An Empirical Study.* Wiley, New York
Fisher R A 1922 On the mathematical foundations of theoretical statistics. *Philosophical Transactions of the Royal Society Series A* 222: 309–68
Haggard E A 1958 *Intraclass Correlation and the Analysis of Variance.* Dryden, New York
Hansen M H, Hurwitz W N, Madow W G 1953 *Sample Survey Methods and Theory,* Vols 1 and 2. Wiley, New York
Kish L 1957 Confidence intervals for clustered samples. *Am. Sociol. Rev.* 22: 154–65
Kish L 1965 *Survey Sampling.* Wiley, New York
Lansing J B, Morgan J N 1971 *Economic Survey Methods.* Institute for Social Research, Ann Arbor, Michigan
Peaker G F 1967 Sampling. In: Husén T (ed.) 1967 *International Study of Achievement in Mathematics: A Comparison of Twelve Countries,* Vol. 1. Wiley, New York, pp. 147–62
Peaker G F 1975 *An Empirical Study of Education in Twenty-one Countries: A Technical Report.* Wiley, New York
Ross K N 1978 Sample design for educational survey research. *Eval. Educ.* 2: 105–95

Ross K N 1983 *Social Area Indicators of Educational Need.* Australian Council for Educational Research, Hawthorn, Victoria

Sudman S 1976 *Applied Sampling.* Academic Press, New York

Yamane T 1967 *Elementary Sampling Theory.* Prentice-Hall, Englewood Cliffs, New Jersey

Sampling Errors

K. N. Ross

The difference between a particular sample estimate and the population parameter obtained from a complete analysis of all members of the defined target population is called the sampling error for that sample. In most practical situations the value of the population parameter is unknown and therefore it is not possible to calculate the sampling error for a particular sample. Instead, through a knowledge of the behaviour of estimates derived from all possible samples, it is sometimes possible to estimate the average, or expected, sampling error even though the value of the population parameter is unknown.

The notion of an average, or expected, sampling error is usually summarized in terms of the mean square error. The mean square error, MSE, is the expected value of the squared difference between a sample value, for example the sample mean $\bar{x}$, and the population parameter, μ, taken over all possible samples. Denoting the expected value of the sampling distribution of sample means by $E(\bar{x})$, the mean square error may be written as:

$$\begin{aligned}\text{MSE}(\bar{x}) &= E(\bar{x} - \mu)^2 \\ &= E[\bar{x} - E(\bar{x})]^2 + [E(\bar{x}) - \mu]^2 \\ &= \text{Variance of } \bar{x} + (\text{Bias of} \bar{x})^2\end{aligned} \tag{1}$$

In most well-designed samples the bias of a sample estimate is either zero or small, tending towards zero with increasing sample size. Therefore, the average sampling error is usually described in terms of the variance.

1. Estimation of Sampling Errors

1.1 Simple Random Samples

The educational researcher is usually dealing with a single random sample of data rather than all possible samples from a population. The variance of a sample estimate therefore cannot be calculated exactly. Instead, by using formulas derived by statisticians, estimates are made of the variance from the internal evidence of a single sample of data.

For a simple random sample of n elements drawn without replacement from a large population, the variance of the sample mean may be estimated from a single sample by using the following formula (Kish 1965 p. 41):

$$\text{var}(\bar{x}) = \frac{s^2}{n} \tag{2}$$

where var($\bar{x}$) refers to the sample estimate of the variance of $\bar{x}$, and s^2 is the unbiased estimate of the variance of the element values. A factor called the finite population correction has been left out of the formula because the population is assumed to be large.

In many practical survey research situations the sampling distribution of the sample mean, and many other sample estimators, is approximately normally distributed. The approximation improves with sample size even though the population of element values is far from normal (Kish 1965). Consequently, by taking the square root of the estimated variance it is possible to obtain an estimate of the standard error of the sampling distribution of these sample estimators and thereby calculate confidence limits for the corresponding parameter.

In the case of the sample mean, the estimate of the standard error would be:

$$\text{SE}(\bar{x}) = (\text{var}(\bar{x}))^{1/2} = \frac{s}{(n)^{1/2}} \tag{3}$$

Although there is general agreement among statistical authors concerning the formula for estimating the standard error of the sample mean for a simple random sample of elements, there are sometimes differences of opinion about the appropriate formulas for calculating the variance of more complex statistics. These differences generally become insignificant for the typically large population and sample sizes which are associated with educational survey research. In Table 1 the formulas for calculating the standard error of several commonly used statistics have been listed. The formulas were selected from one source (Guilford and Fruchter 1978).

Table 1
Formulas for estimation of sampling error when data are gathered by using a simple random sample design

Sample statistic	Estimate of standard error
Mean	$\dfrac{s}{(n)^{1/2}}$
Correlation coefficient	$\dfrac{1}{(n)^{1/2}}$
Standardized regression coefficient	$\left[\dfrac{1 - R_{1,2,3,4,\ldots,m}^2}{(1 - R_{2,3,4,\ldots,m}^2)(n - m)}\right]^{1/2}$
Multiple correlation coefficient	$\dfrac{1}{(n - m)^{1/2}}$

Table 2
Mean values of $(\text{Deff})^{1/2}$ obtained for seven countries participating in the IEA science project at the 14-year-old level

Country	Schools m	Cluster size $\bar{n}$	Value of $(\text{Deff})^{1/2}$		
			Means	Correlation coefficient	Regression coefficient
Australia	225	24	2.4	1.7	1.3
Chile	103	13	2.6	1.6	1.6
Finland	77	30	2.2	1.7	1.3
Hungary	210	33	3.2	1.9	1.5
New Zealand	74	27	1.9	1.4	1.4
Scotland	70	28	2.4	1.5	1.2
Sweden	95	26	1.8	1.2	1.3
Mean $(\text{Deff})^{1/2}$	—	—	2.3	1.6	1.4

The formulas in Table 1 are based on a simple random sample of n elements which are measured on m variables. The symbol s refers to the standard deviation and the symbol $R_{i.jkl}$ refers to the multiple correlation coefficient associated with a regression equation which uses variable i as the criterion and variables j, k, and l as predictors.

1.2 Complex Samples

Educational research is generally conducted by using data obtained from complex sample designs which employ techniques such as stratification, clustering, and varying probabilities of selection. Computational formulas are available to provide estimates of the standard errors of descriptive statistics such as sample means for a wide range of these sample designs. Unfortunately, the computational formulas required for estimating the standard errors for analytical statistics such as correlation coefficients, standardized regression coefficients, and multiple correlation coefficients are not readily available for sample designs which depart from the model of simple random sampling. These formulas are either enormously complicated or, ultimately, they prove to be resistant to mathematical analysis (Frankel 1971).

Due to the lack of suitable sampling error formulas for analytical statistics estimated from complex sample designs, researchers have tended to accept estimates based on formulas which assume that data have been gathered by using simple random sample assumptions. While overestimates of sampling errors may lead to errors of a conservative kind, underestimates have the potential to misrepresent the stability of sample statistics in a fashion which might lead to erroneous conclusions concerning the importance of research findings.

The research evidence which is available concerning the magnitude of sampling errors for statistics such as means, correlation coefficients, regression coefficients, and multiple correlation coefficients suggests that the use of formulas based on the assumption of simple random sampling often results in gross underestimation of sampling errors for many sample designs which are commonly used in educational research (Peaker 1975,

Ross 1978). The degree of underestimation may be summarized by the "design effect" or "Deff" value. In Table 2 some values of $(\text{Deff})^{1/2}$ have been presented for a two-stage sample design employed in seven countries during a cross-national research study carried out by the International Association for the Evaluation of Educational Achievement (IEA)(Peaker 1975). For each country the number of schools selected at the first stage, m, and the number of students selected within the sample schools, $\bar{n}$, has been presented.

The value of $(\text{Deff})^{1/2}$ represents the factor by which sampling errors, obtained from formulas based on simple random sampling assumptions, must be multiplied in order to obtain estimates of the actual value of the sampling error for the complex sample design. For example, from the data presented in Table 2, the standard error of a correlation coefficient for Australia based on the complex two-stage sample of $n_c = m\bar{n}$ elements would be:

$$\text{SE}(r_c) = (\text{Deff})^{1/2}, \quad \text{SE}(r_{srs}) = \frac{1.7}{(n_c)^{1/2}} \quad (4)$$

where $\text{SE}(r_c)$ is the standard error of a correlation coefficient for the complex two-stage sample design of n_c elements, and $\text{SE}(r_{srs})$ is the standard error which would be estimated from the appropriate formula in Table 1, which is based on the assumption that there was a simple random sample of n_c elements.

In Table 2 the values of $(\text{Deff})^{1/2}$ for means are higher than for correlation coefficients and regression coefficients. This result has occurred consistently for other types of sample design in a range of studies (Kish and Frankel 1970, Ross 1978).

2. Empirical Techniques for the Estimation of Sampling Errors

The calculation of the $(\text{Deff})^{1/2}$ adjustment factor requires that the researcher be able to estimate the sampling errors of statistics derived from complex sample designs. In the absence of suitable formulas based on distribution theory for many analytical statistics, a variety of empirical techniques have emerged which provide "approximate variances that appear satisfactory for practical purposes" (Kish 1978 p. 20).

These techniques may be divided into two broad groups: (a) random subsample replication and (b) Taylor's series approximations.

2.1 Random Subsample Replication

In random subsample replication, a total sample of data is divided into two or more independent subsamples, each subsample following the overall sample design except for the sampling fraction and sample size. "A distribution of outcomes for a parameter being estimated is generated by each subsample. The differences observed among the subsample results are then analyzed to obtain an improved estimate of the parameter, as well as a confidence assessment for that estimate" (Finifter 1972 p. 114). The main approaches to this technique have been independent replication (Deming 1960), jackknifing (Tukey 1958), and balanced repeated replication (McCarthy 1966).

The use of independent replication to estimate errors in surveys was first introduced by Mahalanobis (1946) for agricultural surveys carried out in India. Deming (1960) refined this technique as "replicated sampling" and demonstrated that it was useful for estimating the sampling errors of a wide range of statistics. In replicated sampling, a number of subsamples, rather than one full sample, are selected from the population. Each of these subsamples follows the same sample design. Sample estimates, y_i, of the statistic y are then calculated for each subsample. The variation between these independent estimates then provides a means of assessing the sampling error associated with the overall estimate.

For k subsamples the statistic y may be estimated from the mean of the k subsample estimates, $\bar{y}$, and then the variance of y is approximated by the variance of the mean of the subsample estimates:

$$\text{Var}(y) \simeq \frac{\sum (y_i - \bar{y})^2}{k(k-1)} \tag{5}$$

The independent replication technique considers the overall estimate as the mean of an unrestricted random sample of k subsample estimates. Therefore, provided the subsamples represent independent replications of each other, the technique may be used with any complex sample design.

The independent replication technique was used by the International Association for the Evaluation of Educational Achievement (IEA) in their study of the mathematics achievement of students in 12 countries (Peaker 1967). An important feature of this technique is that sophisticated computer programs are not required for the estimation of sampling errors because the analyses required for the overall dataset are simply repeated on each of the subsamples.

Kish (1965 p. 131) has presented a variety of arguments which may be advanced in favour of employing

either large or small numbers of independent replications. Kish favours at least 20 replications, Deming (1960) recommends 10, and Peaker (1967) employed four to estimate errors in the IEA studies. The use of 10 replications provides an appealing result in terms of computational simplicity (Kish 1965 pp. 130, 620). In this case, due to the relationship between the range and the variance of elements in a sample, the variance of the statistic y may be estimated as:

$$\text{Var}(y) \simeq \left[\frac{\text{Range } (y_i)}{10} \right]^2 \tag{6}$$

An alternative approach to the use of independent replications is to use one of the two "pseudoreplication" techniques: jackknifing and balanced repeated replication. The term pseudoreplication refers to the construction of "overlapping" or "interpenetrating" subsamples which are not independent subsamples in the sense described above.

These two techniques do not generally suffer, to the same extent as the independent replication approach, from difficulties associated with having too few cases within a pseudoreplication.

As for the independent replication approach, the necessary calculations may be carried out on a microcomputer—and therefore the maximal number of pseudoreplications should be used. In the case of the jackknife approach this is equal to the number of primary selections.

The development of the jackknife procedure may be traced back to an earlier method used by Quenouille (1956) to reduce the bias of estimates. Further refinement of the method (Tukey 1958, Mosteller and Tukey 1968, Mosteller and Tukey 1977) has led to its application in a range of social science situations where formulas are not readily available for the calculation of sampling errors. The application of the jackknife procedure requires that estimates of parameters be made on the total sample of data, and then, after dividing the data into groups, the calculations are made for each of the slightly reduced bodies of data which are obtained by omitting each subgroup in turn. These subgroups should be constructed according to the same approach used in Deming's technique.

Let y_i be an estimate of a statistic y based on the data which remain after omitting the ith subgroup and let y_{all} be the estimate based on the total sample data. k pseudovalues $y_i^*(i = 1, \ldots, k)$ can be defined based on the k complements:

$$y_i^* = k y_{\text{all}} - (k-1)y_i \tag{7}$$

The jackknife value is defined as:

$$y^* = \frac{1}{k} \sum_i^k y_i^*. \tag{8}$$

The variance of the statistic y may be estimated from the variance of the jackknife value:

$$\text{Var}(y) \simeq \left[\sum_i^k y_i^{*2} - \frac{1}{k} \left(\sum_i^k y_i^* \right)^2 \right] \Big/ k(k-1) \qquad (9)$$

Tukey (1958) set forward the proposal that the pseudovalues could be treated as if they were approximately independent observations and that Student's t distribution could be applied to these estimates in order to construct approximate confidence intervals for y^* or y_{all}. Later empirical work by Frankel (1971) provided firm support for these proposals when the jackknife technique was applied to complex sample designs and a variety of regression-related statistics. The jackknife procedure has been used extensively in the large-scale educational evaluation studies carried out by the International Association for Educational Achievement (Peaker 1975).

A computer program within the OSIRIS statistical software system (SRC 1981) has been designed to carry out jackknife calculations for regression-related statistics. However, even for large samples, provided there are only a few statistics and only a few subsamples it is feasible to carry out the necessary calculations by hand following the preparation of pseudovalues on the computer.

The balanced repeated replication technique was developed by McCarthy (1966) in order to permit variance estimates to be made from sample designs which featured the maximum amount of stratification possible (two primary selections per stratum) and yet still permitted variance estimates to be made from a single sample of data.

Consider a population divided into h strata and the primary sampling units within each of these strata are divided into two random halves of equal size. A primary sampling unit is then selected from each half stratum. A half-sample replicate is formed by randomly choosing one of these primary sampling units for each stratum. The number of independent half samples which can be drawn from the data is 2^{h-1}. Variance estimates are then computed from the squared difference between the total sample estimate and the half-sample replicate estimate.

Thus, if y_{all} is an estimate of a statistic y based on the total sample of data, then the variance of this statistic may be estimated by $(y_i - y_{\text{all}})^2$, where y_i is the estimate based on a half sample (Kish and Frankel 1970).

In order to increase the precision of the variance estimate the researcher may select k repeated replications and then the variance of the statistic y may be estimated from the mean of the k computed variances:

$$\text{Var}(y) \simeq \sum_i^k (y_i - y_{\text{all}})^2 / k \qquad (10)$$

McCarthy's main contribution in this area was to develop a method for choosing a specific subset of half samples which contained all of the information available in the total set of half samples. Frankel (1971) carried out extensive tests of this technique and showed

that it was suitable for generating sampling errors for a variety of statistics employed in multiple regression analysis. A computer program, based on Frankel's research, has been distributed within the OSIRIS statistical software system (SRC 1981). An important feature of this software is that it is capable of producing estimates of sampling errors for both the balanced repeated replication and the jackknife techniques.

2.2 Taylor's Series Approximations

The use of Taylor's series approximations was initially suggested by Kendall and Stuart (1969) and is often described as a more direct method of variance estimation than the "replication" approaches. In the absence of an exact sampling variance formula, the Taylor's series is used to approximate a numerical value of the first few terms of a series expansion of the variance formula. The majority of applications in social science research have been limited to the use of Taylor's series terms up to the first partial derivatives (Kish and Frankel 1970).

If $g(y)$ is a function of the k variates $y_1, y_2, \ldots, y_k$, which have means $\theta_1, \theta_2, \ldots, \theta_k$, then providing $g(y)$ is differentiable, the Taylor's series for $g(y_1, y_2, \ldots, y_k)$ may be written as:

$$g(y) = g(y_1, y_2, \ldots, y_k)$$
$$= g(\theta_1, \theta_2, \ldots, \theta_k) + \sum_{i=1}^k \frac{\partial g}{\partial y_i} (y_i - \theta_i)$$
$$+ \text{ terms of order } n^{-1} \text{ (or less)} \qquad (11)$$

(Kendall and Stuart 1969 pp. 231–32). The partial derivatives in the above expression are calculated at the appropriate expected values.

For large sample sizes, that is, large n values, the approximation is made that $g(y)$ may be expressed as a sum of the first two terms on the right hand side of the above equation.

Then, with this assumption in mind, the sampling variance of $g(y)$ is approximately equal to the sampling variance of the first degree terms of the Taylor's series approximation. That is,

$$\text{Var}[g(y)] \simeq \text{Var} \left[\sum_{i=1}^k \frac{\partial g}{\partial y_i} y_i \right] \qquad (12)$$

since $g(\theta_1, \theta_2, \ldots, \theta_k)$ and $\sum_{i=1}^k (\partial g/\partial y_i) \theta_i$ are both constants (Frankel 1971 pp. 27–28).

The application of this estimator of the sampling variance of $g(y)$ requires that values for the partial derivatives can be obtained, and that the values of these, when they are evaluated for the sample data, are reasonable approximations to their true values.

In the relatively simple situation where $g(y)$ is a ratio mean, y/x, based on two variables, x and y, measured for a simple random sample of intact but unequal sized clusters, the partial derivatives may be obtained readily and it can be shown that:

$$\mathrm{var}\!\left(\frac{y}{x}\right) \simeq \frac{1}{x^2}\Bigg[\mathrm{var}(y) + \left(\frac{y}{x}\right)^2 \mathrm{var}(x) -$$

$$2\left(\frac{y}{x}\right)\mathrm{cov}(y,x)\Bigg] \quad (13)$$

(Kish 1965 p. 207).

The evaluation of partial derivatives when estimates of the sampling variances of correlation or regression coefficients are required becomes a much more unwieldy exercise (Frankel 1971, Mellor 1973). Beyond these elementary analytical statistics, it would appear that very few attempts have been made to tackle the extensive algebra required to make series approximations for more complicated multivariate statistics obtained from complex samples.

A number of computer programs have been produced which employ Taylor's series approximations for the estimation of sampling errors associated with means and proportions (Shah 1981a), ratio means (Shah 1981b, SRC 1981), and regression coefficients (Hidiroglou et al. 1979, Holt 1979). All of these programs are based on subroutines which describe formulas for the partial derivatives of the appropriate statistics. Woodruff and Causey (1976) have produced a more generalized approach in which the partial derivatives of many complicated statistics may be estimated by means of a numerical approximation technique. Wilson (1982) has presented a detailed study of the Woodruff–Causey approach when it is applied to a variety of sample designs which are commonly employed in educational survey research.

See also: Sampling

Bibliography

Deming W E 1960 *Sample Design in Business Research*. Wiley, New York

Finifter B M 1972 The generation of confidence: Evaluating research findings by random subsample replication. In: Coster H I (ed.) 1972 *Sociological Methodology: 1972*. Jossey-Bass, London

Frankel M R 1971 *Inference from Survey Samples: An Empirical Investigation*. Institute for Social Research, University of Michigan, Ann Arbor, Michigan

Guilford J P, Fruchter B 1978 *Fundamental Statistics in Psychology and Education*, 6th edn. McGraw-Hill, New York

Hansen M H, Hurwitz W N, Madow W G 1953 *Sample Survey Methods and Theory*, Vols. 1 and 2. Wiley, New York

Hidiroglou M A, Fuller W A, Hickman R D 1979 *Super Carp*, 4th edn. Survey Section, Iowa State University, Ames, Iowa

Holt M M 1979 *Standard Errors of Regression Coefficients from Sample Survey Data*. Research Triangle Institute, Research Triangle Park, North Carolina

Kendall M G, Stuart A 1969 *The Advanced Theory of Statistics*, 3rd edn., Vol. 1. Griffin, London

Kish L 1965 *Survey Sampling*. Wiley, New York

Kish L 1978 On the future of survey sampling. In: Krishnan Namboodiri N (ed.) 1978 *Survey Sampling and Measurement*. Academic Press, New York, pp. 13–21

Kish L, Frankel M R 1970 Balanced repeated replications for standard errors. *J. Am. Stat. Assoc.* 65: 1071–94

McCarthy P J 1966 *Replication: An Approach to the Analysis of Data from Complex Surveys: Development and Evaluation of a Replication Technique for Estimating Variance*. United States National Center for Health Statistics, Washington, DC

Mahalanobis P C 1946 Recent experiments in statistical sampling in the Indian Statistical Institute. *J. Roy. Stat. Soc.* 109: 326–78

Mellor R W 1973 Subsample replication variance estimators. Unpublished doctoral thesis, Harvard University, Cambridge, Massachusetts

Mosteller F, Tukey J W 1968 Data analysis including statistics. In: Lindzey G, Aronson E (eds.) 1968 *The Handbook of Social Psychology*, 2nd edn. Addison-Wesley, Reading, Massachusetts

Mosteller F, Tukey J W 1977 *Data Analysis and Regression: A Second Course in Statistics*. Addison-Wesley, Reading, Massachusetts

Peaker G F 1967 Sampling. In: Husén T (ed.) 1967 *International Study of Achievement in Mathematics: A Comparison of Twelve Countries*, Vol. 1. Wiley, New York, pp. 147–62

Peaker G F 1975 *An Empirical Study of Education in Twenty-one Countries: A Technical Report*. Wiley, New York

Quenouille M J 1956 Notes on bias in estimation. *Biometrika* 43: 353–60

Ross K N 1978 Sample design for educational survey research. *Eval. Educ.* 2: 105–95

Shah B V 1981a *Standard Errors Program for Computing of Standardized Rates from Survey Data*. Research Triangle Institute, Research Triangle Park, North Carolina

Shah B V 1981b *Standard Errors Program for Computing of Ratio Estimates from Sample Survey Data*. Research Triangle Institute, Research Triangle Park, North Carolina

Survey Research Center (SRC) 1981 *OSIRIS IV User's Manual*, 7th edn. Survey Research Center, Ann Arbor, Michigan

Tukey J W 1958 Bias and confidence in not-quite large samples: Abstract. *Ann. Maths. Stat.* 29: 614

Wilson M 1982 *Adventures in Uncertainty*. Australian Council for Educational Research, Hawthorn, Victoria

Woodruff R A, Causey B D 1976 Computerized method for approximating the variance of a complicated estimate. *J. Am. Stat. Assoc.* 71: 315–21

Bayesian Statistics

H. R. Lindman

Bayesian statistics involve both a philosophy and a set of statistical methods. Their main advantages over traditional statistics are that they encourage thinking about the data in new ways, that they bring prior information and informed opinions explicitly into the data analysis, and that they provide a more realistic philosophical position from which to evaluate the results of statistical procedures.

The principal disadvantages of Bayesian statistics are that the mathematical calculations are sometimes more complicated, prior information and opinions are sometimes difficult to assess in a manner appropriate for Bayesian statistics, and the allowance for prior information and opinions can lead to abuses. For these reasons the methods themselves are probably most valuable with relatively simple data sets (e.g. involving a simple t-test or binomial test, etc.), and where decisions will have practical consequences that will ultimately affect the person making the decisions (so that there are strong motives to separate true opinions from desires). However, a person may be philosophically a Bayesian even when using traditional statistical techniques as a second-best alternative. These issues will be discussed more fully after the basic ideas of Bayesian statistics have been presented.

1. Bayes' Theorem

The term Bayesian statistics is derived from a theorem that was first proved by the Rev. Thomas Bayes and published posthumously in 1763. Then the theorem was novel. Now it can be easily proved in any elementary statistics or probability theory class. Letting $P(A|B)$ represent the probability of event A, given that event B has occurred, and letting B' represent the complement (nonoccurrence) of B, Bayes' theorem can be written in any of several forms:

$$P(B|A) = P(A|B)P(B)/(P)(A) \tag{1}$$

$$P(B|A) = P(A|B)P(B)/[P(A|B)P(B) + P(A|B')P(B')] \tag{2}$$

$$P(B|A)/P(B'|A) = [P(A|B)/P(A|B')][P(B)/P(B')] \tag{3}$$

Equation (3) is called the odds form of Bayes' theorem because it relates the odds of B and B', conditional on A, to the data and the unconditional odds. The first term in brackets on the right-hand side of the last equation is commonly called the likelihood ratio.

The mathematical correctness of Bayes' theorem is unquestioned. The application of Bayes' theorem distinguishes Bayesian from traditional statistics. In traditional statistics it is an interesting but seldom-used formula. In Bayesian statistics it is central.

To see why, consider an ordinary test of a null hypothesis, for example using the normal distribution. Beginning with the null hypothesis, say $H_0: \mu = 50$, and then gathering data a sample mean is obtained of 46. Suppose that on the basis of these data the null hypothesis can be rejected at, say, the 0.05 level, one-tailed. What exactly is meant by that? Specifically, it means that if the null hypothesis were true, then the probability of obtaining a sample mean as small as, or smaller than, 46, would be less than 0.05.

This is a complicated notion, as any student of elementary statistics can testify. It also contains some serious weaknesses. First, it considers the probability of obtaining data that were not actually obtained (i.e. it considers the probability of obtaining sample means smaller than 46 as well as equal to 46), and that therefore should presumably be irrelevant. Second, it considers only the consequences of rejecting the null hypothesis; it ignores the possibility of incorrectly accepting it. To be sure, lip service is given to beta levels of statistical significance in statistics classes, but in practice they are almost universally ignored because there is no simple, direct way to deal with them. Third, it purports to test a null hypothesis in which little faith is put in the first place. In most cases the null hypothesis test is actually an artificial way of deciding whether the mean is really larger or smaller, rather than precisely equal to, the hypothesized value. Fourth, it does not illustrate in any direct way how likely it is that the null hypothesis is true; it tells only how likely the results would be *if* the null hypothesis were true.

The last weakness is especially important, for there are times when the data may be very unlikely, given a particular hypothesis, but a decision is still made to accept the hypothesis in spite of the data. Suppose, for example, that 50 is the mean score on a standardized achievement test for children of age 12, and that 46 was the mean score of students in a local, well-respected college or university. In such a case, the researcher's inclination would be to admit that the data are unlikely under $H_0: \mu = 50$, but to conclude nevertheless that the unlikely has occurred. Of course, one way to deal with this problem is to choose a very small significance level for rejection. However, within traditional statistics there is little guidance in choosing a specific significance level. That is why the 0.05 level, a purely conventional value, is so commonly used as an alpha level of statistical significance.

The same problem arises with confidence intervals. A 95 percent confidence interval is constructed in such a way that it will cover the true population mean in 95 percent of the cases for which it is constructed. However, previous information, unrelated to the experimental data, may suggest that the present experiment is one of the unlucky 5 percent (e.g. if a 95 percent confidence interval of 100 to 105 is obtained for the mean IQ of Oxford University students). The paradoxical situation then exists of having constructed a confidence interval in which it is impossible to have any confidence.

Now consider the alternative using Bayes' theorem. Suppose, in the above equations, that B represents any (not necessarily the null) hypothesis, and A represents the obtained sample data. Then the formula indicates that the probability of the hypothesis, conditional on the sample data, should depend in a specific way on the unconditional probability. The plausibility (i.e. probability) of the hypothesis can thus be calculated directly, avoiding the roundabout methods of traditional statistics. This will be illustrated later with a specific example, but first the principal objection usually given to this approach must be dealt with.

2. Probability Theory

Although Bayes' theorem is accepted by all statisticians, its application to the above example is not. This is because in traditional statistics it is possible to assign probabilities to data but it is not legitimate to assign probabilities to hypotheses. The reason lies in the history of probability theory.

Probability theory was first applied to gambling. As in many areas of mathematics, the procedures were used before the philosophy had been worked out. This caused few problems in gambling situations, in which the appropriate probabilities were usually obvious. However, in scientific applications it led to many abuses, perhaps the most famous being due to Laplace. Applying Bayes' theorem (along with some assumptions that were widely accepted in his day) to the known fact that the sun had risen every day for more than 5,000 years, Laplace stated that the odds in favor of the sun rising tomorrow were higher than 1,826,213 to 1.

The reaction against these abuses came in the form of a theory which limited the assignment of probabilities to the outcomes of rather broadly defined "experiments." An experiment was defined generally as an act or process that led to a single well-defined outcome. Thus the administration of an achievement test to a sample of 12-year-olds is an experiment, as is the toss of an ordinary coin.

However, before probabilities can be assigned to these outcomes, the experiment must have a special property—the experiment must be repeatable, in principle, an infinite number of times under identical conditions. In practice this is generally interpreted to mean that the outcomes must be generated by some random process whose outcomes and probabilities do not change upon repetitions of the experiment. The 12-year-olds must be a random sample from some well-defined population of 12-year-olds, the coin must be randomly tossed, and so on.

This new idea of probability corrected the old abuses. It was adopted by Neyman and Pearson, who developed the foundations of the statistical theory and tests commonly used today. However, it has serious weaknesses. It is extremely limiting; it precludes the assignment of numerical values in the most natural way (i.e. by assigning probabilities) to beliefs about hypotheses because hypotheses are either true or false (i.e. they cannot be "repeated under identical conditions"); and it prevents simple pursuits such as giving odds on horse races. Try to imagine a horse race being repeated an infinite number of times under identical conditions.

Moreover, the philosophical foundations of this view are shaky. No experiment can really be repeated even a finite number of times under exactly identical conditions, and if it could, it would always lead to the same results. If you could toss a coin in precisely the same way every time, you would expect it to land precisely the same way every time. Probabilities exist to the extent that conditions are nonidentical, but under nonidentical

conditions there is no objective way to determine whether the probabilities have remained constant from trial to trial. In fact the very question may be meaningless.

Alternative approaches to probability were proposed in the first half of the twentieth century. Most important were the personalist and necessarist views of probability. According to both, probabilities were assigned not to events but to propositions—statements of fact. A probability represents a "degree of belief" that the statement is true. The personalist and necessarist views differ in that the personalist believes such probabilities are entirely personal—a given person may have any degree of belief whatsoever in a given proposition, while the necessarist believes that there is a "right" probability (usually unknown and unknowable) that one should have for the proposition. Most applied Bayesian statisticians hold the personalist view because the necessarist view gives little practical guidance in searching for the "right" probability.

The personalist view would seem to lead to chaos, letting anyone assign any probability to any proposition. However, this is not the case, at least for reasonable people. The brilliance of the work by the early personalists—Ramsey (1931), de Finetti (1937), Savage (1954), and so on—was that they showed that personal probabilities could not take on just any values whatsoever.

First, the probabilities had to be realistic in that they had to be tied to possible concrete actions by the individual. To oversimplify the problem, if there is a probability of $\frac{3}{4}$ for a given proposition, then it would be reasonable to give three-to-one odds in a bet that the proposition is true. Second, these theorists showed that probabilities, to be consistent, must satisfy the mathematical laws of probability theory. Violation of the laws would lead, in some cases, to the acceptance of sets of gambles which would necessarily result in loss of money (de Finetti 1937).

Requirements such as these are more restrictive than is supposed. For example, it has been shown that if two reasonable people are exposed to a large amount of unambiguously interpretable data bearing on a certain proposition, then those two people should subsequently finish with approximately the same probability for the proposition, even though they began with very different probabilities (Edwards et al. 1963). These approaches to probability are more sound philosophically than the relative frequency approach, and they have the advantage of allowing the assignment of probabilities to hypotheses as well as to outcomes of experiments.

Note, however, that the word "should" is used in the previous paragraph. The theory of personal probabilities is a normative, not a descriptive, theory. It specifies how rational people should behave, not how they naturally do behave. The purpose of Bayesian statistics, if not all statistics, is to more closely approach the rational ideal.

3. Examples

These ideas can now be applied to a relatively simple, concrete problem. Taking an abilities test whose scores are known to be normally distributed with a standard deviation of 10, the next step is to compare two hypotheses, $H_1: \mu = 50$, and $H_2: \mu = 55$. Perhaps the typical score for all children at age 12 on this test is 50, while the typical score for children at age 14 is 55.

The sample consists of children of age 12, but the hypothesis states that their ability level is actually typical of age 14. In fact, the hypothesis states that they are twice as likely to have a mean level of age 14 as of age 12. Therefore a probability of $\frac{1}{3}$ is assigned to hypothesis H_1 and $\frac{2}{3}$ to hypothesis H_2.

Twenty-five students are sampled, and the sample mean obtained is 53. Since the standard error of the mean is then 2, both hypotheses can be rejected at the 0.05 level. However, if these are the only two hypotheses that can be regarded as plausible, both cannot be rejected.

In this case, with continuous normally distributed data, Bayes' theorem can be modified to read:

$$P(B|\bar{X}) = k \, f(\bar{X}|B)P(B) \qquad (4)$$

where $\bar{X}$ is the sample mean, $f(\bar{X}|B)$ is the density function of $\bar{X}$, and k is a constant to be determined later. In the above example, $\bar{X}$ has a normal distribution with a standard deviation of 2, and, given that H_1 is true, a mean of 50. Thus, the regular formula for the normal distribution is:

$$f(\bar{X}|H_1) = (2\pi)^{-1/2}(2)^{-1} \exp[(-1/2)(\bar{X}-50)^2/4] \quad (5)$$

Similarly, $f(\bar{X}|H_2)$ is the same, with 55 substituted for 50 in the exponent. These numbers can be calculated, and the following are obtained:

$$P(H_1|\bar{X}) = k(0.0648)\,(1/3) = k(0.0216) \qquad (6)$$

$$P(H_2|\bar{X}) = k(0.1210)\,(2/3) = k(0.0807) \qquad (7)$$

In each equation, the first number in parentheses is $f(\bar{X}|H_i)$, and the second is the prior probability for the hypothesis. k can easily be found by noting that the two probabilities must sum to one, giving $k = 1/(0.0216 + 0.0807) = 9.775$; $P(H_1|\bar{X}) = 0.21$; and $P(H_2|\bar{X}) = 0.79$.

After obtaining and analyzing the data, the probability for H_2 has increased from $\frac{2}{3}$ to about $\frac{4}{5}$; it is thus possible to say that the prior probability (before the experiment) was $\frac{2}{3}$ and the posterior probability (after the experiment) is about $\frac{4}{5}$.

With a much larger sample, the sample mean would be expected to be very close to either 50 or 55, depending on which hypothesis was actually correct, and the posterior probability for that hypothesis would be very nearly one; in that case the evidence would be overwhelmingly in favor of the correct hypothesis, and, in a sense, uncertainty would be replaced by near certainty. This is a special case of the earlier assertion that large amounts of unambiguous data should lead to near agreement among reasonable people.

Of course in the above simplified example, the possibility that some other hypothesis, such as 52.5, might be correct has been ignored. In practice, any number of hypotheses can be considered at once, with only obvious minor modifications of the procedure just outlined.

Bayesian statistics are most interesting and most useful when all possible hypotheses are considered. In the above example, all points on the real line are considered as possible values for the population mean. As usual in such a case, the probability that the mean is exactly equal to a particular value (that probability is always zero) can no longer be considered but the probability that the mean is between two particular values can be considered. The probabilities can then be described by a density distribution—a curve such that the area under the curve between any two values represents the probability that the mean is between those two values.

To reconsider the previous example, since the children are expected to perform like 14-year-olds, suppose that the most likely value for the mean is felt to be 55. Suppose, further, that a probability of about 0.34 is assigned to the proposition that the mean is between 50 and 55, and the same probability is assigned to the proposition that it is between 55 and 60. Moreover, there is about a 95 percent certainty that the mean is between 45 and 65. The probabilities can then be rather well-represented by a normal distribution having a mean of 55 and a standard deviation of 5.

For this case, Bayes' theorem can be rewritten:

$$f(\mu|\bar{X}) = kf(\bar{X}|\mu)f(\mu) \qquad (8)$$

replacing the probabilities with density distributions. Here $f(\mu)$ is the density distribution representing the probabilities after gathering the data, and k is chosen so that the area under the curve given by $f(\mu|\bar{X})$ is one.

Now the calculations appear even more difficult because two exponentials are involved and the multiplication must be done symbolically. However, the actual calculations are very simple. If, before the experiment is conducted, opinions about μ can be represented by a normal distribution having a mean of m and a standard deviation of σ, and if the sampling distribution of $\bar{X}$ is normal with a mean of μ and a standard deviation of $S/\sqrt{[N]}$, then, after the experiment has been conducted, opinions about μ are represented by a normal distribution whose mean, m^*, and standard deviation, σ^*, are

$$m^* = [(S^2/N)m + \sigma^2 \bar{X}]/(s^2/N + \sigma^2) \qquad (9)$$

$$\sigma^* = \sqrt{[(S^2/N\sigma^2/(S^2/N + \sigma^2)]} \qquad (10)$$

In the example, the posterior probabilities, after gathering and analyzing the data, are represented by a normal distribution having mean, $m^* = 53.3$, and standard deviation, $\sigma^* = 1.9$. The distribution is now much narrower (i.e. has a much smaller standard deviation), indicating that it is possible to be more sure about the true mean for the students. For example, from a simple reference to a normal table it can be seen that the probability that μ is between 50 and 55 has increased from 0.34 before gathering the data, to 0.85 after gathering the data.

A curious but important fact is that the posterior distribution would have been approximately normal with a mean close to 53 and a standard deviation close to 2, even if the prior probabilities had not been well-represented by a normal distribution, or if the prior distribution had had a mean somewhat different from 55. Thus the prior probabilities played only a small role, while the data played a large role, in determining the posterior probabilities. This is always the case when strong data are combined with comparatively vague prior opinions. If the sample had been much larger the posterior mean would have been almost exactly equal to the sample mean, and the posterior standard deviation would have been almost exactly equal to the standard error of the sample mean, as can be seen from the above equations. Thus, once again, with strong data the subjectivity of the probabilities in effect disappears, and reasonable researchers will reach near agreement.

Now that the posterior distribution has been calculated, it can be used for a variety of purposes. It is possible to calculate point estimates and confidence intervals, and test hypotheses about μ. The best point estimate, for general purposes, is the mean of the posterior distribution, 53.3. For a 95 percent confidence interval the upper and lower $2\frac{1}{2}$ percent of the posterior distribution (i.e. at $z = \pm 1.96$) can simply be cut off; it is then possible to be 95 percent confident that μ is between 49.6 and 56.9.

When hypotheses are tested, Bayesian statistics give a choice. Usually when a null hypothesis is tested, interest does not really lie in the null hypothesis itself. For example, if $H_0: \mu = 50$ is tested, the interest is really in whether μ is larger than or smaller than 50; the sample mean indicates whether it is larger or smaller, and the significance level indicates the degree of confidence that can be had in that conclusion. In Bayesian statistics it is possible to assign a probability directly to the hypothesis $H: \mu \le 50$; it is simply the probability that a normally distributed random variable, with a mean of 53.3 and a standard deviation of 1.9, will be less than 50. For the above example, the probability is about 0.04. Note that it is almost, but not quite, possible to reject $H_0: \mu = 50$ by a traditional significance test, at the 0.05 level, one-tailed. With a much larger sample the posterior probability that μ was less than 50 would have been almost exactly equal to the one-tailed significance level. Many Bayesians have argued that the practical value of traditional statistics lies in this fortunate coincidence between traditional and Bayesian results.

Occasionally the interest actually lies in the null hypothesis itself. Perhaps the 12-year-olds really are like typical 12-year-olds (i.e. have a mean of 50). In that case the odds form of Bayes' theorem is most convenient. However, the probability of the data must be known given that the null hypothesis is false as well as given that it is true. Here traditional statistics fail because, in essence, the beta level must be known, and that is usually unknown and unknowable.

The Bayesian approach is described in detail in Edwards et al. (1963). For the above example, the likelihood ratio is about 1.14 against the null hypothesis, meaning that the posterior odds against the null hypothesis are equal to the prior odds multiplied by 1.14. If it had been previously felt that the odds against the null hypothesis were about 2 to 1, then the posterior odds are about 2.28 to 1. Notice that a traditional test would almost reject the null hypothesis at the 0.05 level (one-tailed), yet the data only slightly favor the alternative. The reason is simple. Although these data are not very probable under the null hypothesis, they are not very probable under the alternative either. Therefore they do not give strong evidence for either hypothesis.

4. Other Considerations

The above are just two simple examples of Bayesian procedures. They can be extended to other distributions, such as the binomial and Poisson, with almost equally simple results. They can also be extended to the normal distribution where both the mean and variance are unknown, and to more complicated problems such as analyses of variance and covariance, multiple regression, and so on.

At first Bayesian statistics met with great resistance from statisticians. Today that resistance is disappearing. However, there are four major difficulties preventing the widespread use of Bayesian statistics today.

The first difficulty is computational—the calculations are more complicated in Bayesian than in traditional statistics. The obvious solution is to develop computer programs, and such programs exist, at least for simpler Bayesian problems. CADA, an interactive program available from the University of Iowa, is very good. However, such programs are not widespread. In particular, commonly used general statistics packages, such as SPSS, do not incorporate Bayesian procedures.

The second difficulty involves the problem of ascertaining prior opinions in probabilistic terms. With strong data this problem may not exist—the data may overpower any reasonable prior opinions. For some other cases, this problem can also be solved by computer; CADA, for example, asks the user a series of questions, on the basis of which it derives a reasonable estimate of the user's prior probabilities.

For more complicated problems, such as the case where both the mean and variance are unknown, or analysis of variance is required, the problem is more difficult. Prior opinions of several parameters that are interrelated must then be assessed. Suppose, to take a simple example, the scores of 10-, 12-, and 14-year-old children are being assessed on an abilities test. It may not be possible to have a very clear notion of whether the 14-year-olds have a high or low mean score, yet it may be possible to be quite sure that the 14-year-olds will score higher than the 12-year-olds. In such a case it is not sufficient to evaluate prior opinions for each group separately; a joint distribution must be obtained for the means of all three groups. If the standard deviations are also unknown it complicates the problem still more. Three solutions—none of them completely satisfactory—have been proposed for this problem.

The first is an attempt to remove the subjectivity while retaining the Bayesian mathematics. A set of plausible priors for the parameters is proposed for universal use, relieving the individual researcher of the difficulties of assessing his or her own priors. Occasionally plausible priors can be generated from previously occurring data; the resulting procedures are called empirical Bayes procedures. It is felt by some however that such procedures violate the spirit, at least, of the Bayesian approach, and take away many of its advantages.

The second reduces the more complicated problem to a series of simpler problems. Instead of doing an overall analysis of variance, a number of orthogonal contrasts might be tested, choosing contrasts so that opinion of the value of each contrast is approximately independent of opinions of the values of other contrasts. This works well in theory, but the practical problems of choosing contrasts can be difficult.

The third is "philosophical Bayesianism." It was seen above that with large amounts of data, the results of certain Bayesian tests are nearly the same as those of traditional tests. The traditional tests can therefore be done and interpreted in a Bayesian manner, that is, in terms of posterior probabilities. However, the interpretations are not always clear, nor are they always appropriate.

The third and fourth roadblocks preventing the use of Bayesian statistics are more psychological. The third is that users are reluctant to give up the comfort they receive from having the statistical analyses determine their opinions for them. If the data tell you unambiguously whether to accept or reject a null hypothesis, you are relieved of the responsibility of making that difficult decision yourself. The comfort is of course illusory—you accept the responsibility when you choose a significance level. However, many users are unwilling to give up the illusion. It is perhaps significant that Bayesian statistics are used most widely in business applications, where such illusions cost money.

The fourth is simple inertia. Traditional statistical methods are commonly used. Therefore they must be taught, so that students can understand the existing literature. People then use the statistics that they have been taught, perpetuating the old traditions.

See also: Hypothesis Testing; Decision Theory in Educational Research

Bibliography

de Finetti B 1937 La Prévision: Ses lois logiques, ses sources subjectives. *Annales de l'Institut Henri Poincaré* 7: 1–68 [Foresight: Its logical laws, its subjective sources. In: Kyburg H E, Smokler H E (eds.) 1964 *Studies in Subjective Probability*. Wiley, New York pp. 99–158]

Edwards W, Lindman H, Savage L J 1963 Bayesian statistical inference for psychological research. *Psychol. Rev.* 70: 193–242

Kyburg H E, Smokler H E (eds.) 1964 *Studies in Subjective Probability*. Wiley, New York

Lindley D V 1965a *Introduction to Probability and Statistics from a Bayesian Viewpoint. Part 1: Probability*. Cambridge University Press, Cambridge

Lindley D V 1965b *Introduction to Probability and Statistics from a Bayesian Viewpoint. Part 2: Inference*. Cambridge University Press, Cambridge

Novick M R, Jackson P H 1974 *Statistical Methods for Educational and Psychological Research*. McGraw-Hill, New York

Phillips L D 1973 *Bayesian Statistics for Social Scientists*. Crowell, New York

Ramsey F P 1931 *The Foundations of Mathematics and Other Logical Essays*. Kegan Paul, London

Savage L J 1954 *The Foundations of Statistics*. Wiley, New York

Savage L J 1981 *The Writings of Leonard Jimmie Savage: A Memorial Selection*. American Statistical Association and Institute of Mathematical Statistics, Washington, DC

Schmitt S A 1969 *Measuring Uncertainty: An Elementary Introduction to Bayesian Statistics*. Addison-Wesley, Reading, Massachusetts

Winkler R L 1972 *An Introduction to Bayesian Inference and Decision*. Holt, Rinehart and Winston, New York

Decision Theory in Educational Research

W. J. van der Linden

In most educational situations, tests are used for decision making rather than measurement purposes. The ultimate purpose in these cases is to use test scores not as quantitative ability estimates but merely as data on which qualitative decisions can be based. Examples of such decisions are admissions to training programs, pass–fail decisions, certification, treatment assignment in individualized instructional systems, and the identification of optimal vocational alternatives in guidance situations. In all these examples, decisions are ordinarily based on cutting scores carefully selected with the aim to optimize the actions to be taken.

In spite of the fact that tests are used mostly for decision making, much psychometric research has been aimed at improving the use of educational and psychological tests as means for estimating ability scores from test performances. The first to recognize this paradox were Cronbach and Gleser (1965) in their classical monograph *Psychological Tests and Personnel Decisions*. Their plea for a more decision-theoretic approach to testing had more impact at first on (personnel)

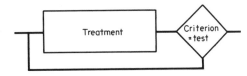

Figure 2
Flowchart of a mastery decision

psychologists than on educators. During the 1970s, however, the situation changed dramatically, and now the use of decision theory in educational testing is one of the main research topics. The major impetus for this has come from the introduction of novel testing procedures in individualized instructional systems, and from politically controversial issues such as culture-fair selection for schools.

The application of decision theory to educational testing falls into two categories. First, decision theory can be used to optimize decisions based on tests. Typically, this takes the form of selecting one or more optimal cutting scores on the test. Second, it can be used for the evaluation of decision rules. Such evaluations show how much room there is for improving decisions by, for instance, redesigning the test.

1. A Typology of Educational Decisions

Decision problems in educational testing can be classified in many ways. A simple typology is the following one, using flowcharts consisting of three basic elements to define each type of decision. In each decision problem, minimally the following elements can be identified: (a) the test that provides the information the decision is based on, (b) the treatment with respect to which the decision is made, and (c) the criterion by which the success of the treatment is measured. "Treatment" is a generic term here, standing for any manipulation aimed at improving the condition of individuals. Examples include training programs, the use of special instructional materials, therapeutic measures, and the like. The criterion may be any type of success measure but is often a test itself. With the aid of these elements, four basic flowcharts can be formed, each defining a different type of decision problem.

1.1 Selection Decisions

In selection problems, the decision in general is whether or not to accept individuals for a treatment. The test is administered before the treatment takes place and only individuals promising satisfactory results on the criterion are accepted for the treatment. Depending on the circumstances, selection decisions may imply that individuals who are rejected are not being admitted to the institute providing the treatment, or have to leave the institute if they were already in. Figure 1 shows the flowchart of a selection problem. Examples of selection

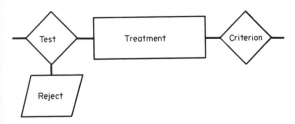

Figure 1
Flowchart of a selection decision

decisions are admission examinations to schools (where grade-point averages are the usual criteria), hiring of personnel in industry, or the intake of students for a special remedial program.

The selection problem is the oldest decision problem recognized as such in the history of educational testing. Traditionally, the problem has been approached as a prediction problem in which regression lines or expectancy tables are employed to predict whether the criterion scores of individuals exceed a certain threshold value. Individuals whose criterion scores exceed the threshold value are accepted. Selection decisions with quota restrictions (see below) have long been evaluated with the aid of Taylor–Russell (1939) tables, which give success ratios for a number of parameters characterizing the selection situation.

1.2 Mastery Decisions

Mastery decisions are made for individuals who have already undergone some treatment. Unlike selection decisions, the question is not whether individuals are qualified enough to be admitted to the treatment under consideration, but whether they have profited enough from the treatment to be dismissed. Figure 2 shows the flowchart of a mastery decision. For this type of decision problem the test and the criterion coincide. The test is an unreliable representation of the criterion or, equivalently, the criterion is to be considered the true score underlying the test. It is the unreliablity of the test that opens up the possibility of making wrong decisions and creates the mastery decision problem.

Mastery decisions usually imply that individuals may leave the institute providing the treatment or proceed with another treatment. Examples of mastery decisions are pass–fail, certification, and successfulness of therapies.

Concern for mastery decisions has grown because of the introduction of modern instructional systems such as individualized instruction, mastery learning, and computer-aided instruction. In the past the main concern has been for issues related to standard setting procedures; that is, to procedures for selecting threshold values on the (true-score) criterion separating "masters" from "nonmasters." The influence of measurement error on decision making was simply ignored. That this may lead to serious decision errors was clearly demonstrated by Hambleton and Novick (1973).

1.3 Placement Decisions

This type of decision problem differs from the preceding two in that alternative treatments are available. The success of each of these treatments is measured by the same

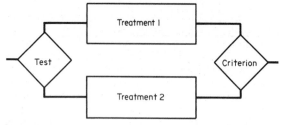

Figure 3
Flowchart of a placement decision (case of two treatments)

criterion. All individuals are administered the same test, and the task is to assign them to the most promising treatment on the basis of their test scores. Unlike the selection problem, each individual is assigned to a treatment. The case of placement decisions with two treatments is represented in Fig. 3. Examples of placement decisions occur in individualized instruction where students are assigned to different routes through an instructional unit or are offered alternative instructional materials.

Interest in placement decisions has emanated from aptitude–treatment interaction (ATI) research which was motivated by the finding that individuals may react differentially to treatments and that treatments that are better on average may be worse in individual cases. The placement decision problem has mostly been approached as a prediction problem to be tackled using linear-regression techniques. For each treatment, then, there is a regression line of the criterion on the test score, and individuals are assigned to the treatment with the largest predicted criterion score. The methodology needed for detecting ATIs is reviewed in Cronbach and Snow (1977).

1.4 Classification Decisions

In classification, the problem also consists of a choice among a number of different treatments. As opposed to placement decisions, however, each treatment has a qualitatively different criterion. The situation is as shown in Fig. 4. In order to be able to compare criterion performances, each criterion may have its own threshold value defining success or it may be clear for each criterion how to transform it on a common scale. Examples are vocational guidance situations in which most

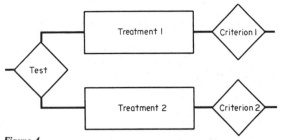

Figure 4
Flowchart of a classification decision (case of two treatments)

promising schools or careers must be identified, and testing for military service.

The most popular approach to classification decisions has been the use of linear-regression techniques again. For each treatment, the regression line of its utility (= transformed criterion) score on the test score is estimated and individuals are assigned to the treatment with the largest predicted utility score. Since more criteria are present, the test is often a whole battery covering relevant aspects of the various criteria. In that case, the use of multiple-regression techniques has been the traditional choice.

1.5 Conclusion

The above four types of problems involve elementary decisions which are not always met in their pure forms. For instance, in some situations, more than one treatment is available, but not all individuals are accepted for a treatment. This creates a combination of a selection and a placement problem. However, all such decisions can be mapped on flowcharts built up with Figs. 1–4 as elements.

Three further distinctions should be made to enable possible refinements to be considered within each type of decision.

(a) *Quota restrictions.* In some situations, the number of vacancies per treatment can be constrained by a quota. Such quotas usually simplify the selection decision (accept individuals with the highest test scores until the quota is filled), but complicate the placement decision.

(b) *Number of tests.* When the criterion is multifaceted or when two or more criteria are present, the single test can be replaced by a test battery. This means that decisions must be made on the basis of multivariate information, which may complicate the decision rule.

(c) *Subpopulations.* In some situations, subpopulations varying on a socially relevant attribute can be distinguished. If the test is biased against any of the subpopulations, the problem of culture-fair decision making arises.

2. Optimizing Decisions Based on Tests

Decision theory is a branch of statistics involving the use of data as an aid to decision making. More specifically, it is concerned with how random data on "true" or future states and utilities of outcomes can be combined into optimal decision rules. In the above decision problems, the data are provided by a test. Since a test may not be a perfectly reliable source of data, it should be considered a random indicator of an individual's criterion performance. For a population of individuals, test and criterion scores relate to each other in a way which is fully specified by their joint probability distribution. In some decision problems, a psychometric model would be needed to specify this distribution.

Several approaches to optimizing decisions can be taken, one of which is Bayesian decision theory. It is indicated below how (empirical) Bayesian theory tackles the four decision problems and provides optimal decision rules (called Bayes rules). First, the Bayesian solution to a classification problem is described. This, in a formal sense, is the most complicated type of decision problem. Then, solutions to the other decision problems are outlined. These problems impose certain restrictions and modifications on the classification model. In order to enhance understanding, some mathematical precision has been sacrificed.

The classification problem is formalized as follows. Suppose a series of individuals, who can be considered as randomly drawn from some population, must be classified into $t + 1$ treatments indexed by $j = 0, \ldots, t$. The observed test scores are denoted by a random variable X with discrete values $x = 0, \ldots, n$. Each treatment leads to a certain performance on its corresponding criterion which is denoted by a continuous random variable Y_j with range R_j. It is assumed that the joint distributions of X and Y_j are given by probability functions $\eta_j(x, y_j)$. Since all individuals are administered the same test, it holds for the marginal probability function $\lambda_j(x)$ of X that

$$\lambda_j(x) = \lambda(x) \tag{1}$$

for all values of j.

Generally, a decision rule is a function that indicates for each possible observation which of the possible actions is to be taken. In the present problem the observations take the form $X = x$, and the possible actions are the assignments to one of the treatments $0, \ldots, t$. It is assumed that the optimal rule takes a monotone form; that is, it can be defined using a series of cutting scores $0 = c_0 \leqslant c_1 \ldots \leqslant c_j \leqslant \ldots \leqslant c_{t+1} = n (t \leqslant n)$, where treatment j is assigned to individuals whose scores satisfy $c_j \leqslant X < c_{j+1}$. For an optimal rule to be monotone, some conditions must be met which are, however, not unrealistic for the present problems (Ferguson 1967).

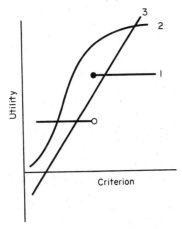

Figure 5
Examples of utility functions: (1) threshold; (2) normal ogive; (3) linear

Suppose that the decision maker is able to express on a numerical scale his or her preferences for the outcomes $Y_j = y_j$ for individuals who were assigned to treatment j. Technically, such an evaluation is known as a utility function. If utility functions can be established for all treatment–criterion combinations, all possible outcomes of the decision have been made comparable on a common scale. To express its dependency on both the criterion and the chosen treatment, utility functions will be denoted as $u = u_j(y_j)$. Figure 5 shows some examples of utility functions that have received some interest in the literature. The threshold function represents the case where a critical value on the criterion discriminates between successful and unsuccessful performances. The other two functions increase more gradually with the criterion performance. The choice of a utility function may be facilitated by varying its form and studying the robustness of the optimal decision rule under these variations (e.g. Vijn and Molenaar 1981).

For each possible series of cutting scores $(c_1, \ldots, c_t)$ the expected utility of the decision procedure can be calculated as

$$B(c_1, \ldots, c_t) \equiv \sum_{j=0}^{t} \sum_{x=c_j}^{c_{j+1}} \int_{R_j} u_j(y_j) \eta_j(x, y_j) \, dy_j \tag{2}$$

The set of optimal cutting scores in the Bayesian sense is the choice of values for $(c_1, \ldots, c_t)$ maximizing the expected utility. A simple procedure to find these values is as follows. Using Eqn. (1) the expected utility can be written

$$B(c_1, \ldots, c_t) = \sum_{j=0}^{t} \sum_{x=c_j}^{c_{j+1}-1} \lambda(x) \int_{R_j} u_j(y_j) \omega_j(y_j | x) \, dy_j \tag{3}$$

where $\omega_j(y_j | x)$ is the conditional probability function of y_j given $X = x$. For known utility and probability functions the integral in this expression only depends on x and j. Since $\lambda(x) \geq 0$, it is apparent that the double sum in Eqn. (3) is maximized if for each possible value of x the value of j is selected for which the integral is maximal. The dependency of the selected value of j on x provides a decision rule which is precisely the Bayes rule for the classification problem. The monotone character of the problem assumed here guarantees that the optimal value of j indeed changes at a series of cutting scores on x.

The Bayesian approach to classification problems in education testing still remains to be elaborated. This would amount to establishing classes of realistic utility and probability functions and studying the properties of their optimal rules.

The placement problem differs from the classification problem in that all treatments lead to the same criterion. Therefore,

$$Y_j = Y \tag{4}$$

$$\omega_j(y_j | x) = \omega_j(y | x) \tag{5}$$

$$u_j(y_j) = u_j(y) \tag{6}$$

for all values of j. These restrictions only simplify the expected utility expression in Eqn. (3), and Bayes rules for the placement problem are found in the same way as for the classification problem. The fact that the utility functions are defined on the same criterion implies that only one criterion needs to be scaled. Differences between the utility functions arise only from their treatment dependency. For instance, each treatment involves a certain amount of costs which may entail differences between the utility curves with respect to the lower asymptote, the intercept, or the location. Solutions to the placement problem for some intuitively appealing utility functions are given in Cronbach and Gleser (1965) and van der Linden (1981).

In the mastery decision problem the true score variable τ underlying the test score is considered as the criterion. Assuming the classical test model, the true score τ_i of a fixed individual i is defined as the observed test score X_i expected across replications: $\tau_i \equiv EX_i$. All individuals have followed the same treatment, so there is no treatment variable modifying the relation of test scores to criterion scores. Hence, the subscript j in $\omega_j(y|x)$ can be dropped. Usually two true states are defined, the mastery ($\tau \geq \tau_c$) and the nonmastery state ($\tau < \tau_c$), τ_c being a true cutting score set on educational grounds. Different utility functions for the mastery and the nonmastery decision are distinguished. In general, the former is a curve that increases in the criterion τ, such as the examples in Fig. 5; the latter usually is its decreasing counterpart (the larger the true test score, the lower the utility of a nonmastery decision). In these utility functions, the true cutting score τ_c is usually treated as a parameter; for example, to govern the location of the jump in the threshold utility function. Formally, the mastery decision model follows if, in addition to Eqns. (4), (5), and (6), the following restrictions are imposed:

$$y_i = \tau_i \equiv EX_i \qquad (7)$$

$$\omega_j(y|x) = \omega(y|x) \qquad (8)$$

with $u_0(y)$ decreasing in y, $u_1(y)$ increasing in y, and where $j = 0, 1$ now denotes the nonmastery and mastery decision, respectively. Cutting scores maximizing the expected utility under these restrictions have been examined for threshold (Huynh 1976), linear (van der Linden and Mellenbergh 1977), and normal-ogive utility functions (Novick and Lindley 1978, van der Linden 1980).

In selection decisions, only one treatment is available for which individuals are either accepted or rejected. Like the mastery testing problem, there is no treatment variable modifying the relation of test scores to criterion scores and the subscript j in $\omega_j(y|x)$ can be dropped. In the usual case, the utility function for the acceptance decision is an increasing function of the criterion, such as the examples in Fig. (5). When an individual is rejected, he or she is of no value to the institute making the selection decisions. This is formalized by putting the utility for the rejection decision equal to zero. In summary, optimal selection decisions follow from maximizing the expected utility in Eqn. (3) if in addition to the restrictions in Eqns. (4–6) the following restrictions are imposed:

$$\omega_j(y|x) = \omega(y|x) \qquad (9)$$

$$u_0(y) = 0 \qquad (10)$$

where $j = 0, 1$ now denotes the rejection and acceptance decision, respectively.

3. Evaluating Decisions Based on Tests

The attractive feature about the expected utility defined in Eqn. (2) is that it can be used not only to find optimal decision rules but also to evaluate any decision rule. Equation (2) is positively related to the quality of the procedure—the larger the expected utility, the better the procedure. Hence, if two decision rules are compared, the one with the larger expected utility is better. Instead of comparing decision rules, it is also possible to evaluate individual rules on a scale defined by the maximum and minimum value of the expected utility possible for the given problem. Such evaluations have been worked out by Livingston and Wingersky (1979), Mellenbergh and van der Linden (1979), and Wilcox (1978).

4. Discussion

As indicated earlier, the four types of decisions discussed above are basic decisions that are not always met in their pure form. In some situations, mixed types of decision must be made. Moreover, within each type of decision further refinements can be made; for example, the presence of restricted numbers of vacancies per treatment, the use of more than one test, or the distinction between relevant subpopulations. The presence of restricted numbers of vacancies entails the necessity to maximize the expected utility under quota restrictions (e.g. Chuang et al. 1981). If more than one test is used, the decision is a function defined on the Cartesian product of their ranges of possible scores, and the probability functions $\omega_j(y_j|x)$ are conditional on points in this product. This leads to corresponding changes in Eqn. (3) which, however, complicate its maximization. If subpopulations must be distinguished, as is the case for instance when the requirement of culture-fair selection must be met, each subpopulation may entail its own utility and probability functions, and cutting scores must be selected for each population separately. Culture-fair decision rules are given in Gross and Su (1975), Mellenbergh and van der Linden (1981), and Petersen (1976). In principle, it is thus possible to deal with all these refinements within the framework of Bayesian decision theory.

Bibliography

Chuang D T, Chen J J, Novick M R 1981 Theory and practice

for the use of cut-scores for personnel decisions. *J. Educ. Stat.* 6: 107–28

Cronbach L J, Gleser G C 1965 *Psychological Tests and Personnel Decisions*, 2nd edn. University of Illinois Press, Urbana, Illinois

Cronbach L J, Snow R F 1977 *Aptitudes and Instructional Methods: A Handbook for Research on Interactions*. Irvington, New York

Ferguson T S 1967 *Mathematical Statistics: A Decision Theoretic Approach*. Academic Press, New York

Gross A L, Su W H 1975 Defining a "fair" or "unbiased" selection model: A question of utilities. *J. Appl. Psychol.* 60: 345–51

Hambleton R K, Novick M R 1973 Toward an integration of theory and method for criterion-referenced tests. *J. Educ. Meas.* 10: 159–70

Huynh H 1976 Statistical considerations of mastery scores. *Psychometrika* 41: 65–79

Livingston S A, Wingersky M 1979 Assessing the reliability of tests used to make pass/fail decision. *J. Educ. Meas.* 16: 247–60

Mellenbergh G J, van der Linden W J 1979 The internal and external optimality of decisions based on tests. *Appl. Psychol. Meas.* 3: 257–73

Mellenbergh G J, van der Linden W J 1981 The linear utility model for optimal selection. *Psychometrika* 46: 283–93

Novick M R, Lindley D V 1978 The use of more realistic utility functions in educational applications. *J. Educ. Meas.* 15: 181–91

Petersen N S 1976 An expected utility model for "optimal" selection. *J. Educ. Stat.* 1: 333–58

Taylor H C, Russell J T 1939 The relationship of validity coefficients to the practical effectiveness of tests in selection: Discussion and tables. *J. Appl. Psychol.* 23: 565–78

van der Linden W J 1980 Decision models for use with criterion-referenced tests. *Appl. Psychol. Meas.* 4: 469–92

van der Linden W J 1981 Using aptitude measurements for the optimal assignment of subjects to treatments with and without mastery scores. *Psychometrika* 46: 257–74

van der Linden W J, Mellenbergh G J 1977 Optimal cutting scores using a linear loss function. *Appl. Psychol. Meas.* 1: 593–99

Vijn P, Molenaar I W 1981 Robustness regions for dichotomous decisions. *J. Educ. Stat.* 6: 205–35

Wilcox R R 1978 A note on decision theoretic coefficients for tests. *Appl. Psychol. Meas.* 2: 609–13

Hypothesis Testing

J. D. Finn and L. Dulberg

The systematic formulation and testing of hypotheses is as essential to the advancement of education and the social sciences as it is to other scientific disciplines. Although the hypothetico–deductive approach to educational research is often difficult to implement, it is particularly important for a field in which causal variables may be multifaceted and imperfectly measured, and rigorous experimental control can be attained only infrequently. This article provides an overview of the ways in which hypotheses are generated, and the logic behind the statistical procedures commonly used to test their veracity.

Hypotheses are informed propositions or speculations about values of two or more variables that may be observed concomitantly. In general, better informed hypotheses contribute more directly to models of social behavior, but it is not necessary that hypotheses derive from a great deal of prior knowledge or extensive theoretical reasoning. The simple observation that more boys than girls enroll in science courses may lead to speculation about a variety of precursors, including different aptitude levels, different interest levels, or various reward structures. Hypotheses may derive from previous empirical findings. For example, it is well-confirmed that greater amounts of "time-on-task" are generally associated with increased levels of learning among elementary- and secondary-school students (Atkinson 1968). Also, high-aptitude students are able to master school-related material at a faster rate than low-aptitude students (Denham and Lieberman 1980). These findings may lead to a further speculation that when instruction is limited to a fixed-time-period class, the achievement difference between high- and low-ability students will be greater than under variable time conditions.

Finally, hypotheses may be derived from a carefully formulated model that attempts to explain a class of outcomes. For example, according to the Getzels (1963) model of observed social behavior, school performance may be explained by an interaction of role expectations defined by the institution and values internalized by the individual. Harrison (1968) extrapolated a set of propositions from this model to explain the performance of children from advantaged home environments whose school performance is poor, and others from disadvantaged homes whose school performance is outstandingly high. These propositions derive entirely from the Getzels conceptualization, and as such were speculative. The empirical testing of the hypotheses contributed both to understanding school performance, and to the adequacy of the original model.

When empirical data are not available or seem contradictory, competing hypotheses may appear equally likely. For example, if there was concern about the effects of teachers' experience on their grading practices, it might be reasoned that as teachers accrue more years of experience, they become more accepting of average or poor performance; thus it would be hypothesized that years' teaching experience is directly related to grades (the more years, the higher the grades tend to be). An inverse but reasonable hypothesis is that more experienced teachers become more rigid and evaluative, and tend to give generally lower grades. These alternatives may be weighed against one another using a two-sided test (described below).

Much educational research is nonexperimental and involves a large number of possible variables, each of which may be an antecedent or an outcome of others. Hypotheses may be formulated to guide the data collection and analysis, or else an "empirical" approach may be taken in which data on many variables are collected and many different analyses are attempted once the data are in (Ellis 1952). In the absence of hypotheses to guide data collection and analysis, the findings that emerge may not be among the more meaningful that the study can provide, and the most important variables may not be given the extra attention they deserve. Complex relationships involving several variables may be overlooked in the attempt to seek out those that are apparent. Through the empirical approach, the relationships that are discovered may have arisen spuriously out of the many that were possible, and may not be replicable. On the other hand, the hypothetico–deductive approach does not preclude exploring a data set for other outcomes that were not anticipated.

Hypothesis formulation and testing are important for yet another reason. No matter how derived, hypotheses are informed propositions. Not only do they direct attention to particular relationships, but they anticipate through logic, theory, or from prior evidence what the nature of those relationships may be. When a hypothesis is confirmed through empirical observations, the outcome is supported not once but twice. Further discussion of the role and logic of hypothesis testing is found in Cohen (1956), Kerlinger (1969), Platt (1964), and Popper (1965).

1. Hypothesis Restatement

Before a hypothesis can be tested empirically, it must be restated in symbolic form. Consider several examples. A mathematics teacher believes that he or she is doing an effective job of teaching students to perform basic operations with fractions. The school principal is willing to grant a salary increment if students actually perform better on a test of fractions than if they were merely guessing the answers. If the test selected has 10 items each with five choices (one choice correct) then the students could guess an average of two items correctly. The teacher, claiming to be effective, hypothesizes that the mean of all students subjected to instruction is higher than 2; symbolically the hypothesis is represented as $H_1: \mu > 2$. H_1 is the research hypothesis being forwarded, and μ is the mean score on the 10-item test.

One consequence of a mastery learning approach to instruction is that the average amount of material learned will be greater than with a nonmastery approach. If μ_1 is the mean achievement score of all grade-eight students learning French as a foreign language through a mastery approach, and μ_2 is the mean of all grade-eight students learning through a traditional lecture approach, then the research hypothesis can be stated as $H_1: \mu_1 > \mu_2$. Additionally, mastery learning is hypothesized to reduce the dispersion of performance scores. This is expected because students who are slow

learners are given additional time and support, and thus are not as far behind the faster students when the unit is complete. If σ_1 is the standard deviation, a measure of dispersion of achievement scores in the mastery condition, and σ_2 is the standard deviation under a traditional approach, this hypothesis is symbolized as $H_2: \sigma_1 < \sigma_2$. Both H_1 and H_2 may be tested in a single investigation of mastery learning.

The hypothesis that more experienced teachers give higher grades asserts that there is a positive relationship between the two variables. If ρ is the correlation of years' experience with average grades given by a teacher, then the hypothesis is represented as $H_1: \rho > 0$ (i.e., the correlation is greater than zero, or positive). The second possibility is that tenure and grades are inversely related, or that the correlation is negative, that is, $H_2: \rho < 0$. Statisticians usually write these together, as $H_1: \rho \neq 0$, but it is important to keep in mind that two distinct possibilities are being tested.

2. Hypothesis Testing Procedures

Hypothesis testing begins with the assumption that the researcher's hypothesis is false. This counterstatement of the original proposition is the "null hypothesis," usually represented as H_0. For example, the null hypothesis regarding the mathematics teacher asserts that students attending his or her class perform at or below guessing level, that is, $H_0: \mu \leq 2$. If mastery learning does not raise mean performance, it may yield the same or lower average scores; this null hypothesis is $H_0: \mu_1 \leq \mu_2$. Both positive and negative correlations between experience and grades are hypothesized. Thus, the null hypothesis is that there is no association between the two variables, or $H_0: \rho = 0$. By comparison to the null hypothesis, the statistical restatement of the researcher's original proposition has come to be termed the "alternate" hypothesis, somewhat of a misnomer for the scientist's best informed judgment.

Systematic observations are made that bear directly on the hypothesis. This involves deciding on an appropriate sample of students, teachers, or other unit, and deciding on appropriate measurement instruments. The data are summarized into a numerical index that indicates the extent to which the null hypothesis is contradicted—the "test statistic." Finally the test statistic is assessed to determine whether the data contradict the null hypothesis to such a great extent that it is very unlikely the null hypothesis is true and thus the researcher's original hypothesis is supported.

2.1 Samples and Populations

Hypotheses describe relationships among variables for a particular "population" of persons (or groups, or institutions) defined by a specifiable set of characteristics. For example, the mathematics teacher claims effectiveness with all groups of children, say, whose ages are 7 through 12 years, who are of normal intelligence, have sound hearing, eyesight, and motor control, and who may have other specific attributes. While certain factors limit the intended population, others, such as locale or time, do not. Thus the hypothesis pertains to last year's class and next year's as well as the present class. However, effectiveness may not be permanent and it may be necessary to reconsider the hypothesis at a later time, or test the original hypothesis by taking samples in each of several years. The population to which the global mastery learning hypothesis applies may be much broader, including children of a wide range of abilities and ages, but a single investigation testing these propositions would specify a number of limiting factors including the school subject area.

It is not necessary to examine the entire population to decide whether a study's hypotheses are supported. Instead an inference may be drawn based on a "representative sample" of observations—that is, a group of subjects that is usually far smaller than the entire population, but whose characteristics approximate those of the population as nearly as is feasible. Still, the hypothesis being tested remains sample free; it is a proposition regarding the population that usually extends far beyond the individuals actually observed. If this were not the case, teachers would have no confidence in the mastery learning approach the following semester or in an untested school, and schools might never invest in new materials "demonstrated" to be effective.

Two principles of sampling are essential, randomization and replication. Randomization is a method of drawing subjects from the larger population such that each subject is as likely to be selected as every other subject, and a particular combination of subjects comprising the entire sample is as likely to be chosen as any other combination of the same number of subjects. Randomization produces an "unbiased" sample in that members of the population with any particular characteristic (e.g., young, old, male, female) are not systematically overselected.

Replication—conducting the study with more rather than fewer subjects—is also necessary to obtain a representative sample. In general, the larger the sample, the more nearly its characteristics will approximate those of the population. However, other factors may be weighed in deciding how large a sample should be, including the information gained by adding additional subjects to a sample. Also, if locating a subject, testing or interviewing, and recording and scoring responses requires extensive time and effort, a balance must be sought between the need for additional subjects and the costs involved.

2.2 Measures

The selection of appropriate measurement instruments is important both because inaccurate measures can produce erroneous decisions about a hypothesis and because measures that are defined too narrowly can limit the generality of the hypothesis test. In addition, a reasonable degree of "referent generality" (Snow 1974) is desirable; that is, the domain of responses should not be limited unduly. For example, in the mastery learning experiment, achievement might be represented by the total score on a test of French vocabulary. Even with a single score, greater generality is obtained by "item sampling"—that is, by choosing a representative sample of easy and difficult vocabulary items from the curriculum. Further, achievement may be defined more broadly to include vocabulary, comprehension, and pronunciation subtests, or both cognitive and attitudinal assessments. A "multivariate" approach to outcome measurement is particularly important when the response variable is somewhat ambiguously defined (e.g., personality traits, affective responses), and employing corresponding multivariate statistical procedures will increase both the replicability and referent generality of the investigation (Finn and Mattsson 1978).

2.3 Summarizing the Data and Deciding

Once the subjects of an investigation have been observed or tested, the quantitative data are summarized through "descriptive statistics," that is, summary indexes that characterize the sample only. These often include simple measures such as the mean scores for the total sample and for each identified subsample, measures of dispersion such as the standard deviation, and measures of the relationships among variables (e.g., differences among means, correlations).

At least one of these statistics must provide direct information regarding the hypothesis being investigated. This statistic is converted to a standardized measure of the extent to which the research hypothesis is supported by the data (and the null hypothesis contradicted), and is called the "test statistic." For example, from a sample of N students taking the 10-item test of fractions, the sample mean $\bar{X}$ and the sample standard deviation S might be obtained. Since the hypothesis is that the population mean is greater than 2, the difference $\bar{X} - 2$ is calculated, and becomes the basic element in the test statistic, $t = (\bar{X} - 2)/(S/N^{1/2})$. The denominator $S/N^{1/2}$ is a scaling factor that puts the t statistic into a standard convenient metric. The more effective the instructor, the larger t will be.

Likewise the test statistics for the two mastery learning hypotheses are measures of the extent to which the hypotheses are supported by data from the sample. Suppose that a sample of N_1 students learn French through the mastery approach and have an average vocabulary score of $\bar{X}_1$ and standard deviation S_1, and N_2 students learn by attending traditional lecture classes and have a mean vocabulary score $\bar{X}_2$ and standard deviation S_2. Then the test statistic for testing the difference between the two population means has the difference between the two samples means as its basic component, $D = \bar{X}_1 - \bar{X}_2$. The test statistic is $t = D/S_D$ where S_D, a function of the standard deviations and the sample sizes, expresses the difference in a convenient standard metric. The test is conducted by determining whether t is sufficiently above zero (i.e., $\bar{X}_1$ above $\bar{X}_2$) to convince us that μ_1 is above μ_2, and mastery learning is generally effective for French vocabulary. The test statistic for comparing the standard deviations is a direct comparison of the dispersions for the two samples, $F = S_1^2/S_2^2$. Since the hypothesis asserts that σ_1 is below σ_2, the F statistic is examined to see if it is enough below unity to be convincing that H_2 is supported for the populations generally.

A test statistic for the correlation of experience with grades is a t statistic that has the sample correlation r as its major component; this is $t = r[(N-2)/(1-r^2)]^{1/2}$. A t value sufficiently above zero (positive correlation) or sufficiently below zero (negative correlation) will convince researchers that one of the research hypotheses is supported. This is termed a "two-sided" or "two-tail" test; the other tests, for which only evidence in one direction will convince researchers that the research hypothesis is supported, are termed "one-sided" or "one-tail" tests.

The decision is made by referring the test statistic to tables that are found in most basic statistics textbooks. The logic by which the tables are formed may be exemplified for the test that $\mu > 2$. It should first be assumed that the null hypothesis is true and that $\mu = 2$. If the study of teacher effectiveness is conducted many times with different samples (e.g., approaching an infinite number of times) a very large collection of $\bar{X}$'s would be obtained. Each sample mean would be a little different, and none would be exactly 2 because samples are not the entire population. Fortunately, it is possible to determine theoretically the point that separates the one percent of the $\bar{X}$'s the farthest above 2 from those closer to 2 or below 2. This value is called the "critical value" of $\bar{X}$. It may also be converted to a t statistic for convenience, and placed into a table of critical values of t that typically has the percentages (one or five) as its column heading, and different sample sizes as the row labels. The percentages (column headings) are usually referred to as α.

The t table described above is assembled from statistical theory based on the assumption that the null hypothesis is true. In reality, the experiment would be conducted only once, a single $\bar{X}$ and t statistic calculated. The test statistic is then compared with the critical value in the table. If it exceeds the critical value, then the sample mean is very unlikely to have arisen from a population in which the null hypothesis is true, and the null hypothesis is deemed false and the instructor effective. The conclusion is expressed by saying that "the null hypothesis is rejected" or "the sample mean is (statistically) significantly different from 2."

The same procedure is followed for the mastery learning hypotheses. In the case of two standard deviations, the critical value would be a fraction below 1, and the null hypothesis is rejected only if the F statistic is smaller than this value. For the two-sided test of the correlation, two critical values would be necessary, one negative and one positive. If the test statistic is lower than the negative critical value or higher than the positive one, one of the research hypotheses is supported and the null hypothesis is rejected. Because of its central role in generalizing from the sample to the population, the test statistic is termed an "inferential statistic."

2.4 The Possibility of Being Wrong

It is likely, but not necessary, that a decision about the entire population based on a single sample is correct. Unfortunately, the actions based on hypothesis tests must often be taken even in the face of this uncertainty—for example, the principal must decide whether or not to award the mathematics teacher a salary increment; curriculum specialists must decide whether or not to invest in mastery learning procedures.

A test statistic that exceeds the respective critical value (e.g., a high mean score for students of the mathematics teacher) is unlikely to have been observed if the teacher were not effective. However, if the sample by coincidence contains only the most able students, then it may be concluded that the hypothesis of effectiveness is correct when in fact it is not. This is a "type I error," that is, rejecting a true null hypothesis. Since the researcher never knows if this has occurred, random sampling and a relatively large sample are particularly important, and pilot testing an investigation an excellent idea. On the other hand, choosing a small α value, thus requiring a larger test statistic before concluding that the research hypothesis is supported, reduces the likelihood of such an error. Thus, when a supported research hypothesis implies an important finding or action (e.g., more money and lifelong employment for the teacher), the investigator may deliberately use a small α level. When the possible benefits of a supported hypothesis are so important that even weak evidence suggests that an action be taken (e.g., a new medication for a formerly incurable form of disease) a larger probability of making a type I error may be acceptable.

If the sample data do not support the research hypothesis and it is concluded that the null hypothesis is true, this too may be erroneous—a "type II error." The probability of a type II error is controlled in practice by taking a sufficiently large number of subjects (Cohen 1977).

3. Conclusion

Hypothesis testing procedures constitute an important methodology for the advancement of the educational and social sciences. The technical formulation of hypothesis testing is detailed in a large number of textbooks including excellent introductions by Glass and Stanley (1970), Mendenhall and Ott (1980), and Shavelson (1980). At the same time, hypothesis tests comprise only part of the results of an empirical investigation. It is also of the utmost importance to inspect as many descriptive data as is feasible to understand a study's major findings, to estimate important population characteristics, and to interpret the relationships that are or are not confirmed.

Bibliography

Atkinson R C 1968 Computer-based instruction in initial reading. *Proceedings of the 1967 Invitational Conference on Testing Problems.* Educational Testing Service, Princeton, New Jersey

Cohen J 1977 *Statistical Power Analysis for the Behavioral Sciences*, rev. edn. Academic Press, New York

Cohen M R 1956 *A Preface to Logic*. Meridian, New York

Denham C, Lieberman A 1980 *Time to Learn*. National Institute of Education, United States Department of Education, Washington, DC

Ellis A 1952 A critique of systematic theoretical foundations in clinical psychology. *J. Clin. Psychol.* 8: 11–15

Finn J D, Mattsson I 1978 *Multivariate Analysis in Educational Research: Applications of the Multivariance Program*. National Educational Resources, Chicago, Illinois

Getzels J W 1963 Conflict and role behavior in the educational setting. In: Charters W W, Gage N L (eds.) 1963 *Readings in the Social Psychology of Education*, 1st edn. Allyn and Bacon, Boston, Massachusetts

Glass G V, Stanley J C 1970 *Statistical Methods in Education*

and Psychology. Prentice-Hall, Englewood Cliffs, New Jersey

Harrison F I 1968 Relationship between home background, school success, and adolescent attitudes. *Merrill-Palmer Q.* 14: 331–44

Kerlinger F N 1969 Research in education. In: Ebel R L (ed.) 1969 *Encyclopedia of Educational Research*, 4th edn. Macmillan, New York, pp. 1127–44

Mendenhall W, Ott L 1980 *Understanding Statistics*, 3rd edn. Duxbury, North Scituate, Massachusetts

Platt J R 1964 Strong inference. *Science* 146: 347–53

Popper K R 1965 *Conjectures and Refutations: The Growth of Scientific Knowledge*, 2nd edn. Basic Books, New York

Shavelson R J 1980 *Statistical Reasoning for the Behavioral Sciences*. Allyn and Bacon, Boston, Massachusetts

Snow R E 1974 Representative and quasi-representative designs for research on teaching. *Rev. Educ. Res.* 44: 265–91

Status Attainment Models

I. Fägerlind

In contemporary industrial societies the process of status attainment, or reaching high-status occupations and well-paid jobs, is a complex one. The main empirical question is to what extent such attainment depends on factors other than the individual's actual competence. In preindustrial societies inheritance or ascription of occupations and status dominate. Industrialism requires a more effective utilization of talent and ideally jobs should be allocated according to needed competence. In order to study this problem effectively it is important to follow the life cycle of different groups of people. The role of formal education in such life cycles is a key question. According to classical liberal conceptions formal education has been looked upon as a useful tool to allocate jobs and status according to individual capacity. In an egalitarian society the right to formal education should accordingly be based on individual merit and not on social background. Social mobility studies have analyzed how these ideas have been functioning in reality.

1. Early Status Attainment Models

Social scientists, who first studied mobility and status attainment, compared current occupations of a sample of subjects with different amounts of education with previous occupations of these individuals or with the occupations of their fathers at a given point in time. Cross-tabulations of later by earlier occupations showed intragenerational mobility, while tabulations by father's occupation gave intergenerational mobility. Comparisons between groups with different amounts of education showed the importance of formal education for occupational promotion. Sometimes occupational information was available for three or more points in time. Status attainment was usually measured by some kind of scale and different techniques were used to analyze the cross-tabulations. Simple percentage analysis was used by Sorokin (1927), Davidson and Anderson (1937),

Lipset and Bendix (1959), and Husén et al. (1969). Contingency table analysis was used by Livi (1950), Rogoff (1953), and Glass (1954), while stochastic matrices were employed in studies by Prais (1955), Carlsson (1958), and Matras (1960). The state of the art of the early research on status attainment is reported in Halsey et al. (1961), and in Lipset and Bendix (1959).

In the early 1960s the status attainment research took important steps forward when Duncan and Hodge (1963) clearly articulated the conceptual framework, and Duncan (1966) applied the technique of path analysis to the socioeconomic career achievement models. Blau and Duncan (1967), and Duncan et al. (1968) developed some basic models that were tested on representative samples in the United States. The Blau and Duncan (1967) "basic model" (see Fig. 1) described important aspects of the process by which family status and education were converted into occupational status through educational attainment. The life course perspective was important for the ordering of the variables. Father's education and occupation were used as exogenous variables, while respondent's education, early occupational status of his or her first job, and present occupational status were used as endogenous in the same causal order. However, as large amounts of variance were still unexplained in the dependent variable of the model, extensions of the model were called for.

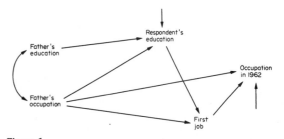

Figure 1
The basic Blau and Duncan (1967) model

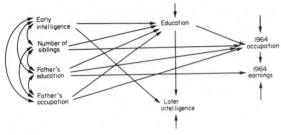

Figure 2
Conceptual model of dependence of socioeconomic
achievement on family background, early and late ability,
and education (Duncan 1968)

2. Inclusion of Cognitive Ability in Status Attainment Models

Only a year after the presentation of the "basic model,"
Duncan (1968) included ability in his model. Early cognitive ability was used as an exogenous variable together
with father's education and occupation, and late cognitive ability was placed after education but prior to occupation (see Fig. 2). The use of early cognitive ability as
an exogenous variable can be interpreted as a belief in
the heredity-oriented conception of ability as presented
by Jensen (1969) in his well-known *Harvard Educational
Review* article. The debate about the determinants of
early cognitive ability or "intelligence" has been considerable, often clearly ideologically anchored. At one
extreme it is argued that ability is almost entirely inherited, almost constant over time, and, therefore, inherently unequal across individuals (Jensen 1969, 1972,
1974, Hernstein 1971). At the other extreme it is argued
that ability is mainly determined by environment,
changes over time, and is potentially about equal for all
individuals (Hunt 1961, Halsey 1959). Between these
two extremes there are many attempts to separate the
effects of genes from the effects of environment. A person's or a child's ability is seen as a result of the interaction between heredity and environment. This thinking
can be found in a model presented by Williams (1973),
where the ability of children is dependent on both
father's and mother's ability combined with parental
status attainments and family environment (see Fig. 3).
In attempting to estimate family effects on cognitive

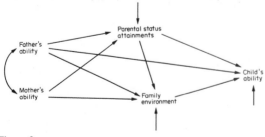

Figure 3
Ability model described by Williams (1973)

ability Leibowitz (1974) included both maternal and
paternal education.

Over and above the variables mentioned, many others
have been included in the basic model as exogenous
variables. Bulcock et al. (1974) included family size and
expected a negative effect of number of siblings on early
cognitive ability. Parental time spent with children, birth
order, family stability, ethnicity, race, religion, urbanization, and region are examples of variables included
and seen as important for early cognitive ability.

3. The Importance of Educational Attainment

In the Blau and Duncan (1967) basic model education
was seen as an intervening mediator between social
background and occupational achievement. The number of years spent in different kinds of formal education
was important for the placement of people on different
steps of the "educational ladder." This measure is used
under the assumption that each year of schooling represents the same additional increment in educational
attainment. In some countries the quality of the same
amount of education can vary considerably between
schools. Also, different types of programs with the same
amount of time can be very different. Attempts have
been made to measure the quality of schooling by such
variables as expenditures per student, particular
resources per student, or conventional achievement
measures (Coleman et al. 1966, Plowden 1967, Morgenstern 1973, Taubman and Wales 1974, Comber and
Keeves 1973, Williams 1980). Highest level of formal
schooling completed can also be used as a substitute for
quality measures (Fägerlind 1975, Dronkers and de
Jong 1979).

Various models have been developed to study the
determinants of educational attainments. The basic Blau
and Duncan (1967) model used father's education and
parental socioeconomic status as the only determinants
(see Fig. 1). The Duncan (1968) model included early
ability and family size as additional exogenous variables
(Fig. 2). Early ability was used as an endogenous variable by Jencks et al. (1972), which mirrors a more
environmentalist view (see Fig. 4). In a model employed
by Bulcock et al. (1974) parental income was included
(see Fig. 5).

Fägerlind (1975) hypothesized a different relationship
between early cognitive ability and educational attainment for individuals from different social backgrounds,
and introduced the interactive effect (Z_a) of early cognitive ability and social background on educational
attainment over and above their combined independent
(additive) effects (see Fig. 6).

In many studies it has been shown that education
exerts a strong influence on the occupational attainment
process. In a meritocratic society education was
assumed to be the dominant factor in social mobility.
However, in the early 1960s the validity of this assumption was challenged by Anderson (1961), who argued
that only a small part of a person's prospects of mobility can be explained by education. Boudon (1973)

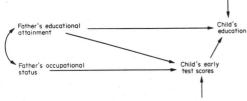

Figure 4
The first two components of the Duncan (1968) model as modified by Jencks et al. (1972)

argued that a highly meritocratic society will not necessarily give those who have reached a high level of education more chances of promotion than those whose level is lower. When using a modification of the Duncan (1968) model, Jencks et al. (1972) also came to the conclusion that education is not as strong a factor in promoting social mobility as traditionally assumed. They claimed that "schools serve primarily as selection and certification agencies, whose job is to measure and label people" (p. 135). When studying the effects of different variables on earnings they reported that education, IQ, family background, and the person's own occupational status together explained only 19 percent of the variance in earnings. They concluded that to a large extent income depends on "luck." When using a similar model on longitudinal data, Fägerlind (1975) showed that the explanatory power of education and the other variables in the model varied according to the stage of the career being considered. Jencks found no direct path from education to earnings, while Fägerlind found such paths significant from the age of 30 to the age of 43, when the last measurement of income was done in his longitudinal study. In a more detailed study Jencks et al. (1979) modified the findings from the earlier publication. Education and the other variables showed more effect and the effect of luck was spelled down.

4. Occupational Status

One measure of socioeconomic success is occupational status. Socioeconomic indices have been used in models of status attainment. The Duncan (1961) index, which is the one most commonly used in the United States, was derived by regressing prestige rankings from a large sample for 45 occupational titles on two summary age-standardized measures from a census: the percentage of male workers in each occupation with a minimum of four years of high school and the percentage with a certain minimum of income. The multiple correlation of the regression was 0.91 and the regression estimates were used as weights to construct an index for 446 detailed occupational categories. Scales of this type have been constructed in other countries and have shown considerable consistency over time and place.

In their book *The American Occupational Structure* Blau and Duncan (1967) expressed a strong belief in the impact of education. They concluded that education, though only one among several factors, "exerts the strongest direct effect on occupational achievement." This finding has been confirmed in many studies using similar models on different kinds of data. Education in most studies is found to be a significant intervening variable between family background and occupation. However, on the basis of longitudinal studies of given birth cohorts, it has been found that the importance of education declines over time. If education, measured by years of schooling or in some other way, shows up in the model as a significant variable this does not imply that schooling leads to social mobility. Many studies show that socioeconomic background has an important impact on years of schooling and for this reason can be considered a primary causal element.

5. Earnings in Status Attainment Models

Earnings are another measure of socioeconomic success commonly used in status attainment models. As mentioned earlier, there is little agreement in the literature concerning the impact of education on earnings. Some researchers find education to be a major determinant of earnings, whereas others find it to be almost insignificant. There is also disagreement as to whether there are significant direct paths from socioeconomic factors to earnings or if the effect of such factors are mediated by education, ability at maturity, or by occupation. In several studies, ability at maturity has been found to be important as a mediator between education and earnings. Other studies have found a weak relationship between ability at maturity and income. Different kinds of results of this sort might be caused by interactions between late ability and occupation.

6. Extensions of the Basic Model

The Blau and Duncan (1967) "basic model" has proved to be a strong and useful one in many countries. It has been extended in four different directions. Additional background variables such as family size and stability, family environment, ethnicity, race, religion, urbanization, and region have been added. Secondly, in addition to education, a number of variables intervening between background factors and socioeconomic attainment factors have been incorporated into the model, including motivation and ambition, aspiration, and other noncognitive traits. Interpersonal influences of wives, husbands, mothers, peers, and significant "others" are also included as intervening variables. Thirdly, there

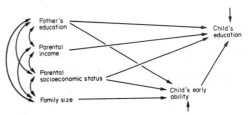

Figure 5
The first two components of the Bulcock et al. (1974) model

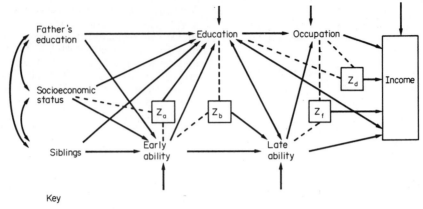

Key

Z_a = Interaction between socioeconomic status and early ability

Z_b = Interaction between early ability and education

Z_d = Interaction between education and occupation

Z_f = Interaction between late ability and occupation

Figure 6
Interaction model (Fägerlind 1975)

have been attempts to examine the effects of proximate career contingencies such as age, first job, and age at first job, and such job characteristics as work experience, size of firm, number of subordinates, and job complexity. Fourthly, the model has been extended to include additional outcome variables such as occupation and income at successive stages in the life cycle.

Although the basic model has mainly been applied to males, extended models have also been used for females. In such models family variables such as number of children, age of children, husbands' education, occupation, and income have been included as intervening variables. The basic model is recursive, which means that the variables are ordered in causal priority. Nonrecursive paths where there are influences between two variables in both directions have been used among intervening variables.

With the advent of latent structure analysis (Jöreskog 1976) many observed variables can be included in the model and errors of measurement can be taken into consideration. Even though many more observed variables are used, the model of latent variables is very close to the basic models described above. The latter are, therefore, still potent ones in attempts to elucidate the status attainment process in highly industrialized societies.

Bibliography

Anderson C A 1961 A skeptical note on education and mobility. In: Halsey A H, Floud J, Anderson C A (eds.) 1961, pp. 164–79

Blau P M, Duncan O D 1967 *The American Occupational Structure*. Wiley, New York

Boudon R 1973 *Education, Opportunity, and Social Inequality: Changing Prospects in Western Society*. Wiley, New York

Bulcock J W, Fägerlind I, Emanuelsson I 1974 *Education and*

the Socioeconomic Career: US–Swedish Comparisons. Report No. 6. Institute of International Education, University of Stockholm, Stockholm

Carlsson G 1958 *Social Mobility and Class Structure*. Gleerup, Lund

Coleman J S et al. 1966 *Equality of Educational Opportunity*. US Department of Health, Education and Welfare, Office of Education, Washington, DC

Comber L C, Keeves J P 1973 *Science Education in Nineteen Countries: An Empirical Study*. Almqvist and Wiksell, Stockholm and Wiley, New York

Davidson P E, Anderson H D 1937 *Occupational Mobility in an American Community*. Stanford University Press, Stanford, California

Dronkers J, de Jong U 1979 Jencks and Fägerlind in a Dutch Way: Report on research on the relationship between social background, intelligence, occupation and income in the Netherlands. *Soc. Sci. Inf.* 18: 761–81

Duncan O D 1961 A socioeconomic index for all occupations. In: Reiss A J (ed.) 1961 *Occupations and Social Status*. Free Press, New York, pp. 109–38

Duncan O D 1966 Path analysis: Sociological examples. *Am. J. Sociol.* 72: 1–16

Duncan O D 1968 Ability and achievement. *Eugenics Q.* 15: 1–11

Duncan O D, Featherman D L, Duncan B 1968 *Socioeconomic Background and Occupational Achievement: Extensions of a Basic Model*. US Department of Health, Education, and Welfare, Office of Education, Washington, DC

Duncan O D, Hodge R W 1963 Education and occupational mobility: A regression analysis. *Am. J. Soc.* 6: 629–44

Fägerlind I 1975 *Formal Education and Adult Earnings: A Longitudinal Study on the Economic Benefits of Education*. Almqvist and Wiksell, Stockholm

Glass D V (ed.) 1954 *Social Mobility in Britain*. Free Press, Glencoe, Illinois

Halsey A H 1959 Class differences in general intelligence. *Br. J. Stat. Psychol.* 12: 1–4

Halsey A H, Floud J, Anderson C A (eds.) 1961 *Education,*

Economy and Society: A Reader in the Sociology of Educa-tion. Free Press of Glencoe, New York

Hernstein R 1971 I.Q. *Atlantic* 228 (September): 43–64

Hunt J McV 1961 *Intelligence and Experience.* Ronald Press, New York

Husén T, Emanuelsson I, Fägerlind I, Liljefors R 1969 *Talent, Opportunity and Career: A Twenty-Six Year Follow-up of 1,500 Individuals.* Almqvist and Wiksell, Stockholm

Jencks C, et al. 1979 *Who Gets Ahead? The Determinant of Economic Success in America.* Basic Books, New York

Jencks D, Smith M, Acland H, Bane M J, Cohen D, Gintis H, Heyns B, Michelson S 1972 *Inequality: A Reassessment of the Effect of Family and Schooling in America.* Basic Books, New York

Jensen A R 1969 How much can we boost IQ and scholastic achievement? *Harvard Educ. Rev.* 39: 1–123

Jensen A R 1972 *Genetics and Education.* Methuen, London

Jensen A R 1974 Kinship correlations reported by Sir Cyril Burt. *Behav. Genet.* 4: 1–28

Jöreskog K G 1976 *Causal Models in the Social Sciences: The Need for Methodological Research.* Acta Universitatis Upsaliensis, Uppsala

Leibowitz A 1974 Home investments in children. *J. Polit. Econ.* 82: S111–S131

Lipset S M, Bendix R 1959 *Social Mobility in Industrial Soci-ety.* University of California Press, Berkeley, California

Livi L 1950 Sur la mesure de la mobilité sociale. *Population* 5: 65–76

Matras J 1960 Comparison of intergenerational occupational mobility patterns: An application of the formal theory of social mobility. *Popul. Stud.* 14: 163–69

Morgenstern R D 1973 Direct and indirect effects on earnings of schooling and socio-economic background. *Rev. Econ. Stat.* 55: 225–33

Plowden A 1967 *Children and their Primary Schools.* A Report of the Central Advisory Council for Education (England) II: Research and Surveys. Her Majesty's Stationery Office, London

Prais S J 1955 Measuring social mobility. *J. Royal Stat. Soc.* Ser. A, 118: 56–66

Rogoff N 1953 *Recent Trends in Occupational Mobility.* Free Press, Glencoe, Illinois

Sorokin P 1927 *Social Mobility.* Harper, New York

Taubman P, Wales T J 1974 *Higher Education and Earnings: College as an Investment and a Screening Device.* McGraw-Hill, New York

Williams T 1973 Cultural deprivation and intelligence: exten-sions of the basic model. (Doctoral dissertation, University of Toronto)

Williams T 1980 *School, Work and Career: 17-year olds in Aus-tralia.* Australian Council for Educational Research, Haw-thorn, Victoria

Models and Model Building

J. P. Keeves

There is a stage in the conduct of inquiry in any field, after variables have been identified as influencing a particular outcome or hypotheses have been advanced for definition, explanation, and prediction in relation to a particular problem, when the interrelations between the variables or the hypotheses which have been formulated need to be combined together into a hypothetical model. The essential characteristic of a model is the proposed structure of the model which is used to investigate the interrelationships between the variables. Research in education is concerned with the action of many factors, simultaneously or in a causal sequence in a problematic situation. Thus it is essential that research in the field of education should increasingly make use of models in the course of its inquiries. This article is concerned with the types of models that are being employed in educational research and the advantages and the dangers of model building. In addition, the article gives examples of some powerful models that have been employed in educational research and considers their contribution to the undertaking of inquiry in areas where prediction or explanation is being sought in relation to particular problems.

1. Theories and Models

It is important to recognize that the term "model" is not synonymous with the term "theory". In the investigation of a problematic situation a set of hypotheses may be proposed in resolution of a problem. The hypotheses

to be investigated are developed from intuition, from earlier studies, or from theoretical considerations. If they are sustained and can be generalized they will contribute to a theory, but until they are confirmed they remain heuristic devices that have been proposed in the course of inquiry. However, as part of an inquiry it may be necessary to consider the hypotheses in abstract and to advance a model that provides a structure for the interrelations which are proposed between the set of hypotheses. The model, like the hypotheses which are contained within it, can be built from accumulated evidence, intuition by analogy, or derived from theory. As Kaplan (1964) has pointed out, a theory may state that the subject matter under investigation should exhibit a certain structure, but the structure is not necessarily part of the theory itself. Kaplan has also stated that the term "model" is useful

only when the symbolic system it refers to is significant as a structure—a system which allows for exact deductions and explicit correspondences. The value of the model lies in part in its abstractness, so that it can be given many interpretations, which thereby reveal unexpected similarities. The value also lies in the deductive fertility of the model, so that unexpected consequences can be predicted and then tested by observation and experiment.

To the research worker, the use of models and model building are merely two of the strategies that can be employed in inquiry. They are not to be confused with either theory or scientific investigation as such.

559

To be useful a model should fulfil the following requirements.

(a) A model should contain structural relationships rather than associative relationships. However, correlational and regression relations which are essentially associative in nature are of value during the early stages of investigation, since they may identify the variables that are important and reveal something about the form of the relationships to be sought. Thus both correlation and regression can contribute to model building.

(b) A model should lead to the prediction of consequences that can be verified by observation. This implies that it should be possible to design critical tests of the model based on empirical data, and if the tests are not sustained, the model should be rejected.

(c) The structure of a model will desirably reveal something of the causal mechanisms which are involved in the subject matter being investigated. Thus the model may contribute not only to prediction, but also to explanation.

(d) In so far as a model contributes to explanation it should become an aid to the imagination in the formulation of new concepts and new relationships and thus be the extension of inquiry.

It will be clear from the above discussion that a model is explicit and definite. Models can be built, tested, and if necessary rebuilt in the course of inquiry. They relate to theory and may be derived from theory, but they are conceptually different from theory itself.

2. The Shortcomings of Models

Several dangers exist in the use of models. The first danger arises from the fact that the model involves simplification. Without the simplification which is associated with the abstractness of the model, there would be nothing to be gained from building the model. However, the danger that arises lies in oversimplification. Kaplan (1964) in this context refers to the well-known principle of the "drunkard's search", in which the drunkard searches under the street lamp for his house key, when he dropped it some distance away, because "it's lighter here". Thus the danger of oversimplification in the use of a model is not that the model is built incorrectly, but that in the process of abstraction, the model has been built with simplification that has extended too far.

The second major danger arising from the use of models is that significance might be attached to aspects of the model which do not belong to the structure of the model but to the particular symbols that have been employed in the model. Likewise, there is a danger arising from an overemphasis on the form in which the model is expressed. A forced analogy, an inappropriate metaphor, the unwarranted use of a mathematical formulation, or the inappropriate use of a diagrammatic representation can all, in certain circumstances, serve to conceal rather than reveal the basic structure of the model which holds underlying relationships that could be tested and verified. Nevertheless, the use of a symbolic or diagrammatic form can often serve to make explicit and definite the structure of the model that would otherwise remain hidden in an excess of words.

3. Testing the Model

Perhaps the greatest danger that is prevalent in educational research today is that of building or developing a single model or perhaps alternative models to serve the purposes of explanation, but without concern for the need for testing the models through the use of empirical data. The purpose of building a model, like that of advancing hypotheses, is that the model should be submitted to the test. Consequently the dangers of model building are not only those of oversimplification or of the inappropriate use of symbols or of form, but rather that the models are not sufficiently realistic for their consequences to be worked out with adequate precision and for an appropriate test to be applied. The strength of certain types of models, for example models expressed in mathematical form, is that they lend themselves more readily to data collection and to testing.

Traditionally in social and behavioural research there has been heavy reliance on the testing of mathematical models by statistical techniques. While in the field of educational research the significance test still has an important place, the shortcomings of testing for statistical significance at the expense of recognition of general consistency and pattern in the results obtained is now being recognized.

In addition, there is another aspect of checking a model against empirical data, namely the estimation of the parameters of the model. From the estimated parameters it becomes possible to make predictions in order to test the generality of the model both from location to location and across time. It is clear that model building, data collection, and the testing of the model must be seen as integrated activities. The structure of the model influences the data to be collected, the data are essential for the verification of the model and the estimation of its parameters, and the testing of the model may lead to rebuilding or reforming. The importance, however, of checking a model against empirical data must be stressed. Without this step the building of the model has been an unprofitable exercise. It is the only means of establishing the validity of the model, of improving realism, and of making an effective contribution through model building to theoretical knowledge. Nevertheless, it is necessary to recognize that the model itself has only heuristic value in the development of theory, it is not essential to the establishment of theory in education or any other fields of scientific knowledge.

4. Types of Models

Several types of models have been identified by Kaplan (1964) and Tatsuoka (1968), and while the classification that follows draws on both these sources it diverges in certain notable ways from them, in part because of developments that have occurred in education and the social sciences in the years that have intervened since these articles were written.

4.1 Analogue Models

A common and important class comprises those models that are related to a physical system, and it is perhaps not surprising that such models should be widely used in the physical sciences, relatively uncommon in the social and behavioural sciences, and rare in the field of education. Such models are referred to as analogue models. The development of the model of the atom through the successive stages of the "currant bun model" to the "planetary model" to the "wave model" has involved the use of appropriate analogues as was consistent with the evidence available at the time. In advancing such models, correspondences are necessary between the elements of the model and the elements occurring in the problem under investigation. Such correspondence which is clear in the use of analogue models, extends to the use of other types of models, although the correspondences are less explicitly defined. It is important to note the presence of one of the dangers associated with the use of models, namely that there is no guarantee that the correspondences will continue to hold beyond those which have been deliberately introduced by the builder of the model. Clearly such models have limited utility, for while they may furnish the research worker with plausible hypotheses for testing, they generally preclude the making of deductions from the model.

A model of a school population. An example of an analogue model used in educational work, which has been taken from the field of demography, is that of a water tank with inlet and outlet pipes to represent the student population of a school system. The inlet pipes correspond to: (a) the intake controlled by the birthrate, (b) the intake as influenced by the rate of immigration, including both external and internal immigration with allowance made for age-specific migration rates, and (c) the reception rate into school at ages below the lower age of compulsory schooling. The outlet pipes correspond to: (d) the rate of emigration, with allowance made for age-specific emigration rates, and (e) the school departure rate at ages above the upper age of compulsory schooling, and with the departure rates taken as the complements of the age-specific retention rates. Estimation of the parameters of the model at a particular point in time using data collected over previous years would enable predictions to be made for the size of the school population of the system at a future time. The main value of the model that has been developed is for the explanation of changes in the student population and the subsequent predictions that can be made to test not so much the validity of the model but the accuracy of the parameters that have been estimated.

4.2 Semantic Models

The essential feature of such models is that they are expressed in verbal form. Frequently such models involve the use of figures of speech or metaphors. Since all language involves the use of metaphors and figures of speech, to a greater or lesser extent, semantic models that are expressed in verbal form can be referred to as figurative or metaphoric models. However, since the figure of speech is not always explicit the use of the term "semantic model" would seem preferable for this very common class of model. It should be noted that semantic models provide a conceptual analogue to the subject matter under consideration rather than a physical analogue. A common deficiency of such models is their lack of precision which renders them not readily amenable to testing. However, because they are expressed in verbal form they provide a valuable explanation of the subject matter that, in general, is readily understood. Semantic models are in common use in the field of educational research. Many are widely disseminated, but few have been subjected to rigorous testing, and hence have failed to serve the heuristic purposes which would justify their construction.

A model of school learning. An example of a semantic model that has served an extremely important function since the early 1970s in so far as it has led to extensive and successful attempts to validate relationships within the model is the "model of school learning" proposed by Carroll (1963). The model contains five elements, three of which are associated with the individual student, and two of which arise from external conditions. Carroll initially formulated the model in the following words:

> Factors in the individual are (1) aptitude—the amount of time needed to learn the task under optimal instructional conditions, (2) ability to understand instruction, and (3) perseverance—the amount of time the learner is willing to engage actively in learning. Factors in external conditions are (4) opportunity—time allowed for learning, and (5) the quality of instruction—a measure of the degree to which instruction is presented so that it will not require additional time for mastery beyond that required in view of aptitude. (Carroll 1963 p. 729)

It should be noted that three of the five factors are expressed in terms of time, and it is this property of the factors contained within the model that has made it relatively easy for the constituent relationships of the model to be submitted to verification with empirical data. Carroll in his presentation of the model also states that both quality of instruction and ability to understand instruction are quantities that are interrelated to variables that can be measured in terms of time. Consequently they can be indexed in terms of time and also submitted to testing. From this model the degree of learning for any individual on a task was tentatively expressed in functional form, as a "ratio of the amount of time the learner actually spends on the learning task to the total amount he needs".

Thus: Degree of learning $= f$ (time actually spent/time needed) (Carroll 1963 p. 730).

Initially, this model was not submitted to verification, but more recently a considerable body of research has been accumulated to provide support for the general validity of the model (Denham and Lieberman 1980). While it is still premature to express the model of school learning in a more precise mathematical form, considerable progress has been made in establishing that the elements of the model are related in the ways that Carroll proposed, thus confirming facets of the structure of the model that Carroll advanced. It is also significant that research workers in education have used the model as a starting point for the development of theories of school learning. Bloom (1976) has advanced a theory in relation to mastery learning; Cooley and Lohnes (1976) have proposed steps towards a theory in relation to the evaluation of schooling; and Harnischfeger and Wiley (1976) proposed a view of the teaching–learning process in elementary schools based upon the concept of time as part of a more general model of schooling.

It should be noted that both Carroll's model and the Harnischfeger and Wiley model identify a set of elements and propose relationships between them. The models do not explain the causal processes which underlie these relationships, and hence they do not contribute to the specification of these relationships in precise functional form. Nevertheless, there is the implicit assumption in their presentations of the existence of causal relationships, and the expectation that from further empirical research it will be possible to express the relationships more explicitly in terms of a mathematical model and hence make a significant contribution towards a theory of school learning.

4.3 Mathematical Models

While mathematical models have been used increasingly since the early 1960s in the behavioural and social sciences, including uses in psychology that have a bearing on educational problems, there have been very few uses of mathematical models directly in the field of educational research. There have, however, been many instances where a measurement model has been used in the field of education, but this involves a generalized model being applied to a measurement problem, rather than the development of a specific mathematical model for use in a problematic situation. Nevertheless, it is being increasingly recognized in the behavioural and social sciences that mathematical models have an important contribution to make in the advancement of theory, and it would seem likely that there will be greater use made of mathematical models in educational research over the coming decades.

Tatsuoka (1968) has drawn attention to the fact that before a mathematical model is advanced there must already exist either an informal theory or a semantic model for the problematic situation. The building of a mathematical model involves a degree of sophistication and a degree of understanding of the problem that is highly unlikely to arise prior to the establishment of informal theory or the confirmation of a semantic model.

The advantages of a mathematical model are many in addition to elegance and parsimony. The model involves the advancement of basic assumptions and postulates that are made explicit and are thus open to scrutiny and questioning. It permits the derivation of explicit quantitative predictions that can be tested with empirical data, and it lays the foundations for a more formal theory built around the causal relationships that are implicitly or explicitly contained within the model.

One of the most successful applications of a mathematical model to an educational problem has been carried out by Zajonc and his co-workers with respect to the birth order problem. The principle of primogeniture is well-established in most societies, and thus there has been long-standing recognition that the first born, especially the first born male child, receives preferential treatment. Furthermore, there is worldwide evidence that increasing family size is consistently related to decreasing intellectual performance. Anomalies which have been observed have tended to disappear after controlling for socioeconomic status. However, much of the evidence that has been collected during the twentieth century from educational and psychological research has shown inconsistent findings for birth order and such characteristics as intellectual development. In 1973, Belmont and Marolla reported data from a very large sample of no fewer than 380,000 cases for male youth aged 19 years showing strong and consistent relationships between birth order and intellectual performance on the Raven Progressive Matrices test for successive family sizes. The magnitude of the effects reported is shown by the fact that the highest of the observed values for the first born of a family of two exceeded the last born of a family of six by approximately two-thirds of a standard deviation. These data on family size and birth order exhibited five important effects: (a) intelligence scores decreased with increasing family size, (b) within family size, intelligence scores declined with increasing birth order, (c) with the exception of the last born child, there appeared to be a reduction in the rate of decline with higher birth orders, (d) the deceleration in the trend with birth order was not observed for the last born who exhibited a discontinuous drop in intellectual performance, and (e) the only child also showed a discontinuity, scoring at a level approximately the same as that of the first born of a family of four.

In explaining the effects of family size on intellectual development, the effect of the educational environment of the home on the individual has been commonly used. It has been generally acknowledged that the educational level of the parents and the number of books in the home contribute to the intellectual home background of the child. Thus, it was within this historical context, based on informal theory concerning the educational environment of the home, that Zajonc and Markus (1975) set out to develop a mathematical model that would account for the strong evidence presented by Belmont and Marolla (1973).

The "confluence model" that Zajonc and Markus (1975) advanced was built around the concept of mutual intellectual influences among children as they develop within the family environment. The primary emphasis was on the intellectual environment of the child during the course of development, and in particular on the intellectual level of the individual's siblings and parents. A reparameterized version of this model was presented by Zajonc et al. (1979) to account for the conflicting results reported in the birth order literature. In the first paper (Zajonc and Markus 1975), it was assumed that the effects of family configuration could be represented by a sigmoid function of age:

$$M_t = 1 - e^{-k^2 t^2} \tag{1}$$

where t is age in years and k is an arbitrary constant associated with the type of intellectual ability involved. In the reparameterized version (Zajonc et al. 1979), rate of intellectual growth was hypothesized to be a function of intellectual development within the family, α, and a factor λ which was associated with the special circumstances of the last children. Thus the level of mental maturity $[M_{ij(t)}]$ achieved at age t by the ith child in a family of j children in a household of n persons was expressed by the equation,

$$M_{ij(t)} = M_{ij(t-1)} + \alpha_i + \lambda_i \tag{2}$$

The two parameters α_i and λ_i are expressed as weighted yearly increments of the sigmoid function M_t where

$$\Delta f(t) = (1 - e^{-k^2 t^2}) - (1 - e^{-k^2(t-1)^2})$$
$$= e^{-k^2(t-1)^2} - e^{-k^2 t^2} \tag{3}$$

Then

$$\alpha_t = \omega_1 \Delta f(t) \left[\frac{\sum_{i=1}^{n} M_{in(t-1)}^2}{n_{(t-1)} + 1} \right]^{1/2}$$

and

$$\lambda_t = \frac{\omega_2 L_t \Delta(f) \Delta(\tau)}{(n_t - 1)^2}$$

The terms ω_1 and ω_2 are weights associated with the two components; τ is the age of the adjacent younger sibling; and L_t is the last child index.

Using simulation procedures, the confluence model predicted accurately the data recorded in six large national surveys of intellectual performance in relation to family configuration factors when all three parameters k_1, ω_1, and ω_2 were used. When the third parameter ω_2 was held constant, little accuracy was lost. The variations in the estimated values of the parameters that reflected the variations in the patterns of effects could be interpreted in a meaningful way in terms of the psychological theory. Thus the confluence model was found to account for the data available on birth order and intellectual performance. The values of the growth constant k were highest for the American data, were very similar for the Dutch, French, and Scottish data, and were nearly twice the size for the Western Israeli sample as for the Oriental Israeli sample. It should be noted that the three Western European samples were cross-sectional samples from the total national population, while the American and the two Israeli samples were selective and not representative of their respective national populations. The values of best fit for the parameter ω_1 associated with the intellectual environment within the family showed a perfect inverse relationship with the ages at testing of the six samples and were consistent with the assumption that the impact of the family intellectual environment decreased as the age of the child increased and with changes in family structure. The values obtained for the parameter ω_2 associated with the handicap for the last born child, indicated how much elder siblings gained from serving as a resource for the intellectual development of the last born. For fuller details of the findings and the interpretation of the results of this study which employed simulation procedures to estimate the parameters of the model, Zajonc and Bargh (1980a) should be consulted. In summary, the findings indicated that when an additional child joined the family, two significant changes could be assumed to take place in the intellectual development of the older child. First, the educative environment of the family was diminished as a consequence of the addition of the new child, and secondly, the older child acquired a teaching role within the family which had positive consequences for the intellectual development of the older child. It is interesting to note that the decline in the quality of the educational environment as a consequence of the addition of a child to the family initially exceeded the benefits that arose from the teaching role. However, the rate of decline was such that the benefits could surpass the losses and a reversal in intellectual performance could arise. Such reversals were shown to occur before the age of 14 years.

The confluence model advanced by Zajonc and his colleagues has also been used to predict changes in achievement test scores over time. Associated with changes in birth rate there will be changes in average order of birth. An increase in birth rate will be accompanied by larger families and a correspondingly lower average birth order. Since the confluence model predicts a decline in intellectual performance with an increase in birth order, there should be changes in average achievement test scores corresponding to changes in the birth rate and the associated variables, family size and average birth order. Data from elementary-school populations for the states of Iowa and New York in the United States, confirmed the predicted relationships. Further confirmation of the confluence model came from the performance of a large sample (nearly 800,000) of high-school students on the National Merit Scholarship Qualification Test in the United States. However, an examination of student performance on the Scholastic Aptitude Test, a test employed for admission to college-level studies in the United States, with respect to family configuration, has shown that only a negligible proportion of the decline in the Scholastic Aptitude Test scores between 1965 and 1977 could be attributed to birth order and family size. However, it was considered possible that the samples used to test the predictions in Scholastic Aptitude Test scores were both too small and not representative enough of the population to show the trends that were predicted (Zajonc and Bargh 1980b).

The confluence model provides an excellent example of a mathematical model that has been developed in the field of educational research from informal theory and from prior research findings to conform to large bodies of data. The use of computer-based simulation procedures to estimate the parameters of the model and to validate the model is of particular interest. Furthermore, the application of this model to predict trends and to explain fluctuations in achievement test data over time illustrates well the manner in which models can be used. It should be noted that the confluence model is not a theory, but its confirmation does provide strong support for theories of the educational environment of the home.

4.4 Causal Models

Since the early 1970s there has been increasing use of causal models in the field of educational research. The employment of causal models derives from work in the field of genetics associated with the analytical technique of path analysis. Rudimentary use was made of path analysis in the field of education by Burks (1928) but the procedure lay dormant for over 40 years in education until used by Peaker (1971) in England. This revival of interest in path analysis was built on the seminal work of Blalock (1961) concerned with the making of causal inferences in nonexperimental research. Subsequent work in sociology drew on earlier developments in the fields of genetics and econometrics and a new approach to models and model building became available for use in educational research.

The procedures employed for the development of causal models enable the investigator to move from a verbal statement or a semantic model of a complex set of interrelationships between variables to a more precise one in which the principles of path analysis are employed. The use of diagrams to portray the interrelations are of assistance but are not essential to the procedures, in which a set of linear equations is constructed to specify the relationships between the variables in the causal model. It is the use of the set of structural equations that has led to the introduction of a further name for the procedures—structural equation models.

The essential idea of a causal model involves the building of a simplified structural equation model of the causal process operating between the variables under consideration. The model is constructed using knowledge gained from substantive theory, and from previous research, and the model is written as a set of linear equations each representing a causal relationship hypothesized to act between the variables. From these structural equations the parameters of the model may be estimated and the model and its component parts evaluated. As an outcome the model is either confirmed or rejected for reformulation to provide an alternative that could be tested with the available data.

For a large class of causal models, such as those advanced in educational research, in which the model is recursive, the procedures of least squares regression analysis can be used to obtain solutions to the set of linear equations of a causal model. There are, however, other analytic procedures that can be used to obtain solutions to more complex models.

Williams (1976) has made a significant contribution to the understanding of the manner in which the home environment operates to influence the development of intellectual ability of a child through the construction and estimation of causal models to describe the situation.

The first model shown in Fig. 1 (from Eckland 1971) is the standard deprivation model which is commonly employed to account for relationships between parental socioeconomic status, the educational environment of the home, and the child's intelligence. This model denies the possibility that the child could inherit from its parents genetic material that might influence the growth of the child's intelligence. Thus while this model is widely used in educational research, although rarely in an explicit form, it must be considered to be deficient.

A second causal model is shown in Fig. 2 in which provision is made for the possibility that the child has inherited from its parents genetic material that will affect in part the intellectual ability of the child.

This second model also denies the possibility that the child might influence the type of educational environment provided by the parents as a consequence of the child's level of intellectual ability. A third causal model is shown in Fig. 3 in which provision is made for the mutual influence between the educational environment of the home and the child's intelligence. However, in order to solve the linear equations of a causal model in which a reciprocating effect is included it is necessary to introduce into the model an instrumental variable which influences one of the reciprocating variables but not the other. It is not always possible to identify an appropriate instrumental variable. However, in this situation the research on the confluence model considered above would appear to indicate that family size is likely to influence the growth of the child's intelligence indirectly through the educational environment of the home

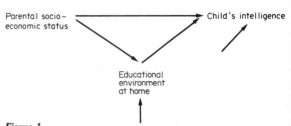

Figure 1
The standard deprivation model

rather than exert a direct influence on the child's genetic composition. Thus family size can be included in the model as an instrumental variable as shown in Fig. 3.

The models shown in Figs. 1 and 2 are both recursive models and can be readily estimated by ordinary least squares regression analysis. The model shown in Fig. 3, is a nonrecursive model because of the reciprocating effect and the linear equations of this model can only be solved by indirect regression analysis procedures. Further, with the inclusion of family size as a variable in the model it is questionable whether parental socioeconomic status exerts a direct causal effect on the child's intelligence, or acts only indirectly through family size and the educational environment of the home. However, this issue is perhaps best left to be determined by the magnitudes of the path coefficients which are estimated for the model from empirical data.

Williams (1976) has measured the dimensions of the environment of the home of a sample of Canadian children and with data on the other components has estimated the parameters of models similar to the ones shown above. He has shown that the environment of the home has a significant influence on the child's intelligence, but more importantly he has shown that the influence of the child's intelligence back on the environment of the home is too large to be ignored. Thus in Williams' model, which is sustained by the data available, not only is a child advantaged or disadvantaged by the socioeconomic status of the parents as is commonly acknowledged, but the child is further advantaged or disadvantaged by inheritance from the parents, and, in addition, the child from a high status home, with parents of high ability is likely to be further advantaged by the influence that a high ability child can exert over the level of the educational environment of the home to benefit his or her further intellectual development.

The causal models analysed by Williams may suffer from oversimplification of an extremely complex problematic situation. Nevertheless they do provide an enhanced understanding of the factors that contribute to influencing the development of a child's intelligence and they provide the means by which attempts can be made to estimate the effects of the major factors that would seem to contribute to the intellectual ability of a child.

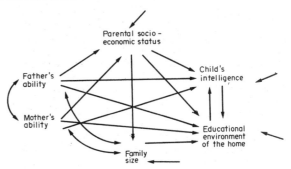

Figure 3
Mutual influence of environment and intelligence model

5. Conclusion

Since the early 1960s there has been an increased use of models and model building in educational research, particularly through the use of causal models. These developments have occurred partly as a result of the availability of computers to undertake the extensive calculation necessary to test quantitative relationships in mathematical and causal models, and, in addition, to obtain estimates of the parameters of such models. In part, too, these developments have taken place as the result of work done in other fields, in particular, the social and behavioural sciences. Nevertheless, the use of semantic models still dominates the field of educational research. As a consequence, the use of causal models is still not common, and the use of mathematical models in educational research is extremely rare.

In this article, models have been referred to that are being investigated in relation to the educational environment of the home and school learning. These are two areas that are central to the process of education, and this work indicates that advances are being made in the development of theory in these two important areas through the use of models and model building. It would seem probable that if further progress is to be made in the development of theory in these and in other areas of the field of education, increased use should be made of mathematical and causal models, and the scientific research methods associated with the use of modelling procedures.

See also: Status Attainment Models

Bibliography

Belmont L, Marolla F A 1973 Birth order, family size, and intelligence. *Science* 182: 1096–101
Blalock H M 1961 *Causal Inferences in Nonexperimental Research.* University of North Carolina, Chapel Hill, North Carolina
Bloom B S 1976 *Human Characteristics and School Learning.* McGraw-Hill, New York
Burks B S 1928 The relative influence of nature and nurture upon mental development: A comparative study of foster parent–foster child resemblance and true parent–true child resemblance. *National Society for the Study of Education Yearbook* 17: 219–316

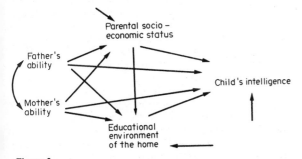

Figure 2
Inheritance of ability model

Carroll J B 1963 A model of school learning. *Teach. Coll. Rec.* 64: 723–33

Cooley W W, Lohnes P R 1976 *Evaluation Research in Education.* Irvington, New York

Denham C, Lieberman A (eds.) 1980 *Time to Learn.* National Institute of Education, Washington, DC

Eckland B K 1971 Social class structure and the genetic basis of intelligence. In: Cancro R (ed.) 1971 *Intelligence, Genetic and Environmental Influences.* Grune and Stratton, New York, pp. 65–76

Harnischfeger A, Wiley D E 1976 The teaching–learning process in elementary schools: A synoptic view. *Curric. Inq.* 6: 5–43

Kaplan A 1964 *The Conduct of Inquiry: Methodology for Behavioral Science.* Chandler, San Francisco, California

Peaker G F 1971 *The Plowden Children Four Years Later.* National Foundation for Educational Research, Slough

Tatsuoka M M 1968 Mathematical models in the behavioral and social sciences. In: Whitla D K (ed.) 1968 *Handbook of Measurement and Assessment in Behavioral Sciences.* Addison-Wesley, Reading, Massachusetts

Williams T H 1976 Abilities and environments. In: Sewell W H, Hauser R M, Featherman D L (eds.) 1976 *Schooling and Achievement in American Society.* Academic Press, New York, pp. 61–102

Zajonc R B, Bargh J 1980a The confluence model: Parameter and estimation for six divergent data sets on family factors and intelligence. *Intelligence* 4: 349–62

Zajonc R B, Bargh J 1980b Birth order, family size and decline of SAT scores. *Am. Psychol.* 35: 662–68

Zajonc R B, Markus G B 1975 Birth order and intellectual development. *Psychol. Rev.* 82: 74–88

Zajonc R B, Markus H, Markus G B 1979 The birth order puzzle. *J. Pers. Soc. Psychol.* 37: 1325–41

Prediction in Research

R. M. Wolf

Prediction represents an effort to describe what will be found concerning an event or outcome not yet observed on the basis of information considered to be relevant to the event. Typically, there is a temporal dimension to prediction when, say, ability test scores are used to forecast future achievement in a course of study.

The information that is used to make a prediction is typically referred to as a predictor. In any prediction study there is at least one predictor variable. Predictor variables can be either quantitative, for example, scores on a test, or qualitative, for example, type of course enrolled in. It is possible to combine qualitative and quantitative variables in a prediction study. The event or outcome to be predicted is typically referred to as a criterion. There are several types of criterion variables. One of the most common is performance on some quantitative continuous variable such as an achievement test or a grade point average. Other criterion variables could be qualitative in nature. When a counselor helps a student make a choice of career or course of study, the counselor is at least implicitly making a prediction about a qualitative variable, career choice or course of study, that the student is likely to succeed in and from which he or she can derive satisfaction. The criterion in this case can be regarded as membership in a particular group. In more complex cases, a criterion may be multidimensional in character as when one is interested in predicting an individual's profile on a number of variables such as a battery of achievement measures. While possible, simultaneous prediction on a number of criterion variables is quite rare.

Prediction studies can be highly varied depending on the nature of the population under study and the number and types of predictor and criterion variables used. However, there are a number of common elements in prediction studies. The first element involves identifying the outcome or event to be predicted. Education, social, or business necessity is usually the basis for such a choice. The second element is to develop or select a measure that will serve as a criterion variable. This crucial step of the process generally receives far less attention than it should. If one decides to use "success in college" as a criterion in a prediction study, then how is success to be defined and measured? Obviously, there are many ways to do this. Unfortunately, there is no clearly correct way to define and measure success. Any definition of success will have its limitations and any measure based on a particular definition will be somewhat deficient. The use of an earned grade point average in college as a measure of success, for example, will only reflect the standards used by a particular group of instructors in a set of courses and will ignore performance in noninstructional aspects of college life. Furthermore, the standards used by a particular set of instructors may not reflect the standards of the institution as a whole. In fact, it is possible that there may be no uniform agreement on a set of standards that will serve to define success across all the instructional areas of the institution. Thus, even a widely used criterion variable such as the grade point average suffers from a number of weaknesses.

The definition and measurement of criterion variables is a formidable challenge. The desired qualities in a criterion variable, whether it is quantitative or qualitative, are: (a) relevancy—standing on the criterion is determined by the same factors that make for success in the situation; (b) freedom from bias—the measure of the criterion variable is free from external factors that provide each individual with the same opportunity to achieve a good score on the criterion; (c) reliability—the measurement of the criterion variable must be stable or reproducible if it is to be predicted; (d) availability—is a measure of the criterion available? How much will it cost to get? While a number of empirical procedures such as task or job analysis, work-sample tests, and factor analysis can be useful in helping to develop measures of criterion variables, the basic ingredient in the definition of criterion variables is judgment. Considerable background and expertise are required to define and develop adequate measures of criterion variables.

A third element in all prediction studies is the identification and measurement of the variable or variables that will serve as predictors. Again, considerable background and expertise is needed. The fourth element in a prediction study is to collect information on both the predictor variable or variables and the criterion for a sample of individuals and to subject these data to analysis. The typical kind of analysis involves some form of least squares procedures. The results will provide an estimate of the extent to which the criterion variable or variables can be predicted from the predictor variable or variables. The results, however, will only apply to the sample that was studied. Consequently, it will be necessary to see if the results obtained with one sample apply to a different sample. This is called cross-validation (Mosier 1951). If it can be shown that the results obtained with one sample apply to a new sample, one can use the results with some confidence. It is necessary, however, to periodically check to see whether the results are holding up. That is, is the level and accuracy of prediction the same for subsequent groups?

Prediction always involves uncertainty. A prediction study is undertaken with a particular sample of individuals, for example, when ability test scores are used to predict subsequent achievement in a learning situation. Once a prediction study has been completed, that is, a group has been followed and their subsequent performance has been assessed, the real purpose of the study is to be able to use the results with a subsequent group of learners. It is in this sense that prediction contains uncertainty since the intent is to use information derived from the study of one group in a prospective way with another group.

The simplest type of prediction study involves the use of a single predictor variable measured on a continuous scale to predict a single criterion variable also measured on a continuous scale. An example of such a study would be the use of an ability test score to predict performance on an achievement test after a period of instruction. To conduct a prediction study involving these two variables would require the administration of the ability test to a group of students prior to the onset of instruction, locking away the results, and the administering of a test of achievement after instruction. Withholding the results of the predictor test until the criterion variable is obtained is necessary to avoid possible contamination of the criterion either consciously or unconsciously by those who provide instruction and develop, administer, and grade the achievement test. Once collected, the data need to be analyzed. In the simple example described here, the usual procedure would be a simple regression analysis of the criterion score on the predictor scores. The analysis would yield a

number of items of information. The first item would be a regression equation of the form:

$$\hat{Y} = a + bX \tag{1}$$

where: $\hat{Y}$ is the predicted score on the criterion variable; a is a constant that would represent the expected score on the criterion variable if the value of X, the score on the predictor variable, were zero; b is the regression coefficient that denotes the number of units of increase in Y, the criterion variable, that is associated with one unit of change on the X variable; and X is an individual's score on the predictor variable.

The regression equation can be used to predict each individual's score on the criterion variable. The chances are that the regression equation will predict few, if any, individuals' criterion scores with perfect accuracy. Thus, it is necessary to have additional items of information to properly evaluate the goodness of prediction. A second item of information that would normally be obtained from a simple regression analysis undertaken in a prediction study would be the correlation coefficient (r) between the two sets of scores. The correlation coefficient is an index number that can take on values from -1.0 to $+1.0$. The magnitude of the correlation coefficient describes the strength of the relationship between the variables while the sign of the correlation describes the direction of the relationship. Correlation coefficients of $+1.0$ and -1.0 describe a perfect relationship while a correlation coefficient of zero denotes no relationship at all between the variables. The square of the correlation coefficient describes the percentage of the variance in the criterion variable that is accounted for by variation in the predictor variable. In a prediction study, the higher the value of r and r^2, the better the prediction.

How high the correlation coefficient should be to be considered satisfactory for predictive purposes is a question that is not easily answered. There are several bases on which the issue can be approached. First, does the use of a particular predictor variable improve prediction over chance levels? If so, there could be a basis for using the particular predictor variable under study. Second, is the use of a particular predictor variable better than other currently available predictors? If the answer is affirmative then there is a basis for using the particular predictor variable. Third, does the use of a predictor variable improve prediction over other currently available predictor variables? This last consideration involves the use of multiple predictors. It requires having information about the population of applicants who will be admitted to a training or employment situation (the selection ratio) and the gain in prediction that is achieved by using the predictor variable under study, the incremental validity of the predictor variable (Anastasi 1982).

The third item of information that would result from a simple regression analysis is the standard error of estimate ($S_{y.x}$). The standard error of estimate is defined as follows:

$$S_{y.x} = S_y(1 - r^2)^{1/2} \tag{2}$$

567

where: S_y is the standard deviation of the criterion variable and r is the correlation coefficient between the predictor and criterion variables.

The smaller the value of the standard error of estimate, the more accurate the prediction. It is clear that if the correlation between the predictor and the criterion variable is $+1.0$, then the standard error of estimate would be zero. If the correlation coefficient were zero, however, then the standard error of estimate would be equal to the standard deviation of the criterion variable. The standard error of estimate is often used in connection with the predicted criterion score ($\hat{Y}$) to establish limits within which an individual's predicted criterion score can be expected to lie with a particular level of confidence. The establishment of such confidence limits is based upon the theory of the normal curve. In much practical prediction work, two standard errors of estimate ($2 . S_{y \cdot x}$) are added and subtracted from $\hat{Y}$ to establish an interval within which one can be 95 percent confident that an individual's predicted score on the criterion variable will lie.

The regression equation is one way of using information from a simple prediction study. Another means of using information from a simple prediction study is an expectancy table. An expectancy table is essentially a form of scatter diagram that displays the relationship between the predictor and criterion variables in percentage terms so that one can estimate the chances of obtaining a particular level of performance on the criterion variable given a particular level of performance on the predictor. An example of an expectancy table is shown in Table 1. Thus, if a student scored in the second quarter on the predictor variable, there are 14 chances in 100 that he or she would score in the lowest quarter on the criterion, 26 chances in 100 of being in the third quarter on the criterion, 32 chances in 100 of scoring in the second quarter on the criterion, and 28 chances in 100 of scoring in the top quarter on the criterion. An individual as well as a research worker can use an expectancy table to estimate the chances of achieving particular levels of performance on the criterion given a particular level of performance on the predictor variable. The values in the cells of an expectancy table will change with changes in the magnitude of the correlation between the predictor and criterion variable. The example in Table 1 is based on a correlation of 0.60 between the predictor and criterion variables.

Table 1
Expectancy table for predictor and criterion variables ($r = 0.60$)

Quarter on predictor	Quarter on criterion			
	Lowest	3rd	2nd	Top
Top	4	14	28	54
2nd	14	26	32	28
3rd	28	32	26	14
Lowest	54	28	14	4

The regression equation and the correlation coefficient in a simple prediction study (one predictor and one criterion variable) are usually estimated by simple linear regression analysis. This statistical procedure assumes that there is a straight line relationship between the two variables. This has been found to be satisfactory for many purposes. However, there is no requirement that the relationship between the variables should be linear. There are a number of nonlinear ways of handling the data from even a simple prediction study (Pedhazur 1982). It is usually recommended that an investigator study the shape of the scatter diagram for the predictor and criterion variables and select a statistical model that will best reflect the nature of the relationship between the variables.

The example described in some detail above—a single predictor variable and a single criterion variable—is the simplest of all prediction paradigms. Yet, as can be seen, it can be rather complex. As one moves towards more complex prediction studies, the situation becomes increasingly complicated. In the next level of prediction study, there are several continuous quantitative predictor variables and a single continuous quantitative criterion variable. The basic procedures of conducting such a study are similar to those for a simple prediction study. The two major differences are: (a) information about several predictor variables is gathered and, (b) multiple rather than simple regression analysis procedures are used. Multiple regression analysis is similar to simple regression analysis except that a weighted composite of the predictor variables is sought that will correlate maximally with the criterion variable. One of the chief tasks in multiple regression analysis is to determine the set of weights that, when applied to the predictor variables, will maximize the correlation between the composite of the predictor variables and the criterion. The analytic procedures for achieving this goal are presented elsewhere (Pedhazur 1982). Multiple regression analysis is a rather general data analytic procedure that can be applied not only to continuous quantitative variables such as test scores but also to qualitative discrete predictor variables such as type of course enrolled in and categories of father's occupation. The special technique that permits handling of such variables is called dummy variable coding (Pedhazur 1982). Multiple regression analysis allows one to estimate the contribution that each predictor variable makes to the estimation of the criterion variable and also allows the development of a prediction equation that will best estimate the criterion variable with the smallest number of predictor variables. The general form of a multiple regression equation is:

$$Y = a + b_1 X_1 + b_2 X_2 + \cdots + b_k X_k \qquad (3)$$

where: Y and a were defined previously; $b_1, b_2, \ldots, b_k$ are regression weights for the predictor variables; and $X_1, X_2, \ldots, X_k$ are values of the various predictor variables for an individual.

Generally, multiple regression analysis is used to develop a linear prediction of a criterion variable from a set of predictor variables. However, regression analysis procedures can be used when the relationships between variables are nonlinear. Various transformations can be readily applied to handle nonlinear variables (Pedhazur 1982). In addition to the regression equation described above, multiple regression analysis will also yield a coefficient of multiple correlation (R) that describes the relationship between the set of predictor variables and the criterion variable and a standard error of estimate that permits one to establish confidence limits for the prediction of individual criterion variable scores.

Both simple and multiple regression analysis have as their goal the prediction of an individual's status on a single continuous quantitative criterion variable. The difference between the two procedures hinges on whether there is one or more than one predictor variable. In contrast, there are prediction situations in which the criterion variable is categorical in nature. Consider a situation in which a counselor is advising a student about a career choice. The counselor would have information about the student such as achievement in various courses, some indicator of ability, and perhaps interest test scores. These would serve as predictor variables. The criterion variable, career choice, consists of a set of categories that do not constitute a continuum. Such categories might be medicine, engineering, commerce, architecture, law, and so on. The goal of prediction is to help the student to select a career choice in which he or she is likely to succeed and achieve satisfaction. Regression analysis procedures would be useless in such a situation because of the categorical nature of the criterion variable. The appropriate statistical procedure for analyzing data from a prediction study in which one wishes to estimate an individual's membership in a group is multiple discriminant analysis. This technique uses a set of predictor variables that can be quantitative or categorical to predict the group to which an individual is most likely to belong. These results can then be compared to the group of which the individual has elected to become a member in much the same way that predicted and actual criterion variable scores on continuous quantitative variables can be compared. While the mathematics of multiple discriminant analysis are fairly complex and require the use of computers, there are standard programs available for such analyses (Nie et al. 1975).

In general, there is considerably more work in predicting group membership than in predicting status on a continuous quantitative variable. The usual reason given for this differential is that the mathematics are rather elaborate and complex and had to await the development of high-speed electronic computers and statistical programs to perform the necessary calculations. The need to make such predictions, however, has long been recognized. Whether there will be more applied work in the area in the future remains to be seen.

One common element in the prediction situations described above is the existence of a single criterion variable to be predicted. Even in the case of predicting an individual's group membership, there is the single criterion variable, group membership. The specific categories of group membership are somewhat analogous to the different score levels of a continuous quantitative criterion variable. In the last situation to be described, there is more than one criterion variable to be predicted. This situation involves the prediction of an individual's profile on a set of criterion variables on the basis of his or her performance on a set of predictor variables. Such prediction is possible using a statistical procedure called canonical correlation analysis (Cooley and Lohnes 1971). Canonical correlation seeks, by appropriate weighting of both the predictor and criterion variables, to maximize the correlation between the two linear composites based on the sets of variables. The computations involved in carrying out a canonical correlation analysis are complex and require the use of a computer although a few heroic studies were done by hand (Thorndike 1949).

In canonical correlation one is concerned with predicting an individual's performance on a set of criterion variables. There has been little use of canonical correlation in prediction work. Besides the arduous computational burden involved, there appear to be few situations in which it has been considered necessary or desirable to predict performance on a number of criterion variables. Rather, the tendency has been to express performance on a single composite criterion and to use this in a multiple regression analysis. This is perhaps unfortunate since the reduction of criterion performance to a single variable undoubtedly results in a loss of information. This is especially true when different aspects of a criterion performance are not highly related to one another. On the other hand, inclusion of a number of criterion variables in a prediction situation can lead to rather strange results sometimes since the weights that are obtained for both the predictor and criterion variables are mathematically derived. If the weights, especially the ones for the criterion variables, do not accord with the weights that would judgmentally be given these variables then the weights given to predictors can be misleading and, in some cases, meaningless. For example, suppose one were interested in predicting a number of aspects of a student's performance in a mathematics course. One would have as predictor variables, say, measures of various abilities. The criterion variables may be scores on tests of mathematical concepts, mathematical computation, and problem solving. A canonical correlation analysis might result in a high correlation between the two sets of variables but this might be due to a high weight being given to the mathematical computation test score and low weights to the other criterion variables. If the instructional goals of the program stressed problem-solving and computational skills only minimally, the prediction would not be useful. Thus, there are some dangers in the blind use of canonical correlation in prediction research.

Prediction has been a major goal of research in education. Institutions all over the world routinely conduct prediction studies and use the results for selection, placement, and classification. Such work can be expected to continue and expand. The goal of all prediction research is to enable educators to make the soundest possible decisions on the basis of empirical evidence.

See also: Validity; Multivariate Analysis

Bibliography

Anastasi A 1982 *Psychological Testing*, 5th edn. Macmillan, New York

Cooley W W, Lohnes P R 1971 *Multivariate Data Analysis*. Wiley, New York
Mosier C I 1951 Problems and designs of cross-validation. *Educ. Psychol. Meas.* 11: 5–11
Nie N H, Hull C H, Jenkins J G, Steinbrenner K, Bent D H 1975 *Statistical Package for the Social Sciences*, 2nd edn. McGraw-Hill, New York
Pedhazur E J 1982 *Multiple Regression in Behavioral Research*, 2nd edn. Holt, Rinehart and Winston, New York
Thorndike R L 1949 *Personnel Selection: Test and Measurement Techniques*. Wiley, New York
Thorndike R L 1982 *Applied Psychometrics*. Houghton-Mifflin, Boston, Massachusetts

Multitrait–Multimethod Analysis

H. W. Marsh

Multitrait–multimethod (MTMM) analysis is used to test the construct validity of interpretations of test scores. Campbell and Fiske (1959) argued that the demonstration of construct validity requires both convergent and discriminant validity. They proposed collecting measures of two or more traits (T1, T2, etc.) each of which is assessed by two or more methods (M1, M2, etc.). Multiple indicators of the same trait should be substantially correlated with each other (convergent validity) whereas indicators of different traits should be sufficiently distinct as to allow differentiation among the traits (discriminant validity). Method/halo effects are inferred when correlations among the different traits are higher when measured by the same method than when measured by different methods. These inferences are based on inspection or analysis of the MTMM matrix of correlations among these measures. In this article the Campbell–Fiske analysis of variance, (ANOVA), and confirmatory factor analysis (CFA) approaches to MTMM analyses are critically evaluated, and new approaches are described.

For purposes of illustration, a MTMM matrix based on the Byrne and Shavelson (1986) study is presented in Table 1. There are three traits: School self-concept (T1), Verbal self-concept (T2) and Math self-concept (T3), and three methods: three different self-concept instruments (M1, M2, M3). The MTMM matrix contains correlations among these M × T measures. It is divided into triangular submatrices of relations among measures assessed with the same method, and square submatrices of relations among measures assessed with different methods. Adopting the Campbell and Fiske terminology, there are four types of coefficients: (a) monotrait–monomethod coefficients: reliability estimates (the values in parentheses along the diagonal of the triangular submatrices) or 1.0s if no reliability estimates are available; (b) heterotrait–monomethod coefficients: the off-diagonal coefficients of the triangular submatrices; (c) monotrait–heteromethod coefficients or convergent validities: the values in the diagonals of the square submatrices; and (d) heterotrait–heteromethod coefficients: the off-diagonal coefficients of the square submatrices.

1. The Campbell–Fiske Guidelines for Evaluating *MTMM Matrices*

Campbell and Fiske (1959) proposed four criteria for evaluating MTMM matrices and inferring support or nonsupport for convergent and discriminant validity. These are applied to the MTMM data in Table 1. An additional criterion designed to infer method effects that was also proposed by Campbell and Fiske but not previously presented as one of their criteria is also presented.

1.1 Convergent Validity Criterion

Criterion 1a: the convergent validity coefficients should be statistically significant and sufficiently large to warrant further examination of validity. Failure of this criterion suggests that different measures are measuring different constructs and implies a lack of validity for at least some of the measures. Satisfaction of this criterion is a prerequisite to the consideration of other criteria. In Table 1 all nine convergent validities are statistically significant, varying between 0.54 and 0.87 (mean $r = 0.70$), thus providing strong support for this criterion.

1.2 Discriminant Validity Criteria

Criterion 2a: the convergent validities should be higher than correlations between different traits measured by different methods. The failure of this criterion implies that agreement on a particular trait is not independent of agreement on other traits, suggesting that agreement can be explained by true trait correlations and/or shared method effects. For T = 3 and M = 3 this criterion requires each convergent validity to be higher than the other four coefficients in the same row and column of the square submatrix. Because convergent validities (mean $r = 0.70$) are higher than the correlations with which they are compared (mean $r = 0.31$) in all 36 of these comparisons, there is good support for this criterion of discriminant validity.

Criterion 2b: the convergent validities should be higher than correlations between different traits assessed by the same method. Violations of this criterion suggest that there are true trait correlations and/or method effects. Where heterotrait–monomethod correlations approach the reliability estimates there is evidence of a strong method effect. In Table 1 this criterion requires each convergent validity to be higher than the four comparison coefficients in the same row and column of the corresponding triangular submatrices. Because the convergent validities (mean $r = 0.70$) are higher than the correlations with which they are compared (mean $r = 0.35$) for 33 of 36 comparisons, there is reasonable support for this criterion. All three failures involve M3 where correlations among the traits (mean $r = 0.44$) are higher than for M1 (0.28) or M2 (0.33).

Criterion 2c: the pattern of correlations among traits should be similar for the same and different methods. Assuming that there are significant correlations, satisfaction of this criterion suggests true trait correlations that are independent of the method of assessment whereas failure suggests that the observed correlations are differentially affected by method effects. When the number of traits is small this criterion is typically examined by inspection of the rank order of correlations (e.g., Sullivan and Feldman 1979), but Marsh (1982) correlated the correlations to obtain a more precise index of similarity when the number of traits was large. In Table 1 all correlations between Math and Verbal self-concepts are small (mean $r = 0.06$) whereas school self-concept is significantly and consistently correlated with both math (mean $r = 0.45$) and verbal (mean $r = 0.42$) self-concepts. These results, particularly since they support a priori hypotheses about the pattern of correlations, provide clear support for this criterion.

1.3 Method Effects

Criterion 3a: Campbell and Fiske (1959 p. 85) stated that "the presence of method variance is indicated by the difference in level of correlation between parallel values of the monomethod block and the heteromethod block, assuming comparable reliabilities among the tests." In operationalizing this criterion for the data in Table 1, for example, the T1–M1/T2–M1 correlation was compared to the T1–M1/T2–M2, T1–M2/T2–M1, T1–M1/T2–M3, and T1–M3/T2–M1 correlations. In this manner each of the nine heterotrait–monomethod correlations was compared to four heterotrait–heteromethod correlations. For 26 of these 36 comparisons heterotrait–monomethod correlations (mean $r = 0.35$) were larger than the heterotrait–heteromethod correlations (mean $r = 0.31$), suggesting weak method effects. However, the method effect for M3 (mean $r = 0.44$, 12 of 12 comparisons larger) is larger than for M2 (mean $r = 0.33$, 10 of 12 comparisons larger) and the method effect for M1 (mean $r = 0.28$, 4 of 12 comparisons larger) is negligible.

2. Problems with the Campbell–Fiske Criteria

The Campbell–Fiske criteria continue to be widely used and inferences based on them will be accurate in many instances. Because of their popularity, ease of application, intuitive appeal, heuristic value, and wide recognition, it is recommended that these criteria should be applied as an initial step in MTMM studies even when more sophisticated approaches are used. If inferences based on the Campbell–Fiske criteria do not agree with those based on other analytic approaches, then the appropriateness of both approaches should be more fully examined. Nevertheless, the following issues represent important limitations to the Campbell–Fiske criteria.

2.1 The Number of Comparisons

For T = 3 and M = 3, criteria 2a and 2b required a total of 72 comparisons between convergent validities and other correlations. However, these comparisons are not

---

Table 1
Multitrait–multimethod correlation matrix [a]

Variables	t1m1	t2m1	t3m1	t1m2	t2m2	t3m2	t1m3	t2m3	t3m3
Method 1									
t1m1	(89)[b]								
t2m1	384[c]	(81)[b]							
t3m1	441[c]	002[c]	(92)[b]						
Method 2									
t1m2	662[d]	368[e]	353[e]	(84)[b]					
t2m2	438[e]	703[d]	008[e]	441[c]	(89)[b]				
t3m2	465[e]	069[e]	871[d]	424[c]	136[c]	(95)[b]			
Method 3									
t1m3	678[d]	331[e]	478[e]	550[d]	380[e]	513[e]	(87)[b]		
t2m3	458[e]	541[d]	057[e]	381[d]	658[e]	096[d]	584[c]	(90)[b]	
t3m3	414[e]	027[e]	825[d]	372[e]	029[e]	810[d]	582[c]	135[c]	(94)[b]

a Source: Byrne and Shavelson (1986)

The nine MTMM variables are scale scores representing all combinations of the three traits corresponding to school self-concept (T1), verbal self-concept (T2), and math self-concept (T3) assessed by three methods corresponding to three self-concept instruments (M1, M2, M3). For $N = 817$, correlations (presented without decimal points) greater than 0.07 are statistically significant ($p < 0.05$).
b Monotrait–monomethod coefficients or reliability estimates
c Heterotrait–monomethod coefficients
d Monotrait–heteromethod coefficients or convergent validities
e Heterotrait–heteromethod coefficients

tests of statistical significance and appropriate significance tests would be difficult to devise for so many non-independent comparisons. Furthermore, the number of comparisons goes up geometrically with the number of traits and methods. For example, 3164 comparisons are required for T = 12 and M = 4 (Marsh et al. 1985). The researcher must then decide what proportion of failures is acceptably low or what mean difference between convergent validities and comparison coefficients is sufficiently large to warrant support of a criterion. This decision is somewhat arbitrary.

2.2 Correlated Traits and Discriminant Validity

Campbell and Fiske (1959) distinguish between method variance, trait variance, and trait covariance. Method variance associated with a particular method of assessment is detrimental to discriminant validity, but does not preclude it. True trait variance, the correlation between different measures of the same trait that is independent of method variance, is good but does not imply discriminant validity. True trait covariation, the true correlation between different traits that is independent of method effects, will increase the likelihood of failures of criteria 2a and 2b. However, criterion 2c specifically tests for true trait covariation and is interpreted as support for discriminant validity. A complete lack of true trait covariation or trait correlations approaching the reliability of the measures makes interpretation simple, but is unlikely. Because true trait correlations are unknown, there is not even a standard against which to judge observed trait correlations. The existence of true trait covariance is typical in MTMM studies and its interpretation in relation to discriminant validity is ambiguous.

2.3 Equally Reliable Measures

Campbell and Fiske (1959) noted that the application of their criteria implicitly assumes the measures to be equally reliable. If the reliabilities differ substantially then inferences based on the criteria may be invalid. For example, correlations among traits assessed with a more reliable method may produce higher intertrait correlations than a less reliable method, and thus give the impression of larger method effects. In some instances the MTMM matrix may be corrected for unreliability (Althauser and Heberlein 1970) but CFA approaches described later may provide a better solution.

2.4 Inferences Based on Observed Correlations

The validity of inferences based on the Campbell–Fiske criteria depends on the behavior of the underlying constructs (Althauser and Heberlein 1970, Alwin 1974, Sullivan and Feldman 1979). These researchers posited causal path models for MTMM data (similar to that in Table 2 which will be discussed later), derived algebraic expressions of the correlations used in the Campbell and Fiske criteria, and specified the conditions under which inferences were likely to be valid.

Convergent validities reflect true trait variance but may also reflect shared method effects. Depending on the assumed causal path model, the influence of shared method effects on an observed convergent validity is the product of the size of each method effect and the correlation between the methods. Inferences will probably be valid only if method effects are small or if method effects are relatively uncorrelated. Even if convergent validity does not reflect shared method effects, it may represent agreement on a trait other than the one intended (Sullivan and Feldman 1979). Hence, criterion 1a provides only preliminary and insufficient evidence that convergent validities reflect true trait variance.

Inferences based on criteria 2a, 2b, and 2c are also complicated by the effects of shared method effects. Inferences based on all three criteria will generally be valid if method effects are small and/or uncorrelated. Alwin (1974) argues that inferences will generally be valid if method effects are approximately equal in size. Sullivan and Feldman (1979, also see Althauser and Herberlein 1970) argued that inferences based on criterion 2b will be valid so long as the direction of the method effects is the same on different measures, but that inferences based on criteria 2a and 2c will typically not be valid. The disagreement between Alwin (1974) and Sullivan and Feldman (1979) apparently stems from their respective interpretations of the intent of the discriminant validity criteria. Sullivan and Feldman argued that criteria 2a and 2c are invalid, and that 2b is valid, in relation to detecting method effects. Alwin argued that the purpose of these criteria is to compare the relative size of true trait variances and covariances so that method effects are nullified so long as they are constant. In support of his contention Alwin noted that Campbell and Fiske (1959) inferred method effects from the comparison operationalized here in criterion 3a.

For criterion 3a inferences about method effects may be complicated by true trait covariation. If trait variance is small, inferences will probably be valid but of little interest. If traits are uncorrelated or if the trait effects are of a similar size, then the inferences probably will be valid. If true trait covariation is large and true trait effects differ substantially, then this comparison is likely to be biased and the direction of the bias will depend on the size of true trait effects. Whereas such a bias for any one comparison may be either positive or negative, this will tend to cancel out for inferences across the entire set of comparisons so that overall inferences will generally be valid.

2.5 Trait/Method Correlations and Interactions

Interpretations of the discriminant validity criteria summarized above are based on the assumption that traits are uncorrelated with method effects. While this assumption may be substantively reasonable in some applications, its justification is primarily pragmatic rather than substantive. Without such an assumption the interpretation of the criteria is more complicated and apparently more problematic, but the effect of its violation on the inferences is not well documented (see Althauser and Heberlein 1970).

Campbell and O'Connell (1967) also proposed that traits and methods may interact. Trait/method interactions are different from trait/method correlations. Trait/method correlations imply that there is an overlap in the variance that can be explained by the main effects of traits and methods, whereas trait/method interactions imply that additional variance can be explained by trait/method crossproducts. Multiplicative relations between traits and methods further complicate the interpretation of the Campbell–Fiske criteria and other approaches to MTMM data. Browne (1984) described a series of product models designed to test such multiplicative relations. Browne's approach is difficult to evaluate because his study is apparently the only application of the approach, and because the computer software for evaluating the parameters is not generally available. Whatever the eventual evaluation of Browne's approach, the concern is an important issue that has been largely ignored in MTMM studies.

3. The ANOVA Model for MTMM Data

Multitrait–multimethod data can be analyzed with a three-factor unreplicated ANOVA and the ANOVA terms can be computed directly form the MTMM matrix (Kavanagh et al. 1981, Marsh and Hocevar 1983, Schmitt and Stults 1986). When measures for all levels of traits and methods are obtained for the same subject, three orthogonal sources of variation can be estimated. The main effect of subjects is a test of whether there are significant differences between subjects for measures averaged across traits and methods, and is used to infer convergent validity. The subject × trait interaction tests whether differences between subjects depend on traits, and is used to infer discriminant validity. If it is nonsignificant then the traits have no differential validity, in that subjects are ranked the same for all traits. The subject × method interaction tests whether differentiation depends on the method of assessment, and is used to infer method effects. If it is significant then the method effects introduce a systematic source of undesirable variance. The three-way interaction is assumed to reflect only random error such that differentiation does not depend on specific trait–method combinations. The main effects due to traits and methods are rarely of substantive interest and are necessarily zero for standardized data.

The advantages of the ANOVA approach are its ease of application and the convenient summary statistics used to infer convergent, divergent, and method/halo effects. Schmitt and Stults (1986) noted that the approach provides only a global evaluation of the variance components and does not allow the evaluation of individual measures. This approach has major limitations in that it assumes that: (a) measures are perfectly reliable (or at least equally reliable); (b) the three-way interaction reflects only random error; and (c) traits are uncorrelated, methods are uncorrelated, and traits are uncorrelated with methods. These assumptions are typically untested, but problems associated with the first

two may be overcome. Particularly if the MTMM variables differ substantially in reliability, analysis of disattenuated data may be justified (Marsh and Hocevar 1983) though significance tests may no longer be justified. Independent estimates of the three-way interaction and the error term can be derived if the MTMM design is replicated (e.g., data are collected for parallel forms or at more than one point in time). There is, however, no apparent resolution to the typically unjustified assumptions of uncorrelated traits and methods, and the implications of such violations are not well known .

The ANOVA model cannot be recommended. Important limitations of the ANOVA model may be overlooked in the model's apparent but deceptive simplicity and precision. The unfortunate linking of the ANOVA effects to the Campbell–Fiske terminology is inappropriate. The convergent, discriminant, and method/halo effects in the ANOVA model are not the same as those inferred from the Campbell–Fiske criteria even though the two approaches may lead to the same conclusions (see Marsh and Hocevar 1983). Further development of the ANOVA model should eliminate use of the Campbell–Fiske terminology, evaluate more fully the validity of inferences in relation to the model's assumptions, and align the approach more closely to the conceptually similar generalizability theory (e.g., Cronbach et al. 1972).

4. Confirmatory Factor Analysis (CFA) of MTMM Data

Multitrait–multimethod matrices, like other correlation matrices, can be factor analyzed to infer the underlying dimensions. Factors defined by different measures of the same trait suggest trait effects, whereas factors defined by measures assessed with the same method suggest method/halo effects. With CFA the researcher can define models that posit a priori trait and/or method factors, and test the ability of such models to fit the data. However, critical problems in the CFA approach are the assumptions underlying the proposed models, technical difficulties in the estimation of parameters, and the validity of inferences based on the parameters.

4.1 The General CFA Model for MTMM Data

In the general MTMM model (Table 1) adapted from Jöreskog (1974) (also see Marsh and Hocevar 1983, Widaman 1985): (a) there are at least three traits (T = 3) and 3 methods (M = 3); (b) T × M measured variables are used to infer T + M a priori factors; (c) each measured variable loads on one trait factor and one method factor but is constrained so as not to load on any other factors; (d) correlations among trait factors and among method factors are freely estimated, but correlations between trait and method factors are fixed to be zero. Alternative models have been proposed when there are only two methods (Kenny 1979) or only two traits (Marsh and Hocevar 1983). While some researchers have estimated correlations between trait and method factors, there are important logical, interpretive, and pragmatic reasons for fixing these correlations to be zero (Marsh and Hocevar 1983, Schmitt and Stults 1986, Widaman 1985). This constraint allows the decomposition of variance into additive trait, method, and error components. When this constraint is not imposed there are typically improper solutions and Widaman suggests that such a model may not be identified. However, as with the evaluation of the Campbell–Fiske and ANOVA approaches, the basis of this assumption is largely pragmatic, the assumption is typically untested, and the implications of its violation are not well known.

Confirmatory factor analysis models for MTMM data can be defined in terms of three design matrices. Adopting the terminology of linear structural relations analysis (LISREL) (Jöreskog and Sörbom 1981), the three design matrices for Model 4D (Table 2) with T = 3 traits and M = 3 methods are: (a) Λ y, a 9 by 6 matrix of factor loadings, where number of rows = M + T = number of measured variables and number of columns = M × T = number of factors; (b) Ψ a 6 by 6 variance–covariance matrix of relations among the six factors; and (c) Θ, a 9 by 9 matrix of error/uniquenesses among the nine measured variables in which the diagonal values are analogous to one minus the communality estimates in exploratory factor analysis. All parameters (Table 2) with values of 0 or 1 are fixed and values for other parameters are estimated so as to maximize goodness-of-fit. Standard errors are estimated for all estimated parameters but not for parameters with fixed values. This model is easily modified to accommodate more traits or methods, or to conform to other models and other parameterizations to be described.

4.2 A Taxonomy of Alternative Models

Researchers have proposed many variations of the general MTMM model to examine inferences about trait or method variance or to test substantive issues specific to a particular study (e.g., Jöreskog 1974, Marsh et al. 1985, Marsh and Hocevar 1983, Widaman 1985). Widaman proposed a taxonomy of models that systematically varied different characteristics of the trait and method factors. This taxonomy was designed to be appropriate for all MTMM studies, to provide a general framework for making inferences about the effects of trait and method factors, and to objectify the complicated task of formulating models and representing the MTMM data. An expanded version of Widaman's taxonomy (see Table 3) represents all possible combinations of four trait structures (trait structures 1 – 4) and five method structures (method structures A – E). The four trait structures posit no trait factors (1), one general trait factor defined by all measured variables (2), T uncorrelated trait factors (3), and T correlated trait factors (4). The five method structures posit no method factors (A), one general method factor defined by all measured variables (B), M uncorrelated method variables (C), M correlated method factors (D), and method effects inferred on the basis of correlated error/uniqueness (E). This taxonomy differs from Widaman's original taxonomy only in the addition of method structure E.

Table 2

Parameters to be estimated for the general MTMM model (Model 4D)

	(a) Factor Loadings (Λ y)						(c) Error/Uniquenesses (Θ)								
Variables	T1	T2	T3	M1	M2	M3	t1m1	t2m1	t3m1	t1m2	t2m2	t3m2	t1m3	t2m3	t3m3
t1m1	LY[a]	0	0	LY	0	0	TE								
t2m1	0	LY	0	LY[a]	0	0	0[b]	TE							
t3m1	0	0	LY	LY	0	0	0[b]	0[b]	TE						
t1m2	LY	0	0	0	LY	0	0	0	0	TE					
t2m2	0	LY[a]	0	0	LY	0	0	0	0	0[b]	TE				
t3m2	0	0	LY	0	LY[a]	0	0	0	0	0[b]	0[b]	TE			
t1m3	LY	0	0	0	0	LY[a]	0	0	0	0	0	0	TE		
t2m3	0	LY	0	0	0	LY	0	0	0	0	0	0	0[b]	TE	
t3m3	0	0	LY[a]	0	0	LY	0	0	0	0	0	0	0[b]	0[b]	TE

(b) Factor Variance/Covariances (Ψ)						
Factors	T1	T2	T3	M1	M2	M3
T1	1[c]					
T2	PS	1[c]				
T3	PS	PS	1[c]			
M1	0	0	0	1[c]		
M2	0	0	0	PS	1[c]	
M3	0	0	0	PS	PS	1[c]

Confirmatory factor analysis (CFA) models to be considered in this investigation can be defined in terms of the three design matrices presented here. The MTMM problem shown here has three traits factors (T1–T3) and three method factors (M1–M3) that are defined in terms of the nine measured variables (t1m1–t3m3). All parameters with values of 0 or 1 are fixed and not estimated whereas all other parameters are estimated without constraint. The parameterization shown here, with factor variances (in Ψ) fixed to be 1, is referred to as the fixed factor variance parameterization.
a For the fixed factor loading parameterization these factor loadings would be fixed to be 1 and factor variances would be freed
b For method structure E (see Table 3) these correlations between error/uniquenesses would be estimated, and the method factors and their associated parameters would be eliminated from Λ y and Ψ.
c For the fixed factor variance parameterization these factor variances would be fixed to be 1 and no factor loadings would be fixed to 1

The general factors may present problems. Widaman (1985) constrained each general factor to be uncorrelated with all other factors and the rationale for this constraint is consistent with the requirement that trait and method correlations be uncorrelated. Models 1B and 2A posit one general method factor and one general trait factor respectively. However, because both models contain one general factor defined by all measured variables, they are identical. Model 2B posits two general factors, but the model is not identified unless other constraints are imposed. Unless there is a substantive basis for imposing these constraints, the interpretation of the general factors may be problematic.

5. Goodness-of-fit

Many indices of a model's goodness-of-fit are used in CFA , but there are no well-established guidelines for what minimal conditions constitute an adequate fit. The general approach is to:

(a) evaluate whether the solution is well-defined by establishing that: the model is identified, the iterative estimation procedure converges, parameter estimates are within the range of permissible values, and the size of the standard error of each parameter estimate is reasonable;

(b) examine the parameter estimates in relation to the substantive a priori model and common sense;

(c) evaluate the χ^2 and subjective indices of fit for the model and compare these to values obtained from alternative models.

In the application of CFA to MTMM data there is an unfortunate tendency to de-emphasize the first two points. If a solution is ill-defined, then further interpretations must be made cautiously if at all. If the parameter estimates make no sense in relation to the substantive a priori model, then fit may be irrelevant. For example, if two indicators of the same trait factor are supposed to load in the same direction, but actually load in the opposite direction, then the results do not support the construct validity of the trait even if the model fits the data well. In this respect, the first criterion is a prerequisite for the next two and the second criterion is a prerequisite for the third.

Goodness-of-fit is evaluated in part with an overall χ^2 test. As typically employed, the posited model is rejected if the χ^2 is large relative to the degrees of freedom (df), and accepted if the χ^2 is small or nonsignificant. However, hypothesized models such as those in Table 3 are best regarded as approximations to reality rather than exact statements of truth, so that any model can be

Table 3
Taxonomy of structural models for MTMM data[e]

Trait Structure	Method Structure				
	A	B[a]	C	D	E[d]
1[a]	1A null model	1B[b]1 general M-factor	1C M uncorrelated M-factors	1D M correlated M-factors	1E T × M correlated errors
2	2A[b] 1 general T-factor	2B[c]2 general factors	2C 1 general T-factor, M uncorrelated M-factors	2D 1 general T-factor, M correlated M-factors	2E T × M correlated errors, 1 general T-factor
3	3A T uncorrelated T-factors	3B 1 general M-factor, T uncorrelated T-factors	3C T uncorrelated T-factors M uncorrelated M-factors	3D T uncorrelated T-factors, M correlated M-factors	3E T × M correlated errors, T uncorrelated T-factors
4	4A T correlated T-factors	4B 1 general M-factor, T correlated T-factors	4C T correlated T-factors, M uncorrelated M-factors	4D T correlated T-factors, M correlated M-factors	4E T × M correlated errors, T correlated T-factors

a General factors are defined to be uncorrelated with other factors in the model. Although general factors are posited to represent either trait variance or method variance, this assumption will not always be accurate and may be difficult to test
b Models 2A and 1B are equivalent, and it is generally not possible to determine whether the one general factor reflects trait variance, method variance or some combination of trait and method variance
c Model 2B requires additional constraints that may be arbitrary and that may not provide equivalent solutions. Hence its usefulness may be dubious unless there is an a priori basis for the constraints.
d Models under method structure E have no method factors. Instead method effects are inferred on the basis of correlated error/uniquenesses (see Table 2). This method structure, particularly when there are three traits, corresponds most closely to method structure C in which there are M uncorrelated methods.
e Adapted from Widaman (1985)

rejected if the sample size is sufficiently large. Conversely, almost any model will be "accepted" if the sample size is sufficiently small. From this perspective Cudeck and Browne (1983) argued that it is preferable to depart from the hypothesis testing approach that assumes that any model will exactly fit the data.

As described by Bentler and Bonett (1980), when two models are nested the statistical significance of the difference in the χ^2s can be tested relative to the difference in their df. Widaman (1985) emphasized this feature in developing his taxonomy of MTMM models and in comparing the fit of different models. However, the problems associated with hypothesis testing based on the χ^2 statistic also apply to tests of χ^2 differences. Furthermore, many important comparisons are not nested and so cannot be compared using this procedure. For example, whereas Models 4A (trait factors only) and 1D (method factors only) are each nested under Model 4D, neither is nested under the other.

6. Poorly-defined Solutions

Identification requires that each unknown parameter (e.g., the free parameters in Table 1) is uniquely determined by the sample covariance matrix (see Kenny 1979). Jöreskog and Sörbom (1981) described checks for indentification that are performed by their LISREL program, but there are no generally necessary and sufficient conditions for establishing that a model is identified, and these checks are fallible. Even when the model is apparently identified, the empirical solution may be poorly defined or "empirically underidentified" (Kenny 1979) such that the iterative procedure used to estimate parameters fails to converge, parameter estimates are outside their permissible range of values, or parameter estimates have excessively large standard errors. Such problems are more likely when: the sample size is small, there are few indicators of each latent factor, measured variables are allowed to load on more than one factor, measured variables are highly correlated, covariance matrices are estimated with pairwise deletion for missing data, and/or the model is misspecified. Knowingly or unknowingly such problems are usually ignored in MTMM studies, and the implications of this practice have not been explored. However, recently developed reparameterizations of CFA models may eliminate some of these problems.

6.1 The Standard Parameterizations

In order for the models in Table 3 to be identified, one parameter for each latent factor must be fixed — typically at a value of 1.0 (see Jöreskog and Sörbom 1981, Long 1983). This is usually done by: (a) fixing the factor loading (in Λ y) of one measured variable for each latent factor to be 1.0 and estimating the factor variance (in Ψ), or (b) fixing the factor variance of each latent factor to be 1.0 so that Ψ is a correlation matrix, and estimating all the factor loadings. So long as the CFA solution is well-defined, both standard parameterizations are

equivalent. The two parameterizations may behave differently, however, when a factor variance estimate is close to zero or negative. Fixing factor loadings may result in an improper solution due to negative estimates of factor variances, whereas fixing factor variance estimates to be 1.0 eliminates this possibility. Consistent with this observation Marsh (1986) reported that solutions were better behaved for the fixed factor variance parameterization than for the fixed factor loading parameterization.

6.2 The Rindskopf Parameterization

Rindskopf (1983) (see also Jöreskog 1981) proposed a solution for negative error/uniqueness estimates that was used by Widaman (1985). With LISREL the error/uniqueness of each measured variable is typically estimated in the Θ matrix (Table 2) but the solution is improper if these variance estimates are negative. Rindskopf proposed an alternative parameterization of the CFA model that forces the error/uniqueness to be positive. So long as the solution is well-defined the standard parameterizations and Rindskopf parameterization should all lead to equivalent results. Because negative error/uniquenesses are frequent for MTMM data, the Rindskopf parameterization may be useful. However, Marsh (1986) found that when this parameterization was used to eliminate negative error/uniquenesses the new parameter estimates were zero (see also Jöreskog 1981) and had extremely large standard errors.

6.3 Method Structure E: an Alternative Conceptualization of Method Variance

Method variance is an undesirable source of systematic variance that inflates correlations between different traits measured with the same method. As typically depicted in MTMM models a single method factor is used to represent the method effect associated with variables assessed by the same method. The effects of a particular method of assessment are assumed to be unidimensional and the method factor loadings provide an estimate of its influence on each measured variable. Alternatively, method effects can be represented as correlated error/uniquenesses in the Θ matrix (method structure E in Tables 2 and 3). The diagonal of Θ represents error/uniquenesses for all the method structures, but in method structure E correlations between these error/uniquenesses are posited instead of method factors. Kenny (1979) proposed this method structure for the special case in which there are only two traits, but it is also reasonable when there are more than two traits.

One important advantage of method structure E is that it apparently eliminates many improper solutions without limiting the solution space or resulting in parameter estimates near the boundaries of the permissible space where estimates are typically unstable. Because method variance is one source of uniqueness, uniqueness is reflected in both method factors and error/uniquenesses. Improper solutions are frequently due to either negative method factor variances or negative error/uniquenesses, but not both. In method structure E all sources of error/uniqueness are contained in the diagonal of Θ, and this combined influence will rarely be negative or even close to zero. Marsh (1986) found no improper solutions with method structure E even when method structures C and D produced improper solutions.

Method structure E corresponds most closely to method structure C (Table 2) in that the method effects associated with one method are assumed to be uncorrelated with those of other methods. When T = 3, method structure E contains $3 \times M$ correlations between error/uniquenesses (see Table 2) and this is the same number of parameters used to define the M method factors in method structure C. So long as the solutions are well-defined method structures C and E are equivalent when T = 3. When T > 3, however, the number of correlations between error/uniquenesses in method structure E [i.e., $M \times T \times (T - 1)/2$] is greater than the number of factor loadings used to define method factors in method structure C (i.e., $T \times M$). Thus method structure C is a special case of method structure E in which one method factor is used to fit all the correlated error/uniquenesses between traits assessed with that method. If models based on method structures C and E fit the data equally well, then this assumed unidimensionality of error/uniquenesses associated with the same method is supported. However, if method structure E provides a substantially better fit, then the assumption may be unjustified. Marsh (1986) demonstrated that Model 4E provided a better fit than did Model 4C and even Model 4D in one application with T = 6.

7. Problems in the Interpretation of Trait and Method Factors

The MTMM models in Table 3 assume that: (a) method factors represent method variance, (b) trait factors represent trait variance, (c) a general factor in combination with trait factors represents method variance, and (d) a general factor in combination with method factors represents trait variance. For present purposes these assumptions are referred to as the traditional interpretation of the MTMM models. These assumptions are probably reasonable when correlations among the trait factors and among the method factors are small, but not when the correlations are substantial. Results from a study by Marsh and Ireland (1984) demonstrated this problem.

Marsh and Ireland (1984) and Marsh (1986) asked six teachers (the multiple methods) to evaluate student essays on six components of writing effectiveness (the multiple traits). In support of convergent validity, teacher agreement was substantial on each trait and on a global rating, and teacher ratings were substantially correlated with an external validity criterion. There was, however, little or no support for discriminant validity. In apparent contradiction of this interpretation, most of the variance in Model 4D was explained by method factors, implying a lack of convergent validity. However, there were large correlations among these so-called

method factors that were substantively inconsistent with a priori hypotheses about the method effects. Furthermore, when the external validity criterion was added to Model 4D, it was substantially correlated to the so-called method factors but much less correlated to the trait factors. These results suggested that the so-called method factors in Model 4D were really general trait factors and that the correlations between the so-called method factors represented agreement on this general trait. This counter-explanation was consistent with interpretations based on the Campbell–Fiske criteria and with teacher agreement on the global ratings, and also accounted for the high correlations between the so-called method factors and the external validity criterion in Model 4D.

In contrast to Model 4D, Models 4C and 4E required method factors to be uncorrelated. For these models most of the variance was explained by trait factors that were very highly correlated. When the external validity criterion was added to Models 4C and 4E, it was substantially correlated with trait factors and nearly uncorrelated with method factors. These results showed that the traditional interpretation of the trait and method factors was apparently wrong for Model 4D but was accurate for Models 4C and 4E. Because the fit of Model 4E was better than 4C, the assumption of the unidimensionality of errors associated with each method was unjustified. For this application, Model 4E was recommended as the most valid interpretation of the method and trait effects.

The traditional interpretation of method factors may be unjustified if:

(a) one or more of the models in Table 3 is poorly defined;

(b) interpretations based on the Campbell–Fiske guidelines and an examination of the MTMM matrix differ substantially from those based on the CFA approach;

(c) the substantive nature of the data dictates that method factors should be relatively uncorrelated (e.g., method effects associated with each of an independent set of judges) but the results show the method factors to be substantially correlated;

(d) substantive theory dictates an expected pattern of correlations among trait factors that is not supported;

(e) Model 4A (trait factors only) and 1D (method factors only) both fit the data reasonably well and Model 4D provides only a modest improvement, or the amount of variance explained by trait factors is substantially reduced by the inclusion of method factors;

(f) external validity criteria collected in addition to the MTMM variables are more substantially correlated with so-called method factors than with trait factors and there is an a priori basis for assuming the external criteria to be independent of method effects.

Violations of these criteria do not necessarily imply that the traditional interpretation is invalid, but provide a warning that the results should be interpreted cautiously. Particularly when there are violations, the substantive interpretation of the results should be given more emphasis than the assessment of fit.

8. Recommendations for the Traditional CFA Approach to MTMM Data

Since the early 1970s there has been a tremendous increase in the number of applications of CFA to MTMM data, and many researchers have argued for its advantages. This approach is epitomized in the elegant taxonomy proposed by Widaman (1985) in which a series of structured comparisons between hierarchically nested models is used to make inferences about the influence of trait and method effects. However, important unresolved problems are the technical difficulties in estimating parameters and the interpretation of so-called method effects that apparently represent the effects of trait variance in addition to, or instead of, method variance.

Most CFA studies of MTMM data posit a separate method factor to represent each method of assessment, whereas method structure E infers method effects from correlated error/uniquenesses. Method structure E has two important advantages over method structure C which it most closely resembles. First, models with method structure C are sometimes ill-defined, whereas models based on method structure E are typically well-defined. Second, when there are more than three traits, method structure E provides a test of the implicit assumption that all the correlated error/uniquenesses associated with a single method of assessment can be explained in terms of a single method factor. Model 4E, because its method effects are assumed to be uncorrelated, will usually provide a poorer fit than Model 4D, but it may better represent the MTMM data. As noted for the Marsh and Ireland (1984) data, so-called method factors from Model 4D represented trait variance so that its traditional interpretation was unjustified whereas the traditional interpretation of Model 4E was apparently valid.

The most serious problem with MTMM models examined here is the implicit assumption that specific and general method factors represent primarily the effects of method variance, whereas specific and general trait factors represent primarily the effects of trait variance. If these assumptions are violated, then the interpretation of trait and method factors in most CFA studies and the detailed comparison of nested models proposed by Widaman (1985) is unjustified. In three MTMM studies described by Marsh (1986), including reanalyses of data examined by Widaman, these assumptions were frequently violated. In all three studies the so-called method factors for at least some of the

MTMM models apparently represented trait variance in addition to or instead of method variance. This problem was particularly serious for models with correlated method factors, but perhaps not when method factors were required to be uncorrelated as in method structures C and E. Because of the potential advantages of method structure E, it is recommended as at least one of the models to be examined in CFA studies of MTMM data.

The choice of the model that best represents the MTMM data should be based primarily on substantive interpretations and secondarily on goodness-of-fit. The purpose of the MTMM models is not necessarily to provide the best fit to the data, but rather to make inferences about trait and method factors. If parameter estimates are substantively unreasonable in relation to trait and method factors, it is better to infer their effects from different models even if the fit is poorer. Particularly when both traits and methods are substantially correlated, the researcher must critically evaluate the MTMM solutions for alternative interpretations. Because the traditional interpretation of trait and method factors is frequently unjustified, the burden of proof lies with researchers to demonstrate the validity of their interpretations. However, if parameter estimates are substantively unreasonable for most of the models in the taxonomy, if the fit of most of these models is poor, or if solutions are consistently ill-defined, then the CFA approach may be inappropriate for the particular MTMM data.

9. The Use of More than One Method Variable in the Same MTMM Study

The method variable in MTMM studies can legitimately be multiple methods that are quite similar (e.g., alternative forms, split-halves, or test–retest data), and convergence refers to a level of generality normally described as reliability or stability. Alternatively, the multiple methods can be quite different (e.g., test scores, teacher ratings, and external observations), and convergence refers to a level of generality typically described as validity. Whereas MTMM studies typically consider only one method variable, Marsh (Marsh et al. 1985, Marsh and Butler 1984) argued that there are important advantages to considering a reliability-like method variable and validity-like method variable in the same study.

Marsh et al. (1985) asked each subject to provide self-ratings on 12 multi-item scales and 12 parallel single-item scales, and then to ask a significant other also to rate the subject with the same materials. Marsh and Butler (1984) examined the construct validity of the multiple scales of a diagnostic reading test by collecting test–retest data for the test and for teacher ratings of the same traits. In both studies the authors distinguished between *internal convergence* (agreement between different response modes when the rater was the same person; stability of test scores or teacher ratings) and *external convergence* (agreement between self-ratings and ratings by significant others; agreement between test scores and teacher ratings). External convergence provides a more demanding test, but if it fails then there is no way to determine whether the failure is due to an inappropriate choice of multiple methods. Internal convergence provides a weaker test, but if it fails then support for the lack of validity is stronger. In this sense internal convergence constitutes a logical upperbound for external convergence in the same way that reliability limits validity. In both studies, assessing internal and external convergence within the same study provided valuable diagnostic information about the measures and a stronger basis for testing construct validity than if only one method variable had been considered. The inclusion of more than one method variable also allows the data to be fit with CFA models that require at least three methods and would also allow the estimation of the trait/method interaction term in the ANOVA model that requires the MTMM design to be replicated.

10. The Application of Hierarchical CFA (HCFA) to MTMM Data

Confirmatory factor analysis as traditionally applied to MTMM data incorporates a single indicator of each scale (i.e., each trait/method combination) even when multiple indicators (e.g., items or subscales) are available. Potential weaknesses of this approach are the failure to: (a) test whether items or subscales accurately reflect the implicit factor structure, (b) correct appropriately for unreliability in the scale scores, (c) separate error due to low internal consistency from uniqueness due to weak trait and/or method effects. However, when analyses begin with multiple indicators of each scale, HCFA can be used to address each of these problems.

In the HCFA approach each trait/method combination is inferred from multiple items or subscales instead of from a single-scale score. First-order factors are posited that correspond to the scale scores (i.e., the trait/method combinations). Correlations among these first-order factors resemble the typical MTMM matrix except that the latent factors are: (a) optimally weighted averages of the item responses, and (b) corrected for measurement error inferred from the internal consistency of the multiple items used to define each scale. Correlations among the first-order factors are then used to infer second-order factors corresponding to trait and method factors. All the models in Table 3 and the different parameterizations for those models can be defined in terms of the HCFA approach.

In the traditional CFA approach, multiple items designed to reflect each scale are typically averaged to form scale scores and the analysis begins with these scale scores. Implicit in this process is the assumption that the actual factor structure accurately reflects the a priori structure (i.e., the one implied by how the items were combined). If this structure is not tested, then the interpretations of the MTMM data may be problematic. The failure to support discriminant validity, for example, may simply reflect an inappropriate combining of items to form scale scores. The problem is relevant to all

approaches that begin with scale scores, but it is particularly ironic that the CFA — but not the HCFA — approach suffers from this weakness.

In the traditional CFA approach to MTMM data the conceptualization of measurement error differs drastically from that of classical measurement theory. Because only one indicator per scale is considered, an internal consistency estimate of the scale's reliability cannot be estimated. Instead, the uniqueness of each scale — its observed variance that cannot be explained by either latent trait or latent method factors — is used to estimate measurement error. Thus measurement error will depend on what other scales are included in the study. In contrast, internal consistency estimates depend on the agreement among multiple indicators and are independent of the other scales included in the analysis. In the traditional CFA approach it is not possible to distinguish measurement error from uniqueness due to a lack of trait and/or method effects. Thus a low loading on a trait or method factor may be due either to substantial measurement error or to a true lack of trait and method effects. This problem will be particularly serious when scale reliabilities differ substantially. Ironically, such issues of reliability are often noted as a weakness in other approaches that are claimed to be resolved in the traditional CFA approach, but this claim may be unjustified.

11. Other Approaches to the Analysis of MTMM Data

The discussion of analysis of MTMM data has emphasized the original Campbell–Fiske criteria, the ANOVA model, and the traditional approach to CFA of MTMM data. It is beyond the scope of this article to examine other approaches that have been proposed, but some may be valuable. Browne (1984) argued that the parameter estimates for method factors in Model 4D may be uninterpretable "wastebasket" parameters that make interpretations of the model dubious. Instead he proposed product models that posit trait-method interactions which he suggests may be more interpretable and more replicable. Browne (1984) also noted that his product model is like Tucker's three-mode factor analysis. Schmitt et al. (1977) described the application of Tucker's three-mode factor analysis for MTMM data, but Schmitt and Stults (1986) found no other applications of this approach. McDonald (1985, see also Browne 1984) also described multimode and multiple battery models that could be applied to MTMM data. Wothke (1984) argued that models such as 4D (Table 3) are prone to poorly-defined solutions and may ignore the fact that variance common to all measures cannot be separated into trait and method variance. Instead he developed an approach based on the covariance structure analysis models by Bock and Bargmann that divided variance into trait components, method components, and a general component that reflected the level of covariance common to all measures. Others researchers (e.g., Hubert and Baker 1978, Levin et al. 1983) have developed nonparametric approaches to the analysis of MTMM data that were reviewed by Schmitt and Stults (1986).

The variety of analytic approaches for MTMM data, the often critical evaluations of existing approaches, and the review presented here, all point to a similar conclusion. There is currently no well-developed, generally accepted approach to the analysis of MTMM data. The most popular approaches are appropriate for only a limited range of applications and the implications of their limitations are generally unknown. New approaches have been proposed but the generality of their appropriateness and claimed advantages are unknown. Thus, no single approach to the analysis of MTMM data can be recommended. Instead, the burden of proof lies with researchers to defend their interpretations in relation to limitations in their selected approaches and to viable counter-explanations of their findings. Because of the popularity of the MTMM design and problems apparently inherent in the analysis of MTMM data, this area of research should continue to attract the attention of methodologically oriented researchers for many years.

See also: Validity; Reliability

Bibliography

Althauser R P, Heberlein T A 1970 Validity and the multitrait-multimethod matrix. In: Borgatta E F, Bohrnstedt W (eds.) 1970 *Sociological Methodology 1970*. Jossey-Bass, San Francisco, California, pp. 151-69

Alwin D F 1974 Approaches to the interpretation of relationships and the multitrait-multimethod matrix. In: Costner H L (ed.) 1974 *Sociological Methodology 1973-4*. Jossey-Bass, San Francisco, California, pp. 79-105

Bentler P M, Bonett D G 1980 Significance tests and goodness of fit in the analysis of covariance structures. *Psychol. Bull.* 88: 588-606

Browne M W 1984 The decomposition of multitrait-multimethod matrices. *Br. J. Math. Stat. Psychol.* 37: 1-21

Byrne B M, Shavelson R J 1986 On the structure of adolescent self-concept *J. Educ. Psychol.*

Campbell D T, Fiske D W 1959 Convergent and discriminant validation by multitrait-multimethod matrix. *Psychol. Bull.* 56: 81-105

Campbell D T, O'Connell E J 1967 Method factors in multitrait-multimethod matrices: Multiplicative rather than additive? *Multivariate Behav. Res.* 2: 409-26

Cronbach L J, Gleser G, Nanda H, Rajaratnam N 1972 *Dependability of Behavioral Measurements*. Wiley, New York

Cudeck R, Browne M W 1983 Cross-validation of covariance structures. *Multivariate Behav. Res.* 18: 147-67

Hubert L J, Baker F B 1978 Analyzing the multitrait-multimethod matrix. *Multivariate Behav. Res.* 13: 163-79

Jöreskog K G 1974 Analyzing psychological data by structural analysis of covariance matrices. In: Atkinson R C, Krantz D H, Luce R D, Suppes P (eds.) 1974 *Contemporary Developments in Mathematical Psychology*, Vol. 2. Freeman, San Francisco, California pp. 1-56

Jöreskog K G 1981 Analysis of covariance structures. *Scand. J. Stat.* 8: 65-92

Jöreskog K G, Sörbom D 1981 *LISREL V: Analysis of Linear Structural Relations by the Method of Maximum Likelihood*. International Educational Services, Chicago, Illinois

Kavanagh M J, Mackinney A C, Wolins L 1981 Issues in managerial performance: Multitrait-multimethod analyses of ratings. *Psychol. Bull.* 75: 34-49

Kenny D A 1979 *Correlation and Causality*. Wiley, New York

Levin J, Montag I, Comrey A L 1983 Comparison of multitrait-multimethod, factor, and smallest space analysis on personality scale data. *Psychol. Rep.* 53: 591-96

Long K S 1983 *Confirmatory Factor Analysis: A Preface to LISREL*. Sage, Beverly Hills, California

Marsh H W 1982 Validity of student's evaluations of college teaching: A multitrait-multimethod analysis. *J. Educ. Psychol.* 74: 264-79

Marsh H W 1986 *Confirmatory Factor Analyses of Multitrait-Multimethod Data: Many Problems and a Few Solutions*. ERIC Document Reproduction Service

Marsh H W, Barnes J, Hocevar D 1985 Self–other agreement on multidimensional self-concept ratings: Factor analysis & multitrait-multimethod analysis. *J. Pers. Soc. Psychol.* 49: 1360-77

Marsh H W, Hocevar D 1983 Confirmatory factor analysis of multitrait-multimethod matrices. *J. Educ. Meas.* 20: 231-48

Marsh H W, Ireland R 1984 *Multidimensional Evaluations of Writing Effectiveness*. ERIC Document Reproduction Service No. ED 242 785. Educational Resources Information Center: National Institute of Education, Educational Resources Information Center, Washington, DC

Rindskopf D 1983 Parameterizing inequality constraints on unique variances in linear structural models. *Psychometrika* 48: 73-83

Schmitt N, Coyle B W, Sarri B B 1977 A review and critique of analyses of multitrait-multimethod matrices. *Multivar. Behav. Res.* 13: 447-78

Schmitt N, Stults D M 1986 Methodological review: Analysis of multitrait-multimethod matrices. *Appl. Psychol. Meas.* 10: 1-22

Sullivan J L, Feldman S 1979 *Multiple Indicators: An Introduction*. Sage, Beverly Hills, California

Widaman K F 1985 Hierarchically nested covariance structure models for multitrait-multimethod data. *Appl. Psychol. Meas.* 9: 1-26

Wothke W 1984 The estimation of trait and method components in multitrait-multimethod measurement. An unpublished dissertation, University of Chicago, Illinois

Single-Subject Research

C. F. Sharpley

Although much of traditional educational research has described the differences in outcomes between at least two groups of children or adults who are undergoing different treatments, there is also a strong stream of research which has focused upon the individual. This type of research is often referred to as "single-subject" research, and has its roots in the clinical study of individual behaviour rather than the "policy" research which may characterize large group designs. Because several of the underlying assumptions of group research designs are not applicable to single-subject research, the analysis of data collected from the latter requires the use of alternative strategies. For example, the process of repeated observations upon the same subject over time ("time-series" research), can invalidate traditional statistical procedures which rely upon the least squares model. While there is a great deal which can be (and has been) written about the design of experiments involving only one subject, and because this information has been well-presented in several other places, it will be treated only briefly here. Following an overview of the basic concepts of such design procedures, the major focus of this article will be upon the development of appropriate and reliable processes for the analysis of the data which may be collected by educational researchers who use single-subject designs when evaluating the effects of interventions with children and adults.

1. The Rationale for Single-Subject Research

In their excellent text on the design of single-subject research, Barlow and Hersen (1984) point out that, while group research has a long tradition in education and psychology, there are several limitations inherent in this sort of research which can confuse and even prevent the development of clear and reliable causal links between intervention and outcomes for all subjects. For example, the averaging of individual results to obtain group scores can lead a researcher to ignore valuable data regarding the effects of treatment(s) upon individual children who may be atypical in the experimental group but widely spread in the general educational community. Secondly, when seeking to generalize from group findings to all individuals within a certain age or grade cohort, the complexity of individual behaviour may be an impediment to the successful implementation of a programme which was an "overall" success within a group-designed study. Thirdly, where the subject population is in some discomfort or disadvantage, the piece-meal application of an intervention to a subsample while the other subjects receive an alternative treatment (or none at all) is difficult to justify on ethical grounds. In this situation, the use of single-subject research designs can allow all subjects to receive the desired treatment, with data being collected from repeated observations in a series over time (the "time-series" experiment) so that each subject acts as its own control (Winer 1971).

2. An Example of Single-Subject Research

The designs used in most single-subject research may be classified as emergent from "interrupted time-series" research. This is because the latter encompasses the collection of data upon the behaviour of subjects over a period of time and under variations in the treatment which subjects receive during that period. This type of

research should not be confused with "repeated measures" research where large groups of subjects are observed within factorial experiments (Kratochwill 1978). These studies are quite valid and the data obtained from them of value to researchers. However, for the purposes of this article, the reader is urged to study those procedures as presented elsewhere.

When considering the collection of data obtained from repeated observations of a subject's behaviour, it is first necessary to obtain a reliable measure of the behaviour in question prior to the implementation of any intervention. This period of pre-intervention data collection is referred to as "baseline", and is a vital aspect of time-series experimentation. Without these data, the researcher is unable to argue for any effects which may have been due to the intervention. When describing this stage of the experiment, the letter "A" is used for baseline, and "B" for intervention, with variations on these stages as "A1", "B1", and so forth. A typical experiment which uses this nomenclature is depicted in Fig. 1. This study was performed by Kirby and Shields (1972), and examined the effects of praise and immediate feedback of results to a seventh-grade boy for correct arithmetic answers. This boy was given a daily 20-problem arithmetic sheet for a total of 24 days. He was allowed 20 minutes to complete the particular sheet for each day (all the sheets were different), and data were collected under the various conditions. As may be seen from Fig. 1, his performance on this task was monitored for five "baseline" (A) days, then for eight days of "intervention" (B) during which period he was given the correct answers and praise after he had completed the sheet for each day.

In order to determine if (a) it was the intervention per se which was having an effect upon the number of correct answers which the subject gave per minute, and (b) this effect was lasting when the praise and feedback

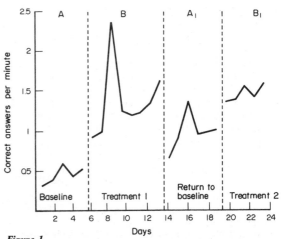

Figure 1
The number of correct arithmetic answers per minute achieved by the subject throughout the study. From Kirby and Shields 1972 p. 82

were withdrawn, a second baseline phase was instituted for five days (this procedure is termed a "reversal"), and this was followed by another period of feedback and praise. The data which are graphed in Fig. 1 suggest that there was an overall increase in the level of correct arithmetic answers given per minute from the first baseline phase to the last baseline phase, and that this increase was most dramatic during the intervention periods. The value of such reversal designs with single subjects is highlighted in this study because the presence or absence of a causal link between the intervention (i.e., the praise and feedback) and the increase in levels of correct arithmetic answers given per minute can be demonstrated.

Some researchers also maintain that the outcomes can be "seen" in a graph of the data. However, as will be shown below, this "visual analysis" is not always a reliable procedure to use when testing for the effectiveness of interventions. This example does show the application of a typical single-subject research design to a fairly common school-based learning problem. For further description and discussion of this and other similar designs, the interested reader is urged to consult the text by Barlow and Hersen (1984).

3. Analysis of Data from Single-Subject Research

3.1 Visual Analysis

As hinted above, the simple graphic presentation of data from much single-subject research is open to misinterpretation. This issue has been discussed elsewhere at greater length than is possible here (e.g., Gottman 1981, Gottman and Glass 1978, Sharpley 1981), but there are several summary points which need to be made.

The methods which researchers use to present their data in graphs require great care if they are not to be open to the sort of misinterpretation which can lead to errors in concluding effects which may be assumed but, in reality, are not present (a Type I error). Conversely, not noticing an effect when one is present in the data (a Type II error) can also occur. If the variables are not graphed with care as to the scales used on the graphs themselves, then misrepresentation of effects can follow. In a dramatic example of this, Campbell (1974 pp. 49–55) has shown that the same data can be quite easily drawn so as to depict major or very minor effects, depending upon the scales used by the researcher when compiling the graph. Even when more sophisticated graphing procedures are used (e.g., lines of progress and semilogarithmic charts), the degree to which two or more persons who are viewing the graphs agree as to the effects shown there can be minimal. This lack of agreement can result in an inability by researchers to decide conclusively if the intervention being tested has effects which are worth noting or not.

Perhaps the most damning account of the lack of reliability which can be present in graphed data such as those depicted in Fig. 1 comes from a study by Jones et al. (1978), who asked a panel of 11 judges who were familiar with graphed data — "full-time researchers, university professors, and graduate students with 3 to 17 years' experience" in graphic analysis (p. 278) — to decide if change had occurred in data sets which had been published in the *Journal of Applied Behavior Analysis* (a major source of graphed data). These experienced judges agreed only 39 percent of the time, hardly arguing for the reliability of this procedure. In a replication of this study, De Prospero and Cohen (1979) used 114 judges who were reviewers and editors of the *Journal of Applied Behavior Analysis* and the *Journal of the Experimental Analysis of Behavior*. The level of interjudge agreement on graphs, which were similar to those used by Jones et al. (1978), was 61 percent. Although the results of the latter study are less condemning of visual analysis, it is worth noting that six of the judges refused to make decisions about the data because of the "absence of circumstantial information" (De Prospero and Cohen 1979 p. 576). This suggests that the decisions which were to be made regarding the effectiveness or not of the intervention depicted in the graphs were based upon more than the actual data themselves, further arguing against reliance upon visual analysis alone when evaluating the outcomes from single-subject research. Finally, White (1972) found that, when examining the same data on the same graph, some judges claimed that there was an acceleration present in the data while others claimed that there was a deceleration in the data. De Prospero and Cohen (1979) concluded that, "A behavioral researcher seeking corroboration on the interpretation of results would not be likely to get the same answer twice", and recommended the use of a statistical "yardstick" instead (p. 578). However, as will be pointed out below, there are some problems in deciding exactly which statistical "yardstick" to use with data from single-subject research.

Before leaving this issue of visual analysis, it is worth commenting that there are some cases when visual analysis is appropriate. For example, where the baseline data indicate a zero or 100 percent occurrence of the behaviour being examined, and this is followed by a dramatic increase (or decrease) in that behaviour, then the effectiveness of the intervention under scrutiny may be accepted as demonstrated. Generalizability is another matter however, and would be enhanced by replication of the effect with other subjects or across other settings, thus demonstrating that the effect noted in one case and under certain circumstances is not selectively confined to that person or those circumstances.

3.2 Statistical Analysis

The statistical procedures traditionally chosen to analyse data collected by repeated observations over time are the *t*-test, the analysis of variance statistic, and regression. All of these are based upon the least squares model which assumes that the data examined are independent of each other. When applied to time-series data, this means that the observations which are repeatedly collected on the subject under scrutiny must all be independent. However, it has been dramatically shown that such data are, in fact, nonindependent. The term used to describe this relationship is "autocorrelation" or "serial correlation", and Glass et al. (1975) found that 72 percent of typical time-series data have high levels of autocorrelation. Jones et al. (1977) noted similar high levels of autocorrelation in 83 percent of the time-series data they surveyed from the *Journal of Applied Behavior Analysis*. Of the 24 data series which the latter authors randomly sampled, nine had autocorrelations of greater than 0.7, and 20 had autocorrelations of 0.4 or greater. As shall be demonstrated below, these levels of autocorrelation can lead to a high incidence of Type I and Type II errors, which invalidate the conclusions drawn by researchers.

Since the use of traditional statistics with autocorrelated data violates an assumption underlying the rationale of traditional statistical procedures, it is relevant to ask just what effect this has upon the results of those analyses. Table 1 presents some figures which have been extrapolated from Hibbs's (1974) formula, and show to how much of its correct value a typical t is inflated when autocorrelation is present in the data. It may be seen from this table that the use of traditional t-tests [the same criticism applies for analysis of variance (ANOVA) and regression] to test for effects with data from time-series experiments can result in mistaken conclusions being drawn by relying upon the inflated values obtained. The reverse (i.e., deflation of the true value) holds true for negative autocorrelations.

Although apparently plausible, it should be noted that the process of testing to determine if the level of autocorrelation present in a data series is significant, and then deciding on the basis of the presence or not of a significant autocorrelation whether traditional statistical procedures can be used to test for effects, is unwise, as well as not in keeping with the methodological rigour which requires that data analysis procedures are stipulated prior to data collection. Even if the autocorrelation was nonsignificant (and this could occur for a quite large autocorrelation if the number of data points was small), the distortion of results can be too high to accept (see Table 1). In addition, as Anderson (1928) has proved, the use of common correlation tables to test for

Table 1
Percentage to which a typical t is inflated when autocorrelation is present

Autocorrelation	Percentage to which t is inflated
0.1	110
0.2	122
0.3	136
0.4	153
0.5	173
0.6	200
0.7	238
0.8	300
0.9	435

the significance of an autocorrelation can lead to erroneous conclusions because these tables are not suited to serially correlated data. The level of correlation necessary for significance is much lower for autocorrelated data than for data which are independent. Finally, since the type of data which is under discussion here is that which arises from repeated performances of a task (such as the arithmetic questions in the example above), it is not realistic to expect that the performance of human subjects at (say) the 20th trial, will not have been affected by their performances on the preceding trials. Thus, to evaluate the effects of an intervention at a particular point in time without taking into account the subject's scores at previous observations is not advisable. Fortunately, there is a statistic which does take previous performances into account when testing for effects — the interrupted time-series statistic.

4. Statistics to Analyse Time-series Data

Based upon the Box and Jenkins (1970) model, Glass et al. (1975) devised a procedure to test reliably autocorrelated data for intervention effects. The output from these procedures is in the form of t-values for changes in the overall level of the data and also for the "slope" or trend of the data. The programme for this procedure (Bower et al. 1974) is reasonably easy to apply and interpretation is aided by study of the Glass et al. (1975) text. A later suite of programmes described in Gottman (1981) and Williams and Gottman (1982), is available for use on an IBM PC. Both of these programmes perform similar activities. The level of autocorrelation present in the baseline data (or any series which is to be compared with any other series) is calculated and then the intervention data are compared with the baseline data and t-values for level and slope changes are presented. Although this is a rather large topic, it is sufficient to say here that researchers will, at different moments in the data analysis process, want to check either level or slope or both as valid measures of change.

5. Issues in the Use of Time-series Procedures

Two major criticisms have been made in regard to the use of time-series procedures. The first of these concerns the number of data points necessary to perform time-series analysis, and the second refers to difficulty in correctly identifying the appropriate model for use in the analysis process. These two criticisms will be discussed below.

5.1 Number of Data Points Necessary

Concerning the number of data points which is necessary before reliable use of the time-series statistics can be assumed, there is an historical accident to be considered. As mentioned above, Glass et al.'s (1975) development of the interrupted time-series procedures was based upon the methods devised by Box and Jenkins (1970). These in turn were derived from a well-established set of procedures to do with extrapolation of data, and closely tied to the prediction of economic variables, sunspot activity, and the probable life of gun barrels! The questions to be answered in this earlier time-series research were all of the type: "if the last *n* occurrences of this phenomenon have been like this, what will the next series of occurrences be like?" The process therefore depended upon the gathering of as much data from the past as possible because the reliable projection of the future depended on accurate examination of all the relevant variations in the data series which were present in the past. Conservatism was predominant, and the researchers who were investigating the likely future of certain phenomena tended to rely upon large numbers of data points (usually 50 to 100) as necessary for accurate prediction of future trends. The result of this conservatism is seen in the resistance of some researchers to adopt interrupted time-series procedures for the testing of intervention effects when there are less than 50 to 100 baseline observations. This rationale relies on the need to have this number of points so that a reliable model of the data can be depicted, thus allowing for the most accurate testing of intervention effects. This rationale is faulty on at least two bases.

First, interrupted time-series procedures are not quite so dependent upon the gathering of long series of preintervention ("baseline") data simply because the reliable and long-term prediction of the future is not the task in hand. By contrast to the need for many data points when trying to make a prediction of the future, the researcher who uses interrupted time-series procedures has, as it were, the future already available in the form of the intervention data collected following baseline. The task here is to test for differences between the two series, not to make (possibly risky) predictions as to the future. Therefore, on the basis of the difference in the rationales underlying these two different tasks (i.e., prediction versus testing for effects in data already collected), there are differences in the number of data points necessary for each task. It simply is a much easier task to test two series for differences than to make predictions about the future, and thus the need for long series is peculiar to the prediction task.

Second, and on an empirical note, it is worth conjecturing as to the effects which using short series (such as those which are typically collected during educational research upon single subjects) will have upon the outcomes of interrupted time-series analysis. Gottman (1981) has addressed this issue from the perspective of the validity of the *t*-value which is obtained from analyses of short series. In order to determine the degree of distortion which would follow the use of interrupted time-series procedures with short series of data, Gottman generated 5,000 series of data which were "*white noise*": that is, these data did not represent actual changes in the mean levels of the data from baseline to intervention. Gottman then examined these series with his interrupted time-series programmes to determine the occurrence of Type I errors. In effect, this was a test of the number of times the interrupted time-series procedures would report a significant change from baseline to intervention when there was, in fact, none actually present in the data series. Gottman performed this test with data series of varying lengths from 5–5 to 60–60 data points. He concluded that the "most important result from these tables is that sample size makes relatively little difference" (p. 355).

What did make a difference was the amount of positive autocorrelation present in the series, a finding of especial note when the results of using five baseline and five intervention points is considered (because this represents the small number of observations often available to educational researchers in the field who are collecting data on the days of the school week). With this number of data points (i.e., 5–5), even an autocorrelation of 0.9 did not result in the likelihood of a Type I error which is in excess of the value commonly accepted by researchers in education (5 percent). This suggests that researchers who are restricted in the number of data points which they can include in a series may gather their data with some assurance that the later use of interrupted time-series procedures to analyse their data will not produce invalid or unreliable results. The use of longer series was recommended by Gottman to avoid Type II errors (i.e., not noting a significant result when there is one present), up to 20 or 30 data points. This latter recommendation should be considered when a null hypothesis is being tested. The researcher can thus check the specific autocorrelation present in the data under examination, and then decide if the degree of likelihood of making a Type I or Type II error is acceptable or not depending upon the methodological and statistical assumptions made prior to hypothesis testing.

5.2 Model Identification

The interrupted time-series procedure which was developed by Glass et al. (1975) required that the researcher correctly identify the underlying "model" of the data series. This was necessary because it was assumed that different data series with different models would be expected to behave differently in any hypothetical extrapolation of the baseline series, and therefore affect testing of baseline versus intervention data. If the incorrect model was assigned to the data, then Bower et al.'s (1974) programme would test intervention data for differences against baseline data which had been incorrectly extrapolated. All of this was based upon the assumption that there was only one correct model for a particular data series (an assumption which will be challenged below), and therefore correct model identification was essential to reliable testing of effects due to intervention. Three parameters were stipulated as requiring identification: the degree of differencing needed to produce a stationary series, the amount of autoregressive component present in the data, and the amount of moving averages component present in the data. Of these three, the amount of differencing required to produce a stationary series was considered most important, with the autoregressive and moving averages components somewhat interchangeable.

Differencing refers to the reduction of a series so that it is stationary, or remains in equilibrium about a constant mean level. Glass et al. (1975 p. 113) recommended that a rule of thumb method to achieve this was to accept the value of differencing which reduced to five percent the number of autocorrelations which were greater than twice the standard errors for those autocorrelations. Several degrees of differencing are produced by the output of the first part of the Bower et al. (1974) programme, and these may be easily tested for their relation to the standard error as suggested above.

Autoregression refers to the "process in which the observation at a time t is predictable to a greater or lesser extent from previous observations" (Glass et al. 1975 p. 74). If the value of t can be predicted by t-1, then this is termed a "first-order" autoregressive process. If the value of t can be best predicted by the point t-2, this is a "second-order" autoregressive process, and so on. Alternatively, the value of t may be most dependent upon a random shock several points previous in the data series, and this is called a moving averages process. Usually these latter two components are mutually exclusive, with the presence of one meaning that the other is not predominant. However, there are some few cases where a mixed model is most appropriate. Gottman (1981) has also dealt with this issue, and the programmes which were developed by Williams and Gottman (1982) provide various methods of forming a model of the data according to the components briefly described above, and then testing for intervention effects.

It is this process of correct model identification which has caused most conjecture as to the applicability of interrupted time-series procedures with the short data series which can be gathered in educational research. There are definitely some series of data which are not easily identified as to their model, and the assumption that correct model identification is essential to the reliable use of the interrupted time-series procedures can lead to hesitation in the use of these procedures. Some critics of the use of interrupted time-series procedures have suggested that the way to avoid incorrect model identification is to collect very long series and to apply this procedure to only those series. However, there are several points which can be made before this rather drastic conclusion is accepted.

First, there is the point that varying the autoregressive and moving averages values should make little difference to the t-statistic obtained, but that the correct identification of the degree of differencing required is very important. In addition, Gottman (1981) has shown that most autoregressive data may be modelled in moving averages terms and vice versa. Finally, Glass et al. (1975) have commented that while the model identification process is somewhat arbitrary, it is not capricious, but instead resembles the same judgmental process undergone in the use of factor analysis, stepwise regression, and even significance testing.

Apart from this degree of latitude which challenges earlier assumptions regarding the need to identify exactly the model underlying a particular series, two recent papers have shown that this issue may not be nearly as important as once thought.

Velicer and Harrop (1983) asked 12 graduate students who had been extensively trained in the model identification process (as described by Glass et al., 1975) to identify 32 different series. All the series had been generated by computer so that they fitted the most common models found in the social and behavioural sciences, and the students were given all of the output relevant to model identification which is provided by the Bower et al. (1974) programme. Of the 384 identifications made (subjects × series), only 109 (28 percent) were correct, with accuracy generally higher (36 percent) for series with 100 data points than for series with 40 data points (20 percent).

From this disappointing result, Harrop and Velicer (1985) decided to test the relative effectiveness of two alternative model identification procedures compared to the "correct" model: (a) a first-order autoregressive model for all series (see above for description of this model); (b) a third-order autoregressive model for all series. Series of 40 and 100 points were generated in this simulation study, with the actual (i.e., correct) model being controlled in the simulation. Each of the two model identification procedures was then tested for agreement with the correct model which was programmed into the data generation. That is, the data were analysed with the correct model and then with the models which arose from application of the first-order autoregressive procedure and the third-order autoregressive procedure. Harrop and Velicer (1985) noted that, "In general, all three approaches provided equivalent results" (p. 39), and concluded that "the model identification process might be eliminated entirely" (p. 42). They recommended that the third-order autoregressive model might have a wider applicability because of the presence of some data series which have a model in excess of the first-order autoregressive model.

6. Summary

Several summary points may be made here. First, single-subject research using time-series designs offers much of value to the educational researcher who is concerned with the effects of interventions upon the academic or behavioural performance of children or adults. Second, the evaluation of these effects via graphs alone is open to some degree of error, or (at best) disagreement between viewers. Third, traditional procedures for the statistical analysis of data collected over time upon single subjects assume independence of observations. The violation of this assumption with autocorrelated data can lead to distortion of the outcome statistic. The interrupted time-series statistic does not assume independence of observations, and calculates the degree of correlation between the points in the data series before testing for intervention effects. This procedure is therefore recommended when data are collected upon the same subject(s) over time and where auto-correlation may be expected.

Finally, the belief that long data series are necessary for the reliable use of interrupted time-series procedures is not justified, and there are strong indications that the troublesome model identification process may be avoided altogether. The result is an affirmation of interrupted time-series procedures as an appropriate statistic for the analysis of data collected from quite short series such as those often gathered by educational researchers.

Bibliography

Anderson R L 1928 Distribution of the serial correlation coefficient. *Ann. Math. Stat.* 13: 1-13

Barlow D H, Hersen M 1984 *Single Case Experimental Designs.* Pergamon, New York

Bower C P, Padia W L, Glass G V 1974 *TMS: Two Fortran IV Programs for Analysis of Time-series Experiments.* Laboratory of Educational Research, University of Colorado, Boulder, Colorado

Box G E P, Jenkins G M 1970 *Time-series Analysis: Forecasting and Control.* Holden Day, San Francisco, California

Campbell S K 1974 *Flaws and Fallacies in Statistical Thinking.* Prentice-Hall, Englewood Cliffs, New Jersey

De Prospero A, Cohen S 1979 Inconsistent visual analysis of intrasubject data. *J. Appl. Behav. Analysis* 12: 573-79

Glass G V, Willson V L, Gottman J M 1975 *Design and Analysis of Time-series Experiments.* Colorado Associated University Press, Boulder, Colorado

Gottman J M 1981 *Time-series Analysis.* Cambridge University Press, London

Gottman J M, Glass G V 1978 Analysis of interrupted time-series experiments. In: Kratochwill (1978) pp. 197-236

Harrop J W, Velicer W F 1985 A comparison of alternative approaches to the analysis of interrupted time-series. *Mult. Behav. Research* 20: 27-44

Hibbs D A 1974 Problems of statistical estimation and causal inference in time-series regression models. In: Costner H L (ed.) 1974 *Sociological Methodology, 1973-1974.* Jossey-Bass, San Francisco, California, pp. 252-308

Jones R R, Vaught R S, Weinrott M 1977 Time-series analysis in operant research. *J. Appl. Behav. Analysis* 10: 151-66

Jones R R, Weinrott M, Vaught R S 1978 Effects of serial dependency on the agreement between visual and statistical inference. *J. Appl. Behav. Analysis* 11: 277-83

Kirby F D, Shields F 1972 Modification of arithmetic response rate and attending behavior in a seventh-grade student. *J. Appl. Behav. Analysis* 5: 79-84

Kratochwill T R (ed.) 1978 *Single-Subject Research.* Academic Press, New York

Sharpley C F 1981 Time-series analysis of counseling research. *Meas. Eval. Guid.* 14: 150-57

Velicer W F, Harrop J W 1983 The reliability and accuracy of the time-series model identification. *Eval. Rev.* 7: 551-60

White O R 1972 Pragmatic approaches to progress in the single case. (Doctoral dissertation, University of Oregon), *Dissertation Abstracts International* 1972 32, 5078A

Williams E A, Gottman J M 1982 *A User's Guide to the Gottman–Williams Time-series Analysis Computer Programs for Social Scientists.* Cambridge University Press, London

Winer B J 1971 *Statistical Principles in Experimental Design.* McGraw-Hill, New York

Statistical Analysis Procedures

Analysis of Variance and Covariance

J. D. Finn

The analysis of variance, introduced by Sir Ronald Fisher near the beginning of the twentieth century, is widely used by behavioral and social scientists. As a class of statistical models, "ANOVA" provides a means for analyzing data that is both rigorous logically and mathematically, and sufficiently broad to address questions posed in a wide spectrum of investigations. This article describes the range of different analysis of variance models, the questions they address, the types of data for which they are appropriate, and the logic by which they operate. Several newer developments and recent thinking about ANOVA procedures are described and demonstrated in an investigation of students' motivation.

The main function performed by ANOVA is to compare systematically the mean response levels of two or more independent groups of observations, or of a set of observations measured at two or more points in time. Analysis of variance techniques are validly applied in each of three types of investigations (Bock 1975): (a) experiments, in which subjects are assigned at random to treatments determined by the investigator; (b) comparative studies, whose purpose is to describe differences among naturally occurring populations; and (c) surveys, in which the responses of subjects in a single population and, if necessary, differential responses of subclasses of the population, are to be described.

Consider several examples. First, an experiment might be conducted in which one randomly assigned group of students receives no formal spelling instruction, a second group receives 15 minutes of spelling instruction per day, and a third group 30 minutes per day. At the end of the experiment, the effectiveness of spelling instruction is assessed by comparing the mean scores of the three groups on a common spelling test. Second, a recent large-scale comparative study examined differences among the achievement levels of students attending American public schools, private schools with religious affiliation, and other private schools. Although many different analyses were employed, ANOVA provides the most direct comparison of mean achievement across the three types of institutions. Third, the International Association for the Evaluation of Educational Achievement (IEA) international survey sampled children in such a way that the final sample represented the entire age cohort attending school within each participating country. Subjects within a country may be subclassified by their responses even after the data are collected, to examine differences in mean response level among subgroups of interest. In an example described below, Swedish 13-year-olds are classified according to their fathers' occupations, and average levels of achievement motivation are compared using ANOVA. In a survey, unlike other types of investigations, removing the researcher-defined subclassifications still yields an intact population (all Swedish 13-year-olds). Nevertheless, whenever mean comparisons are of concern, ANOVA remains an appropriate and powerful analytic tool.

The examples above are described as having one measured response variable. Studies that yield two or more interrelated response measures (i.e., multiple dependent variables) require multivariate analysis of variance ("MANOVA") tests and estimates. For example, the spelling experiment might have included a subtest covering words that were explicitly part of the curriculum and another covering words of similar difficulty that were not taught. Achievement in three types of American schools may have been measured in terms of multiple subject areas (mathematics, reading, social studies, etc.) or in terms of both cognitive and affective outcomes. In each case, summing the measures will obscure important differences among the subscales, while separate analyses of each scale may give contradictory or confusing results and limit the replicability of the investigation. Appropriate MANOVA procedures maintain the integrity of the original measures while providing tests and estimates that pertain to the set of responses jointly.

Repeated measures analysis is employed in investigations in which the same subjects are observed at two or more points in time or under two or more experimental conditions. These include pretest–posttest studies of educational or social interventions, longitudinal studies in which data are collected on the same scale repeatedly, and within-subject experiments in which subjects are measured on the same response variable under several experimental conditions. Both univariate and multivariate analysis of variance models may be used with repeated measures data, depending on the distribution of the multiple measurements. The two types of analysis are described and compared in Bock (1975, Chapter 7) and Finn and Mattsson (1978).

1. Analysis of Variance Models

Analysis of variance procedures are based on linear models that depict the partition of scores on a measure into prespecified components. Consider hypothetical scores of subjects in the spelling experiment who have been exposed to 0, 15, or 30 minutes of instruction per day. The design would be described as a one-way or one-factor design with three "levels"—that is, three different treatment conditions. The ANOVA model describes a typical score as the sum of three components: a response level common to all subjects in the total population of potential subjects (μ); a deviation from μ common to all subjects who receive treatment one (no instruction), treatment two (15 minutes), or treatment three (30 minutes)—α_1, α_2, or α_3, respectively; and a deviation from the average response under a particular treatment unique to the individual subject, ε_{ij}. Thus if Y_{ij} represents the response for typical subject i in treatment group one, two, or three (j), the ANOVA model is:

$$Y_{ij} = \mu + \alpha_j + \varepsilon_{ij} \tag{1}$$

For example, if the final test has 20 spelling words, the average score for all grade-five students might be eight. Further, the average spelling score of all grade-five students who receive 15 minutes of instruction per day might be 10, and one student in this group might obtain a score of 13. Then α_2 is the systematic advantage or "effect" of receiving this instructional treatment, $10 - 8 = 2$, and the unique term for the individual scoring 13 is $13 - 10 = 3$.

Fitting the ANOVA model to empirical data consists of performing two general statistical functions: tests of significance and the estimation of effects. In the spelling experiment, the null hypothesis asserts that the means of the three groups are equal, or equivalently that the three α's are equal; that is,

$$H_0: \alpha_1 = \alpha_2 = \alpha_3 \tag{2}$$

The test of significance provides a sample-based decision as to whether this hypothesis is supported or refuted. If the test reveals that the groups have different means, the researcher may estimate the α's or the differences among them (see Sect. 1.2).

As a more complex example, consider that students are classified by sex and exposed to mastery or nonmastery instruction in simple operations with fractions. The experimental design is pictured in Fig. 1, together with hypothetical mean scores on a test of fractions given at the end of the experiment. The design is a two-way or two-factor design (sex and method) with two levels of sex (M and F) and two levels of method (mastery and nonmastery). There is a total of four "cells" in this design. The ANOVA model for a typical subject in the experiment is:

$$Y_{ijk} = \mu + \alpha_j + \beta_k + \gamma_{jk} + \varepsilon_{ijk} \tag{3}$$

Again, μ is the mean response common to all subjects in all cells, or 35.5 in the example. The effects of being a male or female are α_1 and α_2, respectively; for example, males enjoy an average advantage of $\alpha_1 = 40 - 35.5 = 4.5$ points on the test. Also, β_1 and β_2 are the effects of being exposed to the mastery or nonmastery approach, respectively; for example, mastery students enjoy an average of $\beta_1 = 36 - 35.5 = 0.5$ points. The term γ_{jk}, unlike any in the one-factor model, is the "interaction" or average effect attributable to a particular combination of sex and method. For example, males' 4.5 point advantage and mastery students' 0.5 advantage might lead to the belief that males learning by mastery would have an average score of 40.5 ($35.5 + 4.5 + 0.5$ points). Instead the actual mean is 42, and the interaction for the cell is $\gamma_{11} = 42 - 40.5 = 1.5$. Factors uniquely associated with males learning by this approach appear to elevate the scores further; if the interactions are large, the investigator may wish to explore further what these may be. Finally, an individual subject with a score of 38 would have a unique component (ε) of $38 - 42 = -4$.

Three general tests of significance are obtained under this model, whether the means for males and females are different, whether the means for mastery and nonmastery approaches are different, and whether there is any significant interaction. These are represented symbolically as:

$$H_0(1): \alpha_1 = \alpha_2 \tag{4}$$

$$H_0(2): \beta_1 = \beta_2 \tag{5}$$

$$H_0(3): All\,\gamma_{jk} = 0 \tag{6}$$

If a statistical significance is found, further analysis might include estimating the magnitude and direction of the differences. If significant interaction is found [i.e., $H_0(3)$ rejected], then the mastery–nonmastery difference is not as large (or small) for males as it is for females, and separate differences for males and females must be inspected.

The concept of interaction is all that is necessary to generalize to models with more than two classification factors. Thus most textbooks give limited attention to

	Mastery	Nonmastery	All
Males	42	38	40
Females	30	32	31
All	36	35	35.5

Figure 1
Mean scores for hypothetical mastery learning experiment

higher order designs, and are usually restricted to studies with equal numbers of subjects in the cells. With this (artificial) simplification, tests of significance are easily computed using ordinary scalar algebra and estimated effects are simple differences of the marginal means. Unequal-N designs, although arising frequently in practice, require matrix algebra to obtain the appropriate sums of squares for significance testing and proper estimates of effects and their differences. The study described in the following sections has unequal Ns, and exemplifies the information provided by the more general and realistic application of ANOVA.

1.1 Tests of Significance

The terms μ, α_j, β_k, and γ_{jk} in Eqns. (1, 3) in classical statistical theory represent fixed population constants, while Y and ε are random variables whose distribution may be inferred from the characteristics of the measurement scale (see Sect. 3). The basic ANOVA hypotheses assert that the population constants have particular values or are equal to one another. An inference concerning whether a hypothesis is supported or contradicted may be made from a representative sample of observations.

For example, assume that N subjects are randomly and independently assigned to $J = 3$ different instructional conditions with N_1 students in the no spelling group, N_2 in group 2 (15 minutes), and N_3 in group 3 (30 minutes). At the end of two weeks, a 20-word spelling test is administered and the mean scores for the three groups are found to be some values $\bar{Y}_1$, $\bar{Y}_2$, and $\bar{Y}_3$, respectively. The mean of all subjects is $\bar{Y} = \Sigma N_j \bar{Y}_j / N$. Two measures are obtained from these descriptive data for the test of significance: an index of how different the three means (or the three α's) are from one another in the sample, and a measure of how variable individuals' scores are within the experimental groups. If differences among the group means are large in comparison to differences among individuals, then the groups are clearly distinguishable and it is likely that the null hypothesis [Eqn. (4)] is false. If differences among individuals are relatively large instead, then groups vary no more than random differences among subjects, and the null hypothesis is considered supported.

The measure of differences among means is the "mean square between groups,"

$$MS_B = \frac{\sum N_i (\bar{Y}_j - \bar{Y})^2}{J - 1} \tag{7}$$

The basic component in MS_B is ($\bar{Y}_j - \bar{Y}$), a sample value that estimates the population α_j. The difference between the mean of each group and the mean of all observations, calculated from the sample, is large if the subgroup means are very different from one another and small if they are close in value. Thus MS_B, a summary of these differences, is generally larger when group means are far from one another and smaller if the subgroup means are close together.

The measure of differences among individual subjects within the groups is "mean square within groups."

$$MS_W = \frac{\sum_j \sum_i (Y_{ij} - \bar{Y}_j)^2}{\sum_j (N_j - 1)} \tag{8}$$

The basic component is a sample value for ε_{ij}, that is, the difference of the individual score (Y_{ij}) from the mean in the particular group ($\bar{Y}_j$). These differences are squared and summed across all subjects in all groups, and then divided by $\Sigma(N_j - 1)$. The greater the variation among individuals within the groups, the greater MS_W will be.

The test statistic is the ratio $F = MS_B / MS_W$— the F test, and is referred to in tables of the F distribution found in most statistics textbooks. The parameters needed to look up the F value are the probability of a type I error acceptable to the researcher and the "degrees of freedom" between groups ($J - 1$) and within groups [$\Sigma (N_j - 1)$]. If F exceeds the tabled critical value, MS_B is sufficiently larger than MS_W to conclude that group differences predominate, and H_0 is rejected. If the critical F value is not exceeded, the null hypothesis of no difference is maintained. In the two-way design, in addition to mean square within groups, there is a separate mean square between, and F statistic for, each hypothesis (Eqns. 4, 5, and 6).

1.2 Estimation of Effects

In addition to tests of significance, it is critically important to determine the magnitude and direction of differences among the means, and to locate groups that may not differ from one another even if the overall null hypothesis is rejected. The most straightforward approach is to estimate preselected contrasts among the parameters in the model. In the spelling experiment, if H_0 is rejected, the difference between the no spelling condition and the average of the two instructional conditions [$\alpha_1 - (\alpha_2 + \alpha_3)/2$] might be examined. Also, the difference between 15 and 30 minutes of instruction, $\alpha_2 - \alpha_3$, could be estimated. Common statistical methods allow the determination of these differences in raw and standard deviation units, to draw confidence intervals on the contrasts, or to re-express them in t statistic form. Any contrasts that are required may be estimated. When there is a physical metric underlying the group differences (e.g., time in the spelling experiment) "orthogonal polynomial" contrasts may be particularly useful. These reveal the extent to which a unit increase in time is accompanied by an additional unit increase on the spelling test, and thus results for amounts of time not studied may be predicted. Additional interpretive devices include plots of the estimated differences and "predicted means" obtained by eliminating nonsignificant effects from the ANOVA model (Finn and Mattsson 1978).

1.3 An Example of Two-way ANOVA

A random sample of 102 13-year-old Swedish students whose total school performance placed them among the top 5 percent or lowest 5 percent of students of their age was drawn from the data bank of the IEA international survey of science achievement. The subjects were further subclassified according to their father's occupation, into four levels: professional, manager, skilled laborer, or unskilled laborer. The resulting design had two factors—two levels of school performance and four occupational levels. The investigation focused on differences among the groups in children's achievement motivation. The IEA "need achievement" measure was used for this purpose, obtained by administering a paper-and-pencil attitude questionnaire to each student in the survey. Mean scores and the number of students in each subgroup of the sample are given in Fig. 2. While motivation levels tend to be lower among children of less skilled parents, the difference between the best and poorest students is clearer. A summary of the ANOVA computations is presented in typical "source table" form in Table 1.

The F ratio for performance differences (14.89) exceeds the 0.05 critical value of 3.96; there is a significant difference between the means of the best and poorest students in need achievement, and $H_0(1)$ [Eqn. (4)] is rejected. The F ratio for occupational differences does not exceed the tabled critical value of 2.72; there is not a significant difference among the four means and $H_0(2)$ [Eqn. (5)] is maintained. Finally, the F ratio for interaction does not exceed its critical value and $H_0(3)$ [Eqn. (6)] is maintained.

The direction of the performance difference is obvious from Fig. 2. Since the marginal means for occupational groups decrease monotonically, for purposes of extending the example particular contrasts on that dimension may be examined. Specifically, an estimation may be made of the contrasts between the achievement motivation of children whose fathers are in particular occupational groups and the achievement motivation of children whose fathers are in an occupational group requiring less skill development. That is, the children of professional fathers may be compared with the average of the children of all the other occupational groups; the

Table 1
Analysis of variance source table for need achievement scores

Hypothesis	Degrees of freedom	Mean square	F ratio
Performance [Eqn. (4)]	1	149.73	14.89[a]
Occupation [Eqn. (5)]	3	23.60	2.35
Interaction [Eqn. (6)]	3	1.98	0.20
Subjects within groups	94	10.06	

a Significant at $p < 0.05$

children of managers may be compared with the children of skilled and unskilled laborers; and the children of skilled laborers may be compared with the children of unskilled laborers, on the basis of achievement motivation. The estimates of these contrasts are summarized in Table 2, obtained by employing a general estimation algorithm for unequal-N designs.

The average need achievement of children of professionals is estimated to be 1.12 points above that of other children of fathers in other occupational groups. This is about one-third of a pooled within-group standard deviation ($S = 3.17$). The average need achievement of children of managers is 1.69 points above that of laborers, or slightly over half a standard deviation. The standard error of this difference is 0.99 points so that the difference is 1.70 standard errors in magnitude. This result may be referred to the t distribution with 94 degrees of freedom and exceeds the 0.05 critical value in one tail. The data would support a hypothesis that this particular difference is positive. Thus, while there are no overall differences in need achievement among children whose fathers differ by occupation, the data indicate that children of managers have higher average motivation levels than children of laborers; further research to confirm this finding may be warranted.

2. Analysis of Covariance Models

Many studies obtain data on additional antecedent variables that have well-measured scales. For example, the study to compare three types of American schools may reasonably obtain parents' income, a concomitant of the type of school children attend, as well as individual schooling outcomes. Income need not be subdivided into discrete categories but may be included in the analysis as a "covariate." Likewise, the investigation of spelling performance might include a measure of children's spatial visualization to test whether it partially explains spelling outcomes.

Analysis of covariance is an extension of ANOVA procedures to incorporate one or more measured scales as additional antecedent variables. The "ANCOVA" model is:

$$Y_{ij} = \mu + \alpha_j + \beta(X_{ij} - \bar{X}) + \varepsilon_{ij} \qquad (9)$$

X_{ij} is the score for the individual on the covariate, and $\bar{X}$ is the mean of all observations. β is the regression coefficient reflecting the extent to which scores on the criterion Y are dependent on the covariate X. Three

Father's occupation

		Professional	Manager	Skilled laborer	Unskilled laborer	All
	Best 5%	[22] 13.23	[6] 13.67	[25] 11.28	[4] 12.25	12.35
Performance	Poorest 5%	[6] 10.67	[7] 10.29	[20] 9.10	[12] 8.83	9.42
	Both	12.68	11.85	10.31	9.69	11.06

Figure 2
Mean need achievement scores of 13-year-old Swedish students (sample sizes in upper left inserts)

hypotheses are tested through this model. First, are there differences among the subgroups on response variable Y, eliminating ("holding constant") differences attributable to the covariate? The null hypothesis is identical to Eqn. (2), although adjustments are made to the within and between mean squares for the influence of the covariate. Second, is there a significant correlation of X and Y among individuals within the subgroups, eliminating (holding constant) group mean differences? The null hypothesis is:

$$H_0(2): \beta = 0 \tag{10}$$

Finally, is the relationship of X and Y as strong among individuals in one subgroup as it is in the others? The null hypothesis is:

$$H_0(3): \beta_1 = \beta_2 = \beta_3 \tag{11}$$

where β_1, β_2, and β_3 are separate regression coefficients for each of the three spelling groups. The equivalence of regression coefficients is a necessary condition for the rest of the analysis to be valid, since only one common value of β is included in Eqn. (9). Also, the test may have substantive importance. In the spelling experiment, for example, it may be important to know if more instructional time can lower the dependence of performance on spatial aptitude.

ANCOVA was developed originally for use in experiments. In this application, measurement of the covariate must precede the experimental manipulation. Since groups are assigned at random, their averages on the covariate will not differ. On the other hand, the covariate may be related to differences among individuals within the groups and the residuals (ε_{ij}) are reduced by including X in the model. Thus, mean square within groups will tend to be smaller than in the corresponding ANOVA model, and the sensitivity of the statistical test is increased.

In nonexperimental studies, ANCOVA is a general procedure whenever some antecedent variables define discrete groups of observations and others have well-measured scales. In this context, the covariate(s) may be measured simultaneously with the dependent variables. The availability of general computer programs for ANCOVA obviates the need for such poor data analytic practices as dichotomizing well-measured scales to adapt them to an analysis of variance model, or dummy coding categorical variables to force them into a regression analysis framework.

3. Assumptions Underlying ANOVA and ANCOVA

Four major properties of the distribution of the dependent variable (Y) are important to the validity of the procedures described in this article. First, the units of scale must be well-defined and small relative to the range of the variable, so that a continuous probability function (i.e., the normal distribution) is a reasonable approximation; the scale should have at least ordinal properties and should have nearly equal or equal appearing intervals. Second, the distribution of the response variable should approach normality in the population, although not necessarily in the sample. This is assured by the central limit theorem for the majority of educational and psychological measures, but should be examined whenever departure from normality may become extreme. Third, the variance or standard deviation of the dependent variable should be equal in the populations represented by all of the subgroups in the design (although not necessarily in the samples).

ANOVA is moderately robust to violations of the normality and equal variance requirements, and a program of research summarized in Glass and Stanley (1970) demonstrates the impact of departure from these conditions. On the other hand, the fourth requirement is the *sine qua non* of valid statistical tests with ANOVA models: the observations must be sampled and respond independently of one another. If dependencies arise because the same subjects or groups are measured repeatedly, then multivariate models should be employed. Otherwise, independent observations are essential to all aspects of the analysis, including both sample calculations and theoretical underpinnings, and cannot be compromised.

4. Texts and Computer Programs

Textbooks by Glass and Stanley (1970), Mendenhall (1968), and Shavelson (1980) give particularly clear introductions to ANOVA with examples from the social sciences and education. The text by Scheffé (1959) remains the classic introduction to a wide range of issues related to ANOVA at a more mathematical level. An introduction to MANOVA with real-data examples is given by Finn and Mattsson (1978) and more extensive multivariate presentations are found in Bock (1975) and Harris (1975). ANOVA for unequal-N designs is discussed at length in these multivariate compendia. Good introductions to ANCOVA are given by Gourlay (1953)

Table 2
Contrasts among occupational groups in children's achievement motivation

Contrast	Average difference	Standard error	Difference in standard deviations
Professionals–others $\beta_1 - (\beta_2 + \beta_3 + \beta_4)/3$	1.12	0.77	0.35
Managers–laborers $\beta_2 - (\beta_3 + \beta_4)/2$	1.69	0.99	0.53
Skilled–unskilled $\beta_3 - \beta_4$	−0.17	0.95	−0.05

and Elashoff (1969) although there is a paucity of good textbook coverage.

The computations for any but the simplest ANOVA design require the use of a computer. Several programs will accurately perform the calculations for the widest range of models, including equal and unequal N's, univariate and multivariate responses, analysis of variance and covariance, and complex as well as simple designs. These include MANOVA (Cramer 1974), SAS procedure GLM (Goodnight 1976), and MULTIVARI-ANCE (Finn 1978). All three are readily available from the program publishers.

Bibliography

Bock R D 1975 *Multivariate Statistical Methods in Behavioral Research*. McGraw-Hill, New York

Cramer E M 1974 *Revised MANOVA Program*. Thurstone Psychometric Laboratory, University of North Carolina, Chapel Hill, North Carolina

Elashoff J D 1969 Analysis of covariance: A delicate instrument. *Am. Educ. Res. J.* 6: 383–401

Finn J D 1978 MULTIVARIANCE: *Univariate and Multivariate Analysis of Variance, Covariance, Regression and Repeated Measures: Version 6*. National Educational Resources, Chicago, Illinois

Finn J D, Mattsson I 1978 *Multivariate Analysis in Educational Research: Applications of the MULTIVARIANCE Program*. National Educational Resources, Chicago, Illinois

Glass G V, Stanley J C 1970 *Statistical Methods in Education and Psychology*. Prentice-Hall, Englewood Cliffs, New Jersey

Goodnight J H 1976 SAS *Procedure GLM*. SAS Institute, Raleigh, North Carolina

Gourlay N 1953 Covariance analysis and its applications in psychological research. *Br. J. Stat. Psychol.* 6: 25–33

Harris R J 1975 *A Primer of Multivariate Statistics*. Academic Press, New York

Mendenhall W 1968 *Introduction to Linear Models and the Design and Analysis of Experiments*. Wadsworth, Belmont, California

Scheffé H 1959 *The Analysis of Variance*. Wiley, New York

Shavelson R J 1980 *Statistical Reasoning for the Behavioral Sciences*. Allyn and Bacon, Boston, Massachusetts

The Bootstrap

M. Wilson

Resampling, the use of subsamples of an original sample to estimate statistics and determine properties of the estimator, was first employed to estimate sampling errors in complex sample designs in educational survey research by Peaker (1953) and this has continued as its prime function within educational research until recently (Peaker 1975, Ross 1978, Wilson 1982). Efron (1979) proposed an alternative resampling plan, the *bootstrap*, which has found application to a wider range of issues in statistical data analysis: the estimation of standard errors and confidence intervals in situations where the usual statistical assumptions such as normality and independence are not tenable and where estimators of standard error are unavailable. It is likely to achieve wide acceptance as its power and flexibility become better appreciated by educational researchers. Rao and Wu (1984) have discussed the application of the bootstrap to stratified sampling, unequal probability sampling and to two-stage sampling. Detailed discussion of the relationship between the bootstrap and other resampling plans such as the jackknife and the Taylor's series approximation is given in Efron (1982a).

1. The Technique

Put very generally, the technique is as follows. One is interested in estimating the distribution of a statistic $R(y, F)$ based on some data y and a probability distribution F: R must be well-defined given y; y is of course known; and F is unknown, or at best known for some parameter(s). For example R might be the mean $\bar{y}$, and the aspect of its distribution that is of interest might be the standard error; there are n data points in y but very little is known about their origin. The bootstrap solution is to base an empirical distribution F^* on y, then to sample y^* from F^*. The distribution $R(y^*, F^*)$, where all elements are known, is an estimator of the distribution of $R(y, F)$ and it can be used to investigate the distributional properties of R such as its standard error.

In the example, a large number of bootstrap samples, say 400, would be drawn from y using simple random sampling *with replacement*, each sample of size n (i.e., F^* is a distribution with mass $1/n$ on each data point in y). The mean is calculated for each of these 400 bootstrap samples, and the standard deviation of the 400 bootstrap values is used to estimate the sampling error of the mean. Note that no parametric assumptions about the distribution F of y have been made: the empirical distribution of y has been used as a surrogate for such assumptions. A graphical interpretation of this process is given in Fig. 1, where the double arrow indicates the crucial step in applying the bootstrap.

Some applications of the bootstrap in areas which will be of interest to educational researchers are: standard errors of regression coefficients (Delaney and Chatterjee 1986, Freedman 1981, Freedman and Peters 1982); standard errors for correlation coefficients (Efron 1987b, Lunneborg 1985, Rasmussen 1987); effects and contrasts in the repeated measures design (Lunneborg and Tousignant 1985); standard errors of factor loadings (Chatterjee 1984, Iventosch 1987, Lunneborg 1987); and mean contrasts with covariates, (Lunneborg 1986).

In applying the bootstrap three problems are evident (Hartigan 1986): how does one choose F^*; how many samples y^* from F^* are needed; how close is the distribution of $R(y^*, F^*)$ given F^* to $R(y, F)$ given F? Different answers to these questions motivate different versions of the bootstrap, some of which are discussed below. The bootstrap has generated a lively debate in the statistical literature (Schenker 1985, Efron 1987a) which will ensure rapid progress in resampling theory and applications.

2. An Example

Consider the case of the standard error of the slope in simple linear regression through the origin (the notation follows Efron and Tibshirani 1986). The data consist of observations $y = (y_1, y_2, \ldots, y_n)$ on a criterion variable and $t = (t_1, t_2, \ldots, t_n)$ on an independent variable. The regression model is

$$y_i = \beta t_i + \epsilon_i \quad i = 1, 2 \ldots n \qquad (1)$$

Where β is an unknown parameter to be estimated and the ϵ_i are independent, identically distributed random variables from some distribution F, often assumed to be a normal distribution with mean 0 and variance σ_ϵ^2 [abbreviated $N(0, \sigma_\epsilon^2)$]. The observations on the independent variable t and the sample size n are considered fixed. The least squares estimator of β is $\hat{\beta}$ such that

$$\sum_{i=1}^{n} [y_i - \hat{y}_i]^2 \qquad (2)$$

is minimized where $\hat{y}_i = \hat{\beta} t_i$

An obvious candidate for F^* is given by the distribution of the *residuals* $\hat{\epsilon}_i = y_i - \hat{y}_i$ with a density of $1/n$ on each. Then a bootstrap value for $\hat{\beta}$ can be obtained thus:

(a) estimate $\hat{\beta}$ from Eqn. (2);

(b) make a simple random sample with replacement of n residuals from F^*, call it ϵ^*;

(c) obtain the bootstrap sample as $y_i^* = \hat{\beta} t_i + \epsilon_i^*$;

(d) find the bootstrap value $\hat{\beta}^*$ as in Eqn. (2).

Repetition of (b) through (d) will give an empirical distribution for $\hat{\beta}^*$ called the *bootstrap sample distribution*. The bootstrap estimate of the standard error of β is the standard deviation of the estimates $\hat{\beta}_b^*$ from an infinitely long sequence of bootstrap samples where b indexes the sequence. Of course one cannot take all the bootstrap samples in this infinite sequence of replications, so one

approximates the sequence by stopping at a suitably large number B. Then the bootstrap estimate of standard error of β is

$$\hat{\sigma}^2 = \sum_{b=1}^{B} (\hat{\beta}_b^* - \hat{\bar{\beta}}^*)^2 / B$$

where $\hat{\bar{\beta}}^*$ is the mean of the bootstrap values.

Returning to the three problems mentioned above, one first notes that, although F^* is an obvious candidate for the bootstrap probability distribution, a much simpler approach would be to consider each independent variate-criterion variate pair as a single data point $x_i = (t_i, y_i)$ which has been obtained by simple random sampling from a two-dimensional distribution F_2. Now apply the bootstrap procedure as described using as the bootstrap sample $x^* = (x_1, x_2, \ldots, x_n)$ which is the result of simple random sampling with replacement from F_2. This is conceptually and computationally easier as it eliminates the need to consider a distribution of residuals. It is also more resistant to failure of model assumptions than the first method as it still "gives a trustworthy estimate of β's variability even if the regression model [Eqn. (1)] is not correct" (Efron and Tibshirani 1986). However, it is less like the usual estimate of a regression slope standard error when the regression model is true. Both of these bootstrap procedures are described as *nonparametric* because there are no parametric assumptions made about F^*. Alternatively one could use F^*_{NORM}, the normal distribution with the same mean vector and covariance matrix as the data, in place of F_2^*. This bootstrap procedure is known as the *parametric* bootstrap and has been found to give superior results when the parametric assumptions are justified (Efron 1979, Efron and Tibshirani 1986). The many issues in the design of an appropriate bootstrap probability model for a given situation will most probably ensure that the application of the bootstrap remains an art rather than a science.

Second, the problem of how many bootstrap replications should be taken is one which, in the most general setting, can only be answered by actually finding the bootstrap distributions for a series of large B (say $B = 50, 100, 200, 400, 1,000$) and judging when the resultant series of bootstrap estimates ceases to fluctuate too much (Chatterjee 1984). When some reasonable assumptions about F can be made it will be possible to use Monte Carlo trials of the bootstrap procedure to investigate the appropriate size of B (Efron 1987b). Efron and Tibshirani (1986) advise that 100 replications will often suffice for estimating standard errors, but for estimating confidence intervals they recommend 1,000 replications or more. Sometimes it will prove possible to find the bootstrap distribution analytically, thus eliminating the need to find an appropriate B by eliminating the need to take replications (Lunneborg, in press).

Third, how close is the bootstrap estimate to the true value? In some statistically straightforward situations, such as the simple linear regression discussed above, it is possible to show that the bootstrap estimate and the

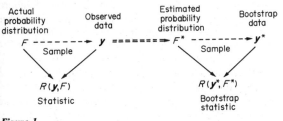

Figure 1
A schematic illustration of the bootstrap process (adapted from Efron and Tibshirani 1986)

classical estimate are asymptotically equivalent (Efron 1979). As above, when reasonable assumptions can be made about F, Monte Carlo trials can be used to investigate the adequacy of various bootstrap procedures (Efron and Tibshirani 1986) and, in situations where the bootstrap has not been applied before, this probably ought to be a standard procedure.

3. Confidence Intervals

The *standard* interval for a parameter θ is the central $1 - 2\alpha$ confidence interval

$$[\hat{\theta} - \hat{\sigma}z(\alpha), \hat{\theta} + \hat{\sigma}z(1 - \alpha)]$$

where $\hat{\sigma}$ is the bootstrap estimate of sampling error and $z(\alpha)$ is the 100α percentile point of a standard normal distribution. This interval will be correct if $\hat{\theta}$ is distributed as $N(\hat{\theta}, \sigma^2)$ for σ constant. In cases where this is not correct, one can use the bootstrap estimator $\hat{\theta}^*$, through the bootstrap cumulative distribution function

$$\hat{G}(s) = \text{Prob*} \{\hat{\theta}^* < s\}$$

where Prob* indicates that the probability is distributed according to the bootstrap distribution of $\hat{\theta}$. There are several different procedures that can be used, each dependent on less strict assumptions than the previous one. The simplest method is the *percentile* method where the $1 - 2\alpha$ central confidence interval for θ is given by

$$[\hat{G}^{-1}(\alpha), \hat{G}^{-1}(1 - \alpha)]$$

That is, for say the 5 percent confidence interval, count in 2.5 percent from each end of the bootstrap distribution. This has been shown to be correct if there exists a normalizing transformation such that $g(\hat{\theta})$ is distributed as $N(g(\hat{\theta}), \sigma^2)$ for σ constant (Efron 1979). An example of such a transformation g is the Fisher's z transform for the correlation coefficient. The bootstrap technique finds this transformation if it exists.

When bias in $\hat{\theta}$ can lead to inaccuracies in this confidence interval the *bias-corrected* percentile (or *BC*) method is recommended (Efron 1982a). To perform the correction calculate

$$z_0 = \Phi^{-1}[\hat{G}(\hat{\theta})]$$

from the bootstrap distribution where Φ is the cumulative distribution function of the standard normal distribution. Then the bias-corrected $1 - 2\alpha$ central confidence interval is given by

$$[\hat{G}^{-1}\{\Phi[2z_0 + z(\alpha)]\}, \hat{G}^{-1}\{\Phi[2z_0 + z(1 - \alpha)]\}]$$

This interval is correct under wider conditions than the percentile method (Efron 1982a). It is often important and it is relatively easy to compute so it would seem reasonable to routinely compute it when the percentile method is used. Efron (1982b) gives a further technique, the BC_a method, which is correct under less restrictive assumptions than the bias-corrected method. A comprehensive discussion of this technique is given in Efron (1987a). Note that each of these methods for confidence interval estimation can be carried out in a parametric or a nonparametric setting.

4. Some Other Developments

A bootstrap technique that is a compromise between the parametric approach and the nonparametric approach is the *smoothed* bootstrap (Efron 1982a). Let s^2 be the sample variance, then the normal (i.e., Gaussian) smoothed bootstrap draws the bootstrap samples from $F* \oplus N(0, as^2)$ where a is some reasonable fraction such as 0.25 and $\oplus$ indicates convolution. Thus each point in the smoothed bootstrap sample y_i^* is the sum of a randomly selected original data point y_i and an independent normal point z_i sampled from a normal distribution with a mean of 0 and a variance of $a \times$ the sample variance. Some other distribution such as the uniform distribution may be more appropriate in a given circumstance (Efron and Tibshirani 1986). The smoothed bootstrap, besides being a useful compromise between the two approaches, can be used to avoid certain degeneracy problems that can occur for small sample sizes.

The fact that the BC_a method works when a certain transformation exists has led DiCiccio and Tibshirani (1987) to propose an approximation to the BC_a confidence interval based upon an estimate of this transformation. This does not entail bootstrap sampling but does involve some cost in terms of assumptions.

5. Computing Bootstrap Estimates

The bootstrap Monte Carlo algorithm is a simple one to program once the appropriate bootstrap procedure has been decided. A few lines of any of the standard computational languages will suffice for the actual sample generation, although access to a sound random number generator is necessary and the storage and book-keeping associated with the bootstrap distribution itself can involve some overhead. Lunneborg (in press) discusses many behavioral science bootstrapping examples in considerable detail and presents listings and a diskette of FORTRAN programs for microcomputers running MS-DOS which provide bootstrap procedures for all of his examples. Several utility subroutines of more general application are also included. He also recommends the microcomputer package PC-ISP for the convenience of programming in a higher level language (Lunneborg 1987). The incorporation of bootstrap procedures into statistical packages has already begun with the addition of the "tboot" command, which calls up a bootstrap procedure with a single line command, to the S statistical computing language at its Stanford University installation (Efron and Tibshirani 1986). In the years ahead we are likely to see extensive use made of the bootstrap procedure in educational research, where highly complex samples are commonly employed.

Bibliography

Chatterjee S 1984 Variance estimation in factor analysis: An application of the bootstrap. *Br. J. Math. Stat. Psychol.* 37: 252-62

Delaney N J, Chatterjee S 1986 Use of bootstrap and cross-classification in ridge regression. *J. Bus. Econ. Stat.* 4: 255-62

DiCiccio T, Tibshirani R 1987 Bootstrap confidence intervals and bootstrap approximations. *J. Am. Stat. Assoc.* 82: 163-70

Efron B 1979 Bootstrap methods: Another look at the jackknife. *Ann. Stat.* 7: 1-26

Efron B 1982a *The Jackknife, the Bootstrap and other Resampling Plans* SIAM, Philadelphia, Pennsylvania

Efron B 1982b Transformation theory: How normal is a one-parameter family of distributions? *Ann. Stat.* 10: 323-39

Efron B 1987a Better bootstrap confidence intervals. *J. Am. Stat. Assoc.* 82: 171-85

Efron B 1987b *Bootstrap Confidence Intervals: Good or Bad.* Technical Report, Department of Statistics, Stanford University, Stanford, California

Efron B, Tibshirani R 1986 Bootstrap methods for standard errors, confidence intervals, and other measures of statistical accuracy. *Stat. Sci.* 1: 54-77

Freedman D A 1981 Bootstrapping regression models. *Ann. Stat.* 9: 1218-28

Freedman D A, Peters S C 1982 *Bootstrapping a Regression Equation: Some Empirical Results.* Technical Report No. 10, Department of Statistics, University of California, Berkeley, California

Hartigan J A 1986 Comment. *Stat. Sci.* 1: 75-77

Iventosch L 1987 An application of the bootstrap technique to variance estimation in factor analysis. Paper presented at the annual meeting of the American Education Research Association, Washington

Lunneborg C E 1985 Estimating the correlation coefficient: The bootstrap approach. *Psychol. Bull.* 98: 209-15

Lunneborg C E 1986 When randomization fails: Bootstrap confidence intervals for mean contrasts with covariates. Paper presented at the annual meeting of the American Psychological Association, Washington

Lunneborg C E 1987 *Bootstrapping Factor Loading Distributions when Factor Structures are Known.* Research Report, Department of Psychology and Statistics, University of Washington, Seattle, Washington

Lunneborg C E *Bootstrap Applications for the Behavioral Sciences.* Research Report, Department of Psychology and Statistics, University of Washington, Seattle, Washington

Lunneborg C E, Tousignant J P 1985 Efron's bootstrap with application to the repeated measures design. *Multivariate Behav. Res.* 20: 161-78

Peaker G F 1953 A sampling design used by the Ministry of Education. *J. Royal Stat. Soc.* 116: 140-65

Peaker G F 1975 *An Empirical Study of Education in Twenty-One Countries: A Technical Report.* Wiley, New York

Rao J N K, Wu C F J 1984 Bootstrap inference for sample surveys. *Proc. Section on Survey Research Methods, Am. Stat. Assoc.* pp. 106–12

Rasmussen J L 1987 Estimating correlation coefficients: Bootstrap and parametric approaches. *Psychol. Bull.* 101: 136-39

Ross K N 1978 Sample design for educational survey research. *Eval. Educ.* 2: 105-95

Schenker N 1985 Qualms about bootstrap confidence intervals. *J. Am. Stat. Assoc.* 80: 360-61

Wilson M 1982 *Adventures in Uncertainty* Australian Council for Educational Research (ACER), Hawthorn, Victoria

Canonical Analysis

J. D. Thomson and J. P. Keeves

Canonical analysis or canonical variate analysis (CVA) is one of the statistical methods used for studying relations between two sets of variables. Each set may contain more than one variable. In this situation, Darlington et al. (1973) envisage three different types of questions that can be asked concerning the correlation matrix of the $(n_x + n_y)$ variables:

(a) Questions about the number and nature of mutually independent relations between the two sets of variables.

(b) Questions about the degree of overlap or redundancy between the two sets. This implies questions about the extent to which one set may be predicted from the other, and vice versa.

(c) Questions about the similarity between the two within-set correlation or covariance matrices.

The use of CVA is often appropriate in answering questions of type (a), sometimes appropriate for those of type (b), and never appropriate for those of type (c).

In order for the purpose of CVA to be more clearly understood, Darlington et al. (1973 p. 439) set out in a table the relationship of CVA to the techniques of analysis of variance, multiple regression analysis, and multi-variate analysis of variance. They also point out that by the appropriate use of dummy variables, CVA can perform multiple discriminant analyses and simple contingency table analyses. Canonical variable analysis is thus a technique to be used when either set X or set Y contains one or more variables, and the variables in either set may be continuous, categorical, or mixed.

In canonical variate analysis, the first canonical correlation is the highest correlation that can be found between a weighted composite of the X variables and a weighted composite of the Y variables (the composites being the first pair of canonical variates). The second canonical correlation is the highest correlation that can be found between the X and Y weighted composites which are uncorrelated (orthogonal) with the first pair of canonical variates. The significance of the first, the second, and each subsequent canonical correlation (there being in all n_{min} correlations where n_{min} is the minimum of n_x and n_y) is tested by Bartlett's chi-square approximation to the distribution of Wilks' lambda.

The canonical correlation coefficient (Rc_i) between each pair of variates describes the strength of the relationship between the two variates. The square of this relationship Rc_i^2 describes the proportion of the variance

ERMM—T*

of one variate predictable from the other variate, both within the same pair of canonical variates.

1. Relationship of CVA with Regression Analysis and Principal Components Analysis

The description of the first and subsequent canonical correlations given above can be compared with two other types of analysis.

First, multiple regression analysis where the Y set contains only one variable and a weighted composite of X variables is obtained to maximize the correlation (R_y) between the Y variable (often called the criterion) and the X composite (called the predictor variate). In this situation R_y^2 can be thought of as the proportion of the variance of the criterion that can be "predicted" (or "accounted for", or "explained") from a knowledge of the set of X variables, in particular, the predictor variate.

Secondly, within each set, the formation of the first, second, and subsequent variates has a univariate analogue in factor analysis, where each factor is a weighted composite of, say, the X variables. In principal components analysis the first composite is formed to maximize the variance extracted. The effect of this first factor is then removed from the original correlation matrix and a second composite formed which is orthogonal to the first composite. The factor loadings of each composite (or variate, or factor), when squared and summed enable the proportion of variance extracted by the factor to be determined.

The relationships between regression analysis and CVA, and between factor analysis and CVA, are discussed by Van de Geer who gives two overviews of multivariate models. The first, a pictorial overview, and the second, an overview in terms of operations on matrices, emphasize "that multivariate techniques do not fall into separate categories as special techniques for special situations, but instead form a close family" (Van de Geer 1971 p. 91).

2. Structure Coefficients and Transformation Weights

Two types of coefficients are available to assist in the interpretation of canonical variates, namely transformation weights and structure coefficients. The interpretation of the factors formed in a canonical analysis has traditionally been based on the standardized transformation weights which are analogous to the beta weights in multiple regression analysis and which are assigned to the original variables in forming each factor as a linear combination of the variables. Alternatively the structure coefficients which are the correlations between each of the derived canonical variates and the original variables may be used. From the view of multiple factor analysis these structure coefficients or factor loadings enable the pairs of canonical variates to be identified and related to the relevant variables in their respective batteries. Moreover, the sum of the squared structure coefficients

enables the proportion of variance (V_i) of each set that is extracted by each factor to be determined. Tatsuoka has commented on the use of structure coefficients:

> That this is a more reasonable approach in attempting to *interpret* the canonical factors (as against assessing the relative contribution of each original variable to the factors) becomes obvious when we recall that the standardized weights (canonical or discriminant) are partial coefficients with the effects of other variables removed or controlled. This is fine when the purpose is to gauge the contribution of each variable in the company of others, but is inappropriate when we wish to give substantive interpretations. (Tatsuoka 1973 p. 280)

Both sets of coefficients are useful, but experience in interpreting canonical factors shows that a more meaningful view is frequently obtained from an examination of the structure coefficients when seeking relationships between the original variables and the derived canonical variates.

3. Variance Considerations

A computer program commonly used for canonical analysis (Cooley and Lohnes 1971) includes in its printout measures of redundancy. These measures combine the proportion of variance of one variate predictable from the other variate (Rc_i^2), with the proportion of variance (V_i) of each test battery extracted by their respective variates to give the (nonsymmetrical) weighted values which indicate how much of the variance of one battery is predictable from a knowledge of scores on the tests in the other battery. This is determined for each variate and is called the factor redundancy: $Rc_i^2 \times V_i$. The factor redundancies are totalled to give the total factor redundancy for each battery given the other battery. Thus it is the redundancy (and not Rc_i^2) that describes how much variance is predictable from one battery to another, whereas for the univariable criterion model of regression analysis, the value of R_y^2 describes this proportion of predictable variance. These measures of redundancy tell much more than do the canonical correlation coefficients about the outcome of the canonical analysis.

4. Partitioning of Redundancy

Mayeske et al. (1969) in their re-examination of the data available from the Equality of Educational Opportunity Survey in *A Study of Our Nation's Schools* partitioned the estimates of variance accounted for into unique and joint effects following a procedure which has been discussed more fully by Wisler (1969) and Mood (1971). This technique had been advanced earlier by Newton and Spurrell (1967) and was employed by Peaker (1971) in the report of the Plowden Follow-up Study. Mood (1971) noted a shortcoming of this measure—under certain circumstances the joint contributions to variance explained could be negative. These effects are similar in kind to suppressor relationships. In spite of this short-coming in the interpretation of the results of partition-ing variance, the technique is a useful one for drawing attention to the confounding which occurs between both individual predictor variables and between domains of predictor variables which account for the variation in the criterion variable.

Recently Cooley and Lohnes (1976) have developed procedures for the partitioning of redundancy in canon-ical analysis. The unique contribution of a domain of predictors to the multivariate prediction of a set of crite-rion measures is that part of the variance of the criteria explained by the full model which cannot be obtained without using the particular domain of predictor vari-ables. It is part of the total redundancy which the partic-ular domain of predictors will account for when they are added to the other predictors included in the canonical analysis. The joint contribution for each predictor domain is the redundancy explained by the full model less the sum of the unique contributions. Thus the total redundancy is partitioned into unique and joint contri-butions, and the commonality or confounded contribu-tion is separated from the contributions which are not so confounded.

The procedures for partitioning variance and redun-dancy are simply those of separating quantities associ-ated with overlapping sets. Where there are more than two domains of predictors the possibility exists of parti-tioning the redundancy into pieces associated with vari-ous subsets of the predictors, but where more than four domains exist, the number of possible partitions becomes large and not very meaningful.

An example of canonical analysis is provided in Keeves (1986) where the results of the analysis of data using this technique may be compared with those obtained through the use of alternative procedures.

5. Some Developments

In both the predictive and descriptive uses of canonical analysis it is possible to employ stepwise procedures for the inclusion of variables in the analysis. However, where such procedures are used some form of cross-validation is desirable if not essential. In addition, by calculating the appropriate matrices of residual correla-tions it is possible to undertake a part (or partial) canonical analysis, but such procedures have not been widely used in substantive studies (Thorndike 1978).

See also: Prediction in Research

Bibliography

Cooley W W, Lohnes P R 1971 *Multivariate Data Analysis.* Wiley, New York
Cooley W W, Lohnes P R 1976 *Evaluation Research in Educa-tion.* Irvington, New York
Darlington R B, Weinberg S L, Walberg H J 1973 Canonical variate analysis and related techniques. *Rev. Educ. Res.* 43: 433–54
Keeves J P 1986 Canonical correlation analysis. *Int. J. Educ. Res.* 10(2): 164–73
Mayeske G W et al. 1969 *A Study of Our Nation's Schools.* United States Government Printing Office, Washington, DC
Mood A M 1971 Partitioning variance in multiple regression analyses as a tool for developing learning models. *Am. Educ. Res. J.* 8: 191–202
Newton R G, Spurrell D J 1967 A development of multiple regression for the analysis of routine data. *Appl. Stat.* 16: 51–64
Peaker G F 1971 *The Plowden Children Four Years Later.* National Foundation for Educational Research, Slough
Tatsuoka M M 1973 Multivariate analysis in educational research. In: Kerlinger F N (ed.) 1973 *Review of Research in Education 1.* Peacock, Itasca, Illinois, pp. 273–319
Thorndike R M 1978 *Correlation Procedures for Research.* Gardner, New York
Van de Geer J P 1971 *Introduction to Multivariate Analysis for the Social Sciences.* Freeman, San Francisco, California
Wisler C F 1969 Partitioning the explained variation in a regression analysis. In: Mayeske G W et al. (1969), pp. 344–60

Change Assessment

R. L. Linn

Change in student knowledge, skills, and performance is obviously a fundamental concern of education. To say that a student has learned something implies that a change has taken place and it is only natural to try to demonstrate this by looking at the difference between scores on measures of achievement obtained at two points in time. Hence, the difference between the score on a posttest and the score on a pretest is a natural, and much used, index of student change. These simple differ-ence scores are often referred to as gain scores or mea-sures of growth as well as change scores. These terms will be used interchangeably here, but it should be recognized that "gain scores" can be negative as well as positive.

Much has been written about measuring change. Fre-quently the focus in discussions of the measurement of change is on various shortcomings of gain scores. As will be discussed below, gain scores tend to be unreliable and to be correlated with initial status. They do not necessarily provide an appropriate measure for compar-ing the results of different educational programs. In addition, there are a variety of technical pitfalls due to limitations of tests that are used to obtain the pre- and post-measures that cause special problems in measuring change. For example, lack of equivalence of pre- and post-tests, ceiling effects, or floor effects can all cause havoc in measuring change.

Before reviewing these criticisms of gain scores it is important to make some distinctions. The force of the various criticisms is quite dependent upon the intended use of the gain scores. For example, poor reliability is a concern if the scores are to be used to make decisions about individuals. On the other hand, if the primary use is in making group assessments and comparing the relative improvement of comparable groups receiving different instructional experiences, then low reliability is of little or no consequence. But if the purpose of using gain scores is to make adjustment for preexisting differences between groups to be compared, then the tendency for gain scores to be correlated with initial status, often in a negative direction, is a major concern. For this, and other reasons, gain scores cannot be counted on to make the desired adjustment for preexisting differences between groups.

In the following sections, salient properties of gain scores and limitations of these scores for particular purposes are reviewed. Brief discussion of variations on gain scores and suggested substitutes is provided next. Growth models and the use of multiple measures across time for assessing growth are then discussed.

1. Properties of Difference Scores

The two most frequently mentioned properties of gain scores are their low reliabilities and the correlation of the scores with their parts, especially the initial measure. These properties can most readily be reviewed by reference to a few basic formulas and, in the case of reliability, assumptions from classical test theory. The score for person i on the pretest is denoted X_{i1} and the score on the posttest by X_{i2}. The difference, or gain, score for person i is simply,

$$D_i = X_{i2} - X_{i1} \tag{1}$$

The resulting difference score typically has low reliability and is correlated with both of its parts, frequently positively with the posttest and negatively with the pretest.

1.1 Reliability

In classical test theory (see, for example, Lord and Novick 1968, Chaps. 2–4) it is assumed that an observed score is the result of the sum of two unobserved parts: a true score and an error of measurement. The latter component is assumed to be uncorrelated with the true score, with true scores on other measures, and with the errors of measurement on other measures. The reliability of a measure is then defined as the ratio of the variance of the true scores to the variance of the observed scores. This ratio may be shown to be equal to the correlation between "parallel measures." Two parallel measures have identical true scores and uncorrelated errors of measurement with equal variances.

Although the above classical model involves a number of strong assumptions, especially when two measures are assumed to be parallel, it is all that is required to derive the expression for the reliability of a difference score. A difference score can be thought of as simply an observed score with two underlying parts: a true difference or change and an error of measurement. The reliability of a difference score is defined like that of any other observed score as the ratio of the variance of the true change scores to the variance of the observed difference scores. These variances are then expressed in terms of their component parts: the difference between the true posttest and true pretest score and the difference between the observed posttest score and the observed pretest score respectively. The result is the following well-known formula for the reliability of a difference score expressed in terms of the correlation between the parts and the reliabilities, and the variances of the parts.

$$\rho_{DD} = \frac{\rho_{11}\sigma_1^2 + \rho_{22}\sigma_2^2 - 2\rho_{12}\sigma_1\sigma_2}{\sigma_1^2 + \sigma_2^2 - 2\rho_{12}\sigma_1\sigma_2} \tag{2}$$

where σ_1^2 and σ_2^2 are the variances of the pre- and posttest respectively, ρ_{11} and ρ_{22} are the reliabilities of the pre- and posttest respectively, and ρ_{12} is the correlation between the pre- and post-test.

The low reliability of a difference score that is typically observed is caused by the influence of the correlation between the pre- and post-test. Other things being equal, the reliability of a difference score will decrease as the correlation between pretest and posttest increases. This tendency can be most readily seen by considering a special case of Eqn. (2) that results when the pretest and posttest have equal variances *and* equal reliabilities. Under these special circumstances, the reliability of a difference score may be expressed as:

$$\rho_{DD} = \frac{\rho - \rho_{12}}{1 - \rho_{12}} \tag{3}$$

where ρ is the reliability of the pretest and of the posttest.

From Eqn. (3) it is clear that the reliability of a difference score approaches zero as the correlation between the pretest and posttest approaches the reliability of each part. Figure 1 shows the reliability of a difference score as a function of the pretest–posttest correlation for four selected levels of reliability for each part.

An inspection of Fig. 1 suggests a strategy for improving the reliability of a difference score would be to obtain pre- and post-test measures with a low intercorrelation. Bereiter (1963) considered this possibility and showed that this seemingly appealing approach is often quite undesirable, because the lower the correlation between the pretest and the posttest the more suspect is a claim that the same characteristic is being measured by the two tests. If different characteristics are indeed measured at the two times of measurement then it becomes meaningless to interpret the resulting difference score as growth. The latter interpretation depends on an assumption that the same characteristic is being

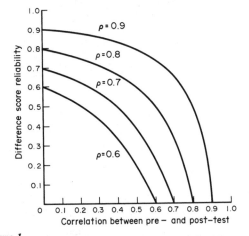

Figure 1
The reliability of difference scores as a function of the correlation between pre- and post-test for four selected levels of pre- and post-test reliabilities, ρ(pre- and post-test are assumed to have equal variances and equal reliabilities)

measured. When the same characteristic is measured, however, the correlation between the two scores tends to be high and hence the reliability of the difference score tends to be low.

For example, for a national sample of sixth-grade students in the United States, the reliability of a measure of reading comprehension administered in the fall was reported to be 0.89 with a variance of 147.6. The corresponding figures in the spring were 0.90 and 152.8 respectively and the correlation between the fall and spring tests was 0.72. The resulting reliability of the fall to spring gain score is only 0.63, a level of reliability that is low for purposes of making individual decisions. But the above reliability is certainly more than adequate for determining the magnitude and direction of change for a group as a whole.

1.2 Correlation of Gain with Initial Status

Gain scores are generally correlated with both the post-test and the pretest. It is the latter correlation that is usually cited as a weakness of gain scores, however. The reason that a nonzero correlation between gain scores and pretest scores is viewed as a weakness involves an implicit assumption that the purpose of the gain score is to provide a means of comparing individuals or groups that is free of initial status. If there is a correlation between gain and pretest, it is reasoned, then the comparison of the gains made by two individuals or by two groups that are at different levels at the time of the pretest will give an unfair advantage to one of the individuals (or groups, as the case may be). If the correlation between gain and pretest is negative, then those who have low pretest scores will gain more, on average, than those with high pretest scores. The converse is true for a positive correlation. Hence, there is a concern for the direction and magnitude of this correlation.

The correlation between gain and a pretest score may be readily shown to be:

$$\rho_{D1} = \frac{\rho_{12}\sigma_2 - \sigma_1}{\sigma_D} \tag{4}$$

where σ_D is the standard deviation of the gain scores.

If the correlation between pretest and posttest is, say 0.75, then the correlation between gain and pretest will equal zero only if the standard deviation of the posttest is one and one-third times as big as the standard deviation of the pretest. If the two standard deviations are more nearly equal in magnitude, as is often the case, then the correlation will be negative, which for comparing gains would give an advantage to those with low pretest scores relative to their higher scoring counterparts.

The sign of the correlation between gain and pretest is dependent on the metric in which scores are reported. If the metric is such that the variance of the scores increases rapidly with age and score level, then the above correlation may be positive. An example of such a metric is the ubiquitous grade-equivalent score that is used for many achievement tests in the United States (Linn 1981, Linn and Slinde 1977). Score metrics for which the variance is fairly stable at different ages, on the other hand, will yield gain scores that are negatively correlated with initial status.

2. Practical Constraints Due to Pre- and Post-test Measures

The components of a gain score obviously determine its properties. The components need to measure a common characteristic and to be free of undesirable features such as floor or ceiling effects if the gain scores are to be interpretable. A few of the major concerns regarding aspects of pre- and post-measures are briefly discussed below.

2.1 Parallel Measures

A primary concern, as has already been mentioned, is that the pretest and posttest measure the same characteristic. One approach to insuring this is to use the same test for both assessments, but this approach has serious drawbacks. Reactivity can be a problem in physical measurements, but is generally more severe for educational and psychological measures. When given for a second time, a test may actually measure something rather different than when given for the first time. Over short periods, memory may be a major factor, for example.

Alternative forms of a test that may be considered interchangeable are usually preferable to repeating a single test. For meaningful comparisons, however, the alternate forms must be essentially parallel or have been carefully equated to adjust for unintended differences in difficulty. This is a stringent but important requirement for adequate assessments of change.

2.2 Floor and Ceiling Effects

When change is studied over a substantial period of time and/or when people are growing rapidly during the period of study, then the tests must provide good measurement over a wide range. Often tests which provide good measurement at one stage of development provide relatively poor measurement at another quite different level. A test that is of appropriate difficulty for 8-year-olds, for example, may be too easy for many of the same children two years later. Due to a low maximum score, or ceiling, many of the 10-year-olds may cluster near the maximum score and have no opportunity to show how much gain has actually taken place in two years. Selecting a test that is appropriate at posttest may only reverse the problem by not discriminating among many students who score near the floor on the pretest.

There are two general approaches to dealing with the problem of floor and ceiling effects. One approach is to select a test that has a sufficiently wide range that there is neither a floor effect on the pretest or a ceiling effect on the posttest administration. Unless the testing is tailored (see, for example, Lord 1981, Chapter 10), as is done for some individually administered tests and in computerized test administrations, then the broad range approach is apt to be rather inefficient and not to provide as good a measurement as is feasible at either the pretest or the posttest.

A second approach to the problem of floor and ceiling effects is to intentionally change the level of the difficulty of the test from pre- to post-test. This second approach is commonly used with standardized achievement tests used in the United States. Such tests are clearly not parallel but an attempt is made to place them on the same scale by means of "vertical equating." There are serious questions about the extent to which such tests can, in fact, be equated (e.g., Slinde and Linn 1977, 1979). It is also possible to question whether or not such tests are actually measuring the same characteristic (e.g., Linn 1981).

3. Alternative Approaches

Residual scores are frequently suggested as an alternative to change scores. These scores have the potential advantage of avoiding problems caused by the pre- and post-tests not having a common metric. They also avoid the problems caused by having an index that is correlated with initial status. Indeed, a primary motivation for residual scores is the creation of an index that is uncorrelated with the pretest.

A residual score is simply the difference between the actual posttest score and the value of the posttest that is predicted from a linear regression equation of posttest on pretest. The resulting residual scores are necessarily uncorrelated with the pretest scores. Residual scores are *not* measures of change, however (Linn 1981). They can be used to indicate whether someone has changed more or less than would be expected based on their pretest performance (Cronbach and Furby 1970), but they cannot be interpreted as simple change.

A variety of other alternatives to simple difference scores have been suggested. Kenny (1975, 1979) proposed the use of differences in standardized scores. Since standardized scores have identical variances, the change in standardized scores necessarily will be negatively correlated with the initial standard score [see Eqn. (4)].

Several authors (e.g., Lord 1958, 1963, McNemar 1958, Cronbach and Furby 1970) have discussed procedures for estimating true gain scores. At a minimum, these procedures require estimates of both pretest and posttest reliabilities for the sample used in the study of change. Cronbach and Furby (1970) also showed how to make use of ancillary information and made distinctions between situations with linked measures (e.g., same test used as pre- and post-test) and unlinked measures. While theoretically elegant, the estimated true gain approach is seldom used, in part, because it is often difficult to obtain the necessary reliability estimates for an appropriate sample.

Tucker et al. (1966) present another formulation based on true-score theory (see also Messick 1981). Their base-free measure of change is a residual of estimated true gain that is unpredictable from true initial status. It is recommended for use in correlation studies involving change measures. Werts and Linn (1971) provide a comparison of several of the above measures based upon a general linear model involving either observed or true scores.

Other than simple difference scores, only residual scores and more recently standardized gain scores have been widely used in assessing change in achievement. The latter approach is the one required under current guidelines for evaluating the effects of the largest federal program of assistance for compensatory education in the United States (Tallmadge et al. 1981).

4. Growth Curves and Approaches to Measurement

Ideally the measurement of change would result in growth curves for individuals and/or groups rather than simple difference scores. Rogosa (in press) has noted that if there are measures at only two points in time then the simple difference score is a sensible measure of the growth curve over that time interval. If the time is treated as one unit, then the difference score is the slope of a linear growth line over that time interval. A curve rather than a straight line is apt to provide a more plausible model of growth. But with only two points a straight line provides a reasonable approximation.

According to Rogosa (in press) the limitations of a simple difference score as a measure of growth "are due to the severe limitations of two-wave data for assessment of change especially when the data are fallible." Implicit in this comment is an important recommendation for those who are interested in studying change. Multiple measures are needed in order to move beyond difference scores and their rather severe limitations.

After a detailed analysis of the limitations of using two-wave data for measuring change, Cronbach and

Furby (1970 p. 80) concluded that "investigators who asked questions regarding gain scores" are well-advised to "frame their questions in other ways." Rather than asking about gain scores, an investigator might ask how the level of performance of an individual or group is functionally related to time, or amount of experience, or hours of instruction. That is, what is the growth curve and what variables alter its rate of acceleration and height. Stated in this way, the need for multiple measures is apparent.

In addition to obtaining measures at more than two points in time, the analysis of change would benefit from the development and use of models of growth. Strong models define measurement needs and approaches to data analysis. The work of Bryk and Weisberg (1976, 1977) and Bryk et al. (1980) provides an illustration of a model-based approach to the assessment of student change and the effect of instructional programs on student growth. Their "value-added" model is based on assumptions about "natural growth" in achievement. The key contribution of this work is not in any particular model of "natural growth," but in the demonstration "that the choice of an appropriate analysis method is highly sensitive to assumptions about the nature of individual growth" (Bryk and Weisberg 1977 p. 960). This suggests that the underlying model of growth is of crucial importance. Measurement at multiple points in time is necessary in order to have any sound basis for distinguishing among models.

Two-wave data have inherent limitations for assessing growth. Although they are clearly superior for this purpose compared to data obtained at a single point in time, such data cannot be expected to solve problems resulting from inadequate experimental design. The hope that difference scores will provide an appropriate measure for comparing groups that are not comparable to start with cannot be realized. When used for this purpose, gain scores "tend to conceal conceptual difficulties and to give misleading results" (Linn and Slinde 1977 p. 147). This is a fault in the logic rather than a weakness of difference scores, however. Yet this is an implicit expectation that is too often held for gain scores when they are used to compare outcomes for systematically formed groups of unknown comparability not only on initial status but on a variety of other factors. Researchers should not expect that gain scores, or any other analysis procedure, will necessarily solve this design problem by providing just the right adjustment.

Bibliography

Bereiter C 1963 Some persisting dilemmas in the measurement of change. In: Harris C W (ed.) 1963 *Problems in Measuring Change*. Proc. of a Conf., Committee on Personality Development in Youth of the Social Science Research Council, 1962. University of Wisconsin Press, Madison, Wisconsin, pp. 3–20

Bryk A S, Weisberg H I 1976 Value-added analysis: A dynamic approach to the estimation of treatment effects. *J. Educ. Stat.* 1: 127–55

Bryk A S, Weisberg H I 1977 Use of the nonequivalent control group design when subjects are growing. *Psychol. Bull.* 84: 950–62

Bryk A S, Strenio J F, Weisberg H I 1980 A method for estimating treatment effects when individuals are growing. *J. Educ. Stat.* 5: 5–34

Cronbach L J, Furby L 1970 How we should measure "change": Or should we? *Psychol. Bull.* 74: 68–80

Kenny D A 1975 A quasi-experimental approach to assessing treatment effects in the nonequivalent control design. *Pscyhol. Bull.* 82: 345–62

Kenny D A 1979 *Correlation and Causality*. Wiley, New York

Linn R L 1981 Measuring pretest–posttest performance changes. In: Berk R A (ed.) 1981 *Educational Evaluation Methodology: The State of the Art*. John Hopkins University Press, Baltimore, Maryland, pp. 84–109

Linn R L, Slinde J A 1977 The determination of the significance of change between pre- and post-testing periods. *Rev. Educ. Res.* 47: 121–50

Lord F M 1958 Further problems in the measurement of change. *Educ. Psychol. Meas.* 18: 437–51

Lord F M 1963 Elementary models for measuring change. In: Harris C W (ed.) 1963 *Problems in Measuring Change*. University of Wisconsin Press, Wisconsin, Madison, pp. 21–38

Lord F M 1981 *Applications of Item Response Theory to Practical Testing Problems*. Erlbaum, Hillsdale, New Jersey

Lord F M, Novick M R 1968 *Statistical Theories of Mental Test Scores*. Addison Wesley, Reading, Massachusetts

McNemar Q 1958 On growth measurement. *Educ. Psychol. Meas.* 18: 47–55

Messick S 1981 Denoting the base-free measure of change. *Psychometrika* 46: 215–17

Rogosa D in press Comparisons of some procedures for analyzing longitudinal panel data. *J. Econ. Business*

Slinde J A, Linn R L 1977 Vertically equated tests: Fact or phantom? *J. Educ. Meas.* 14: 23–32

Slinde J A, Linn R L 1979 A note on the vertical equating via the Rasch model for groups of quite different ability and tests of quite different difficulty. *J. Educ. Meas.* 16: 159–65

Tallmadge G K, Wood C T, Gamel N N 1981 *User's guide: ESEA Title I Evaluation and Reporting System*. RMC Research Corporation, Mountain View, California

Tucker L R, Damarin F, Messick S 1966 A base free measure of change. *Pychometrika* 31: 457–73

Werts C E, Linn R L 1971 Consideration when making inferences within the analysis of covariance model. *Educ. Psychol. Meas.* 31: 407–16

Cluster Analysis

B. S. Everitt

Cluster analysis is a generic term for those numerical and mathematical techniques which seek to produce classifications of objects, people, or whatever is under investigation, from initially unclassified data. Such

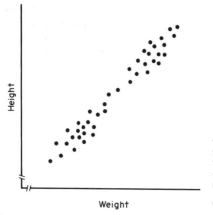

Figure 1
Scattergram of height and weight of a number of individuals

techniques are also referred to by names such as Q-analysis, grouping, clumping, numerical taxonomy, and unsupervised pattern recognition. This variety of names may be due to the importance of the methods in such diverse fields as psychology, zoology, biology, sociology, education, and artificial intelligence.

The ability to classify, that is, to sort similar things into categories, is an essential ability of human beings. If nothing else, early human beings must have been able to realize that many individual objects shared certain properties such as being edible, or poisonous, or ferocious, and so on. Indeed the ability to classify appears to be a prerequisite for the development of language, since each noun in a language is a label used to describe a class of things which have striking features in common. Thus, for example, animals are named as cats, dogs, or horses and such a name collects individuals into groups.

Classification is also of central importance in science. This is because classification involves two basic scientific functions: (a) the description of objects of interest or objects under investigation, and (b) the establishment of general laws or theories by means of which particular events may be explained or predicted. Some areas where classification has played an important role are biology, where the classification of living organisms was a necessary prerequisite for the development of theories of evolution; chemistry, where Mendeleyev's periodic table classifying the elements had a profound influence on the understanding of the structure of the atom; and medicine, where a satisfactory classification of diseases is needed for the investigation of aetiology and the development of treatment.

Many early classifications were arrived at in a rather subjective fashion, but gradually more objective techniques were developed leading eventually to methods of numerical classification based upon the early ideas of Adanson (1727–1806). Such methods use as the basis of the classification a description of the objects in terms of a number of characteristics or variables which can be given numerical values. For example, in attempting to produce a classification of teachers according to their teaching style characteristics, the variables used by Aitkin et al. (1981) included whether pupils were given homework regularly, whether arithmetic tests were given weekly, whether a timetable was used to organize work, and so on.

Most of the newer methods of numerical classification or cluster analysis developed since the early 1960s involve prodigious amounts of arithmetic and their routine use has only become possible with the development of the electronic computer. In some situations, however, a simpler approach may often be sufficient to identify groups or clusters. For example, suppose a number of individuals have had their weight and height recorded. In Fig. 1 each individual is represented by a point whose coordinates are the values of these two measurements. Individuals are similar with respect to these two variables if their corresponding points are close together. In Fig. 1 two distinct clusters of points are clearly visible. Here, of course, the explanation is simple; the groups very likely correspond to males and females.

In many respects the aim of most clustering methods is to imitate and automate the process that can be done well visually for two variables, and extend it to the more usual situation where many more than two variables are recorded for each of the individuals or objects under investigation.

1. Similarity and Distance Measures

Many, though by no means all, methods of cluster analysis operate not on the profile of variable values measured for each object or individual but on the values of an index of similarity, dissimilarity, or distance for each pair of objects or individuals. For example, suppose that the four variables (a) age (above or below 40), (b) depression (depressed or not), (c) anxiety (anxious or not), and (d) delusions (present or absent) had been recorded for each of five psychiatric patients (see Table 1). (Variables having only two possible values such as these are often termed dichotomous or binary variables, and the two possible values are recorded as zero or one.)

One intuitively sensible index of the similarity of two such patients would be the number of variables on which they were given the same rating. However, in general, investigators are happier with similarity indices

Table 1
Hypothetical scores on four dichotomous variables for five psychiatric patients

Patient	Variable			
	a	b	c	d
1	1	1	0	0
2	0	0	1	0
3	1	0	0	1
4	1	1	1	0
5	0	0	0	1

Variable a: 1 = above 40, 0 = below 40
Variable b: 1 = depressed, 0 = not depressed
Variable c: 1 = anxious, 0 = not anxious
Variable d: 1 = delusions present, 0 = delusions absent

Table 2
Similarity matrix for values obtained from Table 1

Individual	1	2	3	4	5
1	1.00	0.25	0.50	0.75	0.25
2	0.25	1.00	0.25	0.50	0.50
3	0.50	0.25	1.00	0.25	0.75
4	0.75	0.50	0.25	1.00	0.00
5	0.25	0.50	0.75	0.00	1.00

ranging from zero to one, and so one could take the number of variables on which the two individuals matched, divided by the total number of variables. Such an index will range from zero for two individuals failing to match on a single variable, to unity for two individuals matching on every variable recorded. The index is easily calculated for the 10 pairs of individuals in the example shown in Table 1, and these values may then be presented in the form of a similarity matrix as shown in Table 2. It can be seen that the entries in this matrix are symmetric, that is, values above the diagonal are the same as those below, and that self-similarities are unity.

Similarities generally take values in the range (0–1), with high values indicating that the two objects or individuals are alike with respect to the variables measured. The complement of similarity is dissimilarity, where high values indicate that the two objects are unalike with respect to the recorded variables. Some dissimilarity indices which have certain mathematical properties are called distances; the most familiar of these is Euclidean distance. For two individuals having measurements on two variables this measure is illustrated in Fig. 2. The extension of this idea to more than two variable values is straightforward.

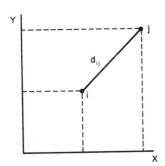

Figure 2
Euclidean distance between two points in two dimensions

2. Methods of Cluster Analysis

Methods of cluster analysis may themselves be classified into a number of groups, for example, hierarchical methods, optimal partition methods, mixture model methods, clumping methods, and so on. Of these, hierarchical methods are perhaps the most widely used. All the methods in this group operate in essentially the same way, building up clusters by combining one or more individuals at a time, starting at the stage where each

individual is regarded as a single-unit cluster and ending with all the individuals combined into a single cluster. Each stage in this procedure corresponds to a partition of the individuals into a particular number of clusters, and choosing that number of groups which best represents a set of data is a difficult problem (Everitt 1979).

Each stage in a hierarchical clustering procedure involves the combination of the closest or most similar individuals, or groups of individuals. Consequently the measures of similarity and distance between individuals have to be extended to measures applicable to groups or clusters of individuals. It is the variety of ways in which this may be done which leads to the variety of hierarchical methods available. Perhaps the simplest between-cluster similarity (distance) measure is to take the similarity (distance) between the most similar (least distant) pair of individuals consisting of one individual from each cluster. This measure is illustrated for distances in Fig. 3. It is known as nearest neighbour distance and is the basis of single linkage cluster analysis. Applying this technique to the similarity matrix for the psychiatric patient example given earlier, gives the following series of steps.

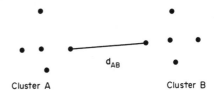

Figure 3
Nearest neighbour distance

Initially there are five "clusters" each containing a single individual. The first step is to combine the most similar pair of individuals. This could be either individuals 1 and 4, or 3 and 5, since both have a similarity value of 0.75. With single linkage clustering either may be chosen, since they will lead to the same final solution. If individuals 1 and 4 are combined at this stage, four clusters (1 4), (2), (3), and (5) are obtained. Now the similarity must be calculated between each of the individuals 2, 3, and 5 and the cluster containing individuals 1 and 4. For example, the similarity between individual 2 and cluster (1 4) is, with single linkage, simply the larger of the similarities for individuals 1 and 2, and 2 and 4; consequently it takes the value 0.50. The results of all such calculations may be presented as a further similarity matrix (see Table 3). The largest entry in this table is the similarity for individuals 3 and 5 and so the next

Table 3
Similarity matrix for combined clusters from Table 2

	(1 4)	2	3	5
(1 4)	1.00	0.50	0.50	0.25
2	0.50	1.00	0.25	0.50
3	0.50	0.25	1.00	0.75
5	0.25	0.50	0.75	1.00

Cluster Analysis

Table 4
Similarity matrix for combined clusters from Table 3

	(1 4)	2	(3 5)
(1 4)	1.0	0.50	0.50
2	0.50	1.00	0.50
(3 5)	0.50	0.50	1.00

step is to combine these and again calculate new individual-to-cluster similarities and also now cluster-to-cluster values. This gives the revised similarity matrix shown in Table 4.

The final stage is the merger of all the individuals into a single cluster. This series of steps may be illustrated by a tree diagram, or dendrogram, which for the above example appears in Fig. 4.

Other measures of intercluster distance lead to other hierarchical methods such as complete linkage, group average, median, and so on.

Another fairly widely used class of cluster analysis techniques operates by attempting to produce a partition of the individuals or objects into a given number of clusters so as to optimize some index measuring the internal homogeneity of the clusters. For example, one such index might be the average within-cluster distance between individuals, which cluster analysis would seek to minimize. Given the number of groups, this would appear at first to be relatively simple since it is only necessary to consider every possible partition of the individuals into the required number of groups and then to select that one with the lowest value of the average within-cluster distance. Unfortunately the number of partitions is very large; for example with 19 individuals and 8 groups there are 1,709,751,003,480 distinct partitions, and consequently complete enumeration is out of

the question. Some modification or restriction is required to reduce drastically the possibilities to be considered, and this has led to what are generally termed hill-climbing algorithms (details of these are given in Everitt 1980 Chap. 3). As with the hierarchical techniques, a difficult problem is that of deciding upon the best number of groups. (A number of generally ad-hoc procedures are described in Dubes and Jain 1979.)

A more statistical approach to clustering involves postulating a probability density function of some form to represent the distribution of variable values within each cluster; this leads to a special type of density function known as mixture distribution for the data as a whole. Such an approach reduces the cluster analysis problem to one of the estimation of the parameters of a probability density function. Details of this approach are given in Wolfe (1970) and Everitt and Hand (1981), and an interesting application of such mixture models in education is given in Aitkin et al. (1981).

3. Evaluating and Interpreting Results

There are many problems associated with using cluster analysis techniques in practice, of which perhaps the most difficult is the assessment of the stability and validity of the clusters found by the numerical technique used. This presents a problem primarily because most (probably all) cluster analysis methods will give clusters even when applied to data sets containing no cluster structure. (For examples see Everitt 1980 Chap. 5.) Consequently a number of questions need to be asked and satisfactorily answered before any given solution can be offered as a reasonable and useful system of classification. Amongst such questions are "Do the same groups emerge when a new sample of individuals is used?" "Do the members of different groups differ substantially on variables other than those used in deriving them?" And in certain situations more specific questions such as "Do the members of the different groups respond differently to the same treatment?" Consideration of such questions may be useful in helping investigators avoid attempting to interpret clusters which are simply artifacts of the numerical methods.

In summary, cluster analysis methods are potentially very useful but they require care in their application if misleading solutions are to be avoided. Users of the techniques must remember that they are essentially "exploratory" in nature so that any indications given of potentially interesting clusters generally need to be confirmed on further data sets.

See also: Q-Methodology

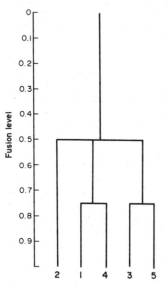

Figure 4
Single linkage dendrogram

Bibliography

Aitkin M, Bennett S N, Hesketh J 1981 Teaching styles and pupil progress: A re-analysis. *Br. J. Educ. Psychol.* 51: 170–86
Anderberg M R 1973 *Cluster Analysis for Applications.* Academic Press, New York

Cormack R M 1971 A review of classification. *J. Roy. Statist. Soc. A* 134: 321–67

Dubes R, Jain A K 1979 Validity studies in clustering methodologies. *Pattern Recognition* 11: 235–54

Everitt B S 1979 Unresolved problems in cluster analysis. *Biometrics* 35: 169–81

Everitt B S 1980 *Cluster Analysis*, 2nd edn. Heinemann, London

Everitt B S, Hand D J 1981 *Finite Mixture Distributions*. Chapman and Hall, London

Hartigan J A 1975 *Clustering Algorithms*. Wiley, New York

Morgan B J T 1981 Three applications of methods of cluster-analysis. *The Statistician* 30: 205–23

Wolfe J H 1970 Pattern clustering by multivariate mixture analysis. *Multiv. Behav. Res.* 5: 329–50

Configural Frequency Analysis

R. Rittich

Configural Frequency Analysis (CFA) was first proposed as an exploratory analysis by Lienert (1969) and then further developed by Krauth and Lienert (1973). Its purpose is to identify overfrequented or underfrequented cells (configurations) in multidimensional contingency tables where overfrequented cells are denoted as "types" and underfrequented cells are denoted as "antitypes". A cell is overfrequented if the number of objects observed in this cell is significantly greater than is assumed under the null hypothesis of independence. In an underfrequented cell, the number of students observed is significantly lower than is assumed under the null hypothesis. For example, if the number of students expected for a certain cell were six and the number of students observed in this cell was 25 this cell would be overfrequented. Whether this is significant is calculated by means of an appropriate statistical test.

For simplicity and brevity of notation the special three-dimensional case of an $I*J*K$-contingency table is considered. If, in the simplest case, the variables used are dichotomous then eight configurations are possible: two to the power of the number of variables, that is, two to the power of three. Let f_{ijk} denote the observed cell frequency in cell (i, j, k), $i = 0 \ldots . I$, $j = 0 \ldots . J$, $k = 0 \ldots . K$. In general, the marginal totals are defined as:

$$N_{i..} = \sum_{j,k} f_{ijk} = a_i$$
$$N_{.j.} = \sum_{i,k} f_{ijk} = b_j$$
$$N_{..k} = \sum_{i,j} f_{ijk} = c_k \qquad (1)$$

Here a_i, or $N_{i..}$, denotes the marginal frequency for the first variable, b_j for the second variable and c_k for the third variable. A cut-off point is used to define whether a criterion is satisfied or not. Those cases which satisfy the criterion or those cases which fail the criterion are summed for the marginal frequency. The sum of both the cases which satisfy and those which fail on the criterion is the total sample size.

The sample size is denoted by N. Let us identify the possible configurations for three criteria with "0" (criterion failed) and "1" (criterion satisfied). Hence, the configurations associated with the eight cells are: 000, 001, 010, 011, 100, 101, 110, 111. For each of the configurations the observed cell frequency f_{ijk} is counted. Then,

for each cell the expected cell frequency under the null hypothesis assumption is calculated. This is done by using the formula:

$$e_{ijk} = a_i b_j c_k / N^2 \qquad (2)$$

Compared with the expected cell frequency, a cell can be observed as overfrequented or underfrequented. Given a certain significance level which must be defined beforehand, it is then calculated whether this overfrequency or underfrequency is significant at the specified level. For this purpose, several possible procedures are available.

1. Pearson's Chi Square

The test which is based upon Pearson's chi square was the first test employed in CFA. Its use was developed by Lienert (1969). The test is similar to the ordinary chi-square test for multidimensional contingency tables. The degrees of freedom for the whole table are $d = IJK - I - J - K + 2$, or $IJK - (I-1) - (J-1) - (K-1) - 1$. For the examination of whether there are types and/or antitypes Lienert assumed that a single cell in the table (CFA) has always one degree of freedom. Also, the chi-square value for a single cell is calculated using the same formula as for the whole CFA and, hence, the overall chi-square value. The formula for both single cells or the whole CFA is given by:

$$\chi^2_{ijk} = \frac{(f_{ijk} - e_{ijk})^2}{e_{ijk}} \quad \text{or} \quad \chi^2_{total} = \sum \frac{(f_{ijk} - e_{ijk})^2}{e_{ijk}} \qquad (3)$$

where e_{ijk} is the expected cell frequency (be it for a single cell or for the sum of all cells), and f_{ijk} is defined analogously for the observed cell frequency. For any particular confidence level one can look up in published chi-square tables whether a cell is significantly overfrequented or significantly underfrequented. Even if no cells were found to be significant the chi-square value for the whole CFA could be significant. Thus, we would know that there is a dependency of variables but we would not know which kind of dependency, if "dependency" is defined as the rejection of the null hypothesis of independence. If types and/or antitypes are found, the variables in a CFA are not independent as assumed under the null hypothesis. The chi-square test is a conservative test, that is, very weak in identifying types or antitypes.

2. Kristof's Test

Kristof has pointed out that not only the cell under investigation but all other cells must be taken into account simultaneously. The formula then becomes:

$$KR^2 = \frac{[e_{ijk}(1) - f_{ijk}(1)]^2}{e_{ijk}(1)} + \frac{[e_{ijk}(2) - f_{ijk}(2)]^2}{e_{ijk}(2)} \quad (4)$$

$e_{ijk}(1)$ here is the expected cell frequency of the cell under investigation and $e_{ijk}(2)$ is the sum of the expected cell frequencies of all other cells. Numbers $f_{ijk}(1)$ and $f_{ijk}(2)$ are defined analogously. The derivation is based on the binomial distribution and is quite straightforward.

To avoid the conservatism of the initial chi-square test, Lehmacher (1981) developed an asymptotic test.

3. Lehmacher's Asymptotic Test

This test leads to less conservative results. The difference to the chi-square test can best be seen from the following formula:

$$Z_{ijk} = \frac{e_{ijk} - f_{ijk}}{s_{ijk}} \quad (5)$$

where e_{ijk} and f_{ijk} have been defined above, and s^2_{ijk} is defined as in Eqn. (6). As can be seen, the numerator is no longer ignored, and the denominator is also calculated in a different way from the denominator in the chi-square formula:

$$s^2_{ijk} = Np_{ijk}[1 - p_{ijk} - (N-1)(p_{ijk} - \tilde{p}_{ijk})] \quad (6)$$

with

$$p_{ijk} = abc/N^3 \quad (7)$$

and

$$\tilde{p}_{ijk} = (a-1)(b-1)(c-1)/(N-1)^3 \quad (8)$$

This test has the disadvantage that occasionally types are identified which are not clearly overrepresented configurations. Lindner (1985) developed an exact test statistic to identify types and antitypes. The method is based on the Fisher–Yates test for the two-dimensional case. However, this method will not be explained in detail in this article because when Wüpper (1985) compared all three methods, he found that the latest version of the Lehmacher test gave nearly the same results as the exact test. Lehmacher later proposed an improvement to his orginial test, which involved a continuity correction of 0.5. With this correction, formula (5) changes to

$$Z_{ijk} = \frac{|f_{ijk} - e_{ijk}| - 0.5}{s_{ijk}} \quad (9)$$

According to Wüpper (1985) this is the better test statistic for the CFA when compared with the exact method developed by Lindner.

4. Alpha Adjustment

To use CFA in a mathematically correct way it is necessary to adjust the chosen alpha value. In our example, eight combinations were possible, that is, there were eight cells which were to be tested simultaneously. In other words, eight tests were carried out at the same time on the same data set. Therefore, the alpha value has to be adjusted such that: Adjusted $\alpha^* = \alpha/r$, where r is the number of tests (i.e., cells) to be carried out simultaneously. In our case, $\alpha^* = \alpha/8$.

It is not always necessary to divide by all cells possible. If the hypothesis for a CFA is such that, for example, only two cells are worth testing, then $\alpha* = \alpha/2$. All other cells which are of no interest and hence are not tested, are then not to be taken into account for the calculation of the alpha adjustment.

Some restrictions are important to note and these must be met in the CFA. The expected cell frequency should not be less than five. If the marginal frequencies are too skewed it might be possible that the CFA does not deliver interpretable or even correct results. This depends on the number of variables which are simultaneously under investigation. Two variables under investigation at one time which are very skewed might result in correct values, while these two variables together with a third skewed variable might give noninterpretable results, because values less than five cannot be automatically assumed to have a chi-square distribution. Consequently, with values less than five a chi-square distribution should not be assumed. Moreover, the observed cell frequency should not be less than five.

5. An Application

An application of configural frequency analysis is provided by a study of student writing which involves the classification of the writers of essays according to the writing styles they exhibit. The first step in identifying types of writers was to establish criteria for the allocation of writing samples to separate categories. The criteria must not only discriminate between writing samples but must also be readily interpretable and have strong face validity. In addition, clearly identified cut-off points must be defined for each criterion. It is plausible to contend that there are simple writers and complex writers with distinctly marked types of writers between these two extremes. The major questions are, however, when can writers be said to be "complex" or "simple", and how can the types of writers in between be identified? The characteristics of writers must be derived from samples of their writing and the criteria developed must necessarily relate to writing samples.

In this exploratory study the first task was to classify clauses in writing samples according to their level of complexity, namely: level 1 involves the use of simple clauses, level 2 involves the use of dependent clauses, level 3 involves the use of interrelated clauses and more complex sentence structures. Six criteria were then identified.

Table 1

Results of configural frequency analysis for independence of DEPTH 1 from DEPTH 3

Cell	Observed	Expected	KR[a]	LEH[b]	Significant at 5% level	
00	87	69.45	6.7	24.5	+	*
01	35	52.46	7.9	24.5	−	/
10	27	44.46	8.8	24.5	−	/
11	51	33.54	10.9	24.5	+	*

Degrees of freedom = 1	Total chi square = 26.1
$\alpha^* = 0.0125$	Critical value = 6.6

a Kristof's test statistic b Lehmacher's asymptotic test statistic

Criterion 1: Simple clause usage (DEPTH 1). If a student uses more simple clauses than clauses at higher levels, code DEPTH 1 = 0. If the student uses more clauses at higher levels than simple clauses, code DEPTH 1 = 1.

Criterion 2: Complex sentence usage (DEPTH 3). If a student uses one or more interrelated clauses or more complex sentences code DEPTH 3 = 1, otherwise code DEPTH 3 = 0.

Criterion 3: Continuations of clauses (CONT). If a student writes at least 5 percent of all clauses as continuations of clauses, code CONT = 1, otherwise code CONT = 0.

Criterion 4: End of sentences (END). If a student ends more sentences with simple clauses at level 1 than with dependent clauses at levels 2 or interrelated clauses at level 3, code END = 0. If a student ends more sentences with dependent or interrelated clauses at level 2 and above than with simple clauses at level 1, code END = 1.

Criterion 5: Beginning of sentences (BEGIN). If a student begins at least 10 per cent of all sentences with dependent or interrelated clauses at level 2 or above, code BEGIN = 1. If a student begins less than 10 per cent of all sentences with dependent or interrelated clauses at level 2 or above, code BEGIN = 0.

Criterion 6: MARKS. If a student uses at least one of the three marks: exclamation mark, question mark, or colon, code MARKS = 1. If a student does not use any of the three marks, code MARKS = 0.

In order to investigate the patterns of student writing and to identify types of writers, a sample of 200 scripts was drawn at random from scripts involving three writing tasks, Task 5, Task 6 and Task 7. The numbers of scripts for Task 5 was 63, for Task 6 was 59, and for Task 7 was 78. Figure 1 records the cross-classification of student usage according to the six criteria listed above for the 200 scripts. Table 1 presents the results of the configural frequency analysis of the data for the first two-way classification in Fig. 1, in order to test the null hypothesis that usage of DEPTH 1 is independent of usage of DEPTH 3.

The table records both the observed and expected values and the total chi-square value of 26.1 for one degree of freedom. In addition, the values of both the Kristof's test and Lehmacher's asymptotic test are recorded. The existence of overfrequented cells is indicated by a "+" sign for Kristof's test and a "*" sign for Lehmacher's asymptotic test, and underfrequented cells are indicated by a "−" or "/" sign. The 95 percent level of significance was used to test the classification of under- and overfrequented cells. However, because in this analysis four cells were being tested simultaneously, the adjusted $\alpha^* = 0.05/4 = 0.0125$ was used with the corresponding critical value of χ^2 of 6.6 in testing for significance both the Kristof's test statistic and the Lehmacher's asymptotic test statistic.

Thus with confidence at the 95 percent level, the entries that are recorded in Fig. 2 indicate underfrequented and overfrequented cells. Where the tests did not indicate significance with a 95 percent level of confidence, a "." is recorded in Fig. 2. In addition, Fig. 2 records below the diagonal the values of chi square for the test of the overall significance of the entries recorded for each two-way classification. Those values of chi square that are significant at the 5 percent level are indicated by an asterisk "*". It should be noted that for the END-CONT cell while there was overall significance, no single cell could be classified as under- or overfrequented using the tests that were applied.

		DEPTH 1		DEPTH 3		CONT		END		BEGIN		MARKS	
All Tasks		1	0	1	0	1	0	1	0	1	0	1	0
DEPTH 1	1			51	35	46	32	60	27	34	49	30	59
	0			27	87	32	90	18	95	44	73	48	63
DEPTH 3	1					43	35	51	36	36	47	39	50
	0					43	79	35	78	50	67	47	64
CONT	1							42	45	28	55	37	52
	0							36	77	50	67	41	70
END	1									29	54	36	53
	0									58	59	51	60
BEGIN	1											38	51
	0											45	66

Figure 1

Cross-classification of student usage according to six criteria

		DEPTH 1		DEPTH 3		CONT		END		BEGIN		MARKS	
		1	0	1	0	1	0	1	0	1	0	1	0
DEPTH 1	1			+	−	+	−	+	−	·	·	·	·
					5		7						
	0			−	+	−	+	−	+	·	·	·	·
DEPTH 3	1	26.1*				+	−	+	−	·	·	·	·
									5				
	0					−	+	−	+	·	·	·	·
CONT	1	21.4*		7.7*				·	·	·	·	·	·
	0												
END	1	58.1*		15.3*		5.6*				−	+	·	·
											6		
	0									+	−	·	·
BEGIN	1	0.2		0.0		1.7		4.2*				·	·
	0											·	·
MARKS	1	1.9		0.0		0.4		0.6		0.9			
	0												

Figure 2
Results of testing of significance of relationships recorded

Further analyses were carried out to determine whether the significance reported for the data associated with each cell in Fig. 2 arose from one or more of the three tasks which were used in the assessment of writing. These analyses were also undertaken for the smaller number of cases associated with the writing samples for each task and involved the use of the tests shown in Table 1. Where a number (5, 6 or 7) is recorded in the centre of a cell in Fig. 2 there was a significant result associated with one specific task, but not with the other tasks. Thus that particular task influenced the overall level of significance recorded.

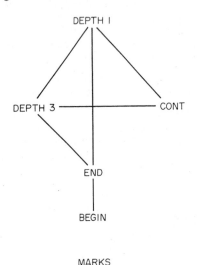

Figure 3
Interdependencies between six criteria from configural frequency analysis

In order to provide a more detailed explanation of the results recorded in Fig. 2, it is of value to take two examples. If we consider the two-way classification of DEPTH 1/END; these two variables are not independent. Underfrequented and overfrequented cells are found which are significant at the 95 percent level of confidence. The "+" sign indicates the presence of an overfrequented cell or the existence of a particular "type" of writing, while a "−" sign indicates the presence of an underfrequented cell or the existence of a particular "antitype" of writing. In general, if one combination of criteria is used by more students than expected, then at least one other combination is used by fewer students than expected. Again, if we consider the two-way classification DEPTH 1/DEPTH 3, the two variables were found not to be independent, but the significance was primarily due to Task 5, and not to Tasks 6 and 7, although there was a trend for these two tasks to be in the same direction as for Task 5.

The results recorded in Fig. 2 have been presented in diagrammatic form in Fig. 3 to show the interdependencies between the six criteria.

It is important to note that Fig. 3 indicates only dependencies of two criteria at a time. Two criteria which are not directly dependent but are each related to a third criterion are not necessarily indirectly dependent because of this relation to the third criterion. In other words, it is possible that they are indirectly dependent but this cannot be proved from the dependencies of two criteria at a time as presented in Fig. 3.

The configural frequency analysis shows that four of the variables can be interpreted as being interdependent, which is a measure of the complexity of the structure or the writing of the essays. These are the variables DEPTH 1, DEPTH 3, END, CONT. The remaining two variables, BEGIN and MARKS, are stylistic measures which were expected to be independent of each other and, in general, independent of complexity. Because of the exploratory nature of this study, plausibility is one of the most important criteria by which to judge these results. Referring to the five criteria mentioned above, it is necessary but not sufficient that a complex writer uses more clauses at deeper levels than level 1. This means implicitly that a complex writer uses more subclauses. In other words, in addition to statements in the main clause a complex writer provides explanations (subclauses) referring to the main clause. Furthermore, the varieties of subclauses enable a complex writer to write in a much more differentiated and precise way than by using only or mostly main clauses.

6. *CFAs with More than Two Variables*

The interrelationship between the three variables DEPTH 1, DEPTH 3 and END recorded in Fig. 3 can be further examined by testing the hypothesis of independence taking three variables at a time. The results of the configural frequency analysis of these three variables taken together are recorded in Table 2. The cell under consideration in the three way classification is recorded in the first column of Table 2 as may be confirmed by comparisons of the entries in Table 2 with those in Fig. 1. There is a strongly significant interdependence between the three variables with cells 000 and 111 being overfrequented and cells 011 and 100 being underfrequented, and with cell 001 significantly underfrequented showing up on Lehmacher's asymptotic test but not on Kristof's test, the latter being a more conservative test. In this analysis the types of writers identified are those writers who meet all (cell 111) or none (cell 000) of the criteria. Clearly these three criteria are closely related to each other. From the results, it can be seen that there are two extreme types of writers: those who satisfy the criteria associated with all three complexity variables, and those writers who satisfy none of the criteria. Each of the 20 three-way combinations of the six variables under consideration can be systematically explored and the underfrequented and overfrequented cells identified. Likewise each of the 15 four-way combinations of the six variables can be examined.

An interesting result from the analysis of the four-way classification of DEPTH 3, CONT, END and BEGIN was that there was only one type of writer contributing to significance, namely those who did not use BEGIN, but who satisfied the other three criteria.

Table 2
Results of configural frequency analysis for independence of DEPTH 1, DEPTH 3, and END

Cell	Observed	Expected	KR[a]	LEH[b]	Significance at 5% level
000	70	39.29	29.9	61.1	+ *
001	17	30.25	6.8	12.1	/
010	25	29.64	0.9	1.3	
011	10	22.82	8.1	12.9	− /
100	8	25.12	13.3	22.5	− /
101	19	19.34	0.0	0.0	
110	10	18.95	4.7	6.7	
111	41	14.59	51.6	73.8	+ *

Degrees of freedom = 4 Total chi square = 101.4
$\alpha^* = 0.00625$ Critical value = 7.6

a Kristof's test statistic b Lehmacher's asymptotic test statistic

7. *Conclusion*

Configural frequency analysis provides a statistical technique by means of which the effects of variables that contribute to the rejection of the null hypothesis in the analysis of contingency tables can be systematically explored. Lienert and von Eye (1984) have extended this procedure for use in the detection of stability and change in longitudinal data and have illustrated its use in this way with examples of the analysis of data from a project on information processing.

Bibliography

Krauth J, Lienert G A 1973 *Die Konfigurationsfrequenzanalyse (KFA)*. Alber, Freiburg
Lehmacher W 1981 A more powerful simultaneous test procedure in configural frequency analysis. *Biomed. J.* 23(5): 429-36
Lienert G A 1969 Die Konfigurationsfrequenzanalyse als Klassifikationsmittel in der klinischen Psychologie. In: Irle M (ed.) 1969 *Bericht über den 26. Kongress der Deutschen Gesellschaft für Psychologie in Tübingen, 1968*. Hogrefe, Göttingen
Lienert G A, von Eye A 1984 Testing for stability and change in multivariate t-point observations by longitudinal configural frequency analysis. *Psychologische Beiträge* 26: 298-308
Lindner K 1984 Eine exakte Auswertungsmethode zur Konfigurationsfrequenzanalyse. In: *Psychologische Beiträge*
Wüpper N 1985 Eine Untersuchung zur Effizienz von Testverfahren bei der Konfigurationsfrequenzanalyse. Diplomarbeit, Universität Hamburg, Hamburg

Contingency Tables

B. S. Everitt

Table 1 shows a sample of 4,353 individuals classified with respect to two qualitative variables, namely occupational group and educational level. Such an arrangement of data is known as a contingency table, and such tables arise very frequently in the social sciences, generally as a result of surveys of one type or

Table 1
Occupational group by educational level

| | Educational level | | | | |
	E1 (low)	E2	E3	E4 (high)	Totals
Self-employed, business:	239 (199.26)[a]	309 (212.28)	233 (237.0)	53 (185.46)	834
Self-employed, professional:	6 (68.33)	11 (72.8)	70 (81.27)	199 (63.6)	286
Teacher:	1 (56.15)	7 (59.82)	12 (66.78)	215 (52.26)	235
Salaried, employed:	794 (716.27)	781 (763.10)	922 (851.95)	501 (666.68)	2,998
Totals	1,040	1,108	1,237	968	4,353

a expected values assuming independence

another. The entries in the cells of Table 1 are counts or frequencies. These may be transformed into proportions or percentages but it is important to note that, in whatever form they are presented, the data were originally frequencies or counts rather than continuous measurements.

Table 1 is known specifically as a two-dimensional contingency table since it involves the classification of the individuals with respect to two variables. Higher dimensional tables arise when a sample of individuals is cross-classified with respect to more than two variables. For example, Table 2 shows a three-dimensional contingency table displaying some data concerning classroom behaviour of school children. The first variable is a teacher's rating of classroom behaviour into deviant or nondeviant. The second is a risk index based on several items of home condition thought to be related to deviance, for example, overcrowding, large family size, and so on; the categories of this variable are considered not at risk for deviant behaviour and considered at risk for deviant behaviour. The third variable is an index of the adversity of school conditions based on items such as pupil turnover, number of free school meals, and so on; this variable is categorized as low, medium, or high.

1. Independent Classifications: Association

The question of most interest about contingency table data is generally whether the qualitative variables forming the table are independent or not. To answer this question, it is clearly necessary to examine just what independence between the classifications would imply. This is most easily seen in 2×2 contingency tables, an example of which appears in Table 3. In this table it is clear that, if the form of tuberculosis from which people die is independent of their sex, then it would be expected that the proportion of males that died from tuberculosis of the respiratory system would be equal to the proportion of females that died from the same cause. If these proportions differ, death from tuberculosis of the respiratory system tends to be associated more with one of the sexes than with the other. Of course, the two proportions might be expected to differ in some measure due solely to chance factors of sampling, and for other reasons which might be attributed to random causes; what has to be ascertained is whether or not the observed difference between the proportions is too large to be attributed to such causes, and to do this the statistical significance test outlined in the next section is used.

Table 2
Data on classroom behaviour of 10-year-old children

| | | Adversity of school condition | | | | | | |
| | | Low | | Medium | | High | | |
	Risk index	Not at risk	At risk	Not at risk	At risk	Not at risk	At risk	Total
Classroom behaviour	Non-deviant	16 (8.72)[a]	7 (11.90)	15 (20.92)	34 (28.57)	5 (4.18)	3 (5.71)	80
	Deviant:	1 (1.85)	1 (2.53)	3 (4.44)	8 (6.07)	1 (0.89)	3 (1.21)	17
Total		17	8	18	42	6	6	97

Table 3
Data on deaths from tuberculosis in males and females

	Deaths from tuberculosis		
	Males	Females	Total
Tuberculosis of respiratory system:	3,534 (3,434.6)[a]	1,319 (1,418.4)	4,853
Other forms of tuberculosis:	270 (369.4)	252 (152.6)	522
Total	3,804	1,571	5,375

a expected value assuming independence

2. Chi-square Test of Independence

To test for an association in a contingency table, the observed cell frequencies are compared with those frequencies that would be expected when the variables forming the table are assumed to be independent. The comparison is via the well-known chi-square test. For example, in Table 3, if sex is independent of the type of tuberculosis causing death, then it can be estimated that the probability of death due to tuberculosis of the respiratory system is 4,853/5,375; consequently, of the 3,804 males in the sample, the number who would be expected to have died from this cause would be 3,804 × 4,853/5,375, that is, 3,434.6. The other expected values could be determined in a similar fashion and are shown in brackets in Table 3. The chi-squared statistic is calculated by finding (observed frequency − expected frequency)^2/expected frequency, for each cell and adding them together. For Table 3 the following can be obtained in this way:

$$\text{chi-squared} = \frac{(3,543 - 3,434.6)^2}{3,434.6} + \frac{(1,319 - 1,418.4)^2}{1,418.4}$$
$$+ \frac{(270 - 369.4)^2}{369.4} + \frac{(252 - 152.6)^2}{152.6}$$
$$= 101.35$$

Since, given the marginal totals, only one of the cells of a 2 × 2 contingency table is not fixed, this statistic is known as a chi-square with a single degree of freedom. To assess whether the observed value of 101.35 should lead to the acceptance or rejection of the hypothesis of independence, it is necessary to compare it to the tabulated chi-square values with one degree of freedom for some chosen significance level. At the 5 percent level,

Table 4
Data on survival of infants for two clinics

		Infants survival			
		Died		Survived	
		less	more	less	more
Amount of pre-natal care:					
Place where care received:	Clinic A:	3	4	176	293
	Clinic B:	17	2	197	23

the requisite value of chi-square with one degree of freedom is 3.84. The calculated value is far above this which leads to the conclusion that the variables are not independent, and that death from tuberculosis of the respiratory system is more common in men than in women.

The extension of the chi-square test of independence to contingency tables with more than two row and column classifications is straightforward. Expected values under independence are calculated as row total × column total/total number of individuals, and the chi-square statistic is calculated again as described previously. For a table with r rows and c columns it has $(r-1)(c-1)$ degrees of freedom. For example, the expected values for Table 1 are shown in brackets beneath the observed values, and the calculated chi-square statistic takes the value 1,254.1. This has nine degrees of freedom and is highly significant, so that occupation and education are clearly related.

Table 5
Data from Table 4 collapsed over clinics

		Infants survival		
		Died	Survived	Total
Amount of prenatal care:	Less:	20	373	393
	More:	6	316	322
Total		26	689	715

3. Three-dimensional Contingency Tables

Three-dimensional contingency tables arise when a sample of individuals is cross-classified with respect to three qualitative variables, and an example has already been given (see Table 2). Many investigators faced with such tables are inclined to analyse separately each of the two-dimensional tables that are arrived at by summing over the remaining variable, using the familiar chi-square test of independence outlined in the previous section. In general this is a far from satisfactory procedure since it can lead to misleading conclusions being drawn about the data. This can be illustrated most simply by means of an example. The data in Table 4 relate to the survival of infants according to the amount of prenatal care received by the mothers at two clinics. Analysing first only the data for clinic A it is found that the chi-square statistic is almost zero. Similarly for the data from clinic B, chi-square is approximately zero. Consequently within each clinic it would be concluded that amount of care was unrelated to survival. If now the data for the two clinics are combined (Table 5), the chi-square statistic takes the value 5.26 which with one degree of freedom is significant beyond the 5 percent level; consideration only of this table would lead to the erroneous conclusion that survival was related to the amount of care received. The reason for this spurious result is that amount of care is related to clinic and so combination over clinics is invalid.

The analysis of three-dimensional contingency tables presents problems not encountered with two-dimensional tables, where a single question is of interest, namely that of the independence of the two variables involved. In the case of higher dimensional tables the investigator may wish to test that some variables are independent of some others, or that a particular variable is independent of the remainder, or some other more complex hypothesis. Again the chi-squared statistic is used to compare observed frequencies with those expected under a particular hypothesis.

The simplest question of interest in a three-dimensional table is that of the mutual independence of the three variables; this is directly analogous to the hypothesis of independence in a two-way table, and is tested in an essentially equivalent fashion. For example, in Table 2 the expected value under independence, for the not at risk, nondeviant, and low adversity of school condition category is given by: total number of children not at risk × estimated probability of being nondeviant × estimated probability of adversity of school condition being low = $41 \times (80/97) \times (25/97) = 8.72$.

Other expected values under independence may be calculated in a similar manner, and are given in brackets below the observed values in Table 2. The chi-square statistic in this case takes the value 17.30 and has seven degrees of freedom. The tabulated value of chi-square with seven degrees of freedom at the 5 percent significance level is 14.07 which consequently leads to the rejection of the hypothesis of mutual independence.

Other hypotheses which might be of interest for three-dimensional tables are those of partial independence, that is, an association exists between two of the variables whilst the third is completely independent, and conditional independence, that is, two variables are independent given the level of the third. (Details of how such hypotheses are tested are given in Everitt 1977 Chap. 4.) Also of interest may be an investigation of whether an association between two of the variables differs in degree or in direction in different categories of the third. Here, however, expected values can no longer be obtained directly from various marginal totals, but instead must be obtained iteratively generally by a procedure known as iterative proportional fitting.

4. Log-linear Models for Contingency Tables

A major development in the analysis of contingency tables which has taken place primarily since the early 1960s is that of fitting models to contingency tables and estimating the parameters in the models. The term model here refers to some "theory" or conceptual framework about the observations, and the parameters in the model represent the "effects" that particular variables or combinations of variables have in determining the values taken by the observations. Such an approach is common in many branches of statistics such as regression analysis and analysis of variance.

For contingency tables, log-linear models are those used most frequently; they may be introduced by considering a two-dimensional table which, in the population, has frequencies m_{ij} for the ij-th cell. (The expected values introduced earlier may be thought of as estimates of the m_{ij}.) If the variables forming the table are independent then it is fairly simple to demonstrate that m_{ij} may be expressed in the form

$$\log m_{ij} = u + u_{1(i)} + u_{2(j)} \tag{1}$$

where u, $u_{1(i)}$ and $u_{2(j)}$ are parameters of the model representing respectively a "grand mean" effect, and "row" and "column" effects. [The similarity of Eqn. (1) to those encountered in the analysis of variance should be clear to those readers familiar with the latter.] Equation (1) is a simple log-linear model; the logarithm of the population frequencies is expressed as a linear function of certain parameters.

If this model fails to provide an adequate fit to the data, an "interaction" term can be added to the independence model, giving

$$\log m_{ij} = u + u_{1(i)} + u_{2(j)} + u_{12(ij)} \tag{2}$$

This term would represent discrepancies between the actual cell frequencies and those to be expected if the two variables were independent. The model given in Eqn. 2 is the most general one for a two-dimensional table.

For a three-dimensional contingency table the most general log-linear model would have the form

$$\tag{3}$$

$$\log m_{ijk} = u + u_{1(i)} + u_{2(j)} + u_{3(k)}$$
$$+ u_{12(ij)} + u_{13(ik)} + u_{23(jk)} + u_{123(ijk)}$$

In this model the parameters $u_{123(ijk)}$ represent the possibility that associations between a pair of variables may differ in degree or direction in each category of the third variable. By dropping parameters for Eqn. 3, models corresponding to the mutual, partial, or conditional independence of the variables may be obtained. For example, the model corresponding to the mutual independence of the three variables has the form

$$\log m_{ijk} = u + u_{1(i)} + u_{2(j)} + u_{3(k)} \tag{4}$$

Procedures are available for fitting log-linear models to contingency tables and testing the adequacy of fit. Such procedures also lead to estimates of the parameters in the model which can be very useful in practical applications.

Log-linear models allow a systematic approach to be taken to discover the relationships that may be present in complex multidimensional tables and provide a powerful addition to methods available for the analysis of contingency table data.

See also: Log-linear Models

Bibliography

Birch M W 1963 Maximum likelihood in three-way contingency tables. *J. Roy. Statist. Soc. B.* 25:220–33
Bishop Y M M 1969 Full contingency tables, logits, and split contingency tables. *Biometrics* 25:383–99
Bishop Y M M, Fienberg S E, Holland P W 1975 *Discrete Multivariate Analysis: Theory and Practice.* MIT Press, Cambridge, Massachusetts

Everitt B S 1977 *The Analysis of Contingency Tables.* Chapman and Hall, London
Fienberg S E 1980 *The Analysis of Cross-classified Categorical Data,* 2nd edn. MIT Press, Cambridge, Massachusetts
Fleiss J L 1981 *Statistical Methods for Rates and Proportions,* 2nd edn. Wiley, New York
Goodman L A 1968 The analysis of cross-classified data: Independence, quasi-independence and interactions in contingency tables with or without missing entries. *J. Am. Statist. Assoc.* 63:1091–131

Correlational Procedures

R. M. Thorndike

In a very general sense, the term correlation refers to a measure of the degree of association between two variables. Two variables are said to be correlated when certain values of one variable tend to co-occur with particular values of the other. This tendency can range from nonexistent [all values of variable $2(Y)$ are equally likely to occur with each value of variable $1(X)$], to absolute (only a single value of Y occurs for a given value of X). A correlation coefficient is a numerical index of the strength of this tendency.

There are many special types of correlation coefficients. All share the characteristic of being measures of association between two variables. The difference lies in how the variables are defined. What is commonly called the correlation coefficient (or, more properly, the Pearson product–moment correlation coefficient or PMC) is an index of association between two variables where both variables are considered as single variables. The association between scores on a reading readiness test and a later measure of reading achievement is an example of such a correlation. Although each measure represents a complex human characteristic, it is treated as a single undifferentiable variable.

At the other end of the spectrum is an index called the canonical correlation coefficient. Like the ordinary PMC, it is a measure of the association between two variables. However, in this case the association is between two unobservable variables: two variables that are weighted additive combinations of multiple measured variables. These are often called latent variables or composite variables. If, for example, the reading readiness and achievement measures each yielded several subscales, the correlation between a weighted combination (composite) of one set of subscales and a weighted combination (composite) of the other would be a canonical correlation.

The mathematical definition of an index of correlation is quite straightforward in most cases, although its actual computation may be very involved and time consuming. Adopting the notation conventions that

X_i is the score of individual i on variable X
Y_i is the score of individual i on variable Y
$\bar{X}$ is the mean of X scores $= \Sigma X/N$
$\bar{Y}$ is the mean of Y scores

where X and Y may be measured variables or composites, the variances of X and Y are both of the general form

$$S_X^2 = \sum_{i=1}^{N} (X_i - \bar{X})^2/N \qquad (1)$$

For any given set of measurements, the mean of the set is a least-squares description of the entire set, that is,

$$\sum_{i=1}^{N} (Y_i - \bar{Y})^2 = \text{minimum} \qquad (2)$$

For a single variable, this is clearly S_Y^2. However, if a second variable (X) is available it may be possible to use that second variable to form subgroups such that some value other than $\bar{Y}$ is a least-squares description within each subgroup. Since for any group or subgroup the mean is the least-squares descriptor, the subgroups must have different mean values if group information is to improve on the overall mean. Letting $\bar{Y}_j$ stand for mean of group j, an individual's deviation from overall mean $\bar{Y}$, may be seen composed of two parts:

$$(Y_{ij} - \bar{Y}) = (\bar{Y}_j - \bar{Y}) + (Y_{ij} - \bar{Y}_j) \qquad (3)$$

The deviation of the ith individual in group j from the overall mean is the sum of the deviation of the group's mean from the overall mean and the individual's score from the group mean.

By going through the process of computing a variance, that is, squaring, summing over N cases, and dividing by N, the above equation becomes

$$\left[\sum_{j=1}^{J} \sum_{i=1}^{N} (Y_{ij} - \bar{Y})^2 \right] \Big/ N =$$
$$\left[\sum_j \sum_i (\bar{Y}_j - \bar{Y})^2 \right] \Big/ N + \left[\sum_j \sum_i (Y_{ij} - \bar{Y}_j)^2 \right] \Big/ N \qquad (4)$$

The term on the left is clearly an ordinary variance of the form found in Eqn. (1). The terms on the right are also variances, but the first is the variance of group means around the overall mean and the second is the variance within groups.

Recall that groups were formed on the basis of the other variable, X. The differences among the subgroup means are due to the X variable in the sense that it was the X variable that led to the identification of groups. Therefore, the second term in Eqn. (4) is the variance in Y that is due to X or is related to X. The third term, then, is the variance in Y that is unrelated to X or independent of X. This is sometimes called the residual variance.

Equation (4) may be rewritten in terms of variances as

$$S_Y^2 = S_{\hat{Y}}^2 + S_{Y.X}^2 \tag{5}$$

where $S_{\hat{Y}}^2$ is the Y variance due to X. $S_{Y.X}^2$ is the residual variance and is the quantity to be minimized in Eqn. (2). With these variance terms defined, the general form for an index of correlation is

$$r = (S_{\hat{Y}}^2/S_Y^2)^{1/2} = [1 - (S_{Y.X}^2/S_Y^2)]^{1/2} \tag{6}$$

That is, an index of correlation is the square root of the proportion of Y variance that is related to X. This mathematical definition of correlation is based on the assumption that Y is measured on an interval scale and has a normal distribution, but X can be a nominal variable. The basic definition in Eqn. (6) is called the correlation ratio and is usually given the symbol η (eta).

1. Product–Moment Correlation

The definition given above is a general definition of correlation in which no assumptions are made about the nature of the X variable. It is frequently the case in educational research that both X and Y variables can be assumed to be measured on interval scales with normal or approximately normal distributions. When both variables are continuous, measured on an interval scale and normally distributed, their joint frequency distribution is bivariate normal.

When X is a discrete or group-membership variable, it is clear that the Y scores of people at any given value of X form a frequency distribution and the mean, $\bar{Y}_j$, is the least-squares description for the group. Likewise, when X is continuous there is a distribution of Y scores for people with a particular X score (X_i), and the mean of these Ys (call it $\hat{Y}_i$), is a least-squares description for these individuals taken as a group. The assumption that X and Y have a bivariate normal distribution means that there is a consistent relationship between changes in X and changes in Y. The graph of X and Y is a straight line of the form

$$\hat{Y}_i = B_{Y.X}X_i + A \tag{7}$$

At any particular value X_i, the variance in Y scores around $\hat{Y}_i$ is the unexplained variance, $S_{Y.X}^2$. The values of $B_{Y.X}$ and A are determined such that, across the entire set of data, $S_{Y.X}^2$ is minimum. By the logic used in developing Eqns. (4) and (5), the total variance of Y may be expressed as

$$S_Y^2 = S_T^2 + S_{Y.X}^2 \tag{8}$$

It can be shown that the value of $B_{Y.X}$ is given by

$$B_{Y.X} = \sum x_i y_i \bigg/ \sum x_i^2 = \sum x_i y_i / NS_X^2 \tag{9}$$

where $x_i = X_i - \bar{X}$ and $y_i = Y_i - \bar{Y}$. When X and Y are expressed in the standard score form

$$B_{Y.X} = \sum z_Y z_X / N \tag{10}$$

The symbol $r_{y.x}$ represents the slope coefficient in Eqn. (7) when X and Y are expressed in standard scores,

$$r_{y.x} = \sum z_Y z_X / N \tag{11}$$

This is one of several definitional formulas for the product–moment correlation. Since the intercept (A) must be zero ($\bar{z}_Y = \bar{z}_X = 0$), Eqn. (7) may be written as

$$\hat{z}_{Y_i} = r_{YX} z_{X_i} \tag{12}$$

Rewriting the least-squares function, Eqn. (2) for z scores produces

$$1/N \sum (z_{Y_i} - \hat{z}_{Y_i})^2 = 1/N \sum (z_{Y_i} - r_{YX} z_{X_i})^2$$
$$= \text{minimum} \tag{13}$$

By squaring, summing, dividing by N, simplifying the result, and recalling from Eqn. (3) the expression for residual variance, the following is obtained:

$$S_{z_Y.z_X}^2 = 1 - r_{YX}^2 \tag{14}$$

In terms of the original raw scores, this equation becomes

$$S_{Y.X}^2 = S_Y^2(1 - r_{YX}^2) \tag{15}$$

Solving for r_{YX} yields

$$r_{YX} = [1 - (S_{Y.X}^2/S_Y^2)]^{1/2} \tag{16}$$

which is identical to Eqn. (6). The following identity is also easy to demonstrate

$$r_{YX}^2 = S_T^2/S_Y^2 \tag{17}$$

A useful computing formula for r is

$$r = \sum xy / NS_X S_Y \tag{18}$$

or its raw-score equivalent

$$r = \left(N \sum XY - \sum X \sum Y \right) \bigg/ \left\{ \left[N \sum X^2 - \left(\sum X \right)^2 \right]^{1/2} \right.$$
$$\left. \times \left[N \sum Y^2 - \left(\sum Y \right)^2 \right]^{1/2} \right\} \tag{19}$$

To this point, three meanings of the product–moment correlation coefficient have been developed. They are

(a) The slope of the least-squares regression line for standard score variables is r [Eqn. (11)].

(b) The strength of association between two variables (S_T^2/S_Y^2) is r^2 [Eqn. (17)].

(c) The residual variance in Y, which may be viewed as the inaccuracy of prediction, is $S_Y(1 - r_{YX}^2)$ [Eqn. (14)].

There are four additional interpretations of the PMC that are discussed by Harman (1976), McNemar (1969), or Thorndike (1978). Interested readers should consult these sources for a complete presentation.

2. Other Bivariate Correlations

The product–moment correlation is the most widely used and understood correlational index. It has several advantages, such as its numerous interpretations, that accrue when the conditions for its use are met. However, there are numerous research situations in which not all variables are continuous, represent an interval scale, and have normal distributions. A number of alternative correlation coefficients are available for situations that do not meet all the requirements of the product–moment correlation.

2.1 Special Product–Moment Coefficients

One of the most common cases investigators encounter is that of dichotomous variables. When one or both of the variables in a correlation is dichotomous, the analysis results in a special PMC with restricted interpretation and perhaps restricted range.

A correlation between one dichotomous variable and one continuous variable is called a point-biserial correlation (r_{pb}). The correlation between two dichotomous variables is called the fourfold point correlation or phi (ϕ). Both of these coefficients are PMCs and may be computed by the usual formulas as well as by special formulas given in some statistics books. They require no special attention on the part of the investigator in that dichotomous variables included in a computer run for correlation analysis will be properly processed by the usual equations and the results will be either r_{pb}s or ϕs. However, the investigator should be aware that neither of these coefficients should be used in Eqns. (11) or (14). They may be interpreted as indicating strength of association and they are the appropriate coefficients to use when dichotomous variables occur in a multivariate analysis.

A second situation that is encountered occasionally in educational research is that the data occur as rankings or other ordinal forms of measurement. While several methods exist for analyzing ordinal data, one popular bivariate procedure is the Spearman rank-order correlation (rho). This index is a PMC that may be computed from two sets of ranks by the usual formulas for r [Eqns. (18) or (19)] or by the classic formula developed by Spearman and given in most statistics texts. Rho is properly interpreted as an index of degree of association only, but it is the appropriate index to use (with caution) when ordinal variables are included in multivariate analyses.

2.2 Estimates of Product–Moment Correlations

It is often the case that a dichotomous variable represents an attribute that reasonably may be considered continuous and normally distributed. A classic example is the multiple-choice test item which dichotomizes the ability continuum into passes and fails. For bivariate situations where it is reasonable to assume an underlying normal distribution in one variable, and the other variable is measured as a continuum (for example, items and total test scores) the appropriate index is the biserial correlation (r_b). This coefficient is an estimate of what

the PMC would have been, had the dichotomous variable been measured as a continuous variable. The biserial correlation, using the subscripts 1 and 2 to indicate the higher and lower portions of the dichotomy, is as follows:

$$r_b = (\bar{Y}_1 - \bar{Y}_2)(p_1 p_2)/h S_Y \qquad (20)$$

where p_1 is the proportion in the upper group, p_2 is the proportion in the lower group, $\bar{Y}_1$ is the mean of the continuous variable in the upper group, $\bar{Y}_2$ is the mean in the lower group, S_Y is the standard deviation of Y, and h is the height of the normal curve at p_1.

The biserial correlation is an appropriate statistic for certain bivariate applications, but it is not a product–moment correlation. It can, on occasion, exceed unity and it is not a directly computable function of the scores themselves. For these reasons, r_b should not be used in multivariate analyses.

Another coefficient, the tetrachoric correlation (r_{tet}), is analogous to ϕ, in that it is based on the assumption that each of two dichotomous variables represents an underlying normally distributed continuous variable. The computation of r_{tet} is very complicated and is only approximate. In addition, the coefficient should not be used in further analyses. It is usually better to ignore r_{tet} and use ϕ instead.

3. Significance Tests

The topic of statistical significance probably is most fruitfully viewed from the perspective of sampling distributions. Assume that there is a population that reasonably approximates infinite size and that every member of this population has or could have a value on every variable of interest. If random samples are drawn from this population, measured on the variables of interest, and summary statistics computed, it is possible to make frequency distributions of these summary statistics. Such frequency distributions are called sampling distributions, and they exist for all statistics.

Of course, the population is never really completely available, and it is unusual to draw more than one sample, but mathematical statisticians have derived theoretical sampling distributions for many statistics. These theoretical distributions form the basis for statistical inference and significance testing.

Tests of statistical significance are usually applied to means, but they may be used with any statistic. The statistic of interest might be a correlation coefficient. Suppose, for example, that an investigator wishes to test the hypothesis that the correlation between two variables such as number of books in the home and reading ability at age 10 is greater than zero. This implies a one-tailed null hypothesis of the standard form that ρ (the correlation in the population) is zero or negative ($\rho \leqslant 0$), and this hypothesis creates a hypothetical sampling distribution of the correlation coefficient, r, for samples of size N. The investigator obtains a sample, computes r and the appropriate test statistic (described below), determines the probability of obtaining this large a value of the test statistic, and reaches a conclusion. If the value of the test statistic is unlikely, given the hypothesized sampling distribution, the investigator concludes that in the population from which the sample was drawn $\rho > 0$.

3.1 Tests for a Single r

Tests of statistical significance are somewhat more complicated for correlation coefficients than for means. The reason for this is that with sufficient sample size the sampling distribution of the mean is symmetric around the population parameter regardless of the value of that parameter, while for the correlation coefficient the shape of the sampling distribution depends on both ρ and N. When ρ is zero or close to zero, the sampling distribution is symmetric; however, when ρ exceeds about $+0.25$ the sampling distribution becomes skewed with the direction of skew toward zero. The degree of skewness increases as ρ increases.

Asymmetry of the sampling distribution is not a problem for most simple tests of hypotheses because for most cases the null hypothesis is $\rho = 0$. However, for nontypical nulls, such as $\rho = 0.60$, and for confidence intervals on larger correlations, the problem is more serious.

When testing the hypothesis that $\rho = 0$, the appropriate statistic depends upon N. For $N > 50$, the standard error of r is $\sigma_r = 1/(N^{1/2})$ and the statistic $z = r/\sigma_r$ is normally distributed. Smaller samples require that $t = r/[(1 - r_y^2)/(N - 2)]$, and that $df = N - 2$ be used instead.

The solution to the asymmetry problem for the PMC was derived by R. A. Fisher. The transformation

$$z_F = \ln(1 + r) - \ln(1 - r) \tag{21}$$

which is known as Fisher's z, results in a statistic that has a sampling distribution that is very nearly normal in shape for any value of ρ. The standard error of z_F is $1/(N - 3)^{1/2}$, and the statistic $z = (z_F - K)/\sigma_{z_F}$ is a normal deviate. In this case K is the value of ρ specified in the null hypothesis.

3.2 Significance of r_{pb}, ϕ, r_b, and rho

For small samples ($N < 100$) the best way to test the hypothesis ($\rho = 0$) for r_b and r_{pb} is to test the significance of the difference between group means. If the value of t exceeds the critical value with $N - 2$ degrees of freedom, it is safe to conclude that the correlation is statistically significant. When $N > 100$, r_{pb} may be treated as any other PMC, while the standard error of r_b is approximated by $\{(p_1 p_2)^{1/2} / [z(N^{1/2})]\}$.

The ϕ coefficient may be tested for significance by the relationship $\chi^2 = N\phi$, where χ^2 has $df = 1$. If the value of χ^2 exceeds the critical value, it is appropriate to conclude that $\phi \neq 0$. When the sample size is fairly large, the approximate standard error of ϕ is $1/N^{1/2}$.

A word of caution is necessary with regard to tests of significance for these coefficients. If the frequencies in the two categories of a dichotomous variable are very unequal, tests of significance may be inappropriate. McNemar (1969) suggests that when the proportion of cases in either category of a dichotomous variable exceeds 0.90 the significance tests should be viewed with caution.

Rank order coefficients such as rho are seldom used with large samples because of the difficulty of obtaining a clear ranking of large numbers of observations. Therefore, the statistic for testing significance will usually be a t test of the form $t = \rho/[(1 - \rho^2)/(N - 2)]^{1/2}$, which is identical to the small sample test for r. Unfortunately, this test only gives satisfactory results when N exceeds 10 and no satisfactory test exists for smaller samples.

3.3 Testing Differences between r's

The situation occasionally arises when it is desirable to test a hypothesis about the equality of two correlation coefficients. Such tests may take either of two forms. The correlations being tested may be correlations between the same variables in different samples, or they may be correlations between one variable and two different variables in the same sample. In the first case, both rs are transformed to z_Fs. The standard error of the difference between two z_Fs is $\sigma_{(z_{F_1} - z_{F_2})} = [1/(N_1 - 3) + 1/(N_2 - 3)]^{1/2}$ and the test statistic $z = (z_{F_1} - z_{F_2})/\sigma_{(z_{F_1} - z_{F_2})}$ is a normal deviate.

The second situation is a little more complicated. Three variables have been measured on a sample of N individuals, so there are three correlations, r_{12}, r_{13}, and r_{23}. If an investigator wishes to test the null hypothesis that $\rho_{12} = \rho_{13}$, the necessary test is

$$t = \frac{(r_{12} - r_{13})[(N - 3)(1 + r_{23})]^{\frac{1}{2}}}{[2(1 - r_{12}^2 - r_{13}^2 - r_{23}^2 + 2r_{12}r_{13}r_{23})]^{\frac{1}{2}}} \tag{22}$$

with $df = N - 3$.

3.4 Other Uses of z_F

There are two other useful applications of Fisher's z transformation in correlational research. The first of these is averaging correlations. Since the correlation coefficient itself does not represent an interval scale, it is not proper to average correlations directly. However, z_F is an interval scale measure of association, so it is appropriate to compute an average correlation, weighted by N. After converting each r to z_F, a mean z_F is found:

$$\bar{z}_F = \frac{(N_1 - 3)z_{F_1} + (N_2 - 3)z_{F_2} + \ldots + (N_j - 3)z_{F_j}}{(N_1 - 3) + (N_2 - 3) + \ldots + (N_j - 3)} \tag{23}$$

The standard error of $\bar{z}_F$, $1/[(N_1 - 3) + (N_2 - 3) + \ldots + (N_j - 3)]^{1/2}$, may be used to test the significance of the mean correlation.

Once $\bar{z}_F$ has been calculated, the mean correlation, r, may be found by reversing the original transformation or, more commonly, by reference to tables found in McNemar (1969), Thorndike (1982), and others. Finding $\bar{z}_F$ to be statistically significant is equivalent to finding $\bar{r}$ significant.

The second application for z_F is the determination of a confidence interval for ρ. Since the sampling distribution of r is not symmetric except when ρ is zero, the confidence interval for any nonzero ρ cannot be symmetric. However, the sampling distribution of z_F is symmetric. A proper confidence interval for any ρ can be obtained by transforming r to z_F, finding the standard error of z_F, multiplying σ_{z_F} by the appropriate critical values from the normal distribution, adding these products to z_F, and finally transforming the resulting limits for z_F back into correlations. For example, if $r = 0.65$ and $N = 19$, then $z_F = 0.775$ and $\sigma_{z_F} = 0.25$. To find the 95 percent confidence interval the critical values are $+1.96$ and -1.96. Multiplying these by 0.25 yields $+0.49$ and -0.49, and adding these values to z_F gives 1.265 and 0.285 as the upper and lower limits for z_F. These are transformed back to correlations, yielding 0.85 and 0.28 as the limits of the 95 percent confidence interval for ρ. Note that this confidence interval is symmetric around r in terms of probability, but not in the scale of r.

4. Partial and Semipartial Correlation

There are many occasions in educational research where it is desirable to control or remove statistically the effect of one or more variables. One way that this can be accomplished is through sampling. A characteristic that is constant for all subjects in a study cannot be a source of variance in the results. The effect of gender can be removed by using only male or only female subjects. Likewise, maturational factors can be controlled, at least in part, by studying children who are all the same age.

However, control at the sampling stage of a study has some definite drawbacks, the most important of which is that the generalizability of the findings may be severely restricted. Also, there are many research situations in which it is not possible to control variables by selection or it may be undesirable to do so because one or more of the questions of interest in the study involve the control variables as independent or dependent variables in the study. For example, in a study of the relationship between pupil attitudes and achievement the investigator might wish to remove or hold constant the effect of differences in age and measured intelligence. Selecting pupils of only a particular age and intelligence level would be wasteful of subjects and might distort the sample on other relevant variables such as socioeconomic status. In addition, the investigator might wish to include one or both of the control variables in a later phase of the analysis.

The solution to this problem is to collect data on an unrestricted sample, a sample that is representative of the population to which generalizations are to be extended, and then remove the control variables statistically. Note that the term control variable is being used in a restricted way in this discussion. Some potential variables such as conditions under which measurements are obtained should be held as constant as circumstances allow. It is to other variables, particularly status characteristics of the subjects, such as age, intelligence, and sex, that this discussion is directed. These variables

may be measured during the data collection phase, and their effects removed during analysis.

If X is a student motivation variable, Y is a performance measure, Z is ability, and S is sex, then it might be of interest to examine the relationship between motivation and performance both with and without controlling for ability and gender. The effect of one variable on another may be removed by analyzing the residual variance. For example, the residual variance in Y after controlling S is the variance in Y within levels of S, pooled across levels of S. The variance is found for males and for females independently, and the weighted average of these two variances is the variance in Y that is independent of S.

The analysis of residual variance is equivalent to using deviation scores of the form $y_{ij} = Y_{ij} - \bar{Y}_j$, or, for continuous variables, $y_i = Y_i - \bar{Y}_i$. Each individual's residual score is his/her deviation from the least-squares prediction made from the variables being removed or controlled. The residual scores are then analyzed like scores on any other variables. For example, the correlation between motivation and performance with the effect of sex differences removed from the motivation variable would involve correlating residual scores on motivation ($X_{ij} = X_{ij} - \bar{X}_j$) with raw scores on performance and is given the symbol $r_{Y(X.S)}$, where the subscript indicates that S is controlled in X but not in Y.

Correlations that involve residual variances are called partial correlations. When residual scores appear on both sides of the equation the term partial correlation or bipartial correlation is used. Semipartial or part correlations are those that involve residual scores on only one side of the relationship.

While the logic of partial correlations involves residual scores, the computations can generally be performed with the ordinary bivariate correlations themselves. Starting with the definitions of the residual scores as deviations from least-squares predictions, it can be shown (McNemar 1969) that the partial correlation of X and Y with Z removed is

$$r_{XY.Z} = (r_{XY} - r_{XZ}r_{YZ})/[(1 - r^2_{XY})^{1/2}(1 - r_{YZ})^{1/2}] \quad (24)$$

There is only one partial correlation between X and Y controlling Z, but there are two possible semipartial correlations, one where Z is controlled in X and one where it is controlled in Y. The formulas for these correlations differ from Eqn. (24) only in the denominator:

$$r_{Y(X.Z)} = (r_{XY} - r_{XZ}r_{YZ})/(1 - r^2_{XZ}) \quad (25)$$

$$r_{X(Y.Z)} = (r_{XY} - r_{XZ}r_{YZ})/(1 - r^2_{YZ}) \quad (26)$$

4.1 Higher Order Partials

There may be occasions when it is desirable to control more than one variable statistically. The logic is a direct generalization of the case of a single variable. That is, the analysis involves residual scores in one or both of the variables being correlated. The difference is that now the residuals are more complex. For example, the partial correlation of motivation and performance with sex and ability controlled (a second-order partial correlation) would first involve the residual scores on X and Y from sex. These residuals would then be entered into analyses with Z and the residuals of the residuals obtained. Finally, the correlation of second-order residuals yields the desired partial correlation. Higher order semipartial correlations can be conceptualized in the same way; however, they are very closely related to the standardized regression weights of multiple regression analysis and are usually obtained in that way.

Partial correlations of any order are correlations between residual scores of that order. As was the case with the first-order partial, the analysis may be performed starting with ordinary bivariate correlations. The procedure is a sequential one involving repeated use of Eqn. (24). First, all first-order partials removing one variable (say Z) are computed. Then Eqn. (24) is repeated for a second control variable, but with each term replaced by the appropriate first-order partial.

For problems involving more than two control variables the procedure described above is quite cumbersome. Although it would be conceptually and computationally sound to continue in such a sequential fashion, the analysis would almost certainly be performed by one of the computer programs that uses a matrix algebra solution.

4.2 Tests of Significance

The statistical significance of a partial correlation may be tested by procedures analogous to those used for simple rs. The z_F transformation is appropriate and with large N the standard error of z_F is $1/(N-p-3)$ where p is the number of variables being partialled out of the relationship. z_F may be used either to test a hypothesis about the partial correlation or to set up a confidence interval for ρ.

An alternative way to test the hypothesis that $\rho = 0$ for small N is available. The statistic $t = r_p/[(1 - r_p^2)/(N - p - 2)]^{1/2}$, in which r_p is the partial correlation and p is as above, is distributed as t with $df = (N - p - 2)$.

Tests of significance for semipartial correlations are closely related to multiple correlation. In general, the significance of a semipartial correlation is tested by testing the significance of the difference between the multiple correlation with the relevant variable included and excluded. If the difference between multiple correlations is statistically significant, the semipartial correlation of the excluded variable with the dependent variable of the multiple correlation analysis is significant.

5. Multiple Correlation

Correlation was defined as an index of the degree of association between two variables. Common bivariate correlations describe the relationship between a pair of observed variables. Partial correlations are PMCs between sets of residual scores after the effect of one or more variables has been removed. In all of these cases the correlation coefficient is an index of maximum relationship in terms of a least-squares criterion.

Multiple correlation extends the concept of least-squares association to the relationship of one dependent

or outcome variable with more than one independent or predictor variable. The multiple correlation coefficient is the bivariate product–moment correlation between the outcome variable (Y) and some combination of the set of predictor variables ($X_1, X_2, \ldots X_p$). The combination of X variables (call it P) is determined in such a way that the multiple correlation (r_{YP}) is the largest possible correlation that could be obtained from the given set of data.

The majority of work with multiple correlation in education and the behavioral sciences defines P as a weighted linear combination of the Xs. That is, if the array ($B_1, B_2, \ldots B_p$) is a set of weights to be applied to the Xs, then P is of the general form

$$P = B_1 X_1 + B_2 X_2 + \ldots + B_p X_p + A \qquad (27)$$

To say that P is a weighted linear combination of the Xs means that no term in Eqn. (27) involves a product of X terms or any X term other than the first power. The restriction of linearity is not a necessary one, and there are some situations where a particular theory may postulate nonlinear relationships, but for most applications the linear model is best for two reasons—its simplicity and its generalizability.

The definition of the best or least-squares composite of the set X is relatively simple, but is most easily accomplished if all variables are expressed as standard scores. In standard score form Eqn. (27) becomes

$$z_P = \beta_1 z_{X_1} + \beta_2 z_{X_2} + \ldots + \beta_p z_{X_p} \qquad (28)$$

It can be shown that for the special case of $p = 2$ the values of β_1 and β_2 are given by

$$\beta_1 = (r_{1Y} - r_{2Y} r_{12})/(1 - r_{12}^2) \qquad (29)$$

$$\beta_2 = (r_{1Y} - r_{1Y} r_{12})/(1 - r_{12}^2) \qquad (30)$$

These equations are very similar to semipartial correlations; β_1 represents the contribution of X_1 to P that is independent of X_2, and β_2 is the independent contribution of X_2 to P. They differ from semipartial correlations only by the scaling factor $(1 - r_{12}^2)^{1/2}$ in the denominator. The squared multiple correlation, r_{YP}^2, can be shown to be equal to the sum of products of the βs and the bivariate predictor–criterion correlations, $r_{YP}^2 = (\beta_1 r_{YX_1} + \beta_2 r_{YX_2})$, and the multiple correlation itself is the positive square root of r_{YP}^2.

Generalization to the multivariable case is most easily handled by using matrix algebra. The solution, which is simply a substitute for solving p linear equations in p unknowns, is given by $\beta_{pY} = \mathbf{R}_{pp}^{-1} \mathbf{r}_{PY}$, where β_{pY} is a $p \times 1$ vector of β-weights for use in Eqn. (28), $\mathbf{R}_{pp}^{-1}$ is the inverse of the $p \times p$ matrix of correlations among the p predictors, and $\mathbf{r}_{Y_p}$ is the $p \times 1$ vector of correlations between the predictor variables and Y. The squared multiple correlation is then given by $r_{YP}^2 = \beta_{yp} \mathbf{r}_{py}$.

The β-weights may be expressed in the metric of the original variables appropriate for use with Eqn. (27) by the transformation $B_p = \beta_p (S_Y/S_{X_p})$. The value of the intercept, A, is given by

$$A = \bar{Y} - \sum_{j=1}^{p} B_j \bar{X}_j \tag{31}$$

Of course, the correlation between Y and P is unchanged by this transformation.

5.1 Asymmetry of Multiple Correlation

There is an important restriction on the interpretation of r_{YP}. Whereas r_{XY} was a symmetric index of the degree of association between two variables, r_{YP} is not. The simple squared bivariate correlation reflects the proportion of variance in Y that is related to X and the proportion of variance in X that is related to Y. It is bidirectional. The multiple correlation is unidirectional in the sense that r_{YP} is the proportion of variance in Y that is related to the set of X variables but not the proportion of variance in the set of X that is related to Y. The relationship is symmetric in the observed variable Y and the latent variable P.

The reason for this asymmetry is the fact that P does not contain all of the variance of the set X. The variance that each X variable shares with P is given by $r_{PX} = r_{YX_p}(1/r_{YP})$. These correlations of observed variables with a latent variable are factor loadings. The mean of squared loadings

$$\left(\bar{r}_{PX} = \sum_p r^2_{PX_p}/p \right)$$

is the proportion of X set/variance that is related to P, and $\bar{r}_{PX} \cdot r_{YP}$ is the proportion of variance in the set X that is related to Y.

5.2 Tests of Significance

There are several types of hypotheses that can be tested in a multiple correlation analysis. The most obvious is $\rho_{YP} = 0$. The appropriate test of this hypothesis is an F test of the ratio of the mean square due to the multiple regression equation (MS_P) to the mean square residual (MS_R). Note that the total sum of squares of Y is

$$SS_Y = \sum_{i=1}^{N} (Y_i - \bar{Y})^2 \tag{32}$$

and that this is a combination of SS due to regression (SS_P) and residual (SS_R). That is, $SS_Y = SS_P + SS_R$.

It can be shown that these SS terms are given by $SS_P = r^2_{YP} SS_Y$ and $SS_R = (1 - r^2_{YP})SS_Y$. Each, divided by its degrees of freedom, is a mean square ($MS_P = SS_P/p$; $MS_R = SS_R/N - p - 1$). The ratio of these MSs, canceling where possible, is an F with $df_1 = p$ and $df_2 = N - p - 1$:

$$F = (r^2_{YP}/p)/[(1 - r^2_{YP})/(N - p - 1)] \tag{33}$$

A second hypothesis of interest relates to the contribution of some subset of the set X. The significance of the contribution of a subset of variables may be determined by the equation

$$F = [(r^2_{YP} - r^2_{YP2})/(p_1 - p_2)]/$$
$$[(1 - r^2_{YP1})/(N - p - 1)] \tag{34}$$

where r^2_{YP} is the squared correlation between Y and a set of $p_{1_i} X$ variables and r^2_{YP2} is for some subset of the variables in the first correlation. If F with $df_1 = p_1 - p_2$ and $df_2 = N - p_1 - 1$ is statistically significant, the contribution of the variables that were omitted from p_1 in p_2 is statistically significant. By applying Eqn. (34) repeatedly with each single variable omitted in turn, the significance of each β-weight in Eqn. (28) can be determined. Equation (34) is also used with the general linear model to perform tests of hypotheses related to the analysis of variance.

5.3 Stepwise Analysis

When a large number of predictor variables are available, a small subset of these variables will usually account for most of the predictable variance in the outcome variable. It is generally desirable to determine the smallest set of predictors that will do a satisfactory job of prediction for reasons of economy and simplicity. The method by which such a minimum subset is identified is stepwise analysis.

A stepwise analysis may be either a step-up or a step-down procedure. In the former, the analysis starts with the best single predictor and additional variables are added in order of the magnitude of their contribution. A step-down analysis begins with the complete set of predictors and deletes those variables that make the smallest contribution at each stage. The decision about which variables to add or delete is usually made by selecting the variable that results in the largest (step-up) or smallest (step-down) F as computed by Eqn. (34).

6. Canonical Correlation

A canonical correlation is the bivariate correlation between two latent variables or composites where each composite has been determined in such a way as to maximize its relationship to the composite of the other set. Given a set of X variables (measures of student achievement, for example) and a set of Y variables (interest or motivation measures) a canonical analysis finds a weighted linear combination, P, of the X set and a weighted linear combination, Q, of the Y set such that the correlation between them, r_{PQ}, is maximized. This is similar to the multiple correlation problem except that it involves the simultaneous solution for two sets of regression weights.

There is an additional complication in canonical analysis. Where there was only one multiple correlation coefficient, there are as many canonical correlations as there are variables in the smaller set. The first canonical correlation (R_{c_1}) is the highest possible correlation between composites of the two sets of original variables. The second correlation, (R_{c_2}), is the highest possible correlation between composites of the two sets of residual variables with the first pair of composites partialled out. In general, R_{c_i} is the correlation between composites of residual variables with all preceding composites partialled out. Thus, each succeeding pair of composites is statistically independent of all other pairs and each R_c describes an independent dimension of association between the sets.

A canonical analysis begins with three correlation matrices: $\mathbf{R}_{PP}$, the within set matrix of correlations among the X variables, $\mathbf{R}_{QQ}$, the within set matrix for the Y variables, and $\mathbf{R}_{PQ}$, the between set correlations of the X variables with the Y variables. The solution of a series of complete matrix equations (Cooley and Lohnes 1971, Thorndike 1978) results in a matrix of standardized regression weights (βs) for each set of variables and the R_cs between the pairs of composites.

However, interpretation of a canonical analysis is complex and requires additional information. While the regression weights indicate the relative contributions of the variables to the composites of their own set, the correlations between the observed variables and the composites, which are akin to factor loadings, may be of greater interest. There are four matrices of such loadings, two matrices of intraset canonical loadings of the X variables on the P composites and the Y variables on the Q composites, and two matrices of interset canonical loadings of the X variables on the Q composites and the Y variables on the P composites. These loadings, both intra- and inter-set, enable the investigator to treat the composites as factors and interpret them in a similar fashion.

6.1 Tests of Significance

The statistical significance of canonical correlations is tested sequentially. If there are J canonical correlations (the number of variables in the smaller set), then the first hypothesis tested is that all of them are zero. A significant value of the test statistic (χ^2) implies that at least R_{c_1} is nonzero. R_{c_1} is removed and the hypothesis that the remaining R_{c_j} are zero is tested. The sequence is repeated, removing the largest remaining correlation, until the hypothesis cannot be rejected. The pairs of composites associated with statistically significant correlations may then be interpreted. The test of statistical significance is an aid to the investigator in determining the dimensionality of the space in which the relationships among the variables will be interpreted.

6.2 Redundancy

The problem of asymmetry in interpreting the relationship described by a canonical correlation is more acute than for multiple correlations because R_c is an index of association between two latent variables, not the observed variables or the sets of variables. Proper interpretation of a canonical analysis requires computation of an index which was given the unfortunate name redundancy (Stewart and Love 1968).

Although there are alternate ways to conceptualize the redundancy index, perhaps the simplest is in terms of the interset canonical loadings. An interset loading is the correlation between a variable of one set and a composite of the other. The square of this loading is the proportion of variance of the observed variable that is related to the composite. The mean of squared loadings across observed variables in the set is the proportion of variance of that set that is accounted for by the composite of the other set. There are therefore two sets of redundancies; those of the X set of variables with the Q composites and those of the Y set of variables with the P composites. The sum of the redundancies for a set is the total redundancy of that set with the other set. In general the redundancy of set X with set Y will not equal the redundancy of Y with X.

Canonical analysis is an extremely general and flexible data-analytic model that has only briefly been described here. It has been shown (Knapp 1978) that most commonly used hypothesis testing procedures such as analysis of variance are special cases of the canonical model. More recently, Bagozzi et al. (1981) have demonstrated that canonical analysis is a special case of the structural relations model. However, proper interpretation of analyses such as these is complex and requires a deeper grasp of its technical aspects than can be developed here. Potential users of canonical analysis should consult Cooley and Lohnes (1971) or Thorndike (1978) for a more detailed explanation and examples.

7. Cross-validation

Whenever an index of relationship is developed on a sample using the least-squares criterion, the result is optimum for that sample. However, a least-squares equation in one sample will not be a least-squares solution for another sample from the same population. In the bivariate case the degree of correlation and the equation of the regression line will fluctuate from sample to sample. In multiple correlation the problem is compounded because the least-squares equation depends not only on the correlations of the predictors with the criterion but also on the correlations among the predictors. To the extent that the pattern of correlations in a sample deviates from the pattern in the population or in other samples, a condition called sample-specific covariation, the equation developed in that sample will give poorer results with new sets of data. Of course, the problem is worse with canonical analysis because two sets of regression weights are being fitted simultaneously.

The tendency of multiple and canonical correlation analyses to capitalize on sample-specific covariation raises two related issues—the degree to which the description (magnitude and pattern) of relationships generalizes to future samples and the accuracy of predictions made from the regression equation itself. A useful response to both of these issues is the procedure called cross-validation.

Cross-validation involves applying the least-squares regression equation from one set of data to a new set of data. The correlations between predicted and observed scores provide a good indication of how well "real" predictions would work if the criterion measures were yet to be obtained. Since the regression equation is not a least-squares equation in the new sample, it will be unaffected by sample-specific covariation in the data.

Likewise, the degree and pattern of relationships in the new set of data as described by the multiple or canonical loadings indicates the generalizability of the original equations as a model for new samples. The multiple or canonical correlations in cross-validation provide an index of the degree of fit of the model. A more complete discussion of issues relating to cross-validation may be found in Thorndike (1978).

Bibliography

Bagozzi R P, Fornell C, Larcker D F 1981 Canonical correlation analysis as a special case of a structural relations model. *Multivariate Behav. Res.* 16(4): 437–54

Cooley W W, Lohnes P R 1971 *Multivariate Data Analysis.* Wiley, New York

Draper N R, Smith H 1981 *Applied Regression Analysis,* 2nd edn. Wiley, New York

Harman H H 1976 *Modern Factor Analysis,* 3rd edn. University of Chicago Press, Chicago, Illinois

Knapp T R 1978 Canonical correlation analysis: A general parametric significance-testing system. *Psychol. Bull.* 85: 410-16

McNemar Q 1969 *Psychological Statistics,* 4th edn. Wiley, New York

Morrison D F 1976 *Multivariate Statistical Methods,* 2nd edn. McGraw-Hill, New York

Stewart D, Love W 1968 A general canonical correlation index. *Psychol. Bull.* 70: 160-63

Thorndike R M 1978 *Correlational Procedures for Research.* Gardner, New York

Thorndike R M 1982 *Data Collection and Analysis.* Gardner, New York

Correspondence Analysis

G. Henry

The factorial analysis of correspondence is one of the procedures recently developed for the analysis of information in the form of contingency tables, where nominal data are presented for examination. This procedure is one of the most efficient for describing and establishing relationships in qualitative data and was initially proposed by Benzecri (1963). It stands alongside contingency table analysis, configural frequency analysis, Galois Lattices, log-linear models and the scaling of nominal data, as one of a battery of new techniques that can be employed for the investigation of qualitative data. This procedure has as its principal characteristic an exchange of the roles of variables and observations and seeks to represent them in the same space. This type of representation was initially suggested by Kendall, but for a long time remained unused.

1. An Illustrative Example

The following hypothetical example was employed by De Lagarde (1983) to illustrate the procedure.

Let us suppose that a store has sold 1,000 records and has filed information on the characteristics of the records (jazz, songs or classical music) and on the characteristics of the buyers (young people, male or female adults, and old people). It is then possible to construct a contingency table (see Table 1) in order to analyse relationships between age, sex and type of music.

Let the proportional frequencies of the cells in the contingency table be denoted by f_{ij} for cell (i,j) where $i = 1, \ldots, I$, $j = 1, \ldots, J$. The marginal frequencies are denoted by

$$R_{i.} = \sum_j f_{ij} = r_i \quad \text{for rows, and}$$

$$C_{.j} = \sum_i f_{ij} = c_j \quad \text{for columns}$$

Table 1

Contingency table of numbers of records and buyers

Type of Music	Buyers				
	Young people	Female adults	Male adults	Old people	Total
Songs	69	172	133	27	401
Jazz	41	84	118	11	254
Classical music	18	127	157	43	345
Total	128	383	408	81	1,000

The values of the proportional frequencies are recorded in Table 2. The variable "type of music" is obviously recorded on a nominal scale. Likewise the variable "buyers" is also on a nominal scale. The aim of correspondence analysis is to represent graphically the data contained in this two-dimensional contingency table.

In this example, it would clearly be possible to use three rectangular axes (songs, jazz, and classical music) to represent the four categories of buyers in this three-dimensional space. However, such a direct representation is limited to small contingency tables and is not very useful. Correspondence analysis permits more complex bodies of data to be represented in simplified form.

Correspondence analysis is based not on the proportional frequencies recorded in Table 2, but on the relative proportions which are obtained by dividing f_{ij} by c_j for columns or f_{ij} by r_i for rows. The relative frequencies for columns are presented in Table 3.

If we denote f_{ij} divided by c_j as x_i, then $\Sigma x_i = 1$ for each value of j. Thus it is possible to state this as the equation of a plane

$$x_1 + x_2 + x_3 = 1 \tag{1}$$

If we have l dimensions with $(l > 3)$ the equation of the corresponding hyperplane will be

$$x_1 + x_2 + x_3, \ldots, x_l = 1.$$

Table 2
Contingency table of cell proportions of records and buyers

Type of music (i)	Buyers (j)				
	Young people	Female adults	Male adults	Old people	Total
Songs	0.069	0.172	0.133	0.027	0.401
	(f_{11})	(f_{12})	(f_{13})	(f_{14})	(r_1)
Jazz	0.041	0.084	0.118	0.011	0.254
	(f_{21})	(f_{22})	(f_{23})	(f_{24})	(r_2)
Classical music	0.018	0.127	0.157	0.043	0.345
	(f_{31})	(f_{32})	(f_{33})	(f_{34})	(r_3)
Total	0.128	0.383	0.408	0.081	1
($N = 1,000$)	(c_1)	(c_2)	(c_3)	(c_4)	

In this example the four points representing young people, female adults, male adults and old people belong to a plane since their three coordinates will satisfy Eqn. (1). Moreover, this plane will intersect the three axes at points A, B and C which are at a distance of one unit from the origin of the three-dimensional space. These three points will therefore form an equilateral triangle. As shown in Fig. 1, it is possible to represent the data for each group of buyers by a circle of area proportional to the value of c_j.

The reciprocal analysis is also possible in which the three points (songs, jazz, and classical music) are located on a hyperplane in four-dimensional space. In the reciprocal analysis, Benzecri (1973) weights the values of x_i by $(r_i)^{1/2}$ for the first analysis, and the values of x_j by $(c_j)^{1/2}$ for the reciprocal analysis.

In the first analysis:

$$x_i = \frac{f_{ij}}{r_i(c_j)^{1/2}}$$

and in the reciprocal analysis:

$$x_j = \frac{f_{ij}}{c_j(r_i)^{1/2}}$$

By proceeding in this way, the three poles of the triangle in the first analysis are no longer equidistant from the origin. The perpendicular line from the origin to the four dimensional hyperplane intersects the plane at a point G. Thus, OG becomes the initial axis of the four-dimensional scatter plot. By considering the reciprocal

Table 3
Contingency table of relative cell proportions (by columns) of records and buyers

Type of music	Buyers			
	Young people	Female adults	Male adults	Old people
Songs	0.539	0.449	0.326	0.333
Jazz	0.320	0.219	0.289	0.136
Classical music	0.141	0.332	0.385	0.531
Total ($N = 1,000$)	1.000	1.000	1.000	1.000

analysis, it is a simple task to identify the second axis. Mathematical procedures have been developed for computing these different axes. In the example concerned with buyers and type of music there are only two axes and the total proportion of variance extracted by these two factors is 100 percent. The four types of buyers and the three types of records can consequently be accurately represented in two-dimensional space as in Fig. 2. It should be noted that G is the centroid at which the proportions would be the same for each buyer or type of music category. When a point is far from G it contributes significantly to the location of the axes. Distances between points are also meaningful. For instance, in the example, note the relative proximity of the positions of female adults and songs, and between old people and classical music. In addition, it is clearly possible to identify the meaning of the two axes. The horizontal axis (axis 1) in Fig. 2 represents the relationship between young people and old people, while the vertical axis (axis 2) distinguishes between jazz and non-jazz music.

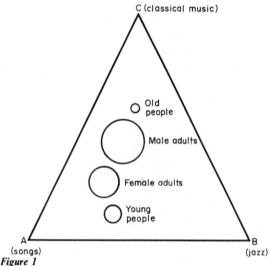

Figure 1
Type-of-music plane with buyer groups shown

One advantage of this procedure is that more complex mathematical operations can be carried out, but they will not be developed in this introductory article. For example, it is possible to calculate the relative contribution of each dimension to each of the factorial axes in order to identify more clearly the nature of the axes. It is also of value to calculate the expression

$$R = \sum_{ij} \left(\frac{f_{ij}^2}{r_i c_j} \right)$$

Since R is distributed with a chi-squared distribution, it is possible to proceed beyond a description of the sample and to employ inferential statistics.

Moreover, it is possible to generalize correspondence analysis to a $m \cdot n$ table. If j is the lowest dimension of the table then $j - 1$ axes of reference can be identified, and as with traditional factor analysis, the first two or three axes generally account for a high proportion of the

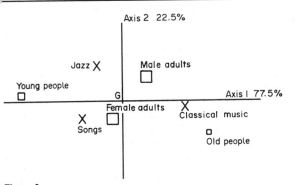

Figure 2
Positions of types of music and buyers represented in two-dimensional space

total variance. These features of the procedure will be illustrated in the following example drawn from educational research.

2. *A Study of Teaching Behaviour*

In a study reported by Crahay[1] of teaching behaviour, 21 lessons were observed of one teacher teaching the same sixth grade class. The verbal interactions between the teacher and the students were recorded on audiotape. The tape recordings of the first 20 minutes of each lesson were transcribed for more detailed analysis. Since the extracts of each of the lessons sampled and examined are of the same duration, the absolute frequencies of teaching behaviour are comparable between lessons.

From an examination of the transcripts, the verbal behaviour of the teacher was coded using a nine-category system developed by De Landsheere (De Landsheere and Bayer 1969, De Landsheere et al. 1973). The directions of the teacher–student interactions were also coded, namely, whether the teacher spoke to the whole class or to a specific student. In addition, the verbal participation of the students was coded into one of three categories. In this system of classification of teacher behaviour there was thus a total of 14 categories of teacher or student behaviour.

Five axes were identified as significant by correspondence analysis. The proportion of the data accounted for by each of the five axes has been recorded in Table 4.

The first two axes account for 63.48 percent of the data, which is sufficient to restrict further analysis to consideration of these two axes only. Distances in this two-dimensional space and the relative contributions of each variable can be calculated, but limitations of space prevent such information being presented here. However, a diagrammatic presentation of the lessons and teaching behaviour variables in the two-dimensional space has been recorded in Fig. 3.

In Fig. 3, each of the 21 lessons is indicated by a number and each of the teaching behaviours by a combination of letters. In the following discussion only those teaching behaviours and lessons which have a relative contribution equal to or greater than 0.20 are considered. Two groups of lessons can be identified and contrasted on the horizontal axis (axis 1). The first group are shown clustered on the left hand side of Fig. 3, namely lessons: 19, 3, 21, 17, 9, 14, and 15. The second group of lessons lie on the right hand side of Fig. 3, namely lessons: 4, 10, 1, 6, 7, and 11. The first group of lessons is associated with five teaching behaviour variables: TC (teacher speaks to the whole class); RSC (a student responds to a request that the teacher has addressed to the whole class, without specifying who has to respond); IMP (imposed instruction); FB$^+$ (positive feedback) and CONC (concretization by the teacher).

The second group of lessons may be characterized by five teaching behaviours: TP (teacher speaks to a specific student); RSP (a student responds to a request that the teacher has addressed specifically to the student); PS (a student spontaneously asks a question or reacts to the teacher's comment without specifically being asked); DEV (content development in the lesson); and A$^+$ (positive affectivity).

The first group of lessons reflect a traditional teaching style. During these lessons, the verbal behaviour of the teacher is mostly directed towards the whole class (TC). The teacher lectures and frequently asks questions of the whole group without specifying who has to respond. We may assume that those students who participate verbally are those who know the correct answer. This would account for the high level of positive feedback (FB$^+$).

The second group of lessons reflects another pattern of interaction: (a) where a specific student questions the teacher (PS); (b) the student responds (RSP); (c) the teacher's verbal behaviour is oriented towards a particular student (TP); (d) the teacher develops (i.e., accepts, classifies and amplifies what the student says) (DEV); and (e) the teacher gives more positive affect than usual (A$^+$). In the first group of lessons verbal participation by the students is quite different in comparison to the second group of lessons where the students participate spontaneously or respond to questions directed to them personally.

Table 4
Proportion of data accounted for by each axis

Axis	Proportion of data explained
1	33.07
2	30.41
3	8.05
4	7.47
5	7.01
Total	86.01

1 This example is extracted from M. Crahay, Stability and variability of teachers' behaviors, A case study. To be published in *Teaching and Teacher Education* Vol. 4, no. 4, Pergamon Press. We thank him for this authorization to use his paper and his data.

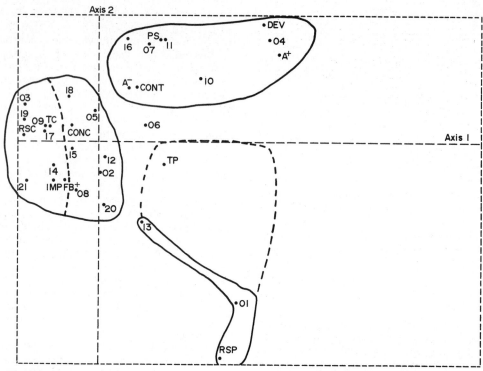

Figure 3
Spatial representation of categories and lessons

Before discussing the second group of lessons in greater detail, it is necessary to examine the vertical axis in Fig. 3 (axis 2). Few teaching behaviour variables show high relative contributions. The axis is clearly polarized on two forms of verbal participation by the students. On the one hand there is a student responding to a request that the teacher has specifically addressed to the student (RSP). On the other hand there is a student spontaneously asking a question or reacting to the teacher's comment without being specifically asked (PS). Four other teaching behaviour variables were found to have substantial loadings along this second axis: imposed instruction (IMP) and positive feedback (FB$^+$) on the negative side; and content development (DEV) and controlling function (CONT) on the positive side. However, the roles that these four teaching behaviour variables play in the definition of the second axis is slight, since their relative contributions do not exceed 0.28.

Five lessons are located on the negative side of this second axis (namely, 1, 8, 13, 20, 21). On the positive side, four lessons (namely, 4, 7, 11, 16) show a high relative contribution on this axis (greater than 0.44) and three others (namely, 3, 10, 18) show a lower positive loading on this axis (between 0.22 and 0.25). The six lessons which belong to the positive side of the first axis are split into three groups by the second axis. Four lessons (4, 7, 10, 11) are characterized by a high frequency of spontaneous participation by the students,

and by a low frequency of personally solicited participation, whereas lesson 1 is characterized by a low frequency of student spontaneous participation, and by a high frequency of personally solicited participation.

3. Conclusion

Correspondence analysis has therefore allowed the construction of a typology of lessons and their characterization according to two main dimensions. These two main dimensions take into account the different types of variables which have been observed. In one sense this technique of correspondence analysis may be compared with factor analysis and the scores assigned along the two axes to the calculation of factor scores, but the mathematical model is very different, and the technique is suitable for use with nominal data, whereas factor analysis is suitable for use with scores associated with an underlying normal distribution. Correspondence analysis seeks to account for the distribution of data in the specified categories, and factor analysis seeks to account for the variance in the scores obtained with respect to specified variables.

Bibliography

Benzecri J P 1963 *Cours de linguistique mathématique*. University of Rennes, Rennes, France

Benzecri J P 1973 *L'analyse des données, Vol. 2, L'analyse des correspondances.* Dunod, Paris

Crahay M 1987 Stability and variability of teachers' behaviors, A case study. *Teach. and Teach. Educ.*, forthcoming issue

De Lagarde J 1983 *Initiation a l'analyse des données.* Bordas and Dunod, Paris

De Landsheere G, Bayer E 1969 *Comment les maîtres enseignent.* Ministère de l'Education Nationale, Brussels

De Landsheere G, Nuthall G, Cameron M, Wragg E, Trowbridge N 1973 *Towards a Science of Teaching.* National Foundation for Educational Research (NFER), London

Lefebvre J 1976 *Introduction aux statistiques multidimensionelles.* Masson, Paris

Detection of Interaction

P. M. O'Malley

Statistical interaction refers to a situation where the effect of one variable on a second variable varies, depending on the values of one or more other variables. The focus of this article is on the detection of interaction effects in a set of data. For simplicity, the basic assumption will be that there is a single dependent variable, and at least two explanatory (or predictor, or independent) variables.

1. Definition

Consider a dependent variable Y, a predictor variable X, and a dichotomous variable C. It can be said that there is interaction present if the relationship between X and Y varies for the different levels of C. Figure 1 illustrates three possible patterns of association between variables X and Y for two levels of variable C. In (a) there is no interaction: the slope (though not the height) of the relationship between X and Y is the same for both levels of C (C-1 and C-2). In (b) the relationship is positive for both levels of C, but is stronger in C-1 than in C-2. In (c) the relationship is positive for C-1, and negative for C-2. The situation in (b) has been termed ordinal interaction because the rank order of means on variable Y is the same for each value of X. (The mean on variable Y for group C-1 is always higher than the mean for group C-2 at any value of X.) The situation in (c) is termed disordinal interaction because the rank order of means actually reverses. Of course, any two nonparallel lines will eventually intersect; therefore ordinal interaction occurs only for certain values of the X variable. The area of research interest defines whether the interaction is ordinal or disordinal. Thus, whether a situation is described as ordinal or disordinal can sometimes depend on which way the data are graphed; in the case where it makes a difference, the term hybrid interaction has been suggested.

There are two very different approaches to the detection of interaction: (a) an empirical search for interactions in a data set, and (b) the inclusion of an interaction effect in a statistical model and a test of its significance.

2. Searching for Interaction

The availability of high-speed computers has made it possible to search algorithmically through large data

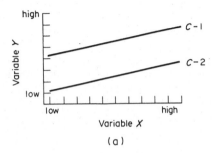

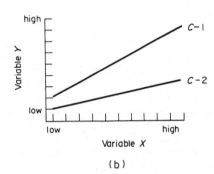

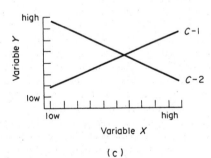

Figure 1
Examples of no interaction, ordinal interaction, and disordinal interaction

sets for interactions. One common automated search procedure is called AID, an acronym for Automatic Interaction Detector (Sonquist et al. 1974). This procedure is essentially a binary segmentation technique.

The program proceeds by first examining a single predictor to determine the binary (dichotomous) split for that predictor which provides the largest reduction in the unexplained sum of squares (or, equivalently, which explains the most variance) in the dependent variable. After every predictor in turn has been examined, the program divides the entire sample into two groups by making the dichotomous split on whichever predictor results in the largest reduction in the unexplained sum of squares. Each resulting subgroup is subjected to the same process until terminal conditions are met. The end result is a defined set of subgroups which is the optimal set for explaining variance in the dependent variable. The final set of subgroups is determined by the number of cases, number of groups, and amount of variance reduction.

If there is no interaction between predictors, then a symmetric set of subgroups would result. For example, suppose that the first predictor variable selected to subset the sample was sex; in this case, the total sample would be split into two groups, male and female. In the absence of interaction, each of these two groups would subsequently be split on some other variable. If they were not split on the same other variable, it would have to be because some variable (variables) had a different effect for males than for females, and that is interaction. A detailed examination of the pattern of splits is necessary to detect the specific interactions.

While this search procedure is intuitively appealing it unfortunately suffers from several problems. One problem is that search procedures such as AID are highly susceptible to error and there is considerable potential for detecting interactions which fail to replicate in new samples. This failure to replicate is because the interactions may be due to sample variability. The usual tests of statistical significance are not suitable in search procedures, and therefore are not very useful in determining significant interactions. Consequently, it is very important to use search procedures only with samples of large numbers of cases (as a rule of thumb, at least 1,000) in order to reduce sampling error. Further, it is advisable that the search procedure be conducted on one sample, and the validity of the resulting model be tested on another sample. However, if only one sample is available, the original can be split into separate search and validation groups.

The original AID was developed for use with a single intervally scaled dependent variable and at least two nominally or ordinally scaled predictor variables. Subsequent extensions have been developed to accommodate nominally scaled dependent variables and multiple intervally scaled dependent variables.

A more traditional technique for searching for interactions is the examination of residuals—the difference between observed values of data and values predicted on the basis of some additive models. In the absence of interaction, there will be no systematic association between the residuals and the variables used in the prediction. While inspection of residuals can be very useful, it is also true, as with the automated search procedure, that results of searches can be misleading. It is usually preferable to have an interaction hypothesized, for which a test can be performed.

3. Testing for Interaction

The classic approach to interaction detection is the analysis of variance (ANOVA). This technique is suitable when the dependent variable is intervally scaled and the independent variables are nominally or categorically scaled. The ANOVA model, in the case of two independent variables or factors in the ANOVA literature, assume that the "true" data (data without any sampling or measurement error) are "caused" by four effects: (a) an overall grand mean (a constant for each cell in the two-way cross-classification), (b) an effect for each level of the first independent variable (without consideration of the second variable), (c) an effect for each level of the second variable (without consideration of the first variable), and (d) an interaction effect for each cell. Stated algebraically,

$$Y_{ijk} = m + a_i + b_j + (ab)_{ij} \tag{1}$$

where the four terms on the right hand side correspond respectively to the four enumerated effects.

In the absence of interaction, the last effect is zero. In that case, a graph of the data generated by such a model (assuming no errors) would always show perfectly parallel lines (as in Fig. 1a). Equivalently, if one were to subtract from the mean in each cell the effects of the grand mean, and the main effects of the two factor variables, then the residual cell values would all equal zero. Any nonzero residual cell values, or any departures from parallelism, reflects the presence of interaction. In practice, of course, there is always some departure from zero, and the question is whether the amount of observed interaction is statistically or substantively significant. In the ANOVA model, the statistical significance is generally assessed by an F-test. Several features of this F-test should be noted.

One feature of the ANOVA model is that the interaction effects are assumed to sum to zero across relevant categories. This imposes certain restrictions on those effects. In the case of two two-level factors (a two-by-two design), for example, each of the four cells is assumed to have the same size effect (except two are negative and two are positive). Therefore, if the theoretical or hypothesized model requires some other pattern of results, then the standard factorial approach is not the most appropriate. Various alternatives exist, either in the analysis stage (for example, testing specific contrasts or using regression), or in the design stage (for example, nesting factors rather than crossing them).

A second point which should be noted is that a significant F-test for interaction, signals that there is some interaction between the data; as with the omnibus F-test for equality among means, it does not indicate specifically where the interaction is. Post hoc contrasts can be used to locate the combinations of cells that are responsible for the rejection of the null hypothesis. However, planned comparisons among interaction terms are valid alternatives, just as they are for equality of cell means.

A third point that should be made is related to the measurement theory involved in the usual ANOVA analyses. Here the concern is whether any observed interaction is "real" if there exists some way to transform the dependent variable so that the interaction is no longer significant. The reasoning is that since many dependent variables in social science research have only ordinal properties, rather than interval properties, the interaction effects should not depend on which particular ordinal scale happened to have been used. Therefore, the only true interactions are those that cannot be made to vanish under any monotonic transformation of the data. The conjoint measurement method and the functional measurement method have been developed to deal with this problem. The essence of the conjoint measurement approach is to determine whether any ordering of the cells in the factorial design is inconsistent with an underlying additive relationship. Only if there exists such an ordering (subject, of course, to assessment of statistical significance) is the presence of interaction accepted (Anderson 1970, 1981). The essence of functional measurement methods is to render the data as additive as possible, to determine the minimal amount of interaction consistent with the data. Only if that minimal amount is significant is the presence of interaction accepted (Krantz et al. 1971, Luce and Tukey 1964).

The major alternative to the ANOVA approach is multiple regression analysis. This is basically an additive technique; that is, it estimates a function of form:

$$Y = a + b_1 X_1 + b_2 X_2 \qquad (2)$$

where a is a constant, and b_1 and b_2 are regression weights to be applied to X_1 and X_2.

However, the model can be easily modified to include a term which reflects interaction between X_1 and X_2 in their effect on Y. If X_3 is the multiplicative product of X_1 and X_2, then the model:

$$Y = a + b_1 X_1 + b_2 X_2 + b_3 X_3 \qquad (3)$$

incorporates interaction between X_1 and X_2. The variables X_1 and X_2 can be either continuous or dichotomous or any combination. The presence of interaction is signalled by the difference in variance explained between the two models. The model which incorporates interaction will virtually always explain more variance than the additive version, and the additional variance must be examined for statistical and substantive significance. This technique is sometimes referred to as hierarchical regression, because the model with the interaction term incorporates the additive terms and the nonadditive term(s).

The interpretation of the interaction is much more complex than its detection. In particular, the estimates of the regression weights (b_i) can be affected by the particular scaling or coding used. Sometimes the product term is thought of as representing the interaction effect, analogous to the ANOVA situation. This is not generally the case, however, because the interaction variable is not orthogonal to (that is, uncorrelated with) the other variables. As a result, the interaction variable ordinarily

contains variance due to the linear effects of both other variables as well. This is an example of the more general problem of multicollinearity. The general technique of product terms can be extended to include three-way or higher order interactions, and in fact, the form of the interaction term can be made quite complex to represent specific hypothesized types of interactions (Southwood 1978).

Conceptually, the task of locating the source of interaction is facilitated by the use of a categorical variable (preferably dichotomous) version of at least one of the interacting variables. For example, variable C might refer to treatment groups and variable X might be aptitude and the researcher may be interested in an aptitude by treatment interaction. The situation then might look like Fig. 1. If (b) or (c) is the result, it becomes important to distinguish where the treatment groups differ significantly in the relationship between aptitude and the dependent variable. These "regions of significance" can be determined by straightforward techniques (Kerlinger and Pedhazur 1973 pp. 256–58), and the result can be some very specific statements of exactly where the interaction is.

If all the variables—including the dependent variable—are nominal, then neither regression nor ANOVA are convenient techniques for detecting interaction. In this case, multiple contingency table analysis (MCTA) is the preferred technique. There are several different general approaches to MCTA, which affects how interactions are detected and, in fact, how they are defined.

One approach is the general log–linear method which does not distinguish between a dependent variable and independent variables. In this approach, ANOVA-like notation is employed, and terms such as main effects and interactions effects are used. However, in this approach the goal is to describe the structural relationships among all the variables. In contrast, the goal in the ANOVA model is to assess the effects of the independent variables on a dependent variable.

When a distinction is made between dependent and independent variables, log-linear models can be converted into logit or linear logistic response models. In this case, the analyst predicts the log-odds of some response using a linear combination of effects of the nominal independent variables (Fienberg 1980).

Perhaps the most general approach in MCTA is the GSK procedure named after its creators (Grizzle et al. 1969, Reynolds 1977). In this procedure, the dependent variable can take any of several forms: means, conditional probabilities, log-odds, among others. A model can be specified, using a very flexible design matrix technique, which might include all main effects of the categorical independent variables, but no interactions. Such a model is analogous to regression, but weighted least squares, rather than ordinary least squares, is the estimation technique. Then, if the additive model provides a satisfactory fit to the data, as indicated by a chi-square statistic, there is no significant interaction. An unsatisfactory fit implies that the simple additive model is inadequate and further specification of the model, including interaction terms, can be used to improve the fit. However, the GSK procedure is more general than the logistic or logit procedure because it can incorporate nonhierarchical models and can also accommodate interval properties on the dependent and independent variables.

Often in the literature on detection of interaction, different terminology is used; conditioner or moderator variables are variables which affect, condition, or moderate the relationship between other variables. This is simply another way to look at interactions. These terms are particularly common in psychometric areas where the relationship between some criterion and some predictor(s) may vary among different types of individuals. Type of individual (for example, male vs. female) would be said to be a moderator of the predictor–criterion relationship. The same procedures as discussed above can be used to test for the presence of such moderator variables.

All the procedures discussed above to detect interaction rely on the concept of relationships between variables differing according to the values on another variable. The concept is clearest when the other variable is categorical, so that the data can be examined for different groupings, though it is by no means necessary that the other variable be categorical. When different groupings can be examined, the detection of interaction becomes an investigation of differences between groups in relationships. Even sophisticated structural equation models can be investigated in this way for different measurement models or for different causal models (Jöreskog and Sörbom 1978).

It is always important in comparing relationships found in disparate groups not to assume, if the relationships are similar in the disparate groups, that a similar relationship must exist at the aggregate level. It is quite possible to observe what is called a Simpson paradox (Simpson 1951).

A well-known example was provided in a study of sex differences in acceptance rates at a large university (Bickel et al. 1975). Females were found to be less likely to be accepted than males, a finding which seemed to provide clear evidence of bias. However, a close look at the data revealed that within each department, there was no evidence of bias. The reason for the overall lower acceptance rate for females was that females tended to apply more than males to departments that had lower rates of acceptance, regardless of sex. The relationship between sex and acceptance was critically dependent on whether the relationship was examined within or across departments. Nevertheless, it should be noted that this type of seeming paradox is not interaction in the sense used in this article, although it would be termed interaction in the log-linear approach.

See also: Interaction Effects

Bibliography

Anderson N H 1970 Functional measurement and psychophysical judgment. *Psychol. Rev.* 77: 153–70
Anderson N H 1981 *Foundations of Information Integration Theory*. Academic Press, New York
Bickel P J, Hammel E A, O'Connell J W 1975 Sex bias in graduate admissions: Data from Berkeley. *Science* 187: 398–404
Fienberg S E 1980 *The Analysis of Cross-classified Data*, 2nd edn. MIT Press, Cambridge, Massachusetts
Grizzle J E, Starmer F, Koch G G 1969 Analysis of categorical data by linear models. *Biometrics* 25: 489–504
Jöreskog K G, Sörbom D 1978 LISREL: *User's Guide*. National Educational Resources, Chicago, Illinois
Kerlinger F N, Pedhazur E J 1973 *Multiple Regression in Behavioral Research*. Holt, Rinehart and Winston, New York
Krantz D H, Luce R D, Suppes P A, Tversky A 1971 *Foundations of Measurement*, Vol. 1. Academic Press, New York
Luce R D, Tukey J W 1964 Simultaneous conjoint measurement: A new type of fundamental measurement. *J. Math. Psychol.* 1: 1–27
Reynolds H T 1977 *The Analysis of Cross-classifications*. Free Press, New York
Simpson E H 1951 The interpretation of interaction in contingency tables. *J. Royal Stat. Soc. (Series B)* 13: 238–41
Sonquist J A, Baker E L, Morgan J N 1974 *Searching for Structure: An Approach to Analysis of Substantial Bodies of Micro-data and Documentation For a Computer Program*, rev. edn. Survey Research Center, University of Michigan, Ann Arbor, Michigan
Southwood K E 1978 Substantive theory and statistical interaction: Five models. *Am. J. Sociol.* 83: 1154–203

Discriminant Analysis

P. R. Lohnes

Discriminant analysis is the special case of regression analysis which is encountered when the dependent variable is nominal (i.e., a classification variable, sometimes called a taxonomic variable). In this case, either a single linear function of a set of measurements which best separates two groups is desired, or two or more linear functions which best separate three or more groups are desired. In the two-group application, the discriminant analysis is a special case of multiple regression, and in those applications where the criterion variable identifies memberships in three or more groups, the multiple discriminant analysis is a special case of canonical regression. However, because of its focus upon the parsimonious description of differences among groups in a measurement space, it is useful to develop the algebra of discriminant analysis separately from that of regression,

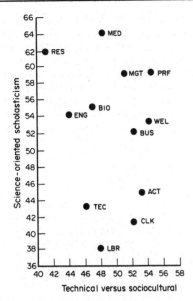

Figure 1
Group centroids in discriminant space

and to have computer programs for discriminant analysis which are rather different in their printouts from general regression programs.

1. Aspects and History

Discriminant analysis has had its earliest and most widespread educational research applications in the areas of vocational and career development. Because education prepares people for a variety of positions in the occupational structures prevalent in their societies, an important class of educational research is concerned with the testing of theories about the causes of occupational placements and/or the estimation of prediction equations for allocating positions or anticipating such allocations. This research is characterized by criteria which are taxonomies of occupations or other placements, and predictors which are traits of the individuals who have been sampled from the cells of the taxonomy. Thus there are many independent variates which can be taken as approximately multivariate normal in distribution, and a dependent variable which is a nominal identifier of the cells of a taxonomy (or the populations in a universe). The resulting discriminant analysis design may be thought of as a reverse of the simple one-way MANOVA (multivariate analysis of variance) design.

Where MANOVA assumes a nominal independent variable and a multivariate normal dependent vector variable, discriminant analysis assumes a multivariate normal independent vector variable and a nominal dependent variable. Both methods share the assumption of equal measurement dispersions (variance–covariance structures) for the populations under study, so that much of the statistical inference theory of MANOVA is applicable to the discriminant design, especially the significance test provided by Wilks' Λ, Pillai's V, Roy's Θ,

and the Lawley–Hotelling U statistics (Tatsuoka 1971 pp. 164–68, Timm 1975 pp. 369–82). There is also a formal equivalence of discriminant analysis to the canonical correlation design with dummy variates representing group memberships (Tatsuoka 1971 pp. 177–83). Discriminant analysis is also closely related to the statistical literature on the classification problem, since a discriminant space may be optimal for classification decisions in some situations (Rulon et al. 1967 pp. 299–319, 339–41). However, a good discriminant program will report interpretive results which will not be obtained from a canonical correlation program, and modern computers so easily compute classifications in original measurement spaces of very large dimensionality that the reduction in dimensionality provided by a discriminant space no longer has great utility when the emphasis is on classification.

Discriminant analysis serves primarily to provide insight into how groups differ in an elaborate measurement space. It is most useful when the number of measurement variates is so large that it is difficult for the human mind to comprehend the differentiation of the groups described by a table of means. Usually it will be found that the major differences can be captured by projecting the group means onto a small number of best discriminant functions, so that an economical model of group differences is constructed as an aid to understanding. Often the discriminant functions will be theoretically interpretable as latent dimensions of the manifest variates. It is even possible to make a rotation of the discriminant dimensions to more interpretable locations, once the best discriminant hyperplane has been located. Thus the goals and procedures are not unlike those of factor analysis.

Barnard (1935) seems to have been the first to describe the discriminant problem clearly. She wanted to classify Egyptian skulls into four dynasties on the basis of four measurements, which was so definitely a discriminant problem that Rao (1952) and Williams (1959) presented her results in their texts. Barnard had the problem but not the optimal solution, as she regressed a single time-line comparison of the skulls on the four measurements, thus making a standard multiple regression. Rao commented, "Barnard maximized the ratio of the square of unweighted regression of the compound with time. It is doubtful whether such a linear compound can be used to specify an individual skull most effectively with respect to progressive changes, since linear regression with time does not adequately explain all the differences in the four series" (1952 p. 271). Fisher (1936) provided the appropriate criterion to be maximized by a discriminant function, as λ equal to the ratio of the between-groups sum of squares to the pooled within-groups sum of squares on the function. He treated only the two-group case, for which weights which maximize λ depend only on the inverse of the pooled within-group dispersion and can be found by regression. His example used four measurements on 50 flowers from each of two species of iris, and is reproduced in the text by Kendall (1957). Tatsuoka (1971 pp. 170–77) gives an outstanding treatment of the special two-groups case.

Bartlett was the first to develop the multiple groups generalization of discriminant analysis. "If the 'most predictable criterion' were to be used as a discriminant function" (1938 p.36) said Bartlett, it would be possible to maximize λ more than once when there were three or more criterion groups, using dummy-coded variates to represent the group membership information. He stated with great clarity and elegance the application of Hotelling's 1935 invention of the canonical correlation method to the multiple discriminant problem. He showed that if there are g groups and p measurements, the number of nonzero λs must be the lesser of $g-1$ and p, and for each nonzero λ the corresponding canonical variable of the measurements is a discriminant function. He had no doubt that the desired discriminant functions should be uncorrelated and should span a hyperplane of minimum dimensionality to get the job done. Today when there is so much hard sell for modeling methods that encourage the use of correlated latent variables, it may be well to consider the motives of the great pioneers, including Pearson, Fisher, Hotelling, and Bartlett, who assumed that good constructed variables should be uncorrelated among themselves. Bartlett's 1938 paper deserves to be reprinted and read widely as a classic argument for parsimonious and mathematically disciplined modeling methods.

Hotelling's and Bartlett's inventions were destined to lie fallow for two decades for lack of computing machinery capable of evaluating the eigenstructures requiring numerical analysis in most practical applications of canonical and discriminant methods. In the interim there was one more major theoretical invention. Rao and Slater (1949) developed the algebra to generalize Fisher's λ criterion directly from the customary MANOVA accumulations matrices, rather than by using dummy variates in canonical regression. Since the Rao and Slater algebra is now accepted standard algebra for presenting the mathematics of discriminant analysis, it is reviewed in the next section of this article. Rao and Slater also originated the mapping of the group centroids in the best discriminant plane which has become the standard display of the model for the data, and is illustrated in the example provided later in this article, as Fig. 1. Strangely, Rao (1952) did not choose to incorporate these developments in his great pioneering textbook, but instead concentrated on the alternative device of using one classification discriminant function for each group, based only on the inverse of the pooled within-groups dispersion. He did reproduce the Rao and Slater (1949) demonstration of this approach (Rao 1952 pp. 307–29). Anderson (1958) also confined his treatment to classification discriminant functions, while Williams (1959) presented only the Barnard-type generalization to an arranged linear placement of the several groups which is then regressed upon the measurements. Rao's classification discriminant functions are mutually

intercorrelated, and while they provide an efficient classification rule they do not provide an elegant and parsimonious descriptive model for the differences among the groups. Kendall seems to have provided the first textbook treatment of Rao and Slater's generalization of Fisher's λ to the multiple discriminants method. Kendall said vividly, "If [the means] are collinear, one discriminator is sufficient; if they are coplanar two are required, and so on" (1957 p. 169). Perhaps Rao and Anderson ignored the multiple discriminants method in their texts because it is not essentially a statistical method. The interesting statistical issues are subsumed under MANOVA and classification. Discriminant analysis is essentially mathematical and geometric modeling of data on group differences. The model provided is a spatial one. The researcher's decisions about the rank of the model (i.e., the number of discriminant dimensions) and the naming and interpretation of the dimensions, which are so critical to the meanings produced, are based more on theoretical or practical considerations than statistical ones. The special value of the discriminant analysis is heuristic, and as Kendall perceived, in this it "links up with component and canonical correlation analysis and our various topics are to be seen as different aspects of the same fundamental structure" (Kendall 1957 p. 169). The difference is that discriminant and canonical analyses involve regression structures which are not viewed by principal components.

2. Mathematics

Letting

$$\bar{x}_j = \bar{X}_j - \bar{X}(j = 1, 2, \ldots, g) \tag{1}$$

where g is the number of populations sampled (i.e., the number of groups), so that $\bar{x}_j$ is the vector of deviations of the jth sample means from the grand means,

$$y_j = V' \bar{x}_j \tag{2}$$

is the desired discriminant model for the centroids, transforming the centroids into discriminant space. The necessary rank of y is the lesser of p (the number of variates in the measurement vector X) and $g - 1$, but often n (the rank of y) will be even smaller by choice of the analyst. Thus the desired transformation matrix V is a $p \times n$ matrix, each column of which contains the discriminant function weights for one of the functions $v_r (r = 1, 2, \ldots, n)$. Fisher's (1956) criterion for v_r is

$$\lambda_r = (v_r' B v_r)/(v_r' W v_r)|_{\max} \tag{3}$$

where

$$B = \sum_{j=1}^{g} N_j \bar{x}_j \bar{x}_j' \tag{4}$$

and

$$W = \sum_{j=1}^{g} \sum_{i=1}^{N_j} (X_{ji} - \bar{X}_j)(X_{ji} - \bar{X}_j)' \tag{5}$$

Table 1
Career plan groups

Acronym	Group name	Sample size
MED	Medicine and Ph.D. biology	279
BIO	Medicine and biology below M.D. and Ph.D.	438
RES	Physical science and mathematics Ph.D.	221
ENG	Physical science and engineering M.S. and B.S.	939
TEC	Technical worker	1297
LBR	Laborer with no post H.S. training	706
CLK	Office worker with no post H.S. training	530
ACT	Accountants and other trained nontechnical	1430
BUS	Business B.A. and B.S.	1214
MGT	Management post baccalaureate training	270
WEL	Sociocultural M.A. and B.A.	1183
PRF	Sociocultural research degree	815

making B the between-groups matrix and W the within-groups matrix. This motivated by the assumption that the populations share a common dispersion Δ estimated by

$$D_w = W/(N - g) \tag{6}$$

where

$$N = \sum_{j=1}^{g} N_k \tag{7}$$

making N the total sample size. Thus by assumption information about population differences is concentrated in the centroids.

The required maxima are provided by the eigenvalues and eigenvectors of

$$(W^{-1} B - \lambda 1) = 0 \tag{8}$$

The resulting discriminant functions are uncorrelated among themselves, but when the column eigenvectors associated with the nonzero eigenvalues are placed in V, V is not column orthogonal. Tatsuoka (1971 p. 169) shows that the angle between two discriminant dimensions has cosine equal to $v_r{}' v_s$, and he remarks that the discriminants are an oblique rotation of the principal components of X (p. 163).

Since $W^{-1} B$ is nonsymmetric, the numerical analysis of its eigenstructure is complicated. In 1962 Cooley and Lohnes published a practical discriminant analysis program supported by a subroutine called DIRNM (diagonalize a real nonsymmetric matrix) which facilitated computation of the eigenstructure of $W^{-1} A$. The DIRNM subroutine lies at the heart of the improved programs for discriminant and canonical analyses they published later (Cooley and Lohnes 1971 pp. 192–98, 258–60).

The discriminant functions can be scaled to unit standard deviation for the total sample by creating the matrix $T = B + W$ and the matrix $D = T/(N - 1)$, then defining the discriminant factors as

$$f_{ji} = (V' \, D \, V)^{-1/2} \, V' \, X_{ji}$$

$$= C' \, X_{ji} \tag{9}$$

Then

$$S = D \, C \tag{10}$$

is the very useful matrix of factor structure coefficients (i.e., correlations of the original variates with the discriminant functions). Users wishing to scale the functions to unit variance within groups may substitute D_w in Eqn. (9) and Eqn. (10).

Choice of scale for a discriminant function is arbitrary, since the weights are determined only with regard their proportionality to each other. Williams (1959 p. 177) suggested that it would be useful to set the variance for the total sample to unity, in order that the pooled within-groups variance on the discriminant function would decrease as further efficient predictors were added to the measurement vector. The complement of this pooled within-groups variance provides a useful index of the discriminating power of the function which is both the correlation ratio for the function and the squared canonical correlation coefficient between the discriminant function and the implicit canonical function of the group-identifying dummy variates. This excellent statistic is calculable as

$$R_r^2 = \lambda_r/(1 + \lambda_r) \tag{11}$$

Cooley and Lohnes liked this argument and scaled the discriminant functions produced by their program this way, so that this convention is represented by the example of the next section, and by Fig. 1. Others have argued that the appropriate scaling would set the pooled within-groups variance to unity, so that the plot of the group centroids in a discriminant plane would display the distances among groups in units of within-groups standard deviation. Isofrequency contours could then be drawn around centroids as circles. Since the model is on the means and is a spatial model, the argument for facilitating the interpretation of distances among centroids is a good one. Bock (1975 p. 405) provides a strong statement of the case for scaling so that the within-groups variance is unity.

Table 2
Discriminant functions

MAP Measurement basis	Discriminant	
	Science-oriented scholasticism	Technical versus sociocultural
Abilities	$R_c = 0.69$	$R_c = 0.37$
Verbal knowledges	0.62	0.20
Perceptual speed and		
accuracy	0.02	0.10
Mathematics	0.73	−0.49
Hunting–Fishing	−0.10	−0.26
English	0.28	0.23
Visual reasoning	−0.01	−0.43
Color and foods	0.08	0.10
Etiquette	0.05	0.07
Memory	0.00	0.01
Screening	−0.33	−0.25
Games	0.10	−0.05
Motives		
Business interests	−0.04	0.31
Conformity needs	0.21	0.12
Scholasticism	0.78	−0.19
Outdoors and shop interests	−0.41	−0.42
Cultural interests	0.25	0.47
Activity level	−0.22	−0.10
Impulsion	−0.01	0.08
Science interests	0.54	−0.36
Sociability	−0.19	0.47
Leadership	0.28	0.22
Introspection	−0.06	−0.03

The Bock (1975) text is especially strong on interpretation of discriminant functions. It asserts that discriminants are most useful when the many measurements available are low in reliabilities and factorially complex in validities. "Working with linear combinations of these variables tends to reduce variation due to measurement error and to enhance the effect of latent sources of variation common to two or more variables" (p. 416). Bock distinguishes between the case where a new measurement increases the reliability of a discriminant function and the case where it sponsors an additional dimension of discrimination. His examples illustrate collinearity of centroids, bipolarity of functions, and suppressor variables. Bock asserts that discriminant functions may be difficult to interpret "until the results of a number of independent studies utilizing the same set of variables become available" (p. 416). This is so, but it would also be helpful if authors of reviews of research would be alert for the appearance of substantially the same discriminant functions in studies using different mixes of measurements. More research studies should also be looked at in which previously discovered discriminant functions are moved intact to new samples. Many years ago Bartlett remarked about discriminants fitted by Hotelling's method to one sample, that "if a function suitable for discriminating species or groups were so devised, any subsequent use *on further data* would simply conform to orthodox analysis-of-variance lines" (1938 pp. 37–38).

3. Example

Cooley and Lohnes remark that the best discriminant plane is very often an adequate model for the data (1971 p. 244). The resulting reduction in rank, or simplification of the measurement basis, is perhaps the most attractive aspect of discriminant research strategy. In their Project TALENT researches, they found that approximately the same discriminant plane was discovered in a series of 14 researches using different samples and different taxonomic criteria but a common measurement basis (Cooley and Lohnes 1968 pp. 5–8). One of their studies can provide an example for this article.

The current career plan of 9,322 young men was collected by questionnaire five years after they left high school. These plans were classified into 12 categories of a careers taxonomy. Table 1 lists the 12 categories, with an acronym for each, and the subsample count. Six years earlier, when they were high-school seniors, these men had taken a battery of 60 ability tests and 38 typical performance scales. Lohnes (1966) created a factor analytic solution for these two batteries, and the measurement basis for the discriminant analysis was his 22 MAP factors. Table 2 lists these 22 factors and locates the two best discriminant functions by their correlations with the 22 scales of the measurement basis. The major discriminant function, called science-oriented scholasticism, is oriented toward mathematics and verbal abilities, and scholastic and science interests. The minor discriminant is bipolar, contrasting technical abilities and interests with sociocultural abilities and interests. Figure 1 maps the 12 group centroids on this plane. Note how it separates the laborer and office workers from the medical and research doctorates.

See also: Regression Analysis

Bibliography

Anderson T W 1958 *An Introduction to Multivariate Statistical Analysis.* Wiley, New York

Barnard M M 1935 The secular variations of skull characters in four series of Egyptian skulls. *Annals Eugenics* 6: 352–71

Bartlett M S 1938 Further aspects of the theory of multiple regression. *Proc. Cambridge Philos. Soc.* 34: 33–40

Bock R D 1975 *Multivariate Statistical Methods in Behavioral Research.* McGraw-Hill, New York

Cooley W W, Lohnes P R 1968 *Predicting Development of Young Adults: Project TALENT Five-year Follow-up Studies, Interim Report 5.* American Institutes for Research, Palo Alto, California

Cooley W W, Lohnes P R 1971 *Multivariate Data Analysis.* Wiley, New York

Fisher R A 1936 The use of multiple measurements in taxonomic problems. *Annals Eugenics* 7: 179–88

Kendall M G 1957 *A Course in Multivariate Analysis.* Griffin, London

Lohnes P R 1966 *Measuring Adolescent Personality: Project TALENT Five-year Follow-up Studies, Interim Report 1.* American Institutes for Research, Palo Alto, California

Rao C R 1952 *Advanced Statistical Methods in Biometric Research.* Wiley, New York

Rao C R, Slater P 1949 Multivariate analysis applied to differences between neurotic groups. *Br. J. Psychol. (Stat. Sect.)* 2: 17–29

Rulon P J, Tiedeman D V, Tatsuoka M M, Langmuir C R 1967 *Multivariate Statistics for Personnel Classification.* Wiley, New York

Tatsuoka M M 1971 *Multivariate Analysis: Techniques for Educational and Psychological Research.* Wiley, New York

Timm N H 1975 *Multivariate Analysis with Application in Education and Psychology.* Brooks/Cole, Monterey, California

Williams E J 1959 *Regression Analysis.* Wiley, New York

Expectancy Tables

G. Morgan

An expectancy table is a tabular device designed to report, in probabilistic terms, the relationship between two or more variables. This may be taken to mean that the relationship between the variables is expressed as a table of expected probabilities of possible values (outcomes) of one of the variables, usually called the criterion, for the sets of observed combinations of values on the other variables, usually called the predictors. In other words, the table provides the conditional distribution of criterion values for different combinations of values of the predictors.

Although many formats have been used for expectancy tables, most of these have, in one way or another, specified the relationships between the variables in terms of cross-tabulations, as in contingency tables. Indeed the usual starting point in the construction of an expectancy table is a scatter plot with a superimposed grid or, equivalently, a contingency table (frequency table). In education, the units of analysis of expectancy tables are persons, and the variables appearing in the tables represent characteristics of the persons or conditions or treatments applied to the persons. The numbers of persons or cases falling in the cells of the cross-tabulations provide the primitive database of an expectancy table, but in practice most expectancy tables report the probabilistic relationship between the variables in terms of relative frequencies, conditional probabilities (proportions), or percentages.

1. Constructing an Expectancy Table

When constructing an expectancy table, the choice of criterion from the set of variables being used must be guided by substantive considerations. As a rule, only one variable from the set is chosen to be the criterion, but the criterion may itself be a composite of two or more variables.

It is common to identify expectancy tables according to the numbers of their predictors. As examples, tables with one predictor are called single-entry expectancy tables, and tables with two predictors are called double-entry expectancy tables. Because of the problems of interpreting tables with more than two predictors, few such tables have been constructed.

In order to illustrate the concepts introduced in the foregoing discussion, two examples are presented here of expectancy tables. Table 1 is a single-entry expectancy table which reports the predictive relationship between scores on a mathematics aptitude test (the predictor) and scores on a mathematics achievement test (the criterion). The purpose of this table was to provide information which could be used to counsel and select future applicants to a university mathematics course, by providing them with measures of their likely chances of scoring satisfactorily in the course, based on their scores on the aptitude test. For this purpose, the variables were categorized as shown in Table 1; both tests allowing a maximum score of 100. Because the table was to be used in a predictive sense, the table's cell entries were expressed as conditional probabilities (raw frequencies shown in parentheses), which were computed by dividing each cell frequency by the total frequency of the row containing the cell. According to Table 1, the expected probability that a future applicant to the mathematics course will obtain a score on the achievement test in the score interval 60–79, given that the applicant's score on

Table 1
Example of a single-entry expectancy table

Aptitude test score	Achievement test score			
	20–39	40–59	60–79	80–100
80–100		0.01 (2)	0.29 (50)	0.70 (120)
60–79	0.02 (5)	0.20 (50)	0.40 (100)	0.38 (93)
40–59	0.11 (29)	0.39 (100)	0.39 (100)	0.11 (30)
20–39	0.48 (85)	0.43 (85)	0.06 (10)	0.03 (5)

the aptitude test falls in the interval 40–59, is 0.39. Also, if the applicant's aptitude score falls in the interval 60–79, the expectancy table states that the probability that the applicant's achievement score will be greater than 59 is 0.78 (0.40 + 0.38).

Table 2 represents a more detailed breakdown of the data on which Table 1 was based. It is a double-entry expectancy table involving two predictors—the aptitude test score reported in Table 1 and a predictor indicating the sex of the applicants. The purpose of this expectancy table was to allow finer predictions for each of the sexes. Table 2 clearly shows that, in general, female applicants have better chances of obtaining higher achievement scores than males, for the same aptitude scores. Consequently selection decisions based on Table 2 would be more favourable to the female applicants than the male applicants, whereas the male applicants would generally be expected to do better if decisions for them were based on Table 1 instead. Table 2 shows that by introducing a second predictor, namely the sex of the applicants, improved information about chances of success in the course can be gained for each applicant.

The above examples suggest how expectancy tables could be employed to predict performance: information which could subsequently be used to select applicants to courses. Typically an applicant could be selected if the applicant's scores on the predictors were greater or equal to cutting scores corresponding to an appropriately chosen level of achievement on the achievement test. It is important to understand that the validity of decisions based on expectancy tables such as Tables 1 and 2 are group dependent, and that tables should be used only with individuals or groups who are sufficiently similar to the group on which the expectancy table was based.

Perhaps one of the most important applications of expectancy tables is in test research and development, where the tables can provide a simple framework in which to report validity studies. Instead of presenting validity data in terms of correlational and regression statistics, which the nonstatistician may find difficult to understand or apply, these data often have been presented just as effectively, for most practical purposes, in tabular form as in expectancy tables. In many instances, one advantage of an expectancy table is that it can provide a picture of validity relationships rather than just a set of summary numbers.

There is no easy answer to the question of whether one, two, or more predictors should be used in an expectancy table. By and large the number of predictors is an arbitrary decision that must be rationalized on substantive grounds, and the question of ease of interpretation should be kept in mind. However, only one criterion is employed in an application of an expectancy table.

The problem of how to categorize the predictors and criterion variables is an important consideration when designing an expectancy table. Should a variable be expressed in terms of points, a dichotomy, or three or more mutually exclusive and exhaustive categories? Often the nature of a variable determines its categorization. Thus variables which are measured at the nominal level, such as the sex of individuals, come already categorized. However variables which are measured at higher measurement levels may not suggest obvious categorizations. In these cases there is no simple answer; the purpose of the table from the points of view of the constructor and user should provide the necessary guidelines. In general, the variables should be categorized in a way that is readily understood and usable by the user of the table. The point form of the variables is advantageous when computing cell entries in the expectancy table on the basis of regression analysis. However, the categorized form can often provide a more meaningful indication of the effectiveness of prediction. The use of few categories may simplify the reporting process, but it may also lead to loss of information through the aggregation of the data. The dichotomous form is useful when decisions are based on cutting scores.

As a rule, variables should not be overcategorized when there are few subjects, because the reliability of the data in an individual cell is proportional to the number of cases that fall in that cell.

The measurement units of the predictors and criterion is another important consideration. Should variables be left in their original form or expressed in terms of relative standing in the defined group? The relative standing may be expressed in terms of quantities such as percentiles and stanines. Use of the original units is recommended when the expectancy table is to apply to a single group, such as the students in a particular school or university. However, if useful comparisons are to be

Table 2
Example of a double-entry expectancy table

	Achievements test score	Aptitude test score			
		20–39	40–59	60–79	80–100
Female applicants	80–100	0.05	0.18	0.45	0.76
	60–79	0.11	0.48	0.39	0.24
	40–59	0.51	0.30	0.16	
	20–39	0.33	0.04		
Male applicants	80–100		0.04	0.29	0.63
	60–79		0.28	0.42	0.35
	40–59	0.35	0.49	0.25	0.02
	20–39	0.65	0.19	0.04	

made between groups it is necessary to convert original units to percentages or other standardized values.

2. Technical Issues in the Construction of Expectancy Tables

Methods for constructing expectancy tables may be concrete in that they make no distributional assumptions about the variables or the relationship between variables, or they may be theoretical in that they do make distributional assumptions.

Concrete methods utilize only the observed frequencies in the cells and margins of the contingency table to construct the expectancy table. Conditional probabilities, corresponding to cells, are computed directly from the cell frequencies and the marginal frequencies. Tables 1 and 2 are examples. The advantage of a concrete approach is its mathematical simplicity: it does not entail making complex transformations of the data to accommodate statistical assumptions. It is suited to decision making without concern for distributional assumptions. It also avoids the introduction of underlying model assumptions, which may be erroneous or unrealistic. Its major disadvantage is that without some kind of summary index, such as the correlation coefficient, which depends on statistical assumptions, it is difficult to evaluate the expectancy table or to compare it with other tables.

In contrast, the theoretical approach permits greater flexibility in the design of tables. Assumptions about the nature of the data may be varied, and different statistical techniques may be employed, in order to construct expectancy tables that serve particular purposes. Statistical techniques which have been used include those that involve the normal distribution, including regression and correlational methods and, more recently, techniques based on Bayesian statistics (Novick and Jackson 1974).

Some advantages of theoretical methods include (a) the facility to "smooth" cell entries so that cell entries display regular progressions, free of idiosyncratic fluctuations, (b) the facility to derive results for extrapolated regions where data are very scanty, and (c) the facility to adjust variables so as to take into account restriction of range.

Of these, perhaps the one of greatest importance is the use of smoothing-of-data techniques. Two reasons are frequently put forward for smoothing the entries in expectancy tables: (a) some cell samples may be small and (b) the relationships between predictors and criterion may not be monotonic, because of reversals in the cell data. Reversals may occur because of sampling fluctuations. Consequently, some have suggested that before expectancy tables are used, the tables should be smoothed by statistical means rather than left in their unsmoothed form. For example, in a counselling situation, it can be argued that it would be unsound to make recommendations that capitalized on sampling reversals in the data. Recent research (e.g. Perrin and Whitney 1976) on smoothing methods has examined methods that are based on (a) linear and multiple regression procedures, (b) isotonic regression procedures, (c) iterative maximum likelihood procedures, and (d) noniterative minimum chi-squared procedures.

In summary, expectancy tables are simple statistical devices useful for summarizing and reporting predictive data. The information conveyed by expectancy tables enables users to see at a glance the probabilistic relationship between criterion and predictors in terms of the pattern of cell entries.

Bibliography

Novick M R, Jackson P H 1974 *Statistical Methods for Educational and Psychological Research*. McGraw-Hill, New York

Owen D B, Li L 1980 The use of cutting scores in selection procedures. *J. Educ. Stat.* 5(2): 157–68

Perrin D W, Whitney D R 1976 Methods for smoothing expectancy tables applied to the prediction of success in college. *J. Educ. Meas.* 13: 223–31

Schrader W B 1967 A taxonomy of expectancy tables. In: Payne D A, McMorris R F (eds.) 1967 *Educational and Psychological Measurement: Contributions to Theory and Practice*. Blaisdell, Waltham, Massachusetts, pp. 209–15

Exploratory Data Analysis

G. Leinhardt and S. Leinhardt

Exploratory data analysis (EDA) is a collection of specialized tools and an approach to the analysis of numerical data which emphasizes the use of graphic displays and outlier resistant methods to detect and model patterns in data. Numerous researchers and statisticians have contributed to the development of EDA but the primary source of ideas is generally acknowledged to be John Tukey. Although many EDA tools have been known for some time, Tukey has created new procedures, improved older ones, and knitted them all together into a systematic method. Tukey's work, only partially described in his book, *Exploratory Data Analysis* (Tukey 1977), provides the data analyst with new capabilities for uncovering the information contained in numerical data and for constructing descriptive models.

Data exploration, as Tukey envisages it, is not simply an exercise in the application of novel tools. It is a phase of the empirical research activity, one which follows data collection (or acquisition) and precedes the application of confirmatory or "classical" inferential procedures (Tukey 1973). It is, thus, part of that twilight zone which experienced researchers find so exciting and challenging, novice researchers fear and misunderstand, and few researchers ever report. The excitement of this phase of research derives in large measure from the prospect of discovering unforeseen or unexpected patterns in the data and, consequently, gaining new insights and understanding of natural phenomena. The fear that novices feel is partly a response to this uncertainty, but it is also partly due to traditional teaching which holds that "playing around" with data is not "good" science, not replicable, and, perhaps, fraudulent. Many experienced researchers pay lip service to this view, while surreptitiously employing ad hoc exploratory procedures that they have learned are essential to research. Exploratory data analysis by making exploration routine and systematic, and by using theoretically justifiable procedures, opens the exploratory phase of research to public review, enhances its effectiveness, and allows for replicability.

Because Tukey's methods exploit the natural behavior of measurements, they allow researchers to rely on their intuitions. The simple logic of the methods helps clarify the process of modeling data and, consequently, makes it easier to detect errors in data or departures from underlying assumptions. Much of this is due to the graphical devices Tukey invented which are central to this approach because of their ability to portray a wide range of patterns that data can take. Well-designed graphics, such as those used in EDA, are useful for the guided searching that characterizes exploration and are also attractive mechanisms for communicating results to nontechnical audiences. As a consequence, EDA can serve in data analysis and for reporting the results of an analysis.

Many of the methods in EDA fall on the frontiers of applied statistics. Two important topics in statistics today are the robustness and resistance of methods, terms which refer to the ability of a procedure to give reasonable results in the face of empirical deviations from underlying theoretical assumptions. Clearly, robust and resistant methods are particularly advantageous in social science research because empirical social science data are so often obtained in an ad hoc fashion, frequently under nonreplicable circumstances, on opportunistically defined variables whose relation to substantive theoretical constructs are vague at best. Exploratory data analysis is especially important in educational research, where many of the variables studied and data collected are brought into analyses not because well-verified, substantive theory demands their inclusion, but rather because investigators "feel" they ought to be, because they are "convenient" to use, or because measurements have been recorded in some assumed "reasonable" manner. Nor are the data typically produced as a consequence of a scientifically designed experiment. It is precisely in such research that EDA can be used to its greatest advantage because it is here that

an open mind is an absolute necessity: the analyst rarely has the support of theoretically based expectations, and the real task confronting the data analyst is to explore—to search for ideas that make sense of the data (Simon 1977).

In the following brief description of EDA, only a few of the more usable techniques and the philosophical essence behind EDA are presented. Mathematical details are avoided but references to more extensive treatments are provided. The general objective of the procedures presented can be easily summarized. The procedures are tools for achieving resistant estimates of parameters for traditional additive and linear models. In this respect, they speak to a common empirical problem, the presence of outliers in data and the sensitivity of traditional methods of parameter estimation to highly deviant observations. Resistant analogs to three cases are presented: (a) a set of observations on a single factor at one level, (b) a set of observations on a single factor with multiple levels, and (c) a set of observations on two factors. In each case, the traditional approach to parameter estimation is mentioned first and then the EDA approach is detailed.

1. Organizing and Summarizing Individual Batches of Data

One of the first tangible products of a quantitative research project is a set of numbers, "data" that might contain information about the phenomenon or process under investigation. In many cases, the sheer amount of data to be analyzed can be overwhelming, leading an investigator to rely on summaries rather than dealing with all the values obtained. In addition to the impact that quantity can have, computer routines often present data values and summary statistics in a printed format which obscures rather than elucidates data properties. Automatically produced by routines designed to handle a wide variety of situations, output listings typically contain much that is distracting (e.g., decimal points, leading and trailing zeros, scientific notation) and little that is fundamental. In addition, such routines are usually designed to present values in what might be called an accounting framework, one that facilitates the location of identified values but provides little insight into the overall behavior of the data.

Even a small collection of data, for example, three variables for 50 cases, is extremely hard to visualize or to get a feel for. What is needed is a technique that preserves the detail of values but eliminates distracting noise and contributes to a first level of understanding. The stem-and-leaf display and the box plot are two such techniques.

2. Visual Organization: Stem-and-leaf Display

The stem-and-leaf display is an immensely useful and easily appreciated exploratory tool which can provide insightful first impressions. It combines the features of a sorting operation with those of a histogram. The basic procedure can be used to organize and provide information on a single batch of values in a wide variety of circumstances. (A batch is a collection of observations on a variable. The term is not meant to convey any notion of sampling from a population.)

Figure 1 presents a stem-and-leaf display of the number of 5-minute segments out of 40 in which each of 53 children was observed to be reading silently and is referred to as "direct silent" in the figure (Leinhardt et al. 1981). The arrows, words, and circles are for explanation only. To construct a stem-and-leaf display, each number in a batch is partitioned into a starting part (to the left of the bar) and a leaf (to the right of the bar). When single digits are used in leaves each starting part will be an order of magnitude larger than each leaf. A set of leaves for a given starting part is a stem. The unit of display records the scaled value.

To reconstruct a data value, juxtapose a starting part with a leaf and multiply by the unit. For example, consider the two leaves that form the first stem of Fig. 1: 6 and 9. To reconstruct the two data values that these leaves represent, simply juxtapose each leaf with the common starting part, 0, and multiply by 0.01, that is, $06 \times 0.01 = 0.06$; $09 \times 0.01 = 0.09$. As another example, consider the bottom-most stem in Fig. 1. It has only one leaf, 3. Juxtaposing the 3 with its starting part, 16, and multiplying by 0.01 yields 1.63. There are three starting parts 13, 14, and 15 that have no stems or leaves. This indicates that no observations have values between 1.27 and 1.63.

The display in Fig. 1 is actually the result of a two-step procedure (assuming the operation is carried out by hand). The first step normally yields a display in which the starting parts are ordered but the leaves on each stem are not. In the second step, each stem's leaves are ordered. This two-step procedure makes sorting a reasonably efficient operation.

Because all values in the display are represented by leaves occupying equal amounts of space, the length of a stem is proportional to the number of observations it contains. Thus, the display is like a histogram and provides information on shape and variation while also retaining information on individual values. This is true after the first step in construction. After the second step, the values are completely ordered and the display takes on the features of a sort. Because the display is like a histogram, anyone studying it can get the same kind of feeling for such elementary batch characteristics as overall pattern, bunching, hollows, outliers, and skewness that histograms provide. Those features that are akin to a sort allow the determination of maximum and minimum values quickly and, from them, the range of the values which can be used as a measure of overall variation.

Adding an inwardly cumulating count (depth) to the display greatly expands its utility. It facilitates finding other order statistics besides the maximum and minimum, such as the overall median and the medians of the upper and lower halves of the batch, which Tukey calls the "hinges." To form such a count, the number of leaves on a stem are cumulated from both ends in towards the middle. The median is located (not its value) at a depth halfway into the batch from either end. The count of the number of leaves on the stem containing the median is given and put between parentheses because it is not cumulative.

To illustrate the use of this column of inwardly cumulating counts, the count column will be used to find the values of the median of the data in Fig. 1. The median will be located at depth $(n + 1)/2$. Since there are 53 values, the median is at depth 27, that is, it is the 27th value in from either the high or low end of the sorted values. Counting into the batch from the low-value end (which happens to be at the top of this display), it can be seen that the 27th value is represented by a leaf on the fourth stem. The value of the median could just as easily have been determined by counting into the batch from the high-value end (at the bottom of the display).

While the stem-and-leaf display is useful for describing data, it can also be an effective exploratory tool. For example, looking at Fig. 1 an asymmetry can be seen skewing the values toward the high end. The clustering between 0.1 and 0.4 is obvious, as are the two groups at 0.6 and 0.8 and the modal group at 0.3. The minimum value, 0.06, and the maximum value, 1.63, are easily determined. There is a gap apparent between 1.27 and 1.63. A researcher might be concerned, even at this point, with the question of why the maximum value seems to straggle out so much.

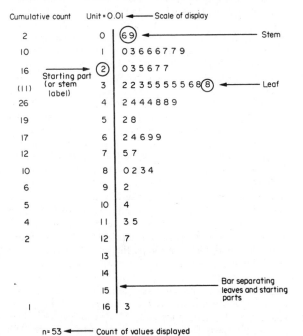

Figure 1
A stem-and-leaf display of direct silent reading data

3. Numeric Summarization: Number Summaries and Letter-value Displays

While the stem-and-leaf display is a convenient and easily understood tool, it has its drawbacks. This is most evident when different batches of values are being compared. Although a simple comparison of the shapes of two batches can be achieved by placing the leaves of one batch on one side and the leaves of the second batch on the other side of a common set of starting parts, simultaneously comparing three or more batches using stem-and-leaf displays is obviously going to be difficult, possibly even confusing. While the visual quality of the stem-and-leaf display is a true asset in any first look at the behavior of a batch, it may be burdensome to continue to work with all the data values at once rather than a set of summary statistics.

The question is which summary statistics to use. The problem with choosing the mean and related statistics, such as the standard deviation, is their lack of resistance to the impact that one or a few deviant data values can have. Because the mean is a ratio of a sum to the number of values making up the sum, it can be made to equal anything by simply changing a single value in the sum. This is not a problem, of course, if the data are reasonably well-behaved. Empirical data, however, often contain deviant values. Indeed, "weird" or "funny" values are rather commonplace occurrences (recall the value of 1.63 in Fig. 1) and, regardless of their source, they can cause traditional summary statistics to misinform.

Other statistics exist which are less sensitive to deviant values than is the mean, and, while they may not yet be fully supported by the inference procedures available for the mean, they may still be preferable at the exploratory stage of an analysis, where inference is not yet a focal issue. Some of the more useful and commonly known resistant measures of location and variation can be derived from the median and other order statistics. Most order statistics are little affected by the presence of a few outliers in a batch. One common resistant order-statistic-based measure of variation is the interquartile range.

Tukey exploits the resistance of order statistics, especially the median, in EDA. His first step in the numerical summarization of a batch for exploratory purposes involves computing five order statistics: the median, the extremes (or maximum and minimum), and the medians of the upper and lower quartiles (i.e., the hinges). When these five numbers are grouped together, they are called a "five-number summary" and can be arrayed conveniently as LE(LH, M, UH)UE, for lower extreme, lower hinge, median, upper hinge, and upper extreme, respectively. Tukey has introduced a truncation rule to avoid the inconvenience of small fractional ranks when finding medians of segments of a batch. The rule is

Depth of next median

$$= (1 + \lfloor \text{depth of prior median} \rfloor /2 \quad (1)$$

The symbols $\lfloor$ and $\rfloor$ refer to the mathematical "floor" function which returns the largest integer not exceeding the number. That is, the fractional component of a value, in this case a fractional depth or rank, is discarded. This means that the only fractional depths used will be those that lie halfway between two consecutive values and, thus, will be easy to compute and understand. As a consequence of this truncation rule, exploratory summary statistics may not be exactly equal to analogous-order statistics whose computation is derived from more mathematically precise definitions.

The notion of a median is easily extended to provide a way of segmenting a batch resistantly. The hinges are themselves medians of segments, the upper and lower halves of the batch. Medians of the upper and lower quarters halve the quarter so that each segment bounds one-eighth of the values; medians of these segments bound 16ths, then 32nds, then 64ths, and so forth. In EDA, this process works outward from the center to the edges of a batch providing more and more detailed information on the behavior of the tails of an empirical distribution.

Although letter-value displays and five-number summaries (and extended number summaries in which medians of further foldings are recorded) provide useful, resistant information on location, their primary analytic use is in facilitating the computation of other features of batches. Differences of values provide information on spread or variation in a batch. For example, the range of silent reading data in Fig. 1 is computed by subtracting the lower extreme from the upper extreme: $1.63 - 0.06 = 1.57$. The range, however, is not a very resistant measure of spread. Obviously, it is very sensitive to deviant values when these appear as extremes, a common occurrence. A more reasonable measure of spread is the range between the hinges. Analogous to the interquartile range, it is called a "hingespread." The hingespread (which is symbolized as *dH*) of the silent reading data is $0.69 - 0.26 = 0.43$.

The hingespread is a statistic of central importance in elementary EDA. It is a useful tool in the search for values that deserve attention because they deviate from most values in a batch. This search can be started by computing another measure of spread, the "step," which is 1.5 times the hingespread. Using this quantity, one literally steps away from each hinge toward the extreme to establish another boundary around the central component of the data. These bounding values are called the "inner fences." Another step beyond these establishes the "outer fences." Note that the fences are not rank order statistics but are computed distances measured in the same scale as the values of the batch. Values that fall between the inner and outer fences are called "outside" values, and beyond these lie the "far outside" values. The two data values (or more if multiple observations occur at the same point) falling just inside the inner fences are called "adjacent values"; they are literally next to or adjacent to the inner fences.

It is useful to re-examine the stem-and-leaf display in Fig. 1 in light of the new information obtained on spread. In examining this display, it was noted that the data were evidently skewed out toward the high end. The numerical information on spread confirms this visual impression and suggests that one value at the high end deserves further attention. This value may be erroneous, or it may have been generated by a process different from that which generated the bulk of the values. Having identified a potential outlier, the problem of deciding what to do about it arises. If data are used which are made to appear highly asymmetric because of a few extreme observations, then it must be realized that many of the usual forms of inference, such as analysis of variance and least squares regression, will be strongly influenced by these few values. These procedures are not very resistant and, while removing values from empirical data should be done with utmost caution, the fact must be faced that unless omission of outliers is explored, fitted parameter values may describe the behavior of only a very small portion of the data. Replicability of findings in such situations is unlikely and generalizability is questionable.

The theoretical rationale underlying this approach to identifying outliers is not explicitly developed in Tukey's book on EDA. Some implicit support is available, however, by examining the properties of a normally distributed population in terms of EDA order-statistic-based measures. In a Gaussian or normal population, 0.75 dH is approximately one standard deviation. Thus, 1.5 dH, a step, is approximately 2σ. Consequently, the inner fences, which are more than 2σ from the median, bound over 99 percent of the values of such populations. Observations drawn from a normal population that lie beyond the population's outer fences, which are an additional 2σ farther out, should indeed be rare.

4. *Schematic Plots as Graphic Summaries*

The quantities contained in number summaries and letter-value displays provide useful information on overall batch behavior. Most analysts, however, and certainly most nonspecialists, find that they can more easily appreciate the nuances of quantitative information when this information is displayed graphically. A schematic plot is an extremely useful graphic representation of the quantities contained in a number summary and, in fact, might well be considered a fundamental EDA summary device. It completely eliminates numbers (leaving them to a reference scale) and selectively obscures the data, drawing attention to some values and not others. Those values that are completely obscured are the values lying between the hinges, on the one hand, and those lying between the adjacent values and the hinges on the other. Attention is drawn by single marks to all values lying beyond the adjacent values. An example using the silent reading data appears in Fig. 2, which also shows the two other techniques that have been previously described.

Several points about schematic plots are worth noting. In the basic schematic plot, the width (or height, depending on orientation) of the box enclosing the central section of the data is arbitrary. However, this dimension can be used to represent information on other aspects of the data, such as batch size and significance of differences between medians (McGill et al. 1978). Whereas vertically oriented schematic plots are traditional and visually appealing, horizontal orientations are more effective for computerized printing operations because they permit a standard width to be used for any number of plots. Although the schematic plot is a visual device like the stem-and-leaf display, it is not as detailed and, indeed, is explicitly designed to reduce the amount of information being displayed. A related but even more elementary display, the box plot (so called because it consists of simply the box portion of a schematic plot and "whiskers" or lines extending to the extremes) obscures all except those in the five-number summary. Even though schematics speak to the issue of shape and spread, they can be somewhat misleading if gaps or multimodality occur between the adjacent values. Consequently, it is not advisable to use schematics as substitutes for stem-and-leaf displays, but rather as adjuncts.

5. *Transformations*

Frequently, naturally occurring data are modestly or extremely skewed, or exhibit some other property that make the data not normally distributed. Tukey emphasizes the need to consider the monotone transformation

Schematic plot

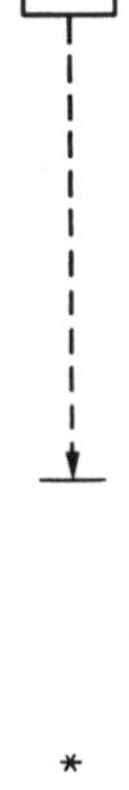

Unit = 10^{-2}

Number summary		Stem-and-leaf display	
LE	0.06	0	6 9
		1	0 3 6 6 6 7 7 9
LH	0.26	2	0 3 5 6 7 7
M	0.38	3	2 2 3 5 5 5 5 5 6 8 8
		4	2 4 4 4 8 8 9
		5	2 8
UH	0.69	6	2 4 6 9 9
		7	5 7
		8	0 2 3 4
		9	2
		10	4
		11	3 5
		12	7
		13	
		14	
		15	
UE	1.63	16	3

Figure 2
Schematic plot, five-number summary, and stem-and-leaf display for direct silent reading data

$y = kx^p$, where y is the transformed value, x is the original value, k is a constant set to -1 when p is less than zero and 1 otherwise. (The constant, k, retains order in the magnitude of the values when the transformation is a reciprocal.) The procedures for determining p are worked out and presented elsewhere and will not be described here (Leinhardt and Wasserman 1978). A summary of transformations is given in Table 1.

Thinking in terms of rescaled data values rather than raw data values is by no means straightforward and, given the central role that power transformations play in EDA, it is important that their rationale and validity is fully appreciated. There are several ways of thinking about transformations. One involves realizing that the well-grounded confirmatory tools of standard inferential statistics make specific assumptions concerning model structure and error properties. In many common procedures these include assumptions about normality of error distributions, additivity in parameters and variables, constancy of error variances, lack of functional dependence between error variance and variable location, and lack of interactions. When these assumptions are invalid, the procedures lose some of their appealing qualities. Their use in such problematic situations can be misleading. Unless procedures that deal directly with the known features of the data are used, one must resort to mathematical modification that adjusts the values so that their properties fit the assumptions of the model and/or estimation procedure. Transformations of scale can often provide the modifying mechanism.

An alternative view is more metatheoretical. In it the theoretical development of the social sciences is seen to trail that of the natural sciences in the sense of not yet having a well-developed, empirically verified, axiomatic and deductive body of theory from which the appropriate scale and dimension for representing a theoretical concept in terms of an empirical variable can be determined. Dimensional analysis in physics is an example of the power inherent in disciplines where such well-developed theory exists. In its absence, analysts must often use variables measured in arbitrary scales or variables defined in an ad hoc manner. Rarely is there any good reason to believe that such measures come in a form best suited to modeling relationships. In the absence of an a priori theory that could specify a model, EDA provides tools to determine whether rescaling a variable will lead to a better analysis.

6. Modeling Data

In EDA, models for data consist of two parts: a part that uses a mathematical statement to summarize a pattern in the data and a part that summarizes what is left over. Each observed value can be decomposed into a part that is typical of the pattern, the "fit," and a part that is not typical of the pattern, the "residual." Tukey constructs a verbal equation to represent a general class of models where the decomposition is additive:

$$\text{Data} = \text{Fit} + \text{Residual} \qquad (2)$$

Other models are not ruled out, but Tukey emphasizes the use of simple models because they are easily understood, are easily estimated, help reveal more complex features, and often provide a good first approximation to these complexities. Additionally, many other forms can be rendered in terms of Eqn. (2) through an appropriately chosen transformation. Consequently, Eqn. (2) plays a fundamental role in EDA.

The computational procedure is straightforward. The median is subtracted from each observed value. This yields a batch of residuals, that is, a batch of adjusted values indicating the amount by which each raw value deviates from the fitted central value. In terms of a horizontally formatted schematic plot, the computation of residuals is analogous to centering the raw data around their median and relocating the zero point on the horizontal axis so that this origin rests exactly on the median.

7. A Model for Multiple Batches

Most research projects are not performed for the purpose of fitting single parameter models or obtaining a single summary statistic such as the mean or median. At the very least, the simplest objective involves comparing several batches in an attempt to determine whether one

Table 1
Summary of transformations: roles, procedures, and failures

Data structure	Problem	Procedure	Failures
(a) Single batch	Asymmetry	Summary table (or equation)	Multimodality large gap
(b) One-way array	Spread heterogeneity	Diagnostic plot of log (dH_1) vs. log (x_1)	Inconsistency in dH_1
(c) Two-way array	Interaction	Diagnostic plot of comparison values	Idiosyncratic interactions
(d) Paired observations	Curvature	Slope ratios or equation	Nonmonotonocity
	Spread heterogeneity	(b above)	(b above)

Note: Sometimes the "correct" transformation is not well-approximated by kx^p for any "reasonable" choice of p

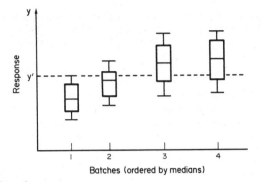

Figure 3
Box plots of multiple batches of hypothesis data

batch differs from another and by how much. A second-order question involves deciding whether an observed difference is important. These questions are traditionally approached through the analysis of variance (ANOVA) using ordinary least squares (OLS) estimation procedures. While OLS has estimable properties when special conditions hold (i.e., the parameter estimates are unbiased, consistent, and have minimal variance), some of these properties are lost when the conditions fail to hold. Such losses can result from the presence of a single outlier. An EDA-based approach which exploits graphical displays to detect data inadequacies is presented here which employs resistant measures in determining effects and provides a useful guide in obtaining a transformation that facilitates the use of classical procedures.

In classical ANOVA, the errors, ε_{ij}, are assumed to be normally distributed random variables with zero mean and constant variance. Thus, the sum of squares for batch effects and the errors are multiples of χ^2 random variables. As a consequence, F ratios can be formed to test zero effect null hypotheses and symmetric confidence intervals can be constructed.

An analogous EDA procedure is presented here; one that is more resistant to outliers than ANOVA but lacking distributional assumptions and, consequently, lacking inferential tests. The purpose is to provide a resistant analysis that can be used in exploration. Furthermore, the EDA procedure provides a useful mechanism for studying the problem of inconsistency of variation in the errors, that is, heteroscedasticity.

The EDA modeling procedure is similar to that pursued in a classical analysis except that common effect and batch effect are estimated by medians and, consequently, involve different arithmetic computations. The model represented by the verbal Eqn. (2) yields a "fit" that is applicable to all batch values. For multiple batches, this model can be further elaborated so as to distinguish a general or common effect across all batches and a set of individual batch effects that are confined within their respective batches. Thus, the general model becomes:

$$\text{Data value}_{ij} = \overbrace{\underbrace{\text{Common effect} + \text{Batch}_j \text{ effect} + \text{Residual}_{ij}}}^{\text{Fit}} \quad (3)$$

Conceptually, the model represents each observed data value as a conditional response determined in part by imprecision, noise, or error. No specific assumptions are made about this last ingredient except that, taken as a batch, the residuals are devoid of an easily described pattern. The information they contain relates solely to the overall quality of the model in terms of its ability to replicate the observed values.

The computational procedure is straightforward. First, consider the hypothetical multiple-batch data set represented by the box plots in Fig. 3. The median of the pooled batches is identified as the "common effect." Next, subtraction is used to "extract" this common effect from all data values. The result is simply a new centering of the adjusted batch values around a new grand median of zero. Second, the individual batch effects are obtained by subtracting the grand median from the individual batch medians. Finally, residuals are obtained by subtracting the batch effects from each adjusted value in the appropriate batch. The residuals are then examined as a whole and as batches. For the hypothetical example, the model is:

$$\text{Data value}_{ij} = \text{Common effect} + \left\{ \begin{array}{l} \text{Batch effect}_1 \\ \text{Batch effect}_2 \\ \text{Batch effect}_3 \\ \text{Batch effect}_4 \end{array} \right\}$$

$$+ \text{Residual}_{ij}. \quad (4)$$

The fitted value for the i, jth observation would simply be:

$$\text{Fit}_{ij} = \text{Common effect} + \left\{ \begin{array}{l} \text{Batch effect}_1 \\ \text{Batch effect}_2 \\ \text{Batch effect}_3 \\ \text{Batch effect}_4 \end{array} \right\} \quad (5)$$

8. A Model for Two-way Classifications

A more complicated but quite common data structure arises when responses can be identified with the levels of two factors. The usual summary layout used to organize such data is the two-way table, an array of "responses" organized on the basis of row (r) and column (c) factors. Such two-dimensional arrays consist of $r \times c$ cells or entries. Each row or column of a factor is referred to as a factor level or factor version. Factors are usually ordinally or nominally scaled but may be interval scaled. Responses are usually ratio scaled. The data are conceived of as triples of values: two classifying variables and a response variable.

The usual approach to such data involves an elaboration of the one-way model. A model, additive in factor-level effects, is posited. The array of responses is decomposed into an overall level or common effect, row effects, column effects, and interaction effects. A two-

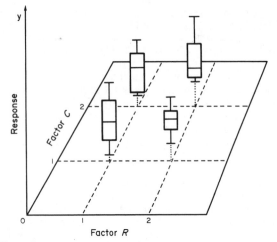

Figure 4
Graphical representation of hypothetical data for a two-way classification of responses (multiple unequal observations in each cell)

way ANOVA using least squares is the traditional method employed to estimate the model's parameters and to test for significance. In ANOVA, the grand mean is used to estimate the common term, and row and column means of the adjusted data estimate the row and column effects.

Once again, the EDA approach is analogous. The differences lie in the lack of distributional assumptions for the errors and the use of medians to estimate model parameters. Because no distributional assumptions are made, the hypothesis tests that are possible with least squares cannot be done. However, the use of medians ensures a result that is more resistant to the impact of deviant values. Furthermore, the EDA procedure provides a useful way to detect interactions even when there is only one observation per cell. When certain kinds of interactions are present, the EDA procedure can lead to a choice of a power transformation of the data that eliminates the interactions, that is, yields a scale in which the additive model provides a reasonable summarization of the data.

The model is in many respects an extension of the one-factor, multiple-level model proposed earlier for multiple batches. Indeed, a two-way table of responses can be thought of as two interwoven sets of multiple batches. Considering the column factor as the only dimension, there is a set of c multiple batches, each containing a maximum of r values. Considering the row factor as the only dimension yields a set of r multiple batches, each containing a maximum of c values.

Because the assumption is that each cell contains multiple observations, these data can be visualized as a two-way categorization of box plots as in Fig. 4. In the display, the vertical or y-axis is the scale on which the numeric response variable is measured. Factors R and C are categorical, so the distances between the levels, as well as their ordering, are arbitrary. The box plots of the

multiply observed responses appear elevated above the origin plane by differing average positive amounts. The mathematical model represented involves a decomposition of the average elevation of each box plot into four parts: (a) an overall level; (b) a contribution from the column level (which occurs regardless of row level); (c) a contribution from the row level (which occurs regardless of column level); and (d) an error or residual. In verbal equation form this appears as:

$$\text{Data} = \overbrace{\text{Common effect} + \text{Row effect}}^{\text{Fit}} \\ + \text{Column effect} + \text{Residual} \tag{6}$$

Whether the grand mean or grand median is used to estimate the common term, the result is conceptually identical. Its removal by subtraction effectively translates the origin plane so that the data are distributed around the origin rather than above it as in the hypothetical example. It is thus analogous to removing the grand median from a set of multiple batches, or the median from a single batch, and using the adjusted values, that is, the raw values with the grand median subtracted out, in constructing a new display.

By assuming that row and column effects are consistent, the model asserts that there will be only one effect for a row level regardless of the number of column levels, their size, and their effects and vice versa. In other words, the effect of row level 1 will be to elevate (or depress) the values in cells (1,1) and (1,2) the same amount, say a_1. Similarly, the effect of column level 2, according to the model, will be to elevate (or depress) the values in cells (1,2) and (2,2) the same amount, say b_2. Thus, any process of fitting this model to data must be constrained to finding these amounts according to a criterion that ensures an additive result. Given some estimate of these effects, the extent to which the data fail to conform can be studied by examining the residuals.

Thinking in terms of multiple observations in each cell gives an opportunity to reflect on the occurrence of weird or deviant cell values in cases where there is only one observation per cell, a common situation. For example, analyses of previously reported data where access to raw values is not possible must usually proceed with cell values reported as averages. In many instances, even when raw values are available, only one observation per cell exists. Finally, in some cases it makes sense to think only in terms of single observations as in a longitudinal sampling frame, and, thus, the observed single cell entry, while drawn from a theoretical distribution of values, is the only observation that will ever be made.

In such cases, it is clear that when a single observation is drawn from the extremes of the cell distributions, a deviant cell results. Means of values, as was demonstrated earlier, provide little protection in such situations because they will be sensitive to any underlying asymmetries. The prospect of deviant observations in the cells as a consequence of poor initial measurement or erroneous data entry is obvious and remains a problem.

The traditional analytic procedure, using means and a least squares minimization criterion, will be highly sensitive to any instance of deviant cell values. As an alternative, Tukey suggests using "median polish." This procedure is relatively resistant and reasonably easy to perform. It involves the repeated (iterated) removal (subtraction) of medians. Several algorithms exist. The following procedure is relatively easy to perform by hand or to program for a computer.

First, the grand median is found and used to estimate the common effect. This term is removed (equivalent to a horizontal translation of the origin plane in Fig. 4) by subtracting the grand median from each cell value. The result of removing the common effect is a new array of positive and negative cell values centered around zero. Now a sweeping operation begins which alternately removes medians from the rows and then from the columns. There is no particular reason to start the steps on rows or on columns. However, because the solution provided by the algorithm is not exact, the results may differ slightly. The operation usually begins by sweeping rows.

In each sweep, each row or column median is found and subtracted out of its respective row and column of cell values. Usually, the process will quickly arrive at a point where row and column medians are zero or near zero. The values remaining in the table at this stage are the residuals. Row and column effects are calculated by adding the row and column medians obtained at each iteration. Individual fitted values can be found by using Eqn. (6) and the appropriate row and column effects. Row and column fits (i.e., estimated values) can be found by adding the common effect to the sum of each row effect and each column effect.

9. Summary and Discussion

The tools and approaches that have been described comprise as much a philosophy of data analysis as a set of specific answers to a number of common data analysis problems. The philosophy is one in which the analyst's first task is viewed as discovery of evidence, not evaluation, and consequently, the tools are designed to reveal unforeseen features rather than to create a decision-analytic framework for judging the importance of expected features. These evaluative tasks are left for another time and for different methods. Exploratory data analysis addresses the need for formulating models and developing hypotheses through the use of empirical data. Using data to test specific models and to determine the precision of parameter estimates remains the province of traditional inference.

There are many procedures associated with EDA which have not been discussed here. Some of these are considered in a number of recent articles and books. Several computer packages now contain EDA procedures. CMU-DAP is an especially versatile package of confirmatory and exploratory procedures. MINITAB, a system widely distributed by Pennsylvania State University, now also possesses some EDA capabilities.

Two features serve as continuous themes in the procedures that have been described. The first is the desire to use resistant procedures rather than to rely solely on traditional least square methods. The solution that Tukey provides in EDA is a set of fitting procedures that use medians instead of means. A good operational rule is to try both resistant and standard methods on a data set and to move cautiously when the two disagree. The second theme deals with deviations from simple models in the form of asymmetry, spread-by-level interaction, and curvilinearity. Tukey's solution here is a standard one, the use of transformations of scale so that in the new scale the data do not exhibit these patterns.

In conclusion, the belief should be reiterated that there is little in the philosophy of EDA that will be new to the experienced scientist. What is new, useful, and timely is the systematic and routine way in which Tukey's procedures allow this philosophy to be put into practice. Furthermore, while research scientists will appreciate these advantages, evidence indicates that EDA can be extremely helpful to students just commencing their education in statistical methods. Using EDA as an introduction to statistics and data analysis provides a refreshingly intuitive and intellectually appealing route to the development of quantitative analytic skills.

Bibliography

Duncan G T in press *Statistical Thinking*. Wiley, New York

Erickson B H, Nosanchuk T A 1977 *Understanding Data*. McGraw-Hill Ryerson, Toronto, Ontario

Hoaglin D C in press *A First Course in Data Analysis*. Addison-Wesley, Reading, Massachusetts

Leinhardt G, Leinhardt S 1980 Exploratory data analysis: New tools for the analysis of empirical data. *Rev. Res. Educ.* 8: 85–157

Leinhardt G, Zigmond N, Cooley W W 1981 Reading instruction and its effects. *Am. Educ. Res. J.* 18: 343–61

Leinhardt S in press *Exploratory Data Analysis: A Primer*. Duxbury, North Scituate, Massachusetts

Leinhardt S, Wasserman S S 1978 Quantitative methods of public management: An introductory course in statistics and data analysis. *Policy Analysis* Fall: 550–75

McGill R, Tukey J W, Larsen W A 1978 Variations of box plots. *Am. Stat.* 32: 12–16

McNeil D R 1977 *Interactive Data Analysis: A Practical Primer*. Wiley, New York

Mosteller F, Tukey J W 1977 *Data Analysis and Regression: A Second Course in Statistics*. Addison-Wesley, Reading, Massachusetts

Simon H S 1977 *Models of Discovery*. Reidel, Dordrecht

Tukey J W 1973 The zig-zagging climb from initial observation to successful improvement. In: Coffman W E (ed.) 1973 *Frontiers of Educational Measurement and Information Systems: 1973*. Houghton-Mifflin, Boston, Massachusetts

Tukey J W 1977 *Exploratory Data Analysis*. Addison-Wesley, Reading, Massachusetts

Factor Analysis

D. Spearritt

Factor analysis is a technique for representing the relationships among a set of variables in terms of a smaller number of underlying hypothetical variables. It aims to describe the variation among a set of measures in terms of more basic explanatory constructs, and thus to provide a simpler and more easily grasped framework for understanding the network of relationships among those measures. Correlations might be computed, for example, among the scores of a group of students on measures of addition, subtraction, multiplication, division, vocabulary, and reading comprehension. A factor analysis of these correlations might show that the relationships among the tests could be almost completely explained in terms of two underlying variables, which might well be interpreted as computational ability and verbal ability.

1. Early Development of Factor Analysis

Although the technique of factor analysis is now applied in a wide variety of disciplines, it originated in the field of psychology. Towards the end of the nineteenth century a number of psychologists turned their attention to experimental studies of intelligence and intellectual abilities. Spearman collected data to test his theory that mental activity could be explained in terms of a single central intellective function, "intelligence". Finding high correlations between estimates of intelligence and students' scores on tests of weight, light, and pitch discrimination, he concluded that

> all branches of intellectual activity have in common one fundamental function (or group of functions), whereas the remaining or specific elements of the activity seem in every case to be wholly different from that in all others. (Spearman 1904)

Subsequently, in his two-factor theory, the fundamental function was described as a general factor, "g", and the element specific to a particular activity as its specific factor, "s".

Spearman had noted that his matrices of correlations among intellectual abilities could be arranged hierarchically, showing a progressive decrease in value from left to right and from the upper to the lower rows of the table. He recognized that this would be the expected pattern of correlations if all mental processes reflected the operation of a single central intellective function, which operated at different levels of complexity. To test whether a set of correlations he had obtained among six variables conformed to this pattern, for instance, he computed the tetrad differences among the correlations, for example $(r_{13}r_{26} - r_{23}r_{16})$. Finding that they were approximately zero, he confirmed the hypothesis that the correlations could be explained by one general factor.

The two-factor theory was challenged by Thomson and other psychologists on both theoretical and empirical grounds. Working with larger batteries of tests and larger numbers of cases, Burt identified verbal, numerical, and practical group factors in school subjects in addition to a general factor; a group factor is one which is represented only in certain similar types of tests but not in others. Spearman later admitted the necessity of group factors, and British factorists adopted a factor model which incorporated both a general factor and group factors.

Hierarchical theories of mental structure had little appeal for American psychologists. They preferred a multiple-factor approach in which several factors were extracted directly from a correlation matrix, without any initial assumption about the need for a general factor. In the early 1930s, Kelley and Hotelling sought a unique and exact mathematical solution to the problem of identifying the underlying factors in a correlation matrix, and developed the general method of principal components analysis put forward earlier by Karl Pearson. This method extracts successive uncorrelated components which account for as much of the variation among the scores of students on a set of variables as is possible at each stage.

Thurstone, the major American contributor to the development of factor analysis, noted that the addition of further tests to a battery could affect the factors identified by the principal components approach. He sought a method of analysis which would lead to the discovery of psychologically meaningful factors which were invariant, that is, supporting the same interpretation, over different test batteries.

In 1931, Thurstone accelerated the development of factor analysis by noting that Spearman's tetrad difference of $r_{13}r_{24} - r_{23}r_{14} = 0$ was the equivalent of setting a second order minor or determinant to be equal to zero. In algebraic form,

$$\begin{vmatrix} r_{13} & r_{14} \\ r_{23} & r_{24} \end{vmatrix} = 0$$

He reasoned that "if the second-order minors must vanish in order to establish a single common factor, then must the third-order minors vanish in order to establish two common factors, and so on" (Thurstone 1947). This allowed him to use matrix algebra procedures to express the problem of determining the number of factors needed to account for an observed correlation matrix. He formulated the problem in terms of the fundamental factor theorem $\mathbf{FF'} = \mathbf{R}$, where $\mathbf{R}$ was the original correlation matrix and $\mathbf{F}$ was the factor matrix to be identified. $\mathbf{F}$ would consist of a matrix of coefficients or "loadings" of the original tests or variables on the "factors", and would usually be a rectangular matrix of lower rank than $\mathbf{R}$. To avoid the then prohibitive calculations of the principal components solution to this equation, Thurstone developed the centroid method of analysis, which although quite tedious, was widely used until the 1950s, when advances in computer technology made other methods feasible.

Thurstone was also responsible for distinguishing two separate phases in the determination of factors—factor extraction and factor rotation. He recognized that the initial extraction of factors by the centroid method or by variants of the principal components method merely provided an arbitrary orthogonal set of reference axes—a set of axes at right angles to each other in two-dimensional, three-dimensional, or higher dimensional space depending upon the number of factors extracted—to represent the correlations among the tests or the relationships among the test vectors, and that any particular set of axes was only one of a very large number which would represent the correlations equally well. He claimed that the factor loadings determined at the factor extraction stage had no psychological meaning until they were rotated in the common factor space. Starting from the psychological assumption that there are some mental functions not involved in every intellectual task, Thurstone developed the criterion of simple structure to locate new positions for the reference axes. This required that the axes be placed so that each test would have significant loadings on only one or two factors and near-zero loadings on the remaining factors, and so that on each factor, a majority of the tests would have near-zero loadings. Unlike the British factorists, he made no initial assumption about the need for a general factor, but sought to determine "how many factors are indicated by the correlations without restriction as to whether they are general or group factors" (Thurstone 1947). It was left to the configuration of the test vectors to determine whether a general factor was needed in addition to other factors to explain the correlations among the tests.

Factor schools differed on the question of acceptable types of rotation. Most of the British factorists and a few of the American factorists insisted on orthogonal rotations; while a given axis could be rotated through any angle, the angle between that axis and other axes should remain at 90°. The factors therefore represented unrelated constructs. Thurstone, however, claimed that the restriction of unrelatedness or orthogonality of factors should not be imposed on the data. Application of the simple structure criterion would reveal whether the data could be represented by an orthogonal axis system. In most cases, however, the simple structure solution would require an oblique rotation of the initial axes, in which the angles between the rotated axes could be smaller or larger than a right angle. The factors emerging from an oblique rotation therefore tended to be themselves correlated. If the factors were correlated, the correlations among the factors could be further analysed to yield second-order or higher order factors, which to the extent that they were represented in all tests in a battery, could be regarded as analogous to a general factor.

The most significant developments during this early period of factor analysis were Spearman's conceptualization of the two-factor theory, its subsequent extension by British psychologists to a general plus group factor model, and a number of crucial contributions from L. L. Thurstone—his generalization of the two-factor notion to a multiple factor analysis model, his recognition of the need to rotate initially-extracted factors to arrive at scientifically interpretable results, and his development of the concept of oblique factors and of criteria for identifying factors. While the basic techniques of factor analysis were well-established by the 1950s, many problems remained. The initial extraction of factors still involved approximate methods, as did the estimation of test communalities, that is, that part of the variance of a test which it has in common with other tests in a battery. Criteria for determining the number of factors needed to explain the correlations were still approximate, and there was a substantial element of subjectivity in the graphical rotational procedures employed by factor analysts. Over the ensuing years, many of these problems have been resolved or considerably refined, with theoretical advances being greatly facilitated by advances in computer technology.

2. The Basic Factor Model

The basic factor model assumes that a score on a variable can be expressed as a linear combination or as a weighted sum of scores on factors underlying performance in that variable. If three hypothetical factors F_1, F_2, F_3 were assumed to underlie performance in test j, scores (expressed in standardized form, that is with a mean of zero and a standard deviation of 1) on test j could be represented by the equation

$$z_j = a_{j1} F_1 + a_{j2} F_2 + a_{j3} F_3 + U_j \tag{1}$$

where the a coefficients represent the loadings of test j on the respective common factors; F_1, F_2, and F_3 represent standard scores on these factors; and U_j represents scores on a factor unique to test j, including error of measurement. The standard scores of two persons on test j, for instance, might be expressed as follows:

$$\text{Person 1: } z_{j1} = a_{j1} F_{11} + a_{j2} F_{21} + a_{j3} F_{31} + U_{j1} \tag{2}$$

$$\text{Person 2: } z_{j2} = a_{j1} F_{12} + a_{j2} F_{22} + a_{j3} F_{32} + U_{j2} \tag{3}$$

Thus the loadings of test j on any one factor are the same for all persons, but the scores on a factor, whether common or unique, differ among persons.

Continuing with the above example, the standard score of Person 1 on test k would be given by

$$z_{k1} = a_{k1} F_{11} + a_{k2} F_{21} + a_{k3} F_{31} + U_{k1} \tag{4}$$

The product of the z scores of Person 1 on tests j and k, that is, $z_{j1} z_{k1}$ can be found by multiplying the expressions on the right-hand side of Eqns. (2) and (4). Summing the product of the standard scores on tests j and k over all N persons in the sample, and dividing the result by N gives

$$\frac{1}{N}\left(\sum_{i=1}^{N} z_{ji}z_{ki}\right) = a_{j1}a_{k1} + a_{j2}a_{k2} + a_{j3}a_{k3} \tag{5}$$

since the scores on the three factors are standard scores and the sum of the squares of standard scores is equal to N, and since product terms involving scores on different factors, whether common or unique, are equal to zero, as the factors are by definition uncorrelated.

The expression on the left-hand side of Eqn. (5) defines the correlation between tests j and k, so that

$$r_{jk} = a_{j1}a_{k1} + a_{j2}a_{k2} + a_{j3}a_{k3} \tag{6}$$

That is, the correlation between any pair of variables can be expressed as the sum of the product of the loadings of those variables on each of the common factors. Using the vector terminology of matrix algebra, Eqn. (6) can be written as

$$r_{jk} = [a_{j1}\,a_{j2}\,a_{j3}]\begin{bmatrix} a_{k1} \\ a_{k2} \\ a_{k3} \end{bmatrix} \tag{7}$$

Generalizing Eqn. (7) to represent the intercorrelations among n variables in terms of the three factors gives

Test

$$
\begin{array}{c}
 \\
\text{Test} \\
1 \\
2 \\
. \\
j \\
k \\
. \\
n
\end{array}
\begin{bmatrix}
1 & 2 & . & j & k & . & n \\
r_{11}^{*} & r_{12} & . & r_{1j} & r_{1k} & . & r_{1n} \\
. & . & . & . & . & . & . \\
. & . & . & . & . & . & . \\
r_{j1} & r_{j2} & . & r_{jj}^{*} & r_{jk} & . & r_{jn} \\
r_{k1} & r_{k2} & . & r_{kj} & r_{kk}^{*} & . & r_{kn} \\
. & . & . & . & . & . & . \\
r_{n1} & r_{n2} & . & r_{nj} & r_{nk} & . & r_{nn}^{*}
\end{bmatrix}
$$

Factors

$$
\begin{array}{c}
\text{Test} \\
1 \\
2 \\
. \\
= \; j \\
k \\
. \\
n
\end{array}
\begin{bmatrix}
F_1 & F_2 & F_3 \\
a_{11} & a_{12} & a_{13} \\
. & . & . \\
. & . & . \\
a_{j1} & a_{j2} & a_{j3} \\
a_{k1} & a_{k2} & a_{k3} \\
. & . & . \\
a_{n1} & a_{n2} & a_{n3}
\end{bmatrix}
\begin{bmatrix}
a_{11} & . & . & a_{j1} & a_{k1} & . & a_{n1} \\
a_{12} & . & . & a_{j2} & a_{k2} & . & a_{n2} \\
a_{13} & . & . & a_{j3} & a_{k3} & . & a_{n3}
\end{bmatrix} \tag{8}
$$

which is conveniently represented by the matrix equation

$$\mathbf{R}_c = \mathbf{F}\,\mathbf{F}' \tag{9}$$

where $\mathbf{R}_c$ is the matrix of correlations among the tests (which differs from the data-generated matrix $\mathbf{R}$ in that the asterisked diagonal entries consist of the correlation shared by the respective test with other tests in the battery and is less than unity), $\mathbf{F}$ is the matrix of test loadings on the factors, and $\mathbf{F}'$ is the transpose of the latter matrix. In Eqn. (8), r_{jk} of Eqn. (7) appears as the product of the jth row of the $\mathbf{F}$ matrix and the kth column of

the $\mathbf{F}'$ matrix. Equation (9) indicates that a given $\mathbf{F}$ matrix would yield a unique $\mathbf{R}_c$ matrix, but that a given $\mathbf{R}_c$ matrix could be analysed to yield many different factor matrices.

Equation (9) represents the common factor model. The complete factor model also incorporates the variance (ψ_j) unique to each test, thus:

$$\mathbf{R} = \mathbf{R}_c + \boldsymbol{\psi} = \mathbf{F}\mathbf{F}' + \boldsymbol{\psi} \tag{10}$$

where $\mathbf{R}$ is the correlation matrix with unities in the diagonal cells, and $\boldsymbol{\psi}$ is the diagonal matrix

$$
\begin{bmatrix}
\psi_1 & 0 & . & 0 & . & 0 \\
0 & \psi_2 & . & 0 & . & 0 \\
0 & 0 & . & \psi_j & . & 0 \\
0 & 0 & . & 0 & . & \psi_n
\end{bmatrix}
$$

Each of the unique test variances (ψ_j) is regarded as consisting of a reliable component (specific variance, s_j^2) and an unreliable component (error variance, e_j^2). The common factor variance or communality for each test is represented by the symbol h_j^2. Thus in the factor model the variance of a test is expressed as the sum of several components:

$$\sigma_j^2 = 1 = \underbrace{(a_{j1}^2 + a_{j2}^2 + \cdots + a_{jm}^2)}_{h_j^2} + \underbrace{(s_j^2 + e_j^2)}_{\psi_j} \tag{11}$$

The reliability coefficient (r_{jj}) of a test is the sum of the reliable components of variance, ($h_j^2 + s_j^2$) or ($1 - e_j^2$).

It was assumed in the derivation of Eqn. (5) that the factors in the $\mathbf{F}$ matrix were uncorrelated, and this assumption is also implicit in Eqn. (10). Regarding this assumption as unnecessarily restrictive, Thurstone advocated the acceptance of oblique or correlated factors if warranted by the configuration of the test vectors. When Eqn. (10) is expanded to accommodate correlated factors, the basic factor equation becomes

$$\mathbf{R} = \mathbf{R}_c + \boldsymbol{\psi} = \mathbf{F}\boldsymbol{\phi}\mathbf{F}' + \boldsymbol{\psi} \tag{12}$$

where $\boldsymbol{\phi}$ represents the matrix of correlations among the factors.

In the present example,

$$\boldsymbol{\phi} = \begin{bmatrix} 1 & r_{F_1F_2} & r_{F_1F_3} \\ r_{F_2F_1} & 1 & r_{F_2F_3} \\ r_{F_3F_1} & r_{F_3F_2} & 1 \end{bmatrix} \tag{13}$$

If the data can be satisfactorily explained by a set of uncorrelated factors, then $\boldsymbol{\phi}$ reduces to an identity matrix,

$$\mathbf{I} = \begin{bmatrix} 1 & 0 & 0 \\ 0 & 1 & 0 \\ 0 & 0 & 1 \end{bmatrix}$$

and Eqn. (12) reduces to Eqn. (10).

3. Exploratory vs. Confirmatory Factor Analysis

Usually, the first objective in carrying out a factor analysis of a correlation or covariance matrix is to arrive at an **F** matrix of the following form:

$$
\begin{array}{l}
\qquad\qquad\qquad\text{Factors}\\
\text{Variables}\quad I\quad II\quad III\quad :\quad p\quad :\quad m\\
\begin{array}{l}
\text{Test 1}\\
\text{Test 2}\\
\;\vdots\\
\text{Test } j\\
\;\vdots\\
\text{Test } n
\end{array}
\begin{bmatrix}
a_{1I} & a_{1II} & a_{1III} & : & a_{1p} & : & a_{1m}\\
a_{2I} & a_{2II} & a_{2III} & : & a_{2p} & : & a_{2m}\\
\vdots & \vdots & \vdots & : & \vdots & : & \vdots\\
a_{jI} & a_{jII} & a_{jIII} & : & a_{jp} & : & a_{jm}\\
\vdots & \vdots & \vdots & : & \vdots & : & \vdots\\
a_{nI} & a_{nII} & a_{nIII} & : & a_{np} & : & a_{nm}
\end{bmatrix}
\end{array}
\tag{14}
$$

This is the matrix of the loadings (a_{jp}) of a set of tests or other variables on a set of m underlying common factors, $m < n$. It is also referred to as a factor structure matrix, representing the correlations of each of the tests with each of the factors. As pointed out earlier, it is only one of a large number of matrices which would satisfy the relationship expressed in Eqn. (10), and some rotation of the axes represented by the factors would be required to arrive at a meaningful representation of the original data.

Both in its early development and in the large majority of its present-day applications, factor analysis has been used in an exploratory manner, to explore the underlying dimensions of a set of data. While there has been some indulgence in blind exploration among the uninitiated, in the sense of seeing what factors emerge from any ill-assorted set of variables, the use of factor analysis to explore the dimensions of an educational or psychological or sociological domain of interest has mostly been in the context of well-designed studies in which hypotheses have been carefully formulated and variables have been carefully selected. Exploratory factor analysis, however, does not place specific restrictions on the number of factors which should appear in the **F** matrix or the subsequent rotated matrix, or on whether particular entries in the factor matrices or factor correlation matrices should be zero or nonzero; it is an unrestricted factor model.

The idea of testing the hypothesis that the relationships among a set of variables might be accounted for in terms of a restricted factor model emerged in the mid-1950s, and following the work of such authors as Howe, Anderson and Rubin, Lawley, Jöreskog and Gruvaeus, had led to the development of procedures for confirmatory factor analysis. In contrast with exploratory factor analysis, confirmatory factor analysis sets out to test whether the original correlation or covariance matrix can be represented by an underlying factor matrix with a specific number of factors and/or specified zero or nonzero entries in factor matrices and/or factor correlation matrices. Instead of extracting an initial arbitrary **F** matrix and subsequently rotating that matrix, confirmatory factor analysis tests the specific hypothesis that the correlation or covariance matrix can be explained by an **F** matrix of a specified form, for example by a matrix

involving exactly three factors with a specified pattern of loadings as in (A) and of factor correlations as in (B) below:

$$
\begin{array}{cc}
\text{(A)} & \text{(B)}\\
\begin{array}{l}
\\
\text{Test 1}\\
\text{Test 2}\\
\text{Test 3}\\
\text{Test 4}\\
\text{Test 5}\\
\text{Test 6}\\
\text{Test 7}\\
\text{Test 8}
\end{array}
\begin{array}{ccc}
I & II & III\\
\end{array}
&
\end{array}
$$

$$
\begin{array}{l}
\text{Test 1}\\
\text{Test 2}\\
\text{Test 3}\\
\text{Test 4}\\
\text{Test 5}\\
\text{Test 6}\\
\text{Test 7}\\
\text{Test 8}
\end{array}
\begin{bmatrix}
x & x & 0\\
x & x & 0\\
x & x & 0\\
x & x & 0\\
x & 0 & x\\
x & 0 & x\\
0 & 0 & x\\
0 & 0 & x
\end{bmatrix}
\qquad
\begin{array}{l}
I\\
II\\
III
\end{array}
\begin{bmatrix}
1 & x & x\\
x & 1 & 0\\
x & 0 & 1
\end{bmatrix}
$$

Maximum likelihood methods are used to estimate the nonzero (x) elements in these matrices, given the original correlations or covariances among the variables. If a goodness of fit test then shows that the observed matrices do not deviate significantly ($p < 0.05$) from the hypothesized factor solutions, the specific theoretical hypothesis is confirmed.

4. Initial Extraction of Factors

Many approaches to the determination of the initial **F** matrix have been developed since Thurstone proposed his centroid method of analysis, and many earlier methods have been superseded as a result of the development of computers. One set of reference axes and its associated **F** matrix have the important property that they enable a set of correlated variables to be described in terms of a set of orthogonal (uncorrelated) axes which account for the maximum amount of variance remaining among the variables as each axis in the new set is determined. The axes in this set are called the principal components of the original correlation matrix.

Equation (15) presents a correlation matrix for three tests: Vocabulary (V), Comprehension (C), Arithmetic problems (A).

$$
\mathbf{R} =
\begin{array}{l}
(V)\\
(C)\\
(A)
\end{array}
\begin{array}{c}
(V)\quad (C)\quad (A)
\end{array}
\begin{bmatrix}
1.0 & 0.6 & 0.2\\
0.6 & 1.0 & 0.4\\
0.2 & 0.4 & 1.0
\end{bmatrix}
\tag{15}
$$

This matrix can be represented by an ellipsoid of points in three-dimensional space, defined by three orthogonal axes X, Y, and Z. The ellipsoid would take the shape of an elongated football oriented from one corner of a room at floor level (the origin of the three-dimensional space) upwards towards the ceiling and outwards to the opposite walls. The first principal axis of the correlation matrix would be the major axis of the football; the second principal axis would pass through the centroid of the set of points and would be perpendicular to the first principal axis; the third principal axis would be perpendicular to both the first and second principal axes, representing the length of the line across the football if it had been flattened in one of its shorter dimensions. These three axes are called the principal components of the correlation matrix. The variances of the principal components are the latent roots or eigenvalues of $\mathbf{R}$ which are determined by solving the characteristic equation

$$|\mathbf{R} - \lambda\mathbf{I}| = 0 \qquad (16)$$

These eigenvalues show the variance of the points along the first, second, and third principal axes of the football to be 1.823, 0.817, and 0.360 respectively.

The orientation of the principal axes with respect to the original axes is given by a set of eigenvectors corresponding to each eigenvalue; these are the direction cosines of each principal axis. By multiplying the elements of the eigenvectors by the square root of the corresponding eigenvalues, the loadings of the tests on the new axes would be found to be

$$
\begin{array}{cccc}
 & \begin{array}{c}\text{1st} \\ \text{principal} \\ \text{component}\end{array} & \begin{array}{c}\text{2nd} \\ \text{principal} \\ \text{component}\end{array} & \begin{array}{c}\text{3rd} \\ \text{principal} \\ \text{component}\end{array} \\
\begin{array}{c}V \\ C \\ A\end{array} & \left[\begin{array}{c}0.800 \\ 0.888 \\ 0.627\end{array}\right. & \begin{array}{c}-0.475 \\ -0.110 \\ 0.762\end{array} & \left.\begin{array}{c}0.366 \\ -0.446 \\ 0.164\end{array}\right]
\end{array}
\qquad (17)
$$

Principal component analysis describes the relationships among the original n variables in terms of n new uncorrelated factors, rather than in terms of a reduced number of factors. Principal axes can be found, however, for the matrix $\mathbf{R}_c$ [see Eqn. (9)], in which the correlations in the diagonal cells represent the variance which each variable has in common with other variables in the set, not including the unique variance. This application of the principal axes method is referred to as principal factor analysis.

The principal factor method will be illustrated with the aid of the fictitious matrix in Eqn. (18), which is based on the correlations among the scores of 200 15-year-old secondary-school students on examinations in English, French, Italian, physics, and chemistry, but in which the diagonal values of unity have been replaced by the communality, h_j^2, [see Eqn. (11)] of each variable. The communality is that part of the variance of each variable which it holds in common with one or more other variables in the set, or that part of the variable's self-correlation attributable to common factor variance in the set of variables. The squared multiple correlation of each variable with all of the other variables in the set is now usually accepted as the communality estimate, and has replaced the original values of unity in the diagonal cells of the matrix in Eqn. (18), which is therefore designated as $\mathbf{R}_c$.

The principal factors for $\mathbf{R}_c$ can be determined by finding the eigenvalues and eigenvectors of the above matrix. As the communality estimates are approximations, however, it is common practice to recompute them from the loadings determined for the principal factors, and to iterate this process until the communality estimates are stabilized. The iterated principal axis factor solution for the $\mathbf{R}_c$ matrix in Eqn. (18) is shown in Eqn. (19).

In this $\mathbf{F}$ matrix, an $(n \times m)$, the values of the communalities are obtained by $\Sigma_{p=1}^{m} a_{jp}^2$ for each test, and the eigenvalues by $\Sigma_{j=1}^{n} a_{jp}^2$ for each factor. It will be seen that the eigenvalues decrease in size from the first to later factors. The question arises as to how many of these factors are worth retaining for subsequent processing. If the original set of correlations or covariances can in fact be expressed in terms of a smaller number of underlying factors, the determination of the rank of the correlation matrix with appropriately chosen communality values would indicate the minimum number of factors needed to describe the original set of relationships among variables. The rank of a matrix is defined as the order of the highest nonvanishing determinant, or geometrically, as the minimum number of linearly independent dimensions or vectors needed to explain the data. If a matrix is of rank 2, the relationships among a set of variables can be expressed in two-dimensional space; if it is of rank 3, a three-dimensional space is required, and so on. With correlation or covariance matrices based on observed data in the social sciences, however, a clear-cut determination of the rank of a matrix is seldom possible. Apart from the problem of estimating communalities, observed data are subject to fluctuations due to the sampling of individuals and errors of measurement in the variables being analysed.

The number of factors of the original $\mathbf{R}$ matrix with eigenvalues greater than or equal to 1 is often taken as an indication of the number of initially extracted factors to be retained for further processing; such factors account for at least the equivalent of the total variance of any of the variables being analysed. In the $\mathbf{R}$ matrix on which Eqn. (18) is based, two eigenvalues are greater

$$
\mathbf{R}_c = \begin{array}{c}
 \\ (1) \\ (2) \\ (3) \\ (4) \\ (5)
\end{array}
\begin{array}{c}
\begin{array}{ccccc}
(1) & (2) & (3) & (4) & (5) \\
\text{English} & \text{French} & \text{Italian} & \text{Physics} & \text{Chemistry}
\end{array} \\
\left[\begin{array}{ccccc}
(0.59) & 0.63 & 0.65 & 0.31 & 0.20 \\
0.63 & (0.41) & 0.45 & 0.27 & 0.18 \\
0.65 & 0.45 & (0.44) & 0.10 & 0.05 \\
0.31 & 0.27 & 0.10 & (0.36) & 0.55 \\
0.20 & 0.18 & 0.05 & 0.55 & (0.31)
\end{array}\right]
\end{array}
\qquad (18)
$$

Variables (j)			Factors (p)			
	I	II	III	IV	V	h^2
English	0.880	−0.239	−0.009	−0.069	−0.017	0.837
French	0.684	−0.129	−0.204	0.068	0.005	0.531
F = Italian	0.642	−0.372	0.190	0.030	0.013	0.587
Physics	0.506	0.588	−0.021	−0.064	0.016	0.606
Chemistry	0.398	0.604	0.091	0.068	−0.013	0.536
Eigenvalues	2.069	0.923	0.087	0.019	0.001	

$$(19)$$

than 1. While this criterion is a useful starting point, it may underestimate the number of factors required to account for the correlational data, and may well be supplemented by other criteria. In Cattell's Scree test (1966), the eigenvalues are graphed from highest to lowest, and factors are accepted only for those eigenvalues above the point on the graph where the eigenvalues level off. Subjective criteria, such as discarding factors which account for less than 5 percent, say, of the total variance, on the grounds of their lack of practical importance, may also be considered. A further useful guide is the number of factors built into a well-designed factor analytic study.

The principal factor method is the most commonly used of the least squares approaches to the estimation of the initial **F** matrix; it is described as a least squares approach, since extracting the maximum variance at each stage is equivalent to minimizing the unexplained variance or residual correlations between the variables. An **F** matrix can also be generated directly from an iterative least squares solution involving the minimization of the residual correlations for an hypothesized number of factors; the Minres method (Harman 1976) is a variant of this approach.

Increasing use is being made of the method of maximum likelihood to determine the initial factor matrix, **F**. The theoretical basis of the method had been given by Lawley in 1940, but its application did not become feasible until the development of new methods of maximum likelihood factor analysis (Jöreskog 1966, 1969, Jöreskog and Lawley 1968). The method is more efficient than other procedures, in the sense that the estimated factor loadings have a smaller sampling variance. It also provides a large sample test of significance for assessing the adequacy of different hypotheses about the number of common factors needed to account for the observed correlation or covariance matrix.

Under the principle of maximum likelihood, the parameter value(s) are sought which maximize the likelihood of a sample result. In its application to factor analysis, the parameter factor matrix **F** is estimated which would have the greatest likelihood, under a given hypothesis about the number of common factors, of generating the observed correlation or covariance matrix. This involves, in the case of uncorrelated factors, the minimization of a function $G(\mathbf{F}, \boldsymbol{\psi})$ where **F** represents the matrix of factor loadings, and $\boldsymbol{\psi}$ the diagonal matrix of unique variances. When the maximum

likelihood estimates of **F** and $\boldsymbol{\psi}$ have been determined, the hypothesis that the n-variable observed matrix can be accounted for by the designated number of common factors (k) can be tested for moderately large N through the χ^2 statistic with $\frac{1}{2}[(n-k)^2 - (n+k)]$ degrees of freedom.

Application of the maximum likelihood factor analysis procedure to the correlation matrix in Eqn. (18) with unities in the diagonal cells showed that one factor was insufficient to account for the correlations ($\chi^2 = 69.487$, d.f. = 5, $p = 0.000$). Maximum likelihood loadings for an **F** matrix were then estimated on the assumption that the **R** matrix could be accounted for by two factors. This **F** matrix is

		Factor	
Variables (j)		I	II
English		0.934	−0.136
French		0.670	−0.033
F = Italian		0.657	−0.257
Physics		0.440	0.739
Chemistry		0.297	0.567
Eigenvalues		2.037	0.953

$$(20)$$

The probability that the observed correlation matrix **R** could have been generated from this **F** matrix is very high, namely 0.998 ($\chi^2 = 0$). The hypothesis that the observed correlation matrix can be accounted for by two underlying factors is therefore accepted. Following Jöreskog, the convention with empirically derived data is to accept the hypothesized number of factors as soon as the probability that the observed correlation matrix can be accounted for by that number of factors exceeds 0.10.

The significance test criterion in the maximum likelihood method tends to overestimate the number of factors when the sample size is large, and can be supplemented by other indices. The appearance of singlet factors, on which only one variable has a substantial loading, may also indicate that too many factors have been extracted. Comparison of the two-dimensional plots based on Eqn. (20) and the first two columns of the matrix in Eqn. (19) shows that the configurations from the maximum likelihood and principal factor solutions are quite similar.

Other approaches to the initial extraction of factors include the canonical factoring procedure, the Alpha factoring procedure, and image factoring. These approaches are available as options in computer packages such as SPSS and SAS.

In matrices with well-defined groupings of variables, as in the 5×5 correlation matrix in Eqn. (18), the various methods for the initial extraction of factors tend to identify the same factors even though factor loadings may differ from one solution to another. Most researchers will find that either the principal factor or maximum likelihood procedures will meet their needs, but it is often instructive to obtain both solutions.

5. Rotation of Factors

As outlined in Sect. 1, Thurstone argued that the initial factors needed to be rotated within the common factor space to arrive at a psychologically meaningful solution. He evolved the concept of simple structure to guide such rotations. As the principles of order implicit in simple structure are germane to a range of disciplines, the rotation of factors in exploratory factor analysis has continued to rely on this general concept.

In searching for new positions to which the original arbitrary orthogonal factor axes should be rotated to give substantive meaning to the factors, the investigator can choose to undertake an orthogonal or an oblique rotation. In the former case, the angles between all of the new factor axes remain at $90°$, and the factors remain uncorrelated. In the latter case, the angles between the new axes can be smaller or larger than $90°$, with the result that rotated factors may themselves be correlated. The difference between the two types of rotation is illustrated in Fig. 1 for the five-variable correlation problem in Eqn. (18), using as the initial factor plots the factor loadings from a two-factor principal factor solution for this matrix, since there were two eigenvalues greater than unity in the original **R** matrix. The principal factor matrix in this case is

$$
\mathbf{F} = \begin{array}{c} \text{English} \\ \text{French} \\ \text{Italian} \\ \text{Physics} \\ \text{Chemistry} \end{array}
\begin{array}{cc} \text{I} & \text{II} \end{array}
\begin{bmatrix}
0.905 & -0.267 \\
0.659 & -0.128 \\
0.615 & -0.349 \\
0.523 & 0.616 \\
0.389 & 0.562
\end{bmatrix} \quad (21)
$$

These loadings are plotted against the original factor axes I and II. The new positions of the axes after an orthogonal rotation are shown as I′ and II′ in Fig. 1(a). Figure 1(b) gives the new positions of the axes, I* and II*, after an oblique rotation.

In Fig. 1(a), the axes have been rotated clockwise through an angle of approximately $30°$. Their placement could be subjectively determined, keeping in mind the need to have some variables with zero or near-zero loadings on each factor. The loadings of the variables on the new axes can be found from the formula $\mathbf{FT} = \mathbf{B}$, where

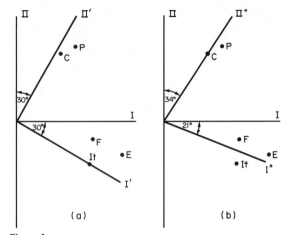

Figure 1
Orthogonal (a) and oblique (b) rotations of initial reference axes in Eqn. (21)

T is the transformation matrix and **B** is the rotated factor matrix. In this particular rotation,

$$
\mathbf{T} = \begin{array}{c} \text{I} \\ \text{II} \end{array}
\begin{array}{cc} \text{I}' & \text{II}' \end{array}
\begin{bmatrix}
\cos(-29°45') & -\sin(-29°45') \\
\sin(-29°45') & \cos(-29°45')
\end{bmatrix}
$$

$$
= \begin{array}{c} \text{I} \\ \text{II} \end{array}
\begin{array}{cc} \text{I}' & \text{II}' \end{array}
\begin{bmatrix}
0.877 & 0.481 \\
-0.481 & 0.877
\end{bmatrix} \quad (22)
$$

$$
\mathbf{B} = \begin{array}{c} \text{English} \\ \text{French} \\ \text{Italian} \\ \text{Physics} \\ \text{Chemistry} \end{array}
\begin{array}{cc} \text{I}' & \text{II}' \end{array}
\begin{bmatrix}
0.92 & 0.20 \\
0.64 & 0.20 \\
0.71 & -0.01 \\
0.16 & 0.79 \\
0.07 & 0.68
\end{bmatrix} \quad (23)
$$

The factor coefficients or factor loadings in Eqn. (23) could be read directly from Fig. 1(a) by measuring the orthogonal projections of the test points on axes I′ and II′ respectively. This matrix of orthogonal projections of the test points on the new axes is known as the factor structure matrix; the entries represent the correlations between the test vectors and the factors. The matrix of coordinates of the test points on the new axes, however, defines the factor pattern matrix; this is the matrix of coefficients which would be needed to estimate the standard scores of each person on the original variables, as set out in Eqn. (1). The factor pattern and factor structure are identical in an orthogonal factor solution but differ in an oblique solution.

In Fig. 1(b), the axes have been placed through the two distinct clusters of points, so that each cluster will have high loadings on one factor and zero or near-zero loadings on the other. Factor I has been rotated clockwise through 21°27′ to the new position I*, and Factor II through 34°28′ to the new position II*. Since the angle of 77° between the two new axes is not a right angle, the rotation is oblique. The orthogonal projections of the end-points of the test vectors on the new axis system is given by $\mathbf{F\Lambda} = \mathbf{S}$ where

$$\mathbf{\Lambda} = \begin{array}{c} \text{I} \\ \text{II} \end{array} \begin{bmatrix} \cos(-21°27′) & \cos(55°32′) \\ \sin(-21°27′) & \sin(55°32′) \end{bmatrix}$$

is the matrix of direction cosines of the new axes with respect to the original axes. In the present example,

	I	II	I*	II*
English	0.905	−0.267	0.9307	0.5659
French	0.659	−0.128	−0.3657	0.8245
Italian	0.615	−0.349		
Physics	0.523	0.616		
Chemistry	0.389	0.562		

$$= \begin{array}{cc} \text{I*} & \text{II*} \end{array} \begin{bmatrix} 0.94 & 0.29 \\ 0.66 & 0.27 \\ 0.70 & 0.06 \\ 0.26 & 0.80 \\ 0.16 & 0.68 \end{bmatrix} \quad (24)$$

The matrix on the right-hand side of Eqn. (24) is the factor structure matrix, $\mathbf{S}$, which represents the correlations of the tests with the factors. The correlation between the two rotated factors is given by the off-diagonal element in

$$\mathbf{\phi} = \mathbf{\Lambda'\Lambda} = \begin{bmatrix} 1.000 & 0.225 \\ 0.225 & 1.000 \end{bmatrix}$$

which represents a moderate degree of correlation. In representing the scores of persons in terms of a smaller number of factors, however, the coordinates of the test vectors with respect to the new oblique axes, which form the factor pattern matrix, are of more interest. These are given by $\mathbf{P} = \mathbf{S\phi}^{-1}$; in the present example, the factor pattern matrix is

$$\mathbf{P} = \begin{array}{c} \text{English} \\ \text{French} \\ \text{Italian} \\ \text{Physics} \\ \text{Chemistry} \end{array} \begin{array}{cc} \text{I*} & \text{II*} \end{array} \begin{bmatrix} 0.92 & 0.08 \\ 0.63 & 0.13 \\ 0.72 & -0.10 \\ 0.08 & 0.78 \\ 0.01 & 0.68 \end{bmatrix} \quad (25)$$

The $\mathbf{S}$ matrix in Eqn. (24) could be read directly from Fig. 1(b) by finding the orthogonal projections of the test vectors on Factors I* and II*, and the $\mathbf{P}$ matrix in Eqn. (25) by finding their oblique projections on these two factors.

A comparison of the matrices in Eqns. (23) and (25) shows the advantages of oblique over orthogonal rotations if the factors are correlated. The factor definition is clearer in the oblique solution; zero or near-zero loadings indicate more clearly that physics and chemistry are not represented in Factor I* and that the three languages are not represented in Factor II*. Some knowledge of the nature of the variables is required to interpret the factors. Each factor must be inspected to determine what the variables with high loadings have in common which is not present in the variables with low loadings, and then named appropriately. The task is deceptively simple in the present example. Since the variables with high loadings on Factor I′/I* are language examinations, and the variables with low loadings are not, this factor can be interpreted as a language ability factor. Similarly, Factor II′/II* can be interpreted as a scientific ability/achievement factor. The task of interpretation can be much more demanding in studies involving many variables and several factors.

The new positions of the axes in Fig. 1 were obtained by analytic methods of rotation, which replaced the subjective graphical methods used prior to the 1950s, in which investigators inspected plots of each pair of factors from the $\mathbf{F}$ matrix. The first fully analytic procedures for rotation developed by Carroll (1953) and other factor analysts became known as quartimax procedures. They aimed to simplify the rows of a matrix of factor loadings, by maximizing the sum of the fourth powers of the loadings or by some equivalent criterion, with communalities held constant. The first factor defined by the quartimax procedures tends to be a general factor, and the procedures are not widely used.

The analytic criterion used to obtain the orthogonal factor solution in Fig. 1(a) was developed and subsequently refined by Kaiser (1958). It is known as the varimax criterion, and aims to simplify the columns of the factor matrix by maximizing over all factors the variance of the squared factor loadings in each column, after first dividing each factor loading by the square root of the relevant variable's communality to give equal weight to the factors in the rotation. It requires the maximization of the function

$$V = n \sum_{p=1}^{m} \sum_{j=1}^{n} \left(\frac{a_{jp}}{h_j}\right)^4 - \sum_{p=1}^{m} \left(\sum_{j=1}^{n} \frac{a_{jp}^2}{h_j^2}\right)^2 \quad (26)$$

The varimax criterion, which is designed to generate factors on which some variables have high loadings and others have low loadings, has been found to be highly satisfactory for orthogonal rotations, and is very widely used.

The placement of the new axes in Fig. 1(b) was determined with the aid of the most widely used oblique analytic rotation criterion, known as the direct oblimin criterion (Jennrich and Sampson 1966). This criterion has replaced oblique analytic rotational criteria based on the factor structure matrix which were developed in the late 1950s, for example, Carroll's biquartimin criterion. Following the same principles as the latter criterion, that is, the minimization over pairs of factors of the cross-products of squared factor loadings, the minimization of the covariances of these squared loadings, and the use of a coefficient to vary the relative weight given to these two components in order to control the degree of obliqueness of the factors, Jennrich and Sampson rotated the **F** matrix directly to the factor pattern matrix, **P**, by minimizing the function

$$G(\mathbf{P}) = \sum_{p<q=1}^{m} \left(\sum_{j=1}^{n} b_{jp}^2 b_{jq}^2 - \frac{\delta}{n} \sum_{j=1}^{n} b_{jp}^2 \sum_{j=1}^{n} b_{jq}^2 \right) \qquad (27)$$

where b_{jp} and b_{jq} are the elements of the matrix **P** and δ is the variable quantity which controls the degree of obliqueness of the factors. Computer packages usually allow the investigator to apply a range of values of δ to facilitate the selection of a solution which best conforms to simple structure. Factors tend to be too oblique when $\delta = 0$, and become less oblique as δ becomes more negative. A delta value of approximately -0.5 has often been found to yield relatively "clean" simple structure solutions.

6. Advances in Confirmatory Factor Analysis

The major advance in factor analysis since the late 1960s has been the development of confirmatory factor analytic procedures. In the course of developing maximum likelihood procedures for exploratory factor analysis, Jöreskog saw their possibilities for testing hypothesized matrices. Recognizing that factor analysts generally wished to specify only some of the parameters in a hypothesized matrix, and to allow others to vary, he reformulated the factor analysis model to incorporate fixed parameters, constrained parameters (unknown in value but equal to one or more other parameters), and free parameters. He expressed the model in terms of a variance–covariance or dispersion matrix which becomes a correlation matrix if the variables are in standardized form. That is,

$$\Sigma = \Lambda \phi \Lambda' + \psi \qquad (28)$$

where Σ is the dispersion matrix of observed scores, Λ is an $n \times m$ matrix of factor loadings, ϕ is the factor correlation matrix, and ψ is the diagonal matrix of unique variances. In confirmatory factor analysis, the investigator is free to specify fixed values for particular parameters in Λ, ϕ, and ψ, given some restriction on the total number of fixed parameters. The matrix $\hat{\Sigma}$ is then estimated by maximum likelihood procedures under these conditions, and a χ^2 test applied to determine whether the observed dispersion matrix Σ differs from the estimated matrix $\hat{\Sigma}$.

The model allows great flexibility for testing a wide variety of hypothesized factor patterns, in which relationships among the factors may be orthogonal or oblique or a mixture of the two. Confirmatory factor analysis has been used, for example, to analyse data

from multitrait multimethod studies (Werts et al. 1972), to illuminate a long-standing controversy on the identification of reading comprehension skills (Spearritt 1972), and to test the simplex assumption underlying Bloom's taxonomy of educational objectives (Hill and McGaw 1981). It has also facilitated the comparison of the factorial structure of different subpopulations, allowing investigators to determine whether the factorial structure of a given set of variables varies, for example, with sex, age, ethnicity, socioeconomic status, or political affiliation, and if so, in what manner (e.g., McGaw and Jöreskog 1971)?

The model set out in Eqn. (28) forms part of a more general model for the analysis of covariance structures, which was subsequently elaborated by Jöreskog to handle a wide range of statistical models for multivariate analysis. The LISREL V suite of computer programs (Jöreskog and Sörbom 1981) which provide for the analysis of linear structural relationships by the method of maximum likelihood, has become a basic tool for studying not only exploratory and confirmatory factor analysis models, but also path analysis models and models relating to cross-sectional and longitudinal data.

7. Some Additional Methodological Aspects of Factor Analysis

7.1 Construction of Factor Scales

When factors are identified as a result of a factor analysis, it is possible to calculate a factor score for each person on the new factors, for example a language score and a science score. With some exceptions, the calculation of factor scores has not been an important feature of educational and psychological studies, in which the emphasis has been mainly on the identification rather than the measurement of factors. In some disciplines, however, the chief concern has been to create composite factor scales to facilitate further study of a topic.

The most widely used method of calculating a person's factor scores has been to regress the factor loadings on each factor in the factor structure matrix against the original set of variables. A matrix of factor-score coefficients or regression weights can be found from the formula

$$\mathbf{W} = \mathbf{S}' \mathbf{R}^{-1} \qquad (29)$$

where **S** is the rotated factor structure matrix and **R** is the original correlation matrix. Factor scores are conventionally presented as standard scores, derived by applying the regression weights to a person's standard score on each of the original variables. Other approaches to the estimation of factor scores are outlined by Harman (1976) and Kim and Mueller (1978).

7.2 Hierarchical Factor Solutions

Hierarchical factor solutions were attractive to early British factorists because of their hierarchical theories of cognitive processes. Accordingly, a general factor was extracted from the correlation matrix as a first step;

group factors were then extracted from the residual correlations (Burt 1950, Vernon 1961). Even without the initial assumption of a general factor, the American oblique rotational methods could still yield an hierarchical factor solution. Provided the data yielded at least three primary factors, the correlations among these factors could themselves be analysed to arrive at second-order factors; if there were sufficient primary factors to yield several second-order factors, the latter could be analysed to yield third-order factors, and so on. If the matrix of primary-factor correlations were of unit rank, a second order general factor would emerge. If desired, such hierarchical solutions could be made orthogonal (Schmid and Leiman 1957).

7.3 Comparison of Factors

Coefficients of congruence designed to measure the degree of similarity between pairs of factors derived from different sets of variables in the same domain, and the degree of similarity between loadings on pairs of corresponding factors derived when the same set of variables is applied to different subpopulations, are summarized in Harman (1976). Comparisons of factor matrices can be made through confirmatory factor analysis procedures.

7.4 Assumptions of Linearity

It is usually assumed in factor analysis (necessarily so with maximum likelihood procedures) that the variables have a multivariate normal distribution in the population which has been sampled, and this implies that the variables are linearly related. Where this is not the case, multivalued variables may be normalized as a first step. Care needs to be taken in applying factor analysis to dichotomously scored variables such as test or scale items (Kim and Mueller 1978, Muthén 1981). Factor analysis models in which factors are not linearly related to variables have been extensively investigated by McDonald (1967).

8. Computer Programs

Widely available statistical packages such as SPSS, SAS, BMDP, and OSIRIS all contain factor analysis programs. For the initial extraction of factors, the researcher usually has the option of selecting the principal factor, maximum likelihood, Rao canonical, Alpha, or image method of factoring. Varimax and direct oblimin rotational solutions with nominated values of δ are available in most programs, along with other rotational methods such as, for instance, Quartimax and Equimax in SPSS and SAS, and Promax in SAS. Two-dimensional plots of the rotated factors, and the necessary matrix of coefficients for producing factor scores, are also usually obtainable.

In addition to the LISREL program mentioned in Sect. 6, another special purpose program, COFAMM, is available for confirmatory factor analysis.

9. Applications of Factor Analysis

Factor analysis has made its most direct contribution to education through its influence on the composition of test batteries used for educational or vocational guidance. Batteries of tests such as the SRA Primary Mental Abilities battery and the Psychological Corporation's Differential Aptitude Tests were designed to yield separate scores for students on aptitudes or abilities such as number computation, verbal reasoning, verbal comprehension, abstract reasoning, clerical speed and accuracy, mechanical reasoning, space relations, language usage, and word fluency. Factor analytic studies have also contributed to the selection of areas to be tested in achievement test batteries, such as reading comprehension, listening comprehension, and comprehension and interpretation in mathematics, science, and social studies. Factor analysis has served to identify skills, abilities, and areas of achievement which are relatively independent, and has thus avoided unnecessary duplication of measurement in providing a profile of a student's performance. Factor studies have also often provided the framework for personality and interest inventories used in guidance and counselling.

The major impact of factor analysis has been in the area in which it was first employed, that is, in the study of intellectual or cognitive abilities. It has been the chief technique for exploring the structure of human abilities. It has been used to map the broad areas of human abilities which are needed to account for the variation which occurs in the performance of subjects on a great variety of mental tasks. A test kit of confirmed factors of cognitive abilities was prepared at the Educational Testing Service (French 1954) and was revised and extended in 1963 and 1976; the kit has been of great value in defining factors for use in further exploratory studies. Abilities isolated at one level, such as reasoning ability or memory, have also been subjected to detailed factor analyses of their infrastructure. Studies of these kinds, supplemented by the very extensive factor studies undertaken in connection with Guilford's Structure of Intellect model (Guilford 1967), and Cattell's theory of "crystallized" and "fluid" intelligence (Cattell 1971), have produced a very considerable body of knowledge about the structure of human abilities.

In applications in education, factor analytic studies have been undertaken in such diverse areas as prose style, administrative behaviour, occupational classification, attitudes and belief systems, and the economics of education. The technique is still in extensive use in the exploration of abilities, in the refining of tests and scales, and in the development of composite variables for use in research studies. Its most promising applications in recent years, however, have been concerned with the testing of explicit hypotheses about the structure of sets of variables, as in the study of growth models and other models mentioned in Sect. 6.

Factor analysis will remain an important technique for reducing and classifying sets of variables as a means of improving theoretical understanding in various disciplines, and for testing hypotheses about structural relationships among sets of variables. Confirmatory factor analysis procedures should assist in the formulation of more precise theories about such structural relationships; current theories about the structure of educational or psychological domains have rarely been formulated in sufficiently explicit terms to attract support from these procedures. In the search for explanations about how and why such structural relationships take the form they do, closer links can be expected to be developed between factor analysis and path analysis models. Methodological developments might be expected in the application of factor analysis to dichotomously scored variables and to categorical variables, and in the development of nonlinear models where linear models prove to be inadequate. Considerable scope remains for research on the emergence of factors, involving neurological, general environmental, and schooling influences; relationships between factorial and information processing models (Sternberg 1977) also need investigation. Finally, comprehensive factor studies of the abilities tested in different school subjects would be highly relevant to the design of school curricula.

See also: Path Analysis; Statistical Analysis in Educational Research; Factorial Modeling

Bibliography

Burt C 1950 Group factor analysis. *Br. J. Psychol. Stat. Sect.* 3: 40–75

Carroll J B 1953 Approximating simple structure in factor analysis. *Psychometrika* 18: 23–38

Cattell R B 1966 The Scree test for the number of factors. *Mult. Behav. Res.* 1: 245–76

Cattell R B 1971 *Abilities, Their Structure, Growth and Action.* Houghton Mifflin, Boston, Massachusetts

French J W (ed.) 1954 *Manual for Kit of Selected Tests for Reference Aptitude and Achievement Factors.* Educational Testing Service, Princeton, New Jersey

Guilford J P 1967 *The Nature of Human Intelligence.* McGraw-Hill, New York

Harman H H 1976 *Modern Factor Analysis*, 3rd edn. University of Chicago Press, Chicago, Illinois

Hill P W, McGaw B 1981 Testing the simplex assumption underlying Bloom's taxonomy. *Am. Educ. Res. J.* 18: 93–101

Jennrich R I, Sampson P F 1966 Rotation for simple loadings. *Psychometrika* 31: 313–23

Jöreskog K G 1966 Testing a simple structure hypothesis in factor analysis. *Psychometrika* 31: 165–78

Jöreskog K G 1969 A general approach to confirmatory maximum likelihood factor analysis. *Psychometrika* 34: 183–202

Jöreskog K G, Lawley D N 1968 New methods in maximum likelihood factor analysis. *Br. J. Math. Stat. Psychol.* 21: 85–96

Jöreskog K G, Sörbom D 1981 *Lisrel V (User's Guide).* National Educational Resources, Chicago, Illinois

Kaiser H F 1958 The varimax criterion for analytic rotation in factor analysis. *Psychometrika* 23: 187–200

Kim J O, Mueller C W 1978 *Factor Analysis: Statistical Methods and Practical Issues.* Sage, London

Lawley D N, Maxwell A E 1971 *Factor Analysis as a Statistical Method*, 2nd edn. Butterworth, London

McDonald R P 1967 *Nonlinear Factor Analysis.* Psychometric Society, Richmond

McGaw B, Jöreskog K G 1971 Factorial invariance of ability measures in groups differing in intelligence and socio-economic status. *Br. J. Math. Stat. Psychol.* 24: 154–68

Mulaik S A 1972 *The Foundations of Factor Analysis.* McGraw-Hill, New York

Muthén B 1981 Factor analysis of dichotomous variables: American attitudes toward abortion. In: Jackson D J, Borgatta E F (eds.) 1981 *Factor Analysis and Measurement in Sociological Research: A Multi-dimensional Perspective.* Sage, London

Schmid J, Leiman J M 1957 The development of hierarchical factor solutions, *Psychometrika* 22: 53–61

Spearman C 1904 "General intelligence" objectively determined and measured. *Am. J. Psychol.* 15(2): 201–93

Spearritt D 1972 Identification of subskills of reading comprehension by maximum likelihood factor analysis. *Read. Res. Q.* 8: 92–111

Sternberg R J 1977 *Intelligence, Information Processing, and Analogical Reasoning: The Componential Analysis of Human Abilities.* Erlbaum, Hillsdale, New Jersey

Thomson G H 1951 *The Factorial Analysis of Human Ability*, 5th edn. Houghton Mifflin, Boston, Massachusetts

Thurstone L L 1931 Multiple factor analysis. *Psychol. Rev.* 38: 406–27

Thurstone L L 1947 *Multiple-factor Analysis: A Development and Expansion of the Vectors of the Mind.* University of Chicago Press, Chicago, Illinois

Vernon P E 1961 *The Structure of Human Abilities*, 2nd edn. Methuen, London

Werts C E, Jöreskog K G, Linn R L 1972 A multitrait–multimethod model for studying growth. *Educ. Psychol. Meas.* 32: 655–78

Factorial Modeling

P. R. Lohnes

Factorial modeling (FaM) provides researchers with a simple method for constructing latent structural variables linking theory with correlational data. Structural variables emphasize construct validity rather than predictive power in the linear components fitted by data analysis to vector variables. At the research design stage, the researcher who is planning to use FaM is required to name the latent variables (hereafter called factors) and to specify each of them by means of an exclusive subset of the independent variates (i.e., the measurements). The researcher is also required to specify an order of extraction of the factors, because the mathematical simplicity and computational efficiency of FaM are purchased at the expense of order dependence of the factors. The FaM data analysis yields a structural equation for every observational variate and attributes all explained variance unambiguously among the factors. This is possible because the factors are constructed to be mutually uncorrelated. Partitioning of criterion variance into independent contributions from uncorrelated factors is particularly useful in educational policy studies, where intervention decisions have to be justified by straightforward causal inferences.

The method was named factorial modeling to encourage comparison with factorial analysis of variance. In the design of experiments, a balanced sampling scheme creates uncorrelatedness of the causal factors to permit unambiguous causal inferences. In observational studies, FaM creates uncorrelated causal factors by analysis where they cannot be created by the sampling scheme. Causal inferences from FaM do not possess the high internal validity of inferences from a randomized factorial experiment, but if the data represent an important natural system in situ, the external validity of the factorial model may be much higher than that of any possible experiment. When the constructs of a theory represent interdependent attributes, the corresponding factors of an FaM model for data represent the partial contents of their constructs which are nonoverlapping with the contents of previously extracted factors. Thus FaM is a method which resembles multiple partial correlation.

FaM does not employ an algorithm derived by the differential calculus of linear systems. The method may appeal to researchers who fear that multivariate regression methods overpower many of the data collections available in education. The rationale for FaM is that using noncalculus multivariate mathematics on data will produce loose fitting models that may not be readily transferred to new situations.

1. Mathematics

Factorial modeling extracts ordered orthogonal factors by the method of matrix exhaustion. Each factor is specified by assignment to it of an exclusive subset of the independent variates. It is weighted by the covariances of those specifying variates with a selected dependent variate in the residual matrix prevailing at the start of that factoring step. For the first factor the weights are simply the bivariate correlations of the specifying variates with the selected criterion, or simple predictive validities. For all later factors, the weights are residual covariances representing residual predictive validities. It is not necessary that every independent variate be assigned to the specification of one of the factors, but it is highly desirable that at least two variates specify each

factor. Otherwise, the total variance for a single variate specifying a factor will be swept out, resulting in $h^2 = 1$ for that variate and a degenerate structural equation for it. The object of modeling is to regress criteria on latent variables, not on observed variates.

Let an idempotent matrix containing ones on the main diagonal in the positions corresponding to the positions in the correlation matrix of the specifying variates for the kth factor, and zeros everywhere else, be identified as $\mathbf{I}_k$. Let

$$\mathbf{v}_k = \mathbf{I}_k \mathbf{r}_c \tag{1}$$

where $\mathbf{r}_c$ is the column of the residual matrix $\mathbf{C}_k$ which belongs to the selected criterion. Then $\mathbf{v}_k$ is a vector of the order of $\mathbf{R}$ (which may be designated p for the count of all the measurement variates, independent plus dependent), but the only nonzero elements of $\mathbf{v}_k$ are predictive validities of the specification variates for the kth factor. For the following equation

$$\mathbf{h}_k = (1\mathbf{v}_k{}' \mathbf{C}_k \mathbf{v}_k)^{-1/2} \mathbf{v}_k \tag{2}$$

when $k = 1$, $\mathbf{C}_1 = \mathbf{R}$, the correlation matrix for the measurements. When $k = 2$, $\mathbf{C}_2$ is the covariance matrix remaining after the first factor has been exhausted from $\mathbf{R}$. In general, $\mathbf{C}_k$ is the residual covariance matrix after $k - 1$ factors have been exhausted.

Then the structural coefficients for the kth factor are

$$\mathbf{s}_k = \mathbf{C}_k \mathbf{h}_k \tag{3}$$

and $\mathbf{C}_k$ is exhausted of $\mathbf{s}_k$.

$$\mathbf{C}_{k+1} = \mathbf{C}_k - \mathbf{s}_k \mathbf{s}_k{}' \tag{4}$$

When all n planned factors have been computed, their column vectors of structural coefficients are assembled in a $p \times n$ matrix $\mathbf{S}$. Now the theory plus error partition of $\mathbf{R}$ is given by

$$\mathbf{R} = \mathbf{S}\mathbf{S}' + \mathbf{C}_{n+1} \tag{5}$$

The elements of the main diagonal of the theory matrix $\mathbf{S}\mathbf{S}'$ are the proportions of the variate variances explained by the theory for the data, called the communalities, h_j^2. The square roots of the elements of the main diagonal of $\mathbf{C}_{n+1}$ are the disturbance weights, d_j, which apply to the combined unknown sources of variance in each of the variates. From these results a structural equation can be written for each variate

$$z_j = s_{j1}f_1 + s_{j2}f_2 + \ldots + s_{jn}f_n + d_j u_j \tag{6}$$

In this equation the f_k are the factor scores and the u_j is a uniqueness score, that is, a score for the combination of all other sources of variance in z_j. Dropping the final addend gives the multiple regression equation

$$\hat{z}_j = s_{j1}f_1 + s_{j2}f_2 + \ldots + s_{jn}f_n \tag{7}$$

Table 1
Correlation matrix for informed condition (N = 111)[a]

MF 1	1.00								
MF 2	0.74	1.00							
E 1	0.31	0.41	1.00						
E 2	0.31	0.40	0.80	1.00					
W 1	0.40	0.46	0.64	0.63	1.00				
W 2	0.40	0.50	0.56	0.57	0.82	1.00			
AA	−0.15	−0.18	−0.22	−0.16	−0.34	−0.34	1.00		
G	−0.20	−0.24	−0.21	−0.18	−0.44	−0.38	0.67	1.00	
AP	−0.06	−0.11	−0.09	−0.06	−0.21	−0.20	0.59	0.64	1.00

a MF = motive to avoid failure; E = emotionality; W = worry; AA = arithmetic/algebra; G = geometry; AP = applied mathematics

This shows that any structural coefficient s_{jk} besides being a product–moment correlation between a variate and a factor, is also a standardized multiple regression weight for the regression of the jth variate on the kth factor, and its square, s_{jk}^2, is the contribution of the kth factor to the explanation of the variance in the jth variate. The squared multiple correlation coefficient is the communality

$$R_j^2 = h_j^2 = s_{j1}^2 + s_{j2}^2 + \ldots + s_{jn}^2 \qquad (8)$$

Thus the canon of unambiguous attribution of variance is satisfied.

Two salient facts emerge from this mathematics. The exact definition achieved for each factor beyond the first is order dependent, in the sense that it depends in part on the order in which the factors are extracted. Also, as factoring continues, the degrees of freedom for arbitrary location of a factor are reduced and the disciplinary force of the uncorrelatedness requirement over the hypothetical location of the factor becomes stronger.

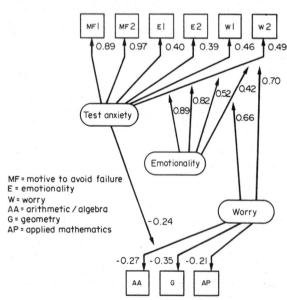

MF = motive to avoid failure
E = emotionality
W = worry
AA = arithmetic / algebra
G = geometry
AP = applied mathematics

Figure 1
FaM model for informed condition

As originally proposed by Lohnes (1979), FaM required the designation of a key criterion toward which all the factors were oriented. Lohnes has modified the algorithm so that when there are multiple criteria, it searches the vectors of residual predictive validities of the specification variates for a factor to find the largest sum of squares of those validities, and orients the factor to that criterion for which it has, in this sum of squares sense, the largest predictive validity. The program provides for the user to override this feature by designating the criterion variate toward which each factor is to be oriented, and it is permissible to designate the same criterion for all the factors, thus restoring the original emphasis on a key criterion.

The current program for FaM also incorporates an improved algebra for computing coefficients defining the latent variables as linear functions of some of the variates. The new algebra supplies true zero coefficients in every possible place. Only the specification variates for the first factor enter its operational definition. Only the specification variates for the first two factors enter the operational definition of the second factor. For any other factor, only the specification variates for it and the previously extracted factors enter the operational definition. Thus the minimum number of nonzero coefficients required to maintain the uncorrelatedness of the factors is employed. For $k = 1, 2, \ldots, n$, and letting $\mathbf{s}_k$ be the kth column of $\mathbf{S}$ and $\mathbf{b}_k$ be the kth column of the factor scoring coefficients matrix $\mathbf{B}$ the coefficients for the kth factor may be computed as

$$\mathbf{b}_k = \mathbf{h}_k - \mathbf{h}_k{}'\mathbf{s}_{k-1}\mathbf{b}_{k-1} - \mathbf{h}_k{}'\mathbf{s}_{k-2}\mathbf{b}_{k-2} - \ldots \qquad (9)$$
$$- \mathbf{h}_k{}'\mathbf{s}_2\mathbf{b}_2 - \mathbf{h}_k{}'\mathbf{s}_1\mathbf{b}_1$$

For the first factor the result is

$$\mathbf{b}_1 = \mathbf{h}_1 \qquad (10)$$

For the second factor

$$\mathbf{b}_2 = \mathbf{h}_2 - \mathbf{h}_2{}'\,\mathbf{s}_1\,\mathbf{b}_1 \qquad (11)$$

Every $\mathbf{b}_k$ will contain true zeros in the positions of all the variates except those variates entering the specification of the first k factors.

In order to explore the possible consequences of an observed or manipulated change in a single independent

Table 2
FaM model for informed condition

| Variate | Factors | | | *d* | *h²* |
	General anxiety	Emotion- ality	Worry		
MF	0.89	−0.05	0.00	0.46	0.79
MF 2	0.97	0.03	0.00	0.24	0.94
E 1	0.40	0.89	−0.02	0.21	0.96
E 2	0.39	0.82	0.04	0.41	0.83
W 1	0.46	0.52	0.66	0.29	0.92
W 2	0.49	0.42	0.70	0.30	0.91
AA	−0.18	−0.15	−0.27	0.94	0.13
G	−0.24	−0.12	−0.35	0.90	0.20
AP	−0.09	−0.05	−0.21	0.97	0.05

MF = motive to avoid failure; E = emotionality; W = worry; AA = arithmetic/algebra; G = geometry; AP = applied mathematics; h^2 = communality

variate, the algebra of the model may be read "backwards" (i.e., reversing the inferred paths of causal influence from the factors to the variates), computing the changes in factors that might be concomitant with a change in a given variate, and then the consequences of such changes in factors for changes in criterion variates. A table with *w* rows representing the criterion variates and *q* columns representing the independent variates (so that $w + q = p$), in which each element ∇_{jm} reports the possible change (in standard deviation units) in the *j*th criterion for a unit change (one standard deviation) in the *m*th independent variate, contains elements

$$\nabla_{jm} = \sum_{k=1}^{n} s_{jk} b_{mk} \qquad (12)$$

where $j = 1, 2, \ldots, w$ and $m = 1, 2, \ldots, q$.

If Δ_m is the fraction of a standard deviation change actually observed or produced in an independent variate, the corresponding possible change in a criterion may be computed as

$$\Delta_j = \Delta_m \nabla_{jm} \qquad (13)$$

This is a highly tenuous interpretation of the model for the data, and the educational policy maker must be very cautious in using it.

The FORTRAN program for FaM should be requested from the author at 379 Baldy Hall, SUNYAB, Amherst, New York 14260, USA.

2. Example

Hagtvet (1981), in an effort to challenge the conventional representation of test anxiety as a unitary construct, hypothesized a three-dimensional hierarchical set of test anxiety factors, which included a general factor (specified by "motive to avoid failure" scales) and two response factors ("emotionality," which refers to self-perceived affective–physiological arousal, and "worry," which refers to focusing of attention on irrelevant cognitions of shortcomings and risks). He also posited that

the general factor would be the dominant source of test anxiety in situations where subjects were surprised with an unannounced test, whereas the response factors would be more psychoactive in situations where subjects had a period of time to prepare for an announced test.

Hagtvet made random assignments of grade nine classes to the two situations. The criterion variates were three tests of the Norwegian national mathematics battery. Two questionnaire scales to specify each of the three anxiety factors were administered one month in advance of the maths tests. Sample sizes of 111 pupils in the informed group and 66 pupils in the uninformed group were available for analysis.

Table 3
Factor scoring coefficients

| Variate | Factors | | |
	General anxiety	Emotionality	Worry
MF 1	0.367	−0.168	−0.143
MF 2	0.696	−0.318	−0.270
E 1	0.000	0.759	−0.529
E 2	0.000	0.393	−0.274
W 1	0.000	0.000	0.758
W 2	0.000	0.000	0.719

MF = motive to avoid failure; E = emotionality; W = worry

Factorial modeling models were computed for each group. Both models confirmed the three-factor theory nicely, and the hypothesis about the effects of the situations was sustained. The uninformed subjects model showed the general factor contributing moderately to variance on all three maths tests while the response factors contributed essentially nothing. In the informed subjects model (Tables 1, 2, 3, and Fig. 1) the "test anxiety" contribution to the maths tests was greatly reduced, whereas the "worry" factor contributed to the variance in all three criteria. The FaM analyses thus tested and supported both the factor structure and the situational effects aspects of Hagtvet's theory.

A further example of this is provided in Lohnes (1986), where the results of the analyses of data using FaM may be compared with those obtained through the use of alternative procedures.

See also: Factor Analysis

Bibliography

Ackerman W B, Lohnes P R 1981 *Research Methods for Nurses.* McGraw-Hill, New York (Chapters 10, 11, 12)

Hagtvet K A 1981 Towards a three dimensional concept of test anxiety: A factorial modeling study. Unpublished paper available from Institute of Psychology, University of Bergen, Bergen

Lohnes P R 1979 Factorial modeling in support of causal inference. *Am. Educ. Res.* 16: 323–40

Lohnes P R 1986 Factorial Modeling. *Int. J. Educ. Res.* 10(2): 181–89

Galois Lattices [1]

Cs. Andor, A. Joó, and L. Mérö

The Galois lattice (*G*-lattice) is a graphic method of representing knowledge structures. The nodes of *G*-lattices represent all the possible concepts in a given body of knowledge in the sense that a notion defines a set of individuals or properties with no exceptions or idiosyncrasies. A *G*-lattice provides a tool to represent all the possible developmental phases to reach a given total knowledge via different partial knowledge structures.

G-lattices are pure algebraic structures and may contain contingent features caused by irregular and random data. In this article some algorithms are proposed to develop the *G*-lattice method so that statistical analyses can be incorporated. These algorithms are based on the possible omissions of individuals or properties from the data so that the resulting *G*-lattice can be reduced as much as possible. The greatly simplified structure represented by the resulting *G*-lattice is still valid for a large percentage of individuals or properties. This is an alternative approach to statistical significance as this approach refers to strict logical relations.

1. On Binary Variables

Binary variables abound in educational research. Right or wrong answers, the presence or absence of certain properties, choices, and rejections in tests can be considered as sets of binary variables. However, there are only a few mathematical procedures that are developed exclusively for binary variables. Statisticians usually propose building up indices from binary variables and then apply common statistical procedures to analyse relationships between the indices.

In many cases, however, one may be interested in the interconnections of the binary variables themselves and when indices are built a great part of these interconnections may be lost. The strength of the connection between any two binary variables can, of course, be measured before composing indices of them. But how can one tell which connections are to be measured? In the case of only 20 binary variables there are more than one million possible connections if all the subsets of the binary variables are considered. Measuring only pairwise connections may be an unreasonable oversimplification.

The Rasch model has been proposed especially for evaluating test data and works well in many cases. A significant restriction of the Rasch model, however, is that it assumes homogeneity of items and, in connection with this homogeneity, that the test items should be ranked unequivocally according to their level of difficulty. The expectation of the test constructor may be different from this.

Task *b* may be easier than task *c* for those who were able to solve task *a*, while task *c* may be easier than task *b* for those who were not able to solve task *a*. This kind of connection may emerge when the solution of task *a* presupposes some kind of knowledge that renders the solution of task *b* obvious but obscures a commonsense solution for task *c*. This implies that the degree of difficulty of the tasks is a partial ordering relation rather than a full one. This means that a lattice model may characterize the connections between the difficulties of the tasks better than a linear model. In such a model it may happen that one task is easier or more difficult than another and it may happen that two tasks are incomparable. However, even two incomparable tasks may prove to be comparable when referenced to other tasks.

The method described in this article is appropriate for these kinds of problems. It has been developed as a purely algebraic model and it will first be presented in its original form, and then developed into a statistical procedure. The procedure is also applicable to problems other than the one described above. It models the way of forming concepts and, therefore, it may be a useful tool in designing instructional materials.

2. The Galois Lattice

Let $I = \{i_1, i_2, \ldots, i_n\}$ denote the set of *n* individuals and $T = \{t_1, t_2, \ldots, t_k\}$ denote the set of *k* features. Let $R \subset I \times T$ denote a relation that is defined in the pair of one individual and one feature. The relation *R* assumes that $i_j \, R \, t_m$ is valid if the individual i_j has the feature t_m, and otherwise, the relation is not valid. The inverse of the relation *R* is denoted by R^{-1} and $t_m \, R^{-1} \, i_j$ is the same as $i_j \, R \, t_m$. Let I_1 be an arbitrary subset of *I* and let $R(I_1)$ denote the set of those features that are valid for all individuals in I_1. Similarly, a subset $R^{-1}(T_1)$ denotes the set of individuals showing all the features in T_1.

The subset of individuals I_1 shall be called a "closed set" of individuals if $I_1 = R^{-1}[R(I_1)]$ is true. Similarly, the subset T_1 of features is called a "closed subset of features" if $T_1 = R[R^{-1}(T_1)]$ is true. The sets I_1 and T_1 are said to be in *Galois connection* (or *G*-connection) if $R(I_1) = T_1$ and $R^{-1}(T_1) = I_1$ are true. Clearly if a set of individuals is in *G*-connection with a set of features then both sets are closed.

The principal aim is to investigate subsets that are in *G*-connection. To illustrate the meaning of a *G*-connection let the individuals be pupils and the features be a set of tasks. In this case a *G*-connection between a set of pupils I_1 and a set of tasks T_1 implies that all the following statements are valid:

1 This is an edited version of the article Galois lattices: A possible representation of knowledge structures, by Cs Andor, A Joó, and L Mérö which was published in *Evaluation in Education*, Vol. 9, no. 2, pp. 207–15. It appears here with permission from Pergamon Press plc. © 1985

Table 1
Model of results of 12 pupils on 12 tasks

Pupils	Tasks 1	2	3	4	5	6	7	8	9	10	11	12
1	−	−	−	+	−	+	−	−	+	−	+	+
2	−	−	−	+	−	+	−	−	−	−	+	+
3	−	−	+	−	−	+	−	−	−	−	+	+
4	−	−	−	−	+	+	−	−	−	+	−	−
5	−	−	−	−	+	+	−	−	−	+	−	−
6	−	−	−	−	+	+	−	−	−	+	−	−
7	−	−	−	+	−	+	−	−	−	+	+	+
8	−	−	−	+	−	+	−	−	−	+	−	−
9	−	−	−	+	−	+	−	−	−	+	−	−
10	−	−	−	+	−	+	−	−	−	+	−	−
11	−	−	+	−	−	−	+	−	−	−	+	+
12	−	+	+	−	−	−	+	−	−	−	+	−

(a) all pupils in I_1 have solved the tasks in T_1;

(b) there is no pupil outside I_1 who solved all the tasks in T_1;

(c) there is no task outside T_1 that was solved by all the pupils in I_1.

It has been proved that the closed subsets of the set I of individuals constitute a lattice if the lattice operations are defined as follows (there are two operations in a lattice, the union and the intersection):

$$I_1 \cup I_2 \overset{\text{def}}{=} I_3$$
  If (a) $I_1 \subset I_3$, $I_2 \subset I_3$ and
  (b) I_3 is the smallest among the closed sets satisfying (a)

$$I_1 \cap I_2 \overset{\text{def}}{=} I_3$$
  If (c) $I_3 \subset I_1$, $I_3 \subset I_2$ and
  (d) I_3 is the largest among the closed sets satisfying (c).

The closed subsets of T constitute a lattice in a similar way, only T is substituted for I everywhere in the previous definition. These two lattices are isomorphic and an isomorphism between them is defined by the *G*-connections. As a consequence of this fact, the two sets can be represented in the same drawing; the union of a pupil set corresponds to the intersection of a task set and vice versa.

Figure 1 presents an example illustrating these notions. Figure 1 is a Galois lattice representation of the data in Table 1. Table 1 contains the results of 12 pupils on 12 tasks; the rows of the matrix correspond to the pupils and the columns of the matrix correspond to the tasks; " + " represents a correct solution and " − " represents a wrong one. Table 2 presents the closed sets of pupils and also the closed sets of tasks. The correspondence between the closed pupil sets and the closed task sets is clear.

There are 19 closed sets in this example including the empty set ($\emptyset$). Figure 1 shows the lattice of the closed sets of tasks. The set of all the tasks (which is obviously closed) is denoted by V and is at the top of the figure. Two elements in the lattice are connected by an edge if one of them includes the other and there is no third closed set which includes one of the two tasks and is included in the other.

The same diagram presents the lattice of the closed sets of pupils, too. In this case the task sets in Fig. 1 can be substituted with the appropriate pupil sets according to Table 2. Then V in Fig. 1 will denote the empty pupil set and $\emptyset$ in Fig. 1 will denote the set of all pupils. Moving upward in the graph of Fig. 1 we find more and more narrow pupil sets and larger and larger task sets. Two closed sets of tasks in the lattice determine their union: the union of two sets in the lattice is the lowest point in the lattice from which a path of edges leads to both given sets. This is apparently not always the same as their set-theoretical union. A similar statement is valid for intersection. For example, the union of the closed sets {4,6,10} and {6,11,12} in the net or lattice

Table 2
Table of closed sets

Set number	Closed sets of pupils	Closed sets of tasks
1	$\emptyset$	1,2,3,4,5,6,7,8,9,10,11,12
2	1	4,6,9,11,12
3	3	3,6,11,12
4	7	4,6,10,11,12
5	11	3,7,11,12
6	12	2,3,7,11
7	3,11	3,11,12
8	11,12	3,7,11
9	1,2,7	4,6,11,12
10	3,11,12	3,11
11	4,5,6	5,6,10
12	1,2,3,7	6,11,12
13	7,8,9,10	4,6,10
14	1,2,3,7,11	11,12
15	1,2,3,7,11,12	11
16	1,2,7,8,9,10	4,6
17	4,5,6,7,8,9,10	6,10
18	1,2,3,4,5,6,7,8,9,10	6
19	1,2,3,4,5,6,7,8,9,10,11,12	$\emptyset$

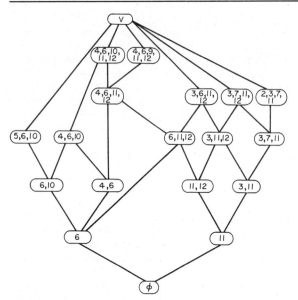

Figure 1
Representation of the Galois lattice

structure is {4,6,10,11,12} and their intersection is {6}. In this case the union and the intersection coincide with the set-theoretical union and intersection. On the other hand, the union of the closed sets {4,6,10} and {5,6,10} in the lattice is the full task set, which is not the same as their set-theoretical union. Their set-theoretical union is the set {4,5,6,10} but this is not a closed set. These kinds of features allow interesting interpretations which will be shown later.

The lattice of closed sets as defined above is called a Galois lattice (or *G*-lattice). If the feature set is interpreted as properties, then a closed set of features can be interpreted as a notion. In this interpretation the concept of a notion is defined in a strict but very logical way: A notion should define a set of individuals with no exceptions and no idiosyncrasies; and conversely, if a set of individuals share a set of properties and no other individual has the same set of properties, then this set of individuals should correspond to a notion. Biologists, for example, narrow down their worlds to special properties of their interest and try to define the species as a notion in the previous sense. They might ask questions like "Is 'horse' a notion in this sense?".

This methodology for creating notions can be witnessed in archaic societies as described by Durkheim (1902), in modern phonetics (here individuals correspond to sounds and the properties correspond to their discriminative features), and recently this way of creating notions emerges in semantics (Katz and Fodor 1963) and in cybernetics (Fay and Takács 1975).

3. Applications in Education

Let us examine Fig. 1 from an educational point of view. There are 12 tasks, so there are 2^{12}, or 4096 pos-

sibilities to investigate subsets of tasks and to measure the strength of connections in the subset. However, there is no need for that many measurement points because Fig. 1 includes all the significant information. It can be readily seen that anybody who solved task 3 also solved task 11, as all the closed subsets containing 3 also contain 11. No pupil solved both task 3 and task 4, because only *V* contains both of these tasks and *V* corresponds to the empty pupil set. There are pupils (at least one) who solved only task 6 and there are pupils who solved only task 11, because these single numbers are closed sets. On the other hand, if a pupil solved task 6 and also solved task 11 then he or she also solved task 12, because the union of {6} and {11} in the lattice is the set {6,11,12}. Some connections of this kind could also have been read from the matrix on Table 1. However, in Fig. 1 *all* connections of this kind can be read without any difficulty. The Galois lattice is a good tool for displaying connections and also for identifying them.

From a Galois lattice it can be immediately stated whether one task is easier or more difficult than another, or whether they are incommensurable. In Fig. 1, for example, task 11 is clearly easier than task 3 or task 12. Task 3 and task 4 cannot be compared as to their difficulty because there was no pupil solving both of them.

The Rasch model aims at setting up an order of the tasks according to their difficulty. This would mean, in the strict sense, that for any two tasks *a* and *b* it should be true that either all the pupils who solved task *a* also solved task *b* (i.e. *b* was easier than *a*) or all the pupils who solved task *b* also solved task *a* (i.e. *a* was easier than *b*). This strict supposition is never fulfilled in large samples, and therefore it is accepted if these statements are true at a particular probability level (e.g. 0.95 or more). Before dealing with statistical matters let us examine the situation in which the Rasch model can properly be applied. It is easy to see that a necessary and sufficient condition of the correct application of the Rasch model (in the strict sense) is that in the *G*-lattice of the task set only one path should lead from the bottom to the top. In other words, the *G*-lattice should look like that in Fig. 2. Figure 2 displays the *G*-lattice of two subsets of the original task set for which the easier/harder relation unequivocally holds between any two tasks.

It was stated above that the *G*-lattice contains all significant information. This raises the question as to how

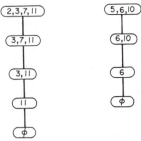

Figure 2
Subsets of the Galois lattice

Fig. 2 can be derived from Fig. 1. There is a very simple way to find all the Rasch-type subsets in the *G*-lattice. One has only to search for all the paths from the top of the graph to the bottom which pass through points fulfilling the following condition: the passed point can be reached from any higher passed points in only one way in the lattice. It can be easily checked that the paths in Fig. 2 have this property.

A figure is always more than just its parts put together. Therefore we may ask what Fig. 1 *in toto* expresses. The claim is that the Galois lattice expresses the structure of knowledge and the possible ways of increasing that knowledge. In Fig. 1 if someone solves task 5, this implies that he or she solves tasks 6 and 10 as well, since the only path to task 5 leads through these two tasks. The knowledge represented by task 4 can be reached in two ways: the shorter path leads immediately through task 6, but the longer path may lead through tasks 11, 12 and only then through tasks 6 and 3. This longer path results in reaching the full knowledge represented in the tasks as a by-product. This kind of information is indispensable, for example, for the designer of instructional materials who wants to know which part of the target knowledge can be reached in several ways, what are the actual paths, what are their lengths, and so forth.

Finally the following theoretical question arises. We have started from a data matrix without any explicit or implicit time parameter. On the other hand, we interpreted the *G*-lattice as the possible paths of increasing knowledge in order to solve some tasks. When, however, the knowledge necessary for solving another task must have been previously acquired, the dimension of time immediately appears in the interpretation. The question is whether we may infer from the result of a process (i.e. the test results) the process itself. In the present case this kind of inference seems to be acceptable and is in accordance with the theory of multilinear evolution (Carneiro 1973). Berlin and Kay (1969) used a similar method for determining the order of appearance

of the names of different colours in more than 100 languages. They treat the problem in a fashion analogous to ours. They state that in all languages the notion of red must have existed before the notion of blue appeared, but the notion of blue never appears immediately after red: either yellow or green (but never both) must exist before the notion of blue appears. These ideas are presented in Fig. 3.

4. Qualitative and Quantitative Methods

The method of *G*-connections can be used only for fairly small samples (e.g. for school classes) in its present form. If the number of individuals increases, the resulting *G*-lattice becomes immensely complex. For 1,000 pupils and 50 tasks the number of nodes in the *G*-lattice may be of the order of the number of neurons in the human brain. The *G*-lattice must be radically simplified, that is, the irrelevant closed sets should be discarded from the lattice. Set theory and abstract algebra in general do not provide any tool for this. Therefore we have to look for statistical methods.

There are two simple methods available. The first possibility is to discard individuals and/or features from the starting matrix according to some relevant point of view (criteria). The other possibility is to discard elements from the final result, from the *G*-lattice, independently from the starting matrix. Neither of these ways seems to lead to satisfactory results. It is almost impossible to define relevant criteria to discard elements without losing important connections.

A satisfactory compromise between the above possibilities is to discard elements from the starting matrix according to the effect of the discarded individual on the *G*-lattice. First of all, if two individuals have the same features, then discarding one of them will not affect the resulting *G*-lattice at all. The next step should result in reducing the *G*-lattice. The basic idea of the following algorithm is to discard as few individuals as possible so

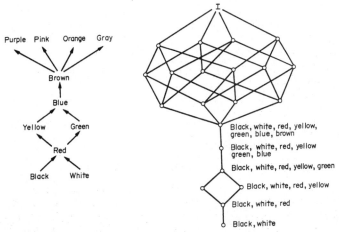

Figure 3
Evolution of colour terminology and its Galois model

that it should result in as big a reduction in the *G*-lattice as possible.

The researcher has first to define a *c* threshold value. This *c* value should express the complexity of the *G*-lattice so that the researcher judges this complexity to be tolerable. The following algorithm results in a *G*-lattice with *c* nodes as a maximum at the price of possibly discarding a few individuals.

Step 1. Compute the number of nodes in the *G*-lattice as a result of discarding the $i_1, i_2, \ldots, i_n$ individuals. Let *k* be the index for which the resulting *G*-lattice is the smallest.

Step 2. Discard the *k*-th individual from the starting matrix.

Step 3. Check whether the *G*-lattice resulting from the present starting matrix consists of more than *c* nodes. If yes, continue with Step 1; if no, the procedure is finished.

The given procedure is very simple, but it takes a lot of computing time. However, if the number of individuals is about 1,000 to 2,000 and the number of features is fairly small (about 20), this algorithm can be performed on personal computers in a few hours. The asymmetry in the features and the individuals is quite logical because in educational research (as in other research areas) the features are stable elements and the individuals are incidental. On the other hand, the best algorithms for computing a *G*-lattice take a computing time in one variable which increases exponentially with the amount of data, while in the other variable the time increases only $N.\log N$ times, where *N* is the number of data in the variable. Thus, asymmetrical data are more favourable from a computing point of view.

We may interpret the above algorithm as if, in every step, the "most disturbing" individual were discarded, namely, the individual who contributed most to the complexity of the given *G*-lattice. In this sense, the pupil who fills out the test in a completely random way is extremely disturbing. This fact suggests the need to devise a tool for filtering out the "random" pupils from the matrix by trying to substitute a pupil by a random pupil, that is, with a test-sheet filled by a random generator. If the resulting *G*-lattice is not more complex than the original one, the pupil, most probably, filled out the test at random. Of course, several trials with different random substitutions will increase the reliability of this method.

A *G*-lattice computed from a random data matrix is usually very much larger than a lattice computed from real data. In the case of a 12 by 12 random starting matrix the resulting *G*-lattice, with a probability greater than 0.95, will consist of more than 100 points. The graph in Fig. 1 consists of only 19 nodes and this is typical for this matrix size. However, some unwanted random effects may also occur in real data. Coding error is a trivial example. A more subtle one is an unimportant computation error made by the pupil.

The proposed algorithm will initially discard those pupils whose results are either unreliable or very uncharacteristic. However, it can sometimes occur that about 30 percent of the pupils must be discarded before the lattice is reduced to the given threshold (e.g. 100-nodes). This is still satisfactory, because it means that 70 percent of the pupils can be described in a fairly simple way. Suppose, for example, that the lattice in Fig. 1 was not the result of Table 1 but represented the result of 1,000 pupils after discarding 300 of them. In this case it can be claimed that the statements read from the *G*-lattice are valid for at least 70 percent of the pupils. This would seem to be a fairly poor result since statisticians usually work with much higher significance levels. Nevertheless, these results refer to strict logical relations like "those who solved tasks 6 and 11 also solved task 12". This is a very different kind of statement from the one that "the correlation of the two variables is 0.68 ± 0.12 at a significance level of 5 percent". It cannot be stated, in general, which of the two statements is stronger.

The method of Galois lattices can be interpreted from both a qualitative and a quantitative point of view. The qualitative train of thought would be: discard the most disturbing individuals to eliminate random effects. Even the most apparent properties of a horse are not valid for all horses. Horses which are perissodactyls have an odd number of toes; but some of them may be injured and have an even number of toes on some legs. It would, however, not be reasonable to form a separate class of this latter type. Rather, it is more reasonable to discard these animals from the system. The described method presents the most stable categories and the aberrant cases should be compared with these stable categories, rather than included in them.

The quantitative approach starts from the fact that the size of the resulting *G*-lattice depends on an a priori decision about what degree of complexity is tolerable. If the structure of the knowledge in a certain domain is in fact more complex than the given threshold, simplifications may bias the result. If this is the case, then one must really work with the traditional statistical methods. However, the Galois method does not exclude statistical analyses; they can still be incorporated in the *G*-lattice. For example, the nodes of the *G*-lattice can be drawn to be proportional to the number of individuals corresponding to the closed set. Also the edges of the *G*-lattice can be labelled with the probability of one pupil belonging to that edge. (In this case in any horizontal line the sum of the probabilities attached to the crossed edges is 1.) In this way, the *G*-lattice is appropriate for deciding whether the test is in accordance with the Rasch model or not. It can also be decided that if the Rasch model can be fitted to 95 percent of pupils, then 5 percent are omitted. And if the test is very far from satisfying the criteria of the Rasch model there is still the possibility, by using the *G*-lattice, of creating a sub-test which is in accordance with the Rasch model at the 95 percent level.

5. *The Complexity of a Relation*

The complexity of a G-lattice has been defined simply by the number of nodes in the lattice. However, it is not self-evident that a lattice with more nodes is really more complex than another lattice with a fewer number of nodes. In fact, it is not even true in the common-sense meaning of complexity. The discarding algorithm described above provides a way of comparing the complexity of two Galois lattices (and of two arbitrary relations) in a sense that is closer to the everyday meaning of complexity. An algorithm for this task is given in the following paragraphs.

Let M_1 and M_2 be two binary matrices both with n rows and k columns. Let the relations induced by the matrices be denoted R_1 and R_2. Let the G-lattices corresponding to the relations be denoted G_{1i} and G_{2i}. The index i means that this is the i-th iteration. Now let us perform the discarding algorithm on both lattices with the threshold chosen as $c = 1$. (This means that all individuals but one are discarded in the consecutive steps as 1 individual can only give 1 closed set.) The lattices obtained in the successive steps are denoted $G_{11}, G_{12}, \ldots,$ $G_{1,n-1}$ and $G_{21}, G_{22}, \ldots, G_{2,n-1}$ respectively. Finally, let the number of nodes in a lattice L be denoted $|L|$.

Thus, the relation R_1 is more complex than the relation R_2 if

$$\sum_{i=0}^{n-1} |G_{1i}| > \sum_{i=0}^{n-1} |G_{2i}|$$

holds. Thus the complexity of the original G_{10} and G_{20} lattices is compared by means of the number of nodes in the consecutive reductions.

This notion of complexity is really closer to the everyday notion of complexity because it also takes into consideration the effect of the individuals on the lattice. If the number of nodes in a lattice is very large only because of a few irregular individuals then the complexity measured in this way will be fairly low. An example of this effect is in Fig. 4 where in the case of relation R_1 the number of nodes decreases only slowly, while in the case of R_2 the number of nodes decreases fairly quickly. Thus, the relation R_1 proves to be more complex than R_2 even if the number of nodes in the starting lattice R_2 involves more nodes than R_1. This measuring algorithm expresses the heuristic that it is reasonable to consider a structure fairly simple if it seems very complex only because of a few irregular elements.

In a similar way we can check whether a relation is more or less complex than another referring to the features instead of the individuals. In this case, of course, the features should be consecutively discarded.

The proposed discarding algorithm discards the individuals one by one, which, theoretically, may result in fewer decreases than if one discards two or more individuals at once. Theoretically, a more "greedy" algorithm could produce a faster decrease of nodes, but this would be fairly hazardous in our case. Such an algorithm would involve the risk that a subset is discarded not because it is really irregular or random but because it is regular but in a different way from the majority, which might change the interpretation. This does not happen if the individuals are discarded one by one.

6. *Conclusion*

In a study of discourse reading, Kádár-Fülöp (1985) used the Galois lattice technique to carry out a detailed investigation of the errors made on a set of five test items by samples of approximately 1,700 Grade 4 and 1,650 Grade 8 students. By comparing the lattice structures for the Grade 4 students and the Grade 8 students, gains in reading skills during the four years of schooling could be examined. While this technique has not been widely used, it has the potential to assist in the teasing out of learning hierarchies and the study of basic learning competencies in a manner that has not been possible with Guttman and Rasch scaling techniques.

See also: Guttman Scales; Cluster Analysis; Partial Order Scalogram Analysis (POSA)

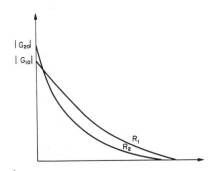

Figure 4
Measuring the complexity of the Galois lattice

Bibliography

Berlin B, Kay P 1969 *Basic Color Terms, Their Universality and Evolution*. University of California Press, Berkeley and Los Angeles, California

Carneiro R L 1973 The four faces of evolution. In: Honigmann J J (ed.) 1973 *Handbook of Social and Cultural Anthropology*. Rand McNally, Chicago, Illinois, pp. 89–110

Durkheim E 1902 De quelque formes primitives de classification. *L'Année sociologique, 1901–1902*. Presses Universitaires de France, Paris pp. 1–72

Fay G, Takács D V 1975 Cell assemblies in cellular space. *J. Cybern.* 5(3): 65–86

Kádár-Fülöp J 1985 CTD reading study. *Eval. Educ.* 9(2): 117–64

Katz J J, Fodor J A 1963 The structure of a semantic theory. *Language* 39: 170–210

Interaction Effects

K. M. Marjoribanks

In his analysis of experimental design, Sir Ronald Fisher proposed that when research is undertaken "we are usually ignorant which, out of innumerable possible factors, may prove ultimately to be the most important, though we may have strong presuppositions that some few of them are particularly worthy of study. We have usually no knowledge that any one factor will exert its effects independently of all others that can be varied, or that its effects are particularly simply related to variations in these other factors" (Fisher 1935 pp. 94–95). Fisher suggested that if investigators confined their attention to any single factor, it might be inferred either that they were the unfortunate victims of a doctrinaire theory as to how experimentation should proceed, or that the time, material, or equipment at their disposal was too limited to allow attention to be given to more than one narrow aspect of the problem. Fisher then challenged investigators to examine not only the possible influences of multiple factors but to design studies that analysed the possible effects of interactions between multiple factors. He observed that such interactions might, or might not, be considerable in magnitude, and it would be of importance in practical cases to know whether they were considerable or not. In this article, some of the issues related to an understanding of interaction effects are examined and studies from educational research that illustrate the analysis of interactions are presented.

1. Ordinal and Disordinal Interaction

It has been suggested (Kerlinger and Pedhazur 1973 p. 245) that "to ask whether independent variables interact is, in effect, to ask about the model that best fits the data. When an interaction is not significant, an additive model is sufficient to describe the data. This means that a subject's score on the dependent variable is conceived as a composite of several additive components. When, however, an interaction is significant, it is necessary to study it carefully in order to decide on a proper course of analytic action." If interaction exists in a set of data, the researcher should not attempt to describe accurately the results with a global statement but through statements describing the results at selected levels. If the interaction is found to be absent, an accurate description of the data can be made by comparing the results across all levels. The global statement of the main effect would describe accurately each of the simple effects if interaction did not exist. If interactions are present in research then it has been proposed that they should be classified as being either ordinal or disordinal (Lindquist 1953). The distinction may be most appropriately illustrated by considering the diagrams in Fig. 1, where each diagram is a representation of fictitious relationships

between measures of aptitudes and achievement outcomes for students in two instructional treatment groups.

In Fig. 1a the parallel lines indicate that across the observed aptitude levels there is a constant difference in outcome scores between the two treatment groups, A and B. Thus, in relation to the outcome measure there is no interaction between the aptitude and treatment variables. Ordinal interaction is represented in Fig. 1b. Although treatment A is relatively more effective at high ability levels, the outcome scores for students in treatment A remain greater than the scores of treatment B students at all aptitude levels. Disordinal interaction is represented by Fig. 1c. At aptitude levels below x_1 the outcome scores of treatment B students are higher than those of treatment A students. The two treatments appear to be equally effective at the aptitude level of x_1. Above x_1, however, students from treatment A have higher outcome scores than students from treatment B. It has been proposed that the decision as to whether an interaction is ordinal or disordinal is based on the point at which the regression lines cross each other. If this point is outside the range of interest, the interaction is considered ordinal. If, on the other hand, the point at

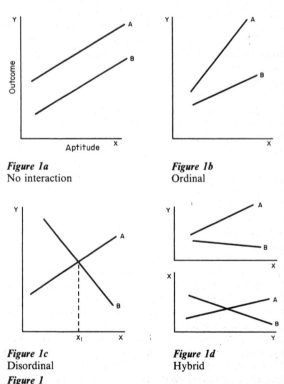

Figure 1a
No interaction

Figure 1b
Ordinal

Figure 1c
Disordinal

Figure 1d
Hybrid

Figure 1
Graphical representation of interaction types

which the lines intersect is within the range of interest, then the interaction is considered disordinal.

In a further classification, interaction effects have been labelled as being either pure ordinal, pure disordinal, or hybrid (Leigh and Kinnear 1980 pp. 842–43). It is suggested that some interactions may be ordinal with one factor as the abscissa and disordinal with the other. Pure ordinal interaction characterizes the situation in which, regardless of the factor used as the abscissa, a consistent rank order relationship exists for levels of a factor or factor combination between levels of the abscissa factor. Pure disordinal interaction occurs when regardless of the factor used as the abscissa, lines connecting treatment combinations for two levels of the other component(s) cross at least once. Hybrid interaction differs from pure ordinal interaction in that the rank order of treatment profiles is invariant between levels of one or more factors, and it varies between levels of one or more remaining factors. The slopes of two or more lines will vary inversely between two or more levels of any of the possible factors, but they do not necessarily have to cross. Because this inverse relationship implies that in a two-factor interaction contrast, the largest and smallest mean values occur at the same abscissa level, the lines must also cross on the graph in which the other factor serves as the abscissa. A graphical representation of such a hybrid interaction is shown in Fig. 1d.

It has been pointed out by Cronbach and Snow (1977 p. 31) that at one time, writers stressed the value of disordinal interactions and tended to dismiss ordinal interactions. The ordinal interaction was regarded as a mere artifact of the choice of measuring scales for the dependent variable. They indicated, for example, that in many studies that examined aptitude–treatment interactions, persons to the right of the crossover point were to be sent to one treatment and persons to the left were assigned to the other. An ordinal interaction (no crossing) would imply the same treatment for all persons. It is claimed by Cronbach and Snow, however, that such an argument about instructional decisions needs to be modified. They have proposed that if the treatment that yields the greater outcome is much costlier than the other, the ordinal interaction effect on outcome becomes a disordinal effect on payoff. The more costly method should be applied only to those who will find it so advantageous that its extra cost is repaid in benefits. Even if the cost-corrected interaction is ordinal, differential assignment will be required when facilities for giving one treatment are limited. The scarce treatment will be given to those persons most likely to profit from it, that is, persons from the end of the range where the payoff differential is greatest. The graphs in Fig. 2 illustrate a change in ordinality when treatment costs are considered. It is assumed in the example that treatment A is much more expensive than treatment B. After outcome scores are adjusted for treatment costs, the ordinal interaction represented in Fig. 2a translates to a disordinal interaction as shown in Fig. 2b. Rather than

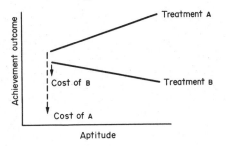

Figure 2a
Ordinal

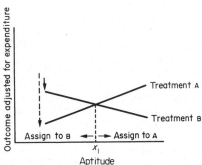

Figure 2b
Disordinal
Figure 2
Ordinality alteration when expense of treatments is considered

assigning all students to treatment A, as Fig. 2a would suggest, the adjusted interaction indicates that a more appropriate instructional decision might be to assign only those students with aptitude scores greater than x_1 to treatment A, and all other students to treatment B. The analysis of ordinal and disordinal interaction indicates the sensitivity that needs to be adopted when interpreting interactions in educational research.

2. Analysis of Interaction Effects

Interaction effects usually come to the attention of behavioural scientists through the analysis of variance. In analysis of variance, which is used generally with nominally scaled research factors, interactions are functions of cell means; usually differences between differences of means. But the idea of interaction is far more general than represented by analysis of variance. Interactions are defined and may be studied using quantitative scales, or using combinations of qualitative and nominal scales. In fact, a single (independent) variable can be formed to carry the effect of the interaction of any aspect of any research factor (nominal or quantitative) with any aspect of another research factor (nominal or quantitative), and so on, for interactions of a higher order. It is useful to point out that both analysis of variance and multiple regression or correlation analysis are realizations of the least-squares general linear model. However, multiple regression/correlation analysis is by far the more general procedure since it incorporates means of representing as sets of independent variables not only nominal scales, but also straight-line and curvilinear (including polynomial) functions, variables with missing data, and interactions among variables of all kinds. Multiple regression/correlation analysis can be used to analyse the data of analysis of variance but the reverse does not hold. In fact analysis of variance can be viewed as a special case of multiple regression/correlation analysis where the conditions are regular, that is, with equal cell sizes in factorial and split-plot designs and with equal sample sizes and intervals in trend analysis. In defining what is meant by interaction when multiple regression models are used, two variables, u and v, are said to interact in their accounting for variance in Y, when over and above any additive combination of their separate effects, they have a joint effect (Cohen and Cohen 1975 p. 292) . This is another way of saying that u and v operate jointly in relating to Y and they also operate conditionally. The relationship between u and Y depends on the value of v, being stronger for some values of v than for others. This conditional relationship is also symmetrical, the relationship between v and Y depending on the value of u. To state the matter more exactly, a nonzero $u \times v$ interaction effect means that the regression of Y on u varies with changes in v and that the regression of Y on v varies with changes in u. Whatever the nature of u and v then, the $u \times v$ interaction is carried in the uv product and can be understood in terms of joint, or conditional, or nonuniform relationships with Y. However, the $u \times v$ interaction "is carried by", not "is" the uv product. This is because, in general, uv will be linearly correlated with both u and v, often quite substantially so. Only when u and v have been linearly partialled from uv does it, in general, become the interaction (independent variable). That is,

$$u \times v = uv \cdot u, v$$

where the $u \times v$ notation is used to represent an interaction and uv indicates a product that only becomes an interaction when its constituent parts are partialled.

Similarly, in a three-way interaction such as $u \times v \times w$, the interaction is carried by the product uvw from which the constituent variables and two-way products of variables are partialled. That is,

$$u \times v \times w = uvw \cdot u, v, w, uv, uw, vw$$

What is being claimed is that the product variable (say) XZ contains the interaction together with variance that is linearly accounted for by X and Z. When this latter variance is removed from XZ by partialling, it is precisely the $X \times Z$ interaction that remains, that is, $XZ \cdot X, Z$. The latter will, of course, correlate precisely zero with X and Z (by construction), and will be correlationally invariant over linear transformations of X and Z, and with an invariant t (or F) value.

The significance of interactions in regression models may most appropriately be examined by analysing hierarchical regression equations in which independent variables are entered in a predetermined order so that prior variables are partialled from later ones. Consider, for example, the regression of Y on the variables X, Z, and their product XZ. Then:

$$Y = b_1 X + b_2 Z + b_3 XZ + a$$

where bs are the raw score regression weights and a the Y-intercept. The amount of variance associated with the addition of an independent variable (its unique contribution) is its squared semipartial r. It is a semipartial r because the other (independent) variables have been partialled from the (independent) variable in question but not from Y. In relation to the product variable, its squared multiple semipartial correlation with Y is:

$$r^2_{Y(XZ \cdot X, Z)} = R^2_{Y \cdot X, Z, XZ} - R^2_{Y \cdot X, Z}$$

which is the increment in Y variance accounted for when the product XZ is added to its constituent variables, X and Z, as a third independent variable.

An illustration of using hierarchical regression models to detect interactions is presented in the following consideration of the correlates of children's affective characteristics.

3. Person–School Environment Correlates of Children's Affective Characteristics: An Analysis of Interactions

Investigations of children's school outcomes have typically adopted either a trait model of explanation in which person variables are considered to have the major associations with outcomes, or a situation framework in which the primary correlates of outcomes are defined by context measures. An alternate approach, labelled the interaction model, that has historical links with conceptual schemes developed by psychologists, has been proposed as a more appropriate framework for examining the complex associations between persons, contexts, and individual outcomes.

An interaction framework was adopted (Marjoribanks 1980) to examine relationships suggested by Bloom's theory of school learning in which learning outcomes are associated with the quality of instruction provided by schools and with the cognitive and affective entry characteristics that children bring to learning tasks (Bloom 1976). Marjoribanks' study examined relations between children's school-related attitudes and measures of intellectual ability, personality, and school environment. Hierarchical regression models of the form: $Y = b_1 X + b_2 Z + b_3 XZ + a$, were examined where Y represented school attitudes; X, school environment; and Z, personality or intellectual ability.

The sample, discussed here, included 255 12-year-old Australian girls selected from eight rural secondary schools, with approximately equal numbers of girls from each school. A simple random sample, however,

Table 1
Regression of school attitudes on person and school environment variables

Predictors	School attitudes	
	b	R^2ch^a
Regulative context	−1.328	0.154
Ability	−0.475	0.022
Context × ability	0.021	0.043
Multiple *R*		0.469
Regulative context	3.348	0.154
Cooperative personality	2.302	0.047
Context × personality	−0.057	0.043
Multiple *R*		0.496
Regulative context	0.776	0.154
Obedient personality	−0.431	0.030
Context × personality	b	
Multiple *R*		0.429
Imaginative context	0.862	0.104
Ability	0.126	0.048
Context × ability	b	
Multiple *R*		0.392
Imaginative context	5.760	0.104
Cooperative personality	5.572	0.043
Context × personality	−0.111	0.054
Multiple *R*		0.449
Imaginative context	−2.296	0.104
Obedient personality	−4.433	0.046
Context × personality	0.085	0.027
Multiple *R*		0.422

a The R^2 change values indicate the variance associated with the addition of each predictor to the regressions
b The added variance associated with the interaction was not significant

was not chosen. Therefore, in the regression models, adjustments were made for design effects. Significance levels for the regression weights were recalculated using the formula: standard error of sample estimate = (design effect)$^{1/2}$ × simple random standard error.

Intellectual ability was assessed using the Otis Intermediate Test, Form AB while the Children's Personality Questionnaire, Form A, was used to measure personality. From the questionnaire, two second-stratum personality scales were isolated and labelled aggressive versus obedient and distant–expedient versus cooperative–conscientious. Items from previous analyses of children's affective characteristics were used to construct a school-related attitude measure.

When discussing the quality of instruction variable in his theory, Bloom suggested that "it is the *environment for learning in the classroom* ... that is important for school learning and that it is the management of learning by teachers rather than the management of learners that is at the center of creating a successful instructional context" (Bloom 1976 p. 111). Although a number of school learning environment scales have been developed, it was decided that a more appropriate measure of Bloom's quality of instruction would be obtained from a schedule that assessed children's perceptions of the quality of teaching and teachers. Also, it was considered that

the conceptual distance between children's affective outcomes and their perceptions of school environments would be greater if an environment scale was used that measured children's perceptions of teachers rather than general perceptions of school. A new school environment scale was constructed that assessed children's perceptions of four interrelated environments that were labelled the regulative, instructional, imaginative, and interpersonal school contexts.

As it is not possible in the space available to examine all the findings from the data, six regression surfaces have been plotted in two figures to provide an indication of the possible nature of interactions. The surfaces were generated from the regression weights shown in Table 1 which indicate the associations between school attitudes, person variables, and the measures of school environment. Low scores on the two personality factors indicated either aggressive or distant–expedient orientations while high values reflected obedient or cooperative–conscientious orientations, respectively. The findings in Table 1 indicated that the interaction variable had a significant association with school attitudes in four of the regression models.

The surfaces in Fig. 3 show the regression-fitted relations between school attitudes, the person variables, and children's perceptions of the regulative context of schools. At low ability levels, increases in the regulative context were associated with decrements in the regression-fitted attitude scores, while at high ability levels increases in the context scores were associated with sizeable increases in attitude scores. At an ability level of 30, for example, the regression-fitted attitude scores were 48 and 42 at regulative context scores of 30 and 70, while the corresponding fitted attitude scores at an ability

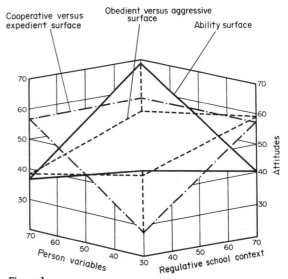

Figure 3
Fitted attitude scores in relation to person and regulative school context variables

level of 70 were 37 and 69. At low context levels, increments in ability were related to decreases in attitude scores, while at high context values increases in ability were associated with large increments in attitude scores. Such an interpretation of the regression surface reflects the quality of conditionality inferred by the presence of significant interactions in educational research.

The surface for the distant–expedient versus cooperative–conscientious personality dimension reflected the presence of a negative interaction. At low regulative scores, changes in personality towards cooperative–conscientious were associated with sizeable increments in attitude scores, while at high context levels there was little relation between the personality and attitude measures. The shape of the surface for the aggressive versus obedient personality dimension indicated the absence of significant interaction. Increases across the range of context scores were related to increments of approximately 13 points in attitude scores, at each aggressive versus obedient personality value, while across the range of personality values changes in the regulative context were associated with increments of approximately seven points in the attitude measure.

In Fig. 4 the surfaces represent associations between school attitudes, person variables, and the perceived imaginative context of schools. The shape of the surface for intellectual ability indicated the absence of interaction while both personality surfaces reflected significant interactions between person and situation variables. Again, the surfaces indicate the possible complexity of relations between person and situation variables when they are related to children's school outcomes. Regression models that neglect an analysis of interactions may generate false interpretations of educational problems.

The study just described illustrates the analysis of interactions in survey educational research. Some of the most elegant analyses of interaction, however, have involved investigations of possible aptitude–treatment interactions in experimental studies. Some methodological developments in aptitude–treatment interaction research are examined in the following section.

4. Aptitude–Treatment Interactions

The following brief examination of aptitude–treatment interaction (ATI) illustrates advances that have occurred in the analysis of interactions.

4.1 Confidence Limits

In their investigation of ATI research, Cronbach and Snow (1977) urged that greater attention should be devoted to the description of effects and less to decisions about the null hypothesis. It is not necessary to choose between the descriptive and the inferential, because by establishing a confidence interval on each effect, it is possible to have both. Research into aptitude–treatment interactions, however, does not place the usual emphasis on the significance of results. The use of confidence limits saves the investigator and his or her readers from premature closure. An illustration of calculating confidence limits, in the analysis of interactions, is provided by Janicki and Peterson (1981). They adopted an extension of the Johnson–Neyman technique, developed by Potthoff (1964), to determine regions of significance. In their study, children were taught a unit of mathematics either by direct instruction or by a small-group variation of direct instruction. Relationships were examined between a set of aptitudes and measures of mathematics achievement and attitude to mathematics. The regression lines in Fig. 5 reveal the nature of some of the significant associations of the investigation. When the confidence level $(1 - \alpha)$ was set at 0.30, a region of significance for the regression of achievement on an attitude/locus of control factor was identified as shown in Fig. 5a. Janicki and Peterson indicated that the students with scores greater than 0.45 on the attitude toward math/locus of control factor (35.5 percent of the students) performed significantly better in the small-group variation than in direct instruction. The achievement of students with factor scores less than 0.45 did not differ significantly in the two approaches.

Regions of significance were also investigated for the regression of attitude towards mathematics on ability. The findings in Fig. 5b indicate that students who had ability scores between -1.64 and -1.0 had significantly more positive attitudes towards mathematics in direct instruction than in the small-group variation. Students who had ability scores between 1.0 and 1.64 also had significantly more positive attitudes in direct instruction than in the small-group variation. Medium-ability students with ability scores between -1.0 and 1.0 did not differ significantly in their attitudes towards mathematics in the two treatments.

The Janicki and Peterson study indicates that a more enriched understanding of the nature of interactions is provided in ATI research by the calculation of confidence levels.

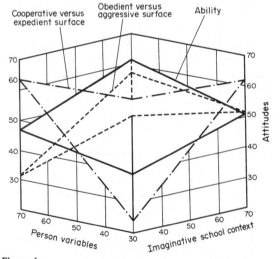

Figure 4
Fitted attitude scores in relation to person and imaginative school context variables

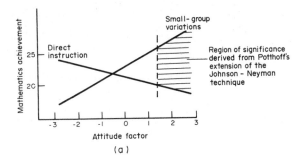

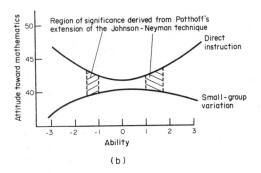

Figure 5
Significance regions: Adapted from Janicki and Peterson (1981) study
a Regression of achievement on attitude showing ATI
b Regression of attitude toward mathematics on ability

4.2 Hierarchical Analysis of Treatment and Aptitude–Treatment Interaction Effects

Corno (1979) has contended that statistical analyses of ATIs typically ignore the hierarchical (students nested within classes) character of classroom data. This problem is particularly important, given that research conclusions may be overturned by reanalyses that take this hierarchical nature of the data into account. It is suggested that in ATI research, analyses need to be conducted at three hierarchical levels: (a) between-classes, (b) pooled within-classes, and (c) overall individuals. For between-class analyses, students are assigned their class mean on each variable which weights each mean by the class size, and the analyses pose the question "Do classes respond to treatments differently depending on the average level of aptitudes?" Pooled within-class investigations adopt student and outcome scores deviated from the class mean and ask, "Does response to treatment depend on where the student is placed on aptitude relative to other students?" Analysis for overall individuals, which is characteristic of most ATI research, ignores class distinctions by regressing raw individual student outcomes onto similarly defined aptitudes to examine whether, "response to treatments depend on individual student aptitudes". That is, regressions and interactions divide—at least in principle—into group

and individual components that have distinct substantive meanings. Recognition of these distinctions forces a radical change in thinking about ATI. Once two distinct interactions are conceived it becomes apparent that previous ATI studies have not asked as penetrating a question as they should. Except for a few studies of teacher effects, the investigator of ATI has reported a single component ATI, calculated either between classes or on pooled classes.

In an investigation of self-appraisal data for students in two treatment groups, Corno et al. (1981) observed that between-class effects accounted for 62 to 81 percent of variation in a number of affective outcome measures while pooled within-class effects accounted for only 11 to 35 percent. Although there were no significant ATIs in the individual overall or within-class pooled analyses there were three significant ATIs for the between-classes analyses. Classes with lower scores on general ability, for example, had more favourable attitudes if they were part of a treatment group in which parents instructed children in classroom strategies. In contrast, classes of higher ability had more favourable attitudes if they were part of a treatment group that received no special parent instruction in strategies. The exploration of between-group and within-group effects generates the possibility of new interpretations for much ATI research. Many analyses of ATI have been based on the assumption that all ATI effects occur independently in different students. However, while this probably is true for instruction administered to students singly, it may not be true when students work side by side, in the classroom.

4.3 Two-aptitude Aptitude–Treatment Studies

In their between-class analysis of self-appraisals, Corno et al. (1981) found two significant three-way ATIs (ability × attitude × treatment and ability × anxiety × treatment). Hedges (1981) has attempted to clarify the interpretation of the outcomes of two-aptitude ATI studies. He indicates that the results of such studies are often represented by drawing the regression surfaces for each treatment as a function of aptitudes. The three-dimensional representations show that the regression surfaces intersect, but they do not provide much insight about the curve on the aptitude plane corresponding to the aptitude where the intersection occurs. It is demonstrated by Hedges that the curve defining the boundary between aptitude regions where one or the other treatment is optimal is usually an hyperbola, while if the regression equation involves quadratic terms, the locus of points on the aptitude plane corresponding to the intersection of the regression surfaces may be either an hyperbola or an ellipse depending on the magnitude of the difference between regression coefficients for cross product $(X_1 X_2)$ and squared $(X_1^2$ and $X_2^2)$ terms.

These brief comments indicate that major refinements are being introduced in ATI studies that, hopefully, will produce more valuable analyses of interactions. In the following section of this article, the refinement of introducing polynomials, as interactions, into educational research is examined.

5. *Polynomials: Special Case of Interactions*

If an $X \times Z$ interaction is interpreted in relation to Y as meaning that the slope of the Y on X regression line varies as Z varies, then it is possible to interpret a partialled power of X as an interaction. It is suggested that when the constituents of a product are linearly partialled there is an interaction, for example, $X \times Z = XZ \cdot X, Z$. Similarly, when the constituents of an integral power are linearly partialled, there is a curve component, for example, $X \times X = XX \cdot X = X^2 \cdot X$. Further, just as $XZ \cdot X, Z$ is necessarily orthogonal to X and Z, whatever the correlations among X, Z, and XZ, so, too, is $X^2 \cdot X$ necessarily orthogonal to X, whatever the correlation between X and X^2 (usually close to unity). Partialled variables (residuals) correlate zero precisely with the variables that have been partialled from them, by construction (or definition). That is, an $X \times X$ interaction $(X^2 \cdot X)$ can be interpreted as meaning that the slope of the Y on X regression line varies as X varies. Polynomials may be analysed in hierarchical regression equations with linear functions preceding quadratic, preceding cubic, and so on, and with main effects preceding two-way, preceding three-way interactions, and so forth, so that terms of lower order are partialled from those of higher order and not vice versa.

As an illustration of an hierarchical model that included linear, two-way interaction, and squared terms, a study (Marjoribanks 1978, 1979) is examined that analysed a model constructed by Bloom (1964) to account for changes in the cognitive, physical, and emotional characteristics of individuals. The model is expressed in the formula $C_2 = C_1 + f(E_{2-1})$, which suggests that the measurement of an individual characteristic at time 2 (C_2) is accounted for by the measurement of the same characteristic at time 1 (C_1) plus some function of the environment between times 1 and 2 (E_{2-1}). From the model it is proposed that "the correlation between measurements of the same characteristic at two different times will approach unity when the environment in which the individuals have lived during the

intervening period is known and taken into account" (Bloom 1964 p. 192). Also, the model proposes that "the environment will have its greatest effects in the period of most rapid normal development of the characteristic and that its effects will be least in the period of slowest normal development, while its effects will approach zero in the period of no normal change in the characteristic" (Bloom 1964 p. 200). In the study being examined, the Bloom model was used to analyse relations between the reading performance of children and measures of their family environment. The data were collected as part of a national survey of elementary-school children in England (Central Advisory Council for Education 1967) and then collected as part of a follow-up study of the same children four years later (Peaker 1971). In the initial survey the sampling procedure had two stages. First, a stratified random sample was taken from all types of government-supported elementary schools in England which resulted in the selection of 173 schools. Then a systematic sample of children was chosen from the schools, which produced three age cohorts each of approximately 1,000 children. The average age of the senior cohort was approximately 11, of the middle group, 8, and of the junior group 7. When the children were surveyed four years later, the number in each cohort was: (a) senior group, 397 girls and 383 boys, (b) middle group, 371 girls and 382 boys, and (c) junior group, 406 girls and 407 boys. The present investigation included those children who were present in both surveys.

During both national surveys, the reading performance of the children was assessed. Also, parents were interviewed in their homes and from responses to the two sets of interviews a family learning environment measure was constructed. The family measure assessed process variables such as parents' aspirations for their children, literacy in the family, parent–teacher interaction, parent–child activeness, parents' knowledge of child's school progress, and parents' pressure for achievement within the family. Relationships between the reading and environment measures were examined by analysing hierarchical regression models of the form:

$$Y = aX + bZ + cXZ + dX^2 + eZ^2 + \text{constant}$$

Table 2
Regression of final reading achievement on initial reading performance and family environment

Predictors	Senior girls		Senior boys		Middle girls		Middle boys		Junior girls		Junior boys	
	b	$R^2 ch^a$	b	$R^2 ch$	b	$R^2 ch$	b	$R^2 ch$	b	$R^2 ch$	b	$R^2 ch$
Reading	1.790	0.441	1.070	0.214	0.201	0.296	0.574	0.196	0.285	0.246	0.417	0.257
Environment	0.070	0.087	0.226	0.197	−0.220	0.064	−0.059	0.104	−0.081	0.046	0.146	0.079
Reading × environment	−0.007	0.049	0.005	0.001[b]	0.012	0.012	0.011	0.043	0.004	0.014	0.002	0.012
(Reading)^2	−0.012	0.133	−0.012	0.326	−0.007	0.089	−0.008	0.199	−0.004	0.066	−0.004	0.094
(Environment)^2	0.002	0.001[b]	−0.002	0.001[b]	−0.001	0.001[b]	−0.001	0.001[b]	0.001	0.001[b]	−0.001	0.001[b]
Multiple R		0.843		0.860		0.679		0.736		0.611		0.665

a The R^2 change values indicate the variance associated with the addition of each predictor to the regression
b The added variance associated with the predictor was not significant

where Y, X, and Z represented measures of final reading performance, initial reading performance, and family learning environment, respectively.

The results in Table 2 indicated that generally, the initial reading × environment interaction was associated with a small additional amount of variation in later reading performance, while (initial reading)^2 was associated with a medium to large percentage of added variance in the later reading scores. The (environment)^2 variable was not related uniquely to the criterion measure.

The nature of the relationships between the variables is shown in the regression surfaces that are plotted in Fig. 6. In the figure the surfaces relate to the senior cohort children and the scores have been standardized with means of 50 and standard deviations of 10. The shape of the girls' surface is representative of those hierarchical regression models in which there was a significant relation between final reading achievement and the interaction between initial reading performance and family environment. At a low initial reading score of 40, for example, the regression-fitted final reading scores at environment levels of 30 and 70 were 37 and 46 respectively. The corresponding final scores at a high initial reading score of 70 were 66 and 67. Also, the curvature of the surface reflected the negative quadratic relationship between initial reading scores and later performance. The boys' surface indicates an absence of a significant initial reading × environment interaction. At an initial reading performance level of 40, for example, the regression-fitted final reading scores at environment levels of 30 and 70 were 34 and 38, while the corresponding fitted values at an initial reading score of 70 were 65 and 68.

The findings from the total study (Marjoribanks 1978, 1979) provided only partial support for the acceptance of Bloom's model of human-development. However, the study was restricted to an analysis of reading performance and did not include an examination of classroom, neighbourhood, and peer group environments nor an investigation of children's perceptions of their family environments. Only when such environment measures are examined in relation to other cognitive and affective measures will the Bloom model be appropriately tested. The purpose of examining the study, however, was to illustrate further the possible complexity of relationships between variables when interactions are included in analyses.

6. Conclusion

Research findings provide support for the adoption of interactionist models in educational research. But the models that have been used in studies should be considered only as an initial approximation of the complexity of interrelationships between measures of person, situation, and outcome variables. In future research, it is hoped that measurement of contexts, persons, and outcomes will be improved. All these characteristics are multivariate, and it is likely to be found that situations and parts of situations will produce different effects on a variety of outcome measures and will produce different effects on different individual characteristics depending on the pattern of their initial states. For subsequent research the following equation might be estimated:

$$I_{j,t_2} = \sum b_j I_{j,t_1}^* + \sum b_k E_{k,t_{1-2}}^* + \sum b_{jk} (I_{j,t_1}^*)(E_{k,t_{1-2}})$$

where I_{j,t_2} is a given individual characteristic. The first term on the right hand side of the model is a weighted composite of a number of antecedent individual characteristics (the asterisk indicates the characteristics are in the optimal mathematical form; for example, linear, quadratic, or logarithmic for prediction). The second term is a similar intervening context composite, and the last term is a weighted composite of products of antecedent characteristics and situations (Marjoribanks 1979).

Research based on the proposed generalized model would allow for the multiplicity of possible causes in the two domains, of persons and situations, and the possibility that initial characteristics interact with context measures, influencing later characteristics. Only by the adoption of such analysis of interaction is it likely that our understanding of the complex nature of educational problems will be enriched.

Bibliography

Bloom B S 1964 *Stability and Change in Human Characteristics*. Wiley, New York

Bloom B S 1976 *Human Characteristics and School Learning*. McGraw-Hill, New York

Central Advisory Council for Education 1967 *Children and Their Primary Schools (Plowden Report)*. Her Majesty's Stationery Office, London

Cohen J, Cohen P 1975 *Applied Multiple Regression: Correlation Analysis for the Behavioural Sciences*. Lawrence Erlbaum, Hillsdale, New Jersey

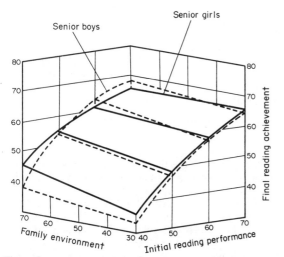

Figure 6
Fitted final reading achievement in relation to initial reading performance and family environment

Corno L 1979 A hierarchical analysis of selected naturally occurring aptitude–treatment interactions in the third grade. *Am. Educ. Res. J.* 16: 391–409

Corno L, Mitman A, Hedges L V 1981 The influence of direct instruction on student self-appraisals: A hierarchical analysis of treatment and aptitude–treatment interaction effects. *Am. Educ. Res. J.* 18: 39–61

Cronbach L J, Snow R E 1977 *Aptitudes and Instructional Methods: A Handbook for Research on Interactions*. Irvington, New York

Fisher R A 1935 *The Design of Experiments*. Oliver and Boyd, Edinburgh

Hedges L V 1981 Illustrating two-aptitude aptitude–treatment interactions: A methodological note. *Am. Educ. Res. J.* 18: 57–61

Janicki T C, Peterson P L 1981 Aptitude–treatment interaction effects of variations in direct instruction. *Am. Educ. Res. J.* 18: 63–82

Kerlinger F N, Pedhazur E J 1973 *Multiple Regression in Behavioral Research*. Holt, Rinehart and Winston, New York

Leigh J H, Kinnear T C 1980 On interaction classification. *Educ. Psychol. Meas.* 40: 841–43

Lindquist E F 1953 *Design and Analysis of Experiments in Psychology and Education*. Houghton Mifflin, New York

Marjoribanks K M 1978 Bloom's model of human development: A regression surface analysis. *Int. J. Behav. Dev.* 1: 193–206

Marjoribanks K M 1979 *Families and their Learning Environments: An Empirical Analysis*. Routledge and Kegan Paul, London

Marjoribanks K M 1980 Person–school environment correlates of children's affective characteristics. *J. Educ. Psychol.* 72: 583–91

Peaker G F 1971 *The Plowden Children Four Years Later*. National Foundation for Educational Research, Slough

Potthoff R F 1964 On the Johnson–Neyman technique and some extensions thereof. *Psychometrika* 29: 241–56

Log-linear Models

E. B. Andersen

Log-linear models are models for describing data given in the form of multidimensional frequency tables or contingency tables. A log-linear model assumes that the expected cell counts are expressed as linear combinations of so-called interaction parameters. Various important hypotheses of independence or conditional independence of the variables can be expressed as certain interactions being zero. The statistical analysis aims at describing the data by as simple a model as possible, that is, with as few interactions as possible.

1. Log-linear Models and Exponential Families

In basic statistical theory the term log-linear model can be used as an alternative name for the very broad family of statistical models, which are usually termed exponential families. Thus let $X_1 \ldots, X_n$ be a set of independent random variables, each with the probability density

$$f(x|\theta) = a(\theta)\exp[g(x)\varphi(\theta)]h(x) \qquad (1)$$

then $\tau = \varphi(\theta)$ is called the canonical parameter and it can easily be shown that

$$t = \sum_{i=1}^{n} g(x_i) \qquad (2)$$

is the minimal sufficient statistic for θ. In addition it can be shown that the maximum likelihood estimate $\hat{\tau}$ for τ [and if $\tau = \varphi(\theta)$ has a unique solution also the maximum likelihood estimate θ for θ] is obtained as the solution to

$$t = E_\theta(T) \qquad (3)$$

where T is the random variable corresponding to t and E_θ is the mean value, when θ is the true parameter. The name exponential family is derived from the exponential form of Eqn. (1). The term log-linear model arises because the logarithm of the likelihood corresponding to Eqn. (1) has the form

$$\log L(\theta) = n \log a(\theta) + t\varphi(\theta)$$

$$+ \sum_{i=1}^{n} \log h(x_i) \qquad (4)$$

that is, the observations and the parameters combine in the linear term $t\varphi(\theta)$.

In the multiparameter case $t \cdot \varphi(\theta)$ takes the form of an inner product $t_1\varphi_1(\theta) + \cdots + t_m\varphi_m(\theta)$.

2. Multidimensional Contingency Tables

The notation $x_{ij\ldots r}$ will be adopted here for the observed count in the cell $(i, j, \ldots, r)$ of an M-way contingency table. It will be assumed that n individuals have been classified according to M categorical variables with I, $J, \ldots, R$ categories, respectively. The probability (constant over the population) of an individual being classified in categories $i, j, \ldots, r$ on the M variables will be denoted by $p_{ij\ldots r}$. Hence the observed value $x_{ij\ldots r}$ of individuals with classification $i, j, \ldots, r$ will have mean value

$$E(X_{ij\ldots r}) = np_{ij\ldots r} \qquad (5)$$

and the distribution of the whole set of x's will be multinomial with count parameter n and probability parameters $p_{ij\ldots r}$; $i = 1, \ldots, I; j = 1, \ldots, J; \ldots r = 1, \ldots R$.

The data in Table 1 of a three-way table with $I = 2$, $J = 3$, $K = 2$ and the data in Table 2 of a four-way table with $I = J = K = R = 2$ will be used as an illustration of log-linear model methods and theory.

Table 1 shows the distribution of nonresponse in a Danish survey on the educational status of young people.

Table 1

Nonresponse classified according to sex and geographical region in a Danish educational survey

Response (R)	Region (G)	Variable	
		Sex (S)	
		Male	Female
	Copenhagen	306	264
Yes	Cities	609	627
	Countryside	978	947
	Copenhagen	49	76
No	Cities	77	79
	Countryside	114	103

For later use the symbols R for response/nonresponse, G for geographical region, and S for sex will be used.

For the data in Table 1, $n = 4,229$ and one has, for example, $x_{111} = 306$; $x_{121} = 609$; $x_{132} = 947$; and $x_{232} = 103$.

The model is 12-dimensional multinomial with parameters $(4229; p_{111}, \ldots, p_{232})$, where $p_{ijk} = P$ [a surveyed person falls in cell (i, j, k)].

The data in Table 2 are from a Danish study of the number of women living 10 years beyond a certain operation for cancer. The variables are S—survives the operation by 10 years or not; X—received x-ray treatment or not; O—the operation was radical or limited; and C—the cancer was at an early or advanced stage at the time of the operation.

For the data in Table 2 one has, for example, $x_{1111} = 10$, $x_{2121} = 38$, and $x_{2222} = 5$, with $n = 299$.

The model assumes that $(x_{1111}, \ldots, x_{2222})$ is 16-dimensional multinomial with parameters $(299; p_{1111}, \ldots, p_{2222})$, where $p_{ijkr} = P$ [a patient falls in cell (i, j, k, r)].

3. Interaction Parameters

For contingency tables like those illustrated in Tables 1 and 2, the statistical analysis should aim at explaining the interrelationships between the variables by as simple a structure as possible. Within the framework of log-

linear models the strategy for pursuing this goal is to first formulate as general a model as possible in terms of convenient parameters, and then reduce the model to one with a simpler structure by testing whether some of these parameters can be omitted. The first model to consider is, therefore, the so-called saturated model, where the basic parameters $p_{ij \ldots r}$ are replaced by a new set of parameters, which represent a reparametrization, that is, the new parameters stand in a one-to-one correspondence with the p's. The new parameters are chosen in such a way that they are canonical parameters for the corresponding exponential family, or as in Eqn. (4), such that parameters and observations enter the likelihood function in linear combinations.

For a four-way table, the saturated log-linear model is obtained by expressing the logarithm of the expected number np_{ijkr} as a linear expression in the following way

$$\log(np_{ijkr}) = \theta_0 + \theta_i^{(1)} + \cdots + \theta_r^{(4)} + \cdots$$
$$+ \theta_{ij}^{(12)} + \cdots + \theta_{kr}^{(34)} + \cdots$$
$$+ \theta_{ijk}^{(123)} + \cdots + \theta_{jkr}^{(234)} + \cdots$$
$$+ \theta_{ijkr}^{(1234)} \qquad (6)$$

This general form was first suggested by Birch (1963) and developed by Goodman in a series of papers, which are reprinted in Goodman (1978). The statistical theory was further developed by Haberman (1974).

The parameters of Eqn. (6) are called interactions. They represent a reparametrization when linear constraints are introduced such that sums over all indices are zero. For example:

$$\theta_{\cdot}^{(1)} = 0$$

$$\theta_{i \cdot}^{(12)} = \theta_{\cdot j}^{(12)} = 0$$

$$\theta_{ij \cdot}^{(123)} = \theta_{i \cdot j}^{(123)} = \theta_{\cdot jk}^{(123)} = 0$$

$$\theta_{ijk \cdot}^{(1234)} = \theta_{ij \cdot r}^{(1234)} = \theta_{i \cdot kr}^{(1234)} = \theta_{\cdot jkr}^{(1234)} = 0.$$

These constraints mean that one has $(I - 1)$ rather than $I\theta_i^{(1)}$'s; $(I - 1) \cdot (J - 1)$ rather than $IJ\theta_{ij}^{(12)}$'s; $(I - 1) \cdot (J - 1) \cdot (K - 1)$ rather than $IJK\theta_{ijk}^{(123)}$'s;

Table 2

Number of women observed in a Danish cancer study for each of four categorical variables

Survived operation by 10 years (S)	Received X-ray treatment (X)	Operation type (O)	Stage of cancer (C)	
			Early	Advanced
No	No	Radical	10	38
		Limited	1	3
	Yes	Radical	17	64
		Limited	3	13
Yes	No	Radical	41	6
		Limited	13	1
	Yes	Radical	64	11
		Limited	9	5

and $(I-1)\cdot(J-1)\cdot(K-1)\cdot(R-1)$ rather than $IJKR\theta_{ijkr}^{(1234)}$'s. In addition θ_0 is determined by the requirement

$$\sum_{i=1}^{I}\sum_{j=1}^{J}\sum_{k=1}^{K}\sum_{r=1}^{R}p_{ijkr}=1 \qquad (7)$$

Observing these constraints, the number of interaction parameters add up to $IJKR-1$, or the same number as the free p_{ijkr}'s when Eqn. (7) is taken into account.

4. Estimation

The log-likelihood function for a multinomial distribution is given as

$$\log L = \text{const.}$$
$$+\sum_{i=1}^{I}\sum_{j=1}^{J}\sum_{k=1}^{K}\sum_{r=1}^{R}x_{ijkr}\log(p_{ijkr}) \qquad (8)$$

Using Eqn. (6) this can also be written as

$$\log L = \text{const.} + \theta_{.}x_{....} + \theta_i^{(1)}x_{i...} + \cdots$$
$$\cdots + \theta_{ij}^{(12)}x_{ij..} + \cdots + \theta_{ijk}^{(123)}x_{ijk.} + \cdots$$
$$\cdots + \theta_{ijkr}^{(1234)}x_{ijkr} \qquad (9)$$

which shows that the interactions are canonical parameters with the corresponding marginals as sufficient statistics. This, by the general result shown in Eqn. (3) also means that the maximum likelihood estimates for the interaction parameters are obtained by equations of the form

$$x_{i...} = E(X_{i...}) = np_{i...} \qquad (10)$$

$$x_{ij..} = E(X_{ij..}) = np_{ij..} \qquad (11)$$

and so on. Because of the constraints imposed, such equations need only be solved when the indices are not equal to their maximum value, that is, Eqn. (10) need only be solved for $i = 1,\ldots, I-1$ and Eqn. (11) for $i < I$ and $j < J$. It is, however, easy to show that the maximum likelihood estimates are obtained when Eqn. (11) is also solved for $i = I$ and $j = J$ if Eqn. (10) is then omitted, as it can now be derived from Eqn. (11) by summation over j.

These results mean that:

(a) Maximum likelihood estimates are obtained by marginal fitting of the form shown in Eqns. (10) and (11).

(b) Any set of marginals which can be derived from other marginals already fitted need not be fitted.

For the saturated model this means that only the trivial "marginals" x_{ijkr} need to be fitted, or that the maximum likelihood estimates are obtained by putting $x_{ijkr} = np_{ijkr}$, for all i, j, k, and r. It would be expected that this would give a complete fit to the observed numbers by the expected numbers. For models which are not saturated, that is, where some of the interactions are zero, it follows from Eqn. (9) that the marginals corres-

ponding to nonzero interactions are still sufficient. As an example, consider a model with no four- and three-factor interactions. The marginals to be fitted are then the two factor marginals $x_{ij..}$, $x_{i.k.}$, $x_{i..r}$, $x_{.jk.}$, $x_{.j.r}$ and $x_{..kr}$. The one factor marginals $x_{i...}$ and so on do not have to be fitted as they can be derived from the two factor marginals.

5. Submodels

A model differing from the saturated model, which will be called a submodel, corresponds to the hypothesis that all interactions not appearing in the submodel are zero. The alternative is often taken to be the saturated model. But a hypothesis may also be considered of certain interactions being zero against the alternative that only some of these are zero. This latter case corresponds to comparing one submodel with another submodel. In the example above, the submodel

$$\log(np_{ijkr}) = \theta_0 + \theta_i^{(1)} + \cdots + \theta_r^{(4)}$$
$$+ \theta_{ij}^{(12)} + \cdots + \theta_{kr}^{(34)} \qquad (12)$$

or the hypothesis

$$\theta_{ijk}^{(123)} = \cdots = \theta_{jkr}^{(234)} = \theta_{ijkr}^{(1234)} = 0 \qquad (13)$$

for all i, j, k, and r can be tested against the saturated model, or the submodel/hypothesis can be tested against the submodel where only the four-factor interaction $\theta_{ijkr}^{(1234)}$ is zero for all i, j, k and r.

The correspondence between interaction parameters and marginals to be fitted is an equivalence relationship, such that a third important result for log-linear models can be formulated.

Each submodel is uniquely described by the *marginals to be fitted*, or *sufficient marginals*.

A convenient notational system which has gained general recognition is to describe a submodel in symbolic form by its sufficient marginals. A marginal is symbolized by those of its indices which are not summed out, that is $x_{i...}$ is written as (1), $x_{.j..}$ as (2), $x_{ij..}$ as (12), $x_{.j.r}$ as (24), $x_{ijk.}$ as (123), and so on. In Table 3, all possible submodels for a three-way table are written in this symbolic form.

6. Applications of Log-linear Models

As regards applications of log-linear models the results from the above examples mean that the various steps of a statistical analysis can be described by listing the sufficient marginals for the submodels under consideration. The solution of the likelihood equations can be considered a technical matter and is conveniently handled today by a number of reliable computer programs. Both the SAS-library and the BMDP-library have such facilities, and maximum likelihood estimates can also be obtained by using the GLIM-library.

An important issue is to determine which submodels are of interest. This was first discussed by Goodman (1978). The theory was further developed by Haberman (1974) and Andersen (1974). The main results are that

Table 3
Hierarchical models for a three-way table

Model	Sufficient marginals	Interpretations
(a) $\theta^{(123)} = 0$	(12), (13), (23)	*
(b) $\theta^{(123)} = \theta^{(12)} = 0$	(13), (23)	$A \otimes B\vert C$
(c) $\theta^{(123)} = \theta^{(12)} = \theta^{(13)} = 0$	(23), (1)	$A \otimes B, A \otimes C$
(d) $\theta^{(123)} = \theta^{(12)} = \theta^{(13)} = \theta^{(1)} = 0$	(23)	$A \otimes B, A \otimes C, A = c$
(e) $\theta^{(123)} = \theta^{(12)} = \theta^{(13)} = \theta^{(23)} = 0$	(1), (2), (3)	$A \otimes B \otimes C$
(f) $\theta^{(123)} = \theta^{(12)} = \theta^{(13)} = \theta^{(23)}$ $= \theta^{(1)} = 0$	(2), (3)	$A \otimes B \otimes C, A = c$
(g) $\theta^{(123)} = \theta^{(12)} = \theta^{(13)} = \theta^{(23)}$ $= \theta^{(1)} = \theta^{(2)} = 0$	(3)	$A \otimes B \otimes C, A = c,$ $B = c,$
(h) $\theta^{(123)} = \theta^{(12)} = \theta^{(13)} = \theta^{(23)}$ $= \theta^{(1)} = \theta^{(2)} = \theta^{(3)} = 0$	(0)	$A \otimes B \otimes C, A = c,$ $B = c, C = c$

some submodels called decomposable models allow for an interpretation in the form of independence, conditional independence, or equiprobability and also allow for explicit solutions of the likelihood equations. For all other models these properties do not hold. Criteria for determining when a model is decomposable are given in Andersen (1974).

Another type of submodel is the hierarchical model. A model is hierarchical if for any interaction which is included in the model, all interactions of a lower order containing combinations of the indices of such an interaction are also included. If, for example, $\theta_{ijk}^{(123)}$ appears in the model then $\theta_{ij}^{(12)}$, $\theta_{ik}^{(13)}$, $\theta_{jk}^{(23)}$, $\theta_{i}^{(1)}$, $\theta_{j}^{(2)}$, and $\theta_{k}^{(3)}$ must also be included. Note that these lower dimension interactions correspond to marginals which can be derived from the marginals $x_{ijk.}$ to be fitted in a submodel with $\theta_{ijk}^{(123)}$ included.

As an illustration of these various concepts, a three-way table can be considered.

In Table 3, the possible hierarchical submodels and their interpretations have been listed with an asterisk denoting a nondecomposable model. The symbolic notations introduced above have been used. The three variables are denoted by A, B, and C and the following notations apply: $A \otimes B$ for A and B being independent; $A \otimes B\vert C$ for A and B being independent given the level of C, and $A = c$ for equiprobability on the levels of variable A.

Submodels obtained from another submodel by exchange of variables are not listed. The indices of the θ's have been omitted in order to facilitate the reading of the table.

The term hierarchical models indicates that a natural procedure is to try to fit the data by a succession of submodels until the most simple model is obtained that gives a satisfactory fit.

In the listing of Table 3 the models form such a natural order except for model (d). It can be seen that the partial hypothesis here is $\theta_{i}^{(1)} = 0$, which is also the partial hypothesis of model (f). It is obvious that there exists this possibility of two strategies, since equiprobability of A can be tested with or without a nonzero interaction between B and C.

Since a submodel and its sufficient marginals are equivalent a model will only be indicated by its sufficient marginals in the following. Most computer programs also use this property. In the BMDP-library, for example, submodel (b) in Table 3 is demanded for execution by the order "MODEL IS AB, BC".

7. Hypothesis Testing

Which model fits the data is determined by a traditional χ^2-test. A Pearson χ^2-test can be used with test quantity:

$$q = \sum_{i=1}^{I} \sum_{j=1}^{J} \sum_{k=1}^{K} (x_{ijk} - n\hat{p}_{ijk})^2/(n\hat{p}_{ijk}) \tag{14}$$

where $n\hat{p}_{ijk}$ are the expected numbers under the given model, or one can use the log-likelihood test quantity

$$z = 2 \sum_{i=1}^{I} \sum_{j=1}^{J} \sum_{k=1}^{K} x_{ijk}[\log x_{ijk} - \log(n\hat{p}_{ijk})] \tag{15}$$

Both quantities are approximately χ^2-distributed with a number of degrees of freedom equal to the number of interactions set equal to zero under the hypothesis. A submodel is thus accepted if the corresponding q-value or z-value is larger than, for example, the 95 percentile in a χ^2-distribution with the given number of degrees of freedom.

If a hierarchical or nested procedure is applied, where one submodel is tested against another, the z-tests for the two submodels are subtracted to give a test quantity which is again χ^2-distributed with a number of degrees of freedom, which is the difference between the number of degrees of freedom for the two involved z-quantities. Thus if submodel M_2, is tested against sub-model M_1, where M_2 has more interactions equal to zero than M_1, and if the z-tests for M_1 and M_2 are z_1 and z_2, respectively, with f_1 and f_2 degrees of freedom, M_1 is tested against M_2 by

$$z_{12} = z_2 - z_1 \tag{16}$$

with $f_2 - f_1$ degrees of freedom.

A hierarchical test procedure is now illustrated with reference to the data in Table 1.

Table 4
Darroch–Lauritzen–Speed graph for the possible submodels of a three-way table

	Graph	Models	Interpretation
(a)		(i) (123)	
		(ii) (12) (13) (23)	*
(b)		(13) (23)	$A \otimes B \vert C$
(c)		(23)	$A \otimes B, A \otimes C$
(d)		(i) (1) (2) (3)	$A \otimes B \otimes C$
		(ii) (1) (2)	
		(iii) (1)	

As the interest here lies with the distribution of the nonresponse, interactions between G and S will be ignored here. An attempt will be made, therefore, to try to fit the models M_1:(12), (23) (which means that response and sex are independent given geographical region) and M_1^*:(13), (23) (which means that response and geographical region are independent given sex). In the former case regional differences explain the variation in nonresponse, while in the latter case there are no regional differences between regions for men and women separately. The two models give for M_1: $z_1 = 8.9$, and $f_1 = 3$; and for M_1^*: $z_1^* = 36.7$, and $f_1^* = 4$. It is thus obvious that regional differences exist but no sex effect exists in the nonresponse pattern.

Alternatively, a hierarchical procedure could have been used by first testing the submodel M_1:(12), (23) and then the submodel M_2:(1), (23) against M_1.

The z-quantity for M_2 is $z_2 = 37.8$, and $f_2 = 5$. Hence the test for M_2 against M_1 should be based on $z_2 - z_1$, $= 28.9$, and $f_{12} = 2$. This again produces a clear rejection.

Actually the model can be further reduced since there is no interaction between region and sex (as should be expected). For testing M_3:(12), (3) against M_1, one gets $z_3 = 10.0$ with $f_3 = 5$ and hence (for M_3 against M_1), $z_{13} = 1.1$ with $f_{13} = 2$. But this latter test is not meaningful in the context and should not be reported. This means that (12), (23) is as good a model as (12), (3) for illustrating the nonresponse pattern.

A graphical technique has been introduced by Darroch et al. (1980), to illustrate the interpretation of a given log-linear submodel. In a diagram all variables are represented by a point and points are connected in the graph if the corresponding variables are related through a nonzero interaction. For a three-way table all possible DLS graphs, the corresponding submodels, and their interpretation are shown in Table 4.

It should be noted that several models can have the same DLS graph and equiprobabilities are not indicated in a DLS graph. More importantly, the models (123) and (12), (13), (23) have no interpretations in terms of independence or conditional independence. For the saturated model (123) this is obviously the case, but for the model (12), (13), (23), where $\theta_{ijk}^{(123)} = 0$, note must be taken of the lack of an interpretation. In fact submodel (12), (13), (23) is a nondecomposable model and the only one in a three-way table.

The interpretation of a given model is easy to establish from a DLS diagram. Two variables are independent if one variable cannot be reached from another variable by a system of connecting lines. Two variables are conditionally independent given a set of variables if one of the variables can only be reached from the other variable by passing through one or more of the conditioning variables. In Table 4, model (b), A cannot be reached from B without passing C. In model (c), A can be reached from neither B nor C.

As a final illustration the data on cancer survival in Table 2 is considered. Here the variable of interest is the survival (S). Interactions between variables O, X and C only tell something about the connections between the observed stage of the cancer and what treatment has been applied, and such interactions are of no particular interest when an attempt is made to predict the chance of survival. A natural first model to fit would, therefore,

Table 5
Test quantities for a sequence of natural submodels for the cancer survival data shown in Table 2

Model	z	f
M_1:(12), (13), (14), (234)	1.9	4
M_2:(13), (14), (234)	2.0	5
M_3:(14), (234)	4.1	6
M_4:(234), (1)	136.7	7

Figure 1
DLS graph for data from Tables 2 and 5

be (12), (13), (14), (234). It would be possible to have started with less simple models like (123), (124), (134), (234), but it is often a good idea to start with a relatively simple model and hope to have it accepted. If it does not fit the data, it is always possible to go back.

Table 5 lists the z-quantities and the corresponding degrees of freedom for the model (12), (13), (14), (234) and subsequent models, where first the interactions between survival and x-ray treatment, then the interactions between survival and kind of operation, and finally the interactions with stage of cancer are removed. There are medical reasons for choosing this order of removal.

Based on the test quantities in Table 5, the submodel M_1 is accepted as the starting point. A test of M_2 against M_1 is then a test for no interaction between S and X, or $\theta_{ij}^{(12)} = 0$. This is clearly accepted with $z = 2.0 - 1.9 = 0.1$ on one degree of freedom.

A test for M_3 against the now accepted M_2 gives a z-value of $4.1 - 2.0 = 2.1$ on one degree of freedom and it can also be accepted that there is no interaction between S and O. But when M_4 is looked at, a very clear rejection is obtained. This means that the data can be described by the model M_3: (14), (234). On a DLS graph, the condition shown in Fig. 1 is obtained, with the interpretation $S \otimes O | C$, $S \otimes X | C$.

Hence when the stage of the cancer is given, neither x-ray treatment nor the kind of operation seems to influence the chance of survival beyond 10 years.

When an appropriate submodel has been chosen and a good fit to the data is established, the parameters of the model should be reported, preferably in their standardized form, that is, divided by their standard errors. For the data of Table 2, some of these parameters are shown in Table 6 for the model (14), (234).

The three-factor interactions between O, X, and C describe which treatment is chosen at different stages of the cancer. The two-factor interactions show that the

Table 6
Standardized interaction estimates for model M_3 of Table 5

$\theta_{jkr}^{(234)}$	X	O	C	
			Early	Advanced
	No	Radical	−2.2	+2.2
		Limited	+2.2	−2.2
	Yes	Radical	+2.2	−2.2
		Limited	−2.2	+2.2

$\theta_{ir}^{(14)}$	S	C	
		Early	Advanced
	No	−10.0	+10.0
	Yes	+10.0	−10.0

survival chance is much less with the cancer at an advanced stage.

8. Other Models

The literature on log-linear models deals with aspects of the general model other than those covered above. The problem of incomplete tables is treated in both Haberman (1974) and Andersen (1974) as well as in most textbooks (for example, Haberman 1978, 1979, Bishop et al. 1975).

Special models have been developed for squared tables such as the model for symmetry, where for an $I \times I$ table $p_{ij} = p_{ji}$, and quasisymmetry or interaction symmetry, where $\theta_{ij}^{(12)} = \theta_{ji}^{(12)}$.

This latter model differs from the full symmetry model in that it is also assumed that $\theta_i^{(1)} = \theta_i^{(2)}$ for the full symmetry model. For squared tables which thin out towards the corners, a log-linear model of the form

$$\log p_{ij} = \begin{cases} \theta_i^{(1)} + \theta_j^{(2)} + \delta |i - j|, & i = j \\ \theta_i^{(1)} + \theta_j^{(2)} + \epsilon_i, & i = j \end{cases} \quad (17)$$

was suggested by Haberman (1974) in connection with British and Danish social mobility data. All these models are also treated in Haberman (1978, 1979) and Bishop et al. (1975).

Among the many textbooks now available with a treatment of the log-linear model, the reader is also referred to Plackett (1981), Everitt (1977), Andersen (1980), and Fienberg (1977).

See also: Contingency Tables; Configural Frequency Analysis

Bibliography

Andersen A H 1974 Multidimensional contingency tables. *Scand. J. Statist.* 1: 115–27
Andersen E B 1980 *Discrete Statistical Models with Social Science Applications.* North Holland Publishing, Amsterdam
Birch M W 1963 Maximum likelihood in three-way contingency tables. *J.R. Statist. Soc. B.* 25: 220–33
Bishop Y M M, Fienberg S E, Holland P W 1975 *Discrete Multivariate Analysis: Theory and Practice.* MIT Press, Cambridge, Massachusetts
Darroch J N, Lauritzen S L, Speed T P 1980 Markov fields and log-linear interaction models for contingency tables. *Annu. Statist.* 8: 522–39
Everitt B S 1977 *The Analysis of Contingency Tables.* Chapman and Hall, London
Fienberg S E 1977 *The Analysis of Cross-classified Categorical Data.* MIT Press, Cambridge, Massachusetts
Goodman L A 1978 *Analyzing Qualitative/Categorical Data: Log-linear Models and Latent-structure Analysis.* Addison Wesley, London
Haberman S J 1974 *The Analysis of Frequency Data.* University of Chicago Press, Chicago, Illinois
Haberman S J 1978 *Analysis of Qualitative Data,* Vol. 1. Academic Press, New York
Haberman S J 1979 *Analysis of Qualitative Data,* Vol 2. Academic Press, New York
Plackett R L 1981 *The Analysis of Categorical Data,* 2nd edn. Griffin, London

Meta-analysis

B. McGaw

For many questions in education there is a large body of empirical research findings from which answers might be sought. Single studies can seldom provide a definitive answer so it is essential to integrate all the studies to determine whether they support any overall conclusions. Such integration has typically been undertaken intuitively but, if the studies vary substantially, the task becomes overwhelming and almost inevitably produces a conclusion that the studies' findings are equivocal. There are, however, strategies for making the integration of the findings of empirical research itself an empirical task rather than an intuitive one. It thus becomes an "analysis of analyses" or "meta-analysis" in the term coined by Glass (1976). The findings of the separate studies becomes the data for a synthesizing meta-analysis.

1. Approaches to Research Integration

1.1 Narrative Integration

The traditional process of integrating a body of research literature is essentially intuitive and the style of reporting narrative. Because the reviewer's methods are often unspecified, it is usually difficult to discern just how the original research findings have contributed to the integration. A careful analysis can sometimes reveal that different reviewers use the same research reports in support of contrary conclusions (see Miller, cited in Glass et al. 1981 pp. 18–19). Inconsistencies less gross than these are difficult to detect, because the reviewer's strategies are not explicit, but they may still bias the reviewer's conclusions.

The most serious problem for reviewers to cope with is the volume of relevant research literature to be integrated. Most reviewers appear to deal with this by choosing only a subset of the studies. Some take the studies they know most intimately. Others take those they value most highly, usually on the basis of methodological quality. Few, however, give any indication of the means by which they selected studies for review (Jackson 1980).

1.2 Frequency Counts of Significant Findings

Some reviewers count the relative frequencies with which reported results fall into three categories: statistically significant in one direction, not significant, and significant in the other direction. One serious weakness of this strategy is that the level of significance of a study depends not only on the magnitude of the observed effect but also on the sample size. Trivial findings from large studies will be counted as revealing an effect simply because they achieve statistical significance. More substantial findings from small studies will be treated as showing no effect simply because they fail to achieve statistical significance.

A further problem arises in the interpretation of the frequency counts. A common strategy is to conclude that there is a consistent significant finding in the literature if more than one-third of the findings reveal a significant effect in one direction. Hedges and Olkin (1980) have developed a precise formulation of the probability of significant results occurring in individual studies comparing experimental and control groups. Where the difference between the population means for the experimental and control conditions is 0.30 standard deviations, for example, the probability of means from samples of 20 persons per condition being significantly different at the 0.05 level is only 0.238. The more studies there are to be integrated, the more likely it is that the proportion reporting a significant difference will be close to 0.238 and below the criterion of 0.33. With study sample sizes of 20, the probability of significant results in studies is less than 0.33 for population mean differences as large as 0.50 standard deviations. With sample sizes of 50, it is less than 0.33 for population mean differences as large as 0.36. Simply counting the relative frequency of significant findings across studies and comparing it with some arbitrary criterion such as 0.33 is, therefore, a misleading way to integrate findings.

1.3 Aggregated Indices of the Strength of Findings

An alternative to frequency counts of significant findings is an aggregation of the probability values associated with reported significance tests (Rosenthal 1978). The aggregation produces an estimate of the probability of the observed pattern of individual study results occurring when there is no underlying population effect. The reviewer can use this probability to decide whether to reject the null hypothesis common to the studies but it provides no indication of the magnitude of the effect. It also allows no investigation of the relationship between study characteristics and study findings.

An alternative is to use some index of the size of effect revealed in each study and to aggregate its values across studies. Glass (1976), for the integration of studies making experimental comparisons, suggested as an "effect size" for study i the standardized difference between experimental and control group means

$$d_i = (\bar{Y}_i^E - \bar{Y}_i^C)/s_i \qquad (1)$$

where $\bar{Y}_i^E$ and $\bar{Y}_i^C$ are the sample means and s_i the within-group standard deviation. For studies of the relationship between variables, Glass (1976) suggested the correlation coefficient as the index for aggregation. Schmidt and Hunter (1977) independently proposed the aggregation of correlation coefficients. In other sets of studies, alternative common indices, such as proportion of individuals improved due to treatment, may be available.

1.4 Meta-analysis

The term meta-analysis is used to describe any quantitative integration of empirical research studies. It involves both the aggregation of effect size estimates across studies and the analysis of their covariation with features of the studies. The techniques developed by Glass and his associates are fully described in Glass et al. (1981). Those of Schmidt and Hunter, generalized from their work on correlations to include standardized mean differences, are described in Hunter et al. (1982).

With the separate study findings quantified and the study characteristics classified, the meta-analyst does not have to hold the complex pattern of study variations in memory for integration as the narrative reviewer does. The pattern is captured and preserved in an explicit fashion, open to both checks and challenges. The task of integration is one of data analysis with no limit to the number of studies which might be included.

2. Scope of the Literature for Integration

2.1 Location of Studies

For any literature review, location of relevant research studies is an important task. Strategies for finding studies are discussed by Glass et al. (1981 Chap. 3) and Hunter et al. (1982 Chap. 7). Details of the search should be reported to allow others to judge the comprehensiveness of literature included and subsequent reviewers to see most readily where the review might be extended. Jackson's (1980) analysis of 36 published reviews revealed that the reviewers paid little attention to the work of prior reviewers. It may well have been that these prior narrative reviewers gave too little information about their procedures for their experiences to illuminate the path for their successors.

One criticism of meta-analysis is that the capacity to cope with large bodies of literature causes the net to be cast too broadly and encourages the attempted integration of studies which are insufficiently similar. Blind aggregation of studies is certainly not justified in any review but it is appropriate to count "apples" and "oranges" together as long as the concern is with "fruit". In any case, differences among the studies need not be ignored. They can be coded and their relationship with study findings systematically examined in the meta-analysis.

2.2 Considerations of Methodological Quality

An important consequence of the meta-analyst's capacity to cope with large volumes of literature is that there is no need for arbitrary exclusion of studies to make the task manageable. Some critics claim that the result is the arbitrary inclusion of studies which ought, on the grounds of methodological deficiencies, to be discarded. Smith and Glass's (1977) meta-analysis of experimental studies of the efficacy of psychotherapy was criticized because the conclusions were based on an integration of all available studies and not just the methodologically

strongest ones. Smith and Glass had actually first established that methodological quality made no difference to study findings before ignoring it in their aggregation. Landman and Dawes (1982), using only methodologically sound studies from the total set used by Smith and Glass, subsequently confirmed the correctness of the Smith and Glass estimates of effect size from all studies. In a body of literature, such as that dealing with the effects of class size on learning, where the methodological quality of the studies was shown to make a difference to study findings, the meta-analysis results were based on the sound studies only (Glass and Smith 1978).

By treating the influence of methodological quality as something to be examined empirically rather than as something to be ruled on a priori, meta-analysts may actually be avoiding a further problem. Narrative reviewers may have a tendency not just to ignore a study judged to be methodologically flawed but to treat it as evidence against the research hypothesis its results apparently support.

2.3 Potential Biases in Published Literature

An important consideration for any reviewer is whether the accessible literature is itself biased. If statistically significant findings are more likely to be published, published studies will be biased against the null hypothesis. The most extreme view is that the published studies are the 5 percent of studies reflecting Type 1 errors. Rosenthal's (1978) method for combining probabilities can be used to estimate how many unpublished nonsignificant studies there would need to be to offset a group of published significant ones. For a set of 311 published studies with an average standardized mean difference of 1.18, Rosenthal (1979) showed that 50,000 unpublished studies with an average standardized mean difference of zero would need to exist to nullify the published ones.

Such calculations can dispel much of the doubt about the credibility of published results but cannot dispel all fears of some bias in the published literature. Completed meta-analyses have tended to find stronger effects in studies published in journals than in studies reported in theses and dissertations (Glass et al. 1981 pp. 64–68). One cannot hope, therefore, to summarize adequately what research says on a particular topic by examining only journal articles.

3. Quantification of Study Findings

3.1 Standardized Mean Differences

The definition of effect size as a standardized mean difference between treatment and control groups, proposed by Glass (1976), is given in Eqn. (1). Glass proposed standardization with the control group standard deviation. Since this standard deviation frequently is not reported, the pooled within-group standard deviation is an alternative. This pooled estimate is actually to be preferred since it has less sampling error and since its use is justified by the assumption of homogeneity of variance required for the original experimental comparison.

The effect size defined by Eqn. (1) is implicitly an estimate of a population effect size, defined in terms of population parameters, for study i, as

$$\delta_i = (\mu_i^E - \mu_i^C)/\sigma_i \tag{2}$$

where μ_i^E and μ_i^C are the population means for the treatment and control conditions and σ_i the common variance within the two populations. Hedges (1981) showed that d_i of Eqn. (1) is a biased estimator of δ_i of Eqn. (2) but that an unbiased estimator d_i^U can be obtained from it as

$$d_i^U = d_i c(m) \tag{3}$$

where $m = (n_i^E + n_i^C - 2)$ is the degree of freedom for the pooled estimate of σ obtained as s for Eqn. (1), and $c(m) = \Gamma(m/2)/\{(m/2)\Gamma[(m-1)/2]\}$ in which $\Gamma(x)$ is the gamma function. Hedges (1981) provided, as an alternative to Eqn. (3) the approximation

$$d_i^U \simeq d_i[1 - 3/(4m - 1)] \tag{4}$$

Since $m > 1$, it can be seen that the unbiased estimate is always smaller than the biased estimate, that is $d_i^U < d_i$, but the correction makes very little difference in practice. If the sample sizes, n_i^E and n_i^C, are both 20, the unbiased estimate d_i^U will be 0.98 of the biased estimate d_i.

In many research reports the sample means and standard deviations required for direct calculations of d_i are not provided. In some cases, d_i can be obtained directly from reported information such as t or F test values. In others, it can be approximated from information such as proportions of subjects improving under treatment and control conditions. Details of these types of transformations to retrieve effect sizes are given in Glass et al. (1981 pp. 126–47).

There are some variations among studies, however, which cause the effect size estimates immediately retrievable from them not to be directly comparable. Some perfectly satisfactory statistical analyses produce arbitrary changes in the metric on which effect sizes are expressed. Covariance adjustments, for example, increase the power of the statistical test but, from the point of view of effect size estimation, arbitrarily decrease the estimate s and thus arbitrarily increase the estimates d and d^U. The use of change scores, either raw or residual, has the same consequences. Similar lack of comparability occurs with studies which provide, not a simple comparison of experimental and control conditions, but a factorial analysis of variance in which the treatment factor is crossed with other factors. The within-treatments variance is reduced by the removal of main and interaction effects variance attributable to the other factors. As a consequence, the effect size estimate for the experimental treatment is arbitrarily increased. Strategies for adjusting the initial effect size estimates derived from such studies are given by McGaw and Glass (1980) and by Glass et al. (1981 pp. 114–26).

A further respect in which studies may differ arbitrarily is in the selectivity of the sample investigated. A restriction of range on some selection variable will reduce the variance of criterion scores and lead to an increased estimate of effect size. In the literature on the educational effects of ability grouping, for example, some studies use only gifted children in the homogeneous grouping condition and, from the heterogeneous condition, report data only for the gifted subgroup. If the proportion of the population represented in the sample were the top p, selected on the basis of some variable X, the ratio of the estimated standard deviation for the full population, s_x, on this measure to that for the restricted population, s_x^p, would be

$$u = s_x / s_x^p$$
$$= 1/[1 + \mu_x^p(c^p - \mu_x^p)]^{1/2} \tag{5}$$

where c^p is the standard score above which the proportion of a normal distribution is p and μ_x^p is the mean standard score for the segment of the population in the top p, given by

$$\mu_x^p = \phi(c)/p$$
$$= \{[\exp(-c^2/2)]/[(2\pi)^{1/2}]\}/p \tag{6}$$

where $\phi(c)$ is the ordinate of the unit normal distribution at the point of the cut. The ratio of the estimated standard deviations on the criterion measure Y, for the full and restricted populations, will be

$$s_y / s_y^p = [(u^2 - 1)(r_{xy}^p)^2 + 1]^{1/2} \tag{7}$$

where r_{xy}^p is the correlation between the selection and criterion variables in the restricted sample. An effect size calculated with s_y^p will be arbitrarily enhanced; s_y should be used as McGaw and Glass (1980) suggest.

The arbitrary differences among studies discussed so far all lead to overestimates of effect sizes because of underestimates of the within-groups standard deviation. Hedges (1981) and Hunter et al. (1982) suggest that the initial effect size estimate, d^U, be corrected for an underestimate due to unreliability of the criterion measure. This unreliability produces an over-estimate of the standard deviation. The correction is

$$d^{UR} = d^U / (r_{yy})^{1/2} \tag{8}$$

where r_{yy} is the criterion reliability. Since $r_{yy} < 1$, then $d^{UR} > d^U$.

The correction in Eqn. (8) expresses the effect size in terms of the estimated standard deviation of true scores instead of that for observed scores. When the observed score values are used, arbitrary differences among studies in the reliabilities of measures cause arbitrary differences in the studies' effect sizes. The sense in which reliability is defined and the way in which it is estimated, however, are crucial to the meaning of corrections of this sort. Information about test reliabilities is needed but similar information is needed for all studies. Different reliability coefficients, such as test–retest and inter-consistency, are based on different conceptions of error. Consistent correction of effect size estimates requires a common form of the coefficient.

In an attempt to minimize some of the influence of arbitrary scale variations on effect size estimates, Kraemer and Andrews (1982) proposed a nonparametric effect size estimate. Their procedure requires pretest and posttest scores for individuals in experimental and control conditions or, in some circumstances, for those in the experimental condition alone. They determine the median pretest score for all subjects in a condition, the median posttest score for the subgroup of persons within the range of two distinct scores either side of the pretest median, and then the proportion of all pretest scores $P(D)$ which were exceeded by the subgroup's posttest median. For a study with only an experimental group, the effect size is obtained by reexpressing this proportion as a z-score. This standardizes the difference between the pretest and posttest medians as

$$D_E = \Phi^{-1}[P(D_E)] \qquad (9)$$

where Φ is the standard normal cumulative density function. For a study with pretest and posttest scores on both experimental and control groups, separate estimates are derived for both groups and the effect size estimated as

$$D = D_E - D_C \qquad (10)$$

Although the development of a robust nonparametric effect size estimate may prove valuable, the version offered by Kraemer and Andrews is of limited use. In addition to requiring complete individual data for each study, it is likely to give very imprecise estimates of D with extreme proportions $P(D)$. Kraemer and Andrews (1982) give an example with $P(D) = 19/20$ and $D = 1.64$. A shift to $P(D) = 18/20$ reduces D to 1.28 and a shift to $P(D) = 17/20$ reduces D to 1.14. More needs to be known about the standard error of the estimates of D before any serious use of this index can be encouraged.

3.2 Correlations

If a meta-analyst's concern is with a body of literature in which the relationship between a pair of variables is investigated, then the index to be aggregated over studies is the correlation coefficient. Alternatives such as covariances or regression coefficients can be used only if the same tests are used in all studies. The aggregation should be undertaken directly with the correlation coefficient r and not with the Fisher transformed Z. Hunter et al. (1982 p. 42) point out that Fisher's nonlinear transformation gives greater weight to large correlations, appropriately if one is concerned as Fisher was with establishing confidence intervals around individual r's, but inappropriately if one is concerned with estimating the mean of a number of r's.

Analyses of the relationships between two variables may not always be reported in terms of correlation coefficients. Procedures for converting from the results of various parametric and nonparametric significance tests to correlation coefficients are summarized by Glass et al. (1981 pp. 149–50).

Hunter et al. (1982), who developed their meta-analytic procedures in cumulations of studies of test validities, suggest that all meta-analyses can be undertaken in terms of correlations. Experimental comparisons of treatment and control conditions on some criterion measure can be expressed as a point biserial correlation between categorized group membership and the criterion measure. For the case with equal experimental and control sample sizes, $n^E = n^C = N/2$, the relationship between the point biserial correlation coefficient r_{pbis} and the standardized mean difference d is

$$r_{pbis} = d/[d^2 + 4(N-2)/N] \qquad (11)$$

In their cumulations of studies reporting validity coefficients, Schmidt and Hunter (1977) correct the reported correlations for any attenuation due to study artifacts such as unreliability of the variables and restriction in the sample due to selection on one of the variables. Variations in test reliabilities and in the degree of sample selectivity produce arbitrary differences in the reported correlations. Removing these effects is intended to ensure that, however a study is undertaken and reported, its findings will be an estimate of the correlation between true scores on the variables in the whole population.

Where there is a restriction in range, due to the selection of only the top proportion p on the selection variable X, the observed correlation for the restricted sample, r^p_{xy}, can be disattenuated by

$$r_{xy} = u r^p_{xy}/[(u^2 - 1)(r^p_{xy})^2 + 1]^{1/2} \qquad (12)$$

where u is as defined in Eqn. (5).

The correction for unreliability of the variables, using the notions of classical test theory, produces an estimate of the true score correlation, $\rho(T_x, T_y)$, from the observed correlation r_{xy}, as

$$\hat{\rho}(T_x, T_y) = r_{xy}/(r_{xx}r_{yy})^{1/2} \qquad (13)$$

where r_{xx} and r_{yy} are the reliabilities of the two variables. If the sample is restricted by selection on the basis of observed scores on one of the variables, Hunter et al. (1982 pp. 88–91) suggest the reliability correction be made only for the other variable. The correction of an observed correlation for unreliability, defined by Eqn. (13), parallels that for correction to a standardized mean difference defined by Eqn. (8). The concern expressed, in connection with that correction, about the need to use comparable definitions of reliability for all studies is also relevant here.

In a study where both corrections are to be applied, the correction for restriction in range, Eqn. (12), is applied before the correction for unreliability, Eqn. (13), unless the reliability estimates are for the restricted subpopulation rather than for the full population.

In practice, many studies do not report data on test reliability or the extent of sample restriction. Adjustments to each finding could be made only if some estimates were used in the absence of information. Hunter et al. (1982 pp. 73–92) describe an alternative. They use the distributions of reliabilities and range restriction in studies where they are reported to correct estimates of the mean and variance of the correlations obtained from the full set of studies.

3.3 Other Effect Sizes

In some sets of studies other effect size measures than standardized mean differences and correlations can be used. Studies of the treatment of alcoholism, for example, may all express their results as the difference between proportions of individuals in treatment and control conditions reaching some criterion level of improvement. With these studies, this difference could be used as the effect size measure without transformation. In other sets of studies some measure such as IQ may provide a common index for use as an effect size without transformation.

4. Coding Study Characteristics

4.1 Choice of Study Characteristics

The ultimate purpose of meta-analysis, in seeking the integration of a body of literature, is both to determine what average effect size is reported in the studies and to establish whether variability in the effect sizes across studies can be accounted for in terms of covariability with characteristics of the studies. The relevant study characteristics can be either substantive or methodological.

Hunter et al. (1982 p. 140) suggest that, before any coding of study characteristics is even undertaken, the distribution of effect sizes should be examined to determine whether 75 percent of the observed variance can be accounted for by sampling error and the influences of other artifacts. If it can be, then they claim that the labour of coding can be avoided. Procedures for partitioning variance in study findings into real and artifactual components and the wisdom of such a doctrinaire rejection of further analysis of covariation between study characteristics and findings are discussed in Sect. 5.

Characteristics to be coded should be chosen carefully. Coding is time consuming and it is not worth the effort to code trivial study variations though, of course, the value of a characteristic cannot always be anticipated in advance. Another important reason for careful choice of coding categories is that, in the analysis of the covariation between study characteristics and findings, the degrees of freedom are limited. Analyses with many study characteristics run the risk of capitalization on chance variations in the data.

4.2 Substantive Characteristics

Which substantive features of studies are most important to code depends on theoretical considerations. The research literature itself should reveal the characteristics such as form of treatment, type of population sampled, and type of outcome measured which are most likely to produce variability in study findings. A helpful initial source of suggestions can be earlier reviews of the same literature. Application of a preliminary version of a coding schedule to key research studies in the field can also facilitate the development of the final version. Some sample coding schemes, developed for a variety of bodies of literature, are given in Glass et al. (1981 Chap. 4).

Nonreporting can cause problems for the coding. If variations in a particular characteristic appear to be related to systematic differences in findings, the variations in that characteristic over studies can usefully be coded only if it is reported in a reasonable proportion of the studies. A "not known" category can be used, but if too many studies are coded into it the characteristic will be doomed to insignificance in the subsequent analyses.

4.3 Methodological Characteristics

For the coding of methodological characteristics of studies, previous meta-analyses can be helpful. Characteristics such as type of experimental design, including method of assignment of subjects to treatments, dropout rates of subjects during treatment, and reactivity of the outcome measures, are important for assessing studies in most fields. Samples of coding schemes for such characteristics are included in Glass et al. (1981 Chap. 4).

The problem of nonreporting in studies is seldom as great with the methodological as with the substantive characteristics. It is perhaps a sad commentary on the state of the field in such educational and other social research that, in reporting, more attention is given to the methods of research than to the precise conditions of the experiment.

4.4 Validity and Reliability of Coding

Since much of the explanatory power of a meta-analysis depends on the coding of study characteristics, considerations of validity and reliability are important. The validity of the codings depends on the definitions of the coding categories and on the objectivity with which they can be used in practice. The definitions can be included in the report of the meta-analysis to allow other reviewers to judge their validity. Even careful definition of the categories, however, cannot avert the precarious inferences about the precise details of a study which must be made when there is incomplete or imprecise reporting. Decision rules for such inferences which minimize interjudge disagreement cannot guarantee valid codings.

Lack of agreement among coders and inconsistency of individual coders are the sole sources of unreliability since the objects to be coded are themselves stable. Some index of coder consistency should be reported for any meta-analysis. Even if only one coder is used in a modest review, an index can be obtained from repeated codings of the same studies after a suitable time lapse. Where more than one coder is used, unreliability due to inconsistencies between and within coders can be separately estimated and reported.

5. Cumulation of Findings

5.1 Averaging Effect Sizes

The first question is whether a nonparametric estimate such as the median or a parametric estimate such as the mean should be used. More powerful statistical analyses can be used in conjunction with parametric estimates, and that is a reason for preferring them, but initial exploratory analyses can give useful information about the distribution of the set of effect sizes and the appropriateness of proceeding with parametric analyses.

Many meta-analyses have used a simple mean of the obtained effect sizes as the summary statistic but this takes no account of the variation in precision of the estimates obtained from different studies. A weighted mean of the estimates derived from k studies could be obtained as

$$\bar{d} = \sum_{i=1}^{k} w_i d_i^U \bigg/ \sum_{i=1}^{k} w_i \qquad (14)$$

Hunter et al. (1982) suggest the use of the sample sizes as the weights, $w_i = N_i$. Hedges (1981, 1982) and Rosenthal and Rubin (1982) suggest the use of the weights which minimize the variance of $\bar{d}$, that is

$$w_i = (1/v_i) \bigg/ \left(\sum_{j=1}^{k} v_j \right) \qquad (15)$$

where v_i is the variance of the estimate d_i^U and can be estimated by

$$v_i = (n_i^E + n_i^C)/(n_i^E n_i^C) + (d_i^U)/2(n_i^E + n_i^C) \qquad (16)$$

Hedges (1982) points out that, though the d_i^U are unbiased estimators of δ, the weighted mean defined by Eqns. (14) and (15) is not. It provides a consistent but small underestimate of δ but can be improved by a recalculation using weights obtained from Eqn. (16) with the first weighted mean $\bar{d}$ replacing the d_i^U to give a more nearly unbiased estimate $\bar{d}^U$ from Eqn. (14). The adjustment makes little difference. Indeed, use of the N_i as the weights is as good in practice as those defined by Eqn. (15).

Where direct effect size estimates are not available for all studies, an overall mean effect size (as a standardized mean difference) can be estimated using only information about the relative frequency of significant findings in the studies (Hedges and Olkin 1980). The method requires the assumption that the sample sizes are the same in all studies and equal for control and experimental conditions. Where they are not the same for all studies, Hedges and Olkin recommend the use of their geometric mean or their square mean root. Although these procedures are not strictly applicable to studies using correlations but reporting only significance levels, because correlation coefficients are not distributed normally, they provide a reasonable approximation. The

reporting of significance without the accompanying value of the statistic, however, is less likely with correlation coefficients than standardized mean differences.

5.2 Estimating Variation in Effect Sizes

Again the first question is whether to use parametric or nonparametric procedures for examining the variation in estimates of effect size from a body of literature. Nonparametric indices such as the interquartile range are less sensitive to skewing of the distribution. Associated exploratory analyses can expose the shape of the distribution and the presence of outliers which might better be excluded as the likely products of error in the original research reports. The more typical procedure in meta-analysis, however, has been to use parametric procedures and to calculate the variance of the effect size estimates and then, in many cases, to establish a confidence interval around their mean.

Some research studies report more than one finding and so can yield more than one effect size. Within the total set of effect sizes obtained from a body of literature, however, subsets obtained from the same studies do not satisfy the usual assumptions of statistical independence of data for statistical analyses. The problem also extends across research reports where a common sample yields the data for more than one report. Even without common subjects or data, there can be a degree of nonindependence among studies conceived under a common influence and using perhaps similar designs and measures.

The most conservative approach with studies reporting more than one effect size is to use only an average from each study and thus to treat "study" as the unit of observation for the meta-analysis. The most liberal approach is to use all effect sizes as though they were independent. Smith and Glass (1977) took the liberal approach in their meta-analysis of the psychotherapy outcome literature but examined the consequences of both methods of analysis in their meta-analysis of the literature examining the effects of class size (Glass and Smith 1978). In this latter case, they found little difference. Landman and Dawes' (1982) replication of the meta-analysis of the psychotherapy studies showed, for that body of literature also, that essentially the same results were achieved by both methods.

If effect sizes are averaged within studies before aggregation, any differences among them in their substantive or methodological characteristics will be lost. If some of these characteristics covary significantly with the magnitude of the effect size, that information will be lost in the averaging.

The statistical problems of multiple findings from single studies are essentially the same as those of cluster sampling. The standard error of the mean from a cluster sample is larger than that from a simple random sample of the same size. For the case of a meta-analysis, if k studies each yield j effect sizes with a variance of s_d^2, the variance of the mean, treating the effect sizes as a simple random sample (SRS) of kj, would be estimated as

$$\text{Var}(\bar{d}^{\text{SRS}}) = s_d^2/kj \tag{17}$$

If the effect sizes were treated as a cluster sample (CS), the variance of the mean would be estimated as

$$\text{Var}(\bar{d}^{\text{CS}}) = \text{Var}(\bar{d}^{\text{SRS}})[1 + (j-1)r] \tag{18}$$

where r is the within-cluster correlation. Treating the effect sizes as a simple random sample would put too narrow a confidence interval around the mean. Glass et al. (1981 p. 203) present evidence from six meta-analyses that the average intrastudy (i.e., within-cluster) correlation of effect sizes was about $r = 0.6$. With two effect sizes per study, treating the effect sizes more correctly as a cluster sample would give a standard error estimate of $[1 + (2-1)(0.6)]^{1/2} = 1.26$ times that estimated for a simple random sample. With 10 effect sizes per study, the cluster sample estimate of standard error would be 2.53 times as large.

In a particular meta-analysis, where the number of estimates per study is not constant, Eqn. (18) could be used with j taken as the total number of effect sizes divided by the number of studies. For all cases then, it is possible to use the more conservative estimate of the standard error of the mean effect size given by Eqn. (18) to establish a confidence interval around the mean. An alternative is to use a jackknife procedure (Glass et al. 1981 pp. 202–8).

5.3 Testing Homogeneity of Effect Sizes

Hunter et al. (1982) take the view that, if the effect sizes can be considered a homogeneous sample from a single population, only the estimation of an overall mean effect size is justified. Along with Hedges (1982), and Rosenthal and Rubin (1982) they have developed χ^2 tests of the homogeneity of a sample of effect sizes. These tests are very powerful. With a large body of studies, small variations in study findings will lead to statistical significance and rejection of the null hypothesis of homogeneity. As a consequence, Hunter et al. (1982) recommend against the use of their statistic and Hedges (1982) suggests that, if the number of studies is large, the size of the variance in effect sizes be examined directly.

Hunter et al. (1982) propose an alternative to such significance testing as a way of deciding whether the analysis can stop with the estimate of an overall mean. They estimate the variance in effect sizes which could be due to sampling error, range restriction, and unreliability. Only if it is less than 75 percent of the total do they explore the covariation between effect sizes and study characteristics to account for the remaining variance.

For a meta-analysis of studies reporting correlations, they estimate the sampling error variance as

$$s_e^2 = k(1 - \bar{r}^2)^2/N \tag{19}$$

where k is the number of studies (assuming one correlation per study) and N is the sum of the sample sizes in all studies. For meta-analyses of studies reporting standardized mean differences, they use the large sample approximation

$$s_e^2 = 4k(1 + \bar{d}^2/8)/N \tag{20}$$

In either case, the true variance of effect sizes is then estimated from the observed variance s_0^2 as

$$s_\tau^2 = s_0^2 - s_e^2 \tag{21}$$

where o represents the d and r of earlier formulas and τ the δ and ρ. If the individual study effect sizes are corrected for restriction of sample range with Eqns. (7) or (12), and for test unreliability with Eqn. (8) or (13), the sampling error variance will be increased. The estimate of the corrected variance (Hunter et al. 1982 pp. 68–71) is

$$s_{e(c)}^2 = \overline{\alpha^2} s_e^2 \tag{22}$$

where $\bar{\alpha}$ is the mean of all correction ratios used, with that for range restriction α_1 being given by Eqn. (7) for standardized mean differences and by

$$\alpha_1 = r_{xy}/r_{xy}^p \tag{23}$$

for correlations, and that for test unreliability being

$$\alpha_2 = 1/(r_{xx}\, r_{yy})^{1/2} \tag{24}$$

with r_{xx} replaced by unity in the case of standardized mean differences. Since the data for making these corrections are seldom available for each study, Hunter et al. (1982) also provide an alternative to correction of the separate effect sizes. Their procedure allows for (a) estimating the variance in effect sizes due to artifacts directly from the distributions of the artifacts in those studies where information is provided, and (b) making corrections to the total distribution of effect sizes.

5.4 Analysing Covariation of Study Characteristics and Findings

Hunter et al. (1982) recommend that the analysis of the covariation of effect sizes and study characteristics be undertaken only if most of the observed variance in effect sizes cannot be accounted for by sampling error and the influence of other artifacts. This is a hardline, even doctrinaire, position to adopt given the assumptions required for their estimate of sampling error and their adjustments to it for the influence of artifacts. A more flexible position is to allow for the discernment of meaningful covariation even in data where purely statistical considerations such as theirs would provide a counsel of no examination.

Hunter et al. (1982) and Hedges (1982) suggest only a single strategy for further analysis. This is to divide the data into subsets on the basis of some characteristic and then to test whether each of the subsets is homogeneous. Other more exploratory strategies are also available. Several classifications can be used simultaneously to provide displays of cell and marginal means and variances (or corresponding nonparametric indices). If too many factors are involved there can be problems with empty cells. On the other hand, if factors which have an effective relationship with effect size are excluded, analyses of the remaining factors will be biased if studies in different levels of the excluded factor are unevenly represented.

The use of ANOVA opens up the possibilities of all the extensions of that technique developed for the analyses of subject data. Miller (cited in Glass et al. 1981 pp. 165–70) estimated main and interaction effects for drug therapy and psychotherapy using the general linear model for a two-way design. Rosenthal and Rubin (1982) provide a χ^2 test for preplanned contrasts among effect sizes.

The relationship between study characteristics and findings can also be explored by regression procedures. The use of too many study characteristics, however, can result in the traditional problem of capitalization on chance variations in the data. Where a simple correlation is computed between a study characteristic and effect size, the correlation can be corrected for attenuation due to sampling error in the effect size estimates (Hunter et al. 1982). The corrected correlation with study feature f is given by

$$r_{\tau f} = r_{of}/(s_\tau/s_o) \qquad (25)$$

For multiple regression analyses, all entries in the matrix of simple correlations could first be corrected by Eqn. (25).

In some studies involving the comparison of two conditions, the differences between the conditions can be measured (e.g., class size or volume of drug) rather than just classified (e.g., treatment and control). Meta-analyses of such studies present special problems of analysis and have generated some interesting solutions. For the case of class size, these are discussed in Glass and Smith (1978), Glass et al. (1981 pp. 174–97, 206–16) and Slavin.

6. Prospects for Meta-analysis

Meta-analysis offers some important prospects for educational research. In some substantial bodies of empirical research, it has already exposed consistency of findings where narrative reviewers could discern only enormous variation. More was already established by existing research than had been recognized. Meta-analysis may help to reestablish public faith in the efficacy of empirical research in education by making clearer what

has already been achieved. It may also expose more clearly the questions for which further research is most needed.

Bibliography

Glass G V 1976 Primary, secondary and meta-analysis. *Educ. Res. AERA* 5: 3–8

Glass G V, Smith M L 1978 *Meta-analysis of Research on the Relationship of Class-size and Achievement*. Far West Laboratory for Educational Research and Development, San Francisco, California

Glass G V, McGaw B, Smith M L 1981 *Meta-analysis in Social Research*. Sage, Beverly Hills, California

Hedges L V 1981 Distribution theory for Glass's estimator of effect size and related estimators. *J. Educ. Stat.* 6: 107–28

Hedges L V 1982 Estimation of effect size from a series of independent experiments. *Psychol. Bull.* 92: 490–99

Hedges L V, Olkin I 1980 Vote-counting methods in research synthesis. *Psychol. Bull.* 88: 359–69

Hedges L V, Olkin I 1985 *Statistical Methods for Meta-analysis*. Academic Press, New York

Hunter J E, Schmidt F L, Jackson G B 1982 *Meta-analysis: Cumulating Research Findings Across Studies*. Sage, Beverly Hills, California

Jackson G B 1980 Methods for integrative reviews. *Rev. Educ. Res.* 50: 438–60

Kraemer H C, Andrews G 1982 A nonparametric technique for meta-analysis effect size calculation. *Psychol. Bull.* 91: 404–12

Landman J T, Dawes R M 1982 Psychotherapy outcome: Smith and Glass' conclusions stand up under scrutiny. *Am. Psychol.* 37: 504–16

McGaw B, Glass G V 1980 Choice of the metric for effect size in meta-analysis. *Am. Educ. Res. J.* 17: 325–37

Rosenthal R 1978 Combining results of independent studies. *Psychol. Bull.* 85: 185–93

Rosenthal R 1979 The "file drawer problem" and tolerance for null results. *Psychol. Bull.* 86: 638–41

Rosenthal R, Rubin D B 1982 Comparing effect sizes of independent studies. *Psychol. Bull.* 92: 500–4

Schmidt F L, Hunter J E 1977 Development of a general solution to the problem of validity generalization. *J. Appl. Psychol.* 62: 529–40

Slavin R E 1984 Meta-analysis-education: How has it been used, and a rejoinder to Carlberg et al. *Educ. Res. AERA* 13(8): 6–15, 24–27

Smith M L, Glass G V 1977 Meta-analysis of psychotherapy outcome studies. *Am. Psychol.* 32: 752–60

Missing Data and Nonresponse

D. Holt

One of the problems with survey research is that no matter how carefully the survey is designed, the actual outcome is imperfect. Survey design is concerned with taking advantage of the population structure through techniques such as stratification and multistage sampling so as to yield a sample which will permit efficient estimation of the various population characteristics. Problems occur because responses are not obtained from all of the selected sample and the sample which is

actually achieved is therefore deficient in comparison to what was intended. The reasons for this are complex and depend to some extent on the nature of the study, the survey procedures, and the relationship between the subjects and the researcher. How serious a problem this is and the effect on the survey objectives will depend on the level of nonresponse and how much respondents differ from nonrespondents in the variables of interest in the particular study.

In the simplest case, in schools for example, it may simply be the case that some selected subjects are unavailable on the day of the survey because of illness or absenteeism. Alternatively it may be the conscious choice of some selected individuals or their parents not to respond. A third situation, which can affect not just one subject but many, occurs when a third party, a headteacher for example, decides on behalf of a whole school, not to cooperate in a particular study. This creates a cluster of nonresponses from the selected subjects in that school. In the wider context of research studies which involve direct contact with individuals rather than via a school or other similar institution, the situation is much more like other social surveys. Nonresponse can now result from direct refusal to cooperate, failure to contact the chosen subject or, more rarely, failure to collect the required information because of communication, language, or other similar problems. Failure to make contact is a broad category which includes a variety of situations. This failure may be due to prolonged absence of the subject or because the subject is simply unavailable on each occasion when contact is attempted. Alternatively, the subject may no longer be living at the last known address if the available information is out of date. This description relates to "unit nonresponse" where no information is obtained for some selected individuals. In other cases, answers to some questions are not given in an otherwise complete response. These may, for example, be more sensitive or personal questions which the respondent chooses not to answer. This is known as "item or question nonresponse".

Thus no matter how carefully the original sample design was made to achieve a sample properly representative of the population of interest, the final data yielded will represent a loss of some of the originally chosen subjects. How much effect this will have depends heavily on the type of study, the means of data collection, the nature of the data required and the purposes of the study, the quality and age of sampling frames used, and the level of cooperation achieved with the various levels of authority such as headteachers and administrators where appropriate. At one extreme a well-designed study with carefully executed methodology and the full support of education authorities may achieve almost complete response. Here nonresponse could be such a small problem that it is felt unlikely to significantly affect any of the conclusions drawn from the survey data. At the other extreme, poorly chosen methodology with poor follow-up using out-of-date information could result in a wholly inadequate response rate of 20 percent or less. It is the first responsibility of researchers to strive for as high a response rate as possible but it is nevertheless common for well-designed social surveys with good methodology to achieve response rates of only 75–85 percent. Surveys based on schools or similar institutions are often carried out in favourable circumstances and might be expected to yield a higher response rate than this. It must be emphasized that the overall response rate, whilst important, is not a complete guide.

It is quite possible that even when this is high, the level of response for particular subgroups may still be too low. Different ethnic groups, for example, may yield different response rates and if the research objectives call for separate statistical analyses for each ethnic group or a comparison between them, a low response rate in one group would still cause concern even though the response rate for all ethnic groups taken together was satisfactory.

Nonresponse may affect the survey results in two ways. First there is the effect of reducing the achieved sample below that intended. This alone will decrease the precision of estimates. If this were the only effect it could be overcome by enlarging the initial sample size and so allowing for a reduction in sample size due to nonresponse. The second and potentially more important, and more intransigent, effect is due to the fact that nonrespondents may differ systematically from respondents. The achieved sample is no longer fully representative of the original population and may result in biased population estimates. There is a substantial social survey literature showing that response rates differ with various factors such as social class and urban/rural location, in particular whether the population includes people in inner cities.

Consider the simple case of estimating the mean reading test score of a population of school children. Imagine that the population consists of two groups (a) potential respondents R who if they happen to be selected into the sample would be available on the survey day and (b) potential nonrespondents NR who if selected would be unavailable on survey day perhaps through illness or absenteeism. It is assumed that the two groups have mean reading test scores of μ_R and μ_{NR} respectively and that in the whole population the proportion of potential respondents is P_R. The proportion of potential nonrespondents is $P_{NR} = 1 - P_R$.

The mean reading age for the whole population is μ,

$$\mu = P_R \mu_R + P_{NR} \mu_{NR} \tag{1}$$

but the achieved sample will contain only respondents and, subject to sampling fluctuation, will have a mean reading age of μ_R. The bias in using only the respondents is B,

$$B = P_R \mu_R + P_{NR} \mu_{NR} - \mu_R$$
$$= P_{NR}(\mu_{NR} - \mu_R) \tag{2}$$

Thus the bias is proportional to the difference in mean reading age between respondents and nonrespondents and to the proportion of the population who are potential nonrespondents. It should be noted that this bias is not reduced simply by increasing the sample size. The hopeful dictum that a large enough sample solves all problems does not apply to this situation. Researchers sometimes try to overcome the nonresponse problem by replacing nonrespondents with extra sampled individuals. This will overcome the reduction in overall sample size but the above analysis shows that nonresponse bias will remain. The basic difficulty has been illustrated above in the simplest of all cases when trying to estimate the population mean. In more complex situations such as estimating a correlation coefficient the same principle applies although the systematic difference between respondents and nonrespondents is concerned with characteristics other than just the mean of each group. Under appropriate assumptions, the work of Pearson (1903) and Anderson (1957) on the effects of selection when estimating population characteristics is relevant.

1. Data Collection Methods to Reduce Nonresponse

It is generally held that the best way to attack the nonresponse problem is at source by achieving as high a response rate as possible. The methods used to do this are varied but all involve careful attention to procedures and a willingness to devote a disproportionate amount of the resources and effort available to potential nonrespondents. The basic data collection method may be crucial and it is usually the case that direct contact involving an interviewer will yield a higher response rate than a mail questionnaire although the latter is considerably cheaper in most situations. For interview surveys, refusals can be minimized by improved training for interviewers and sometimes a second contact by a more senior and experienced member of the field force. It is an obvious help if the objectives of the survey are clearly presented and may be seen to be of benefit. There is some evidence from social surveys that some refusals represent a situational response made by people for whom the particular moment of contact is inconvenient or who happen at that moment to be less responsive than they might otherwise be. For such people a second contact on another occasion will often meet with success. It is the interviewer's task to minimize the influence of factors which might lead to refusal and so promote the likelihood of a successful outcome. For mail surveys, response rates are typically lower but reminder cards, repeat mailing, or interview follow-up will often improve this although not so far as to compare with the response rate from interview surveys. In the usual situation in schools, the respondent is the student who is not approached directly. In this case the same principles apply to parents, administrators, and teachers who control access to the child. In other cases, such as higher education, it is more likely that the eventual respondent will be approached directly. Even in this case the active cooperation of authorities in providing address lists and other materials can minimize subsequent frame and response problems.

The question of noncontact is separate from refusal. Clearly people who are completely unavailable at the time of the survey through prolonged absence may be contacted later if this is practicable. People who are simply difficult to contact need to be sought at a variety of times on different days both in the daytime and evenings in order to maximize the possibility of successful contact. Call-backs and finding out from others when a person is likely to be available are both important parts of good fieldwork. Mail questionnaires and telephone interviews often overcome this initial contact problem although for mail surveys at least the motivation to respond is not as strong which more than offsets the gain.

The case of movers is sometimes a particularly difficult problem. If each mover is followed to a new address which is distant from the original, the field organization needs to be exceptionally well-controlled. The cost of such follow-ups can be very great. For wide-scale surveys, the sample is often designed using multistage sampling techniques so that the chosen samples cluster into locations saving considerably on travel costs. If this clustering relies on outdated information then movers will be located outside of the selected clusters and heavy costs will be incurred for each respondent who is followed to a new address. This problem is often overcome to a large degree by a conceptual change in the sampling unit so that it is not the individual but some other more stable unit, linked to individuals that is used. Thus the sampling unit might be addresses or schools which are located at fixed points and the final sample is taken from the de facto membership of each selected unit at the time of the study. In this way a sample is achieved which is still representative of the whole population (including recent movers for example) without having to trace specific individuals who have moved. Such a method may be suitable for school children or general population surveys but will have limited use if the target population is only associated with a small proportion of the general population of units to be sampled. For example, if the survey is concerned with graduates, then a sample of all addresses will yield relatively few university graduates. A sampling frame provided by the university of the last known address of each graduate, however outdated, may be the best information available.

2. Other Fieldwork and Analytic Methods

However good the fieldwork procedures are, and however great the effort made, a residual nonresponse problem will remain. Good survey methods are the first line of attack and will reduce the problem but not eliminate it. The second line of attack is concerned with special data collection methods or statistical analysis techniques to correct for nonresponse bias. The essential difficulty is that nonrespondents by their very nature are unobserved and the proposed methods all depend to a greater or lesser extent on assumptions which are difficult to verify directly. All of the methods assume that in some way respondents and nonrespondents are alike in the sense that data from respondents may be used in such a way as to make allowance for nonrespondents. In some situations these essential assumptions are intuitively reasonable since the nonresponse mechanism is well-understood. In other situations this is not the case. In a survey of school children for example, nonresponse may be caused by absenteeism on survey day. In this case attendance records of all children may be available and so long as it is assumed that absenteeism on survey day is not abnormal (and in particular not related to the survey taking place), then some adjustment involving attendance records might be easily justified. The adjustment made can take various forms such as (a) duplicating the survey data from a child with a similar attendance record to the nonrespondent's, (b) giving greater weight in the analysis to children with similar attendance records to nonrespondents, or (c) some more sophisticated form of statistical adjustment using the attendance record as a covariate. The exact form of this will depend upon the type of statistical analysis required and assumptions about the relationship between the survey variables and attendance. The duplication of an individual data record as described in (a) is known as "hot-decking" (Madow 1979). This is more widely used in large-scale surveys.

Bartholomew (1961) proposed a simple form of adjustment which is primarily concerned with failure to make contact in social surveys and requires a single recall. He argued that successful first calls were clearly biased since they favoured people who spent much of their time at home. Bartholomew suggested that at the time of the first unsuccessful call, as much information as possible should be obtained from other members of the household, neighbours, and so on, so as to yield as good a chance of success at the first recall as possible. He then suggested that successful interviews at the first recall could be weighted to represent also the failures at the first recall stage. The essential assumption is that the additional information collected at the first call helps in the assumption that successes and failures at the first recall are similar and to provide the link between respondents and nonrespondents.

Politz and Simmons (1949) were also concerned with noncontact and suggested that data could be collected from respondents to allow adjustment for nonresponse without making any recalls. The essential idea is that contact is directly related to the availability of the subject during the survey period and people who are more often unavailable during the survey period will be underrepresented in the achieved survey data. Each respondent is asked about the periods when they were available for interview during the survey period and these data can be used to reweight the survey data. For example, someone who was at home on two days during the survey period is twice as likely to have been contacted as someone at home on only one day. The implicit assumption is that for any given level of availability, respondents can represent nonrespondents with whom no contact was made.

Algebraically, the Politz–Simmons method is a special case of the general situation when some auxiliary information is known which may be used to adjust estimation methods to allow for nonresponse. Suppose, for example, that it was known that response rate varied with age of subject and the proportions W_h in each age group (h) were known for the whole population. Then

the population proportions W_h may be used to reweight the sample data for each age group in a form of poststratification to eliminate nonresponse bias. Thus the population mean would be estimated by $\Sigma W_h \bar{y}_h$ where $\bar{y}_h$ is the sample mean for the hth age group. The essential assumption being made is that whilst the response rate is known to vary with age, within any particular age group the respondents and nonrespondents are similar. Eqn. (2) is modified so that with the obvious extension to the notation, the nonresponse bias is given by

$$B = \sum_h P_{NR,h}(\mu_{NR,h} - \mu_{R,h}) \tag{3}$$

Nonresponse bias now depends on the difference between the mean of respondents and nonrespondents within each age group and the implicit assumption is that this leads to smaller nonresponse bias when age is taken into account. Here it has been assumed that the auxiliary information, age group, is a categorical variable and this leads to adjustment through the population weights W_h by poststratification. Conceptually there is no further difficulty if the auxiliary information is not grouped but is treated as a continuous variable. If age is known for each respondent and the average age for the entire population is known then the adjustment could take the form of a ratio or regression estimate but the basic principle is the same.

This method depends on knowledge of the auxiliary information for the population as a whole to provide the link between the sample data and the population estimate required. If the auxiliary information was unknown for the population as a whole but was known for the sample including nonrespondents, then similar methods could be adopted. Now poststratification, ratio, or regression estimates as appropriate could be used to make "estimates" for the original selected sample including nonrespondents and the estimation procedure from this point to the whole population is that which would have been used had there been no nonresponse at all. In practice, of course, the two stages of estimation are combined. In the case of question nonresponse, the other responses on the questionnaire are available as auxiliary information. This provides a much richer source of information for regression or poststratification adjustments for nonresponse.

The procedures have been described here in terms of estimating the simplest characteristic of the population, the overall mean. The same principles may be applied to more complex statistical procedures (Anderson 1957). Thus if auxiliary information is available as variable x and an estimate is required of the regression coefficient of variable y on variable z then a modification to the usual statistical formula would be

$$B_{yz} = \frac{s_{yz} + \dfrac{s_{yx}s_{zx}}{s_{xx}}\left(\dfrac{\sigma_{xx}}{s_{xx}} - 1\right)}{s_{zz} + \dfrac{s_{zx}^2}{s_{xx}}\left(\dfrac{\sigma_{xx}}{s_{xx}} - 1\right)} \tag{4}$$

Here s_{yz} is the sample covariance between variables y and z based on the data achieved from respondents and similarly for s_{xx}, s_{zx} and so on. For the auxiliary variable x, σ_{xx} is the known population value of the variance. Thus if x were the attendance record for school children, s_{xx} would be the sample variance for respondent school children, and σ_{xx} would be the corresponding variance calculated from all the school children's attendance records whether they were in the sample or not.

The cases described here represent relatively simple situations. Little (1980) and Rubin (1976) and also both authors in Madow (1979) have developed a comprehensive framework describing the basis of statistical inference in the presence of nonresponse. In all the cases described here it has been assumed that the response mechanism is such that the distribution of data from respondents is the same as that for nonrespondents given the same value of the auxiliary variables. When this assumption cannot be made, the situation becomes much more complex. Heckman (1979) has considered this situation in the context of econometric models. Related work is reported by DeMets and Halperin (1977) in epidemiology, and Nathan and Holt (1980) in sample survey theory. Thomson and Siring (1979) have used the number of call-backs required for a successful interview to model the response mechanism in terms of an auxiliary variable (household size). By using Norwegian data where the true responses are obtainable from other sources, they are able to investigate the success of their methods and the extent to which call-backs are needed. For their empirical studies they show that their attempts to remove nonresponse bias are an improvement and secondly that a substantial number of call-backs are worthwhile.

This article has been focused on cross-sectional studies although many of the general principles apply to longitudinal studies where selected individuals are followed over time. In addition, such studies involve other methodological problems of nonresponse. Sample attrition over time and the increasing efforts which must be made to maintain contact are the most obvious. An account of these problems specifically related to longitudinal studies is given by Goldstein (1979).

See also: Survey Studies, Cross-sectional

Bibliography

Anderson T W 1957 Maximum likelihood estimates for a multivariate normal distribution when some observations are missing. *J. Am. Stat. Ass.* 52: 200–03
Bartholomew D J 1961 A method of allowing for "not-at-home" bias in sample surveys. *Appl. Stat.* 10: 52–59
Cochran W G 1977 *Sampling Techniques*, 3rd edn. Wiley, New York
DeMets D, Halperin M 1977 Estimation on a simple regression coefficient in samples arising from a sub-sampling procedure. *Biometrics* 33: 47–56
Goldstein H 1979 *The Design and Analysis of Longitudinal Studies: Their Role in the Measurement of Change*. Academic Press, New York
Heckman J 1979 Sample selection bias as a specification error. *Econometrika* 47: 153–61
Kalton G 1983 *Compensating for Missing Survey Data*. Survey Research Center, Institute for Social Research, University of Michigan, Ann Arbor, Michigan
Kish L 1965 *Survey Sampling*. Wiley, New York
Krewski D, Platek R, Rao J N K (eds.) 1980 *Current Topics in Survey Sampling*. Symp., Carleton University, May 7–9, 1980. Academic Press, New York
Little R J A 1980 Models for non-response in sample surveys. Invited paper, European Conference of Statisticians, Brighton
Madow W G (ed.) 1979 *Symposium on Incomplete Data: Preliminary Proceedings*. United States Department of Health, Education and Welfare, Washington, DC
Moser C A, Kalton G 1971 *Survey Methods in Social Investigation*, 2nd edn. Heinemann, London
Nathan G, Holt D 1980 The effect of survey design on regression analysis. *J. Roy. Stat. Soc. B* 42: 377–86
Pearson K 1903 On the influence of natural selection on the variability and correlation of organs. *Phil. Trans. Roy. Soc. A* 200: 1–66
Politz A, Simmons W 1949 I. An attempt to get the "not at homes" into the sample without callbacks. II. Further theoretical considerations regarding the plan for eliminating callbacks. *J. Am. Stat. Ass.* 44: 9–31
Rubin D B 1976 Inference and missing data. *Biometrika* 63: 581–92
Steeh C G 1981 Trends in non-response rates, 1952–79. *Public Opinion Q.* 45: 40–57
Thomson I, Siring E 1979 On the causes and effects of nonresponse: Norwegian experiences. In: Madow W G (ed.) 1979
Yates F 1981 *Sampling Methods for Census and Surveys*, 4th edn. Griffin, London

Multilevel Analysis

J. P. Keeves and N. Sellin

Many investigations into educational problems are concerned with two basic types of variables, namely, measures of the properties of individual students, and measures of the properties of groups of students. This occurs because students are customarily brought together into classes for the purposes of instruction by teachers; because classes are grouped together in schools; and schools are linked together into larger units, such as school districts, for administrative purposes. Problems arise in the analysis of data collected at two or more levels as a consequence of the fact that it is rarely possible to assign students randomly to treatment or control groups in an experimental study, or to allocate the groups by random selection to receive the treatment or stand as the control. In addition, naturally occurring groups of students are found, in general, to contain members who are more like each other than they are like the members of other groups. The clustering of students with similar characteristics into groups means that unless it can be shown that the groups do not differ significantly from each other it is inappropriate to pool students from different groups into a combined group for the purposes of analysis. The problems that occur in the analysis of the data do not arise only because it has been necessary to sample first schools or classrooms and then to sample students within schools or classrooms, but also because the characteristics of the students commonly influence the treatments they receive in the groups (Keeves and Lewis 1983).

In truly experimental studies, where random allocation of students to treatment and control groups has taken place, analysis of variance and covariance procedures can be employed. However, since random assignment can rarely be fully carried out, in both quasi-experimental studies and those in which data are collected from natural situations, statistical control must be exercised in the analysis of data through regression and related procedures in order to examine the effects of both individual and group level variables. Formerly the issue associated with the appropriate level of analysis was considered to be influenced largely by the nature of the research questions to which answers were sought, for example, whether the problem was concerned with individual students or with classroom groups, as well as by the level at which sampling had taken place and at which generalization to other situations was sought. More recently it has become apparent that a multilevel analysis strategy is required if appropriate answers are to be obtained. Many aspects of this problem have been addressed by Burstein (see *Units of Analysis*). In addition, they have been admirably treated by Finn (1974) in the analysis of data from rigorous experimental studies, where unequal numbers of students are clustered in treatment and control groups. These issues were examined further by Cronbach (1976). However, it is becoming increasingly apparent that strategies of multilevel analysis are required for the effective examination of data collected in schools and classrooms. This article seeks to expose the nature of these analytical problems, and to develop a multilevel approach to analysis for the examination of such data, where regression and related statistical procedures are involved.

1. Levels of Analysis

Since the publication of the article by Robinson (1950) on the problems associated with ecological correlations and the making of inferences about the behaviour of individuals from data analysed at the group level, there has been a general awareness that consideration had to be given to the appropriate level of analysis to be employed in data in which correlation and regression coefficients were reported. Three different levels of analysis have been available, and the question has been

which of these three levels should be employed [a detailed discussion of the terms employed and the principles involved can be found elsewhere (see *Regression Analysis*)].

1.1 Between Students Overall

In this level of analysis the data from different groups are pooled and a single analysis is carried out between all students in the total sample. In symbols a regression analysis of this type with two predictor variables can be stated as follows

$$Y_{ij} = b_0 + b_1 X_{ij} + b_2 G_{ij} + \epsilon_{ij} \tag{1}$$

where Y_{ij} is the criterion variable, X_{ij} is a student predictor variable, G_{ij} is a group predictor variable (G_j), $j = 1, \ldots, J$ for groups, $i = 1, \ldots, n_j$ for students within groups, $N = \Sigma_{j=1}^{J} n_j$ for the total number of students, and ϵ_{ij} is the random error.

It should be noted that the group variable G_j has been disaggregated to the student level. This type of analysis was used exclusively in the First International Mathematics Study (Husén 1967), and has been widely used in many investigations during the past two decades.

1.2 Between Groups

In this type of analysis data are aggregated by group, and the mean value for each group forms the criterion variable. Likewise, the student data for each predictor variable are aggregated by group, and group data for a group level predictor variable need not be disaggregated. In symbols a regression analysis of this type with two predictor variables can be stated as follows:

$$Y_{.j} = c_0 + c_1 X_{.j} + c_2 G_j + \alpha_j \tag{2}$$

where $Y_{.j}$ is the mean value of the criterion variable (Y_{ij}) for group j, $X_{.j}$ is the mean value for the predictor variable (X_{ij}) for group j, G_j is a group predictor variable, and α_j is the random error.

This level of analysis was used together with the between students overall analysis in the examination of the data collected in the International Association for the Evaluation of Educational Achievement (IEA) Six Subject Study (Peaker 1975), and has been relatively widely used in other investigations.

1.3 Between Students Within Groups

In this type of analysis the measures for each student are subtracted from the group mean and thus the deviation values from the group mean are employed. Moreover, the data for all groups are pooled for a combined analysis. It is clearly not possible to include group level variables in such analyses. In symbols a regression analysis of this type with two predictor variables can be stated as follows:

$$(Y_{ij} - Y_{.j}) = w_1(X_{1ij} - X_{1.j}) + w_2(X_{2ij} - X_{2.j}) + \delta_{ij} \tag{3}$$

where X_{1ij} and X_{2ij} are two student predictor variables and the remaining symbols are defined above.

This type of analysis together with the between groups type of analysis were used in the examination of the data collected in the Plowden National Survey in England (Peaker 1967).

1.4 Contextual Analysis

A fourth mode of analysis is sometimes employed that examines the contextual effects of a student level variable. In this mode of analysis the criterion variable at the student level is regressed on both a student level predictor variable and a variable which involves the mean values of that student predictor variable, which has been aggregated by groups and then disaggregated for analysis to the student level. In symbols a regression analysis of this type can be stated as follows:

$$Y_{ij} = b_0 + b_1 X_{ij} + b_2 X_{\cdot j} + \epsilon_{ij} \qquad (4)$$

where the symbols employed are as previously defined with $X_{\cdot j}$ being the contextual variable.

Analyses using the first three models have been undertaken by Larkin and Keeves (1984) in a study of the effects of class size on achievement. Differences were recorded in the magnitudes of the regression coefficients obtained for the same measure analysed at the three different levels of analysis. These differences, in general, were not inconsistent with an intuitive understanding of classroom processes and it was argued that with careful interpretation of the evidence, meaningful results were obtainable at each level. This view is contrary to the view that the differences arise at different levels of aggregation because of specification error (Cooley et al. 1981). There is no doubt that errors in the specification of the models used at different levels will give rise to erroneous results. Nevertheless, it is also possible that differences in model specification may be appropriate at different levels, according to the differences in the research questions being examined, and may give rise to different estimates of effect. This does not necessarily involve specification error. As Cooley et al. (1981) correctly point out, the differences are a consequence of grouping effects, when factors influencing group membership are related to one of the variables involved in the analysis.

Aitkin and Longford have examined in some detail the results of analyses employing all four models outlined above. They dismiss the fourth mode of analysis because there is no reliable interpretation of a context effect "since it can be arbitrarily large or small". Moreover they state, "It will be found quite generally that the standard errors of individual level variables aggregated to the school level are very large, when the individual level variables are also included" (Aitkin and Longford 1986 p. 12).

2. Grouping Effects

The divergent and sometimes contradictory results that arise in regression and correlation analyses conducted at different levels stem from the effects of grouping. Sellin

(1986) has examined the factors which determine grouping effects for both simple and complex regression models in ordinary least squares regression analysis. He has shown that the cross-level differences between the regression coefficients obtained in analyses at the three different levels are essentially due to one factor, namely the differences between individual level and aggregate level variances of individual level predictors. In comparing model (1) with model (3), it should be noted that the calculation of deviation scores for analyses using model (3) automatically reduces the variances of both the criterion and the predictor variables. In comparing model (1) with model (2) the results established by Sellin apply to analyses that use not only individual-related predictors, but also to more complex analyses that employ both individual-related predictors and group-related predictors. Since the group level variances are necessarily smaller than their individual level counterparts, because of the loss of information associated with the calculation of the group means, a strong case must be argued before the aggregation of data to the group level takes place. Moreover, it cannot always be argued that aggregation implies improved measurement of group characteristics and that the estimate of the group level effect is to be preferred, since this would assume that within-group variance of student measures was error variance. For example, in obtaining measures of classroom climate, such an assumption would mean that the differences in the perceptions of different students were essentially error. If such a view could be explicitly defended then the group level analysis would be appropriate, but the choice between the student and group level use of a variable should be made in advance and a comparison of the estimates of effect at the two different levels would not be made.

It is of interest to examine the relationship associated with the difference between an aggregated group level regression coefficient and the corresponding student level regression coefficient namely $(c_1 - b_1)$ when expressed in the symbols of Eqns. (1,2), and the between-group variance expressed as a fraction of the total variance. The grouping effect is sometimes referred to as 'aggregation bias' and the use of this term is probably not inappropriate. In Fig. 1 this relationship is illustrated in a sketched diagram that shows how aggregation bias will generally tend to change as the proportion of between-group variance to total variance changes.

It will be seen that when the between-group variance is small compared with the total between-student variance then the aggregation bias is small. This corresponds to random grouping. However, the aggregation bias increases as the proportion of variance associated with between-group variance increases to reach a maximum value but falls again to zero as the proportion approaches 1.0. Peaker (1975 p. 120) has shown, using data from the IEA Six Subject Study, conducted in 13 countries, in three subject areas, and at three grade levels, that this proportion is commonly of the order of 20 percent. Consequently in most studies undertaken in

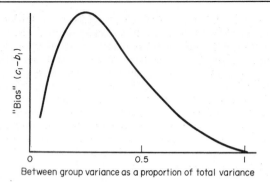

Figure 1
Relationship between aggregation bias and proportion of group variance to total variance

different parts of the world the existence of such bias must be expected.

For those 12 countries that tested in science at the 14-year-old level in 1970, the average bias for the standardized partial regression coefficients when science achievement was regressed on an index of socioeconomic status at the between-school and student levels of analysis was 0.28. The average proportion of the school variance to the total student variance for science achievement test scores for those 12 countries was 0.21. Generally speaking, the regression coefficients doubled in size from student to school levels of analysis. The average size of the clusters was 24 students per school, and the average values of the design effects were for correlation coefficients -2.6 and for regression coefficients -1.7. This would imply intraclass correlation coefficients for the correlations of 0.07, and for the regression coefficients of 0.03. While these measures of clustering are not large they can be associated with quite substantial proportions of between-school variance to total between-student variance and substantial aggregation bias. Since clustering has such important consequences for the estimates of regression coefficients when aggregated data are used, it would seem important that further work should be done to assess the extent of clustering associated with particular predictor and criterion variables in different situations in the analysis of data.

In addition, it would seem very dubious to undertake the disaggregation of a variable from the group level to the individual student level unless it could be argued convincingly that the measure obtained at the group level applied equally to each individual student in the group. For example, it would not be inappropriate to disaggregate the variable, size of class, from the group level to the individual student level in analysis, but measures of teacher–student contact, which involved classroom practices and that influenced individual students in different ways, probably could not be meaningfully disaggregated for student level analyses. It would seem necessary for teacher–student contact to be assessed at the student level and the information related in analysis to each student involved. However, the disaggregation of data does not lead directly to a loss of information in

the way that the aggregation of data does, and as a consequence does not introduce bias into the analysis. Nonetheless, both aggregation and disaggregation require careful justification, and the comparison of the coefficients obtained from different levels of analysis would appear to make little sense.

3. The Framework of Multilevel Analysis

The discussion in the previous section leads to the conclusion that for data collected at more than one level, for example the student and school levels, an analyst must consider the desirability of examining the data at both levels in a way that the two analyses are complementary with the separate components of variance at the two levels being partitioned and subjected to analysis. In this treatment of multilevel analysis the formulation advanced by Mason et al. (1983) has been followed. The data are collected at two levels: the student or micro level and the group or macro level.

The micro level equation may be stated:

$$Y_{ij} = b_{0j} + b_{1j} X_{1ij} + b_{2j} X_{2ij} + \epsilon_{ij} \qquad (5)$$

where Y_{ij} is the criterion variable, X_{1ij} and X_{2ij} are two student predictor variables, and ϵ_{ij} is random error at the micro level.

At the macro level the equations may be stated:

$$b_{0j} = c_{00} + c_{01} G_{1j} + \alpha_{0j} \qquad (6)$$

$$b_{1j} = c_{10} + c_{11} G_{1j} + \alpha_{1j} \qquad (7)$$

$$b_{2j} = c_{20} + c_{21} G_{1j} + \alpha_{2j} \qquad (8)$$

where G_{1j} is the macro level or group predictor variable and α_{kj} is random error at the macro level for $k = 0, 1, 2$.

These equations are written with the usual assumptions associated with the rank condition, and with the error terms at the micro level independent of the errors at the macro level. Equations (6) to (8) represent the effects of the macro level predictor variable (G_1) on the three parameters of the micro level model and it is assumed that once the systematic component associated with this variable has been removed from b_0, b_1 and b_2 the resulting variability is strictly random.

A single equation can be stated for the multilevel model by substituting Eqns. (6) to (8) in Eqn. (5).

$$Y_{ij} = c_{00} + c_{01} G_{1j} + c_{10} X_{1ij} + c_{11} X_{1ij}G_{1j}$$
$$+ c_{20} X_{2ij} + c_{21} X_{2ij} G_{1j} +$$
$$[\alpha_{1j}X_{1ij} + \alpha_{2j}X_{2ij} + \alpha_{0j} + \epsilon_{ij}] \qquad (9)$$

The term in brackets represents a combination of random effects of the micro level variables, namely $\alpha_{1j}X_{1ij}$ and $\alpha_{2j}X_{2ij}$, and random error components, namely α_{0j} and ϵ_{ij}. The random coefficients associated with X_{1ij} and X_{2ij} require special statistical treatment that will be discussed below in connection with the hierarchical linear model (HLM). If, however, $\alpha_{1j} = \alpha_{2j} = 0$ is assumed, Eqn. (9) reduces to a regression model that has no unusual estimation or computational problems.

4. Conditions for Pooling Data

In research situations where groups form the primary sampling unit and students within groups are studied with or without sampling at a second stage, consideration must be given as to whether it is appropriate to pool data across groups. If, however, sampling has occurred at the individual student level the problems associated with the pooling of data are clearly less acute, since some of the effects of grouping have been reduced by random sampling procedures.

Pedhazur (1982) has argued that the critical issues to consider in the pooling of data for analysis at the between-students overall level or the between-students-within-groups level as stated in Eqns. (1, 3) above are:

> ...such an analysis is valid only after it has been established: (1) the b's are not significantly different from each other (the b's are homogeneous); and (2) there are no significant differences among the intercepts of the separate groups. In short, when r_t or b_t is calculated it is assumed that a single regression equation fits the data of all groups. (Pedhazur 1982 p. 537)

Four possible situations arise which influence the analyses. It should be noted that the b_{0j} and b_{1j} coefficients in Eqn. (5) are considered to be random variables whose variability can be examined and tested using the error variance associated with the micro level measures. These situations are:

Case 1. Both the b_{0j} and b_{1j} coefficients are not significantly different from each other.

Case 2. The b_{0j} coefficients are significantly different, but the b_{1j} coefficients are not.

Case 3. The b_{0j} coefficients are not significantly different, but the b_{1j} coefficients are.

Case 4. Both the b_{0j} and b_{1j} coefficients are significantly different from each other.

These four situations can be shown in a 2×2 contingency table (see Table 1).

(a) *Case 1.* In this case there are no significant differences between the b_{0j} and b_{1j} coefficients. Since there are not significant differences between groups, and since the b_{0j} coefficients do not differ, analyses at the between-group level are inappropriate. Moreover the analyses can be carried out by pooling the student data and using the between-students overall model since the b_{1j} coefficients are equal.

Table 1
Contingency table for coefficients b_{0j} and b_{ij}

b_{1j}	b_{0j}	not significantly different	significantly different
not significantly different		Case 1	Case 2
significantly different		Case 3	Case 4

(b) *Case 2.* In this case there are significant differences between b_{0j} coefficients and hence between groups. However, there are no significant differences between the b_{1j} coefficients and under these circumstances it is appropriate to pool the data in a between-students-within-groups analysis and obtain an estimate of the b_1 coefficient. Thus a pooled between-students-within-groups analysis can be conducted as well as a between-groups analysis as suggested by Cronbach and Webb (1975). It has been proposed by Wiley (1976) that the effect of the student level variable can be included in the between-groups analysis as indicated in the following equation:

$$Y_{.j} - b_1 X_{.j} = c_0 + c_1 G_j + \alpha_j \qquad (10)$$

Equation (10) is appropriate if it can be assumed that the effects of X and Y operate at the within-group level and that b_1 represents the appropriate estimate for the effects of X on Y. However Eqn. (10) corresponds to a model that does not specify the effects of X on G or G on X.

(c) *Case 3.* In this case there are no significant differences between the b_{0j} coefficients and under these circumstances a between-groups analysis is inappropriate. However, since there are significant differences between the b_{1j} coefficients it is inappropriate to pool the data at the micro or between-student level and separate analyses for each group should be carried out. Macro level analyses of the b_{1j} coefficients could also be carried out.

(d) *Case 4.* In this case there are significant differences between the b_{0j} coefficients and the b_{1j} coefficients and under these circumstances a full multilevel analysis should be undertaken.

In educational research, where the investigation of differences between schools and classrooms is of primary interest, it would seem that Case 4 would be the situation occurring most frequently in practice. It is, however, unsafe to test simply for statistical significance. Specht and Warren (1976 p. 60) have warned against unwarranted recognition of differences which are small and although statistically significant are substantively slight. This advice should be heeded if trivial analyses are to be avoided when very large samples are employed.

For simplicity, and without loss of generality the data for variables at the individual level are commonly subtracted from the corresponding group mean values. Thus deviation scores are employed in the analysis at this level, and the micro level equation may be stated:

$$(Y_{ij} - Y_{.j}) = b_{1j} (X_{1ij} - X_{1.j}) + b_{2j} (X_{2ij} - X_{2.j}) + \epsilon_{ij}$$
$$(11)$$

It should be noted that the intercept term b_{0j} is no longer included in the equation. However, this does not prevent a multilevel analysis being carried out. It should also be recognized that while deviation scores have been calculated, the scores have not been standardized, so that metric or unstandardized coefficients are employed which can be compared across groups in the analyses.

Table 2
Partitioning of variance in regression analyses with the criterion regressed on the predictors

Level of Analysis	Sum of Squares	df^a	Mean Square	F-Ratio
Between students overall (Y_{ij})				
Due to Regression on X_1	t_1	1	t_1	$t_1 \dfrac{(N-2)}{T_1}$
Residual	T_1	$N-2$	$T_1/(N-2)$	
Total	$t_1 + T_1 = t_2 + T_2 + t_3 + T_3$	$N-1$		
Between groups ($Y_{\cdot j}$)				
Due to Regression on G_1	t_2	1	t_2	$t_2 \dfrac{(J-2)}{T_2}$
Residual	T_2	$J-2$	$T_2/(J-2)$	
Total	$t_2 + T_2$	$J-1$		
Pooled between students within groups ($Y_{ij} - Y_{\cdot j}$)				
Due to Regression on X_1	t_3	1	t_3	$t_3 \dfrac{(N-J-3)}{T_3}$
Residual	T_3	$N-J-3$	$T_3/(N-J-3)$	
Total	$t_3 + T_3$	$N-J-2$		
Unpooled between students within groups ($Y_{ij} - Y_{\cdot j}$)				
Due to Regression on X_1	t_4	J	t_4	$t_4 \dfrac{(N-2J-2)}{T_4}$
Residual	T_4	$N-2J-2$	$T_4/(N-2J-2)$	
Total	$t_4 + T_4 = t_3 + T_3$	$N-J-2$		
Testing for Significance of differences between b_{ij}s				
Unpooled – Pooled SS	$t_4 - t_3$	$J-1$	$(t_4 - t_3)/(J-1)$	$(t_4 - t_3)\dfrac{(N-2J-2)}{T_4(J-1)}$
Residual	T_4	$N-2J-2$	$T_4/(N-2J-2)$	
b_{ij}s regressed on G_1				
Due to Regression on G_1	v_1	1	v_1	$v_1 \dfrac{(J-2)}{V_1}$
Residual	V_1	$J-2$	$V_1/(J-2)$	
Total	$v_1 + V_1$	$J-1$		

a degrees of freedom, i.e., the number of values that are free to vary, given the number of constraints imposed on the data. The interrelations between the number of degrees of freedom in different analyses in this Table should be noted

5. Testing for Significant Differences

Before proceeding to consider the hierarchical linear model it is necessary to obtain the variance components at the micro and macro levels and test the multilevel data for significance. A series of regression analyses at different levels can be undertaken in which the criterion is regressed on one or more predictors using ordinary least squares regression analysis. In the analysis at the group level the aggregated measures are weighted by the number of students within each group. This maintains the orthogonality of the analyses at the different levels. The results of such a series of analyses are given in Table 2.

In analysis 1 at the between-students overall level, the total variance is partitioned into a sum of squares due to regression and a residual sum of squares and the effects of regression are tested for significance. In analysis 2, the regression analysis has been carried out at the between-groups level with a group level predictor G_1. In the analysis 3, the regression analysis has been carried out at the pooled-between-students-within-groups level. In this manner the total variance can be seen to have been partitioned into a between-groups component and a between-students-within-groups component. In analysis 4, the regression analysis is carried out at the unpooled-between-students-within-groups level. In analysis 5, using the results of analysis 3 and analysis 4, a test is applied to determine whether the slopes of the within-group regression lines differ significantly from each other or from a common slope that could be fitted. In analysis 6, a test is applied to determine whether the variation between the slopes of the regression lines is due to a group level variable. The different variance components and the corresponding degrees of freedom, together with the statistical tests are given. An example of this analysis of variance components is given by Keeves and Larkin (1986). For simplicity, this discussion has been presented for only one predictor variable, but could be readily extended for two or more predictor variables at the different levels, although analyses 3 and 4 should be carried out with the same regressors. The tests applied are similar to those used for homogeneity of variance in analysis of covariance (Ferguson 1966 pp. 337-38). Consideration should not only be given to the statistical significance of the tests applied but also to the proportion of the total variance associated with the various components of variance so that trivial effects are not given unwarranted recognition.

In Case 2 where the tests applied in analysis 2 indicate both significant and substantial effects, but where the tests applied in analysis 5 do not, a pooled-between-students-within-groups analysis can be employed to estimate the common regression slope across groups and the components of variance due to the significant student level variables removed before a more detailed between groups analysis is undertaken. This is the group level analysis employed by Wiley (1976) and also illustrated with simulated data by Tate and Wongbundhit (1983). However, it is Cases 3 and 4 discussed above that are of particular interest in school and classroom studies, where significant and substantial differences are detected between groups in the regression slopes since these results are associated with effects that research into educational problems must seek to explain.

6. Hierarchical Linear Models (HLM)

The task facing educational research workers which is of vital importance in the study of classrooms, schools and school districts, as well as in cross-national studies of educational achievement, is the development of appropriate procedures for the analysis of multilevel data. The general framework for such procedures is that of multiple regression, with the outcome variables regressed on variables which measure student as well as teacher, classroom and school characteristics. The procedures must take into consideration the nesting of students within classrooms, and possibly classrooms within schools, and make full provision for the clustering or grouping effects of the micro units within the macro units. In order to ensure generality of findings it is customary for random sampling of both the macro units and the micro units to take place. Thus where such sampling has occurred the effects at both micro and macro level should be regarded as "random" rather than "fixed" effects. The general class of models which have been developed for the analysis of multilevel data has become known as "hierarchical linear models" (HLM), although such terms as "variance components analysis models" and "multilevel models" have been used. At the time of writing this field was passing through a stage of rapid development, and in this article the different approaches are presented, and the issues which have been raised are briefly discussed.

A major problem, as can readily be envisaged, is not only that of formulating the analyses to be carried out but also the inversion of large and complex matrices. As a consequence three different algorithms have been developed with different computing routines and with different analytical strategies. These strategies are:

(a) a general EM algorithm (Mason et al. 1983),

(b) a Fisher scoring algorithm (Aitkin and Longford 1986), and

(c) a generalized least squares algorithm (Goldstein 1986a, Goldstein 1986b).

Each approach is discussed below.

6.1 The General EM Algorithm

This approach involves a two stage process. In the first stage a criterion variable at the micro level is regressed on micro level predictor variables. At the second stage the regression coefficients from the micro stage, including the intercept terms, where meaningful, are regressed on the macro level predictor variables. The major difficulty in this strategy is that the estimation of the regression slopes is associated with considerable error. The issue in the macro level analysis is that of separating the variability in the regression coefficients into their "real" and "random error" components. Mason et al. (1983) developed a restricted maximum likelihood Bayesian estimation procedure, and Raudenbush and Bryk (1986) have extended and applied this procedure to the re-analysis of the data from the 1982 follow-up of the *High School and Beyond Study*. The major problem that Raudenbush and Bryk consider is the error variance in the estimation of the regression coefficients. Since the sampling precision of these regression coefficients varies across units of different sizes and with different extent of variation in the micro level predictor variables, the basic assumptions of ordinary least squares regression analysis would have been violated. Raudenbush and Bryk proposed that the variability in these regression coefficients should be divided into two components, namely, variance due to sampling and the variance of the parameter itself. Following the partitioning of the variance of these regression coefficients into the sampling and parameter components, the parameter variance is estimated as accurately as possible. This permits the macro level effects to be more accurately estimated from an analysis using the parameter component of the variance.

A Bayesian estimation procedure is employed to obtain values of the micro level regression coefficients with reduced error variance, that is, the sum of the parameter variance and the sampling variance. These weights are obtained by an iterative process in which the initial estimate of each micro level regression coefficient is compared with the mean value of these coefficients. Outlier values which are unreliable are successively weighted down and the group coefficient is weighted down more until convergence is obtained. The procedure "shrinks" these micro level regression coefficients and reduces the variance of the estimates prior to the macro level analysis. Since the micro level regression coefficients have been estimated more accurately, the estimates of the effects of the school level variables on these coefficients might be expected to be stronger. While this procedure is computationally complex, it is relatively straightforward conceptually and can be applied where specific models for micro level and macro level effects are being examined.

This approach to hierarchical linear modelling involves two major assumptions, namely, (a) the criterion variable at the micro level is normally distributed, and (b) the regression coefficients obtained from the analysis at the micro level are normally distributed. The first assumption is generally satisfied when achievement tests are used as criterion measures. However, the second assumption could be more problematic, since little experience has been gained from the examination of the distributions of such coefficients. The other assumptions that are necessary do not differ from those required for ordinary least squares (OLS) regression analyses, which have been found to be generally robust. Indeed it might be asked whether OLS regression analysis could be employed. If the condition of homogeneity of the variances of the micro level regression coefficients is satisfied then it might be expected that the use of OLS regression

analyses would yield similar results. One problem encountered in the analysis of the micro level regression coefficients is that the intercept terms (b_{0j}), which are obtained when scaled predictor variables are used, for example, a pretest score of achievement, have no clear meaning since the position of the axis to obtain the intercept is arbitrary. The situation is simplified if, as Raudenbush and Bryk (1986) propose, the within-group data for the micro level analyses are centred around the group mean values of the micro level variables. Where significant differences exist between the group means of the micro level criterion variable, then a macro level analysis using these group means would appear to be necessary, but allowance cannot readily be made for the effects of the student level predictor variables in the analyses at the group level.

6.2 The Fisher Scoring Algorithm

Aitkin and Longford (1986) have reported on the use of the Fisher scoring algorithm in the context of statistical modelling problems connected with British school effectiveness studies. The Fisher scoring algorithm provides maximum likelihood estimates and standard errors for the regression coefficients and group parameter effects of the model:

$$Y_{ij} = b_0 + b_1 X_{ij} + d_j + \epsilon_{ij} \qquad (12)$$

where the symbols are defined as in Eqn. (1) except that d_j are the school or group effects assumed to be a random sample from distribution $N(0,\sigma_I^2)$, and σ_I^2 is the group parameter variance.

It should be noted that this model is in many ways equivalent to the inclusion of a dummy variable for each group and the fitting of a single intercept and regression coefficient for the total set of data. Group level predictor variables that explain the variation in the estimates of d_j can subsequently be sought. However, the micro level regression coefficients are assumed not to vary, and this strategy would appear to be a variation of Case 2 rather than a true HLM analysis required by Case 4.

In fitting the model, weights are employed that are estimated from the variance component estimates. As with the previous procedure which used the general EM algorithm, because the within-group observations are correlated, a coefficient for the ratio of the parameter variance to the sum of the parameter variance and the sampling variance is obtained from the estimates of the parameter variance and the sampling variance. The weights are a maximum when the estimates of the parameter variance are zero, and reduce to zero when the parameter variance is large compared to the sampling variance. This model can be extended to include additional "fixed effect" micro level predictor variables.

Aitkin and Longford (1986 p. 16) note:

school level variables cannot reduce the pupil level component since these variables are constant within school. The failure to distinguish between pupil and school variance components has led in the past to attempts to 'increase R^2' by including school level variables in individual level regressions. When the school variance component is zero or very small such attempts are bound to be fruitless, when it is appreciable, a serious overstatement of significance of such variables is almost inevitable, because the standard errors of the parameter estimates for such variables are seriously understated by individual level regressions.

While certain points are well made, it has long been recognized that simple random sample estimates of error are inappropriate for the testing of such estimates of not only regression coefficients but also mean values, correlation coefficients and multiple *R*'s. More appropriate procedures are widely used (see *Sampling Errors*). The variability in the micro level regression slopes across groups would seem to be an issue of greater consequence.

Consequently, Aitkin and Longford (1986 p. 19) extended their model to include a term in the equation to account for variation in the regression slopes.

$$Y_{ij} = b_0 + b_1 X_{ij} + d_j + f_j X_{ij} + \epsilon_{ij} \qquad (13)$$

Where b_0 and b_1 are the mean intercept and regression slope and d_j and f_j are the random intercept and slope for group j, and where d_j and f_j are not assumed to be independent of each other.

The data which they examined provided an example where one school had a markedly different slope to the others after appropriate adjustments had been made as a result of this analysis. This was a finding of considerable interest.

The general strategies of analysis that they advanced have been employed in the re-analysis of the data obtained in the study of *Teaching Style and Pupil Progress* (Aitkin, Anderson and Hinde 1981; Aitkin, Bennett and Hesketh 1981). The existence of substantial intraclass correlations for the mean score estimates of clustering effects ranging from 0.17 in English and 0.35 in reading indicated the need to undertake a multilevel analytical approach.

Aitkin and Longford (1986 p. 23) also make the valuable point that the clustering effects are not simply a consequence of the sampling design but result from the inherent nature of the grouping of students with similar characteristics within schools.

6.3 Generalized Least Squares Algorithm

Goldstein (1986a) employed the statistical model presented in Eqn. (9) which included an interaction term associated with a micro level predictor variable and a macro level predictor, in order to analyse multilevel data. Moreover, he recognized that if such an approach were adopted then the number of levels involved in an analysis was not necessarily limited to two. In this way the groupings of students within classrooms, classrooms within schools and schools within districts could all be taken into account in a single analysis. The overall variance of the criterion variable was partitioned into components for each level in the ensuing analysis, hence the term "variance component model" was used.

Goldstein proposed that iterative generalized least squares procedures should be employed to obtain estimates of the parameters of the model associated with

both "fixed" and "random" coefficients. Like the two other procedures described above generalized least squares weighted the data according to the accuracy of the estimates at the group level. Goldstein argued that this analytic strategy could also be applied to models for time-related data, with a set of measurements for each individual on a particular variable at different ages or time points. Moreover, there is no requirement that the measurements at each time point should involve the same variable. This approach would appear to be a very powerful and highly flexible one for the efficient analysis of data gathered in educational research. In addition, the use of generalized least squares, while yielding estimates equivalent to maximum likelihood estimates in cases with normal errors, also provides efficient estimates for other distributions. The application of this approach to a range of analyses of educational data is awaited.

7. Some Analytical Issues

De Leeuw and Kreft (1986) have considered many of the recent developments discussed in this article and have raised several analytical issues. In addition they have undertaken the analysis of the same data set using four different approaches: (a) ordinary least squares regression analysis using the two stage estimation procedure represented by Eqns. (5, 6) to (8), (b) ordinary least squares regression analysis using a one stage estimation procedure represented by Eqn. (9), (c) weighted least squares with Swamy weights, and (d) weighted least squares with maximum likelihood weights.

7.1 Random or Fixed Variables

Many studies have been undertaken that have paid insufficient attention to whether or not the regression coefficients from the micro level analysis should be regarded as random variables or as fixed coefficients. Not only should the nature of the sampling process be taken into consideration, but as Tate and Wongbundhit (1983) have argued: (a) the micro level regression coefficients can reflect particular policies and strategies associated with the groups, (b) they are also influenced by unspecified factors associated with the groups, (c) these disturbance factors are commonly considered as giving rise to random variability and, (d) failure to specify these coefficients as random variables annuls attempts that might be made to adjust for such error. It should be noted that ordinary least squares regression analysis treats these regression coefficients as fixed, when there is clearly a very strong case to consider such measures as random variables.

A further question is concerned with whether or not the micro level and macro level predictor variables should be considered as random regressors or fixed regressors. De Leeuw and Kreft (1986) acknowledge that the models they have employed regard the predictor variables as fixed regressors, when random variables are probably involved. They argue for the development of procedures that deal with both mixed regressor models and fully random regressor models.

7.2 Estimation Procedures

The two important aspects of any consideration of estimation procedures are whether the estimates of the parameters are unbiased and whether the estimates of error are efficient. There are, however, further questions as to whether the sampling distributions of the estimates of error are known so that significance tests can be applied. It should be recognized that jackknifing strategies are always available for the estimation of errors in complex models (see *Sampling Errors*). Their use is not uncommon in educational research where ordinary least squares regression procedures are employed, and where allowance has to be made for the effects of clustering. Moreover, ordinary least squares is known to be robust for the data that are obtained in the examination of educational research problems.

(a) *Least squares estimation.* Ordinary least squares regression procedures are widely used in educational research and have been employed in multilevel analysis. For example, Larkin and Keeves (1984) have used least squares regression analysis without weighting, arguing that the appropriate weights which might have been used would be given by the numbers of cases in each group involved in the analysis at the micro level. Consequently, the use of weighted least squares regression analysis (Chatterjee and Price 1977), would have contaminated the analysis with respect to the variable of interest, namely class size. Under these circumstances it was considered inappropriate to weight the data. While the estimation of parameters by ordinary least squares produces unbiased estimates, the estimation of errors of these estimates is inefficient. Clearly in analysis the most efficient estimation procedures available should be employed. However, De Leeuw and Kreft (1986 p. 72) contend that "the weighted estimate will generally improve on the unweighted estimates, although this is by no means certain".

(b) *Weighted least squares.* De Leeuw and Kreft (1986) argue that the weighted least squares estimate has the same asymptotic distribution as the unweighted separate equation estimate. However, since the weighted estimates are generally more efficient and thus improve on the unweighted estimates at least with relatively small numbers of groups and group sizes the use of weighted estimates is to be preferred.

(c) *Separate or single equation estimation.* There is little doubt that separate equation analyses are easier to interpret and to understand and are less likely to be contaminated by problems of multicollinearity than are single equation analyses. However, both approaches lead to unbiased estimates.

(d) *Maximum likelihood or weighted least squares estimation.* In general, maximum likelihood estimation procedures lead to smaller estimates of error and are thus more efficient, although in the example presented by De Leeuw and Kreft (1986) the gains were slight. It must be recognized, however, that the use of maximum likelihood procedures in general requires that the variables included in the analysis are normally distributed.

(e) *Generalized least squares.* Although generalized least squares is an analytic strategy that was advanced more than 50 years ago, and has been treated by Johnston (1972), it would appear that the variance estimates obtained are not distributed as a chi-square distribution and no proper methods are available to provide confidence limits about the values predicted by regression analysis.

7.3 Contextual Effects

A common problem in educational research is concerned with the assessment of school and classroom climates. Measures of climate are obtained from the views and perceptions of students with respect to the situations that they experience. While it is recognized that individuals within a particular group will view a common situation differently and that their different perceptions will influence differentially their behaviour, there is expected to be a high degree of commonality within the group with respect to their views of the situation which they jointly experience. Thus the variability in individual perceptions can also be regarded as error in the measurement of a shared climate. Under such circumstances it might be expected that there would be regularity both within and between groups with regard to the influence of perceptions on behaviour. This expectation can be tested empirically by the analysis of data at the micro level of analysis using Eqn. (5) and by examining whether the differences between regression slopes (b_{1j}) across groups are significant. If there are significant effects of the perceptions of climate on the criterion as assessed by the regression coefficients at the micro level of analysis, but nonsignificant or trivial differences between the regression slopes, then a common slope can be estimated using Eqn. (3) through a pooled between-individuals-within-groups regression analysis. This common slope, it is argued, not only applies to all individuals within their particular groups, but must also logically apply across groups. There is no reason to expect that the group effects differ in any way from the individual effects. Any such differences that have been previously reported are an artefact of analysis using grouped data and must be regarded as aggregation bias. As a consequence before undertaking any analysis at the group level to examine the effects of group level variables on the criterion measure a partial adjustment has been proposed by Wiley (1976) and presented in Eqn. (10).

If significant differences exist in the values of b_{1j} from the micro level analysis using Eqn. (5), it would seem important to examine why such differences existed using a strategy of multilevel or HLM analysis. Only when an answer was known to that question could the group mean values or the micro level equation intercepts (b_{0j}) be examined. It would seem essential to adjust at least in part each group mean value of the criterion measure as in Eqn. (10) in those situations where intercepts (b_{0j}) have no identifiable meaning. The equation for this partial adjustment can be stated as follows:

$$Y_{\cdot j} - b_{1j}\, X_{1\cdot j} = c_0 + c_1\, G_j + \alpha_j \qquad (14)$$

where b_{1j} represents the micro level regression slopes for variable X_{1ij} as in Eqn. (5).

This equation involves the adjustment of the outcome mean values for each group by specific within group effects, using the same logic as in Eqn. (10) with b_1 replaced by b_{1j}.

No adjustment of this type has been reported. It would seem that the use of an iterative approach such as that employed in partial least squares path analysis would provide an appropriate analytical strategy to undertake adjustments of this type based on micro and macro levels of analysis.

8. Conclusion

Multilevel analysis is a field where a number of highly significant papers have recently been published. Much has been accomplished towards the solution of a critical problem in the analysis of educational research data in the short period of time since Mason et al. (1983) suggested to research workers in the social sciences that the problem might be addressed using multilevel analysis procedures. De Leeuw and Kreft (1986 p. 79) conclude with the following statement:

Our first and foremost recommendation is that if one uses contextual analysis, or slopes as outcomes analysis, then one should try to specify the statistical model as completely as possible. This does not necessarily mean that one must adopt the specification we have investigated here. In fact, we believe that our model, although certainly a step ahead, is not quite general enough. It must be generalized in such a way that it can deal with recursive models, in which there are several dependent variables and the regressors are random. Moreover, for many school career analysis situations it must have provisions for incorporating categorical variables. These seem to be developments that are needed from the modeling point of view.

Recently, Wong and Mason (1985) have also developed a hierarchical logistic regression model for multilevel analysis where a categorial criterion variable is employed. We must await with interest the applications of these principles and procedures not in simulation studies but in the detailed analysis of the extensive bodies of data in educational research that are multilevel in nature and that are concerned with real problems.

Bibliography

Aitkin M, Anderson D, Hinde J 1981 Statistical modelling of data on teaching styles. *J. Royal Stat. Soc.* A, 144: 419-61

Aitkin M, Bennett N, Hesketh J 1981 Teaching style and pupil progress. A re-analysis. *Br. J. Educ. Psychol.* 51 (2): 170-86

Aitkin M A, Longford N 1986 Statistical modelling issues in school effectiveness studies. *J. Royal Stat. Soc.* A,149 (1): 1-26

Chatterjee S, Price B 1977 *Regression Analysis By Example.* Wiley, New York, Chap. 5

Cooley W W, Bond L, Mao B-J 1981 Analyzing multilevel data. In: Berk R (ed.) 1981 *Educational Evaluation Methodology: The State of the Art.* The Johns Hopkins University Press, Baltimore and London

Cronbach L J 1976 *Research on Classrooms and Schools: Formulation of Questions, Design and Analysis,* Occasional Paper of the Stanford Evaluation Consortium. Stanford University, California

Cronbach L J, Webb N 1975 Between-class and within-class effects in a reported aptitude × treatment interaction: Re-analysis of a study by G.L. Anderson. *J. Educ. Psychol.* 67: 717-24

De Leeuw J, Kreft I 1986 Random coefficient models for multilevel analysis. *J. Educ. Stat.* 11 (1): 57-85

Ferguson G A 1966 *Statistical Analysis in Psychology and Education.* McGraw Hill, New York

Finn J D 1974 *A General Model for Multivariate Analysis.* Holt, Rinehart and Winston, New York

Goldstein H 1986a Multilevel mixed linear model analysis using iterative generalized least squares. *Biometrika* 73 (1): 43-56

Goldstein H 1986b Statistical modelling of longitudinal data. *Ann. Hum. Biol.* 13: 129-42

Husén T (ed.) 1967 *International Study of Achievement in Mathematics,* 2 Vols. Almqvist and Wiksell, Stockholm

Johnston J 1972 *Econometric Methods,* 2nd edn. McGraw Hill, New York

Keeves J P, Larkin A I 1986 The context of academic motivation. *Int. J. Educ. Res.* 10 (2): 205-14

Keeves J P, Lewis R 1983 Data analysis in natural classroom settings. *Aust. J. Educ.* 27 (3): 274-87

Larkin A I, Keeves J P 1984 *The Class Size Question: A Study at Different Levels of Analysis.* Australian Council for Educational Research (ACER), Hawthorn, Victoria

Mason W M, Wong G Y, Entwisle B 1983 Contextual analysis through the multilevel linear model. In: Leinhardt S (ed.) 1983 *Sociological Methodology 1983-84.* Jossey-Bass, San Francisco, California

Peaker G F 1967 The regression analyses of the national survey. In: Central Advisory Council for Education 1967 *Children and Their Primary Schools: A Report of the Central Advisory Council for Education,* (Plowden Report), Vol. 2, Appendix 4. Her Majesty's Stationery Office, London

Peaker G F 1975 *International Series in Evaluation,* Vol. 8: An Empirical Study of Education in Twenty-One Countries. Almqvist and Wiksell, Stockholm

Pedhazur E J 1982 *Multiple Regression in Behavioral Research.* Holt, Rinehart and Winston, New York

Raudenbush S, Bryk A S 1986 A hierarchical model for studying school effects. *Sociol. Educ.* 59: 1-17

Robinson W S 1950 Ecological correlations and the behavior of individuals. *Am. Sociol. Rev.* 15: 351-57

Sellin N 1986 On Aggregation Bias in Educational Research. Paper presented to the 28th IEA General Assembly, Stockholm

Specht D A, Warren R D 1976 Comparing causal models. In: Heise D R (ed.) 1976 *Sociological Methodology 1976.* Jossey-Bass, San Francisco, California

Tate R L, Wongbundhit Y 1983 Random versus nonrandom coefficients models for multivariate analysis. *J. Educ. Stat.* 8 (2): 103-20

Wiley D E 1976 Another hour, another day: Quantity of

schooling, a potent path for policy. In: Sewell W H, Hauser R M, Featherman E L, (eds.) 1986 *Schooling and Achievement in American Society.* Academic Press, New York

Wong G Y, Mason W M 1985 The hierarchical logistic regression model for multivariate analysis. *J. Am. Stat. Assoc.* 80: 513-24

Multivariate Analysis

J. P. Keeves

Educational research is necessarily concerned with many variables in its attempts to predict and explain educational processes. It is rare that attempts are made to predict educational outcomes using a single variable, and it is rare that there is concern for only one outcome. Likewise in descriptive studies, researchers seldom seek to describe only in terms of a single variable. The many-faceted nature of educational processes demands that measurements should be made on many variables, and that the procedures of analysis employed should be capable of the simultaneous examination and analysis of the many variables on which data have been collected. Until the mid-1960s educational research workers were largely denied the opportunity to analyse in full the rich bodies of data that they were able to collect. However, with the availability of the high-speed computer, the tedious repetitive tasks associated with data analysis were largely eliminated and it was possible to undertake the analysis of data that involved a large number of cases and many variables. The mathematical and statistical procedures associated with such analyses had, in general, been available for many years and simply awaited the arrival of the computer to facilitate calculation. However, the widespread use of these procedures has inevitably led to further developments in the field of multivariate analysis.

Some research workers have, nevertheless, been reluctant to make use of these techniques of multivariate analysis and have continued to employ simpler and frequently inappropriate procedures involving univariate analysis only. Other research workers have rejected the research paradigm associated with accurate measurement and the analysis of quantitative data and have endorsed the use of qualitative, ethnographic, and anthropological approaches. Whilst the use of such approaches in the initial and exploratory examination of a problem is not inappropriate, in general, greater exactness in the making of observations increases their potential usefulness (see *Research Methodology: Scientific Methods*).

Multivariate analysis is primarily concerned with the study of relationships between and within one, two, or more sets of variables that are sequentially ordered with respect to time. The first measured set of variables forms the predictor set; the second measured set forms the criterion set. Where a third set of variables forms the criterion set, the second set, being located with respect to time of measurement between the predictor and the criterion sets, forms a mediating or intervening set. Sometimes a strict time sequence associated with the measurement of the sets of variables cannot be adhered to, and a logical sequence, customarily associated with an underlying temporal relationship, is employed to order the sets of variables.

Darlington et al. (1973) have pointed out that certain general types of question may be asked about sets of variables ordered in this way:

(a) questions about the similarity between variables within one set, which will be referred to as the internal analysis of a set of variables;

(b) questions about the number and nature of mutually independent relationships between two sets of variables, which will be referred to as the external analysis of sets of variables; related to these questions are further questions about the degree of overlap or redundancy between the two sets of variables; and

(c) questions about the interrelations between more than two sets of variables, which will be referred to as the structural analysis of the relationships between the sets of variables.

The different procedures for multivariate analysis will be considered in this article under these three headings, internal analysis, external analysis, and structural analysis.

1. The Multivariate Normal Distribution

The main theory of multivariate analysis is based upon the multivariate normal distribution. The use of this distribution as the mathematical model for multivariate analysis, together with the use of the large sample theory of probability and the multivariate central limit theorem, enable the testing of the significance of relationships between variables obtained from multivariate analyses. While there is much remaining to be learnt about the sensitivity of the multivariate model to departures from the assumptions of the distribution, in general, the model would appear to be relatively robust. The major assumptions associated with the use of the model are first, that observations on a predictor set of variables must be independent of one another, with respondents being both independently sampled and providing information without reference to one another. Secondly, the variance–covariance matrix among the criterion set of variables must exhibit homogeneity regardless of sampling from the population or of the values of the predictor set of variables. While the former assumption cannot wisely be ignored, testing for a violation of the latter assumption is often neglected. It would seem desirable that in analysing data, tests should be applied for the homogeneity of the variance–covariance matrix and a warning recorded if departure from homogeneity is large. Commonly an examination of residuals will provide information on marked departures from homogeneity on the variance–covariance matrix.

2. Variables in Multivariate Analysis

The variables examined in multivariate analyses may involve nominal data with two categories (dichotomous data), or with more than two categories (polychotomous data), or the variables may involve ordinal, interval, or ratio scaled data. Where the variables involve nominal data, they may be submitted to scaling to permit the examination by certain procedures of multivariate analysis (see *Scaling of Nominal Data*). Where the variables involve ordinal data, it is possible to scale the data using rank-scaled scores, through which an appropriate integer score value is assigned to each category. Alternatively, criterion scaling procedures may be used. Commonly, in criterion scaling regression weights are assigned to categories which have been obtained from regression analysis using an appropriate criterion measure (see *Measurement of Social Background*). It is also commonly necessary to transform variables that are members of the criterion set to ensure that they are normally distributed and that the use of the multivariate normal distribution model is appropriate. Where the variables are dichotomous in nature the logit transformation is used (Snedecor and Cochran 1967). In addition, where variables show a high degree of skewness the variables are normalized, as the procedure is commonly referred to, or more accurately, transformed using the probit transformation (Fisher and Yates 1963).

3. Tests of Significance

The fundamental question in testing for significance is concerned with calculating the probability that some sample statistic is representative of a particular population parameter. The techniques employed assume both multivariate normality of distribution and homogeneity of the variance–covariance matrix. Several different approaches have been advanced with regard to testing for significance in multivariate analysis. However, the principles of testing employed in multivariate analysis are parallel to those used in univariate analysis. Nevertheless, there is considerable difference of opinion between statisticians with regard to which test statistic is the most appropriate one to use in a particular situation. Thus while there is agreement that Bock's generalized F statistic and Roy's largest root criterion are of value in the detection of group mean differences along a single dimension, the most commonly used tests for the significance of effects on all criterion measures simultaneously are Wilk's likelihood ratio criterion, and Hotelling's trace criterion, and the step-down test (Bock and Haggard 1968).

In recent years increased use of distribution free procedures, e.g., jackknifing procedures, have been made to obtain estimates of sampling errors in which tests of significance can be based.

4. Estimation in Multivariate Analysis

Two general approaches to multivariate analysis have been developed. The one most commonly employed involves the reduction of the ordered collections of numbers in the matrices associated with sets of variables in accordance with certain specified rules, typically with respect to minimizing errors of prediction or description. In this approach, the principle of least squares is used to determine regression weights in multiple regression analysis and canonical correlation analysis, and the initial position of factors in some types of factor analysis. A second approach has been to obtain maximum likelihood estimates. The task is to find a factor matrix in the sample data most like that which exists in the population. Lawley (1940) was the first to derive the necessary equations, but unfortunately the equations could not be solved by direct computation. Subsequently Lawley (1943) proposed an iterative solution to these likelihood equations. However, the best solution, at present available, has been developed by Jöreskog (1967). This procedure involves the obtaining of an iterative solution to the complex set of equations based on the assumption that there is a particular number of factors. At the end of the analytic procedure a test is applied to determine whether the solution involving this number of factors is adequate to describe the sample data. Other approaches have been employed in multivariate analysis, such as the centroid method of factor analysis and the iterative procedures employed in multiple classification analysis, but these procedures do not have widespread use (see *Factor Analysis; Survey Research Methods*).

5. Internal Analysis Techniques

These techniques seek interrelations between the variables within a single set.

(a) *Contingency table analysis*. In contingency table analysis information is obtained on a set of variables within discrete categories with respect to a number of persons or events. Initially the analysis carried out tests for the independence of the qualitative variables by means of a chi-square test. Where statistical significance is observed it is necessary to undertake a more detailed investigation of the reasons for the significant association between the variables.

(b) *Cluster analysis*. Cluster analysis is a general term for those analytical techniques which seek to develop classifications of variables within a set. The cluster analysis of a set of variables commences with the correlations between the variables, obtained by summing across persons. It is however, possible to obtain correlations or indices of similarity between persons, summing across variables, and this is a more commonly used form of cluster analysis.

(c) *Smallest space analysis.* Smallest space analysis is a technique of data analysis for representing geometrically the pairwise similarities between variables in a set as indicated by the correlations or other measures of distance between the variables of the set. However, smallest space analysis is also used to describe the similarities which exist between persons or with respect to the measured variables.

(d) *Principal components analysis.* In principal components analysis, the problem is that of the reduction of the number of variables used to describe a set of persons, by the derivation of a smaller set of significant components that are statistically unrelated (orthogonal) to each other. The extraction of principal components is the first step in one commonly employed form of factor analysis.

(e) *Factor analysis.* There are many forms of factor analysis, each employing a different analytical procedure. In one procedure it is possible, following the extraction of the principal components from the data on a set of variables to rotate the principal axes while keeping them orthogonal, in order to maximize the distribution of variance across the factors. Rotation of the axes under other conditions is also possible. Through the use of such procedures, sometimes carried out under apparently arbitrary conditions, it is possible to obtain what would seem to be a more meaningful reduction of the original set of variables.

(f) *Log-linear models.* Log-linear models are used in the analysis of contingency tables through the fitting of multiplicative models to sets of data and estimating the parameters of the models. Subsequently, the main effects and interaction effects are tested for significance. These procedures may be extended to use in the analysis of causal models with categorical data, by analysing change over time, for examining panel data, and for the investigation of Markov chain models. Such uses of log-linear models in essence involve structural analysis techniques.

6. External Analysis Techniques

These techniques seek not only interrelations between the variables within two sets but also the interrelations between the two sets of variables.

(a) *Regression analysis.* Perhaps the most widely used of the multivariate procedures of analysis is multiple regression analysis. Although multivariate regression may be considered to involve more than one variable in the criterion set, the analytical procedures employed when there is only one criterion variable and when there are more are essentially the same. In regression analysis linear combinations of both the variables in the predictor set and the criterion set are sought in order to minimize the residual variance. It is common that there are more variables in the predictor set than are necessary for a parsimonious solution to the problem, and stepwise selection procedures are frequently employed before the inclusion of a variable from the predictor set in the regression equation. Where the predictor variables are polychotomous, dummy variable regression procedures are commonly employed, so that each category is considered as a separate variable in the analysis.

(b) *Canonical correlation analysis.* In canonical correlation analysis the nature and number of relationships between two sets of variables are examined. The analysis is carried out in such a way that linear and orthogonal combinations of variables from the set of predictor variables are related to linear and orthogonal combinations of variables from the set of criterion variables. In addition, the analysis provides information on the degree of overlap in variance or redundancy between the variables in the predictor set and the variables in the criterion set. Since the method of analysis maintains full reciprocity between the two sets of variables, in a manner that does not occur in multivariate regression analysis, it is not necessary to identify one set of variables as the predictor set and the other as the criterion set although it is frequently meaningful to do so.

(c) *Multivariate analysis of variance and covariance.* Multivariate analysis of variance and covariance are analytical techniques that can only be properly applied where subjects have been assigned at random to treatments which form the predictor set of variables. The associated variables in the predictor set are thus categorical and not scaled variables. Analysis of covariance differs from analysis of variance in so far as the former is associated with the regression of the criterion variables on one or more variables in the predictor set. Thus the variables in the criterion set are adjusted for the effects of the predictor variables which are considered to be covariates. However, it is important to note that such an adjustment is inappropriate if the covariate variables influence systematically the nature of the treatment received by the subjects. Although analysis of covariance is widely used in research in education and the behavioural sciences, its use is commonly inappropriate, since subjects have not been randomly assigned to treatments and the subject's standing on the covariate has influenced the treatment given.

(d) *Discriminant analysis.* In discriminant analysis, identification of membership of particular groups is considered to be associated with one set of variables, and measures of the characteristics of the groups provide information on the other set of variables. The analysis seeks to obtain one or more composites of the continuous variables such that the composites show maximum differences between group means with respect to these composite scores and minimum overlap in the distributions of these scores. This technique can also be viewed in such a way that membership of the groups forms the criterion set of variables, and the continuous variables form the predictor set. From this perspective the analysis seeks to maximize the prediction of membership of the criterion groups using information on the continuous variables in the predictor set.

(e) *Factorial modelling.* In factorial modelling the analyst is required to name latent variables or factors and to specify each by means of an exclusive subset of predictor variables. The variance associated with the variables in the criterion set is then partitioned among the latent variables or factors which have been identified. The strength of the technique is in its capacity to partition the criterion variance into independent contributions from uncorrelated factors or latent variables.

(f) *Automatic interaction detection* (AID). As a consequence of the search for interaction effects among predictor variables, the technique known as the automatic interaction detection subdivides persons into groups and subgroups, by successively splitting the total sample so that there is maximum variation between groups and minimum variation within groups with respect to the criterion variable. The criterion variable must be either an interval-scaled variable or a dichotomous variable. The identification of groups of persons who are either high or low on the criterion is frequently of very considerable value.

(g) THAID. The technique employed in THAID is similar to that used in automatic interaction detection (AID), except the criterion variable is associated with membership of one of a number of mutually exclusive groups. Again the sample is split into subgroups so that the number of correct predictions of membership of each group is maximized and the differences between the groups is also maximized with respect to the proportion of persons in each group category (Morgan and Messenger 1973).

(h) *Multiple classification analysis* (MCA). Multiple classification analysis uses an iterative procedure to obtain estimates of the effects of several predictor variables, in nominal or ordinal form, on a criterion variable in dichotomous or interval form, so that each of the predictor categories has been adjusted for its correlations with the other predictor categories. The technique does not make provision for the obtaining of information on interaction effects. However, the interaction problem can be handled in appropriate ways, if knowledge of the existence of an interaction effect is available from the use of automatic interaction detection, and the correct cross-classification terms are introduced into the analysis. While this technique is equivalent to the use of dummy variable multiple regression, the procedure would appear to be less vulnerable to multicollinearity problems as well as providing information that is more directly interpretable.

7. Structural Analysis Techniques

(a) *Path analysis.* Path analysis is a technique that in its simplest form employs multiple regression analysis in order to trace the causal links between a series of predictor and mediating variables and a criterion variable. In the analysis of more complex models which are nonrecursive in nature, the techniques of indirect regression and two-stage least squares regression analysis may be used.

(b) *Linear structural relations analysis* (LISREL). This analytic technique may be used for the analysis of causal models with multiple indicators of latent variables, measurement errors, correlated errors, correlated residuals, and reciprocal causation. LISREL is based on maximum likelihood statistical theory and is associated with the analysis of the variance–covariance matrix by maximum likelihood procedures. If a sound fit of the data to the model is obtained then a highly meaningful interpretation is produced. However, many difficulties are commonly encountered in the use of the technique and in obtaining a significant solution. In addition, the multivariate normal distribution or some other known distributions must be assumed for the variables included in an analysis.

(c) *Partial least squares path analysis* (PLS). Partial least squares path analysis like LISREL, may be used for the analyses of causal models with multiple indicators of latent variables. However, it does not require such rigid specification of the error terms and from its use estimates of parameters for a complex model are readily obtained. Since it is an iterative least squares method of analysis, it does not demand the rigid distributional and independence assumptions necessary in maximum likelihood methods. As a consequence the same level of statistical inference cannot be attained with partial least squares path analysis as with linear structural relations analysis.

8. Some Problems of Analysis

There are five problems in educational research associated with the analysis of data by multivariate analytic procedures which are both persistent and widespread. It is common in a very high proportion of investigations in educational research to sample first by schools or classrooms and then by teachers or students within schools or classrooms. Furthermore, in quasiexperimental studies the school or classroom becomes the unit of treatment although data are collected from individual students. Unfortunately students are commonly viewed as the appropriate unit of analysis. In this approach to investigations lie the foundations of some of the problems (Keeves and Lewis 1983).

(a) *Units of analysis.* The data collected can be analysed at one of several levels; between schools, between classrooms, between classrooms within schools, between students within classrooms, between students within schools, and between students. Commonly analyses are carried out at the between student level only and inferences are drawn that are inappropriate to the school as a whole or to the classroom as a unit. Where analyses are undertaken at the between-school or between-classroom level, it is generally recognized as inappropriate to make inferences that apply to students. Consequently, it is necessary that greater care should be taken in stating the propositions to be examined and the hypotheses to be tested so that the appropriate unit of analysis can be employed.

(b) *Effective number of units.* Even where it is appropriate to undertake analyses at the between-student level, it is important to recognize that in investigations in natural settings the student was not the primary unit of sampling and, where the school or the classroom was the primary unit of sampling, effects of sampling may be expected to be substantially greater than if the student was the primary sampling unit. As a consequence of the clustering of students within classrooms and schools, it is inappropriate to use simple random sample formulas for the calculation of errors, and it is necessary to use a correction factor to allow for the design effect of the sampling procedures employed. Fortunately relatively effective and efficient procedures are now available to estimate the sampling errors of statistics estimated from complex samples (Ross 1975b, Wilson 1983).

(c) *The effect of prior performance on treatment*. In investigations in a natural setting it is frequently inevitable that the prior characteristics of the students should influence the treatment provided by the teacher and by the school. As a consequence the measures obtained on school and classroom variables can be influenced significantly by such characteristics of the student as prior achievement. Only when there has been fully random assignment of students to classrooms and to treatments in an experimental study is it likely that the prior achievement of the student will have been adequately controlled. Thus, only when the design of the study makes the necessary provision for random allocation are the procedures of analysis of variance and covariance appropriate. It is clear that where treatment is influenced by prior performance, analysis of covariance provides an unsatisfactory statistical control. Under such circumstances regression analysis must be used. Moreover, it is now possible to undertake regression analysis of data at more than one level of analysis using multilevel analysis models or hierarchical linear models, and the use of such procedures is likely to increase.

(d) *Overfitting of data*. The use of a large number of students at the between-student level of analysis frequently conceals the fact that there are insufficient numbers of classrooms and schools from which data have been collected. Thus in multivariate analysis where data derived from relatively few classrooms and schools are being included in the analysis, the introduction of many classroom or school variables to the analysis is likely to lead to problems in the multicollinearity of the data that are not immediately evident because of the substantial number of students involved.

(e) *Suppressor variables*. One of the signs associated with problems arising from the overfitting of data can be observed when variables change from the expected sign of their relationship with the criterion variables or when variables change markedly the magnitude of their relationship with the criterion as the number of variables included in the analysis is increased. The occurrence of suppression effects must be viewed with great caution.

9. Computer Programs

It is now rare in educational research to find data sets that can readily be analysed by hand or by a simple calculator. This has led to reliance on a range of statistical packages. Each of the large commercial packages has advantages and disadvantages for the analysis of multivariate data sets. Comment is provided briefly on the packages that are widely used.

(a) Statistical Programs for the Social Sciences (SPSS): the SPSS package provides a set of interrelated programs that have considerable flexibility of data management, editing, and analysis. The programs are particularly easy to use, and a very clear manual is provided (Nie et al. 1975).

(b) BMDP: the BMDP package provides a set of programs for a very wide range of analytical techniques, but the procedures for data management and editing are not as straightforward as in other packages (Dixon and Brown 1979).

(c) OSIRIS: the OSIRIS package was well-designed for use with very large data sets and is particularly appropriate for the merging of files and for building files to be used at different levels of analysis. While there is a wide range of multivariate procedures available, and while these programs make economical use of the computer, the individual programs have some deficiences and are sometimes not particularly easy to use (University of Michigan 1976).

(d) SAS: the SAS package has a variety of programs as well as procedures for matrix manipulation, although the package requires a greater degree of sophistication in computing from the user than do the three packages mentioned above. The flexibility thus gained is considerable (Helwig and Council 1979).

(e) Generalized Linear Interactive Modelling (GLIM): the GLIM system is particularly useful for the interactive testing of a wide variety of linear and log-linear models. However, considerable mathematical and statistical sophistication is needed in order to utilize its advantages fully. (Baker and Nelder 1978).

(f) MULTIVARIANCE: the MULTIVARIANCE package is particularly suited to the analysis of nested designs by analysis of variance and covariance procedures. The multivariate analysis programs provided are very sophisticated and require considerable statistical skill to use (Finn 1974).

In order to analyse large bodies of data it is no longer necessary for the educational research workers to spend long hours on tedious calculations, nor is it necessary to become a master of computer programming. However, it is important to have a firm understanding of statistical principles and to maintain a preparedness to consult an experienced statistician concerning the analyses to be undertaken.

10. Comparison of Methods of Analysis

The *International Journal of Educational Research* in 1986 published a series of articles comparing different methods of analysis, including: path analysis, canonical analysis, LISREL, factorial modeling, partial least squares analysis, and multilevel analysis. The differences in the results obtained were very informative (Keeves 1986).

Bibliography

Baker R J, Nelder J A 1978 *The GLIM System Release 3: Generalized Linear Interactive Modelling.* Numerical Algorithms Group, Oxford

Bock R D, Haggard E A 1968. The use of multivariate analysis of variance in behavioral research. In: Whita D K (ed.) 1968 *Handbook of Measurement and Assessment in Behavioral Sciences.* Addison-Wesley, Reading, Massachusetts

Darlington R B, Weinberg S L, Walberg H J 1973 Canonical variable analysis and related techniques. *Rev. Educ. Res.* 43: 433–54

Dixon W J, Brown M B (eds.) 1979 BMDP-*79: Biomedical Computer Programs.* University of California Press, Berkeley, California

Finn J D 1974 *A General Model for Multivariate Analysis.* Holt, Rinehart and Winston, New York

Fisher R A, Yates F 1963 *Statistical Tables for Biological, Agricultural, and Medical Research*, 6th edn. Oliver and Boyd, Edinburgh

Helwig J T, Council K A (eds.) 1979 SAS *User's Guide*, 1979 edn. SAS Institute, Raleigh, North Carolina

Jöreskog K G 1967 Some contributions to maximum likelihood factor analysis. *Psychometrika* 32: 443–82

Keeves J P 1986 Aspiration, motivation and achievement. Different methods of analysis and different results. *Int. J. Educ. Res.* 10(2): 117–243

Keeves J P, Lewis R 1983 Three issues on the analysis of data in natural classroom settings. *Aust. J. Educ.* 27(3): 220–40

Lawley D N 1940 The estimation of factor loadings by the method of maximum likelihood. *Proc. Roy. Soc. Edinburgh* 60: 64–82

Lawley D N 1943 The application of the maximum likelihood method to factor analysis. *Br. J. Psychol.* 33: 172–75

Morgan J N, Messenger R C 1973 THAID: *A Sequential Analysis Program for the Analysis of Nominal Scale Dependent Variables.* Survey Research Center, Institute for Social Research, Ann Arbor, Michigan

Nie N H, Hull C H, Jenkins J G, Steinbrenner K, Bent D H 1975 *Statistical Package for the Social Sciences*, 2nd edn. McGraw-Hill, New York

Ross K N 1976 *Searching for Uncertainty: An Empirical Investigation of Sampling Errors in Educational Survey Research.* Australian Council for Educational Research, Hawthorn, Victoria

Snedecor G W, Cochran W G 1967 *Statistical Methods*, 6th edn. Iowa State University, Ames, Iowa

University of Michigan Institute for Social Research 1976 *OSIRIS IV Manual.* University of Michigan, Ann Arbor, Michigan

Wilson M 1983 *Adventures in Uncertainty.* Australian Council for Educational Research, Hawthorn, Victoria

Nonparametric Statistics

M. Cooper

The most commonly used and best known methods of statistical inference employed in educational research assume a knowledge of the nature of the probability distributions of variables in the populations from which samples are drawn. The tests of significance employed in making statistical inferences are in a majority of cases dependent upon the assumption of an underlying normal distribution, although other underlying distributions are sometimes assumed. However, in practice many situations arise where little is known about the nature of the distribution of a variable in the population, or where it is known that wide departures occur from the commonly used distributions. Under these circumstances it may be desirable to use what is known as a distribution-free statistical procedure.

Distinctions must be made between variables in educational research according to the properties of the measurements that can be made on the variables. Measurement commonly provides data of four classes: nominal, ordinal, interval, and ratio data. Nonparametric statistical procedures are appropriately used with nominal and ordinal data. Parametric statistical procedures are applicable to interval and ratio data. However experience has shown that nonparametric procedures can sometimes be used very effectively in situations where parametric procedures would normally be applied. This requires that the interval and ratio data are reduced to a form such that the methods which are appropriate only for nominal and ordinal data can be employed.

There are two major classes of nonparametric statistical procedures. The first class employs only the sign properties of the data, and all observations above a chosen fixed value are assigned a plus or one (1) while all those at or below the fixed value are assigned a minus or zero (0). The second class of nonparametric statistics employs the rank properties of the data, and all observations are assigned a rank order value. The subsequent statistical procedures involve the making of inferences based on the ranks assigned. It is evident that when nonparametric methods are applied to interval and ratio data, only part of the information available is used. Although it was initially believed that a heavy price would be paid for the loss of efficiency in the application of a statistical test under these conditions, there may be gains made in the robustness and validity of the test employed. This is particularly true where small samples are being used or where little is known about the underlying distribution of the variable under investigation.

1. Methods

The terms nonparametric and distribution free tend nowadays to be used interchangeably. A nonparametric test is, generally speaking, one in which no hypothesis is made about the value of a parameter in a statistical density function. In many so-called nonparametric tests, the value of the test statistic is derived from ranks or frequencies, which are sample-dependent quantities that cannot be specified by a single observation. The distribution of the observation characteristic used in such a test thus tends to be discrete and specifiable exactly; this makes the test free of the distribution of the population from which the observations were drawn.

Because nonparametric tests do not use ratio or interval data, they do not test directly for parameters calculated from magnitudes. Rather, tests using ranks and frequencies would test for relationships between parameters such as medians and proportions. Many of the more common parametric tests for use with ratio or interval data have nonparametric analogues for use with ordinal or categorical data.

Many tests using ordinal data are based on expressions applicable to unbroken sequences of positive integers. Tied observations therefore render such tests somewhat inaccurate and corrections have to be applied.

A number of nonparametric tests use discrete sampling distributions constructed by Fisher's method of randomization. In a typical two-sample test, the test statistic might be the sum S_i, of the n_i ranks in sample i. In Fisher's technique, the value of S_i for each of the $\left[\begin{smallmatrix} n_1 + n_2 \\ n_i \end{smallmatrix}\right]$ combinations of the data is found, the distribution of S_i being formed. Under the assumption of equal probability of occurrence of each such combination, the corresponding probability distribution is determined.

Since the distributions of many test statistics approach normality when samples are large, exact probability tests usually have large-sample normal approximations.

The first application of a nonparametric technique appears to have been when Arbuthnott (1710) used the sign test. The latter is based on the binomial distribution developed by Bernoulli in 1713, which as de Moivre showed in 1733 approaches the normal distribution when samples are large in size. Brief details of many nonparametric tests are presented below.

2. Correlation

There are two general classes of correlation coefficient used in nonparametric statistics: those dealing with variables measured ordinally and those for use with categorical data.

2.1 Ordinal Data

When two variables, X and Y, are measured by ranks, either Spearman's correlation index or Kendall's correlation index may be used to indicate the intercorrelation of X and Y. If the difference of ranks for subject i is

represented by d_i, Spearman's index (ρ) is given (assuming no tied observations) by

$$\hat{\rho}_S = 1 - 6 \sum_i d_i / (n^3 - n) \tag{1}$$

where n is the size of the sample. The hypothesis of independence may be tested using Fisher's method of randomization, $\hat{\rho}_S$ being calculated for each pair of rank sets possible for the given n. For large samples, the standard normal deviate may be used as the test statistic. This is given by

$$z = \left(6 \sum_i d_i - n^3 + n \right) \Big/ [n(n+1)(n-1)^{\frac{1}{2}}] \tag{2}$$

Kendall's index of rank correlation (τ) is based on his general theory of rank correlation. For subject i, an indicator variable a_i is assigned the value $+1$, 0, or -1 depending on whether performance on one variable is better, equal to, or worse than that on the other. The formula for τ is

$$\tau = \sum_i a_i \Big/ \binom{n}{2} \tag{3}$$

The sampling distribution of τ is constructed by Fisher's method of randomization. When samples are large, it approaches normality with zero mean and variance equal to $\frac{1}{18} n(n-1)(2n+5)$ (Kendall 1970).

2.2 Categorical Data

If both variables are dichotomies, the appropriate correlation index is the phi coefficient (ϕ). When either variable has more than two categories, the mean square contingency coefficient C should be used. Both indices are related to chi-squared (χ^2). For a sample of size n, the relationships are $\phi^2 = \chi^2/n$ and $C^2 = \chi^2/(\chi^2 + n)$. The absolute values of both ϕ and C can exceed unity.

Since the above indices are related to χ^2, this statistic may be used to test the hypothesis of independence. If the number of subjects lying in category i of the one variable and category j of the other is represented by f_{ij} (the observed frequency), the expected frequency for this combination of categories is $f_{i.} f_{.j}/n$ where $f_{i.}$ is the number of subjects in category i of the first variable and $f_{.j}$ is the number in category j of the second. The value of χ^2 is then given by

$$\chi^2 = \sum_{ij} \sum [n(f_{ij} - f_{i.} f_{.j}/n)^2 / f_{i.} f_{.j}] \tag{4}$$

If the variables have m and k categories, respectively, χ^2 is associated with $(m-1)(k-1)$ degrees of freedom.

The above general formula for χ^2 is often replaced by formulas which are specific to the statistical design. In many cases, Yates's correction for continuity is applied so that discrete data may be tested by reference to the continuous χ^2 distribution.

2.3 Coefficient of Concordance

A technique which addresses the relationship among many ordinally measured variables results in Kendall's coefficient of concordance (W). In this procedure, each subject is ranked across all variables, a rank sum for each variable being obtained. W is the ratio of the sum of squares among the rank totals to the sum of squares that would be obtained if all subjects ranked identically across all variables.

If the rank sum for variable j is T_j, a formula for W is

$$W = \left[\left(12 \sum_j T_j^2 \right) \bigg/ n^2 k (k^2 - 1) \right] - 3(k + 1)/(k - 1) \tag{5}$$

where n subjects are ranked across k variables (Kendall 1970).

3. Two Independent Samples

Nonparametric analogues of Student's t test for independent samples include the Mann–Whitney (Wilcoxon) test, the normal scores tests, and Fisher's exact test.

3.1 Mann–Whitney (Wilcoxon) Test

For this test, all subjects are ranked across both samples, the rank sum for one sample being determined.

If this sample contains n_1 of the N subjects, Fisher's method of randomization may be used to determine a value of the rank sum T_1 for each of the $\binom{N}{n_1}$ possible sets of n_1 ranks selected from the N ranks available. Under the assumption that all such sets have equal probability of occurrence, the probability distribution for T_1 may be determined.

The Mann–Whitney version of the test employs the statistic U, defined as $\min(U_1, U_2)$ where, for example i

$$U_i = T_i - \tfrac{1}{2} U_i (U_i + 1) \tag{6}$$

For large samples, a normal approximation is available, where

$$z = (U - n_1 n_2 / 2) / [n_1 n_2 (n_1 + n_2 + 1)/12]^{1/2} \tag{7}$$

Where there are tied observations, a correction term may be applied (Hays 1973).

3.2 Normal Scores Tests

Under certain conditions, greater power may be achieved by the substitution of normal scores for ranks (Marascuilo and McSweeney 1977).

The van der Waerden test replaces ranks with inverse normal scores. For rank i, the inverse normal score W_i is the value of z corresponding to the $100_i/(N + 1)$ centile point in the normal distribution, there being N subjects in both samples together. The sum of the W_i, s, in one sample is the test statistic. Fisher's method of randomization may be used to construct a sampling distribution of S. Under the assumption of equal probability of occurrence of each set of normal scores, the probability distribution for S may be determined.

For large N, a normal approximation is available, where

$$z = S \bigg/ \left\{ [n_1 n_2 / N(N - 1)] \sum_i W_i^2 \right\}^{\frac{1}{2}} \tag{8}$$

The Terry–Hoeffding test uses the expected values of the corresponding normal-order statistic, usually referred to as expected normal scores. These have been likened (Marascuilo and McSweeney 1977) to the best guess as to the value of the original scores as reconstructed from the ranks. The sampling distribution of S is constructed as for the van der Waerden test.

For large N, the normal deviate may be used, z being given by

$$z = S \bigg/ \left\{ [n_1 n_2 / N(N - 1)] \sum_i W_i^2 \right\}^{\frac{1}{2}} \tag{9}$$

The Bell–Doksum test employs random normal scores and may be used with large samples only. N values of z are randomly selected from normal distribution tables, ordered, and matched with the ordered ranks 1 to N. In each sample, each rank is replaced by the corresponding random normal score. The test statistic is standardized from

$$z = D / [(1/n_1) + (1/n_2)]^{1/2} \tag{10}$$

where

$$D = (S_1 / n_1) - (S_2 / n_2) \tag{11}$$

3.3 Fisher's Exact Test

Fisher's exact test may be used when two independent populations are dichotomized into those having a characteristic of interest and those not having it. If x_i of the n_i subjects in sample i have the characteristic, the proportion having it in population i is estimated by $\hat{p}_i = x_i / n_i$. The probability of occurrence of (x_1, x_2) given their sum, based on the hypergeometric distribution, is

$$P[(x_1, x_2) | x_1 + x_2] = \begin{bmatrix} n_1 \\ x_1 \end{bmatrix} \begin{bmatrix} n_2 \\ x_2 \end{bmatrix} \bigg/ \begin{bmatrix} n_1 + n_2 \\ x_1 + x_2 \end{bmatrix} \tag{12}$$

A probability distribution associated with the set of all $x_1 x_2$ pairs possible given n_1 and n_2 and holding $x_1 + x_2$ constant is constructed and used for testing the hypothesis $p_1 = p_2$. A modification to Fisher's exact test has been proposed by Overall (1980).

For large samples, a normal approximation is available, where

$$z = (\hat{p}_1 - \hat{p}_2) / \{ \hat{p}_0 (1 - \hat{p}_0) [(1/n_1) + (1/n_2)] \}^{1/2} \tag{13}$$

where

$$\hat{p}_0 = (x_1 + x_2)/(n_1 + n_2) \tag{14}$$

The two-sample median test is an application of Fisher's exact test, in which lying above (or below) the median is the characteristic of interest. Observations lying at the median may be discarded, or assigned to cells so as to make the test more conservative, or less.

3.4 Other Tests

Included among two-sample tests are a number which will not be elaborated upon. Examples are the Kolmogorov–Smirnov test, the Wald–Wolfowitz runs test, and the Moses test of extreme reactions (Siegel 1956).

4. Matched-pair Tests

If observation j in sample 1 is X_j, the match in sample 2 being y_j, the difference is $d_j = X_j - Y_j$. The test statistic for the sign test, $S = \Sigma(d_j | d_j > 0)$, has a binomial probability distribution.

The Cox–Stuart (1955) S_2 and S_3 tests for monotonic increase (or decrease) in a sequence of observations are an extension of the sign test; corresponding observations in earlier and later sections of the sequence form the matched pairs.

For the Wilcoxon matched-pairs signed-ranks test, pair j is assigned a "signed rank" $r_j = a_j R_j$, where $a_j = 1$ if $d_j > 0$, $a_j = -1$ if $d_j < 0$, and R_j is the rank of $|d_j|$ in the set of absolute observation differences. The test statistic is $T_P = \Sigma(r_j | r_j > 0)$, or $T_N = \Sigma(r_j | r_j < 0)$. The probability distribution of T_P (or T_N) is determined by Fisher's randomization method. For large numbers of paired-observations (n), the test statistic for the normal approximation is

$$z = [T_P - n(n+1)/4]/[n(n+1)(2n+1)/24]^{1/2} \quad (15)$$

In a normal-scores version of the Wilcoxon test, positive normal scores are assigned to the unsigned ranks and re-signed according to the signs of the ranks. The test statistic is $T_P = \Sigma(w_j | w_j > 0)$ where w_j is the signed normal score for pair j. The exact test is based on Fisher's method of randomization, the normal approximation for large n uses

$$z = (2T_P - \Sigma w_j)/(\Sigma w_j^2)^{1/2} \quad (16)$$

(Marascuilo and McSweeney 1977).

5. Tests for Many Independent Samples

Nonparametric analogues of the one-way analysis-of-variance test include the Kruskal–Wallis test, normal scores versions, and a test for homogeneity of k proportions (Marascuilo and McSweeney 1977).

5.1 Kruskal–Wallis Test

For the Kruskal–Wallis test, all N observations are ranked across all k samples. The test statistic, which is approximately distributed as χ^2 with $k - 1$ degrees of freedom, is

$$H = 12 \sum_j (S_j^2/n_j)/N(N+1) - 3(N+1) \quad (17)$$

where S_j is the sum of the n_j ranks in sample j. Scheffé-like post hoc procedures are available, as are tests for polynomial trend. Tobach et al. (1967) have evolved a post hoc procedure for use with small samples. Steele (1960) has proposed post hoc procedures for pairwise

comparisons, in which two-sample Wilcoxon tests are used at the $2\alpha/k(k-1)$ level of significance. Bradley (1968) has presented a method of collapsing data in a factorial design so that the Kruskal–Wallis test may be used to test for main interaction effects.

5.2 k-Sample Normal-scores Tests

The ranks in the Kruskal–Wallis design may be replaced by normal scores, the test statistic for this test being

$$W = (N-1) \sum_j (S_j^2/n_j)/T \quad (18)$$

where S_j is the sum of the n_j normal scores in sample j and T is the sum of all N squared normal scores. Scheffé-like post hoc procedures are available (Marascuilo and McSweeney 1977).

5.3 Homogeneity of k-Proportions

The design used for the Fisher exact test may be extended to k samples each dichotomized on a variable of interest. The homogeneity of the population proportions having the characteristic of interest may be tested by use of χ^2. Post hoc procedures exist, as do tests for polynomial trend. When samples are small, an arcsine transformation may be applied to proportions, the test statistics being,

$$U_0' = \sum_j n_j \left[\phi_j - \left(\sum_j n_j \phi_j \right) \middle/ \sum_j n_j \right]^2 \quad (19)$$

where

$$\phi_j = 2 \sin^{-1} p_j^{1/2} (0 < p_j < 1) \quad (20)$$

p_j being the proportion of the n_j subjects in sample j having the characteristic (Marascuilo and McSweeney 1977).

5.4 Multivariate Analysis of Variance

A nonparametric analogue of one-way multivariate analysis of variance has been proposed by Katz and McSweeney (1980). Two post hoc procedures are provided; one, the multivariate Scheffé-like technique, allows examination of as many contrasts as desired, the overall error rate being established at a specified value for the entire set. The other, the univariate Scheffé-like technique, limits examination to within-variable contrasts.

5.5 Analysis of Covariance

Techniques for the analysis of data in a k-sample design with p dependent variables and q covariates have been proposed by Quade (1967), Puri and Sen (1971), and McSweeney and Porter (see Marascuilo and McSweeney 1977). All use ranks; the second may be based on normal scores also.

In the Quade test, observations for each variable are ranked across all subjects, the ranks being subjected to linear regression techniques to generate errors of estimate, which are then subjected to conventional analysis of variance. The McSweeney–Porter test, which has about the same power as the Quade test, performs conventional analysis of covariance on the ranks.

6. Repeated Measures

6.1 The Friedman Model

The Friedman test may be used to test for homogeneity of rank means in a one-way design in which n subjects are each ranked over k occasions. The test statistic, which is associated with $k - 1$ degrees of freedom is

$$\chi^2 = 12 \sum_j T_j^2/nk(k + 1) - 3n(k + 1) \qquad (21)$$

where T_j is the rank sum for occasion j. Scheffé-like post hoc procedures exist.

A normal-scores version (Marascuilo and McSweeney 1977) is also available.

6.2 Tests for Change

Among tests for change in behaviour, in which a sample is measured on a categorical variable on two occasions, are the Bowker test and the McNemar test. The former, used for dichotomous variables, is based on the binomial distribution; the latter uses a χ^2 statistic.

The Cochran Q test is an extension of the McNemar test in which n subjects are measured on k occasions by means of a dichotomous dependent variable scoring 0 or 1. The test statistic is

$$Q = \left[k(k - 1) \sum_j (T_j - T/k)^2\right]\Big/\left(k \sum_i S_i - \sum_i S_i^2\right) \quad (22)$$

where T_j is the sum of "scores" for example j, S_i is the total score for subject i, and T is the total score for the sample. Scheffé-like post hoc procedures exist (Marascuilo and McSweeney 1977).

7. Nonparametric Tests in Blocking Designs

7.1 Two-sample Tests

In the Hodges–Lehmann test, scores are replaced by deviations from block means. These deviations are then ranked across all N subjects, thus "aligning" the observations. If S_i of the n_i subjects in block i are in sample A, the sum of their S_i ranks being W_i, the test statistic is $W = \Sigma_i W_i$. A sampling distribution of W may be formed by a tedious method of randomization, leading to an exact test.

In block i, the expected value and variance of W_i are

$$E_i = S_i \sum_j (R_{ij}/n_i) \qquad (23)$$

$$V_i = [S_i(n_i - S_i)/(n_i - 1)]$$

$$\times \left\{\left[\left(\sum_j R_{ij}^2\right)\Big/n_i\right] - \left[\left(\sum_j R_{ij}\right)\Big/n_i\right]^2\right\} \qquad (24)$$

For the normal approximation for large samples, therefore, the test statistic is

$$Z = \left(W - \sum_i E_i\right)\Big/\sum_i V_i \qquad (25)$$

A correction for continuity may be applied.

A test referred to by Marascuilo and McSweeney (1977) as a multiple Wilcoxon test may be used as an alternative. Here observations are ranked within blocks, ranks for sample B being discarded. For this large-sample test,

$$E_i = S_i(n_i + 1)/2 \qquad (26)$$

$$V_i = S_i(n_i + 1)(n_i - S_i)/12 \qquad (27)$$

7.2 Many-sample Tests

For the k-sample design with m blocks, an extension of the Hodges–Lehmann test may be used. The test statistic, which is distributed approximately as χ^2 with $k - 1$ degrees of freedom is

$$W = m^2(n - 1) \sum_j [\bar{R}_i - (N + 1)/2]^2/k \sum_i V_i \qquad (28)$$

where $\bar{R}_j$ is the rank mean for sample j, N is the total number of subjects, and V_i is the variance of the ranks in block i. Post hoc simultaneous confidence intervals may be constructed.

Alternatively, Marascuilo and McSweeney (1977) present a technique in which ranks in the above test are replaced by normal scores.

8. Nonparametric Tests for Interaction

8.1 Multisample Design with Two Dichotomous Variables

When subjects in a k-sample design are classified on two dichotomous variables, a series of k 2×2 tables results. If $\hat{p}_{ij}$ subjects in sample j are classified into the first category of the first variable and the ith category of the second, the difference of the proportions is $\hat{\Delta}_j = \hat{p}_{1j} - \hat{p}_{2j}$. Homogeneity of the Δ_j, indicating no interaction, may be tested by a χ^2 test. Components of interaction in the populations may be identified by means of post hoc procedures.

8.2 Second-order Interaction in a One-sample Design

Interaction involving a multicategory variable (A) and two dichotomies (B and C) on which a single sample is classified may be tested by means of a χ^2 test. If a proportion $\hat{p}_{ijk}$ of the subjects in category k of A are classified into category i of B and category j of C, a measure of the association of B and C in A_k is Goodman's index of association (γ), estimated by

$$\hat{\gamma}_k = \ln(\hat{p}_{11k}\hat{p}_{22k}/\hat{p}_{12k}\hat{p}_{21k})$$

$$= (\ln \hat{p}_{11k} + \ln \hat{p}_{22k}) - (\ln\hat{p}_{12k} + \ln\hat{p}_{21k}) \qquad (29)$$

The hypothesis for the test of second-order interaction is that of homogeneity of γ across all categories of A (Marascuilo and McSweeney 1977).

9. Relative Efficiency of Nonparametric Tests

Many of the nonparametric analogues of classical tests have high relative efficiency. The Mann–Whitney (Wilcoxon) test, the Wilcoxon signed-ranks test, and the Kruskal–Wallis test, for example, all have an asymptotic relative efficiency (ARE) of about 0.955 relative to their analogues when assumptions of normality and homogeneity of variance are made for the parametric test (Marascuilo and McSweeney 1977). When underlying distributions are nonnormal, the efficiency is never below 0.864 and can exceed unity. Blair and Higgins (1980) report that the Wilcoxon rank-sum test generally holds "very large power advantages" over the t-test. The substitution of normal scores for ranks can boost the efficiency considerably.

10. Computer Packages

The NPAR TESTS subprogram of the *Statistical Package for the Social Sciences* (Nie et al. 1975) offers analysis for a number of the more common techniques. The programme BMDP 3S from *Biomedical Computer Programs* (Dixon 1975) provides analysis for nine procedures. Perhaps the most comprehensive set of interactive nonparametric computer routines is available in EASYSTAT (Cooper 1982).

Bibliography

Arbuthnott J 1710 An argument for Divine Providence, taken from the constant regularity observ'd in the births of both sexes. *Philosophical Transactions* 27: 186–90

Blair R C, Higgins J J 1980 A comparison of the power of Wilcoxon's rank-sum statistic to that of Student's *t* statistic under various nonnormal distributions. *J. Educ. Stat.* 5: 309–66

Bradley J V 1968 *Distribution-free Statistical Tests*. Prentice-Hall, Englewood Cliffs, New Jersey

Cooper M 1982 *EASYSTAT: Non-parametric Section*. University of New South Wales, Sydney

Cox D R, Stuart A 1955 Some quick tests for trend in location and dispersion. *Biometrika* 42: 80–95

Dixon W J (ed.) 1975 *BMDP: Biomedical computer programs*. University of California Press, Berkeley, California

Hays W L 1973 *Statistics for the Social Sciences*, 2nd edn. Holt, Rinehart and Winston, New York, p. 780

Katz B M, McSweeney M 1980 A multivariate Kruskal–Wallis test with post hoc procedures. *Multivariate Behav. Res.* 15: 281–97

Kendall M G 1970 *Rank Correlation Methods*, 4th edn. Griffin, London

Marascuilo L A, McSweeney M 1977 *Nonparametric and Distribution-free Methods for the Social Sciences*. Brooks-Cole, Monterey, California

Nie N H, Hull C H, Jenkins J G, Steinbrenner K, Bent D H 1975 *Statistical Package for the Social Sciences*. McGraw-Hill, New York

Overall J E 1980 Continuity correction for Fisher's exact probability test. *J. Educ. Stat.* 5: 177–90

Puri M L, Sen P K 1971 *Nonparametric Methods in Multivariate Analysis*. Wiley, New York

Quade D 1967 Rank analysis of covariance. *J. Am. Stat. Ass.* 62: 1187–200

Savage I R 1962 *Bibliography of Nonparametric Statistics*, Harvard University Press, Cambridge, Massachusetts

Siegel S 1956 *Nonparametric Statistics for the Behavioral Sciences*. McGraw-Hill, New York

Steele R G D 1960 A rank-sum test comparing all pairs of treatments. *Technometrics* 2: 197–207

Tobach E, Smith M, Rose G, Richter D 1967 A table for making rank and sum multiple paired comparisons. *Technometrics* 9: 561–67

Partial Least Squares Path Analysis

R. D. Noonan and H. Wold

In modeling large and complex social systems, such as school systems, the model builder works in a research situation with massive amounts of data but relative scarcity of theoretical knowledge. In such a problem area, partial least squares (PLS) path analysis with latent variables is useful. Its scope and flexibility make it a superior statistical tool for treating large systems. This article will describe the PLS basic design, discuss some features pertinent to research on school system structure and performance, and present an application involving a simple model using real-world data. The most complete and authoritative exposition of PLS is given in Wold (1982). Educational applications are given there and in Noonan and Wold (1983).

1. The Historical Origins of PLS: The Merger of Econometrics and Psychometrics

Sociology entered a new era in the early 1960s when latent (indirectly observed) variables from psychology were merged with path modeling with manifest (directly observed) variables from econometrics. The econometric models included multiple ordinary least squares regression, causal chain systems, and interdependent systems whereas the psychological models included factor analysis, principal components, and canonical correlations. In econometrics there were the new developments in interdependent (ID) systems with Wold's introduction of the REID (reformulated ID) and

GEID (general ID) systems and the FP (fix-point) iterative method for the estimation of REID and GEID systems (Wold 1965). In psychometrics there were the related iterative methods for assessing principal components and canonical correlations (Wold 1966).

Path modeling with latent variables posed entirely new statistical problems, which in the sociological literature were dealt with throughout the 1960s by ad hoc devices. In the early 1970s Jöreskog launched his LISREL algorithm for maximum likelihood estimation of path models with latent variables (e.g., Jöreskog 1973). When LISREL was introduced, it became clear to Wold that principal components and canonical correlations could be interpreted as path models with one and two latent variables respectively, with each latent variable explicitly estimated as a weighted aggregate of its indicators. This led Wold to extend his iterative algorithm for principle components and canonical correlation to general path models with latent variables indirectly observed by multiple indicators. By the early- to mid-1970s, a general algorithm for iterative PLS estimation of path models with latent variables was available (Wold 1975). By late 1977 the basic design for PLS estimation of path models with latent variables was established (Wold 1977).

2. Exposition of PLS Soft Modeling

PLS estimation of path models with latent variables indirectly observed by multiple indicators is often described as "soft modeling," because it does not involve the "hard" assumptions about a specific distribution subject to independent observations which are characteristic of maximum likelihood methods. A unique feature of PLS is the explicit estimation of each latent variable as a weighted aggregate of its indicators. Hence PLS involves a twofold aggregation, that is, over both cases and variables.

2.1 Arrow Scheme

Some fundamental notions can be illustrated by a path diagram. Figure 1 represents a simple path model with six latent variables. The arrow scheme of a path model specifies its theoretical–conceptual design. The formal definition of the model, and the PLS algorithm for its estimation, can be written directly from the arrow scheme.

As illustrated in Fig. 1, a PLS model has inner and outer variables. The core of the model is a set of hypothetico–predictive inner relations among the inner variables. The inner variables may be manifest or latent (directly or indirectly observed). Each latent variable is indirectly observed by a block of manifest outer variables treated as indicators of the latent variable. The manifest variables are illustrated by squares or rectangles, and the latent variables by circles. A PLS model can be interpreted as a give-and-take of causal–predictive information. Thus information is conveyed by inner relations between inner variables, and by outer relations between the latent variables and their indicators.

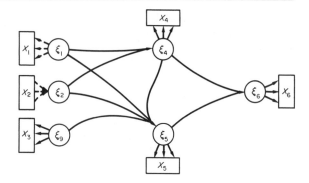

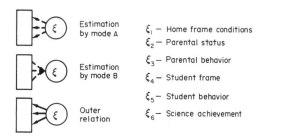

Figure 1
A simplified model of influences on science achievement

2.2 Formal Specification

A PLS model is formally defined by its inner and outer relations. The formal specification further includes the relations for substitutive prediction of the latent and manifest variables. Inner and outer relations are subject to predictor specification, and all outer residuals are assumed to have zero correlations across the blocks and with all latent variables.

Suppose that the manifest variables are observed over time or cross-section on N cases; $n = 1, N$. Latent variables ξ_j; $j = 1, J$, are represented by their estimates X_{jn}. Each estimated latent variable is measured by manifest variables x_{jkn}; $k = 1, K_j$. In the discussion below the ranges of the subscript n will often be tacitly implied. For example, consider the model illustrated in Fig. 1. The exogenous latent variables are ξ_1, ξ_2, ξ_3; their estimates are X_1, X_2, X_3. The endogenous latent variables are ξ_4, ξ_5, ξ_6; their estimates are X_4, X_5, X_6.

Partial least squares is general and can be used with either raw data or product data, such as correlation matrices or variance–covariance matrices (plus a vector of means where location parameters are of interest). In school survey research it is common to work with large samples, ranging in size from a few thousand students upward. Since the estimation procedure is iterative, it is most appropriate to use product data with samples of this size. In school survey research, the focus is on population results, not individual results. Moreover, many of the measures lack an intrinsically meaningful scale. Because of these characteristics of the school survey research situation, multivariate analyses are typically carried out on correlation matrices. For such reasons and for the sake of brevity, location parameters will be ignored in the expositions that follow.

(a) *Outer relations.* In soft modeling, the outer relations take the form:

$$x_{jk} = \pi_{jk} \xi_j + \varepsilon_{jk} \tag{1}$$

with predictor specification

$$E(x_{jk} | \xi_j) = \pi_{jk} \xi_j \tag{2}$$

which implies

$$E(\varepsilon_{jk}) = 0; \quad r(\varepsilon_{jk}, \xi_j) = 0 \tag{3a, 3b}$$

As an idealization subject to testing against the estimated model, it is assumed that all information conveyed between the blocks of indicators is conveyed through the inner relations via the inner variables. This ficticious assumption should make the residuals uncorrelated between blocks:

$$r(\varepsilon_{gh}, \varepsilon_{jk}) = 0; \quad g \neq j; \quad g = 1, G;$$
$$h = 1, H_g; \quad k = 1, K_j \tag{4a}$$

The residuals within blocks, in contrast to LISREL and factor analysis, are *not* assumed to be uncorrelated. Accordingly:

$$r(\varepsilon_{jh}, \varepsilon_{jk}) \neq 0; \quad h \neq k; \quad h = 1, H_j; \quad k = 1, K_j \tag{4b}$$

Since both π_{jk} and ξ_j in Eqn. (1) are unknown, scale standardization is necessary in order to avoid ambiguity. The choice of scale does not affect the substantive results of the analysis. In PLS, scale unambiguity is achieved by standardizing all latent variables and their estimates to unit variance:

$$\text{Var}(\xi_j) = 1; \quad \text{Var}(X_j) = 1 \tag{5a, 5b}$$

(b) *Inner relations.* In the basic design for PLS soft modeling, the inner relations are linear and additive, and form a causal chain. The inner relations, involving the predictand ξ_m and predictors ξ_h, have the general form:

$$\xi_m = \sum_h (\beta_{mh} \xi_h) + v_m; \quad h = 1, H_m \tag{6}$$

The general inner relation shown in Eqn. (6) has the predictor specification

$$E(\xi_m | \xi_1, \xi_2, \ldots, \xi_{H_m}) = \sum_h (\beta_{mh} \xi_h) \tag{7}$$

which implies

$$r(v_m, \xi_h) = 0; \quad h = 1, H_m \tag{8}$$

2.3 Substitutive Prediction

For the indicators of any endogenous latent variable, PLS modeling gives relations for prediction of case values, obtained by substitutive elimination of the latent variable from the outer relations, using the corresponding inner relations. For example, the general form of the predictive relation for the estimation of the manifest variable x_{jkn} in the model shown in Fig. 1 is given by:

$$x_{jkn} = \pi_{jk} \sum_h (\beta_{jh} \xi_{hn}) + v_{jkn};$$
$$j = 4, 5, 6; \quad h = 1, H_j \tag{9a}$$

with residual given by

$$v_{jkn} = \epsilon_{jkn} + \pi_{jk} v. \tag{9b}$$

Inner relations and substitutive predictions are two key tools for prediction in PLS soft modeling. An inner relation predicts an endogenous inner variable in terms of explanatory inner variables. Substitutive prediction provides prediction of an endogenous indicator in terms of the explanatory variables in the corresponding inner relations.

2.4 Partial Least Squares Estimation

Each latent variable is estimated explicitly as a weighted sum of its indicators:

$$X_j = \text{Est } \xi_j = f \cdot \sum_h w_{jh} x_{jh}; \quad h = 1, H_j \tag{10}$$

where f is a standardizing scalar giving all latent variables unit variance [see Eqns. (5a) and (5b)]. If the data apply to individual cases, subscripts n can be added to Eqn. (10) to give explicit estimates of case values.

Weight relations involve estimates of adjacent or contiguous latent variables. In the model shown in Fig. 1, for example,

$$C_4 = S_{41} X_1 + S_{42} X_2 + S_{54} X_5 + S_{65} X_6 \tag{11}$$

where S_{ij} is either $+1$ or -1, depending on whether $r(X_i, X_j)$ is positive or negative.

The investigator may choose between two estimation modes, A and B.
Mode A:

$$x_{jh} = w_{jh} C_j + d_{jh} \tag{12a}$$

Mode B:

$$C_j = \sum_h x_{jh} x_{jh} + d_j \tag{12b}$$

The iterative process begins with the first latent variable, sweeps through to the last, back to the first, and so on until the system converges.

2.5 Some Extensions of the Basic PLS Design

In addition to linear additive models, PLS has been extended to a wide variety of applications, such as models involving categorical data and multidimensional contingency tables, interdependence, two-way observations, that is, over both time and cross-section, latent variables with several dimensions, and hierarchically structured latent variables.

3. Hypothesis Testing

Usually, predictive relations are intended to yield predictions beyond the data used for estimating the relations. Three kinds of tests are available, of which only the first can be used if raw data are not employed.

3.1 F-test with Classical Estimation of Sampling Errors

Since the latent variables are estimated as exact linear combinations of their indicators, there is nothing to prevent the application of the distributional assumptions upon which the classical estimates of the standard errors and corresponding *F*-tests are based. The estimated standard errors of the regression coefficients for the inner relations can be computed from the diagonal element of the inverse matrix of the predictor variables (Draper and Smith 1981). Then the *F*-test can be applied, the nonsignificant paths can be removed, and the simplified model can be re-estimated. In school survey research, where cluster sampling is routine, the design effect, DEFF (Kish 1965), can be used to adjust (upward) the standard errors estimated by the classical formula for single stage sampling.

3.2 Tests of Predictive Relevance through Sample Reuse

With the Stone–Geisser test of predictive relevance (Stone 1974, Geisser 1974) the predictive relations are validated by "blind-folding," omitting *m* observations at a time, each time re-estimating the model using the remaining $N - m$ observations. An adaptation of Ball's Q^2 serves as a test criterion. In the special case of multiple ordinary least squares regression, the test criterion for the prediction of y_n (ignoring location parameters), is given by:

$$Q^2 = 1 - \frac{\sum_n \left(\sum_h (b_h^{(n)} x_{hn}) - y_n \right)^2}{\sum_n (\bar{y}^{(n)} - y_n)^2};$$

$$n = 1, N; \quad h = 1, H \tag{13}^1$$

where $b_h^{(n)}; h = 1, H$ are the coefficients of the multiple ordinary least squares regression when re-estimated after omitting y_n from the data, and $\bar{y}^{(n)}$ is the trivial prediction of y_n given by the mean $\bar{y}$ after omitting y_n. The predictive relation under test has more predictive relevance the higher Q^2 is. The Stone–Geisser test for multiple regression allows straightforward extension to PLS models.

3.3 Jackknife Estimation of Sampling Errors

Tukey's jackknife (Tukey 1977) is a general device for assessing standard errors of parameter estimates. It gives *m* estimates for each parameter in the model, and from these estimates the jackknife estimate of the standard error can be computed (Miller 1974). For large samples, such as those typical in school survey research, each parameter might be estimated using 10 samples, each omitting one-tenth of the total sample, and this process repeated at least six times. The Stone–Geisser test gives the jackknife estimates of the standard error of

Table 1
Inner variables in the PLS path model

Block	Name	Latent variable	No. MVs	Estimation mode	Weight multipliers
1	PARENSTA	Parents' socioeducational level	3	Mode A	—
2	SIBLINGS	Number of siblings and sibling position	1	Tied to 4	—
3	HOMERESC	Home reading resources	3	Tied to 4	—
4	*HOMEFRM	Home frame	4	Mode A	0.1
5	PARENBEH	Parents' instructional and motivational behavior	2	Mode B	—
6	STUDSEX	Student's sex	1	Tied to 14	—
7	STUDMATR	Student's maturity (age and grade)	2	Tied to 14	—
8	STUDVERB	Student's verbal ability	3	Tied to 14	0.1
9	REASONL	Student's reasoning level (Piagetian)	1	Tied to 14	—
10	*STFRMCG	Student frame: cognitive	4	Tied to 14	0.1
11	ATTEDUC	Student's attitudes toward education	7	Tied to 14	0.1
12	ATTSCIEN	Student's attitudes toward science	6	Tied to 14	0.1
13	*STFRMAF	Student frame: affective	13	Tied to 14	0.1
14	**STFRM	Student frame	20	Mode A	0.1
15	LEISACT	Science-related leisure activities	4	Tied to 21	—
16	LEISREAD	Leisure reading activities	4	Tied to 21	—
17	*STBEHH	Student home behaviors	8	Tied to 21	0.1
18	TEXTBOOK	Use of textbooks in school	4	Tied to 21	—
19	LABWORK	Laboratory work in science instruction	8	Tied to 21	—
20	*STBEHS	Student school behaviors	12	Tied to 21	0.1
21	**STBEH	Student learning behaviors	20	Mode B	0.1
22	SCIENACH	Science achievement	5	Mode A	1.0
Total			135		

---

1 Eqn. (13) was given incorrectly in an earlier publication (Noonan and Wold 1983)

the parameter estimates of the predictive relations as a by-product.

For an example of the use of jackknife error estimation procedures with partial least squares path analyses, see Sellin (1986).

4. An Application Involving Hierarchically Structured Latent Variables

An application is presented here of PLS with hierarchically structured latent variables. The most complete discussion of PLS with hierarchically structured latent variables is given in Noonan and Wold (1983).

4.1 The Data

The data were collected in Sweden by the International Association for the Evaluation of Educational Achievement (IEA) in their 1970 survey of student achievement in science (Comber and Keeves 1973) and other subjects [see Walker (1976) for an overview]. The data cover 14-year-old students, the schools they attend, and the science teachers in those schools. It should be noted that in Sweden, relatively small differences prevail between schools in terms of physical resources and personnel compared with many other countries, and these differences tend not to be related to the social-class composition of the schools (Noonan 1976). This low and non-systematic between-school variation in Sweden can be expected to lead to relatively small observed effects of the school variables on achievement.

In the application that follows, the student was the unit of analysis. Each student was represented in the files by a record containing the student's responses to test and questionnaire items as well as responses from the school principal and the aggregated responses of the science teachers in the school.

4.2 The Variables

A total of 22 inner variables appear in the model, as shown in Table 1. The inner variables are represented by from one to 20 manifest variables. There are three classes of variables: (a) frames, representing characteristics or states of students, their homes, and their parents; (b) behaviors, representing student and parent behavior of relevance to schooling; and (c) goals, representing student science achievement.

Nineteen of the 22 variables were organized into hierarchical structures. Latent variables which represent a hierarchical aggregation are denoted in the variable name by "*" for the first level of aggregation and by "**" for the second. Variables representing the higher, more general level of the hierarchy appear in Table 1 immediately below the variables representing the lower, more specific level. For example ATTEDUC and ATT-SCIEN represent the basic latent variables making up the higher level variable *STFRMAF, while STUDSEX and STUDMATR, together with *STFRMCG and *STFRMAF make the still higher level variable **STFRM. These variables are referred to collectively as the student frame

hierarchy. Two other hierarchies are represented in Table 1, namely home frame and student learning behaviors. Variables not appearing in a hierarchical structure are PARENSTA, PARENBEH, and SCIENACH. The measurement of PARENSTA and PARENBEH is not sufficiently elaborate conceptually to enable a hierarchical structuring. The measurement of SCIENACH is based on a highly elaborate topic-by-level grid (Comber and Keeves 1973), and the formation of subscores used here as indicators represents a hierarchical structuring.

4.3 The Model

The model is defined by its inner and outer relations. The outer relations follow from the definition of the blocks of manifest variables, as shown in Table 1. The inner relations are defined by a set of structural equations, which may be expressed in functional form as follows:

Hierarchical relations

$$*\text{HOMEFRM} = f_1 \text{ (SIBLINGS, HOMERESC)}$$
$$*\text{STFRMCG} = f_2 \text{ (STUDVERB, REASONL)}$$
$$*\text{STFRMAF} = f_3 \text{ (ATTEDUC, ATTSCIEN)}$$
$$**\text{STFRM} = f_4 \text{ (STUDSEX, STUDMATR,}$$
$$*\text{STFRMCG,} *\text{STFRMAF)}$$
$$*\text{STBEHH} = f_5 \text{ (LEISACT, LEISREAD)}$$
$$*\text{STBEHS} = f_6 \text{ (TEXTBOOK, LABWORK)}$$
$$**\text{STBEH} = f_7 \text{ (}*\text{STBEHH,} *\text{STBEHS)}$$

Hypothetico–predictive relations

$$\text{STUDVERB} = f_8 \text{ (PARENSTA, }*\text{HOMEFRM, STUDSEX,}$$
$$\text{STUDMATR)}$$
$$\text{REASONL} = f_9 \text{ (PARENSTA, }*\text{HOMEFRM, STUDSEX)}$$
$$\text{ATTEDUC} = f_{10} \text{ (PARENSTA, }*\text{HOMEFRM,}$$
$$\text{PARENBEH, STUDSEX, STUDMATR,}$$
$$*\text{STDFRMCG)}$$
$$\text{ATTSCIEN} = f_{11} \text{ (PARENSTA, }*\text{HOMEFRM,}$$
$$\text{PARENBEH, STUDSEX, STUDMATR,}$$
$$*\text{STDFRMCG)}$$
$$\text{LEISACT} = f_{12} \text{ (PARENBEH, }**\text{STFRM)}$$
$$\text{LEISREAD} = f_{13} \text{ (}*\text{HOMEFRM, }**\text{STFRM)}$$
$$\text{SCIENACH} = f_{14} \text{ (}**\text{STFRM, }**\text{STBEH)}$$

The hierarchical relations are algebraic and are not given a causal interpretation, while the hypothetico–predictive relations are stochastic and are given a causal interpretation.

For each latent variable, the investigator has a choice of two modes of estimation, A and B. The distinction between modes A and B is parallel to Hauser's (1973) distinction between reflective and productive indicators. Thus mode A is typically used for blocks containing manifest variables treated as reflecting some underlying factor, whereas mode B is typically used for blocks containing manifest variables treated as producing or forming some underlying latent variable. In the present model a sharp conceptual distinction is maintained between frames and behaviors. This distinction, given

Table 2
Path (structural form) coefficients and R² for hypothetico–predictive relations (decimal points omitted)

Predictand	Predictor								R²
	PARENSTA	*HOMEFRM	PARENBEH	STUDSEX	STUDMATR	*STFRMCG	**STFRM	**STBEH	
STUDVERB	23	24	—	7	16	—	—	—	16
REASONL	12	9	—	−15	—	—	—	—	5
ATTEDUC	19	9	21	5	−12	34	—	—	30
ATTSCIEN	7	8	17	−19	−8	25	—	—	17
LEISACT	—	—	8	—	—	—	18	—	5
LEISREAD	—	9	—	—	—	—	36	—	16
SCIENACH	—	—	—	—	—	—	62	19	55

the measurements used in the present study, corresponds to the distinction between reflective and productive indicators. Hence frames are estimated using mode A and behaviors are estimated using mode B. Estimation mode is relevant here only for the highest level of the hierarchically structured latent variables. Weights for the lower level latent variables in a hierarchy follow algebraically from the weights of the highest level and from the hierarchical relations.

Table 1 also shows a set of weight multipliers which are assigned to each inner relation, in practice to each latent variable which serves as a regressand. These weight multipliers are used by the investigator to steer the analysis so as to give greater weight to the relations of primary interest and less weight to relations of secondary interest. The relationship of primary interest here is that predicting SCIENACH, and it is given a weight of 1.0. All other hypothetico–predictive relations are given a weight of 0.1. Weight multipliers are relevant only for hypothetico–predictive relations. In Table 1, weight multipliers for hierarchical relations are undefined and given as " — ."

4.4 The Results

The analysis was completed in nine iterations and required 3.6 seconds of CPU time on an IBM 360/90 system. It is not possible within the space available to present more than a small portion of the results even for a comparatively simple model such as the one analyzed here. Some illustrative examples are provided but substantive aspects are not studied deeply here.

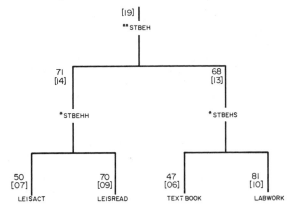

nn   Hierarchical relation
[nn]   Disaggregated effect on SCIENACH

Figure 3
Hierarchical relations and hierarchical disaggregation of effects of student behavior on science achievement

The coefficients of the hierarchical relations for the student frame and student behavior hierarchies are given in Figs. 2 and 3. They are computed as structural form coefficients and interpreted as scaling factors. Figures 2 and 3 also show in brackets the reduced form coefficients, which are interpreted as the total effect of the given latent variable on SCIENACH. From Fig. 2 it can be seen that the most important student frames are the cognitive and affective characteristics, especially verbal ability. From Fig. 3 it can be seen that learning behaviors in the home and at school are equally important. Among the home behaviors, leisure reading is most important, but among school behaviors, laboratory work is most important.

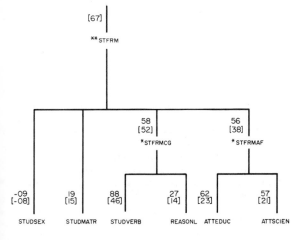

nn   Hierarchical relations
[nn]   Disaggregated effects on SCIENACH

Figure 2
Hierarchical relations and hierarchical disaggregation of effects of student frames on science achievement

Table 3
Total (reduced form) coefficients for hypothetico–predictive relations (decimal points omitted)

Predictand	Predictor							
	PARENSTA	*HOMEFRM	PARENBEH	STUDSEX	STUDMATR	*STFRMCG	**STFRM	**STBEH
STUDVERB	23	24	—	7	16	—	—	—
REASONL	12	9	—	−15	—	—	—	—
ATTEDUC	27	17	21	6	−7	34	—	—
ATTSCIEN	12	14	17	−19	−4	25	—	—
LEISACT	5	4	11	—	4	14	18	—
LEISREAD	10	18	5	−4	8	28	36	—
SCIENACH	18	17	9	−8	15	52	67	19

Tables 2 and 3 show the path (structural form) and total effect (reduced form) coefficients of the hypothetico–predictive relations. The path coefficients are based on the simplified model after nonsignificant paths were deleted. The reduced form coefficients follow as a corollary from the entire set of equations (hierarchical as well as hypothetico–predictive) in the simplified model.

In Table 2 it can be seen that the influence of student frames on science achievement is much greater than the influence of student behaviors. Girls tend to have more favorable attitudes toward education but less favorable attitudes toward science. Parental behavior has an important influence on attitudes. The strongest influence on attitudes is shown by student cognitive characteristics. In Table 3 it can be seen that the total effect of the home and parental variables is as powerful as the effect of student behavior. These home and parental variables influence science achievement mainly through their effects on verbal ability and attitudes.

5. Conclusions

Partial least squares path analysis with latent variables carries over the whole range of least squares regression from manifest variables to latent variables. As an iterative least squares method, it does not involve the hard distributional and independence assumptions which are characteristic of maximum likelihood methods. Because of its simplicity (compared with maximum likelihood methods), it is a powerful and flexible tool for the causal modeling of large and complex social systems.

The basic PLS design is established and a number of extensions of the basic design are now available. Research and development work now under way is opening up vast new areas for PLS path modeling methods. With this, PLS is evolving into a general tool for least squares analysis.

See also: Path Analysis; Regression Analysis; Multivariate Analysis

Bibliography

Comber L C, Keeves J P 1973 *Science Education in Nineteen Countries: An Empirical Study*. Almqvist and Wiksell, Stockholm
Draper N, Smith H 1981 *Applied Regression Analysis*, 2nd edn. Wiley, New York
Geisser S 1974 Contribution of the written discussion of the article by M. Stone. *J. Royal Stat. Soc.* Series B 36: 134–47
Hauser R M 1973 Disaggregating a social–psychological model of educational attainment. In: Goldberger A J, Duncan O D (eds.) 1973 *Structural Equation Models in the Social Sciences*. Seminar Press, New York, pp. 255–84
Jöreskog K G 1973 A general method for estimating a linear structural equation system. In: Goldberger A S, Duncan O D (eds.) 1973 *Structural Equation Models in the Social Sciences*. Seminar Press, New York, pp. 85–112
Kish L 1965 *Survey Sampling*. Wiley, New York
Miller R G 1974 The jackknife: A review. *Biometrika* 61: 1–15
Noonan R D 1976 *School Resources, Social Class, and Student Achievement: A Comparative Study of School Resource Allocation and the Social Distribution of Mathematics Achievement in Ten Countries*. Almqvist and Wiksell, Stockholm
Noonan R D, Wold H 1983 Evaluating school systems using partial least squares. In: Choppin B, Postlethwaite T N (eds.) 1983 *Evaluation in Education: An International Review Series*, Vol. 7, No. 3. Pergamon, Oxford
Sellin N 1986 Partial least squares analysis. *Int. J. Educ. Res.* 10(2): 189–200
Stone M 1974 Cross-validatory choice and assessment of statistical predictions. *J. Royal Stat. Soc.* Series B 36: 111–33
Tukey J W 1977 *Exploratory Data Analysis*. Addison-Wesley, Reading, Massachusetts
Walker D A 1976 *The IEA Six Subject Survey: An Empirical Study of Education in Twenty-one Countries*. Almqvist and Wiksell, Stockholm
Wold H 1965 A fix-point theorem with econometric background. *Arkiv för Matematik* 6: 209–40
Wold H 1966 Nonlinear estimation by iterative least squares procedures. In: David F N (ed.) 1966 *Research Papers in Statistics: Festschrift for J. Neyman*. Wiley, New York, pp. 411–44
Wold H 1975 From hard to soft modelling. In: Wold H (ed.) 1975 Modelling in complex situations with soft information. Group report presented at the Third World Congress of Econometrics, Toronto, 21–26 August
Wold H 1977 Open path models with latent variables. In: Albach H, Halstedter E, Henn R (eds.) 1977 *Kvantative Wirtschaftsforschung: Wilhelm Krelle zum 60. Geburtstag*. Mohr, Tübingen, pp. 729–54
Wold H 1982 Soft modelling: The basic design and some extensions. In: Jöreskog K G, Wold H (eds.) 1982 *Systems under Indirect Observation: Structure, Prediction, Causality*, Vol. 2. Amsterdam, North Holland, Proc. of Conf., Oct. 18–20 1979, Cartigny, Switzerland

Partial Order Scalogram Analysis (POSA)

S. Shye

Partial order scalogram analysis is one of the newer multivariate data analytic techniques for processing and graphically depicting nonmetric data. It is characterized by its focus on order relations that exist among objects, where the objects, in most usages, are the score profiles of individual subjects to be scaled. When analyzing a set of objects, the term order relations means that in some well-defined sense any one of the following relations holds:

(a) Object A is comparable to object B (in symbols: $A \gtrless B$; and then further specification should tell whether
  (i) A is greater than B $(A > B)$; or
  (ii) A is equal to B $(A = B)$; or
  (iii) A is smaller than B $(A < B)$.

(b) Object A is incomparable to object B (in symbols $A \nleqgtr B$).

POSA is employed in order to scale individual subjects according to the scores each has received on a set of tests or variables. Hence POSA is an extension of the unidimensional scale known as the Guttman scale (Guttman 1950) to configurations of higher dimensionalities. Much of the mathematical development of POSA and all of its published applications have been so far with respect to two-dimensional scalogram configurations.

The geometrical depiction afforded by POSA yields the following desiderata for empirical data:

(a) a new profile, of shorter length (fewer scores) than the original one, is assigned to every individual;

(b) the possibility of abstracting fewer (and possibly more "fundamental") variables for the contents investigated.

POSA has been referred to as "nonmetric factor analysis" by Coombs and his associates in their works on partial order models (Coombs and Kao 1955, Coombs 1964). Guttman observed that POSA is but a special case of his multidimensional scalogram analysis (Shye 1978, Zvulun 1978) and applied it to attitude research and to content classification problems (Guttman 1954, 1959, 1972). Since then Guttman's approach to POSA has been employed in various social studies (e.g., Shye and Elizur 1976, Levy 1980). Mathematical studies of POSA and of its relationship to smallest space analysis (SSA) have been carried out by Shye (1976, 1985). A specially developed computer program, POSAC/LSA, permits the processing of empirical data by POSA by computing the best two-dimensional configuration.

The present article covers the following:

(a) An illustration of the essential idea of POSA.

(b) A mathematical formulation of partial order scalograms.

(c) The uses of POSA for structuring concepts and scaling individuals.

1. The Essential Idea of POSA: An Illustration

Suppose each individual in a particular population is observed as to whether he or she possesses each of three traits, T_1, T_2, T_3. An individual receives a score $T_1 = 1$ if he or she possesses trait T_1, and $T_1 = 0$ if not, and similarly for T_2 and T_3. A profile 101, for example, would be assigned to an individual who is observed to possess traits T_1 and T_3 but not T_2. If the three specific traits conceptually represent a single general trait such as health (or sociability, or intelligence, or any other), then an individual with profile 011 may be said to be healthier (or more sociable, etc.) than the one with profile 010 because he has all the specific health traits of the latter $(T_2 = 1)$ as well as additional one(s) $(T_3 = 1)$. Hence 011 and 010 are comparable profiles. These relationships between the two profiles can be represented schematically by a directed graph thus:

If in a given set of profiles all profile pairs are comparable, the set constitutes a perfect scale or a Guttman scale. For example,

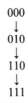

However, two individuals with profiles 110 and 011 are incomparable with respect to their health because the specific health traits of each are different: the former exceeds the latter in one trait (T_1) but falls short of the latter in another trait (T_3). For the same reason, 110 and 001 are incomparable (even though 110 has two specific health traits and 001 only one). (Note that in this analysis the specific traits are not assumed to be of equal weights; in fact their relative weights may be unknown or undefined.)

In a schematic representation, incomparability between profiles is characterized by the absence of a directed line between them. The relations among the four profiles 010, 011, 110 and 001 are representable thus:

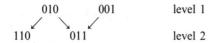

In such partial order diagrams it is customary and helpful to locate all profiles having a similar total score (i.e., the sum of the scores on all tests—here the number of traits possessed) on the same horizontal level of the scalogram. This permits the omission of the arrow heads without causing misunderstanding: the line segments are assumed to point downwards.

In POSA the absence of profiles from the empirical data is presumed to reflect something about the structure of the investigated traits for the population in question. Such absence can often lead to a more economic representation of the data.

Suppose, for example, that in studying a particular population with respect to the three dichotomous traits T_1, T_2, and T_3 the following profiles have been observed:

	T_1	T_2	T_3
profile a	0	0	0
profile b	0	0	1
profile c	0	1	0
profile d	1	0	0
profile e	0	1	1
profile f	1	1	0
profile g	1	1	1

Note that in this list the profile 101 is missing. Under appropriate experimental conditions and with certain assumptions this may mean that this profile is impossible; in other words that the mechanism investigated is such that the occurrence of $T_1 = 1$ and $T_3 = 1$ implies the occurrence of $T_2 = 1$. This structural interdependence among the three traits permits a simplification in the data representation in that the order relations among observed profiles can be illustrated in a two-dimensional space (see Fig. 1) instead of a three-dimensional space, which three traits are expected to produce when they are not interdependent.

That the configuration is indeed two-dimensional is evidenced by the fact that the diagram could be drawn without crossings among the lines segments that

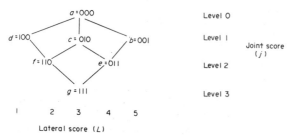

Figure 1
A two-dimensional partial order configuration of three dichotomous traits. Note that if the location of any two profiles (say, 100 and 010) were interchanged, lines would cross

represent comparability relations (note that if the missing profile 101 is added to the diagram, crossings are unavoidable).

Since the seven profiles (*a–g*) contain profiles that are incomparable, they do not form a perfect scale and so their dimensionality cannot be one. Hence two is the minimum partial order dimensionality for that set of profiles.

Given the configuration of Fig. 1, two scores are sufficient to identify a profile (and reproduce all three original scores): one score, the joint score, specifies the level to which the profile belongs; the other, the lateral score, locates the profile within the level. Moreover (in contrast to an arbitrary assignment of identity scores to profiles), the two new scores are likely to have substantive meaning. The question of interpreting the joint and lateral axes will be taken up below.

A more general way of thinking about (and determining) the partial order dimensionality of a given set of observed data is by answering the following question: What is the smallest coordinate space (i.e., the space with the minimum number of coordinates) into which observed profiles can be mapped (as points) such that all original order relations among profiles ("greater than," "smaller than," "incomparable to") are preserved in the coordinate space? For example, the seven profiles, *a–g*, can be mapped into a space of just two coordinates X and Y as shown in the minimal space diagram in Fig. 2.

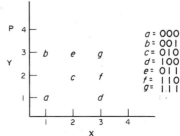

Figure 2
Minimum space diagram for profiles *a* through *g*

As may be verified, the mapping transforms the original three-variable profiles into new two-variable profiles in such a way that the relation between every pair of profiles remains the same after the transformation. For instance, the three-variable profiles $c = 010$ and $e = 011$ are transformed by the mapping (see Fig. 2) into the two-variable profiles 22 and 23 respectively (the XY coordinates of *c* and *e*); and indeed the relation between the original profiles (010 is less than 011) is preserved (22 is less than 23). Considering another pair, the profiles 011 and 110 are incomparable and indeed so are their transformations 23 and 32. The mapping similarly preserves all other order relations among profile pairs.

Although Fig. 1 is essentially topological (the exact profile locations are immaterial), it may be viewed as a rotation of Fig. 2. In well-designed research or assessment excercises, the axes X and Y can be found to correspond to essential factors of the investigated contents.

The concepts discussed above (comparability, partial order dimensionality, etc.) apply to any number (n) of tests (variables) having any number of ordered categories. The partial order dimensionality m may be anywhere between 1 and n ($1 \leq m \leq n$). Since much of the experience with POSA has been with $m = 2$, this article is confined to two-dimensional analysis.

When the number of profiles is small, a two-dimensional POSA can be carried out by hand. For a large number of profiles a computer program, the POSAC/LSA, is available. For a given set of profiles, the program seeks an optimal two-dimensional minimal space diagram as well as a spatial mapping of the analyzed variables in accordance with the role they play in structuring the scalogram (Shye and Amar 1985).

2. Partial Order Scalograms: A Mathematical Formulation

Suppose each of N subjects $p_1, \ldots, p_N$ in a population P receives a score in each of n tests $v_1, \ldots, v_n$ where the range of each test is $A_i = (1, 2, \ldots, \alpha_i)$, where $i = 1, \ldots, n$; and $a_i \geq 2$. Let A_i be regarded as a set ordered by the relations $\alpha_i > , \ldots, > 2 > 1$ and let the cartesian set $A = A_1 \ldots A_n (n \geq 2)$ be looked at. Each component set A_i is called a facet and each element $a \epsilon A$ ($a = a_1 a_2 \ldots a_n$, $a_i \epsilon A_i$) is a profile in the n tests. $a' > a$ if $a_j' \geq a_j$ for all $j = 1, \ldots, n$ and if there exists j', $1 \leq j' \leq n$ with $a_{j'}' > a_{j'}$ (where $a = a_1 \ldots a_n$ and $a' = a = \ldots a_n'$). a' and a are comparable ($a \lessgtr a'$) if $a' > a$, or $a > a'$, or $a' = a$, and otherwise are incomparable ($a' \nleqgtr a$). The score $S(a)$ of a profile a is

$$S(a) = \Sigma_{j=1}^n a_j$$

A scalogram is a mapping $P \to A$ from a population P to the cartesian set A. The subset A' of profiles of A onto which elements of P are mapped, is called the scalogram range, or briefly scalogram. The subset $A(s) \subset A'$ of all profiles having the score s is a level of the scalogram.

If every two profiles in the range A' of a scalogram are comparable, the scalogram is a Guttman scale.

A (and therefore also $A' \subset A$) is a partial order set with respect to the relation $\leq$.

The partial order dimensionality of a scalogram A' is the smallest m ($m \leq n$) for which there exists an m-faceted cartesian set $X = X_i \ldots X_m$, $X_i = 1, 2, \ldots, \xi_i$, $i = 1 \ldots m$ and there exists a 1–1 mapping, $Q: X' \to A'$ from a subset X' of X onto A' so that if $Q(x') = a'$ and $Q(x) = a$ then $a > a' \Leftrightarrow x > x'$.

Figure 3
Partial order diagram of a double scale, for $n = 4$

The function Q is called a conversion and the cartesian set X is called the minimal space of A'. A function $Q^*: X \to A'$ from the entire cartesian set $X = X_1 X_2$ onto A' is a full conversion if it is an extension of a conversion and if for every $x, x' \epsilon X'^c$, $x > x' \Rightarrow a \geq a'$ whenever $Q^*(x) = a$ and $Q^*(x') = a'$.

Some elementary results are shown below.

THEOREM 1. *Let $A' \subset A$ be any scalogram, and let $a' \epsilon A$. The dimensionality of the scalogram $A'' = A' \cup \{a'\}$ is no smaller than that of A'.*

In certain senses (such as reproducibility of the original n scores from a smaller number of scores) the two-dimensional analogues of the one-dimensional Guttman scale are identifiable families of scalograms which can be determined for every given n.

A scalogram in n tests is a double scale if it is made up of exactly two complete scales. If the tests are all dichotomous ($\alpha_i = 2$, $i = 1, \ldots, n$), the scalogram can be characterized as follows: there exists a permutation of the tests which results in the profiles being all of at most two "runs" of digits (and the scalogram contains all such profiles). For example, if $n = 4$ the partial order diagram of a double scale is as shown in Fig. 3.

THEOREM 2. *Double scales are two dimensional for every n.*

A scalogram in n dichotomous tests belongs to the family of diamond scalograms if it contains (after a suitable permutation of the tests) all profiles of n 1's and 2's with at most three runs of digits. For example, if $n = 4$ the partial order diagram of a diamond scalogram is as shown in Fig. 4.

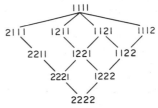

Figure 4
Partial order diagram of a diamond scalogram for $n = 4$

THEOREM 3. *Diamond scalograms are two dimensional for every n.*

Important notions in scalogram theory are those of dense scalograms and standard scalograms. A two-dimensional partial order scalogram is dense if each of its levels can be uniquely ordered so that if two profiles, say $a = a_1 a_2 \ldots a_n$ and $a' = a'_1 a'_2 \ldots a'_n$ are adjacent in that order, then firstly the profile $a \cup a' \equiv \max (a_1, a'_1)$ $\max (a_2, a'_2) \ldots \max (a_n, a'_n)$ and the profile $a \cap a' \equiv \min (a_1, a'_1) \min (a_2, a'_2) \ldots \min (a_n, a'_n)$ are of scores $s + 1$ and $s - 1$ respectively; and secondly, both

$a \cup a'$ and $a \cap a'$ are in the scalogram. For example, double scales are not dense, but diamond scalograms are.

A two-dimensional partial order scalogram is a standard scalogram if it is dense and if every pair of its tests (out of the n tests), crosses (that is, forms a two-dimensional scalogram, or, in other words, no pair of its tests form a Guttman scale). The scalogram shown in Fig. 5, for example, is two-dimensional and dense but is not standard, because two of its tests (the first and second) do form a scale.

In two-dimensional standard scalograms, exactly two tests, the polar tests, can be singled out as being in a sense the "farthest apart" among all test pairs. For instance, the correlation between them (if all profiles occur with equal frequency) is the smallest. This observation is the first step in the analysis of the structural relationship between the "profile (subject) space" (such as the partial order configuration) on the one hand, and the space of tests [such as the space obtained by smallest space analysis (SSA)] on the other hand. The value of polar tests in theoretical applications is that in contrasting their contents a "first approximation" of the meaning of the scalogram lateral axis is afforded.

Mathematical analyses show (Shye 1976, 1985) that in standard scalograms the other (nonpolar) tests further refine the structure of the lateral axis (as well as the X, Y axes) of the scalogram, with a corresponding refinement in the interpretability of these axes. The scalogram axes (J and L; or alternatively X and Y, of Sect. 1 above) are the factors of the contents analyzed, and in this sense scalogram analysis merits the name of "nonmetric factor analysis" proposed by Coombs.

Partial order scalograms structure the observed profiles so that individual subjects may be classified and rated. A structural analysis of the scalogram tests (i.e., variables) on the other hand, can result in a test space that is merely a special version of the smallest space analysis of the tests. Smallest space analysis, that maps tests according to a principle anchored in the roles these tests play in structuring partial order scalograms, is of particular value. Two such versions [termed lattice space analysis (LSA) 1 and 2] have been proposed and applied through the use of the POSAC/LSA computer program.

(a) *LSA 1*. This procedure for mapping scalogram tests is based on the observation that in a standard scalogram considerable information concerning the structure of the interrelationships among scalogram tests is

embodied in the two boundary scales of the scalogram, namely, the scales that envelop the scalogram's partial order diagram. LSA 1 maps the tests in a two-dimensional array so that the polar tests are relatively far apart while all other tests are located in the space according to the order in which they change their values on the boundary scales. This procedure, illustrated below, has been shown to be equivalent to a version of smallest space analysis in which the coefficient of similarity is a newly defined structural (not distributional) coefficient and the metric employed is the lattice ("city block") distance.

(b) *LSA 2*. This procedure is based on the observation that in the minimal space of a two-dimensional partial order scalogram, each test has partitioning lines that divide the space into regions according to the values of that test. For instance, in the minimal space shown in Fig. 2, the vertical line that separates profiles a, b, c, and e from profiles d, f, and g pertains to test T_1. It divides the space into a region where $T_1 = 0$ (profiles a, b, c, e) and another region where $T_1 = 1$ (d, g, f). Similarly, an L-shaped partitioning line separates the region where $T_2 = 0$ (profile a, b, d) from the region where $T_2 = 1$ (profiles c, e, f, g). Now, in the analyses of empirical data involving many variables and possibly some "noise," the partitioning lines do not usually have simple shapes. In LSA 2, each of the scalogram tests is characterized by its similarity (assessed by correlation coefficients) to each of four ideal-type tests. The latter are "pure content" tests which could conceivably be devised for the content universe. They are defined by the shapes of their partitioning lines in the scalogram minimal space diagram: vertical (representing one polar test), horizontal (representing another polar test), L-shaped (representing a moderating test—one whose high values tend to concentrate in the middle of the lateral axis), and inverted L-shaped (representing a polarizing test—one whose high values tend to concentrate in the ends of the lateral axis). The resemblance of each scalogram test to these four ideal types helps determine to what extent it plays the role of one or the other of the two polar tests, or of a moderating test, or of a polarizing test.

3. The Uses of POSA for Structuring Concepts and Scaling Individuals

POSA/LSA is a new and valuable tool for tackling theoretical and practical problems of assessment. Perhaps more than other multivariate procedures it requires the researcher to formulate a clear definition of the concept involved (with respect to which individuals are to be assessed) and to construct variables or tests that cover the definition reasonably well. If that concept (or a well-defined aspect of it) turns out to be two-dimensional in the sense of the partial order scalogram (or even nearly two-dimensional) the pay-off may be considerable: through LSA, variables making up the concept may be characterized according to their role in shaping the concept and in determining the meaning of the scalogram

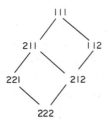

Figure 5
Two-dimensional dense, nonstandard scalogram

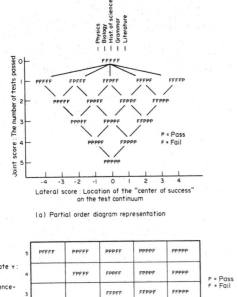

(a) Partial order diagram representation

(b) Minimal space representation

Figure 6
The diamond scalogram hypothesis for passing a series of ordered tests

axes; and the partial order scalogram itself provides an efficient two-score scaling of the individual observed.

POSAC/LSA is a computer program that produces pictorially the best (two-dimensional) minimal space for empirical data, and, in addition, relates that diagram to external variables (variables that are not included in the scalogram itself). Lattice space analysis (LSA) aids the investigator in interpreting the scalogram axes and in testing regional hypothesis.

To demonstrate the interplay between concept definition and scalogram structure, a hypothetical example can be considered.

Suppose a researcher is interested in assessing the educational level of individuals of a given population. One procedure might be to devise n tests which represent, in his or her opinion, the notion of education sufficiently well. The tests may be graduated with respect to their difficulty for the population in question and then a Guttman scale may be expected. If indeed one is empirically obtained, the structure of the concept, as represented by the tests, is the simplest: LSA identifies no polar tests, and exhibits no interpolar spread so the dimensionality of the tests space is, in a sense, 0 and the concept is monolithic. This could occur perhaps if education is defined as general knowledge representable by a series of tests ordered by their difficulty, so that if an

individual passes any one test he or she is sure to pass all easier tests (Elizur and Adler 1975).

However, a more structured definition of "education" may result in a selection of variables whose interdependence is neither so high nor so simple. For instance, the tests may be selected to represent a range of topics such as those taught in schools; and, moreover, the topics may be found to be ordered by some substantive criterion, for example, from the sciences to the humanities (say, physics, biology, history of science, grammar, literature). A possible hypothesis—and a possible result for such a test sampling—could be that pass or fail scoring of the tests would produce a diamond scalogram. The logic of such a scalogram is that if a person passes any two tests in the series he or she also passes all tests that are in between these two in the order specified above. For $n = 5$ tests, the scalogram is given in Fig. 6. Figure 6(a) shows the partial order diagram with its joint (J) and lateral (L) axes; and Fig. 6(b) presents the minimal space diagram with its X and Y axes. Note that here the figures facilitate a clear interpretation for each of the scalogram axes. These interpretations for the J and L axes, or alternatively the X and Y axes, are indeed more fundamental than the original tests and qualify as factors of "education" as constructed and represented by the tests.

Lattice space analysis for the above scalogram identifies the first and the last tests in the series as the two scalogram poles and places all other tests in the expected order on a straight line between the two. The test space for the diamond scalogram is of dimensionality one (akin to Guttman's 1954 simplex) as shown in Fig. 7.

The diamond scalogram is characteristic for certain linear processes. It has been found empirically to accommodate data in a study of exposure to evening television programs (Levinsohn 1980) (the series of tests was: "do you watch television at 7.00 p.m.? at 7.30 p.m.?...at 10.30?"), reflecting the fact that the population investigated tended to switch their television sets on just once, watch for varying lengths of time, and then switch off (and only few switch it on and off more than once).

A more complex definition of education can lead to a more structured scalogram. For instance, it may be

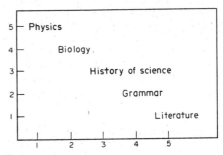

Figure 7
LSA of the diamond scalogram of Fig. 6, hypothesized for a series of tests

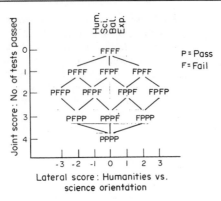

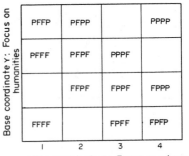

(a) Partial order diagram representation

(b) Minimal space representation

Figure 8
A hypothesized four-test scalogram for "education"

desirable to define education to include not only tests of knowledge but also a test of balanced exposure to areas of knowledge and perhaps also a test of the individual's tendency to study in depth whatever area he or she is knowledgeable in. For simplicity, let just four tests be considered and let it be assumed that they are dichotomous pass/fail tests (each test in turn could be made up of many items having their own internal structure).

Test T_1:	knowledge in the humanities	P/F
Test T_2:	knowledge in the sciences	P/F
Test T_3:	tendency to balance knowledge in the two areas	P/F
Test T_4:	expertise (tendency to study in depth) areas of knowledge	P/F

Given an appropriate design, it may be hypothesized that the profiles FFFP and FFPP in the test $T_1 T_2 T_3 T_4$ respectively would not be observed since lack of knowledge in both the humanities and the sciences could not go together with expertise in any of them. Also the profiles PPFF and PPFP are unlikely to be observed because knowledge in both the humanities and the sciences does indicate—let it be assumed—a balanced exposure to the two areas. A partial order scalogram of the remaining 12 profiles turns out to be two-dimensional. Figure 8 shows this and offers interpretations to the scalogram axes.

Passing T_1 (knowledge in humanities) characterizes the left-hand side of the partial order diagram while passing T_2 (knowledge in sciences) characterizes its right-hand side. Profiles with passing grade in T_3 (balanced knowledge) tend to occur in the middle range of the lateral axis and profiles with passing grade in T_4 (expertise) characterize the extreme ends of that axis. In the language of Sect. 2, T_1 and T_2 are the polar tests of the scalogram; T_3 is a moderating test and T_4 is its polarizing test. The LSA 1 diagram (Fig. 9) describes these roles graphically.

This scalogram, made up of what may be called four ideal-type tests, has been found empirically, for example, in a study of job rewards, the loss of which was feared by a sample of government accounting unit workers, following the introduction of computerized procedures (Shye and Elizur 1976). Fear of loss of job and of loss of interest in work constituted the two polar variables. Fear of encountering difficulties in performing the job and of being transferred to another unit constituted the moderating and the polarizing variables, respectively.

In another example, Antonovsky (1981) relates health to feeling of coherence which in turn he breaks down into (a) manageability; (b) comprehensibility; and (c) meaningfulness, of life situations. Questionnaire items constructed a priori to represent each of the three conceptual categories were found empirically to occupy separate regions in the LSA 2 space, reproduced in Fig. 10. This diagram helped infer the meaning of the lateral axis of the scalogram (obtained by the POSAC/LSA computer program) of the 80 interviewed individuals: manageability and meaningfulness tended to play a polar role, while comprehensibility tended to play a polarizing role.

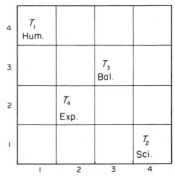

Figure 9
LSA of the scalogram of Fig. 8, hypothesized for four education indicators

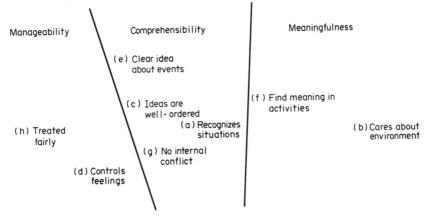

Figure 10
LSA 2 of Antonovsky's "coherence" depicting regional separation of items by three prespecified aspects of coherence

Thus comprehensibility, when present, served to accentuate whatever pole—manageability or meaningfulness—was dominating the other.

See also: Scaling Methods; Scaling of Nominal Data

Bibliography

Antonovsky A 1981 The sense of coherence as a determinant of health. In: Matarazzo J P et al. (eds.) 1981 *Behavioral Health: A Handbook of Health Enhancement and Disease Prevention.* Wiley, New York

Coombs C H 1964 *A Theory of Data.* Wiley, New York

Coombs C H, Kao R C 1955 *Nonmetric Factor Analysis.* University of Michigan Press, Ann Arbor, Michigan

Elizur D, Adler I 1975 *Information Deprivation.* Israel Institute of Applied Social Research, Jerusalem

Guttman L 1950 The basis for scalogram analysis. In: Stauffer S A et al. (eds.) 1950 *Measurement and Prediction,* Vol. 4. Princeton University Press, Princeton, New Jersey

Guttman L 1954 A new approach to factor analysis: The Radex. In: Lazarsfeld P F (ed.) 1954 *Mathematical Thinking in the Social Sciences.* Free Press, New York

Guttman L 1959 A structural theory for intergroup beliefs and action. *Am. Sociol. Rev.* 24: 318–28

Guttman L 1972 A partial-order scalogram classification of projective techniques. In: Hammer M, Salzinger K, Sutton S (eds.) 1972 *Psychopathology: Contributions from the Social, Behavioral, and Biological Sciences.* Wiley, New York

Levinsohn H 1980 *Patterns of TV Viewing and Radio Listening Among the Arab Population in Israel.* Israel Institute of Applied Social Research, Jerusalem

Levy S 1980 *Partly Ordered Social Stratification.* Israel Institute of Applied Social Research, Jerusalem

Shye S 1976 *Partial Order Scalogram Analysis of Profiles and its Relationship to the Smallest Space Analysis of the Variables.* Israel Institute of Applied Social Research, Jerusalem

Shye S 1978 Partial order scalogram analysis. In: Shye S (ed.) 1978 *Theory Construction and Data Analysis in the Behavioral Sciences.* Jossey-Bass, San Francisco, California, pp. 265–79

Shye S 1985 *Multiple Scaling.* North-Holland, Amsterdam

Shye S, Amar R 1985 Partial order scalogram analysis by base coordinates and lattice mapping of the items by their scalogram roles. In: Canter D (ed.) in press *Facet Theory: Approaches to Social Research.* Springer, New York

Shye S, Elizur D 1976 Worries about deprivation of job rewards following computerization: A partial order scalogram analysis. *Human Relations* 29: 63–71

Zvulun E 1978 Multidimensional scalogram analysis: The method and its application. In: Shye S (ed.) 1978 *Theory Construction and Data Analysis in the Behavioral Sciences.* Jossey-Bass, San Francisco, California, pp. 237–64

Path Analysis

J. P. Keeves

Since the 1960s there have been considerable advances in the procedures available for examining complex causal relationships in sociological and educational investigations through the use of the technique of path analysis. The developments follow those undertaken earlier in the field of genetics and more recently in economics. These techniques have been introduced into studies in the social sciences by Blalock (1961), Duncan (1966), and Blalock (1968). Articles by Land (1969), Heise (1969), and Duncan (1969) have served to systematize the procedures being used and to clarify some of the issues involved. Rudimentary use was made of path analysis in the field of educational research by Burks (1928), but the procedure lay dormant for over 40 years in education until used by Peaker (1971) in England.

The approach employing these techniques enables the investigator to shift from verbal statements of a complex set of interrelationships between variables to more precise mathematical ones and to estimate the magnitudes of the causal links involved. In this article the development of a causal model for the home environment is considered and some of the principles and assumptions of the method are discussed. This treatment draws heavily on articles by D. E. Stokes under the title "Compound Paths in Political Analysis" in Volume 5 of *Mathematical Applications in Political Science* and "Compound Paths: An Explanatory Note" in *American Journal of Political Science*. The article is not intended to be an exhaustive discussion of either the problems associated with the use of path analysis in interpreting multivariate systems or of gains to be made in educational research from its use.

1. Towards a Causal Model of the Educational Environment of the Home

The example considered is taken from a study reported by Keeves (1972). A model of the educational environment of the home contains causal relationships between the structural, attitudinal, and process dimensions of the home and the achievement of the child at school. The structural characteristics of the home, such as the occupational status of the head of household, the level of education of the parents and the income of the head of household influence the attitudes and ambitions of the parents for the child. Furthermore, both the structural and attitudinal dimensions of the home influence the processes of the home which assist the child at school.

The causal paths in the model can be viewed as three connected steps: first, the structural characteristics influence the attitudes of the parents; secondly, the attitudes affect the processes of the home; and thirdly, the structural characteristics of the home may directly influence the processes. Figure 1 shows these relationships.

Each of these three dimensions may influence educational outcomes, and of these three the influence of the processes of the home is beyond question. The evidence available from other studies also shows that the attitudes of parents influence the child's performance. However, it is questionable whether structural characteristics of the home independently exert an influence, or

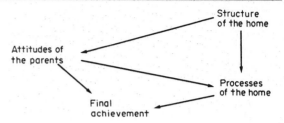

Figure 2
Effects of the educational environment of the home on student achievement

whether their effects only take place indirectly through the attitudes and processes of the home. For simplicity a causal link will not be assumed in this model.

This discussion has developed a more elaborate pattern of relationships for the effects of the educational environment of the home on student achievement (see Fig. 2). These relationships suggest a simple causal model of the influence of the environment of the home on student achievement.

Let X_1 denote the structure of the home, X_2 the attitudes of the parents, X_3 the processes of the home, and X_4 the final achievement of the student.

It will in addition be of value to show explicitly the operation of the disturbance or residual forces which arise from outside the model itself. Let the parts of the attitudes of the parents, the processes of the home, and the final achievement of the student which are not determined by the variables included in the system be denoted by R_u, R_v, and R_w respectively. Figure 3 employs this notation.

The following conventions are employed in the path diagram:

(a) A causal relationship is indicated by a unidirectional arrow from the determining variable to the variable dependent on it.

(b) A noncausal correlation between variables that are not dependent on other variables in the system is indicated by a bidirectional curved arrow. The magnitude of a noncausal correlation is indicated by the zero-order correlation coefficient between the two variables (r_{ij}), but such a correlation is not present in the model.

(c) Causal relationships which involve disturbance variables and represent forces outside the system, not correlated with the variables immediately determining the dependent variables, are indicated by unidirectional arrows from the disturbance variables under consideration.

(d) The magnitude of the relationship associated with an arrow, indicating one-way causation in the path diagram, is given by a path coefficient (p_{ij}), where i denotes the dependent variable and j denotes the independent or determining variable.

Figure 3 shows that in this system there are no non-causal relationships between the variables that are not

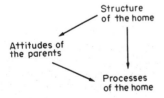

Figure 1
Causal model of the educational environment of the home

dependent on other variables. Those variables not dependent on other variables are known as "exogenous variables", while the variables that are dependent on others are known as "endogenous variables". In addition, in this system there are no variables that are linked by reciprocal causation or feedback. A model where there is a hierarchical arrangement of variables and where there is no feedback is known as a "recursive" model.

While the type of diagram shown in Fig. 3 is an aid to investigators in clarifying their thoughts, it is more than a heuristic device of this kind, because from it mathematical relationships between the variables can be derived and stated in the form of a set of simultaneous equations exhibiting the structure of the model.

2. Formulating the Mathematical Equations

To begin with, variable X_2, the attitudes of the home, will be considered and the structural equation stated:

$$X_2 = p_{21} X_1 + p_{2u} R_u \qquad (1)$$

This equation states that X_2 is determined partly by X_1 and partly by the influence of disturbance variables outside the model represented by the unmeasured residual variable R_u. Several points should be observed with respect to this equation.

First, the relationship between the variables is linear. Whether a linear relationship is acceptable must depend on the assumptions made in setting up the model. If a more complex relationship is hypothesized then appropriate transformations must be used.

Secondly, the equation does not include an "intercept" term. Such a term has been removed by adjusting each variable to a zero mean. The variables X_1 and X_2 will satisfy this requirement if they are scored in standard form with a mean of zero and with unit variance or standard deviation. Thus the expected value $E(X_i)$ of X_i for any i under such a method of scoring will be zero, that is, $E(X_i) = 0$. An assumption which is similar must be made for R_u, so that the mean or expectation of R_u vanishes; that is, $E(R_u) = 0$.

Thirdly, a further advantage obtained from the use of standard scores is that the covariance of any two variables will be equal to their product–moment correlation that is $E(X_i X_j) = r_{ij}$ for any i and j. By extension for all i, $E(X_i X_i) = E(X_i^2) = 1$.

It is also assumed that the disturbance variables have unit variance so that $E(R_u^2) = 1$. The advantage of this

is that the path coefficient p_{2u} associated with this disturbance variable may be compared directly with the other path coefficients of the model.

Although it simplifies the mathematical treatment to use variables which are expressed in standard form it is not essential that this should be done. An alternative approach using the covariance matrix instead of the correlation matrix employs partial regression coefficients (c_{ij}). In such cases the variables are expressed in terms of units with a clear substantive meaning. This may be preferred to the expression of the variables in standard form.

Fourthly, it is also necessary to assume that a residual or disturbance variable is uncorrelated with the predetermined variables which are included in the same equation. It is therefore assumed that the correlation between R_u and X_1 vanishes, that is, $r_{1u} = E(X_1 R_u) = 0$. The investigator must rely on his or her understanding of the research problem to know whether such an assumption is reasonable.

It is also possible to write down a structural equation for the second endogenous variable, the processes of the home:

$$X_3 = p_{31} X_1 + p_{32} X_2 + p_{3v} R_v \qquad (2)$$

This indicates that the processes of the home are partly determined by the structure of the home, partly by the attitudes of the home, and partly by the disturbances given by R_v.

In addition it is possible to write down the structural equation for final achievement in terms of the attitudes of the home, the processes of the home, and the appropriate residual variable:

$$X_4 = p_{42} X_2 + p_{43} X_3 + p_{4w} R_w \qquad (3)$$

The fact that X_1 is not included in this equation arises from the assumption that the structure of the home does not directly influence the achievement of the student at school.

It should be noted that not only is the residual term R_w assumed to be uncorrelated with X_2 and X_3 variables appearing in Eqn. (3), but it must also be assumed to be uncorrelated with X_1, since X_2 and X_3 are partially built from X_1.

The strength of the procedure outlined above lies not in the stating of these three equations, but in the fact that the terms for p_{ij} included in the equations can be expressed in ways that allow their estimation from observed data.

3. Estimating Path Coefficients

The method employed in estimating the path coefficients involves multiplying each structural equation of the model by the predetermined variables in the equation, taking expectations, and examining each term to see whether it will vanish or whether it can be estimated from observed data.

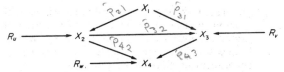

Figure 3
Operation of the disturbance or residual forces arising from outside the model shown in Fig. 2

Consider the structural equation for X_2 given by Eqn. (1). Multiplying this equation by X_1, the only pre-determined variable included in it gives

$$X_1 X_2 = X_1(p_{21}X_1 + p_{2u}R_u) \tag{4}$$
$$= p_{21}X_1^2 + p_{2u}X_1 R_u$$

Taking the expectations of each term gives

$$E(X_1 X_2) = E(p_{21}X_1^2 + p_{2u}X_1 R_u)$$
$$= p_{21}E(X_1^2) + p_{2u}E(X_1 R_u) \tag{5}$$

Since the variables X_1 and X_2 are expressed in standard form, $E(X_1 X_2) = r_{12}$ and $E(X_1^2) = 1$. Moreover, since R_u is uncorrelated with X_1 then $E(X_1 R_u) = 0$. Equation (5) reduces to $\hat{p}_{21} = r_{12}$.

The estimate of the parameter has been derived in terms of the observed correlation between X_1 and X_2. Since, however, in the bivariate case when both variables are expressed in standard form the correlation and regression coefficients have identical values, the estimate of p_{21} is given by the standardized partial regression coefficient β_{21}. The derivation of the estimates of p_{31} and p_{32} is complicated by the presence of two predetermined variables X_1 and X_2 in the structural equation for X_3.

First, the structural equation given in Eqn. (2) above is multiplied by X_1 giving

$$X_1 X_3 = X_1(p_{31}X_1 + p_{32}X_2 + p_{3v}R_v)$$
$$= p_{31}X_1^2 + p_{32}X_1 X_2 + p_{3v}X_1 R_v \tag{6}$$

Taking the expectations of each term gives

$$E(X_1 X_3) = E(p_{31}X_1^2 + p_{32}X_1 X_2 + p_{3v}X_1 R_v)$$
$$= p_{31}E(X_1^2) + p_{32}E(X_1 X_2) \tag{7}$$
$$+ p_{3v}E(X_1 R_v)$$

Since the variables are expressed in standard form, then

$$E(X_1 X_3) = r_{13}, \ E(X_1^2) = 1, \text{ and } E(X_1 X_2) = r_{12} \tag{8}$$

Moreover since R_v is uncorrelated with X_1, then $E(X_1 R_v) = 0$. Equation (7) simplifies to

$$r_{13} = p_{31} + p_{32}r_{12} \tag{9}$$

This gives a relation between the parameters p_{31} and p_{32} in terms of the two observed correlations r_{12} and r_{13}.

In a similar manner by multiplying Eqn. (2) for X_3 by the second of its predetermined variables X_2 the following equation is obtained:

$$X_2 X_3 = p_{31}X_1 X_2 + p_{32}X_2^2 + p_{3v}X_2 R_v \tag{10}$$

Taking the expected values of each term gives

$$E(X_2 X_3) = p_{31}E(X_1 X_2) + p_{32}E(X_2^2)$$
$$+ p_{3v}E(X_2 R_v) \tag{11}$$

Since the variables are in standard form and since R_v is uncorrelated with X_2, Eqn. (10) simplifies to

$$r_{23} = p_{31}r_{12} + p_{32} \tag{12}$$

This gives the relation between the same two parameters p_{31} and p_{32} in terms of the two observed correlations r_{12}

and r_{23}. The two equations (9) and (12) have two unknowns and may be solved by simple algebra to give the following two estimates:

$$\hat{p}_{31} = \frac{r_{13} - r_{12}r_{23}}{1 - r_{12}^2} \tag{13}$$

$$\hat{p}_{32} = \frac{r_{23} - r_{12}r_{13}}{1 - r_{12}^2} \tag{14}$$

These expressions are identical to the formulas for the standardized partial regression coefficients $\beta_{31.2}$ and $\beta_{32.1}$.

If it were inappropriate to express the variables in standard form, similar formulas could be derived for a metric path coefficient c_{ij}, for example

$$\hat{c}_{31} = \frac{b_{31} - b_{32}b_{21}}{1 - b_{12}b_{21}} \tag{15}$$

where b_{21}, b_{31}, b_{12}, and b_{32} are regression coefficients computed from observed data. In this form $\hat{c}_{31}$ is identical to the last squares estimator for the partial regression coefficient in raw or deviation score form. Under these circumstances the path regression coefficients can be derived from a regression analysis based on the covariance matrix, where the partial regression coefficients are not in standard score form.

In order to estimate the parameters of the structural equation for the third endogenous variable, X_4, given in Eqn. (3) above, each term is multiplied by X_2, expectations are taken, and the resulting terms are interpreted to obtain the equation

$$r_{24} = p_{42} + p_{43}r_{23} \tag{16}$$

Similarly, multiplying by X_3 instead of X_2, the following is obtained:

$$r_{34} = p_{42}r_{23} + p_{43} \tag{17}$$

Equations (16) and (17) may be solved for their two unknowns giving the following estimates:

$$\hat{p}_{42} = \frac{r_{24} - r_{23}r_{34}}{1 - r_{23}^2} = \beta_{42.3} \tag{18}$$

$$\hat{p}_{43} = \frac{r_{34} - r_{23}r_{24}}{1 - r_{23}^2} = \beta_{43.2} \tag{19}$$

If Eqn. (3) is multiplied by X_1 instead, the following is obtained:

$$X_1 X_4 = p_{42}X_1 X_2 + p_{43}X_1 X_3 + p_{4w}X_1 R_w \tag{20}$$

Moreover, since all variables are in standard form and R_w is uncorrelated with X_1 as well as with X_2 and X_3, on taking expectations and simplifying the equation further, the following is obtained:

$$r_{14} = p_{42}r_{12} + p_{43}r_{13} \tag{21}$$

The equation gives the parameters p_{42} and p_{43} in terms of certain observed correlations. Under these circumstances a check can be applied to the validity of the assumptions, particularly concerning the independence of the disturbance variables and the appropriateness of excluding the path between variables X_4 and X_1 from the path model by substituting in Eqn. (20).

In cases where the model is overdetermined in this way a check on the adequacy of the causal model can be applied.

If it were found from a check that an inconsistency existed then the causal path between variables X_4 and X_1 could be inserted and the structural equation for X_4 rewritten to include a term for X_1:

$$X_4 = p_{41} X_1 + p_{42} X_2 + p_{43} X_3 + p_{4w} R_w \qquad (22)$$

With this term included, the structural equation for X_4 is now fully determined, and by multiplying through by X_1, X_2, and X_3 in turn, taking expectations, and simplifying, relationships for p_{41}, p_{42}, and p_{43} can be obtained in terms of observed coefficients. It should be noted that the estimates are again equivalent to the standardized partial regression coefficients, and the use of regression analysis procedures simplifies the computational work required.

Using these procedures the assumption could be checked that the causal path between the variables X_4 and X_1 could be deleted without loss, by calculating a value for p_{41}, and arguing that if it were nonsignificant or negligible it could be safely dropped.

To obtain the path coefficients associated with the disturbance variables, the methods already used can be extended. If Eqn. (1) for X_2 is multiplied by R_u, the following is obtained:

$$X_2 R_u = p_{21} X_1 R_u + p_{2u} R_u^2 \qquad (23)$$

Taking expectations gives

$$E(X_2 R_u) = p_{21} E(X_1 R_u) + p_{2u} E(R_u^2) \qquad (24)$$

Since R_u is uncorrelated with X_1, then $E(X_1 R_u) = 0$. Equation (24) can be simplified by noting further that if X_2 and (by assumption) R_u are expressed in standard form, then $E(X_2 R_u) = r_{2u}$ and $E(R_u^2) = 1$. The equation becomes

$$r_{2u} = p_{2u} \qquad (25)$$

Although Eqn. (25) is not of direct assistance in evaluating p_{2u} because R_u is unmeasured and r_{2u} is unobserved, Eqn. (1) containing X_2 can be multiplied by X_2 itself:

$$X_2^2 = p_{21} X_1 X_2 + p_{2u} R_u X_2 \qquad (26)$$

Taking expectations and simplifying gives

$$E(X_2^2) = p_{21} E(X_1 X_2) + p_{2u} E(R_u X_2) \qquad (27)$$

hence

$$1 = p_{21} r_{12} + p_{2u} r_{2u} \qquad (28)$$

Since $p_{2u} = r_{2u}$,

$$p_{2u}^2 = 1 - p_{21} r_{12} \qquad (29)$$

$$p_{2u} = (1 - p_{21} r_{12})^{1/2} \qquad (30)$$

In a similar manner the following relationship could be derived from Eqn. (22):

$$1 = p_{41} r_{14} + p_{42} r_{24} + p_{43} r_{34} + p_{4w} r_{4w} \qquad (31)$$

If $p_{4w} = r_{4w}$ is substituted, the following is obtained:

$$p_{4w}^2 = 1 - (p_{41} r_{14} + p_{42} r_{24} + p_{43} r_{34}) \qquad (32)$$

It should be noted, however, that $p_{41} = \beta_{41.23}$, $p_{42} = \beta_{42.13}$, and $p_{43} = \beta_{43.12}$ whence

$$p_{4w} = (1 - r_{14} \beta_{41.23} - r_{24} \beta_{42.13} - r_{34} \beta_{43.12})^{1/2} \qquad (33)$$

Furthermore it is known that

$$r_{14} \beta_{41.23} + r_{24} \beta_{42.13} + r_{34} \beta_{43.12} = R^2$$

$$\text{whence } p_{4w} = (1 - R^2)^{1/2} \qquad (34)$$

Equation (34) is more convenient to use in practice than any other equation because the multiple correlation coefficient R has commonly been calculated. In addition, it should be noted that R^2, the square of the multiple correlation coefficient, is the proportional variance in the criterion variable X_4 accounted for by the three predictor variables X_1, X_2 and X_3. R^2 is called the coefficient of multiple determination.

4. The Basic Theorem of Path Analysis

The above approach from first principles can be summarized in terms of the basic theorem of path analysis. It may be stated in the general form

$$r_{ij} = \sum_k p_{ik} \cdot r_{jk} \qquad (35)$$

where i and j denote two variables in the system and the index k includes all variables from which paths lead directly to X_i. This allows the mathematical relations between the variables to be expressed as a set of linear equations, called the path model:

$$r_{12} = p_{21}$$
$$r_{13} = p_{31} + p_{32} r_{12}$$
$$r_{23} = p_{32} + p_{31} r_{13}$$
$$r_{14} = p_{41} + p_{42} r_{12} + p_{43} r_{13}$$
$$r_{24} = p_{42} + p_{41} r_{12} + p_{43} r_{23}$$
$$r_{34} = p_{43} + p_{41} r_{13} + p_{42} r_{23}$$

These equations can be solved to obtain the six path coefficients in terms of the observed correlation coefficients.

An important extension of the theorem expressed in Eqn. (35) is when $i = j$, then

$$r_{ii} = 1 = \sum_k p_{ik} \cdot r_{ik} \qquad (36)$$

This relationship enables the path coefficient of a disturbance variable to be calculated as discussed above.

5. A Necessary Extension of the Model

If interest exists in the influence of the educational environment on change in achievement, allowance must be made for initial achievement. Experience suggests that not only does initial achievement influence the final achievement of the child, but it also influences the attitudes of the parents and their practices, and so affects the home environment in which the child lives. Although it appears improbable that the prior achievement of the child would influence the structural characteristics of the home, a causal link between the structure of the home and initial level of achievement contains many ambiguities. Consequently the relationship between these two components of the model is best represented by a noncausal correlation.

These further complexities can be incorporated into the path diagram for the causal model of the home environment. According to these conventions the path diagram for the causal model of the home environment is shown in Fig. 4.

The relationships between these variables are expressed in terms of the path model which is the set of linear equations. This set of equations can be solved and the path coefficients can be derived in terms of the zero-order correlations between the variables. The model associated with Fig. 4 represents a completely identified system of linear equations, and under these conditions the path coefficients are the partial regression coefficients obtained from a regression analysis of the variables expressed in standard form. From an analysis of the data associated with the three dimensions of the home environment and initial and final performance, it is possible not only to estimate the parameters of the model but also to test the causal relationships in the model for significance and consistency.

5.1 An Example

Table 1 shows the intercorrelation between the three home variables and scores on the mathematics and science tests administered at both time 1 and time 2.

The data collected at time 1 were used for calculating the measures for both the structural and attitudinal dimensions and data gathered at time 2 were used for

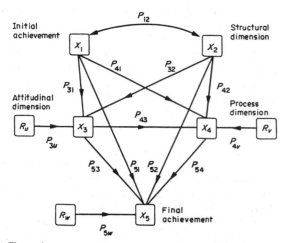

Figure 4
A path diagram for a causal model of the home environment

728

Table 1
Correlations between the structural, attitudinal, and process dimensions and the mathematics and science test scores

No.	$N = 215$ Variable	1	2	3
1	Structure dimension (t_1)	1.00	0.67	0.45
2	Attitudes dimension (t_1)	0.67	1.00	0.63
3	Process dimension (t_2)	0.45	0.63	1.00

	1	2	3	
Mathematics (t_1)	0.43	0.52	0.54	*Maths* (t_1)
Mathematics (t_2)	0.45	0.56	0.52	0.83
Science (t_1)	0.35	0.49	0.48	*Science* (t_1)
Science (t_2)	0.40	0.55	0.45	0.76

the process dimension of the home. In this way a temporal sequence was maintained between the variables in the causal path diagram.

5.2 Results

(a) *Achievement in mathematics.* Since a causal path had not been proposed for the relationship between the structural dimension of the home and prior achievement, the association between these measures was given by the correlation coefficient ($r = 0.43$). The path coefficients were estimated by multiple regression analysis and the following values were obtained. For the endogenous variables: $p_{31} = 0.28$; $p_{32} = 0.54$; $p_{41} = 0.28$; $p_{42} = 0.01$; $p_{43} = 0.48$; $p_{51} = 0.73$; $p_{52} = 0.03$; $p_{53} = 0.15$; $p_{54} = 0.02$. For the disturbance variables: $p_{3u} = 0.70$; $p_{4v} = 0.73$; $p_{5w} = 0.54$.

These values have been inserted in the path diagram shown in Fig. 5.

The estimated path coefficients showed that neither the structural dimension nor the process dimension made a significant contribution to final achievement test scores in mathematics although their influence was positive. Furthermore, the process dimension depended little on the structural characteristics of the home, being influenced mainly by the prior achievement of the child and the attitudes of the home. However, the attitudes of the home were influenced both by the structural variables and by prior achievement in mathematics.

Seventy-one percent of the variance in the achievement test scores in mathematics was accounted for by the components of this model. In part, the unexplained variance could be attributed to error, but some might well be accounted for by practices of the home that were not included in this analysis.

(b) *Achievement in science.* The correlation between the structural dimension of the home and initial achievement in science was found to be 0.35, and gave the association between characteristics of the home background and performance in science at the beginning of the first year in secondary school.

The path coefficients were estimated by multiple regression analysis and the values obtained have been recorded below. For the endogenous variables: $p_{31} = 0.29$; $p_{32} = 0.56$; $p_{41} = 0.22$; $p_{42} = 0.04$; $p_{43} = 0.50$;

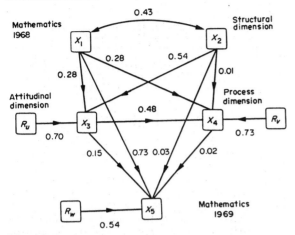

Figure 5
Path diagram for achievement in mathematics with estimates of the path coefficients

$p_{51} = 0.61$; $p_{52} = 0.02$; $p_{53} = 0.15$; $p_{54} = 0.14$. For the disturbance variables: $p_{3u} = 0.69$; $p_{4v} = 0.75$; $p_{5w} = 0.61$. These values have been inserted in the path diagram shown in Fig. 6.

The estimated path coefficients for achievement in science were similar to those obtained for achievement in mathematics except that prior achievement in science was less strongly related to final achievement, and the process dimension made a significant contribution. While the structural variable strongly influenced the attitudes of the home, it had little effect on both the process dimension and final achievement. Furthermore, initial achievement had a clear influence on both the attitudes of the home and the process dimension.

Only 63 percent of the variance in the achievement test scores in science was accounted for by the variables included in this analysis, and it was probable that other characteristics of the home environment influencing achievement could be identified and assessed.

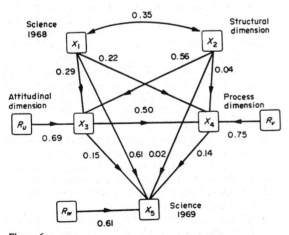

Figure 6
Path diagram for achievement in science with estimates of the path coefficients

In the path models considered above, all causal links have been specified and their path coefficients estimated. These models could be reexamined and the nonsignificant causal paths deleted in order to simplify the models.

6. *The Examination of Compound Paths*

It is of interest to analyse the compound paths and to estimate the contributions of the various paths to the outcomes. In a recursive system, wherever an endogenous variable is determined in part by other variables that are endogenous it is possible to express the structural equation for a variable later in the system in terms of path coefficients associated with variables that are earlier in the system. The procedure is straightforward. The structural equation for X_3 includes one endogenous variable X_2. The relation given by the structural equation for X_2 [Eqn. (1) above] can be used to substitute for X_2 in Eqn. (2) for X_3:

$$
\begin{aligned}
X_3 &= p_{32} X_2 + p_{31} X_1 + p_{3v} R_v \\
&= p_{32}(p_{21} X_1 + p_{2u} R_u) + p_{31} X_1 + p_{3v} R_v \\
&= (p_{31} + p_{32} p_{21}) X_1 + p_{32} p_{2u} R_u + p_{3v} R_v \quad (37)
\end{aligned}
$$

Equation (37) shows that X_3 can be written as a linear combination in which X_1 enters twice, each time with a weight equal to the product of the elementary path coefficients associated with one of the possible traverses between X_1 and X_3. The remaining portion of X_3 is shown by the equation to be a linear combination of the disturbance influences R_u and R_v.

If each term is now multiplied by X_1 the following is obtained:

$$
\begin{aligned}
X_1 X_3 &= (p_{31} + p_{32} p_{21}) X_1^2 + p_{32} p_{2u} R_u X_1 \\
&\quad + p_{3v} R_v X_1 \quad (38)
\end{aligned}
$$

Taking expectations gives

$$
\begin{aligned}
E(X_1 X_3) &= (p_{31} + p_{32} p_{21}) E(X_1^2) \\
&\quad + p_{32} p_{2u} E(R_u X_1) + p_{3v} E(R_v X_1) \quad (39)
\end{aligned}
$$

This simplifies to

$$
r_{13} = p_{31} + p_{32} p_{21} \quad (40)
$$

In a similar manner the correlation between X_1 and X_4 in the simpler case considered above where there was no direct causal path between X_1 and X_4 can be expressed in terms of path coefficients as follows:

$$
r_{14} = p_{42} p_{21} + p_{43} p_{31} + p_{43} p_{32} p_{21} \quad (41)
$$

In this way the correlation between the structural dimension of the home and final achievement can be written as the sum of three terms which correspond to the three alternative pathways of influence originally proposed. Each term is the product of the elementary path coefficients associated with the individual steps along the pathways.

Duncan has shown that the expression in Eqn. (35) can be expanded by successive applications of the formula itself to r_{jk}. Expressions in expanded form can be read directly from the path diagram by using the following rule:

> Read back from variable *i*, *then forward* to variable *j*, forming the product of all paths along the traverse; then sum these products for all possible traverses. (Duncan 1966 p. 6)

This rule allows the investigator to express any correlation between coefficients associated with each of the admissible traverses between the variables. It may, however, be more instructive to derive from first principles such expressions of the relationship between two variables.

To express the relationship between two variables in this way is particularly illuminating when:

(a) the correlation is built up completely from indirect effects of one on the other as has been indicated in the case between variables X_1 and X_4;

(b) the correlation of the earlier variable with the later is only partly the result of the influence of the first on the second and partly the result of the common influences on both of still earlier variables of the system;

(c) the correlation of two variables in a recursive system is entirely the result of common influences on both and not the result of the influence of one on the other.

7. Errors of Measurement

One of the major difficulties facing the use of path analysis in sociological and educational research may, however, be the errors of measurement that appear inevitable in the investigations carried out. Both random errors which typically lead to an underestimation of correlation and regression coefficients as well as nonrandom errors, which since they may be contrary to the assumption that disturbance variables are uncorrelated with variables earlier in the model may have a serious distorting effect. It is not difficult to believe that bias and errors of response associated with survey measurement have distorted some of the results of tests of structural models which have employed interview data.

The problems of such errors can be faced in several ways. First, the design of the measuring instruments can be improved, so that they have greater validity and reliability. Secondly, the error may be measured well enough to include its effects in more complex but more realistic structural models. Thirdly, a more systematic study of error may be undertaken so that corrections for attenuation can be applied to correlation coefficients, and more accurate estimations for missing data, which are inevitable in survey studies, can be utilized. With additional information on the reliability of the measures included in an analysis it is possible to examine a complex model using maximum likelihood procedures instead of the least squares regression procedures outlined in this article.

7.1 Alternative Models and Procedures

Jöreskog and Sörbom (1982) have employed structural equation modeling to reexamine the path model developed and tested above for the influence of the home environment on achievement in mathematics. In their alternative model, errors of measurement in the home variables are taken into account, and the three dimensions of the home environment are treated as fallible indicators of an aggregate construct variable "home". In addition, they have assumed that the achievement measures have a reliability of 0.90 in order to estimate both the direct effects of "home" on final achievement as well as the indirect effects of "home" mediated through initial achievement. An acceptable level of fit is obtained with this model. In addition, Keeves (1986) has examined different models and different procedures of analysis, including regression analysis, canonical analysis, LISREL, factorial modeling, partial least squares path analysis and hierarchical linear modeling, using the same set of data. It is apparent that using path analytic approach, models derived from theory can be tested by a variety of statistical techniques. The conditions under which the different techniques should be employed have yet to be clarified.

See also: Multivariate Analysis; Regression Analysis

Bibliography

Blalock H M 1961 *Causal Inferences in Nonexperimental Research.* University of North Carolina Press, Chapel Hill, North Carolina

Blalock H M 1968 Theory building and causal inferences. In: Blalock H M, Blalock A B (eds.) 1968 *Methodology in Social Research.* McGraw-Hill, New York, pp. 155–98

Burks B S 1928 *The Relative Influence of Nature and Nurture upon Mental Development: A Comparative Study of Foster Parent–Foster Child Resemblance and True Parent–Child Resemblance.* National Society for the Study of Education, Chicago, Illinois, pp. 219–316

Duncan O D 1966 Path analysis: Sociological examples. *Am. J. Sociol.* 72: 1–16

Duncan O D 1969 Contingencies in constructing causal models. In: Borgatta E F (ed.) 1969 *Sociological Methodology 1969.* Jossey-Bass, San Francisco, California

Heise D R 1969 Problems in path analysis and causal inference. In: Borgatta E F (ed.) 1969 *Sociological Methodology 1969.* Jossey-Bass, San Francisco, California

Jöreskog K G, Sörbom D 1982 Recent developments. *J. Marketing Res.* 19: 404–16

Keeves J P 1972 *Educational Environment and Student Achievement.* Almqvist and Wiksell, Stockholm

Keeves J P 1986 Aspiration, motivation and achievement: Different methods of analysis and different results. *Int. J. Educ. Res.* 10(2): 117–243

Land K C 1969 Principles of path analysis. In: Borgatta E F (ed.) 1969 *Sociological Methodology 1969.* Jossey-Bass, San Francisco, California

Peaker G F 1971 *The Plowden Children Four Years Later.* National Foundation for Educational Research, Slough

Stokes D E 1968 Compound paths in political analysis. *Mathematical Applications in Political Science* 5

Stokes D E 1974 Compound paths: An explanatory note. *Am. J. Polit. Sci.* 18: 191–214

Profile Analysis

J. P. Keeves

In analysing and recording the findings of many investigations in the field of education, comparisons are made between persons or groups of persons in terms of a set of measurements on specific related characteristics. Thus for each person or group of persons a profile is obtained on a set of variables. The comparison between profiles for persons or groups on the same set of variables is known by the generic term "profile analysis". The term "profile" is derived from the practice, common in educational research, of plotting as a graph or profile, the scores of a person or a group on a battery of tests, expressed either as raw scores or as standard scores which have been standardized separately for each variable over all persons in the investigation. The investigator who wishes to make comparisons between persons or between groups should pay particular attention to the choice of variables to be used in the set making up the profile.

Nunnally (1967) has drawn attention to the fact that there are three major features of the score profile for any person or group of persons: level, dispersion, and shape. Level is defined as the mean score of the person or group over the set of variables in the profile. The concept of level can only be employed if the variables are concerned with similar properties of an individual or group and it is appropriate to add together the scores and calculate a mean. Dispersion of a score profile is related to the scatter or spread of the scores and indicates the extent to which the scores of the profile diverge from the average. A measure of dispersion is the standard deviation of the scores for each person or group from the mean score or level. The third characteristic of a profile is its shape, and an indicator of shape is the rank order of scores for each person or group. Thus it would be possible for two persons or groups to have profiles at the same level and with the same dispersion, but to differ markedly in shape.

Studies in which profiles have been compared have used a large number of techniques for assessing profile similarity (Cronbach and Gleser 1953). A common approach to the assessment of profile similarity is to consider the measurements which have been made on the set of variables as coordinates, and the scores of a person on the variables as a point in the space defined by ordinates or dimensions associated with the variables. The distance between any two points, given k variables, may be calculated by the generalized Pythagorean formula:

$$D_{12}^2 = \sum_{i-1}^{k} (X_{i1} - X_{i2})^2$$

D^2 can be used as a measure of similarity. The use of D is generally preferred to other possible measures because it gives less weight to larger differences, although the measure of similarity D is not normally distributed. D as an index of profile similarity considers level, dispersion, and shape, and it has the advantage of being the basis for other more powerful techniques of profile analysis.

A second commonly used index of profile similarity is the Pearson product–moment correlation coefficient. It should be noted that the product–moment correlation coefficient based on raw scores provides the same result as that obtained using scores standardized within profiles. The product–moment correlation coefficient used in this way is a special case of the D measure, which ignores the differences in level and dispersion between the two sets of measures. It follows that the product–moment correlation coefficient is only sensitive to differences in shape between the two profiles. Cronbach and Gleser (1953) have provided a weighted similarity index which can be used when the sets of scores on the variables do not have a very strong first principal component.

It is important that before using the techniques of profile analysis, consideration should be given to the strength, assumptions, and limitations associated with the indexes of similarity that are available because different indexes will lead to different conclusions. If correctly used profile analysis is a powerful technique which can be employed in multivariate analysis, as well as in the simple comparison of the profiles obtained from two persons or groups. Where the groups are known in advance of the analysis, the multivariate technique of discriminant analysis may be used to compare the groups. However, when the grouping of persons is not known in advance of the analysis, the function and purpose of the analysis is to cluster persons in terms of their profiles on the set of variables. Here the multivariate techniques of cluster analysis and multidimensional scaling may be applied to cluster the persons into groups.

See also: Multivariate Analysis

Bibliography

Cronbach L J, Gleser G C 1953 Assessing similarity between profiles. *Psychol. Bull.* 50: 456–73

Nunnally J C 1967 *Psychometric Theory*. McGraw-Hill, New York

Q-Methodology

R. M. Wolf

Q-methodology had its origins in factor-analytic work of the 1930s but did not emerge as a fully developed approach to the study of individuals until the early 1950s when Stephenson published *The Study of Behavior*. This seminal work systematized a considerable body of both conceptual and empirical work and claimed that *Q*-methodology was, "...a comprehensive approach to the study of behavior where man is at issue as a total thinking and behaving being" (Stephenson 1953 p. 7).

1. Q-Sorts

While *Q*-methodology is regarded as a general approach to the study of individuals and consists of a variety of techniques, *Q*-sorts lie at the heart of the method. A *Q*-sort consists of a number of stimuli which an individual is called on to sort into piles along some dimension. The stimuli can be verbal statements, or single words, pictorial material or figures. The task for a subject is to sort the stimuli along a particular dimension such as "prefer most" to "prefer least," "most like me" to "least like me," and so forth. Usually, a *Q*-sort will involve from about 40 to 120 stimulus items and about 7 to 12 categories into which the stimuli are to be sorted. Often, the instructions to an individual require that a specified number of objects be sorted into each category. Such prespecified distributions are often quasi-normal distributions. Figure 1 sets forth one possible prespecified distribution for a *Q*-sort.

The result of a *Q*-sort is a rank ordered set of stimuli along a particular dimension. What is done with these statements depends, of course, on the purposes of a particular investigation. The earliest uses of *Q*-sorts, and the basis for naming it *Q*, was to obtain correlations among the individuals. If several individuals perform a *Q*-sort, it is possible, using the scale values of the categories, to obtain correlations between individuals over the stimulus items. This is in direct contrast to typical correlations between variables over individuals. The latter correlations, summarized in a matrix are referred to as "*R*" while the former, to signify the difference, were dubbed "*Q*".

Correlations between individuals can be inspected to identify whether there appear to be clusters of individuals that serve to define particular *types*. Such correlation matrices have also been subjected to factor analysis for

	Most prefer									Least prefer	
Categories	11	10	9	8	7	6	5	4	3	2	1
No. of stimuli		3	4	7	10	13	16	13	10	7	4	3 = 90

Figure 1
Possible prespecified distribution for a *Q*-sort

the purpose of analytically identifying clusters or types of people.

It is also possible to compare a single individual's *Q*-sort under varying instructions. For example, before beginning therapy, clients might be instructed to rank order a set of statements along the dimension of "most like me" to "least like me" in order to describe their perception of themselves. They could then be instructed to sort the same set of statements along the dimension of "what I want to be like" to "what I don't want to be like" in order to describe an ideal self. Finally, the same individuals could be instructed to re-sort the statements along the dimension "how others see me" to "how others don't see me" so as to describe how they perceive themselves to be seen by others. The three sortings can be correlated and represented in a 3×3 correlation matrix *for a single individual*. Repetition of the procedure over the course of therapy could be used to trace how the relationships between real self, ideal self, and perceived self change over time. As long as the set of stimulus variables are reasonably homogenous, that is, they measure one broad variable such as "self," they are serviceable in such work.

A distinction is made between *unstructured* and *structured Q*-sorts. The *Q*-sort that was described above is an unstructured one. The stimulus items are selected because they measure a single broad variable. The single variable might be the self, paintings, or adjectives describing an object. In selecting a set of stimuli, the presumption is that the stimuli are representative of the domain of interest.

In a structured *Q*-sort, the items to be sorted are carefully selected to represent different categories of a particular domain. For example, Stephenson (1953 pp. 69-79) illustrates how a set of 10-15 statements for each of Jung's four major personality types could be generated and used in a *Q*-sort. Similarly, Kerlinger (1986 pp. 512-14) shows how a *Q*-sort could be developed for Spranger's six types of men. In each case, the category values into which statements were classified could be used to produce a mean for each type. The standard deviation for each type can also be computed. Inspection of the means can reveal the individual's standing on each type. In addition, Stephenson recommends that analysis of variance be used to test for the significance of difference between types in order properly to characterize an individual.

The above description illustrates what is called a structured one-way *Q*-sort. Stephenson extended structured *Q*-sorts into two-, three-, and four-way sorts. Consider the design shown in Fig. 2, in which, two traits are represented: dominant–submissive and introvert–extrovert. Stephenson would seek to develop or select an equal number of statements (15-20) with which dominant introverts might describe themselves, and so

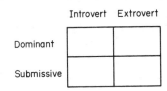

Figure 2
Structured two-way Q-sort

on, for each cell of the design. More than two levels on a dimension and more than two dimensions may be used. The statements are then assembled into a deck for sorting into a predetermined quasi-normal distribution and administered to a subject. The resulting information can then be analyzed, using a two-way analysis of variance, to test for the main effects of dominance/submission and introversion/extroversion and the interaction between the two according to Stephenson.

Q-methodology relies heavily on comparative judgments and ranking. An individual who is presented with a *Q*-sort is required to order a set of stimuli along a particular dimension. If a prespecified distribution is used, such as quasi-normal distribution, the result is a rank ordered set of statements. Two individuals ranking the same set of statements could obtain the same mean and standard deviation on all dimensions being measured by a *Q*-sort and yet be markedly different with regard to their actual standing on each dimension. This is due to the comparative nature of the sorting process and the use of a prespecified distribution. For these reasons, some writers have questioned the use of forced distributions while others have advocated the abandonment of ranking procedures and the use of normative measurements where an individual is asked to rate stimuli according to particular value labels.

2. Evaluation of Q-Methodology

It is not easy to evaluate the arguments that have swirled around *Q*-methodology. The reason for this is that *Q* refers to a loosely related bundle of techniques and not to a single procedure. Thus, if one were to try to evaluate the criticism about the relative nature of rankings in *Q* and the use of a forced distribution, one's position would largely depend on what aspect of *Q* is being considered and what one will be doing with the resulting data.

For example, if the object of a particular investigation is to compare an individual's ranking of a set of self-descriptive statements with what he or she would like to be (ideal self) then the exact distribution form has little effect on the kinds of analyses which are made of the data. Correlation coefficients, and the factors obtained from them, are largely insensitive to changes in distribution shapes.

On the other hand, if one wanted to estimate an individual's actual level of, say, self-esteem, then *Q*-methodology would be inappropriate. This is not a criticism of *Q*-methodology. It is simply a recognition of the fact that different procedures are used for different purposes.

Nonetheless, it is possible to make some evaluative comments about *Q*-methodology. The general approach has been part of the research scene for over 50 years, and a systematic treatment (Stephenson 1953) has been available for over 30 years.

One of the most notable features of *Q*-methodology is the prominent role given to theory. Any investigator who undertakes to use *Q* is forced, from the outset, to consider how a theory or aspects of a theory can be expressed in categories or levels, and if stimulus items can be selected or devised to express those categories or levels. In such use, *Q* can be a powerful way to test theories. Even the most severe critics of *Q* (Cronbach and Gleser 1954), acknowledge the importance of these newer ways in which questionnaire items can be used. *Q* simultaneously allows for flexible use of questionnaire items and for the standardization of descriptions of complex phenonema in a theoretically relevant way. Proponents of *Q* suggest that the attention to theory and the importance of content sampling may be among its most important contributions (Nunnally 1970). A second major feature of *Q* is its suitability for the study of the individual. The same individual can be studied under different conditions of instructions (real self, ideal self, etc.) as well as over time in order to assess the impact of therapy or other program interventions. The approach is not free of pitfalls, however. Although rank ordering is used in connection with forced distribution, the effects of response sets are not totally eliminated.

A third claim regarding *Q*-methodology regards its use in testing the effects of independent variables on complex dependent variables. The use of structured *Q*-sorts offers the possibility of sensitively assessing the effects of variables through the use of analysis of variance procedures on an individual by individual basis. Although this has been done rather infrequently, the promise remains.

Finally, *Q* offers considerable promise for exploratory studies as well as for its heuristic value. Intensive study of a single case or a few individuals can help in generating new ideas, formulating hypotheses and examining relationships. Stephenson's own work (Stephenson 1953) perhaps illustrates this quality better than any treatise would. One gets the impression of a lively mind at work while engaged in working with *Q*.

3. Criticisms of Q-Methodology

Q-methodology has also drawn strong criticism. One suspects that some of the criticism stems from the way in which Stephenson presented *Q*. Strong claims were made for *Q*. There was also a general neglect of a number of issues that make *Q* somewhat methodologically dubious.

One major set of criticisms of *Q* has been statistical in nature. Since *Q*-sorts are ipsative in nature and most statistical tests assume independence, there is an inherent conflict between *Q*-procedures and most forms of data analysis that are used to analyze the data resulting from Q-sorts. Technically, the statisticians are on sounder grounds than the proponents of Q. However, the important question is whether the violation of statistical assumptions is serious enough to invalidate the use of factor analysis of variance. Proponents of Q (Kerlinger 1986, Nunnally 1970) say they are not, while critics (Cronbach and Gleser 1954, Sundland 1962) say they are. Given the unresolved nature of the issue, it would seem that caution should be exercised in the use of Q.

A more basic criticism centers on the issue of external validity or generalizability. Studies using Q are invariably based on very small samples: from 1 to 20 individuals. To what populations can results obtained from such small samples generalize? The small sample sizes simply do not provide the basis for generalizations. Since this is the case, what uses can be made of Q? A partial answer is that Q can be used in exploratory studies. Q can also be used in clinical work in the study of individual cases. Beyond that, normative studies using much larger (and representative) samples are needed to test theoretical propositions adequately.

Other technical issues surrounding the use of Q involve the use of forced versus unforced distributions and the loss of information through the lack of elevation and scatter because of the ipsative nature of Q procedures. These issues have received considerable attention in the literature but have not been fully resolved. It is doubtful if they ever will. The issue of lack of elevation and scatter because of the ipsative nature of Q is not an issue that can be resolved. If elevation and scatter are important considerations, Q cannot be used. If they are not considerations, Q can be used.

4. Conclusion

Q-methodology, as a systematic approach to the study of human behavior, has been available in a systematized form for over 30 years. Its general lack of use over the past two decades is probably the best testament to its limited utility. Why it has not been used more than it has is not entirely clear. It would seem that the areas in which Q has its greatest utility, for example, clinical work, are largely staffed by people who do not have the statistical and psychometric expertise to develop and use Q, while people who have the requisite statistical and psychometric competence have little need for Q.

Bibliography

Cronbach L J, Gleser G 1954 Book review of William Stephenson's "The study of behavior: Q-technique and its methodology." *Psychometrika* 19: 327–30
Kerlinger F N 1986 *Foundations of Behavioral Research*, 3rd edn. Holt, Rinehart and Winston, New York, pp. 507–21
Nunnally J C 1970 *Introduction to Psychological Measurement.* McGraw-Hill, New York, pp. 447–58
Stephenson W 1953 *The Study of Behavior: Q-technique and its Methodology.* University of Chicago Press, Chicago, Illinois
Sundland D 1962 The construction of Q sorts: A criticism. *Psychol. Rev.* 69: 62–4
Wittenborn J R 1961 Contributions and current status of Q methodology. *Psychol. Rev.* 58: 132–42

Reciprocal Effects, Analysis of

D. R. Rogosa

The analysis of reciprocal effects consists of the study of mutual influences between two (or more) variables. Often, researchers attribute causality to the influences among variables and speak of reciprocal causal effects. Examples from educational research include analyses of the reciprocal effects between: teacher expectations and student achievement, student self-concept and academic achievement, and vocabulary and comprehension skills. Also, among the many studies of reciprocal effects in psychology are analyses of mother–child interactions, infant intelligence and behavior, and aggressive behavior and viewing of violent television shows. Often, research questions about reciprocal effects have been simplified to, does X cause Y or does Y cause X? Consequently, many researchers have sought only determinations of causal predominance or of *the* causal ordering of the variables.

Longitudinal data are crucial to the analysis of reciprocal effects, because the temporal ordering is needed to unravel the influences linking the variables. Typically, observations on a large number of cases are obtained for each variable on a few (two or more) occasions. (Each case may be an individual or a unit such as a student–teacher or mother–child dyad.) Much of the empirical research and methodological discussion on reciprocal effects has been limited to the two-wave, two variable (2W2V) panel design, in which measures of X and Y are available on each of two occasions

Four different approaches and statistical methods for quantitative data have been used in analyses of reciprocal effects. These methods are cross-lagged correlation, structural regression models, continuous-time feedback models, and multiple time series. Separate methods for dichotomous and categorical data, which have not been much used in educational research, are Lazarsfeld's 16-fold table, log-linear models for contingency tables, and continuous-time Markov models.

1. Cross-lagged Correlation

Cross-lagged correlation has been the most popular procedure in educational and psychological research for the analysis of reciprocal effects. Most often, cross-lagged correlation is used to determine a predominant causal influence. Figure 1, which presents the population correlations among the variables in a 2W2V panel design, is

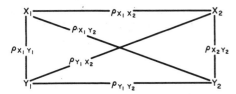

Figure 1
Population correlations for a 2W2V panel. The variables at time 1 are X_1 and Y_1 and the variables at time 2 are X_2 and Y_2

the diagram that accompanies expositions of cross-lagged correlation. The population cross-lagged correlations are $\rho_{X_1Y_2}$ and $\rho_{Y_1X_2}$.

The difference between the population cross-lagged correlations, $\rho_{X_1Y_2} - \rho_{Y_1X_2}$, is the basis for attributions of a predominant causal influence. If the data indicate that $\rho_{X_1Y_2} - \rho_{Y_1X_2}$ is positive, the predominant causal influence is concluded to be in the direction of X causing Y. If the data indicate that $\rho_{X_1Y_2} - \rho_{Y_1X_2}$ is negative, the predominant causal influence is concluded to be in the direction of Y causing X. Usually, attributions of predominant causal influences are made only when the null hypothesis of equal population cross-lagged correlations is rejected. If this null hypothesis is not rejected, the usual interpretation is that no direct causal influences exist between X and Y; in particular that a common causal influence may be responsible for their observed associations. This interpretation has been adopted as a null hypothesis of spuriousness, which is represented through a model allowing no direct influences between X and Y but with an unmeasured third variable influencing both X and Y at each time (Kenny 1979 Fig. 12-2, Rogosa 1980 Fig. 3).

The extension of cross-lagged correlation to determinations of causal predominance when more than two waves of data are available is to compare the cross-lagged correlations from all possible two-wave combinations. Rogosa (1980) showed that this strategy of using the multiple waves for replication of differences between the cross-lagged correlations is more likely to generate confusion than corroboration.

A related statistical procedure for 2W2V panel data, which has seen a number of applications in educational research, is the frequency-in-change-in-product–moment procedure developed by Yee and Gage (1968). Although the Yee–Gage procedure differs from cross-lagged correlation in many important details, this procedure for the analysis of reciprocal effects suffers from the same basic deficiencies as cross-lagged correlation.

Cross-lagged correlation does not provide dependable information as to the causal structure underlying the data. Building upon earlier analyses by Duncan (1969) and Heise (1970), Rogosa (1980) demonstrated that, when there are no reciprocal causal effects, the difference between the cross-lagged correlations may be small or may be large; and when there are considerable reciprocal causal effects, the difference between the cross-

lagged correlations may be small or may be large. Furthermore, a zero difference between the cross-lagged correlations (indicating spuriousness in cross-lagged correlation) is consistent with large reciprocal causal influences or with small or nonexistent causal influences between the variables. Moreover, cross-lagged correlation may indicate a causal predominance opposite to that of the actual causal structure of the data. Hence, neither determinations of spuriousness nor causal predominance can be trusted.

A basic deficiency in cross-lagged correlation is the lack of an explicit definition of a causal effect. Without a clearly defined quantity to be estimated, it is not surprising that cross-lagged correlation fails to provide sound inferences. Also, the emphasis on causal predominance in cross-lagged correlation is unwise. The reciprocal nature of many social and educational processes makes determination of only causal predominance a serious oversimplification of the research problem. Measures of the strength and duration of the reciprocal relationship and of the specific causal effects are needed.

2. Structural Equation Models

Structural regression formulations of reciprocal effects in longitudinal panel data were originally introduced in the path analysis literature (Wright 1960, Duncan 1969, Heise 1970). The term causal model is popular for describing both the path analysis and the more general structural equation models. In these models, a causal effect is represented by the change in an outcome variable that results from an increment to an antecedent variable. For two variables, X and Y, the reciprocal influences are represented by the regression parameters of the path from a prior X to a later Y and from a prior Y to a later X.

Previous formulations of regression models for panel data with reciprocal causal effects have focused on models for 2W2V data. Figure 2 represents a specific regression model for 2W2V data, given by the regression equations:

$$X_2 = \beta_0 + \beta_1 X_1 + \gamma_2 Y_1 + u \tag{1}$$

$$Y_2 = \gamma_0 + \beta_2 X_1 + \gamma_1 Y_1 + v \tag{2}$$

The parameters β_2 and γ_2 represent the lagged, reciprocal causal effects between X and Y and thus are of central importance in the investigation of reciprocal causal effects.

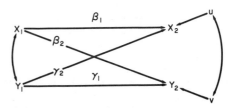

Figure 2
Representation of a regression (path analysis) model for 2W2V data

Although the structural regressions do provide a model that defines reciprocal effects among the variables, the validity of inferences about the reciprocal effects depends crucially on the validity of the model. Foremost among the important assumptions built into Fig. 2 and Eqns. (1) and (2) is that X and Y constitute a closed system so that no important influences have been omitted from the regression model. Also important is the assumption that all causal influences are lagged; simultaneous causal influences between X and Y are not included. With only 2W2V data, frequently it is not possible to distinguish between different underlying models, which makes the determination of reciprocal effects very difficult. Additional observations can aid the formulation and testing of the regression models; one example of the use of regression models for three waves of data is the analysis of the influences between economic development and educational expansion in Hannan et al. (1974).

A generalization of these path analysis models is to specify X and Y to be latent variables having multiple indicators at each time point. The influences among the variables are represented by the parameters of the structural regression equations that relate the latent variables. (A measurement model connects the latent variables with their indicators.) For example, recasting Eqns. (1) and (2) in terms of latent variables, β_2 and γ_2 would then represent the reciprocal effects between the latent variables X and Y. Examples of the use of structural equation models for the analysis of reciprocal effects are: the analysis of attitudes and behaviors in Bentler and Speckart (1981), the analysis of intellectual flexibility and complexity of work in Kohn and Schooler (1978), and models for home environment and intellectual development in Rogosa (1979).

3. Continuous-time Feedback Models

An alternative formulation of reciprocal effects is to model the rates of change of the variables. A simple two variable continuous-time model that incorporates reciprocal influences between X and Y is:

$$\frac{dX(t)}{dt} = b_0 + b_1 X(t) + c_2 Y(t) \tag{3}$$

$$\frac{dY(t)}{dt} = c_0 + c_1 Y(t) + b_2 X(t) \tag{4}$$

Equations (3) and (4) are coupled differential equations which stipulate that the rates of change of X and Y at any time depend linearly on the levels of X and Y. The parameters b_2 and c_2 represent the cross effects or couplings between X and Y. Note that Eqns. (3) and (4) are deterministic. Similar models for change can be formulated which include stochastic components, exogenous variables, and other generalizations. Many applications of these models are presented in Hannan and Tuma (1983).

Rates of change are not directly observable. However, the solution of the system of differential equations in

Eqns. (3) and (4) yields equations, in terms of the observable variables, of the same form as Eqns. (1) and (2). The parameters β_2 and γ_2 in Eqns. (1) and (2) are nonlinear functions of the time between observations and the parameters of Eqns. (3) and (4). That the solutions of Eqns. (3) and (4) have the same form as the regression model for 2W2V data allows models for 2W2V data to be thought of as reflecting a more general process, that of causal influences and resulting adjustments that are continuous in time.

4. Multiple Time Series

The statistical analysis of reciprocal effects, or feedback, between two time series has been an active area in econometrics, with most applications investigating reciprocal effects between money supply and income or those between advertising and sales. The statistical methods are based on predictability criteria. Loosely speaking, one time series, $X(t)$, is said to cause another time series, $Y(t)$, if present Y values can be predicted better using past values of X than by not using past values of X, other relevant information (including past values of Y) being included in the prediction. This definition encompasses both lagged and instantaneous influences between X and Y. A comprehensive classification of the possible patterns of causal influences was provided by Pierce and Haugh (1977) who also presented data analysis procedures based on the correlations of residuals between the separately filtered time series for detecting these reciprocal effects. In addition, useful measures of linear dependence and feedback among multiple time series were developed by Geweke (1982).

In most economic research on reciprocal effects, the data consist of a single extensive time series of observations for each variable. The minimum number of observations over time needed for the application of time series statistical models is far beyond the usual design of longitudinal research in education. The longitudinal data for which methods commonly used in education (cross-lagged correlation, structural regression, and continuous-time feedback models) are applicable consist of a collection of many replications of very short time series (often with only two observations). Of course, such limited temporal data cannot support the complex time-series models used in the econometric analyses of reciprocal effects. One psychological application of models and analyses of reciprocal effects in time series data is the analysis of play behavior of individual mother–infant dyads in Gottman and Ringland (1981).

5. Methods for Categorical Data

Analyses of reciprocal effects using dichotomous or polychotomous variables have not been common in educational research. Lazarsfeld's 16-fold table for analyzing reciprocal effects among dichotomous variables is the best-known method for categorical data; Lazarsfeld

(1978) provided a history of the development and application of this procedure. A natural extension of the 16-fold table analysis is the application of log-linear models for contingency tables (Goodman 1973). A third approach to the analysis of reciprocal effects is the use of continuous-time stochastic models, in particular, discrete-state, continuous-time Markov models. For additional references and for applications of these methods, see Coleman (1968), Hannan and Tuma (1979, 1983), and Markus (1979).

6. Conclusion

The investigation of reciprocal effects is an extremely difficult enterprise. Questions about reciprocal effects are some of the most complex in the design and analysis of longitudinal research. A humbling reality for research on reciprocal effects is that much simpler, preliminary research questions, namely those connected with the measurement of individual change and the assessment of correlates of change, remain controversial and unsolved. Clearly, reciprocal effects cannot be studied cheaply. Extensive, high-quality longitudinal data and theoretically based, explicit models of the reciprocal effects are absolutely necessary.

See also: Longitudinal Research Methods

Bibliography

Bentler P M, Speckart G 1981 Attitudes "cause" behaviors: A structural equation analysis. *J. Pers. Soc. Psychol.* 40: 226–38
Coleman J S 1968 The mathematical study of change. In: Blalock H M, Blalock A B (eds.) 1968 *Methodology in Social Research*. McGraw-Hill, New York, pp. 428–78
Duncan O D 1969 Some linear models for two-wave, two-variable panel analysis. *Psychol. Bull.* 72: 177–82
Geweke J 1982 The measurement of linear dependence and feedback between multiple time series. *J. Am. Stat. Ass.* 77: 304–24
Goodman L A 1973 Causal analysis of data from panel studies and other kinds of surveys. *Am. J. Sociol.* 78: 1135–91
Gottman J M, Ringland J T 1981 The analysis of dominance and bidirectionality in social development. *Child Dev.* 52: 393–412
Hannan M T, Tuma N B 1979 Methods for temporal analysis. *Annu. Rev. Sociol.* 5
Hannan M T, Tuma N B 1983 *Social Dynamics: Models and Methods*. Academic Press, New York
Hannan M T, Rubinson R, Warren J T 1974 The causal approach to measurement error in panel analysis: Some further contingencies. In: Blalock H M Jr (ed.) 1974 *Measurement in the Social Sciences: Theories and Strategies*. Aldine, Chicago, Illinois, pp. 293–323
Heise D R 1970 Causal inference from panel data. In: Borgatta E F, Bohrnstedt G W (eds.) 1970 *Sociological Methodology*. Jossey-Bass, San Francisco, California
Kenny D A 1979 *Correlation and Causality*. Wiley, New York
Kessler R C, Greenberg D F 1981 *Linear Panel Analysis: Models of Quantitative Change*. Academic Press, New York
Kohn M L, Schooler C 1978 The reciprocal effects of the substantive complexity of work and intellectual flexibility: A longitudinal assessment. *Am. J. Sociol.* 84: 24–52
Lazarsfeld P F 1978 Some episodes in the history of panel analysis. In: Kandel D B (ed.) 1978 *Longitudinal Research on Drug Use*. Wiley, New York, pp. 249–65
Markus G B 1979 *Analyzing Panel Data*. Sage, Beverly Hills, California
Pierce D A, Haugh L D 1977 Causality in temporal systems: Characterizations and a survey. *J. Econometrics* 5: 265–93
Rogosa D R 1979 Causal models in longitudinal research: Rationale, formulation, and interpretation. In: Nesselroade J R, Baltes P B (eds.) 1979 *Longitudinal Methodology in the Study of Behavior and Development*. Academic Press, New York, pp. 263–302
Rogosa D R 1980 A critique of cross-lagged correlation. *Psychol. Bull.* 88: 245–58
Wright S 1960 The treatment of reciprocal interaction, with or without lag, in path analysis. *Biometrics* 16: 423–45
Yee A H, Gage N L 1968 Techniques for estimating the source and direction of causal influence in panel data. *Psychol. Bull.* 70: 115–26

Regression Analysis

M. M. Tatsuoka

Regression analysis refers to a broad class of statistical techniques that are designed to study the relationship between a criterion (or dependent) variable, Y, and one or more predictor (or independent) variables, X_1, $X_2, \ldots, X_p$. The means by which such study is effected is a regression equation, which is an equation of the general form

$$\hat{Y} = f(X_1, X_2, \ldots, X_p) \qquad (1)$$

where the circumflex on the Y denotes that what is represented by the function of the X's is a "predicted" or "modeled" Y-value rather than one that is actually observed.

The function $f(\ )$ may, at one extreme, be a simple linear function of a single predictor (i.e., $b_0 + b_1 X$). At the other extreme it may be a complicated weighted sum of several predictors raised to various powers and include also products of two or more predictors (e.g., $b_0 + b_1 X_1 + b_2 X_2 + b_3 \ X_1^2 + b_4 X_1 X_2 + b_5 X_1 X_2^2$). The terms may even include transcendental functions such as $\log X_j$, e^{aX_j}, and so forth. However, such a term may be defined as a separate predictor, and the task of determining the combining weights (or regression coefficients) will become more involved but no new principle will have to be invoked.

What is the general principle involved in determining the regression coefficients? It is desirable that the modeled Y-values, $\hat{Y}_i$ (where i represents the i-th individual in the sample), should "be as close as possible" to their actually observed counterparts Y_i. More specifically, "closeness" can be defined so as to mean small total (or average) squared discrepancies between Y_i and $\hat{Y}_i$. That is, the quantity

$$Q = \sum_{i=1}^{N} (Y_i - \hat{Y}_i)^2 \equiv \sum_{i=1}^{N} e_i^2 \qquad (2)$$

can be defined as the "loss function," which is to be minimized by appropriate choice of the regression-coefficient values. (Here N is the sample size, and e_i is simply another symbol for $Y_i - \hat{Y}_i$, known as "error" or "lack of fit" of the i-th observation to the model.) This is the famous least-squares principle.

Of course, invoking the least-squares principle, by itself, does not completely solve the problem of determining the regression coefficients. Before that, a decision must be made on what particular functional form to adopt for $f(\ )$; that is, the regression model must be chosen. Until this choice is made, the very task of minimizing the loss function is ill-defined. For instance, the minimum Q attainable by adopting the class of linear functions $f(X) = b_0 + b_1 X$ as the regression model and determining the optimal b_0 and b_1 values will, in general, be "undercut" if one allows a quadratic function $f(X) = b_0' + b_1' X + b_2' X^2$ as a candidate and determines the optimal values of b_0', b_1', and b_2'. Thus, the choice of a type of regression model is the crucial first step before one can even apply the least-squares principle.

Ideally, there should be some theoretical grounds for making this choice. A substantive theory in the field of research should dictate whether to adopt, say, a linear, quadratic, or exponential regression model. Unfortunately, it is seldom the case in behavioral science that there is a substantive theory precise enough to specify a particular type of regression model. It is thus frequently necessary to proceed by trial-and-error. In this case, the decision is guided by another principle of scientific endeavor: the canon of parsimony, which holds that a more complicated model should not be used when a simpler one will suffice.

In the context of choosing a regression model, this usually means that a linear model should be tried first, and only if this proves not to yield an "adequate" fit should a sequence of more complicated models be tried successively. A crucial point here is how to decide whether the fit offered by a given regression model is adequate or not. One way is to test whether or not a significant decrease would be obtained in the loss function Q if one were to go from the simpler to the more complicated model. Only if the decrease $Q_1 - Q_2$ (say) is significantly greater than zero would there be justification for using the second model. To ignore this and jump suddenly to a complicated, well-fitting model would be to commit the error of "overfitting" the sample at hand. An excellent fit may be obtained to the current dataset, but this would more likely than not

incur a drastic drop in the extent of fit in a future sample from the same population, when an attempt is made to replicate (cross-validate) the finding or utilize the regression equation.

What was said above concerning the choice of a class of regression models holds equally well with regard to the number of predictor variables to include. Even when the mathematical form of a model is fixed, say to a multiple linear regression form, the fit can generally be improved by adding more and more predictor variables. But the more that is added, the less likely it will be that the extent of fit achieved in the sample at hand will hold up in future samples. Hence, a predictor variable should not be added to an existing multiple regression equation unless the addition results in a significant decrease in the loss function Q—or, as is shown below—a significant increase in the squared multiple correlation coefficient.

In the forgoing, nothing was said about the purposes of regression analysis, since it was assumed that the reader was familiar with at least the simplest (or most practical) of the purposes served; namely the prediction of such things as college or job performance for the screening or guidance of candidates. However, regression analysis is coming more and more to be used for a purpose that has traditionally been served by analysis of variance (ANOVA) and analysis of covariance (ANCOVA). This usage will be discussed below after a description of several models, their properties, and some problems inherent in regression analysis.

It should also be pointed out here that a regression model, properly speaking, requires the values of the independent variable(s) to be fixed by the researcher. Examples would be ages of the subjects to be used, dosages of a drug to be administered, and so on. This is in counterdistinction to the correlation model, in which dependent and independent variables alike are random variables, whose values are "brought along" by the subjects sampled—for example, course grades and pretest scores; height and weight. Most of the techniques of regression analysis are applicable equally to the regression and correlation situation, although some differences in significance tests and so on do exist. This article will speak for the most part in the language of the regression model; this allows one to refer to groups defined by values of the independent variable(s), and hence to subgroup means of Y.

1. Models, Properties, and Problems

1.1 Simple Linear Regression

The simplest regression model takes the form of a single-predictor linear equation,

$$\hat{Y} = b_0 + b_1 X \qquad (3)$$

where the constants are determined, as mentioned earlier, so as to minimize the loss function $Q = \Sigma(Y - \hat{Y})^2$. The results turn out to be

$$b_1 = \Sigma x_i y_i / \Sigma x_i^2 \qquad (4)$$

and

$$b_0 = \bar{Y} - b_1 \bar{X} \tag{5}$$

(Here $x_i = X_i - \bar{X}$ and $y_i = Y_i - \bar{Y}$ are deviations from the means.) b_1 is called the coefficient of regression of Y on X—or, simply, the "regression coefficient"—while b_0 is the Y-intercept. These constants are unbiased estimates of the corresponding population constants β_1 and β_0.

When b_1 and b_0 as defined by Eqns. (4) and (5) are substituted back into the expression for Q with $\hat{Y}$ replaced by $b_0 + b_1 X$, after doing some algebra, the following is obtained:

$$Q_{\min} = \Sigma y^2 - (\Sigma xy)^2 / \Sigma x^2 \tag{6}$$

This is called the residual sum of squares of Y, denoted SS_{res}. Factoring out Σy^2 in the right-hand expression yields

$$SS_{res} = (\Sigma y^2)[1 - (\Sigma xy)^2 / (\Sigma x^2 \Sigma y^2)] \tag{7}$$

The reader may recognize the fraction in the brackets to be equal to the square of the product–moment correlation coefficient r_{xy}. Thus,

$$SS_{res} = (\Sigma y^2)(1 - r_{xy}^2) \tag{8}$$

Recalling that SS_{res} is another symbol for $Q_{\min}$, the minimum value of the loss function that can be achieved for the given regression model by using the optimal b_0 and b_1, it can be seen that the larger r_{xy} is in absolute value, the smaller $Q_{\min}$ is. (Of course $0 \leqslant |r_{xy}| \leqslant 1$, as the reader probably knows.)

Equation (8) may also be written as $SS_{res} = \Sigma y^2 - r_{xy}^2 \Sigma y^2$, and it may further be shown that

$$r_{xy}^2 \Sigma y^2 = \sum_{i=1}^{N} (Y_i - \bar{Y})^2 \tag{9}$$

which is called the sum of squares due to linear regression, symbolized $SS_{lin.\ reg.}$. It therefore follows that

$$r_{xy}^2 = SS_{lin.\ reg.} / SS_{tot} \tag{10}$$

where SS_{tot} has been written for Σy^2 (since this is the total sum of squares of ANOVA). This is the mathematical formulation of the well-known statement that "the squared correlation is the proportion of the variability of the dependent variable that is associated with its linear regression on the independent variable."

The reader may recall that the t statistic for testing the significance of a correlation coefficient is $t = r(N-2)^{1/2} / (1 - r^2)^{1/2}$, which follows a t distribution with $N-2$ degrees of freedom when the null hypothesis is true. The square of this statistic, which may be rearranged slightly to read

$$F = \frac{r^2/1}{(1 - r^2)/(N-2)} \tag{11}$$

follows an F distribution with 1 and $N-2$ degrees of freedom. Substituting for r^2 and $1 - r^2$ from Eqns. (10) and (8), respectively, the following is obtained:

$$F = \frac{SS_{lin.\ reg.}/1}{SS_{res}/(N-2)} \tag{12}$$

or, upon rewriting the numerator and denominator as mean squares,

$$F = \frac{MS_{lin.\ reg.}}{MS_{res}} \tag{13}$$

which bears an obvious resemblance with the customary F ratio in one-way ANOVA: $F = MS_b / MS_w$.

1.2 Multiple Linear Regression

One way in which the simple linear regression Eqn. (3) can be complexified by one step is to add a second predictor variable to get

$$\hat{Y} = b_0 + b_1 X_1 + b_2 X_2 \tag{14}$$

The constants b_0, b_1, and b_2 are again determined by minimizing $Q = \Sigma(Y - \hat{Y})^2$ with $\hat{Y}$ replaced by the second member of Eqn. (14). Setting the appropriate partial derivatives equal to zero results in the equations,

$$(\Sigma x_1^2)b_1 + (\Sigma x_1 x_2)b_2 = \Sigma x_1 y \tag{15}$$

$$(\Sigma x_2 x_1)b_1 + (\Sigma x_2^2)b_2 = \Sigma x_2 y \tag{16}$$

and

$$b_0 = \bar{Y} - b_1 \bar{X}_1 - b_2 \bar{X}_2 \tag{17}$$

The first two of these equations, called the normal equations, may be written in a compact form by defining the sum-of-squares-and-cross-products (SSCP) matrix of the predictor variables,

$$S_{xx} = \begin{bmatrix} \Sigma x_1^2 & \Sigma x_1 x_2 \\ \Sigma x_2 x_1 & \Sigma x_2^2 \end{bmatrix} \tag{18}$$

the vector of regression coefficients (more precisely, partial regression coefficients),

$$b = \begin{bmatrix} b_1 \\ b_2 \end{bmatrix} \tag{19}$$

and the vector of sums of cross products (SCP) between predictors and criterion,

$$S_{xy} = \begin{bmatrix} \Sigma x_1 y \\ \Sigma x_2 y \end{bmatrix}. \tag{20}$$

The normal equations then become

$$S_{xx} b = S_{xy} \tag{21}$$

which may be solved to yield

$$b = S_{xx}^{-1} S_{xy} \tag{22}$$

(provided that S_{xx} is nonsingular). The similarity between this and Eqn. (4) for the one-predictor case is evident—especially if the latter is deliberately rewritten in the form

$$b_1 = (\Sigma x^2)^{-1}(\Sigma xy) \tag{23}$$

Those who are not familiar with matrix algebra may either simply follow the formal analogy with the one-predictor situation described in the previous subsection or refer to a reference such as Green (1976) or to the matrix-algebra chapter in any of several multivariate analysis texts (e.g., Tatsuoka 1971).

If Eqn. (14) is generalized to

$$\hat{Y} = b_0 + b_1 X_1 + b_2 X_2 + \ldots + b_p X_p \qquad (24)$$

one has only to define a larger SSCP matrix (with p rows and p columns) $\mathbf{S}_{xx}$ and larger (p-dimensioned) vectors $\mathbf{b}$ and $\mathbf{S}_{xy}$ to go into Eqn. (21). The equation for the Y-intercept b_0 is not worth rewriting in matrix notation. The general case can be simply written as

$$b_0 = \bar{Y} - b_1 \bar{X}_1 - b_2 \bar{X}_2 - \ldots - b_p \bar{X}_p \qquad (25)$$

The index which measures how well (or poorly) a multiple linear regression model fits a given set of observations—that is, how small the minimum value of Q can be made by choosing regression coefficients and intercepts that satisfy Eqns. (21) and (25)—is defined as the product–moment correlation coefficient $r_{Y\hat{Y}}$ between the observed and modeled criterion scores Y and $\hat{Y}$. This is called the multiple correlation coefficient and is symbolized as $R_{y \cdot 123 \ldots p}$ (or simply R if the context makes it clear what the criterion and predictor variables are). R may be computed by actually determining each person's "predicted" (i.e., modeled) Y score, $\hat{Y}_i$, from Eqn. (24) and correlating it with the observed Y score, Y_i. This, however, would be extremely tedious to do, and in practice one of several algebraically equivalent formulas is used that gives the same result. One of these is $R^2 = \mathbf{S}'_{xy}\mathbf{b}/\Sigma y^2$, where $\mathbf{S}'_{xy}$ (or $\mathbf{S}_{yx}$) is the transpose of $\mathbf{S}_{xy}$—that is, a row vector with the same elements as the $\mathbf{S}_{xy}$ defined before. Nevertheless, it is important to keep in mind that $R = r_{Y\hat{Y}}$.

A test of the null hypothesis that the population multiple correlation coefficient is zero may be carried out by using an F statistic that is a direct generalization of that displayed in Eqn. (11) for the one-predictor case;

$$F = \frac{R^2/p}{(1 - R^2)/(N - p - 1)} \qquad (26)$$

which follows an F distribution with p and $N - p - 1$ degrees of freedom under the null hypothesis.

A more important test, in view of the earlier admonition against proceeding to a more complicated regression model than warranted by the data, is one that allows a test to be carried out to determine whether the addition of a new predictor results in a significant decrease of the loss function. This may now be restated in terms of an increase in the squared correlation coefficient, by using the relation between $Q_{\min}$ (i.e., SS_{res}) and r^2 given by Eqn. (8) and its multiple-predictor extension. For if the residual SS using one predictor X_1 is denoted by $SS_{res(1)}$ and that using two predictors, X_1 and X_2, by $SS_{res(2)}$ then the decrease in Q, $SS_{res(1)} - SS_{res(2)}$, is, by Eqn. (8) and its two-predictor extension, equivalent to

$(\Sigma y^2)(R^2 - r^2)$. Hence, the F statistic for testing the significance of the increase from r^2 to R^2 is

$$F = \frac{(R^2 - r^2)/1}{(1 - R^2)/(N - 3)} \qquad (27)$$

The divisor, 1, in the numerator is the difference, 2–1, between the numbers of predictors; the $N - 3$ dividing the denominator is $N - p - 1$ with $p = 2$. The degrees of freedom of this F statistic are 1 and $N - 3$. More generally, the statistic for testing the significance of the increase in R^2 (or the "incremental R^2" as it is often called) in going from a p-predictor model to a $(p + 1)$-predictor model is

$$F = \frac{(R_{p+1}^2 - R_p^2)/1}{(1 - R_{p+1}^2)/(N - p - 2)} \qquad (28)$$

which has an F distribution (under the null hypothesis) with 1 and $N - p - 2$ degrees of freedom.

The incremental R^2 is sometimes used in the reverse (then called the decremental R^2) as a measure of how much the predictability of the criterion decreases when a particular predictor variable is removed from a multiple regression equation. This was called the "usefulness" of that predictor by Darlington (1968) in an article that compares the advantages and disadvantages of several measures of the relative importance of each predictor variable in predicting or "expanding" the criterion. The best known of such measures is, of course, the standardized regression weight b_j^* (or "beta weight") associated with each variable, which is related to the corresponding raw-score regression weight b_j by the equation $b_j^* = (s_j / s_y) b_j$ where s_j and s_y are the standard deviations of X_j and Y, respectively. However, Darlington points out several drawbacks of the beta weight as a measure of each variable's contribution to the predictability of the criterion.

1.3 Polynomial Regression

Another way in which the simple linear Eqn. (3) may be complexified is to add, successively, a term in X^2, X^3, and so on, while holding the number of actual predictor variables to one. Such a regression equation is called a polynomial regression equation of degree m, when X^m is the highest degree term involved. The effect of adding higher degree terms is to enable the modeling of datasets in which the Y means corresponding to the distinct values of X trace curves of more and more complicated forms.

Once again, it cannot be overemphasized that the mistake should never be made of overfitting the data at hand by using a polynomial equation of a degree higher than warranted. In fact, it can be seen without too much difficulty that, if there are K distinct values of X in the dataset (and hence at most K distinct Y-means), the subgroup Y-means $\bar{Y}_1, \bar{Y}_2, \ldots, \bar{Y}_K$ can be fitted perfectly by a polynomial regression equation of degree $K - 1$. (This is because the number of constants whose values can be chosen in a polynomial equation of degree $K - 1$ is K, which is the number of Y-means to be fitted.) Clearly such a fit is spurious and would never begin to hold up in a subsequent sample.

The determination of the regression coefficients and the successive significance testing may be done by precisely the same methods that were described for multiple linear regression in the preceding subsection. This should not be difficult to see, because in a cubic regression equation (for instance) the successive powers X, X^2, and X^3 may be regarded as three different predictor variables, X_1, X_2, and X_3, respectively. Thus, the SSCP matrix for the normal equations may be written by the simple device of starting out with the SSCP matrix appropriate to the three-predictor linear model case, then moving the subscripts upwards to the position of exponents, and finally using the rule of exponents $(x^m x^n = x^{m+n})$. The SSCP matrix then becomes

$$\mathbf{S}_{xx} = \begin{bmatrix} \Sigma x^2 & \Sigma x^3 & \Sigma x^4 \\ \Sigma x^3 & \Sigma x^4 & \Sigma x^5 \\ \Sigma x^4 & \Sigma x^5 & \Sigma x^6 \end{bmatrix} \qquad (29)$$

Similarly, the predictor-criterion SCP vector $\mathbf{S}_{xy}$ becomes

$$\mathbf{S}_{xy} = \begin{bmatrix} \Sigma xy \\ \Sigma x^2 y \\ \Sigma x^3 y \end{bmatrix} \qquad (30)$$

With $\mathbf{S}_{xx}$ and $\mathbf{S}_{xy}$ thus, constructed, the normal equations [Eqn. (21)] are written and solved in exactly the same way as before.

The multiple correlation coefficient, defined as $R = r_{Y\hat{Y}}$ in the context of multiple linear regression, can be used in conjunction with polynomial regression equations just as well. Hence, it can be computed as $R = \mathbf{S}'_{xy}\mathbf{b}/y^2$ with the newly defined $\mathbf{S}_{xy}$ and $\mathbf{b}$ solved from the redefined normal equations.

The significance tests, both for a given multiple correlation coefficient itself and for the residual from the polynomial regression equation of a given degree, can likewise be conducted in the ways described in the previous subsection. For the former the F statistic given in Eqn. (26) is used, where the p used for the number of predictors may be replaced by m to denote the degree of the polynomial. Similarly, for testing, if it is warranted to go from an m-th degree equation to an $(m + 1)$-th, Eqn. (28) may be used, again with p replaced by m.

Although the forgoing significance tests are generally adequate and commonly used, there is one troublesome thing about them. This is that, in using these formulas, it is tacitly being assumed that the residual sum of squares, $(1 - R^2)\Sigma y^2$ or $(1 - R^2_{m+1})\Sigma y^2$ as the case may be, is attributable to "pure sampling error." This would be true if it was known that the degree of the regression equation entertained at any given stage is indeed the correct population model (in which case there would be no need to conduct a significance test). Otherwise, SS_{res} would be an overestimate of pure sampling error, since it would include also a portion due to regression of Y on a higher degree term of X. For this and other reasons, it

is often advisable to use an alternative approach to constructing and testing polynomial regression equations, which is known as the method of orthogonal polynomials. Very briefly, this approach uses a sequence of polynomials $P_1(X)$, $P_2(X)$, $P_3(X)$, and so on, instead of pure powers of X as the terms of the regression equation. Thus, for example, a cubic regression equation would be written as $\hat{Y} = a_0 + a_1 P_1(X) + a_2 P_2(X) + a_3 P_3(X)$.

For situations when the values that X can take are equally spaced (and hence can, by a suitable linear transformation, be transformed into 1, 2,..., K) and each of these X values is taken by the same number of cases, there is a specific sequence of orthogonal polynomials $P_1(X)$, $P_2(X)$,..., $P_{K-1}(X)$ for each K. These were originally derived by R. A. Fisher, and tables of their values are available in many textbooks on experimental design (see, e.g., Winer 1971). As explained in these books, orthogonal polynomials have the important property that, for each K their values for $X = 1$, 2,..., K sum to 0. Hence, the polynomial values may be used as coefficients of a contrast among the subgroup means of Y. For example, with $K = 5$ and $j = 1$,

$$\hat{\psi}_1 = P_1(1)\bar{Y}_1 + P_1(2)\bar{Y}_2 + \ldots + P_1(5)\bar{Y}_5 \qquad (31)$$

is a contrast of the five subgroup means of Y "attributable" to the first-degree polynomial, $P_1(X)$.

A further important property is that, associated with each contrast $\hat{\psi}_j$ for any given K, there is a sum of squares $SS(\hat{\psi}_j)$, with one degree of freedom, that constitutes an additive component of the between-groups sum of squares in the following sense:

$$SS(\hat{\psi}_1) + SS(\hat{\psi}_2) + \ldots + SS(\hat{\psi}_{K-1}) = SS_b \qquad (32)$$

Moreover, the partial sums of these $SS(\hat{\psi}_j)$'s are related to the SS due to regressions of successive degrees:

$$SS(\hat{\psi}_1) = r^2 \Sigma y^2 = SS_{lin.\ reg.} \qquad (33)$$

$$SS(\hat{\psi}_1) + SS(\hat{\psi}_2) = R^2_2 \Sigma y^2 = SS_{quad.\ reg.} \qquad (34)$$

$$SS(\hat{\psi}_1) + SS(\hat{\psi}_2) + SS(\hat{\psi}_3) = R^2_3 \Sigma y^2 = SS_{cubic\ reg.} \qquad (35)$$

and so forth. (Here each $R_m = r_{Y\hat{Y}m}$ is the correlation of Y with the m-th degree regression.)

Consequently, the question of whether or not the m-th degree regression equation is "adequate" for modeling the K subgroup means of Y may be tested by

$$F = \frac{\left[SS_b - \sum_{j=1}^{m} SS(\hat{\psi}_j) \right] \Big/ (K - 1 - m)}{MS_w} \qquad (36)$$

With $K - 1 - m$ and $N - K$ degrees of freedom. If this is significant, it is possible to proceed to the $(m + 1)$-th degree equation; if not, it can be concluded that the m-th degree equation is adequate.

1.4 Multiple Nonlinear Regression

This combines the complexities of multiple-linear and polynomial regression models. That is, higher degree terms of each of several predictors, and possibly products among two or more predictors, constitute the terms of the regression equation. Geometrically, this would represent a curved surface or "hypersurface." Such an equation can again be treated like a multiple linear regression, with each term regarded as a separate predictor. Hence, nothing new in the way of determining the regression coefficients, computing multiple correlation coefficients, and conducting significance tests needs to be added.

However, the presence of product terms (which could go beyond the simple $X_1 X_2$ type and include such monstrosities as $X_1^2 X_2 X_3$) does introduce a considerable difference in interpretation. To illustrate the point, the simplest case will be examined:

$$\hat{Y} = b_0 + b_1 X_1 + b_2 X_2 + b_3 X_1 X_2 \qquad (37)$$

By collecting the last two terms, this may be rewritten as

$$\hat{Y} = b_0 + b_1 X_1 + (b_2 + b_3 X_1) X_2 \qquad (38)$$

which somewhat resembles a multiple linear regression equation with two predictors X_1 and X_2, except that the coefficient of X_2 is not a constant but is itself a linear function of X_1. What this means is that the effect of X_2 on the criterion Y depends on the value of X_1. Assuming $b_3 > 0$, it can be seen that the larger X_1 is, the larger the coefficient $b_2 + b_3 X_1$ of X_2 becomes, hence the greater the effect of X_2 on Y. This, as the reader may have recognized, is what is known as interaction in ANOVA. The effects of the two independent variables are not simply additive, but are exerted jointly—each enhancing the effect of the other.

2. ANOVA and Multiple Regression

Since the mid-1960s or so, the writings of Darlington (1968), Kerlinger and Pedhazur (1973), Cohen and Cohen (1975), and others, have done much to popularize, in the behavioral and social sciences, the use of multiple regression analysis in situations where analysis of variance has traditionally been the main if not the sole analytic tool. This has been hailed by many as a recent innovation, but in point of fact some early writings of R. A. Fisher indicate that he invented ANOVA as a computational tool to get around the intractable computational difficulties, in the precomputer era, that arose when multiple regression was applied to designed experiments—that is, when the independent variables were qualitative variables (such as different fertilizers, different varieties of corn, etc.) that were manipulated by the experimenter.

The nature of the difficulty is not hard to see even in the case of one-way designs with qualitative independent variables having a large number of "levels"—for example, five or six different instructional methods for teaching some subject matter. Since there is no a priori ordering to the different teaching methods, it will not do to define a variable called "method," denoted X, give it the values $1, 2, 3, \ldots, 6$ (say), and use it as the independent variable in a simple linear regression analysis. Rather a technique has to be used known as "coding," of which there are several varieties.

Perhaps the most widely used type is that known as "dummy variable coding." Suppose there are K categories (K different teaching methods, K different religions, etc.) to the independent variable. $K - 1$ dummy variables $X_1, X_2, \ldots, X_{K-1}$ are then introduced and values assigned to members of the different categories as follows:

$X_1 = 1$ and $X_2 = X_3 = \ldots = X_{K-1} = 0$
 for Category 1 members;

$X_2 = 1$ and $X_1 = X_3 = \ldots = X_{K-1} = 0$
 for Category 2 members:

.
.
.

$X_{K-1} = 1$ and $X_1 = X_2 = \ldots = X_{K-2} = 0$
 for Category $K - 1$ members;

$X_1 = X_2 = X_3 = \ldots = X_{K-1} = 0$
 for Category K members.

A multiple (linear) regression analysis of the criterion variable Y (a suitable measure of achievement in the subject matter, observed on the entire sample) is then carried out. The test of significance of the multiple correlation coefficient thus obtained gives results identical to those given by the familiar F-test of ANOVA;

$$F = \frac{R^2/(K-1)}{(1 - R^2)/(N - K)} = \frac{MS_b}{MS_w} \qquad (39)$$

where the first ratio comes from Eqn. (26) with p replaced by $K - 1$. The curious reader will no doubt wonder why this should be so. Why do two techniques so seemingly different as multiple regression and ANOVA yield identical results?

Before answering this question, it is useful to look at how the technique of coding is extended to designs involving two or more factors. For specificity, suppose it is desirable to handle a 3×4 factorial-design ANOVA by the multiple regression approach via dummy-variable coding. Two dummy variables U_1 and U_2 (say) would be used for coding the three categories of factor A, and three dummy variables X_1, X_2, and X_3 for the four levels of B. How is the interaction A $\times$ B expressed? The reasoning introduced in Sect. 1.4 has simply to be applied so that the product of two variables represents an interaction between them. It is thus necessary to form all possible products between one of the U's and one of the X's—that is, $U_1 X_1, U_1 X_2, U_1 X_3, \ldots, U_2 X_3$ and treat these as six additional predictor variables. There would therefore be a total of $2 + 3 + 6 = 11$ "dummy" predictor variables in the multiple-regression version of the 3×4 ANOVA problem. It is easy to see that the number of predictor variables increases rapidly with the complexity of the design; so it is not surprising that Fisher should have striven, and succeeded, in inventing the alternative computational routines of ANOVA. Without the benefit of a computer, the solution of the normal equations (21) is a formidable task even when $p = 4$ or 5.

Returning now to the question of identity of the results obtained by the usual ANOVA method and the multiple-regression approach, just outlined, it can be recalled that a set of K group means of Y, $\bar{Y}_1$, $\bar{Y}_2$, . . ., $\bar{Y}_K$ can be perfectly fitted by a polynomial regression equation of degree $K - 1$. Hence, as pointed out earlier, the sum of squares $R^2_{K-1} \Sigma y^2$ due to the regression equation of degree $K - 1$ is equal to SS_b, since $\Sigma n_k (\hat{Y} - \bar{Y})^2 = \Sigma n_k (\bar{Y}_k - \bar{Y})^2$ when $\hat{Y} = \bar{Y}_k$ for each group. It therefore follows that $(1 - R^2_{k-1}) \Sigma y^2 = SS_w$, and hence that Eqn. (26) becomes

$$F = \frac{R^2/(K-1)}{(1-R^2)/(N-K)} = \frac{MS_b}{MS_w} \tag{40}$$

which is the customary F-test of ANOVA.

Consequently, in order to show that the same holds for the multiple correlation of Y with the $K - 1$ dummy variables X_1, X_2, . . ., X_{K-1} introduced above, it need only be shown that

$$R_{Y \cdot X_1 X_2 \ldots X_{K-1}} = R_{Y \cdot XX^2 X^3 \ldots X^{K-1}} \tag{41}$$

Although a general proof of this relation requires some background in linear algebra, it is a simple matter to verify that it holds for, say $K = 3$.

It stands to reason (and it can be proved both algebraically and geometrically) that the criterion variable Y has the same multiple correlation with X_1 and X_2 as it does with X and X^2. This reasoning can be extended to the general case of $K - 1$ dummy variables for K groups. Each dummy variable may be shown to be a linear function of X, X^2, . . ., X^{K-1} where X may be given the values 0, 1, . . ., $K - 1$ (or 1, 2, . . ., K or any K distinct values for that matter) for members of the K groups, respectively. Hence Y has the same multiple correlation with X_1, X_2, . . ., X_{K-1} as it does with X, X^2, . . ., X^{K-1}, and since it is already known that $r^2_{Y \cdot \hat{Y}_{K-1}} \Sigma y^2 = SS_b$, it follows that the significance test of $R_{Y \cdot X_1 X_2 \ldots X_{K-1}}$ is equivalent to the F test MS_b/MS_w of ANOVA.

Two other coding systems that are often used are effect coding and contrast coding. In the former, which is a special case of the latter, all members of a particular group (usually the Kth) are given the value -1 in all the $K - 1$ coding variables, while members of one and only one of the other groups are given a $+1$ on each coding variable in turn, members of all other groups getting 0's. Thus, for instance, with $K = 4$:

1	0	0 for Group-1 members
0	1	0 for Group-2 members
0	0	1 for Group-3 members
-1	-1	-1 for Group-4 members.

Note that the columns here constitute the coding variables. This system has the advantage that the resulting regression coefficients $b_1, b_2, \ldots, b_{K-1}$ represent the successive treatment effects $\bar{Y}_1 ms \bar{Y}, \bar{Y}_2 - \bar{Y}, \ldots, \bar{Y}_{K-1} - \bar{Y}$

(assuming that members of Group j got the 1 on the j-th coding variable).

In the more general contrast coding system, it is usual to use—as the values of each coding variable for the several groups—any set of numbers that add up to zero, with the further condition that no column (listing the values for one coding variable) be a linear combination of the other columns. Thus, the first three columns below qualify as values for a set of contrast coding variables, but the last three columns do not, because $VI = IV + V$.

	I	II	III	IV	V	VI
Group 1:	3	0	0	1	0	1
Group 2:	-1	2	0	-1	1	0
Group 3:	-1	-1	1	-1	0	-1
Group 4:	-1	-1	-1	1	-1	0

Each contrast coding variable asks a specific question. For example, I above asks whether $\bar{Y}_1$ differs significantly from the average of $\bar{Y}_2$, $\bar{Y}_3$, and $\bar{Y}_4$; II asks whether $\bar{Y}_2$ differs significantly from the average of $\bar{Y}_3$ and $\bar{Y}_4$. When the contrasts further satisfy the condition of orthogonality—that is, when the products of corresponding values of any pair of coding variables sum to zero (as do those in the set I, II, III)— the resulting analysis has an interesting property. Namely the coding variables are then uncorrelated among themselves, and hence the squared multiple R is the sum of the squares of the zero-order r's of the several coding variables with the criterion: $R^2_{Y \cdot 12 \ldots (K-1)} = r^2_{Y1} + r^2_{Y2} + \ldots + r^2_{Y, K-1}$

2.1 Advantages of the Multiple Regression Approach

The advantages of the multiple regression approach to ANOVA are implicit in the above discussions. The main advantage is that, with a judicious choice of coding variables, it is possible to dispense with the two-stage procedure of carrying out "global" significance tests and then going on to more specific, "fine-grained" significance tests that address specific issues, and go directly to the latter.

Another advantage is that a mixture of quantitative and categorical variables can be used as the independent variables in multiple regression whereas in ANOVA the independent variables must all be categorical or deliberately categorized (e.g., "high," "medium," "low" in mechanical aptitude), thus resulting in a loss of information.

Also, there is a greater flexibility available to the researcher in the order in which the independent variables are entered into the analysis. Since, at each stage, the significance of the increase in R^2 is tested, this corresponds to asking whether or not the later entered variable affects the criterion over and above the effects associated with the earlier entered variables.

Finally, and somewhat ironically, the "simplified" computational routines that Fisher developed in the precomputer days for ANOVA are mixed blessings at best in the computer age. Multiple regression offers a unified approach that dispenses with having to use specific formulas for specific designs.

An approach that further formalizes, generalizes, and routinizes the multiple regression approach is called the general linear model approach. This avoids (at least initially) an explicit coding of members of different subclasses by using coding variables and, instead, utilizes what is called the design matrix to specify the structural equation of the design being used. The interested reader is referred to treatises by Bock (1975), Finn (1974), and to a brief, introductory booklet by Tatsuoka (1975).

3. Concluding Remarks

Space limitations have precluded the discussion of several ancillary but nevertheless noteworthy topics in the forgoing. Cursory mention will therefore be made of some of them here, and the reader will be referred to suitable sources.

3.1 Correction for Shrinkage

One consequence of using the least-squares principle in determining the regression coefficients (more precisely, estimating the population regression coefficients) and the multiple correlation coefficient is that the latter is necessarily "inflated" for what can reasonably be expected as the correlation $r_{Y\hat{Y}}$ when the equation is used in a subsequent sample. A correction is therefore called for, and one that is commonly used is Wherry's shrinkage formula,

$$R_w^2 = 1 - \frac{N-1}{N-p}(1-R^2) \tag{42}$$

where N is the sample size, p the number of predictor variables, and R and R_w are the observed and "corrected" (or deflated) multiple-R, respectively.

This formula, however, is not the most appropriate one, for it is actually an estimate of what the population R^2 would be if the regression coefficients were optimized in the population as a whole. A better shrinkage formula is that developed by Stein (1960), which reads

$$R_s^2 = 1 - \frac{N-1}{N-p-1}\frac{N-2}{N-p-2}\frac{N+1}{N}(1-R^2) \tag{43}$$

What this equation gives is an estimate of the cross-validated $r_{Y\hat{Y}}^2$ in the population, using the sample-based regression equation. It therefore is closer to what is being looked for, that is the $r_{Y\hat{Y}}^2$ in a subsequent sample, using the current regression equation.

3.2 Alternative Predictor-weighting Schemes

By the same token as the sample R^2 is an overestimate of the population R^2 and the cross-validated $r_{Y\hat{Y}}^2$ in the population, the observed regression coefficients b_j or b_j^*, as the case may be, are extremely unstable from one sample to the next. Several authors have therefore proposed alternative weighting schemes, the most recent of which is Wainer's (1976) unit-weight system, which holds that not much predictive power is lost by simply

giving every standardized predictor a weight of one. While this has considerable intuitive appeal, some cautions against uncritical acceptance of the proposal are given by Laughlin (1978) and by Pruzek and Frederick (1978), to which Wainer (1978) responds in defence.

3.3 Ridge Regression

A different problem occurs when one predictor has a high multiple correlation with some of the others. In this situation the sample SSCP matrix $\mathbf{S}_{xx}$—or correlation matrix $\mathbf{R}_{xx}$ if the standardized predictors are being used—becomes close to singular, and the solution of the normal equations for $\mathbf{b}$ or $\mathbf{b}^*$ becomes extremely inaccurate. One method designed to cope with this problem (often called the problem of multicollinearity) is known as ridge regression, and it consists essentially of modifying the correlation matrix by subtracting a suitable constant from the diagonal elements. Marquardt and Snee (1975) present a good exposition of this method.

3.4 Applications

Applications of multiple regression analysis in educational research—especially those of the "technological" variety designed for practical prediction purposes—are too numerous even to think of reviewing in the limited space available. A highly selective, minuscule set of abstracts of some of the more innovative and research-oriented applications is given here, and the reader is referred to other sources of research examples.

An often cited and early example of the "ANOVA qua multiple regression" type of research is Cronbach's (1968) reanalysis of Wallach and Kogan's (1965) study of creativity in young children. The original researchers did a 2×2 ANOVA for each sex separately, using dichotomies on indices labeled "intelligence" and "creativity" as the independent variables and measures of social interaction and confidence in schoolwork as the criteria. Cronbach used the sequential multiple regression approach entering intelligence [renamed "achievement" (A) to avoid "surplus connotations"] and creativity [likewise renamed "flexibility" (F)] first and then adding sex (S), AS, FS, and AFS, testing the incremental R^2 each time. Outcomes that contradicted Wallach and Kogan's original results were that a significant $A \times F$ interaction was found on several dependent variables while the $A \times S$, $F \times S$, and $A \times F \times S$ interactions were in general nonsignificant.

In a study of the effects of classroom social climate on learning, Anderson (1970) included quadratic and product terms of the predictors, using samples at random from about 110 high-school physics classes. The criteria were posttest–pretest gain scores on a physics achievement test, a test on understanding science, and two other tests. Treating males and females separately, a total of eight multiple regression equations were constructed, entering IQ, LEI (learning environment inventory), IQ × LEI, (IQ)^2 and (LEI)^2 sequentially as predictors in each case. Not surprisingly, the IQ × LEI interaction was found significant in many cases, but the detailed graphical presentations of the resulting response surfaces are well worth careful study.

Another ingenious study relating environmental forces to cognitive development was that by Marjoribanks (1972), who was interested also in the possible effects of ethnic background (Canadian Indians, French Canadians, Jews, southern Italians, and WASPs). Specifically, eight "environmental variables" (P) (press for achievement, press for intellectuality, press for independence, etc.) plus ethnicity (E) served as the independent variables, and four subtests (verbal, number, spatial, and reasoning) of the SRA Primary Mental Abilities Test constituted the dependent variables. The main results for the verbal subtest (which was the most highly affected by the independent variables) was that $R^2_{V \cdot P_1 P_2 \ldots P_8 E_1 E_2 \ldots E_4} = 0.61$ while $R^2_{V \cdot P_1 P_2 \ldots P_8} = 0.50$ and $R^2_{V \cdot E_1 E_2 \ldots E_4} = 0.45$ (Note that there are eight variables in the environmental press set, since each is a quantitative variable in its own right, while there are four coding variables for the five ethnic groups.) From these three R^2 values, it may be inferred that the proportion of variability in verbal ability attributable to environmental press alone is $0.61 - 0.45 = 0.16$, while that attributable to ethnicity alone is $0.61 - 0.50 = 0.11$. This subtraction of squared multiple R's is in the same spirit as that of incremental (or decremental) R^2's, described above. Note, however, that the differencing is here done for sets of variables (the eight environmental variables as a set, and the four ethnic variables as a set) rather than individual variables. The systematic study of the separate effects of single sets of independent variables and the joint effects of two or more sets, when the independent variables fall into natural clusters as they do here, was called commonality analysis by Mayeske and his co-workers (1969) who used it as a prominent tool in a reanalysis of the well-known Coleman Report (*Equality of Educational Opportunity* 1966).

More than one study in the area of detection and correction of salary inequalities (between the sexes, among ethnic groups, etc.) have used multiple regression as their main analytic tool.

Birnbaum (1979), however, argues that it is fallacious to conclude, on the basis of a regression analysis of salary on merit (as measured by the typical indices of number of journal articles and other publications, ratings of teaching, years of experience, etc.), that discrimination exists whenever the actual salaries (Y) for a minority group fall short of the predicted salaries ($\hat{Y}$) based on the regression equation for the majority group (e.g., white males). He contends that the opposite regression—that of merit on salary—should also be considered. Group bias should be inferred only if a particular group is shown to have a lower mean salary holding merit constant and to have higher mean merit holding salary constant. An equitable system is proposed in which part of the salary increase is based on merit alone while another part is based on both merit and current salary in a compensatory manner (i.e., with current salary fixed, a person with greater merit gets a larger raise,

whereas with merit fixed, a person with lower current salary gets a larger raise).

Besides Kerlinger and Pedhazur (1973) and Cohen and Cohen (1975), the following are excellent sources for discussions of illustrative research studies using regression analysis—and, in the second case, related techniques such as canonical correlation, covariance structure analysis, factor analysis, and path analysis: Pedhazur (1982) and Kerlinger (1977).

3.5 Computer Programs

No account of regression analysis would be complete without some mention of the available computer programs. Briefly, all the well-known computer packages such as BMD, BMDP, OSIRIS, SAS, and SPSS include one or more multiple regression and/or general linear model programs. A package that is not typically implemented at a computer center but requires one's own typing in the FORTRAN file is the package included in Cooley and Lohnes' textbook (1971). In addition, a stand-alone program for the general linear model, called MULTIVARIANCE, is available from International Educational Resources, Inc.

Each of these programs has its advantages and disadvantages, so it is not feasible to rate them from "best" to "least desirable." One thing that all these programs have in common is the stepwise multiple regression (Draper and Smith 1966) capability—something that was implicit through all the forgoing discussions but never explicitly mentioned; that is, adding predictors one at a time so that the incremental R^2 at each step is as large as possible and terminates the adding when the resulting incremental R^2 is not significant at a prescribed level. A related procedure is that of adding the independent variables successively in a predetermined order—not necessarily that which will maximize the incremental R^2—having to do with some sort of priority ordering either chronological or theoretical. It will be recalled that all the research examples alluded to, utilized this procedure.

Finally, it is almost trite to say that, with the increasing availability and popularity of microcomputers, one should become cognizant of the availability and efficiency of software capable of carrying out multiple regression and other statistical analysis that is proper to or compatible with each machine. A short-range economy may prove to be a long-term waste unless a brand is carefully selected to match its capabilities with a person's needs and plans.

See also: Statistical Analysis in Educational Research

Bibliography

Anderson G J 1970 Effects of classroom social climate on individual learning. *Am. Educ. Res. J.* 7: 135–52

Birnbaum M H 1979 Procedures for the detection and correction of salary inequities. In: Pezzullo T R, Brittingham B F (eds.) 1979 *Salary Equity: Detecting Sex Bias in Salaries Among College and University Professors.* Lexington Books, Lexington, Massachusetts, pp. 121–44

Bock R D 1975 *Multivariate Statistical Methods in Behavioral Research.* McGraw-Hill, New York

Cohen J, Cohen P 1975 *Applied Multiple Regression/Correlation Analysis for the Behavioral Sciences.* Erlbaum, Hillsdale, New Jersey

Coleman J S et al. 1966 *Equality of Educational Opportunity.* United States Government Printing Office, Washington, DC

Cooley W W, Lohnes P R 1971 *Multivariate Data Analysis.* Wiley, New York

Cronbach L J 1968 Intelligence? Creativity? A parsimonious reinterpretation of the Wallach–Kogan data. *Am. Educ. Res. J.* 5(4): 491–511

Darlington R B 1968 Multiple regression in psychological research and practice. *Psychol. Bull.* 69: 161–82

Draper N R, Smith H 1966 *Applied Regression Analysis.* Wiley, New York

Finn J D 1974 *A General Model for Multivariate Analysis.* Holt, Rinehart and Winston, New York

Green P E 1976 *Mathematical Tools for Applied Multivariate Analysis.* Academic Press, New York

Kerlinger F N 1977 *Behavioral Research: A Conceptual Approach.* Holt, Rinehart and Winston, New York

Kerlinger F N, Pedhazur E J 1973 *Multiple Regression in Behavioral Research.* Holt, Rinehart and Winston, New York

Laughlin J E 1978 Comments on "Estimating coefficients in linear models: It don't make no nevermind". *Psychol. Bull.* 85: 247–53

Marjoribanks K 1972 Ethnic and environmental influences on mental abilities. *Am. J. Sociol.* 78: 323–37

Marquardt D W, Snee R D 1975 Ridge regression in practice. *Am. Statistician* 29: 3–20

Mayeske G W et al. 1969 *A Study of Our Nation's Schools.* United States Office of Education, Washington, DC

Pedhazur E J 1982 *Multiple Regression in Behavioral Research: Explanation and Prediction,* 2nd edn. Holt, Rinehart and Winston, New York

Pruzek R M, Frederick B C 1978 Weighting predictors in linear models: Alternatives to least squares and limitations of equal weights. *Psychol. Bull.* 85: 254–66

Stein C 1960 Multiple regression. In: Olkin I, Ghurye S G, Hoeffding W, Madow W G, Mann H B (eds.) 1960 *Contributions to Probability and Statistics: Essays in Honor of Harold Hotelling.* Stanford University Press, Palo Alto, California, pp. 424–43

Tatsuoka M M 1971 *Multivariate Analysis: Techniques for Educational and Psychological Research.* Wiley, New York

Tatsuoka M M 1975 *The General Linear Model: A "New" Trend in Analysis of Variance.* Institute for Personality and Ability Testing, Champaign, Illinois

Wainer H 1976 Estimating coefficients in linear models: It don't make no nevermind. *Psychol. Bull.* 83: 213–17

Wainer H 1978 On the sensitivity of regression and regressors. *Psychol. Bull.* 85: 267–73

Wallach M, Kogan N 1965 *Modes of Thinking in Young Children: A Study of the Creativity–Intelligence Distinction.* Holt, Rinehart and Winston, New York

Winer B J 1971 *Statistical Principles in Experimental Design,* 2nd edn. McGraw-Hill, New York

Regression Discontinuity Analysis

R. M. Wolf

Regression discontinuity analysis is a quasiexperimental design and analysis procedure that can be used to estimate the effectiveness of an educational treatment that is dispensed to all students who are deemed eligible for it. It differs from a true experimental design in two important respects: first, there is no random assignment of students to a treated and untreated group, and second, the treatment being studied is not withheld from anyone deemed eligible. Also, the procedures for analyzing data from studies employing regression discontinuity differ in important ways from traditional comparative studies of the effectiveness of educational treatments.

Consider that a school decides to institute a remedial reading program for students found to have deficiencies in reading skills at a particular grade level. A reading test is administered to all students in the school at the grade level in question. A certain score on the test is used as a cutoff so that all students scoring at or below the cutoff score are placed in the remedial program while all students who score above the cutoff score are placed in classes of regular instruction. Strict adherence to the use of a cutoff score is required for regression discontinuity analysis.

After the establishment of the groups, remedial and regular, appropriate instruction is dispensed to each group. At the conclusion of the treatment period, all students in both the remedial and regular groups are again administered a reading test. The results can then be represented in graphical fashion as shown in Fig. 1.

The analysis of the data proceeds as follows. First, a regression analysis of posttest scores on pretest scores is carried out and a best-fitting regression line is obtained for the group receiving the experimental treatment. In this case, it is the group of students in the remedial reading program. Second, a separate regression analysis of posttest scores on pretest scores is carried out and a

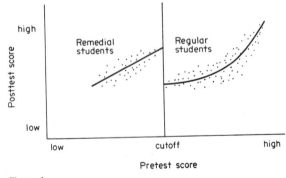

Figure 1
Graph to show results of remedial reading program following regression discontinuity analysis

best-fitting regression line is obtained for the group receiving the regular treatment. The term "best fitting" refers to a regression line that minimizes the sums of squares of deviations of the points from the regression line. Standard regression analysis procedures are routinely employed to obtain such lines. While usual practice is to obtain straight lines, there is no reason why this has to be. Curved regression lines may fit the data better than straight lines. In Fig. 1, the regression line for the students in the regular program is a curved one. The third step in the analysis of data from a regression discontinuity design involves a comparison of the lines at the cutoff point. To accomplish this, the prediction equation produced by each of the regression analyses is used to compute the estimated posttest score for a pretest score at the cutoff point. Since there are two regression equations, there will be two estimated posttest scores, one for each group. A comparison of these two scores provides an estimate of the effectiveness of the treatment.

In the example presented above, the estimated posttest score for the remedial group is higher than the estimated posttest score for the regular group. This difference or discontinuity is represented by the vertical distance between the lines at the cutoff point and suggests a positive augmenting effect for the remedial program. If there had been no difference or discontinuity between the regression lines at the cutoff point, this would be taken as evidence of no effect. If the regression line for the regular group had, in fact, been higher than the line for the regular group, then this would be taken as evidence of a decremental effect of the remedial treatment.

The special feature of regression discontinuity analysis is that it permits the use of a nonequivalent group for comparison purposes. Normally, this is not done. The reason it can be done in regression discontinuity analysis is that the nature of the comparison involves comparing the intersection of regression lines at a particular point in the score distribution rather than simply comparing the means or even adjusted means of noncomparable groups.

The example used in this article involved a remedial treatment. Regression discontinuity analysis can also be used to estimate the effects of treatments that are given to the most deserving students, for example, a program for gifted students. Again, all that is needed is to administer a pretest or some selection procedure, formulate and strictly adhere to a decision rule for placement, and obtain a posttest measure. The design should be quite serviceable when policy or administrative decision decrees that all who are eligible for a particular treatment should receive it and yet it is necessary to obtain an estimate of the effectiveness of the treatment.

See also: Regression Analysis

Bibliography

Cook T D, Campbell D T 1979 *Quasi-experimentation: Design and Analysis Issues for Field Settings.* Rand McNally, Chicago, Illinois, pp. 137–46
Wolf R M 1984 *Evaluation in Education: Foundations of Competency Assessment and Program Review*, 2nd edn. Praeger, New York, pp. 145–47

Smallest Space Analysis

S. Shye

Smallest space analysis (SSA) is a data analytic technique for representing geometrically pairwise similarities existing within a set of observed items (e.g., correlation coefficients computed between observed variables). As such, it belongs to the class of paired comparisons techniques, including factor analysis, which, in a sense, constitutes a special case of SSA. The term smallest space analysis (SSA) was coined by Guttman (1968) to indicate that a solution of smallest dimensionality to the geometrical representation problem is sought. When the given information about the pairwise similarities is treated as nonmetric, that is, only the relative degrees of similarity are represented, the dimensionality attained can be smaller than would otherwise be the case. Guttman (1968) presents computational procedures (algorithms) for solving a family of SSA problems within a unified mathematical formulation. These procedures have been programmed for the computer by Lingoes (1973). Smallest space analysis, then, often refers to any of these programs (most often SSA-I and its modifications). Along with similar procedures, such as Kruskal's (1964a, 1964b) multidimensional scaling and M-D-SCAL

computer program, SSA is sometimes referred to as a multidimensional scaling (MDS) technique. Indeed, whenever some correlation coefficient (calculated on a population of individuals) is used as the similarity criterion between observed variables, a central issue of these techniques is that of ranking or scaling the individuals. The scaling is done with respect to a number of derived variables (factors) and hence is multidimensional. But it is anticipated that these derived variables will be fewer (and have more fundamental meanings) than the original set of observed variables. The study of relationships between the SSA of the variables on the one hand and the space in which individuals are scaled on the other, while not sufficiently developed, is of theoretical and practical importance.

Smallest space analysis is often used as a technical device for visually representing a similarity (or dissimilarity) matrix but, more importantly, to aid in the formulation of theories. In conjunction with Guttman's facet technique it suggests a strategy for theory construction in the behavioral sciences. This strategy hinges on identifying correspondences between defined research contents and recognizable patterns observed in the empirical space of SSA (e.g., the simplex, the circumplex, the radex). It has implications for scientific lawfulness and for the scaling of tested individuals.

1. The Representation of Similarity Data by SSA

Suppose A,B,C,... are objects such as variables, people, social groups, ideas, or countries. And suppose that for each pair of objects there are empirical data about how similar (or dissimilar) the pair is. The similarity may be expressed in the form of correlation coefficients, preference indicators, conditional probabilities, panel judgment scores, or any other quantified measure. It is desirable to represent these data in a geometrical space in such a way that each object is represented by a point in that space, and the empirical similarity within each pair of objects is represented by the geometrical proximity of their respective points: the more similar two objects are, the closer the points representing them in the geometrical space. It is sought to attain such a representation simultaneously for all objects pairs, within a space whose dimensionality is the smallest possible. In practice, however, the problem is this: given a particular dimensionality m, ($m = 1,2,3$, etc.) what distribution of the points (each representing an object) in an m-dimensional space would best fit the similarity data?

A solution to this complex problem requires, first, its mathematical formulation, specifying the loss function to be minimized; the treatment of ties in the similarity data; and the distance function to be used in the geometrical space. Following contributions by Guttman and by Shepard (1962) a solution was found by Kruskal (1964a, 1964b) and in a rather general way by Guttman (1968) who proposed a loss function (Kruskal's stress or Guttman–Lingoes' alienation coefficient) and a computational procedure was developed for solving the problem.

1.1 The Essential Idea: An Illustration

Suppose the pairwise similarities between three objects A, B, and C have been found to be as shown in Table 1. A,B,C, could be, for example, three different schools and similarity could be assessed and scored, (e.g., with respect to their educational philosophies) by a panel of judges.

An empirical procedure for scoring the degrees of similarity between objects might produce the numerical scores shown in Table 1, which are commonly written in a matrix form, as shown in Table 2.

Table 1

Pairwise similarities between three objects, A, B, and C

Object pairs	Similarity	Possible similarity score (range 0–100)
A and B	Not similar	5
A and C	Very similar	85
B and C	Somewhat similar	30

Table 2

Matrix form of degrees of similarity between objects from numerical scores given in Table 1

	A	B	C
A	100	05	85
B	05	100	30
C	85	30	100

The essential information used in SSA is simply the ranking of the similarities. Thus, when the similarity scores 85, 30, and 5 are ranked 1,2, and 3 respectively (ignoring the diagonal values), the matrix of similarity ranks between A, B, and C will be as shown in Table 3. This matrix is the effective input of the SSA algorithm in its most popular version, SSA-I, for symmetric matrices.

Table 3

Matrix of similarity ranks between A, B, and C from Table 2 data

	A	B	C
A	—		
B	3	—	
C	1	2	—

In a two-dimensional Euclidean space with the familiar Euclidean distance function, A, B, and C can be easily mapped so that the similarity between any two of them is reflected by their proximity in the space, as shown in Fig. 1. The largest distance, between A and B, represents the fact that they are the least similar pair; B and C, being somewhat similar, are a little closer in the diagram; and the most similar pair A and C, are the closest in the diagram. Thus, the rank order of the pairwise similarities is correctly represented by the (inverse) rank order of the respective pairwise distances. That this could be done on the flat page means that a space of dimensionality two is sufficient. But is it necessary? Could one-dimensional space suffice? As Fig. 2 shows, the three objects can be placed on a straight line (a Euclidean, one-dimensional space) and yet all relative similarities are still correctly represented. This is, indeed, a solution of smallest dimensionality for the given similarity matrix.

In the above simple illustration it was a simple task to find a perfect geometrical representation for the matrix since it contained only three similarity coefficients. But in general, the task of constructing a geometrical representation for a similarity matrix becomes increasingly more complex when the number of objects, n, increases. Then the number $n(n-1)/2$, of coefficients to be ranked and represented by ranked distances, is much larger (e.g., if $n = 10$, it is 45; if $n = 50$, it is 1,225). Hence the need for computer programs.

In general, the larger the number of objects, n, the larger the dimensionality required for a perfectly faithful representation. But a dimensionality $m = n - 2$ (the number of objects minus 2) will always suffice (provided the untying in the output of ties in the input is permitted). Often, however, empirical interdependencies

Figure 1
A two-dimensional mapping representing similarity relationships between the three objects

Figure 2
A one-dimensional mapping representing similarity relationships between the three objects

among objects (schools, variables, etc.) produce a pattern of similarities that can be represented fairly faithfully within a space of much lower dimensionality, thus facilitating a parsimonious interpretation of the space, linking it with predefined research content.

2. Versions of SSA

Versions of SSA differ both with regard to the kind of input they can take (i.e., the matrix to be analyzed) and with regard to the specifications of the analysis itself (the treatment of tied values in the similarity matrix, and the choice of distance function for representing the similarity data). Some of the possibilities are reviewed briefly here.

2.1 Input Matrix

The similarity (or dissimilarity) matrix can be symmetric, corresponding to the situation where the similarity of A to B (A and B being any two of the analyzed objects) is by definition equal to the similarity of B to A. Examples of symmetrical similarity relations include: product–moment correlation coefficients between two variables; judgmental scores directly assessing the (symmetrical) similarity of two objects, A and B. This is the case illustrated above, where in fact only half of the (off-diagonal) matrix entries are considered. This is perhaps the most popular version nowadays and is often referred to as SSA-I, the name given to the corresponding computer program in the Guttman–Lingoes series (Lingoes 1973).

Often, however, similarity is neither defined nor observed as a symmetrical relation: The similarity of A to B may differ from that of B to A. (Recall that similarity in this article is a generic, umbrella concept for any relation that connotes affinity of any kind and that needs to be defined and quantified in any particular application.) Examples of asymmetrical relations are: conditional probabilities or conditional relative frequencies (probability of A given B does not equal probability of B given A; or, if A and B are social groups, say, the rich and the smart, respectively, then the relative frequency of A in B is not that of B in A); preference of association (if A and B are students, the extent to which A prefers to associate with B does not necessarily equal the extent to which B prefers to associate with A). Such

data sets can be analyzed by SSA with the interpoint distances reflecting similarities based on either the matrix columns or the matrix rows. In the above illustration these choices would correspond to the ranking by active preference (preferring) versus ranking by passive preference (being preferred). This version of SSA, too, has a corresponding computer program, SSA-II.

For further varieties of input matrices there are further versions of SSA including SSAR for analyzing rectangular matrices and others (Lingoes 1973).

2.2 Treatment of Ties

In SSA, the mapping of objects into a geometrical space is done subject to (or accommodating as best as possible) the condition that the greater the similarity between two objects the smaller the distance between their point-images in the space.

In symbols, this condition for SSA-I: if

$$v_{ij} < v_{kl} \text{ then } d_{ij} > d_{kl}$$

where v_{ij} and v_{kl} are the coefficients of similarity between objects (e.g., variables) i and j, and between objects k and l, respectively, as provided by the empirical data. d_{ij} and d_{kl} are the distances in the geometrical space between the points representing objects i,j and objects k,l respectively. This condition, however, does not specify what representation should be attempted if $v_{ij} = v_{kl}$. Two main possibilities may be considered: (a) it is possible to insist on representing equal similarities by equal distances, that is, if $v_{ij} = v_{kl}$, then $d_{ij} = d_{kl}$. That is, equality in similarity coefficients is represented by equality in distance relations.

In conjunction with the first condition stated above, this is the strong monotonicity condition.

The strong monotonicity condition is appropriate when importance is attributed to the equality in similarities as such, and when it is desirable to preserve the information about equality in the spatial representation. This is the case in the lattice space analysis (LSA) version which emphasizes structural aspects of the data and association with the individual profile space. (b) Alternatively, it may be possible to allow equality in similarity coefficients to be represented freely with any of the two distances being larger than the other ("untying of ties"). SSA solutions based on this weaker condition of so-called semistrong monotonicity could be of lower dimensionality which is consistent with the general aim of the analysis. Indeed, this semistrong monotonicity condition is the choice made in the most current applications of the SSA program series.

2.3 Distance Functions

There are a variety of distance functions that may be used in SSA: Minkowsky, Euclidean, or other and even semimetrics (functions which do not obey the triangle inequality); the exact functional form for the common SSA versions is given in Guttman's (1968) original paper. So far, however, the familiar Euclidean distance function has been the most widely used.

In recent years a new version of SSA, the lattice space analysis (LSA), has been proposed [Shye 1976, 1985b] in which lattice ("city block") distance function is employed. This version seems appropriate when the concern is with structural issues such as the connection between SSA and partial order scalogram analysis.

3. Comparison with Other Techniques

Several writers have reviewed multidimensional scaling (MDS) techniques. Carroll and Arabie (1980), taking Coombs' (1964) *Theory of Data* as a point of departure, have developed a general taxonomy for the numerous MDS models and methods advanced in recent years. Others compare MDS computational procedures for their technical merits (e.g., Lingoes and Roskam 1973). Here only a brief comparison of SSA with the more traditional technique, factor analysis, is made (Guttman 1982).

Both SSA and factor analysis are used to represent correlation matrices in a geometrical space for the purpose of formulating the essential concepts (dimensions) of the contents sampled by the observed variables. Both represent each variable as a point and vary the distances d_{ij} between the points inversely with the correlation coefficients r_{ij} between the corresponding variables i, j. In factor analysis, as in SSA-III output, the points are the termini of vectors extending from a common origin and the distances are the scalar products of these vectors. In that, SSA-III is the SSA version closest to factor analysis.

However, in factor analysis, the distances are related to correlations by an exact function, and if the vectors are all corrected to be of unit length, that inverse relation is $d_{ij} = 2(1 - r_{ij})^{1/2}$. In SSA, distances can be related to correlations by any monotone decreasing function. The exact relation is determined by the data and is provided in the SSA programs by a graphical plot ("Shepard diagram"). This a priori restriction to a particular function in factor analysis constitutes a strong constraint in the analysis and in this sense factor analysis is a specialized case of SSA. The result is that for a given set of data the dimensionality of the SSA solution cannot be larger, and often is smaller than that of the factor analytic solution (see Schlesinger and Guttman 1969, for an empirical example).

Another important difference is that factor analysis requires the r_{ij} to be product–moment coefficients. This is because it uses regression analysis for relating the individual factors scores to their variables scores. In this exercise, however, the analysis suffers from the indeterminacy of the relation of the desired score space to the calculated space for the variables. For a review of the indeterminacy problem see Steiger and Schönemann (1978).

In SSA, any real numbers, interpretable as similarity coefficients, can be used for r_{ij}. The space of individuals is left to be treated in its own right according to any relevant theoretical or technical consideration. This, of course, does not preclude attempts to relate the two spaces mathematically or substantively.

The SSA-I with its Euclidean distance function is further contrasted with factor analysis by its coordinate-free representation which is conducive to the discovery of patterns of regional contiguity (e.g., simplex, circumplex, radex).

4. Relating the Space of Variables to the Space of Individual Profiles

Since SSA is concerned directly with similarity among objects (which could, as a specialized case, be correlation among variables) it is not based on, nor does it assume, the existence of individuals' scores. Nevertheless, in cases where SSA is carried out with reference to some statistical coefficient computed on a population of individuals, it is of interest to characterize relationships between structural and interpretational features of the SSA space of the variables, on the one hand, and the associated space of the individuals' space (ordering them by their score profiles), on the other. In relating to two spaces there are a number of specifications that need to be made concerning the principle of structuring the two spaces; the exact nature of the statistical coefficients to be employed (whether product–moment or any other); the version of SSA employed; the technique for ordering individuals; and so on. Initial mathematical results on this question have been obtained by Shye [1976, 1985b, Shye and Amar 1985] with reference to partial order scalograms of individuals' scores (a multidimensional generalization of the unidimensional Guttman scale) and a special version of SSA, lattice space analysis, LSA.

5. The Uses of SSA for Theory Construction

Beyond being a mere device for visually displaying the multiple similarity relationships among objects, SSA can help in exploratory or confirmatory studies and aid in theory construction. Several examples from recent literature will illustrate that the utility of SSA hinges on the identification of reliable correspondences between clearly defined objects and interobject similarities, on the one hand and patterns of partitioning the SSA space into regions, on the other.

5.1 The Uses of SSA: Examples

(a) *Sociogram of a community elite.* Some 50 members of a community elite of a small city in the Federal Republic of Germany played the role of objects in an SSA carried out by Laumann and Pappi (1973). In one of the analyses, reproduced in Fig. 3, the similarity criterion was interpersonal professional or business contact. Since each person was characterized by institutional sector (as well as the political party and religion) to which he or she belonged and each was ranked as to his or her influence in the community, correspondences could be sought, and to a large extent were found, between these

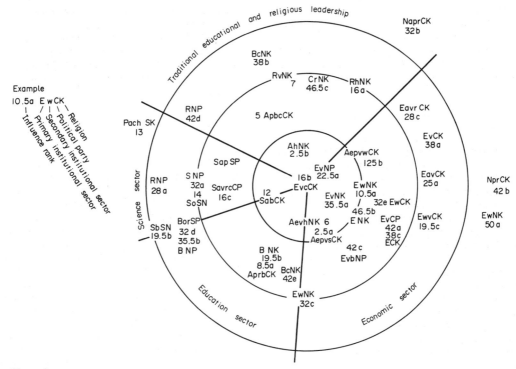

Figure 3
Business/professional network (Guttman–Lingoes coefficient of alienation = 0.148)[a]

a Source: Laumann and Pappi (1973)

characteristics and the location in the SSA map; a person's influence was found to be related to proximity to the center of the map, and membership in the institutional sector was found to correspond to circularly ordered sections of the SSA map, as shown in Fig. 3. The resulting business/professional network helped structure the community influence system and contributed to the theory of community decision making.

That interest or professional sectors are circularly ordered in SSA has also been found in a sociogram of experts, mapped by proximity of values (Shye 1982).

(b) *Testing a hypothesis on the structure of achievement motive*. SSA was used by Shye (1978a) to confirm the hypothesized structure of the concept of achievement motive. On the basis of a content analysis using the facet technique (Jordan 1978), the concept of achievement motive was structured; 18 variables for assessing achievement motive were derived; and a hypothesis concerning the structure of achievement motive was formulated. The hypothesis stated how the conceived structure of the concept would be manifested in an empirical SSA in terms of prespecified regions; spatial arrangement of the regions; and the dimensionality of the arrangement. Subsequently, the 18 variables were observed on a sample of executive managers and the intercorrelations among them were taken as the similarity measure for SSA. The resulting SSA (see Fig. 4) confirmed the anticipated structure by exhibiting regions that correspond to

the preconceived aspects ("factors") of achievement motive and arranging these aspects in space according to a rationalized criteria.

An analogous picture was obtained also in a study of the wider concept of achievement orientation in school children (Shye 1980).

(c) *The structure of visual and audio stimuli*. Reviewing many studies by himself and others, Shepard (1978)

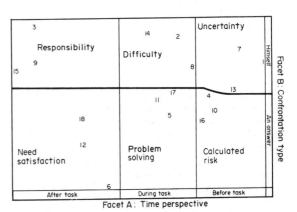

Figure 4
The empirical structure of achievement motive. Space diagram of intercorrelations among 18 variables. Two-dimensional SSA: coefficient of alienation = 0.17

found that when certain sets of stimuli are spatially represented according to the perceived similarity between them, they form a circle (circumplex). This is true, in particular, of colors differing in hue, and of musical sounds differing in chroma. This is especially noteworthy because from the purely physical point of view the stimuli are linearly ordered by their wavelengths. Hence the observed circularity could well be an instructive indication of the way in which the human mind tends to structure these sets of stimuli.

Circularity can be often regarded as the outcome of two (or more) polarities. This is illustrated in the nonmetric modeling of behavioral systems (Shye 1985a).

(d) *The structure of intelligence.* An important contribution of SSA to solving a theoretical problem is its application to the field of intelligence test theory. Since Binet introduced the notion of individual intelligence scores, the need to define intelligence has led to theories about its structure. Among these, Spearman's TFT (two factor theory) with its general factor ("g") of intelligence, and Thurstone's multiple factor generalization of Spearman's theory, are especially noteworthy. By employing SSA (together with an appropriate definition of intelligence items) Schlesinger and Guttman (1969) confirmed the radex as the pattern that best structures intelligence tests, thereby not only identifying factors of intelligence but also depicting their interrelationships through their spatial arrangement.

In the intelligence radex the one partitioning, into concentric rings, is according to the nature of the task required by the intelligence item: whether rule inferring (center), rule applying (ring around center), or achievement (outer ring). The other partitioning, into circularly ordered wedge-like sections, is according to the "language" of the intelligence items: whether figural, numerical, or verbal (see Fig. 5). Since then, refinements of this

structure, using spaces of higher dimensionalities and finer classifications of tests, have been studied.

5.2 Generalizations for Research and Theory Construction

The above examples as well as numerous applications of SSA in the study of intelligence, attitudes, personality, and social organization, illustrate that SSA focuses on stable aspects of data and hence can aid in scientific research and theory construction. In working with SSA it is useful to identify recurring patterns of regional contiguity and spatial arrangements by labeling them. Simplex denotes a linear arrangement of the analyzed objects; in circumplex objects are circularly ordered [see example (c) above]. Radex denotes a double partitioning of a two-dimensional SSA space (a) into rings by concentric circles and (b) into sections by radii emanating from the center [see example (a) above]. Duplex is a double partitioning of two-dimensional SSA by two sets of parallel lines [example (b)]. The question of comparing empirical structures, specifically in the context of educational research is discussed by Shye (1981).

See also: Scaling Methods; Factor Analysis; Partial Order Scalogram Analysis (POSA); Guttman Scales

Bibliography

Carroll J D, Arabie P 1980 Multidimensional scaling. *Annu. Rev. Psychol.* 31: 607–49

Coombs C H 1964 *A Theory of Data.* Wiley, New York

Guttman L 1968 A general nonmetric technique for finding the smallest coordinate space for a configuration of points. *Psychometrika* 33: 469–506

Guttman L 1982 Facet theory, smallest space analysis and factor analysis. Addendum to Guttman R, Shoham I. The structure of spatial ability items: A faceted analysis. *Percept. Mot. Skills* 54: 487–93

Jordan J E 1978 Facet theory and the study of behavior. In: Shye S (ed.) 1978 *Theory Construction and Data Analysis in the Behavioral Sciences.* Jossey-Bass, San Francisco, California, pp. 192–209

Kruskal J B 1964a Multidimensional scaling by optimizing goodness of fit to a nonmetric hypothesis. *Psychometrika* 29: 1–27

Kruskal J B 1964b Nonmetric multidimensional scaling: A numerical method. *Psychometrika* 29: 115–29

Laumann E O, Pappi F U 1973 New directions in the study of community elites. *Am. Sociol. Rev.* 38: 212–30

Lingoes J C 1973 *The Guttman–Lingoes Nonmetric Program Series.* Mathesis, Ann Arbor, Michigan

Lingoes J C, Roskam E E 1973 A mathematical and empirical analysis of two multidimensional scaling algorithms. *Psychometrika* 38(4 pt. 2)

Schlesinger I M, Guttman L 1969 Smallest space analysis of intelligence and achievement tests. *Psychol. Bull.* 71: 95–100

Shepard R N 1962 The analysis of proximities: Multidimensional scaling with an unknown distance function (parts I and II). *Psychometrika* 27: 125–40, 219–46

Shepard R N 1978 The circumplex and related topological manifolds in the study of perception. In: Shye S (ed.) 1978 *Theory Construction and Data Analysis in the Behavioral Sciences.* Jossey-Bass, San Francisco, California, pp. 29–80

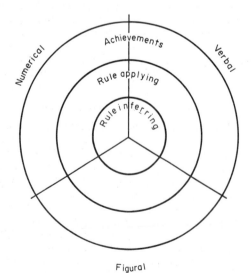

Figure 5
The radex of intelligence (schematic diagram)

Shye S 1976 *Partial Order Scalogram Analysis of Profiles and Relationship to Smallest Space Analysis of the Variables.* The Israel Institute of Applied Social Research, Jerusalem

Shye S 1978a Achievement motive: A faceted definition and structural analysis. *Multivariate Behav. Res.* 13: 327–46

Shye S 1978b On the search for laws in the behavioral sciences. In: Shye S (ed.) 1978 *Theory Construction and Data Analysis in the Behavioral Sciences.* Jossey-Bass, San Francisco, California, pp. 2–24

Shye S 1980 A structural analysis of achievement orientation derived from a longitudinal study of students in Israeli schools. *Am. Educ. Res. J.* 17: 281–90

Shye S 1981 Comparing structures of multidimensional scaling (SSA). *Stud. Educ. Eval.* 7: 105–09

Shye S 1982 Compiling expert opinion on the impact on environmental quality of a nuclear power plant: An application of a systemic life quality model. *Int. Rev. Appl. Psychol.* 31: 285–302

Shye S 1985a A nonmetric multivariate model for behavioral action systems. In: Canter D (ed.) 1985 *Facet Theory: Approaches to Social Research.* Springer Verlag, New York

Shye S 1985b *Multiple Scaling.* North-Holland, Amsterdam

Shye S, Amar R 1985 Partial order scalogram analysis by base coordinates and lattice mapping of the items by their scalogram roles. In: Canter D (ed.) 1985 *Facet Theory Approaches to Social Research.* Springer Verlag, New York

Steiger J H, Schönemann P H 1978 A history of factor indeterminacy. In: Shye S (ed.) 1978 *Theory Construction and Data Analysis in the Behavioral Sciences.* Jossey-Bass, San Francisco, California, pp. 136–78

Sociometric Methods

L. J. Saha

Sociometry and sociometric methods are concerned with the study of the ways people interact with one another. Knowledge about how people in groups choose one another for friendship, work, and other activities tells us much about group structures and the ways they change.

The origins and development of sociometry are inextricably linked with educational research. Moreno, the originator of sociometry and the sociometric method, based many of his early observations on studies of student classroom structure, and his work on the evolution of groups in *Who Shall Survive?* Moreno (1934) clearly documented the structures of groups from kindergarten to the eighth grade. The analysis of group properties is facilitated by the sociometric test, which "requires an individual to choose his associates for any group of which he is or might become a member." The individual is expected to make the choices without restraints and is not limited to members of his or her own group. In order to be sociometric, the test must determine according to specified criteria (sitting or working together, etc.) the feelings of individuals toward each other (attraction or rejection). The representation of these choices in two-dimensional space is called a sociogram, which portrays in graphic form the sociometric "stars," the "isolates," "the cliques," and other patterns of group structure.

Virtually no aspect of the educational process has been unexplored by sociometric research, including cognitive development, creativity and innovativeness, school success, and teacher effectiveness.

1. Early and Recent Uses of Sociometric Methods

Both the techniques of designing a sociometric test as well as the statistical procedures for analyzing the results have undergone considerable change over the years.

In its original form, the sociometric test was deceptively simple. In *A Primer of Sociometry*, Northway (1967) suggests that in any test, three or four criteria should be used as the basis for choices, the choices should be limited in number, and the choice questions should be stated in the conditional mood. Hence, the appropriate question is not "With whom do you associate," but "If all things were possible and you could associate with anyone you liked, with whom would you choose to associate?" Although Northway argued that three criteria and three choices for each individual were desirable, others contend that an unspecified number of choices is necessary to locate the full range of choice patterns (Lindzey and Byrne 1968).

There have been many variations in the standard sociometric question. One has been the self-rating method whereby the subject predicts how he or she will be chosen by others, or how all members of the group will relate to each other through their choices. Other methods include scaling instruments which are designed to elicit ratings of members of groups in terms of capacity to meet certain needs, such as affiliation and recognition. More complex approaches have combined sociometric data with other information to more accurately portray the group structure, while the time spent with individuals on certain tasks and interpersonal attractiveness have also found their way into sociometric tests.

1.1 Quantitative Methods in Sociometric Analysis

The earliest approach to the quantification and organization of sociometric data was the matrix whereby all choices are recorded and then summed. The names of individuals are listed along the vertical and horizontal axes and the choices are recorded in the cells for each criterion which is being tested. According to Northway (1967) the total number of choices for all criteria provides a social acceptance score or an indication of sociometric status. The actual number of persons choosing the subject gives a social receptiveness score, while the number of individuals chosen by the subject gives a social expansion score. It is also possible to identify groups of individuals for whom choices are or are not reciprocated, as well as the social isolates who neither choose nor are chosen.

Other methods have been applied to sociometric data. Of considerable use has been the probability model which identifies individuals who receive greater or fewer choices than they would ordinarily receive by chance. More complex matrix approaches consist of reordering rows and columns, by trial and error, until the clique structure of the group is located. Likewise, factor analysis has been used to identify and isolate underlying dimensions of group structure (Proctor and Loomis 1951, Lindzey and Byrne 1968, Hallinan 1974).

1.2 Graphic Presentation of Sociometric Data

The sociogram provides a graphic portrayal of sociometric information. It is constructed on the principle that choices between individuals may be symmetric (reciprocated), asymmetric (not reciprocated), or nonexistent. The major limitation of the sociogram is that it cannot adequately deal with large groups. Some researchers have argued, for example, that 20 persons is the ideal size for sociometric analysis, although more have been used.

In its original form, group members were designated by symbols with lines and arrows to indicate the direction of choice (Moreno 1934 pp. 33–44). Northway (1967) introduced the notion of the "target sociogram" which contained four concentric circles similar to an archery target. Each circle represented four quartiles or the four levels of probability, significantly above chance, above chance, below chance, and significantly below chance, from the center outwards. The "stars" were placed in the center circle and the "isolates" in the

outside circle. A vertical line through the center of the diagram was used to separate males and females, and the choice levels for each circle were usually indicated below each circle line (Northway 1967, Gronlund 1959).

The sociogram can sometimes be misused or misinterpreted. Gronlund (1959) has identified four common errors: (a) the sociogram usually depicts a graphic picture of desired associations, not actual associations, (b) the sociogram depicts the internal structure of the group, and therefore provides an incomplete depiction of group structure, (c) the choice patterns are sometimes seen as representing a fixed group structure rather than a changing social process, and (d) the sociometric structure will appear different when constructed by different individuals.

Recent usage of the sociogram has tended to focus on cliques rather than individuals. An early example of this clique-oriented structure is found in Coleman's analysis of adolescent friendship groups and their value systems in *The Adolescent Society* (1961). For example, in *Social Relations in a Secondary School*, Hargreaves (1967) focuses his attention on the clique structure of groups rather than individual "stars" or "isolates." Figure 1 reproduces a sociogram from Hargreaves' analysis of Form 4A boys in Lumley Secondary Modern School for Boys in England. Here it can be seen that clique A dominates the group structure but with cliques B and C also prevalent. The "star" of clique A is Adrian (number 29) who is also school captain.

2. Sociometrics and Educational Research

The importance of sociometry for educational research rests on the recognition that individual behavior is

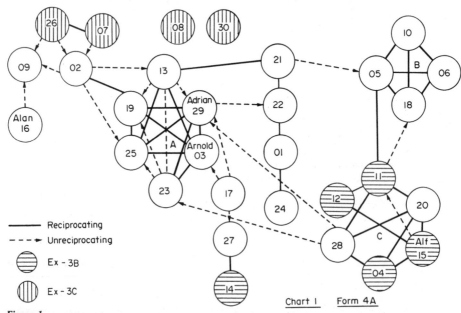

Figure 1
Sociogram depicting group structure of Form 4A (hatched circles represent students not in form 3A the previous year)

profoundly influenced by the group of which the individual is a member. Within the classroom, motivation, achievement, conduct, pupil–pupil and pupil–teacher relations are affected by group social composition and particularly informal group structure. A selective discussion of the findings of educational research using sociometric techniques points to some patterns of classroom behavior resulting from the sociometric context.

2.1 Intelligence and Achievement

There are distinct sociometric differences between students with extremely high or low intelligence (Gronlund 1959). Low intelligence may interfere with social acceptance by a person's peers, but high intelligence is not sufficient for high sociometric status. Pupils tend to choose those who are similar in intelligence, and a high deviation from group norms results in low peer acceptance. Gronlund (1959) identifies many studies which suggest that high levels of achievement are related to high social acceptance, but the direction of causality is not clear. However, the relationship is strongest where achievement is most highly valued by the group. The same pattern seems to hold for other skills which are highly valued, for example, in sport, playing an instrument, or social skills.

2.2 Social Factors

Social factors influence sociometric choice. Hollingshead's study, *Elmtown's Youth* (1949), pointed to high class homophily with regard to adolescent friendship patterns: two-thirds of all girls' clique relations and more than half the boys' were between members of the same social class. A reanalysis of recent data from Elmtown showed less choice between class equals, which suggests that over time the class structure in Elmtown had become more open and flexible, and hence less a criterion for sociometric choice (Cohen 1979). Similar patterns have been found regarding other social factors, such as family status and residential proximity.

2.3 Classroom Interaction

It is generally recognized that greater involvement in group activity and satisfactory social relationships leads to less emotional tension and thus provides a better environment for classroom learning. Shared group activities tend to promote greater affective ties, and teachers can manipulate the classroom situation to promote greater interaction and thus more interpersonal relationships. Classroom organization, both controlled and uncontrolled by the teacher, has a pronounced effect on the social development of students.

3. The Applicability of Sociometrics to the Improvement of Social and Cognitive Development

The knowledge derived from sociometric research is directly applicable to the improvement of social and cognitive development. Sociometric grouping whereby each individual is best placed for his or her own social

and cognitive development, is fundamental. Sociodrama and the use of roleplaying have also received attention for promoting beneficial classroom structures. Finally a recognition of the importance of power and influence, leadership and headship, both between students, and between teacher and student, facilitates the utilization of group structures already present in the classroom setting.

4. Future Directions in Sociometric Research

New developments in sociogram construction include three-dimensional models based on a number of variables. Recently Klovdahl (1982) has used computer programs to create and manipulate visual, including stereoscopic, representations of sociometric data and has suggested that the increasing availability of sophisticated interactive computer graphics promises to stimulate the development of theory about complex relational data. Many of these developments are taking place in the broader field of social network research, which includes the study of communities and organizations, as well as schools and other educational institutions.

Hallinan (1974) finds the traditional quantitative techniques of sociometric analysis too weak for an adequate analysis of the complexity of group sentiment and structure, and argues that there is more promise in the use of powerful mathematical theories and methods, such as Markov chains, matrix algebra, abstract algebra, game theory, and differential equations. With respect to schooling, greater attention to the process of group formation, its development and decline, is required to better understand the dynamics of classroom interaction and their consequences. Finally there is need to utilize what is now known about sociometrics in educational practice, particularly classroom pedagogy to further improve classroom learning and general school effectiveness.

Bibliography

Cohen J 1979 Socioeconomic status and high school friendship choice: Elmtown's youth revisited. *Social Networks* 2(1): 65–74
Coleman J S 1961 *The Adolescent Society: The Social Life of the Teenager and its Impact on Education*. Free Press, New York
Gronlund N E 1959 *Sociometry in the Classroom*. Harper and Row, New York
Hallinan M T 1974 *The Structure of Positive Sentiment*. Elsevier, New York
Hargreaves D H 1967 *Social Relations in a Secondary School*. Routledge and Kegan Paul, London
Hollingshead A B 1949 *Elmtown's Youth: The Impact of Social Classes on Adolescents*. Wiley, New York
Klovdahl A S 1981 A note on images of networks. *Social Networks* 3(3): 197-214
Lindzey G, Byrne D 1968 Measurement of social choice and interpersonal attractiveness. In: Lindzey G, Aronson E (eds.) 1968 *The Handbook of Social Psychology,* 2nd edn. Vol. 2:

Research Methods. Addison-Wesley, Reading, Massachusetts, pp. 452–525

Moreno J L 1934 *Who Shall Survive? A New Approach to the Problem of Human Interrelations*. Nervous and Mental Disease, Washington, DC

Northway M L 1967 *A Primer of Sociometry*. University of Toronto Press, Toronto, Ontario

Proctor C H, Loomis C P 1951 Analysis of sociometric data. In: Jahoda M, Deutsch M, Cook S W (eds.) 1951 *Research Methods in Social Relations: With Special Reference to Prejudice*, Pt. 2: *Selected Techniques*. Dryden, New York, pp. 561–85

Sociometry: A Journal of Interpersonal Relations 1937–1978 (since 1978 known as *Social Psychology*)

Statistical Analysis in Educational Research

G. F. Peaker

This article is a fictitious account of the happenings in a school in which two teachers became interested in improving their teaching and the work of the school and sought to check whether the things that they did were effective in increasing the learning of their students. Fortunately, the headmaster of the school had taken a degree in mathematics, and had read courses in statistics, in the days before the ready availability of calculators and computers and was well-able to give advice on some of the statistical issues that were raised. In this account the methods and procedures of elementary statistics are considered in a way in which the principles of statistics are advanced for consideration and the calculations are reduced to a minimum in an attempt to make clear the statistical principles involved. The statistical principles which are commonly applied in educational research are presented in a form that, hopefully, persons who like the two teachers in the article have not undertaken courses in statistics or educational research methods, can follow and understand.

1. Experiments

Miss Brown, who taught one of two parallel classes in the school, had given a good deal of thought to improving the presentation of part of the curriculum through the use of some visual aids that she had devised. The headmaster was mildly impressed, but being old enough to have lived through many tides of fashion, said that he would like some cogent evidence that the new method was really an improvement. Miss Green who took the other parallel class, was more doubtful, but was willing to take part in an experiment to see whether the claims for the new method had solid support. They agreed that, during a trial period of six weeks, Miss Brown would use the new method with her class while Miss Green covered the same field with her class in the customary way. At the end of the period the progress made in the field by the two classes would be assessed, and the results compared. But how could they be compared, and what sort of result would be convincing? They turned to the headmaster for advice.

The headmaster pointed out to Miss Green and Miss Brown that the existence of the two parallel classes was a fortunate circumstance, because an implication of the word "parallel" used in this sense was that if the numbers in the two classes were equal every Brown child could be a matched pair with a Green child of roughly the same ability and general standing. Consequently in the assessment of progress it would be possible to compare each of these pairs so that, at any rate roughly, like could be compared with like. But what if the numbers were not equal? What if Miss Brown had two more children than Miss Green? In that case two children in the middle of Miss Brown's class could be left out of the pairing, without bias to the results.

The headmaster went on to explain that if at the end of the agreed period the assessment was made, and that it turned out that in 19 of the 30 pairs the Brown child had made more progress, that in 9 cases, the Green child had done so, and that there were two ties, this would be 19 to 9. What were they to conclude? Was this result evidence of real superiority on the part of the Brown method, or was it a chance result that could easily be reversed on another occasion?

Some light on this could be gained by considering a case where they had no doubt that chance was at work. The tossing of coins would provide such a case. If they tossed 30 coins repeatedly in a box the average number of heads would fluctuate round 15, drawing closer to it as the number of times the box was shaken increased. This is a very easy, though rather noisy, experiment to make, and sceptical readers must perform it for themselves. They will find, if they persist, that on about two occasions in three the score does not depart from 15 all by more than three, and that on about 19 occasions out of 20 it does not depart by more than six. The general rule is that the odds are about 19 to 1 against a departure by more than the square root of the number of coins, and about 2 to 1 against the departure by more than half this number.

The headmaster continued to explain to Miss Green and Miss Brown that if they ignored the ties, they would have a departure of five from the even balance of 14 each. The square root of 28 is 5.3, so that the departure would be almost equal to the square root, and they would have therefore rather strong evidence that something more than chance had been at work. If they had 24 to 4 instead of 19 to 9 the departure would have been practically double the square root, and the evidence would have been very strong indeed. The headmaster explained that this was perhaps the simplest instance of the general rule that a result would be convincing to the extent that it exceeded its own standard error, a term

Table 1
Results of experiment for matched pairs of students. Scores recorded are Brown student minus Green student

Classroom rows		A	B	C	D	E	F	Total
				Classroom columns				
Scores	1	2	−2	8	4	−1	−3	8
	2	−3	4	10	10	−5	0	16
	3	6	2	2	2	−1	1	12
	4	5	4	−1	−1	4	4	15
	5	2	−1	0	2	1	1	5
Total		12	7	19	17	−2	3	56
Average		2.4	1.4	3.8	3.4	−0.4	0.6	11.2
Positive entries		4	3	3	4	2	3	19
Negative entries		1	2	1	1	3	1	9
Range in column		9	6	11	11	9	7	53

used to describe the variability of a measure over repeated sampling. In this case the standard error was half the square root of the number of matched pairs, and the departure from the even balance was about double this amount. The odds against this being a chance result were about 19 to 1. The odds against a chance departure of three or more standard errors would be very large indeed.

The headmaster now suggested that if the circumstances were such that each child could be given a reliable test the experiment would be more sensitive. When they had merely said that the Brown child had done better than the Green, or vice versa, they were ignoring the question of how much better? And it was plainly possible that if they could assess this it might tip the balance more, or less, towards Miss Brown. Before long Miss Green and Miss Brown had agreed to develop an appropriate test and give it to both their classes at the end of the experimental period of six weeks, but they wondered whether they could analyse the results without buying a calculator and learning how to use it.

The headmaster explained to them that they could do all the calculations necessary on the chalkboard, if they used some simple statistical techniques. It was perhaps fortunate that in each of their classrooms there were 30 desks arranged in five rows and six columns and at the beginning of the school year the students had been assigned to their seats in an alphabetical order. Of course, if the students had not been arranged in seats in this way, or had not been seated in alphabetical order, they could still have proceeded to analyse the test scores they had collected by using procedures that would have the same effect. However, in this case because the students had been randomly assigned to their seats the procedures suggested were sound. If each student in Miss Green's class was matched with a student in Miss Brown's class according to where they sat in the classroom, and if for each pair of matched students the score for a Green student was subtracted from the score for a Brown student, the results could be set out on the chalkboard as shown in Table 1.

In Table 1, the 30 differences have been set out in six columns and five rows. Altogether the 30 pairs have given Miss Brown's class a total superiority of 56 or an average superiority of 1.87 per pair. To see how convincing this result would be, it must be compared with its standard error. This can be found by looking at the row of ranges at the foot of the table. The range is the difference between the highest and the lowest entry in each column. To find the standard deviation, or scale, of the differences, it is necessary to divide the average range by the range factor for groups of five, which is 2.33. The total of the six ranges is 53, and dividing 53 by six times 2.33 gives 3.8 as the standard deviation or scale. To obtain the standard error, the scale 3.8 is divided by the square root of the number of pairs, which is 30 in this case, producing 0.69. So the average superiority of the Brown method is given by the average score plus or minus the standard error: 1.87 ± 0.69. The estimate is 2.7 times its standard error. This is stronger than the evidence from merely counting the signs, as would be expected, since more information has been used (Hartley 1950, David 1951).

The headmaster explained that although this use of the range was not included in many statistical textbooks, provided the items were in a random order the standard deviation, or scale, could always be obtained with enough accuracy, and the minimum of arithmetic, by the use of ranges. The range factors—that is, the factors by which the average range should be divided to give the standard deviation—are 2.04, 2.33, and 2.53 for batches of four, five, and six respectively. For larger batches the method would be less accurate, but could be used to give a check on the usual working by summing squares. The factor is 3.09 for batches of 10, and roughly four, five, and six in batches of 25, 100, and 500, and the procedures described are the basis for analysis of variance.

2. Replication of Experiments

The headmaster then explained, with some hesitation, that the apparent superiority of the new method could have nothing to do with the method as such, but might merely represent the fact that Miss Brown could be a better teacher than Miss Green, in the enthusiasm of her new discovery. And might it not be the case that the parallelism of the classes was to some extent a delusion, and the matching very imperfect? These were substantial objections, but they had to be considered before any very firm conclusions could be reached. They amounted to saying that one small experiment could not by itself be very convincing. The answer was replication—that is the repetition of the experiment, preferably under different conditions. To secure the most appropriate variation of the conditions was the object of experimental design. While more could be said about this, it must be noted that any replication was better than none, and that progress need not be delayed because the circumstances were not propitious for a good experimental design.

The advantage of replication can be seen by looking at the columns in Table 1. No single column by itself was particularly convincing. Apart from the fact that one of them (E) gave the palm to Green and not to Brown it would be quite easy to get four heads in five tosses of a coin. But when the six columns were aggregated the evidence was seen to be stronger. In the same way the evidence might be greatly strengthened by a sixfold repetition of the experiment. Or of course, it might be wiped out. Consequently, if three or four other schools could be found who were willing to try the experiment there was a better prospect of reaching firm conclusions. The prospect would be enhanced if the schools differed widely in their circumstances. Common sense suggests, and large-scale surveys have confirmed, that a child's school achievement must be affected by a very large number of varying circumstances, which are called variables for short. By comparing matched groups in the same school it has been possible to get rid of interschool variation, since only one school has been involved. This could be seen to be both a strength and a weakness. It would strengthen the evidence for that school, but it provided weak grounds for generalizing to the other schools. If there was a plan to bring in more schools, should these be as like the first school as possible, or as unlike?

There were arguments on both sides. If the evidence from the first school was rather weak it would perhaps be better to try the experiment again in other schools that were like it, in the hope of getting stronger evidence for this kind of school. If the first evidence was rather strong there would be grounds for thinking that it should not be repeated in other schools of the same kind, and in this case it would be better to widen the range of reference and generalization by seeking rather different schools for the replication. In practice, of course, the question could be settled by the fact that there were only three or four schools that were in communication with the first and willing to repeat the experiment. It would be a mistake to reject the proffered assistance of these volunteers in the hope of getting a better experimental design. But if there were a choice the

strength of the initial evidence would be a useful guide in making it.

Matching the children had done something to reduce the clouding variation within each school, and matching the teachers would do more. The headmaster explained that the clouding variation was the variation in the factors that were left out of account, and therefore tended to blur the results of the experiment. But the matching of teachers could only occur through good fortune, since the organization of the school could hardly be upset to produce it. Here there was a real clash between what was desirable as a matter of school policy and what was desirable for experimental design. Teachers were more likely to work effectively with methods they believed in. On the other hand if the better teachers were all on one side then the apparently greater success of a new method might merely be evidence of this, and not evidence that the new method was intrinsically better than the old. Another insidious possibility was what is known (from the name of the works where it was first noted) as the Hawthorne effect. Merely taking part in an experiment tended to increase the zeal of those concerned. This had a well-known parallel in medicine, where patients given placebos and patients given treatment alike made better progress than those who were left untreated. The fact that experiments generated enthusiasm was itself a strong argument in their favour, even if nothing else were gained. Holidays do people good, even though after the holiday they return to their starting point.

Some light could be obtained by considering whether there were marked differences in the results from different schools taking part, and if so whether these could be linked with known circumstances. But what would be considered as marked differences? As in the case of the single school the thing to look at is the standard error. The results above showed that the average superiority of the Brown method came out at 1.87 ± 0.69. Since standard errors could be added by Pythagoras' theorem, the standard error of a difference would be the root mean square of the standard errors of the items. If the standard error were the same in a second school the standard error of the difference would be 0.98, so that differences would not be remarkable until they exceeded two. If there were several schools in the experiment, it would be possible to look at the range instead of at the separate differences.

With four, six, and ten schools the critical factors were 3.6, 4.0, and 4.5. That is, if with four schools the difference between the highest and the lowest Brown superiority exceeded 3.6 times the average standard error it would be useful to look for something to account for this, which it would not be with a smaller range. If the range were not excessive it might be concluded that the new method was successful to about the same extent in all the schools, and that this would make it rather improbable that its apparent superiority was illusory and really reflected only differences between teachers.

3. Repeated Surveys and Contingency Tables

The next time Miss Green and Miss Brown met with the headmaster to discuss the experiment that Miss Brown had planned to undertake, Miss Green suggested that the major factor that influenced the performance of the students in her class appeared to be parental attitudes towards encouraging higher school achievement. As a consequence she argued there was more to be gained from persuading parents to adopt more encouraging attitudes than from undertaking the proposed experiment. Miss Brown, however, suggested that common sense and general experience would seem to indicate that a higher level of performance at school would produce more favourable parental attitudes and to her the effect that Miss Green had proposed would appear to operate in the opposite direction. Under these circumstances it was more desirable for her to undertake the proposed experiment and in this way raise the level of achievement of the students in her class, and as a consequence improve the attitudes of the parents towards their children's schooling and towards the school. The headmaster saw quickly that it was necessary for him to explain some of the problems that were likely to arise when data were collected in a nonexperimental study, and since data were not available, he made up some data so that they could together discuss what might happen if at the beginning of the year they set out to measure not only student achievement for all students in the school but also to assess parental attitudes. Of course it was clear that to throw some light on this perplexing question it would be necessary to carry out a repeated study for all students in the school 12 months later. Without the repeated study there would be no chance of teasing out whether parental encouragement had led to higher achievement or whether higher achievement had influenced parental attitudes.

The results that the headmaster used in their discussion of this problem are recorded in Table 2. In the table the first sign (+ or −) relates to parental attitudes and the second sign to student achievement. A positive sign is associated with an encouraging attitude, or an above average level of achievement, and a negative sign a neutral or negative attitude and an average or below average level of achievement. The rows are associated with the first survey and the columns are associated with the

second survey carried out a year later. There were data for both occasions for 491 of the 521 students in the school. By adding the entries on the leading diagonal in the table the number of students for whom there had been no changes in sign would be obtained. There were 363 such students who could be described as "steadies". By adding together the entries on the other diagonal, it can be seen that there were six cases in which both parental attitudes and achievement had changed signs. Thus there were six "double-crossers". From the addition of the entries in the eight remaining cells of the table it can be noted that there were 122 cases where one sign had changed. These students have been referred to as the "crossers". The information contained in Table 2 could be seen more readily if the table were rewritten with the entries in the diagonals removed as in Table 3.

The rows and the columns have been labelled as convergent or divergent according to whether the crossing brings parent and child closer together or further apart. There were 106 cases of convergence and only 16 cases of divergence. Furthermore, there were 100 (58 + 42) cases where the child followed the parent and only 6 (3 + 3) cases where the parent followed the child. Thus, the headmaster explained, if these numbers had been obtained there would be strong prima facie evidence in favour of the view that it was the attitudes that produced the achievement rather than vice-versa. If the figures in the table were reversed, a strong case would exist for a reversal of the interpretation, while if the number of divergent cases was very large neither interpretation would suffice. However, it would be necessary to count the number of divergent cases, if only to be satisfied that the number was small.

4. Correlation

The headmaster explained that for the purposes of simplification, a comparison had been made with both attitudes and achievement reduced to variables with two values only. It would, however, have been preferable to use data in which attitudes and achievement had been assessed along an interval scale. If the data had been in interval form it would have been necessary to use correlation coefficients. But the statistical principles associated with the use of correlation coefficients could be well-illustrated by using data assessed in two nominal categories (+ or −) instead of being measured along an interval scale. With two categories, the tetrachoric correlation coefficient could be employed to express the relationship between the two variables.

In Table 2 the data in the right hand column giving the totals for the categories used in the first survey could be set out in a two-by-two contingency table as shown on the left-hand side of Table 4. Likewise the totals for the categories used in the second survey, obtained from the final row of Table 2 could also be set out in a two-by-two contingency table, as shown on the right-hand side of Table 4.

From the two halves of Table 4, a tetrachoric correlation coefficient can be obtained. The calculation of the

Table 2
Results of surveys of parental attitudes and school achievement

| | | Second survey | | | | |
		+ +	+ −	− +	− −	Total
First	+ +	170	5	4	1	180
survey	+ −	58	11	2	3	74
	− +	3	2	10	42	57
	− −	1	4	3	172	180
Total		232	22	19	218	491

Numbers changing:
  Steadies—363, Crossers—122, Double crossers—6

Table 3
Crossers in the results of survey

		Second survey					
		+ +	+ −	− +	− −	Total	Category
First	+ +		5	4		9	Divergent
survey	+ −	58			3	61	Convergent
	− +	3			42	45	Convergent
	− −		4	3		7	Divergent
Total		61	9	7	45	122	
Category		Convergent	Divergent	Divergent	Convergent		

tetrachoric correlation is complex, but tables and an ABAC are readily available which permit the values to be read off very quickly. For the first survey the correlation is 0.67 and for the second 0.96.

The headmaster went on to show that four other correlation coefficients could be derived from Table 2:

(a) Parents in the first survey with parents in the second survey = 0.99.

(b) Children in the first survey with children in the second survey = 0.75.

(c) Parents in the first survey with children in the second survey = 0.98.

(d) Parents in the second survey with children in the first survey = 0.67.

The contingency tables used for the calculations of these correlation coefficients have been recorded in Table 5. They were obtained by combining the appropriate rows and columns in Table 2.

If the correlation coefficients were all collected together and set out in a table as in Table 6, the patterns amongst the correlations would become clearer and would reveal the relationships that were argued to exist from Table 2.

The headmaster then explained that the following conclusions could be drawn from Table 6.

(a) Correlation $P_1 P_2$ (0.99) is greater than correlation $C_1 C_2$ (0.75), that is, children shift more than their parents.

(b) Correlation $P_2 C_2$ (0.96) is greater than correlation $P_1 C_1$ (0.67), that is, the shift among parents is more towards agreement.

(c) Correlation $P_1 C_2$ (0.98) is greater than correlation $P_2 C_1$ (0.67), this suggests that children move

towards their parents rather than parents moving towards their children.

At this point in the discussion Miss Brown who had been following the argument very carefully said that she was very uneasy about drawing the final inference from the difference between the correlation coefficients, and the discussion was adjourned until a later occasion while Miss Brown sought to consult her nephew David who was undertaking research into statistical procedures (Rogosa 1980).

5. Simple Regression and Analysis of Covariance

On the next occasion when Miss Green and Miss Brown met with the headmaster to discuss the study that Miss Brown had planned, Miss Green raised the question of how their previous discussions would be modified, if the data they had used for both attitudes and achievement had been measured along an interval scale, and how the procedures would change if additional factors were introduced. She suggested to the headmaster that perhaps it would be better to undertake the study in several schools instead of using students from only one school. The headmaster did not wish to be drawn away from a discussion about the experimental study, but quickly saw the relevance of the issues being raised. In his reply, which we now quote, he made reference back to the design of the experimental study.

When we have parallel classes matching, it is the natural procedure to give each side of an experiment a fair chance. How can we replace it in the case where parallel classes do not exist? The inquiries that would be needed to match children in different schools would be too extensive to be practicable, unless the circumstances are very favourable. It will usually be easier to replace them by giving each child in the experiment an initial and a final assessment in the subject

Table 4
Contingency tables for results of first and second surveys

First survey		Parent			Second survey		Parent		
		+	−	Totals			+	−	Totals
Child	+	180	57	237	Child	+	232	19	251
	−	74	180	254		−	22	218	240
Totals		254	237	491	Totals		254	237	491

Table 5
Combined tables for calculation of tetrachoric correlation coefficients

$r = 0.99$		Parent second survey (P_2)			$r = 0.75$		Child second survey (C_2)		
		+	−	Total			+	−	Total
Parent first (P_1) survey	+	244	10	254	Child first (C_1) survey	+	187	50	237
	−	10	227	237		−	64	190	254
Total		254	237	491	Total		251	240	491

$r = 0.98$		Child second survey (C_2)			$r = 0.67$		Parent second survey (P_2)		
		+	−	Total			+	−	Total
Parent first (P_1) survey	+	234	20	254	Child first (C_1) survey	+	180	57	237
	−	17	220	237		−	74	180	254
Total		251	240	491	Total		254	237	491

matter. The exact form of these two assessments, examinations, or tests will need careful discussion among the teachers concerned, but this will not be a waste of time, since it will do much to clarify what it is hoped that the children will learn during the progress of the experiment.

When the final test has been given, the success of the experiment can be judged by plotting the final marks vertically against the initial marks horizontally. We can use colour to distinguish the methods that are being compared; let us say red for the new method and blue for the old. We can distinguish schools by indicating the position of a pupil by a distinct shape for each school, such as circles, triangles, clubs, hearts, spades, and diamonds. These will be enough to cover the case where six schools are taking part, with three on the side of the new method and three on the other side. Let us suppose that on the average there are 30 pupils in each of the six classes. If so, our diagram will include 180 points or markers, of which 90 will be red and 90 blue, while there will be 30 or thereabouts for each of the six shapes. The 180 points or markers will make a roughly elliptical cloud.

There will be two smaller clouds, coloured red and blue, and six little ones, each distinguished by the characteristic shape of its points. The clouds will be elliptical because, if the tests have been well-chosen, the abler and more knowledgeable children will tend to do rather better in both the initial and the final test, and the less able and less knowledgeable rather worse. The greater this tendency the slimmer the elliptical shapes.

We can now find the average increase in the final test that corresponds to unit increase in the initial test. We can do this by dividing the paper into eight (say) vertical strips and drawing a short horizontal line across each strip in a position such that half the points in the strip are above the horizontal

Table 6
Summary of correlations

	P_1	P_2	C_1	C_2
P_1	1	0.99	0.67	0.98
P_2	0.99	1	0.67	0.96
C_1	0.67	0.67	1	0.75
C_2	0.98	0.96	0.75	1

and half below. We then mark the middle of each horizontal line and draw a line through all these eight points. This is the regression line. It tells us what is the average score on the final test corresponding to any given score on the initial test. It also tells us, and this is what we want to know, whether the red children have on the whole been more successful than the blue. This will be the case if the points above the line are preponderantly red, and the points below preponderantly blue.

Miss Brown was clearly interested in the possibility of analysing data from six schools, and she sought clarification at this point. "What do you mean by preponderantly?", she asked, "How much preponderance is needed for evidence in favour of red?" The headmaster replied,

To answer this question with the least amount of arithmetic, we can merely count the red points above and below the line. With 90 points the even break would be with 45 above and 45 below. The square root of 90 is 9.5, so that if we have 55 or more red points above the line, and therefore 35 or fewer below the line we have firm evidence in favour of the new method. But 50 above and 40 below would be only rather weak evidence. As a check we can carry out the complementary count on the blue points. This should give the reverse result, since, if we have drawn the regression line properly, there will be about as many points (red and blue) above it as below.

By making similar counts and calculations for each of the six schools individually we can find whether there is any evidence of marked differences between the success of the two methods in different schools. If there is little difference it is more likely that the new method will be equally successful in other schools. If there is a great deal of difference the interesting question is why?

The procedure that the headmaster described, he said was a simple form of the analysis of covariance, just as in the earlier discussion he had described a simple form of the analysis of variance. He went on to say that while it would be easy to undertake such an analysis using a programmable calculator or a computer, there was still a great deal to be gained from actually plotting the evidence on paper and taking a good look at it. Moreover, the test which was available for examining data in this way, of measuring the departure from the even break against the square root of the number of cases involved, was a very simple one to apply.

6. *Multiple Regression Analysis*

Miss Green, who at this point considered that the headmaster had not fully answered the question that she had asked, once again raised the issue of examining data for more than two variables, and also commented that the sizes of classes were less than 30 in most of the neighbouring schools and in his discussions the headmaster had only considered cases in which the classes were equal in size with 30 students. The headmaster took up these two points as he continued with the discussion.

If you have taken care to draw a probability sample and have obtained numerous measures from its members, it would clearly be wasteful to stop short of a full analysis of the results. However, a salient feature of the results will be that the variables are all intercorrelated, so that each blurs the effect of the others. For example, consider the question of the effect of the size of the teacher's class. It is very hard to believe that, if other things were equal, merely adding several more children to the class will improve the average achievement. Yet most surveys show mild positive simple correlations between the average size of class in school and the average achievement for that school. But this can hardly be the whole story. The result has only to be stated to arouse the conjecture that there must be various favourable circumstances, associated with large classes, to explain a result that would otherwise be incredible. But what can these circumstances be?

To answer such questions we need multiple regression analysis, which discloses what is left of a simple correlation when the effects of other correlated variables are removed. This is only one of several forms of multivariate analysis, but it is perhaps the most generally useful.

Until the advent of the electronic computer the sheer weight of the arithmetic made extensive applications impracticable. This difficulty has now been overcome, owing to the extreme rapidity with which computers can do arithmetic, and particularly the kind of arithmetic needed here, which consists only of the repeated application of the same short series of steps. Work that would be intolerably tedious and lengthy to do by hand can be done by the computer in a few minutes or even seconds. None the less, if you are to make a sensible use of the computer output you must understand the nature of the process. However, the computations are sufficiently complex to leave for a discussion at another time. It is perhaps more important for us to consider the interpretation of the results.

The first step in the interpretation is easy. We are entitled to say that the variables that have not survived the regression are irrelevant, on the evidence of the sample, though, even here we have to keep in mind that some of them might have survived on the evidence of another sample, so that it is important to have a proper estimate of sampling error. For some of the variables, however, the difficult question of cause and effect may arise. For example, are the attitude variables mere proxies for more fundamental attitudes that we ought

to have measured but have not? If there is a causal relation, in which sense does it work? For example, does parental encouragement produce better achievement in school, or does better achievement in school produce more parental encouragement? The analysis can show the existence and the strength of a relation, but cannot tell us how or why in what sense it works. For this we must rely on our general experience of parents, teachers, children, and schools. Consequently we have a sort of double sieve. Some explanations compatible with the analysis may not be compatible without judgment from our general experience; on the other hand some explanations compatible with our general experience may not be compatible with the analysis. Those that are compatible with both have a higher probability than they had before the surveys were carried out. This double sieving is the ordinary way of scientific progress.

The question of cause and effect is a great deal simpler if a sound experiment has been carried out. However, in educational research there are very severe ethical restrictions upon experiment. Thus in education it is rarely justifiable to apply the method of artificial randomization to control for unknown factors that might influence the results, as has been so successful in agricultural and industrial work. In our earlier discussion you were teaching parallel classes, which can in fact be regarded as an example of artificial randomization, since in this context the word "parallel" implies the random allocation of students to classes. The subsequent matching of the students is an example of the use of what are called, in the technical language of factorial experiments, randomized blocks, each block being a pair of students in this case. "Blocking" in the language of the design of experiments corresponds to "stratification" in survey design. In each case the object is to get as much of the variation as possible between the blocks or strata, in order to reduce the sampling fluctuation.

The use of parallel classes in the experiment that you are planning eliminates the wide range of ability and background between the children from the uncertainty in the comparison of the two methods. But cases like this, where randomization already exists, are in the nature of fortunate accidents. To apply artificial randomization in other cases would generally result in the disruption of school organization, to an extent that would make the game not worth the candle. We can be the more confident about this when we remember that the distribution of relationships, like that of characteristics, exists only in a framework of specific populations, and that inferences derived from the experimental testing of several treatments are restricted to the population included in the experimental design. In general, we cannot solve simultaneously all the problems of measurement, representation, and control; we have to compromise and do the best we can, and in educational work this compromise will only rarely include the devices of artificial randomization.

7. *The Scale of Inquiry*

So far in the discussions that they had had, the headmaster and Miss Green and Miss Brown had discussed the small-scale experimental study in only one, or at most six schools that the enterprising teacher could carry out to test the ideas that had emerged from experience and reflection. The headmaster explained that such small-scale experiments could be among the most useful. Successful innovation in teaching method was more likely to begin in the classroom than elsewhere. Only rudimentary experimental design was needed, and, if the experiment was successful, a simple statistical test of the kind discussed would provide prima facie evidence of this. While it would be a mistake to attach great weight to the results of one small experiment it would always be possible to replicate what looked like a successful experiment to see whether the success was repeated.

Nevertheless, he pointed out as he continued, there were a very large number of different influences interacting to advance or retard a student's learning in very complicated ways. It was plain that there might be a great number of factors influencing a student's school achievement that might never have been thought of. Quite a large number had been thought of, and some of them had been measured, but even so there remained a formidable problem of trying to disentangle them and estimate their several effects. Broadly speaking, there were two ways of tackling this problem. The first was to try to set up an experimental situation in which it was reasonable to hope for success in balancing all the variables but two, and then to observe the effect of one of these two on the other. This is called a bivariate experiment. The second was to measure the other variables instead of attempting to balance them. This is called a multivariate experiment. In the first case there was a criterion variable and a predictor variable, and observations could be made of the effect of the predictor on the criterion. In the second case there was again a criterion variable, but now there were several predictors, and the object was to estimate what the effect of each would be if it acted in isolation. In the first case the other variables could be controlled by the experimental design. In the second case each predictor could be taken in turn and controlled statistically.

Whether a variable would be regarded as a predictor or a criterion depended upon what was being attempted. The same variable could play both parts although not of course simultaneously. A variable could be considered as a criterion when an attempt was being made to estimate the influence of other variables on it. When an attempt was made to estimate its influence on other variables it would be called a predictor. Predictors are sometimes spoken of as independent variables, and criteria as dependent variables. While both usages were well-recognized, neither was totally satisfactory. Independent variables did not need to be independent in the statistical sense, and predictors often did not predict in the everyday sense of making a forecast about the future.

In planning a study in educational research a choice must be made between undertaking a simple experiment in the classroom setting and replicating the experiment in other classrooms or schools if it proved to be successful, or undertaking a large-scale inquiry in a random sample of schools. In a simple experiment it was only possible to investigate two variables at a time. In a large-scale inquiry it was possible to examine the effects of many factors simultaneously. Large-scale inquiries had two advantages that could be set against the much greater flexibility and intimacy of small-scale work.

First, they could be carried out with random samples of students, parents, teachers, and schools, and greater generality could be claimed from the findings. Secondly, the numbers could be made large enough to stand multivariate analysis so that much more could be done in the way of disentangling the effects of the different variables. However these advantages were bought dearly at the expense of both flexibility and intimacy. The sacrifice of intimacy and flexibility that was entailed by large-scale work would only be justified if there was a compensating advantage of representativeness. The only sure way of obtaining this compensating advantage, would be to apply probability sampling to a large and important population, such as the population of children aged 14 in all the government schools of a country. The main point that distinguished this form of sampling from others, such as selecting the sample by expert judgment or by the "quota" method, was that only with probability sampling could the accuracy of the estimates be found from the material evidence of the sample itself.

At this stage in the discussion Miss Green and Miss Brown asked the headmaster further questions on probability sampling. But since this topic was well-removed from the topic under discussion of planning the experiment, he offered to find an essay that he had written many years before on probability sampling and pass it to them so that they could read about the subject at their leisure. The text of this essay follows.

8. Probability Sampling

The essence of probability sampling is that every member of the population to be sampled should have a specifiable, nonzero, chance of appearing in the sample. To ensure this requires a good deal of careful organization, which is totally absent, for example, from the methods by which members of the public are frequently chosen for television interviews. It is a consoling reflection that some of the sillier statements made in such interviews are likely to arise from the fact that the idle and the exhibitionist have an unduly large chance of being selected for interview.

Humankind has acquired enough knowledge of the world to invest in a considerable technology that often produces dramatic effects. All this knowledge has been acquired from samples, since only minute portions of space and time have ever been scrutinized. This suggests that nature tends to offer fair samples for inspection, and that the problem of fairness cannot therefore be very important. But this is altogether too easy. It ignores the immense amount of experience that has gone into the recognition of natural kinds and the invention of manufacturing processes so that in the upshot one bit of copper wire is very like another bit. Furthermore, it ignores the fact that in classical physics the only concern is with averages reckoned over enormous numbers of unit particles. But in educational research concern is with the unit—the individual boy or girl, or man or woman—and not merely with the aggregate or population.

Fairness in the sample can be secured by giving every member of the population a specifiable chance of appearing in it. The accuracy of representation depends upon the size of the sample, and the size is given not by the number of members in the sample, but by the number of independent selections that have been made.

Suppose it is desirable to obtain a fair and reasonably accurate sample of the boys and girls in some specified population. Let the population be specified as the population, in January 1984, of boys and girls in the last year of primary education in England. In principle, though plainly not in practice, the simplest way of doing this would be to write the name of every pupil in the population on a ping pong ball and then whirl the balls in an enormous churn, as in the Irish sweep, and take the names on the winning balls as the sample. If there were N balls altogether, and n were selected, every member of the population would have a specifiable chance (n/N) of being selected.

This is plainly impracticable. The churning process could be replaced by the use of random numbers, which are, so to speak, prechurned, but the labour of collecting the relevant names from all the primary-school registers in England would be enormous. None the less there are several practicable methods by which a close approximation to this simple, single stage, sampling could be made. But since these methods would take some time to describe, and are unlikely to be used, they need not be gone into.

A method that has been used in practice is to select the boys and girls by specifying a date, and taking those whose birthdays fall on this date. This is quite different in principle, since only one independent choice, namely the choice of the date, is made. The selection is not a probability sample, but a subpopulation. It is not the case that every boy and girl in the full population has a specifiable nonzero chance of entering the sample. The chance is zero for all except those born on the given date. However, it is reasonable to think that the subpopulation will be like the general population in those respects that do not depend on the date. But there are some important respects, such as the age of entering and leaving school, and of taking examinations, in which children born in March differ from those born in October. This could be overcome by taking several birthdays, spread uniformly round the year—for example, the first of every month. This would, of course, produce a very large sample, but large samples are needed for some purposes. Another way of obtaining a large simple sample is to take one child in 10 in the relevant population in every school, making the selection not by birthdays but by the use of random numbers or some other lottery process. For example, a number not exceeding 10 could be allotted to each school. A school that drew the number eight would take the eighth, eighteenth, twenty-eighth, and so on, name on the registers for its sample. It is to be noted that while this process would be fair over all schools the results might look unfair in particular schools. According to the starting number allocated to the school the school sample might be untypically good, about right, or untypically bad. It would be, and has been, fatal to the fairness of the whole sample if the schools that drew numbers rejected them, on the grounds that they were unfair to the school, and chose for themselves more typical samples.

So far the simplest types of sampling have been looked at, where the selection is made directly in terms of the final unit, in this case the child. This single stage sampling is only suitable for very large enquiries which can bear the weight of corresponding with and carrying out the work in every school in the country. For enquiries on a smaller scale two-stage sampling is needed. The two stages are first the selection of schools and secondly, the selection within selected schools. The preliminary selection of schools has two advantages. In the first place it greatly reduces the amount of field work. Secondly, it gives more information about schools as such. These are the advantages of complex sampling. The price to be paid for them is that a complex sample has to be larger, in terms of the number of boys and girls, than a simple sample of the same accuracy. The reason for this is that students, parents, and teachers in the same school tend to resemble one another more than they resemble students, parents, and teachers in other schools, just as apples on the same tree tend to resemble one another more than they resemble apples on other trees, particularly if the trees are of different kinds. The point about "different kinds" can be overcome by stratification—that is, by sampling the kinds separately. Thus in sampling secondary schools, the draw is made after a preliminary separation into comprehensive, grammar, modern, technical, and other types, and into boys, girls, and mixed. This ensures that the sample estimates are not blurred by the differences between types. The practice has been to make a further stratification by region, though this is not very important, since regional differences (in contrast to neighbourhood differences) are generally small. It is to be noted that in a complex sample of the two-stage type the number of independent choices is the number of schools. A student's chance of selection is conditional upon whether or not the school attended is selected in the first instance. This makes no difference to the method of making the estimates. In each case the sample can be treated as though it were the population if the chances of selection have been everywhere the same, while compensating weights are needed if the chances have been unequal from one class to another. It does however make a difference to the method of estimating error, which is equally important. It should be noted that sampling errors are not mistakes; they are fluctuations or wanderings, as in "knight errant", or "we have erred and strayed like lost sheep". They represent the average variation between one sample and another when the same method of drawing the sample is used in each case. The point about probability sampling, as distinct from other forms of sampling, is that these errors can be estimated. A sample chosen by expert judgment, or a quota sample, as used in some forms of public opinion polls, may be an excellent sample or may not; in either case the extent of its departure from representativeness cannot be ascertained from the internal evidence of the sample itself. With a probability sample this can be done.

The rules for estimating standard errors for single-stage samples are simple and well-known. For complex samples they are much more complicated, and for the multivariate analysis of complex samples it is not practicable to estimate the reliability directly. It is however possible to obtain reasonably satisfactory estimates of error by subsampling. For example, if a quantity, such as a correlation coefficient or a regression coefficient is calculated first from the whole sample and then from a half sample, the difference between the two estimates is itself an estimate of the error in the whole sample estimate. By comparing a large number of such estimates with the corresponding estimates calculated as though the sample were a simple sample, the design effect can be obtained, which is the ratio of the size of the complex sample to that of a simple sample with the same reliability. In splitting off the half sample the full complexity of the complex design must be followed. Thus if the complex sample is a stratified sample of schools, half the schools in each stratum must be taken for the half sample, for example by taking every alternate school. The size of the design effect increases with the number of children taken from each school. Experience has shown that a good rough preliminary rule for estimating, in two-stage stratified sampling, is to assume that about 10 percent of the variation lies between schools and 90 percent between students within schools. This enables preliminary estimates to be made for any allocation of the sample, either of the standard errors or of the simple equivalent sample. Thus if a sample of 2,000 students comes from 100 schools the simple equivalent sample would be 690, while if the 2,000 were drawn from 200 schools instead of 100 the simple equivalent sample would be 1,050. This can be extended to three-stage sampling, in which the first stage is to draw local authorities, the second to draw schools within selected authorities, and the third to draw students within selected schools. In this case about 3 percent of the variation lies between authorities, about 7 percent between schools within authorities, and the remainder between students within schools. A sample of 2,000 students from 100 schools in 20 local authority areas gives a simple equivalent sample of 380 pupils, but if the 100 schools came from only five areas the simple equivalent sample would fall to 140.

In sampling the key is "probability". In sampling schools, parents, teachers, and students "probability" is used in the same restricted sense as in games of chance. Each member of a specified population is given a specifiable, nonzero, chance of being drawn in the sample, and other chances, such as that of a particular error of estimate exceeding a certain size, are calculated by the rules of combinatorial algebra, or by resorting to approximations, when the algebra becomes too complicated to be manageable.

By applying the rules to the evidence given by past experience, it is possible to determine the size of sample that is needed if the results obtained are not to be vitiated by uncertainty. Then by applying the rules to the new evidence it is possible to see whether the posterior estimate confirms the prior estimate of the magnitude of the sampling fluctuation.

9. Statistical Inference

When Miss Green and Miss Brown returned to talk to the headmaster after they had read his essay on sampling, the head drew attention to the key word "probability" in the last paragraph. He said

In all educational research, there is another important aspect of probability. In this sense it is more akin to "credibility". This sense is not only much wider. It is also much vaguer, since our judgment of credibility often depends upon a great range of imperfectly remembered experience. This accounts for the facts that each of us has his own system of credibilities, and that the systems often agree but sometimes do not. For this reason different persons may draw different conclusions from the same evidence, which gives scope for the legal profession.

Both kinds of probability deserve due respect, and failure to recognize this is responsible for some needless disputes between champions of teacher opinion and partisans of educational research.

Research results depend on both kinds of probability, and probability changes when the evidence changes. If all we know of Smith is that he is an Englishman the probability that his right eye is blue is about a half. But this probability is completely changed if we now learn that his left eye is blue.

The champions of "objectivity" sometimes tend to overlook the fact that our inferences about other people begin with introspection, memory, and testimony. Their opponents, on the other hand, tend to underrate the extent to which these inferences can be strengthened by observing regularities of behaviour. To strike a good balance needs temperate judgment.

Regularities of behaviour can be observed intimately, on a small scale, by teachers in their classrooms. They can also be observed, less intimately but on a much larger scale, by sampling whole populations. In the first case the scale may be extended by subsequent replication. In the second the broad generalizations may be refined by later work. Thus there is a part for everyone to play, and, while it is plain that we know very little about the immense variety of human nature, it is reasonable to hope that if we apply ourselves to the task we may learn more.

The headmaster went on to explain that as the study of a particular research question progressed it would be possible to plan a more detailed investigation to test specific relationships. In such a study a decision is commonly required as to whether an observed relationship could be ascribed to *sampling error* or whether it could be argued with confidence that it was the result of an experimental condition. The statistical techniques involved in making inferences of this kind are referred to as *tests of statistical significance*, and the procedures employed are known as *significance testing*. Sometimes such tests can be applied between the estimates made for independent samples, or between the estimates obtained under different conditions with the same sample. Sometimes, however, a test of significance is used to examine the difference between the estimate made for a single sample and a fixed value.

9.1 Hypothesis Testing

Consider the situation where previously established theory has led to the design of an experiment which uses an *experimental group* and a *control group*. Measurements are made on both groups. Since a treatment is applied to the experimental group, and the treatment is absent from the control group, it can be assumed that any significant difference between the two groups can be ascribed with confidence to the application of the treatment and not to other causes. If $\bar{X}_t$ is the estimate of the population mean μ_t for the treatment group and $\bar{X}_c$ the estimate for the population mean μ_c for the control group, the trial hypothesis may be advanced for testing that no difference exists between μ_t and μ_c. This *null hypothesis* may be written

$$H_0 : \mu_t - \mu_c = 0$$

It is, however, also necessary to specify an *alternative hypothesis* which is to be accepted if the null hypothesis is rejected by the testing procedures employed. An appropriate alternative hypothesis may be written

$$H_1 : \mu_t - \mu_c \neq 0$$

The logical steps that are applied by the investigator in significance testing are:

a) the null hypothesis is assumed to be true, this involves the population values μ_t and μ_c;

b) the empirical data are examined, and the difference between the observed mean values $(\bar{X}_t - \bar{X}_c)$ is obtained;

c) the question is asked, what is the probability of observing a difference equal to or greater than the one obtained by drawing samples at random from the populations involved, when it is assumed that the null hypothesis is true?;

d) if this probability is small, the investigator may be led to reject the null hypothesis; if the probability is not small, then it must be accepted that the observed difference could be accounted for by sampling variations; and

e) if the null hypothesis is rejected, then the alternative hypothesis may be accepted, which implies that the observed difference is a result of the application of the treatment.

At this point in the discussion Miss Green, who had been following the argument very closely asked whether there was also a chance that the alternative hypothesis was true even though the null hypothesis was accepted. The head agreed that it was clearly possible to have two types of error.

9.2 Type I and Type II Errors

If the alternative hypothesis H_1 is accepted when the null hypothesis H_0 is true, the error is referred to as a *Type I error*. However, it is also possible that the null hypothesis H_0 might be accepted when the alternative hypothesis H_1 is true. This error is known as *Type II error*. The total situation is represented diagrammatically in Fig. 1. In the cases where we accept H_1 and H_1 is true or we accept H_0 and H_0 is true, a correct decision has been made. However, there is a probability of accepting H_1 when H_0 is true, given by α, and a probability of accepting H_0 when H_1 is true given by β.

9.3 Levels of Significance

In discussing hypothesis testing above it was assumed that H_0 was true, and since the probability of observing a difference equal to or greater than the one obtained was small the alternative hypothesis had been accepted. Commonly a level of significance of either 0.05 or 0.01 is adopted for this probability, which is indicated in Fig. 1 by α. If the observed probability is less than the chosen value of α, namely 0.05 or 0.01, then the null hypothesis is rejected, and, in general practice, this decision is made without reference to the Type II error of probability β. However, the danger of applying too stringent a test associated with the error of Type I, or too small a value of probability α, is that the value of β can become large. In advanced work in statistics the levels of significance of both α and β are examined and the power of the testing procedure is considered for samples of different sizes and differences between population mean values of different magnitudes.

Miss Brown, who was more concerned with establishing that the treatment applied in the experiment that she wished to conduct was beneficial than with those situations where there was no difference between mean values and the null hypothesis was true, asked whether it was possible to make allowance for the fact that the mean value of the experimental group was expected to exceed the mean value for the control group. The head replied, that if she had confidence in her treatment, then it would be advantageous to use a *one-sided test* or *one-tailed test* instead of a *two-sided test* or *two-tailed test*.

9.4 Directional and Non-directional Tests

If an investigator wished to examine and choose between the null hypothesis $H_0 : \mu_t - \mu_c = 0$, and the

Decision	Truth	
	H_0 is true	H_1 is true
Accept H_1	α	Correct decision
Accept H_0	Correct decision	β

Figure 1
The two types of error

alternative hypothesis $H_1 : \mu_t - \mu_c \neq 0$, there is no implication that the treatment group mean μ_t is greater than the control group mean μ_c. The statistical test used is a two-sided or two-tailed, or *non-directional test*. If the 5 percent probability level is employed in testing for significance, then 2.5 percent probability is associated with $\mu_t - \mu_c > 0$, and 2.5 percent probability is associated with $\mu_t - \mu_c < 0$. With these probabilities the difference between the means must exceed 1.96 times the standard error of the difference for significant effect to be present. This non-directional test is appropriate where there is concern for the absolute magnitude of the difference between the mean values for the treatment and control groups, without regard for the sign of the difference. However, it is possible to hypothesize the direction of the difference, for example $H_1 : \mu_t - \mu_c > 0$, namely where the difference is positive in sign because the nature of the treatment leads to a greater treatment mean value μ_t being expected. Under these circumstances the null hypothesis can be reformulated to become $H_0 : \mu_t - \mu_c \leqslant 0$ and the 5 percent probability is assigned in one direction and a one-sided or one-tailed test is employed. Here the treatment mean must exceed the control mean by 1.64 times the standard error of the difference for a significant effect to be reported. The use of a *directional test* leads to smaller differences between mean values being reported as significant, provided that the difference is in the expected direction. If the treatment mean value is significantly greater than the control mean value, the null hypothesis is rejected and the alternative hypothesis is accepted.

10. Conclusion

The head, in concluding the discussion, pointed out that the use of probabilities in *statistical inference* demanded different approaches according to the level of expectation for the differences being tested, that arose from substantial theories. Where much was known about the introduction of a treatment and where a value in dollars could be assigned both to the costs of implementation, as well as to the benefits derived from the gains associated with the treatment, then statistical *decision theory*, that provided a guide for choosing an effective decision-rule, should be employed. Failure to take account of such costs could lead to disastrous errors in practice. Thus it would not be merely a question as to whether Miss Brown's treatment was superior, but rather an issue of what the cost benefits associated with its use were when weighed against the costs of implementation, that should determine whether a decision was made to proceed with the introduction of the treatment on a widespread basis. Advanced procedures of statistical inference sought to take these matters into account. On the other hand it could be argued that in the field of education, since each teacher commonly has to decide what actions he or she should take, personal probabilities should be taken into account. If *personal probabilities* were taken into consideration then a Bayesian approach should be employed.

See also: Unintended Effects in Educational Research; Sufficient Statistics in Educational Measurement; Nonparametric Statistics; History of Educational Research

Bibliography

David H A 1951 Further applications of range to the analysis of variance. *Biometrika* 38: 393–409
Ferguson G A 1976 *Statistical Analysis in Psychology and Education*, 4th edn. McGraw-Hill, New York
Guilford J P 1954 *Psychometric Methods*, 2nd edn. McGraw-Hill, New York
Hartley H O 1950 The use of range in analysis of variance. *Biometrika* 37: 271–80
Hays W L 1963 *Statistics for Psychologists*. Holt, Rinehart and Winston, New York
Kish L 1965 *Survey Sampling*. Wiley, New York
Rogosa D 1980 A critique of cross-lagged correlation. *Psychol. Bull.* 88: 245–58
Thorndike R L (ed.) 1971 *Educational Measurement*, 2nd edn. American Council on Education, Washington, DC

Structural Equation Models

T. H. Williams

Structural equation models are mathematical formalizations of theories. Theories in this sense are simply explanations developed to account for the observed covariation among phenomena. Thus, if X_1 and X_2—educational achievement and aspirations, for example—are observed to covary among students, explanations tend to be offered in terms of some underlying process; X_1 influences X_2; X_2 influences X_1; X_1 and X_2 influence each other; X_1 and X_2 are joint products of some other factor. Structural equation models capture such explanations as a system of equations which specify "the process underlying the joint distribution of a set of observable variables" (Bielby and Hauser 1977 p. 141). In much of the literature models of this kind are called simultaneous equation models, causal models, or path analysis. The term structural equation models subsumes these and related approaches and, as the more generic term, is adopted here.

Consider the first of the explanations developed to account for the covariation between X_1 and X_2, namely that X_1 influences X_2—students who do well in school aspire to higher levels of education. This situation is pictured in Fig. 1 and represented in the accompanying equation.

Structural equation models are often pictured in this way as a system of cause and effect with unidirectional arrows representing the (hypothesized) effect of one variable upon another. In the simple system picture in

Fig. 1, X_1 is *a* cause (not *the* cause) of X_2, as indicated by the arrow. p_{21} is a structural parameter which captures the magnitude of the influence of X_1 on X_2. Since X_1 will only rarely explain all of the variation in X_2, that part of X_2's variation which is unexplained by the specified causes is represented by an error term X_u which accounts for influences on X_2 unrelated to X_1. Such terms are often referred to as residuals or errors in equations. p_{2u} is the structural parameter that captures the effects of X_u on X_2. Between them, X_1 and X_u partition the variance in X_2 into respectively, explained and unexplained components.

Structural equation :
$$X_2 = p_{21} X_1 + p_{2u} X_u$$

Figure 1
X_1 influences X_2

Since the structural parameters are measures of effect they are asymmetrical terms in which the order of the subscripts has meaning. By convention the structural parameter for the effect of X_1 on X_2 in Fig. 1 is written as p_{21}; the first subscript refers to the effect, the second to the cause. To write this coefficient as p_{12} would imply a different model, one in which X_2 affects X_1. In contrast, correlations or covariances are symmetric measures of association and thus the correlation between X_1 and X_2 may be written as either r_{12} or r_{21}.

With X_1, X_2, and X_u standardized to a mean of zero and standard deviation of one, the structural equation can be written as

$$Z_2 = p_{21} Z_1 + p_{2u} Z_u p \tag{1}$$

Multiplying through this equation by Z_1 and summing over N leads to the following:

$$(\Sigma Z_1 Z_2)/N = p_{21}(\Sigma Z_1 Z_1)/N + p_{2u}(\Sigma Z_u Z_1)/N \tag{2}$$

$$r_{12} = p_{21} r_{11} + p_{2u} r_{1u}$$

$$= p_{21} \tag{3}$$

(since $r_{11} = 1$ and $r_{1u} = 0$ by assumption). Thus, according to this theory the observed correlation between X_1 and X_2 (r_{12}) comes about because X_1 affects X_2 to a degree represented in the structural parameter p_{21}.

Of course, if a theory dictated that r_{12} arises because X_2 affects X_1—students who aspire to high levels of education are motivated to do well in school—then the appropriate structural equation would be

$$X_1 = p_{12} X_2 + p_{1w} X_w \tag{4}$$

and

$$r_{12} = p_{12} \tag{5}$$

Similarly, in the spurious correlation case which argues that X_1 and X_2 are the joint products of some other factor (X_3), if the covariation between aspirations and achievement comes about not because they influence each other, but because they are both products of a common antecedent, for example social origins, then the model and equations would be as shown in Fig. 2.

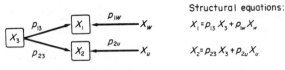

Figure 2
X_1 and X_2 are joint products of some other factor X_3

Using the same logic as in Eqns. (1, 2, 3), and multiplying the first structural equation by X_2 and X_3 and the second by X_1 and X_3, a rearrangement of terms produces the following three equations:

$$r_{12} = p_{13} r_{23} = p_{23} r_{13} \tag{6}$$

$$r_{13} = p_{13} \quad \text{and} \quad r_{23} = p_{23} \tag{7}$$

$$r_{12} = p_{13} p_{23} \quad \text{(by substitution)} \tag{8}$$

Thus, if the model is correct, the observed correlation r_{12} comes about because X_3 affects X_1 and X_2, not because either X_1 or X_2 influence each other directly.

The same logic applies to less trivial models. For example, take the argument that the observed covariation between social origins, educational attainment, occupation status, and income comes about because: an individual's social origins (X_1) affect his/her educational attainments (X_2); both affect occupational status (X_3); and all three influence economic attainments (X_4). The model would be as shown in Fig. 3.

With the variables standardized it follows that

$$r_{21} = p_{21} r_{11} + p_{2u} r_{1u}$$

$$= p_{21} \tag{9}$$

$$r_{31} = p_{31} r_{11} + p_{32} r_{21} + p_{3w} r_{1w}$$

$$= p_{31} + p_{32} r_{21} \tag{10}$$

$$r_{32} = p_{31} r_{21} + p_{32} r_{22} + p_{3w} r_{2w}$$

$$= p_{31} r_{21} + p_{32} \tag{11}$$

$$r_{41} = p_{41} r_{11} + p_{42} r_{21} + p_{43} r_{31} + p_{4v} r_{1v}$$

$$= p_{41} + p_{42} r_{21} + p_{43} r_{31} \tag{12}$$

$$r_{42} = p_{41} r_{21} + p_{42} r_{22} + p_{43} r_{32} + p_{4v} r_{2v}$$

$$= p_{41} r_{21} + p_{42} + p_{43} r_{32} \tag{13}$$

$$r_{43} = p_{41} r_{13} + p_{42} r_{23} + p_{43} r_{33} + p_{4v} r_{3v}$$

$$= p_{41} r_{13} + p_{42} r_{23} + p_{43} \tag{14}$$

By substitution, the following equations are produced to express the underlying processes responsible for each observed correlation:

$$r_{21} = p_{21} \tag{15}$$

$$r_{31} = p_{31} + p_{21} p_{32} \tag{16}$$

$$r_{32} = p_{21} p_{31} + p_{32} \tag{17}$$

$$r_{41} = p_{41} + p_{21} p_{42} + p_{21} p_{32} p_{43} + p_{31} p_{43} \tag{18}$$

$$r_{42} = p_{21} p_{41} + p_{42} + p_{21} p_{31} p_{43} + p_{32} p_{43} \tag{19}$$

$$r_{43} = p_{31} p_{41} + p_{21} p_{32} p_{41} + p_{21} p_{31} p_{42}$$

$$+ p_{32}p_{42} + p_{43} \qquad (20)$$

Thus, the process generating each observed correlation is specified in terms of the underlying theory and the following illustrative interpretations become possible:

(a) r_{21} comes about because X_1 affects X_2—social origins influence educational attainments (p_{21});

(b) r_{31}, the correlation between social origins and occupational status, is observed because social origins affect occupational status directly (p_{31}) and because social origins affect educational attainment which, in turn, affects occupational status ($p_{21}p_{32}$)—processes of ascription and achievement, respectively;

(c) analogously, a correlation is observed between educational attainment and occupational status (r_{32}) because placement within the occupational structure depends in part on educational attainment (p_{32}) and because social origins influence both of these attainments ($p_{21}p_{31}$).

1. Direct and Indirect Effects

Terms like p_{21}, p_{31}, p_{32}, and p_{42} are referred to as direct effects. For example, p_{32} represents the influence of X_2 on X_3 controlling for the influence of X_1 on X_3. As such, this parameter offers a *ceteris paribus* interpretation; other things equal (X_1), the effect of X_2 on X_3 is captured in p_{32}. Similarly, p_{43} is the effect of X_3 on X_4, other things (X_1, X_2) equal. Compound terms such as $p_{21}p_{32}$ represent indirect effects, in this case the effect of X_1 on X_3 via X_2. Thus, the model specifies explicitly the social processes assumed to generate the observed correlations.

2. Exogenous and Endogenous Variables

In Fig. 3, X_1 is an exogenous variable, one whose variation is not explained within the system. By contrast, X_2, X_3, and X_4 are endogenous variables whose variation is explained completely within the system by hypothesized causes and by the respective error terms.

Most structural models contain several exogenous variables and the correlations between these are unexamined, in the sense of not being explained by the model. Thus, if a researcher was unwilling to postulate that X_1 affected X_2 in the model above, X_2 might be shown as an exogenous variable correlated with X_1, as

in Fig. 4. Correlations between exogenous variables are shown traditionally by curved double-headed arrows.

Under these circumstances the equations specifying the decomposition of each correlation are analogous to Eqns. (15–20) but with p_{21} replaced by r_{21}. The consequences for interpretation are that each correlation is now decomposed into three components: direct effects, indirect effects, and causally unanalysed components. Take the equation for r_{41} as an example:

$$r_{41} = p_{41} + p_{42}r_{12} + p_{32}p_{43}r_{12} + p_{31}p_{43} \qquad (21)$$

p_{41} captures the direct effect and $p_{31}p_{43}$ represents the indirect effect of X_1 on X_4 through X_3. The remaining terms contain the exogenous correlation r_{12} and, thus, constitute causally unanalysed components of r_{41}.

An examination of the literature cited in Bielby and Hauser (1977) and Bentler (1980) will show the variety of other theoretical configurations possible within models of this kind. These include: causally unspecified relationships among endogenous variables, correlated error terms, reciprocal causation, unmeasured variables, in fact almost anything that a theory might suggest.

3. Identification

While structural models may be developed to reflect almost any set of theoretical considerations, the fact that the structural parameters would be estimated from data on variances and covariances imposes some limitations on these developments. In the simplest case, the number of parameters to be estimated cannot be greater than the number of variances and covariances. For example, while it might be argued that two variables affect each other in a feedback relationship, and while this argument might be represented by the structural equations $X_1 = p_{12}X_2 + p_{1u}X_u$ and $X_2 = p_{21}X_1 + p_{2\,w}X_w$, given only r_{12}, unique estimates of p_{12} and p_{21} are not possible (unless assumptions are made about the magnitude of one or both of these parameters). This, basically, is the issue of identification.

Identification is a condition of parameters within models rather than models as a whole. Thus, it is possible to have a model in which some parameters are identified and some not. Individual parameters may be just identified, overidentified, or underidentified. If a parameter can be estimated by one function of the observed variances and covariances, and one function only, it is just identified (degrees of freedom are zero). If two or more functions provide estimates of the parameter, it is overidentified and must provide consistent estimates in

Structural equations:

$$X_2 = p_{21}X_1 + p_{2u}X_u$$

$$X_3 = p_{31}X_1 + p_{32}X_2 + p_{3w}X_w$$

$$X_4 = p_{41}X_1 + p_{42}X_2 + p_{43}X_3 + p_{4v}X_v$$

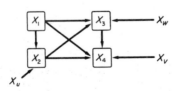

Figure 3
X_1 affects X_2; X_1 and X_2 affect X_3; X_1, X_2, and X_3 affect X_4

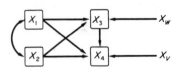

Structural equations :

$$X_3 = p_{31} X_1 + p_{32} X_2 + p_{3w} X_w$$

$$X_4 = p_{41} X_1 + p_{42} X_2 + p_{43} X_3 + p_{4v} X_v$$

Figure 4
When X_2 is an exogenous variable correlated with X_1

the several functions (degrees of freedom are greater than or equal to one). Underidentified parameters arise when it is not possible to obtain unique parameter estimates from the estimating function (the number of "unknowns" is greater than the number of "knowns"). These three conditions are illustrated respectively in the following equations:

$$x + 6 = 9 \text{ (just identified)} \tag{22}$$

$$\left.\begin{array}{l} x + 6 = 9 \\ x - 3 = 0 \end{array}\right\} \text{(overidentified)} \tag{23}$$
$$\tag{24}$$

$$x + y = 9 \text{ (underidentified)} \tag{25}$$

4. Model Specification

One of the critical assumptions of any structural equation model is that it contains all the variables of consequence and, moreover, in their correct functional form. Parameter estimates are biased to the extent that, for example, a structural equation (a) omits important causes of the phenomenon of interest; (b) includes variables that are, say, consequences rather than antecedents of this phenomenon; or (c) specifies a linear relationship when the true form is nonlinear.

5. Parameter Estimation

There are a number of statistical models that might be used to estimate the parameters of structural equation models. For the types of models discussed to this point, the use of ordinary least squares regression is common and the structural parameters are estimated as partial regression coefficients. This approach reflects a direct transformation of structural equations into structural regression equations. In estimating these equations the usual assumptions of multiple regression apply.

Consider the following equation from Fig. 3:

$$X_4 = p_{41} X_1 + p_{42} X_2 + p_{43} X_3 + p_{4v} X_v \tag{26}$$

Cast in standard multiple regression terminology this has the form

$$Y = a + b_1 X_1 + b_2 X_2 + b_3 X_3 + e \tag{27}$$

or

$$Y = \beta_1 X_1 + \beta_2 X_2 + \beta_3 X_3 + e \tag{28}$$

when the variables are standardized.

The parameter estimates denoted b_i are metric partial regression coefficients because they retain their original units of measurement. Thus, if Y were measured in dollars and X_2 in years of education, b_2 is interpreted as:

other things equal, a one-unit difference in X_2 is associated with a b_2-unit difference in Y—each additional year of education is worth b_2 additional dollars income. By contrast the metric of the standardized partial regression coefficients is standard deviation units and thus they do not offer concrete interpretations of this kind. However, because the β_i have the same metric they can be compared within an equation and, thus, provide a relative effects interpretation (β_1 has twice the influence of β_2, for example) which the b_i do not because of their (usually) differing metrics. Comparisons of effects across groups involve direct comparisons of analogous b_{ij}. Between-group comparisons of β_{ij} are not legitimate as the coefficients are likely to have been standardized to different variances in the different groups.

A point worth making again in this context is that structural equation models are not statistical models. While they are associated with several statistical models for the purposes of parameter estimation they do not provide a technique that can be applied mechanically to data. Since the same data will yield different parameter estimates depending on the structural model postulated, theory comes first and statistics later: "one cannot even get started...without a firm grasp of the relevant scientific theory, because the starting point is, precisely, the model and not the statistical methods" (Duncan 1975 p. 6).

6. Goodness-of-fit

Historically, questions of the fit of the model to the data have not received much attention. To provide tests of goodness-of-fit, overidentifying restrictions are needed and, for the most part, structural models of this type have been specified with just-identified parameters. Theoretical arguments strong enough to specify in advance the size of an effect have been rare and, typically, these models have proceeded from the just identified to the overidentified through the elimination of statistically insignificant effects, and reestimation. Under these circumstances comparisons between observed and implied correlations were often reported. Statistically more defensible model testing procedures for structural equation models were reported in the mid-1970s and are discussed below.

7. A Short History

More recent developments in the formulation and estimation of structural equation models are the product of a merging of sociological, econometric, and psychometric approaches and are introduced here in historical perspective.

Structural equation models seem to have evolved somewhat independently in several disciplines, notably economics, where they are known as simultaneous equation models, and biometrics, where Sewell Wright is identified with the development of the method of path coefficients now known as path analysis—"a flexible means of relating the correlation coefficients between variables in a multiple system to the functional relations among them" (Wright 1934 p. 161).

Though well-developed and exploited by econometricians, simultaneous equation models of econometric origin did not penetrate other social sciences until the late 1960s. Instead, structural equation models in sociology, psychology, and education developed from the path analysis tradition. One of the first applications of path analysis in the social sciences was in educational research, in a dissertation by Barbara Burks published in 1928, not long after Wright's original formulation of path analysis. However, nothing more was heard of structural equation models until the 1960s when sociologists became interested in the development and estimation of these models. Duncan (1966) provided an explicit introduction to path analysis for sociologists in the mid-1960s and started something of a methodological revolution in that discipline, something he commented on 10 years later: "these models provided a tool that only facilitated the genuinely scientific enquiry that sociologists were already engaged in ... the models responded to an implicit need for formalisms that would help in maintaining order and coherence in increasingly complicated lines of investigation and theorizing" (Duncan 1975 p. 151).

Some four years after Duncan's "Path analysis: Sociological examples", Werts and Linn (1970) introduced structural equation models to psychology in their article "Path analysis: Psychological examples". Four years later Anderson and Evans (1974) published a paper that might have been called "Path analysis: Educational examples" introducing the topic formally to educational research.

In the late 1960s a number of sociologists, sometimes in collaboration with economists, began to draw on the psychometric literature in an attempt to formulate structural models involving latent variables and thus to address the issues of measurement error and unmeasured variables within these models. At about the same time several psychometricians extended their longstanding concerns with measurement error and measurement models to the development of structural models linking the latent variables of several measurement models. Jöreskog and Werts among others led in the development of the approaches to combined structural and measurement models.

The end result of these efforts was an approach to structural equation models which specified each element of the structural model as a latent variable usually with one or more indicators, though sometimes with none. In such models each latent variable is defined by an explicit measurement model specifying the relationships between the latent variable and its indicators. Within this context Jöreskog generalized his concerns with measurement model estimation and testing in the form of restricted factor analysis to develop a more general approach to the analysis of covariance structures and hence a general method that allowed the estimation of both measurement and structural models from the variance–covariance matrix defined by the measured variables (Jöreskog 1973). Jöreskog's model is known as LISREL (LInear Structural RELationships) and is implemented in a computer program known as LISREL VI in its latest version (Jöreskog and Sörbom 1983).

8. Measurement Error and Structural Models

As the forgoing suggests, structural equation models in the path analysis tradition typically have not distinguished between latent variables and their observable indicators. For the most part the variables in structural models have been measured by single indicators assumed to have perfect reliability (and validity). Since the level of measurement in most path analytic type models has been fairly crude, the parameter estimates for these models are attenuated by measurement error. More problematic though is the matter of differential attenuation of these parameters due to differences in the reliability with which variables are measured. What this means is that real differences in the magnitude of effects may be confounded with differences that arise solely from variability in the reliability with which variables are measured. The consequences of this are obvious; substantive meaning is likely to be assigned to differences in effect estimates when these differences are produced by variability in the precision with which variables are measured. See Bielby et al. (1977) for further discussion of this issue.

It is only since the early 1970s that an explicit treatment of measurement error has become a part of structural equation models. This has taken the form of treating the structural model as a system of relationships among latent variables each measured less than perfectly by several indicators. Goldberger (1973 p. 1) identifies the three fundamental characteristics of these second-generation structural equation models:

(a) for the most part they involve the analysis of nonexperimental data and hence substitute statistical controls for experimental controls;

(b) they contain hypothetical constructs or latent variables which are not directly observed; and

(c) they are formulated as multiequation systems.

9. Structural Models with Latent Variables

Structural equation models which incorporate latent variables tend to adopt the nomenclature characteristic of LISREL. Figure 5 and the accompanying structural

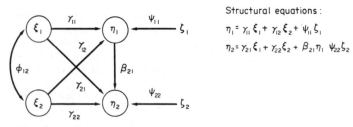

Structural equations :

$$\eta_1 = \gamma_{11}\xi_1 + \gamma_{12}\xi_2 + \psi_{11}\zeta_1$$

$$\eta_2 = \gamma_{21}\xi_1 + \gamma_{22}\xi_2 + \beta_{21}\eta_1 \; \psi_{22}\zeta_2$$

Figure 5
Structural equation model incorporating three categories of latent variables: exogenous (ξ); endogenous (η); and error terms (ζ)

equations are illustrative. The model contains three categories of variables: exogenous variables (ξ); endogenous variables (η); and error terms (ζ).

The γ_{ij} are structural coefficients representing the effects of the exogenous variables (ξ) on the endogenous variables (η). Similarly, the β_{ij} are structural coefficients capturing the influence of one endogenous variable upon another. ϕ is a variance–covariance matrix which contains estimates of the variances of the ξ_i and their covariances—ϕ_{12} in Fig. 5. ψ is also a variance–covariance matrix. It contains the variances and covariances of the error terms for the latent variables.

10. Measurement Models

The measurement models which specify the relations between latent variables and their indicators tend to have the general form shown in Fig. 6, although other forms are possible. In this model the covariation among the three observed indicators (y_i) is accounted for by a single latent variable (η_1). Measurement models of this kind are isomorphic with factor analysis models: η_1 is the factor; the λ_{ij} are the factor loadings; and the ε_{ii} are the unique variances of the indicators, called errors in variables in contrast to the previously mentioned errors in equations.

Models of this kind are sometimes called reflective models because the theory behind the model sees the measured indicators (the y_i) as the observable reflections of an underlying, unmeasured latent variable—a psychological trait, for example, inferred from the covariation among items in a psychological test.

Occasionally, productive rather than reflective models are postulated. In these, indicators are seen to be causes of the latent variable rather than reflections of it. It might, for example, be argued that the latent variable socioeconomic status is the product of an individual's educational, occupational, and economic attainments rather than these being a reflection of this underlying status position. Models of this kind pose some estimation problems that hinge on the assumptions necessary to identify the measurement model (Munck 1979).

Information additional to that contained in the variances and covariances can also be introduced into the model. A common instance is one where a composite score on a test is used as the single indicator of a latent variable. If the reliability of this test is known this information may be included in the model. For example, if the η_1 in Fig. 6 had only one indicator, a composite score y_1, with known reliability, this information could be included within the model by constraining the parameter λ_{11} to equal a function of this reliability.

11. Combined Structural and Measurement Models

Some of the theoretical flexibility possible in these models is indicated in Fig. 7 which includes for the structural model:

(a) the effects of the exogenous variables (ξ_1 and ξ_2) on the endogenous variables (η_1 and η_2) shown as γ_{11} and γ_{22};

Measurement equations

$$y_1 = \lambda_{11}\eta_1 + \varepsilon_{11}$$

$$y_2 = \lambda_{21}\eta_1 + \varepsilon_{22}$$

$$y_3 = \lambda_{31}\eta_1 + \varepsilon_{33}$$

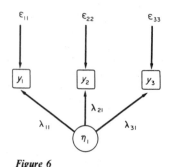

Figure 6
Measurement model specifying relations between latent variables and their indicators

(b) postulated zero effects, γ_{21} and γ_{12}, indicated by the absence of arrows linking ξ_1 and η_2 on the one hand, and ξ_2 and η_1 on the other;

(c) the effects of the endogenous variables (η_1 and η_2) on each other, β_{21} and β_{12}, shown as a reciprocal influence—simultaneous causation or feedback;

(d) correlated exogenous variables (ξ_1 and ξ_2) whose correlation (covariance) is shown as ϕ_{12}; and

(e) error terms (ζ_1 and ζ_2) whose variance is shown as ψ_{11} and ψ_{22} and whose covariance (correlation) is shown as ψ_{12}.

The measurement models for ξ_1, ξ_2, η_1, and η_2 are specified as follows:

(a) The latent exogenous variable ξ_1 has two observable indicators, x_1 and x_2. The factor loading of x_1 on ξ_1 is shown as λ_{11} and that of x_2 on ξ_1 is shown as λ_{21}. δ_{11} and δ_{22} are the unique variances of these two indicators—the error terms in the measurement model equations. With the exception of the measurement model for η_2, the measurement models for the other latent variables are similarly specified.

(b) The measurement model for η_2 specifies a single indicator (y_4) whose loading on the latent variable is constrained to be 0.9. This is illustrative of the situation noted above where x_4 might be a composite test score of known reliability.

(c) The measurement model for η_1 shows the error terms for y_1 and y_2 (ε_1 and ε_2) to be correlated and this correlation (covariance) is expressed as ε_{12}.

Such a situation could occur if y_1 and y_2 were repeated measures of η_1.

12. Parameter Estimation

Models of the kind shown above may be estimated with LISREL VI and the estimation is essentially that of fitting the covariance matrix implied by the model to the sample covariance matrix (Jöreskog and Sörbom 1983). This fitting is achieved by an iterative process which minimizes a fitting function to successively improve parameter estimates. LISREL VI provides estimates by five methods—instrumental variables, two-stage least squares, unweighted least squares, generalized least squares, and maximum likelihood.

Systems of this kind may also be estimated using similar statistical models implemented in other computer programs; see McDonald (1980), for example. Somewhat different statistical procedures have also been applied to the estimation of these combined structural and measurement models—partial least squares, factorial modelling, and normalized ridge regression are examples.

13. Goodness-of-fit

LISREL provides three measures of the overall fit of the model to the data: a likelihood ratio test statistic with a χ^2 distribution; a goodness-of-fit index (GFI) based on the relative amount of variance and covariance accounted for by the model; and, the root mean square

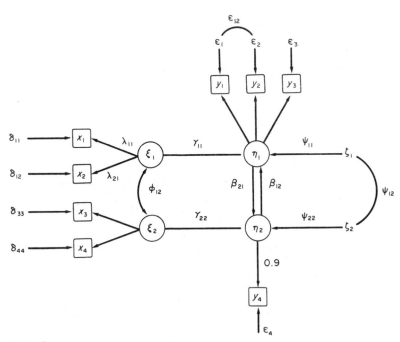

Figure 7
A combined structural and measurement model

residual, a measure of the average of the residual variances and covariances. These are supplemented by several other statistics which give an indication of the reasonableness of the model (see Jöreskog and Sörbom 1983). The LISREL VI program also provides indications of where a model is not fitting the data, in the form of normalized residuals and a modification index for each fixed parameter. COSAN (McDonald 1980) provides similar statistics on which judgments about goodness-of-fit can be made.

See also: Path Analysis; Partial Least Squares Path Analysis

Bibliography

Anderson J G, Evans F B 1974 Causal models in educational research: Recursive models. *Am. Educ. Res. J.* 11: 29–39
Bentler P M 1980 Multivariate analysis with latent variables: Causal modeling. *Annu. Rev. Psychol.* 31: 419–56
Bielby W T, Hauser R M 1977 Structural equation models. *Annu. Rev. Sociol.* 3: 137–61
Bielby W T, Hauser R M, Featherman D L 1977 Response errors of black and nonblack males in models of the intergenerational transmission of socioeconomic status. *Am. J. Sociol.* 82: 1242–88
Duncan O D 1966 Path analysis: Sociological examples. *Am. J. Sociol.* 72: 1–16
Duncan O D 1975 *Introduction to Structural Equation Models.* Academic Press, New York
Goldberger A S 1973 Structural equation models: An overview. In: Goldberger A S, Duncan O D (eds.) 1973 *Structural Equation Models in the Social Sciences.* Conf., Madison, Wisconsin, 1973. Seminar Press, New York
Jöreskog K G 1973 A general method for estimating a linear structural equation system. In: Goldberger A S, Duncan O D (eds.) 1973 *Structural Equation Models in the Social Sciences.* Conf., Madison, Wisconsin, 1973. Seminar Press, New York
Jöreskog K G, Sörbom D 1983 LISREL VI: *Analysis of Linear Structural Relationships by Maximum Likelihood and Least Squares Methods.* National Educational Resources, Chicago, Illinois
McDonald R P 1980 A simple comprehensive model for the analysis of covariance structures: Some remarks on applications. *Br. J. Math. Stat. Psychol.* 33: 161–83
Munck I M E 1979 *Model Building in Comparative Education: Applications of the LISREL Method to Cross-national Survey Data.* Almqvist and Wiksell, Stockholm
Werts C E, Linn R L 1970 Path analysis: Psychological examples. *Psychol. Bull.* 74: 193–212
Wright S 1934 The method of path coefficients. *Ann. Math. Stat.* 5: 161–215

Suppressor Variables

J. P. Keeves

A special problem that has arisen in both studies of prediction and of explanation in educational research is associated with the presence of suppressor variables. The presence of suppression effects can be observed both with partial correlation coefficients and partial regression coefficients. An example of a suppression effect is where the partial correlation coefficient between a predictor variable and a criterion variable after controlling for a second predictor variable is larger than the corresponding zero-order correlation coefficient. It should be noted that the effect may be an interrelated one and the second predictor variable may also exhibit a substantial change in its partial correlation with the criterion.

Horst (1966) has reported an example of the phenomenon of a suppression effect from a study of the prediction of success in the primary training of pilots during the Second World War. It was found that mechanical, numerical, and spatial ability tests had significant positive correlations with the criterion, success as a pilot. However, while verbal ability had relatively high positive correlations with these three predictor variables, it had a very low positive correlation with the criterion. It is perhaps not surprising that verbal ability should correlate highly with the other predictors which were measured by pencil and paper tests, and should act as a suppressor variable, with a negative weight, in the combined prediction equation. In this case the verbal ability test was used to partial out reading factors which were serving to attenuate the relationships associated with the mechanical, numerical, and spatial ability tests.

Conger has developed a definition of suppression effects:

A suppressor variable is defined to be a variable which increases the predictive validity of another variable (or set of variables) by its inclusion in a regression equation. This variable is a suppressor only for those variables whose regression weights are increased. (Conger 1974 pp. 36–37)

In addition, Conger (1974) and Cohen and Cohen (1975) have identified three kinds of suppression effects that can occur in regression analyses between two predictor variables and a criterion variable.

(a) *Classical suppression.* This occurs when one predictor has a correlation with the criterion of zero but has a significant regression coefficient when the criterion is regressed on both predictors. The regression coefficient of the other predictor variable will also be increased by the inclusion of the suppressor variable in the regression equation.

(b) *Negative suppression.* This effect was identified by Darlington (1968) and occurs when both predictor variables are correlated positively with the criterion variable and are correlated positively with each other. However, when the criterion variable is regressed on both predictors the suppressor variable has a negative regression coefficient. Thus the direction of the relationship between the predictor and the criterion has changed as a consequence of the suppression effect.

(c) *Reciprocal suppression.* This effect was identified by Conger (1974) and occurs when both predictor variables are correlated positively with the criterion variable and are correlated negatively with each other. Alternatively, it occurs when one predictor is correlated positively with the criterion variable and the other predictor is correlated negatively with the criterion, but the two predictors are correlated positively with each other. When the criterion variable is regressed on both predictor variables, the suppression effect operates to increase the magnitude of the regression coefficients of both predictor variables.

Tzelgov and Stern (1978) have examined the range of possible relationships which exist between the three variables and have identified the mathematical conditions existing between the three variables that give rise to the three different types of suppression effects as well as the situation under which no suppression effects occur.

Cooley and Lohnes (1976 p. 160) have drawn attention to a phenomenon which all who have used multiple-regression analysis extensively, whether for the estimation of path coefficients in path analysis, or for studies of explanation, through the use of stepwise regression analysis, or for the purposes of prediction with a theoretically based prediction model, are well-aware. They refer to the phenomenon as one of "bouncing betas". The "bouncing" of standardized partial regression coefficients can arise in several ways. Firstly, through the inclusion of an additional variable in the regression analysis that acts as a suppressor variable, and it should be noted that under certain circumstances a regression coefficient will exceed 1.0 when a suppression effect is present. Secondly, the "bouncing" can occur in a replicated study, where sampling variations change the interrelationships between the variables. Thirdly, "bouncing" can occur in a study where measurement error can distort the interrelations between the variables. The results of "bouncing" can be of considerable significance not only where suppression effects are operating but also where there is a substantial degree of multicollinearity between the predictor variables.

In developing a prediction equation many have argued that suppressor variables should be used to refine the prediction model. Cronbach (1950) was among the first to suggest that response sets in achievement testing could be allowed for by the use of a suppressor variable measuring a tendency to answer "true" to objective test items. In the same way it has been proposed that in personality assessment, scores on personality inventories could be corrected by the inclusion of a measure of response style for socially desirable responses as a suppressor variable in the prediction equation. However, the evidence available over a long period with respect to the predictive effectiveness of suppressor variables in personality assessment (Thorndike 1949, Wiggins 1973) is not impressive and suppressor variables that operate consistently to improve prediction are rare. In practice it would seem wise not to include a suppressor variable in a prediction equation unless the inclusion of the variable was strongly supported on theoretical and rational grounds. Nevertheless, the idea of using a suppressor variable in prediction models must remain an interesting possibility.

In explanation studies, the research worker must be extremely wary that suppressor variables are not being introduced into the analyses without a sound theoretical basis. The dangers are particularly great when stepwise regression analysis is employed, and where a suppressor variable is introduced with a marginal increase in the variance accounted for, but with a marked influence on the partial regression coefficients arising from the inclusion of the variable.

See also: Regression Analysis; Validity; Prediction in Research

Bibliography

Cohen J, Cohen P 1975 *Applied Multiple Regression/Correlation Analysis for the Behavioral Sciences.* Erlbaum, Hillsdale, New Jersey

Conger A J 1974 A revised definition for suppressor variables: A guide to their identification and interpretation. *Educ. Psychol. Meas.* 34: 35–46

Cooley W W, Lohnes P R 1976 *Evaluation Research in Education.* Irvington, New York

Cronbach L J 1950 Further evidence on response sets and test design. *Educ. Psychol. Meas.* 10: 3–31

Darlington R B 1968 Multiple regression in psychological research and practice. *Psychol. Bull.* 69: 161–82

Horst P 1966 *Psychological Measurement and Prediction.* Wadsworth, Belmont, California

Thorndike R L 1949 *Personnel Selection: Test and Measurement Techniques.* Wiley, New York

Tzelgov J, Stern I 1978 Relationships between variables in three variable linear regression and the concept of suppressor. *Educ. Psychol. Meas.* 38: 325–35

Wiggins J S 1973 *Personality and Prediction: Principles of Personality Assessment.* Addison-Wesley, Reading, Massachusetts

Units of Analysis

L. Burstein

"Units of analysis" are those entities or objects whose behavior one is trying to understand or describe; they are the explanatory focus of an investigation (Burstein 1980a, 1980b, Cronbach 1976, Haney 1980, Wiley 1970). The typical units of analysis in educational investigations are students, classrooms, teachers, schools, and so on, which are the entities from the various levels of the multilevel educational hierarchy. A pupil's test score, the size of the class, the teacher's chosen instructional method, and the availability of a school library are examples of measured variables based directly on units at a given level. The units for other measured variables, for example, teacher–student interaction, are less obvious since they can characterize behavior at more than one level.

Data collected on units at a lower level (students) can be aggregated to yield a characteristic of a unit at a higher level (e.g., class average, class standard deviation, school average). This characteristic may take on special meaning at the higher level or simply be indicative of aggregated lower level properties. While a student test score is an individual (student) characteristic, the average test score for students in a given class is a class characteristic.

A variable measured strictly at a higher level such as the class or school (e.g., teacher's previous years of experience) cannot be disaggregated to yield a student characteristic. Such variables are often called global properties of groups as opposed to aggregated properties like average test scores. Though they cannot be disaggregated, global properties do represent a particular kind of variable, the context, associated with lower levels. Thus students are said to be learning in a "high inquiry" context if their teachers use instructional methods that emphasize inquiry.

Aggregated characteristics can also represent the context of lower level units. Thus, a student in a class with a high mean pretest score can be said to be in a "high ability" context. Similarly, when the performance of students within the same class varies substantially, the student is in a "heterogeneous ability" context.

The hierarchical structure of educational data results in yet another class of measures, relative standing or status, that are properties of lower level units. That is, the deviation of a student's score from the class average is a student-level measure of relative or comparative ability. Similarly, the deviation of the teacher's years of experience from the school average is a teacher or class measure (relative experience of the teacher). These characteristics are typically labeled within-group or pooled within-group measures.

While the literature is somewhat confusing on this point, the "level of analysis" is typically defined in terms of the units of the dependent variable or outcome in a study. Thus if posttest scores of students are the data used as outcomes, the analysis is said to be conducted at the student level; on the other hand, analyses with the class mean posttest scores as dependent variables are class-level analyses.

In many educational investigations, there is interest in explaining the behavior of units from more than one level. For example, the investigator may wish to estimate the relationship between students' entering ability relative to their classmates and their relative posttest performance and may also want to estimate the effects of teacher's time allotments for a given topic to the average posttest performance of the class. Separate analyses conducted at two or more levels are termed multilevel analyses.

A much broader category of multilevel analyses, encompassing much of the literature on school and educational effects, employs a set of explanatory variables that are characteristics from two or more levels. For example, the regression of students' posttest scores on their own pretest scores, the average pretest scores for the class, and the teachers' reports of emphasis on whole-class instruction is a multilevel analysis because explanatory variables from multiple levels are included.

The apparent ease with which units and levels of analysis were defined above masks the often difficult task of selecting the appropriate units and levels in a given context. Educational researchers typically assume that only one unit is appropriate. They then attempt to justify their choice of unit and thereby the level at which the analysis should be conducted.

The desire to determine a single "correct" unit is perhaps a natural reaction to the results from various empirical studies involving multilevel educational data. In particular, attempts at cross-level inference, that is, using group-level data to infer about individual behavior and vice versa, are likely to be futile. Analyses of educational effects at different levels consistently reveal different results across levels (Burstein 1980a, Cronbach 1976). While the treatment of such differences as evidence of aggregation bias or cross-level bias has subsided in recent years, there are lingering doubts about the wisdom of mechanically choosing the units that serve as outcomes. The conduct of routine analyses at any level without concern for the general investigative intent and for possibly confounding technical considerations is also beginning to disappear.

The remainder of the discussion of unit and levels of analysis focuses on the kinds of issues that arise in selecting units, on an alternative perspective (which is termed multilevel) regarding unit and level considerations, and on major measurement and analysis issues that can be examined once this alternative perspective is adopted. Readings which provide more comprehensive discussions of these topics include Burstein (1980a, 1980b), Cronbach (1976), Haney (1980), Roberts and Burstein (1980), Treiber (1980), and Wiley (1970).

1. Issues in Selecting Units

Traditionally, a variety of conceptual and technical arguments have been cited as justification of the choice of either students or groups (classes, schools, etc.) as the appropriate units of analysis. There are several extensive discussions of units of analysis issues. The major conceptual and technical issues are highlighted below.

1.1 Research and Decision Contexts

Clearly, the results of an educational study are more salient and supportable when substantive questions of interest guide the investigation. The specific research paradigm employed can, however, complicate the selection of units by constraining the type of information collected and the manner of collection. That is, whether specific conceptual or technical considerations are pertinent in selecting a unit of analysis is dependent, in part, on the type of study being conducted and the types of outcomes and processes of interest.

For the purposes of this article, the types of studies that warrant consideration are empirical investigations involving units from multiple levels where quantifiable data are collected about specific outcomes (test scores, attitudes, occupational or educational attainments, etc.), specific educational processes and practices (instructional characteristics, educational treatments, structural characteristics of schooling context, etc.), and perhaps about specific background or entry characteristics (home circumstances, entering abilities, community circumstances, etc.). The units under investigation may be either a random, stratified random, purposive, or nonrandom sample from some population of units (students, classrooms, teachers, schools, etc.) or they may be the entire population of possible units (e.g., all schools in a given state). To further complicate matters, the sampling units may be the units of interest or perhaps a higher level unit.

The contrast of a well-defined and implemented treatment randomly assigned to units with a loosely defined and implemented treatment or with naturally occurring educational "treatments" is also relevant in understanding the salience of various unit selection criteria. In an experimental context where units are assigned at random to different treatment conditions, the choice of a unit would appear to be straightforward. Unless, however, the units assigned to treatments are also the focus of the investigation, in which case the decision is no longer clear cut. For example, assigning intact classrooms or schools to treatments when the intent is to investigate individual student behavior can introduce statistical and substantive dependencies among the observations on individual students that cause many investigators to shift to a higher level for analysis. Even under random assignment conditions, the nature of the treatment contrasts (e.g., individualized instruction versus whole-group lecture) and the possibility of interactions among student attributes and treatments may point toward students as units despite the assignment of intact classes to treatments. The differential implementation of treatments in an experiment can also have a bearing on which units are considered appropriate.

The above concerns multiply in the quasiexperimental and nonexperimental investigations that dominate large-scale empirical inquiry in education. The heart of the matter is that investigators typically are studying the educative process within the context of the sociopolitical multilevel organizational settings. Neither the context nor the levels can be ignored without risk of misinterpretation.

Two other generic study attributes condition the choice of units in nonexperimental contexts. First, the type of data collection concerning educational processes impacts on the choice. Survey data gathered from school principals and teachers represent a different depth of description than an observational study of classroom practices (e.g., teacher–student and student–student interactions). Even when the variables of interest are the same, collection by one method (questionnaire, interview, observation) as opposed to another and/or from one source (student, teacher, principal) as opposed to another introduce different amounts of surplus meaning and analytical complexity. A student's report of his or her own opportunities to learn a specific topic involves different kinds of information than would a teacher's or observer's report of the individual's learning opportunities. Decisions about units of analysis and interpretations of results are obviously influenced by these distinctions.

The second consideration is the purpose of the investigation. The distinction between research and evaluation is relevant here. In research contexts—that is, research on school effects, educational effects, teacher effectiveness, classroom instruction, student learning, process–product relationships, educational production functions, contextual effects, aptitude–treatment interactions, and so forth—the intent is to clarify the linkages among the various attributes of the educational system and the behavior of the entities (students, teachers, classrooms, principals, schools, administrators) within the system. The products of such investigations are presumably a better understanding and further explanations about how the system and its elements work.

In contrast, there may be little concern for explaining how things work in many evaluations. The emphasis is upon generating information that contributes to some decision (e.g., Should handicapped children be mainstreamed? Does the scope and sequence for middle schools need revision? What happens to instructional programs when schools are allocated more or less funds? Will instructional decision making improve if criterion-referenced testing systems are substituted for norm-referenced systems?). Arguments can be made that the salience of information for a particular decision is affected by the closeness of the units from which it was collected (or the level at which it was analyzed) to the organizational level at which the decision is to be made. Yet these units may be either the same or different from those required to provide a valid explanation of why a particular program works the way it does.

The points emphasized in this discussion of research and decision contexts barely mention, much less elucidate, the specific conceptual and technical considerations that an investigator can expect to encounter in selecting units of analysis. Nonetheless, they presumably caution the reader against assuming that the discussion of conceptual and technical considerations represents general as opposed to context-specific aspects of the decision process regarding units and levels of analysis. Moreover, it foreshadows a later argument for an altered approach to decisions about units.

1.2 Conceptual Considerations

Conceptual considerations pertain to the purpose of an investigation. As such, they incorporate the first stage of empirical inquiry—question identification and formulation and theory specification—in other words, what is to be examined and how it fits within the broader scheme of things. These considerations are fundamental in determining units of analysis. Indeed, Haney (1980) and others view the purpose of the investigation as the pre-eminent consideration.

In investigations involving multilevel data, the alignment of the purpose with a single unit is seldom clear cut. While at times a particular analyst may consider a given unit as central, another analyst approaching the same empirical situation from a somewhat different perspective might find a different unit better serves his or her purpose.

There are several ways to better delineate this dilemma. A comparison of the primary units in various lines of empirical inquiry highlights historical disciplinary alignments with choice of focus. For example, schools and even school districts were typically the primary units for the economists and sociologists conducting large-scale school effects and educational production function research during the 1960s and early 1970s. In some cases they were guided by data availability considerations; many used district-reported school-level outcome (e.g., mean test scores) and schooling characteristics (availability of libraries, average teacher salary, experience, or education, pupil–teacher ratios, etc.). Others believed that the manipulable elements of educational programs were those factors controllable at the school or district level; that is, it is possible to "buy" better educated or more experienced teachers, smaller class sizes, and more science equipment.

Much of the process–product research on teaching from the 1970s, on the other hand, employed either classes or students as their units of analysis (Burstein 1980a). These studies typically involved observations of teacher behavior and teacher–student and student–student interactions. Thus activities in the classroom—what the teacher does and how it affects student behavior—were central. While not always clearly stated, the choice between classes and students as units in such studies typically depended on whether the investigator was more interested in teaching behaviors or student learning. For instance, when there was interest in possible aptitude–treatment interactions, students were typically the units of analysis.

In much of the large-scale program evaluation activities, the determination of a specific unit is more complicated. As Haney (1980) points out, "social interventions have complex goals aimed at different levels of social life" (p. 3). In his examination of units of analysis issues in Project Follow Through (FT), Haney explains why different choices are possible. Even though "the ultimate goal of FT was to develop educational processes and environments that would enable children to develop to their full potential...intermediate goals were...the

promotion of changes in individual students, teachers, and educational institutions" (Haney 1980 pp. 3–4). Clearly the student is a fundamental unit in such circumstances. But questions about the ability of teachers to implement a specific curriculum faithfully and the school to target and administer program resources appropriately identify classes and schools as relevant foci for the evaluation. These same concerns were implicit in the earlier units of analysis debate generated by Wiley's (1970) presentation at a 1967 conference on evaluation of instruction sponsored by the Center for the Study of Evaluation (see Wittrock and Wiley 1970 for a detailed and illuminating account of the conference).

To further document the dilemma implied above, a subset of the appealing but competing conceptual perspectives in support of either students or groups as units can be paraphrased:

(a) Since the ultimate aim is to determine the effects on pupil outcomes of the educational resources that an individual pupil receives, his or her background, and the influence of his or her community setting and peers, pupils are the units for which questions must be finally addressed.

(b) Pupils react as individuals, and the effects on them should be the focus (Bloom in Wittrock and Wiley 1970).

(c) Effects in classrooms (schools) are essentially the effects of environmental arrangements on individuals (Wittrock and Wiley 1970).

(d) In classroom interaction research, teacher behavior is typically directed at individual students rather than at the whole class and student individual differences affect such teacher behavior.

(e) The effects of a treatment on a classroom (school) are fundamentally different from the effects of the treatment on the individuals within it. Thus the appropriate unit of study is the collective—class or school—rather than the individual (Wiley 1970).

(f) The utility of evaluation data depends on the number of organizational levels between the action the data describes and the decision processes they are intended to influence. Each decision maker should choose analysis units at his or her organizational level or at immediately adjacent levels.

The points cited are generally compelling and disagreements are unresolvable if a choice of a single unit is required.

1.3 Technical Considerations

While resolution of conceptual complexities is a necessary condition for appropriate selection of units, it is not necessarily sufficient in the presence of complicating technical considerations. Haney (1980) cites three types of technical considerations—evaluation (research) design, statistical considerations, and practical considerations—that also arise in unit selection decisions.

Evaluation or research design considerations encompass issues of units of treatment and independence of units, among others. The concerns about units of treatment are derived from the classical conception of experimental units as the smallest units (lowest level) which can receive different treatments or different replications of the same treatment. For example, if the teacher or the specific program of study implemented by the teacher were considered to be the "treatment" in a given investigation, then the classroom would be judged the appropriate unit of analysis (Wittrock and Wiley 1970). Likewise, if the program were instituted schoolwide (e.g., a violence prevention program in secondary schools), schools would be the units. But if the program were so organized that each student received a distinct replication of the treatment, as might be possible in a laboratory study or in a highly individualized learning setting, then the pupil might qualify as the unit under this criterion.

The independence of unit issue is closely related to the units of treatment concern but focuses on the independence of the response rather than on the treatment per se. Experimental canons caution that "experimental units should respond independently of one another...[there should be] no way in which the treatment applied to one unit can affect the observation obtained from another unit" (Cox 1958). Dependencies among units of the type described confound treatment effects and complicate the estimation of the within-treatment error.

Obviously, both types of design concerns are likely to arise in the typical nonexperimental investigation. In fact, literal adherence to classical experimental canons can virtually paralyze many educational studies since the presumably statistically required unit (because of dependency problems) might be very different from units associated with the research purpose (Hopkins 1982).

While the consequences of dependencies among observations and contaminated treatments are certainly real, their role in educational research and thus the means of handling them are best understood by a specification of their statistical and substantive manifestations. For example, the statistical consequences of dependency have to do primarily with complications in specifying the correlation structure among disturbances (errors) which in turn yield spuriously liberal tests of treatment effects in many instances (Burstein 1980a). Yet the most direct way to resolve this problem is to devote more attention to specifying an appropriate error structure and adjusting the analysis accordingly. The substantive manifestation is that dependencies among observations within groups (classes, schools, etc.) are a function of the treatment or processes under investigation as well as the manner in which groups are formed and their composition. Thus within-group dependency is information about substantive educational processes and should be examined accordingly (Bidwell and Kasarda 1980, Webb 1980).

The statistical considerations cited by Haney (1980) include measurement reliability, degrees of freedom, and analysis considerations. Conventional wisdom is that aggregation to higher levels produces more reliable measures but reduces degrees of freedom for analysis. The analysis considerations focus on the unreliability problem as it affects estimation of treatment effects in the analysis of covariance. But these concerns are often erroneously applied, especially on the degree of freedom question, and are certainly peripheral to more immediate questions about the substantive focus of the investigation. Moreover, there is a clear tradeoff between reliable measurement of the wrong variable and less reliable measurement of the right one. Similarly, practical considerations such as missing data problems and the change in setting in multiple-year investigations are nuisances rather than central elements in unit selection, albeit highly visible ones. Haney's conclusion that the purpose of the investigation should guide choice rather than these other technical matters is eminently sensible.

2. A Multilevel Perspective

An alternative perspective on the selection of units is that the attention given to the selection of the unit of analysis is misdirected (Burstein 1980a, 1980b, Barr and Dreeben 1977, Rogosa 1978). As Rogosa (1978) points out, "no level is uniquely responsible for the delivery of and response to educational programs...confining substantive questions to any one level of analysis is unlikely to be a productive research strategy" (p. 83). Similarly, Barr and Dreeben (1977) contend that "school events should be observed where they occur; school, track, classroom, or whichever....A full range of organizational levels and their interconnections" (pp. 101–02).

A multilevel perspective shifts the investigative focus toward the development of adequate theories of educational processes and analytical strategies for assessing their effects. The multilevel structure of the data is not merely a nuisance; it reflects reality. What is needed is an appropriate model of the educational phenomena of interest and analytical strategies that disentangle effects from a variety of sources so that the interface of the individuals and the "groups" to which they belong and the implications of this interface for educational effects can be examined.

The shift to a multilevel perspective offers the possibility of important benefits by focusing attention on key measurement and analytical issues that naturally arise in investigating data on individuals in social structures. Certain of these issues are discussed below.

2.1 Measurement Issues

The measurement issues most salient from a multilevel perspective are those associated with the possibility of change in the meaning of variables across levels and with indices of group-level performance. The former conveys more than the fact that relationships among variables may be specific to particular levels of aggregation. More importantly, the relationship between a theoretical construct and its measurable indicator may also be level specific; the aggregation of the manifest variable will not always lead to an aggregate indicator of the original construct operationalized by the disaggregated measure.

The principle that the same observable variable can measure different constructs at different levels of aggregation is well-established (Burstein 1980a, 1980b, Burstein et al. 1980, Cronbach 1976, Sirotnik 1980, Sirotnik and Burstein 1985). A few examples serve to emphasize its ubiquity in educational research. Take, for instance, the standard measures of socioeconomic background typically found in school effects research. At the individual level, they may properly convey the parental investment in the individual child's learning. Once aggregated to the school level, social background measures also reflect the community context (e.g., wealth, urbanism, commitment to quality education) which in many countries determines the resource allocations to schools. Within an educational level, relative social background positions students within a potential status hierarchy (e.g., a big fish in a small pond) that can affect their experiences. All three measures of social background may be important in understanding the experiences and performances of students but they do represent distinctly different mechanisms.

In a reanalysis of data from an observational study of the factors influencing student learning, Burstein (1980a) demonstrated how the interpretation of a measure of the relative amounts of student learning tasks judged easy changed as the analysis shifted from the student to the class level. Students' success rates in learning tasks at the individual level captured proximal student ability and thus were positively related to student performance. At the class level, this same observational variable reflected teachers' policies with regard to task difficulty and in many instances exhibited negative relationships with student outcomes.

The problems of change in variable meaning across levels are particularly evident in the literature on organizational and educational climate (Sirotnik 1980, Sirotnik and Burstein 1985). The distinction between a specific student's perception of classroom climate, which reflects both absolute and comparative aspects of individual personality and perception, and the average perception of the class, a normative measure of the instructional environment, is an important one. Whether the "organizational" or the "psychological" aspect of the climate is most salient in a given context is unclear. For instance, aggregate responses of teachers within schools on scales purported to measure the degree of innovation and teacher influence have been construed as indicators of the atmosphere and organizational structure of the school program. In contrast, the individual teacher responses, relative to the responses of other teachers in the school, were interpreted as indicators of the teachers' sense of personal efficacy. That the effects of aggregated and individual measures on pupil outcomes were

opposite in sign and consonant with expectations reinforces the need for a better understanding of how aggregation affects the measurement of program and process characteristics.

The other measurement issue, alternative indicators of group-level outcomes, reflects the concern that the decision to examine group-level phenomena leaves the question of relevant measures of group-level indices unresolved. The most typically investigated group-level index is the group (class, school) mean. While interest in overall level of performance, as captured by means or medians, is certainly reasonable in most contexts, means alone cannot capture the full detail that is contained in individual-level scores. Some of this additional detail may reflect student achievement differences that vary as a function of educational process variables. For example, in schools and classrooms with a high proportion of children with poor entering performance, say in the bottom quartile, an effective school or teacher might be one which manages to shift a significant proportion of the pupils above the bottom quartile when instructional outcomes are measured.

The main alternative to group means in the literature is measures of the distribution of performance within groups such as the within-group standard deviation. The "tastes" of the educational organization might cause schools or programs to reduce the spread of test performance rather than concentrate solely on shifting the overall level. Advocates of mastery learning and individualized instruction are often interested in such outcomes and their chosen indicators of group-level performance should be sensitive to the consequences of their programs.

An analogous case has recently been made for treating within-group regressions of outcomes on inputs as measures of group-level performance (Burstein 1980a, Burstein et al. 1978).

The logic of within-group slopes as indicators is that they can potentially convey within-group processes in a group-level analysis. For a given distribution of entering student abilities, different teachers and different programs, through their choice of instructional processes, can relatively benefit either initially low-achieving or high-achieving students or provide equal benefits regardless of initial abilities. These differences across instructional settings can be reflected by variation in the within-group slopes. Whether the use of slopes as indicators of group-level outcomes is a fruitful investment of investigative resources remains a relatively unexplored question (Rachman-Moore and Wolfe 1984).

2.2 Analysis Issues

Once a multilevel perspective is adopted, a salient concern is how to conduct an analysis that considers effects at all pertinent levels. Multilevel analyses, that is, separate analyses at two or more levels or a combined analysis containing explanatory variables at two or more levels, are typically necessary. The central issues, then, focus on the development of strategies that combine the features of analyses at more than one level.

While earlier forays into estimating educational effects at multiple levels concentrated on the estimation of variance components or proportions of variation, current emphasis is on the decomposition of relationships (covariances, correlations, regression coefficients). Certain methods are basically direct extensions of widely used regression methods for handling multilevel data. Cronbach (1976), for example, decomposes the individual-level regression relationships into between-group and within-group components and recommends that between-group and pooled within-group regressions be separately estimated. On the other hand, there is the danger of the confounding of compositional effects (aggregated individual effects) with true group-level effects in the analysis of means when individuals are nonrandomly assigned to groups. Alternative analytical procedures which purportedly adjust estimates of group effects for within-group composition should be considered. Whether these adjustments are the proper ones is the subject of continuing debate, however.

A set of more elaborate multilevel estimation procedures have been proposed recently (Aitkin et al. 1981, Aitkin and Longford 1986, Erbring and Young 1979, Goldstein 1986, Mason et al. 1984, Rachman-Moore and Wolfe 1984, Raudenbush and Bryk 1986, Schneider and Treiber 1984). These methods are intended to model multilevel processes and outcomes more conscientiously and involved more powerful estimation procedures. To date, however, their application to actual educational data has been limited. Further conceptual, analytical, and empirical work on these methods is clearly warranted as they have yet to be subjected to the kinds of analytical and empirical tests that could identify their properties, much less their range of utility.

In summary, treating the analysis of multilevel data as simply a matter of selecting an appropriate unit and, thereby, level of analysis is too narrow a conception of the issues. Rather, the focus should be on the identification of the appropriate set of substantive research questions at and within various levels and the specification of appropriate models for analyzing multilevel data. Once this shift occurs, the measurement and analytical problems that typically arise in multilevel settings rightfully dominate the examination of interrelations among units at and within various levels of the educational system. As a consequence, progress in the understanding of educational phenomena will accelerate.

See also: Multilevel Analysis

Bibliography

Aitkin M, Anderson D, Hinde J 1981 Statistical modeling of data on teaching styles. *J. R. Statist. Soc. A*. 144: 419–61
Aitkin M, Longford N 1986 Statistical modeling issued in school effectiveness studies. *J. R. Statist. Soc. A*. 149: 1–26
Barr R, Dreeben R 1977 Instruction in classrooms. In: Shulman L S (ed.) 1977 *Review of Research in Education*, Vol. 5. Peacock, Itasca, Illinois, pp. 89–162
Bidwell C E, Kasarda J D 1980 Conceptualizing and measuring the effects of school and schooling. *Am. J. Educ*. 88: 401–30
Burstein L 1980a Analysis of multilevel data in educational research and evaluation. In: Berliner D (ed.) 1980 *Review of Research in Education*, Vol. 8. American Educational Research Association, Washington, DC, pp. 158–233
Burstein L 1980b The role of levels of analysis in the specification of educational effects. In: Dreeben R, Thomas J A (eds.) 1980 *The Analysis of Educational Productivity*, Vol. 1: *Issues in Microanalysis*. Ballinger Press, Cambridge, Massachusetts, pp. 119–90
Burstein L, Fischer K, Miller M D 1980 The multilevel effects of background on science achievement: A cross-national comparison. *Sociol. Educ*. 53: 215–52
Burstein L, Linn R L, Capell F J 1978 Analyzing multilevel data in the presence of heterogeneous within-class regressions. *J. Educ. Statist*. 3: 347–83
Cox D R 1958 *Planning of Experiments*. Wiley, New York
Cronbach L J 1976 *Research on Classrooms and Schools: Formulation of Questions, Design, and Analysis*. Occasional Paper, Stanford Evaluation Consortium, Stanford, California
Erbring L, Young A A 1979 Individuals and social structure: Contextual effects as endogenous feedback. *Soc. Meth. Res*. 7: 396–430
Goldstein H 1986 Multilevel mixed linear model analysis using iterative generalized least squares. *Biometrika* 72: 43–56
Haney W 1980 Units and levels of analysis in large-scale evaluation. In: Roberts K H, Burstein L (eds.) 1980
Hopkins K D 1982 The unit of analysis: Group means versus individual observations. *Am. Educ. Res. J*. 19: 5–18
Mason W M, Wong G Y, Entwisle B 1984 Contextual analysis through the multilevel linear model. In: *Sociological Methodology 1983/1984*. Jossey-Bass, San Francisco, California
Rachman-Moore D, Wolfe R G 1984 Robust analysis of a nonlinear model for multilevel educational survey data. *J. Educ. Statist*. 9: 277–93
Raudenbush S, Bryk A S 1986 A heirarchical model for studying school effects. *Soc. Educ*. 59
Roberts K, Burstein L (eds.) 1980 *New Directions in Methodology of Social and Behavioral Sciences*. Jossey-Bass, San Francisco, California
Rogosa D 1978 Politics, process, and pyramids. *J. Educ. Statistics* 3: 79–86
Schneider W, Treiber B 1984 Classroom differences in the determination of achievement changes. *Am. Educ. Res. J*. 21: 195–211
Sirotnik K A 1980 Psychometric implications of the unit-of-analysis problem (with examples from the measurement of organizational climate). *J. Educ. Meas*. 17: 245–81
Sirotnik K A, Burstein L 1985 Measurement and statistical issues in multilevel research on schooling. *Educ. Adm. Quart*. 21: 169–85
Treiber B 1980 Mehrebenenanalysen in der bildungsforschung. *Z. Entwicklungspsychol. Paedagog. Psychol*. 12: 358–86
Webb N M 1980 Group process: The key to learning in groups. In: Roberts K H, Burstein L (eds.) 1980
Wiley D E 1970 Design and analysis of evaluation studies. In: Wittrock M C, Wiley D E (eds.) 1970 *The Evaluation of Instruction: Issues and Problems*. Holt, Rinehart and Winston, New York, pp. 259–88
Wittrock M C, Wiley D E (eds.) 1970 *The Evaluation of Instruction: Issues and Problems*. Holt, Rinehart and Winston, New York

Contributors Index

Contributors are listed in alphabetical order together with their affiliations. Titles of articles which they have authored follow in alphabetical order, along with the respective page numbers. Where articles are co-authored, this has been indicated by an asterisk preceding the article title.

† deceased

† deceased

Name Index

The Name Index has been compiled so that the reader can proceed either directly to the page where an author's work is cited, or to the reference itself in the bibliography. For each name, the page numbers for the bibliographic citation are given first, followed by the page number(s) in parentheses where that reference is cited in text. Where a name is referred to only in text, and not in the bibliography, the page number appears only in parentheses.

The accuracy of the spelling of authors' names has been affected by the use of different initials by some authors, or a different spelling of their name in different papers or review articles (sometimes this may arise from a transliteration process), and by those journals which give only one initial to each author.

Aaron J H, 177 (175)
Ackerman W B, 657
Acland H, 456 (455), 559 (557)
Adams E, 365 (365)
Adams R J, 297 (296), 403 (399), 418 (417)
Adams R N, 510
Adams R S, 495
Adelman C, (44), 81 (80), 478 (475)
Ader H J, 403 (402, 403)
Adler I, 723 (721)
Adorno T W, (151)
Agassi J, 225 (221)
Ainley J G, 150 (149)
Airey C, 107 (101)
Aitkin M, 604 (602, 604), 699 (697), 781 (781)
Aitkin M A, 699 (691, 696, 697)
Ajzen I, 426 (421, 423, 426)
Akinsanya S K, 63
Albach H, 716
Alder T F, 487 (486)
Alexander S, 431 (430)
Algina J, 282
Alker H R, 456 (455)
Allal L, 277 (274, 275, 276)
Allport G W, 260 (258), 426 (421, 423)
Altbach P G, 205 (204)
Althauser R P, 580 (572)
Alwin D F, 451 (448), 580 (572)
Amar R, 723 (719), 753 (750)
Amidon E J, 478
Amin F, (151)
Anastasi A, 487 (482), 497, 570 (567)
Anderberg M R, 604
Andersen A H, 677 (674, 677)

Andersen E B, 292 (287), 322 (321, 322), 677 (677)
Anderson C, 225 (222)
Anderson C A, 451, 558 (555, 556)
Anderson D, 699 (697), 781 (781)
Anderson G J, 451 (449), 745 (744)
Anderson H D, 558 (555)
Anderson J, 231 (229)
Anderson J E, 260 (259)
Anderson J F, 482
Anderson J G, 774 (771)
Anderson L W, 426 (421, 422, 423, 425, 426), 428 (427), 429 (428, 429)
Anderson N H, 628 (627)
Anderson R C, 363 (362)
Anderson R L, 586 (583)
Anderson S B, 188 (186), 492 (491)
Anderson T R, 74 (73, 74)
Anderson T W, 633 (630), (647), 689 (687, 688)
André M E D A, 74 (73, 74)
Andrews F M, 113 (112), 513 (511)
Andrews G, 685 (681)
Andrich D, 260 (258), 286, 292 (287), 297 (295, 296), 302 (300, 301, 302), 306 (305)
Angoff W, (396)
Angoff W H, 403 (399), 418 (410, 413, 414)
Antonovsky A, 723 (722)
Apel K-O, 69 (63, 68)
Appelbaum M I, 260 (257)
Apple M W, 58 (54)
Arabie P, 316 (306), 320 (317, 318, 319), 752 (750)
Arbuthnott J, 710 (706)
Argyris C, 225 (223)

Aristotle, 81 (79)
Aronson E, 541, 755
Arter J A, 252 (251)
Arzi H J, 74 (74)
Ashenden D J, 526 (525)
Asplund J, (68)
Atkinson R C, 554 (551), 580
Auden G, (262)
Averill M, 403 (398)
Ayres L P, (13)

Babad E Y, 492
Bacher F, 354 (346)
Bagozzi R P, 621 (620)
Bailey K D, 93
Bailyn B, 42 (38)
Bain A, (10)
Bain R K, 510 (509)
Baird J R, 74 (71, 73, 74)
Baker D N, 42
Baker E L, 113 (112), 372, 628 (625)
Baker F B, 252 (251), 580 (579)
Baker R J, 705 (704)
Balch G I, 205
Ball S, 188 (186), 492 (491)
Ball S J, 53 (52)
Baltes P B, 125, 126 (114, 115, 119, 125), 737
Bancroft G, 465 (459)
Bane M J, 456 (455), 559 (557)
Bannister D, 490
Bardouille R, 129 (129)
Bargh J, 566 (563, 564)
Bargmann, (579)
Barker L L, 354 (352)

789

Subject Index

The Subject Index has been compiled as a guide to the reader who is interested in locating all the references to a particular subject area within the Encyclopedia. Entries may have up to three levels of heading. Where the page numbers appear in bold italic type, this indicates a substantive discussion of the topic. Every effort has been made to index as comprehensively as possible and to standardize the terms used in the index. Given the diverse nature of the field and the varied use of terms throughout the international community, synonyms and foreign language terms have been included with appropriate cross-references. As a further aid to the reader, cross-references have also been given to terms of related interest.